12372409

Historical Dictionary of France from the 1815 Restoration to the Second Empire

Historical Dictionaries of French History

This five-volume series covers French history from the Revolution through the Third Republic. It provides comprehensive coverage of each era, including not only political and military history but also social, economic, and art history.

Historical Dictionary of the French Revolution, 1789–1799
Samuel F. Scott and Barry Rothaus, editors

Historical Dictionary of Napoleonic France, 1799–1815
Owen Connelly, editor

Historical Dictionary of France from 1815 Restoration to the Second Empire
Edgar Leon Newman, editor

Historical Dictionary of the French Second Empire, 1852–1870
William E. Echard, editor

Historical Dictionary of the Third French Republic, 1870–1940
Patrick H. Hutton, editor-in-chief

Historical Dictionary of France from the 1815 Restoration to the Second Empire

A-L

Edited by
EDGAR LEON NEWMAN

ROBERT LAWRENCE SIMPSON,
Assistant Editor

Greenwood Press
New York
Westport, Connecticut

Library of Congress Cataloging-in-Publication Data
Main entry under title:

Historical dictionary of France from the 1815 restoration
 to the Second Empire.

 Bibliography: p.
 Includes index.
 1. France—History—Restoration, 1814–1830—
Dictionaries. 2. France—History—Louis Philip, 1830–
1848—Dictionaries. 3. France—History—Second
Republic, 1848–1852—Dictionaries. I. Newman, Edgar
Leon.
DC256.H57 1987   944.06′03′21   85–17728
ISBN 0–313–22751–9 (lib. bdg.: alk. paper)
ISBN 0–313–26045–1 (lib. bdg. : alk. paper : v.1)
ISBN 0–313–26046–X (lib. bdg. : alk. paper : v.2)

Library of Congress Catalog Card Number: 85–17728
ISBN: 0–313–22751–9 (set)
ISBN: 0–313–26045–1 (v.1)
ISBN: 0–313–26046–X (v.2)

First published in 1987

Greenwood Press, Inc.
88 Post Road West, Westport, Connecticut 06881

Printed in the United States of America

The paper used in this book complies with the
Permanent Paper Standard issued by the National
Information Standards Organization (Z39.48–1984).

10 9 8 7 6 5 4 3 2 1

FOR MY FATHER

Contents

Contributors

Albury, W. R., University of New South Wales, Kensington, New South Wales, Australia

Aldrich, Robert, University of Sydney, Sydney, New South Wales, Australia

Allen, James Smith, Phillips University, Enid, Oklahoma

Bailey, Charles R., S.U.N.Y.-Geneseo, Geneseo, New York

Beach, Vincent, University of Colorado, Boulder, Colorado

Beck, Thomas, Chapman College, Orange, California.

Bertier de Sauvigny, Guillaume de, Paris, France

Brown, Robert, Pembroke State University, Pembroke, North Carolina

Caron, Jean-Claude, Nogent-sur-Marne, France

Castelli, Helen, East Stroudsberg, Pennsylvania

Chandler, David, Royal Military Academy Sandhurst, Camberley, Surrey, Great Britain

Chastain, James, Ohio University, Athens, Ohio

Collins, Irene, University of Liverpool, Liverpool, Great Britain

Comeau, Paul, New Mexico State University, Las Cruces, New Mexico

Connor, Susan, Tift College, Forsyth, Georgia

Cook, Bernard, Loyola University, New Orleans, Louisiana

Creighton, John K., University of Texas at El Paso, El Paso, Texas

Crosland, Maurice, University of Kent at Canterbury, Great Britain

Day, C. Rod, Simon Fraser University, Burnaby, British Columbia, Canada

de Luna, Frederick A., University of Alberta, Edmonton, Alberta, Canada

Earls, Irene, Orlando, Florida

Ehrenberg, John, Long Island University, Brooklyn, New York

Elwitt, Sanford, University of Rochester, Rochester, New York

Frader, Laura, Northeastern University, Boston, Massachusetts

Freedeman, Charles E., S.U.N.Y.-Binghamton, Binghamton, New York

Fuchs, Rachel, Arizona State University, Tempe, Arizona

Grubb, Alan, Clemson University, Clemson, South Carolina

Gullickson, Gay L., University of Maryland, College Park, Maryland
Guthrie, Christophe E., Tarleton State University, Stephenville, Texas
Gutman, Sanford, S.U.N.Y.-Cortland, Cortland, New York
Harrigan, Patrick J., University of Waterloo, Waterloo, Ontario, Canada
Higgs, David, University of Toronto, Toronto, Ontario, Canada
Johnson, Christopher H., Wayne State University, Detroit, Michigan
Kaiser, Thomas E., University of Arkansas at Little Rock, Little Rock,
   Arkansas
Kieswetter, James K., Eastern Washington University, Cheney, Washington
Klinck, David M., University of Windsor, Windsor, Ontario, Canada
Kors, Alan C., University of Pennsylvania, Philadelphia, Pennsylvania
Kselman, Thomas, University of Notre Dame, Notre Dame, Indiana
Latta, Claude, Professor of History, Lauréat de l'Académie Française
Lehning, James, University of Utah, Salt Lake City, Utah
Longfellow, David, Baylor University, Waco, Texas
Loubère, Leo A., S.U.N.Y.-Buffalo, Buffalo, New York
McBride, Theresa, College of the Holy Cross, Worcester, Massachusetts
McPhee, Peter, Victoria University of Wellington, Wellington, New Zealand
Moon, S. Joan, California State University, Sacramento, California
Moss, Bernard H., University of Auckland, Auckland, New Zealand
Necheles, Ruth F., Long Island University, Brooklyn, New York
Neely, Sylvia, Indiana University-Purdue University at Fort Wayne, Fort
   Wayne, Indiana
Newman, Edgar L., New Mexico State University, Las Cruces, New Mexico
O'Brien, Patricia, University of California-Irvine, Irvine, California
Outlaw, Shelby A., Atlanta, Georgia
Pinkney, David H., University of Washington, Seattle, Washington
Popkin, Jeremy, University of Kentucky, Lexington, Kentucky
Porch, Douglas, The Citadel, Charleston, South Carolina
Rader, Daniel, San Diego State University, San Diego, California
Ratcliffe, Barrie M., Université Laval, Quebec, Quebec, Canada
Reedy, W. Jay, North Dakota State University, Fargo, North Dakota
Reid, Donald, University of North Carolina, Chapel Hill, North Carolina
Rooney, John W., Marquette University, Milwaukee, Wisconsin
Rose, Robert Barrie, University of Tasmania, Hobart, Tasmania, Australia
Sandstrom, Roy E., University of Northern Iowa, Cedar Falls, Iowa
Schleifer, James T., College of New Rochelle, New Rochelle, New York
Schmidt, Daniel P., Marquette University, Milwaukee, Wisconsin
Sibalis, Michael, Brock University, St. Catherines, Ontario, Canada
Simpson Robert L., New Mexico State University, Las Cruces, New Mexico
Smith, Bonnie G., University of Rochester, Rochester, New York
Smith, Don, Oakland, California
Smith, Robert J., S.U.N.Y-Brockport, Brockport, New York
Staum, Martin S., University of Calgary, Calgary, Alberta, Canada

Strumingher, Laura S., University of Cincinnati, Cincinnati, Ohio
Sussman, George D., Delmar, New York
Truant, Cynthia, University of California-San Diego, La Jolla, California
Weber, William, California State University-Long Beach, Long Beach, California
Weissbach, Lee Shai, University of Louisville, Louisville, Kentucky
Weisz, George, McGill University, Montreal, Quebec, Canada
Welch, Marcelle Maistre, Florida International University, Miami, Florida
Zhang Zhilian, Peking University, Peking, People's Republic of China

Preface

The period from 1 January 1815 to 31 December 1852 began and ended with a Napoleon Bonaparte as emperor of the French. It included two major revolutions and several revolts, an experiment with parliamentary government and an independent press, the dawn of socialist ideology, the golden age of romanticism, and the beginning of the Industrial Revolution. But this was an age dominated by memories, not events.

The conflicts of the great French Revolution grew in stature as time passed. They seemed larger than life, like the ancient wars between gods and giants. The Republic and the Terror had proven that France was not ready for democracy, and the men associated with the Republic and the Terror were generally despised. The memory of Napolean, however, was more and more the one source of excitement in a lackluster world. France was a divided nation, and only the army was a truly national institution. The legend of its conquests could confer glory upon the most ordinary shopkeepers and peasants. While the surface of political life kept changing, Bonapartism remained the constant undercurrent in France during the first half of the nineteenth century. It surfaced as soon as it could. In the first democratic presidential election, which took place on 10 December 1848, the common people cast their votes for Louis-Napoleon Bonaparte. Meanwhile the memory of Napoleon and the Revolution had affected every event, every trend in literature and art, and every mind in France. Frenchmen of the nineteenth century had a sense of being dwarfs who lived in the shadow of giants. Each current event was seen as the product of the Revolutionary past. Leftists, however moderate, could be made to appear dangerous if they were presented as reincarnations of Maximilien Robespierre. The memory of Voltaire was a living force; his books were best-sellers, and his ideas were at the height of their influence. Consequently figures from the past like Robespierre and Voltaire have been included in this book because of their influence on France between the two Napoleons. And the system of cross-references, which has been used in all the volumes of this Greenwood Press series of French historical dictionaries, is especially appropriate for this one in which so many entries are interrelated.

Readers who follow the cross-references from one entry to another will become aware of the wide spectrum of viewpoints included in this book. There are more than 950 articles written by 75 scholars from countries throughout the world. Some of these scholars are conservatives, some Marxists, and some are not part of either school. Because there is no definitive interpretation of most issues, I have tried to present a balance of several prevailing viewpoints and to allow each author enough space to defend his or her conclusions. Each entry has a brief bibliography of works for further reference.

Although this book is called a historical dictionary, it is intended to serve as a useful reference guide in many fields. Several authors are specialists in literature, art, music, sociology, and other disciplines. Our goal has been to include as wide a variety as possible of academic fields and political points of view.

This historical dictionary reflects the time in which it was written: the 1980s. In addition to the standard entries on writers, politicians, kings, battles, newspapers, scientists, philosophers, generals, artists, revolutionaries, laws, and schools, there are entries that reflect the triumph of social history, the *Annales* school, and Fernand Braudel, such as: Childrearing Practices; Children, Abandoned; Children, Institutions For; Child Labor; Wet Nursing; Public Welfare; Liberty of Education; Public Instruction; Singing Societies; Domestic Servants; Silk Industry; Women's Newspapers; Worker Poets; Railroads; Banking; Jews; Coal Industry; Peasants; Popular Religiosity; Fertility; Migration; Mortality; Nuptiality; Population; Banking; and of course, Bonapartism. There is more about women, more about economic and social matters, and more history-from-the-bottom-up than there would have been in a book written twenty years ago. On the other hand, political leaders are given relatively little space, and military leaders are often left out unless they participated in a popular revolution. It was all but impossible to find somebody to write the entry on the battle of Waterloo. Everyone seemed to be working on demographics, economic and social change, and popular mentality. Just a few weeks before I wrote this preface, an angry President François Mitterand complained that schoolchildren in France know the price of wheat in 1789 but they have never heard of the marquis de Mirabeau. Indeed there are indications that historians may be responding to Mitterand's complaint and turning back to the study of great leaders and important events. In any case, this dictionary includes and cross-references both the traditional dictionary items and subjects of interest to the *Annales* school of history-from-the-bottom-up.

It includes extensive articles on the principal movements of the period. This was the Romantic age: Victor Hugo, Honoré de Balzac, René de Chateaubriand, Alphonse de Lamartine, George Sand, Hector Berlioz, Eugène Delacroix. There was an explosion of literature accompanied by the appearance of an independent press; newspapers like the *Constitutionnel* and the *Journal des débats* during the Restoration and like the *National* and the *Réforme* during the July Monarchy had a powerful influence on public opinion. Although their circulation was less than 50,000, they could launch political careers for their editors and ignite the spark of popular revolution.

French politics have never been more interesting than in the years between the two Napoleons. Only a few men could vote: there were fewer than 100,000 electors during the Restoration (1814–30) and about 300,000 electors during the July Monarchy (1830–48). Nevertheless France achieved a workable parliamentary government based on free elections, a comparatively free press, and the rule of law. The nation was learning to deal with the divisions that caused and were caused by the French Revolution without suspending its constitutional guarantees of individual freedom. All of this would be swept away after the June Days of 1848 and during the plebiscitary dictatorship of Napoleon III (1852–70), but it laid the basis for the constitutional parliamentary democracy of the Third, Fourth, and Fifth Republics.

The relative success of constitutional government in France from 1815 to 1852 was remarkable in view of the differences between the rulers and the ruled. The common people were an Anglophobic, aggressively nationalistic mass of peasants, artisans, and shopkeepers ruled by a pusillanimous élite of frightened landowners and bourgeois. Support for constitutional liberty was narrow and thin, and the liberal politicians and journalists who supported it were true heroes. They deserve the large amount of space devoted to them because of the weakness of their cause, not because of its strength.

Far stronger than constitutional liberalism were the resurgent conservative movements centered around the Bourbon monarchy and the Catholic church. Guillaume de Bertier de Sauvigny, the leading historian of the Restoration, has contributed a number of articles on these movements, which dominated life in the south and west of France and were second only to Bonapartism as a political force among the masses. The power of clericalism and conservatism in nineteenth-century France should never be underestimated. No government could stand against them and survive. This was the creative golden age of conservatism, which inspired Balzac, Alexandre Dumas, Chateaubriand, the young Lamartine, the young Lamennais, and the young Victor Hugo. The works of the great English constitutional conservative, Edmund Burke, exercised a powerful influence on French political and social thought affecting both liberals and conservatives from Pierre-Paul Royer-Collard to François Guizot to Alexis de Tocqueville. Less influential were the paternalistic clerical monarchists Bonald and de Maistre and their socialist counterpart, Saint-Simon, who insisted that the nation was not capable of governing itself. The failures of the great French Revolution had cast doubt upon the powers of human reason and upon the ability of the individual to live in freedom. The legacy of the Revolution was conservatism and self-doubt.

Of course, there were two revolutions, one in 1830 and one in 1848, during this great conservative age. These revolutions made heroes of a variety of malcontents and misfits who wrote revolutionary tracts and led revolutionary movements, and who consequently occupy a great deal of space in this dictionary. France was still divided and disorderly enough so that any loudmouthed scofflaw could hope to emerge as a popular leader. Revolutions can turn ridiculous people into powerful ones and vice-versa. The years between the two Napoleons saw the birth of socialism and the rebirth of revolutionary republicanism, and both movements have been covered here. Bernard Moss, who wrote the article on the Society of the Rights of Man, sees republicanism as a democratic and socialistic revolutionary movement that clung at first to the memory of the First French Republic and then expanded to capture the imagination and the loyalty of the working classes. Christopher Johnson's entry on socialism follows the same argument: that revolutionary socialism became the dominant ideology of the proletariat. Michael Sibalis's entry on Bonapartism also sees the popular devotion to the memory of Napoleon as essentially republican and socialistic, dominated by the tricolored flag of the democratic Republic rather than the eagle of the nationalistic and militaristic Empire. The entries by Bertier de Sauvigny, on the other hand, see the masses as concerned essentially with their own material needs, and David Pinkney's entry on the July Revolution does not see the crowd as motivated by a particular ideology. My entry on the republicans views the French people as Bonapartist and nationalist and consequently unimpressed by either republican or socialist ideas. In the end, it is crucial but impossible to know the mentality of the French people during the years between the two Napoleons. The period ended with a democratic republic in February 1848, a democratic and socialist uprising in June 1848, a massive vote for Louis-Napoleon Bonaparte in December 1848, followed by socialist electoral victories, then a Bonapartist military coup d'état, and finally a plebiscite massively endorsing that coup. The populace went through many moods, and we can only guess which of its faces showed its true inner nature.

France during the years between the two Napoleons was more disunited and disorderly than it would ever be again but more harmonious and peaceful than it had been in the past. Despite the revolutionary upheavals of 1830 and 1848–52, the wounds of the great French Revolution had begun to heal so that the nation could begin to deal with the changes that the Revolution had produced. In addition, the new means of production, especially in manufacturing and mining, and the new means of transportation like steamships and the first railroads would have to be absorbed into a nation that was still politically unstable. To its credit, France in this period coped with its problems by means of constitutional government, elected parliaments, a relatively free press, and the rule of law. Liberals, conservatives, nationalistic Bonapartists, and socialist revolutionaries each laid the groundwork for their nation's future, each hoping to pull it in a different direction. The result of their efforts has divided, confused, and enriched France ever since, through the near-miss of the Dreyfus Affair, the age of a Herculean Clemenceau, through the reforms of Léon Blum, the shame of Vichy, the napoleonic pride of de Gaulle, the dashed hopes of Mitterand, and beyond.

This book was made possible by the imagination and devotion to scholarship of the Greenwood Press and especially of Cynthia Harris, the editor of reference books. The years betwen the two Napoleons have not attracted a large number of scholars, but the high quality, style, and thoughtfulness of these entries attests to the vitality of the field. Those who took the time to contribute their work deserve, along with Ms. Harris and Greenwood Press, the thanks of everyone who will benefit from this dictionary. Finally, this volume was made possible only by the hard work and dedication of Robert Simpson, the assistant editor. He compiled the cross-references and the index, carried on the bulk of the correspondence with six dozen authors, and made my life much easier for the past four years.

Edgar Leon Newman

The Dictionary

A

ABRANTES, DUCHESSE D'. See JUNOT.

ACADEMIE FRANCAISE, the oldest and most prestigious of the French learned academies. It numbered among its forty "Immortals" the leading figures of nineteenth-century intellectual life. The *Moniteur universel* of 26 March 1816 published a royal ordinance dated 21 March 1816 that decreed the reorganization of the four existing French learned societies. Introduced by a preface in which Louis XVIII clearly echoed sentiments expressed in the preamble of the Charter of 1814, it stated his wish to restore to each learned body its original name so that the link with the past would be renewed. The ordinance declared that henceforth the Institut would be composed of four academies, that these four would be listed in the order of their foundation, that the Académie française would resume its pre-Revolutionary name and statutes, and that the remaining three academies would retain their organization and rules from the Institut of 1803. The ordinance also listed the membership of the four academies; a careful reading of the roll of the Académie française reveals that eleven members had been purged from its ranks.

Both the First Restoration and the Hundred Days were too short and too filled with events of greater moment for much attention to be paid to the Institut, though Louis XVIII probably contemplated reforms as early as March 1815. With the Second Restoration, however, came the third major restructuring of the French learned institutions in just over twenty years; it has endured with but minor changes to the present. One ambition of the restored Bourbons, made patent in the preamble to the Charter of 1814, was to renew the thread of French history, broken by some twenty-five years of war and revolution. This intention clearly underlay the provisions of the ordinance of 21 March 1816 that once again revamped the Institut. In addition to restoring the traditional names to the academies, thus giving formal confirmation to a common practice, the ordinance ranked the academies by their date of foundation, thus restoring the French

Academy to its original primacy. Following it, in order, came the Academy of Inscriptions, the Academy of Science, and the Academy of Fine Arts. Each academy enjoyed the right to select its own permanent secretary, the privilege of electing its own membership, and the independence resulting from possession of its own statutes. The Académie française readopted its pre-Revolutionary rules. Still housed in the former Collège de quatre-nations, the building Napoleon had presented to the Institut, the four academies were obligated to hold a common session once a year on 24 April, the day of Louis XVIII's return to France in 1814. While these structural reforms failed to arouse much controversy, the provisions of the ordinance of 21 March 1816 with regard to the membership of the Academy unleashed a furious controversy. Issued when the political atmosphere in France was poisoned by the White Terror and the Chambre introuvable and when royalist thirst for vengeance had yet to be slaked, the ordinance purged from the Academy eleven prominent regicides and Napoleonic figures and replaced them with nine royalist appointees. The forty academicians named in the ordinance of 21 March thus included six members of the Academy of the Old Regime, fifteen from the Second Class of the Institut, eight elected during the waning years of the Empire, and the nine royal appointees. Excluded from the Academy were comte Dominique-Joseph Garat (1749–1833), Jean-Jacques-Régis de Cambacérès (1753–1824), comte Philippe-Antoine Merlin [de Douai] (1754–1838), the abbé Emmanuel-Joseph Siéyès (1748–1836), comte Pierre-Louis Roederer (1754–1835), Charles-Guillaume Etienne (1777–1845), Antoine-Vincent Arnault (1766–1834), Cardinal Jean-Siffrein Maury (1774–1817), Lucien Bonaparte (1775–1840), the duc de Bassano (1763–1839), and comte Michel-Louis-Etienne Regnault Saint Jean d'Angely (1762–1819). Etienne and Arnault were reelected to the Académie in 1829. Appointed to replace these men were Cardinal de Bausset (1748–1824), comte Louis-Gabriel-Ambroise Bonald (1754–1840), comte Antoine-François-Claude Ferrand (1751–1825), Joseph-Henri-Joachim Lainé (1767–1865), the marquis de Lally-Tollendal (1751–1830), the duc de Lévis (1764–1830), comte Marie-Gabriel-Florent-Auguste de Choiseul-Gouffier (1752–1817), the duc de Richelieu (1766–1822), and the abbé de Montesquiou-Fezensac (1757–1832). Resentment at the government's cavalier attitude toward the traditions of the Academy no doubt helped prevent the comte de Vaublanc, who as minister of the interior had signed the ordinance, from gaining election to the Academy. Within a month, Louis-Simon Auger (1772–1829) and the marquis de Laplace, the famed astronomer, had been elected to fill the two vacant seats. The first session of the reorganized Academy took place on 24 April 1816.

On at least two notable occasions during the Restoration, the French Academy took sides in disputes of the day. Of these, the first, which concerned the famous battle between the advocates of romanticism and the defenders of classicism, is the more important. By the early 1820s, French romanticism, the complex product of historical, political, social, literary, and cultural forces, had clearly begun to effect a radical transformation of French literary taste, and its advent on the

French literary scene touched off the strongest literary debate since the famous battle of the Ancients and the Moderns. In this early stage of the conflict, the French Academy assumed the role of the champion of France's classical past, labeling romanticism an enemy that needed to be mercilessly crushed. Auger, who later became permanent secretary of the Academy, spoke in a famous public address of April 1824 of a schism in literature and of romanticism as a new heresy; he also charged that romanticism not only called into question the rules of literature and insulted the great works of the past but that it also dangerously inflamed the passions of the mob. His colleague, the playwright Jean-Louis Laya, reviled the newcomers on the literary scene, calling them *les factieux* and *les barbares*. The divisions of the mid–1820s were so bitter and the lines of battle so sharply drawn that the elections of Alexandre Soumet (1824) and Casimir Delavigne (1825) were considered by some to be victories for the romantics. The romantics had time as their ally, and 1830, the year of the celebrated battle of Hernani and the July Revolution, witnessed the reception of Alphonse de Lamartine, noted romantic poet and author of the *Méditations*, elected on 5 November 1829. Within the course of the next twenty-two years, most of the major champions of the romantic movement won election to the Academy, though many had to overcome considerable difficulties placed in their path by the dwindling number of classicists. Charles Nodier (1833), François Mignet (1836), Victor Hugo (1841), Prosper Mérimée (1845), Charles-Augustin Sainte-Beuve (1845), Alfred de Vigny (1846), and Alfred de Musset (1852) all entered the Academy during the July Monarchy and the Second Republic. Victor Hugo, without a doubt the dominant personality on the French literary scene in the nineteenth century, however, stood for election five times before becoming one of the Immortals in 1841.

Of the rare and notable occasions when the French Academy has involved itself directly in contemporary political controversies, one took place during the Restoration. At issue was the repressive press law introduced by the comte de Peyronnet late in 1826. At the instigation of Jean-Charles de Lacretelle and Abel-François Villemain and with the support of Chateaubriand, members of the Academy, after overcoming the opposition of conservative members and after pointedly ignoring a royal threat, availed themselves of one of their privileges and directly addressed Charles X with a protest against the law. Lacretelle, Villemain, and Joseph-François Michaud drafted the appeal and suffered immediately the impact of the king's wrath when all three lost their government posts. From the Academy came a feeble protest, but it also elected to fill a vacant seat Pierre-Paul Royer-Collard, the noted politician whose speech in the Chamber of Deputies had virtually assured the defeat of the Peyronnet law.

The French Academy also resumed work during the Restoration on its principal public work, the *Dictionnaire*. Begun in 1639, the *Dictionnaire* went through four editions during the *ancien régime*. When the Convention abolished the learned academies in 1793, work on the *Dictionnaire* had been turned over to the Committee on Public Instruction. Despite the turmoil of the Revolutionary years, a fifth edition, carefully edited to reflect Revolutionary ideology, appeared in 1798. Publication of the sixth edition, once more the work of the Academy, occurred in 1835.

The twenty-two years from the Revolution of 1830 to the start of the Second Empire remain a period remarkable in the history of the Academy, for it elected to its ranks not only the leading proponents of romanticism but also a notable number of men who have achieved a permanent place in the history of French culture. Included among the thirty-six academicians elected during these years are Victor Cousin (1830), Adolphe Thiers (1833), François Guizot (1836), Eugene Scribe (1834), Narcisse-Achille Salvandy (1835), Alexis de Tocqueville (1841), Pierre-Simon Ballanche (1842), Ludovic Vitet (1845), Charles de Rémusat (1847), and the comte de Montalembert (1851). Despite the impressive number of luminaries chosen to occupy an academic bench, public interest and curiosity had also been aroused by a mere listing of the eminent French thinkers and writers who never received the right to call themselves one of the Immortals. Of all such lists, Arsène Houssaye presented the most famous in his *Histoire du 41e fauteuil de l'Académie française* (1882). Notable by their absence from the ranks of the Academy during the nineteenth century were, among many others, Benjamin Constant, Stendhal, Honoré de Balzac, Gérard de Nerval, Théophile Gautier, Jules Michelet, Charles Baudelaire, Gustave Flaubert, and Emile Zola. They join, nonetheless, a most exalted company, which includes René Descartes, Blaise Pascal, Molière, Jean-Jacques Rousseau, and Denis Diderot.

The present-day division of the Institut into five academies came about in 1832 when Louis-Philippe, acting on a recommendation of Guizot, revived the Academy of Moral and Political Sciences, originally founded in 1795 and abolished by Napoleon Bonaparte in 1803.

F. Aucoc, *L'Institut de France. Lois, statuts et reglements concernant les anciennes académies et l'Institut de 1635 à 1889* (Paris, 1889); G. R. Beale, "Academies to Institut," *Consortium on Revolutionary Europe, 1750–1850,* pp. 110–127 (1972); Duc de Castries, *La Vieille Dame du Quai Conti. Une Histoire de l'Académie française* (Paris, 1978); D. M. Robertson, *A History of the French Academy* (New York, 1910).

Robert Brown

Related entries: ACADEMY OF FINE ARTS; ACADEMY OF SCIENCES; AUGER; BALLANCHE; BALZAC; BAUDELAIRE; BAUSSET; BONALD; CAMBACERES; CHATEAUBRIAND; CONSTANT; COUSIN; DAUNOU; DAVID; FERRAND; FLAUBERT; GARAT; GAUTIER; GREGOIRE; GUIZOT; HUGO; LAINE; LAMARTINE; LAPLACE; MERIMEE; MICHAUD; MICHELET; MIGNET; MONTALEMBERT; MONTESQUIOU; MUSSET; NERVAL; NODIER; PEYRONNET; REMUSAT; REVOLUTION OF 1830; RICHELIEU; ROUSSEAU; ROYER-COLLARD; SAINTE-BEUVE; SALVANDY; SCRIBE; SIEYES; SOUMET; STENDHAL; THIERS; TOCQUEVILLE; VIGNY; VILLEMAIN.

ACADEMY OF FINE ARTS, the French academy of painting and sculpture, known also as the Académie royal de peinture et sculpture. Founded in 1648 and strengthened under Colbert (1661–83) and later under Charles le Brun (1683–90), the academy played a major role in taste and in the training of French artists. Under Louis XIV the academy held a virtual dictatorship over artists, requiring attendance and membership and allowing no life drawing outside its studios. Its main purpose was to school students in the accepted court style, classicism. In 1795 it was replaced by the Institut national des arts et sciences, which was to take the place of the old academies (Académie française, Académie des inscriptions et belles-lettres, Académie des sciences, Académie des sciences morales et politiques, and the Académie des beaux-arts). Initially the Institut had three classes (Sciences morales et politiques, Sciences, and Litterature et beaux-arts); in 1803 a fourth class was announced when the fine arts were separated from literature. The classes of the Institut were renamed ''académies'' with the return of the monarchy, but the Institut itself was kept, including the best French intellects from every category.

The Académie des beaux-arts received its definitive organization in 1819. There were five sections—painting, sculpture, engraving, music, and architecture—and forty members (who were also members of the Institut). Members held tremendous powers. They presented the candidates for new professorships at the *école*. They controlled the path to success with a variety of state commissions, a multitude of prizes, and coveted certificates. The Prix de Rome and the more important awards were given without exception to the most traditional artists, while all innovations were ignored. Most of the important painters of the nineteenth century attended the *école*, including Henri Matisse, Claude Monet, Edouard Manet, and Edgar Degas. Finally, under Napoleon III, Nieuwerkerke instituted a major reform in 1863. The reform resulted in a more varied program and less classical bias. Much of the academicians' authority over the *école* was removed during the Second Empire because of its earlier abuse and its stultifying effect on the development of art. The demand for art after this became so complex and taste so varied that art students found concentration on a single style absurd.

A. Boime, *The Academy and French Painting in the Nineteenth Century* (London, 1971); B. S. Myers, ed., *McGraw-Hill Dictionary of Art*, vol. 5 (New York, 1969); G. Norman, *Nineteenth-Century Painters and Painting: A Dictionary* (Berkeley, 1977); N. Pevsner, *Academies of Art: Past and Present* (Cambridge, England, 1940).

Irene Earls

Related entries: ACADEMIE FRANCAISE; ACADEMY OF SCIENCES.

ACADEMY OF SCIENCES, the official body of science originally founded under the patronage of the French crown in 1666, consisting of some seventy elected resident members, constituting an elite. The Académie royale des sciences of the *ancien régime* was restored in 1816, in place of the First Class of the

National Institute, which is what the official body of science had been called from 1796 to 1815. The membership of the First Class was continued with the notable exception of the Bonapartist Gaspard Monge. The government's decision to nominate to his place the royalist mathematician Augustin Cauchy caused indignation among the scientists, despite Cauchy's undisputed mathematical genius, since it bypassed the normal means of election and suggested political favoritism. Also the primacy of esteem held by the leading scientists as the First Class came to an end, and the Académie française (founded 1635) was given special privileges as the senior academy. The new royal academy also reintroduced the category of *académiciens libres*, or honorary academicians, who received no salary and were men of considerable social standing often chosen from the nobility. The Academy of Sciences continued its subdivision of scientists into eleven sections (Mathematics, Mechanics, Astronomy, and others).

Elections became more and more competitive in the nineteenth century as the size of the scientific community grew without any corresponding increase in the membership of the academy. Thus for the burgeoning science of chemistry, there were still only six places, the same as for the more static science of botany. Occasionally a chemist of broad interests might be elected to one of the other sections (such as Agriculture or Physics), but the general effect of the restricted number of places was to raise the age of election. Candidates submitted lists of their qualifications, and particularly their publications, and the section in which the vacancy occurred drew up a list of candidates in order of merit in preparation for the ballot of the full academy. Even the most able candidates usually had to submit to the election process several times before they were successful. Election to the academy came to be regarded as the ultimate accolade in a scientific career and could lead to further salaried appointments since the academy also acted as a nominating committee to several institutions of higher education. There was also the position of corresponding member, to which provincial and foreign scientists were elected. The greatest honor that the academy could bestow on a foreign scientist was to elect him as one of the eight *associés étrangers*.

The academy met regularly in the center of Paris on Monday afternoons. The meetings were widely reported, but not always accurately or sympathetically, and this helped to lead to the establishment in 1835 of the *Comptes rendus hebdomadaires des séances de l'Académie des sciences*, a weekly journal published by the academy itself, which created a major precedent in scientific publication and came to overshadow the annual volume of *Mémoires*, which the academy continued to publish in the eighteenth-century tradition. The leading figure in the establishment of the *Comptes rendus* was D. F. J. Arago (1786–1853), who had been elected one of the two permanent secretaries in 1830. Arago believed in bringing science to the people, but the *Comptes rendus* were even more effective in bringing the work of the Paris academy to the attention of scientists throughout the world. To receive recognition in France, research had to be presented to the academy and was automatically reported in its *Comptes rendus*. The academy followed the practice of appointing small commissions to examine major papers presented by nonmembers. These commissions often gave encouragement to promising young scientists but, with the ever-increasing number of memoirs presented, after the 1830s it became the exception rather than the rule to receive a report.

Another way in which the academy exercised the function of judgment of merit was in the award of prizes. Although some prize money was included in the annual budget of the academy, a substantial private legacy from Baron Montyon began to overshadow the official government-funded prizes and from the 1820s began to provide the academy not only with a series of large prizes, mostly relating to medicine, but also provided it with an independent source of income deriving from prize money not awarded. This was one of the ways in which the academy escaped the tight control of the Ministry of the Interior, or from 1824 the Ministry of Public Instruction, to which it was responsible. The minister had to approve its accounts, as well as its elections. Occasional political interference can be seen in some cases, such as that of the republican J. N. P. Hachette (1769–1834), elected in 1823, but whose election Louis XVIII refused to confirm. Hachette was finally accepted after reelection in 1831. In the 1820s the academicians François-Pierre-Charles Dupin and Louis-Jacques Thenard were members of the Chamber of Deputies, and in the 1830s Joseph Gay-Lussac and François Arago were elected to the Chamber. Thenard and Dupin were soon made peers, as were Gaspard-François de Prony and Siméon-Denis Poisson. Both Dupin (1834) and Arago (1848) briefly held ministerial rank. The academy included many senior civil servants with the rank of *inspecteur général* and also a few admirals and senior army officers. It therefore constituted something of a social elite as well as an intellectual elite. Many of its members were graduates of the Ecole polytechnique, and later, of the Ecole normale supérieure. The majority of the academicians were professors at one or more of the many Paris institutions of higher education. The elite was reinforced by intermarriage. There was some nepotism in the politics of the academy, as exemplified in such families as those of Alexandre Brongniart, Etienne-Geoffroy Saint-Hilaire, and Antoine-Laurent de Jussieu.

The academy had no laboratories in which scientific research could be carried out, but it served as the stage on which research done elsewhere could be presented and received. There were occasional vigorous debates, such as that between Georges Cuvier and Geoffroy Saint-Hilaire in March 1830 on Jean-Baptiste Lamarck's theory of transformism or evolution. The academy held an annual public meeting in which a report was often made on recent scientific developments and *éloges* were read of recently deceased academicians. The public meeting was also used to announce the results of prize competitions and the subjects for future prizes. It was through its prize competitions and its elections that the academy exercised greatest influence within the scientific community. It also gave technical advice to the government when asked. There was always the danger that the academy would be prejudiced in favor of established theories and not be fully receptive to new ideas. In some ways, therefore, it exercised a conservative influence on science, but there was always freedom of expression and even of publication. No major French scientist of the nineteenth century who lived a normal span of years failed to be elected.

M. P. Crosland, *Gay-Lussac, Scientist and Bourgeois* (London, 1978), "The French Academy of Sciences in the Nineteenth Century," *Minerva* 16 (1978), and *The Society of Arcueil* (London, 1967); E. G. Saunders, "The Archives of the Academie des Sciences," *French Historical Studies* 10 (1977–78); A. J. Tudesq, *Les Grands notables en France, 1840–1849*, 2 vols. (Bordeaux, 1964).

Maurice Crosland

Related entries: ACADEMIE FRANCAISE; ACADEMY OF FINE ARTS; ARAGO FAMILY; CAUCHY; CHAMBER OF DEPUTIES; CHAMBER OF PEERS; CUVIER; DUPIN, FRANCOIS-PIERRE-CHARLES; ECOLE POLYTECHNIQUE; GAY-LUSSAC; LAMARCK; MIGNET; MONGE.

L'ACCUSATEUR PUBLIC (June 1848), a radical republican newspaper founded in Paris by H. F. Alphonse Esquiros and published from 11 June to 25 June 1848. Alphonse Esquiros was a member of the Club de la Montagne; an ardent social republican; a former editor of *La Commune de Paris*, the journal of the Club of Clubs; and a member of Armand Barbès' Comité révolutionnaire. When *La Commune* fell to the wave of reaction following the demonstration of 15 May, Esquiros, who had attempted to rally the remnants of the Club Blanqui and the Club Raspail into a new Club du peuple, set up *L'Accusateur public*. He was assisted by his wife, Adèle Bettanchon, a radical feminist; Paul de Flotte; Pierre Lachambeaudie; and Pierre Bry.

In *L'Accusateur public* Esquiros and his associates attempted to keep alive the spirit of radical republicanism and to warn against the rising reaction, the policies of which they equated with those of François Guizot. Esquiros in *L'Accusateur public* advocated the social republic that would destroy privilege and liberate the workers. The paper's fourth and final issue appeared on 25 June.

J. P. van der Linden, *Alphonse Esquiros, De la bohème romantique à la république sociale* (Paris, 1948).

Bernard Cook

Related entries: CLUB OF CLUBS; *LA COMMUNE DE PARIS*; ESQUIROS; GUIZOT.

ACTE ADDITIONNEL, the constitution of Napoleon's restored Empire during the Hundred Days in 1815. At Lyons, on 10 March, while en route from Elba to Paris, Napoleon promised a new constitution. To avoid the delays involved in convoking a constituent assembly, he appointed to advise him a small committee on the constitution composed of notables of the Revolution and Empire, including Lazare-Nicholas-Marguérite Carnot, Jean-Jacques de Cambacérès, Michel-Louis-Etienne Regnault de Saint-Jean d'Angély, and Joseph Boulay de la Meurthe. But he chose a well-known liberal opponent, Benjamin Constant, to draft the new constitution in order to attract the support of bourgeois liberals, rather than to become the emperor of the Revolution by appealing to a more democratic and popular constituency. As he explained to Constant, "I do not wish to be the king of a *jacquerie*. . . . I am getting older; one is no longer at forty-five what he was at thirty. The repose of a constitutional king suits me, and it will suit my son even better."

In its main lines, the Acte additionnel resembled Louis XVIII's Constitutional Charter of 1814 more than the constitutions of the Consulate and Empire, and on the whole the Acte additionnel was more liberal than the Constitutional Charter. There was a hereditary Chamber of Peers, modeled after the English House of Lords, whose members were initially appointed by the emperor, with no limitation on numbers. Napoleon objected to a hereditary upper house but gave way to Constant's insistence on this point. The 629 members of the Chamber of Representatives were to be elected, 368 by arrondissement colleges and 238 by departmental colleges. The remaining 23 were special representatives to represent commerce and industry, to be elected by departmental colleges from lists submitted from 13 chambers of commerce. Representatives were to be at least twenty-five years old, and no property qualification was required, in contrast to the forty years and high property qualifications that the Constitutional Charter of 1814 required. Only the government could initiate legislation, which had to be drafted by the Conseil d'état. No taxes could be levied or monies borrowed without the approval of the chambers. The ownership of property confiscated during the Revolution was guaranteed to current holders. Freedom of the press, freedom of religion, and jury trials for criminal offenses were guaranteed. Judges were appointed for life and could not be removed.

Constant wanted to call his work simply "Constitution," but Napoleon wished to emphasize the continuity of the new regime with the Empire, so it was entitled "Acte additionnel aux constitutions de l'Empire." Like the constitutions of the Consulate and Empire, the Acte additionnel was submitted to a plebiscite for final approval, but the election of the Chamber of Representatives and the selection of the Chamber of Peers proceeded at the same time as the plebiscite. The number of eligible electors participating in arrondissement colleges and departmental colleges to elect members of the Chamber of Representatives was small, and liberals emerged with a large majority in the new chamber. The turnout for the plebiscite was also small, with only a little more than 1.3 million in favor and 4,206 against as compared with over 3.5 million votes cast in earlier plebiscites. Over 5 million eligible voters abstained. The small turnout reflected the unsettled conditions in many parts of the country, as well as apathy and opposition to the new regime. The chambers met on 3 June; on 21 June, three days after the battle of Waterloo, the Chamber of Representatives demanded the abdication of Napoleon, and they later recognized the succession of his son as Napoleon II in an effort to prolong the new regime.

I. Collins, *Napoleon and His Parliaments, 1800–1815* (London, 1979); B. Constant, *Mémoires sur les Cent-Jours* (Paris, 1829); J. Godechot, ed., *Les Constitutions de la France* (Paris, 1970); H. Houssaye, *1815* (Paris, 1893); E. LeGallo, *Les Cent Jours*

(Paris, 1923); L. Radiguet, *L'Acte additionnel aux Constitutions de l'Empire* (Caen, 1911); R. Warlomont, "La représentation économique dans l'Acte additionnel aux Constitutions de l'Empire (1815)," *Revue internationale d'histoire politique et constitutionnelle* (1954).

Charles E. Freedeman

Related entries: CAMBACERES; CARNOT, LAZARE-NICOLAS-MARGUERITE; CHARTER OF 1814; CONSTANT; COUNCIL OF STATE; HUNDRED DAYS; WATERLOO, BATTLE OF.

ADDITIONAL ACT. See ACTE ADDITIONNEL.

ADELAIDE, MADAME (EUGENE ADELAIDE LOUISE D'ORLEANS), also known as MADEMOISELLE D'ORLEANS (1777–1847); daughter of Philippe Egalité (Philippe, duc d'Orléans); sister and confidante of Louis-Philippe I. Born in Paris 25 August 1777, Adélaïde was one of twin girls. Her sister, Françoise, died in 1782. Adélaïde was entrusted to a governess, the comtesse de Genlis, her father's mistress. Young Adélaïde became close to Mme. de Genlis, who instilled liberal egalitarian doctrines in her charges. In the spring of 1789 Adélaïde became engaged to the duc d'Angoulême, the son of the comte d'Artois, but the engagement was broken during the summer of that year, in part because of the opposition of the king and queen. In October 1791 Mme. Genlis took Adélaïde to England, ostensibly to improve the latter's health by taking the waters at Bath. Adélaïde returned to Paris in November 1792 but was unable to obtain exemption from the laws on *émigrés*. Thus she and Mme. de Genlis went to Tournai in the Austrian Netherlands, and in April 1793 after the French defeat at Neerwinden they fled to Switzerland. They ultimately found shelter in the convent of Bremgarten. Subsequently separated from Mme. de Genlis by the intervention of Louis-Philippe, Adélaïde went to live with her great aunt, the princesse de Conti, in Fribourg in 1794. Then she moved to Bavaria, where she remained for two years before going to Pressburg, Hungary.

In November 1802 she joined her mother at Figuieres, Spain. But disillusioned by her mother's subservience to Rouzet de Folmont and none too fond of her anyway, Adélaïde found her brother and rejoined him at Portsmouth in 1808. Together they sailed for Sicily in October 1808, although she remained on Malta until September 1809.

Plain of visage, Adélaïde was nevertheless poised and dignified. She was gifted with a keen mind and a strong character, which she henceforth devoted to Louis-Philippe and quickly became a close adviser to him. She was present at his marriage on 25 November 1809 to Marie Amélie of Naples, with whom she initially enjoyed the friendliest of relations. After the defeat of Napoleon, Adélaïde followed her brother to Paris on 22 September 1814. They regained their home, the Palais Royal, where the wealth and size of the Orléans family quickly expanded and their popularity increased, as did their role of royal liberal opposition. Together they regained possession of the family estates that had not been sold. Adélaïde left Paris on 20 March 1815 for London, not for Ghent with Louis XVIII with whom there was now considerable enmity. She returned to Paris in April 1817, her role as social leader and political mastermind ever increasing. In 1821 her mother died, leaving a large legacy, one-third to Adélaïde and two-thirds to her brother. Their fortune was further increased by their inheritance from the duchesse de Bourbon in 1822. In 1824 Charles X granted the Orléans family the title "royal highness." Then in 1825 they jointly applied for and received compensation of 17 million francs for property they had lost during the Revolution, the largest settlement granted to any family.

Throughout the Restoration Adélaïde constantly advised her brother on political, legal, and financial interests. While he generally waited for time to bring him political opportunity, she actively prepared for it, cultivating useful contacts everywhere. She largely guided the Orléanist course during the 1830 July Revolution. While other members of the family vacillated, shortly after Charles X's ill-fated ordinances appeared on 26 July, Adélaïde saw the opportunity they presented and urged her brother to seize it. On 28 July when Adolphe Thiers went to Neuilly to sound Louis-Philippe on the offer of the crown, it was Adélaïde, in the absence of her brother, who committed the Orléans family to participating in the revolution. She and the princesses immediately set to sewing tricolor cockades, and she helped arrange the transformation of the lieutenant general of the kingdom into the king of the French. With the establishment of the July Monarchy, she worked to consolidate the king's position and popularize the new regime. She maneuvered to ensure the king's power against politicians such as Casimir Périer. She also undertook works of charity and reconstruction to aid the victims of the 1830 revolution.

As king, Louis-Philippe consulted her extensively on political and diplomatic affairs. Fully at home in high state affairs, her influence was significant in the handling of matters such as the Spanish and Portuguese uprisings, the Belgian succession in 1834, and the Spanish marriages in 1846. She also was the subject of some of the same vicious caricature and gossip that assailed the king, among the accusations being alcoholism and incest. In her later years she may have urged Louis-Philippe to adopt a more flexible political position.

For some years she had suffered from asthma and a heart condition, but her sudden and unexpected death on 31 December 1847 was a grievous personal blow to the king. Deprived of her counsel, he turned increasingly to the queen and to François Guizot for advice, with consequences that soon became disastrous.

R. Arnaud, *Adélaïde d'Orléans* (Paris, 1908); T. E. B. Howarth, *Citizen King, The Life of Louis-Philippe King of the French* (London, 1961); R. Recouly, *Louis-Philippe, roi des francais: le chemin vers le trone* (Paris, 1930).

James K. Kieswetter

Related entries: CHARLES X; FOREIGN POLICY OF LOUIS-PHILIPPE; GUIZOT; INDEMNITY BILL OF 1825; LOUIS XVIII; LOUIS-PHILIPPE; MARIE-AMELIE DE BOURBON; PERIER; REVOLUTION OF 1830; THIERS.

AFFRE, DENIS-AUGUSTE (1793–1848), archbishop of Paris. Affre was not the first choice of the king to succeed Hyacinthe-Louis de Quélen as archbishop of Paris in 1840. When the bishop of Arras turned down the appointment, Affre— as head of the vicar-generals and recently named *bishop in partibus*—was named to the post, perhaps as a consequence of his excellent speech made at the king's birthday celebration.

The bishop had been almost unknown outside clerical circles, although his family had pretensions of nobility. A simple, almost timid, priest, Affre had disagreed often with the legitimist Quélen, and his appointment was a blow to other legitimists, especially to those in high ecclesiastical offices. In 1840, of eighty bishops and archbishops, forty were members of noble families and twenty-eight were former *émigrés*. Thirty-eight had been appointed throughout the Restoration. Of these, twenty-six had been invested under Charles X.

Anticlerical violence marked the early days of the July Monarchy, but gradually the relationship between church and state improved. After 1840 Louis-Philippe had a policy of making ecclesiastical appointments more democratic. The Gallican Affre's appointment was thus a symbolic one. It was followed by those of sons of merchants, farmers, and lawyers.

In 1845 Monsignor Affre and Louis-Philippe backed the movement to disperse the Jesuits, and Affre wrote in secret to urge Pope Gregory XVI to break up the Congrégation. Although he had always been a supporter of the Jesuits, the weak pope gave in and issued the order for the closing of their houses and the dissolution of their novitiates. The orders were never fully carried out.

Affre and other Catholic liberals were involved in educational reform and freedom of instruction, although in 1844 he complained that in the universities, men of all religions, or no religion, were teaching. Protestants were teaching history, and Jews were teaching philosophy, he said. In 1845 Affre established a school for advanced instruction in the old Carmelite convent, opening with classes for six young men studying for the priesthood. Les Carmes evolved into the Institut catholique de Paris in 1875. In 1845, also, in an effort to deal with the lack of religion among workers, the archbishop started classes in history in the churches. That same year he founded a medical insurance company with 15,000 members.

Cognizant of the many social problems of his day, Affre hoped that the February Days of 1848 would bring about social change. The spirit of the revolutionaries was not altogether one of anticlericalism, and the new constitution declared that the Republic would guarantee religious freedom. The workers themselves, after sacking the Tuileries, took sacred items from the chapel to the Church of St. Roch, and the National Guard bore its colors to the archbishop for his blessing. Thus the church had a reason to back the Provisional Government, and Affre sang a *Te Deum* for the new order. The bishops and lower clergy followed suit in their praise of the Revolution, and the trees of liberty were planted everywhere and blessed by the prelates. In his pastoral letter of 3 March, Affre stated that Christ "neither commands nor prescribes any form of government.'' On 6 March he formally presented to Jacques-Charles Dupont de l'Eure, president of the Provisional Government, the support of his clergy.

In April 1848 the *Ère Nouvelle*, begun with the purpose of "reconciling the Church and democracy" and supported by the younger clerics, received the approval also of Affre, although the papal nuncio expressed his disapproval. As conditions for the proletariat worsened, the publication advocated social reforms, but the proposals were not generally accepted by the conservative clerics, who were concerned primarily with the salvation of their flocks and the preservation of order. The breach grew wider between church and workers, who poured into the streets, perhaps encouraged by troublemakers, when the National Workshops closed in June.

On 25 June the archbishop bravely set out with two vicars-general to talk to the insurgents in an attempt to bring about peace. He first went to seek the advice of General Eugène Cavaignac who had become the quasi-head of government. The general advised him of the danger and said he could not promise him any protection. Dressed in his purple robes, with a pectoral cross further identifying him, Affre made his way into the last stronghold of the insurgents. Although there was much tension in evidence, primarily because General François de Négrier had just been killed and a wounded deputy was dying, the archbishop managed to obtain the agreement of both factions to a truce. He was well received, and one report even says the soldiers and insurgents fraternized. But drumbeats resounding from another quarter were misinterpreted as marking the end of the truce, and firing began again.

The crowd was horrified when the peacemaker fell. It is believed that a shot fired by a member of the *garde mobile* hit the archbishop from behind and not one from the ranks of the workers since he was facing the insurgents at the time. He died the following day despite the tender care of many of the workers and soldiers.

L. Alazard, *Denis-Auguste Affre* (Paris, 1905); H. Daniel-Rops, *The Church in an Age of Revolution, 1789–1870*, trans. John Warrington (New York, 1965); G. Duveau, *1848: The Making of a Revolution*, trans. Anne Carter (New York, 1967); Le Marquis de Normanby, *Une Année de Revolution d'après un journal tenu à Paris en 1848*, vol. 2 (Paris, 1958).

Helen Castelli
Related entries: ANTICLERICAL CAMPAIGN; CAVAIGNAC, EUGENE; CONSTITUTION OF 1848; DUPONT DE L'EURE; *GARDE MOBILE*; JUNE DAYS; NATIONAL GUARD; NATIONAL WORKSHOPS; PROVISIONAL GOVERNMENT; QUELEN.

AGOULT, MARIE-CATHERINE-SOPHIE DE FLAVIGNY, COMTESSE D' (pseud. DANIEL STERN) (1805–1876), writer. Marie de Flavigny was born in Frankfort-am-Main to a French *émigré* viscount and the daughter of a German banker. Convent educated, she returned to France with her family at the Restoration and married the count of Agoult in 1827. A monarchist turned liberal, Agoult

ran a salon in Paris, which included Frédéric Chopin, Franz Liszt, and Nicolò
Paganini, until her support for the Revolution of 1830 led to her separation from
her husband in the same year. (Her only brother, Maurice, shared her liberal
sympathies and was raised to the peerage under the July Monarchy, later serving
as a deputy from Indre-et-Loire under the Second Republic and Napoleon III.)
In 1835, Agoult embarked on an affair with Liszt, which lasted, with interruptions,
until 1844. Following a quarrel and temporary separation in 1839, she took up
writing under the pseudonym Daniel Stern and published two novels (*Hervé* and
Valentia) and reviews of the Paris art salons between 1841 and 1843. Her German
background stimulated an interest in German romantic literature and philosophy,
and she wrote studies of Heine and Friedrich Freiligrath, and her *Etudes politiques
sur l'Allemagne* in the late 1840s.

Her growing enthusiasm for republican ideas was reflected in an *Essai sur la
liberté* (1846) and *Histoire de la Révolution de 1848* (3 vols., 1850–53), a good
contemporary account that attributed the revolution to a spontaneous union of
the common people and the bourgeoisie, based on the political traditions of the
Great Revolution and popular misery. Later works of fiction included the novel
Julien (1866) and a play about Joan of Arc (1857), and her history of republicanism
in the Low Countries was honored by the French Academy. Her memoirs (1877)
are a valuable source of information on French society and politics in her lifetime.
Agoult's daughter married Emile Ollivier.

G. de Bertier de Sauvigny, *La Restauration* (Paris, 1955, 1963); M.-C. d'Agoult,
Mémoires, 5th ed. (Paris, 1937); J. Vier, *La Comtesse d'Agoult et son temps*, 6 vols.
(Paris, 1955–63); T. Zeldin, *France 1848–1945*, vol. 1 (Oxford, 1973).

David Longfellow

Related entries: LISZT; OLLIVIER; REVOLUTION OF 1830; REVOLUTION
OF 1848.

AGRICULTURE. During the first half of the nineteenth century, France was
a rural country. Three-quarters of the population lived in communes with fewer
than 2,000 inhabitants. A majority of the population was employed in agriculture,
and the absolute number of farm workers grew as the period progressed. This
was a period of gradual agricultural progress in some regions of France and of
stagnation in others, but in no region was change dramatic.

As the size of urban areas grew, peasants in the rich grain-producing regions
were drawn more and more into production for the market. This was made
possible by two agricultural developments that were gradually adopted in the
more fertile regions. Traditional French agriculture was based on a three-field
rotation system, with peasants owning or working land in each of three zones.
The fields in each zone rotated together into spring grain, winter grain, and
fallow. During the fallow year, cattle and other animals grazed the land, fertilizing
it and improving its grain-producing ability for the following year. Grazing was
communal, and the fields in each zone were unenclosed. Landowners and tenants

were bound by communal decisions about when to plant and when to harvest the crops. Innovation was difficult and generally discouraged.

Between 1814 and 1852 some owners began to consolidate their landholdings and to enclose them, which allowed individual owners to participate in the agricultural revolution that had begun in England in the eighteenth century. The consolidated fields were fenced or hedged and closed to animal grazing. Then instead of rotating into fallow, they were planted with root crops (especially clover). Variations on the three-year rotation cycle were introduced. The clover or other crop could be mowed twice during the year and fed to stalled cattle. In autumn the owner's livestock could be turned out to pasture on it, and then it could be plowed under, a process that released nitrogen into the soil and increased the size of the following grain harvests.

Only peasants who could afford animals could participate in the new agriculture since it required much larger amounts of manure for fertilizer than traditional agriculture had. Once established, the artificial meadows or green fallow improved the size and health of livestock and allowed the consumption of meat to increase. Farmers who consolidated and enclosed their fields and planted artificial meadows gradually moved to more complicated crop rotations. In a properly chosen rotation each crop on a field used different nutrients and returned to the soil part of what the preceding crop had taken from it. These practices increased the size of the grain harvests, as well as the harvests of the alternating crops.

The major new crop to make advances during this period was the potato. Until the late eighteenth century the French regarded the potato as inedible. Following a serious grain shortage in 1793, however, it began to be accepted as a substitute for bread, and its cultivation spread slowly.

In areas of poor soil or isolation from urban areas, agricultural practices saw few advances. The difficulty of transporting grain into any area before the late 1840s and the arrival of the railroad meant that geographical specialization was impossible, and all regions tried to produce their own grain. In these areas peasants continued to use a three-field rotation system, with the land lying fallow every third year. Communal obligations remained strong, and the peasants remained poor. Farming was done on a subsistence basis, with families producing grain only for themselves since the land was not capable of producing grain surpluses and the market was inaccessible.

Rye was often the dominant crop in subsistence regions since it was the least demanding of the major cereals in its soil requirements. It needed less fertilizer, was more resistant to drought and excessive moisture in the soil, required less sunshine, could survive lower winter temperatures, provided more straw, and required less labor than wheat. In some areas a mixture of wheat and rye called *meteil* was sown, reducing the risk of a total crop failure from late frost if only wheat was planted.

The major innovations in planting, harvesting, and threshing occurred in the second half of the century. Before 1850 grain was still sown broadcast, harvested with sickles and scythes, and threshed with flails. In grain regions, agricultural work was highly seasonal. Enclosure created some new year-round jobs in agriculture but also increased the size of the harvest and the imbalance between harvest labor needs and off-season labor needs continued. Only in the vineyard regions of central and southwestern France was agricultural labor demand constant and year round.

There were no significant improvements in treating plant and animal diseases during this period, and peasants frequently watched their animals and crops suffer from sheep foot rot, hoof and mouth disease, potato blight, ergot, and other problems. Agronomists urged improvements throughout the period, but advances were slow. Those who wished to improve their cultivation were hampered not only by communal norms and local suspicions but also by the impossibility of borrowing money for less than usurious interest rates and difficult and expensive transportation of crops to markets.

J. Blum, *The End of the Old Order in Rural Europe* (Princeton, 1978); M. Morineau, *Les faux-semblants d'un démarrage économique* (Paris, 1971); J. W. Shaffer, *Family and Farm* (Albany, 1982); E. Weber, *Peasants into Frenchmen* (Stanford, 1976).

Gay L. Gullickson

Related entries: MIGRATION; PEASANTS; POPULATION.

AIDE-TOI, LE CIEL T'AIDERA, society formed to aid opposition candidates for election to the Chamber of Deputies, 1827–1834. Aide-toi, le ciel t'aidera (God helps those who help themselves) was an organization active from 1827 to 1834 in supporting opposition candidates for the Chamber of Deputies. It was directed by a central committee in Paris and operated through a network of local committees and agents throughout the country.

Young liberals in Paris associated with *Le Globe*, including François Guizot, Charles de Rémusat, and Odilon Barrot, organized the society in 1827 for the specific purpose of aiding liberal candidates and electors in contesting the government's efforts to keep their names off the ballot or off lists of electors. In the electoral campaign of 1827, the group published an elector's manual on the legal requirements for inclusion on lists and on procedures for formation and revision of lists, issued pamphlets, and organized meetings of voters. The increase in the liberal deputation in the chamber from fewer than twenty to nearly two hundred gave the founders reason to continue the organization.

In the winter of 1829–30, when apprehension grew among liberals over the plans of the Polignac ministry, Aide-toi alerted its members, and when the king dissolved the chamber in May 1830 and ordered new elections, Aide-toi was ready to direct the opposition's campaign. It concentrated on reelecting the 221 deputies who had voted in favor of the censorious reply to the royal address to the opening session on 2 March. The central committee reissued its elector's manual and with its affiliates in the provinces organized receptions for returning members of The 221 and made certain that no liberal rivals entered the races. Members personally solicited votes and provided transportation to electoral college meetings. The effectiveness of its efforts is suggested by the election results:

201 of The 221 were reelected, and the total of liberal deputies in the chamber rose to 270.

After the Revolution of 1830, the original directors of the society withdrew, and leadership passed to young republicans, including Godefroy Cavaignac, Etienne Garnier-Pagès, and Louis Blanc. Under their direction the society published pamphlets, distributed letters of political intelligence and advice to members, and furnished political articles to local newspapers. It took an active part in the election of 1834 but was severely handicapped by association in the public mind with the insurrections in Lyons and Paris earlier that year. A few weeks later the society, found in violation of the new Associations Law of 1834, was dissolved.

G. de Bertier de Sauvigny, *La Restauration* (Paris, 1955); S. Kent, *Electoral Procedure under Louis-Philippe* (New Haven, 1937), and *The French Election of 1827* (Cambridge, 1975); D. H. Pinkney, *The French Revolution of 1830* (Princeton, 1972); C. Pouthas, *Guizot pendant la Restauration: Préparation de l'homme d'état* (Paris, 1923).

David Pinkney

Related entries: BARROT; BLANC; CAVAIGNAC, G.; CHAMBER OF DEPUTIES; CHARLES X; GARNIER-PAGES; *LE GLOBE*; GUIZOT; LYONS, REVOLTS IN; POLIGNAC; REMUSAT; REVOLUTION OF 1830.

AIX-LA-CHAPELLE, CONGRESS OF, a meeting in October 1818 of the principal sovereigns and heads of government who had signed the 1815 treaties of Paris. The avowed purpose of the powers (France, Russia, Austria, Prussia, and Great Britain) meeting at the Congress of Aix-La-Chapelle was to decide if the military occupation of France, which had been imposed in order to guarantee the political stability of that country and the payment of war indemnities, should be lifted. By means of certain financial arrangements, the conference was able to inform the duc de Richelieu, representative of the king of France, that the occupation would end; indeed this decision had been reached before the conference met.

Although the conference was not supposed to take up other topics, it did discuss many other problems: quarrels among the German princes, the suppression of the slave trade, the repression of the Barbary pirates, and the fate of the Spanish colonies in America. But the most serious and delicate question concerned relations between France and the four major Allied powers of 1814. France asked for the dissolution of the Quadruple Alliance of 1815, which had been directed against itself, and its admission as an equal partner in the Concert of Europe. Austria and England, however, wanted to maintain the Quadruple Alliance in its original form as a guarantee against instability in France and also as a means of controlling Russian ambitions for hegemony. The solution was a compromise put forward by the English foreign secretary, Lord Castlereagh. The clauses of the Quadruple Alliance of 1815 aimed at keeping France under control were confirmed in a secret protocol, while at the same time France was officially invited to participate in all future meetings called under article 6 of the treaty to discuss the general interests of Europe. Thus the original four were replaced, at least as far as the public was concerned, by a kind of pentarchy whose mission harked back to the Congress of Vienna and whose inspiration was the Holy Alliance.

G. de Bertier de Sauvigny, *Metternich et la France après le Congrès de Vienne*, vol. 2 (Paris, 1968); C. K. Webster, *The Foreign Policy of Castlereagh*, vol. 2 (London, 2d ed., 1931).

Guillaume de Bertier de Sauvigny, trans. E. Newman

Related entries: HOLY ALLIANCE; PARIS, SECOND TREATY OF; QUAD-RUPLE ALLIANCE; QUINTUPLE ALLIANCE; RICHELIEU; VIENNA, CONGRESS OF.

ALBERT (1815–1895), pseudonym of ALEXANDRE MARTIN, "the worker," member of the provisional government of 1848. Born at Bury (Oise), son of a peasant, Alexandre Martin was apprenticed to his uncle, a machinist in Paris, and settled in the capital. Details are obscure, but under the alias Albert, he became active in the revolutionary movement, especially the new Society of the Seasons, which he led in the 1840s. He later wrote: "I have always been a revolutionary; I fought in June 1832; in 1834, on the rue Transnonain; in 1839, with Barbès; and, in 1848, I was . . . recognized head of the secret societies." He was no intellectual, however, and the claim by some biographers that he contributed anonymously to *L'Atelier*, the workers' newspaper, is unfounded.

In February 1848, Albert was a tool-and-dye maker in a button manufactory. His reputation as a genuine proletarian and a veteran of the republican cause earned him a place in the Provisional Government. The crowd gathered at the offices of *La Réforme* on 24 February put forward his name, which Louis Blanc added to the radical list imposed on the moderates of *Le National*, already meeting as a government at city hall. Albert's inclusion was a symbol of popular sovereignty and a promise of social reform.

Albert demonstrated common sense and modesty in his new role but he had little influence within the government. He rarely spoke up at meetings and usually voted with Louis Blanc. He headed the Commission on National Compensation, created to reward political victims of the July Monarchy, and served as Louis Blanc's vice-president on the Luxembourg Commission. The Seine Department elected Albert to the Constituent Assembly on 23 April 1848, but on 15 May he joined the popular insurrection against the Assembly, leaving his seat to march with the crowd to city hall, where he and Armand Barbès signed the proclamation of a new provisional government. Arrested that evening and imprisoned at Vincennes, he was later tried before the high court at Bourges (7 March–2 April 1849) for his attempts "to change or destroy the government" and "to foment civil war." He refused to defend himself. He was condemned on both counts and sentenced to deportation. He spent four years on Belle-Ile, then, after falling sick, five years in prison at Tours.

Amnestied in 1859, Albert returned to Paris and found work as an inspector for the gas company. He took no part in politics during the Second Empire, since he would take no oath of loyalty to Napoleon III. He failed in bids for election to the National Assembly in February 1871 and the Senate in 1879. His name made the newspapers once more in 1884 when an adventurer, claiming to be the real Albert, sued him as a fraud. The court affirmed Albert's right to his identity. He died in retirement at Mello (Oise). The Third Republic gave him a national funeral and paid for a monument over his grave.

Albert (letters from), to *Le Moniteur*, May 5, 1848, and *Le Figaro*, May 22, 1895; M. Alhoy, *Biographie parlementaire des représentants du peuple à l'Assemblee nationale constituante de 1848* (Paris, 1848); A. Bataille, "Les trois Alberts," in his *Causes criminelles et mondaines de 1884* (Paris, 1885); L. de la Hodde, *Histoire des sociétés secrètes et du parti republicain de 1830 à 1848* (Paris, 1850); *La République au donjon de Vincennes: Biographies d'Albert, Barbès, Raspail* (Paris, 1848).

Michael Sibalis

Related entries: L'ATELIER; BARBES; BLANC; CLUBS, POLITICAL; CONSTITUTION OF 1848; LUXEMBOURG COMMISSION; *LE NATIONAL*; PROVISIONAL GOVERNMENT; *LA REFORME*; REPUBLICANS; REVOLUTION OF 1848; SOCIALISM; SOCIETY OF THE SEASONS; TRANSNONAIN, MASSACRE OF THE RUE.

ALBIN, SEBASTIEN. See CORNU.

L'ALBUM (1821–1823), satirical and literary magazine in opposition to the Restoration government. This first *Album* was founded by Jean-Joseph Magallon in July 1821 as a literary magazine, but from the start it emphasized political attacks on the regime, always satirical and often bold. In 1823 Magallon was indicted under the law of 9 June 1819, which had been designed to trap such "little" magazines. Among his offenses was ridicule of the unpopular military campaign in Spain. Although his sentence was only three months and a heavy fine, Magallon became a liberal martyr for the treatment he received: arrested during the night and chained with a galley convict as he went to prison. His magazine lapsed but was reborn as *L'Ancien album* five years later. A close collaborator on both *Albums* was L. M. Fontan.

A. Germain, *Martyrologie de la presse* (Paris, 1861); C. Ledré, *La presse à l'assaut de la monarchie* (Paris, 1960); D. Rader, *The Journalists and the July Revolution* (The Hague, 1973).

Daniel Rader

Related entries: L'ANCIEN ALBUM; SPAIN, 1823 FRENCH INVASION OF.

ALGIERS, EXPEDITION TO (May–July 1830), the first step in the French colonization of Algeria. Algiers in 1830 was a tributary state of the Ottoman Empire. Officially termed a regency, Algiers was governed by a *dey*, chosen by the militia (*odjaq*) and janissaries of the capital. Although the *dey's* authority was confirmed by the sultan in Constantinople, Algiers was largely autonomous, and its rulers governed the capital and the subordinate territories (*beyliks* of Titeri, Constantine, and Mascara) through appointed governors (*beys*) who sought the cooperation of the chieftans (*douads*) of the indigenous tribes. Changes in rulers tended to be abrupt (half of the twenty-eight *deys* since 1515 had been assassinated), and the central authority was regularly menaced by conspiracies, tribal revolts, and outbreaks of Muslim fanaticism. Although the *dey* controlled the military and collected taxes, the source of Algiers's wealth in the early nineteenth century remained piracy, the principal activity of powerful coastal *reis* (captains), and the resulting trade in captives (more than 35,000 after 1800), ransoms, and tribute paid by other states seeking to purchase immunity for their merchant ships. Although piracy was declining in the first decades of the century, it remained an indispensable source of income, and treaties (with the United States in 1815), bombardments of the capital (by the English in 1816 and 1824), and Spanish invasions had failed to stop it entirely. In 1815, seven European states still paid annual tribute to the *deys* to protect their Mediterranean commerce.

The finances of the regency were largely controlled by Livornese Jewish families, who were resented by the governing Turkish minority and occasionally killed in outbreaks of popular violence that resulted in the pillage of the Jewish quarter of the city. Between 1804 and 1830 the regency was increasingly threatened by tribal uprisings and revolts by Islamic sects, never entirely repressed, and the authority of the *deys* (Hadj Mohammed ibn Ali [1815–17], Ali ibn Ahmed [1817–18] and Hussein ibn Hassan [1818–30]) became steadily more fragile.

In 1796, two wealthy Jewish merchants, Baki and Busnach, contracted with the Directory to supply France with wheat, which was largely drawn from government reserves in the *beyliks* and not from individual merchants. The debt remained unpaid until the Restoration, which fixed it at 7 million francs and received authorization to make payment from the Chamber in 1820. French merchants owed money by Baki and Busnach then sued for the payment of 5 million francs, and the French consul in Algiers (Deval) explained to the *dey* that these debts would be settled out of the repayment, with the balance going to the regency, a policy that both confused and annoyed Hussein.

On 30 April 1827, at the end of the Islamic holy days of Ramadan, Deval requested an interview with the *dey* to ask for the release of a French-flag ship (owned by a resident of the Papal States) recently captured by Algerian pirates. The *dey*, angered by the French position on the debt and by the blockade of Algerian ships supporting the Turkish effort to repress the Greek war of independence by British, Russian, and French warships, struck Deval three times with his flywhisk and poured out his grievances. On 11 June, French warships evacuated the French citizens living in Algiers, and the government of Charles X declared a blockade of Algerian ports. The Villèle ministry rejected calls for more aggressive action. The blockade was expensive, and the liberal opposition in the Chamber regularly criticized its cost, but negotiations brought no settlement, and on 9 August 1829 Algerian gunners fired on a French frigate carrying delegates under a flag of truce. The Polignac ministry (October 1829) discussed punitive action, with the minister of the navy (Charles de Haussez) urging an invasion. Efforts to apply pressure on the *dey* through the sultan or by the use of Egyptian troops under Mehemet Ali having failed, the ministry authorized an expeditionary force in December.

Haussez and Louis-Auguste-Victor de Bourmont (minister of war) revived plans made under the Empire and overcame opposition from naval and army officers and by May 1830 had organized a fleet of 100 warships, 500 transports, and 37,000 troops in Mediterranean ports. A circular letter to the major powers stressed the punitive nature of the expedition, though English demands that the French disavow any intention of conquering or colonizing Algeria were fended off without direct answers. In fact, French goals were unclear. Public statements by the ministers stressed insults to the French flag, the freeing of Christian captives and stopping piracy, but the possibility of capturing an estimated 150 million francs in the *dey's* treasury and displaying energy in foreign policy clearly played a role. There was little domestic support for the expedition (French merchants were largely uninterested), but it does not appear to have been launched as a deliberate distraction from Charles's domestic political problems.

The French forces (under Bourmont's direct command) sailed on 25–27 May and landed (after delays caused by storms) on the peninsula of Sidi-Ferruch (12 miles from Algiers) on 14–16 June. After a victory in the field on 19 June, the French laid siege to the city, which capitulated on 4 July. Hussein surrendered the regency and left with his family, while the French gained political control and seized about 48 million francs in treasure at a cost of 415 dead. The success of the operation may have strengthened Charles's resolve in his struggle with the liberal opposition at the end of July, but it fell to the provisional government (the Marquis de Lafayette, Adolphe Thiers, François Guizot, and Casimir Périer) to decide on French occupation for the immediate future.

Between 1830 and 1834, the July Monarchy imposed a restrained occupation limited to the coastal cities and implemented by a series of military governors (Bertrand Clausel, Jean-Marie de Savary, Pierre Berthezène, and Jean-Baptiste Drouet d'Erlon). An "arab bureau" was created to negotiate with tribal chieftains, but there was no coherent policy before the Muslim revolt led by Abd-el-Kader, which broke out in 1834. The subsequent pacification campaign in the interior (1834–47), brought to a successful conclusion by General Thomas-Robert Bugeaud, extended French control, brought in 100,000 European settlers by 1846, and transformed Algeria into a French colony.

G. de Bertier de Sauvigny, *La Restauration* (Paris, 1955, 1963); P. Boyer, *L'évolution de l'Algérie médiane de 1830 à 1856* (Paris, 1960); H. Celarie, *La prise d'Alger* (Paris, 1929); J. Debu-Bridel, *La guerre qui paye: Alger, 1830* (Paris, 1930); M. Emerit, "Une cause de l'expédition d'Alger," *Actes* du 79e congrès national des sociétés savantes (Algiers, 1954); G. Gautherot, *La conquête d'Alger, 1830*, Bourmont papers (Paris, 1929); C. d'Haussez, *Mémoires*, 2 vols. (Paris, 1896–97); C.-A. Julien, *Histoire de l'Algérie contemporaine*, vol. 1: *Conquête et colonisation* (Paris, 1964); H. Nouguères,

L'expédition à Alger, 1830 (Paris, 1962); P. Serval, *La ténébreuse histoire de la prise d'Alger* (Paris, 1980).

David Longfellow

Related entries: BOURMONT; BUGEAUD; HAUSSEZ; HUSSEIN; MEHE-MET; POLIGNAC; PROVISIONAL GOVERNMENT; VILLELE.

ALMANACH ROYAL, official publication listing government officials, government organizations, ruling family members, French and foreign diplomats, high clergy, and other notables. Beginning as an unofficial work in 1636, the *Almanach royal* became the official compendium of government data in 1700. From 1700 to 1792 it was known as the *Almanach royal* and from 1793 to 1804 the *Almanach national de France.* In 1805 it appeared under the title *Almanach royal,* and from 1806 to 1813 it was the *Almanach impérial.* From 1814 to 1830 it reverted to *Almanach royal,* becoming the *Almanach royal et national* from 1831 to 1847. From 1848 to 1852 it was entitled *Almanach national annuaire de la république française.* In 1853 it became again the *Almanach impérial* until 1870. From 1872 on it appeared as the *Almanach national.*

During the early nineteenth century the *Almanach* was usually published early in the year of its title; thus, the *Almanach* for 1818 reflected changes through 1817 and perhaps the very early weeks of 1818. The *Almanach* usually began with a calendar, followed by a section on the French royal family, the royal failies of other European countries, cardinals of the church, foreign ambassadors in France and French ambassadors abroad, and the members of the households of the various French royal princes and princesses. The section on the government included the members of the councils and the chambers, the various ministries and their internal organization and personnel, the Academy, and so forth. Also included might be a section on the administration of Paris and other such miscellany as currency exchange rates, weights and measures, and the etiquette of mourning. Each ministerial section listed the jurisdiction and duties of the ministry, its internal organization and personnel, and the personnel in the field. Thus the sections on the Ministry of the Interior listed not only the more important personnel in Paris but also the bishops, archbishops, and even parish priests for Paris, the Protestant clergy throughout France, the members of the various councils of the ministry, the prefects and subprefects of each department, all mayors appointed by the king, the administration and faculty of the various colleges and academies, the administrators and engineers of the department of roads and bridges, the members of the various orders such as the Order of the Holy Ghost and the Legion of Honor, and other groups under the jurisdiction of the ministry. Thus the *Almanach,* which is usually cataloged under the classification of *Almanach national,* is an invaluable source of information on the organization and personnel of the French government, as well as containing various other useful items such as currency exchange rates.

James K. Kieswetter

ALTON-SHEE, EDMOND DE LIGNERES, COMTE D' (1810–1874), left-wing aristocrat and political reformer. Alton-Shée entered the Chamber of Peers in 1836 but became increasingly critical of the July Monarchy. He was one of the leaders of the reformist banquets that preceded the Revolution of February 1848. He became a colonel in the National Guard during the Second Republic. After 1870 he founded two left-wing newspapers, *Le Peuple souverain* and *Le Suffrage universel*.

E. Alton-Shée, *Mémoires* (Paris, 1868).

Douglas Porch

Related entries: BANQUET CAMPAIGN; CHAMBER OF PEERS; NATIONAL GUARD; REVOLUTION OF 1848.

L'AMI DE LA CHARTE, liberal and anticlerical newspaper of the Restoration. In 1814 a local printer, Victor Mangin, founded at Nantes a news sheet to carry notices of local events. During the freer atmosphere of 1819, a group of local politicians turned Mangin's *Feuille d'annonces* into a liberal newspaper with the title *L'Ami de la charte*. When censorship was established in 1820, the paper found itself in difficulties but learned to show sufficient moderation to survive. During the ultraroyalist ministry of Joseph de Villèle the paper showed extreme anticlerical tendencies and was the source of some of the information reproduced in the *Constitutionnel*, which led to the latter's famous trial in 1825. *L'Ami* played an important part in the elections of 1827 and 1830; having established local editorship committees at Rennes and Angers, it also opened consultative bureaux for electors in those two towns, as well as at Nantes. It had thus become a truly regional paper, and during the July Monarchy it appropriately took the title *Le National de l'Ouest*.

C. Bellanger et al., *Histoire générale de la presse francaise*, vol. 2 (Paris, 1969); S. Fizaine, *La Vie politique dans la Côte d'Or sous Louis XVIII* (Dijon, 1931); F. Libaudière, ''La presse à Nantes sous la Restauration,'' *Annales de la Société Académique de Nantes* (1903).

Irene Collins

Related entries: ANTICLERICAL CAMPAIGN; CENSORSHIP; *LE CONSTITUTIONNEL*; ELECTIONS AND ELECTORAL SYSTEMS; ULTRA-ROYALISTS; VILLELE.

AMI DE LA RELIGION ET DU ROI (1816–1824), only regularly issued Catholic periodical, ultramontane and pro-Jesuit. During the reign of Louis XVIII, *Ami de la religion* was the principal magazine of the clerical ultra faction. Although it had a very small list of subscribers, its attacks on the "revolutionary atheism" of the opposition served as grist for liberal journalists in their continuing exposure of a *parti-prêtre* and an alleged Jesuit conspiracy.

E. Hatin, *Histoire de la Presse*, vol. 8 (Paris, 1859–61).

Daniel Rader

Related entries: JESUITS; ULTRAMONTANES; ULTRAROYALISTS.

L'AMI DU PEUPLE EN 1848, democratic-socialist newspaper of 1848. On 6 March 1848 the Provisional Government of the Second Republic abolished or suspended almost all the restraints that the previous regime had placed on the press, including the need to deposit caution money. In Paris, over a hundred newspapers appeared within a few weeks. Many were produced by amateur politicians who had also founded political clubs. In spite of their cheapness, they could not compete with the more popular professional newspapers, and many disappeared after a few days. *L'Ami du peuple*, whose title deliberately evoked memories of the more radical trends in the Revolution of 1789, was one of the few that lasted throughout the year. Its success was mainly due to the vigor of its editor François Raspail, who was also president of a democratic socialist club of the same name.

P. H. Amann, *Revolution and Mass Democracy: The Paris Club Movement in 1848* (Princeton, 1975); H. Izambard, *La Presse Parisienne: statistique bibliographique et alphabetique* (Paris, 1853).

Irene Collins

Related entries: CLUBS, POLITICAL; PROVISIONAL GOVERNMENT; RASPAIL.

AMIS DE LA LIBERTE DE LA PRESSE. See SOCIETY OF FRIENDS OF THE FREEDOM OF THE PRESS.

AMIS DE LA VERITE, SOCIETE DES. See SOCIETY OF THE FRIENDS OF TRUTH.

AMNESTY BILL OF 1816, effective 12 January 1816, this law specified who would and, most important, who would not receive amnesty from the Bourbon government for their activities during the Hundred Days. After Waterloo but before his return to France, Louis XVIII found himself pressured, especially by those extreme royalists at his court who viewed the successful return of Napoleon Bonaparte as both a result of royal leniency during the First Restoration and a Bonapartist conspiracy, to issue a statement vowing punishment to all those who had chosen once again to serve the emperor. While a first royal proclamation issued at Cateau-Cambrésis threatened only in the vaguest terms, military and civilian leaders who had joined the Napoleonic cause during the Hundred Days, a second and more important statement, drafted with the aid of Talleyrand and proclaimed by Louis XVIII at Cambrai on 28 June 1815, promised a pardon for service during the Hundred Days to all Frenchmen who had joined the imperial cause after 23 March 1815 and who had abandoned it before 28 June 1815; excluded from any hope of a pardon were those thought to have made the Hundred Days possible. Bowing to additional pressure from an aroused public opinion and from the victorious Allies, especially the British, Louis XVIII abandoned the prudent idea of postponing the issuance of a more specific statement on the question of amnesty until the two chambers could meet.

He appointed Joseph Fouché (1759–1820), once minister of police under the First Empire who had rallied to the emperor during the Hundred Days and now again minister of police, to draw up a list of those responsible for Napoleon's return to France. Fouché, probably selected by Louis XVIII for this task because the king did not favor a massive purge, sought at first to avoid sole responsibility for compiling this list while nonetheless agreeing that the issuance of such a list was necessary, if only to quiet rumors that greatly exaggerated the potential number of proscribed and to check a flood of arrests in the south of France. The resulting amnesty decree of 24 July 1815, more important as an indicator of the limits of amnesty than as a statement of royal leniency, was in effect an indictment for treason of fifty-seven men who had served Napoleon in either a military or civilian capacity before 23 March or after 8 July 1815. Of the fifty-seven, nineteen were military officers who, the government claimed, had used violence to overthrow royal authority; most prominent of the men on this list was Marshal Michel Ney. In the second category came thirty-eight civilian and military leaders, all charged with making public statements advocating the emperor's return; ordered to quit Paris, these men were placed under police supervision. Fouché, to give credit where it is due, did much to assist the nineteen officers charged with treason in fleeing France. Marshal Ney, who had refused to flee, was captured, returned to Paris, and tried before the Chamber of Peers in November and December 1815. Convicted of treason, he was shot on 7 December 1815.

The duc de Richelieu, concerned about royalist excesses in southern France and availing himself of public disgruntlement with the Ney execution and of a decline in the thirst for vengeance, introduced on 7 December a generous amnesty bill. Supported by Louis XVIII, it pardoned all Frenchmen who had taken part in the Hundred Days, except the fifty-seven named in the decree of 24 July 1815, members of the Bonaparte family, and those against whom criminal proceedings had already begun. The ultraroyalists who dominated the so-called Chambre introuvable evinced considerable displeasure at the government's proposal. In fact, a committee of the Chamber of Deputies had been meeting secretly since mid-November in an effort to formulate a harsh bill. In these discussions, the ultraroyalist François de la Bourdonnaye (1767–1839) took a leading role, proposing on 10 November that a significantly larger group be excluded from amnesty. To be denied amnesty and to face the death penalty were all who had corresponded with the exiled emperor with the intent of assisting his return, military officers, prefects, and others who had accepted ministerial appointments prior to 23 March, and generals who had led troops against royalist forces during the Hundred Days. In keeping with the procedures of the Chamber, Richelieu's bill was referred to a committee, from which it was reported out, despite heavy lobbying by Richelieu, carrying not only amendments reflecting La Bourdonnaye's views but two additional ones: an exclusion of all regicides from amnesty and a provision making these men financially responsible for the cost of the Hundred Days. Estimates of the number of Frenchmen affected by the chamber's bill varied widely, ranging from some 850 to over 1,200. Debate on this controversial amnesty bill took place on 2–6 January 1816; before it was over, fifty-four deputies had spoken either for or against the bill. The final vote came on 6 January. Passage of articles 1 and 2 posed no problem, for they confirmed the exemptions from amnesty included in the decree of 24 July 1815 and exiled the Bonaparte family and its descendants in perpetuity. When the question of La Bourdonnaye's amendments arose, a clever parliamentary maneuver by the moderate deputy Jean-Marie Duvergier de Hauranne forced a vote that resulted in their rejection by a mere nine votes. On the question of exemption from amnesty for regicides who had joined Napoleon, Richelieu and the government had to back down and accept it. However, the proposal that held these men financially responsible for the cost of the Hundred Days failed. Following acceptance of the amnesty bill by the crown and its passage by the Chamber of Peers, it became law on 12 January 1816.

Estimates of the impact of the amnesty bill vary. Henry Houssaye noted that of the nineteen soldiers named in the first category of the decree of 24 July, fifteen were condemned to death, that of the thirty-nine named in the second category, all (or almost all) went into exile, and that of the regicides, most left France. Further, ultraroyalists, disappointed at the leniency of the amnesty bill, pressured the minister of war to expedite judicial proceedings against some thirteen officers to ensure that they would not be granted amnesty; seven of these men ultimately received a sentence of death.

The bitter controversy occasioned by the amnesty bill raised a major constitutional question to which the Charter of 1814 supplied no ready answer, thus engendering in the press a curious debate over the nature of the new constitution: in the case of an unresolvable conflict between the will of the king and his ministers and the will of the chambers, to which branch of the government belongs the final authority? Had the debate been conducted according to widely accepted political principles, the liberals would have argued in favor of the chambers, and the ultraroyalists would have championed the prerogatives of the crown. However, since the ultras controlled the Chambre introuvable and since Louis XVIII favored moderation, both sides in the debate reversed their customary positions and, despite attempts to clothe their rhetoric in the guise of principle, argued on no other base than political expediency. These debates supplied a foretaste of many Restoration political controversies to come.

Archives parlementaires de 1787 à 1860, 2ème série, vol. 15 (Paris, 1859); H. Houssaye, *1815: La seconde abdication—La terreur blanche* (Paris, 1905); D. Resnick, *The White Terror and the Political Reaction after Waterloo* (Cambridge, Mass., 1966).

Robert Brown

Related entries: CHAMBER OF DEPUTIES; CHAMBER OF PEERS; CHAMBRE INTROUVABLE; CHARTER OF 1814; FOUCHE; HUNDRED DAYS; LA BOURDONNAYE; NEY; RICHELIEU; TALLEYRAND; ULTRAROYALISTS.

AMPERE, ANDRE-MARIE (1775–1836), scientist, physicist, mathematician, chemist, botanist, and philosopher after whom the international unit of electrical current is named. Ampère, born in Lyons and raised in the nearby village of Poleymieux-les-Mont-d'Or, was a child prodigy. By age twelve he had mastered all known mathematics and by fourteen had read all twenty volumes of the *Encyclopedia* of Diderot and d'Alembert. At age eighteen he developed a universal language. That same year, 1793, his father, a moderately wealthy retired merchant, was guillotined for his cooperation with the Lyons resistance to the Revolutionary Paris government.

In 1801 Ampère was named professor of chemistry and physics at Bourg. The next year he wrote his first scientific work, *Considerations on the Mathematical Theory of Games*. In 1804 he was a professor of mathematics and astronomy at Lyons and two years later became secretary of the Bureau of Arts and Sciences. He became professor of mathematical analysis and mechanics at the Ecole polytechnique in 1809 and in 1814 was elected to the Royal Institute of France for his work in geometry. Also in 1814 he independently developed Avogadro's hypothesis: that the number of molecules of any gas at a given temperature and pressure is proportional to the volume.

In 1820 Ampère heard of the discovery by the Danish physicist Oersted that a magnetic needle is deflected by an electric field. Within a week Ampère wrote the first of several papers on this phenomenon, including a mathematical description of the force between two currents. This is known as Ampère's law and was restated by Maxwell: the line integral of the magnetic field around an arbitrary path is proportional to the net electric current enclosed by the path. Ampère also explained and predicted other electrodynamic phenomena and is considered the founder of the science of electromagnetism. In 1826 he wrote *The Theory of Electrodynamic Phenomena Based Exclusively on Experiment*.

Inventions that Ampère made or improved on include the electromagnet, the galvanometer, and the commutator. He proposed an electric telegraph in which each letter was to be represented by a particular strength of current.

Ampère married twice. His son by his first wife, Jean-Jacques (1800–64), became a prominent historian and writer. The death of his first wife, Julie Carron, in 1804 is said to have plunged Ampère into a depression that lasted the rest of his life.

There are several legends that, if true, show Ampère as a true absent-minded professor. He is said once to have picked up a pebble in the road, examined it, checked the time, and then tossed his watch into a river while putting the pebble back in his pocket. Another time while waiting in a station, he suddenly thought of a possible answer to a mathematical problem he had been pondering. Pulling chalk from his pocket he wrote several formulas on the nearest flat surface. Unfortunately the horse-drawn bus he was writing on the side of pulled away before he reached the solution. Another time he challenged the credentials of a man sitting with the French Academy. The man turned out to be the Emperor Napoleon, who was not offended but even invited Ampère to have dinner with him and the empress the next night. Ampère accepted but forgot to go.

"La Oeuvre et la vie d'Ampere," *Revue général de l'electricité* (November 1922).

Don Smith

Related entries: ACADEMIE FRANCAISE; ECOLE POLYTECHNIQUE.

L'ANCIEN ALBUM (1828–1829), satirical and literary magazine, successor to the earlier *L'Album* of J. Magallon. The later *Album* was called *L'Ancien Album* and subtitled *Tribune of the Literary Opposition*. It emerged in the world of little journals (literary-cum-satirical magazines) in November 1829. Its coeditors, as in the first version, were Joseph Magallon and Louis-Marie Fontan. Despite recent passage of a more lenient press law, the second *Album* was to experience among the harshest prosecutions of any other periodical of the Restoration. Magallon, as owner, was sentenced (February 1829) to a year in prison for an editorial in praise of Karl Sand, executed assassin of Kotzebue in Germany, and a martyred tyrannicide to liberals since 1819. The editor's crime was defined as glorification of a murderer. Magallon again lost in an appeal trial where it became obvious that the rescinded tendency law was the basis of the prosecution. The actual writer of the piece was jailed for only two months. Magallon was taken from prison in July to stand trial for two *Album* articles. One had denounced the foreign minister, Joseph-Marie Portalis, for extraditing an Italian patriot back to Naples and certain death. In this case, Magallon was given a token fine, and Fontan, the author, only fifteen days. The judge even upheld the general right of citizens to criticize royal ministers. On another charge, both men were acquitted.

After this near victory, the *Ancien album*, now under Fontan's direction, grew even more rash and provocative. When Jules-Armand de Polignac's ministry was chosen, the journal on 10 August 1829 predicted not only a royal violation of the charter but a holocaust in Paris when the people would rise to resist the coup. This bold editorial appeared in spite of another recent conviction and unprecedented punishment of Fontan. A transparently artless satire, "The Mad Ram," had appeared in the 20 June issue. Fontan had depicted a ram amid his sheep and ewes, a ram who is growing increasingly mad and whose attempts at dominance fail because he has "only sheep's blood" in his veins. The ram's name is Robin. Charles X's popular nickname was Robin Hood. Mad rams, Fontan concluded, are put to death. For direct offense to the king's person, Fontan was ordered to five years in prison, five years of exile, and a fine of 10,000 francs, enough to justify seizure of the journal. Young Fontan's grandly aloof behavior during his trial may have weighted his penalties. Although he managed to flee to Belgium, he grew so depressed there that he returned to Paris to be incarcerated. Much was made of his treatment by the opposition because of his youth, as well as the generally lenient justice toward humorists. For example, in 1830, the *Silhouette*'s publisher received only a six-month term for Philipon's portrait of Charles X with fangs and wearing a Jesuit's collar.

A. Germain, *Martyrologie de la presse* (Paris, 1861); C. Ledré, *La presse a l'assaut de la monarchie* (Paris, 1960); D. Rader, *The Journalists and the July Revolution* (The Hague, 1973).

Daniel Rader

Related entries: L'ALBUM; CHARLES X; CHARTER OF 1814; POLIGNAC; PRESS LAWS; *LA SILHOUETTE.*

ANGOULEME, LOUIS-ANTOINE DE BOURBON, DUC D' (1775–1844), eldest son of King Charles X. After living with his father as an *émigré* in England, he left in the spring of 1814 to join Wellington's army, which was pushing across the Pyrenees into France. Under the protection of that army, he was able on 12 March 1814 to have the restoration of the Bourbons proclaimed in Bordeaux, a proclamation that greatly influenced the decisions of the Allies when they entered Paris at the end of that month. When Napoleon returned to France in March 1815, the duc d'Angoulême was given the task of organizing royalist resistance in the south of France, and he did this courageously and well. In 1823 he commanded the French army sent to Spain to reestablish the absolute power of Ferdinand VII, the king of Spain. When his father became king of France, the duc d'Angoulême became the dauphin, heir to the throne.

The 1830 Revolution sent him into exile once again. When Charles X died, though the majority of legitimists recognized his grandson, Henry V, as his heir, the duc d'Angoulême took the title of Louis XIX because he believed that the act of abdication signed by Charles X at Rambouillet in July 1830 had become null and void. Although he had been held back by an inferiority complex and although his looks never worked to his advantage, the duc d'Angoulême was nevertheless a man of common sense, moderation, and generosity. He had married his cousin, the daughter of Louis XVI, and they had no children.

R. Dugourg, *Le 12 mars à Bordeaux* (La Rochelle, 1930); E. de Guichen, *Le duc d'Angoulême* (Paris, 1909); O. Monge, *La campagne du duc d'Angoulême dans le Vaucluse (mars-avril 1815)* (Avignon, 1894); J. Sarrailh, *Le duc d'Angoulême en Espagne* (Paris, 1930).

Guillaume de Bertier de Sauvigny, trans. E. Newman

Related entries: ANGOULEME, DUCHESSE D'; BORDEAUX; CHARLES X; HUNDRED DAYS; REVOLUTION OF 1830; SPAIN, 1823 FRENCH INVASION OF.

ANGOULEME, MARIE-THERESE-CHARLOTTE DE BOURBON, DUCHESSE D' (1778–1851), daughter of Louis XVI. Known at first by the title Madame Royale, she was imprisoned with her parents in the Temple in August 1792. She was liberated when she was exchanged in 1795 by the French government for some members of the National Convention who had been captured by the Austrians. From that moment on, she stayed near her uncle, the exiled King Louis XVIII, who married her off to her own cousin, the duc d'Angoulême. In March 1815 when Napoleon returned to France from Elba, she was in Bordeaux, and there she was given the task of organizing the resistance against Napoleon's latest usurpation. She demonstrated such courage that the emperor called her "the only man in her family." During the reigns of Louis XVIII and Charles X, Madame, or the Dauphine (as she was called after September 1824), marked by the terrible trials of her youth, remained implacably hostile to everything that suggested the Revolution. Her piety and her great spirit of charity made her the protectress of numerous works of assistance.

A. Castelot, *Madame Royale* (Paris, 1974); J. Evans, *Madame Royale* (London, 1959).

Guillaume de Bertier de Sauvigny, trans. E. Newman

Related entries: ANGOULEME, DUC D'; CHARLES X; HUNDRED DAYS; LOUIS XVIII.

ANNEAU, SOCIETE DE L'. See CHEVALIERS DE LA FOI.

ANTICLERICAL CAMPAIGN, a powerful movement of the mid- and late 1820s that opposed certain aspects of Roman Catholicism, such as the Jesuits, ultramontanism, and clerical influence in government, and that contributed significantly to the July Revolution. The French Restoration, like other periods of French history, experienced its share of anticlerical sentiment. It was not, however, generally as radical as its counterparts in other periods, for much of its thrust was aimed at curtailing perceived abuses by the church rather than destroying religion or Catholicism in France. The anticlericalism of the Restoration drew on a mixed heritage, including the rationalism of the Enlightenment, the legacy of the Revolution, which ranged from simple religious freedom to de-Christianization, and the heritage of the Consulate and the Empire. Although the major anticlerical movement of the Restoration did not begin until after 1825, some aspects and motivations of it appeared much earlier.

Early in the Second Restoration, the ultras proposed that article 5 of the Charter, which guaranteed religious freedom, be revoked. Some high churchmen, like many nobles, clamored for the return of confiscated property, disquieting the purchasers of that property. Simultaneously the abbé de Rauzan and the abbé de Forbin-Janson established the Society of Missionaries in France, whose purpose was to proselytize among the masses. This organization, which enjoyed government favor, employed such tactics as processions, book burnings, and denunciations of men of the Revolution and Empire. The vulgarity, absurdity, and fanaticism of such acts disenchanted many genuinely Catholic French. Unfortunately such religious practices and the backlash they generated were linked politically, both in fact and in popular perception, with the ultraroyalists and their leader, the comte d'Artois, and thus by extension with the monarchy itself. Furthermore, many ultras were otherwise linked with the Congrégation and the secret Knights of the Faith. Some such as Gabriel Donnadieu even argued in the Chamber of Deputies for church supremacy over the secular state. Conditions and attitudes such as these, which seemed to enjoy government favor, were bound to cause resentment not only among those already inclined against the church but also among many moderate, devout Catholics, especially as the accession of Artois to the throne approached. These doctrines were challenged by the new liberal philosophical and political doctrines of the times, by the rise of interest in science, and by new religious concepts. These liberal ideas were for some time propagandized in the *Globe*. Shortly before his death, Louis XVIII created the new Ministry of Ecclesiastical Affairs and Public Instruction, and he appointed two archbishops to the Council of State. Then the government halted the lectures of Victor Cousin and François Guizot at the Sorbonne. The coronation at Rheims of Charles X was a revival of the religious panoply of the Old Regime. The ultraroyalists now pushed more than ever their program, which included a law on sacrilege and the revocation of the Revolutionary religious legislation still on the books. Many clergy adopted a reactionary attitude, refusing burial to liberals or Jansenists, declaring void all marriages made during the Revolution, and advocating repressive measures such as absolute press censorship. Charles gave the Order of the Holy Ghost to Antoine de Clermont-Tonnerre, archbishop of Toulouse, who in 1823 had denounced the secular state and demanded the abolition of the Concordat. Then in 1826 the king participated ostentatiously in processions celebrating the papal jubilee, carrying candles, proceeding on foot, and dressed in purple, the color of mourning for French kings. But purple was also the color of bishops' vestments, and the rumor spread that Charles had become a bishop and said Mass in the Tuileries. Much liberal antagonism focused on the Jesuits, who had illegally reappeared in France but were certainly not the ubiquitous force as rumor would have it. The anticlerical campaign was stimulated by the 1825 debates on a sacrilege law involving the death penalty. The law was amended so that it was unenforceable, and its basic accomplishment was to stir controversy. The ultras themselves began to split between ultramontanism and Gallicanism. The liberals fostered this, and, perhaps being short of issues to arouse the public, they also used the religious question to stimulate popular interest in their views. Furthermore, they appealed to French nationalism to support the Gallican aspect of their position. Many began to believe in a Jesuit-ultra conspiracy to restore the Old Regime, a belief furthered by government attempts to prosecute newspapers for anticlerical articles. The unsuccessful government prosecutions of the *Courrier français* and the *Constitutionnel* for attacks on religion aroused much public interest, and their acquittal was popularly cheered. The ultramontane newspapers were usually even more acrimonious than the anticlerical ones, yet they generally escaped prosecution. The anticlericals also utilized songs, cartoons, and doggerel verse in addition to newspapers and pamphlets. In addition to the political liberals, the anticlericals included various moderate monarchists, peers, university faculty, lawyers, and judges. One of the most devastating attacks on the church came from an ultra of impeccable credentials, the comte de Montlosier, a former *émigré*, a devout Catholic, and a staunch monarchist. In 1826 Montlosier published a *Mémoire* attacking the Jesuits, alleging that they controlled the cabinet and 105 deputies and that they were ruining religion. The Peers ultimately approved Montlosier's denunciation of the Jesuits, who became the special target of the anticlericals. This made a strong contrast with the continuing publication of the works of Lamennais supporting the Jesuits and ultramontanism. Furthermore, in 1826 the duc de Rivière, a friend of the Jesuits, was appointed governor of the duc de Bordeaux, heir presumptive to the throne. It was little wonder that on one plane men like Pierre Royer-Collard, Pierre-Jean de Béranger, Paul-Louis Courier, and Benjamin Constant dueled in print with the defenders of ultramontanism and the Jesuits, such as Louis de Bonald, Joseph de Maistre, and initially Félicité de Lamennais. On another level, firecrackers were thrown at religious processions, and ink was poured in the holy water. The elections of 1827 were a victory for the moderate monarchists, hence a defeat for the clericals. The attacks on the church, especially the accusations of religious control of the government, declined somewhat in 1828 when the moderate Martignac cabinet replaced the ultra government of Joseph de Villèle. But the Martignac ministry stirred new controversy when it prohibited seminaries from taking in students who were not destined for the priesthood and when it closed eight Jesuit-run schools and halted meetings of the Congrégation. The clericals struck back, denouncing Martignac as Julian the Apostate and Jean-Francois Feutrier, Martignac's minister of ecclesiastical affairs, as Marat.

The religious controversy that swirled around the Martignac government was a major factor in its replacement in 1829 by the Polignac cabinet. To a great extent in the eyes of many, this cemented the link between crown and clerical factions, for Polignac was a member of the Congrégation and an extreme ultraroyalist. Furthermore, in 1830 many priests used their office to oppose liberal candidates at elections. Thus there should be no surprise that at the July Revolution, although churches in general remained intact, the Paris archbishop's residence was sacked, as were the Jesuit novitiate at Montrouge and the headquarters of the Mission Society. Various archbishops were forced to flee, including Forbin-Janson; priests wore mufti; and Roman Catholicism lost its privileged position as the state religion. The real tragedy of the anticlerical campaign and the conditions that brought it about was not just that such a campaign existed but rather that certain church institutions had become so closely identified with a particular political faction. The anticlerical campaign of the 1820s contributed to the formation of the anticlericalism of the later nineteenth century.

A. Coutrot and F. G. Dreyfus, *Les Forces religieuses dans la société française* (Paris, 1965); A. Dansette, *Religious History of Modern France* (New York, 1961); A. Latreille and R. Rémond, *Histoire du catholicisme en France* (Paris, 1962); C. S. Phillips, *The Church in France, 1789–1848* (New York, 1966).

James K. Kieswetter

Related entries: CHAMBER OF DEPUTIES; CHEVALIERS DE LA FOI; CLERMONT-TONNERRE; CORONATION OF CHARLES X; DONNADIEU;

JESUITS; LAW OF SACRILEGE; MARTIGNAC; MISSIONS; MONTLO-
SIER; POLIGNAC; QUELEN; ULTRAMONTANES; ULTRAROYALISTS;
VILLELE.

L'APOSTOLIQUE (July 1829–July 1830), ultraclerical religious periodical.
L'Apostolique, a small periodical of the extreme ultraclerical faction of the Right,
was alleged to be backed by the enigmatic Congrégation, a religious society
falsely believed to be a front for a right-wing secret society. It was less temperate
and erudite than the *Mémorial Catholique* and was often ridiculed in the anticlerical
campaign of the liberal press. At the start of 1830, it had only eighty paid
subscriptions, but its sustained attack on the ''atheism'' of the opposition and
its defense of the Jesuits made it a useful target for the Left. When the Polignac
ministry indicted *Le Figaro* (28 August 1829) for some devastating satires
against the new government, it also charged *L'Apostolique* with press violations
in a crude attempt to appear evenhanded. The latter's editor, Louis Mercier,
had written that the Charter, sworn to by two kings, was the ''impious and
atheist'' source of all France's troubles and called for its destruction. He
received the minimum sentence of a light fine and thirty days in jail. The editor
of *Figaro*, by contrast, received a sentence of 1,000 francs and a six months'
term.

E. Hatin, *Histoire de la presse* (Paris, 1859–61).

Daniel Rader

Related entries: ANTICLERICAL CAMPAIGN; CHARTER OF 1814; CON-
GREGATION; *LE FIGARO*; JESUITS; *LE MEMORIAL CATHOLIQUE*;
POLIGNAC; ULTRAROYALISTS.

APPONYI, THERESE NOGAROLA, COUNTESS (?–1873), wife of the
Austrian ambassador to Paris; leading socialite of the late Restoration and July
Monarchy. Born to an old family of Verona, Thérèse Apponyi was the wife of
Antoine Rudolphe Apponyi, Austrian ambassador to Paris from 1826 to 1848.
Apponyi and his wife arrived in Paris in February 1826. They quickly turned
their residence, the Hôtel d'Eckmühl on the rue St. Dominique, into a center of
the social life of the elite of Paris. Her charm, elegance, and grace played no
small role in his diplomatic success and lengthy tenure. She quickly earned
renown for her beauty, her rich and elegant dress, and her elaborate hair styles.
Her nephew Rodolphe, a junior official of the embassy, described her as ''the
divine Theresa.'' They were social friends and associates of such as the duchesse
de Berry, the duc d'Orléans and his sister Mme. Adélaïde, and Mme. Récamier.
After the July Revolution they became especially good friends with Louis-
Philippe, who invited them on vacation to Neuilly, to receptions at Fontainebleau,
and on a royal tour of Versailles. The Apponyis were frequent hosts of cardinals,
kings, and emperors and were frequently hosted by them.

Countess Apponyi was best known as a hostess. She helped establish the
vogue for morning dances and afternoon musicals at which leading members of
the diplomatic community and high society played or sang. The countess herself

sang solos in her early years but later preferred to perform either in ensembles or as an accompanist. The fame of her hospitality grew so great that by 1829 she was forced to stay home almost every evening to receive. By 1835 her large evening receptions might include 700 to 800 guests. In the 1840s she began hosting tea dances. Her hospitality was so gracious that even when she had to go out during the day, she continued to receive until the moment of her departure. Invitations to her gatherings were highly sought, and failure to receive an invitation sometimes provoked formal protest. Thus she was perhaps the leading arbiter of Paris social life during this period.

The countess was also a woman of firm determination. When Louis-Philippe's son, Ferdinand, duc d'Orléans, criticized her for hosting legitimists, the pressure was delicately resisted. In fact for twenty-two years she equally received Bonapartist marshals, Bourbon supporters, and Orléanists. She and her family were in Dieppe during the July Revolution. But they experienced the riots of the following December, and while others panicked, the countess was determined to defend the embassy from possible attack. She remained in Paris during the 1848 Revolution, albeit not without apprehension. After she and her husband left Paris later that year, her former associates spoke highly of her and remembered her as a model ambassador's wife.

R. Apponyi, *Vingt-cinq ans à Paris* (Paris, 1913–26); H. Contamine, *Diplomatie et diplomates sous la restauration* (Paris, 1970); G. de Sauvigny, *The Bourbon Restoration* (Philadelphia, 1966).

James K. Kieswetter

Related entries: ADELAIDE; BERRY, M.; LOUIS PHILIPPE; RECAMIER.

ARAGO FAMILY, a Catalan family that played a remarkable role in the political, intellectual, and cultural life of nineteenth-century France. The four brothers of the first generation were born in Estagel, a small town in the Pyrénées-Orientales, sons of a man from peasant stock who had won a senior position in the finance administration in nearby Perpignan during the Revolution.

The oldest of the brothers, François (1786–1853), had a brilliant scientific and teaching career in the Ecole polytechnique, the observatory, and, from the age of twenty-three, in the Academy of Science, of which he was named permanent secretary in June 1830. His political life commenced after the 1830 Revolution, and from then almost until his death he was a deputy; one of the few republicans in the chamber under the July Monarchy, he became a member of the Provisional Government and minister for war in 1848. It was Arago who organized the return of the army to Paris in anticipation of the June civil war, but he consistently voted with the Left after 1848.

Jean (1788–1836), the second of the brothers, spent much of his adult life in Mexico, fighting for Mina in the insurrection of 1817 and subsequently filling important posts in the Mexican army and administration from which he was able to protect French economic interests. Jacques (1790–1855) was a productive historical novelist, historian, and playwright, even after going blind in 1837.

He was an enthusiastic voyager, dying in Brazil on his fifth trip there, and his best works are travelogues, notably *Souvenirs d'un aveugle*.

Etienne (1802–92), the youngest of the four, was a prolific novelist and dramatist (notably *Les Aristocraties*, 1847), and director of the Vaudeville (1829–40). Politically the most radical of the family, Etienne was an active carbonaro under the Restoration, fought in the risings of 1830, 1832, and 1834, and wrote for *La Réforme*. He was appointed director of the Post Office in 1848 but resigned after Louis-Napoleon's election in December. After his heavy involvement in the rising of 13 June 1849, he had to flee the country, returning only after the amnesty of 1859. He was later mayor of Paris in 1870 but devoted his life thereafter to the fine arts.

The two sons of François were also important literary and political figures. Emmanuel (1812–96) began his working life as a writer, from which developed a long and close friendship with George Sand, but then he became a lawyer and acted for the defense in the major political trials of the July Monarchy. He fought in February 1848 and, as *commissaire* at Lyons, expelled religious orders and imposed an emergency tax on the wealthy to pay for unemployment relief. He represented the new regime in Berlin but resigned after Louis-Napoleon's election; he voted consistently with the Left between 1848 and 1851. He was a deputy and senator from 1869 until his death and ambassador to Switzerland from 1880 to 1894. The second son, Alfred (1816–92), was a talented artist, a pupil of Ingres and Paul Delaroche, and filled important posts in the Ministry of Fine Arts.

D. F. J. Arago, *Histoire de ma jeunesse*, vol. 1 of *Oeuvres complètes*, 17 vols. (1854–62); *Dictionnaire de biographie française* (Paris, 1933-); R. Gossez and J. Vienney, *Francois Arago* (Perpignan, 1952); G. Sand, *Correspondance* (Paris, 1964-); G. Weill, *Histoire du parti républicain en France de 1814 à 1870* (Paris, 1900).

Peter McPhee

Related entries: ACADEMY OF SCIENCES; CARBONARI; CHAMBER OF DEPUTIES; ECOLE POLYTECHNIQUE; JUNE DAYS; PROVISIONAL GOVERNMENT; *LA REFORME*; REVOLUTION OF 1830; REVOLUTION OF 1848.

ARC DE TRIOMPHE DE L'ETOILE, triumphal arch in the place de l'Etoile, Paris. The proposal to erect a monument in this location, a major crossroads just outside the Etoile barrier in the Paris wall in the early nineteenth century, dates from the reign of Louis XV. The Directory solicited plans for a monument as part of the decoration of the square, although nothing was built. After returning from the Austerlitz campaign, Napoleon on 18 February 1806 ordered the construction of a large triumphal arch to honor the victories of the French armies. Thus the arch was originally known as the Austerlitz arch. Napoleon at first intended it to be built on the site of the Bastille, but the Etoile location was accepted as a compromise. The design by Jean François Chalgrin was accepted, although it was later modified. Construction began 15 August 1806. The project was only one-tenth finished, however, by early 1810, and so for the ceremonial entry of Marie Louise into Paris by this route, painted canvas over a wooden scaffold was used to give the appearance of the completed arch. With Chalgrin's death on 20 January 1811 and Napoleon preoccupied, work on the arch slowed.

The restored Bourbons initially did nothing more with the arch than remove the scaffold. In 1823, however, Louis XVIII ordered construction resumed in honor of the French victory in Spain. The work proceeded slowly, and the basic structure was not finished until 1831. In August 1833 Adolphe Thiers, then Louis-Philippe's minister of the interior, assigned commissions for the major groups of sculpture, which were to symbolize the military achievements of the Revolution and the Empire. Antoine Etex designed the figures representing Resistance and Peace; Jean Pierre Cortot did the Triumph of 1810. The most famous of the groups, The Departure of 1792, was designed by François Rude. Other artists created the six bas-reliefs and the frieze, while other surfaces were ultimately inscribed with the names of 660 generals and 128 battles. The arch measures 164 feet high and 148 feet wide.

The Arc de triomphe was officially opened by Louis-Philippe I on 29 July 1836, and it has been the scene of many ceremonies since that time. The remains of Napoleon I passed through the arch when they were returned to France in 1840. The coffins of numerous French heroes have been honored there before being interred in their final resting places, including Gambetta, Victor Hugo, Foch, Joffre, and Lyautey. The French unknown soldier of World War I was buried beneath the arch in 1921, and an eternal flame was installed in 1923.

J. Hillairet, *Dictionnaire historique des rues de Paris* (Paris, 1963); G. Poisson, *Napoléon et Paris* (Paris, 1964).

James K. Kieswetter

Related entries: SPAIN, 1823 FRENCH INVASION OF; THIERS.

ARCHBISHOPS OF PARIS. Between 1814 and 1850 the see of Paris was occupied by the following individuals: Alexandre-Angélique de Talleyrand-Périgord (1817–21); Hyacinthe-Louis de Quélen (1821–39); Denis-Auguste Affre (1840–48); and Marie-Dominique-Auguste Sibour (1848–57).

Guillaume de Bertier de Sauvigny

Related entries: AFFRE; QUELEN.

ARCHIVES PHILOSOPHIQUES, POLITIQUES, ET LITTERAIRES, a *doctrinaire* periodical of the Left-Center during the Restoration, offering cultural and intellectual articles, frequently with political emphasis. Among the first of those ideologically oriented literary reviews that were to proliferate in the Restoration, the *Archives* was begun in 1817 by François Guizot and Pierre Royer-Collard. The political stance of these *doctrinaires* of the earlier Restoration was to be objective, aloof, and above the clash of faction but still to promote its ideals. The journal stood for the Charter, a free press, free elections, and a pan-European cultural outlook. Under such rubrics as archaeology, natural science, and political science, there often appeared translations from foreign journals like the *Edinburgh Review*. Until the later creation of the *Globe* and *Revue française*, the *Archives* was the most significant periodical of its type.

E. Hatin, *Histoire de la presse* (Paris, 1859–61).

Daniel Rader

Related entries: CHARTER OF 1814; DOCTRINAIRES; *LE GLOBE*; GUI-ZOT; *REVUE FRANCAISE*; ROYER-COLLARD.

ARGOUT, ANTOINE-MAURICE-APOLLINAIRE. See D'ARGOUT.

L'ARISTARQUE FRANCAIS (1815–1827), newspaper of varied political orientations. Founded in May 1815 in an attempt to encourage Napoleon to rule as a constitutional monarch, the *Aristarque* had a checkered career. At the second Restoration of Louis XVIII, newspapers came once more under the law of 21 October 1814, which obliged them to seek government permission to appear. This was interpreted by the government as placing them under police control. Joseph Fouché exercised this control by appointing to each newspaper (including the *Aristarque*) a responsible editor whose role was virtually that of internal censor. Duke Elie Decazes, who succeeded Fouché as minister of police, withdrew the responsible editors and judged newspapers in accordance with the law of 9 November 1815 against seditious cries and writings. The *Aristarque* was in consequence suppressed during 1816. In 1819 a more liberal press law encouraged a group of left-wing writers to revive the *Aristarque*; it appeared in December 1819, only to be suppressed by the censorship of 1820. A further press law of 1822 revived the rule whereby anyone who wished to found a new journal must seek government permission but stated that journals already in existence did not need permission to continue publication; whereupon a group of extreme royalists who wished to attack the more moderate royalist policy of Joseph Villèle conceived the idea of buying up the title of the defunct *Aristarque* and publishing the paper again, without permission, as a newspaper already in existence in 1822. The *Aristarque* kept up continuous opposition to Joseph Villèle from 1824 until it collapsed under accumulated lawsuits and fines in January, 1827.

C. Bellanger et al., *Histoire generale de la presse française*, vol. 2 (Paris, 1969); I. Collins, *The Government and the Newspaper Press in France, 1814–1881* (Oxford, 1959).

Irene Collins

Related entries: DECAZES; FOUCHE; LAW ON SEDITIOUS SPEECH; LOUIS XVIII; PRESS LAWS; VILLELE.

ARSENAL, SALON OF (1824–1830), famous meeting place for romantic personalities. The appointment of Charles Nodier to succeed abbé Crozier as librarian of the Arsenal—property belonging to the comte d'Artois—was made 3 April 1824. At the time the appointment was made, Charles was forty-four and by far the eldest and most experienced of the group of royalist romantics who assembled at Emile Deschamps' under the banner of *La Muse française*.

In less than two weeks, Nodier had moved his family. Having extended his hospitality for several years to a limited group at the rue de Choiseul, he could now, in his spacious apartment at the old Arsenal with its vast dining room and attractive salon, invite a broad spectrum of friends. During more than five years of its existence, practically all major romantic writers were regular guests, at first Victor Hugo and Alfred de Vigny, later Honoré de Balzac, Alexandre Dumas, Prosper Mérimée, Gérard de Nerval, Théophile Gautier, finally Alfred de Musset and Charles-Augustin Sainte-Beuve and even prominent women poets such as Marceline Desbordes-Valmore and Delphine Gay and her mother Sophie. The presence of philosophers, artists, travelers, and miscellaneous friends added a special stimulus to the activities.

The first reception was held on Sunday, 14 April 1824, and henceforth Sunday gatherings were always the liveliest and the most congenial in an atmosphere of gracious informality. The evenings typically consisted of two major activities. Promptly at 8 P.M., Nodier would usually extricate his tall frame from his chair and make his way to the fireplace. As he leaned against it, a hush would fall over the assembly, and he would hold them spellbound with tales of elves and fairies or memories of his youth. His conciliatory ways and tolerant attitude coupled with a keen and respected aesthetic judgment made him the perfect choice during those years to be the pilot of the movement. He preferred to guide rather than lead, to keep the ambitious, energetic young writers on a true course. He injected substance into the movement by urging the young authors to write rather than argue. Therefore his soliloquies were often followed by free-wheeling literary discussions. The participants, mainly the old *Muse française* group, were expected not to attack (since theirs was a salon and not a *cénacle*) but to react to some article wherein a classicist had criticized them. Occasionally Lamartine, Hugo, or Musset read poems. Désirée Nodier, beautiful, intelligent, sensitive and friendly, and her attractive, graceful, charming daughter, Marie, had much to do with making the Arsenal a happy place and a social success. The wife, promptly at 10 P.M., would discreetly have Marie move to the piano where an arpeggio would warn of the time for entertainment, which usually stretched to the early morning hours. The salon was taken over by dancers, while the husband, with Baron Isidore Taylor and a few other cronies, played *écarté* or *bataille*. A few more serious guests, Hugo usually among them, would seek an alcove to continue discussions.

Other evenings, guests were normally welcomed in Désirée's room, where she and Charles sat facing each other, striving to make guests of all means, position, and social condition feel that their presence was appreciated. Dinner was served at 6:00. There were always dinner guests, often up to fifteen, and unexpected guests were always warmly received.

When Hugo asserted his leadership in 1827 by opening his own Notre Dame des Champs *cénacle*, the importance of the Arsenal dwindled. Serious discussions took place at Hugo's, while one went to Nodier's for relaxation. Nevertheless, for nearly four years, the salon had played a crucial role as a center for the *romantique* conservative (royalist-Catholic) faction, which would join with the liberals of the *Globe* and the regulars (Stendhal and Mérimée) of the Delécluze-Stapfer-Viollet-le-duc salons to orchestrate the triumph of French romanticism. It had provided a unifying environment conducive to the production of literary works, which would enable romanticism to make immense progress and to create for itself a true identity. It was a necessary intermediate step, a critical transition between the faltering, uncertain *Muse française* group and the militant, confident band of the Hugo *cénacle*.

J. Bertaut, *L'Epoque romantique* (Paris, 1947); M. Salomon, *Charles Nodier et le groupe romantique* (Paris, 1908); L. Séché, *Le Cénacle de la Muse française, 1823–1827* (Paris, 1908).

Paul Comeau

Related entries: BALZAC; DELECLUZE; DESBORDES-VALMORE; DES-CHAMPS; DUMAS, A.; GAUTIER; GAY, D.; GAY, S.; HUGO; LAMAR-TINE; MERIMEE; *LA MUSE FRANCAISE*; MUSSET; NERVAL; NODIER; ROMANTICISM; SAINTE-BEUVE; SALON D'EMILE DESCHAMPS; STAP-FER; STENDHAL; VIGNY.

L'ARTISAN (1830), moderate working-class newspaper. The Revolution of 1830, which replaced the monarchy of Charles X with that of Louis-Philippe, took place during a period of economic crisis. In Paris where many workers, particularly artisans, had fought on the barricades, there was much disappointment with the conservative outcome of the revolution. During the autumn, artisanal groups expressed their discontent by striking and by founding newspapers, of which three appeared: the *Artisan*, the *Peuple*, and the *Journal des ouvriers*. They were moderate in their views, asking only for better wages and conditions within the new political structure. Nevertheless they were short-lived, the *Artisan* lasting only from 26 September to 13 October 1830.

E. Dolléans, *Histoire du mouvement ouvrier, 1830–1870* (Paris, 1936); H. J. Hunt, *Le Socialisme et le romanticisme en France* (Oxford, 1935).

Irene Collins

Related entries: LE JOURNAL DES OUVRIERS; LE PEUPLE; REVOLUTION OF 1830.

ARTOIS, COMTE DE. See CHARLES X.

ARTS ET METIERS. See CONSERVATOIRE NATIONAL DES ARTS ET METIERS.

ASSIZE COURTS. See COURTS OF ASSIZE.

L'ATELIER (1840–1850), important workers' newspaper, appearing monthly September 1840-July 1850 (weekly February-June 1848) under the subtitle *Organ of the Moral and Material Interests of the Working-Class, Edited Exclusively by Workers*. It was edited by about seventy-five skilled workers, including twenty-six printing workers, and its articles were written by a collective of printers, hat makers, jewelers, and other skilled workers. Among its founders and writers were Philippe Buchez, Claude-Anthime Corbon, Alexandre Martin (the "Albert" of the 1848 Provisional Government), Henri Leneveux, François Chevé, Agricol Perdiguier, Pascal, Alexandre Lambert (editor of *Le Travailleur de l'Indre* in 1849), and the worker-poets Marie-Eléonore Magu, Charles Poncy, and Eugène Pottier (later author of the *Internationale*). The paper usually printed fewer than 1,000 copies; subscriptions increased from 550 in 1847 to 896 in June 1848, though it claimed to have printed 40,000 copies on 15 June 1849 to protest the Roman expedition.

L'Atelier is of central importance as a mouthpiece of workers' demands for state-financed producers' cooperatives and associations and for its class analysis of relations of production and surplus labor. However, it stressed its hostility to violence, expropriation, and collective or "communist" solutions. Louis Blanc was criticized on both the last issue and for his appeals to the rich to help emancipate the workers. The paper called for shorter hours and the reorganization of work, for accident compensation and old-age pensions, and for the abolition of *marchandage, livrets*, child labor, and work in prisons and convents.

While anticlerical, the paper emphasized religion as the "cement of social unity"; in 1837 the printing workers had published a popular edition of the gospels. It was consistently democratic and called for political solutions to workers' grievances. Admiration was expressed for Napoleon but only as a republican soldier. The editors were in contact with English workers and Italian refugees in London and corresponded with the Chartists.

The paper welcomed the 1848 Revolution while condemning the accompanying wave of machine breaking. Its political reformism was reflected in the election of Buchez and Corbon as president and vice-president of the National Assembly. The paper supported Cavaignac in the June civil war, though criticizing the repression that followed, and campaigned for his election in December 1848 in appreciation of his government's encouragement of cooperatives and reform of working hours and conciliation boards (*conseils de prud'hommes*). It regarded the planned colonization of Algeria as of equal importance to the proclamation of the Republic.

Louis-Napoleon's ending of state funding of cooperatives and limits to working hours and his foreign policy pushed *L'Atelier* into an increasingly hostile position. The increase of caution money forced its closure in July 1850, with its quip about 1848, immortalized in Gustave Flaubert's *Sentimental Education*, that "we should have set fire to the four corners of Europe."

A. Cuvillier, *Un journal d'ouvriers: "l'Atelier" (1840–1850)* (Paris, 1954); F. A. de Luna, *The French Republic under Cavaignac, 1848* (Princeton, 1969); E. Dolléans, *Histoire du mouvement ouvrier*, vol. 1 (Paris, 1967).

Peter McPhee

Related entries: ALBERT; BUCHEZ; MAGU; PERDIGUIER; POTTIER; WORKER POETS.

ATELIERS NATIONAUX. See NATIONAL WORKSHOPS.

AUBER, DANIEL-FRANCOIS-ESPRIT (1782–1871), composer, noted for his *opéras comiques*. Born in Caen, Auber showed an early talent for music and studied piano under Ignaz Ladurner and composition (after 1805) under Luigi Cherubini. His early compositions included solo instrumental, chamber, and vocal works, and his career was largely financed by his father (an art dealer) until the older Auber's bankruptcy in 1819. Forced to support himself, Auber turned to the composition of light dramatic vocal works and enjoyed some success with *La bergère châtelaine* (1820) and *Emma* (1821). His collaboration with librettist Augustin-Eugène Scribe began in 1821, ending only with Scribe's death in 1861, and the influence of Giacomo Rossini marked much of his work in the early 1820s. Auber sought to adapt Rossini's melodic innovations to the traditional French *opéra comique*, developing a distinctive national style of composition in this form that was alert, lyrical, unpretentious, and gently mocking. *Le maçon* (1825), *Fiorella* (1826), *Fra Diavolo* (1830), *Le Domino noir* (1837), and *La sirène* (1844) demonstrated the fruitful marriage of Scribe's sophisticated lyrics and plots with Auber's "French style" and established their reputations. Auber made an effort at grand opera (a form dominated in France by Louis Véron and Giacomo Meyerbeer) in his *La Muette de Portici* in 1828, which featured huge choruses, crowd scenes, processions, a volcanic eruption in the final act, and a mute heroine who expressed herself in pantomime. Based loosely on the Neapolitan insurrection of 1647, *La Muette* was performed in Brussels on 25 August 1830, and the resulting riot is usually considered the beginning of the Belgian revolution for independence from the Netherlands. Despite this spectacular (if unintended) success, Auber's other grand operas were less appreciated.

In the 1840s, Auber's compositions became more serious in tone (*Haydée*, 1847, and *Manon Lescaut*, 1856) and harmonically richer, and in his later years he turned increasingly to nonoperatic music, particularly motets, hymns, and fragments of Masses, but these remained suffused with operatic elements that lessen their value. The success of Auber's *opéras comiques*, however, soon brought the diminutive and modest composer (who could never bear to hear or see his works performed) myriad honors. He was awarded the Legion of Honor (1825), elected to the Institut (1829), named to replace Cherubini as head of the Conservatory (1842–70), and appointed musical director of the imperial chapel (1852). Given stipends and government commissions, Auber was regarded by successive regimes (Bourbon, Orleanist, and Bonapartist) as a major national asset, and other composers (Rossini and Wagner) praised his talents. His work was instrumental in setting the musical and social tone associated with mid-nineteenth-century Paris, and several of his productions remain in the current repertory of light opera companies.

B. J. B. Jouvin, *D. F. E. Auber* (Paris, 1864); R. M. Longyear, "Daniel François-Esprit Auber (1782–1871)" (Ph.D. diss., Cornell University, 1957); C. Malherbe, *Auber* (Paris, 1911); E. de Mirecourt, *Auber* (Paris, 1867); A. Pougin, *Auber* (Paris, 1873).

David Longfellow

Related entries: BELGIAN REVOLUTION OF 1830; SCRIBE.

AUDRY DE PUYRAVAULT, PIERRE-FRANCOIS (1773–1852), deputy of the Restoration and July Monarchy and representative in the Constituent Assembly of 1848. Audry was born 27 September 1773 at Puyravault (Charente-Inférieure). His home department first elected him to the Chamber of Deputies in 1822. He staunchly opposed the policies of Charles X in the late Restoration and was among the 221 deputies who on 13 March 1830 voted an address to the crown that criticized Charles and his government. After the issuance of the July Ordinances, Audry became one of the most ardent of deputies in pressing the conflict and refusing negotiation with Charles. His house on the rue du Faubourg-Poissonnière became a meeting place for some of those leading the revolution, including Jacques Laffitte, the marquis de Lafayette, and Casimir Périer. Frustrated by the inactivity of many deputies, on the night of 28 July Audry published the appointment of Lafayette as commander of the Paris National Guard. It was said that he gathered arms for distribution to the people and that he gave his wagons to the barricade builders. Certainly the crowd that gathered in his courtyard did nothing to restrain the men meeting with him. Although he urged the establishment of a republic, Audry was a member of the provisional municipal commission that assumed the leadership of the revolution and played a significant role in offering the crown to the duc d'Orléans.

Audry was reelected to the Deputies in 1831. But he regarded the July Monarchy as too conservative and thus participated in the founding of the Society of the Rights of Man in 1832. He was one of the defenders of those tried by the Peers for the Lyons uprising of April 1834, and he signed the famous address to the accused that concluded, "The infamy of the judge glorifies the accused." For this the Deputies approved the prosecution of Audry. But he refused to appear before the Peers and was not troubled further. Defeated at the polls in 1837, Audry attempted to rebuild his personal financial position, which had suffered during his political career. The Revolution of 1848 brought him back into politics, with election by the department of Charente-Inférieure to the National Constituent Assembly on 23 April. There he followed a generally moderate course. Audry died on 6 December 1852 at Maisons-Laffitte (Seine-et-Oise).

Archives parlementaires; J. L. Bory, *La Révolution de juillet* (Paris, 1972); D. Pinkney, *The French Revolution of 1830* (Princeton, 1972); A. Robert et al., *Dictionnaire des parlementaires français* (Paris, 1889–91).

James K. Kieswetter

Related entries: MUNICIPAL COMMISSION; SOCIETY OF THE RIGHTS OF MAN; THE 221.

AUGER, LOUIS-SIMON (1772–1829), journalist, defender of classicism, and member of the French Academy. Born in Paris on 29 December 1772, Louis-Simon Auger appeared at first to be headed for success in a bureaucratic career. After entering in 1793 an office responsible for the provisioning of the army, he joined the Ministry of the Interior in 1799 and remained there until 1812. During the founding of the University, Auger served on the commission charged with the examination and composition of classical texts. Having literary ambitions, Auger used his leisure time to write numerous comedies and vaudevilles and to submit essays to the *Décade philosophique* and the *Journal de l'Empire*. His literary efforts won recognition from the Institut in 1805 and 1818.

During the Bourbon Restoration, Auger gained a notorious reputation as a dedicated champion of monarchism in government, Catholicism in religion, and classicism in literature. Named royal censor in 1814, he lost his post when Napoleon returned for the Hundred Days. Further, a contribution to the royalist *Journal général de France* before the emperor's return brought him three days of detention. When the Bourbons returned in 1815 for the Second Restoration, Auger reclaimed his position as royal censor. His election to the French Academy on 12 April 1816 aroused, perhaps unjustly, the wrath of those academicians eliminated from their seats by the ordinance of 21 March 1816. Auger soon became a member of the Commission of the Dictionary, and he acquired an influential role in the French literary world. As a result of his prominence, a bitter polemic erupted between Auger, who continued to write for government influenced newspapers, and such organs of the liberal opposition as *La Minèrve* and *Les lettres normandes*.

Following the abolition of freedom of the press in 1820, an event occasioned at least in part by the assassination of the duc de Berry, Auger became a member of the commission on censorship. He also began to take a leading role in the reigning literary debate of the day, the battle between the classicists and the romantics. A founding member of the Société des bonnes lettres in 1820, which, after some initial enthusiasm for Victor Hugo's *Odes*, turned against the new movement, Auger regularly championed the dictates of the classical taste. In the famous session of the French Academy on 24 April 1824, he severely taxed the romantics in his "Discours sur le romantisme." Of Auger's literary works, the most important are his many editions of French authors, Boileau, Racine, and Molière, to name but a few, most prefaced with helpful introductions. Auger also made a number of contributions, including entries on Molière and Voltaire, to Michaud's famous *Biographie universelle*. His work on Michaud's great encyclopedia brought him into a bitter and public polemic with Mme. de Genlis.

Elected as perpetual secretary of the French Academy on 20 July 1826, Louis-Simon Auger proved to be a capable administrator. He also had the honor to welcome, among others, Abel Villemain and Casimir Delavigne to the Academy. Frequently serving as an intermediary between members of the Academy and the government, he managed to block, for example, an attempt by a minority of the academicians to address a protest to Charles X on the controversial press law proposed by Peyronnet.

Louis-Simon Auger died by his own hand on 2 January 1829.

L. S. Auger, *Mélanges philosophiques et littéraires*, 2 vols. (Paris, 1828); *Biographie universelle*, vol. 2.

Robert Brown

Related entries: ACADEMIE FRANCAISE; CENSORSHIP; CHARLES X; HUGO; HUNDRED DAYS; *LE JOURNAL GENERAL DE FRANCE*; *LES LETTRES NORMANDES*; MICHAUD; *LA MINERVE*; PEYRONNET; LA SOCIETE ROYALE DES BONNES LETTRES; VILLEMAIN.

L'AVANT-GARDE (1848–1850), radical student newspaper. This newspaper was founded by a group of students in January 1848 to support the Banquet Campaign, which had been started by left-wing deputies in 1847 to promote extension of the franchise. The campaign was intended to culminate in a great procession and banquet in Paris on 22 February 1848. When the government banned the demonstration, most of the politicians who had been involved in the arrangements backed out. On the night of 21 February, however, the editors of the *Avant-Garde* held a meeting in their office on the Left Bank of the Seine, and it was agreed that students should lead the people in defying the government. After a hectic night collecting ammunition, the group from the newspaper met outside the Madeleine and persuaded passers-by to join them in the procession. During the two days leading up to the abdication of Louis-Philippe, the office of the *Avant-Garde* acted as headquarters for student agitators. During the presidency of Louis-Napoleon Bonaparte, the government grew increasingly suspicious of the radical press, and the *Avant-Garde* disappeared in March 1850.

I. Collins, *The Government and the Newspaper Press in France, 1814–1881* (Oxford, 1959); A. Crémieux, *La Révolution de février 1848* (Paris, 1912).

Irene Collins

Related entries: BANQUET CAMPAIGN; REVOLUTION OF 1848.

L'AVENIR (1830–1831), liberal Catholic newspaper. In August 1830 the prospectus of a new Catholic paper, the *Avenir*, announced the beginning of a campaign to unite the Catholic church with the new liberalism: the liberalism that turned its back on the skepticism of the eighteenth century. The *Avenir* appeared as a daily paper on 16 October, with Félicité de Lamennais as its leading writer. It welcomed the pope's recognition of Louis-Philippe and condemned legitimist demonstrators for promoting the sack of the church of Saint-Germain l'Auxerrois, calling on Catholics to break with men who compromised religion by connecting it with an unpopular political creed. This anticarlist attitude pleased the government, but not so the demands for freedom Lamennais said had been promised by the Charter of 1830: the separation of church and state and freedom of the press, association, and education. The *Avenir* also published a series of outstanding articles by Charles de Coux defending artisans against the advance of industrialization. In November 1830 the paper contained scathing comments on Louis-Philippe's new episcopal nominations, and on 31 January 1831 Lamennais and his young colleague, Henri Lacordaire, were charged with provoking hatred and mistrust of the government. Both were acquitted, and the incident brought such renown to the *Avenir* that another young writer, Charles-Forbes de Montalembert, joined its editorial staff.

Lamennais meanwhile had advanced from seeing liberty merely as a means of defending the church to loving it for its own sake as part of God's gift to humanity. In this mood he fearlessly demanded universal suffrage. Laffitte's government, which was courting a reputation for liberalism, could not openly attack the *Avenir* for its criticisms of the restrictive electoral law of 1831, but the police watched the newspaper with grave suspicion and hindered its publication in every way. For instance, the minister of the interior refused permission for new presses to be installed in the offices of the paper. In spite of (and perhaps because of) the hostility of the bishops, the *Avenir* caused a great stir among the young priests and students who formed the main body of its supporters, but its subscribers never numbered more than 2,000. It ceased publication of its own accord in November 1831.

I. Collins, *The Government and the Newspaper Press in France, 1814–1881* (Oxford, 1959); J. B. Duroselle, *Les débuts du catholicisme social en France, 1822–1870* (Paris, 1950); R. Rémond, *Lamennais et la démocratie* (Paris, 1948); A. R. Vidler, *Prophesy and Papacy* (London, 1954).

Irene Collins

Related entries: CHARTER OF 1830; ELECTIONS AND ELECTORAL SYSTEMS; LACORDAIRE; LAFFITTE; LAMENNAIS; LOUIS PHILIPPE; MONTALEMBERT; SAINT-GERMAIN L'AUXERROIS.

AVIAU DUBOIS DE SANZAY, CHARLES-FRANCOIS D' (1736–1826), archbishop of Bordeaux. The scion of a noble family from Poitou, he had been made archbishop of Vienne in January 1790. His opposition to the schismatic reorganization of the French church by the Constituent Assembly compelled him to go into exile. In spite of the penalties incurred by *émigré* priests, he secretly reentered France in 1797 and while disguised as a peasant ministered to his flock. Bonaparte appreciated his courage, and after the reconciliation of state and church (1801) named d'Aviau as archbishop of Bordeaux; there he won the respect and affection of all. When on 12 March 1814 the duc d'Angoulême entered Bordeaux under the protection of British forces, the archbishop greeted him with the warmest expressions of devotion to the Bourbon family. Thereafter he enjoyed many tokens of the gratitude of the regime, among which was a seat in the Chamber of Peers (1821).

J. Dissard, *Monseigneur Charles-François d'Aviau* (Bordeaux, 1953); Lyonnet, *Histoire de Mgr. d'Aviau du Bois de Sancay, successivement archévêque de Vienne et de Bordeaux*, 2 vols. (Lyons, 1847).

Guillaume de Bertier de Sauvigny

Related entries: ANGOULEME, L.; CHAMBER OF PEERS.

AYLMER, LOUISA ANNE WHITWORTH, LADY (?–1862), English observer and diarist of the July Revolution. In the spring of 1830 Matthew Whitworth, Baron Aylmer, and his wife Louisa Anne left Naples to journey northward. At Soleure, Switzerland, Baron Aylmer was notified to return to London immediately for he had just been named governor-general of Upper and Lower Canada and should assume his duties there before winter. He hastened to London, leaving his wife with Whitworth and Mary Lloyd. Lady Aylmer remained to take the waters at Schinznach with Mary Lloyd. On 22 June she received word from her husband, advising her to remain in Europe through the winter. However, she left immediately in order to sail with him, traveling with Mary Lloyd via Paris where she had stayed several times before. She arrived in Paris on the morning of 27 July 1830, the day after the July Ordinances became public knowledge. The ensuing revolution trapped her there for a week. Fluent in French, having a keen and inquisitive mind, and with friends in high places, she was able to observe and record with a certain objectivity some of the conditions in Paris, especially since she frequently ventured out onto the streets. She ultimately arrived safely in England, complaining that English customs officials were less polite than the Paris revolutionaries who had helped her through the barricades. Somewhat of a diarist, she wrote down her observations on the revolution, apparently during the voyage to Quebec, where she arrived on 13 October. Her husband remained governor-general of Canada until 1836. Lady Aylmer died on 13 August 1862. Extracts from her journal dealing with the July Revolution were published in the *Revue d'histoire moderne* 6 (1931).

James K. Kieswetter

Related entries: JULY ORDINANCES; REVOLUTION OF 1830.

B

BAILLEUL, JACQUES CHARLES (1762–1843), politician and journalist. Born in 1762 Bailleul was the son of a bourgeois cultivator. He decided for the law and was received as an *avocat* at the Parlement of Paris just before the Revolution began. He was elected as a deputy to the Convention where, though supporting a Republic, he opposed the execution of Louis XVI. In the Convention Bailleul became an ardent opponent of the Mountain and the Terror. Later he was elected to the Council of 500 and became one of the leaders of the Directory. He also served Napoleon in a minor post.

Although Bailleul frequently ran for election during the Restoration and July Monarchy, he was never elected and remained in private life between 1814 and 1843. During these years, he published a great number of works on politics, finance, and geography and even wrote a few plays.

As a political journalist and pamphleteer, Bailleul was a strong critic of the ultraroyalists. He generally sided with the liberals in their support of freedom of the press, extension of the suffrage, opposition to clerical influence in government, and especially to the ultraroyalists' attempt in 1826 to reinstitute primogeniture. With his brother he founded and published the *Journal du commerce*, purchased in 1817 by the staff of the *Constitutionnel*.

Among his writings in history and politics, his *Examen critique des considerations de Madame . . . de Staël* was probably the most famous. In that work he criticized Mme. de Staël's *Considérations* for glorifying the aristocracy of the Old Regime. He found little redeeming value in any part of it and rejected de Staël's contention that the great aristocracy had contributed to the growth of liberty in France from the Middle Ages through the end of the Old Regime by limiting royal power. Where de Staël had seen the protection of liberty, Bailleul saw the protection of selfish interests. This hostility to the privileged corps of nobles extended to the provision in the Restoration Charter, which restored nobles to their titles. Bailleul also gave only lukewarm support to the institution of a hereditary Chamber of Peers.

Still, he did favor some kind of intermediary corps to protect against "extreme" individualism and mobility. In his pamphlet on successions and substitutions (primogeniture), he proposed his own novel hierarchy of "high councils," which would serve as the eyes and ears of the crown and people. Recognizing the force of tradition he recommended a moderator or *duc* to head each council. But such councils were to be made largely of men of the middle class with proved talent and service. Though a supporter of the Revolution of 1830, he feared further disorders and called for maintaining the heredity of the Chamber of Peers as the last political symbol of continuity and counterweight to democracy. He continued to write during the July Monarchy but played no important part in the debates of the regime. He died in obscurity in 1843.

J.-C. Bailleul, *Doctrines religieuses et politiques* (Paris, 1824), *Espirit de la Révolution* (Paris, 1814), *Examen critique des "Considerations . . ." de Madame de Staël* (Paris, 1824), and *Petites lettres sur les grandes questions* (Paris, 1831); E. Cappadocia, "The Liberals and Madame de Staël," in *Ideas in History* (Durham, N.C., 1965); S. Gutman, "Justifications for an Aristocracy," (Ph.D diss., University of Michigan, 1976).

Sanford Gutman

Related entries: CHAMBER OF PEERS; CHARTER OF 1814; *LE CONSTI-TUTIONNEL*; ELECTIONS AND ELECTORAL SYSTEMS; HEREDITY LAWS; PRESS LAWS; REVOLUTION OF 1830; STAEL; ULTRAROY-ALISTS.

BALLANCHE, PIERRE-SIMON (1776–1847), religious and social philosopher. Born in Lyons, the son of a printer, Ballanche was distressed by the civil war and the Terror in his native city during the Revolution and embraced the Catholic revival after 1800. Though a monarchist and a Christian, Ballanche was never an ultraroyalist, and in his philosophical works and epics (*Antigone* [1814], *L'homme sans nom* [1820], *Orphée* [1827–29], *La Vision d'Hébal* [1831] and *La Ville des Expiations* [1832–35]) worked out an original view of human history that permitted active encouragement of social reform. Ballanche's basic idea, which he believed was inherent in all theologies and myths, was that of palingenesis (*Essais de palingénésie sociale* [1827–29]), whereby fallen mankind is progressively redeemed through successive historical epochs. Each epoch sees a new group of people (roughly identified with social classes) pass through a process of initiation, testing, and expiation, guided by a great initiator (Prometheus, Oedipus, Cicero, Moses, Christ), who is martyred at the hands of those he has illuminated. The final stage of this process culminates in a world of universal brotherhood, charity, and eternal calm. Because each epoch is progressive, Ballanche rejected Rousseauist ideas of the corruption of an earlier state of nature and proclaimed the death of neoclassical art and literature. Each man could attain the dominant thought of his epoch through individual inspiration (illuminism), and because the rehabilitation of humanity was collective, not individual, the initiation of his own century could include factory legislation, penal reform, an end to war, and the extension of property rights to the lower classes.

Although scholars disagree on the influence of Ballanche's ideas, they seem to be reflected in the writings of Francois-René de Chateaubriand, Edgar Quinet, Alphonse de Lamartine, Victor Hugo, Félicité de Lamennais, Alfred de Vigny, and the Saint-Simonians.

D. O. Evans, *Social Romanticism in France, 1830–1848* (Oxford, 1951); A. J. George, *Pierre Simon Ballanche* (Syracuse, 1945); H. J. Hunt, *The Epic in Nineteenth-Century France* (New York, 1941); R. Picard, *Le Romantisme social* (Paris, 1944).

David Longfellow

Related entries: CHATEAUBRIAND; HUGO; LAMARTINE; LAMENNAIS; QUINET: ROUSSEAU; SAINT-SIMONIANISM; THEOCRATS; ULTRA-ROYALISTS; VIGNY.

BALZAC, HONORE DE (1799–1850), prolific French novelist who established the genre as a major literary art form. Born in Tours of meridional and peasant stock, Balzac bore the marks of this dual heredity in his physical appearance and his vitality, his incredible capacity for work, and his attachment to money. He had almost no family life. His mother, thirty-two years younger than his father, called him "the fruit of duty and chance" and put him immediately out to nurse until age four when he was sent to the first of a succession of boarding schools. Little wonder that, nourished in this stony ground of indifference, the young Balzac failed to show promise or any special gifts.

The year 1819 marked the beginning of ten years of bitter apprenticeship in the literary and business world. After clerking in a law office while pursuing his studies, he announced that he was abandoning the law for literature. He proved that he could subsist on the meager allowance with which his family hoped to starve him into submission, but there was born in those years a passion for instant riches that would provide him the luxury and leisure to pursue his writing in comfort and style. One can only wonder what place Balzac would occupy in the history of literature had any of his schemes succeeded, for the fact is that by age twenty-nine a failed publishing venture had left him so deeply in debt that he was obliged to write furiously all his life simply to keep pace with his creditors.

Ironically literary success came to him in the midst of financial ruin. After a series of mediocre novels that gave little or no indication of Balzacian genius, the year 1829 saw his first moderate success with *Le Dernier Chouan*, a historical novel.

His muse during the apprentice years was Mme. Laure de Berny, a married woman twenty-three years his senior. She was the prototype of Balzac's ideal woman, wealthy, living her last love, grateful for youthful ardor and attention, and willing to lavish money and passion, as well as the maternal affection he had never known. This first love was to be always "La Dilecta," and his idealized portrait of her in *Le Lys dans la vallée* was, he said, but a pale reflection of her grace and goodness.

By 1834 Balzac had determined that the novels he was churning out at a prodigious rate were to form an ensemble. He divided them into studies of manners, philosophical studies, and analytical studies. The bulk of his work actually falls into the first category. It was also about this time that he conceived of the idea of reappearing characters, which he announced to his family, saying, "Take your hat off to me, for I am about to become a genius." He utilized the principle systematically for the first time in 1834–35 with *Père Goriot*. He had also determined by this time that his particular gift was that of a sociologist, acutely observing and describing the contemporary scene. To him "a generation is a drama of four or five thousand dominant characters." And that drama was to be his life's work.

He chose the title *La Comédie humaine* in conscious opposition to Dante, emphasizing a sociological rather than theological orientation. He reduced human motivation, with rare exception, to money and pleasure. He projected that the complete work would include approximately one hundred fifty novels with several thousand characters. Such an ambitious project was beyond even Balzac's energy and indomitable will to work, and the fact that he produced some ninety novels and pieces with over two thousand characters is an unparalleled feat, a godlike impulsion to creation.

Balzac's prolific output is the more remarkable in that writing never came easily to him. His inventiveness outraced his pen so that he practically rewrote every work on the galley proofs, resulting on occasion in books that cost more to produce than he received in revenue. The human cost was even greater; Balzac wrote with intense concentration for twelve to fourteen hours or longer at a stretch, working through the night and subsisting on black coffee. He literally worked his heart out, always writing to juggle the demands of his creditors, always accumulating more debts through his passion for ill-fated speculation and his mania for collecting bricabrac. The endless indulgence and prodigality of lady friends was all that saved him from imminent ruin many times.

Balzac had confided to his sister, Laure, in 1822 that he dreamed of marrying a rich widow. His first contact with the woman who fulfilled that dream, Eveline Hanska, occurred when she wrote him an admiring letter in 1832, signed "L'Anonyme." She was the unhappily married Polish wife of a Russian nobleman, and until her husband's death in 1841, their affair proceeded through correspondence and occasional trysts, which in no way hindered the numerous other relationships Balzac juggled like his debts. Even after she gained her freedom, the marriage was inexplicably delayed until 1850, and in the spirit of dreams that can never be fully realized, Balzac died only five months later.

He had opted for a life lived at full tilt, consumed like so many of his characters by his own energy, his passion for life, his devouring ambition. He drew on a broad canvas with bold strokes yet with the finesse of an infinite accumulation of minute detail. His writing is romantic in its melodrama, its effusion, its use of the fantastic, the grotesque, even the mystic. Yet his absorption with mundane detail, with sordid materialism, with acute, analytical documentation announces realism and paves the way for the naturalists. His work is infused with the rare insight of a poetic visionary, which enabled him to paint the surface and reveal the substance, the motor, the inner mechanisms of the human heart and psyche. In face of the scope, the creativity, the sheer bulk of *The Human Comedy*, as Henry James said, criticism simply drops out. Balzac stands alone, an enduring standard of measurement for the novel and the novelist.

A. Allemand, *Honoré de Balzac, création et passion* (Paris, 1965); R. Barthes, *S/Z*, trans. Richard Miller (New York, 1974); A. Béguin, *Balzac lu et relu* (Paris, 1965) and *Balzac visionnaire* (Geneva, 1946); F. Marceau, *Balzac and His World*, trans. Derek Coltman (London, 1967); A. Maurois, *Prometheus: The Life of Balzac*, trans. Norman Denny (London, 1965); V. S. Pritchett, *Balzac* (New York, 1973); S. Zweig, *Balzac* (New York, 1946).

Shelby A. Outlaw

Related entry: ROMANTICISM.

BANKING. The nineteenth-century French banking system has been the object of two kinds of criticism. The one is mainly an ideological—and more rarely anti-Semitic—critique, chiefly from the Left but also from the extreme Right. Already in the 1840s, for instance, there appeared attacks on the supposedly nefarious powers of the Parisian financial oligarchy, as in Alphonse Toussenel's pamphlet, *Les Juifs rois de l'époque* (1845). The other criticism is concerned with the efficacy of the system. Already in the early nineteenth century the conservatism of the Bank of France was frequently decried and extending credit facilities advocated, most notably by the Saint-Simonians and the Pereires. This second criticism appeared all the more justified in the light of the banking developments—and especially the establishment of mixed banks—after the midcentury and in view of the role that banks were destined to play in the French and other capitalist economies. Many scholars have subsequently repeated these allegations. They have rightly pointed out that one aspect of economic growth in the nineteenth century was the spread of bank money (notes and deposits) and the creation of complex banking networks, but they have wrongly treated banking as an independent variable.

Recent research and a more sensitive approach to banking history has led to a radical revision of these traditional strictures. The question of the relationship between banking and economic growth—is the one a cause or a consequence of the other, or is there a complex servomechanism?—is still open, for neither theory nor history offers a clear-cut answer. It is now clear, though, that the banking system is closely dependent on the economy, social structures, and attitudes and especially on demand for banking services. In the France of the early nineteenth century, for instance, it was the widespread attachment to gold and silver that limited the use of bank notes. And it was the desire of French industrial firms, both large and small, to remain independent of outside financing—a desire made practicable in this period by the low capital requirements even of industries undergoing technical innovation and by the practice of ploughing back profits—that limited the demand for bank credit. Self-financing as a motor of growth, indeed, was to remain the pattern for French firms throughout the century.

Even regarding the much-criticized policies adopted by bankers at the time, there is little evidence that these were not flexible and profit maximizing. By their nature, bank resources are mobile, and on general grounds it is difficult to conceive of French banking in the early part of the nineteenth century as ill adapted to the needs of the economy or as a hindrance to growth.

What, then, was the structure of banking in the first half of the nineteenth century? Any answer has to be prefaced by a proviso: though an understanding of many aspects of banking at this time has been greatly advanced by work done in the last quarter-century, we still do not have enough quantitative evidence on bills of exchange, bank deposits, the funds and functions of merchant bankers in provincial centers, interest rates, and indebtedness in the agrarian sector. We do know, however, that interest rates were markedly higher in the rest of France than they were in Paris and that extremely high rates were prevalent in agriculture. We know that specie continued to dominate the stock of money. In 1803 specie in circulation made up 95 percent and bank notes a mere 5 percent of this stock. By 1845 specie still constituted 82 percent, while bank notes had risen to 8 percent and bank deposits to 10 percent. Silver constituted the greater portion of this coin, though France maintained a bimetallic standard. As for bank notes, the smallest denomination until 1847 was for 500 francs, and only under the pressure of crisis were smaller notes issued. We also know that it was in the capital that banking structures were the most developed and powerful and that Paris acted as a magnet that drew in funds from the provinces.

The Bank of France, established in 1800, was at the center of the Parisian banking system. In this period, however, the status of the institution that was to become the country's central bank was ambiguous and its powers relatively limited. On the one hand, it was a private bank, which had stockholders and a board composed of the Parisian business elite. On the other, it was subject to tight control by the government, which from 1806 appointed its governor and deputy governors and periodically renewed—and revised—its privileges. It was the banker of last resort, discounted high-quality commercial paper, and was a note-issuing bank whose monopoly until 1836 was limited to the Seine department and thereafter extended only slowly to the provincial centers in which it established branches. The Bank of France's discount and note-issuing functions were supplemented by provincial banks, nine of which were set up before 1840. These new banks, though, enjoyed only restricted powers, and their notes had currency only in departments in which the banks were situated. In the economic crisis from 1847, all of them collapsed, and their functions were assumed by the Bank of France. It was only then—in 1848—that its monopoly of note issue was extended to the whole country.

The bank worked closely with, and its board was dominated by, leading Parisian merchant bankers. Known collectively as the *haute banque*, the strength of the some twenty-five firms that made up this group lay in the relatively large funds—their own capital and customers' deposits—they had at their disposal and their high standing in the national and international financial community.

Theirs was not only an open rather than closed group—new members from the early century included Jewish firms like the Rothschilds, d'Eichthals, and Foulds—but one that was getting richer.

Even more than structures, the policies adopted by bankers—and here there was a margin of maneuver where banks could have an impact on growth—were criticized by some contemporaries, and many historians have echoed them. The Bank of France, for example, has traditionally been castigated for a discount policy deemed too exigent, a note issue policy considered too timorous, and what was seen as a reluctance to set up provincial agencies. However, at least two major arguments can be invoked to explain and defend the bank's policies. The one is the control exercised by a government anxious to protect its interest in the bank as a lender of short-term funds and to protect its loan flotations and the national debt. The other is that memories of the collapse of the John Law scheme in 1720, and of the *assignats* and inflation of the Revolutionary and Napoleonic periods, engendered powerful fears that an overextension of credit and imprudent note issue would cause economic crises and inflation. Nor were the policies adopted out of step with what was happening across the Channel. Similarly conservative policies were being followed in England at this time, as evidenced in the Bank Act passed in 1844. Besides, even if they were prudent, bank policies were not inflexible; they were modified during economic crises and discount policy relaxed from the early 1830s.

A second facet of the reputedly Malthusian policies pursued by the *haute banque* at this time has been revealed to be false by the research of Bertrand Gille and Maurice Lévy-Leboyer. Their research shows that Parisian bankers were flexible and innovative in their search for profits. In the first half of the century, indeed, they expanded their activities in five new directions. They established insurance companies; by the midcentury thirty of these were listed on the Paris Stock Exchange. They took a leading role in government loan flotations in France and abroad. They increasingly invested in real estate, buying urban property, forest land, and estates. More important, since many members of the *haute banque* had begun their careers as industrialists, and all of them, as merchant bankers and importers of raw materials, had close ties with industrial firms, it was not surprising that they increasingly invested in industries like textiles and even heavy chemicals, metallurgy (especially the modern integrated concerns set up in the 1820s), sugar refining and mining. The *haute banque* played a major role, finally, in transport developments: canal building from the 1820s, in which they collaborated with the government, and railway construction, in which they became heavily—perhaps too heavily—committed in the 1840s.

There were also innovations and experiments in types of banks in this period. From 1818 savings banks were established, and by midcentury there were 272 *caisses d'épargne* (and 81 branch offices) with over half a million depositors with average balances of 53 francs. This, though, was but modest success compared with the subsequent expansion of savings banks, and the working class in 1850 was still largely untouched either by banks and bank notes or even by the savings banks set up for its use. There was also an attempt to improve mortgage credit with the creation in 1820 of the *caisse hypothécaire*. This institution did not secure the capital it had hoped for and, after a checkered and largely unsuccessful career, was wound up in 1847. More successful were the institutions known as *caisses* that were set up from 1837 onward. Their purpose was industrial promotion and the granting of short-term commercial and long-term industrial credit. By 1847 there were five such *caisses* in Paris and at least twenty in the provinces. Finally, in 1848 short-term credit facilities were extended by the creation by business and government of the *comptoirs d'escompte*. Though originally intended as temporary expedients in a crisis, some of these acquired permanent status. It is because of these innovations, and others elsewhere in Europe, that the so-called Banking Revolution of the Second Empire period was only quantitative and not qualitative, since it invented nothing in terms of technique or forms.

Banking in the first half of the century was thus not static but changing and responsive to the needs of the economy. Structures and functions then, as later, were largely dependent on the needs of the economy, savings, investment habits, and attitudes toward money. Banking indeed reflected the dualism to be found in the economy, the economic geography, and the society of France. Although bankers began to invest in some modern sectors and larger concerns in industry and transportation, medium and small enterprises and many sectors of the economy received no services at all from financial institutions. Banking facilities—notes, deposits, commercial credit—were still restricted to the capital and some large towns, though there was a discernible acceleration in the spread of bank notes in the 1840s. The great majority of the population in town and country still lived beyond the pale of banking and were long to continue to do so.

R. Bigo, *Les banques en France au cours du XIXe siecle* (Paris, 1947); F. Braudel and E. Labrousse, eds., *Histoire économique et sociale de la France*, vol. 3, pt. 1 (Paris, 1976); R. E. Cameron et al., *Banking in the Early Stages of Industrialisation: A Study in Comparative Economic History* (Oxford, 1967); B. Gille, *La banque et le crédit en France de 1815 à 1848* (Paris, 1959); B. M. Ratcliffe, ''Some Banking Ideas in France in the 1830s: The Writings of Emile and Isaac Péreire, 1830–1835,'' *Revue internationale d'histoire de la banque* 6 (1973).

Barrie M. Ratcliffe

Related entries: CAISSES D'EPARGNE; ECONOMIC CHANGE; JEWS; PEREIRE BROTHERS; ROTHSCHILD FAMILY; SAINT-SIMONIANISM.

BANQUET CAMPAIGN (1847–1848). In June 1847, a Paris committee supporting the parliamentary opposition under the July Monarchy decided on a campaign of political banquets to pressure the government into reform. Between July and the following February, approximately sixty banquets were held, and the fate of the last of them was central to the outbreak of the Revolution of 1848.

The campaign was engendered by the frustration of the opposition in the

Chamber of Deputies—the Center Left, dynastic Left, and the handful of republicans—and their supporters at the refusal of Louis-Philippe and the Guizot ministry to contemplate electoral and parliamentary reform. The government's success in the August 1846 elections added to their frustration. Their specific demands were for an extension of the franchise and for a reform to end the right of government officials to retain their positions if elected as deputies. In practice, however, there was disagreement within the opposition over the extent to which the franchise should be widened and on the need for other reforms of a social nature. This friction was echoed in the opposition press, which to varying degrees supported the campaign: *Le Constitutionnel, Le Siècle, Le National, La Réforme*.

The first banquet was held on 9 July in a Paris public garden, the Château Rouge, where 1,200 subscribers dined to the sound of patriotic tunes under the gaze of a crowd of onlookers. Among the speakers were Adrien-Barnabé Athanase de Recurt, L.-A. Pagnerre, Alexandre-Thomas Marie, Odilon Barrot, and Prosper Duvergier de Hauranne. This alliance of moderate republicans and liberal monarchists was to dominate the campaign. The Center Left was divided (Adolphe Thiers, Alexis de Tocqueville, and Jules Dufaure remained aloof) while radical republicans organized fewer, if more controversial, banquets.

After the close of the parliamentary session on 9 August, opposition deputies joined with constituency committees to organize provincial banquets, often with distinctly local issues paramount. While most of these banquets were small, others were substantial, such as that at Saint-Quentin in September where 750 attended and another 300 were turned away. A loose national cohesion was imposed by the presence of keynote speakers such as Barrot or Adolphe Crémieux. Momentum was sustained by anger at a series of scandals during the winter of 1847–48: the murder involving the duc de Choiseul-Praslin, the Teste-Cubières affair, which implicated a former minister, and finally the Petit scandal, which touched François Guizot himself.

Only with the Lille banquet on 7 November did radical republicans enter the campaign in earnest. Tension developed when Alexandre-Auguste Ledru-Rollin accepted an invitation and Barrot failed to convince the organizing committee to make the explicit purpose of the banquet the preservation of the principles of 1830. However, only about 60 of the 1,250 guests followed Barrot and the Center Left deputies from the hall; the rest, though of middle-class background, applauded Ledru-Rollin's openly democratic toast to the working class.

The radicals held two other large banquets, at Chalon-sur-Saône and Dijon, where about 1,300 guests listened to Etienne Arago, Ferdinand Flocon, Louis Blanc, Ledru-Rollin, and others. However, after Lille the coalition of moderate republicans and the dynastic Left had felt impelled to counter the radicals and organized a series of less militant banquets, notably at Lyons and Rouen; the latter, on Christmas Day, was the largest banquet of the campaign, with about 1,800 present.

Quite different was the revolutionary and socialist banquet at Limoges on 2 January, organized by Théodore Bac and Pierre Leroux, calling for democracy and the organization of labor. While hitherto government responses to the banquets had been limited to petty harassment, now it became more hostile. In his address at the opening of the new parliamentary session, Louis-Philippe criticized the "blind and hostile passions" opposed to his regime. Henceforth, as in the stormy debate over the address in reply between 7 and 12 February, the issue was to be the right of association.

Acting independently of the Paris organizing committee, National Guard officers in the Latin Quarter had been preparing a large banquet for 22 February designed to unite all shades of the opposition. The government and parliamentary opposition, both concerned at the prospect of up to 4,000 subscribers—including for the first time delegations of students and workers—meeting in Paris, decided on a compromise whereby the right to hold such a banquet would be tested in the courts.

However, this was thwarted by the publication in *Le National* and *La Réforme* on 21 February of a proclamation drawn up by Armand Marrast; this laid down details of a mass march from the Madeleine along the Champs-Elysées to precede the banquet. On the grounds that this proclamation had usurped its prerogative to call out the National Guard, the government banned the banquet outright. Meetings of all the opposition groups on the evening of 21 February also decided that it was too risky to proceed. But by the next morning, as groups of students and workers began to assemble on the place de la Madeleine, it was apparent that the banquet campaign had been unsuccessful in another sense: not only had it failed to pressure the government into reform, but the parliamentary opposition now found itself outflanked by other groups for whom piecemeal reform was inadequate.

O. Barrot, *Mémoires posthumes*, 4 vols. (Paris, 1876); J. J. Baughman, "The French Banquet Campaign of 1847–1848," *Journal of Modern History* 31 (1959); F. A. de Luna, *The French Republic under Cavaignac, 1848* (Princeton, 1969); G. W. Fasel, "The French Moderate Republicans, 1837–1848" (Ph.D diss., Stanford University, 1965); J. Vidalenc, "A propos de la campagne des banquets (1847–1848)," *Actes du 81e congrès national des sociétés savantes* (Paris, 1956).

Peter McPhee

Related entries: ARAGO FAMILY; BARROT, C.; BLANC; *LE CONSTITU-TIONNEL*; CREMIEUX; FLOCON; GUIZOT; LEDRU-ROLLIN; LEROUX; MARRAST; *LE NATIONAL*; *LA REFORME*; *LE SIECLE*; THIERS.

BARAGUAY D'HILLIERS, ACHILLE (1795–1878), French general, deputy, and ambassador. Baraguay d'Hilliers, son of the famous French General Louis Baraguay d'Hilliers, was a famous and highly decorated general who began his military career in 1813 at the end of the First Empire at the battle of Leipzig, where Napoleon's new army was defeated. During the course of this battle, he was severely wounded in the head by a saber and at the same time lost his left hand in a blast of cannon fire. At this time he held the rank of patrol lieutenant of the artillery and was considered extremely capable.

By 1823 he was distinguished and promoted to the rank of captain as part of an expedition in Spain. In 1830 he became lieutenant colonel and participated in the African expedition that ended with the taking of Algeria. Algeria became legally part of France in 1848 as a result of these and later military operations. Algeria earned him the epaulets of colonel.

After the Revolution of 1830, Baraguay d'Hilliers continued his military service under Louis-Philippe during the July Monarchy, and he was charged with heading the famous military school of Saint-Cyr. By 1843 he was back in Algeria commanding troops. The natives named him Father of Arms, making reference to the loss of his forearm. He was an active participant in the Revolution of 1848 and remained on the side of Napoleon III as an elected deputy. He stayed at the side of Napoleon III after the coup d'état of 1851 and gained a reputation as being bellicose. Later he was ambassador to Rome, selected by the emperor to "preach peace" for the French government during the Crimean War. After the defeat of Russia, he was nominated to the Senate. During the campaign in Italy in 1859, he was head of the French Army after the entrance of Franco Sardi into Milan. He had received so many honors "there were no more." By 1870 when the French established the Third Republic, he was too old for combat, but because of his previous record and extraordinary leadership capabilities, he was made head of the military post of Paris. Despondent over the new fate of France and his own failing health, Baraguay d'Hilliers killed himself with a pistol on 6 July 1878.

Enciclopedia Italiana Ristampa Fotolitica Del., vol. 6 (1930); *Nouvelle biographie générale depuis les temps les plus recules jusqu'à 1850–1860* (Copenhagen, 1964).

Irene Earls

Related entries: ALGIERS, EXPEDITION TO; COUP D'ETAT OF 2 DECEMBER 1851; ECOLE MILITAIRE; REVOLUTION OF 1830; REVOLUTION OF 1848; SPAIN, 1823 FRENCH INVASION OF.

BARANTE, AMABLE-GUILLAUME-PROSPER BRUGIERE, BARON DE (1782–1866), moderate royalist politician and author, deputy and peer of the Restoration and the July Monarchy. Barante was born 10 June 1782 at Riom (Puy-de-Dôme). Educated at the Ecole polytechnique, Barante entered Napoleon's bureaucracy, serving in the Ministry of the Interior in 1802, as auditor in the Council of State in 1806, and on special missions in Spain, Danzig, and Warsaw in that same year. In 1807 he became subprefect at Bressuire (Deux-Sèvres) and in 1809 was appointed prefect of the Vendée at age twenty-seven. During this period he became close friends with Mme. de la Rochejaquelein, Mme. Récamier, and Mme. de Staël, to whom he proposed marriage. In 1809 he married Mlle. Houdetot. In 1813 he became prefect of Loire-Inférieure, remaining there until his resignation on 20 March 1815. At the Second Restoration the Bourbons appointed him a councillor of state and secretary-general of the Ministry of the Interior, where he fulfilled the duties of the minister until Vincent de Vaublanc was named to that post. Barante then became director-general of indirect taxes.

In August 1815 two departments, Loire-Inférieure and Puy-de-Dôme, elected him to the Chamber of Deputies where he was part of the faction led by Pierre Royer-Collard and Pierre-François de Serre. As a deputy Barante opposed conservative efforts to reduce the number of courts, although he gave significant support to the government's budget and to the use of indirect taxes. But when Louis XVIII dissolved the Chambre introuvable on 5 September 1816, he also raised the minimum age for deputies to forty, thus excluding Barante. Nevertheless Barante continued to appear in the Chamber as a government commissioner, speaking on the army recruiting law of Gouvion Saint-Cyr and supporting the tobacco monopoly.

Barante's appointment to a peerage on 5 March 1819 did not dampen his liberal sentiments, and he continued to speak out, most notably on a proposed draconian press law and against special privileges for the Roman Catholic church. The more conservative second Richelieu ministry removed Barante from the Council of State but offered him the Copenhagen embassy, which he refused.

Although he continued to appear in the Chamber of Peers, he now turned his attention to writing history. His first work, on the dukes of Burgundy of the house of Valois, published between 1824 and 1828, won him a seat in the French Academy for its style and quality. The July Monarchy was more to his political taste than had been the Bourbons, and in the Peers he consistently supported the government. In 1830 he went as ambassador to Turin and in 1835 to Saint Petersburg. His political career came to an end with the February Revolution of 1848. Thereafter he turned increasingly to writing and died at Dorat (Puy-de-Dôme) on 21 November 1866. His other major works include histories of the National Convention and of the Directory and biographies of Royer-Collard, Mathieu Molé, and Joan of Arc. The eight volumes of his own *Souvenirs* were published by his grandson, Claude de Barante, in 1890–91.

Archives parlementaires; J. Regnier, *Les Préfets du consulat et de l'empire* (Paris, 1907); N. Richardson, *The French Prefectoral Corps, 1814–1830* (Cambridge, 1966); A. Robert et al., *Dictionnaire des parlementaires français* (Paris, 1889–91); J. Savant, *Les Préfets de Napoléon* (Paris, 1958).

James K. Kieswetter

Related entries: ACADEMIE FRANCAISE; CHAMBER OF DEPUTIES; CHAMBER OF PEERS; CHAMBRE INTROUVABLE; ECOLE POLYTECH-NIQUE; MOLE; PRESS LAWS; RECAMIER; RICHELIEU; ROYER-COL-LARD; SERRE; STAEL.

BARBE-MARBOIS, COMTE FRANCOIS DE (1745–1837), Napoleonic and Restoration minister. Son of the director of the royal mint in Metz, Barbé-Marbois served under Louis XVI as a consul-general in the United States and as intendant in Santo Domingo, returning to a post in the foreign ministry in 1789. He retired from national politics in 1791, becoming mayor of Metz. His royalist sympathies led to his deportation to Guyana after the Fructidor coup (4 September 1797). Released after Napoleon's seizure of power in 1799, he served the Emperor and was made president of the Cour des comptes in 1808 and Senator in 1813. One of the authors of Napoleon's act of abdication in 1814, Barbé-Marbois rallied to the Bourbons and was named to the commission that drafted the Charter. He was made a peer (June 1814) and continued as president of the Cour des comptes. Napoleon removed him from this post during the Hundred Days, but the Second Restoration saw his appointment as keeper of the seals and minister of justice (August 1815) in the first Richelieu ministry. He defended the "exceptional laws," which penalized seditious speech and writing and reestablished the *cours prévôtales*, against ultra opposition in the Chamber (October 1815–January 1816). The ultras, who never forgave his service to Napoleon, voted down his proposed reform of the Cour des comptes, and Louis XVIII, eager to placate his right-wing opponents, dropped him from the ministry in May 1816. He returned to his customary position of president of the Cour des comptes until his retirement for reasons of health in April 1834. He devoted his last years to composing his memoirs.

Never sympathetic to the Revolution, Barbé-Marbois served Bonaparte and the Bourbons with equal loyalty and obsequiousness. A better financial bureaucrat than politician, he was described by contemporaries as possessing a gruff demeanor that inadequately concealed an inner weakness and general mediocrity.

F. de Barbé-Marbois, *Journal d'un déporté non-jugé* (Paris, 1835); L. Bergeron, *L'episode napoléonien* (Paris, 1972); G. de Bertier de Sauvigny, *La Restauration* (Paris, 1955, 1963); J. F. Bosher, *French Finances, 1770–1795* (Cambridge, 1970); G. Lefebvre, *Napoléon* (Paris, 1936); P. Mansel, *Louis XVIII* (London, 1981).

David Longfellow

Related entries: COURS PREVOTALES; LAW ON SEDITIOUS SPEECH; RICHELIEU; ULTRAROYALISTS.

BARBES, SIGMUND-AUGUSTE-ARMAND (1809–1870), republican militant under the July Monarchy and club leader during the Revolution of 1848. Barbès was born in Guadeloupe 18 September 1809, the son of a French father and Creole mother. He went to France with his parents at age five and lived in the Midi near Carcassonne, where his father practiced medicine. Barbès began to study law but soon joined the republican opposition to the July Monarchy. A member of the Société des droits de l'homme, Barbès was briefly arrested in 1834 on a charge of inciting to insurrection. In 1835 he was chosen as one of the legal defenders of the 164 republicans arrested following the abortive Parisian insurrection of 1834 and also helped 28 of the prisoners to escape.

Soon thereafter Barbès began a close association with Louis-Auguste Blanqui in the secret Société des familles; arrested in 1836 along with Blanqui, with whom he shared a residence, Barbès was sentenced to a year in prison for illegal possession of arms. Shortly after serving his term, Barbès, a resident of Carcassonne once more, published a brochure, *Quelques mots à ceux qui possedent en faveur des prolétaires sans travail*, which brought upon him a new charge of an attack on property. Though acquitted, he was imprisoned for a month for contempt of court.

In 1838, Barbès along with Blanqui organized a new secret society, that of the Seasons, which on 12 May 1839 attempted an uprising in Paris. Barbès was wounded at the Hôtel de ville where he had attempted to proclaim a provisional government. Tried with eighteen colleagues before the Cour des pairs, Barbès alone was sentenced to death, but King Louis-Philippe commuted the sentence to life imprisonment following student demonstrations and appeals by Victor Hugo and Alphonse de Lamartine. Barbès remained in prison for nine years, until he was freed following the February Revolution of 1848.

Disdaining the post of governor of the Luxembourg Palace offered by the Provisional Government, Barbès instead chose to play an active political role, as president of the Club de la révolution and as commander of the National Guard in the twelfth arrondissement of Paris. Relations with his old colleague Blanqui, who now led a rival club, were embittered by the publication on 31 March 1848 of the Taschereau document, which purportedly proved that Blanqui had betrayed his fellow conspirators of 1839. On 16 April 1848, Barbès played an important part in thwarting an antigovernment demonstration by workers when he massed his Twelfth Legion of the National Guard at the Hôtel de ville.

During the elections to the National Constituent Assembly on 23 April 1848, Barbès was elected in the Aude and sat at the extreme Left. After demonstrators invaded the assembly on 15 May and declared it dissolved, Barbès along with Albert, the worker member of the former Provisional Government, led the insurgents to the Hôtel de ville, where they proclaimed a new provisional government that included Barbès. But within an hour the reviving governmental forces had arrested Barbès and his colleagues.

Barbès was thus in prison during the climax and dénouement of the revolution: the abortive workers' insurrection in June, the stern government of Eugène Cavaignac, and the election of Louis-Napoleon Bonaparte to the presidency in December 1848. Tried along with Albert, Blanqui, and others in 1849 at Bourges, Barbès was once more sentenced to life imprisonment. The Emperor Napoleon III pardoned him in 1854, but Barbès preferred to remain in exile. He was living at the Hague when French republicans asked him to pose his candidacy in the elections of 1869; he refused for reasons of health and died 26 June 1870, just ten weeks before a republic was once more proclaimed in France, on 4 September 1870.

P. H. Amann, *Revolution and Mass Democracy* (Princeton, 1975); F. F. Jeanjean, *Armand Barbès* (1809–70); I. Tchernoff, *Le Parti républicain sous la monarchie de juillet* (Paris, 1905); S. Wassermann, *Les Clubs de Barbès et de Blanqui en 1848* (Paris, 1913); G. Weill, *Histoire du parti républicain en France, 1814–1870* (Paris, 1928).

Frederick A. de Luna

Related entries: ALBERT; BLANQUI; CAVAIGNAC, L.-E.; CLUBS, PO-LITICAL; CONSTITUTION OF 1848; HUGO; JUNE DAYS; LAMARTINE; NATIONAL GUARD; PROVISIONAL GOVERNMENT; REVOLUTION OF 1848; SOCIETY OF THE RIGHTS OF MAN; SOCIETY OF THE SEASONS.

BARERE DE VIEUZAC, BERTRAND DE (1755–1841), revolutionary politician, *conventionnel*, terrorist, and man of letters. The future terrorist and colleague of Maximillian Robespierre on the Committee of Public Safety was born in Tarbes on 10 September 1755, the first of the five children of Jean Barère, procurator to the *seneschal* of Digorre. During the 1770s, he acquired the *seigneurie* of Vieuzac (or Biéouzac) and the title *seigneur* of Vieuzac from a relative of his noble-born wife. During the Revolution he served with Robespierre on the Committee of Public Safety, then turned against Robespierre when he lost power. Later he supported Napoleon Bonaparte.

When in early 1814 the invasion and defeat of France seemed imminent, Barère, fearing for his life, fled Paris in February, returning only in April. Declaring himself satisfied with both the Declaration of Saint-Ouen and the Charter of 1814, he began a campaign for a place in the new government. To this end, he wrote one pamphlet denouncing Napoleonic despotism, another appealing for loyalty to the Bourbon government and the Charter, and a series of anonymous articles in the *Gazette de France*. All of Barère's effort availed him nought. When the emperor returned in 1815, Barère again made it known that he was willing to serve France. Elected to the chamber as a deputy from the Hautes-Pyrénées in May 1815, Barère adhered to a group directed by Joseph Fouché that sought to curb Napoleon's despotic tendencies. In this cause, Barère endeavored to make the Additional Act more democratic, to influence public opinion, and to gain the emperor's attention with his purported translation of *Théorie de la constitution de la Grande-Bretagne*. Not only did Barère author this work, he also wrote for the *Moniteur* a laudatory review of it. From Barère's pen also came the *Considérations sur la Chambre des Pairs*, a plea for a hereditary peerage, and *Les Epoques de la nation française*, which presented a history of the tradition of popular sovereignty in France. All Barère's efforts came to nothing when Napoleon's armies met defeat at Waterloo.

During the political crisis of late June and early July 1815, when Fouché attempted to play the role of king maker, Barère participated in several futile efforts to impose conditions on the return of the Bourbons. Along with fifty-two other deputies, he signed a protest on 8 July that denounced the closing of the Chambers by foreign troops. Although he had felt relatively secure up to this point, for he had Fouché's protection, Barère found his name on the ordinance of 24 July and immediately went into hiding. When it became clear that the Bourbon government would not suffer the presence in France of Barère, with his reputation as a terrorist and a regicide, he decided to evade the provisions of the amnesty bill of 1816, fleeing France under a false name on 1 March 1816. For the next fourteen years, the old terrorist, afflicted with poor health, lived in fear and poverty, first in Mons (1816–22) and then in Brussels (1822–30). In the latter city, he maintained close contacts with the community of exiled *revolutionnaires*, which included Jacques-Louis David and, curiously, Filippo Buonarroti, former Babouvist and now prophet of communist revolution.

Following the July Revolution, Barère, together with others proscribed during the Restoration, returned to France. Between 1833 and 1844, he served in the Departmental Council of the Hautes-Pyrénées. Toward the end of his life, he completed the arrangements for the publication of his *Mémoires*; edited by Lazare Hippolyte Carnot, the four volumes appeared between 1842 and 1844. At the age of eighty-five, Bertrand Barère died on 13 January 1841. The bulk of his papers may be found in the Archives departementales des Hautes-Pyrénées.

B. Barère de Vieuzac, *Mémoires de Barère*, 4 vols. (Paris, 1842–44); L. Gershoy, *Bertrand Barère: A Reluctant Terrorist* (Princeton, 1962); R. Palmer, *Twelve Who Ruled* (Princeton, 1941).

Robert Brown

Related entries: ACTE ADDITIONNEL; AMNESTY BILL OF 1816; BU-ONARROTI; CARNOT, L.-H.; CHARTER OF 1814; DAVID; FOUCHE; *LA GAZETTE DE FRANCE.*

BARRES, JEAN-BAPTISTE-AUGUSTE (1784–1846), officer under Napoleon and the Restoration, grandfather of Maurice Barrès. J. B. A. Barrès was born at Blesle in the Haute-Loire on 25 July 1784 to Jean-Francois Barrès and Antoinette-Christine Cheminard. Barrès studied medicine but in June 1804 joined the Imperial Guard. He fought at Austerlitz and at Eylau and Friedland. He was made a second lieutenant on 31 December 1807 and after serving in Spain and Portugal was promoted to captain on 19 April 1812. He was wounded at Lutzen and decorated by Napoleon on 18 May 1813. He fought in the final campaigns and was then furloughed. Although he rallied to Napoleon during the Hundred Days, he was appointed commander of the Departmental Legion in the Haute-Loire in October 1815. In December 1820, he was transferred to the Pyrénées-Orientales. On 14 November 1827, he became a battalion commander of the Fifteenth Infantry, and during the July Revolution he led his unit in defense of Charles X's regime in the Pantheon district. On 19 June 1831, Barrès was appointed to the Legion of Honor. He retired on 6 June 1835 to Charmes, where he died in January 1846.

On 3 July 1827, he married Marie-Reine Barbier of Charmes. Their son, Joseph-Auguste, was the father of Maurice Barrès. Maurice Barrès edited his grandfather's journal, and it was published in 1923 as *Souvenirs d'un officier de la Grande Armée.*

R. D'Amat in *Dictionnaire de biographie française*, vol. 5 (Paris, 1951); T. de Lamathière, *Panthéon de la légion d'honneur*, (Paris, 1875–1911).

Bernard Cook

Related entries: CHARLES X; REVOLUTION OF 1830.

BARROT, CAMILLE-HYACINTHE-ODILON (1791–1873), lawyer, politician, and leader of the dynastic Left during the July Monarchy. Although born in the southeastern village of Planchamp (Lozère), Odilon Barrot received his education in Paris and spent most of his adult life in the capital as a political figure during the Restoration, the July Monarchy, and the Second Republic. His father, Jean-Antoine Barrot (1753–1845), a lawyer before the Revolution, served in the Convention as a deputy from the Lozère and took part in the trial of Louis XVI, voting against the death penalty. As a representative of Lozère in the Corps legislatif, he supported the overthrow of Napoleon and the return of the Bourbons in 1814, but he welcomed the emperor's return during the Hundred Days. When appointed a judge by Louis XVIII, Barrot's past political associations prevented him from taking office. His son Odilon, who had arrived in Paris in 1795, attended Saint-Cyr, the Lycée Napoléon (1806–8), and the Faculty of Law; having passed his examinations, he swore the required oath before the imperial court in 1811 and began his career as secretary to the old *conventionnel* and regicide Jean Mailhe, lawyer to the Council of State and the Cour de cassation. During the First Restoration, Barrot replaced his mentor at the Council of the King. Unlike many of his compatriots, Barrot sided with the Bourbons during the Hundred Days. A member of the National Guard, he watched both the departure from the Tuileries of Louis XVIII and the arrival of Napoleon; he later refused to recognize the Additional Act, and he welcomed the Second Restoration. Short-lived was his enthusiasm, however, as Barrot saw his patron Mailhe exiled and his father forced from a judgeship granted him by Louis XVIII. To the fortunate young lawyer, Mailhe had ceded his position at the Cour de cassation, a post Barrot used in 1816–18 to build a reputation as an ardent defender of liberal men and causes.

During the White Terror, Barrot defended men brought before the special *cours prévôtales* who had appealed their cases, notably Colonel Auguste Lepeletier de Chambure. He also participated in two notorious cases of 1817, that of Wilfrid Regnault and that of the Tapestries. One year later, he defended the liberal journal *Le Censeur européen* when it was prosecuted in Rennes on the pretext that it had slandered the local prosecutor. To the rightist reaction that followed the assassination of the duc de Berry (13 February 1820), prominent liberals responded with a committee of protest, and Barrot, along with Charles Comte of the now-defunct *Censeur européen* and others whose names were linked to it, found himself brought before the Cour d'assises (29 June 1820). Acquitted, Barrot prudently shunned involvement in the various liberal conspiracies that flourished in France between 1820 and 1822. He did, nevertheless, defend two men accused in the Bazar français conspiracy of 1820, attend the funeral of the student Lallemand killed in June 1820, and unsuccessfully argued the appeal of Lieutenant-Colonel Caron, tried and executed for his complicity in a carbonari plot at Colmar in 1822. For the remaining eight years of Restoration, Barrot continued to plead liberal causes, and he maintained a close association with various opposition movements. By marrying Agathe Desfossez (10 June 1824), he gained a tie with the important Labbey de Pompières family. In addition, he took a prominent role in the activities of the electoral society Aide-toi, le ciel t'aidera, founded in 1827 to encourage qualified voters in the exercise of their rights, by serving with other noted opposition leaders on its executive committee.

With the advent of the Polignac ministry, described by Barrot as a "pealing of the tocsin in all France," he took a more active but still moderate role. At a banquet held for the 221 deputies who had voted for the reply critical of Charles X's address of 2 March 1830, Barrot offered a toast ("To the constitutional monarchy and the two chambers; to the cooperation of the three powers") in place of an effort by more radical elements to ban altogether the toast to the crown.

In the July Revolution and the regime created by it, Odilon Barrot took an active part. Like most of his fellow Frenchmen, Barrot read with surprise the announcement of the royal ordinances in the *Moniteur* of 26 July 1830. At about 11 A.M., in response to questions put to him by the publishers of the *Constitutionnel*, he agreed with fellow lawyers André Dupin, Joseph Mérilhou, and Félix Barthe that the ordinances were illegal. Upon learning of this opinion, the journalists retired to the offices of the *National*, where Adolphe Thiers drafted the famous protest, which over forty of them signed. During that same evening, Barrot received a delegation of students, led by a nephew, from the Ecole polytechnique; to them, Barrot counseled resistance to the government. Trapped by the fighting in his home for two days, Odilon Barrot managed to establish contact on 29 July with the leading opposition deputies; when they named a municipal commission to assume control of the capital, Barrot became its secretary. By 30 July Barrot was ready to take a more active role, advising Lafayette and the group at the Hôtel de ville to accept a constitutional monarchy with the duc d'Orléans at its head. Barrot watched while Lafayette and the duke embraced on the balcony of the Hôtel de ville the next day.

While events in the capital worked themselves out, Charles X fled to Rambouillet, where he signed on 2 August a letter of abdication. The duc d'Orléans, now lieutenant-general of the kingdom, immediately dispatched a delegation that included Odilon Barrot to persuade Charles to quit France; the mission failed. Barrot returned, accompanied this time by a force of National Guardsmen and a motley band of armed Parisians, and he succeeded in convincing the ex-king to depart. Barrot accompanied Charles to Cherbourg, from whence the last of the Bourbons sailed into exile on 16 August. Barrot returned to Paris to assume his new duties as prefect of the Seine.

During Barrot's short but eventful tenure as prefect of the Seine (20 August 1830–22 February 1831), he faced two major crises—the disturbances accompanying the trial of Charles X's ministers and the sack of the palace belonging to the archbishop of Paris—and a host of minor ones. Out of the struggle of Barrot and the other men who formed the first government of the July Monarchy came the first indications of a difference in attitude that would first lead to Barrot's resignation and eventually to his long career as leader of the dynastic opposition to the Orléans regime. Demonstrations by Parisians demanding the death penalty for the last ministers of Charles X began in late September and reached a critical point in mid-October. Within the government a serious split developed over how to deal with these disturbances. François Guizot, Casimir Périer, and Achille de Broglie favored harsh repression, while

Jacques Laffitte, Jacques-Charles Dupont de l'Eure, Barrot, and others inclined toward appeasement of the crowd. Late in December, the forced resignation of the marquis de Lafayette as commander of the National Guard gave an indication of the course favored by the government. Barrot, although disturbed enough by the direction in which events were moving to call publicly for a more liberal electoral law and a more representative Chamber of Peers, remained in office, though not for long. In February 1831, a crowd of Parisians, provoked by legitimists who unwisely sought to organize a memorial service on the anniversary of the assassination of the duc de Berry, ransacked the church and presbytery of Saint-Germain-l'Auxerrois and pillaged the archbishop's palace. Sharply criticized by the government for failing to take measures to prevent these events, Barrot, together with the prefect of the police, was dismissed. Odilon Barrot's last direct connection with the government was severed when he left the Council of State in April 1831.

Between 1831 and 1848, Odilon Barrot, from his position in the Chamber of Deputies, representing first the Eure (1830–31), then the Bas-Rhin (1831–34) and, finally, the Aisne (1834–48), steadfastly opposed the July Monarchy, emerging as the leader of the dynastic Left.

With its origins during his months as prefect of the Seine, Barrot's opposition to the dominant political tendencies of the July Monarchy became a fixed feature of the French political scene. He opposed the ministry of Casimir Périer, the strong-willed banker who, between March 1831 and May 1832, insisted to France that the days of revolution were over and that demands for future changes would be resisted. Barrot later joined the unlikely coalition of Guizot and Thiers and helped bring down the government of the comte Molé, who had been head of the ministry since 1836; behind this marriage of convenience of usually opposed forces was a distaste for the strong personal role taken by Louis-Philippe in the government. Once successful, Barrot, Thiers, and Guizot failed to find enough common ground for the creation of a government, and the king appointed Marshal Soult, a famed general who occasionally served as the head of various governments in the 1830s. After 1840, when Guizot became the leading figure in French politics, Barrot spoke without restraint as a vocal and bitter opponent of the government. In his role as an opposition leader, Barrot took a prominent part in the famous Banquet Campaign that began in 1847 and that helped to trigger the Revolution of 1848.

As the recognized leader of the dynastic Left during the 1830s and the 1840s, Odilon Barrot articulated in his many speeches before the Chamber of Deputies and in several published and unpublished works a relatively consistent set of views on what shape French domestic and foreign policy should assume. A defender of the notion that the Revolution of 1830 corrected and completed the Revolution of 1789, Barrot also accepted Thiers' classic dictim of 1830: "le roi regne et ne gouverne pas." Throughout the July Monarchy, he advocated moderate electoral and parliamentary reform, though by no means advocating democracy or even universal suffrage. Barrot firmly supported the necessity for a bicameral legislature, and his ideas on the question of the peerage derived from this conviction. Opposing both a hereditary peerage and a peerage named by the king, Barrot favored instead direct election of members of the upper house by the municipal councils. He also supported the decentralization of the government and reductions in government spending. When the question of the nature of the French army arose, Barrot opposed a professional army, defending instead an army built on a citizen reserve. On one of the major social questions of the day, Barrot favored the reintroduction of divorce. In foreign affairs, he took a moderate position, balanced between those who favored military action to regain what they considered France's natural frontiers and a propaganda war in favor of the struggles of oppressed peoples, and those who advocated a cautious policy of complete nonintervention. While expressing great sympathy for the plight of oppressed peoples, especially the Poles, who rose up in rebellion, and while favoring French efforts to restrain outside powers from intervening to crush such revolutions, Barrot did not advocate active French support for foreign revolutionary movements.

Following Guizot's major electoral victory of 1846 and his decisive defeat of proposed electoral and parliamentary reforms in March 1847, his major parliamentary opponents, Thiers, Barrot, and the radical Left, decided upon a campaign of propaganda and peaceful agitation. In the ensuing Banquet Campaign, which was modeled on the efforts of Richard Cobden and the English Anti-Corn Law League, Barrot had a prominent role, the cautious Thiers remaining for the most part out of the limelight. The first of some seventy banquets took place at the Château Rouge near Paris on 9 July 1847 and attracted about 100 opposition deputies and some 1,200 electors. During the next three months, Barrot became the principal spokesman of the campaign, addressing twenty such banquets, including the one held at Rouen that counted among its 1,800 guests a disgruntled Gustave Flaubert. Writing with undisguised disgust of the rhetorical clichés favored by politicians, Flaubert found offensive "the righteous bellowing of M. Odilon Barrot." By early 1848, Barrot found that the speeches being given at the banquets were becoming too radical for his taste, but he and the other opposition leaders could not distance themselves from them without doing damage to their political credibility. The gigantic banquet planned by the twelfth arrondissement of Paris for early February 1848 hence placed the opposition in an awkward predicament. Barrot negotiated with the government to find a peaceful solution to a potentially explosive situation, but the complex agreement they reached was fraught with danger. Although the government would ban the banquet, it would allow the participants to assemble, and, following a brief, perfunctory protest, they agreed to disperse at the order of the police. Such a charade would save face for all concerned and allow the courts to settle the question of the legality of the banquets. This complex plan dissolved on 21 February when Armand Marrast, the republican editor of the *National*, published a plan of march for participants in the banquet. Viewing this scheme as a direct challenge to its authority, the government demanded the immediate cancellation of the banquet. While assembled at Barrot's house, a group of opposition deputies voted to cancel their plans for the march and the banquet and, in an effort to protest feebly, to attempt to impeach the ministry. A large and unruly crowd nonetheless assembled on 22 February at the Madeleine and the place de la Concorde. Meanwhile Barrot placed before the Chamber of Deputies a petition accusing the ministry.

On 23 February, following a night of barricade building and sporadic violence, Louis-Philippe dismissed the unpopular Guizot and attempted to rally the National Guard with the promise of a reform program and with a new cabinet headed by Thiers and Barrot. The next day, the two men, in an attempt to avoid additional bloodshed, ordered the army to withdraw from the streets, leaving the maintenance of order in Paris to the National Guard. Barrot tried unsuccessfully to rally the insurgent Parisians to the new government. Faced with the inevitable, Louis-Philippe abdicated on 24 February in favor of his grandson. Barrot then hastened to the Palais Bourbon and appealed to the Chamber of Deputies to save the monarchy and to accept the count of Paris as king, with his mother, the duchesse d'Orléans, as regent. Lamartine, who followed Barrot to the podium, carried the day, however, with a demand for the creation of a provisional government. Barrot, meanwhile, turned aside a request for support from a group of republicans. Only with reluctance did Barrot come to support the Second Republic.

During the Second Republic, Barrot played a minor but important role. Elected in April to the new Assembly, he served, along with Alexis de Tocqueville, among others, on the committee that drafted the Constitution of 1848; owing to his displeasure with the completed document, Barrot abstained when the final vote came. In the aftermath of the June Days, Barrot headed the parliamentary commission of inquiry that investigated the insurrection of May and June. Throughout much of 1848, Barrot associated with the Réunion de la rue de Poitiers, a group that brought together such men as Thiers and Remusat to defend Orleanist and legitimist interests. Following the elections for the presidency of the Second Republic, the newly elected Louis-Napoleon, whom Barrot had not supported, made him head of his first government.

In domestic affairs, Barrot's ministry, largely a coalition of Orleanists and legitimists, because it had as its principal goal the restoration of order, closed the clubs, opposed amnesty proposals, and sought to hasten the dissolution of the Constituent Assembly. The most noteworthy and controversial event of Barrot's government came, however, in foreign affairs, and it entangled France in Roman and Italian affairs for the next twenty years. After a revolution chased the pope from Rome in November 1848, Italian republicans proclaimed in February a Roman republic. Louis Napoleon, seeking to anticipate the other Catholic powers who wanted to restore the pope, sent an expedition to Italy. But because the government rightly feared an outcry on the part of French republicans, who could not be expected to remain silent while a French army destroyed a sister republic and restored an absolutist sovereign, it asked for the needed funds without specifying the true purpose of the expedition. While a first assault on Rome failed, a second succeeded in June, and Pius IX returned to his city. However, despite French entreaties, he refused to reform the abuses that had lead to his ouster. French troops remained in Rome until 1871. Barrot's ministry, which increasingly came into conflict with the prince-president, ended on 30 October 1849.

Following the fall of his government, Barrot returned to the Assembly, voting mainly with the Right and seeking to defend the prerogatives of the Assembly against Louis-Napoleon's encroachments. Although he had no part in the coup d'état of 2 December, Barrot participated in the protest of the deputies at the mairie of the tenth arrondissement. Arrested, he passed a few days of imprisonment in Vincennes.

Between 1851 and his death on 6 August 1873, Barrot lived in retirement, devoting himself to his *Mémoires* and to the work of the Académie des sciences morales et politiques. He refused a position in Emile Ollivier's government. At the insistence of Thiers, he returned to public service in 1872, becoming president of the Council of State.

C. Alméras, *Odilon Barrot avocat et homme politique (19 juillet 1791–6 août 1873)* (Paris, 1951); O. Barrot, *Memoires posthumes de Odilon Barrot*, 4 vols. (Paris, 1875–76); A. Lebey, *Louis-Napoleon Bonaparte et le Ministere Odilon Barrot, 1849* (Paris, 1912).

Robert Brown

Related entries: BANQUET CAMPAIGN; BARROT, V.-F.; BARTHE; BAZAR CONSPIRACY; CARON; *LE CENSEUR EUROPEEN*; COMITE DE LA RUE DE POITIERS; *LE CONSTITUTIONNEL*; DIVORCE, ABOLITION OF; DUPIN, A.-M.-J.-J.-; DUPONT DE L'EURE; GUIZOT; LABBEY DE POMPIERES; LAFAYETTE, MARQUIS DE; LAFFITTE; LALLEMAND; LAMARTINE; MARRAST; MERILHOU; MOLE; MUNICIPAL COMMISSION; PERIER; ROMAN EXPEDITION; SAINT-GERMAIN L'AUXERROIS, RIOT OF; SOULT; THE 221; THIERS.

BARROT, VICTOR-FERDINAND (1806–1883), lawyer, politician, and prominent Bonapartist. Son of the *conventionnel* Jean-Antoine Barrot (1753–1845) and the younger brother of the diplomat Adolphe Barrot (1801–70) and the politician Odilon Barrot (1791–1873), Ferdinand Barrot was born in Paris on 10 January 1806. His legal studies completed, he entered the Parisian bar before the July Revolution, an event in which he did not participate. During the July Monarchy, Barrot served first as a *procureur du roi* (1830–36), and then, after his return to private life, he made his reputation as a defense attorney in a number of celebrated political trials. His successful defense of Colonel Vaudry, implicated in Louis-Napoleon's abortive coup of 1836, and his unsuccessful defense of Louis-Napoleon before the Chamber of Peers after the Boulogne affair (1841), tied his political future to the fate of Bonapartism. Elected to the Chamber of Deputies in 1842, Barrot sat with the opposition, although his political position remained more moderate than that of his brother, the leader of the dynastic Left during the July Monarchy. Having obtained property in Algeria, he took a great interest in matters concerning this area.

During the Second Republic, Ferdinand Barrot's political fortunes rose with those of Louis-Napoleon. Elected to both the Constituent Assembly (1848) and the Legislative Assembly (1849), he regularly voted with the Right. In the campaign for the presidency of the Second Republic, Barrot supported Louis-Napoleon, making public his views in an article in the *Siècle* of 19 November 1848. Following the collapse of his brother's cabinet, Ferdinand Barrot became minister of the interior in the new government. Appointed an ambassador to Turin (March 1850), he played an important part in Franco-Italian relations.

Ferdinand Barrot enjoyed considerable political prominence during the Second Empire. He served in the Council of State and became a senator in 1853, and he took a special interest in matters concerning public assistance. He also collaborated with Baron Haussmann in the rebuilding of Paris. Excluded from political life by the events of 1870, he retained his Bonapartist faith. Late in his life, Barrot returned to the Senate but took no active role in French political life. He died on 12 November 1883.

A. Robert, E. Bourloton, and G. Cougny, *Dictionnaire des parlementaires français* (Paris, 1891).

Robert Brown

Related entries: BARROT, C.-H.-O.; BONAPARTISM; CHAMBER OF DEPUTIES; CHAMBER OF PEERS; CONSTITUTION OF 1848; COUNCIL OF STATE; LEGISLATIVE ASSEMBLY; *LE SIECLE.*

BARTHE, FELIX (1795–1863), opposition lawyer and member of the carbonari during the Restoration; politician and minister during the July Monarchy. Born 28 July 1795 in Narbonne, Félix Barthe began his schooling in his native town, then studied law in Toulouse, and completed his studies in Paris. In 1817, the same year that Barthe arrived in Paris determined to conquer the capital, he was inscribed as a lawyer at the royal court.

Outspoken as a critic of the Bourbon regime, Barthe took an active role, both as a participant and as a defense lawyer, in the bitter and often violent political tumults of the years 1820–23. In the conservative reaction of the ultraroyalists that followed the murder of the duc de Berry in February 1820, the Decazes government attempted to modify the press and electoral laws. On 3 June 1820, Barthe took part in the large demonstrations provoked by a proposed electoral law; during this demonstration, a soldier shot and killed a student named Lallemand. Not only did Barthe speak at Lallemand's funeral and publish protests in the press, he also had the soldier responsible for the student's death brought before a court-martial. Not long after, he defended two men accused of having tried to frighten the duchesse de Berry, the pregnant widow of the assassinated duke, so that she would abort.

In the various conspiracies that erupted between 1820 and 1822, Barthe took a prominent role. It is not unlikely that he had some part in the abortive conspiracy of 19 August 1820, for Barthe had as acquaintances many of the young men known to have participated in the Bazar français plot. He also defended and won the acquittal of Lieutenant-Colonel Caron, tried before the Chamber of Peers for his role in the military side of the August conspiracy. Known to have been a member of the French carbonari, Félix Barthe most likely sat on the Haute vente, the governing body of this conspiratorial group. Details about his actual role in the plots remain unknown. He did, however, serve as a defense attorney in two of the three great carbonari trials. At the Colmar trial in July 1822, his efforts were largely successful, for most of the accused won acquittal. In the more famous trial of the four sergeants of La Rochelle, held in Paris in August 1822, Barthe did not repeat his earlier success; the four sergeants, all implicated in the carbonari plots, were convicted and then guillotined on 21 September 1822. Barthe's third and final effort as a defense attorney in the trials related to the outbreak of carbonarism in 1823. He defended Jacques Koechlin, the liberal deputy from Mulhouse, who had been indicted for publishing a pamphlet, *Relation historique des événements qui ont eu lieu à Colmar et dans les villes et communes environnantes, les 2 et 3 juillet 1823*, that denounced the trial and later execution at Strasbourg of the same Lieutenant-Colonel Caron whom Barthe had defended in 1821. Conducted with a vehemence that resulted in his suspension from the court, Barthe's defense failed to save Koechlin from a conviction and a short prison term.

Throughout the remaining years of the 1820s and in the Revolution of 1830, Barthe continued to figure in political circles where opposition to the Bourbon regime flourished. In 1827, with François Guizot, Odilon Barrot, and the youthful editors of the *Globe*, he served on the executive committee of the Aide-toi, le ciel t'aidera, a society organized to promote the liberal cause in the elections of that year. Three years later, when Charles X attempted a coup of sorts by issuing the ordinances of July 1830, the thirty-five-year-old Barthe took an active part in fomenting the July Revolution. On 26 July he participated in two crucial gatherings: in the morning, he assembled with other noted liberal lawyers in the offices of André Dupin and heard the ordinances denounced as illegal; shortly after, Barthe was in the offices of the *National* when the journalists drafted and signed their protest. Three days later, he appeared at the Hôtel de ville and joined the work of the Municipal Commission.

As recompense for his faithful participation in the opposition movements of the 1820s and in the July Revolution, Barthe entered the service of the Orleanist monarchy. In the process, he abandoned the radicalism of his youth and became not only a solid supporter of the July Monarchy but one of its principal beneficiaries. Appointed royal prosecuter by Dupont de l'Eure, Barthe also won election to the Chamber of Deputies in October 1830. In the Laffitte ministry, he became minister of public instruction in December and in this capacity ordered the repression of disorders at the Schools of Law and Medicine. When the ministry of Casimir Périer succeeded that of Laffitte, Barthe remained in the government, exchanging his old office for that of Justice. As minister of justice, he had a major role in the drafting of important legislation, notably the laws of 31 August 1831 and 17 January 1832. Barthe also had a hand in the reform of the Penal Code in 1832, which provided for a general mitigation of the penal laws and for greater discretion to the courts in the application of penalties. When the Broglie ministry fell in April 1834, Barthe temporarily retired from political life. Named a peer of France, he became first president of the Audit Office. Félix Barthe took back the portfolio of Justice in the second Molé government of 15 April 1837, holding this office until the coalition of François Guizot, Adolphe Thiers, and Odilon Barrot toppled the ministry. While minister of justice, Barthe had to deal with a number of sensitive religious questions, including the return to France of the Dominicans.

As a result of the Revolution of 1848, Barthe lost his post at the Audit Office. Within a year, however, he managed to win favor with the new government and have himself reinstated. Following the creation of the Second Empire, Barthe entered the Senate, where his most visible act was a speech given on 7 March 1861 concerning the Roman question. In it, he criticized the activities of Garibaldi and the attitude of Piedmont and defended the temporal power of the pope. In 1855, he was named to the Academy of Moral and Political Sciences. Félix Barthe died in Paris on 27 January 1863.

F. Barthe, *De l'esprit de notre révolution de celui de la Chambre et du premier ministère* (Paris, 1831); *Dictionnaire de biographie française*, vol. 5.

Robert Brown

Related entries: AIDE-TOI, LE CIEL T'AIDERA; BARROT, C.-H.-O.; BAZAR CONSPIRACY; CARBONARI; CARON; JULY ORDINANCES; LALLEMAND; LA ROCHELLE, FOUR SERGEANTS OF; MUNICIPAL COMMISSION; PERIER; REVOLUTION OF 1830.

BARTHELEMY, AUGUSTE MARSEILLE (1796–1867), Bonapartist-liberal poet and satirist who wrote in collaboration with J. P. A. Méry in opposition to the Bourbons and Louis-Philippe. Auguste Barthélemy and his collaborator, J. P. A. Méry, were among the creators of the Bonaparte legend. Both poets worked so closely together that authorship of many works is unclear. Only Pierre-Jean de Béranger had a wider reputation as a Napoleonic bard. The work of all of these poets reflects the exploitation of Bonapartist glories in order to discredit the existing regimes of the Restoration and July Monarchy. Nevertheless, the legend that led to a second Empire was rooted in the sentiments of popular writers such as Barthélemy.

Like Béranger, Barthélemy often used the mock-epic style. He deflated and trivialized his monarchist and ultra targets in *La Villeliade* and *La Peyronneide* in 1827, the former printed in fifteen editions within the year. In 1828 a poem on Napoleon's Egyptian campaign was equally popular, but in 1829 Barthélemy was prosecuted for his *Le fils de l'homme* in praise of Napoleon's son, the duke of Reichstadt. This trial stirred great interest, and under the press laws, newspaper accounts of the proceedings were not subject to censorship. In addition, the defendant presented his testimony entirely in verse, amid the amused toleration of spectators, judges, and prosecutor.

Barthélemy's defense even brought an admission from the royal prosecutor, who had earlier accused him of "corrupting" youth, that he too admired the poet's spirit and ability. Because the incriminating poem included a plea to Napoleon's son to trade his present title for a "future scepter," the charge involved provocation to alter the form of government. In addition, the defendant had recently visited Vienna, vainly seeking an interview with the duke. In the verses for his own support, Barthélemy cleverly implied that since Bonapartism was only a memory, it could hardly be subversive. The judgment was a victory of sorts: a minimum sentence of three months in prison and a 1,000 franc fine. He appealed in vain to the royal court of Paris six months later. Both trials received wide publicity and increased the poet's popularity.

Immediately following the July Days of 1830, he and Méry wrote a brilliant paen to that revolution, *L'Insurrection*. In March 1831 the two poets started a weekly periodical of verse under the title *Nemesis*, attacking the new regime. A year later, Louis-Philippe purchased Barthélemy's silence with a generous pension. When he returned to satire in 1844, his poems were not well received.

J. Garson, *Barthelemy et Méry* . . . with *Oeuvres* (Paris, 1831); D. Rader, *The Journalists and the July Revolution* (The Hague, 1973).

Daniel Rader

Related entries: BERANGER; LOUIS PHILIPPE; PRESS LAWS; REICHSTADT; REVOLUTION OF 1830; ULTRAROYALISTS.

BASTIDE, JULES (1800–1879), republican militant under the Restoration and the July Monarchy and foreign minister for the Second Republic during most of 1848. Born 21 November 1800 in Paris, Bastide studied law before joining the republican movement under the Restoration. In 1821 he was one of the early members of the carbonari, and a few years later he helped found another secret organization, the Société des francs-parleurs. During the July Revolution of 1830, Bastide was one of the leaders of a column of insurgents who captured the Tuileries Palace on 29 July.

Bastide soon turned against the July Monarchy and joined the abortive insurrection of 1832 in Paris. Condemned to death, he escaped to England where he lived for two years before receiving amnesty and returning to France. In 1835 he was among those chosen to defend the 164 republicans arrested after the abortive Paris insurrection of 1834. Bastide also began to write for the Parisian republican newspaper, *Le National*, of which he became editor upon the death of Armand Carrel in 1836. Bastide soon joined the movement to reconcile republicanism with Catholicism and as a result of differences with Armand Marrast left *Le National* in 1846. The following year he helped found *La Revue nationale* with Philippe Buchez, a leading exponent of social Catholicism.

Bastide was one of several republican journalists to come to power in the February Revolution of 1848. On the crucial day of 24 February, Bastide helped influence Alphonse de Lamartine to oppose a regency and advocate a provisional government. When Lamartine became foreign minister, Bastide on 28 February assumed the second position in the ministry, as secretary-general. In the elections to the National Constitutent Assembly in April, Bastide was successful in three departments and sat with the moderate republicans following the lead of *Le National*. He became foreign minister in his own right on 11 May after Lamartine became a member of the new Executive Commission.

During the June Days, Bastide played a dramatic role in the move to replace the Executive Commission with the dictatorship of General Eugène Cavaignac; in the midst of debate on 24 June, Bastide urged a speedy decision on the ground that the insurgents were about to capture the Hôtel de ville. The assembly immediately granted full powers to Cavaignac, who thereafter crushed the insurgents (who never did take the Hôtel de ville). After the insurrection, Bastide remained as foreign minister in Cavaignac's new government of 28 June; he retained that position until Louis-Napoleon Bonaparte became president of the Republic on 20 December 1848, and thus he was the only prominent man of February to remain in power throughout the year of revolution.

As foreign minister, Bastide continued the pacific foreign policy of Lamartine while attempting to implement the National Assembly's pledge of fraternal support to the peoples of Germany, Poland, and Italy. During the last half of 1848, Bastide formulated policy jointly with General Cavaignac. Although many in France and Italy advocated or expected French military intervention against Austria in northern Italy, Bastide and Cavaignac preferred joint diplomatic mediation with England. Bastide did, however, dispatch two warships to protect the new Venetian republic. When the pope fled from a turbulent Rome in November, Bastide and Cavaignac prepared to send French troops to ensure his personal safety though not to restore his temporal rule; they even invited the pontiff to France, but instead he fled to neighboring Gaeta.

After Louis-Napoleon became president, Bastide as a member of the National Assembly on 11 May 1849 protested in vain against the president's plan to send a military expedition against the new Roman republic to restore the pope to power. Bastide was unsuccessful in his bid for election to the Legislative Assembly in 1849 and failed again when he stood for the Legislative Body in 1857. The following year, in reply to criticisms by the Piedmontese prime minister, Count Cavour, of French foreign policy in 1848, Bastide published a detailed apology, *La République française et l'Italie en 1848*. He soon after also published a two-volume work, *Les Guerres de religion en France*, but eschewed politics. He died in Paris in March 1879.

J. Bastide, *La République française et l'Italie en 1848* (Brussels, 1858); F. A. de Luna, *The French Republic under Cavaignac, 1848* (Princeton, 1969); L. C. Jennings, *France and Europe in 1848* (Oxford, 1973).

Frederick A. de Luna

Related entries: BUCHEZ; CARBONARI; CAVAIGNAC, L.-E.; EXECUTIVE COMMISSION; PIUS IX; ROMAN EXPEDITION; SOCIAL CATHOLICISM.

BAUDE, JEAN-JACQUES, BARON (1792–1862), liberal journalist, politician, and deputy of the July Monarchy. Jean-Jacques Baude was born 19 February 1792 in Valence (Drôme), the son of the local attorney-general. He entered Napoleon's service, holding subprefectures at Confolens (Charente) in 1813, Roanne (Loire) in 1814, and Saint-Etienne (Loire) in the Hundred Days. At the Second Restoration, Baude began his career of attacking the Bourbon government and became an editor of the liberal newspaper *Le Temps* after its establishment on 15 October 1829. In that capacity, on 27 July 1830 Baude signed the protest drafted by opposition journalists, and *Le Temps* published it in defiance of the new requirement for prior authorization. When the police arrived to wreck the presses, Baude confronted them with a copy of the Code, threatening burglary charges against every locksmith they brought and gaining much popular support. As immediate popular enthusiasm for the revolution seemed to wane, Baude urged better organization of the people. Baude himself led a bourgeois mob to the Hôtel de ville on 29 July, where he became secretary to the Paris Municipal Commission and was given the task of provisioning Paris. Although Baude became the center of a group of radicals opposing the continuation of the Charter, his designs were thwarted by the assumption by the marquis de Lafayette of a more active role in leading the revolution. Nevertheless, he was instrumental in getting the Paris government functioning again and in summoning the deputies to meet at the Hôtel de ville.

On 1 August Baude was appointed secretary-general of the Ministry of the Interior, which he ran until 11 August. On 10 November he became under secretary of state at that ministry, having in the meantime also been charged with directing the departments of Roads and Bridges and of Mines. He also was appointed to the Council of State. On 26 December 1830 he was named prefect of police, an appointment intended to reassure the liberals. He then immediately wrote to Louis-Philippe, advocating a more democratic election law and transformation of the Peers into a more representative body. However, the antilegitimist violence that surrounded religious services commemorating the death of the duc de Berry resulted in Baude's dismissal as prefect. In October 1830 he had won election to the Chamber of Deputies from the department of Loire. On 15 March 1831 in the Deputies, he proposed a measure banishing the Bourbons from France and depriving them of the right to own property there. He was defeated at the polls in 1831 but reelected in 1832. Although he initially voted with the ministerial majority, by 1835 he had shifted somewhat to the liberal opposition and lost his position on the Council of State. During this period he supported measures in favor of political prisoners of the Restoration, generals' widows, and the Bonaparte family. He also tried to intervene on behalf of Eugène Raspail when Raspail was attacked for an article on the legislature. Although reelected in 1837, Baude was absent from the Deputies from 1839 until 1842 when he won his last election. During the next four years, he ceased opposing the government and especially voted in support of the Guizot ministry of 1840.

Baude's political career came to an end when he was defeated in an election on 1 August 1846. He retired to private life, dying in Paris on 6 February 1862.

Archives Parlementaires; J. L. Bory, *La Révolution de juillet* (Paris, 1972); D. Pinkney, *The French Revolution of 1830* (Princeton, 1972); A. Robert et al., *Dictionnaire des parlementaires français* (Paris, 1889–91).

James K. Kieswetter

Related entries: BERRY, C.-F.; CHAMBER OF DEPUTIES; GUIZOT; HUNDRED DAYS; LAFAYETTE; *LE TEMPS*.

BAUDELAIRE, CHARLES-PIERRE (1821–1867), poet, translator, and critic. Charles-Pierre Baudelaire, later to gain fame and notoriety as the author of *Les Fleurs du mal*, was born in Paris on 9 April 1821, the son of Joseph-François Baudelaire (1759–1827) and Caroline Archimbaut-Dufays (1794–1871). His father, a former schoolmaster, imperial civil servant, and amateur painter who taught his small son the rudiments of art, died in 1827, leaving alone his young wife, who was intensely devoted to her son. In November 1828, she remarried, choosing as her second husband a Major Aupick, a veteran of Waterloo who would become a general, an ambassador, and a senator. With this marriage, Baudelaire, who had apparently enjoyed up to this point a happy childhood, began to undergo a change in personality; his hatred of his stepfather grew to such proportions that during the Revolution of 1848 he supposedly called out for the assassination of General Aupick. Baudelaire received his education from the Collège royal in Lyons (1832–36) and the famous Lycée Louis-le-Grand in Paris. Expelled from the latter school for outrageous and immoral behavior, he completed his studies at a small pension and passed his final examinations in 1839.

Rejecting the diplomatic career offered him by his stepfather, he proclaimed to his family that he wished to become a writer and took up the bohemian life-style of the Latin Quarter, where he probably began experimenting with drugs, contracted the venereal disease that would help kill him, and mixed in the company of Henri de Latouche, Honoré Balzac, and Gérard de Nerval. In 1841, the Aupick family, hoping to separate Baudelaire from his chosen life-style, sent him on a voyage to India. Baudelaire left the voyage shortly after its departure, returning to Paris in 1842 with a wealth of new images and experiences. The same year, having come of age, he claimed a substantial inheritance, amounting to some 100,000 gold francs, much of which he quickly spent to support a life of extravagant luxury and decadence in an elegant apartment on the Ile Saint-Louis. During these two years, he commenced his tumultuous liaison with Jeanne Duval, the mulatto who would become the Black Venus of his poetry. Baudelaire also pursued during these years his interest in art, making the acquaintance of both Eugène Delacroix and Gustave Courbet, artists he later defended in his art criticism. Many of the poems later published in *Les Fleurs du mal* date from this period.

Baudelaire's brief fling with luxurious and extravagant living came to an abrupt end in 1844 when his family obtained a legal judgment that prevented him from squandering the remainder of his inheritance. This judgment, which allowed Baudelaire a small monthly stipend, deprived him of his independence and left him heavily in debt, a condition he never succeeded in escaping; plunged into despair, he even attempted suicide in 1845. From these bleak years date some of the great "spleen" poems, later collected in *Les Fleurs du mal*. Despite the difficulties of his life, Baudelaire embarked in the mid–1840s on a brilliant career as an art critic, publishing important reviews of the Salon of 1845 and the Salon of 1846 in which he not only championed the works of Delacroix and Courbet but also advanced various original theories about the nature of art and painting. By the end of this decade, Baudelaire had published in small journals his first poems, and he had seen his autobiographical novel *La Fanfarlo* in print.

Baudelaire, who before 1848 had entertained sympathies with the suffering of oppressed peoples, supported with enthusiasm the revolution of that year, taking a small part in both the February Revolution and the June Days. He then collaborated in the publication of a short-lived journal, *Le Salut public*, in 1848, and he openly sympathized with the ideas of Pierre-Joseph Proudhon. While Baudelaire's whereabouts between June 1848 and the early months of 1850 remain a mystery, he spent 1850 and 1851 undertaking but never completing a number of ambitious projects. The coup d'état of 1851, by releasing Baudelaire from any further interest in politics, freed him to begin a short but remarkably fruitful period of creative activity.

Between 1852 and 1857, when *Fleurs du mal* finally appeared, Baudelaire published the first of his famous translations of Edgar Allan Poe, several important critical articles on Poe, and the first extensive collection of his own poems. In the nine years after 1856, Baudelaire, who had learned English as a child and who had discovered his affinity with Poe in the late 1840s, published five volumes of translations, beginning with the *Histoires extraordinaires* of 1856. He also wrote the first major critical study of Poe in any language; it appeared in the *Revue de Paris* (1852). Meanwhile he began to see more of his poems in print; a group of eighteen appeared under the title "Les Fleurs du mal" in the June 1855 issue of the conservative *Revue des deux mondes*, poems that immediately won for Baudelaire considerable notoriety and that brought upon him charges of obscenity; more poems followed in the *Revue de Paris* and *L'Artiste*. Finally, in June 1857, came the first edition of *Les Fleurs du mal*, dedicated to Théophile Gautier, a collection of one hundred poems written during the previous decade and a half, published by his friend Auguste Poulet-Malassis. Divided into five sections, the poems chart a spiritual journey that begins with a realization of the horror of life and a frantic search for some sort of redemption and ends with an escape into death. Among these poems is also found the famous "Correspondances," in which Baudelaire set out his theory of art. Not only did the publication of this volume unleash a storm of hostile criticism, it also brought Baudelaire, his publisher, and the printer into court. Charged and convicted of the charges of offending religion and public morality, Baudelaire was fined 300 francs, a sum later reduced to 50 francs. In addition, six of the poems in *Les Fleurs du mal* were banned, a ban lifted only in 1949. Despite the great impact this conviction had on Baudelaire, a second and enlarged edition of *Les Fleurs* appeared in 1861; a third and posthumous edition, which was published in 1868, contained 151 poems. Baudelaire also published in Belgium in 1866 a collection of verse under the title *Les Epaves*.

For Baudelaire, the ten years of life that remained to him after the failure of *Les Fleurs du mal* were filled with economic hardship and continual disappointment. Nevertheless, he continued to write a number of fine works, including an essay on the Salon of 1859 and the perceptive "Richard Wagner et Tannhauser à Paris," a hymn of praise to another of his artistic heroes. In 1861, he stood briefly as a candidate for the French Academy. Plagued by money problems and by legal difficulties resulting from the bankruptcy of his publisher, Baudelaire in 1864 undertook a lecture tour in Belgium. The failure of this tour notwithstanding, he stayed in Belgium until 1866, when a sudden illness compelled his return to Paris, where he died on 31 August 1867. Charles Baudelaire lies buried in the Montparnasse Cemetery. Largely unappreciated at the time of his death, Baudelaire's reputation as a poet and a critic has grown steadily since.

L. J. Austin, *L'Univers poétique de Baudelaire* (Paris, 1956); C. Baudelaire, *Les Fleurs du mal* (Paris, 1857); A. Brookner, "Baudelaire," in *The Genius of the Future: Studies in French Art Criticism* (London, 1971); Jacques Crépet, ed., *Oeuvres complètes*, 19 vols. (Paris, 1922–53); A. Fairle, *Baudelaire: Les Fleurs du mal* (London, 1960); L. B. Hyslop, *Baudelaire, Man of His Time* (New Haven, 1980); E. Starkie, *Baudelaire* (London, 1957).

Robert Brown

Related entries: ACADEMIE FRANCAISE; BALZAC; COUP D'ETAT OF 2 DECEMBER 1851; DELACROIX; GAUTIER; LATOUCHE; NERVAL; PROUDHON; REVOLUTION OF 1848; *LA REVUE DE PARIS*; *LA REVUE DES DEUX MONDES*.

BAUSSET, LOUIS-FRANCOIS DE (1748–1824), cardinal, historian, and administrator. Bausset had been bishop of Alès since 1784 when his diocese was suppressed in the reorganization of the ecclesiastical map of France. After a short emigration in Switzerland, he returned to France and shortly after was arrested. Freed by the Thermidorian Reaction, he was able thereafter to lead a secluded and laborious life, one fruit of which were his two large biographies of Fenelon (1808–9) and Bossuet (1814). Napoleon wanted him in the higher administration of his University (1809). Under the Bourbon Restoration, rewards and dignities were heaped on him: president of the Royal Council of Public Instruction (1814), peer of France (1815), member of the French Academy (1817), cardinal (1817), minister of state, and duke. In the higher Chamber he was the leader of a group known as La Réunion cardinalice, which favored Right-centrist policies.

H.-L. de Quélen, *Recueil des discours . . . de l'Académie francaise*, (Paris, 1843).

Guillaume de Bertier de Sauvigny

BAVOUX, JACQUES-FRANCOIS-NICOLAS (1774–1848), jurist, journalist, and republican political figure of the Restoration and July Monarchy. Under Napoleon I, Bavoux was a member of the faculty of law at Paris and was appointed a judge on the Tribunal de la Seine. In 1819 he was named professor of criminal law, but the course was suspended because of his political views against the Restoration, and he was indicted for subversive lectures. Defended by Jean-Charles Persil and André Dupin, he was triumphantly acquitted and successfully ran for deputy of the Seine in the opposition ranks. As cofounder in 1828 (with baron de Schonen) and editor of the small republican *Nouveau Journal de Paris*, Bavoux advocated social reform, social democracy, and a broad franchise. He also engaged in personal journalistic encounters with an opposite member on the Right, Alphonse Martainville of the *Drapeau Blanc*, who tried unsuccessfully to have Bavoux prosecuted for sedition. The July Monarchy, as a sop to the moderate republicans, elevated him to prefect of police and later counselor in the Cour des comptes. Bavoux's paper had defected from the more ardent republicans, accepting the new order in 1830 without enthusiasm. As the regime became more reactionary, Bavoux resigned his official posts and was soon elected a deputy of the Jura. He died too soon to see the Second Republic established. His writings, other than polemics, were chiefly on the criminal law and the practice of law.

E. Hatin, *Histoire de la presse française*, vol. 8 (Paris, 1859–61).

Daniel Rader

Related entries: DE SCHONEN; *LE DRAPEAU BLANC*; DUPIN, A.-M.-J.-J.; MARTAINVILLE; *NOUVEAU JOURNAL DE PARIS*.

BAZAR CONSPIRACY, a conspiracy to overthrow the Bourbons, planned for 19 August 1820, involving republicans, Bonapartists, discontented soldiers and officers, and perhaps partisans of the houses of Orléans and Orange; also known as the Conspiracy of 19 August. In the spring and summer of 1820, opposition to the Bourbon government increased due to overall discontent among soldiers and civilians, a series of reactionary measures adopted that spring, and the outbreak of revolutions in Spain and Naples. A coalition of revolution-minded leaders began seeking ways to overthrow the government. Included in their number were the marquis de Lafayette, Jacques Laffitte, Jacques-Antoine Manuel, Marc-René de Voyer d'Argenson, Jacques-Charles Dupont de l'Eure, and Jean-Joseph Tarayre. Simultaneously there formed a group of disgruntled ex-army officers who met at the French Bazar, a large store managed by ex-Colonel Sauset at No. 11 rue Cadet in Paris. Sauset's co-conspirators included Colonel Charles-Nicolas Fabvier, who was the real leader of the plot, and Captain Nantil,

Major Bérard, ex-Lieutenant Colonel Maziau, and others. Even the duc de Rovigo (Savary) may have been involved. These two groups ultimately established contact. By July 1820 they had developed a plan that called for uprisings by sympathetic officers and garrisons in Amiens, Cambrai, Vitry, Epinal, Belfort, Lyons, Grenoble, Nantes, and Rennes. These would distract the government from the revolt that would then occur in Paris, where, counting on student support, the revolutionaries would seize the fortress of Vincennes, the Tuileries, and other key locations. They agreed on overthrowing the Bourbons but apparently not on what would succeed them. The uprisings were originally scheduled for 10 August, but delays in the provincial revolts and other factors caused a general rescheduling for the night of 19–20 August. This delay was detrimental to any possibility of success. On the night of 18 August, a powder magazine exploded in Vincennes, drawing large numbers of Royal Guard to the fortress. But in fact, as early as 15 August, several officers and sergeants had already revealed the plot to the government. Some in the cabinet advocated letting the affair proceed to catch the conspirators in the act. Richelieu and Auguste de Marmont, however, wanted to move quickly to avoid the inevitable bloodshed. Then on the afternoon of 19 August, Marmont announced that he had doubled the guard at the Tuileries Palace and had put other units on alert, unavoidably warning the conspirators. On 19 and 20 August the disaffected army units were transferred elsewhere, and many of the conspirators were arrested. But many, such as Lafayette and d'Argenson, discreetly retired to the provinces, and some escaped abroad or went into hiding. The Court of Peers, which tried the accused, apparently did not wish to press the case into its upper circles. Thus on 16 July 1821 only six, none of them high ranking, were sentenced to light prison terms, although three were condemned to death in absentia.

E. Guillon, *Les Complots militaires sous la restauration* (Paris, 1895); A. B. Spitzer, *Old Hatreds and Young Hopes* (Cambridge, 1971); A. T. Vaulabelle, *Histoire des deux restaurations* (Paris, 1874).

James K. Kieswetter

Related entries: CHAMBER OF PEERS; FABVIER; MARMONT; ROYAL GUARD; SAVARY; VOYER D'ARGENSON.

BAZARD, SAINT-ARMAND (1791–1832), carbonarist conspirator and Saint-Simonian. As a captain in the National Guard in 1815, Bazard fought against the Allied attack on Paris at the end of the Hundred Days and was named to the Legion of Honor. With the Second Restoration he found a job as a clerk in the *octroi* bureau of the Paris prefecture and took classes in the law faculty of the university. With three fellow clerks and students (Philippe Buchez, J. T. Flotard, and Nicholas Joubert), Bazard organized the Friends of Truth Masonic lodge in 1818 or 1819 to serve as a cover for opposition activity against the Bourbon regime. Bazard was a committed republican and particularly resented the Empire's destruction of the goals of the Revolution and reestablishment of the Catholic church. When the Friends of Truth became the center of carbonarist conspiracy in France in 1821–22, Bazard was serving as its president (*Vénérable*) and had worked with Flotard and Buchez on adapting the Italian carbonarist model to French conditions. The most influential of the younger members of the conspirators' central committees (the *Haute vente* and the *Vente suprème*), which met initially in his rooms in Paris, Bazard was reputed to have rebuked liberal supporters from the Chamber of Deputies (the Marquis de Lafayette, Marc-René de Voyer d'Argenson, Jacques-Antoine Manuel) for their hesitation in organizing armed revolts against the regime. Bazard traveled frequently outside Paris to coordinate the various carbonarist conspiracies (of Belfort, Besançon, Nancy, Metz, Strasbourg, and la Rochelle) and succeeded in warning Lafayette in December 1821 when the marquis was on his way to join the Belfort conspirators, who had just been arrested. Despite a possible membership of nearly 50,000, the carbonarist cells were crushed by the regime in the winter of 1821–22, and Bazard went into hiding when he was sentenced to a prison term in absentia.

In 1825, Bazard met several disciples of Saint-Simon (who had died on 19 May of that year), and their ideas provided a new outlet for his idealism. Saint-Simon's theories of industrial progress and technocracy appealed to several wealthy French bankers and entrepreneurs who agreed to finance a Saint-Simonian newspaper, *Le Producteur*, in October 1825, on which Bazard served as an editor and principal writer. The paper failed to flourish, soon became a monthly, and closed in 1827 for lack of funds. The Saint-Simonian movement (led by Bazard, Buchez, and Barthélemy Enfantin, a graduate of the Ecole polytechnique) continued and began a series of public lectures (written collectively but usually read by Bazard). These were presented biweekly in meeting halls in the rues Taraine and Taitbout and in the place de la Sorbonne and were printed in a new paper (*l'Organisateur*), which began to appear in August 1829. In the process, Saint-Simon's ideas were considerably modified. The Saint-Simonians, while retaining the original vision of a government based on an aristocracy of talent that would create a corporatist society through unlimited credit and education of the masses, stressed the need for the development of a new moral system with religious overtones. A general priest would guide the activities of Saint-Simon's *industriels*, and a new organic view of society, propounded by visionary intellectuals, would create collective harmony and abolish private property, inheritance, competition, and war. This new society was not to be egalitarian, however, and a natural hierarchy (based more on a kind of pantheistic illuminism than technological skill) would guide humanity to perfection. Although it was hoped that this new world could be created by education and persuasion, coercion was not ruled out.

The Saint-Simonian movement took on the character of a lay church or confraternity by 1829, with Enfantin and Bazard acknowledged as "fathers of the doctrine" who led a "family" of believers, who listened to sermons and sang Saint-Simonian hymns. Manifestoes were posted around Paris in 1830, and Pierre Leroux, the owner of the opposition daily *Le Globe*, "converted" and turned his paper over to the society in January 1831. Although Saint-Simonian clubs spread (attracting perhaps 40,000 adherents) and sympathizers included Franz Liszt, Heinrich Heine, J. S. Mill, Thomas Carlyle, Balzac, Lammenais, and Lamartine, the movement was denounced in the Chamber of Deputies for promoting common ownership of property and free love. The leaders of the sect began to quarrel over the proper interpretation of the master's theories, the best means to liberate the working class, and the role of women in the new order. Enfantin, who with other members of the society was beginning to undergo convulsions and utter infallible prophecies, particularly insisted on a stronger feminist focus for the movement and urged the replacement of marriage with nonbinding sexual unions and the "sanctification of the flesh." Bazard, who was older and married, strongly opposed these innovations and was expelled from the movement in a chaotic meeting on 19 November 1831, the complete transcript of which, with typical Saint-Simonian theatricality, was published in the movement's paper. Enfantin's victory was confirmed by his successful seduction of Bazard's wife, and Bazard retired to the countryside outside Paris, dying a year later. The movement became increasingly other-worldly, with members pursuing transcendent experiences at a small monastic community at Ménilmontant and organizing expeditions to Egypt in the mid–1830s to locate a female messiah. The *Globe* ceased publication in April 1832 and Enfantin was jailed in the same year for "outraging public morality."

While Bazard's desire for social and political reform clearly provides a link between his carbonarist and Saint-Simonian careers, the failure of the anti-Bourbon conspiracies of the 1820s and the relative weakness of the republican opposition in the early years of the July Monarchy help to explain the more abstract character of his later ideas.

S.-A. Bazard, *Doctrine de Saint-Simon* (Paris, 1829) and *Introduction* (to his translation of Jeremy Bentham's *Defense of Usury-Défense de l'usure*) (Paris, 1828); S. Charléty, *Histoire du Saint-Simonisme* (Paris, 1931); G. Iggers, *Introduction* to *Doctrine of Saint-Simon* (New York, 1958); F. Isambert, *De la Charbonnerie au Saint-Simonisme* (Paris, 1936); F. Manuel, *The New World of Henri Saint-Simon* (Cambridge, 1956); *Oeuvres de Saint-Simon et d'Enfantin*, 47 vols., 41–42 by Bazard (Paris, 1865–78); *Paris révolutionnaire*, 4 vols. (Paris, n.d.); A. B. Spitzer, *Old Hatreds and Young Hopes* (Cambridge, 1971).

David Longfellow

Related entries: BUCHEZ; CARBONARI; ENFANTIN; LA ROCHELLE, FOUR SERGEANTS OF; LEROUX; *L'ORGANISATEUR*; SAINT-SIMON; SAINT-SIMONIANISM; SOCIETY OF THE FRIENDS OF TRUTH.

BEAUX ARTS, ACADEMIE DE. See ACADEMY OF FINE ARTS.

BECQUEY, FRANCOIS-LOUIS (1760–1849), legislator and administrator of the Revolution, Empire, and Restoration. Becquey was born 24 September 1760 at Vitry-le-François (Marne) into a bureaucratic family. He was elected to the Legislative Assembly by the department of Haute-Marne in August 1791. There he joined the constitutional monarchist faction, criticizing legislation against the nonjuring clergy and against the *émigrés* and opposing the declaration of war in 1792. He was in frequent contact with the king and royal family and succeeded in freeing several noble prisoners. During the Reign of Terror Becquey remained undisturbed at Vitry and Saint-Dizier, but he returned during the Directory to work for the restoration of Louis XVIII. Although remaining a crypto-royalist, he was elected to the Corps législatif in December 1803, and in 1810 he was appointed a councillor of the university. At the first Restoration he became director-general of agriculture, commerce, arts, and manufactures, as well as receiving appointments to the Council of State and the Legion of Honor. He advocated some government intervention in trade but not prohibitive tariffs. In August 1815 the department of Haute-Marne elected him to the Chamber of Deputies, and he consistently won reelection until in 1831 he chose not to stand again. Initially a moderate royalist after 1814, he opposed the extreme measures of the ultras although supporting with some hesitation the conservative measures of 1820 such as the law of the double vote. But he opposed the increasing liberal trend of the late 1820s, especially as represented by the Martignac ministry. He voted against the Deputies' address to the throne in March 1830. He was nevertheless reelected to the Deputies on 3 July 1830 and retained his seat during the first months of the July Monarchy, although he took little part in debate until his retirement in 1831.

In 1816 the Richelieu ministry appointed him director of roads and bridges, a post he held until 1830. In this area he probably made his greatest contribution. He somewhat reorganized his department, reclassified roads, and more vigorously enforced the classifications. Under Becquey the condition of the royal roads greatly improved, and many bridges were built or rebuilt. When he resigned in May 1830, Charles X made him a minister of state, appointed him to the Privy Council, and promoted him to commander in the Legion of Honor. After his retirement from the Deputies in 1831, Becquey lived quietly until his death in Paris on 2 May 1849.

Archives parlementaires; H. Cavailles, *La Route française* (Paris, 1946); A. Robert et al., *Dictionnaire des parlementaires français* (Paris 1889–91).

James K. Kieswetter

Related entries: BRIDGE AND ROAD SERVICE; CHAMBER OF DEPUTIES; CHARLES X; DOUBLE VOTE, LAW OF THE ; MARTIGNAC; RICHELIEU; ULTRAROYALISTS.

BEDEAU, MARIE-ALPHONSE (1804–1863), French general, considered among the most humane of the Algerian generals. In 1840, he became the youngest brigadier in the French army after having distinguished himself in several actions, including the siege of Constantine. In 1844, he was promoted to lieutenant general for his conduct in the battle of Isly, where he commanded the French right wing against the Moroccans. As governor of the province of Constantine, he opposed the wholesale eviction of Arabs from the best agricultural land. He was disliked, but respected, in the armée d'Afrique for his strict discipline and opposition to looting by French soldiers and to the lavish life-styles of some officers. During the Second Republic, he became war minister, military governor of Paris, and vice-president of the Constituent Assembly. Exiled after the coup d'état of December 1851, he returned to France following the amnesty of 1859.

P. Azan, *Grands soldats d'Algérie* (Paris, 1831); C.-A. Julien, *Histoire d'Algérie contemporaine* (Paris, 1964).

Douglas Porch

Related entries: CONSTITUTION OF 1848; COUP D'ETAT OF 2 DECEMBER 1851; REVOLUTION OF 1848.

BEETHOVEN, LUDWIG VAN (1770–1827), composer. To a French historian, the myth of Beethoven is more important than the life itself. As Leo Schrade demonstrated in *Beethoven in France* (New Haven, 1947), French romantic poets seized upon Beethoven as a culture hero who epitomized their aesthetic ideals. Few of the poets, of course, had heard much, if any, of the music; the point was the mythology of his heroic role in breaking off the shackles of social constraint, freeing music to express human emotions.

In the concert world as well, Beethoven took on an enduring fame that no other Western composer, not even Wagner, has yet matched. In 1828 the Société des concerts was established, the orchestra supported by the Conservatoire de musique, which became known as Europe's best such ensemble and whose programs were focused on Beethoven's music. Although subscription lists are not extant for the early decades, the series was extraordinarily prestigious, probably including the Orleanist nobility and certainly the leading figures in the arts, and we do know that by the 1860s its subscribers were primarily from families of the highest government officials. The quasi-official status of the orchestra, performing for state occasions in some instances, gave Beethoven an odd kind of official role in a country he never visited. The rise of popularly priced orchestral concerts from the 1860s on—with programs centered around his symphonies—gave Paris as broad a classical music public as anywhere else in Europe.

W. Weber, *Music and the Middle Class* (London, 1975).

William Weber

Related entries: LISZT; ROMANTICISM.

BELGIAN REVOLUTION OF 1830, the struggle that, with French help, resulted in the independence of Belgium. In 1815, the great powers at Vienna united the former Austrian Netherlands (Belgium) with the former United Provinces (Holland) to create the United Kingdom of the Netherlands. The representative of Great Britain to the Congress, Viscount Castlereagh, acted on the premise that European tranquillity would be best served by the establishment of a series of buffer states on the eastern frontier of France, which would restrain any future military activity by that Jacobin state. The new United Kingdom of the Netherlands was to be the foremost of these buffer zones, laced as it was throughout with a series of awesome fortresses.

Castlereagh and his Vienna colleagues insisted that there were many natural advantages in a Belgian-Dutch union. Belgian industry under the Empire had expanded far beyond Belgium's domestic needs, while Holland possessed a large merchant fleet and farflung empire. From the standpoint of economic compatibility, this blend of commerce and industry made the United Kingdom of the Netherlands a financial success.

There remained in this amalgamation a few rough edges, which were apparent to the perceptive viewer from the outset. In 1815, there were 3.5 million Belgians and 2 million Dutchmen, yet King William I of the house of Orange-Nassau insisted on a constitution that granted equal representation in the Estates General to each section of his kingdom. Without question King William, a Dutchman, favored his fellow Hollanders over the Belgians when it came to important government and army appointments. Traditional religious differences between the Belgians and the Dutch hovered in the background.

Unfortunately, since all Belgians were Roman Catholics and a third of all Dutchmen also professed that faith, good politics on the part of the king dictated that a special relationship should have existed between the Roman church and the government. This he finally conceded in the Concordat of 1828, a document he never fully implemented, thus causing even further alienation of his Catholic subjects. Linguistic differences also produced friction between the two parts of the kingdom. Despite the fact that at least one-third of the Belgians spoke French, William moved toward having Dutch established as the national language.

These political, religious, and linguistic grievances simmered for fifteen years in the Belgian community. Although the Belgians might not have appreciated their new sovereign, Europe's great powers had vested interests in the preservation of the United Netherlands. Although William's policies appeared at times to be rash, the leaders of Europe agreed that this was one of the unpleasant realities that the Belgians had to learn to endure in the interests of peace.

On 25 August 1830 the situation changed drastically. After attending a performance of Auber's inspiring patriotic opera, *La Muette de Portici*, wherein an aria *L'Amour sacré de la patrie* was sung to the melody of "La Marseillaise," the audience, composed largely of middle-class youth, took to the streets of Brussels and began rioting against the Dutch. These youthful rioters were led only by romantic dreams of national liberty, emanating from hazy reports of events then transpiring in Paris. Their ranks swelled because of a bizarre chain of events. William's birthday was 25 August, and the authorities in Brussels had planned a gigantic fireworks display to honor the king. An enormous crowd had gathered in anticipation of this extravaganza. When the streets of Brussels became the scene of riots, local authorities cancelled all entertainment fearing further violence. Many, disappointed by this cancellation, vented their frustration by joining the opera-going rioters. They burned a few houses and smashed a few machines in the suburbs.

Almost 60 percent of the Brussels streetfighters were drawn from the ranks of the unemployed. Their common denominator was their hatred of Dutchmen. Most of them had been reduced to poverty by the 1825–30 recession. Not understanding the causes of their plight, they vented their anger against the dynasty, an unpopular minister of justice, C. F. van Maanen, and against Dutchmen in general. Day laborers did most of the fighting during the famous September Days (23–27 September) while middle-class leaders like Charles Rogier articulated the goals of the moment. By 27 September, the Brussels' streetfighters had driven an army under the command of the king's second son, Prince Frederick, from the city. Immediately other cities throughout the south revolted and expelled the Dutch. From that moment Belgium was effectively lost to the House of Orange.

William reacted by calling on his allies to help him preserve his kingdom. On 3 November, representatives of Great Britain, France, Austria, Russia, Prussia, and the Netherlands gathered at the Foreign Office in London and constituted themselves the Conference of London. This body was to meet off and on over the next nine years.

Simultaneously a Belgian National Congress, dominated by middle-class representatives, met in Brussels. It proclaimed Belgian independence, established a constitutional monarchy, and excluded the house of Orange. In January 1831, the Congress elected the duke of Nemours, second son of Louis-Philippe, to be king. Palmerston threatened war if Nemours accepted. On 4 June 1831, the National Congress satisfied all elements by electing Leopold of Saxe-Colburg to be the monarch.

The Conference of London eventually accepted Belgium's independence conditioned on the permanent neutrality of Belgium. William I did not easily accept the loss of Belgium. He sought the restoration of the provinces by force in August 1831. In that month he launched a military attack aimed at recapturing Belgium. The Belgian Army under Leopold collapsed, but the French Armée du nord under the command of Marshal Etienne-Maurice Gérard drove the Dutch back. Only Antwerp remained in Dutch hands. In November 1832, the French intervened—again with the permission of the conference—to expel the remaining Dutch troops from that city. In 1839, William finally accepted the situation and formally acknowledged the independence of Belgium; then he abdicated.

The Belgian Revolution of the 1830s demonstrates the power of the working class when directed by a determined, enlightened leadership. It also shows how an unlikely series of occurrences can cause latent discontent to crystallize into revolutionary upheaval. Despite the careful planning that went into the construction of the United Kingdom of the Netherlands at Vienna, flaws in the design, compounded by William's personality and questionable political decisions, resulted in the dissolution of a state.

John W. Rooney Jr., *Belgian-American Diplomatic and Consular Relations: 1830–1845* (Louvain, Belgium, 1969), "Profil d'un Combattant," *Revue Belge d'histoire con-*

temporaine (Winter 1982), and *Revolt in the Netherlands . . . Brussels . . . 1830* (Lawrence, Kan., 1982).

John W. Rooney

Related entries: GERARD; REVOLUTION OF 1830; VIENNA, CONGRESS OF.

BELLIARD, AUGUSTE-DANIEL (1769–1832), general and diplomat. Born in Fontenay-le-Comte (Vendée), he began to distinguish himself at the battle of Jemmapes, under Charles-Francois Dumouriez. Thereafter he was in almost all the important campaigns and battles of the Napoleonic era, including those of Italy, Egypt, Spain, and Russia. He was made a brigadier general in 1796 and a divisional general two years later. In 1814, Louis XVIII included him in the Chamber of Peers as one of the most glorious soldiers of the time and appointed him major-general of the army. But he too easily rallied to Napoleon in March 1815 and after the return of the king was punished by a short imprisonment. In 1820, however, Duke Elie Decazes had him reinstated in the Peers. In 1830, he warmly supported the advent of Louis-Philippe, and the new king sent him to Vienna with the delicate mission of explaining the change of regimes to Metternich. After that he was the first French envoy to Belgium, and in that capacity he signed the treaty establishing the independence and neutrality of the new country. He died while still on mission in Brussels, where one of the finest streets perpetuates his name.

J. Garson, *Le Général Belliard* (Paris, 1936); *Mémoires du comte Belliard, recueillies par M. Vinet* (Paris, 1842).

Guillaume de Bertier de Sauvigny

Related entry: BELGIAN REVOLUTION OF 1830.

BELLUNE, CLAUDE-VICTOR-PERRIN. See VICTOR.

BEQUET, ETIENNE (1796–1838), a Parisian literary figure of the Restoration and early July Monarchy. Etienne Béquet was born in Paris around 1796. For fifteen years he contributed a weekly article of literary criticism to the *Journal des débats*. Jules Janin said that Béquet knew how to say everything without offending anyone. Béquet in particular gave his support to Casimir Delavigne, and he was the first to applaud the comedies of Eugène Scribe.

His writings were very popular in his day. He wrote *Marie ou le mouchoir bleu* (1823) and *L'abbaye de Maubuisson* (1831). He also translated Lucian's *History*.

In August 1829, Béquet was tried for his attacks on the government but was acquitted. He consequently supported the July Revolution but did not profit from its success. His intemperate life-style has been blamed for shortening his life. He died 30 September 1838.

M. Prevost. *Dictionnaire de biographie française*, vol. 5 (Paris, 1951); note by E. Racot in the reprinted *Marie ou le mouchoir bleu* (Paris, 1884).

Bernard Cook

Related entries: JANIN; *JOURNAL DES DEBATS*; SCRIBE.

BERANGER, PIERRE-JEAN DE (1780–1857), poet and songwriter. This son of a petit-bourgeois family of Paris had in 1809 obtained a modest place as secretary in the office of grand master of the university. Later he would systematically refuse all places and honors offered by successive governments, preferring to maintain his independence. Not until 1815, when his first collection of songs was published, did he achieve notoriety. Two other collections, published in 1821 and in 1825, brought him glory and money; everywhere he was considered the greatest national poet and courted by the world of letters. The mediocrity of Béranger's poetry and the ordinary lowness of his inspiration, which displays a conventional Epicureanism, cannot explain his success. No doubt this success was due to the fact that song was the principal means of political expression for the people, and Béranger's songs furnished the best way to express opposition to the monarchy and the church. His songs also contributed to the spread of the Napoleonic legend.

J. Touchard, *La gloire de Béranger*, 2 vols. (Paris, 1968).

Guillaume de Bertier de Sauvigny, trans. E. Newman

Related entries: BONAPARTISM; SINGING SOCIETIES.

BERARD, AUGUSTE-SIMON-LOUIS (1783–1859), liberal deputy of the Restoration and July Monarchy and leader of the 1830 July Revolution. Bérard was born 3 June 1783 in Paris to a Protestant family of Provençal origin. His father, a merchant and founder of the last Company of the Indies, was executed in 1794. Bérard graduated from the Ecole polytechnique and became an auditor in the Council of State in 1810 and a master of requests in 1814. He returned to Napoleon's service in the Hundred Days, thus incurring dismissal from the Council at the second Restoration. He was restored to it in 1817 and dismissed again in 1820 by the Richelieu ministry. In 1825 he founded a bank in Paris, and he also was involved in the Compagnie des forges d'Alais. A staunch political liberal, Bérard was elected a deputy from Arpajon (Seine-et-Oise) in November 1827. He joined the liberal opposition but was most active in committees and elsewhere rather than on the floor of the Chamber. Bérard was one of the 221 deputies who in March 1830 voted the Deputies' address that criticized Charles X. Reelected in July 1830, he was in Paris when Charles issued the July Ordinances. He quickly became one of the strongest advocates of opposition to the ordinances, first proposing a protest by the Deputies on 26 July. This proposal met with what he regarded as a timorous response from his colleagues. Nevertheless, his house on the rue de la Ville-l'Evêque, behind the Church of the Madeleine, was the scene of one of the important meetings of deputies opposing the king on 28 July. He also led in the efforts to win over Marshal

Auguste Marmont. When public ardor seemed to falter, he exhorted the people, who looked to him for leadership, to build more barricades and continue the uprising. Although Bérard urged the duc de Mortemart, Charles X's emissary to Paris, to meet with the Deputies, it was he who told Mortemart that Charles's proposed concessions were unacceptable and that the king could not return to Paris.

Having presided over the Deputies, Bérard was among those sent to offer to Orléans the post of lieutenant-general of the kingdom, and he urged Orléans to accept the offer on 31 July. To prevent further radical action by the advocates of a republic, whose success appeared possible, Bérard and other deputies then quickly published a declaration announcing the Chamber's invitation to Louis-Philippe. On 3 August at a meeting with Jacques Laffitte, Bérard and Louis Cauchois-Lemaire suggested proposing to the Deputies that Orléans become king, albeit under very stringent conditions, which many others found to be too harsh. Later Bérard proposed to the Chamber a declaration that Charles X and his family had abdicated the throne and that Louis-Philippe be named king of the French. Thus Bérard played a significant role in influencing the outcome of the July Revolution toward a monarchy instead of a republic. He then participated in revising the Charter, supporting a more liberal position on matters such as a new election law. But in fact Bérard may have been duped into presenting as his own the moderate changes wanted by Guizot and Broglie, thus ensuring their success with the liberals in the Chamber. Later in August Bérard became director-general of roads, bridges, and mines, and still later he was named once again to the Council of State. Reelected to the Deputies from Seine-et-Oise in July 1831, for the next three years he was part of the conservative majority in the Chamber. However, differences with the cabinet led to his retirement from political life after 1834. He then became involved with the textile industry in Touraine, until Louis-Mathieu de Molé appointed him receiver general for the department of Cher. Bérard died 23 January 1859 at la Membrolle (Maine-et-Loire).

Archives parlementaires; A. Bérard, Souvenirs historiques sur la revolution de 1830 (Paris, 1834); J. L. Bory, La Révolution de juillet (Paris, 1972); D. Pinkney, The French Revolution of 1830 (Princeton, 1972); A. Robert et al., Dictionnaire des parlementaires français (Paris, 1889–91).

James K. Kieswatter

Related entries: BROGLIE, A.-L.-V.; CAUCHOIS-LEMAIRE; GUIZOT; LAFFITTE; MORTEMART; RICHELIEU.

BERGASSE, NICHOLAS (1750–1832), lawyer, politician, and writer. Born in Lyons to a bourgeois family, Bergasse became a lawyer and in 1775 began pleading cases before the Parlement of Paris. At first he mixed in the circles of the *philosophes*, but he increasingly came to emphasize the religious bases of society. He first came to public attention in 1787 when, in a celebrated case, he defended a wealthy financier, Guillaume Kornmann, who had accused his wife of adultery and had her exiled for infidelity. As a delegate to the Constituent Assembly he joined the monarchist party, but in 1790 he left the Assembly in opposition to the limitation on royal power. He did not serve Napoleon, advocating instead the return of the Bourbons.

Bergasse reentered the political scene in 1814. He welcomed the return of the Bourbons but deplored the initial limitations imposed by the Napoleonic Senate. In general, he opposed the Charter as too liberal and insufficiently cognizant of the divine origin of power. His political importance in the Restoration was limited since Louis XVIII had little sympathy for his ultraroyalism and because Bergasse detested the political moderation of the Richelieu and even of the Villèle ministries. Bergasse, however, found a mutual admirer in Czar Alexander. Their considerable correspondence reveals that Bergasse had an important influence on the creation of the Holy Alliance and on the principle of intervention against internal revolt adopted by the Alliance at the Congress of Troppau.

He published several pamphlets during the Restoration reflecting ultraroyalist tendencies. Although not one of its most famous adherents, Bergasse did gain considerable notoriety with his *Essai sur la propriété*, which Richelieu seized in 1815, and for which he was tried and acquitted. In its original form the *Essai* advocated the return of *émigré* property, which, he argued, had been seized unjustly during the Revolution. By 1821, when the work was finally published, he recognized the impossibility of the return of *émigré* property and instead recommended a large indemnity so that the *émigrés* might buy the land back. In this work and others, he sought a hierarchical social and political system controlled by great landowners, though not necessarily noble, who would defend stability and morality.

An octogenarian in 1830, he opposed the new regime, was dropped from the Council of State and lost his pension. He died in 1832.

L. Bergasse, *Un defenseur des principes traditionnels* (Paris, 1910) and *Un philosophe Lyonnais* (Lyons, 1942); N. Bergasse, *Essai sur la loi* (Paris, 1817) and *Essai sur la propriété* (Paris, 1821); S. Gutman, "Justifications for an Aristocracy" (Ph.D diss., University of Michigan, 1976).

Sanford Gutman

Related entries: CHARTER OF 1814; COUNCIL OF STATE; HOLY ALLIANCE; LOUIS XVIII; RICHELIEU; TROPPAU, CONGRESS OF; ULTRAROYALISTS; VILLELE.

BERLIOZ, LOUIS-HECTOR (1803–1869), composer. Berlioz was born in the Isère to the family of a distinguished and moderately wealthy doctor. After being enrolled in the Ecole de médecin in 1821, he shifted to the Conservatoire de musique. In the course of his musical training, which his parents did not condone, he made music journalism his principal source of income until his father died in 1848. During the late 1820s his creative output grew increasingly strong, reaching its first major peak in the *Symphonie fantastique* in 1830. That year the Conservatoire finally admitted his stature with the award of the Prix de Rome (his fourth try).

During the ten years after his return from Italy in 1832, he put himself in the forefront of his generation of artists with the daring originality of his compositions and the power of his prose. He gained some recognition from state commissions for the *Grande messe des morts* in 1837 and the *Grande symphonie funèbre et triomphale* in 1840. As a bold concert promoter, he put on a program primarily of his own works almost every year, sometimes using large halls and orchestral resources as great as could be marshaled (a thousand performers in 1845). Most Frenchmen, however, knew him as the principal writer on musical subjects for *Le Journal des débats* between 1834 and 1863. But his main goals eluded him. The Société des concerts, the city's extremely prestigious orchestral series, ignored his works as it slipped into a repertory of classical masterpieces, and the Opéra never looked at him again after the failure of his *Benvenuto Cellini* in 1838. Soon known as the bad boy (or, more justifiably, the revolutionary) of French musical life, he won wide fame but little sympathy and few performances.

From 1842 on he sought—and to a considerable extent gained—fuller recognition outside France, traveling to England, Russia, Austria, and Germany. In the course of these trips, he emerged as one of the most important conductors in Europe; he in fact helped define the new role of the conductor as an interpreter. But operatic success still eluded him. Although half of his opera *Les troyens* was done at the Théâtre lyrique with some success in 1863, he spent the last years before his death in 1869 largely in seclusion and with a bitter sense of failure.

Although the word *romantic* was not commonly used in musical life, Berlioz embodied some of the most important principles of the movement. His belief in the unbridgeable authority of the composer over his work—over any attempts to alter or ornament his music—made him a raving idealist in his time. His *Les Soirées de l'orchestre* (1852), a biting satire on the musical tastes of the period, as well as his newspaper articles, show the romantic traits that the artist expressed as fully, powerfully, and wittingly as any other artist. One of the bigger ironies of the time is that these pieces originally appeared in the newspaper of the *juste milieu*, the *Journal des débats*, thanks to the enlightened musical views of the Bertin publishing family.

Musically Berlioz had a style that was probably more idiosyncratic than that of almost any other major composer of the century. He went his own way and had few followers. There are quite conservative traits in his music, his concern with contrapuntal voice leading, and his use of a harmonic language, which is essentially that of Gluck and Beethoven. But his use of chords to expressive and dramatic purposes pointed in a drastically new direction, and his autobiographical and poetic tendencies have a modern flavor. Poetic interests indeed lie behind much of what is going on in his music, formed by the reading of Goethe, Shakespeare, and Byron and close contact with Nerval, de Musset, and Vigny. Still, his links with romanticism were nonetheless indirect, for he never identified his music with the movement. He also refused to take sides with Franz Liszt and Richard Wagner when they formed the first musical avant-garde in the 1850s for the cause of progressive music. While Liszt encouraged him and Wagner was deeply influenced by his values and writings, Berlioz remained an individualist to his unhappy end.

J. Barzun, *Berlioz and the Romantic Century* (New York, 1955); *New Groves Dictionary of Music and Musicians* (London, 1980).

William Weber

Related entries: BERTIN DE VAUX, "AINE,"; BERTIN DE VAUX, L.-F.; BYRON; *JOURNAL DES DEBATS*; JUSTE MILIEU; LISZT; MUSSET; NERVAL; ROMANTICISM; VIGNY.

BERNADOTTE, JEAN-BAPTISTE-JULES (1764–1844), general of the Revolution, marshal of the Empire, king of Sweden as Charles XIV John. Born at Pau (Basses-Pyrénées) 26 January 1764, Bernadotte enlisted in 1780. His promotion was rapid, rising from sublieutenant in 1791 to division commander in October 1794 after serving at Fleurus. After campaigning in Germany in the winter of 1798–99, Bernadotte served as war minister from July to September 1799, actively reorganizing the French forces. But his republicanism resulted in his removal by Sieyès. Although he did not defend the Directory, he did not support the coup of 18 Brumaire. In January 1800 he became a councillor of state and in April was given command of the army of the west.

Having proclaimed his loyalty to the Empire, Bernadotte became a marshal of France in May 1804, and in June he was appointed governor of Hanover. There he demonstrated considerable administrative skill and attempted to reform the tax structure.

Meanwhile, in 1809 the Swedes had overthrown their king, Gustavus IV. The crown went to Charles XIII, who was aged and childless. The Swedish Baron Otto Mörner, impressed by Bernadotte's military, administrative, and humanitarian record, approached Bernadotte, and on 21 August 1810 the Riksdag, also impressed, elected him crown prince of Sweden. Napoleon gave his approval, and Bernadotte, having converted to Lutheranism, landed in Sweden in October. He quickly gained control of the government. Relations between France and Sweden gradually worsened, although Bernadotte apparently preferred the role of mediator to that of belligerent. In January 1812 Napoleon occupied Swedish Pomerania. In April Sweden allied with Russia and in 1813 with Britain and Prussia. Bernadotte may have had hopes of becoming ruler of France at Napoleon's defeat. Instead he was drawn back to Sweden because the Norwegians had adopted a liberal constitution and refused to recognize their annexation by Sweden. Bernadotte defeated them but again demonstrated his generosity by allowing them to keep the constitution. Although Austria and France supported the rival claims of the son of the deposed Gustavus IV, Britain and Russia successfully backed Bernadotte. Thus when Charles XIII died on 5 February 1818, Bernadotte succeeded him as Charles XIV John. Although as king he was rather autocratic and opposed some political reforms, his reign was a period of peace and economic growth, especially in shipping and in agriculture. At Bernadotte's death in Stockholm on 8 March 1844, he was succeeded by his son, Prince Oscar.

D. P. Barton, *Amazing Career of Bernadotte* (Boston, 1930), *Bernadotte and Napoleon, 1799–1810* (London, 1921), *Bernadotte, Prince and King* (London, 1925), and *Bernadotte: The First Phase, 1763–1799* (London, 1914); T. T. Höjer, *Bernadotte maréchal de France* (Paris, 1945); P. de Pressac, *Bernadotte, un roi de suède francais* (Paris, 1942); F. D. Scott, *Bernadotte and the Fall of Napoleon* (Cambridge, 1935).

James K. Kieswetter

Related entry: SIEYES.

BERNARD, CLAUDE (1813–1878), experimental physiologist and theorist of the scientific method. After receiving his doctorate from the School of Medicine in Paris in 1843, Bernard devoted the rest of his career to the study of physiology. His experimental approach to this study was shaped by his association with François Magendie, under whom he served at the Collège de France as *préparateur* from 1841 to 1844 and as *suppléant* from 1847 to 1855. Upon the death of Magendie in 1855, Bernard succeeded his mentor in the chair of medicine at the Collège, but he had effectively been carrying out the duties of that position since Magendie's retirement in 1852.

Like Magendie, Bernard emphasized the value of experiments in physiological research and especially experiments involving animal vivisection. In the course of his early work, he sought to define an experimental method for physiology that would distinguish it from the discipline of anatomy and from that of animal chemistry, as the biochemistry of his day was known. Unlike Magendie, however, Bernard was not content with the accumulation of often incompatible empirical results, and he insisted that the phenomena be reduced to some systematic order. In this respect, Bernard stood closer to the positivism of Auguste Comte than to Magendie's extreme skepticism.

Bernard's early physiological research included studies of the gastric juice (his M.D. thesis in 1843), the nervous system (1843–45), the secretions of the liver (1848), and the pancreatic juice (1849). The most significant outcome of this work was his discovery in August 1848 that the liver normally synthesizes sugar and secretes it into the bloodstream (the glycogenic function of the liver).

Bernard actively pursued his research between 1850 and 1860, receiving scientific and governmental recognition for his distinguished achievements in physiology. After a serious illness in 1860, he began to work toward a theoretical synthesis, the first expression of which was published in 1865 under the title *Introduction à l'étude de la médecine expérimentale*. The success of this book as a philosophical discussion of scientific method secured for Bernard election to the Académie française in 1869. He was made a senator of the empire in that same year. When he died in 1878, he became the first French scientist to receive the honor of a state funeral.

F. L. Holmes, *Claude Bernard and Animal Chemistry* (Cambridge, Mass., 1974); J. Schiller, *Claude Bernard et les problèmes scientifiques de son temps* (Paris, 1967).

W. R. Albury

Related entries: ACADEMIE FRANCAISE; COLLEGE DE FRANCE; COMTE, A.; MAGENDIE; PARIS FACULTY OF MEDICINE.

BERRY, CHARLES-FERDINAND DE BOURBON, DUC DE (1778–1820), heir to the French throne whose assassination in 1820 provoked a political crisis. The second son of the comte d'Artois (who became King Charles X in 1824), he lived with his emigrant father in England until 1814, where he resided with an English woman, Amy Brown, and had two illegitimate daughters by her. Under Louis XVIII he played only a limited role in politics, occupied as he was with his own pleasures, but his place as third in line to the throne made him important. His assassination by a fanatic named Louvel on 13 February 1820 set off a political crisis that brought down the Decazes ministry and finally brought to power the right-wing royalists. His posthumous son, the duc de Bordeaux, later known as the comte de Chambord, was the last of the senior branch of the Bourbon family.

A. Castelot, *Le duc de Berry et son double mariage* (Paris, 1950); J. Lucas-Dubreton, *Louvel le régicide* (Paris, 1923).

Guillaume de Bertier de Sauvigny

Related entries: BERRY, M.-C.; BORDEAUX; CHARLES X; DECAZES; LOUIS XVIII.

BERRY, MARIE-CAROLINE DE BOURBON, DUCHESSE DE (1798–1870), royalist conspirator and mother of the Legitimist Pretender to the French throne. This granddaughter of King Ferdinand I of Naples had married her cousin, the duc de Berry, second son of the future King Charles X of France, in June 1816. Her friendly disposition and interest in literature and the arts made her the only popular member of the royal family, and this popularity increased when on 29 September 1820 she gave birth to a son, the duc de Bordeaux, seven months after the assassination of her husband. After the 1830 Revolution she tried to reconquer the throne for her son, but she found when she landed in Marseilles that the help promised by her partisans was not forthcoming. She then went to the Vendeé, where her maladroit efforts at revolution were quickly crushed by the July Monarchy. She hid for five months in Nantes, but she was betrayed and seized by the police. She was imprisoned at the fortress of Blaye and became a source of embarrassment to the government because of the popular sympathy for her, which was inspired by her courage and her misfortunes. But soon it was learned that she was pregnant. To save her honor, she claimed that she had been secretly married in Italy to a Count Lucchesi-Palli. Consequently she lost the confidence of the former royal family and the title of regent, which she had assumed in the name of her son, the Bourbon pretender. She was freed and lived out her life uneventfully in Italy.

A. Castelot, *La duchesse de Berry, d'après des documents inédits* (Paris, 1963); A. de Reiset, *Marie-Caroline, duchesse de Berry* (Paris, 1906).

Guillaume de Bertier de Sauvigny, trans. E. Newman
Related entries: BERRY, C.-F.; BORDEAUX; REVOLUTION OF 1830.

BERRYER, PIERRE-ANTOINE (1790–1868), barrister and politician. Son of Pierre-Nicolas, he at first supported his father in the defense of Marshal Michel Ney and other victims of the royalist reaction of 1815–16. But he soon turned against Elie Decazes and became a favorite defender of royalist and religious causes, building a reputation as an excellent orator. He entered the Chamber of Deputies in January 1830 through a by-election in Haute-Loire; his only speech there was to defend the crown's prerogative against the majority in the debate of March, which was the starting point of the final crisis of the Bourbon Restoration. After the revolution, he was one of the few legitimist deputies to decide it was an acceptable formality to take the oath to the new king so that the voice of legitimism could still be heard. For years, almost single-handedly he was the herald of the traditional monarchy, which he wanted to blend with a dose of democracy. So popular was he that in 1834 four different constituencies elected him; he chose to represent Marseilles, where he was to be reelected constantly. In 1848 he was elected to the Constituent Assembly of the Second Republic and after that to the Legislative Assembly. There he strove to achieve some collaboration among conservative factions, meeting in the so-called Comité de la rue de Poitiers. His open opposition to Louis-Napoleon interrupted his parliamentary career. When he was elected to the French Academy (1855), he accepted the appointment on the condition that he would not have to pay the ritual visit to the emperor. In 1863, he was reelected in Marseilles and resumed, until his death, his role of speaker for the royalist opposition. Berryer was universally admired as one of the greatest orators in French parliamentary assemblies and courts; he was also respected for his generous and high-minded character.

C. de Lacombe, *Vie de Berryer*, 3 vols. (Paris, 1894–95).

Guillaume de Bertier de Sauvigny
Related entries: ACADEMIE FRANCAISE; BERRYER, P.-N.; CHAMBER OF DEPUTIES; COMITE DE LA RUE DE POITIERS; CONSTITUTION OF 1848; DECAZES; LEGISLATIVE ASSEMBLY; LEGITIMISM; NEY; REVOLUTION OF 1830; REVOLUTION OF 1848.

BERRYER, PIERRE-NICOLAS (1757–1841), lawyer. The defender of Marshal Michel Ney at his trial before the Chamber of Peers in November 1815, he was the father of the great orator and legitimist parliamentarian, Antoine B. He left some interesting memoirs.

P.-N. Berryer, *Souvenirs*, 2 vols. (Paris, 1839).

Guillaume de Bertier de Sauvigny
Related entries: BERRYER, P.-A.; CHAMBER OF PEERS; NEY.

BERTIER, ANNE-FERDINAND-LOUIS, COMTE DE (1782–1864), son of the last intendant of Paris, who was murdered in an atrocious manner on 22 July 1789. He pledged his life to fight against everything that had anything to do with the Revolution. He refused to serve Napoleon, and, to combat the emperor, he created in 1810 the secret society of the Chevaliers de la foi. He took an active personal role in the events in the Midi that helped to bring the Bourbons to power in 1814 and 1815. At the beginning of the Restoration he was prefect of the Calvados and then of the Isère. But his opposition to the policies of Elie Decazes forced him to resign in order to devote himself to carrying on the activities of the Chevaliers de la foi, the secret motor of the ultraroyalist party. When that party came to power at the end of 1821, Bertier entered the Council of State and then the Chamber of Deputies as deputy of the Seine (March 1824). Here he was one of the leaders of the counteropposition of the Right against Joseph de Villèle, which earned him a temporary disgrace. In 1828, however, he regained the confidence of Charles X and prepared the formation of the unfortunate ministry of 8 August 1829. Under Jules-Armand de Polignac, he was director general of the Department of Streams and Forests and minister of state, but he had no role in preparing the coup d'état that was the Four Ordinances of July 1830. An implacable enemy of the Orléans dynasty, he gave up all his official positions and threw himself into the legitimist conspiracy of the duchesse de Berry. After its lamentable failure, he abstained from further political activity.

G. de Bertier de Sauvigny, *Le comte Ferdinand de Bertier et l'enigme de la Congré-gation* (Paris, 1948).

Guillaume de Bertier de Sauvigny, trans. E. Newman
Related entries: BERRY, M.-C.; CHEVALIERS DE LA FOI; CHAMBER OF DEPUTIES; COUNCIL OF STATE; DECAZES; JULY ORDINANCES; LEGITIMISM; POLIGNAC; REVOLUTION OF 1830; ULTRAROYALISTS; VILLELE.

BERTILLON, LOUIS ADOLPHE (1821–1883), pioneer demographer and sociologist, born in Paris on 2 April 1821. His father Jean Baptiste operated a chemical distillery near Montargis. Bertillon studied medicine in Paris, became a friend of Michelet, and an avowed enemy of Catholicism. In the wake of 1848 he became a socialist and cared for casualties of the June Days. At the time of the coup d'etat in 1851 he was subjected to preventive detention.

Bertillon received his medical degree on 6 August 1852 and took up residence in Montmorency. He had studied under Achille Guillard, who had stimulated his interest in sociology and demography. Bertillon viewed these as the natural science of human aggregates. In 1857 he published *Un Essai sur la méthode statistique appliquée à l'étude de l'homme*, which introduced his *Conclusions statistiques contre les detracteurs de la vaccine*. One of his first studies concerned the very high rate of infant mortality in the Paris area, which he ascribed to wet-nurses.

Bertillon was among the first members of the Societé de statistique and the Société d'anthropologie. He wrote *La méthode en anthropologie*, and articles on marriage, birth-rates, mortality, and migration, which appeared in the *Dictionnaire encyclopédique des sciences medicales*. In 1874 he published *La Démographie figurée de la France*.

With the collapse of the Empire, he was named mayor of the fifth arrondissement of Paris on 4 September 1870 and became the inspector general of charitable institutions. In 1876 he assumed the chair of demography at the Ecole d'anthropologie, of which he was a founder. In 1880 he was placed in charge of the statistical and demographic research for Paris and wrote the introduction of the *Annuaire statistique de la ville de Paris*. In 1882 he was named honorary president of the Geneva Congress on Health and Demography.

He died at Neuilly on 1 March 1883.

E. Duché, *Notice sur le Dr. Bertillon* (Paris, 1883); M. Prevost, *Dictionnaire de biographie française*, vol. 6 (Paris, 1954), 6:240.

Bernard Cook

Related entries: MIGRATION; MORTALITY; NUPTIALITY; POPULATION; WET NURSING.

BERTIN DE VAUX, "AINE," LOUIS-FRANCOIS (1766–1841), journalist. The revolution of 1789 turned Bertin away from an ecclesiastical career, and he became prominent as a royalist journalist before in 1800 buying *Le Journal des débats* with his brother. Shortly after he was imprisoned for nine months for involvement in a royalist plot.

Bertin, with his contributors François-René de Chateaubriand, Pierre Royer-Collard, and Louis de Bonald, was engaged in a running battle with the Empire, and the paper was closed in 1811. He welcomed the Restoration and followed Louis XVIII into exile. With 23,000 subscriptions the new *Journal* was by far the most popular paper under the Restoration. Bertin supported the regime until the dismissal of Chateaubriand in 1824; his criticisms resulted in a major trial in 1829 in which he was acquitted.

Under the July Monarchy Bertin used the paper to support uncritically Casimir Périer and François Guizot, but sales never again passed 12,000. The paper was also important as a review of literature and the arts, publishing Jules Janin, Berlioz, Saint-Marc Girardin, and Sue's *Les Mystères de Paris*.

C. Bellanger, J. Godechot, P. Guiral, and F. Terrou, eds., *Histoire générale de la presse francaise*, vol. 2 (Paris, 1969); *Le livre du centenaire du Journal des débats, 1789–1889* (Paris, 1889); *Nouvelle biographie générale* (Paris, 1855–66); A.-J. Tudesq, "Le Journal des débats au temps de Guizot," *Politique* (April-June 1959).

Peter McPhee

Related entries: BERLIOZ; BERTIN DE VAUX, L. F.; BONALD; CHATEAUBRIAND; GUIZOT; JANIN; *JOURNAL DES DEBATS*; PERIER.

BERTIN DE VAUX, LOUIS-FRANCOIS (1771–1842), founder and editor of the *Journal des débats*; deputy of the Restoration and peer of the July Monarchy. A member of a well-known family of journalists, Louis-François Bertin de Vaux was born in Paris on 18 August 1771. His elder brother, also named Louis-François, was distinguished from him by the name ''Bertin l'Aîné.'' Bertin de Vaux appears to have begun his journalistic career at *L'Eclair*, which first appeared in Vendémiaire Year IV (October 1795). It continued into Fructidor Year V when, as part of the antiroyalist reaction, it was closed because of its royalist, anti-Jacobin outlook, and its directors were condemned to deportation. In 1799, after Napoleon's coup of 18 Brumaire, Bertin de Vaux and his brother acquired the *Journal des débats* and completely changed its appearance and its substance. Both men actively engaged in publishing their paper. Bertin de Vaux also entered the banking business in 1801 and served as a judge and vice-president in 1805 of the tribunal of commerce of the department of Seine. In July 1805 the name of the newspaper was changed to *Journal de l'empire*, and, after a conflict of some length, Napoleon confiscated it on 18 February 1811.

At the Restoration in 1814, the journal was returned to the Bertin brothers, and its name was changed to *Journal des débats politiques et littéraires*. It ultimately became the most influential paper of the Restoration. In 1815 Bertin de Vaux served as president of one of the electoral colleges in Paris, and in the first Richelieu cabinet he became secretary-general to Elie Decazes at the Ministry of Police. He resigned, however, in 1818 because of what he regarded as the vacillating policy of the cabinet. On 14 November 1820 the department of Seine-et-Oise elected him to the Chamber of Deputies. He became a leader of the royalist opposition. When the Villèle ministry was formed in December 1821, Bertin de Vaux entered the Council of State, but he resigned when Chateaubriand, his collaborator at the *Journal*, lost the Ministry of Foreign Affairs on 6 June 1824. In fact the *Journal des débats* had already joined the constitutional monarchist opposition. Now Bertin de Vaux, reelected to the Deputies in February 1824 after a brief absence, became an opponent of Villèle and company. He especially spoke out against the various financial measures of the government. Remaining in the Deputies until the end of the Restoration period, he reentered the Council of State in 1827 during the Martignac ministry but resigned when the Polignac cabinet was formed. He was one of the 221 deputies who voted the critical address to Charles X in March 1830. In July 1830 he was reelected to the Chamber, where he remained until 1832. After the issuance of the July Ordinances, he participated to some extent in the meetings of deputies and journalists. He also assisted in the formation of a provisional municipal council on 29 July. Bertin staunchly supported the July Monarchy, which recalled him to the Council of State and in September 1830 sent him as minister plenipotentiary to the king of the Netherlands. On 11 October 1832 Louis-Philippe named him to the Chamber of Peers, where he joined the liberal majority. He participated frequently in debates and continued to be active in the management of the *Journal des débats*, which benefited from the uniquely wide acquaintance of the Bertin brothers in high government circles. Bertin de Vaux and his brother also differed from most other newspaper owners in that they did not write for their paper but rather constantly supervised its production, the result being a quality of journalism envied by other editors. Bertin de Vaux died in Paris on 23 April 1842.

Archives parlementaires; I. Collins, *The Government and the Newspaper Press in France, 1814–1881* (London, 1959); E. Hatin, *Histoire du journal en France, 1631–1853* (Paris, 1853) and, *Histoire politique et littéraire de la presse en France* (Paris, 1859); A. Péreire, *Le Journal des Débats politiques et littéraires, 1814–1914* (Paris, 1914); A. Robert et al., *Dictionnaire des parlementaires francais* (Paris, 1889–91).

James K. Kieswetter

Related entries: BERTIN DE VAUX, "AINE"; CHAMBER OF DEPUTIES; CHAMBER OF PEERS; CHATEAUBRIAND; DECAZES; *JOURNAL DES DE-BATS*; LOUIS PHILIPPE; MARTIGNAC; POLIGNAC; THE 221; VILLELE.

BERTON, JEAN-BAPTISTE (1769–1822), Napoleonic general and liberal conspirator in 1821–22. Born at Cullyer (Ardennes) on 15 June 1769, Berton was educated at Brienne and Châlons. He served in the revolutionary and imperial armies under Jean-Victor Moreau, Jean-Baptiste-Jules Bernadotte, and Claude-Perrin Victor, with an outstanding record at Austerlitz, in the Prussian campaign, at Friedland, and in Spain. He also was governor of Malaga. In 1813 he was promoted to brigadier general. Placed on half-pay by the Bourbons in 1814, Berton commanded a cavalry brigade under Rémi-Isidore Exelmans at Waterloo. He remained with the army of the Loire until it was disbanded. Then he returned to Paris. Unemployed under the Restoration, Berton became well known to the police for his liberal attitudes and was imprisoned in 1815 for a year as a suspect. Thus he joined the ranks of disgruntled former imperial officers.

In 1821 there developed the charbonnerie, a French version of the Italian carbonari, devoted to achieving a republican uprising. Spurred by revolutions in Spain and Naples, its members joined forces with the Knights of Liberty, another secret society, and with many former officers. Led by men such as the Marquis de Lafayette and Marc-René de Voyer d'Argenson, they hatched a plot for simultaneous uprisings in Alsace and in the west at Saumur, location of the army cavalry school. Although various aspects of the plot miscarried, especially in Alsace, and the authorities at Saumur were alerted, the conspirators pressed on. They agreed to a virtually new and independent conspiracy on 9 February 1822. Berton volunteered his services and was accepted into the plot, which had links with Paris and other local groups. However, Berton's presence in Brittany had alerted the authorities to the extent of the plot. On 17 February 1822 Berton and his colleagues at Saumur decided to seize the nearby town of Thouars, proclaim a provisional government, and capture the castle at Saumur. On 24 February Berton and his followers seized Thouars, arresting various local royalists and announced the formation of a government in Paris under Lafayette, d'Argenson, Maximilien-Sebastien Foy, Benjamin Constant, and others. After some delay, they marched on Saumur, but there the authorities had been alerted and closed the gates, and the people did not rise to support Berton as he had expected. Having lost much time reaching Saumur and even more negotiating with the authorities there, Berton finally dispersed his small force early the next morning. Berton's own weak leadership had greatly contributed to the failure, for success depended on daring and rapid execution, of which Berton proved incapable. Berton fled to La Rochelle where he unsuccessfully attempted to stir a revolt among carbonarists in the Forty-fifth Regiment. Then he went on to Rochefort and finally back to Saumur, where he and others continued to plot from hiding. He made contact with a sergeant who pretended to be a carbonaro but who, on 17 June 1822, handed Berton and his comrades over to the authorities. Tried with numerous others, Berton was sentenced to death and guillotined on 5 October 1822 at Poitiers. The Saumur conspiracy was the last of the extensive plots against the Bourbons.

M. Berthon, *Les Conspirations de Saumur* (Paris, 1940); C. Gauchais, *Histoire de la conspiration de Saumur* (Paris, 1832); E. Guillon, *Les Complots militaires sous la restauration* (Paris, 1895); H. Pontois, *La Conspiration de général Berton* (Paris, 1877); A. B. Spitzer, *Old Hatreds and Young Hopes* (Cambridge, 1971).

James K. Kieswetter

Related entries: BAZAR CONSPIRACY; CARBONARI; *DEMI-SOLDES*; FABVIER; HUNDRED DAYS; LAFAYETTE; LA ROCHELLE, FOUR SERGEANTS OF; VOYER D'ARGENSON.

BESLAY, CHARLES-VICTOR (1795–1878), politician, participant in three revolutions (1830, 1848, 1871), and industrialist friend of Proudhon. Charles-Victor Beslay followed his father into politics. His father, Charles-Hélène-Bernardin (1768–1839), was a deputy to the Corps législatif (1802–14), the Chamber of Representatives (1815), and the Chamber of Deputies (1815–24, June 1830–1839), where he sat on the constitutional Left and continued his opposition under Louis-Philippe. The young Charles-Victor studied science, worked as an engineer on the Brest-Nantes canal, and engaged in commerce as a *négociant* before he joined the carbonari. He avoided the attention of the police in the insurrections of the early 1820s as the first public notice of his political activity was in quieting worker unrest in Pontivy in July 1830.

Upon this notoriety, he was elected to the Chamber of Deputies from Pontivy (Morbihan) in July 1831. He listed his occupation as *entrepreneur*, and his taxes placed him among the top quarter of the electorate. He took his seat on the far Left and voted with the democratic opposition. In the elections of 1834 he defeated General Gabriel-Jean Fabre, but by the elections of 1837 his advanced opinions were no longer in favor in the Morbihan.

After his defeat, Beslay set up a machine manufacturing shop in the Popincourt quarter of Paris. Here he developed his own ideas on the proper relationship between an employer and his workers. He believed in association of the two so that each would benefit from the work performed. Under the Child Labor Law of 1842, he was named an inspector.

His reputation for support of democratic principles led him to be named commissioner-general for the Morbihan by the Provisional Government in 1848.

From this position he was elected first of the twelve deputies from the Morbihan to the Constituent Assembly in April 1848. A moderate of somewhat uncertain opinions, he became a member of the Labor Committee and its important Subcommittee on the National Workshops headed by the comte de Falloux. Beslay played an insignificant role as Falloux forced through a report designed to lead to the abolition of the National Workshops. When the workers revolted against this, General Eugène Cavaignac turned to Beslay as someone well-known among the workers to calm the faubourg Saint-Antoine. Beslay himself claimed to have voted against Cavaignac in the Assembly, but no such opposition vote is recorded in the official record.

In the Assembly, Beslay maintained an independent attitude. He voted against the banishment of the Orléans family, against the proposition of Proudhon, against the abolition of capital punishment, against progressive taxes, for the pursuit of Louis Blanc, and for the credits for the Roman expedition, all supported by the Right. Yet he also voted against reestablishment of caution money for newspapers, against replacements in the draft, and for the suppression of the salt tax. He took a neutral position on Louis-Napoleon, and since he was not reelected in May 1849, he never had to face this issue directly.

After returning to industrial pursuits, he found the ideas of Proudhon more attractive. He had met Proudhon by chance one rainy day on the way to the Assembly. Proudhon, in need of an umbrella, shared Beslay's and asked him what he thought about the Banque du peuple. Beslay responded, "It is not viable." Proudhon invited him to lunch the next day, and a lifelong friendship developed.

Beslay played no political role under the Empire, although he had allowed protesters of the coup d'état of 2 December 1851 to take refuge in his home. Instead of engaging in politics, he became involved in new developments in business. He founded a *banque d'escompte*, and he took part in the early years of the First Workers' International.

Patriotism was an intricate part of Beslay's mentality. At the age of seventy-five he volunteered to fight the Prussians in 1870, though he had to be satisfied with running for the new Assembly in February 1871. The voters of Paris did not support this republican, but he was successful when he ran for a seat on the council of the Paris Commune from the sixth arrondissement in March 1871. Because of his age, he presided at the opening session of the Commune. Revolution, however, was not in his thoughts, so he soon found himself isolated. His moderation during the Commune gained him the support of Adolphe Thiers; therefore in the repression of the Commune, Beslay was allowed to leave France unharmed. He lived in Switzerland until his death.

C.-V. Beslay, *Mes souvenirs: 1830–1848–1870* (Paris, 1874, and Geneva, 1979).

Thomas Beck

Related entries: BLANC; CARBONARI; CAVAIGNAC, L.-E.; CHILD LABOR; CONSTITUTION OF 1848; COUP D'ETAT OF 2 DECEMBER 1851; NATIONAL WORKSHOPS; PRESS LAWS; PROUDHON; PROVISIONAL

GOVERNMENT; REVOLUTION OF 1830; REVOLUTION OF 1848; ROMAN
EXPEDITION; THIERS.

BEUGNOT, JACQUES-CLAUDE, COMTE (1761–1835), member of the
Legislative Assembly; deputy, minister, and peer of the Restoration. Jacques-
Claude Beugnot was born at Bar-sur-Aube (Aube) on 25 July 1761. He was
active in public affairs before the Revolution and in its early years. In September
1791 the department of the Aube elected him to the Legislative Assembly, where
he was a constitutional monarchist. After 10 August 1792 he vanished from the
Assembly. He was arrested in 1793 but was released after the fall of Robespierre.
He did not reappear in public life until after 18 Brumaire, when he became
secretary to Lucien Bonaparte, minister of the interior.

The Provisional Government appointed him commissioner of the interior on
3 April 1814. In this capacity Beugnot was responsible for rewriting a long,
turgid speech by the comte d'Artois on 12 April, replacing it with the well-
known catchy comment, "Nothing has changed in France except that there is
now one Frenchman more." Beugnot also arranged the successful reception of
Louis XVIII in Paris on 3 May and played a key role in drafting the Charter.
Louis XVIII subsequently transferred him to the directory-general of police.
Remaining there throughout most of the first Restoration, Beugnot was responsible
for measures providing for public religious processions and reestablishing Sunday
as a day of rest. Both measures caused considerable opposition. Later in 1814
Beugnot became minister of marine. He followed the king to Ghent, functioning
in the government in exile during the Hundred Days. On their return to Paris,
he was appointed director general of posts on 9 July 1815; however, he quickly
left this post and received instead the honorary title of minister of state.

In October 1816 the department of Seine-Inférieure elected him to the Chamber
of Deputies where he joined the doctrinaire royalists, a group known for their
intelligence and integrity. As in the Legislative Assembly twenty-five years
earlier, he was a fluent speaker, known for his ready wit. In April 1817 he was
promoted to grand officer of the Legion of Honor, and on 16 June he became
director general of the sinking fund. In 1818 he led in debates on the army bill,
insisting that the legislature vote on the army annually. He was reelected to the
Deputies by a close vote in September 1819. During this, his last term in office,
he supported the Decazes ministry, helping to defeat a proposal by the ultraroyalist
Francois de Barthélemy to change the election laws to defeat the liberals. He
also supported freedom of the press. In 1820 after the assassination of the duc
de Berry, Beugnot changed his position on the press. But he attempted to restrain
the reaction. Later in 1820 he resigned from the Chamber of Deputies, thus
ending his political career. He died in Bagneux (Seine) on 24 June 1835.

Archives parlementaires; J. C. Beugnot, *Mémoires du comte Beugnot* (Paris, 1889);
E. Dejean, *Un Préfet du consulat: Beugnot* (Paris, 1897); N. Richardson, *The French
Prefectoral Corps, 1814–1830* (Cambridge, 1966); A. Robert et al., *Dictionnaire des
parlementaires français* (Paris, 1889–1891); B. Saint-Edme, *Biographie des lieutenans-*

généraux, ministres, directeurs-généraux . . . de la police (Paris, 1829); J. Savant, *Les Préfets de Napoléon* (Paris, 1958).

James K. Kieswetter

Related entries: CHARTER OF 1814; DOCTRINAIRES.

BEURNONVILLE, PIERRE RIEL, MARQUIS DE (1752–1821), general and minister of the Revolution, senator of the Empire, and peer of the Restoration. Beurnonville, born 10 May 1752 at Champignol (Aube), enlisted in the grenadiers of the queen and served in the Indies. He stayed in the army during the Republic and became minister of war from 4 February to 11 March 1793. Captured by the Austrians in April 1793, he was not released by them until 19 December 1795 when he resumed his military career and became commander of the Army of the North.

Beurnonville supported Napoleon's coup of 18 Brumaire and the Empire, becoming a senator, ambassador, and Grand Eagle of the Legion of Honor. Nevertheless, as a senator in April 1814 he voted for the dethronement of Napoleon and the recall of the Bourbons.

Beurnonville became a member of the 1814 provisional government led by Talleyrand. Later in April the comte d'Artois named him to the Council of State, and Louis XVIII appointed him minister of state and a peer on 4 June 1814. As a peer he sat in judgment on Marshal Michel Ney in 1815, voting for execution. In October 1815 Beurnonville was appointed to preside over one of the two commissions established to evaluate former imperial officers to decide which should continue on active service. Beurnonville's commission specifically had the task of evaluating claims by royalist officers who had served in various irregular units. The acceptance by this commission of many outrageous pretensions and its harsh treatment of many imperial army officers caused extensive resentment among officers and civilians alike. On 3 May 1816 Beurnonville was made a marshal of France, and on 3 July he was named a marquis. In 1816 he also became a commander in the Order of Saint Louis, and at the birth of the duc de Bordeaux he received an appointment to the Order of the Holy Ghost. Beurnonville died in Paris on 23 April 1821.

L. Graux, *Le Maréchal Beurnonville* (Paris, 1929); R. W. Phipps, *The Armies of the First French Republic* (London, 1926–39); A. Robert et al., *Dictionnaire des parlementaires français* (Paris, 1889–91); A. Vaulabelle, *Histoire des deux restaurations* (Paris, 1874); E. Whitcomb, *Napoleon's Diplomatic Service* (Durham, 1979).

James K. Kieswetter

Related entries: NEY; TALLEYRAND.

BEYLE, HENRI. See STENDHAL.

LA BIBLIOTHEQUE HISTORIQUE, Bonapartist journal of the Restoration. In the years immediately following 1815, left-wing journals were often described by their opponents as Bonapartist. The *Bibliothèque historique* was probably, however, the only genuinely Bonapartist journal of the Restoration period. Founded in December 1817 by two ardent admirers of Napoleon, Chevalier and Reynaud, it was in many respects like other left-wing newspapers. There were the usual anecdotes illustrating the pretensions of priests and nobles and the vexatious behavior of prefects and mayors. One of the editors, probably Antoine-Vernier Benoit, introduced an original note, however. In order to present Napoleon in as favorable a light as possible, he edited documents supposed to have been written by Napoleon as first consul and emperor. A number of them were fictitious, but they were sufficiently plausible to mislead not only contemporary readers but Bonapartist historians for many years.

The *Bibliothèque historique* evaded the press laws, which required police authorization for periodicals, by appearing at irregular intervals. In July 1818 Chevalier and Raynaud were charged under the law against seditious cries and writings and condemned to six months imprisonment and 3,000 francs fine, but the government got little credit from the proceedings, since Benjamin Constant was able to write one of his most powerful pamphlets accusing the minister of police of stretching the law. The circulation of the *Bibliothèque* never reached more than 2,500; nevertheless, prefects cited it as one of the most influential newspapers in the provinces, and Chevalier figured in police reports as one of the government's most dangerous enemies.

Under the liberal press laws of 1819, the editors were charged with offense to the king in an article that compared the king's Swiss Guards to the sultan's janissaries. Mérilhou, for the defense, said that the article could have implied no tyranny on the part of the king since the latter's name was never mentioned. The editors were acquitted. On 24 January 1820 they were acquitted again of any offensive intent in an article that described the state religion as "full of corruption, machiavellianism, and tyranny." The censorship law of 31 March 1820, imposed after the murder of the duc de Berry, covered periodicals appearing at both regular and irregular intervals. The *Bibliothèque*, after threatening revolution, disappeared of its own accord, though the publisher Corréard continued for two months to sell brochures that escaped the censorship.

I. Collins, "Liberalism and the Newspaper Press during the French Revolution," *History* 46 (1961); P. Gonnard, "La Légende napoléonienne et la presse libérale," *Revue des etudes napoléoniennes* 1 (1912).

Irene Collins

Related entries: BERRY, C.-F.; CENSORSHIP; CONSTANT; LAW ON SEDITIOUS SPEECH; MERILHOU; PRESS LAWS; SWISS GUARD.

BIGNON, LOUIS-PIERRE-EDOUARD, BARON (1771–1841), Napoleonic diplomat and liberal Restoration deputy. The well-educated son of a Rouen dyer, Bignon enlisted in the army in 1797, but his real talent was in the diplomatic service, where Charles-Maurice de Talleyrand's support helped him rise to prominence during the Republic and the Empire. Captured by the allied armies at Dresden (1813), he was released by virtue of his diplomatic immunity and returned to Paris. Napoleon made him under-secretary of the foreign ministry during the Hundred Days, and as foreign minister in the provisional government that followed Waterloo, Bignon signed the capitulation of Paris to the allies (3 July 1815).

Ignored by the Bourbons, Bignon secured election to the Chamber in 1817 (initially from the Eure, later the Haut-Rhin) and became a leading orator of the liberal opposition. His steady opposition to the Holy Alliance and vigorous denunciation of government repression in the wake of the carbonarist conspiracies of 1822 won him a wide following, and he was named foreign minister after the Revolution of 1830. Although Louis-Philippe would have preferred to keep him in that post, Austrian and Russian pressure forced his reappointment as minister of public education in October 1830. He soon resigned and returned to the Chamber, where he championed the causes of Polish and Italian independence. Elevated to the peerage, he began work on a diplomatic history of the Napoleonic era, a task for which Napoleon had specifically left him 100,000 francs in his will. The work was completed after his death in 1841 by his son-in-law Alfred Ernouf.

L. P. E. Bignon, *Histoire de France sous Napoléon*, 14 vols. (Paris, 1829–50), *Les cabinets et les peuples depuis 1815* (Paris, 1822), and *Proscriptions anciennes et modernes* (Paris, 1820); E. Harpaz, *L'Ecole libérale sous la Restauration* (Paris, 1968); O. Connelly, *Napoleon's Satellite Kingdoms* (New York, 1965); A. B. Spitzer, *Old Hatreds and Young Hopes* (Cambridge, 1971).

David Longfellow

Related entries: CARBONARI; TALLEYRAND.

BIGOT DE MOROGUES, PIERRE-MARIE-SEBASTIEN, BARON DE (1776–1840), agronomist, philanthropist, political writer, and member of the Chamber of Peers. Bigot described himself as religious by conviction, a philosopher by virtue of reason, a patriot and royalist by affection, a monarchist and constitutionalist out of principle, an enemy of despotism and anarchy, a nobleman by birth, and philanthropic by sentiment. This is a useful self-description of a man who dedicated his life more to philanthropy and agronomy than politics and whose writings and practical efforts were aimed at bridging the two worlds of the Old Regime and the Revolution.

Born into a family who had long served in the navy, Bigot was also destined to follow this career. The Revolution, however, intervened, and in 1794 he entered the School of Mines and traveled widely in France in conjunction with his research. His career took another turn with his marriage to Claudinne de Montaudouin. Since she held one of the largest domains in Sologne, the Chateau de la Source, Bigot decided to leave mineralogy for agronomy. For the next forty years he wrote numerous articles and pamphlets on specific agricultural improvements. Both on his own estates and in local agricultural societies he encouraged the use of new techniques to better the lot of the local peasantry. Bigot believed that it was the responsibility of the great landowners and the government to encourage the peasants to use new agricultural methods and to educate them in a more scientific outlook.

More broadly, Bigot was interested in the social, economic, and moral conditions of the poor. He emphasized the need for society to educate the young in basic skills so that they could function better in the modern world, but also to perfect their judgment "by putting into their heart a morality fashioned by wisdom and enlightenment." In several works on the wealth of nations and the poverty of workers written at the end of the Restoration and in the early July Monarchy, he was critical of Adam Smith and the political economists whose works he believed increased pauperism. Bigot saw luxury and the inequality of wealth as necessary causes and by-products of modern civilization, but he also recognized the negative effects of industrial capitalism. Economic progress might raise the level of civilization in both the arts and morality, but something had to be done to help the poorer classes who frequently suffered under such progress. Indeed, Bigot maintained, these disenchanted classes were largely responsible for the July Revolution.

His solutions to the social problems connected with industrialization, however, did not go much beyond reminding the upper classes of their responsibility to the poor and warning society of the dangers of an excessive concentration of wealth. Bigot advocated diversification into smaller industries and the continuing division of large estates. In this way, small producers, whether peasants or workers, would have reason to be more ambitious and would gain increased responsibility. For those workers who lost their jobs because of machines, he recommended the creation of agricultural colonies.

The guarantee of the sense of social responsibility needed to bring all this about was to fall on what Bigot called a "constitutional nobility." Although *La Noblesse constitutionelle . . .* was written before most of his social and economic works, it is clear from this work that Bigot felt that only a well-constituted elite could bring progress and social harmony. Unlike that of the Old Regime, his nobility was to be open to all according to merit, but, paradoxically, it was to be passed on hereditarily. Thus, for him, individual merit and social mobility would be joined with the basis for social cohesion and order. This constitutional nobility would stretch hierarchically from the local village to the central state and would serve as a philanthropic and political elite guiding the social and moral condition of all Frenchmen. His fantasies about such an elite faded with the Revolution of 1830 but not his writings about industrial capitalism.

In recognition of his writings and good works, Bigot was rewarded with appointment to the Legion of Honor (1834) and one year later to the Chamber of Peers. The local citizenry of Sologne had earlier recognized his contributions by electing him mayor of their commune and later to the Conseil général of the department of Loiret. In the last few years of his life, Bigot suffered from frequent bouts of the gout but still took an active part in the debates of the Chamber of Peers.

P. M. Bigot de Morogues, *Essai sur les moyens d'améliorer l'agriculture* (Paris, 1822), *Influences des sociétés littéraires, savants et agricoles* (Orleans, 1823), *La noblesse constitutionnelle* (Paris, 1825), and *Du pauperisme* (Paris, 1834); L. Epsztein, *L'Économie et la morale au début du capitalisme industriel* (Paris, 1966); S. Gutman, "Justifications for an Aristocracy in Restoration France" (Ph.D. diss., University of Michigan, 1976); J. Wyslouch, *Notice biographique et historique* (Paris, 1841).

Sanford Gutman

Related entries: AGRICULTURE; CHAMBER OF PEERS; PEASANTS; PHILOSOPHY OF INDUSTRIALISM; PUBLIC WELFARE; REVOLUTION OF 1830.

BIXIO, JACQUES-ALEXANDRE (1808–1865), intellectual and political figure, who initiated gatherings of intellectuals at the Restaurant Philippe. Bixio was born on 20 November 1808 at Chiavari, located at that time in the department of Apennins. He studied medicine at Paris and received his doctorate around 1830. While a student, he joined the French carbonari. As a proponent of liberalism, he took part in the Revolution of 1830.

In 1831 he and Francois Buloz founded the *Revue des deux mondes*. In 1831, with Jean-Augustin Barral he founded the *Journal d'agriculture pratique et de jardinage*, which he edited for eleven years. He also published the *Maison rustique du XIXe siècle*, the *Almanach du jardinier*, and the *Almanach du cultivateur*.

He wrote for the *National* and took part in the reformist campaign that led to the Revolution of 1848. When the revolution erupted in February, he joined the defenders of order, and supported the establishment of a regency after Louis-Philippe's abdication. Nevertheless, when the Republic was established, Bixio was sent as its ambassador to Piedmont. He was elected to represent the department of Doubs in the Constituent Assembly. He had not yet returned to Paris when he heard of the invasion of the Assembly on May 15. He denounced the radical Left, and, upon arriving in Paris, associated with the moderate Left. He gave his support to Eugène Cavaignac. During the June Days he was on the rue St. Jacques with General Marie-Alphonse Bedeau. After the general was wounded, Bixio led the troops in an attack but was himself seriously wounded. Upon recovering, he returned to the Assembly, where he was chosen vice-president. He served for a short time as minister of agriculture. In March 1849, as a member of the Committee on Foreign Affairs, he proposed French military intervention in Italy.

He was elected from both the Seine and Doubs to sit in the Legislative Assembly. He opted for the seat from Doubs and voted with the moderate republicans against the monarchists. On 8 December 1851, he joined with the representatives who denounced Louis-Napoleon's coup. He was arrested and detained at Mazas for a month. After his release he devoted himself to industrial and agricultural affairs. He was an associate of the Pereire brothers and became an administrator of the Crédit mobilier and the Crédit foncier.

In 1856, he and a number of friends began regular gatherings at the Restaurant Philippe. Among the authors and artists who gathered for these "academic diners,'' called Dîner Bixio, were Eugène Delacroix, Alexandre Dumas père, Léon Halévy, Prosper Mérimée, François Ponsard, and Charles-Augustin Sainte-Beuve. Bixio died in Paris, 16 December 1865.

J. Claretie, *Souvenirs du dîner Bixio* (Paris, 1924); M. Prevost, article in *Dictionnaire de bibliographie française*, vol. 6 (Paris, 1954); L. Wetzel, *A Bixio* (Paris, 1869).

Bernard Cook

Related entries: BEDEAU; CARBONARI; CAVAIGNAC, L.-E.; DELA-CROIX; JUNE DAYS; LEGISLATIVE ASSEMBLY; MERIMEE; *LE NA-TIONAL*; *LA REVUE DES DEUX MONDES*; SAINTE-BEUVE.

BLACAS D'AULPS, PIERRE-JEAN-LOUIS-CASIMIR, COMTE, then **DUC** (1770–1839), politician and diplomat. An *émigré* since 1789, he had become after 1810 the confidant of Louis XVIII, and after that king regained his throne, Blacas became minister of the Maison du roi. In 1815 he followed his royal master into temporary exile in Ghent. Because he was blamed for certain measures that had alienated public opinion during the First Restoration, Louis XVIII had to distance himself from his favorite by naming him ambassador to Rome, and in this capacity Blacas negotiated a new concordat with the Holy See. He played an important role at the Congress of Laibach and from 1823 to 1830 was ambassador to Naples, trying to block Austria's attempts to attain hegemony in Italy. He was also interested in archaeology, and he gave strong protection to the young Jean-François Champollion's work in Egyptology.

E. Daudet, *Joseph de Maistre, Leur correspondance inédite* (Paris, 1908).

Guillaume de Bertier de Sauvigny, trans. E. Newman

Related entries: CHAMPOLLION; TROPPAU, CONGRESS OF.

BLANC, LOUIS (1811–1882), socialist theorist, deputy, journalist, and historian. Louis Blanc was born into a royalist family that had rallied to Napoleon I. His mother's connections with the restored Bourbons secured a scholarship for both him and his brother Charles, enabling them to receive a good classical education in the Collège de Rodez. The Blanc brothers, like so many other provincials, arrived in Paris in 1830, almost penniless after the fall of the Bourbons. Aided by relatives, they eked out a meager existence until Louis found a job as a journalist with a rather small Parisian paper, the *Bon sens*. Having given up his ambition to become a poet, he now developed his prose style into a means of spreading the ideas that were fermenting in his generous mind. The 1830s were the truly formative years in his long life. Abandoning the royalism of his youth, he developed a political philosophy that showed the strong influence of the Jacobins and a social view that blended the collectivist ideals of the Babeuvians and the cooperatism of Robert Owen. He was not a highly original thinker, and yet he reoriented the socialist movement toward the political arena. He founded the *Revue du progrès*, a periodical in which he began the publication of his most famous work, *Organisation du travail*, in 1839. In 1840 he put out an expansion of these articles in book form, and this little work brought him almost instant success.

His philosophy can be easily summarized. The workers, with sympathetic members of the middle class, are to create a democratic state similar to the First Republic of 1793–94. The duty of this new state is to finance the establishment of social workshops (*ateliers*), which the workers will own collectively. The term *factory*, however, would be more appropriate than *workshop* because Louis Blanc envisioned large-scale, mechanized production, not the preservation of the handicrafts of artisans. He also called for cooperation among centers of production as a means of ending competition, the true evil of society in his mind. Eventual abolition of wages would also end competition among workers within each *atelier social*, for only when each worker produces according to his strength and consumes according to his needs will the era of social fraternity begin.

When another revolution broke out in February 1848 Louis Blanc attained the high point of his career. He became, in the new Provisional Government, a minister without portfolio; however, he was without power and a budget. His more conservative colleagues appointed him to head the Luxembourg Commission set up to study labor problems. Nothing went right for him; he lacked a solid base of support, and the reaction following the 15 May invasion of the National Assembly and the June Days forced him to flee into exile.

The next twenty-two years of his life were spent in England. He completed his massive *History of the French Revolution* and continued his career as a journalist. Not until the fall of the Second Empire in 1870 did he return. The next twelve years of his life were spent in politics as a deputy. He helped to found the Third Republic and influenced the social ideas of a new generation of the left wing, both authentic socialists like Benoît Mâlon and radicals like George Clemenceau. Democratic socialism owes much to him.

L. A. Loubère, *Louis Blanc* (Evanston, Ill., 1961); E. Renard, *Louis Blanc* (Toulouse, 1922).

Leo A. Loubère

Related entries: *LE BON SENS*; JUNE DAYS; LUXEMBOURG COMMISSION; PROVISIONAL GOVERNMENT; REVOLUTION OF 1848; *LA REVUE DU PROGRES*.

BLANQUI, JEROME-ADOLPHE (1798–1854), economist and economic historian, brother of the Revolutionary, Louis-Auguste Blanqui. Born in Nice, the eldest of ten children (of whom Louis-Auguste was the third, and next-eldest brother), Jérôme-Adolphe Blanqui was the son of Jean-Dominique Blanqui (1759–1832) and Sophie Brionville. The father had been elected from Nice to the Convention in May 1793 and was subsequently imprisoned for ten months during the Terror when he dared to protest the Jacobin coup of 31 May–2 June. Released after Thermidor, Jean-Dominique served in the Council of 500 (1795–97) and was then named subprefect of the Alpes-Maritimes in 1798. Jérôme-Adolphe was born in Nice on 21 November 1798, shortly before his father took up his post at Puget-Théniers, where the family remained until 1814. Young Adolphe attended the local collège and a lycée in Nice and had moved to Paris to pursue his studies when his father was dismissed from his post by the restored Bourbon government. Though returned briefly as subprefect of Marmonde during the Hundred Days, Jean-Dominique was discharged again under the Second Restoration, and the family moved to an inherited property of Adolphe's mother near Aunay (Eure-et-Loire). Adolphe returned from Paris to help a family burdened by his father's unemployability and his mother's increasingly erratic behavior and mental instability. He taught briefly in an unauthorized primary school his father had started but returned to Paris in 1818 to find work when the school was closed by the prefect. His brother Louis-Auguste soon followed, and the two lived together while Auguste attended the Lycée Charlemagne, winning honors as a brilliant student, and Adolphe worked as an assistant teacher and tutor in humanities in a succession of private schools. Both were politically liberal, contributing articles to the opposition *Courrier français* and *Journal du commerce*, but Adolphe did not follow his younger brother into the conspiratorial underground of the carbonari in the 1820s.

In 1824, Adolphe attended a course in industrial economy presented at the Conservatoire des arts et métiers by Jean-Baptiste Say and was soon taken on by the economist as a protégé and colleague. In 1825, he was able to present his own public course at the Athénée, and the resulting acclaim won him a joint professorship of history and industrial economy at the Ecole supérieure de commerce. In 1830, he became director of the school, which was attended by sons of well-to-do business families and run as a profit-making enterprise by Blanqui. At the time of his brother Auguste's first trial for plotting against the July Monarchy in April 1831, the two were still close enough for Adolphe to protest publicly the reading of his brother's confiscated correspondence on the floor of the Chamber, but Adolphe's growing acceptance of Louis-Philippe's regime led to their permanent estrangement by 1832.

At Say's death in 1833, Blanqui took over his chair at the Conservatoire (Say's chair at the Collège de France went to P. L. E. Rossi) and in 1837 published his widely praised *Histoire de l'économie politique en Europe, depuis les anciens jusqu'à nos jours* (1837–38, 2 vols.), the earliest formal economic history of Western Europe. Most contemporary writers traced the development of economic theory no further back than Adam Smith and François Quesnay, but Blanqui argued that the conscious elaboration and management of economic systems (political economy) began with the ancient Greeks. As Blanqui traced the economic history of Europe, he devoted considerable attention to the condition of the poor and working classes in various societies and did not hesitate to praise institutions and political leaders who sought a more equitable distribution of wealth. This concern for social justice and the condition of labor characterized most of Blanqui's writings, and his willingness to accept government action on behalf of working men and women to some extent separates him from his mentor Say, whom the *History* criticizes for ignoring the social abuses created by industrialism and uncritically adopting a Malthusian perspective on the plight of the poor. Blanqui nonetheless remained an ardent advocate of laissez-faire economics, condemning mercantilism and government intervention in most other areas of the economy. The *History* also proved to be a pioneering work in its analysis of the historical interaction of political practice and economic theory, as when Blanqui attributed the physiocrats' emphasis on agriculture and land as the primary sources of wealth and investment to the earlier failure of John Law's financial system under the Regency.

In 1838, Blanqui was elected to the Academy of Moral and Political Sciences and in subsequent years traveled extensively to study contemporary economic systems. These trips (to England, Italy, Spain, Austria, Germany, Serbia, Algeria, and the Middle East) resulted in newspaper and magazine articles, scholarly papers, and published studies, which were widely read and added to Blanqui's reputation. A trip to the department of the Nord in 1840 and the resulting report on the conditions of the working class there provoked widespread pressure for reforms. Blanqui was a cofounder of the *Journal des économistes* and was elected as a deputy to the legislature from Bordeaux in 1846–48 (not reelected).

The news of Blanqui's death on 28 January 1854 led to fulsome tributes from colleagues throughout Europe and profoundly upset his brother Auguste (then serving a ten-year term for subversion at Belle-Isle). The professional revolutionary wrote of the respected economist that their differences had always been political, not personal, and that the day he learned of his elder brother's death was the worst of his life. Blanqui's writings have been criticized for failing to distinguish between economic systems (which can be traced to antiquity) and economic theory (as opposed to general ideas), which some feel begins in the eighteenth century. Joseph Schumpeter found Blanqui's research on working-class conditions and labor economics considerably more significant than the famous *History*. A number of scholars, however, credit Blanqui with the first use of the term *industrial revolution* in an 1837 essay. He had begun to write his memoirs, but these were unfinished at the time of his death.

J.-A. Blanqui, *History of Political Economy in Europe* (translation in New York, 1880) and ''Souvenirs d'un étudiant sous la Restauration,'' *Revue de Paris* (November–December 1918); W. B. Catlin, *The Progress of Economics: A History of Economic Thought* (New York, 1962); L. Cossa, *An Introduction to the Study of Political Economy* (London, 1893); G. Geoffroy, *L'Enfermé*, 2 vols. (Paris, 1926); R. W. Postgate, *Out of the Past: Some Revolutionary Sketches* (New York, 1923); A. Renouard, *Histoire de l'école supérieure de commerce de Paris* (Paris, 1898, 1920); J. Schumpeter, *History of Economic Analysis* (New York, 1954).

David Longfellow

Related entries: ACADEMY OF SCIENCES; BLANQUI, L.-A.; CARBONARI; CHAMBER OF DEPUTIES; COLLEGE DE FRANCE; CONSERVATOIRE NATIONAL DES ARTS ET METIERS; *LE COURRIER FRANCAIS*; *JOURNAL DES ECONOMISTES*; *JOURNAL DU COMMERCE*; LOUIS PHILIPPE; SAY.

BLANQUI, LOUIS-AUGUSTE (1805–1881), revolutionary socialist and militant anticlerical. Auguste Blanqui was born on 1 February 1805 at Puget-Theniers, near Nice, where his father, a former member of the Convention, was imperial subprefect. At the Restoration the family moved to Paris, where Auguste was educated. During the 1820s he worked as a private tutor and as a journalist, particularly on the *Globe*, and studied both law and medicine. Blanqui joined the carbonari, the radical underground movement, in 1824 and began a long career of militant opposition to a succession of French governments that earned him more than twenty-seven years' imprisonment and the popular nickname *L'Enfermé*. He took part in the fighting in Paris during the July Revolution against Charles X in 1830 but regarded the new constitutional monarchy of Louis-Philippe as a bourgeois usurpation. In the 1830s he supported the Amis du peuple and the Droits de l'homme societies in their campaigns for universal suffrage and pressed for full implementation of the republican Jacobin constitution of 1793.

When the repression of 1834 drove the republican opposition underground, Blanqui helped to organize two revolutionary secret societies, the Société des familles (1834–36) and the Société des saisons (1837–39). In May 1839, with Armand Barbès and Martin Bernard, he led the abortive attempt of the Société des saisons to seize power in Paris and was captured, spending the years 1840–47 in prison or in exile in consequence. Blanqui was prominent in the agitation of the Parisian popular societies that followed the February Revolution of 1848, and on 15 May he was named member of a revolutionary provisional government by an insurgent crowd at the Hôtel de ville. When the coup collapsed, he was again imprisoned, this time until 1859. Agitation against the Second Empire resulted in a further four years in jail (1861–65) and a period of exile in Belgium. Returning to Paris, in August 1870 Blanqui led a premature and farcical coup against the declining Empire. After the fall of the Empire, he was involved in yet another abortive uprising, on 31 October, when he was again named a member of an ephemeral provisional government at the Hôtel de ville. His subsequent arrest prevented Blanqui from playing any part in the Paris Commune of 1871, and there followed a final seven years of incarceration before a pardon freed him, in 1879, to spend the last months of his life in open political campaigning. He died on 1 January 1881.

Blanqui sought always to overthrow private property and to introduce a regime of complete equality. Although he paid tribute to the new socialist principles of association, he framed no clear plans for the postrevolutionary society. In his analysis all modern revolutions had followed the same pattern: they were made by the proletarian masses, only to be captured by the bourgeoisie. Therefore it was essential to organize a determined revolutionary elite for the capture and consolidation of political power. The elite would then supervise the reeducation of the people, under a revolutionary dictatorship, so that they would ultimately, freely, and gradually choose communism. This process would take many years. The central role of the clergy in the existing educational system, and their ideological domination, coupled with Blanqui's own atheism, made Blanqui and his followers violently anticlerical, and this was for many sympathizers their most notable appeal.

In his writings and speeches Blanqui contributed substantially to the developing class analysis of society as divided between a propertyless proletariat and an exploiting capitalist bourgeoisie, and is credited with first formulating the notion of the dictatorship of the proletariat, which was subsequently adopted by Marx and Engels. The Blanquists were always centrally concerned, however, with the techniques of political revolution rather than organizing a broader working-class movement. Their coups all failed, in Blanqui's view, either through mistakes in timing or inadequate preparation. They were an important party in the Paris Commune of 1871, however, and formed one of the influences ultimately absorbed into the organized socialist movement under the Third Republic. Through his disciple P. N. Tkachev (1844–85) Blanqui also influenced the Russian revolutionary movement and, arguably, Lenin's tactical ideas.

S. Bernstein, *Auguste Blanqui and the Art of Insurrection* (London, 1971); *Dictionnaire de biographie française*, vol. 6 (Paris, 1954); M. Dommanget, *Auguste Blanqui des origines à la révolution de 1848* (Paris, 1969); A. B. Spitzer, *The Revolutionary Theories of Louis-Auguste Blanqui* (New York, 1957).

Robert Barrie Rose

Related entries: ANTICLERICAL CAMPAIGN; BARBES; BLANQUI, A.; CARBONARI; CLUBS, POLITICAL; *LE GLOBE*; REVOLUTION OF 1848; SOCIETY OF THE RIGHTS OF MAN; SOCIETY OF THE SEASONS.

BOE, JACQUES. See JASMIN.

BOIGNE, LOUISE-ELEONORE, CHARLOTTE-ADELAIDE D'OSMOND, COMTESSE DE (1781–1866), political hostess and memoirist. After emigrating with her mother, who was *dame d'honneur* to Mme. Adelaide of France, she spent part of her youth in Naples, where she befriended the princess who would become in 1830 queen of the French. In 1798 in London she married General Benoit le Borgne de Boigne, a self-made man who had made a huge fortune in the Indies, and this misalliance, whose purpose had been to put an end to her family's poverty, would soon be broken by an amicable separation.

During the Restoration, she ran her father's house while he served as ambassador to Turin and then to London. During the July Monarchy she kept a popular political salon. Her intimate liaison with the minister and chancellor Etienne-Denis Pasquier furnished her with abundant material for the copious memoirs that she wrote and that would be published in 1907–8 under the title *Récits d'une tante*. An English edition, published in London and New York, was entitled *Recollections of a Great Lady* (1912). These amusing recollections should be used with great caution.

Matuxchek, *Die Gräfin von Boigne und ihre Memoiren* (Weimar, 1932).

Guillaume de Bertier de Sauvigny, trans E. Newman

Related entries: ADELAIDE; MARIE-AMELIE DE BOURBON; PASQUIER.

BONALD, LOUIS-GABRIEL-AMBROISE, VICOMTE DE (1754–1840), philosopher and politician. Before emigrating, this scion of an old family of Roumergue had served in the Musketeers. He wrote his first work, *Théorie du pouvoir politique et religieux dans la société civile* (Constance, 1796), while he was in exile in Heidelberg. In that book his fundamental doctrine, which he would constantly repeat ever after, emerged: there is only one true and natural constitution in political society—that of pure monarchy—and only one constitution for religious society—that of Catholicism, and that true civil society is the result of the union of the altar and the throne, outside of which there is no stability and no salvation.

After his clandestine return to France at the end of the Directory, Bonald was able under the Consulate to develop further his political theories in a series of works, of which the best known is *La Législation primitive considérée par les seules lumières de la raison* (1802). Bonaparte, believing that the theories of Bonald could contribute to the restoration of monarchical power, made him a member of the Superior Council of the University in 1808. Under the Restoration, Bonald was deputy from Aveyron and then in 1823 peer of France. In 1816 he was named a member of the Académie française. He became the oracle of the royalist party, respected all the more because his thought was difficult to understand. In politics he was the intransigent defender of the most reactionary measures and a faithful supporter of Joseph de Villèle. The 1830 revolution ended his political career.

H. Moulinié, *De Bonald, La vie, La carrière politique, la doctrine* (Paris, 1916); M. H. Quinlan, *The Historical Thought of the Vicomte de Bonald* (Washington, 1953).

Guillaume de Bertier de Sauvigny, trans. E. Newman

Related entries: ACADEMIE FRANCAISE; THEOCRATS; VILLELE.

BONAPARTISM. Bonapartism at its simplest meant support for the claims of the Bonaparte family to the French throne. The claimants were Napoleon Bonaparte himself until his abdication in June 1815 or his death in May 1821; his son, the king of Rome (Napoleon II), until his own death in July 1832; and Louis-Napoleon Bonaparte thereafter. As a political doctrine, Bonapartism is much more difficult to define; it was inconsistent, shifting, and often opportunistic. The general theme of Bonapartism, however, was the reconciliation of the fundamental principles of the French Revolution with a strong government to maintain law, order, and property. As practiced by Napoleon I, Bonapartism was centralizing, authoritarian, and antiparliamentary, subordinating legislative to executive power. But it was also egalitarian in its rejection of privileges of birth and its acceptance of social mobility ("the career open to talent"). It acknowledged the principle of popular sovereignty but in fact limited its expression to the occasional plebiscite or undemocratic election. The emperor himself was first representative of his people. "Sovereignty resides in the French people," according to Napoleon I, "in the sense that everything . . . must be done for its happiness and glory."

Two variant forms of Bonapartism emerged during the Hundred Days (1815). Napoleon officially adopted liberal Bonapartism, embodied in the Additional Act, a constitution drawn up by Benjamin Constant that guaranteed parliamentary government and civil rights. A neo-Jacobin version of Bonapartism also appeared spontaneously among urban workers and the peasantry of certain regions. This portrayed Napoleon as defender of the French Revolution against the clerical and aristocratic enemy within France and the leagued foreign despots without.

There was no Bonapartist party after 1815, apart from the group of malcontents later recalled by Chévremont, a prefect under the Second Empire, as "few in number but compact . . . , composed of former soldiers wounded in their nationalism and their personal interests, and of several families who had lost positions and honors when the Empire fell." But the Napoleonic legend was developing rapidly in these years: a veritable cult of Napoleon that exalted him as the incarnation of the French Revolution and celebrated his civil achievements and military glory. Inevitably Napoleon became a potent symbol for anyone unhappy with the Restoration. A vague Bonapartism consequently suffused all political opposition to the Bourbons. Anticlericals, nationalists, liberals, and republicans—few of whom had any wish to resurrect the Empire—nonetheless expressed Bonapartist sympathies. Genuine Bonapartists meanwhile worked alongside the men of other parties, and many Napoleonic generals or prefects emerged as leading liberals.

Bonapartist sentiments also spread among the lower classes. This was in part the result of offended national pride after the defeats of 1814–15 and in part the consequence of declining agricultural prices and real wages from 1817 to 1852. Police reports show that Parisian workers in the 1820s frequently grumbled that wages had been higher and work more plentiful under Napoleon. Any severe economic crisis, such as the high bread prices of 1816–17 and the depression of the late 1820s, aroused this latent popular Bonapartism. The Napoleonic legend also had a profound effect among the masses; a million demobilized soldiers were influential propagandists. According to a police report of 1829, the songs of Pierre-Jean de Béranger, which evoked Napoleon's glory, "are sung in all the workshops." Police throughout France repeatedly seized Napoleonic prints, busts, medallions, and songsheets, as well as an incredible variety of other objects bearing the portrait of Napoleon or his son.

The July Revolution of 1830 demonstrated the weakness of Bonapartism as an independent political force. Napoleon II was a virtual prisoner in Vienna, and there was no organized party in France to take advantage of the political crisis. The Parisian crowd shouted Bonapartist slogans, but these expressed little more than a desire for steady work and renewed French glory. Prominent Bonapartists rallied quickly to Louis-Philippe, who rewarded them well for their allegiance. The Chamber of Peers that condemned Louis-Napoleon Bonaparte in October 1840 included at least 127 men who had once served Napoleon I. The July Monarchy appropriated the Napoleonic legend for itself; it restored Napoleon's statue to the Vendôme Column in Paris (1833), completed his Arch of Triumph (1836), and brought his ashes from St. Helena to rest in the Invalides Church (1840).

The republican and socialist opponents of the regime also used Napoleon's name to add luster to their cause; their newspapers printed articles and poems that praised the great man. But their attitude toward Napoleon was ambivalent in that they accepted only the Revolutionary component of the Napoleonic heritage. *L'Atelier*, a workers' newspaper, expressed this opinion when it described the ceremonies for the arrival of Napoleon's ashes in Paris:

> It was not the restorer of the nobility . . . or the ambitious conqueror that the crowd came to salute, but the artillery lieutenant of 1793, the victor of Arcoli and the Pyramids. . . . Above all it was revolutionary France, represented at this ceremony by the veterans of the armies of the Republic and Empire, that the people of Paris came to salute.

In the 1830s and 1840s, Louis-Napoleon Bonaparte sought to take advantage of the widespread but nebulous Bonapartist sentiments and tried to organize a party. Unable to win over the political elites, who remained loyal to Louis-Philippe, he turned instead to the masses. His attempt to raise the garrison at Strasbourg (30 October 1836) and his landing at Boulogne (6 August 1840) were ridiculous failures that damaged his cause. He did, however, formulate a coherent Bonapartist doctrine, albeit one that owed more to the traditions of the Napoleonic legend than to historical fact. His pamphlet *Napoleonic Ideas* (1839) argued that the main achievement of Napoleon I had been "a reconciliation of Order and Liberty, the rights of the people and the principles of authority." Napoleon I had done this by creating a powerful centralized state embodied in a hereditary dynasty that ruled only by popular consent. "The base [of the imperial system] is democratic, because all power comes from the people; while the organization is hierarchical." This state transcended all political factions. It protected equality and liberty yet maintained law and order. It guided social progress by an active promotion of agriculture, industry, and commerce. It ameliorated the condition of the masses through charitable institutions for the poor, public works projects for the unemployed, and general economic prosperity for all. As for foreign policy, the pamphlet insisted that Napoleon had fought purely defensive wars; his armies advanced the cause of nationalism and aimed to create a European association among the nations to replace international disorder. A later pamphlet, *The Extinction of Pauperism* (1844), was vaguely socialist in its denunciation of modern industrial capitalism and its promotion of state-subsidized agricultural colonies as a solution to unemployment.

The Revolution of 1848 unexpectedly opened the road to power to Louis-Napoleon and to Bonapartism. Louis-Napoleon's victory in the partial elections of 4 June to fill seats in the Constituent Assembly stunned the other parties. He won it with propaganda that appealed to the lower classes. In subsequent elections, including the presidential election of 10 December, his appeal was wider. The propaganda put out by newly established Bonapartist committees and newspapers delivered contradictory messages. Bonapartism was for property rights but against the "aristocracy of money"; for the Republic but against the "Red Republic"; for national glory but in favor of peace. Above all, Bonapartist propaganda stressed national unity. Louis-Napoleon, wrote one newspaper, "is the hyphen between the parties . . . [and] he will reconcile them on the terrain of liberty and nationality." In other words, he was all things to all men, as the results of the presidential election proved. Louis-Napoleon won almost 75 percent of the vote. The Party of Order supported him (principally because they thought his victory inevitable), but so did many on the Left. He won the votes of Orleanist and legitimist notables and of conservative, Catholic peasantry. Urban and rural radicals preferred him to Eugène Cavaignac, and, in voting for him, discontented workers, artisans, and peasants registered their disapproval of the Republic that had prolonged the economic crisis and raised their taxes.

As president, Louis-Napoleon distanced himself from the Party of Order. During the legislative elections of May 1849, Bonapartist candidates in many (but not all) constituencies ran independently of the Party of Order and local notables. They spoke somewhat less than the conservatives did about traditional values (family, religion, property) and somewhat more about economic development and social measures for the masses. This was a social, though not a socialist, Bonapartism—a revival of the themes of the 1840s. The tactic failed, however, and conservatives dominated the new Assembly, committed to reactionary politics and opposed to presidential authority. In 1849–51, therefore, Bonapartism was stridently antiparliamentary: a strong executive alone, went the argument, could save France from the reds on the one side and the royalists on the other. This was the justification for the coup d'état of 2 December 1851, but it was clearly less a move against the dormant Left than a blow against the conservatives, who had refused the president the second term in office that he wanted. Indeed Louis-Napoleon hoped to have the support of the social democrats, which is why he repealed the law of 31 May 1850 that limited universal suffrage. But the leftist insurrections in Paris and the provinces compelled the president to take severely repressive measures against the social democrats and to reaffirm his old alliance with the conservatives. Social Bonapartism was set aside once more, and Bonapartism became again a doctrine of law and order. The plebiscite of 21–22 December demonstrated continued support for Bonapartism in almost all the country, especially among the peasantry of the northeast. There were serious rates of abstention only in the legitimist west and south and in some pockets of left-wing opposition, such as the working-class quarters of Paris.

This shift after 2 December was evident in a closer alliance between Bonapartists and notables at the local level. Since 1848, the work of organization, the distribution of propaganda, and the selection of candidates had been carried out by a central Bonapartist committee in Paris with the help of affiliated correspondents, agents, and electoral committees in the provinces. The committees were staffed by dedicated political activists, often former soldiers, small businessmen, professionals, journalists, and even workers. After 10 December 1848, they had the help of government bureaucrats; indeed the prefects played an increasingly dominant role in Bonapartist politics. In 1852, Louis-Napoleon effectively ignored his own party organization, preferring to rely entirely on the prefects and the notables. In the parliamentary elections of 1852, the president designated official candidates, selected by his ministers from local notables, usually on the recommendation of the prefects. They secured election with the assistance of the bureaucracy.

Bonapartism was to undergo further transformations under the Second Empire and beyond. Such twists and turns were perhaps inevitable given the inherently ambiguous, even contradictory, themes of Bonapartism. As François Guizot once remarked, "It is quite a feat to be at one and the same time a national glory, a guarantee of the Revolution, and a principle of authority."

F. Bluche, *Le Bonapartisme: Aux origines de la droite autoritaire* (Paris, 1980); H. A. L. Fisher, *Bonapartism* (Oxford, 1968); R. Pimienta, *La propagande bonapartiste en 1848* (Paris, 1911); R. Rémond, *The Right Wing in France from 1815 to de Gaulle*, 2d ed. (Philadelphia, 1969); A. Tudesq, "La légende napoléonienne en France en 1848," *Revue historique* 218 (1957); T. Zeldin, *The Political System of Napoleon III* (New York, 1958).

Michael Sibalis

Related entries: ARC DE TRIOMPHE DE L'ETOILE; *L'ATELIER*; BERANGER; CAVAIGNAC, L.-E.; COUP D'ETAT OF 2 DECEMBER 1851; PARTY OF ORDER; REICHSTADT; REPUBLICANS; REVOLUTION OF 1848.

BONNELIER, HIPPOLYTE-MARIE-LOUISE-PHILIBERT (1779–1868), novelist and political figure. Bonnelier (or Bonnellier) ran a private literature and public speaking school in Paris in the 1830s and acted at the Odéon theater (under the pseudonym of Max). Politically liberal, he was one of three secretaries to the Municipal Commission that assumed control of the Paris government in the Revolution of 1830. He served briefly as *sous-préfet* of Senlis (1831) and Sceaux (1849) and married the daughter of Francois de Neufchateau. His reputation in the nineteenth century rested largely on his popular novels (*Eliza Tarrakonoff* [1822], *Urbain Grandier* [1825], *La Fille du libraire* [1828], *Calomnie* [1832], *L'Anneau de paille* [1836], *Le Vicomte d'Arché* [1837], *Sous la lampe* [1847] and others), but these were largely forgotten by the 1900s.

D. Pinkney, *The French Revolution of 1830* (Princeton, 1972); J. Querard, *La France litteraire* (Paris, 1827).

David Longfellow

Related entries: MUNICIPAL COMMISSION; REVOLUTION OF 1830.

LE BON SENS (1832–1839), democratic newspaper, appearing weekly and at times daily under the subtitles "The Voice of the People Is the Voice of God" and "Everything for and by the People." Its founding editor was Cauchois-Lemaire, an experienced journalist who had had to flee France in 1817 following the suppression of his paper *le Nain jaune*. Contributors included Martin-Maillefer, Jean-David Richard, Victor Rodde, and Louis Blanc, who became chief editor in 1835. Although an average of 1,650 copies were printed in 1836, this figure had fallen to below 700 by 1838, largely because of declining provincial subscriptions.

Le Bon Sens was democratic in its politics though increasingly outflanked by more militant rivals. It consciously saw its role as educative of workers and used a regular supplement, the *tribune des prolétaires*, to encourage workers' letters. In the last four months of 1832, ninety such letters were published. Like Cabet's *Le Populaire*, there were imaginative efforts to attract readers, with uniformed street hawkers selling copies at 5 centimes; it sold sustaining subscriptions at 20 francs to cover the losses on these sales. No complete collection exists of this paper.

J. P. Aguet, "Le tirage des quotidiens de Paris sous la Monarchie de Juillet," *Schweizerische Zeitschrift für Geschichte* 10 (1960); R. Gossez, "Presse parisienne à destination des ouvriers (1848–1851)," in J. Godechot, ed., *La Presse ouvrière, 1819–1850*; *Bibliothèque de la Révolution de 1848*, 23 (1966), 123–90.

Peter McPhee

Related entries: BLANC; CABET; CAUCHOIS-LEMAIRE; *LE NAIN JAUNE*; *LE POPULAIRE*.

BORD DE L'EAU, CONSPIRATION DU. See CONSPIRACY AT THE WATER'S EDGE.

BORDEAUX, HENRI-CHARLES-FERDINAND-MARIE DIEUDONNE D'ARTOIS, COMTE DE CHAMBORD, DUC DE (1820–1883), grandson of Charles X, last direct male heir of the elder branch of the Bourbon family, legitimist pretender. The duc de Bordeaux was born in Paris on 29 September 1820, the posthumous son of the duc de Berry, who was assassinated on 14 February, and of Caroline of Naples. His birth—their only male child—gave new hope to the royalists that the male line would continue. Elaborate preparations, many of which failed, were made to ensure appropriate official witnesses to the birth. The royalists regarded him as a miracle child, and he was baptized with elaborate ceremony with water brought from the Jordan River by Chateaubriand. Nevertheless, rumors immediately appeared questioning the legitimacy of the child. The legitimists attributed these stories to the duc d'Orléans and the jealous cadet branch of the family. In 1821 a public subscription purchased the chateau of Chambord and gave it to the infant; in May 1839 he took the name comte de Chambord from this chateau. He was raised in the traditions of the Old Regime monarchy by his governors, the dukes of Montmorency, Rivières, and Damas, and by Frayssinous, the bishop of Hermopolis. When the July Revolution forced Charles X from the throne, he abdicated on 2 August in favor of Bordeaux and proclaimed him king under the name of Henry V at Rambouillet. Charles also instructed the duc d'Orléans, then lieutenant general of the kingdom, to proclaim him in Paris. This Orléans refused to do. But Charles and his family left Rambouillet for England, still believing his grandson would be king.

They settled first at Holyrood Palace in Edinburgh, where Charles had stayed before the Restoration. There he attempted to prepare his grandson's restoration by establishing legitimist networks and contacts in France. Bordeaux continued his education in exile, proving inept at languages but showing an inclination toward history and military art. He was very attached to his grandfather and to the old king's ideas, which definitely guided the prince's actions as late as the 1870s. In October 1832 Charles, who felt humiliated by the English and unwelcome, moved his small court to the Hradschin Palace outside Prague. Meanwhile, Bordeaux's mother, the widowed duchesse de Berry, had returned to France in May 1832 to attempt unsuccessfully a legitimist uprising without Charles' approval. She was captured, imprisoned, and found to be pregnant once again. She was later released after the birth of her child. Her cause was now temporarily discredited in France, and Bordeaux was forbidden to see her.

In the fall of 1836 Charles again moved his family, this time to Goritzia, where he died on 6 November 1836. Bordeaux subsequently visited the countries of central Europe and Italy, which received him as a visiting monarch. He caused a bit of a sensation on 27 October 1843 when he established himself on London's Belgrave Square, hoping Victoria would receive him. Advancing his claim to the French throne, he began receiving with all the etiquette of a royal court the various legitimists who came from France to pay their respects, among them François-René de Chateaubriand, Pierre-Antoine Berryer, and Amedée Pastoret. The death in 1844 of his uncle, Louis, duc d'Angoulême, made him head of the Bourbon family in fact as well as in practice. On 16 November 1846 Bordeaux, now called Chambord, married a Habsburg archduchess, Marie-Therese-Beatrice Gaétane, daughter of the duke of Modena. She brought with her a large dowry, but no issue resulted from this union. They subsequently established their residence at Frohsdorf, near Salzburg, living in an atmosphere of unrealistic expectations.

Chambord remained aloof from the events of 1848. Nevertheless, he and his partisans hoped the situation would soon lead to a restoration. To this end some of them joined forces with the Orleanists and even with some Bonapartists. To them the presidency of Louis-Napoleon was merely a means to a restoration. For his part, Chambord followed a moderate policy. He occasionally appeared in German cities near the border such as Ems, Cologne, or Wiesbaden, where his followers came to pay him court. The establishment of the Second Empire temporarily ended these hopes. But Chambord did seek to capitalize by attacking Napoleon III's Italian war. He also maintained a legitimist high command in Paris, and at the fall of the Empire he renewed his efforts. On three occasions (9 October 1870 and 8 May and 5 July 1871) he publicly advanced his pretensions to the throne and declared he would accept a parliamentary government, the third declaration being made at the chateau of Chambord. However, he also rejected the tricolor flag, and much of France was immediately disillusioned. Furthermore the July 1871 parliamentary elections returned republicans. By the summer of 1873, with the distasteful business of dealing with the German indemnity and occupation all arranged, and with a royalist, Marie-Edme-Patrice-Maurice MacMahon as president, the royalists thought the time had come to make their move. The Orleanist and legitimist factions agreed on a formula, accepted by the Orleanist pretender, that Chambord would ascend the throne, and when he died the Orleanist comte de Paris would succeed him.

The combined royalists, who still controlled a majority in the Chamber, sent a delegation to see Chambord at Salzburg on 14 October 1873. They returned with word that Chambord would accept a constitutional government and would, at least temporarily, maintain the tricolor flag, which Louis XVIII had rejected in 1814 and Louis-Philippe had restored in 1830. However, on 27 October 1873 Chambord wrote to Paris that he would insist on the white flag of the Bourbons and would return to Paris without any conditions. Even Pope Pius IX unsuccessfully urged him to abandon the white flag. But his insistence effectively ended his chance for a restoration, and the Chamber ultimately turned to other solutions. In November 1873 Chambord came clandestinely to Versailles, hoping to meet with MacMahon to persuade him to use the army to effect a restoration. But MacMahon would have none of it. Chambord returned to Frohsdorf after the Assembly voted the Law on the Septennate, establishing a seven-year presidential term and thus rejecting the monarchy. At Frohsdorf he continued to lead his followers until his death on 24 August 1883. He was buried at Goritzia, alongside his grandfather. The leadership of the royalist cause then passed to the Orleanist family. Chambord himself published *Mes idées* in 1872; his *Correspondence* was published in 1859 and 1871.

V. Beach, "The Education of the Comte de Chambord," *Journal of Modern History* 20 (1958); E. Beau de Loménie, *Le Restauration manquée: l'affaire du drapeau blanc* (Paris, 1932); M. L. Brown, *The Comte de Chambord: The Third Republic's Uncompromising King* (Durham, N.C., 1967); A. Nettement, *Henri de France* (Paris, 1875); G. de Nouvion, *Le Comte de Chambord 1820–1883* (Paris, 1884); A. de Saint-Albin, *Histoire d'Henri V* (Paris, 1874).

James K. Kieswetter

Related entries: ANGOULEME, L.-A.; BERRY, C.-F.; BERRY, M.-C.; BERRYER, P.-A.; CHARLES X; CHATEAUBRIAND; DAMAS; FRAYSSINOUS; LEGITIMISM; LOUIS PHILIPPE; MONTMORENCY; PARTY OF ORDER.

BORIES, JEAN-FRANCOIS-LOUIS LECLERC (1795–1822), soldier and Carbonarist conspirator, leader of the Four Sergeants of La Rochelle. Bories was born in Villefranche (Aveyron) and in 1821 was a sergeant-major in the Forty-fifth line infantry regiment. While the regiment was stationed in Paris (May 1821–January 1822), Bories became a member of the Friends of Truth

Masonic Lodge, a Carbonarist front whose members were mostly students and Parisian radicals of his own age. As a member of the society and chief of a Carbonarist *vente centrale*, Bories organized a cell among the soldiers and noncommissioned officers of his regiment. A tavern brawl with royalist soldiers in Orléans prevented him from making contact with other conspirators in western France while his unit was en route to la Rochelle in February 1822. Bories and his fellow conspirators (including Sergeants G. P. Goubin, J. J. Pommier, and M. Raoulx) were arrested in February and March 1822, interrogated by General H. F. J. Despinois (the commander of the military district), brought to trial in Paris (August–September 1822), and sentenced to death. They were executed by guillotine on 21 September.

Bories was the only one of the principal conspirators not to confess his role and name his comrades during the investigation. His calm demeanor and generally heroic behavior at the trial excited widespread admiration, pleas for clemency, and a posthumous cult as a republican martyr. Many witnesses vouched for his gentle character, firm sense of purpose, and idealism. A popular story holds that during the trial, Bories wrote to his aged parents in Villefranche, concealing his predicament and reporting that he would soon leave France for the colonies. The kind-hearted citizens of the town conspired for several years to keep the news of his fate from his parents.

A. B. Spitzer, *Old Hatreds and Young Hopes* (Cambridge, 1971).

David Longfellow

Related entries: CARBONARI; LA ROCHELLE, FOUR SERGEANTS OF; REPUBLICANS; SOCIETY OF THE FRIENDS OF TRUTH.

BOSIO, FRANCOIS-JOSEPH, BARON (1768–1845), sculptor. Born in Monaco, he learned his art under Augustin Pajou and spent seventeen years in Italy perfecting his style. He was influenced by Antonio Canova so much as to be called the French Canova. Back in Paris in 1808, he was kept busy by a continuous stream of commissions from numerous sources. Many celebrities of the time had their portraits executed by him. He was involved in a number of monumental projects of the Restoration period, some of which are still visible today: the statue of Louis XIV restored on the place des Victoires, the equestrian group on top of the Arc de triomphe of the Carrousel courtyard, and the statue of Louis XVI in the Chapelle expiatoire. For these Bosio received the title of royal sculptor and that of baron.

L. Barbarin, *Etude sur Bosio et son oeuvre* (Paris, 1916).

Guillaume de Bertier de Sauvigny

Related entries: ARC DE TRIOMPHE DE L'ETOILE; RESTORATION, SECOND.

LES BOULETS ROUGES, journal of the Peaceful Club of the Rights of Man, a socialist periodical that lasted only one number, dated 22–25 June 1848. This periodical wanted to be the voice of all the democratic and socialist clubs, the spokesman for the poor, and, according to its president and editor, Citizen Pelin, it wanted to "walk peacefully down the path of progress."

Three mottoes appeared on its masthead: "The abolition of sinecures, privileges, and poverty." (Consequently it protested against the closing of the National Workshops and asked the government to see to it that the right to work would be respected.) "Economy, work, and the moralization and education of the masses": from this second motto flowed the third, which stated "order is the consequence of freedom and of civilization." The revolutionary newspaper defended the democratic and socialist republic and asked that property rights be limited by law.

Les Boulets rouges attacked Victor Hugo as a "phrasemaker and posturer, an orator who speaks grandiose and empty words." The editor concluded, "Politics are not like plays and novels; we need socialists and thinkers in the Chamber, and not actors and mountebanks."

Les Boulets Rouges, feuille du Club pacifique des droits de l'homme. B. N. Fol. Lc^2, 1908; E. Hatin, *Bibliographie historique et critique de la presse periodique française* (Paris, 1866); H. Izambard, *La presse parisienne, statistique bibliographique et alphabetique de tous les journaux; revues et canards periodiques, nes, morts, ressuscites ou metamorphoses a Paris depuis la 22 fevrier 1848 jusqu'a l'Empire* (Paris, 1853).

Jean-Claude Caron, trans. E. Newman

Related entries: CLUBS, POLITICAL; HUGO, VICTOR; NATIONAL WORKSHOPS.

BOURBON, LOUIS VI HENRI-JOSEPH, DUC DE (1756–1830), courtier, *émigré*, and last of the Condé branch of the royal family. Louis, duc de Bourbon, was born at Chantilly in 1756, the son of Louis V Joseph, prince de Condé. Bourbon, who at age fifteen married Louise-Bathilde d'Orléans, experienced a riotous youth. Revolution and exile did not change him. During his long stay in England, he took as his mistress Sophy Dawes, a servant and fisherman's daughter from the Isle of Wight. He married her to one of his courtiers, and took her back to France when he returned in 1814, dreadfully embarrassing the royal family by his doting on her.

Bourbon returned to France in 1814 and on 3 May rode into Paris in the same carriage with Louis XVIII, along with the duchesse d'Angoulême and Condé, all of whom had accompanied Louis from Hartwell. When Napoleon returned from Elba, Bourbon was sent to try to raise the Vendée. But finding little enthusiasm and fearing arrest, he sailed from Nantes for Spain on 27 March 1815. Although the Restoration made Bourbon the grand master of the royal household, he devoted himself primarily to sports and to various nefarious acquaintances and played little role in public affairs. At the death of his father in 1818, he inherited the title prince of Condé. In 1829 Bourbon named the seven-year-old Henri duc d'Aumale, fifth son of Louis-Philippe d'Orléans, as the sole heir to the chateau of Chantilly and his huge fortune.

On the night of 26 August 1830, the duc de Bourbon hanged himself from a window in his other chateau, Saint Leu. He was buried in the Abbey of Saint Denis, the royal necropolis, in spite of his wish to lie next to his son, the duc d'Enghien, at Vincennes. The circumstances of his death gave rise to accusations against Mme. de Feuchères. The official inquest, however, ruled the death a suicide, and the investigation of her was closed on the order of Louis Philippe.

V. Beach, *Charles X* (Boulder, 1971); C. Robert, *Expédition des émigrés à Quibéron* (Paris, 1899); D. Seward, *The Bourbon Kings of France* (New York, 1976); H. Vrignault, *Généologie de la maison de Bourbon* (Paris, 1957).

James K. Kieswetter

Related entries: ANGOULEME, M.-T.-C.; CHARLES X; LOUIS XVIII.

BOURDONNAYE. See LA BOURDONNAYE.

BOURMONT, LOUIS-AUGUSTE-VICTOR, COMTE DE (1773–1846), soldier and politician. During the Revolution he served in the counterrevolutionary army of *émigrés* under the prince de Condé, and he slipped into France clandestinely to join the royalist partisans fighting in the west. He was one of the leaders who negotiated the pacification of the west with the first consul, Bonaparte. Nevertheless, he continued to conspire and was imprisoned. In 1805 he escaped and took refuge in Portugal. He was able to return to France in 1810 and agreed to serve in Napoleon's army. By 1814 his military valor had caused him to be raised to the rank of general commanding a division. During the Hundred Days his behavior was ambivalent: placed under the command of Marshal Michel Ney, he deserted, along with his commander, from the armies of Louis XVIII and rallied to the emperor, even asking Napoleon for the command of a division, but on the eve of the battle of Fleurus (14 June 1815) he abandoned his troops to rejoin Louis XVIII in Ghent. This defection, even if it did not give useful intelligence to the duke of Wellington as one might have supposed it would, no doubt helped to demoralize French troops at Waterloo. It also earned Bourmont the undying hatred of Napoleon's supporters. Bourmont increased their hatred by the pitiless manner in which he testified against Marshal Ney at his trial in December 1815 before the Chamber of Peers. Bourmont later held several high commands and was named by Charles X as minister of war in Polignac's ministry, and this added still more to his unpopularity. At his request, he was given command of the expedition against Algiers, which he led with decisiveness and success, and consequently he was promoted to the rank of marshal. He refused to serve Louis Philippe, and instead he joined the adventurous royalist attempt at a coup led by the duchesse de Berry in 1832. After he went to Portugal to support the cause of the absolutist party of Dom Miguel. He did not return to France until 1840, and he ended his life in his chateau of Bourmont in Anjou.

G. Gautherot, *Un gentilhomme de grand chemin, le maréchal de Bourmont* (Paris, 1926).

Guillaume de Bertier de Sauvigny, trans. E. Newman

Related entries: ALGIERS, EXPEDITION TO; BERRY, M.-C.; CHAMBER OF PEERS; CHARLES X; HUNDRED DAYS; NEY; POLIGNAC.

BOURRIENNE, LOUIS-ANTOINE FAUVELET DE (1769–1834), diplomat of the Revolution and Napoleonic periods, secretary to Napoleon, and deputy of the Restoration. Born on 9 July 1769 at Sens (Yonne), Bourrienne attended the military academy at Brienne where he claimed he became a friend of Napoleon, who studied there at the same time. Bourrienne, however, lacked the four quarterings of nobility necessary for military promotion. The Revolution freed him from this obstacle, and his star rose with that of Napoleon Bonaparte, who made him his private secretary in 1797. He was director-general of posts when the Bourbons returned in 1814.

Although Bourrienne now professed to be a royalist and offered his services to the Bourbons, Louis XVIII did not retain him at the post office. The king did, however, appoint him an honorary councillor of state and gave him the Legion of Honor. On 12 March 1815, while still en route to Paris from Elba, Napoleon named him prefect of police. One of the new prefect's first acts was to order the arrest of Joseph Fouché. Shortly after, however, Bourrienne himself fled to Ghent. He returned to France after Waterloo and in August 1815 was elected a deputy from the department of Yonne, over whose electoral college he presided. He was defeated in the 1816 elections but was reelected in November 1820 and remained a deputy until 1827. During his terms as a deputy, he sat with the ultraroyalists, voting against liberal measures and staunchly supporting the Villèle ministry. In 1826 he was peripherally involved in the trial of a political adventuress, Mme. Benoit, who styled herself the marquise de Campestre. He lost his fortune in the July Revolution, whose effects also left him deranged. In 1832 he was hospitalized in an asylum in Caen, where he died on 7 February 1834. Bourrienne's memoirs, written in collaboration with Villemarest and first published from 1829 to 1831, contain numerous details and insights and are rather critical of Napoleon. They are not, however, totally reliable.

Archives parlementaires; L. A. F. de Bourrienne, *Mémoires* (Paris, 1829); A. Robert et al., *Dictionnaire des parlementaires français* (Paris, 1889–91); B. Saint-Edmé, *Biographe des lieutenans-généraux, ministres, directeurs-généraux . . . de la police* (Paris, 1829).

James K. Kieswetter

Related entries: FOUCHE; HUNDRED DAYS; REVOLUTION OF 1830; ULTRAROYALISTS; VILLELE.

BOURSE, PARIS, the Paris stock exchange located in the place de la Bourse in the second arrondissement. The present location of the Paris Bourse was originally the site of the convent of the Daughters of Saint Thomas, established in Paris in 1626. The convent was closed during the Revolution and demolished in 1807–8. In March 1808 construction began on the present Palais de la Bourse under the direction of the architect Alexandre-Théodore Brongniart. At his death in 1813, Lebarre took over the project, which, after an interruption from 1814–21, was completed in 1827. It was officially opened a bit prematurely on 4 November 1826. It was expanded to its present size in 1902 and 1907.

The first stock exchange (Bourse) in Paris was established in 1724 in a gallery of the Mazarin palace. It subsequently resided in the Louvre, the Palais Royal, the church of Notre Dame des Victoires, and finally in a building on the location of the convent of the Daughters of Saint Thomas, before settling in its new and present quarters in 1827. In the early nineteenth century, the operations of the Bourse were on a very small scale. Under the Restoration it was open only two hours per day, from 2 until 4 P.M., and most of the dealings were in various French government bonds, both national and municipal, and in the shares of the Bank of France and the Mortgage Bank. Corporations based on the mobilization of capital through common stock were quite rare. Under the 1807 Commercial Code, such a company could be formed only on the recommendation of the Council of State. Thus it is not surprising that from 1815 through 1829, only 120 new corporations (*sociétés anonymes*) were established, a total of 129 authorized since the 1807 Code. But between 1840 and 1848, 177 were created. Not all were listed on the Paris Bourse, which in fact tended to specialize during this period in government rents and *anonyme* shares. Trading in such securities was even more limited, in part because the price of shares ranged from a low of 1,000 francs ($200) to ten times that amount. Only the wealthy could afford to invest. Furthermore, government bonds were in such demand that when a new issue was authorized, frequently the cabinet ministers themselves met to decide which of the would-be purchasers should be allowed to buy them. Hence there was relatively little trading in those securities that did exist. By 1830 only 38 securities were listed on the Paris Bourse, and these included government bonds as well as corporate stock. Nevertheless, prices of issues such as the shares of the Bank of France and especially the 5 percent consolidated government bonds (the *consols*) were a commonly used barometer of the reaction of the public, at least of the investing public, to various policies and developments, just as modern indicators such as the Dow Jones industrial averages or the *London Times* financial index are used for somewhat similar purposes. By 1847, however, 198 stocks were listed on the Bourse, including some foreign stocks, and under the Second Empire corporations greatly increased, numbering 307 by 1869.

F. B. Artz, *France under the Bourbon Restoration 1814–1830* (Cambridge, 1931); S. B. Clough, *France: A History of National Economics* (New York, 1939); C. E. Freedman, *Joint-Stock Enterprise in France, 1807–1867* (Chapel Hill, N.C., 1979); J. Hillairet, *Dictionnaire historique des rues de Paris* (Paris, 1963); H. Sée, *Histoire économique de la France* (Paris, 1942).

James K. Kieswetter

Related entry: BANKING.

BREA, JEAN-BAPTISTE DE (1790–1848), political activist and general in the National Guard. On 25 June 1848, he was assassinated as he tried to negotiate with a group of insurgents at the barrière de Fontainebleau in Paris. His death was used as an argument to intensify the repression of the insurgents.

L. Girard, *La IIe république* (Paris, 1968).

Douglas Porch

Related entries: JUNE DAYS; NATIONAL GUARD; REVOLUTION OF 1848.

BRETON ASSOCIATION, for the Mutual and Legal Defense of the Civil and Political Rights of the Inhabitants of Morbihan was founded 25 November 1832 in Vannes. The republican tradition had been carried on by the Breton bourgeoisie since 1789. A Breton association to refuse the payment of taxes had already been established in 1829. Breton students in Paris, who met each year at a banquet, carried on an active role during and after the July Revolution.

After the insurrections of 5–6 June 1832 had been put down, the government adopted a hard line against republican societies. Consequently the bourgeoisie of certain towns (Nantes, Niort, Vannes) formed associations to defend the civil and political rights of the French. But behind the title of this Breton Association hid a republican club.

Its initial prospectus, published in November 1832, emphasized the arbitrary and illegal acts of the government against the people of the Morbihan and especially against the poor farmers "whose animals and harvests are seized and sold, and whose lands are completely ruined."

But the Breton Association had a larger goal: "to defend all the constitutional rights of the French citizens of the West and principally of the Morbihan." The six articles of its statutes also proclaimed that the society would come to the legal defense "of the poor class, which is suffering and oppressed by the government" (articles 2 and 3). Funds came from voluntary gifts received by M. de Quenechquivillic, a lawyer in Vannes. Members were ranked, according to their importance, into founders, associates, and adherents.

The association was to form a council, which would receive the complaints of farmers "by a knowledgeable inhabitant of their commune" and would take action against the responsible government agents. This council of seven members would take charge of all costs and would give to the plaintiffs any compensation for damages that they might win. This Breton Association does not seem to have left any other documents beyond its prospectus of November 1832.

"Association bretonne pour la défense mutuelle et légale des droits civils et politiques des habitants du Morbihan," prospectus (Vannes, 25 November 1832), B. N. Lb51 1602.

Jean-Claude Caron, trans. E. Newman

Related entries: CLUBS, POLITICAL; *JOURNAL DU COMMERCE*; REVOLUTION OF 1830.

BRIDGE AND ROAD SERVICE, the agency charged with building and maintaining roads and bridges. In 1669 Colbert created the first separate French government agency specifically charged with looking after highways when he appointed a commissioner for roads and bridges under the controller general of finances. Gradually the Bridge and Road Service was able to achieve its independence from the financial administration. The era of the Revolution was to expand greatly the concept of road building and maintenance as a public service of benefit to all. However, the administration of roads and bridges was maintained by the Revolution almost exactly as it was inherited from the Old Regime. Napoleon modified the administration in some ways. The director general was now made a member of the Council of State, with direct access to the emperor. Thus his status was greatly enhanced, and the office of director general even came to be known as one of the little ministries. Under the Empire the director general of roads and bridges was responsible not only for highways but also for interior waterways, commercial seaports, lighthouses and signal lights, and telegraph lines (the Chappe semaphore system).

The Restoration maintained with little change the imperial administrative and classification system for roads and bridges. The responsibilities of the director general now expanded, however, to include other areas, such as supplying Paris with fuel, supervising mills and factories, and controlling mining and its related affairs. Etienne-Denis Pasquier, the Restoration's first director general, undertook to limit wagon weights and regulate wheel sizes, abuses in these matters being a major cause of road damage. One of the greatest directors was Louis Becquey, who held office from 1816 to 1830. Not only did he restore some order to the legacy of damage left by Napoleon, but Becquey was also responsible for introducing English (Macadam) road-building methods and metal bridges into France. Under the July Monarchy, foreign peace and greatly improved domestic economic conditions benefited highway construction and maintenance. The administrative position of the Department of Bridges and Roads, however, suffered in comparison with former regimes. From 1831 to 1833 its functions were transferred from the Ministry of the Interior, to which it had been subject since the Empire, to the Ministry of Commerce and Public Works. In May 1836 a new law drew a new distinction between local roads and main through highways, the latter being placed more under the prefect and general council of each department for funding and supervision. In May 1839 the Ministry of Public Works was established, and the separate directory general of roads and bridges and of mines was abolished. The new ministry included roads, railroads, internal navigation, and mines. This basic arrangement lasted until 1960 when the Ministry of Public Works and Transport was created.

H. Cavilles, *La Route française* (Paris, 1946); J. Petot, *Histoire de l'administration des ponts et chaussées* (Paris, 1958); F. Ponteil, *Les Institutions de la France, 1814 à 1870* (Paris, 1966).

James K. Kieswetter

Related entries: BECQUEY; ECOLE POLYTECHNIQUE; PASQUIER; TELEGRAPHY, AERIAL.

BRILLAT-SAVARIN, JEAN-ANTHELME (1755–1826), magistrate, writer, and gastronome. Brillat-Savarin was born in Belley (Ain) into a large family of lawyers and reputed gourmets. He undertook legal studies at Lyons and (perhaps)

Dijon and returned to his native town as a magistrate. A deputy of the Third Estate at Versailles in 1789, he opposed most of the Revolutionary reforms, particularly the institution of the jury system and the proposed abolition of the death penalty. Successively president of the departmental tribunal and mayor of Belley in 1791–92, he emigrated in 1793, spending several years in New York. Returning to France under the Directory, he became a judge on the Supreme Court of Appeals under the Empire and moved in Mme. Recamier's social circle. His reputation today rests almost entirely on his publication of the *Physiology of Taste* in December 1825, an engaging mixture of autobiography, recipes, and gastronomical anecdotes and aphorisms. It set a standard of moderation, education, and refinement in dining, and included speculations on the nature of thirst, taste and appetite, the influence of diet on dreams, lyrics of songs, and comparisons of national cuisines and dining customs.

J.-A. Brillat-Savarin, *Physiologie du goût* (Paris, 1825, Eng. trans. in 1925).

David Longfellow

Related entries: RECAMIER.

BROGLIE, ACHILLE-LEONCE-VICTOR, DUC DE (1785–1870), statesman, diplomat, and political thinker. Born in Paris on 28 November 1785, Broglie was the descendant of an aristocratic family that had served the Bourbons with distinction as *ducs et pairs*, marshals, diplomats, and high ecclesiastics. The Revolution shattered his childhood and changed the family's political orientation and area of service. At eight his father, a liberal nobleman who supported the Revolution, was executed under the Terror; his subsequent education was completed by his stepfather, Marc-René Voyer d'Argenson, whose radical politics he never embraced but whose influence reinforced his ties to the new society. It was through d'Argenson's influence and Napoleon's desire to attract the old nobility to his regime that he became a Napoleonic *auditeur* and served the Empire in various minor capacities. With the Restoration he was named peer for life. In the Chamber of Peers he began his parliamentary career as the only peer to vote against Marshal Michel Ney's execution for treason in 1816. In that year he also married Albertine, the daughter of Mme. de Staël. These two acts completed his break with the old aristocracy and reinforced his liberal orientation.

Thereafter he distinguished himself as one of the more articulate critics of the Bourbons, particularly of the reactionary politics of Charles X and the ultraroyalists. Although originally associated with the Left, he was never comfortable with the revolutionary politics of the marquis de Lafayette and the republicans and in 1819 joined the *doctrinaires*, the small but influential group of Pierre Royer-Collard, Camille Jordan, Jacques-Claude Beugnot, and François Guizot, whose moderate liberal philosophy he shared and helped to shape. An ardent Anglophile, he was greatly influenced by English political ideas and institutions, and through his interest in the abolitionist cause, he established contacts with English reformers like William Wilberforce and Bruxton, Whig politicians, and reform philosophers like Jeremy Bentham and James Mill. In the Chamber of Peers he played an important role in the liberal opposition, most notably concerning liberty of the press, the electoral law, the law on sacrilege, the *milliard des émigres*, and the abolition of slavery.

With the Revolution of 1830, which he accepted but did nothing to encourage, Broglie became one of the founders of the Orleanist system of monarchy. He was minister of public instruction and president of the Conseil d'état in the Laffitte ministry in 1830, minister of foreign affairs in the Soult cabinet from 1832 to 1834, and president of the council and minister of foreign affairs in 1835–36. A strict legalist, he was wary of revolutions and revolutionaries and supported the conservative strain in Orleanism, first under Casimir Périer and later Guizot. In 1835, after Giuseppe Fieschi's attempt on Louis Philippe's life, he introduced the repressive September Laws (*lois scélérats*), which in his effort to guarantee public order abridged some of the provisions of his own press bill of 1819. A model of political virtue, he was unpopular in Orleanist milieus, his curt, arrogant manner putting off king and colleagues alike. He was, in fact, always a reluctant *homme d'état*, and in 1836, after an unfavorable vote in the Chamber and a quarrel with Louis Philippe, he resigned as prime minister and thereafter eschewed ministerial rank.

He returned briefly to political activity in 1849–50 as one of the leaders of the Party of Order in the National Assembly and one of the so-called Burgraves who endeavored, by a conciliatory attitude regarding Louis-Napoleon's term of office, to avert a coup d'état. Briefly arrested in 1851, he belonged to the liberal opposition during the Empire, and, though not politically active, it was he who brought together the Union libérale in 1862. During that time he wrote his *Souvenirs* and various political treatises, most notably *Vues sur le gouvernement de la France*. The latter, the product of his lifelong concern for his country's political instability and his disdain for ideologues and faith in the value of institutions, contained an outline of future policy for liberal monarchists in the event that the monarchy could not be restored. Often appealed to by political moderates, Broglie's book greatly influenced liberal conservative policy after 1871, many of his ideas finding their way into the Constitution of 1875. He died in Paris on 25 January 1870.

Archives Nationales, Fonds Guizot, 42AP-214; D. de Broglie, *Les Broglie* (Paris, 1972); V. de Broglie, *Souvenirs*, 4 vols. (Paris, 1886–87) and *Vues sur le gouvernement de la France* (Paris, 1870); F. Guizot, *Le duc de Broglie* (Paris, 1872); P. Meuriot, "La Constitution de 1875 et ses parrains: Prévost-Paradol et Victor de Broglie," *Séances et travaux de l'Académie des Sciences morales et politiques* 194 (1920); J. de la Varende, *Les Broglie* (Paris, 1950).

Alan Grubb

Related entries: BEUGNOT; BROGLIE; *DOCTRINAIRES*; FIESCHI PLOT; GUIZOT; JORDAN; NEY; PARTY OF ORDER; PERIER; PRESS LAWS; ROYER-COLLARD; STAEL.

BROGLIE, ALBERTINE DE STAEL, DUCHESSE DE (1797–1838),
celebrated hostess of the Restoration and July Monarchy. Born at Coppet,
Switzerland, on 8 June 1797, the daughter of Germaine de Staël (and reputedly
Benjamin Constant), the granddaughter of Jacques Necker, she bore a famous,
if controversial, name, one closely associated with French Revolutionary politics.
Despite her upbringing, she grew up to be beautiful, highly cultured, intelligent,
but extremely sensible and serious minded, quite unlike her famous mother. She
revered her mother but never tried to emulate her. Instead, modest about her
own gifts, she devoted herself to perpetuating the memory and political tradition
of Mme. de Staël, which she did through her encouragement of her husband
and the political salon she presided over. Widely admired by some of the principal
political and literary figures of her day, she exercised considerable influence
over men as different as Francois-René de Chateaubriand, Alphonse de
Lamartine, Odilon Barrot, Louis-Mathieu de Molé, Alexis de Tocqueville, and
François Guizot. The memoirs of the period are full of tributes to her charm,
her persevering virtue, and her great beauty, the last captured in 1820 by Francois-
Pascal-Simon Gérard in his portrait of her.

In 1816 she married Victor de Broglie, the young liberal peer celebrated for
his recent vote against Michel Ney's execution for treason. Their marriage, which
united two prominent political families, one bourgeois and the other aristocratic,
one Protestant and the other Catholic, forged the link between Mme. de Staël's
moderate liberalism and the *juste milieu* philosophy of the *doctrinaires* and the
July Monarchy. The Broglies were the epitome of the liberal patrician notables
of the period. Their salon, built around the remnants of Mme. de Staël's, was,
in contrast to the faubourg Saint-Germain, a salon of ideas: cosmopolitan,
respectably liberal, a place where the important political and constitutional issues
of the day were discussed, and, after 1819, when her husband joined the
doctrinaires, it became the center of that small but influential group. The *Revue
française*, their journal, was an offshoot of the Broglie salon, and there the
leaders of the *doctrinaire* party met, along with a host of foreign, especially
English, visitors.

Known also for her piety and religious fervor, she was, like Guizot, her close
friend, inspired by a rigidly orthodox Calvinism and active in Protestant mission
work. She made of the Broglie chateaux in Normandy and Coppet important
centers of French Protestantism in the early nineteenth century. After 1830 she
inclined increasingly to religious melancholy, a state of mind not uncommon to
the period or her co-religionists but which caused her, as did her husband's
retreat from active politics, to withdraw from society.

She died on 22 September 1838, of cerebral fever, her sudden and unexpected
death greatly saddening her contemporaries. Besides her role in Restoration and
July Monarchy politics, she also influenced, through her son, Albert, the liberal
Catholic movement of the 1850s and 1860s which largely embraced the
doctrinaire liberalism of her salon. Her daughter Louise married Othénin

d'Haussonville, a prominent Orleanist. Her letters, published in 1896, give an excellent picture of the milieu of the parliamentary *notables* of the period.

A. de Broglie, *Mémoires*, 2 vols. (Paris, 1938); and Albertine de Broglie, *Lettres* (Paris, 1896); C. Herold, *Mistress to an Age* (New York, 1958); G. Stenger, *Grandes dames du xix*siècle* (Paris, 1911).

Alan Grubb

Related entries: BARROT, C.-H.-O.; BROGLIE, A.-L.-V.; CHATEAU-BRIAND; CONSTANT; *DOCTRINAIRES*; GUIZOT; *JUSTE MILIEU*; LA-MARTINE; MOLE; *REVUE FRANCAISE*; STAEL; TOCQUEVILLE.

BROTHERS OF THE CHRISTIAN SCHOOLS, society of religious laymen devoted to elementary education. The first and principal society known by this name was founded in the last years of the seventeenth century by Jean-Baptiste de LaSalle, a canon of the cathedral of Reims. At the time of its legal suppression in 1792, it numbered around 800 subjects. Some of them were able to pursue their activities as private school teachers under the protection of local authorities. Napoleon Bonaparte recognized the educational value of an organized body of devoted teachers. In 1803 he authorized the restoration of the society and in 1808 put it under the control of the grand master of the university. For the Bourbon monarchy, Christian education was a high priority, and the government warmly encouraged the development of the brothers. Their number grew from about 300 in 1814 to 1,420 in 1830, when they served 380 schools.

But the LaSalle Brothers, or *grands frères*, as they were called, adhered strictly to the rule that demanded that they live in communities of at least three individuals, and because of this, their activities were practically limited to city schools. In order to provide a Christian education to villagers, many local groups—at least a score of them—organized under their bishop's authority to start similar societies of religious teacher brothers. They were sometimes designated by the name *petits frères*. Some of these societies used the title Brothers of the Christian Schools so as to be covered by the napoleonic legislation. From this, much confusion arises for historians, a confusion compounded by the frequent splitting or consolidation of those smaller societies. In 1830, mainly the following societies were well organized and active:

Frères de l'Instruction chrétienne de Ploërmel, founded by Gabriel Deshayes and Jean-Marie de Lamennais.

Frères de Marie, or Marianistes, established in Bordeaux by Guillaume-Joseph Chaminade.

Frères de Saint-Gabriel or du Saint-Espirit, founded by Gabriel Deshayes, in Vendée.

Petits frères de Saint Joseph, founded by Jacques-François Dujarié, in Le Mans.

Frères de Saint-Joseph of Ruillé-sur-Loire, founded also by Dujarié.

Petits frères de Marie, founded by Marcellin Champagnat, in Lyons.

Petits frères du Sacré-Coeur, founded by André Colin in Lyons.

Frères de la doctrine chrétienne de Nancy, established by Father Fréchard.

G. Rigault, *Histoire generale de l'Institut des frères des écoles chrétiennes*, 9 vols. (Paris, 1935–52); P. Zind, *Les nouvelles congregations de Frères Enseignants en France, de 1800 a 1830* (Saint-Genis-Laval, 1939).

Guillaume de Bertier de Sauvigny

BROUSSAIS, FRANCOIS-JOSEPH-VICTOR (1772–1838), physician. Born in 1772 in Saint-Malo, Broussais was the son of a health officer. After schooling in Dinan, where he was a friend of Chateaubriand, he became a soldier in 1793. He then studied medicine in Saint-Malo, Brest, and Paris and served as a surgeon for the navy. In 1803, Broussais received his doctorate in medicine and continued his military career with the Napoleonic armies in central Europe and Spain. In 1814, he was appointed to the Val-de-Grâce hospital in Paris, becoming head doctor six years later. Also in 1820, he became professor of pathology in the Paris medical faculty. In 1823, he was elected to the Académie de médecine and in 1832 to the Académie des sciences morales et politiques.

Broussais published a number of works on medicine, including a study of circulation and the nervous system, an examination of medical doctrine, and books on physiology and mental illness and on cholera. He became well known (and controversial) for a theory on the irritation of nerve tissues. Broussais thought that moderate irritation of the nerves produced good health; weak irritation produced debility, while strong irritation resulted in illness. Broussais was respected for his progressive views on medicine, since he insisted that medical theory must follow scientific observation and denied any spiritual or metaphysical explanations of physiology and disease.

P. Bonnette, *Broussais* (Paris, 1939); M. Prévost and R. d'Amat, "Broussais," *Dictionnaire de biographie française*, vol. 7 (Paris, 1956).

Robert Aldrich
Related entries: CHATEAUBRIAND; PARIS FACULTY OF MEDICINE.

BRUNE, GUILLAUME-MARIE-ANNE (1763–1815), marshal of France, senior French commander of strong republican convictions. From October 1807 Brune, a marshal of the first Napoleonic creation, languished in imperial disfavor for publicly expressing his republican views, and in consequence he received no important military appointments for seven successive years. Ironically, Brune saw fit to adjust his political attitudes in 1814 and rallied to the cause of the restored Bourbons, who appointed him a chevalier of the order of Saint Louis. Even more strangely, Napoleon was prepared to reemploy him following his return from Elba in 1815 and appointed him governor of Provence and commander of the Eighth Military Division (or district) in succession to Marshal André Masséna. On 17 April he was given command of the Var Corps of Observation, and on 1 June he was made a peer of France.

When the campaign of 1815 opened, Brune found himself at the head of barely 5,500 men facing over four times that number in the Army of Naples on the

Riviera coast. He fought a staunch withdrawal in the face of superior enemy forces and eventually shut himself up in the fortress and naval arsenal of Toulon. This he defended staunchly until late July—five weeks beyond Napoleon's second abdication—before finally surrendering to the royal commissioner, the marquis de Rivière.

Placed under arrest, he set out for Paris under escort on 31 July. While passing through Avignon, he was attacked by royalist sympathizers who shot him dead, stabbed his body a hundred times, and then used it for target practice in the River Rhône for a further hour.

R. F. Delderfield, *The March of the Twenty-six: The Story of Napoleon's Marshals* (London, 1962); Le Barrois d'Orgeval, *Le Maréchalat de France des origines a nos jours*, 2 vols. (Paris, 1932); G. Six, *Dictionnaire biographique des Généraux & Amiraux français de la Revolution et de l'Empire*, vol. 1 (Paris, 1934).

David Chandler

Related entries: HUNDRED DAYS.

BUCHEZ, PHILIPPE-JOSEPH-BENJAMIN (1796–1865), philosopher, historian, and social reformer who from the early 1830s on attempted to draw together in a new synthesis apparently disparate traditions: the Catholic, the democratic, and the Saint-Simonian. Most historians (with the notable exception of François-André Isambert) have underestimated the originality and the importance of Philippe Buchez. Three reasons explain their attitude. One is that his published works are badly written and long-winded, a curious mixture of platitude and prophetic insight. Yet difficult to penetrate and little read though they are, his writings contain much more than the proposal for workers' producer cooperatives and the idealistic Christian socialism for which Buchez is usually remembered. They contain, above all, his brave attempt to create a science of society—the most elaborate after that of Comte—and to understand society in a historical perspective. A second reason why he has not been given the recognition he deserves is that his career seems to consist of a series of abrupt turns. He was first a revolutionary actively plotting the overthrow of the regime, then an early member of the Saint-Simonian sect that eschewed political violence, and finally the leader of his own school that itself evolved toward a neo-Catholicism and a more moderate reform position. Nevertheless, the complex itinerary he followed does not set him apart from contemporaries. On the contrary, it makes him representative of many of those who came to intellectual maturity during the Restoration. Moreover, by dint of his lower-middle-class origins (and even his chosen profession as a doctor) and his attitudes toward capitalist society and revolution, he was not untypical of the socialist theorists who flourished in the Paris of the July Monarchy. What sets him apart is less the evolution of his thought than the synthesis he attempted. There is a third reason why Buchez has not been given the attention he deserves: his failure in 1848. Not only did he fail in the National Assembly, but his influence began to wane. It must be said in his defense, though, that Buchez was not the only social reformer to be disappointed by the course of events after February 1848.

The formative phase of Buchez's career down to 1830 saw him choose a career, abandon his religious faith, and seek commitment, first in carbonarism and then in Saint-Simonianism. Son of an official in the Paris *octroi* administration, Buchez left school when he was fifteen to follow in his father's footsteps. In 1817, however, he began studies at the Faculty of Medicine in Paris. He graduated in 1825 and until 1847 practiced medicine. It was while he was a student that he became a republican. Already in 1818 he helped set up a student discussion group, and, soon after, a Masonic lodge (the Loge des amis de la vérité) that was a cover for discussing liberal ideas. In May 1821 he went further when he helped found the French carbonari movement, a secret organization bent on the overthrow of the Bourbons that was to attract many of the future leaders of republicanism. Buchez, given the task of establishing carbonarism in eastern France, was arrested in January 1822 when the authorities discovered and easily suppressed an ill-conceived plan for an insurrection. By the following August, when a jury found him innocent and he was released from prison, the movement had suffered setbacks elsewhere, and Buchez returned to his studies. This failure convinced him of the futility of political violence, and his conviction was reinforced by his experience in the Saint-Simonian sect, which he joined in 1825.

He was attracted to the newly founded sect because of his growing awareness of the sufferings of the working class, a concern shared by other Saint-Simonians, and because he felt the religious void of his time and was touched by the *Nouveau christianisme*, which had been Saint-Simon's last publication. His involvement in the sect was to be the crucial formative influence on his mature thought. It was, indeed, his first creative intellectual experience, for he contributed articles to the *Producteur* in 1826 and participated in the discussions that led up to the important lectures Saint-Simonians gave in 1828–29. His break with the sect at the end of 1829 was important in the evolution of the sect since it was the first major schism; Buchez took at least five others with him. With these followers, he began his career as an independent thinker. It is testimony to the impact Saint-Simonianism had on him that he did not consider he had left the sect as a schismatic but as the true heir of Saint-Simon, whose mission it was to carry on the master's work.

In the first years of the July Monarchy, Buchez quickly developed and propagated his ideas. He did this in three ways. First, like the Saint-Simonians and Comte, he gave a series of lectures. Significant numbers of Parisian artisans attended these lectures, and Buchez was always to maintain contacts with those whom he called, in a phrase that was to be used by others, the laboring aristocracy. Second, and more important, he founded a newspaper, the *Européen* (for its first four issues, it had the title *Journal des sciences morales et politiques*), which ran from December 1831 to October 1832 and again from 1835 to 1838. In collaboration with Jules Bastide, Buchez edited a second journal, the *Revue nationale* in 1847–48. Third, Buchez began to publish philosophical and historical studies. In 1833 appeared his first work, *Introduction à la science de l'Histoire, ou science du développement de l'humanité*, and in the following year appeared the first volume of the *Histoire parlementaire de la Révolution française*, which he wrote with J.-C. Roux-Lavergne. Five years later, when the series was complete, it comprised no fewer than forty volumes. Buchez also wrote *Essai d'un traité complet de philosophie du point de vue du Catholicisme et du progrès* (1838–40 in three volumes). Among his later works the most notable is the two-volume *Traité de politique et de science sociale*, which was published posthumously in 1866.

His thinking has three major and related aspects: his attempt to lay the bases of a science of society; his attempt to fill the religious vacuum of his time and his gradual reconciliation with Catholicism; and his attempt to find a peaceful and democratic solution for the problem of working-class suffering and alienation. Regarding the first of these, Buchez believed that to understand politics and society as a whole, it was necessary to study the secular evolution of profound forces. These forces, he argued, could be studied scientifically. The study of the past, then, was the key to understanding contemporary society and human destiny. This explains the title of his first published work, which refers not to the philosophy but the science of history. Buchez believed there was a pattern in the past and that this pattern was progress toward a Christian goal. He also accepted the notion of the alternation of critical and organic epochs proposed by Saint-Simon and the Saint-Simonians. But Buchez was more than a metahistorian. He also published a remarkable and influential study of the recent French past. His *Histoire parlementaire de la Révolution française* has often been mistakenly seen as little more than a compendium of parliamentary speeches and newspaper articles. It was, in fact, one of the first works to insist that the conflicts of the 1790s were class struggles. The idea that the Revolution as a whole had been a conflict between the people—that is, the bourgeoisie and the populace—and privilege had already been put forward, but Buchez dared to go further than his liberal contemporaries: he tried to explain and even defend Jacobinism. He not only treated the Jacobins as representing working-class and hence democratic interests but praised their achievements. He even insisted that Christians and Catholics should regard the Revolution as a progressive force.

His attempt to find a new spiritual and moral force for society is the second major strand of his thought. The Saint-Simonians made a comparable effort, and a number of other ex-Saint-Simonians were to continue the quest. In the early 1830s Buchez thought that Catholicism, which had failed to fulfill its mission since the beginning of the modern era, was not capable of providing this new faith. In succeeding years, however, he gradually moved back to the Catholic church. New collaborators, who joined him from the later 1830s on and who were less radical and closer to Catholicism than the first groups of Buchezians, helped bring about this reconciliation.

The third strand in his thinking is the one that is best remembered and had the most easily traceable influence: his concern to improve the workers' lot. Like other Saint-Simonians, he characterized society as divided into two antagonistic classes: those who owned the means of production and those who had only their labor. Like the other Saint-Simonians too, he believed inheritance transmitted inequalities and should be limited, but he laid greater stress than they had on the need to reform education and introduce universal suffrage. However, his best-known, though perhaps not his most original, proposal was that for the establishment of workers' producer cooperatives. These, he believed, would allow workers to work democratically together toward a common goal and enable them to liberate themselves (rather than being liberated from above) from dependence on capitalists—"pure parasites," as he called them. It should be pointed out that others in both Britain and France at this time were also advocating producer cooperatives. The most noteworthy elements in Buchez's proposal were that these associations would be voluntary when they involved skilled trades that needed little capital and given government aid when large inputs of capital were necessary and that a proportion of the annual income of a cooperative was inalienable, belonging not to members but to the association itself.

Buchez's reform proposals, together with his contacts with skilled workers in Paris, had three practical consequences. One was the setting up, by workers influenced by his ideas, of the *Atelier*, the most successful workers' journal of the period. Another was the jewelery workers' cooperative that Buchez helped set up in the capital in 1834. This was moderately successful (though it never had more than seventeen members at any one time) and lasted until 1873. Finally, Buchezians were the principal promoters of the decree of 5 July 1848 that created a parliamentary committee to help promote workers' producer cooperatives and gave it a budget of 3 million francs. Buchez himself achieved fleeting prominence in 1848 when the National Assembly chose him as its first president. When the crowd invaded the Assembly on 15 May, however, he first sent for the National Guard and then apparently anxious to avoid bloodshed, rescinded the order. His vacillation cost him his presidency. Thereafter Buchez played no prominent role in national affairs and, though he continued to write, gradually lost most of his erstwhile collaborators.

A. Cuvillier, *Hommes et idéologies de 1840* (Paris, 1956), *Buchez et les origines du socialisme chrétien* (Paris, 1948), and *Un journal d'ouvriers, "L'Atelier," 1840–1850* (Paris, 1954); J.-B. Duroselle, *Les débuts du catholicisme social en France (1820–1870)* (Paris, 1951); F.-A. Isambert, *Christianisme et classe ouvrière* (Paris, 1961), *De la charbonnerie au saint-simonisme: étude sur la jeunesse de Buchez* (Paris, 1966), and *Politique, religion et science de l'homme chez Philippe Buchez (1796–1865)* (Paris, 1967); R. Reibel, "Les idées politiques et sociales de P.-J.-B. Buchez," in R. Reibel and P. Rougère, *Socialisme et ethique* (Paris, 1966).

Barrie M. Ratcliffe

Related entries: L'ATELIER; CARBONARI; COMTE, A.; FREEMASONRY; NATIONAL GUARD; PARIS FACULTY OF MEDICINE; REPUBLICANS; REVOLUTION OF 1848; *REVUE NATIONALE*; SAINT-SIMONIANISM; SAINT-SIMON; WORKERS' COOPERATIVES.

BUGEAUD, THOMAS-ROBERT (1784–1849), marquis de la Piconnerie, duc d'Isly, soldier, conservative politician, agricultural reformer, and marshal of France. Born into an impoverished noble family in the Périgord, Bugeaud received little formal education before he joined the army in 1804. Most of his early military service was spent in Spain, where he experienced the difficulties of guerrilla fighting and learned lessons he was later to apply in Algeria. Put on half-pay by the Bourbon Restoration in 1815, he retired to his estate, which he transformed into a model farm. In 1831, he was elected deputy for the Dordogne and reintegrated into the army with the rank of brigadier. He supervised the captivity of the duchesse de Berry in the chateau of Blaye and in 1834 killed in a duel the young deputy Charles Dulong who criticized the severity of his wardenship.

In 1836, Bugeaud was sent to Algeria for a brief campaign, which ended with the signing of the treaty of Tafna. Despite his strongly anticolonialist opinions, François Guizot made him governor-general of Algeria in 1840. For the next seven years, Bugeaud pursued a relentless campaign against Abd el-Kader, the chief of the Algerian resistance. He abandoned the policy of fixed posts in favor of a series of mobile columns of between 6,000 and 8,000 men, which would often converge on an enemy concentration. In this respect, he can be called the Father of Colonial Warfare. But the brutality of his methods, in particular that of the *razzia* (or punitive raids on Algerian villages) which devastated great parts of Algeria and caused much unnecessary loss of life among the Arabs, led to violent criticism at home, criticism that Bugeaud countered with typically callous and intemperate language. In 1843, he was promoted to marshal of France and the following year named duc d'Isly in honor of his victory over the Moroccans in 1844. His policy of founding military colonies and his general neglect of administration made him unpopular among Algerian colonists. He resigned in 1847 after facing severe criticism in the French parliament. He died of cholera in 1849.

T. R. Bugeaud, *Par l'epée et par la charrue, Ecrits et discours* (Paris, 1948); C.-A. Julien, *Bugeaud—Les techniciens de la colonisation* (Paris, 1946) and *Histoire de l'Algérie contemporaine* (Paris, 1964); A. Thrall-Sullivan, *Thomas-Robert Bugeaud, France and Algeria 1784–1849* (Hamden, Conn., 1983); P. Thureau-Dangin, *Histoire de la Monarchie du Juillet*, 7 vols. (Paris, 1884–92).

Douglas Porch

Related entries: BERRY, M.-C.; *DEMI-SOLDES*; GUIZOT.

BUONARROTI, FILIPPO-MICHELE (1761–1837), French revolutionary, communist, and Italian patriot. Buonarroti was born in Pisa on 11 November 1761, a member of a noble Florentine family. Educated at the University of Pisa, he graduated doctor of laws in 1782 and began a career as a journalist in Florence. Exiled in 1789 for his enthusiastic welcome to the French Revolution, during 1790–92 he worked to consolidate the Revolution in Corsica and to expand its influence in Sardinia and Italy. He became a French citizen in 1793 and in

1794 was appointed an administrator of French occupied territories in Liguria, in north Italy; he imposed Jacobin policies of social welfare and educational indoctrination. Recalled and jailed for revolutionary excesses in 1795, Buonarroti was soon freed and became, with Babeuf, one of the organizers of the communist Conspiracy of the Equals in Paris in 1796. The collapse of the conspiracy resulted in a new arrest and six years' imprisonment. Released in 1802, Buonarroti eventually settled in Geneva, where he lived until 1823. He attempted to make Geneva the center of an underground international revolutionary opposition to the Empire, uniting Jacobin survivors, new disciples, and dissident Bonapartist officers. Sometime between 1809 and 1811 he founded the Sublimes maîtres parfaits, a secret society on quasi-Masonic lines, for this purpose. This society was destroyed in 1823 but was replaced by a similar secret organization, the Monde. Buonarroti now moved to Brussels until the 1830 revolution made possible his return to France.

In 1828 Buonarroti published his account of the 1796 conspiracy. His *Conspiration pour l'égalité* was a vindication both of Jacobin radicalism and Babouvist communism and exercised considerable influence on the new generation of radicals and socialists in France during the 1830s and 1840s, for whom Buonarroti became a charismatic elder statesman figure. Marx and Engels paid tribute to his role in transmitting the ideas of the Enlightenment and French Revolutionary pioneers of communism to the nineteenth century. After returning to Paris, Buonarroti continued his activities as a conspirator until his death in 1837. Meanwhile he collaborated with Marc-René Voyer d'Argenson and Charles Teste in helping to create an open democratic and socialist movement in opposition to Louis Philippe.

Buonarroti's 1828 account of the conspiracy of 1796 shows that his fundamental objectives remained those of the conspirators and had not changed over three decades: a regime of communism based on the complete equality of labor and goods, to be brought about by the conquest of political power and the subsequent dictatorship of an enlightened revolutionary elite. Buonarroti's communism was essentially moral in inspiration. He had no understanding of, or rejected as irrelevant, the new possibilities created by the Industrial Revolution, and he criticized the Saint-Simonian doctrine of material progress; nor did he regard the new industrial proletariat as possessing any distinctive revolutionary role. He sought instead a universal return to the spirit of equality and fraternity of Maximilien Robespierre's Republic of Virtue of 1794. Presenting Robespierre as a true democrat, at heart an enemy of private property, and generally minimizing the differences between the Jacobins of 1793–94 and the Equals of 1796, he did much to create the powerful Robespierrist myth around which radical democrats and socialists united after 1830. Buonarroti's political tactics showed a greater flexibility than his fundamental thought. After 1815 he envisaged his followers less as conspirators urgently preparing for an actual uprising after the pattern of 1796 than as an inner circle of true believers, keeping their long-term aims intact but pragmatically adjusting compromise policies to suit circumstances. Thus he publicly advocated such limited reformist objectives under the July Monarchy as universal suffrage (although not for women, without extensive reeducation) and a single, graduated income tax, and he gave his support to the reform campaigns of the political Society of the Rights of Man. The renewed emphasis of Louis-Auguste Blanqui, Armand Barbès, and others on the revolutionary seizure of power by a coup d'état did not therefore mark a direct continuation of Buonarroti's influence so much as a return to the common inspiration of the 1790s.

E. L. Eisenstein, *The First Professional Revolutionist: Filippo Michele Buonarroti* (Cambridge, Mass., 1959); P. Onnis Rosa, *Filippo Buonarroti e altri Studi* (Rome, 1971); A. Saitta, *Filippo Buonarroti*, 2 vols. (Rome, 1950–51).

Robert Barrie Rose

Related entries: BARBES; BLANQUI, L.-A.; LOUIS PHILIPPE; MARX; REVOLUTION OF 1830; ROBESPIERRE; SAINT-SIMONIANISM; SOCIETY OF THE RIGHTS OF MAN; VOYER D'ARGENSON.

BYRON, GEORGE GORDON, LORD (1788–1824), English romantic poet whose legendary life-style and inspired poetry gave rise to *Le Byronisme* in France and exerted tremendous lasting influence throughout the Continent. Byron's style of writing was as varied, complex, and even paradoxical as his personality. The qualities that catapulted him to instant fame with the publication of the first two cantos of *Childe Harold* in 1812 are generally contrary to those appreciated by modern readers in *Don Juan*. To the impassioned introspective Byronic hero in perpetual revolt that inflamed European romantic consciousness in his early verse and the remorselessly lucid satirist and realist of his mature work must be added the libertarian idealist in order to capture a complete image. His death in the cause of Greek freedom affixed the seal of sincerity to his complicated, turbulent character and echoed the sentiments concerning George III's reign expressed in his last work, *The Vision of Judgement*.

Byron the man and Byron the poet burned like a brilliant comet across the European literary scene, leaving an indelible and enduring impression despite his early death. His father, "Mad Jack" Byron, a notorious rake and gambler, died when he was three. His grandfather, Admiral "Foulweather Jack" Byron, had cut one of the most colorful figures in the eighteenth-century navy, and his great-uncle, from whom he inherited the title when he was only ten, was the "wicked lord" who led a strange, secluded life. This heredity, sprinkled with traces of insanity and marriages between cousins, and the birth defect that caused him to walk with a limp, weighed on his consciousness and his imagination. It planted seeds that were nourished when Byron toured Europe in 1809.

This voyage produced incredible consequences. In addition to *Childe Harold*, which made him famous in mythic proportions, *The Giaour*, *The Bride of Abydos*, *The Corsair*, and *The Siege of Corinth* all resulted directly from this trip, but even scenes in *Don Juan* and his later political involvement with the *risorgimento* movement in Italy and the liberation of Greece have their origin in the life-transforming experiences of this year of travel.

Byron's raffish reputation forced him to leave England in 1816. After travels in Switzerland, where he met Percy Shelley, Byron resided in Italy, where he continued to write, and where he participated in the carbonari, a liberal secret society. He left Italy in July 1823 to join in the war for Greek independence, and accounts of his presence and participation range from extremely laudatory to highly critical. The sincerity of Byron's motivation, however, is undoubted, and his death from fever on 19 April 1824, though it spread a pall throughout Europe, was the missing capstone to the legend he had created of the noble impetuous hero in perpetual revolt.

Among Byron's biographers and critics are his prominent French contemporaries, Victor Hugo, Charles Nodier, Stendhal and Alfred de Vigny. Alphonse de Lamartine was particularly in his debt, and the course of French romanticism might well have run quite differently had there been no Byron. His later satirical pieces translated with difficulty, both in form and content, however, and it remained for André Maurois, among French writers, to seize on Byron's enduring greatness: "It is in the letters, in the journals, in *Don Juan* . . . that the greatest of English romantics reveals himself, not far behind Voltaire and Swift, as one of the greatest classic writers."

L. A. Marchand, *Byron: A Biography*, 3 vols. (New York, 1957) and L. A. Marchand, ed., *Byron: Letters and Journals*, vols. 1–7 (1981); A. Maurois, *Byron*, trans. Hamis Miles (New York, 1930); A. Rutherford, *Byron, A Critical Study* (Palo Alto, 1962) and *The Letters of Lord Byron* (1948).

Shelby A. Outlaw

Related entries: HUGO; LAMARTINE; NODIER; ROMANTICISM; STENDHAL; VIGNY.

C

CABANIS, PIERRE-JEAN-GEORGES, COMTE (1757–1808), physician, senator (1799–1808), and a leader of the *idéologue* philosophical circle. With the Catholic revival and anti-empiricist philosophy dominant in the Restoration, the survivors of the *idéologue* circle were in complete disarray. In 1818, to the ultraconservative political theorist Louis de Bonald and to Jacques-Henri Bernardin de Saint-Pierre's biographer, Louis Aimé Martin, Cabanis represented the stereotypically dangerous materialist and atheist. Yet in 1824, publication of Cabanis's manuscript "Letter on First Causes" (written probably in 1806 to C. Fauriel) by the Montpellier physician F.-E. Bérard made possible a more subtle philosophical appraisal. Cabanis had there advocated the probable existence of a universal intelligence, source of all forces, and even the possible existence of an immortal soul. His metaphysic was still monist, though more akin to panpsychism than to mechanical materialism. While Bérard and the historian of philosophy J.-P. Damiron in 1828 hailed this alleged conversion of Cabanis, most readers were wary of exchanging a materialist for a pantheist heresy.

In 1842 the secretary of the Academy of Medicine, F. Dubois d'Amiens, still viciously attacked Cabanis's "materialism," and the next year the Dijon philosopher Joseph Tissot warned that nerves cannot sense. The physicians L. Cérise and L. Peisse, who edited the seventh and eighth editions of Cabanis's *Rapports du physique et du moral de l'homme* (1802) in 1843 and 1844, stressed their uncompromising dualism and revulsion at Cabanis's stomach-brain analogy. Peisse at least recognized that some sentences of the *Rapports* anticipated passages of the *Letter* to Fauriel and that Cabanis's physiology derived partly from the animist-vitalist tradition of Stahl and the Montpellier school.

If Cabanis's philosophy of life and matter had few advocates, his suggested method for clinical practice and his unwittingly statistical orientation (*Coup d'oeil sur les révolutions et sur la réforme de la médecine*, 1795; published 1804) won adherents in the Paris Clinical School such as P. Pinel or the surgeon Louis. Cabanis's views on the nervous system still won the plaudits of the famous physician F.-J.-V. Broussais in 1826, while even politically conservative physicians J.-L. Alibert and B.-A. Richerand were indebted to Cabanis's physiology and theory of perfectibility by habit. Cabanis was no experimentalist, but his views on nervous sensitivity, internal impressions, and organic brain function helped stimulate the research of F. Magendie and M.-J.-P. Flourens.

J.-J. Moreau de la Sarthe was an advocate in 1821 of Cabanis's plans to use hygiene to improve character and intelligence (see the article "Moral" in the *Encyclopédie méthodique*). These views gained support among the writers of the *Annales d'hygiène publique et de médecine légale* (founded 1829) and in the statistical social research of L.-R. Villermé in the 1830s and 1840s. Saint-Simon and Auguste Comte praised Cabanis for aspiring to establish a science of man, but their organic view of society owed more to the physiology of Bichat.

P.-J.-G. Cabanis, *Oeuvres complètes*, ed. P. Thurot, 5 vols. (Paris, 1823–25), *Oeuvres philosophiques*, ed. C. Lehec and J. Cazeneuve, 2 vols. (Paris, 1956), *On the Relations between the Physical and Moral Aspects of Man*, ed. G. Mora (Baltimore, 1981), and *Rapports du physique et du moral de l'homme* (Paris, 1844; reprint, Geneva, 1980); A. Guillois, *Le salon de Madame Helvétius* (Paris, 1893); G. Gusdorf, *La conscience révolutionnaire, les Idéologues* (Paris, 1978); S. Moravia, *Il pensiero degli Idéologues* (Florence, 1974); M. Staum, *Cabanis* (Princeton, 1980).

Martin S. Staum

Related entries: BONALD; BROUSSAIS; COMTE; *IDEOLOGUES*; MAGENDIE; PINEL; SAINT-SIMON; VILLERME.

CABET, ETIENNE (1788–1856), radical and utopian. Recent research has revealed the depth and breadth of the Icarian communist movement during the 1840s. Its founder, or rather father, was Etienne Cabet, a lawyer born into a Dijon artisan family in 1788 who thereafter traveled a typically Jacobin political path until his conversion to communism in 1837–38. First active in the carbonari conspiracies of 1823–25, he followed the disillusioned-liberal trend toward republicanism in the early 1830s, writing a popular account of the Revolution of 1830 and founding associations and newspapers promoting democratic reform. At that point he was to the right of many neo-Jacobins, however, for he failed to challenge the idea of property as a natural right, though he decried the poverty and degradation of the people, specifically the urban laboring classes. His diatribes against the king in his newspaper, *Le Populaire de 1833*, brought him a conviction on 28 February 1834 that led to a five-year exile in London.

Influenced by Robert Owen, More's *Utopia*, and a new understanding of French history based on an intensive reading of those in the Jacobin and Babouvist traditions, Cabet moved directly to "the logical consequence" of Maximilien Robespierre's view of property as a "social convention," to what he termed *la communauté*, a society based on complete economic equality. His *Histoire de la Révolution française* (1839), a primer on how easily France might have become a communist nation had 9 Thermidor not intervened, laid out the moral imperatives and the teleology behind Cabet's new vision, while the *Voyage en Icarie* (1840) provided a blow-by-blow description of the new revolution through which *communauté* might be established and, above all, a detailed and quite fascinating plan for Icaria, the perfect communist society. He imagined a highly centralized nation-state where decision making was democratic but where overwhelming majorities were always achieved because all tasks were essentially "the administration of things," as another communist would put it. The problems surrounding the General Will and Jacobin democracy were thus simply ignored. But it was the vision of the happy, materially abundant, familial, peaceful, and almost genteel life that inspired the tens of thousands of French working people who became aware of Cabet's utopia during the following decade. It is important to note, however, that while Cabet proclaimed total economic and social equality, he stressed the need for variety in style and content of goods actually used. Differences in individual taste were assumed even though he argued that all human beings are essentially equal in capacities; they develop differing proclivities through experience, and these should not be thwarted.

The essential social unit in Icaria was an idealized version of an extended rural family. Education provided fully equal opportunity, but Cabet naively assumed that differing interests would carry individuals into occupational slots that would be sufficient to staff the diverse needs of a modern economy. Icaria was a fully industrialized, technologically advanced society. Cabet saw modern industry as the foundation for general prosperity. Work would be totally nonexploitative and as "pleasant and easy" to do as possible. But Cabet seemed little concerned about its creative side, taking an interesting position therefore on a critical issue of the day. Perhaps it is no accident that his greatest appeal was among the poorest and most threatened artisans for whom most work was drudgery, no matter how it was performed.

The impact of Cabet's new outlook was immediate. After his return to France in 1839, he dedicated himself with unbounded energy to the propagation of his ideas. In 1840 a variety of polemics against both the government and the moderate reformists helped regain his fame, and when he launched the new *Populaire* in March 1841, he began to build the nucleus of a veritable workers' party through the distribution system of his newspaper. He emphasized the use of legal means—propaganda and discussion groups—rather than secret societies in building the worker movement, though he remained equivocal on the idea of revolution. Violence he condemned, but the voices of revolutions past and future, if not present, rang through his writings during the 1840s. These were voluminous and repetitive. Thousands of pages of Icarian propaganda poured out of his office on the old rue J.-J. Rousseau in the Latin Quarter. The total number of Icarians will never be known, but a guess of 100,000 is not outlandish, and although Paris and Lyons were its principal seats, Icarian communism ultimately reached seventy-eight of France's eighty-nine departments. Its supporters came overwhelmingly from what had come to be called the working class, principally in the artisanal trades such as tailoring and shoemaking that were traditionally poor and now being ravaged by new capitalist practices.

The movement peaked in 1846–47 as Cabet's dictatorial bearing and his public pronouncements against violence were opposed by more and more of his adherents. He personally had developed an analysis of French society that appears vaguely Marxist, but his reputation had been built on social pacifism and legal means. Thus, through a complex process, Cabet decided to attempt an experimental community, an idea that he had consistently rejected in the past. He coupled his call for the emigration to "the promised land" of Texas with a new focus on Icarian communism as the "true Christianity." Both ideas found widespread enthusiasm, but the movement experienced a massive turnover in personnel as a result, with Christian experimentalists moving in and many revolutionaries moving out. The actual size and scope of the movement remained roughly the same. The Revolution of 1848 occurred just after the avant-garde (not including Cabet) sailed for Texas, and Cabet quickly recognized that an entirely new situation had arisen. "Quelle Révolution!" He was among the first and most ardent of its supporters, and he and many of his followers and former followers went on to play important roles in it. But the hopes of building an Icaria in France were quickly dashed, and, indeed, anticommunism became an instrument in the conservative arsenal and a significant influence on the reactionary outcome of the 23 April elections. Even before the June Days, Cabet therefore decided to revive the American venture. The Texas situation turned out disastrously, but the Icarians were able to purchase the abandoned Mormon village at Nauvoo, Illinois, and then build a fairly solid community rooted in Cabet's main principles. Cabet returned to France in 1850–51 to help fight the reaction and recruit for the colony but went back forever to the United States after the coup d'état. Nauvoo grew and maintained considerable stability, but Cabet's authoritarianism wore thin. In 1855, the colonists split, with a majority opposing the leader. To his credit, he moved on to St. Louis in order to found a new community, but death overtook him in 1856 before it was well established. Nevertheless, Nauvoo and other experiments in Iowa and finally on the West Coast survived longer than any other secular utopian experiment, the last, small group in California finally breaking up in 1898. This, however, was not Cabet's main inheritance. Rather, it was his indefatigable work in building the first communist workers' party in history and helping to set the stage for the explosive events of the Second Republic.

R. Aminzade, *Class, Politics, and Early Industrial Capitalism* (Albany, N.Y., 1981); C. H. Johnson, *Utopian Communism in France: Cabet and the Icarians, 1839–1851* (Ithaca, 1974); J. Prudhommeaux, *Icarie et son fondateur, Etienne Cabet* (Paris, 1907).

Christopher H. Johnson

Related entries: CARBONARI; COUP D'ETAT OF 2 DECEMBER 1851; JUNE DAYS; *LE POPULAIRE*; REPUBLICANS; REVOLUTION OF 1830; REVOLUTION OF 1848; ROBESPIERRE.

CAISSES D'EPARGNE. The first *caisse d'épargne et de prévoyance*, or savings bank, was created in 1818 by the duc de la Rochefoucauld-Liancourt, Michel Frédéric Pillet-Will, and Benjamin Delessert. Delessert (1773–1847), the prime initiator of the project, was the son of a Lyons banker; he also created the first refinery for sugar beets in France, owned a cotton spinnery, and was a regent of the Bank of France. The *caisse d'épargne* was designed as a depository institution for the modest savings of ordinary Frenchmen; it was modeled on a similar British institution. Individuals could deposit a maximum of 300 francs at one time, and the maximum total for each account was set at 3,000 francs. (The average deposit was 575 francs.) The money was invested in state securities, and depositors were paid 3.5 percent interest.

The savings banks were very successful during the first half of the nineteenth century because of their active recruitment of clients and because of the suppression of the royal lottery in 1836. By 1829, the savings banks had 6 million francs in deposits and by 1845, almost 400 million francs. Meanwhile, the number of depositors had risen to 150,000, and over 350 savings banks had been established around France. In 1835, the interest rate was raised to 4 percent. The greater government expenditures on interest, however, led to a reduction in the maximum deposit to 1,500 francs in 1845.

The 1848 Revolution created a crisis for the *caisses d'épargne*. Less than a sixth of the banks' deposits were held as liquid assets, and the government faced the task of reimbursing depositors. Only 100 francs was paid in cash, the rest in paper money issued at par value; however, the notes were often exchanged for as little as half their face value. During 1848, the *caisses d'épargne* lost four-fifths of their depositors.

The savings banks revived during the Second Republic and the Second Empire and were once again prosperous by the late 1800s. In an effort to recruit more savers, particularly the residents of rural areas where no *caisses d'épargne* existed, the government in 1881 created a national savings bank. This was administered by the post office, and deposits could be made at any post office. The *caisses d'épargne* had established a pattern for savings and provided a source of money for the government, but they also had retarded the development of private savings institutions and the diversification of investments.

A. Cormont, *Les Caisses d'épargne en France* (Paris, 1922); B. Gille, *La Banque et le crédit en France de 1815 à 1848* (Paris, 1959); R. Laurent, *Les Caisses d'épargne dans la formation de l'épargne nationale* (Paris, 1951); H. Sée, *Histoire économique de la France: les temps modernes (1789–1914)* (Paris, 1951).

Robert Aldrich

Related entries: BANKING; DELESSERT, J.-P.-B.; LA ROCHEFOU-CAULDT-LIANCOURT; REVOLUTION OF 1848.

CAMBACERES, JEAN-JACQUES-REGIS DE (1753–1824), Duc de Parme, member of Revolutionary legislatures and imperial archchancellor. Born into a family of the *noblesse de robe* of Languedoc, Cambacérès studied the law and in 1771 succeeded his father as *conseiller* in the Cour des comptes of Montpellier. Following service as a popular local official during the early days of the Revolution, he won election to the Convention, where he voted for the guilt of Louis XVI, avoided committing himself on the death penalty, and supervised the burial of the king's remains. Cambacérès continued to serve in the Revolutionary Legislatures, both before and after 9 Thermidor, until, suspected of un-Revolutionary moderation, he was eliminated from the government during the Directory.

Following a brief return to private life as a lawyer, Cambacérès became minister of justice after 30 Prairial, a position he occupied during the coup of 18 Brumaire. Napoleon Bonaparte rewarded Cambacérès for his support by naming him second consul and by charging him with important judicial and legislative functions. Between 1799 and 1814, Cambacérès faithfully served as an adviser to Napoleon, taking, for example, an important role in negotiating the Concordat of 1801 and in drafting the Civil Code. He also exercised important executive functions when Napoleon was absent from France, especially in 1806 and 1812. For these and other services, Napoleon made Cambacérès archchancellor, president of the Senate, grand-eagle of the Legion of Honor, and duke of Parma.

During the First Restoration (1814–15), Cambacérès withdrew from public life. He took no part in the events of April 1814, avoiding the Senate's futile efforts to draft a constitution and absenting himself from both the delegation that welcomed the comte d'Artois to Paris and the senatorial commission that accompanied Talleyrand to greet Louis XVIII at Saint-Ouen. To nobody's surprise, Cambacérès' name did not appear on the list of peers announced by Louis XVIII on 4 June 1814. Just as he avoided displays of approbation for the Bourbons, so he refused, even when requested by a crowd of demonstrators at the Eglise Saint-Roche, to speak out against the new ruling family. Despite his efforts to pursue a private life in peace, Cambacérès' name was frequently linked to pro-Bonapartist activities.

Napoleon's landing on the French coast on 1 March 1815 elicited from Cambacérès not enthusiasm but dismay. After the emperor's arrival in Paris on 20 March, Cambacérès' evident reluctance to join his former master was overcome only by Napoleon's insistence that he become minister of justice. During the Hundred Days, Cambacérès urged Napoleon to issue the Additional Act (23 April 1815), and when the emperor left for the front on 12 June, he fulfilled his assigned duties with his customary diligence. Following the defeat at Waterloo, Cambacérès, although he participated in the animated discussions about the fate of Napoleon and the future of France, avoided taking a major role, allowing Joseph Fouché to maneuver freely and, at least in part, to mastermind the return of the Bourbons for a second restoration.

In the reaction that accompanied the Second Restoration, the Bourbons exiled the regicides, and Cambacérès was forced to leave France and seek asylum in Brussels. A royal ordinance of 13 May 1818 permitted a return to France; shortly after, the government restored to Cambacérès his civil and political rights. Until his death on 8 May 1824, he lived a quiet and private life, avoiding all political entanglements. His remains lie in Pére Lachaise.

Following the former archchancellor's death, the Bourbon government made a claim to all his papers. His nephew, assisted in 1824 by the liberal lawyer André Dupin, opened a long legal battle that ultimately gave possession of Cambacérès' correspondence and memoirs to his family. Although selections from these papers have appeared from time to time, the present location of Cambacérès' *Mémoires*—known to Adolphe Thiers and others in the 1820s—is unknown.

A. Aubriet, *Vie de Cambacérès, ex-archichancelier* (Paris, 1824); P. Duvivier, *Les Anciens conventionnels sous la Restauration. L'exil de Cambacérès à Bruxelles, 1816–1818* (Paris, 1923); F. Papillard, *Cambacérès* (Paris, 1961); J. Thiry, *Cambacérès, archichancelier de l'Empire* (Paris, 1934); P. Vialles, *L'Archichancelier Cambacérès, 1753–1824, d'après des documents inedits* (Paris, 1908).

Robert Brown

Related entries: ACTE ADDITIONNEL; DUPIN, A.-M.-J.-J.; FOUCHE; HUNDRED DAYS; LOUIS XVIII; RESTORATION, FIRST; RESTORATION, SECOND; TALLEYRAND; THIERS; WHITE TERROR.

CAMBRAI, DECLARATION OF (28 June 1815), a statement made by King Louis XVIII at the start of the Second Restoration promising to adhere to the liberal policies of the First Restoration. Soon after Napoleon's defeat at Waterloo, Louis XVIII had reentered France. From his first stop at Cateau-Cambresis, he had issued a short declaration (25 June), the terms of which could have had threatening interpretations. Charles-Maurice de Talleyrand, arriving from Vienna, suggested the issuing of another proclamation that would help to reassure public opinion. In this document the king went so far as to admit having made some mistakes in the past years; he promised to maintain and strengthen the concessions and guarantees granted by the Charter of 1814; he promised forgiveness for all who had rallied to Napoleon after the departure of the king. Other culprits to be punished were to be designated by the Chambers.

Guillaume de Bertier de Sauvigny

Related entries: CHAMBER OF DEPUTIES; CHAMBER OF PEERS; CHARTER OF 1814; HUNDRED DAYS; LOUIS XVIII; RESTORATION, FIRST; RESTORATION, SECOND; TALLEYRAND; WATERLOO, BATTLE OF.

LES CANCANS (1831–1834), ephemeral newspaper of the July Monarchy. During the early years of the July Monarchy, the former dynasty was supported not only by serious newspapers such as the *Quotidienne* but by a number of squibs such as Pierre-Clément Bérard's *Cancans* (1831–34), which was condemned ten times in the law courts for attacks on Louis-Philippe.

C. Bellanger et al., *Histoire générale de la presse française*, vol. 2 (Paris, 1969).

Irene Collins

Related entries: LA *QUOTIDIENNE*

CANROBERT, CERTAIN (1809–1895), soldier and politician, marshal of France. Canrobert went straight from Saint-Cyr to Algeria, where he quickly gained a reputation for audacity and rapid promotion. Louis-Napoleon Bonaparte made Canrobert his aide-de-camp in 1850, and he took an active part in the coup d'état of 2 December 1851. He succeeded Saint-Arnaud as French commander in the Crimea but was replaced by Pelissier in 1855 after several disagreements with Lord James Raglan. On his return to Paris, he was named marshal of France. In 1870, he commanded the VI Corps, took part in the battle of Saint-Privat, and was captured at Metz. After the war, he was elected senator for the Lot. His memoires, published by Bapst, offer a useful first-hand view of Algerian warfare and of many of the Algerian generals.

G. Bapst, *Le maréchal Canrobert, Souvenirs d'un siècle* (Paris, 1898); B. Gooch, *The New Bonapartist Officers in the Crimean War* (The Hague, 1959); Commandant Grandin, *Le dernier maréchal de France: Canrobert* (Tolra, 1895); M. Howard, *The Franco-Prussian War* (London, 1961); A. Rastoul, *Un soldat, Le maréchal Canrobert* (Lille, 1897).

Douglas Porch

Related entries: COUP D'ETAT OF 2 DECEMBER 1851; ECOLE MILI-TAIRE; PELISSIER; SAINT-ARNAUD.

CANUEL, SIMON, BARON DE (1767–1840), general of the Empire, ultraroyalist deputy of the Restoration and July Monarchy. Canuel was born on 29 October 1767 at Trois-Moutiers (Vienne). In 1792 he volunteered for the army and served as an aide-de-camp to Jean-Antoine Rossignol. In 1793 he fought in the Vendée where he earned a reputation for brutality toward the royalists. He participated notably in the battles of Doué and Savenay where, in December 1793, Jean-Victor Moreau halted the chouans' major offensive. After the latter battle, Canuel, who now avowed staunchly republican doctrines, became a division commander. He was compromised by the fall of Maximilien Robespierre and did not see active service again until the Year V. The Directory, which suspected royalist conspiracies at Lyons, gave Canuel command of the city with authority to place it in a state of siege. After 18 Brumaire he rallied to Napoleon, who named him to the Legion of Honor and in 1805 made him commander of the Second Military Division at Mézières. In 1806 he became commander of the Twenty-Fifth Division at Liège. However, his profane language helped earn him the disfavor of Napoleon, who ordered him home and stripped him of active command.

The disfavor of Napoleon served to recommend him to the Bourbons, who at the Restoration restored him to active duty and gave him the Order of Saint Louis. He now professed support for the monarchy just as strongly as twenty years earlier he had advocated revolution. During the Hundred Days he attempted to raise the department of Vienne and revive the Vendéan uprising. As the major general of Louis de La Rochejaquelein's corps, Canuel was once again appointed to command Lyons. In August 1815 the department of Vienne elected him to the Chamber of Deputies, where he joined the ultraroyalist majority. When the

Chamber was dissolved in September 1816, he returned to command the Nineteenth Division at Lyons. There he brutally repressed a small uprising in June 1817, even resorting to firing on jailed prisoners, treating the residents like a conquered enemy, and establishing a reign of terror of nearly three months. When Paris received his report that a "major Bonapartist insurrection" had been suppressed, Louis XVIII named him a baron. In fact, Canuel was later accused of fomenting the insurrection to win advancement by suppressing it. These accusations by Sébastien-Claude-Salicon Charrier-Sainneville, a police official at Lyons, and by Colonel Charles-Nicolas Fabvier, Auguste de Marmont's aide who was sent to Lyons to investigate, resulted in the removal from command of Canuel on 6 October. Nevertheless, he subsequently won a civil suit against his accusers.

He was involved in the enigmatic ultraroyalist Conspiracy at the Water's Edge, which came to the light in June 1818, and he was to be a member of the cabinet the conspirators hoped to force on the king. As a result of this conspiracy, Canuel was jailed until November 1818 during a long investigation that resulted in the dropping of the charges. The government recalled Canuel to active duty as inspector general of infantry and gave him command of a division in time for the 1823 Spanish campaign. His final military assignment was to command the Twenty-first Division at Bourges. He retired at the time of the July Revolution, during which his life was endangered. Canuel died at Loudun (Vienne) on 11 May 1840, leaving his published memoirs on the 1815 Vendéan war.

Archives parlementaires; S. Charléty, "Une Conspiration à Lyon en 1817," *Revue de Paris* 4 (1904); E. Guillon, *Les Complots militaires sous la restauration* (Paris, 1895); A. Spitzer, *Old Hatreds and Young Hopes* (Cambridge, Mass., 1971).

James K. Kieswetter

Related entries: CHABROL DE CROUZOL; CHAMBER OF DEPUTIES; CONSPIRACY AT THE WATER'S EDGE; FABVIER; HUNDRED DAYS; LA ROCHEJAQUELEIN, L.; MARMONT; REVOLUTION OF 1830; SPAIN, 1823 FRENCH INVASION OF; ULTRAROYALISTS.

CANUTS, Lyons silk workers. The term *canut*, which was originally peculiar to the spoken *patois* of Lyons, is of obscure origin. It may be derived from *canette* (one synonym for *bobine*, or "bobbin") or *canne* (a hollow reed or tube), which together suggest the weaver's shuttle, or *navette*, which held a bobbin of thread in its hollow center. The term did not enter into general usage until the early 1800s (it first appears in a dictionary in 1838), as eighteenth-century weavers were consistently referred to as *maîtres-fabricants, ouvriers en soie* or, more generally, *soyeux*. It acquired wide usage and historical significance as a result of the Lyons weaver uprisings of 1831 and 1834, the *révolte des canuts*, and is still employed today for anyone working in the Lyons silk industry.

R. Bezucha, *The Lyon Uprising of 1834* (Cambridge, 1974); J. Godart, *L'ouvrier en soie* (Paris, Lyons, 1899); J. Vaschalde, *Les Industries de la Soierie* (Paris, 1961).

David Longfellow

Related entries: LYONS, REVOLTS IN; SILK INDUSTRY.

CAPELLE, GUILLAUME-ANTOINE-BENOIT (1775–1843), administrator and minister. He had at first heartily embraced the Revolution and served in the National Guard of his native department of Aveyron and later in the army. Under the Consulate, Jean-Antoine-Claude Chaptal employed him in his Ministry of the Interior. Capelle was appointed prefect at Livorno (February 1805) and Geneva (November 1810). Under Louis XVIII he was prefect of the Ain (June 1814) and the Doubs (July 1815). In January 1816 he entered the Council of State, and in 1823 he became secretary general of the Ministry of the Interior, where the listlessness of Jacques-Joseph-Guillaume Corbière left him in charge of business. When Jean-Baptiste de Martignac took over that department in January 1828, he removed Capelle by making him prefect at Versailles. Jules-Armand de Polignac and Charles-Ignace de Peyronnet, who wanted his help as an expert on electoral manipulation, created for him a special Ministry of Public Works (May 1830). Thus he was one of the signers of the fatal July Ordinances (1830). He managed to escape to England, where he was member of a council set up by Charles X, with Casimir de Blacas d'Aulps and Louis-Auguste-Victor de Bourmont.

G. de Maisonfort, *Notice . . . sur le baron Capelle* (Paris, 1846).

Guillaume de Bertier de Sauvigny

Related entries: BLACAS D'AULPS; BOURMONT; CHARLES X; COR-BIERE; COUNCIL OF STATE; JULY ORDINANCES; LOUIS XVIII; MAR-TIGNAC; NATIONAL GUARD; PEYRONNET; POLIGNAC.

LE CAPITOLE (1839–1840), ostensibly bonapartist newspaper of the July Monarchy. During the latter half of the reign of Louis-Philippe, a great many newspapers were founded with the simple intention of making money. The *Capitole*, founded on 15 June 1839, hoped to take advantage of the bonapartist sentiment prevailing at the time when the government was arranging for Napoleon's body to be brought from St. Helena to Paris. The paper was prosecuted for bonapartism at the time of Louis-Napoleon's landing at Boulogne and ceased publication on 3 December 1840.

C. Bellanger et al., *Histoire générale de la presse française*, 2 vols. (Paris, 1969).

Irene Collins

Related entry: BONAPARTISM.

CARBONARI or CHARBONNERIE, a secret revolutionary group opposed to the Bourbon Restoration government, most active from 1821 to 1823. The group took its name and much of its ritual and organization from an Italian revolutionary group of the time, which had named itself for the medieval supporters of the Guelphs who met secretly in the cabins of charcoal makers (*carbonari*) in the woods.

The first years of the Bourbon Restoration saw several plots against the government, as well as its short overthrow in the Hundred Days when Napoleon returned. In February 1820 the heir to the throne, the duke of Berry, was assassinated. The response of the government was repression, including tightened press censorship and an electoral law change that strengthened the very rich voters. In August 1820 the government found evidence of a conspiracy when soldiers at several places reported having been approached by officers and outsiders with talk of a proposed national uprising. A trial was held, and three men were condemned to death, including Captain Noel Nantil of Meurthe and the liberal attorney Joseph Rey of Grenoble. All three had fled the country, as had several others involved, including Nicolas Joubert and Pierre Dugied, who made contact with the Italian carbonari. This Italian secret group had just carried out the revolution of July 1820 in Naples. Returning to France, Joubert and Dugied started a French carbonari in May 1821 with a pyramidal organization like their Italian model. The local group or *vente* (''stand of timber'') had from eight to twenty members and sent one to the next higher level. The *ventes* on the second level each sent one member to the third level, and so on. Thus most members did not know the identity of the central *vente* at Paris. Each member promised to keep the secret, pay 1 franc per month, keep a gun and twenty-five cartridges ready, and obey the next higher *vente*. Initiation was an elaborate ritual, with the new member promising to keep the secret under pain of death and being presented with the secret dagger. But unlike the Italian model, the French carbonari ritual was largely devoid of religion, with the initiate promising to uphold equality before the law and freedom of the press and never to usurp the sovereignty of the French people. Most members supported a republic, and the bonapartists were further weakened with Napoleon's death in May 1821. Members often spoke in code—with, for example, ''purging the forest of wolves'' meaning ridding the country of tyrants and oppressors.

The carbonari grew rapidly, merged with another secret revolutionary group, the Knights of Liberty, and had perhaps 50,000 members within two years. Prominent political leaders were members, including liberal legislators the marquis de Lafayette (of American Revolution fame), Jacques-Antoine Manuel, and Nicolas Koechlin the industrialist. Other members were the philosopher Victor Cousin and possibly writer Honoré de Balzac. However, the carbonari were remarkably unsuccessful at revolution. Most of their conspiracies were nipped in the bud with quick trials and the execution of the leaders. In only one case was there an actual uprising.

That uprising was led by General Berton who, like many other carbonari, had attained glory under Napoleon but was retired at half-pay by the Restoration government. In February 1822 Berton, aided by a section of the National Guard, seized control of the town of Thouars. He issued a proclamation stating that ''all France has risen to recapture its independence,'' and telling soldiers that they would remain permanent slaves in the lowest ranks in the king's army. He signed the proclamation as the general commanding the National Army of the West. Leading a band of 100 semiuniformed followers, Berton marched on the city of Saumur, where he was persuaded to wait overnight before crossing the bridge into the fortified city. The band dispersed overnight, but forty-three were later arrested. Berton was caught four months later and sentenced to death along with five others. One of the others was apparently condemned because he had carried the tricolor flag from Thouars to Saumur, a task he had been chosen for more because of his size and strength than his political fervor.

Of the other carbonari plots, all stopped before they reached armed uprisings, usually when soldiers reported seditious proposals to their officers. The most famous was that of the four sergeants of La Rochelle. These unfortunate young soldiers, too open with their comrades about a planned uprising, were executed on 21 September 1822. They could probably have saved themselves by cooperating with the government in tracking down the carbonari leadership. Their silence earned them liberal sainthood. Their case and other carbonari trials led to criticism of the leaders, who took little risk themselves while their subalterns died. One conservative of the time compared the carbonari leaders to the Romans watching their gladiators. It was learned much later that Lafayette was on his way to a planned uprising in Belfort in January 1822 but turned back when a messenger told him of its failure.

There were more than a dozen trials of carbonari plotters. In general, the defense tried to keep the accused from implicating higher-ups, switched the blame to those conspirators who had fled to safety, and characterized key government witnesses as agents provocateurs. At least one case, that of Colonel Caron, was clearly entrapment. He was assigned two squadrons infiltrated with officers disguised as ordinary troopers. He was arrested after being tricked into leading a march for "the emperor," tried, and executed in October 1822.

The carbonari was effectively dead by the end of 1822. Although few former carbonari fought in the Revolution of July 1830, many served the bourgeois monarchy. Despite the carbonari dedication to republicanism, former members served the new king as minister of the interior, a prefect of police, prosecuting attorneys, and the first three ministers of justice. Perhaps this was because of the overwhelmingly middle-class membership of the carbonari. Studies have found very few wage earners in the group. Some historians see the carbonari's elaborate rituals and organization as evidence of its isolation from a true mass movement. To a large degree it was the tool of a new elite, largely bourgeois and military, in its struggle against the old aristocratic elite back in power in the Restoration. However, some carbonari, more truly dedicated to republicanism, were later active in leftist and socialist causes, including several key figures in the Saint-Simonian collectivist movement.

A. Spitzer, *Old Hatreds and Young Hopes, The French Carbonari against the Bourbon Restoration* (Cambridge, 1971).

Don Smith

Related entries: BERTON; CARON; COUSIN; *DEMI-SOLDES*; KOECHLIN, N.; LAFAYETTE; LA ROCHELLE, FOUR SERGEANTS OF; MANUEL; REY; SAINT-SIMONIANISM.

LA CARICATURE (1830–1835), republican newspaper of the July Monarchy. This weekly paper was founded on 4 November 1830 by Charles Philipon, a republican who believed that Louis-Philippe had betrayed the revolutionaries to whom he owed his throne by appointing moderate rather than radical ministers. Philipon's increasing hatred of the July Monarchy greatly influenced the chief artist working on the journal, Honoré Daumier. In 1831 Daumier began to depict Louis-Philippe in the shape of a pear. The whole of the satirical press took up this theme, and although Louis-Philippe professed to be amused by it, the *Caricature* sustained three heavy penalties in the law courts. It ceased publication on 27 August 1835 when a press bill (which became law on 9 September 1835) proposed that no drawing should be published without government permission.

I. Collins, *The Government and the Newspaper Press in France, 1814–1881* (Oxford, 1959); H. Marcel, *Daumier* (Paris, 1907).

Irene Collins

Related entries: DAUMIER; PRESS LAWS; REPUBLICANS.

CARNOT, LAZARE HIPPOLYTE (1801–1888), opposition deputy under the July Monarchy, republican minister of education in 1848. Second son of Lazare Carnot, Organizer of Victory in 1793–94, Hippolyte was born at St. Omer, 6 April 1801. Imbued from an early age with the ideals of his father, Carnot during the 1820s helped organize the republican Société des francs-parleurs, along with Jules Bastide and Godefroy Cavaignac. Carnot also was an early disciple of Henri de Saint-Simon, wrote for Saint-Simonian journals including *Le Producteur, Le Globe*, and *L'Organisateur*, and opened his home to Saint-Simonian lectures in 1828.

An insurgent during the July Days of 1830, Carnot thereafter continued writing for Saint-Simonian periodicals but broke away from the group led by Père Enfantin at Ménilmontant. Carnot also edited *La Revue encyclopédique* and began to write on educational topics. In 1837 he attempted unsuccessfully to win election to the Chamber of Deputies; in 1839, however, he was elected in Paris, a seat that he retained to the end of the July Monarchy. In 1847, to the dismay of his fellow republicans, Carnot published a pamphlet, *Les Radicaux et la Charte*, in which he advocated close cooperation with the dynastic opposition; he also participated in the 1847 Banquet Campaign for electoral and parliamentary reform.

Although Carnot played no active role in the February Revolution of 1848, the Provisional Government immediately appointed him minister of education, a position that he retained under the Executive Commission and briefly under the government of Eugène Cavaignac. Among a number of innovations Carnot introduced was the creation of a short-lived Ecole d'administration, modeled on the Ecole polytechnique and intended to prepare career governmental administrators. Carnot also sponsored evening classes for workers in the cities and small libraries in some rural communes. He increased the salaries of school teachers, whom he exhorted to educate the new mass electorate in the principles of democratic republicanism. Carnot's major project was a comprehensive plan to make the French primary school system free, compulsory, and secular. But the proposal was not ready for formal introduction until after the June Days, when the reviving forces of reaction in the National Assembly, unable to persuade General Cavaignac to dismiss him, on 5 July 1848 voted nonconfidence in Carnot, after which he resigned; by 1850 the Legislative Assembly had supplanted his plan with the Falloux Law, which reflected conservative and religious principles.

Unsuccessful in the parliamentary elections of 1849, Carnot regained a seat in a partial election in 1850 and was one of the deputies who sought unsuccessfully to oppose the coup d'état of Louis-Napoleon Bonaparte on 2 December 1851. In the first balloting under the rigorous system of the Second Empire in 1852, Carnot was one of only three republicans elected, but all three surrendered their seats after refusing to take the oath of loyalty to the prince-president. Carnot again won election in 1857 but again lost his seat for refusing to take the oath. He finally took a seat in the Legislative Body in 1864 after winning a by-election in Paris. After the fall of the empire on 4 September 1870, Carnot became mayor of the seventeenth arrondissement of Paris and in February 1871 was elected to the National Assembly from the department of Seine-et-Oise. President of the group of the republican Left, Carnot was one of the first senators elected under the Constitution of 1875, in December of that year. He lived to see his son Sadi Carnot become president of the Third Republic in 1887 and was the eldest member of the Senate when he died in Paris on 16 March 1888.

H. Carnot, *Le Ministère de l'instruction publique et des cultes* (Paris, 1848); G. Cogniot, *La Question scolaire en 1848 et la loi Falloux* (Paris, 1948); F. A. de Luna, *The French Republic under Cavaignac, 1848* (Princeton, 1969).

Frederick A. de Luna

Related entries: BASTIDE; CARNOT, L.-N.-M.; CAVAIGNAC, G.-E.-L.; CAVAIGNAC, L.-E.; *LE GLOBE; L'ORGANISATEUR;* PROVISIONAL GOVERNMENT; SAINT-SIMONIANISM.

CARNOT, LAZARE-NICOLAS-MARGUERITE (1753–1823), soldier, engineer, republican revolutionary, member of the Committee of Public Safety, Organizer of Victory, and minister of war. Lazare Carnot was born in Nolay (Côte d'Or), the second son of Claude Carnot, a lawyer and notary, and Marguérite Pothier, who had eighteen children (seven surviving to adulthood). Carnot was admitted to the engineering school at Mezières after he had established that his family had lived nobly for several generations. Nevertheless he espoused radical ideas and served on the Committee of Public Safety during the Terror. A lifelong republican, he opposed the establishment of the Empire in 1804. Nevertheless, the brilliant military engineer offered his services to Napoleon when the Allies invaded France in 1814. He was promoted to general of division, charged with defending Antwerp (his first real military command). He held the city for three months, until ordered to surrender it by Louis XVIII, and presented the king with a widely read memoir on organizing the Bourbon government. During the Hundred Days, Carnot served as minister of the interior and was made a count and peer. He founded the Society for Elementary Instruction in April 1815 and advised against the Waterloo campaign. Chosen as a member of the Provisional Government (22 June) after Napoleon's second abdication, he urged the emperor to go to the United States and resigned on 8 July. Proscribed by the Bourbons on 24 July, he secured a passport from Alexander I and traveled through Brussels, Vienna, and Warsaw with his son Hippolyte, finally settling in Magdeburg with the permission of the Prussian government in early 1816. He lived there until his death on 2 August 1823. His remains were returned to France and buried in the Pantheon in August 1889.

Carnot was a good republican, a remarkably gifted military administrator, and one of the uncontrovertibly great figures of the Revolution. Absolutely honest, he suffered from a certain political naiveté, which largely accounts for the low points in his career. Justly remembered as the Organizer of Victory in 1793–94, with statues in Nolay and Antwerp, he founded a republican dynasty in France. His son Hippolyte (1801–88) was a leading opponent of the July Monarchy, minister of education under the Second Republic, and a senator under the Third. Another son, Nicolas (1796–1832) became a noted physicist and pioneer in thermodynamic theory. His grandson (Hippolyte's son), Sadi, was a minister and president (1887–94) of the Third Republic.

E. Arago, *Biographie de Lazare-Nicolas-Marguérite Carnot* (Paris, 1850); F. Aulard, *Receuil des Actes du Comite de Salut Public avec la correspondance officielle des representants en mission*, 27 vols. (Paris, 1895); A. Chuquet, *Les Guerres de la Révolution*, 11 vols. (Paris, 1914); H. Depasse, *Carnot* (Paris, 1883); H. Dupré, *Lazare Carnot* (Oxford, Ohio, 1940); M. Lyons, *France under the Directors* (Cambridge, 1975); M. Reinhard, *Le Grand Carnot*, 2 vols. (Paris, 1950–52); S. Ross, *Quest for Victory* (Cranbury, N. J., 1973).

David Longfellow

Related entries: CARNOT, L.-H.; HUNDRED DAYS; SOCIETY FOR ELEMENTARY INSTRUCTION.

CARON, AUGUSTIN-JOSEPH (1774–1822), army officer and leader of a carbonarist conspiracy. Caron was a native of Alsace and dragoon lieutenant colonel, a veteran of the Revolutionary and Napoleonic wars, retired on half-pay at the Restoration. He was active in anti-Bourbon conspiracies in the Haut-Rhin by 1820 and soon came to the attention of the political police. Acquitted of involvement in the Paris military conspiracy of August 1820, he devised a plan to free the imprisoned leaders of the conspiracy of Belfort (December 1821-January 1822) from the fortress of Colmar. Encouraged by army officers in the pay of the government, who overcame Caron's hesitations and even supplied several squadrons of regular cavalry to carry out the plan, Caron was arrested the night of 2 July 1822. He was tried by a military tribunal in Strasbourg (18–23 September) and sentenced to death, despite charges of entrapment and attacks on the government's methods in the Chamber by General Maximilien-Sébastien Foy and other liberal deputies. He was shot by firing squad on 1 October. The government's agents were promoted and given a cash reward of 1,500 francs. Caron's entire enterprise was marked by a surprising indifference to the possibility of government surveillance and infiltration.

E. Guillon, *Les Complots militaires sous la Restauration* (Paris, 1912); *Procès d'Augustin-Joseph Caron* (Strasbourg, n.d.); A. B. Spitzer, *Old Hatreds and New Hopes* (Cambridge, Mass., 1971); H. Wahl, "Les manifestations de l'opposition libérale et les complots militaires dans le Haut-Rhin sous la Restauration (1820–1824)" *Revue d'Alsace* 92 (1953).

David Longfellow

Related entries: BAZAR CONSPIRACY; CARBONARI; *DEMI-SOLDES;* FOY.

CARREL, NICOLAS ARMAND (1800–1836), journalist, soldier, historian, essayist, and coeditor of *Le National* (1829–1836). Within an adventurous life of thirty-six years, Armand Carrel's roles ranged from guerrilla fighter to philosopher of history. Although a classicist by conviction (he once challenged the romanticist Victor Hugo to a duel), the handsome Carrel's personal life was laden with a tragic love affair, futile heroics, and other romantic ingredients.

Carrel, as a young soldier and Bonapartist-tinged liberal, took part in a carbonari plot among the troops at Belfort in December 1821. At the same time a more famous French carbonari plot was unmasked at La Rochelle. Both conspiracies were exposed, and Carrel, lucky to escape with his life, went underground for a time with some fellow plotters, including Joseph Mérilhou, later a prominent liberal deputy and lawyer. He associated closely with leading philosophers, academicians, and artists, including Victor Cousin, Augustin Thierry, André Ampère, and the Scheffer brothers, Ary, Charles-Arnold, and Henry.

In 1823, Carrel embarked on a new illegal adventure: to join the international guerrilla forces in Catalonia opposed to King Ferdinand, who was supported by Louis XVIII of France. Carrel, landing near Barcelona with his boatload of Bonapartist, Polish, and Piedmontese expatriates, found the rebel force too disunited for an effective liaison. He was able, however, to witness the struggle at close range. The alliance of France with Spain's reactionary king was deemed shameful by French liberals, and Carrel's articles in the press concerning it rekindled the embarrassment for several years. Carrel played upon his own patriotism and honor as a soldier to attack French foreign policy. His 1830 articles in the *National*, which scorned Jules-Armand de Polignac's Algerian campaign as a wasteful and opportunistic ploy, also praised the virgin honor of the new Restoration army.

Carrel turned to writing articles for the Saint-Simonians' socialist journal *Le Producteur* in 1825 but broke with them shortly. Having discovered he was not a socialist and having never felt a strong sense of social equality, he grew by 1830 to appreciate the working class for the first time as the heart of the nation. By 1826, he was working on a new, but short-lived, republican journal sponsored by the marquis de Lafayette, the *Revue américaine*. Also in that year he had written in the *Constitutionnel* (14 January 1826), a widely acclaimed review of his friend Adolphe Thiers' history of the French Revolution. Most of the liberal historians by this time were popularizing two themes: to rescue the French Revolution from the calculated stigma of the Terror and to educate French readers in the history of England's Glorious Revolution, heavy with implied analogies. Carrel's politics were now established, republican, and liberal but with no hope of a stable republic. He moved naturally into the Orleanist orbit.

Carrel's tendentious, propagandistic history of England's Restoration era was published by his friend A. Sautelet (later manager of the *National*) in 1827. The work, which came close to sedition by nearly suggesting that James II could be taken for Charles X, was popular enough to receive an English translation in 1846. Carrel's overly candid preface to the first edition had to be edited to pass the censorship panel. Carrel continued to write his barbed historical sketches and antigovernment editorials in the *Temps* and the *Revue de Paris* until 1829, when he was invited to join a proposed Orleanist newspaper, to be called *Le National*.

With François Mignet and Thiers, Carrel completed the *National*'s brilliant triumvirate of journalistic kingmakers. During the final seven months of the Restoration, Carrel's articles in the *National* concentrated on three ideas: to warn of an impending ultra coup against the Charter and thus to fortify against it; to hint broadly of the Orleans alternative as the only sensible one; and to discredit the government's patriotic pretensions in regard to Algeria, in the last case even flaunting his latent Bonapartist coloration. During the July Days of 1830, Carrel signed the journalists' manifesto and later declared that those three days made a democrat of him.

When his chosen king, Louis-Philippe, did ascend the throne, Carrel's disappointment grew rapidly. As he continued on the *National*, replacing Thiers, who joined the government, both Carrel and the paper became republican. The *National* endured repeated prosecutions under the new regime, which had promised a press truly free. The notorious September Laws of 1835 provided for guilt by indirect association, and Carrel and other republicans, as well as royalists, were imprisoned.

On 24 July 1836, Carrel died of a wound taken in a duel with rival journalist Emile de Girardin, editor of *La Presse*, whose cheap and popular newspaper had offended Carrel's honor. Neither man really wanted the meeting, and Carrel was said to have misfired deliberately. His fellow republican Lafayette said of him, "He was the master of us all."

C. F. Brown Jr., "Armand Carrel, His Historical and Political Ideas" (master's thesis, 1949); R. Nobécourt, *Armand Carrel, journaliste* (Rouen, 1935), and *La vie d'Armand Carrel* (Paris, 1930); C. Sainte-Beuve, *Causeries du Lundi*.

Daniel Rader

Related entries: CARBONARI; COUSIN; GIRARDIN, E.; LA ROCHELLE, FOUR SERGEANTS OF; MERILHOU; *LE NATIONAL*; REPUBLICANS; *LA REVUE DE PARIS*; SAINT-SIMONIANISM; *LE TEMPS*; THIERS.

CASSATION, COURT OF. See COURT OF CASSATION.

CASTELLANE, ESPRIT-VICTOR-ELISABETH-BONIFACE, COMTE DE (1788–1862), officer of the Empire and Restoration, peer of the July Monarchy, senator and marshal of the Second Empire. Castellane was born in Paris on 21 March 1788. He enlisted in the army as a common soldier in 1804 and rose to sublieutenant in February 1806. He served in the army of Italy and in December 1807 became aide-de-camp to Georges Mouton in the Pyrenees. He campaigned in Spain in 1808, especially participating in the battles of Rio-Socco and Burgos. In 1809 he fought in Germany, for which Napoleon named him a chevalier of the Empire. He was promoted to captain in 1810 and given the Legion of Honor. Castellane participated in the Russian campaign from Smolensk to Moscow to the Berezina. At Moscow on 3 October 1812, he was promoted to major. On 1 June 1813 he became commander of the first regiment of honor guards and fought in this post until the end of the Empire.

At the fall of Napoleon, Castellane rallied to the Bourbons and on 27 September 1815 was made colonel of the hussars of Bas-Rhin. Louis XVIII also gave him the Order of Saint Louis and promoted him in the Legion of Honor. In 1822 he became colonel of the hussars of the guard, and on 14 January 1824 he was promoted to *maréchal de camp*. He participated in the Spanish campaign, where he gained some attention for his generous treatment of the Spanish population. He was recalled from Spain in 1827, allegedly because he refused to sanction the political persecution demanded by the king of Spain, Ferdinand VII. In 1829 Castellane became inspector of seven regiments. He also served on the general council of the department of Allier. But in early July 1830 he was dismissed for having supported an opposition candidate, and he subsequently condemned the July Ordinances.

Bourbon disfavor, however, helped bring him success under the July Monarchy, which in 1831 appointed him to command the department of Haute-Sâone and in April 1832 made him commander of an infantry brigade in the Army of the North. As such he participated in the siege of Antwerp, which earned him promotion to lieutenant general on 9 January 1833. On 3 October 1837 he was appointed to the Chamber of Peers where he generally supported the government, participating actively in debates on military subjects and child labor. He carried out assignments in Africa and in 1847 became commander of the Fourteenth Military Division based at Rouen. That year he also received the grand cross of the Legion of Honor. At Rouen he learned of the proclamation of a Republic on 24 February 1848. He initially refused to accept the Republic and took his troops to seize control of the high ground near Rouen. But on 28 February, after the workers of Rouen rose up, he recognized the Republic. He was quickly relieved of his command and retired on 17 April 1848.

Louis-Napoleon recalled Castellane in 1849 to command first at Lyons and then at Nantes and Rennes. He strongly supported the policies of the prince-president and the coup of 2 December 1851. A few days after the coup, he was appointed general in chief of the army at Lyons. On 26 January 1852 he became a senator, and on the following 2 December Napoleon III promoted him to marshal in consideration of the aid he had given the 1851 coup. He became commander of the Fourth Army Corps in 1859.

Throughout his career he was noted for his flamboyance, his eccentricity, and his harshness. Castellane died in Paris on 16 September 1862, leaving a journal that was published in 1895–97.

J. Monteilhet, *Les Institutions militaires de la France* (Paris, 1936); A. Robert et al., *Dictionnaire des parlementaires français* (Paris, 1889–91).

James K. Kieswetter

Related entries: CHAMBER OF PEERS; COUP D'ETAT OF 2 DECEMBER 1851; JULY ORDINANCES; REVOLUTION OF 1830; REVOLUTION OF 1848; SPAIN, 1823 FRENCH INVASION OF.

CATHOLICISM, LIBERAL. See LIBERAL CATHOLICISM.

CATHOLICISM, SOCIAL. See SOCIAL CATHOLICISM.

CATHOLIC SOCIETY OF GOOD BOOKS (1824–1830), a society to distribute books favorable to the Catholic church. The abbé Julien Barrault, assistant in a parish of Bordeaux, had created a sort of circulating library, expanding its operations all over the diocese. The leaders of the Paris congrégation took up the idea, establishing a formal association with the government's permission (August 1824). The *Société catholique des bons livres* also later received the approval of the Holy See (1827). The proclaimed purpose was to provide a counterweight against the flood of impious and anticlerical literature pouring from the Parisian presses. For a yearly subscription of 25 francs, members received three volumes; the rest of the proceedings would be used to distribute moral literature cheaply and to promote by competitive awards the writing of books of Christian inspiration. The first president was Mathieu de Montmorency, the grandmaster of the secret society of the Knights of the Faith and, after his death (March 1826), the pious duc de Rivière. In December 1825, the society claimed to have enlisted 7,900 subscribers and to have distributed 300,000 volumes in a year. But by 1829 its activities seemed to have waned, and after 1830 it survived only locally.

J.-B. Duroselle, "Les Filiales de la Congrégation," *Revue d'histoire ecclésiastique* 50 (1955); *Moniteur universel*; 6, 8 August 1824, 9 December 1825, 28 November 1826, 30 January 1827, 21 February, 17 December 1829.

Guillaume de Bertier de Sauvigny

Related entries: CHEVALIERS DE LA FOI; CONGREGATION; MONTMORENCY.

CAUCHOIS-LEMAIRE, LOUIS-AUGUSTE-FRANCOIS (1789–1861), liberal journalist and politician, first openly to propose an Orléans alternative during the Restoration, republican during July Monarchy. Cauchois-Lemaire traveled nearly the entire course of French opposition journalism from a near-Bonapartist liberal in 1814 to Orleanist in the later Restoration, to republican under Louis-Philippe. From December 1814 to October 1815 he edited and published the impudent satirical journal, *Le Nain jaune*, during which period he gave this periodical two other titles to evade suppression. Although King Louis XVIII read it with amusement and was said to have given it financial support, it finally became too brazen for the ministry of police and the ultra legislature and was suppressed. Among its sins was a eulogy of Lazare-Nicolas-Marguérite Carnot and a suggestion that the duke of Orléans was France's William III.

Cauchois-Lemaire sought refuge in Brussels, where he soon edited and exported le *Nain jaune réfugié*, edited by a society of "anti-Extinguishers." This term refers to a custom of the *Nain* of granting awards: "order of the extinguisher" for extreme reactionaries and "order of the weathervane" for those judged hypocrites. Cauchois-Lemaire, however, abused his asylum by attacking Dutch-Belgian authorities and was soon a fugitive from the police of those jurisidictions and even of Prussia, to which he was extradited for trial. Escaping his Prussian escort, he sought refuge in the Hague and other cities. He returned to Paris in 1819, as the laws of the press, though severe, were now less arbitrary and began publishing again. Almost immediately he faced prosecution anew for a book glorifying the Hundred Days as well as a brochure exposing the "secret government" of the Jesuits. He was acquitted on these charges but nevertheless spent the next year in St. Pélagie prison for a published anthology of previously censored *Nain* articles. Even in prison, he managed to have several anonymous pamphlets smuggled out by visitors.

Upon his release in 1821, he started his collaboration with the staff of the *Miroir des spectacles*, ostensibly cultural and literary but, like *Nain*, a political lampoon at heart. From 1823 to 1828, it was called *La Pandore* and enjoyed a steady popularity.

Cauchois-Lemaire, along with Jacques-Antoine Manuel, Jacques Laffitte, Charles-Guillaume Etienne, and others, also helped launch the largest of the liberal newspapers opposed to the Bourbon Restoration, the *Constitutionnel*. This giant of the Left also bore several titles on its masthead before making a final choice in 1819. When young Adolphe Thiers joined the paper, a clique grew around him and quarreled with the older group. Among these divisions, besides ideology and policy, was an attempt by Cauchois-Lemaire to purchase a controlling interest in the paper. Cauchois-Lemaire's wealthy backers included Antoine Gévaudan, an entrepreneur of stagecoach lines. In a paper whose policy was limited to anticlericalism and attacking ultra designs, Cauchois-Lemaire's signed editorials were vigorous but predictable.

Then in December 1827, as Joseph de Villèle's government was starting to collapse following an episode of rioting and street barricades, Cauchois-Lemaire produced a propaganda sensation. A pamphlet, appearing under his name alone, bore the title *On the Current Crisis, Letter to his Royal Highness, the Duke of Orléans*. Its sixty-nine pages energetically attacked not only Villèle but the entire

Restoration. As a conclusion, Cauchois-Lemaire addressed the duke of Orléans in what he termed "parables" but that clearly called on the duke to prepare himself for the throne, to replace the existing dynasty. Everyone in the opposition, from Lafayette to Chateaubriand, either denounced the pamphlet or dismissed it as an aberration of taste. The duke pretended it did not exist.

Cauchois-Lemaire was put on trial, along with the publishers of the booklet, Ponthieu and Schubart. The latter received sentences of three months and fines of 500 francs. The writer, charged with attempting to change the order of royal succession, among other crimes, was ordered to La Force for fifteen months and to pay a 2,000 franc fine. The court rejected the prosecutor's plea for a maximum term (four years) because no tangible effects had resulted. But the Orléans kite had been sent aloft for all to see, and it would fly more easily henceforth. The trial itself, as with all other Restoration trials, was allowed wide publicity under the press laws, and this enhanced the pamphlet's message. During the later part of his term, Cauchois-Lemaire formed a close friendship with a new fellow inmate, the poet Pierre-Jean de Béranger, and many stars of the opposition, including Benjamin Constant and Laffitte, visited both men on several Sundays.

When the July Ordinances appeared in 1830, Cauchois-Lemaire was one of the group with Thiers who wrote the manifesto of the journalists against Polignac's edicts, the first overt act of resistance in the Revolution of 1830.

In the new reign of Louis-Philippe, Cauchois-Lemaire rejected a 6,000 franc pension to protect his independence and was among the first of the recent Orleanist kingmakers to defect. In 1832, he began to edit *Bon sens*, which, while not wholly republican, advocated a more liberalized monarchy and greater popular representation. *Bon sens* stood between René-Théophile Chatelain's liberal *Courrier* and Francois-Vincent Raspail's democratic and socialist *Réformateur*. The heated feuds among these opposition papers were in contrast to the united front the Left had presented in 1830 and encouraged the government to suppress *Bon sens* in 1834. Cauchois-Lemaire remained active in the opposition through the Aide-toi electoral society, where he associated with Armand Carrel.

He was acquitted at a trial in 1835 for articles in *Bon sens* and joined in founding another paper in 1836, *Le Siècle*. *Bon sens* was revived under Louis Blanc's editorship, but in 1839 Cauchois-Lemaire, worn out by a life of losing battles, retired from the journalistic wars. Long a student of history, he accepted a position as royal archivist in 1840 and undertook a history of the July Revolution. Only one volume of this work appeared: a collection of memoirs and documents.

E. Hatin, *Histoire de la presse française* (Paris, 1859–61); D. Rader, *The Journalists and the July Revolution in France* (The Hague, 1973); P. Thureau-Dangin, *Le parti libéral sous la Restauration* (Paris, 1876); G. Weill, *Histoire du parti républicain en France, 1814–1870* (Paris, 1928).

Daniel Rader

Related entries: BERANGER; *LE BON SENS*; CARREL; *LE CONSTITU-TIONNEL*; MANUEL; *LE MIROIR DES SPECTACLES*; *LE NAIN JAUNE*; PO-LIGNAC; PRESS LAWS; RASPAIL; *LE REFORMATEUR*; THIERS.

CAUCHY, AUGUSTIN-LOUIS (1789–1857), mathematician. As a student at the Ecole polytechnique, he astounded his masters by his precocious gift for the most abstract mathematics, so much so that he passed immediately from the student bench to a professor's chair and was a member of the Academy of Sciences at the age of twenty-seven. The five hundred learned papers he produced in his lifetime made him by far the most prolific mathematician of his time. This scientific activity did not prevent him from devoting much time and effort to works of Christian charity as a member of the Congrégation. In 1830, he held the chair of mechanics at the Ecole polytechnique, but because he was a staunch legitimist, he refused to take the oath of fidelity to the new regime and lost the position. He went first to Turin, where a chair of mathematics had been created for him by King Carlo-Alberto. In 1832, he responded to the call of his old master, King Charles X, then exiled in Prague, who asked him to supervise the scientific education of his grandson and heir. In 1838, he was able to return to France, but, being denied any official appointment, he taught in private schools. In their attitude toward this stubborn legitimist, the Second Republic and Louis-Napoleon were more tolerant than the July Monarchy. In 1848 Cauchy was given a chair of mathematical astronomy in the University of Paris, and after 1852 the emperor let him hold it despite his refusal to take the oath demanded from all office-holders.

M. d'Ocagne, *Hommes et choses de science*, vol. 1 (Paris, 1930); C. A. Valson, *La vie et les travaux du baron Cauchy* (Paris, 1868).

Guillaume de Bertier de Sauvigny

Related entries: ACADEMY OF SCIENCES; BORDEAUX; CHARLES X; CONGREGATION; ECOLE POLYTECHNIQUE.

CAULAINCOURT, ARMAND-LOUIS-AUGUSTIN, MARQUIS DE (1773–1827), Duc de Vicence, general, diplomat, and minister of the Empire. The future duc de Vicence was born on 9 December 1773 at Caulaincourt (Aisne), the son of a lieutenant general and scion of one of the best French noble families. He began a military career at age fifteen and by 1791 was a general staff captain. Caulaincourt and his father both shortly lost their ranks due to their noble lineage, and Caulaincourt was imprisoned in 1793. But he quickly gained his freedom and joined a Paris battalion as a grenadier, rising to become Napoleon's foreign minister in 1813. In 1814 when the emperor could no longer avoid unconditional abdication, it was Caulaincourt who negotiated the terms of the treaty of Fontainebleau. It was to his influence with czar Alexander I that Napoleon owed even his sovereignty over Elba.

Charles-Maurice de Talleyrand offered Caulaincourt a position in the new Bourbon government, which he refused. During the first Restoration, Caulaincourt returned to his home department and married Mme. de Canisy, a marriage he had delayed because of Napoleon's opposition. During the Hundred Days, Caulaincourt returned as foreign minister, continuing his futile efforts to preserve the peace. On 2 June 1815 Napoleon named him a peer. After Waterloo he served briefly in the provisional government commission, although still remaining loyal to Napoleon. Then he left Paris at the return of Louis XVIII. Had it not been for the influence of Alexander I, Caulaincourt undoubtedly would have been proscribed by the Bourbons. He henceforth retired and devoted much effort to clearing himself of blame in the Enghien affair. He died in Paris on 19 February 1827, leaving several volumes of memoirs, three of which were published in 1933. Caulaincourt had been one of Napoleon's most able, honest, and loyal servants, as well as one who refused to advance himself by sycophancy.

H. Butterfield, *The Peace Tactics of Napoleon, 1806–1808* (Cambridge, 1929); A. Frangulis, *Dictionnaire diplomatique comprenant les biographies des diplomates du moyen age à nos jours* (Paris, 1933); H. Nicolson, *The Congress of Vienna* (New York, 1961); A. Vandal, *Napoléon et Alexandre Ier* (Paris, 1891–96); E. Whitcomb, *Napoleon's Diplomatic Service* (Durham, 1979).

James K. Kieswetter

Related entries: HUNDRED DAYS; LOUIS XVIII; TALLEYRAND.

CAUSSIDIERE, LOUIS-MARC (1808–1861), artisan, revolutionary, and prefect of police (February-May 1848). Son of an artisan and veteran of the First Republic, the tall, robust, and energetic Marc Caussidière first became involved in politics in the workers' violence in St.-Etienne in 1831. A silk worker by trade, he was also active as a cloth merchant. His father helped to organize the insurrection of 1834 in St.-Etienne, a brother was brutally killed, and Marc was singled out with 163 other supposed leaders for prosecution. After being found guilty by the Cour des pairs, he was imprisoned at Mont-St.-Michel. He would have escaped, except that his regard for a fellow prisoner, who broke his leg in the attempted escape, led to his recapture. He was released in the general amnesty of 1837.

Caussidière's magnetic personality pushed him into commerce in Paris. He gained the backing of well-known radical politicians for his business adventures, while also apparently belonging to Auguste Blanqui's Society of the Seasons. He was not involved in the Seasons' attempted insurrection in May 1839, and he became a wine salesman and a hawker for the new journal *La Réforme*. He is credited with gaining 2,000 new subscribers for this radical journal.

Events in Paris in the winter of 1847–48 were volatile. Caussidière had formed a secret revolutionary group near the end of 1847, and the funeral of his father, as a veteran of the First Republic and of the workers' revolts of the 1830s, drew a huge crowd in January 1848. At the first hint of revolt in February, the son set to work to found the Second Republic. Caussidière grabbed his rifle, occupied the prefecture of police on 24 February, and refused to relinquish his position to anyone. Recognizing the devotion of Caussidière and his place among the men of *La Réforme*, the members of the Provisional Government confirmed him as the new prefect of police on 17 March, the same day he demonstrated his loyalty to the new government by resisting the attempts of Blanqui to organize antigovernment demonstrations.

Although a staunch supporter of the government, Caussidière had strong ties to the workers of Paris and the men of the secret societies. He organized his own police force (*garde du peuple*) from among these groups. This force allowed him some freedom of action, kept order in Paris, and frightened the middle class and conservative elements of society. He put these former political criminals in consular-guard blue uniforms with red facing and named the companies after revolutionary heroes. One was called the company of Saint Just. With this guard he made good his claim, "I brought order with disorder."

The flamboyant Caussidière enhanced his image by acting the part of the policeman; he roamed Paris wearing a helmet, two pistols in his belt, and a saber at his side. A romantic, Caussidière believed the people of Paris should see the prefect of police in the proper light. His desire to impress carried over into his political career. At the first meeting of the Constituent Assembly, he arrived dressed in the brilliant white waistcoat of a deputy of the Convention.

In the politics of the early days of the revolution, Caussidière tried to maintain a center position. He opposed Blanqui for his tactics, including the poor effect it had on his *garde du peuple*. He urged the government not to postpone the elections, since he believed any delay would worsen the government's situation, yet he was a fast friend of Alexandre-Auguste Ledru-Rollin. By the first week in May, Caussidière was the only socialist left in the government, partly because he had managed to remain out of the limelight in the events of 16 April. At the same time, Caussidière won the backing of the clubs of Paris for election to the Constituent Assembly. He was elected twentieth among the thirty-four deputies for the Seine. It was not in the Assembly, however, that he was to make his mark.

On 9 May he refused to issue a proclamation condemning the proposed demonstration, planned for the fifteenth, in favor of the revolution in Poland on the grounds that it would only give the backers of the demonstration more publicity. He downplayed the importance of the demonstration, so when the hall of the Assembly was invaded by Blanqui and friends, Caussidière's lack of precautions seemed to implicate him in this threat to the government. Although he made an elegant defense of his activities as prefect of police before the Assembly, he was forced to resign. His *garde du peuple* was also disbanded.

Caussidière resigned his seat in the Assembly at the same time and appealed to the people in the by-elections of 4 June. His middle position between the socialists and neo-Jacobins and his success in maintaining order in the difficult days of March and April allowed him to finish first among the eleven deputies elected in the Seine. Although he sat with the Montagnards and did his best to prevent the conflict that developed over the disbanding of the National Workshops, his general attitude in favor of order led him to support General Eugène Cavaignac in repressing the workers in June.

As the conservatives gained full control during the summer of 1848, they moved against those allied with the people. Louis Blanc and Caussidière were accused of complicity in the events of 15 May and of June. Neither contemporaries nor historians have believed the charges, but to the men of the Assembly, Caussidière represented the potential power of the people. He had harnessed this power in support of the government, but the riots of the fifteenth showed the dangers involved. The Assembly voted to remove the parliamentary immunity of Blanc and Caussidière. The government itself was more sympathetic to both, and they were allowed to leave for England.

After fifteen years of insurrectionary politics, this romantic yet practical man had failed to bring his vision of government to France. He spent the prosperous 1850s being a merchant of wines and spirits to the British aristocracy in London. He was allowed to return to Paris shortly before his death.

M. Caussidière, *Mémoires de Caussidière, ex-préfet et répresentant du peuple* (Paris, 1849), also published as *Memoires of Citizen Caussidière* (London, 1849).

Thomas Beck

Related entries: BLANC; BLANQUI, L.-A.; CAVAIGNAC, L.-E.; CLUBS, POLITICAL; CONSTITUTION OF 1848; LEDRU-ROLLIN; NATIONAL WORKSHOPS; PROVISIONAL GOVERNMENT; *LA REFORME*; REVOLUTION OF 1848.

CAUTION MONEY. See PRESS LAWS.

CAVAIGNAC, GODEFROY-ELEONORE-LOUIS (1800–1845), republican insurgent leader during the Revolution of 1830 and prominent opponent of the July Monarchy. The son of Jean-Baptiste Cavaignac, Jacobin member of the National Convention, Godefroy Cavaignac from an early age was imbued with the republican convictions of his father. After Jean-Baptiste was exiled by the Second Restoration in 1815, Godefroy spent some time with him in regicide circles in Brussels. Upon his return to Paris to study law, he became active in student secret societies and was an early member of the carbonari. During the 1820s Cavaignac together with Hippolyte Carnot, Jules Bastide, and other young republicans formed the Société des francs-parleurs, which affiliated with the liberal organization Aide-toi, le ciel t'aidera. Following the violent street demonstrations in Paris in November 1827, Cavaignac and other republicans tried to organize secret municipalities in each of the twelve arrondissements of Paris to prepare for an eventual revolution.

In the spring of 1830, Cavaignac was among those republicans who joined with the liberals in the campaign against the Polignac ministry, appearing notably at a banquet in April honoring the 221 deputies who had voted nonconfidence. During the Revolution of 1830, Cavaignac was one of the leaders of the column of insurgents that invaded the Tuileries Palace on 29 July. After the dramatic acceptance of Louis-Philippe by the titular republican leader, the marquis de Lafayette, at the Hôtel de ville, Cavaignac was also one of the young republican leaders whom the Orleanists sought to placate; thus Cavaignac had an audience with the duc d' Orleans the evening of 31 July and soon thereafter with Charles-Maurice de Talleyrand.

In the wake of the revolution, Cavaignac became a captain in the newly constituted National Guard and a prominent member of the Société des amis du peuple, a new organization of republicans that advocated universal suffrage and also sought to appeal to the workers by introducing a mild social program.

Within a few months of the July Revolution, Cavaignac was one of those republicans who actively showed their displeasure with the new regime. He participated in the Parisian demonstrations in October 1830 demanding the execution of Jules de Polignac and other former ministers of Charles X, as well as those in December during the trial of the ministers. Brought to trial himself with others involved in these activities, Cavaignac in April 1831 created a stir with his proud public declaration of his republican faith, inspired by the memory of the Convention, and was acquitted. Cavaignac was tried once more for involvement in the abortive Parisian insurrection of June 1832 and once more was acquitted. In December 1832 the government sought to crush the Amis du peuple by charging the leaders with being members of an illegal organization. Cavaignac as their spokesman defended the right of association, and once more the jury acquitted the republicans. And when the Amis du peuple was officially suppressed shortly afterward, Cavaignac helped found a new secret Société des droits de l'homme, of which he became president in 1833. Cavaignac in the early 1830s also wrote for republican periodicals such as *La Tribune* and the *Revue républicaine*, edited a collection of articles, *Paris révolutionnaire*, and wrote some romantic novels.

Following the abortive Parisian insurrection of 1834, Cavaignac was once more arrested along with other republican leaders and was one of the principal spokesmen at the mass trial held in 1835 before the Chamber of Peers. In July 1835, after spending a year in prison, Cavaignac and several other republicans escaped and went into exile in England. There he became a correspondent for the republican newspaper, *Le National*, but on his return to France after receiving amnesty in 1840, he found *Le National* too moderate and in 1842 became editor of the more radical though ephemeral *Journal du peuple*. The following year Cavaignac became editor of Alexandre-Auguste Ledru-Rollin's new radical journal, *La Réforme*; he also wrote for Louis Blanc's *La Revue du progrès*. In addition to articles on domestic political and social issues, Cavaignac wrote on Algeria, after visiting his brother Louis-Eugène there in 1841 and 1843. Upon his death in 1845, republicans commissioned François Rude to produce a remarkable bronze statue of Cavaignac for his tomb in Montmartre Cemetery. Another statue of Cavaignac adorns the Hôtel de ville in Paris.

F. A. de Luna, *The French Republic under Cavaignac, 1848* (Princeton, 1969); G. Perreux, *Au Temps des sociétés secrètes* (Paris, 1930); I. Tchernoff, *Le Parti républicain sous la monarchie de juillet* (Paris, 1905); G. Weill, *Histoire du parti républicain en France, 1814–1870* (Paris, 1928).

Frederick A. de Luna

Related entries: BASTIDE; CARBONARI; CARNOT, L.-H.; CAVAIGNAC, L.-E.; *LE JOURNAL DU PEUPLE*; *LE NATIONAL*; *LA REFORME*; REPUB-

LICANS; *LA REVUE DU PROGRES*; *REVUE REPUBLICAINE*; SOCIETY OF THE RIGHTS OF MAN.

CAVAIGNAC, LOUIS-EUGENE (1802–1857), army general who crushed the insurrection of the Paris workers during the June Days of 1848 and remained chief executive of France until the election of Louis-Napoleon Bonaparte as president in December 1848. Second son of Jean-Baptiste Cavaignac, *conventionnel*, and younger brother of Godefroy Cavaignac, Louis-Eugène under the influence of both adopted the republican faith at an early age. Directed into a military career by his father, Eugène entered the Ecole polytechnique in 1820 and while there became a carbonaro. Although he played no active role in the abortive uprisings of 1822, Restoration authorities planned to prohibit his entry into the army upon graduation from the Polytechnique in 1822, until Cavaignac's uncle, General Jacques-Marie Cavaignac, who had rallied to the Restoration, interceded for him. As an officer in the corps of engineers, Cavaignac in 1828 served with the French expeditionary force sent to support the Greek revolutionaries and was stationed at Arras when the Revolution of 1830 broke out. He played no role in the July Days but shared the disappointment of his brother and other republicans in the outcome. Already under suspicion in the army for his republican views, Cavaignac nevertheless expressed sympathy for the workers of Lyons who were suppressed by the army in 1831. He was stationed at Metz at the time of the abortive Parisian uprising of 1832; after Cavaignac told his commanding officer that he would refuse to fight against republicans, he was transferred to Algeria in August 1832.

Cavaignac spent most of his mature life in Algeria, participating in all aspects of the brutal war of conquest. He first won renown as commanding officer at Tlemcen during a sixteen month siege in 1836–37. Although he at first opposed the tactic of the *razzia*, or punitive raid, on Arab villages, Cavaignac later practiced it himself and in 1844 was probably the first French officer to resort to the *enfumade*, or asphyxiation by smoke, of Arabs who had taken refuge in a cave. The Cavaignac incident of 1844 did not arouse much comment, but in the following year French public opinion was outraged by another *enfumade* on a larger scale—with at least 500 deaths—carried out by Colonel Aimable-Jean-Jacques Pélissier at Dahra. Curiously, despite his own *enfumade*, Cavaignac retained his reputation among the French and Arabs alike as one of the most humane of the "Africains."

Cavaignac also retained his reputation as one of the few republican officers. Although he abstained from political activity, he invited his brother Godefroy, a noted republican militant, to visit him in Algeria in 1840 and again in 1843, and Eugène contributed 2,000 francs to Godefroy's short-lived radical *Journal du peuple* in 1842. Nevertheless, Cavaignac was promoted to brigadier general in 1844 and in January 1848 became commander of the province of Oran.

After the February revolution, the Provisional Government appointed Cavaignac to be governor-general of Algeria, to succeed the son of Louis-Philippe, the duc d'Aumale, and Cavaignac officially proclaimed the republic in Algeria. Soon after he was appointed minister of war, but on the advice of his mother in France, Cavaignac refused. He posed his candidacy for the National Constitutent Assembly, however, and was elected both in Paris and in the Lot, the department that had sent his father to the Convention. Even before the election, Cavaignac had informed Alphonse de Lamartine that he would now accept the Ministry of War, and he assumed that position immediately upon his return to Paris on 17 May. Determined to avoid a repetition of the invasion of the Assembly two days earlier, Cavaignac immediately began to recall more army units to the capital.

When on the morning of 23 June, following demonstrations at the place de la Bastille and at the Panthéon, barricades began to go up, the Executive Commission put Cavaignac in full command of all military forces in Paris and accepted his plan to concentrate his troops instead of trying to prevent the insurrection from spreading. Cavaignac assembled troops near the National Assembly at the Palais Bourbon and near the Hôtel de ville, then sent out three columns against the insurgent areas of eastern Paris—two on the Right Bank and one on the Left. Fighting became so intense during the afternoon of 23 June that Cavaignac himself led a relief column to the faubourg du Temple. On the morning of 24 June, when the insurgents seemed to be about to capture the Hôtel de ville, the National Assembly declared Paris in a state of siege and delegated full executive authority to General Cavaignac. While continuing the military operations, Cavaignac also used his dictatorial powers to close the political clubs, disarm National Guardsmen who had not responded to the call to arms, and seize certain newspapers suspected of fomenting the uprising. He also sought to discourage men from the National Workshops from joining the insurrection by continuing to pay them during the fighting, and he issued a series of proclamations urging the insurgents to lay down their arms.

Once the insurrection was vanquished, Cavaignac surrendered his dictatorial powers, but a grateful National Assembly immediately reinvested him with the executive power as president of the Council of Ministers. He retained this position and also functioned as effective head of state until the election of Louis-Napoleon Bonaparte as president of the Republic in December 1848; thus, of the three provisional governments that stemmed from the revolution of February, that of Cavaignac was the most durable. In the immediate aftermath of the June Days, most of Cavaignac's policies were of a reactionary nature: he dissolved the National Workshops, reinforced the army in Paris, maintained the state of siege, and sponsored legislation imposing controls on the clubs and establishing financial bonds for newspapers. But the moderate republican government of Cavaignac also preserved and consolidated the democratic institutions that derived from February, extending universal suffrage to local government and attempting to democratize the educational institutions of France. Above all, the National Assembly during the Cavaignac period drew up the first democratic constitution since the abortive one of 1793.

Although Cavaignac and his ministers were hostile to socialism, post-June policies also reflected the moderate republicans' support of mild social reforms. The Cavaignac government not only substituted direct relief for the dissolved National Workshops and sponsored a number of job-creating public works projects, but it also provided a moderate amount of state funding for producers' cooperatives, preserved maximum hours legislation for adult male factory workers, and introduced postal reform.

In foreign affairs also, the Cavaignac administration essentially continued the policies of the preceding revolutionary governments; in general, this meant expressing sympathy for the liberal national movements, especially in Italy, Germany, and Poland, while remaining at peace. Continuity was maintained in the person of Jules Bastide, who had been Lamartine's close associate since February, had become foreign minister in May, and remained in that position during the Cavaignac period. The general himself, however, took a personal interest in international affairs and worked out jointly with Bastide a foreign policy with certain distinctive features. For example, Cavaignac took advantage of the Russian emperor's favorable attitude toward his victory in the June Days to seek recognition of the French Republic and even to propose an alliance with Russia, though both efforts were unsuccessful.

But Italy was the chief problem for the Cavaignac government. Lamartine had been reluctant to aid Piedmont-Sardinia in its war against Austria, and Piedmont had insisted on fighting alone. After the Austrian victory at Custozza on 25 July, however, the issue of possible French intervention was posed once more. Cavaignac readied an army of 60,000, but in the absence of a formal request from the king of Piedmont preferred to avoid military involvement in Italy, partly out of concern for internal security in France. France then offered joint diplomatic mediation with England, a policy that aroused bitter criticism in French radical circles. Near the end of the Cavaignac regime, in November, a new crisis in Rome led Cavaignac to prepare a military expedition to aid the pope. Cavaignac even invited Pius IX to come to France; instead he fled to Gaeta in the Kingdom of Naples. Insisting that his military mission was to ensure the personal safety of the pontiff and not to restore papal authority in Rome, Cavaignac cancelled the expedition once he learned that the pope was no longer in danger.

One motive for the invitation to the pope was undoubtedly an attempt by Cavaignac to win the support of French Catholics in the forthcoming presidential election. But in the election held 10 December Cavaignac came in a weak second to Louis-Napoleon Bonaparte, winning 1,448,302 votes to Bonaparte's 5,534,520. Although Bastide and other republicans advised Cavaignac to carry out a coup d'état to prevent Bonaparte from assuming power, Cavaignac refused and formally handed over power on 20 December.

General Cavaignac retained his seat in the National Assembly, however, and was also one of the few moderate republicans elected to the Legislative Assembly in May 1849. Distrusted by the monarchist majority as well as by the strong democratic-socialist minority and the president, Cavaignac played a minor role in the later Second Republic but opposed both the law of 31 May 1850 that mutilated universal suffrage and the movement in 1851 to revise the constitution to permit Louis-Napoleon to succeed himself. At the time of the coup d'état of 2 December 1851, Cavaignac was one of the opposition leaders arrested during the night; he was released from prison several weeks later. In the first elections held after the coup, in 1852, Cavaignac was one of only three republicans who were successful, but all were denied their seats because they refused to take the oath of loyalty to Louis-Napoleon. Thereafter Cavaignac lived in retirement near Le Mans. In the elections of 1857, he was once again successful but once again resigned his seat. A few months later he died of a heart attack.

Few Frenchmen or historians have accepted Alexis de Tocqueville's opinion that General Cavaignac "was the only great figure" to emerge in 1848. His historical reputation remains essentially that of the executioner of the workers during the June Days.

F. A. de Luna, *The French Republic under Cavaignac, 1848* (Princeton, 1969); Le General Ibos, *Le General Cavaignac* (Paris, 1930); L. C. Jennings, *France and Europe in 1848* (Oxford, 1973).

Frederick A. de Luna

Related entries: ALGIERS, EXPEDITION TO; BASTIDE; CARBONARI; CAVAIGNAC, G.-E.-L; EXECUTIVE COMMISSION; JUNE DAYS; LAMARTINE; LYONS, REVOLTS IN; NATIONAL WORKSHOPS; PIUS IX.

CAYLA, COMTESSE. See DU CAYLA.

LE CENSEUR (1814–1815), liberal newspaper of the First Restoration and Hundred Days. Shortly after the Restoration of Louis XVIII, royalist newspapers found themselves under attack by a liberal journal. Although the new *Censeur* had only 4,500 subscribers, compared with their own 5,000 to 6,000, they disliked its criticism of the power that the Charter had left in the hands of the king, and its warnings against the pretensions of church and aristocracy. Founded as a weekly journal on 12 June 1814, the *Censeur* disappeared in September and reappeared in November with a different format and at irregular intervals, thus evading the police control prescribed for periodicals by the law of 21 October 1814. Thereafter the importance of liberty of the press became one of the leading themes of the *Censeur*. The two editors, Charles Comte and Charles Dunoyer, were denounced in royalist newspapers as Bonapartists, but the accusation was belied by their hostility to Napoleon during the Hundred Days. Volume 5 of the *Censeur* was seized by Napoleon's police, but the paper was allowed to reappear as a result of the intervention of Benjamin Constant. It nevertheless criticized the Acte additionnel and the ceremony of the Champ de mai, protesting the impossibility of establishing a constitutional monarchy under a military leader such as Napoleon. In spite of this record, the *Censeur* was suppressed in September

1815 during the period of general repression following Napoleon's Hundred Days.

E. Harpaz, ''*Le Censeur*: histoire d'un journal,'' *Revue des sciences humaines* (1958).

Irene Collins

Related entries: ACTE ADDITIONNEL; *LE CENSEUR EUROPEEN*; CHARTER OF 1814; CONSTANT; DUNOYER; HUNDRED DAYS.

LE CENSEUR EUROPEEN, liberal opposition periodical; appeared as *Le Censeur* at irregular intervals, 1814–1815; reappeared as *Le Censeur européen*, February 1817–April 1819; became daily 15 June 1819–22 June 1820; merged with *Le Courrier français* June 1820. The original *Censeur* was published June 1814 to September 1815 by Charles-Louis Comte and the economist Charles Dunoyer, a disciple of J.-B. Say. An important collaborator was Paul-François Dubois, creator of the *Globe*. Before the periodical was suppressed, it had begun to appear in book form at odd intervals to evade suppression as a periodical. The ruse was not successful but was nevertheless used again in the second *Censeur*, founded in February 1817, under the title *Le Censeur européen*. The magazine became a daily newspaper under the more liberal press laws of 1819 and enjoyed a short but brilliant career until suppressed in the reaction of 1820.

In addition to Comte and Dunoyer, its editorial columns included André Dupin, Augustin Thierry, and Paul-Louis Courier. The journal's policy was outspoken and fearless. Dupin asserted a clear distinction between attacks on the king's person and on his government; Courier condemned the designs of clericalists, and the managers were prosecuted in 1818 for reporting outbreaks of Chouan violence in Brittany. This was part of a campaign by liberal papers and pamphlets (1818–20) to accuse the government of complicity in an ultra conspiracy, said to be nourished in the provinces. Comte was sentenced to five months in La Force Prison and in 1820 to another two months on a similar charge. He became an exile in Switzerland and later in England. The second conviction led to total suppression of the newspaper under the reactionary press law of 1820. Both the *Censeur* and the *Renommée* devoted their last issues (2 April 1820) to denouncing the alleged secret government. Both papers, however, merged their stock with that of Benjamin Constant's new daily, *Le Courrier français* (June 1820).

The *Censeur européen* was too radical and forthright for its perilous times: Alfred Nettement called it the ''banner of the stoic school.''

E. Hatin, *Histoire de la presse* (Paris, 1859–61); C. Ledré, *La presse à l'assaut de la monarchie* (Paris, 1960).

Daniel Rader

Related entries: LE CENSEUR; COMTE, F.-C.-L.; CONSTANT; COURIER; *LE COURRIER FRANCAIS*; DUBOIS; DUNOYER; DUPIN, A.-M.-J.-J.; *LA RENOMMEE*; THIERRY.

CENSORSHIP. Official censure of books, newspapers, and magazines existed between 1815 and 1830 under different laws and governments. At times some laws were in abeyance. At other times censorship was only one of several methods of control. Censorship was abolished in the Charter of the July Monarchy (1830), but other restraints were applied to published writings, often with great severity.

The ideal of a free press had been capricious in the Old Regime, perilous in the Revolution, and fraudulent under Napoleon. Except for the Hundred Days interlude, when Napoleon was forced to liberal concessions, the Restoration of 1815 gave the first promise of a stable regime of limited press freedom. In spite of fifteen years of abuses, suppressions, bribery, and censorship, a free press not only survived but flourished and became a major political factor of the Restoration.

Although article 8 of the Charter of 1814 declared the freedom of the press, it also provided that such freedom was subject to laws that "should repress its abuse." Censorship was first provided as one such means of repression during the First Restoration (law of 21 October 1814) and applied to everything printed of fewer than twenty pages, meaning most periodicals and pamphlets but not books. Joseph Fouché's police ministry enforced this provision arbitrarily, although newspapers could be suppressed altogether by rescinding official authorization. During the Hundred Days the press was free of censorship, but the 1814 law was revived by an edict of Louis XVIII (8 August 1815) at the start of the Second Restoration, applying now only to the periodical press, but still under police jurisdiction.

Police censorship continued in the period 1815–19 and so threatened the newspaper press that even loyal monarchist editors such as Francois-René de Chateaubriand and Joseph-Francois Michaud began to oppose it. Three laws in May and June 1819 resulted from this clamor and from the moderate outlook of the king and the new Elie Decazes ministry. These laws, although inaugurating the "rich man's bond" or *cautionnement* and a stricter definition of press crimes, abolished the hated arbitrary censorship. In spite of more frequent prosecutions, the larger newspapers were at last on firmer ground, and the press began to prosper.

In the wake of the assassination of the duc de Berry in 1820, however, came more reactionary press laws, including severe censorship provisions. The law of 31 March 1820 provided a six-month jail term and up to 1,200 francs fine for each instance of failure to present all copy to the censor prior to printing. This crippling form of preliminary censure also provided for closure of the offending newspaper in case of a conviction. It applied to all periodicals that were even partially political or periodically irregular and included cartoons. Its reign of repression was short; it expired with the end of the Chambers sessions of 1820. A panel of twelve censors, of whom five formed a quorum and all chosen by the king, replaced the more secretive police jurisdiction. In the provinces, each prefect was to name a panel of three censors. Wide publicity of these nominations resulted in great controversy. Students at Paris struck their classes and forced the suspension of a professor who had accepted the post of censor; another who refused to serve was paraded as a hero. Censored articles began to appear "legally" in pamphlet form and circulated widely.

Liberals regained some advantage in a new law (26 July 1821) that restricted the application of censorship only to periods when the Chambers were in session, but much of this victory was lost through the laws of 17 and 25 March 1822, part of Joseph de Villèle's new strategy. Along with the infamous tendency definition of press offenses, censorship was augmented by a provision that under grave circumstances, it could be invoked even during the months of intersession. In addition, a proof of each printed sheet of every periodical had to be deposited with the royal prosecutor, an onerous requirement tantamount to preliminary censorship. These 1822 provisions remained in force throughout Villèle's administration. Censure was actually decreed during the "free" intersession periods twice under Villèle: 15 August–29 September 1824 and 24 June–5 November 1827.

The ultras' zeal for censorship suffered a defeat early in 1827 when a majority of the Chamber of Peers, including some ultras and led by Chateaubriand, amended so broadly an extreme proposal by the comte de Peyronnet that Villèle was forced to withdraw it. This bill, among other provisions, would have required preliminary censorship of all printed works of any kind. The debates over this proposal, ironically nicknamed the law of justice and love, created such heat and publicity as to discredit Villèle's regime further.

The vicomte de Martignac's moderate government of 1828–29, under liberal pressures, proposed a new law, which, heavily amended, passed 18 July 1828 and was, relative to the previous thirteen years, the most liberal press legislation of the Restoration. The worst provisions of earlier laws were abolished along with censorship, and only trial in open court could now be used to control the expression of editors and contributors to periodicals. The era of liberty thus begun contributed to the overthrow of the Bourbons; a hatred of the press led to Jules de Polignac's 25 July 1830 ordinances, which sparked the insurrection. Polignac's attempted coup would have made immediate suppression of all newspapers possible and restored censorship as well.

Louis-Philippe's new charter of 9 August 1830 guaranteed a free press and abolished censorship, yet the press became more rigidly controlled in the July Monarchy than it had been in the Restoration. Five laws between 1830 and 1834 created much harsher penalties and more frequent prosecutions for an expanded list of press offenses. In 1835 (9 September) the Chambers passed the notorious September Law, designed to annihilate the opposition press and restore a special censorship for those caricatures and cartoons that had so ridiculed the monarchy.

The Second Republic, after a period of arbitrary censorship and intervention, established limits on the press without censorship but returned (June 1849) to laws of arbitrary suspension, reflecting bourgeois and liberal fears of socialists and democrats.

In general, censorship was not effective as a political weapon of governments. Criminal press statutes vaguely enunciated and zealously prosecuted could with more certainty destroy or intimidate newspapers and periodicals.

I. Collins, *The Government and the Newspaper Press in France, 1814–1881* (London, 1959); A. Germain, *Martyrologie de la presse, 1789–1861* (Paris, 1861); C. Ledré, *La presse à l'assaut de la monarchie* (Paris, 1960).

Daniel Rader

Related entries: CHATEAUBRIAND; DECAZES; FOUCHE; LABBEY DE POMPIERES; LAW ON SEDITIOUS SPEECH; MARTIGNAC; MICHAUD; POLIGNAC; PRESS LAWS; ULTRAROYALISTS; VILLELE.

CENT JOURS. See HUNDRED DAYS.

CHABROL DE CROUZOL, CHRISTOPHE-ANDRE-JEAN, COMTE DE (1771–1836), magistrate and administrator of the Empire; deputy, peer, and minister of the Restoration. Born at Riom on 16 November 1771, Chabrol de Crouzol was the elder brother of Chabrol de Volvic. He was educated for the clergy but refused to swear the oath to the civil constitution. Imprisoned with his family during the Terror, he was freed in 1795 and retired to private life. In August 1803 he became an auditor in the Council of State and was promoted to master of requests in 1809. After serving on the Tuscan debt commission, he was named to the imperial court of Paris in March 1811. Then in August 1811 Napoleon appointed him intendant-general of the Illyrian provinces, where his ability attracted Napoleon's praise. With his provinces overrun by the Allies in 1813, Chabrol returned to Paris where in 1814 he rallied to the Bourbons. In July 1814 they appointed him to the Council of State and then in November named him prefect of the Rhône. When Napoleon returned from Elba, Chabrol at first attempted to rally Lyons against him, but realizing the futility, he abandoned the city to join Artois.

Chabrol resumed his prefectoral functions in July 1815 when the Austrians occupied Lyons. Perhaps unwittingly he became involved in the excessive reaction to the conspiracy invented by Simon de Canuel in 1817. After Auguste de Marmont intervened at Lyons to halt the excesses and Canuel was dismissed, Chabrol was recalled from his prefecture. But in September 1817 he became under secretary of state at the Ministry of the Interior, remaining there until December 1818. In July 1820 Chabrol was reappointed to the Council of State, and in November of that year the department of Puy-de-Dôme elected him to the Deputies. He voted with the supporters of the Richelieu ministry, which in January 1821 appointed him director general of recording of estates. He won reelection to the Deputies in October 1821, but in December 1823 Louis XVIII named him a peer of France. From August 1824 to March 1828 he served as minister of marine in both the Villèle and Martignac cabinets. Under his administration, an admiralty council was formed, and the maritime prefectures were reestablished. A naval school was founded, the construction of warships was expanded, and line crews were trained and organized. He extended to the French colonies the application of the laws of metropolitan France. Chabrol's moderation in the Villèle cabinet—for example, he had opposed the abolition of the National Guard—resulted in his retention in the Martignac ministry. He resigned in March 1828, however, over criticism of the Villèle cabinet by Martignac and the Chamber.

In August 1828, at the insistence of Charles X, he accepted the Ministry of Finance in the Polignac ministry. But he warned Charles of the dangers inherent in the composition of the cabinet. While minister of finance, Chabrol was able to effect certain reforms and economies. In an effort to defuse the crisis in the spring of 1830, he urged that Villèle be brought in to replace Polignac. But he resigned in May 1830 rather than participate in the radical measures he knew Polignac and the king would take in the event the forthcoming elections returned a hostile Chamber. Under the July Monarchy, he took some part in the affairs of the Peers, while devoting himself extensively to farming, literature, and science. He especially spoke in opposition to the measures exiling the Bourbons and against the Bonapartes. Chabrol de Crouzol died in the chateau of Cabannes in Puy-de-Dôme on 7 October 1836.

Archives parlementaires; E. Daudet, Le Ministère de M. de Martignac (Paris, 1875); A. Kleinclausz, Histoire de Lyon (Lyons, 1952); N. Richardson, The French Prefectoral Corps, 1814–1830 (Cambridge, 1966); A. Robert et al., Dictionnaire des parlementaires français (Paris, 1889–91); J. Savant, Les Préfets de Napoléon (Paris, 1958).

James K. Kieswetter

Related entries: CANUEL; CHABROL DE VOLVIC; CHAMBER OF DEPUTIES; CHAMBER OF PEERS; CHARLES X; HUNDRED DAYS; MARMONT; MARTIGNAC; NATIONAL GUARD; POLIGNAC; REVOLUTION OF 1830; RICHELIEU; VILLELE.

CHABROL DE VOLVIC, GILBERT-JOSEPH-GASPARD, COMTE DE
(1773–1843), administrator and prefect of the Empire, prefect and deputy of the Restoration, deputy of the July Monarchy. Chabrol de Volvic, the younger brother of Chabrol de Crouzol, was born at Riom (Puy-de-Dôme) on 25 September 1773. He fought in the ranks in the early days of the Revolution, but under the Terror he was imprisoned and not released until 1795. After studying at the Ecole polytechnique, in April 1796 he became an engineer in the Department of Roads and Bridges. He subsequently served on the Commission on Arts and Sciences that accompanied the Egyptian expedition, where he showed great diligence and courage. Back in Paris he assisted in the publication of the commission's work on Egypt. Napoleon assigned him as subprefect at Pontivy (Morbihan), which he planned and rebuilt as the emperor wanted and which was renamed Napoléonville. In January 1806 Napoleon sent Chabrol to Savona as prefect of Montenotte, where the emperor desired an ambitious public works program. There Chabrol was responsible for beginning the well-known coastal corniche road. He also had to deal with Pope Pius VII who was imprisoned at

Savona in 1809–10. In his relations with the pope, Chabrol exercised considerable tact and courtesy in spite of the constraints placed on him by Napoleon. During the Russian campaign the prefect of Seine, Nicolas-Thérèse-Benoît Frochot, allowed himself to be duped by the Malet conspiracy. Thus on his return, Napoleon in December 1812 dismissed Frochot and replaced him with Chabrol, who remained prefect of the Seine until the end of the Empire.

Chabrol apparently supported, albeit tacitly perhaps, the return of Louis XVIII. The restored Bourbons maintained him at his post and in 1814 named him councillor of state and gave him the Legion of Honor. He did not rally to Napoleon during the Hundred Days and after Waterloo returned to his prefecture. Due to his competence and flexibility, he remained there until the 1830 July Revolution. During his long tenure as prefect of Seine, Chabrol was involved in the construction or completion of numerous public works, including the canal de l'Ourcq, the Saint Martin and Saint Denis canals, the Halle aux vins, the Bourse, and various churches, bridges, slaughterhouses, and sewers. Based on a similar study he had done in Italy, he published a statistical survey of the Seine, which, with his similar compilation of Montenotte, became models for such surveys. He established primary schools, supported the arts, and invented a new enameling technique (*émaille sur lave*) that earned him admission to the Institute in 1820. In addition to his prefectoral duties, he was elected to the Deputies by the department of Seine in 1816 and reelected by Puy-de-Dôme in 1824, 1827, and 1830. Deprived of instructions from his superiors during the July Revolution, he escaped the insurrection by hiding in the cellar of the Hôtel de ville. On 11 August 1830 he retired as prefect of Seine, but he did not altogether abandon politics. In 1839 the department of Puy-de-Dôme once again elected him a deputy and reelected him in 1842; however, he died in Paris on 30 April 1843 in the midst of his term.

Archives parlementaires; D. Pinkney, *The French Revolution of 1830* (Princeton, 1972); N. Richardson, *The French Prefectoral Corps, 1814–1830* (Cambridge, 1966); A. Robert et al., *Dictionnaire des parlementaires français* (Paris, 1889–91); J. Savant, *Les Préfets de Napoléon* (Paris, 1958).

James K. Kieswetter

Related entries: BRIDGE AND ROAD SERVICE; CHABROL DE CROUZOL; CHAMBER OF DEPUTIES; ECOLE POLYTECHNIQUE; HUNDRED DAYS; LOUIS XVIII; REVOLUTION OF 1830.

CHAMBER OF DEPUTIES, lower house of the French legislature from 1814 to 1848; elected by limited manhood suffrage. The Constitutional Charter of 1814 provided for a Chamber of Deputies of the departments, the members being elected by electoral colleges. Each department would keep the same number of deputies that it had had before 1814. Each deputy's term was to be five years, and the Chamber was to be renewed annually in fifths. Only men at least forty years of age and paying 1,000 francs direct tax were eligible. Eligibility to vote for the deputies required a minimum age of thirty and a direct tax of 300 francs.

Only half the deputies of each department actually had to be residents of that department.

The president of the deputies was selected by the king from a list of five candidates named by the Chamber. The sessions of the Deputies were public but could be closed on the vote of five members. The Deputies, like the Peers, had no right of legislative initiative, although they could petition the king to propose legislation. Amendments had to be proposed or accepted by the king. The Deputies had priority of action on tax bills; only after acceptance by the Deputies could tax measures be presented to the Peers. The king was required to convoke both chambers every year and could prorogue them. He could also dissolve the Deputies, but he was then required to convoke a new session within three months. Deputies were immune from bodily constraint during sessions and for six weeks preceeding and following a session. Furthermore, they could not be arrested or charged on a criminal charge during a session unless the Chamber approved or they were caught *in flagrante delicto*. Cabinet ministers could sit in either chamber and had to be heard on demand. The Charter specified that the ministers were responsible, but it did not specify to whom. Nevertheless, the Deputies had the right to accuse the ministers and to prosecute them before the Chamber of Peers for treason or peculation.

These legislative provisions of the Charter reflected the French experience since 1789 and current French political thought. More important, they reflected the current vogue for bicameralism and for English institutions, which stemmed from the Enlightenment. The new arrangement also resulted from the English exile of Louis XVIII and other *émigrés* and from a preference for English institutions by those now in power in France. Many of the constitutional provisions were, however, subsequently changed by legislation.

The number of Deputies fixed by the Charter was ambiguous. Napoleon's Corps législatif, reduced by territorial losses, had 258. In July 1815 Louis XVIII increased that to 402 (actually 395 after the Second Peace of Paris) but lowered it to 258 in September 1816. The 1820 Law of the Double Vote added 172 new seats, bringing the total to 430 where it remained until in April 1831 it was changed to 459 and in 1839 to 460. One of Charles X's July Ordinances reduced the Deputies to 258, but this was never put into effect. Other changes more clearly violated the letter of the constitution. In June 1824 the ultras, seeking to perpetuate their majority, extended the five-year term of a deputy to seven years. The July Revolution restored the five-year term. The mandated annual renewal of one-fifth of the chamber was already violated by the provision in the constitution for total dissolution of the chamber and then again by the addition of 172 new seats in 1820. It was definitively replaced by integral renewal in 1824 when the Septennial Law was passed, and it was retained by succeeding regimes. The means of electing deputies and the qualifications for deputies and for voting changed over the years.

The Charter provided for two-stage indirect election of deputies through an electoral college system. In 1817 direct election from a departmental list was adopted. Then in 1820 the Law of the Double Vote provided for arrondissement lists for all the electorate and departmental lists for the double voters. The July Monarchy restored direct election from arrondissement lists. The 300 franc tax requirement to vote was maintained through the Restoration, but the July Monarchy lowered it to 200 francs. The 1,000 franc qualification for deputies was lowered in 1830 to 500 francs. The Restoration, however, changed the age qualification for voting from thirty in the Charter to twenty-one in 1815 and then raised it back to thirty in 1817. The July Monarchy lowered it to twenty-five. The Restoration changed the minimum age for deputies to twenty-five in 1815 and then raised it to forty in 1816. The minimum age for a deputy after 1830 was thirty years.

The prohibition of salary for deputies, maintained until 1848, was specifically intended to constrain the liberal professional classes; however, many deputies held salaried government posts, and their tenure was dependent on their political, not their administrative, performance. The chambers of both the Restoration and the July Monarchy had the right to verify the credentials of their members, a right granted by law, not by the respective constitutions. They also established their own internal rules of procedure. Voting in secret and organization of the Deputies into commissions (*bureaux*) were common to both regimes.

Some changes awaited the July Revolution. Under the July Monarchy a deputy who accepted a bureaucratic post was required to stand for reelection, and a few posts were declared incompatible with membership in the Deputies. Under the Restoration the Deputies prepared a list of nominees from which the king selected their president each session. The 1830 constitution allowed the Deputies to elect their president. Prior to 1830, the king in theory held an exclusive right to initiate legislation. The July Revolution gave that power to both Chambers and the king, along with freedom of amendment. Although both chambers of the Restoration theoretically enjoyed the right to veto royal legislation, article 14 of the Charter allowed the king himself to legislate in certain circumstances. This article, used by Charles X in 1830, was abolished after the July Revolution. Under the Restoration, the deputies did not enjoy any real right to interpellate the ministers; under the July Monarchy, a limited right was practiced. During the Restoration, political parties in the modern sense were basically unknown. Rather, factions with shifting membership existed, making for considerable confusion in the political organization of the Deputies. This situation, if anything, worsened from 1830 to 1848. Finally, perhaps the most important criterion of political power, the question of ministerial responsibility to the legislature, remained unsettled through the Restoration. Nor was it completely resolved even by 1848. Nevertheless, after 1815 the Chamber of Deputies quickly became the center of political activity and generally overshadowed the Peers.

P. Bastid, *Les Institutions politiques de la monarchie parlementaire française, 1814–1848* (Paris, 1954); T. Beck, *French Legislators, 1800–1834* (Berkeley, 1974); H. Bergasse, *Histoire de l'assemblée* (Paris, 1967); P. Campbell, *French Electoral Systems and Elections since 1789* (London, 1965), P. Duvergier de Hauranne, *Histoire du gouverne-*

ment parlementaire en France, 1814–1848 (Paris, 1857–71); F. Ponteil, *Les Institutions de la France de 1814 à 1870* (Paris, 1965).

James K. Kieswetter

Related entries: CHAMBER OF PEERS; CHARLES X; CHARTER OF 1814; CHARTER OF 1830; DOUBLE VOTE, LAW OF THE; ELECTIONS AND ELECTORAL SYSTEMS; ELECTORS; JULY ORDINANCES; LOUIS XVIII; PARIS, SECOND TREATY OF; REVOLUTION OF 1830; REVOLUTION OF 1848; ULTRAROYALISTS.

CHAMBER OF PEERS, upper house of the French legislature from 1814 to 1848; composed of peers appointed by the king. Louis XVIII's Constitutional Charter established a Chamber of Peers, which was required to meet concurrently with the Deputies. The peers were appointed exclusively by the king without limitation of numbers, and their peerages could be either life or hereditary. A peer could be named at age twenty-five but had to be at least thirty before he could participate in the Chamber. The chancellor, appointed for life by the king, presided over the Peers. The Peers included members of the royal family and princes of the blood, who took precedence immediately after the chancellor and who could participate at age twenty-five; however, the princes could appear only on specific order of the king. The Chamber of Peers deliberated in secret. They had criminal jurisdiction over high treason and attacks on the security of the state. They also had the right to try ministers accused of treason or peculation by the Deputies. Peers themselves could be arrested and tried on criminal matters only by their own chamber. These constitutional provisions remained virtually unaltered throughout the Restoration and were only slightly amended after the July Revolution. The 1848 Revolution destroyed the Chamber of Peers, although it reappeared in somewhat similar form as the Senate of the Second Empire and in less similar form as the Senate of the early Third Republic.

The concept of the peerage dates back at least to Charlemagne. Under Philip II Augustus, there were recognized six lay and six ecclesiastical peers, and by 1789 their numbers had increased to forty-three lay but still six ecclesiasticals. Although ostensibly they had served as councillors to the king, they were never organized into a chamber until 1814. This clearly reflected the vogue for bicameralism and the fondness for English political institutions, which also influenced the formation of the Deputies. In the preamble to the Charter, Louis XVIII spoke of a renewed peerage, a national institution to bind past and present together. Virtually the only real analogy between the old and new peerages was immunity from criminal prosecution except by their own colleagues. In fact, of the 154 peers appointed in 1814, 84 were senators of the Empire, while the others were nobles of the Old Regime, returned *émigrés*, and others. The Restoration Peers shared almost identical powers with the Deputies, the exceptions being the Peers' judicial functions and immunities and the requirement that the Deputies act first on tax bills. The Hundred Days had no impact on the Peers, except for the destitution of twenty-nine men who served in Napoleon's Chamber of Peers. One difficulty with the initial Restoration peerages was their lack of endowments. On 25 August 1817 the king decreed that all peerages except clerical ones must be endowed with a *majorat*, to provide a specified minimum income for each of the various noble ranks that all peers received. These *majorats* were to be inherited by primogeniture, a clear deviation from existing legislation on property division. The intention was to recreate a noble, landed aristocracy as a bulwark against liberalism. It did not succeed.

Ostensibly appointments to the Peers were to be made on an individual basis. In fact, most were appointed in large groups for ulterior reasons. After Waterloo the Chamber had decreased to only 115. Therefore on 17 August 1815 Louis XVIII appointed 94 new peers, ranging from former Vendéans to the sons of imperial marshals. Subsequent large appointments were more directly politically motivated. In response to the Peers' opposition to government policy on elections and finances, Elie Decazes persuaded the king to appoint 59 new peers in March 1819 and 8 more in November. Liberal in nature, they included virtually all those excluded after the Hundred Days. Villèle attempted a similar but more discreet move to benefit the Right, nominating 8 ecclesiastical peers in October 1822 and 28 more in December 1823. The most notorious such packing of the Peers was Villèle's appointment in November 1827 of 76 conservatives. Yet the Peers were not always under crown control. On other occasions peerages were awarded for past services by a current government that did not necessarily appreciate those services. Thus members of the outgoing second Richelieu ministry were named peers in the fall of 1821, and Villèle was appointed to the upper chamber by Jean-Baptiste de Martignac. In March 1830 the Chamber of Peers, which then numbered 365, was sufficiently independent minded that although it did not vote an address like that of the Deputies, it protested that it was attached to the Constitutional Charter. Thus in its own restrained way, it too rebuked the king.

The July Revolution brought several changes in the composition of the Peers but not in their power. All peers named by Charles X were excluded, and many others resigned rather than accept the new regime. The king was now required to select peers from certain categories, especially the army and politics, which in fact reflected the composition of the Restoration's Peers anyway. This was intended to deemphasize the nobility of birth, a change that led peers between 1830 and 1848 to be more concerned with material affairs and less with privilege and prestige. In December 1831 the abolition of the hereditary peerage, a major demand in July and August 1830, furthered this trend. It also led to a more aged Chamber, for no longer could a young man inherit a peerage and enter the Chamber at age twenty-five. Rather peerages now usually came as a reward for a life's career at a more advanced age. The inheritance of *majorats* was limited, and in 1835 the creation of new ones was prohibited. The Peers of the July Monarchy devoted proportionally more time to their judicial functions as the Court of Peers, especially trying the perpetrators of the frequent attacks on Louis

Philippe and those of their own members involved in crime and corruption. Furthermore, with only certain exceptions, the Peers' sessions were now public.

Nevertheless the Peers' constitutional power was not really altered. As before 1830, the monarch tried to control the Peers, but from 1837 on, a constitutional opposition party functioned within the Chamber. Louis-Philippe, however, did have sufficient influence with the Peers that he was frequently able to use them to defeat legislation rather than having to attempt to veto it himself. In general the Peers of the July Monarchy attracted less public attention than those of the Restoration and did not enjoy the popularity that some of their actions before 1830 had earned them. When the February 1848 Revolution broke out, the Peers, unlike the Deputies, were utterly unprepared for it. On 24 February, after the Republic was proclaimed, they were suspended *sine die*. One of the first acts of the new provisional government was to prohibit further meetings of the Peers.

P. Bastid, *Les Institutions politiques de la monarchie parlementaire française, 1814–1848* (Paris, 1954); P. Duvergier de Hauranne, *Histoire du gouvernement parlementaire en France, 1814–1848* (Paris, 1857–71); L. Labes, *Les Pairs de France sous la monarchie de juillet* (Paris, 1938); F. Ponteil, *Les Institutions de la France de 1814 à 1870* (Paris, 1965).

James K. Kieswetter

Related entries: CHAMBER OF DEPUTIES; CHARLES X; CHARTER OF 1814; CHARTER OF 1830; DECAZES; ELECTIONS AND ELCTORAL SYSTEMS; ELECTORS; HUNDRED DAYS; LOUIS XVIII; MARTIGNAC; RICHELIEU; VILLELE.

CHAMBERS OF COMMERCE. A few chambers of commerce had existed in the France of the *ancien régime*, but they disappeared in 1791. A decree of 3 Nivose, Year XI (23 December 1803) established twenty-two chambers; it stipulated that each department would have one, and as many as one per arrondissement could be set up. They were composed of five to fifteen businessmen, selected by cooptation from among the merchants, financiers, manufacturers, and masters of coastal vessels. Their purpose was to promote business interests, provide a forum for businessmen to exchange information, and act as consultative bodies to the government. The organizations grew in number and influence in the nineteenth century, the Paris Chamber of Commerce becoming a sort of national center for businessmen. The Paris chamber also owned and administered certain sections of the stock exchange, reserved the right to test and regulate the production of various products (such as diamonds and firearms), operated port facilities and business schools, and maintained a library. In addition to the chambers of commerce in France, several were established overseas to encourage French export trade. The semiofficial status of the chambers of commerce was recognized by a government charter issued on 9 April 1898.

S. B. Clough, *France, A History of National Economics, 1789–1939* (New York, 1939); A. Fournier, *La Chambre de commerce de Marseille d'après ses archives historiques* (Marseilles, 1910); G. Pariset, *La Chambre de commerce de Lyon* (Lyons, 1887).

Robert Aldrich

Related entry: BOURSE, PARIS.

CHAMBORD, COMTE DE. See BORDEAUX.

CHAMBRE INTROUVABLE, a name that Louis XVIII gave to the royalist Chamber of Deputies elected in August 1815. The name, which is difficult to translate into English, means "peerless," "unexpected," and "so good as to be improbable."

Guillaume de Bertier de Sauvigny, trans. E. Newman

Related entries: CHAMBER OF DEPUTIES; *CHAMBRE RETROUVEE*; LOUIS XVIII; RESTORATION, SECOND; ULTRAROYALISTS.

CHAMBRE RETROUVEE, the name given by Louis XVIII to the chamber elected in March 1824. The large majority of ultraroyalists present reminded many of the *chambre introuvable* of August 1815.

Guillaume de Bertier de Sauvigny

Related entries: CHAMBER OF DEPUTIES; CHAMBRE INTROUVABLE; LOUIS XVIII; RESTORATION, SECOND; ULTRAROYALISTS.

CHAMP-DE-MARS DEMONSTRATION (16 April 1848), a mobilization of Parisian workers, opposition to which marked a decisive shift in political forces. The occasion for the demonstration was an election, to be held on the Champ-de-Mars in western Paris, of fourteen National Guard officers representing organized labor. After the election, other workers from railways workshops and from another meeting at the Hippodrome joined the march, which was to present a donation and petition to the Provisional Government at the town hall. The march was composed of about 30,000 workers, led by an editor of *L'Atelier* and the printing workers carrying banners calling for the organization of labor and the end of exploitation. Along the quai du Louvre they encountered heavily armed National Guards and Mobile Guards and at the town hall were forced to march through a gauntlet of troops shouting anticommunist slogans. The workers' petition and donation was received by only a deputy mayor of Paris, whereas Alphonse de Lamartine and other members of the government had earlier welcomed the Guards.

Although there is no substantive evidence that the unarmed demonstrators had planned anything more than a show of strength to remind the government of its social obligations, the context of the march created a situation electric with rumors. The gathering was just one week before the national elections, which had already been postponed once; Louis-Auguste Blanqui had recently been angered by the release of the famous Taschereau documents; and in the sixteenth *Bulletin de la République*, George Sand had warned of further revolution if the elections were conservative. In such a situation, many radicals became more concerned about an attempt to seize power by Blanqui, perhaps with Etienne Cabet and Francois-Vincent Raspail, than they were about growing reaction on the right. Alexandre-Auguste Ledru-Rollin ordered the National Guard onto the streets, and two key club leaders, Marie-Joseph Sobrier and Armand Barbès, energetically supported the government.

The precise intentions of many key figures on 16 April remain uncertain. Most significant, however, was that the National Guard, including many workers, supported the Provisional Government. At the same time, not all of those enrolled in the National Workshops obeyed orders to leave the Champ-de-Mars after the election to join their National Guard units. Caught between support for a government that was giving them subsistence and the political polarization of the nation, increasing numbers of unemployed workers were opting for the radical cause. Despite the huge Festival of Fraternity four days later, the *journée* of 16 April prefigured the social cleavages that were to tear Paris in two in June.

P. H. Amann, *Revolution and Mass Democracy* (Princeton, 1975); R. Gossez, *Les ouvriers de Paris*, vol. 1, "Bibliothèque de la Révolution de 1848," 24 (Paris, 1967); D. C. McKay, *The National Workshops* (Cambridge, Mass., 1933); G. Sand, *Correspondance*, vol. 8 (Paris, 1971).

Peter McPhee

Related entries: L'ATELIER; BARBES; BLANQUI, L.-A.; CABET; CLUBS, POLITICAL; DEMONSTRATIONS OF 1848–1849; JUNE DAYS; LEDRU-ROLLIN; NATIONAL WORKSHOPS; PROVISIONAL GOVERNMENT; RASPAIL; SOBRIER.

CHAMPOLLION, JEAN-FRANCOIS, LE JEUNE (1790–1832), Orientalist, Egyptologist, decipherer of the Rosetta stone, and museum curator. Born at Figéac on 23 December 1790, Champollion followed the lead of his elder brother, Jacques-Joseph Champollion, an archaeologist and paleographer, in the study of ancient history. When he was only sixteen he presented to the Academy of Grenoble a paper arguing that Coptic was the language of ancient Egypt. In 1809 he became professor of history at the lycée of Grenoble. In 1814 he published *L'Egypte sous les pharons*, a two-volume geographical study of ancient Egypt based on classical as well as Arabic and other sources. But his most notable contribution to scholarship was the deciphering of Egyptian hieroglyphics, using as a key the Rosetta stone, which was discovered in 1799 during the French campaign in Egypt.

Champollion's first work with decipherment was done in 1821, and the following year he presented a paper that laid the foundation of his deciphering of hieratic and hieroglyphic writing. His work reached fruition in 1823 when he published *Précis du système hieroglyphique des anciens Egyptiens*. He established a list of the Greek equivalents of the ancient symbols, and he was the first to recognize that these signs variously represented letters of the alphabet, syllables, or complete ideas. This accomplishment, in connection with his work in museology, was instrumental in establishing the science of Egyptology. In 1824 Charles X sent him to Italy to visit collections of Egyptian antiquities. The holdings of the king of Sardinia especially impressed Champollion, and he managed to acquire the Salt collection, which formed the basis of the Egyptian collection of the Louvre.

Champollion soon became curator of this acquisition, which enjoyed the support of Charles X, and in 1827 he prepared a catalog of it. In 1828 he went on a scientific expedition to Egypt. In March 1831 he was appointed to a chair of Egyptian antiquities at the Collège de France, a post created especially for him, and that same year he entered the Academy of Inscriptions. He died of an attack of apoplexy on 4 March 1832 while engaged in publishing the results of his Egyptian trip. His private papers were acquired by the French state, which commissioned his brother to publish them.

A. Champollion-Figéac, *Les Deux Champollions: leur vie et leurs oeuvres* (Grenoble, 1887); C. Gordon, *Forgotten Scripts: The Story of Their Decipherment* (London, 1968); H. Hartleben, *Champollion sein Leben und sein Werk* (Berlin, 1906), and *Lettres et journaux de Champollion jeune* (Paris, 1909); M. Pope, *The Story of Archeological Decipherment* (New York, 1975); H. Sottas, *Centenary Edition of Champollion's Lettre à M. Dacier* (Paris, 1922).

James K. Kieswetter

Related entries: CHARLES X; COLLEGE DE FRANCE.

CHAMPS-ELYSEES, a famous Parisian playground and thoroughfare. At the end of the reign of Louis XIV, some tree plantations were started to give a more stately appearance to the empty ground beyond the Tuileries gardens toward the west. It was at first called the Grand cours. Further plantations and levelings during the eighteenth century, and, above all, the creation of the monumental Place Louis XV (first name of place de la Concorde) gave shape to the ensemble of alleys and playgrounds that came to be called the Champs-Elysées. The large driveway cutting through these grounds and leading toward the place and barrière de l'Etoile continued to be called avenue de Neuilly until at least 1840. But it was only in 1864 that the name of avenue des Champs-Elysées was formally sanctioned for the whole length of the road between Concorde and Etoile.

P. d'Ariste and M. Arrivetz, *Les Champs-Elysees, la place de la Concorde, etc.* (Paris, 1913).

Guillaume de Bertier de Sauvigny

CHANGARNIER, NICOLAS-ANNE-THEODULE (1793–1877), general who made his career in Algeria during the July Monarchy and played an important political role during the Second Republic. Born in Autun 26 April 1793, he was the son of a royalist magistrate imprisoned during the Terror. After solid studies at the collège of Autun, Nicolas Changarnier was sent to Paris to study law, and there he saw the Empire fall. Because he was not interested in the law, his family in November 1815 got him a place as a lieutenant in the king's Gardes du corps.

This unit, composed entirely of sons of good families, failed to interest him, and so in that same month of November 1815 he was enrolled in the Departmental Legion of the Yonne, which became the Sixtieth Line Regiment. He participated brilliantly in the Spanish campaign in 1823, obtained two citations, and was named a chevalier in the Legion of Honor. In 1825 he transferred to the Royal Guard with the rank of captain, and he remained at that rank until 1835. In 1828 he entered the Second Regiment of the Light Infantry, and he went with this unit to Algiers in 1830.

The July Revolution delayed the conquest of Algeria, and so Changarnier returned to France and stayed on garrison duty in Perpignan for almost five years. Here, in the city of the liberal Arago brothers, he gained a reputation as a Legitimist, challenging and sometimes dueling with Bonapartists and republicans. Nevertheless, he was well thought of by his commander, the comte de Castellane.

In 1835 his regiment returned to Africa, and Changarnier would take part in all of the campaigns there until 1843, receiving two minor bullet wounds, seven citations, and the rank first of officer, then of commander of the Legion of Honor, an honor he was given in 1841. Within the army, his advancement, which had been slow, would become lightning fast. Named as a battalion commander in 1835, he distinguished himself the following year under Marshal Bertrand Clauzel, and especially during the expedition to Constantine, where he covered the army's retreat to Bône. This earned for him the rank of lieutenant colonel in 1839, and then the battles of Mouzáià and Chéliff earned him the supreme accolade: he was named a maréchal de camp on 21 June 1840 and he received his insignias on 3 July, the same day as Louis de Lamorcière.

In 1837, his birthplace, the city of Autun, had commissioned Horace Vernet to paint *The Retreat from Constantine* to honor the feats of arms of its local hero.

Changarnier, now commander of the provinces of Milianah and Médéah, distinguished himself in 1843 by subduing tribes in the Ténès region who were supporting Abd-el-Kader. But this success, which won him the rank of lieutenant general, ended his first sojourn in Africa. He did not get along with Thomas-Robert Bugeaud, the governor-general of Algeria, and so he returned in that same year (1843) to France, where he was inspector general in various infantry units until 1847.

Several times he refused to go back to Africa. In 1846 he was an unsuccessful candidate for the Chamber of Deputies from Autun. But when Bugeaud gave up his command in Algeria, Changarnier accepted a command in Africa from the duc d'Aumale, who succeeded Bugeaud. The Revolution of February 1848 found Changarnier commander of the Algiers division, a post to which he had been named on 6 October 1847.

Despite his attachment to the duc d'Aumale, he offered his services to the Provisional Government, asking to be posted "to the most threatened frontier." He refused the post of ambassador to Berlin, which Alphonse de Lamartine, president of the Provisional Government, offered him, and remained in Paris, where he advised the Provisional Government during the revolutionary demonstration of 16 April 1848. He was named governor-general of Algeria on 29 April 1848, replacing Eugène Cavaignac, who had been elected to the Constituent Assembly, but his stay there was short. On 4 June he was elected a deputy from the Seine department, and he returned to Paris. He would never go back to Algeria.

On June 29 Cavaignac named him commander in chief of the National Guard of the Seine. He was also put in command of the troops stationed in the First Military Division following the presidential elections of 10 December 1848. Changarnier was thus master of all troops in the capital. On 5 April 1849, he received the plaque of grand officer in the Legion of Honor. Because he was close at that time to President Louis-Napoleon Bonaparte, Changarnier was attacked by the Constituent Assembly, especially by Alexandre-Auguste Ledru-Rollin, and then by the Legislative Assembly, which replaced him with another National Guard commander. But on 13 June 1849, Changarnier got this job back and repressed the riot of that month. This increased his popularity, and he distanced himself more and more from Prince-President Bonaparte and moved closer to the conservatives, who believed that he would use his power as a military commander to restore the monarchy.

Upon learning of the death of Louis-Philippe in 1850, Changarnier ordered a Mass in his memory. Bonapartist newspapers attacked Changarnier, and he was called before Prince Jerome Bonaparte. On 9 January 1851, he was relieved of his two commands. He now drew closer to the Assembly and spoke against "the era of the Caesars," expressing his confidence in the loyalty of the army to the Republic, and on 3 June 1851, he ended his speech by declaring, "Voters of France, deliberate in peace!"

On the morning of 2 December 1851, Changarnier was arrested and brought to Mazas, where he stayed until he was banished by a decree of 9 January 1852. He refused to take the oath given to all functionaries and soldiers and was forcibly retired on 4 August. He moved to Malines and tried to reconcile the Bourbon and Orleans pretenders to the throne. Following the wars in the Crimea and in Italy, he carried on a long-distance polemic with his critics concerning his political conduct during the Second Republic. He returned to France as a result of the amnesty of 1859 and played no part in politics during the second Empire.

In 1870, when war was declared between France and Prussia, Changarnier offered his services to the government. Napoleon III refused at first but on 8 August called him to the command post at Metz. After the fall of France he became active in politics as a Legitimist during the Third Republic until his death in Paris on 14 February 1877.

Biographies du XIXe siècle, 7eme série: le général Changarnier (Paris, 1891); T. Changarnier, *Le Comte d'Antioche* (Paris, 1891) and *Memoires (Campagnes d'Afrique)* (Nancy, Paris, Strasbourg, 1930).

Jean-Claude Caron, trans. E. Newman

Related entries: ALGIERS, EXPEDITION TO; BUGEAUD; CASTELLANE; DEMONSTRATIONS OF 1848–1849; ROYAL GUARD; SPAIN, 1823 FRENCH INVASION OF.

CHANTELAUZE, JEAN-CLAUDE-BALTHAZAR-VICTOR DE (1787–1859), judge and statesman. Born in Montbrison (Loire), he had a brilliant career in the judiciary: deputy prosecutor at Montbrison, attorney general in Lyons (1815), at Douai (1826), and at Riom (1826). In November 1827 he was elected to the Chamber of Deputies, where he stood as a staunch champion of the right wing. Jules de Polignac, when he formed his ministry of August 1829, wished to include him, mainly because of his recognized talent as a public speaker, but Chantelauze declined and instead was given the office of president of the royal court of Riom. In May 1830, however, under the pressing orders of Charles X, he reluctantly joined the faltering administration of Polignac as keeper of the seals (that is, head of the Justice Department). In this capacity he and his colleagues signed the fateful July Ordinances (1830). It was he who wrote the preamble, which remains as a remarkable indictment of the abuses of the freedom of the press. He was arrested while trying to escape and judged by the Chamber of Peers with Polignac and Charles de Peyronnet. Sentenced to life imprisonment, he recovered his freedom in 1838.

E. de Sauzet, *M. de Chantelauze* (Paris, 1860).

Guillaume de Bertier de Sauvigny

Related entries: CHARLES X; JULY ORDINANCES; PEYRONNET; POLIGNAC.

CHARBONNERIE. See CARBONARI.

LE CHARIVARI (1832–1902), satirical newspaper, appearing daily from December 1832 until 1902, with interruptions. Its cofounders were Charles Philipon, who also worked on other satirical papers such as *La Silhouette, La Caricature* and *Le Journal pour rire*, and Louis Desnoyers. Other contributors included Arnould Frémy (vice-president of Louis-Auguste Blanqui's club in 1848), Jules Simon, Taxile Delord, Marie-Michel Altaroche (a republican deputy in 1848 and director of the Odéon 1850–53), and the famous caricaturists Amédée-Charles de Cham and Honoré Daumier. The paper's average print run increased from 918 in 1836 (408 provincial subscriptions) to 2,740 in 1846 (1,705 provincial subscriptions), and, as one of the few papers to survive the upheavals of 1848–51, it was still printing 2,875 copies in 1866.

The biting satire of *Le Charivari*, and especially Daumier's justly famous caricatures of Louis-Philippe, bourgeois life-style, and legal and political corruption, made it fight a running battle with the July Monarchy, and it was repeatedly fined. While some of its subscribers were legitimists who relished the ridiculing of the Orléanist *juste-milieu, Le Charivari* was itself a reformist paper. It welcomed the democratic Republic in 1848 and supported Eugène Cavaignac in the elections in December. While its satire under the Second Republic was aimed chiefly at Bonapartists and social reaction, it did not spare the Left, mocking the women's movement and Eugène Sue, who stood for election as a *démoc-soc* in April 1850 from his chateau in the Loiret.

J.-P. Aguet, "Le tirage des quotidiens de Paris sous la Monarchie de Juillet," *Schweizerische Zeitschrift für Geschichte* 10 (1960); C. Bellanger, J. Godechot, P. Guiral, and F. Terrou, eds, *Histoire generale de la presse francaise*, vol. 2 (Paris, 1969).

Peter McPhee

Related entries: LA CARICATURE; DAUMIER; *JUSTE MILIEU*; LA SILHOUETTE; SUE.

CHARLES X (1757–1836), king of France (earlier, the comte d'Artois). Charles was the fourth son of the dauphin Louis and Marie-Josèphe of Saxony, and grandson of Louis XV. Artois, with his friendly, generous, and impulsive character and with his elegance of stature (which distinguished him from his brothers), was soon the spoiled child of the court, and he gave himself over without restraint to every pleasure. When he began to take an interest in affairs of state in 1785, he was the champion of all the absolutist ideas. This attitude, added to his scandalous reputation, made him a principal target of the Revolutionaries in 1789, and so on the advice of his brother Louis XVI, he emigrated along with his two sons from his marriage to Princess Marie-Thérèse of Savoy: Louis-Antoine, duc d'Angoulême, and Charles-Ferdinand, duc de Berry.

In the following years Artois visited most of the courts of Europe trying to mobilize the forces of monarchy against Revolutionary France.

In March 1805 the death of the countess of Polastron, who had been his *maîtresse en titre* for twenty years, precipitated a deep spiritual crisis in him, and henceforth he showed himself to be just as religious and as irreproachably moral as he had been libertine. When the military defeats of Napoleon in 1813 offered a new chance for the Bourbons, Artois got the permission of the English to go to the Continent and try to influence the leaders of the coalition whose armies were getting ready to invade France. But the allies, who still hoped to negotiate with Napoleon, refused to give him any aid and forbade him to take any action. He was in Nancy, where the population had welcomed him warmly, when on 6 April he heard that Paris had been taken and Napoleon had abdicated. He hastened to the capital, where he made his entry on 12 April amid manifestations of enthusiasm. The Napoleonic Senate recognized him as lieutenant general of the Kingdom, and he took as his ministers the members of the Provisional Government that the Senate had designated when the emperor had abdicated. The leader of this ministry was Charles-Maurice de Talleyrand. During the First Restoration, Artois was kept away from important matters. He was given only the task to stimulate by his presence the royalist sentiments of the provinces of the southeast. When Napoleon returned from Elba, he was sent to Lyons, and there, despite the devotion of Marshal Etienne MacDonald, he could not prevent the troops from rallying to the emperor. He had to flee before he himself was made prisoner. He rejoined Louis XVIII at Ghent and remained there during the interregnum.

At the end of 1815 Artois became the leader and the hope of the ultraroyalist party. His residence, the Pavillon de Marsan, in the Louvre, was denounced by the liberals as the seat of an "occult government" that was undermining the policies of the king throughout the country through a network of secret societies. But all his efforts were blocked by the more powerful influence of Elie Decazes, the royal favorite, who gave a more and more liberal orientation to successive governments. Relations between the king and his brother became so strained that Artois spoke of leaving the country. The assassination of the duc de Berry brought about the fall of Decazes. At the urging of Artois, Richelieu regained power, and the ultraroyalist party regained the terrain it had lost. Meanwhile the comtesse du Cayla, the current favorite of the king, arranged a lasting reconciliation between the two brothers. Louis XVIII ended up accepting in December 1821 a ministry composed entirely of royalists devoted to Artois. Until the end of the reign of Louis XVIII, Joseph de Villèle, president of the Council, governed in perfect agreement with the heir to the throne. The death of Louis XVIII on 16 September 1824 thus caused no change in the government. The coming to the throne of Charles X, which had been feared as a cause of troubles, was carried out in an atmosphere of reconciliation and general good feeling. Henceforth the biography of Charles X becomes more or less the history of the realm.

The new king had conserved, at the age of sixty-seven, his elegant stature and a physical activity that contrasted with the immobility of his predecessor. Friendly and generous, he gave a certain luster to life at court, though his tastes were quite simple, his only hobby being hunting. A large proportion of his civil list went to charitable aid and to the arts and letters. He made it his conscientious duty to follow very closely the affairs of state and did not conceive the role of a constitutional monarch in the British manner. Consequently he became engaged in unpopular and imprudent policies that would lead to the Revolution of July 1830.

When the fallen king left France at Cherbourg, he at first found asylum in the castle of Lulworth (Dorsetshire) and then at Holyrood in Scotland. The growing friendship between the new French government and England made the presence of the Bourbons in Scotland an embarrassment, and the emperor of Austria offered him asylum in his Estates. From the end of 1832 to the start of 1836, Charles X lived in Prague in the castle of Hradschin, where his only concerns seemed to be the preservation of the unchanging forms of royal etiquette and the education of his grandson, the duc de Bordeaux. At the end of 1836 he went to live in Gorizia. He had hardly arrived when he died there from an attack of cholera. He was buried, according to his wish, in the crypt of the church of the Franciscans of Castagnavizza.

V. W. Beach, *Charles X of France, His Life and Times* (Boulder, Colo., 1971); J. Cabanis, *Charles X, roi Ultra* (Paris, 1972); J.-P. Garnier, *Charles X, le roi le proscrit* (Paris, 1967).

Guillaume de Bertier de Sauvigny, trans. E. Newman

Related entries: ANGOULEME; BERRY, C.-F., BORDEAUX; CORONATION OF CHARLES X; DECAZES; DU CAYLA; JULY ORDINANCES; LOUIS XVIII; MACDONALD; RESTORATION, SECOND; REVOLUTION OF 1830; RICHELIEU; TALLEYRAND; ULTRAROYALISTS; VILLELE.

CHARRAS, JEAN-BAPTISTE (1810–1865), colonel. Like many other Polytechniciens of his generation, Charras was swept up in the opposition tide in 1830. He served on the barricades and wrote for the *National*, a left-wing newspaper. Commissioned in the artillery, he was sent to Algeria but soon abandoned that arm for the more active service of the combat units. Considered among the most republican of the officers, he was elected deputy for Puy de Dôme in 1848 and named under secretary of state in the War Ministry. In this capacity, he helped Eugène Cavaignac put down the Revolution of June 1848. An opponent of Louis-Napoleon Bonaparte, he was exiled after the coup d'état of 2 December 1851. He died in Basel. He is the author of *Histoire de la campagne de 1815, Waterloo*.

Douglas Porch

Related entries: CAVAIGNAC, L.-E.; COUP D'ETAT OF 2 DECEMBER 1851; ECOLE POLYTECHNIQUE; JUNE DAYS; *LE NATIONAL*; REVOLUTION OF 1830; REVOLUTION OF 1848.

CHARTE, LA. See CHARTER OF 1814; CHARTER OF 1830.

CHARTER OF 1814, the constitution "granted" by Louis XVIII. On 3 April 1814, the French Senate and Legislative Body declared Napoleon dethroned, and on 6 April, after much discussion and under pressure from the victorious Allies, the French restored the Bourbons in the person of the comte de Provence (as Louis XVIII) on condition that he accept a constitution. They wrote one for him that contained a ludicrous attempt by the imperial Senate to give itself job security by making itself permanent. Louis XVIII ignored this document, but in his Charter of 1814 he accepted its main provisions. (Later he even mollified the senators by including many of them in his Chamber of Peers.) In essence, the king accepted the Revolutionary settlement while insisting that nothing had changed. In the preamble he said that "all authority in France resides in the person of the king" and that the Charter was merely a "grant and concession" offered by an absolute monarch to his subjects. But then he accepted the principal changes achieved by the Revolution: equality before the law, taxation in proportion to ability to pay, freedom of religion, and freedom from arbitrary arrest and prosecution.

The Charter did not grant these rights absolutely. Although it granted freedom of worship, it also established Roman Catholicism as the religion of the state. Although Frenchmen were to have the right to publish and to have their opinions printed, they could do so only "while conforming to the laws which are necessary to restrain abuses of liberty." There was to be a two-chamber legislature, but it must share its power with the king: "The legislative power is exercised collectively by the king, the Chamber of Peers, and the Chamber of Deputies." Furthermore, the legislature could not initiate laws; it could only petition the king to initiate them. No bill could become law without the concurrence of the two chambers and the signature of the king. The ministers were responsible, but the Charter did not say to whom. Article 14 of the Charter stated that the king "makes the necessary regulations and ordinances for the execution of the laws and the security of the state," and this gave the king an opening to justify absolute rule in the name of the security of the state. Thus there was enough of the Old Regime in the Charter to make the document ambiguous.

But it quickly gained the support of liberals because of the essential concessions that it did make. Most important, it ratified the Revolutionary land settlement. It declared all property to be inviolable, including the so-called national lands, which had been confiscated from the church and the *émigrés* and sold by the Revolutionary government. The national debt, including government securities sold during the Revolution, was also guaranteed. The Legion of Honor was maintained.

In addition, conscription was abolished, and this won support from the common people. The Restoration would have been even more popular had it carried out its promise to abolish the *droits réunis*, or sales taxes, on wine and necessities, but it needed the money to pay off government bonds, and thus the Charter preferred the interests of middle-class bondholders to those of ordinary taxpayers.

Article 68 of the Charter provided that "the Civil Code *(Code Napoléon)* and the laws actually existing which are not in conflict with the present charter remain in force until legally abrogated." Thus, Revolutionary legislation, such as the decree abolishing feudalism, remained the law of the land throughout the Restoration era. The Concordat of 1801, which Napoleon had negotiated with Pope Pius VII, also survived Napoleon's downfall and was not repealed until 1905.

The Charter of 1814 enjoyed wide respect and even reverence throughout the Restoration. When in 1830 King Charles X tried to use article 14 as a device to become an absolute monarch, his opponents based their stand on the Charter, and "Long live the Charter!" was the shout most frequently heard in the streets during the Revolution of 1830. The new Charter of 1830, which was the result of that revolution, was little more than a refinement of the Charter of 1814, which provides the basis of the French political and legal structure even today.

F. Anderson, ed., *Constitutions and Other Select Documents Illustrative of the History of France, 1789–1901*, 2nd ed. (Minneapolis, 1904); V. Beach, *Charles X of France: His Life and Times* (Boulder, 1971), "The Fall of Charles X of France: A Case Study of Revolution,'' *University of Colorado Studies*, History Series 2 (1961), and ''The Polignac Ministry: A Reevaluation,'' *University of Colorado Studies*, History Series 3 (January 1964); G. de Bertier de Sauvigny, *The Bourbon Restoration* (Philadelphia, 1966); E. L. Newman, ''The Blouse and the Frock Coat: The Alliance of the Common People of Paris with the Liberal Leadership in the Middle Class during the Last Years of the Bourbon Restoration,'' *Journal of Modern History* 46, (1974); D. Pinkney, *The French Revolution of 1830* (Princeton, 1972).

Vincent Beach

Related entries: CHAMBER OF DEPUTIES; CHAMBER OF PEERS; CHARLES X; CHARTER OF 1830; *DROITS REUNIS*; LOUIS XVIII; NATIONAL LANDS; REVOLUTION OF 1830.

CHARTER OF 1830, the revised version of the Charter of 1814, which substituted a limited constitutional monarchy for the divine right monarchy of the Bourbons. During a simple ceremony held on 9 August 1830, the duc d'Orléans appeared before a joint session of the Chamber of Deputies and the Chamber of Peers and formally accepted a declaration that called him to the throne as king of the French and swore to observe the Constitutional Charter of 1830. This event, in many ways the symbolic conclusion of the Revolution of 1830, brought to an end eleven days of frantic political activity and maneuvering during which moderate leaders struggled to endow France with a form of limited constitutional monarchy that would replace the divine right monarchy of the recently overthrown Bourbons. The Charter of 1830, a revised version of the Charter given to France in 1814 by Louis XVIII, embodied in its seventy articles the fruits of these efforts.

Two major constitutional problems and a host of lesser ones confronted French politicians in Paris when the fighting of the ''Three Glorious Days'' ended. The first centered on the question of who would head the new government, and the second concerned the form that government would assume. The issuance of the July Ordinances and the fighting in Paris provoked by them made it clear that the Bourbon king Charles X could not remain on the throne. Further, republicans, encouraged by the victory won in the streets, were prepared to demand the abolition of the monarchy altogether and its replacement by a republic. In this unsettled situation, moderate deputies and politicians had to act quickly and decisively to ensure that their choice of a monarch, the duc d'Orléans, the head of the younger branch of the Bourbon family, would be placed on the French throne. Called on by a proclamation of the deputies, which also contained a list of proposed changes in the structure of the government, to become lieutenant general of the kingdom on 31 July, he agreed to accept, declaring on 1 August, ''The Charter henceforth shall be a reality.'' But on the date of this declaration, Charles X had not yet abdicated, and no consensus existed on how a revised Charter should read.

While the duc d'Orléans moved with dispatch to consolidate his hold on the executive power, discussions concerning the future of the Charter of 1814 began in the Chamber of Deputies. On 3 August, the duke read a short speech, written by himself but carefully edited by François Guizot and the lawyer André Dupin, to the assembled peers and deputies. It reflected a conservative interpretation of the July Revolution, one of three emerging conceptions of the Revolution, and it called for preservation of the 1814 Charter with but minor alterations. Opposing this conception of the revolution were the republicans, men who wanted, if not to abolish the monarchy, to surround it with republican institutions, and the moderate majority, who favored retention of the Charter with significant modifications. Auguste Bérard, who emerged as the spokesman for this latter group made up largely of deputies from the Laffitte circle, suggested in a draft proposal of 3 August that the Charter be revised so as to base the new government on the venerable social contract theory. Bérard's group wanted to impose special conditions on the new king that were too radical for the duc d'Orleans. Orléans and his advisers did not reject Bérard's proposal outright; instead they assigned Guizot and the duc de Broglie to prepare an alternate draft. Completed on the fourth and the fifth, this text eliminated the contract theory, called for changes in about one-third of the Charter's articles, and enumerated a list of pressing matters on which the Chambers would promise to legislate. After making revisions in the Guizot-Broglie text, most notably the deletion of language that might have allowed the duc d'Orléans to make a legitimate claim to the throne, Bérard presented this text to the Chamber, and, with a few additional changes made in committee and on the floor, the deputies adopted the revised Charter of 1830 by a vote of 219 to 33. Before the Peers could vote on the new text, the deputies had marched to the Palais-Royal and presented the duc d'Orléans with a proclamation that declared the throne vacant, detailed the changes in the Charter, listed areas in which legislation was still necessary, and invited the duke to become king; Orléans accepted with alacrity. Meanwhile, the Peers approved the Charter by a vote of 88 to 10. On the next day, the duke announced his decision to take the title of Louis-Philippe I, not the expected Philippe VII; this new title symbolized the beginning of a new dynasty and distanced it from the Bourbons. On the ninth, Louis-Philippe stood before members of both chambers, accepted the crown, and swore to defend the Charter.

Of the many differences between the Charter of 1814 and that of 1830, the most important concerned the nature of the monarchy and the relation between the monarch and the constitution. In 1814, the monarchy's existence was independent of that of the nation, and Louis XVIII based his claim to the French throne on the theory of legitimacy. The Charter, as both the name given to the document and the notorious preamble make patently clear, was nothing more than a royal gift to the nation, a generous grant of specified liberties and guarantees. In contrast, the Charter of 1830 was the work of a legislative assembly, although significantly not one elected to draft a constitution, and it was then accepted by the king. Reviving, albeit tentatively and with notable caution, the doctrine of the sovereignty of the nation, these representatives of the people arbitrarily declared the throne vacant and called Louis-Philippe to it not as a divine right king, but as king of the French, a title chosen to emphasize the break with the old monarchy. The new monarchy was thus, in a limited sense, both elective and contractual; it was the work of the elected representatives of the nation, and it was imposed on the king.

The remaining modifications in the Charter of 1814 were drafted largely to remove areas of controversy that had arisen during the Restoration and to eliminate provisions considered offensive to the French nation. Into this last category fell the preamble of 1814, which had, in addition to describing the Charter as a royal gift, and to emphasizing the divine origin of regal power, underscored the continuity of the French monarchy, thus virtually eliminating the Revolutionary and imperial periods from French history. The new preamble stated simply that Louis-Philippe, as king of the French, ordered the publication of the Charter as amended by the two chambers; the preamble thus emphasized the role of the monarch as executor of the laws made by the chambers.

Other revisions to the Charter may be briefly summarized. In the first section, "Public Laws of the French" (articles 1–11), two articles underwent major alterations. Article 6, which had established the Catholic religion as the religion of the state, was changed so as to state that Catholicism was the religion of the majority of Frenchmen. Modifications made in the wording of article 7 guaranteed freedom of the press and absolutely prohibited the reestablishment of censorship. Changes in articles 12–19, "Forms of the Government of the King," affirmed the role of the king as executor of the laws and stated unequivocally that he could neither suspend nor fail to execute the laws passed by the Assembly. The provisions of article 14 of the 1814 Charter that had permitted Charles X to issue ordinances, such as the July Ordinances of 1830, in the case of national security were eliminated. In the revised Charter, the king had to share the right to initiate laws with both chambers (article 15). Only minor changes were made to the articles (20–29) relating to the Chamber of Peers; one stated that sessions of the Chamber had to be henceforth public. However, the role of the peerage in the government, the method by which peers were created, and the question of whether the peerage should be hereditary were questions that stimulated passionate debate in 1830. Some spokesmen even demanded that the peerage be completely abolished. The authors of the Charter prudently avoided committing themselves on this volatile issue and, although they allowed the inclusion in the new Charter of the article from the 1814 document concerning royal appointment of peers, they also provided (article 68) that the whole question of the peerage would be considered during the legislative session of 1831.

Substantive changes in the articles (30–45) relating to the Chamber of Deputies ensured that France after 1830 would be slightly more democratic. The electoral term for a deputy was fixed at five years, and all members were required to stand for reelection at the same time. Both the minimum age required for election as a deputy and for the right to be an elector were reduced, the former from forty to thirty and the latter from thirty to twenty-five. Although a minimum tax payment was required of a candidate or an elector, the actual amount of this tax was not specified until the law of 19 April 1831. The Chamber of Deputies also gained a measure of independence from the crown by the provisions of article 35, which declared that presidents of departmental electoral colleges were to be chosen by the electors, and article 37, which permitted the Chamber to elect its own president. With regard to the ministers (articles 46–47), the Charter made them legally accountable for all their acts, not just for acts of treason and peculation as before. In the articles (48–59) relating to the judiciary, only one change was made; eliminated was the sentence that allowed the establishment of provost courts (article 54).

Completing the Charter of 1830 were two sections, one that contained a seemingly random collection of guarantees (articles 60–67) and the other a number of special provisions (articles 68–70). According to the vague and ambiguous language of article 66, the Charter and the rights guaranteed by it were placed under the special protection of the National Guard and patriotic French citizens. The following article declared that France adopted once again the tricolor; just as Louis XVIII had linked his regime with the *Ancien régime* by resurrecting in 1814 the fleur-de-lys, so the authors of the July Monarchy symbolically linked the new government with the colors of Revolutionary and imperial France. Completing the Charter of 1830 was a group of three articles, the contents of which had originally appeared in the Proclamation of the Deputies of 31 July 1830 that had called upon Louis-Philippe to assume the office of lieutenant general, and the declaration of 7 August 1830 that had declared the throne vacant and had invited Louis-Philippe to accept the crown as king of the French. Article 68 pronounced void all the nominations to the peerage made by Charles X and provided for a prompt examination of the whole question of the peerage. The penultimate article provided that nine separate items, including jury trials for press and political offenses, ministerial responsibility, the reelection of deputies appointed to public office, the recruitment of the army, the organization of the National Guard and the election of its officers, the legal status of army and navy officers, the creation of an electoral basis for department and municipal government, the questions of public instruction and freedom of teaching, the abolition of the hated double vote, and the establishment of minimum requirements for electors and candidates would be examined by the chambers in the near future. The framers of the Charter of 1830 completed their work by abolishing all laws and ordinances contrary to the new constitution.

That article 68 and the penultimate article of the Charter listed important items requiring the immediate attention of the two chambers clearly indicates that the process of government making was far from complete on 14 August 1830, the day of the promulgation of the Charter of 1830. Over the course of the next seventeen months, the chambers would debate and pass four fundamental laws that would largely complete the work left undone by the Charter, laws that Félix Ponteil calls the legal basis of the July Monarchy. Of these four laws, the important electoral law of 19 April 1831 specified the conditions that had to be met before a man could be inscribed on the voting rolls or could stand as a candidate for election to the Chamber of Deputies. It abolished the double vote, and it reduced both the minimum age of a voter from thirty to twenty-five, and the minimum direct tax from 300 to 200 francs, unless the voter belonged to the Institute or was a retired army officer, in which case the minimum tax was fixed at 100 francs. To be eligible for election to the lower chamber, a man had to be at least thirty, reduced from forty in the Charter of 1814, and he had to pay a minimum direct tax of at least 500 francs, reduced from 1,000 francs. In the circumstance where the number of voters and/or candidates fell below a certain number, the rolls could be filled by men paying a lower tax. While this law certainly provided for a younger and more broadly based electorate, it did not move France dramatically along the road to true democracy. Although the number of electors rose from about 94,000 before the Revolution of 1830 to almost 169,000 in 1831, the voting rolls inscribed a significantly smaller portion of the French population than did the English ones after the Reform Bill of 1832. By 1848, the number of electors had risen to a mere 241,000.

Three other fundamental laws—the Law on Municipal Organization (21 March 1831), the Law on the National Guard (22 March 1831), and the Law on the Peerage (29 December 1831)—all adopted before 1831 came to an end, completing the process of constructing a legal basis for the July Monarchy. The Law on Municipal Organization based local government on the electoral system, for it gave to the electors the right to choose the municipal council, from which either the king or the prefect, depending on the size of the commune, appointed the mayor. Of this law, which virtually ensured control over the local government by men of property, Louis Blanc remarked that it based municipal power on 34,000 small bourgeois oligarchies. The Law on the National Guard provided a legal basis for the Guard, abolished during the Restoration and provisionally reestablished on 29 July 1830, charged it with the maintenance of internal order and with assisting the army in the national defense, and ensured, by allowing only taxpayers to enroll, that its members would come from the middle classes. The Law on the Peerage abolished hereditary seats in the Chamber of Peers and replaced them with life peers appointed by the king from certain categories. Not abolished, as many revolutionaries wanted in 1830, the peerage was transformed so the upper middle class could enter its ranks.

The revised Charter of 1830 left intact much of the governmental edifice constructed in 1814. Of the significant modifications made in it, those concerning the nature of the Charter itself and those concerning the role of the monarch are most important. No longer the gift of the monarch, the Charter of 1830 was the work of the representatives of the nation, and they imposed it on the king. The French nation nonetheless was never asked to approve, by a plebiscite or otherwise, the completed Charter. And although the exact legal basis for the new monarchy was ambiguous, for Louis-Philippe was neither a legitimate sovereign nor an elected king, the king of the French was clearly a constitutional monarch. The Revolution of 1830, in short, revived the revolutionary doctrine of national sovereignty.

F. M. Anderson, *The Constitutions and Other Select Documents Illustrative of the History of France, 1789–1901*, 2d ed. (Minneapolis, 1904); P. Bastid, *Les Institutions politiques de la monarchie parlementaire française, 1814–1848* (Paris, 1954); A. Bérard, *Souvenirs historiques sur la Révolution de 1830* (Paris, 1834); M. Deslandres, *Histoire constitutionelle de France de 1789 à 1870*, 3 vols. (Paris, 1932); L. Duguit, H. Monnier, and R. Bonnard, *Les Constitutions et les principales lois politiques de la France depuis 1789*, 7th ed. (Paris, 1952); M. Duverger, *Constitutions et documents politiques*, 6th ed. (Paris, 1971); D. Pinkney, *The French Revolution of 1830* (Princeton, 1972); F. Ponteil, *Les Institutions de la France de 1814 à 1870* (Paris, 1965).

Robert Brown

Related entries: BERARD; BROGLIE, A.–L.–V.; CHAMBER OF DEPU-TIES; CHAMBER OF PEERS; CHARTER OF 1814; ELECTIONS AND ELEC-TORAL SYSTEMS; LAFFITTE; LOUIS PHILIPPE; REVOLUTION OF 1830.

CHARTRES, ROBERT-PHILIPPE-LOUIS-EUGENE-FERDINAND D'ORLEANS, DUC DE (1840–1910), son of the duke of Orléans and grandson of Louis-Philippe. Robert d'Orléans, duke of Chartres, was born in Paris on 9 November 1840, the second son of the duke of Orléans and Hélène of Mecklenburg–Schwerin, and the grandson of King Louis-Philippe. The duke of Orléans died 13 July 1842 as the result of a carriage accident, and Hélène, a devoted Lutheran, oversaw the education of their son.

During the February Revolution in 1848, in a vain attempt to preserve an Orleanist monarchy, Robert and his brother, the count of Paris, were brought into the Chamber of Deputies after Louis-Philippe's abdication on 25 February. Robert, ill at the time, was separated from his mother in the tumult, and they were not rejoined until 26 February at the chateau of Bligny, near Limour. Hélène then left France with her children, traveling by rail from Amiens to Belgium. They stayed first at Eisenach and then moved to England, where they were attended to by a little entourage of Frenchmen.

There Robert d'Orléans continued his education. As a soldier, he fought for Piedmont, the Union Army during the American Civil War, and, as Robert Lefort, for France during the Franco–Prussian War. He commanded a band of thirty to forty men, dubbed the Scouts of the Seine–Inférieure. He fought with the army of Normandy at Longchamps and Etrépagny, and on 2 December joined the staff of General Briand. Still known as Robert Lefort, he was nominated for the Legion of Honor. The subterfuge no longer necessary, Robert, the duke of Chartres, made his real identity known. He was retained in the army and given the rank of regular major. On 18 July 1878 he was appointed colonel of the Twelfth Light Infantry at Rouen. He was, however, removed from active service on 23 February 1883 and on 23 June 1886 stripped of his rank in virtue of a law excluding the members of former French ruling families from military service.

He spent the rest of his life traveling, hunting, and studying history and the military. He amassed a library of five thousand volumes and was chosen president of the Sociètè des bibliophiles français. He died at the chateau of Vineuil–S.–Firmin near Chantilly, on 5 December 1910.

P. Leguay, article in *Dictionnaire de biographie française*, vol. 8 (Paris, 1959); P. de Lessert, *Le duc de Chartres* (Paris, 1914).

Bernard Cook

Related entries: JOINVILLE; LOUIS PHILIPPE; NEMOURS; PARIS, COUNT OF; REVOLUTION OF 1848.

CHATEAUBRIAND, FRANCOIS-RENE, VICOMTE DE (1768–1848), writer and statesman. His choice of style and subject matter was perhaps the single greatest influence on the rise of French romanticism. Although influenced by Jean-Jacques Rousseau, his particular blend of Breton melancholy, overweaning egotism, and flamboyant prose was an entirely personal invention. Although he spent half his life contemplating and composing his posthumous memoirs, it is almost impossible to discover the factual reality from his personal perceptions of the remembered past.

Chateaubriand called himself the chevalier de Combourg, and the ancient chateau occupies a central place in his published recollections of childhood, but in fact he did not discover it until 1777, and after his father's death he returned only four times for brief visits. He was born and for the most part raised in St. Malo, the sickly youngest son of a merchant shipowner of the old nobility. Proud and hypersensitive, Chateaubriand suffered from the indifference of his stern, forbidding father. Of his four sisters, he was devoted to and identified most with Lucile. He described her as having a funereal imagination, and it was she who introduced him to the bittersweet joys of melancholy reminiscences.

The last-born son faced an uncertain future, and after studies at Dol, Rennes, and Dinan, he obtained a commission as second lieutenant in the Navarre regiment. It is possible that his father, fatigued with his depressive moods, which had culminated in an attempted suicide, determined this move. Although only five feet four inches tall, Chateaubriand wore the uniform with flair. He was presented at court in 1787 and began to benefit from the patronage of the minister, Chrétien-Guillaume de Malesherbes. The Revolution found his sympathies divided between the intellectual doctrines of the *philosophes* and the royalist sympathies that were part of his family heritage. He abhorred violence, and undoubtedly the turn of Revolutionary events in 1791, combined with his thirst for adventure and new sensations, determined his decision to set sail for America to seek the Northwest Passage.

In fact, Chateaubriand remained only five months in the New World, and considerable scholarship has been devoted to proving that he could not have seen the Mississippi or made the extensive overland voyages that he described with such meticulous eye-witness authority. The writings spawned by this voyage, however, are a tribute to the amplification of memory and the imaginative transposition of his prodigious readings and remembered experiences. There is no question that those few months played a capital role in the later development of his literary career.

When word of the arrest of Louis XVI reached him, he returned precipitously to France. In March 1792, he entered into a marriage of convenience with Céleste Buisson de la Vigne, a friend of his sister Lucile. He left her shortly after to join the army of *émigrés* in Brussels. Wounded in the siege of Thionville, he made his way to England and spent seven years (1793–1800) in exile, enduring great hardship. His study of English law convinced him, as it had his admired predecessor Montesquieu, that a constitutional monarchy was the preferred form of government.

During the years in England, he also began to meditate a dramatic reappraisal of the Christian faith. Here again, Chateaubriand's account of his new-found religious fervor differs from the historical. Upon receiving news simultaneously of the deaths of his mother and his sister Julie, he wrote, "I wept and I believed." According to contemporary accounts, however, the bookseller Dulau, a former Benedictine monk, advised him that the way to draw the spotlight to himself was to declare war on the religious philosophies of Voltaire and Rousseau. By the time he received word of the deaths in his family, he was already hard at work on a Christian apologetic, which would take advantage of the French religious reaction to the Terror.

Le Génie du christianisme was almost ready for the publisher when Chateaubriand returned to France in 1800, but in order to acquaint the public with his name, he published *Atala,* a tale of the love of "two savages in the desert" in 1801. It was an instant success. The following year, concurrently with Napoleon's Concordat with the pope, he published *Le Génie,* which at that time included *Réné,* another illustration of man's spontaneous natural religious sentiment. *Le Génie* enjoyed an immediate and astounding success and brought him favor with Napoleon, who appointed him to the embassy at Rome. Chateaubriand was ideologically incapable of long remaining in Napoleon's camp, however, and he resigned his appointment in protest after the execution of the duc d'Enghien in 1804.

During the Napoleonic era, he traveled in Greece, the Near East, and Spain (1806–7), which provided color and material for later fiction, and he lived outside Paris in his small property of La Vallée aux loups, where he devoted himself to writing. Somewhat surprisingly, considering his open hostility to the Empire, Napoleon neither exiled him nor blocked his election to the French Academy in 1811, but he was never allowed to read his politically provocative reception speech.

The rise of Chateaubriand as a statesman coincided with the downfall of Napoleon. His vituperative pamphlet, *De Buonaparte et des Bourbons*, published in 1814, did more for the Restoration, in Louis XVIII's words, than 100,000 soldiers. Chateaubriand's political star rose: he became minister to the king (1815), peer of France, ambassador to Berlin (1821) and to London (1822) and minister of foreign affairs (1823). However, Chateaubriand's ambitious political behavior, which provoked the fall of the Decazes ministry, and his success in obtaining the right to French intervention at the Congress of Verona and in organizing the Spanish expedition, spawned jealousy and hostility. His star waned under Charles X, both politically and financially, and he took refuge in writing. *Les Natchez* was finally published (1826), incorporating *Atala* and *Réné*.

Chateaubriand's last two decades were spent primarily in the daily company of his long-time respected friend, Mme. Récamier, and his memories. Financial necessity obliged him to take "a mortgage on his grave," as he termed the payment in advance for his posthumous *Mémoires d'outre-tombe*. His long lifetime spanned the Old Regime, the Revolution, the Empire, the Restoration, and the July Monarchy. The memoirs offered him the perfect forum to indulge his cult of the self against the background of an epic vision of the passage of the Old Regime to the modern world.

Of his contributions to the state, he wrote, "Had there been no Chateaubriand, what a difference in the world." Politically the claim may be debatable, but it is incontestable that his writing opened a new era of personal, poetic, evocative prose and that such giants of melancholy romantic poetry as Byron, Lamartine, and Hugo are deeply indebted to him. Chateaubriand's voyages infused his writing with vibrant color and the mystery and excitement of the exotic, revolutionizing the world of letters as Eugène Delacroix had revolutionized painting.

Chateaubriand extended his superb isolation beyond the grave. He was buried according to his wishes on the island of Grand-Bé, facing his perennial consolation and inspiration, the romantic, melancholy Breton sea.

M. Levaillant et al., *Chateaubriand, prince des songes* (Paris, 1960); A. Maurois, *Chateaubriand: Poet, Statesman, Lover*, trans. Vera Fraser (New York, 1938); G. Painter, *Chateaubriand: a Biography* (New York, 1978).

Shelby A. Outlaw

Related entries: HUGO; RECAMIER; ROMANTICISM; SPAIN, 1823 FRENCH INVASION OF; VERONA, CONGRESS OF.

CHAUSSEE D'ANTIN, a fine street built at the end of the eighteenth century, leading north from the boulevard des Italiens. It became a fashionable site for the luxurious, modern houses built for the emerging aristocracy of financiers and merchants. The neighborhood benefited from the construction of these homes, and an entire quarter of the second arrondissement took the name d'Antin. The name also came to designate by metonymical association the higher, wealthy bourgeoisie, for whom the quarter was a favorite place of residence.

Guillaume de Bertier de Sauvigny

CHEVALIER, MICHEL (1806–1879), Saint-Simonian socialist theorist and journalist who became an adviser to Napoleon III under the Second Empire. Socialism was a flexible doctrine during the years between the two Napoleons. Radicals like Louis Blanc might wave it as a flag of revolt, but conservatives like Michel Chevalier could hide behind it and use it as a cover to justify their inactivity. Yet Chevalier's socialism was no less sincere than that of his radical comrades.

Chevalier was born in Limoges (Haute-Vienne) on 3 April 1806, one of seven children of a bureaucrat. He was a good student at the Collège royal of Limoges and in 1823 went on to the Ecole polytechnique in Paris. It seems that his lifelong dream of engineering a better society was formed at the Polytechnique. Shortly after his graduation thirteenth in his class in 1825, Chevalier, now a mining engineer, began to contribute articles to the Saint–Simonian newspaper *L'Organisateur*. The success of these articles brought him to the attention of Prosper Enfantin, a fellow Polytechnicien who had become the Father of the Saint-Simonian church. In the first months after the July Revolution of 1830, Chevalier left his job and became editor of the *Globe,* which the Saint-Simonians had just bought. He lived with Enfantin in the Saint-Simonian monastery in Ménilmontant. In this Parisian setting he helped to edit the bible of the new sect, served at table, and scrubbed the floor.

The growing success of the sect and its advocacy of free love brought Chevalier before the assize court of the Seine in 1832 along with Enfantin. Condemned to a year of prison and a fine of 100 francs, Chevalier and the other Saint-Simonians were released after six months. Chevalier went to the United States for two years in order to study the communications system, also visiting Canada, Mexico, and Cuba. The letters he wrote back were published in the influential *Journal des débats* during his voyage and then in his two-column *Lettres sur l'Amérique du Nord* (Paris, 1836) after his return.

The ex-prisoner enjoyed a rapid rise in influence. In 1836 he was named a chevalier of the Legion of Honor, then Maître des requêtes to the Council of State, and in 1840 professor of political economy at the Collège de France. He pushed hard to reverse the protectionist policies of Louis-Philippe and to establish free trade, which he saw as the only means to improve the condition of the working classes. In 1844 he advised the Saint-Simonian banker Olinde Rodriguès when he set up his retirement funds for workers.

Chevalier was strongly opposed to the nationalization of the means of production advocated by socialists like Louis Blanc. He favored producer cooperative associations. In the *Revue des deux-mondes* of 15 March 1848, he opposed both Blanc's National Workshops and Charles Fourier's phalansteries, but he recommended that the government appropriate 5 million or 10 million francs to each scheme because they were "fashionable nowadays." In May 1848, Chevalier was appointed an officer of the new bank of the revolutionary Provisional Government.

He became a close adviser to Napoleon III after his coup d'état and was able to push the Second Empire toward a policy of free trade. He negotiated the landmark Cobden–Chevalier Treaty with England in 1860 and organized the French exposition at the London fair of 1862. He remained a socialist, albeit in imperial uniform, and tried to end the growing separation of rich from poor by lending government money to small businessmen and artisans. He died near Lodève (Hérault) in November 1879.

S. Charléty, *Histoire du saint-simonisme* (Paris, 1825–64); S. Nicard des Rieux, *Michel Chevalier et Saint-Simon* (Poitiers, 1912).

Edgar L. Newman

Related entries: COLLEGE DE FRANCE; ECOLE POLYTECHNIQUE; EN-FANTIN; FOREIGN TRADE AND TARIFF POLICY; FOURIER; *LE GLOBE*; *JOURNAL DES DEBATS*; *L'ORGANISATEUR*; *REVUE DES DEUX MONDES*; SAINT-SIMONIANISM; SOCIALISM; WORKERS' COOPERATIVES.

CHEVALIERS DE LA FOI (KNIGHTS OF THE FAITH), a royalist and Catholic secret society founded in mid–1810 by Count Ferdinand de Bertier. The founder had been convinced by the ideas of Father Augustin Barruel that the French Revolution had begun as a Freemason conspiracy, and consequently he had decided to fight Freemasonry with its own arms by creating an anti-Masonic secret society at the service of the throne and the altar. This society would also revive the virtues and organization of the old knighthood, and its founders even wanted to make it into a military religious order similar to the Knights of Malta. They asked the pope twice for his approval, and both times he refused. At the end of the Empire, the society had been able to create a real resistance network in several provinces to prepare public opinion for a restoration of the Bourbons. In the spring of 1814 it set off a series of demonstrations, including the uprising of 12 March 1814 in Bordeaux, that allowed Charles-Maurice de Talleyrand to assure the Allies that the only possible alternative was the restoration of Louis XVIII.

During the Second Restoration the society, which had eliminated its most liberal elements, became the soul of the ultraroyalist party. It was directed by a supreme council of nine people presided over by a grand master, Mathieu de Montmorency. Known at that time as the Société de l'anneau, it included many priests, and the liberals denounced it as an occult government opposed to the government of the king. Protected by the comte d'Artois, it fought fiercely against the royal favorite, Elie Decazes. But when its leaders came to power at the end of 1821, they were soon divided, especially on the question of French intervention in Spain. Joseph de Villèle, although a member of the group, caused the minister of foreign affairs, Montmorency, grand master of the secret society, to resign. Yet the society continued to strengthen its influence: the sympathy of Charles X for its leaders and the number of its members elected to the *Chambre retrouvée* in 1824 (there were more than a hundred of them) allowed it to force Villèle to put forth several reactionary laws, such as the law against sacrilege. After Villèle, president of the Council, had forced the society to follow his policies, its founders brought about its dissolution at the start of 1826. They hoped thereby to put an end to the polemic that the liberals were directing against the Congrégation, which was wrongly being held responsible for the actions of the Chevaliers de la foi. But their hopes were dashed and the polemic continued unabated.

G. de Bertier de Sauvigny, *Le comte Ferdinand de Bertier et l'énigme de la Congrégation* (Paris, 1948).

G. de Bertier de Sauvigny, trans. E. Newman
Related entries: BERTIER; CONGREGATION; DECAZES; FREEMA-
SONRY; LAW OF SACRILEGE; MONTMORENCY; TALLEYRAND,
CHARLES-MAURICE DE; ULTRAROYALISTS; VILLELE.

CHILD LABOR. French children were commonly put to work from a very
young age, and although their work experiences in agriculture and in handicraft
production in the early nineteenth century remained much as they had been in
the past, their participation in new forms of industrial labor became a matter of
concern and the subject of legislation.

In the family economies of traditional French society, the initiation of children
into productive activity from the age of six or seven was an accepted practice.
Child labor had always played an integral role in agricultural production and in
small-shop manufacturing. Commonly, very young children fed the poultry and
fetched the water, herded the cows and gleaned in the fields, cleaned the wool
and carded it for spinning. Thus, as France began to industrialize in the early
decades of the nineteenth century, it seemed natural for children to find work in
the new factories as well. Children served most commonly in textile mills, where
they tied broken threads, replaced bobbins, and cleaned machines, but youngsters
were found also in many other industries. By the mid–1840s there were some
144,000 children under sixteen employed in French industry, and these children
constituted about 12 percent of the industrial work force.

From very early in the century, there were a few individuals who noticed the
great differences between the traditional uses of children in productive activity
and their use in factory labor. Factory labor was far more intense and highly
disciplined than traditional labor, and it was devoid of the personal relationships
that existed between youngsters and their elders in traditional work situations.
It was only in the late 1820s, however, that serious suggestions for the regulation
of industrial child labor began to be heard. The very first broadly conceived plan
for national child labor reform was that proposed by Jean Jacques Bourcart, an
Alsatian industrialist. Bourcart's plan won the support of many in the Industrial
Society of Mulhouse, and soon that body placed itself at the forefront of the
child labor reform movement.

In the first decade of the July Monarchy, the concept of national legislation
to control child labor gained further backing. By the middle of the decade several
influential propagandists, most notably Alban de Villeneuve-Bargemont and
Louis Villermé, had registered their support for child labor reform, and in 1837
the government acknowledged the growing concern over child labor by initiating
its own inquiry. The inquiry of 1837 was itself the catalyst for further interest
in the child labor problem, and the crusaders for reform were able to increase
their pressure on the government. Although their number remained quite small,
the champions of reform were effective because they focused their attention on

forcing the government to act rather than on bestirring public opinion. In January 1840, the administration submitted a child labor bill to the Chamber of Peers. The most active champions of child labor reform within the legislature, led by Baron Charles Dupin, greatly strengthened the bill placed before them, and although the revised measure faced some opposition from champions of laissez-faire and much apathy from those with little interest in industrial matters, it was adopted by both houses of the legislature and enacted early in 1841.

The Child Labor Law of 1841 established eight as the minimum age for employment and eight hours as the maximum workday for children under the age of twelve. The law allowed children twelve to sixteen a maximum workday of twelve hours, and it severely restricted the employment of youngsters at night and on Sundays and holidays. Minimal requirements for school attendance were also incorporated into the law, and the measure was made applicable in mechanized shops and in those employing more than twenty workers. Perhaps the major weakness of the 1841 law was its lack of serious provisions for enforcement. Largely because of the mixed feelings in the legislature over factory reform, enforcement of the law was left in the hands of locally constituted child labor commissions composed of volunteers. Still, the 1841 law was extremely important, as it represented a major first step toward state intervention in industrial affairs and a major first step toward state protection of the welfare of children.

Throughout the final years of the July Monarchy, implementation of the 1841 Child Labor Law remained problematic. Many of the provisions of the law were generally observed: few children under eight were put to work in factories; the prohibition of night and Sunday labor was widely observed. But these practices were rare in the first place. Restrictions that manufacturers considered inappropriate or burdensome were often ignored; it was not uncommon for children under twelve to work more than eight hours a day, and the regulation concerning schooling for factory children was often ignored.

The most active champions of reform, both inside the government and out, saw the limitations of the 1841 law from the outset, and they did not hesitate to press for a strengthening of factory legislation. The efforts to bring about further reform were bolstered by the appearance of poetry and literature with the problem of working children as a theme. By 1847 the legislature was considering a new child labor bill that sought to improve on the existing law by extending its provisions to more shops and by instituting a system of salaried factory inspectors. The bill passed the Chamber of Peers, but before it could be acted on in the lower house, revolution brought the July Monarchy to an end.

Despite the interest in child labor expressed by some within the bureaucracy and within the National Assembly during the early months of the Second Republic, no action was taken on national child labor reform between 1848 and 1852. Indeed, at the end of this period, the departmental government of the Nord, despairing of any action on the matter in Paris, appointed its own salaried factory inspector. Nonetheless, under the Second Republic, there was action taken on a matter closely related to child labor: the regulation of apprenticeship. The

French Revolution had destroyed the guild system that once controlled apprenticeship training, and at least since the passage of the 1841 Child Labor Law there had been discussion of apprenticeship legislation as a necessary complement to factory legislation. The apprenticeship law adopted in 1851 defined the mutual obligations of masters and apprentices and mandated written apprenticeship contracts. Like the Child Labor Law of 1841, however, the Apprenticeship Law of 1851 remained difficult to enforce. Although state protection of factory children had been initiated under the July Monarchy and state protection of apprentices had been initiated under the Second Republic, the level of that protection was still minimal on the eve of the Second Empire.

L. Gueneau, "La legislation restrictive du travail des enfants," *Revue d'histoire économique et sociale* 15 (1927); S. Touren, *La loi de 1841 sur le travail des enfants dans les manufactures* (Paris, 1931).

Lee Shai Weissbach

Related entries: DUPIN, F.-P.-C.; VILLENEUVE–BARGEMONT; VILLERME.

CHILD-REARING PRACTICES. They varied with the stages of childhood and socioeconomic position of the family. During the nineteenth century, throughout all stages of childhood, mothers had primary responsibility for child rearing. Fathers alone, however, exercised paternal authority as head of household and legal guardian of the children. In the absence of the father due to death or disappearance, mothers inherited this authority, but by law the family council (composed of six relatives by blood or marriage—half from the paternal and half from the maternal side) had decisive control and confirmed the assignment of guardianship, whether to the mother or to another relative. Thus, the family council assumed importance in the rearing of a minor child in all circumstances in which the father was unable to fulfill his obligations.

Infancy, the first stage of childhood, comprised the first two years, and feeding the infant assumed paramount importance. Since the beginning of the nineteenth century, educated upper-class and upper-middle-class mothers either nursed their own babies or hired wet nurses to come from the countryside, live in their homes, and nurse their babies. Mothers, and sometimes their attending physician, frequently selected such live-in wet nurses with care and supervised them well. The wet nurses' own children, however, suffered. If a wet nurse nursed in another woman's home, she arrived with her child to prove her value and then sent her own child back to the countryside to be immediately weaned or placed with a relative or neighbor. Mortality for wet nurses' babies sent home was estimated at 64 percent; whereas in the same area, the mortality for babies nursed by their own mothers was 16 percent.

Throughout the nineteenth century, the well-to-do increasingly tended toward maternal feeding, but wet nursing continued, and the demand for rural wet nurses was strong, especially in the cities and among shopkeepers, craftsmen, artisans, single parents, and public authorities responsible for abandoned children. Unlike the elite who could afford to bring a wet nurse into their home and pay them well, the public authorities, artisans, shopkeepers, and those less financially secure sent their babies out of the cities to the homes of the rural wet nurses. There the babies stayed until they were weaned and walking—about one to two years. Wet nursing activity varied with the locale in France; the main centers were at Paris and Lyons. In midcentury, approximately 50 to 60 percent of all Parisian babies were nursed by their mothers, while 40 to 50 percent were wet nursed.

Unregulated placement bureaus for wet nurses were common in large cities. There the parents hired the wet nurses and entrusted their babies to the women, who were usually strangers, although some had been recommended by acquaintances. Once back in the countryside, the wet nurses and their charges were unsupervised. A high infant mortality rate existed in regions where wet nursing was common. The mortality of infants sent to wet nurses by their parents was between 30 and 40 percent, and most died of gastroenteritis and diarrhea (symptons of artificial feeding). Artificial feeding consisted of unsterilized and unrefrigerated cow's or goat's milk in a glass, metal, or wooden baby bottle or stored in little pots from which women fed the babies. In this era before pasteurization and sterilization, milk frequently became contaminated. Women also fed babies *bouillie*, a pap of flour and milk, water, or other liquid. *Sucettes*, a rag dipped in *bouillie* or wine, functioned as pacifiers. Feedings were not scheduled or regularized. Wet nursing continued because pervasive poverty made artisan families dependent on the labor of all family members. Women found it more convenient and less costly to send their babies to rural peasant women than to try to nurse their babies themselves at home or at work. Both women and doctors believed that wet nursing was superior to feeding a baby artificially.

Clothing for infants varied with socioeconomic status. Swaddling was declining in practice among the educated and upper classes but continued among the rural peasants well into the nineteenth century. Sometimes the baby's arms were freed at three months. Rural mothers believed that swaddling kept babies' legs and bodies straight. Furthermore, an unsupervised swaddled child would be safer and avoid more accidents than one who crawled. If the mother worked near the house, she often left the infant inside, either alone or with older siblings. All children, both male and female, wore dresses until after age three and often until age five or six. Toilet training was expected to be completed around the age of three; until that time, mothers changed infants two or three times a day. Public assistance supplied the last set of diapers for its wards when the children were two years old. They expected these diapers to last until the children were at least three; by that age they could be trained.

For children aged two to six, the family was the educative and moralizing milieu, and the mothers were primarily responsible for teaching. Parents, especially mothers, concerned themselves with their children's health, but they rarely summoned doctors. Given the state of medical knowledge, there was little doctors could do. Superstitions and home remedies prevailed among both the elite and peasants. In the poorer, rural parts of France, one child in four did not reach its sixth birthday; in the richer areas, one in five or six died before age six.

From ages six through twelve, child rearing consisted of further education and training of the children, either at home or at a school. At this stage of childhood, children joined groups of peers their own age either at school, at work, or in the countryside.

Private initiatives in education occurred in 1815 with the founding, by J.-M. de Gérando, of the Société pour l'instruction élémentaire. In 1820 there were 1,300 mutual schools that received 150,000 boys. Girls attended the church-run primary schools, if they went at all. An ordinance of 29 February 1816 prefigured the Guizot Law of 1833. The Guizot Law required each commune to educate its children, to establish a school, and to assure free education to the indigent in the belief that education would prevent revolution and preserve the monarchy. In 1821, as a result of these first tentative efforts in education, 1 million boys out of 2.8 million attended school. Thus at least three-fifths were not literate. For girls, 500,000 out of 3 million attended school; thus at least five-sixths were illiterate. Primary education increased, and during the years 1833 to 1850 about 2,176,000 boys and 1,354,000 girls attended school each year, but frequency of attendance and degree of literacy are unknown. There were, however, 3,213 communes still without schools by 1850. The northeast third of France had the highest percentage of school attendance. Formal schooling was predominantly for upper-class boys. Rural parents were reluctant to send their children to school because they needed their children's labor at home. Rural parents also kept their children out of school because the distance to the nearest school was great, the children had insufficient clothing, they were too poor to buy their own required school supplies, they perceived school as worthless since what it taught had little relationship to life and needs, and there was pressure from local landowners who did not want their future work force to be diminished by education.

Christian education was in the hands of the local priest and the parents. Child rearing included two years of catechism classes followed by a first communion usually at age twelve. The first communion was a crucial *rite de passage*. Schools and parents paid almost no attention to children's physical education until the second half of the nineteenth century.

Child-rearing practices differed among the bourgeoisie, urban workers, and peasants. Family respectability meant that upper bourgeois wives did not work for wages outside the home. Their main role was to manage the household and supervise the education of their children. Governmental authorities sentimentalized the functions of motherhood and saw the education of children as a means to inculcate certain personality traits useful to society. Middle-class parents believed that constant surveillance of the children was essential. They did not believe in striking the child; they wanted discipline and good behavior to be internalized. Bourgeois children in the six to twelve age bracket engaged less in mutual education with their peers than did the children of other social groups, and they spent more time with their families, especially their mothers. They were to imitate and emulate adults more readily. Parents chose their children's acquaintances, and their mothers supervised their homework. The family and schools complemented each other in establishing rules of discipline for children.

The working-class and rural peasant family, on the other hand, was a unit for economic survival. Unlike the women in the bourgeois household, working-class wives frequently held wage-earning positions outside the home, as well as having responsibility for household management and work responsibilities in and around the home. Working-class and rural mothers could not engage in constant surveillance of their children. They had few abstract rules for their children other than demanding specific work. They believed that corporal punishment was essential for raising a well-behaved child. For urban working-class children, factories competed with the schools for the children's time, just as in rural areas farm work competed with school.

Rural children had gender-related tasks. Girls tended the small animals, gleaned the fields, had domestic chores (which included caring for the younger children, sewing, and embroidering), and in general worked alongside their mothers. Boys tended the larger animals such as sheep, goats, and cows, worked in the fields, and in general served alongside their fathers and grandfathers.

From ages twelve to twenty-one, youths no longer were reared solely by their parents and teachers. Elite boys continued their education at lycées or colleges. Rural and working-class youths learned a trade or took a job. Girls worked as domestic servants, either at home or in another household. They also entered the garment trade either as day laborers or in trades that required some short-term apprenticeship. Boys frequently assumed the same occupation as their fathers—as agriculturalists, artisans, or laborers. Sometimes they were apprenticed with another artisan to learn a trade. In 1848 there were 19,114 apprentices in Paris, of whom 5,600 were under sixteen years old. Most of the apprentices had only a verbal contract. Many children worked in factories from age eight. They had no education. In 1841 factory legislation fixed the length of the workday. Children ages eight to twelve legally could work no longer than eight hours a day; children twelve to sixteen no longer than twelve hours a day; night work was forbidden for those under thirteen. This law was not enforced. An estimated 1.3 million children ages eight to sixteen worked in factories each year in the 1840s.

Socially segregation of the sexes remained throughout the teen-age years but with numerous occasions for the youths to get together at church functions, fairs and other social events, and at work. During the 1820s and 1830s youths assembled, primarily at carnival times, to mete out justice to each other and to others in the community. Marriages were primarily endogamous, and people usually married those in similar occupations. Prebridal pregnancies ranged from 2.8 percent in the stable population of the Basses-Pyrénées to 50 percent in some areas of the Nord. Boys up to age thirty and girls to age twenty-five who wanted to marry needed the consent of both parents (or, if the father was dead, of the family council). If the parents disagreed, the consent of the father sufficed. In general, child rearing ended when the youths married or reached their majority.

M. Crubellier, *L'Enfance et la jeunesse dans la société française, 1800–1950* (Paris, 1979); J. Donzelot, *The Policing of Families* (New York, 1979); F. Fay–Sallois, *Les nourrices à Paris au XIXe siècle* (Paris, 1980); R. G. Fuchs, *Abandoned Children* (Albany, N.Y., 1984); M. Perrot, *La mode de vie des familles bourgeoises* (Paris, 1961); G. D. Sussman, *Selling Mothers' Milk* (Urbana, Ill., 1982); L. Tilly and J. Scott, *Women, Work and Family* (New York, 1978); E. Weber, *Peasants into Frenchmen* (Stanford, Calif., 1976).

Rachel Fuchs

Related entries: AGRICULTURE; CHILD LABOR; CHILDREN, ABAN-DONED; COTTAGE INDUSTRY; DOMESTIC SERVANTS; ECOLE MU-TUELLE; GERANDO; GUIZOT LAW ON PUBLIC EDUCATION; PEASANTS; PUBLIC INSTRUCTION; PUBLIC WELFARE; SOCIETY FOR ELEMENTARY INSTRUCTION; WET NURSING.

CHILDREN, ABANDONED. Children, usually newborn infants, who were left by their mothers at state-run foundling homes, became wards of the state and were sent to wet nurses or foster parents by public welfare officials. In nineteenth-century France, parents abandoned their children in overwhelming numbers: up to 20 percent of live births in the Parisian area and 3 percent in the country as a whole. For all of France, one in 38 live births, or 25,000 babies, were abandoned annually in the years from 1838 to 1845. The proportion of children abandoned each year varied with the department and locale, ranging from one abandoned child per 10 births in the department of the Seine to one per 752 live births in the Haute-Saone. From 1824 to 1833 approximately 119,000 abandoned children under age twelve lived in France each year. This means that there was one abandoned child under twelve years of age for each 350 inhabitants of the country. The number decreased to about 96,000 each year in the period 1844–53.

These abandoned babies, almost all newborn and over 80 percent illegitimate, were left at state-run foundling homes that by the provisions of the National Decree of 1811 existed in the major city of almost every department in France. That decree gave the Ministry of the Interior and departmental governments full control over abandoned children. The national government allocated a fixed amount of 4 million francs annually divided among the departments for the maintenance of these children. Decrees of 1817–19, 1823, and subsequent years gave the departments more fiscal responsibility for the expenses engendered by the abandoned children. The decree of 1811 further stipulated that each foundling home should have a *tour*—a revolving cradle in a window-like aperture of the building—to allow parents to abandon the babies anonymously. Abandoned babies then became wards of the state until they were twelve years old. Babies were left at the *tour*, were brought to the admissions office of the foundling home by a person (usually the mother), or came directly from a free public hospital in which they were born. The period prior to the 1830s was one of complete, open, unrestricted, and anonymous admission of children to foundling homes. During these years the rate of abandonment increased and correlated with several economic indexes, such as the cost of living, price of bread, and price of various grains. After the 1830s, when admissions became more restrictive, the correlation of abandonment with economic indexes was less conclusive. Most babies were abandoned by their mothers, and the women who abandoned their babies were about twenty-two years old, unwed, and working as domestic servants, day laborers, or seamstresses. Leaving a baby at the foundling home was an acceptable strategy of survival for women living on the brink of poverty who could not afford to keep a baby or hire a wet nurse.

As soon as possible after abandonment—usually within one week—foundling home authorities sent babies to government-paid wet nurses (or foster parents) who lived in rural France. The departments, with a fixed supplement from the state, bore the expenses for the children with the wet nurses and foster parents. Payments averaged 75 to 80 francs per child per year for the period 1834–43 and increased to about 90 francs a year in 1853. The payments to the wet nurses decreased after the children reached their first birthday and gradually diminished over the next five years; at age seven they fell sharply again, followed by another gradual decrease until the children reached their thirteenth birthday. At this time regular payments to the foster parents stopped. As the children got older, their labor was to compensate the foster parents for the care received.

Between 1815 and 1833 the number of abandoned children in France increased from 84,000 to 129,000, a rate greater than that of the population. In the 1830s the state and departments endeavored to reduce the number of abandoned children and their consequent expense by four measures. First, between 1833 and 1844 many *tours* were closed or watched by police officers, and admissions offices operated during the daytime in an effort to prevent surreptitious and anonymous abandonment. Second, in departments other than the Seine, *déplacement*, or the moving of abandoned babies from the department in which they were abandoned to wet nurses in other jurisdictions, was first proposed in 1827, reached its peak in the early 1830s, and declined after 1837. Officials advocated this measure to prevent mothers from abandoning their babies and then presenting themselves as wet nurses to care for their own children with payment from the government. The measure died because of its ineffectiveness in significantly reducing abandonment (fewer than 25 percent of the babies who were destined for relocation were reclaimed by their parents), the trouble and expense involved in transporting them, and the large public outcry in the provinces against it. Third, in the department of the Seine private charity, with departmental support, offered a small-scale program of aid to unwed mothers to prevent abandonment. Finally, in the dual effort to decrease abuses in the system and expenses for the state and departmental governments, the July Monarchy inaugurated a departmental inspection system in the 1830s.

Mortality of abandoned children was high. Depending on the department, from one in three (33 percent) to one in seventeen (6 percent) of abandoned children under twelve years of age died per year. Infant mortality was higher. For children abandoned in the department of the Seine and sent to wet nurses in rural departments several hundred kilometers away, infant mortality decreased from 78 percent in 1830 to 62 percent in 1852. Not all the deaths occurred with the wet nurses. Approximately 25 percent of the infants who died during their first twelve months died in a public foundling home, and 40 to 45 percent died with wet nurses. Gastrointestinal disorders and diarrhea (indicative of artificial feeding) prevailed as causes of infant mortality. Respiratory diseases caused most deaths in children between one and seven years. Children who survived worked with their foster parents usually until they were thirteen years old, when all payments from the government stopped. Then they either stayed with their family in the countryside or went to work for someone else either as a domestic servant, field hand, or apprentice if their foster families could not afford to keep them. Although biological parents could reclaim their abandoned child, fewer than 10 percent of children abandoned per year in all of France were reclaimed. For children abandoned in Paris, 0.8 percent were returned to their parents in 1816. That percentage increased to 1.3 percent in 1852.

Societal attitudes toward abandoned children changed from the Restoration to the July Monarchy to the Second Republic. During the Restoration, officials paid little attention to either the morality or welfare of the abandoned children. They primarily concerned themselves with the expense. During the July Monarchy, reformers considered the abandoned children and their mothers as part of the larger social question. Officials sought to contain child abandonment and other forms of perceived social deviance while restricting the role of state institutions. They saw the abandonment of children as a symptom of the perceived immorality and potential dangerousness of urban masses. During the 1830s, reducing the numbers of abandoned and limiting expenses of the state, departments, and communes were two themes of debate and discussion. The Second Republic's legislators discussed the state's moral obligation to the abandoned children and implemented their beliefs by the creation of L'Assistance publique, a bureau of public assistance. Bureaucrats designed this governmental organization to administer to the abandoned children. It gave full recognition to their existence, and the state took more responsibility for their maintenance.

R. G. Fuchs, *Abandoned Children* (Albany, N.Y., 1984).

Rachel Fuchs

Related entries: CHILD-REARING PRACTICES; CHILDREN, INSTITUTIONS FOR; DOMESTIC SERVANTS; PUBLIC WELFARE; WET NURSING.

CHILDREN, INSTITUTIONS FOR. State authorities and social reformers from the Restoration through the Second Republic believed that the family was the proper milieu to socialize the young. The few institutions for children—

hospitals, hospices, day-care centers, children's shelters, farm colonies, prisons—were slow to develop and housed few children.

Infant day-care facilities (*crèches*) were private or communal establishments that received legitimate infants of working mothers to enable the women to work outside the home. F. Marbeau opened the first one in 1844 in Paris, and within two years there were eleven, although some soon closed. Each had fewer than twenty children. They accepted only legitimate infants still in cribs and were devised to prevent child abandonment, encourage maternal feeding, and increase the availability and productivity of female labor. Some were located in working-class districts so the mothers could come and nurse their infants at least once during the day. The Ministry of the Interior encouraged the establishment of *crèches*. Subventions from the commune in which the *crèche* was located provided about 14 percent of the income; the department contributed about 2 percent and the state 1.5 percent. The rest of the funds came from private sources, particularly from philanthropic women who directed and inspected the *crèches*. Only a small proportion of the income came from those who used the *crèche*. The organizers set the fees at what they felt were affordable rates. In midcentury, a working mother paid 20 centimes per day for one child and 30 centimes per day for two children. In 1853, there were eighty-four *crèches* in thirty-five departments receiving 6,279 infants. The department of the Seine had twenty-five.

Philanthropic individuals of particular communes founded *salles d'asile*, or children's shelters, designed to receive legitimate children who were not yet old enough to attend primary school or work and were too old for a *crèche*. Nuns and philanthropic women who directed and staffed these shelters were to teach the children "in accordance with their intelligence" and prepare them for school in a manner that they could not receive at home because they came from poor, working-class families where both parents worked outside the home. In 1853 there were 2,203 *salles d'asile*; 1,345 were founded by specific communes, and 858 were created by particular private philanthropy.

Schools may be considered as institutions for children, especially those where the children boarded. The Guizot Law of 1833 called for the establishment of public elementary schools in each commune. Urban centers had more schools than rural areas, and those in the cities were better attended. Technical school education began under the Restoration. The Brothers of the Christian Schools expanded by the 1830s; the Association polytechnique was founded in 1848; and the Ecoles des arts et métiers was established at Châlons-sur-Marne, Angers in 1811 and Aix in 1843. In addition municipal technical schools and classrooms associated with factories increased during the 1840s. Upper-class boys attended lycées and collèges. In 1842 the total number attending lycées was 18,697, of whom 43 percent lived at the school. During the same year, 26,584 boys attended collège while 46 percent lived there. Some young girls lived in convents for an education that was not necessarily to prepare them to take vows. Strict religious and disciplinary surveillance prevailed at lycées, collèges, and convents.

Numerous hospitals or hospices housed ill, infirm, incurable, or abandoned children. In every major city of each department foundling homes, or special areas of a *hôtel dieu*, accepted abandoned infants. Infants stayed in the institutions less than a week, at which point they went to wet nurses in the countryside. Only infants who were ill stayed in the foundling home or hospital until they were cured or died. In Paris, the Hôpital des orphelins accepted abandoned children and poor orphans aged two to twelve years. In 1837 authorities closed that institution, and the children were sent either to the foundling home (Hospice des enfants trouvés) or, if sick, to the Hôpital des enfants malades. Hospitals for the blind, the deaf, and those with incurable diseases existed in major cities. They sheltered, at public expense, indigent children ages eight to fourteen, as long as they were of good conduct and free from contagious diseases and mental retardation. In all institutions children were to be taught reading, writing, music, and a trade.

Special institutions housed those youths, boys and girls, whom authorities or parents felt were disciplinary problems. *Ouvroirs* were institutions designed to give free, or almost free, education to young girls. Most had been founded by private charity and were run by women of religious congregations. Twenty-seven percent of their resources came from subsidies from the national, departmental, or communal budgets; 15 percent came from donations and legacies; and the rest came from fund-raising events and private philanthropy. In many departments the *ouvroir* had been annexed to the *salle d'asile* and partook of its resources. Parents or public authorities placed most of the girls in *ouvroirs* for disciplinary problems. In 1853, 27,292 young girls had been admitted to *ouvroirs*, which existed in sixty-two departments.

Colonies (or *asiles*) *agricoles* (prison farm colonies or reformatories) founded in the early 1840s, and funded by the private charity of religious orders, with some aid from the state and a few departments, housed boys from ages eight to twenty needing discipline. The largest, most well-known, and with the greatest state subsidy was that at Mettray, founded in 1840 by the magistrate Frédéric Demetz. It began with only nine boys but increased to six hundred by the end of the century. Twelve *colonies agricoles* existed by 1845; some housed only twenty boys. They were a rehabilitative alternative to prison for juvenile delinquents, beggars, boys judged too rebellious or deviant to remain with either parents, foster parents, or those offering apprenticeship positions, and others sent there for discipline by their parents or the courts. The regimented life at a *colonie agricole* included severe discipline, moral instruction, basic schooling, and hard work—most of it in the open air. *Colonies agricoles* were designed to rid the streets of major cities of juvenile delinquents and at the same time make farmlands more productive by putting into use lands that had not been cultivated. In 1852 in all of France, there were eighteen *colonies agricoles*.

Youths too incorrigible for *colonies agricoles* were placed in prison, either together with the adults in *maisons centrales* or, after 1834 and especially after 1850, in special prisons for young offenders. During the 1830s government administrators, spurred on by reformers, carried out a number of changes in prisons for juvenile offenders. The most radical was the idea of separate cells and total isolation of the offenders from each other day and night. La Petite roquette, completed in 1836, housed male juvenile offenders in Paris and kept them in cellular isolation day and night. Since 1834 Saint Lazare combined aspects of both a prison and a hospital for girls and young women deemed undisciplined or criminal. It had four divisions. One area served as a place of detention for young girls sent there by their fathers or guardians for discipline and crime prevention. A second area housed those under detention, sometimes while awaiting trial. The third section was for girls sentenced to a prison term of less than one year. The fourth area functioned as a hospital for prostitutes, especially those with venereal disease. Due to an increase in the population and increased efforts of police, from 1837 to 1847 the number of children detained in correctional prisons increased steadily from 1,334 to 4,276.

A law of 1850 pertaining to juvenile delinquents specified the separation of juveniles from adults in prisons and provided for public and private *colonies pénetentiaires* similar to *colonies agricoles* for children needing discipline. It also established *colonies correctionnelles* for children sentenced to long-term imprisonment or judged incorrigible. The law further mandated that children in detention and in other institutions receive moral, religious, and occupational training. Although reformers and government authorities still viewed a family as the proper socializing environment for children, they were beginning to recognize the special needs of children in institutions.

E. Ackerknecht, *Medicine at the Paris Hospital, 1799–1848* (Baltimore, 1967); L. Berlanstein, "Vagrants, Beggars and Thieves: Delinquent Boys in Mid-Nineteenth Century Paris," *Journal of Social History* (Summer 1979); M. Crubellier, *L'Enfance et la jeunesse dans la société française, 1800–1950* (Paris, 1979); R. G. Fuchs, *Abandoned Children* (Albany, N.Y., 1984); H. Gaillac, *Les Maisons de correction* (Paris, 1971); G. Wright, *Between the Guillotine and Liberty* (New York, 1983).

Rachel Fuchs

Related entries: CHILD LABOR; CHILDREARING PRACTICES; CHILDREN, ABANDONED; ECOLES NATIONALES DES ARTS ET METIERS; GUIZOT LAW ON PUBLIC EDUCATION; PUBLIC INSTRUCTION; PUBLIC WELFARE; WET NURSING.

CHOPIN, FREDERIC (1810–1849), Polish composer. Frédéric Chopin was born into a family of pure French blood that had emigrated to Poland in 1787. His father, an official on an aristocratic estate, stayed to avoid conscription into the Revolutionary army, and the family quickly laid down strong roots in Polish society in general. Frédéric learned the social customs of fashionable salons at an early age, earning wide acclaim performing there and in public concerts. He then sought his fortune by trips, first to Vienna and then to Paris in 1831, and was rapidly accepted there in the highest salons (by the Rothschilds especially) as the most popular piano teacher among that milieu. As a result of this unusual patronage, as well as his enjoyment of teaching, he lived handsomely from the high prices he charged for lessons.

Chopin's career was quite atypical of his age. The goal of most performers was to settle down as a teacher to wealthy families, since touring the concert circuit was debilitating and not always reliable financially. But Chopin skipped the initial period of public concerts and tours, which was usually necessary for a performer to establish a reputation (and annual concerts to maintain it), for in his whole career he gave only thirty concerts, many of them semiprivate in nature. The devotion of his patrons was thus quite exceptional. While he felt obliged to carry on an often exhausting round of visits to salons, never seemingly of the mind that he was above that world, he was nevertheless revered there as an artistic genius in the full romantic manner.

His music was also special in its time for its intimacy and sophistication. Although all of Chopin's works involve the piano, the premier instrument of the virtuoso age, few of them are typical of the most popular numbers of the age: flashy medleys of well-known opera tunes. The internal lines in his works are far more complex and significant than was conventional then, and his command of melodic subtlety places his music on a plane of its own. Most important, his experiments in harmony—the use of chromatic chords, unusual scales, and remote modulations in key—were revolutionary in impact, profoundly influencing the course of piano literature, and even the dramas of Richard Wagner.

Chopin's health first weakened in 1836, and while he seemingly recovered well, the damage done limited his contacts with the musical world from that time on. In 1836 he initiated a close liaison with George Sand, which, though cooling romantically after a few years, remained at the center of his life until 1847. Following a year's stay in England, he returned home to die of tuberculosis in 1849.

William Weber

Related entries: ROMANTICISM; ROTHSCHILD FAMILY; SAND.

CHRISTIAN SCHOOLS. See BROTHERS OF THE CHRISTIAN SCHOOLS.

CLASS STRUGGLE, THEORY OF. A mistaken notion has long prevailed that the theory of class and class struggle was originated by Karl Marx. As early as 1852 Marx pointed out that "no credit is due to me for discovering the existence of classes in modern society, nor yet the struggle between them. Long before me bourgeois historians had described the historical development of this struggle of the classes." Frederick Engels later specified that the historians of the Restoration period, from Augustin Thierry to François Guizot, Auguste Mignet and Adolphe Thiers, spoke of it (the struggle between the landed aristocracy and the bourgeoisie) everywhere as the key to the understanding of all French history since the Middle Ages. Karl Marx even labeled Thierry the Father of Class Struggle in French Historiography.

These four French historians who began their career under the Restoration and experienced the acute struggle between the bourgeoisie and the aristocracy were keenly aware of the significance of class antagonism and its interpretative value. Thierry tried to demonstrate that the history of England and of France was dominated by the revolt of the conquered against the conquerors for emancipation and liberty. It began as a conflict between races but turned into a struggle between social classes, which led finally to the victory of the Third Estate. For Thierry the "communal revolution" of the twelfth century, the peasant movements of the fourteenth and fifteenth centuries, and the "national revolution" of the eighteenth century constituted the mainstream of French social history.

Guizot was also of the opinion that the political history of France was composed of the struggle between estates and that modern Europe was in effect born out of the contention among various social classes. His *History of the English Revolution* (1850) exposed to a certain extent the class character of that epoch-making event.

Both Mignet and Thiers used the French Revolution to serve their liberal political principles. They stressed the historical inevitability of the Revolution, which they explained by the conflict of interest between the privileged classes and the Third Estate. Mignet went even further by saying that the Reign of Terror and Napoleonic dictatorship were also the product of class struggle; he predicted that by the play of class forces, the Bourbon monarchy was bound to fall.

The theory of class and class struggle as conceived by the Restoration historians is rather superficial and ambiguous, however. Thierry, for example, explained the origins of class and class oppression in terms of Germanic conquest. Guizot went a step further by attributing them to property relations but failed to clarify how these relations arose. While recognizing the role of class struggle in history prior to the French Revolution of 1789, these historians were reluctant to admit the continuation of the struggle in the conflict between the proletariat and the bourgeoisie under the July Monarchy and after. For both Thierry and Guizot, class struggle no longer existed, because to them French society after 1830 had become a unified whole; any rising from below against the governing classes could thus play only a destructive role. The hostile attitude of Mignet toward the Paris Commune of 1871 and its fiercely violent repression by Thiers testified to the bourgeois nature of their conception of class struggle.

Y. Knibieler, *Naissance des sciences humaines: Mignet et l'histoire philosophique au XIXe siècle* (Paris, 1973); G. V. Plehanoff, "The Early Stage of the Theory of Class Struggle," in *Selected Philosophical Works*, vol. 2 (Moscow, 1956); B. Reizov, *L'Historiographie romantique française* (Moscow, n.d.).

Zhang Zhilian

Related entries: GUIZOT; MARX; MIGNET; THIERRY, J.-N.A.; THIERS.

CLAUSEL DE COUSSERGUES, JEAN-CLAUDE (1759–1846), ultraroyalist politician. A scion of the robed aristocracy, he emigrated and served in the Condé army. After his return to France under the Consulate, the friendship of Jean-Jacques de Cambacéres provided him a seat in the court of appeals of Montpellier. In 1808 he was sent to the Legislative Corps by the electors of his native province of Aveyron. In 1814 he greeted with enthusiasm the return of the Bourbon dynasty. He represented Aveyron in the *chambre introuvable* and all the subsequent legislatures, except between November 1820 and August 1821. There he voiced the most reactionary opinions. He won a temporary and dubious fame when, after the murder of the duc de Berry, he proposed to indict the minister Elie Decazes for complicity. He had two brothers, both of whom had made a name for themselves as prominent clergymen: Michel (1763–1833) was a polemicist and administrator in the University; Claude-Hippolyte (1769–1857) was an orator, bishop of Chartres, and prolific writer.

H. de Barrau, *Documents . . . sur les familles et les hommes remarquables du Rouergue*, vol. 4 (1853–60).

Guillaume de Bertier de Sauvigny

Related entries: BERRY, C.-F.; CAMBACERES; CHAMBRE INTROU-VABLE.

CLERMONT-TONNERRE, ANNE-ANTOINE-JULES, DUC DE (1749–1830), deputy in the Estates General; extremely reactionary prelate of the Restoration; cardinal archbishop of Toulouse. Clermont-Tonnerre was born in Paris on 1 January 1749 to an old noble family. As the second son, he was intended for a clerical career. He earned his doctorate at the Sorbonne and in 1782 became bishop of Châlons-sur-Marne. Elected a deputy of the First Estate in the Estates General, he defended the Old Regime and protested against the civil constitution of the clergy. He subsequently emigrated to Germany. In accordance with the Concordat, Clermont-Tonnerre resigned his bishopric and returned to France during the Consulate, remaining inactive until 1814. In June 1814 Louis XVIII named him to the Chamber of Peers and on 1 July 1820 appointed him archbishop of Toulouse. He received his cardinal's hat on 2 December 1822.

Clermont-Tonnerre quickly became known for his challenges to the secular state and for his support of ecclesiastical supremacy, as well as for his pride and class consciousness. In October 1823 while in Rome for a conclave, he published a rather intemperate pastoral letter in his archdiocese, demanding the abrogation of the Concordat and insisting on the supremacy of the church over the secular state. This caused a furor among the liberal newspapers and others suspicious of clerical intentions. The government referred the matter to the Council of State, which in essence censured Clermont-Tonnerre by concluding that a pastoral letter was not the appropriate means to suggest improvements in religion. The king ordered the letter suppressed. In July 1824 Clermont-Tonnerre published in the *Quotidienne* a challenge to the government's authority to regulate seminaries. The journal was fined by the courts; the author went unpunished. Nevertheless, Charles X subsequently awarded him the Order of the Holy Ghost and in November 1826 appointed him a minister of state and member of the Privy Council, thereby causing a furor.

On 16 June 1828 at the insistence of the Martignac cabinet, Charles X signed two ordinances aimed against the Jesuits, one restricting teaching by unauthorized orders and the other limiting enrollment in seminaries to students genuinely studying for the priesthood. The extremists among the prelates reacted strongly, especially Clermont-Tonnerre who wrote and published in his diocesan newsletter a blunt letter to Jean-François Feutrier, minister of ecclasiastical affairs. He also refused to provide the documentation to prove compliance with these decrees. For this opposition Charles X forbade him to appear at court and exiled him to his diocese. Clermont-Tonnerre then sent his grand vicar to Paris and after weeks of negotiation provided the minister simply with a signed blank form. His conflict with the government now ended, however, and he busied himself with the establishment at Toulouse of a savings bank and a newspaper to propagate orthodoxy. In 1829 he published an episcopal letter attacking the now-fallen Martignac ministry and supporting the Polignac government. Clermont-Tonnerre died on 21 February 1830 at Toulouse.

G. de Bertier de Sauvigny, *The Bourbon Restoration* (Philadelphia, 1966) and *Le Comte Ferdinand de Bertier et l' énigme de la congrégation* (Paris, 1948); A. Dansette, *Religious History of Modern France* (New York, 1961); F. Hoefer, *Nouvelle biographie générale* (Paris, 1852–66); A. Latreille et al., *Histoire du catholicisme en France* (Paris, 1962).

James K. Kieswetter

Related entries: FEUTRIER; MARTIGNAC; POLIGNAC; *LA QUOTIDIENNE*.

CLUB OF CLUBS (1848), a Parisian club that tried to federate all Parisian clubs. It was founded in March 1848 and dissolved after the elections to the Constituent Assembly in April 1848. During its brief existence, this club tried to realize what historian Peter H. Amann has called "the mirage of unity." Amid the proliferation of clubs following the February Revolution, several attempts were made to unite republican clubs of all political tendencies. Auguste Blanqui tried to do this in his Central Republican Society, but it was his person rather than any particular program that made for unity.

As the elections to the Constituent Assembly on 23 April approached, leaders of republican clubs saw the need for an instrument of propaganda to ensure the success of authentically republican candidates in Paris and the provinces. After the demonstration of the Bearskin Buskins (conservative members of the National Guard) and the republican counterdemonstration of 17 March, a call for a meeting of several club leaders, including Marie-Joseph Sobrier and Cahaigne, was published: "We now have only the name of a Republic, we need the thing.

Political reform is the only means to a social reform." It was decided that the Club of the Revolution would be created. This club, sometimes called the Barbès Club after its principal orator, held its first meeting on 21 March. Among its first members were the Dufraisse brothers, Martin Bernard, Sobrier, Pierre Leroux, Pierre-Joseph Proudhon, Félix Pyat, Charles Delescluze, and N. Lebon.

From the first meeting, Marc Dufraisse suggested the creation of "a central club of all clubs." This began a struggle with Blanqui, who also wanted to federate the Parisian clubs. Blanqui's appeal of 25 March "to the democratic clubs of Paris" wanted to create a central committee for the elections, but it had only a limited success. After the Taschereau Affair broke out a few days later, the Club of the Revolution called on all Parisian clubs to send three delegates to a meeting set for 26 March. About sixty clubs were represented, and Amable Longepied, a member of the Club of the Revolution, was elected president of the group, which now called itself the Club of Clubs. This club, with a maximum of 200 members, elected an executive commission that met permanently in the house of Sobrier, director of the Paris Commune. Its members were Longepied, Delaire, Gadon, Thiele, Lebreton, Armand Barbès, Sobrier, Cahaigne, Laugier, Louis Deplanque, N. Lebon, and Aloysius Huber.

It decided to print 30,000 copies of Maximilien Robespierre's Declaration of the Rights of Man and of the Citizen and to send delegates to the provinces to work in the elections. Alexandre-Auguste Ledru-Rollin, minister of the interior, granted the commission 120,000 francs. About 500 delegates were sent to the provinces, and each was paid between 6 and 10 francs a day. Laugier wrote the instructions sent to the delegates, and, at the same time, a circular notice was sent to provincial clubs asking them to help the delegates. Delegates were also sent to the republican regiments of the army.

On 2 April, the Club of Clubs elected new leaders, and Huber replaced Longepied as president.

Daniel Stern (Marie d'Agoult) was correct when she said, "It was in this club that the police were most active." Its president, Huber, had worked for the police under Louis-Philippe and was the principal leader of the uprising of 15 May. According to Stern, Ledru-Rollin, Alphonse de Lamartine, Armand Marrast, and Marc Caussidière all had moles working inside this club. Pierre-Joseph Proudhon's judgment was more severe: "I have just left the Club of Clubs. It is laughable, it is distressing, it is frightful. A pseudo-education has driven everyone crazy" (8 April 1848).

As the elections approached, the Club of Clubs printed a proclamation: "Vote only for known republicans. . . . Don't believe in these belated republican professions of faith."

Following the demonstrations of 16 April, attacks against the Club of Clubs reached the ears of Lamartine. Longepied met him to explain the activities of the club, and the two men reached an accord. But Huber and N. Lebon resigned when they heard about this meeting. Their resignations were refused, and a second meeting with Lamartine took place. The Club of Clubs was worried that the government was betraying the republican ideal, and within the government it supported Louis Blanc, Ledru-Rollin, Albert, and Ferdinand Flocon.

The Club of Clubs drew up a list of thirty-four candidates for the elections in Paris, including Albert, E. Arago, Louis Blanc, Caussidière, Flocon, Huber, N. Lebon, Ledru-Rollin, P. Leroux, Martin Bernard, A. Perdiguier, Proudhon, Francois-Vincent Raspail, and Sobrier. This list had been drawn up in conjunction with the Luxembourg Commission.

This was one of the last acts of the Club of Clubs. On 28 April, Huber declared it dissolved and replaced by the new Committee for the Centralization of Clubs, of which he remained president, but neither Barbès nor N. Lebon nor Sobrier was a member.

The principal mission of the Club of Clubs—the election of leftist deputies—was a failure in both Paris and the provinces. We can thus conclude with Peter Amann that "the history of the Revolutionary Committee, Club of Clubs, is the history of a political failure."

P. H. Amann, *Revolution and Mass Democracy* (Princeton, 1975); F. A. de Luna, *The French Republic under Cavaignac, 1848* (Princeton, 1969); A. Longepied and Laugier, *Comité révolutionnaire, Club des Clubs et la Commission* (Paris, 1850); J. M. Merriman, *The Repression of the Left in Revolutionary France, 1848–1851* (New Haven, 1978); R. Price, *The French Second Republic, A Social History* (London, 1972); D. Stern (Marie d'Agoult), *Historie de la Révolution de 1848*, vol. 2 (Paris, 1851).

                                    Jean-Claude Caron, trans. by E. Newman
Related entries: AGOULT; BARBES; BLANC; BLANQUI, L.-A.; CAUSSIDIERE; CLUBS, POLITICAL; DELESCLUZE; DEMONSTRATIONS OF 1848–1849; DEPLANQUE; FLOCON; HUBER; LEDRU-ROLLIN; LEROUX; LONGEPIED; MARRAST; PERDIGUIER; PROUDHON; PYAT; RASPAIL; REPUBLICANS; SOBRIER.

CLUBS, POLITICAL, public meetings in a predetermined place designed for the purpose of discussing political or social problems. There was a large number of clubs in Paris and in the big cities of the provinces, but they were repressed after the riots of June 1848 and June 1849. All contemporaries of the 1848 Revolution were struck by how quickly clubs were formed (Auguste Blanqui started his on 25 February) and by their great number, especially in Paris. Etienne Garnier-Pagès published a list drawn up by a commission of inquiry of the National Assembly that named 145 in Paris on 30 March 1848; Daniel Stern published a list of 236. Their total number exceeded 300.

There are two reasons why this phenomenon is not surprising. First, the 1848 revolution was made in part to win the right to assemble, which the July Monarchy refused to grant. Even so, a few secret societies existed on the eve of the 1848 Revolution.

Second, the revolutionaries of 1848 saw themselves as the successors of the Revolutionaries of 1789. As in the first revolution, the revolutionaries of 1848 hastened to found clubs, either for their own political ambitions or to put forth their point of view. According to Garnier-Pagès, "Paris had club fever," and Pierre Larousse described the movement: "Hardly had the 1848 Revolution begun when in Paris and throughout France innumerable clubs formed. In public halls, cafés, ballrooms, and concert halls, clubs met where men, women, and children came to discuss public affairs and to hear them discussed."

There were clubs at every level: arrondissement, neighborhood (like the Club du faubourg Saint-Antoine), suburban (like the Club de Charenton and the Club de Neuilly), and at every social level: working class (Fraternal Club of Washerwomen), students (Central Committee of the Schools), artists (Club of Dramatic Artists), shopkeepers (Club of Grocers). Every political tendency was represented: Auguste Blanqui guided the Central Republican Society, Armand Barbès the Society of the Rights of Man and then the Club of the Revolution, Francois-Vincent Raspail the Club of the Friends of the People, Etienne Cabet the Central Fraternal Society. Women had their clubs, especially the Society of the Voice of Women, founded in April 1848 and led by Eugénie Niboyet and Pauline Roland. Political refugees, who were numerous in Paris, founded their clubs, from the Democratic German Society to the Club of Italian Emigrants, and including the Club of Polish Emigrants. Several provincials, such as those from Alsace, the Nord, and Provence, also founded their own clubs in Paris. Admirers of 1789 united around their ideals: there were two Jacobin Clubs and at least six clubs of the Mountain or of Montagnards.

Most of the big provincial cities had their own clubs, as the works of A. M. Gossez, Philippe Vigier, Maurice Agulhon, and A. Corbin have shown. These clubs generally followed the patterns set by Paris, and sometimes they were started by men who had come out from the capital. The workers of Lyons met in the Society of the Voracious, which had been the name of a secret society repressed by the police during the July Monarchy. Montagnard clubs, like the one in Lille, were also founded. Cities with big working-class populations (Marseilles, Limoges, Rouen, Le Havre) had clubs of various tendencies. It seems that the Provisional Government, especially Alexandre-Auguste Ledru-Rollin, counted on these clubs to spread the idea of the republic and to get ready for the coming elections. The Club of Clubs sent out a circular to the provincial clubs concerning these elections.

Not all clubs were of the same duration or importance. Some claimed several thousand members and were built around a newspaper, whose editor was president of the club. Some were merely professional or regional associations, while others had larger goals. Conservatives, monarchists, Orleanists, and others created their own electoral associations. Few had permanent organizations with a president, officers, membership cards, and a fixed meeting place. The novelist Gustave Flaubert felt distaste for the clubs, where, he said, "the worker's blouse attacked the dress suit and the rich conspired against the poor." In the fictional "Club of Intelligence" where Frédéric and his friends met in Gustave Flaubert's *A Sentimental Education*, everything was grotesque. But some clubs, essentially those in Paris with well-known leaders, were means of political action that could attempt to influence the course of events.

The clubs tried to influence the elections first of the National Guard commanders and then of the deputies to the Constituent Assembly. When on 5 March a decree was published announcing legislative elections for 9 April, Blanqui and his Central Republican Society asked at once that these elections be postponed. Then the conservative demonstration of the Bearskin Buskins on 16 March provoked a massive and unified response from the clubs. Indeed several clubs, including Cabet's Central Fraternal Society, had been calling for a big popular demonstration since 13 March. On 14 and 15 March several club leaders met to fix the date, and at the same time they began to think in terms of forming a federation of clubs. The conservative demonstration of 16 March galvanized them into action.

The demonstration of 17 March was at once a day of glory for the clubs, whose leaders were received by the Provisional Government, and the only example of their unity. Cabet, Marie-Joseph Sobrier, Blanqui, and Barbès, whose personal rivalries would later divide the club movement, were all there. Soon afterwards, the rivalry between Barbès and Blanqui, each of whom tried to unite the clubs under his own leadership, split the movement. Barbès, with the help of Ledru-Rollin, Sobrier, and Amable Longepied, replaced Blanqui as leader of the Club of Clubs at its 26 March meeting, which united about sixty clubs. Shortly afterward, the Taschereau document of March 31 temporarily alienated Blanqui from his Central Republican Society. When the leaders of several well-known clubs formed a jury to shed light on the Taschereau document, Blanqui refused to serve on it.

By the middle of April the Club of Clubs had become the strongest in Paris. It wanted to influence the elections of 23 April for the Constituent Assembly, and it received government funds from Ledru-Rollin to send delegates to the provinces. But its role in preparing the demonstrations of 16 April had discredited it and the other clubs. The National Guard, made up of the middle class, tried to sabotage evening meetings of several clubs, especially the Central Republican Society. Not only conservative bourgeois but also moderate republicans were beginning to see the clubs as a cause of political and economic disorder. After the elections of 23 April, conservatives began to speak up both within and without the Constituent Assembly, while even Montagnard deputies (with the exception of Barbès) stopped appearing at the clubs. The clubs, sensing that they were losing their influence, seized upon the issue of French foreign policy for the demonstration of 15 May.

The clubs intended to march to the Assembly to present a petition in favor of Poland. They were divided: Blanqui, Barbès, Raspail, and Sobrier were hesitant, but Aloysius Huber, president of the Committee of Centralization, insisted that the manifestation take place. Its failure, which should have been foreseen, ended with the arrest of Barbès, Raspail, Blanqui, and many other club leaders, who were brought to trial before the high court at Bourges in March 1849.

Henceforth the legal status of the clubs would be called into question. When the June uprising began on 23 June 1848, the Assembly decided to get rid of the clubs. The clubs of Blanqui and Raspail were closed, and Barbès's was brought under police surveillance. By June, many clubs had ceased to exist, while others were hesitant to side with the rebels.

On 23 June Ariste-Jacques Trouvé-Chauvel, prefect of Paris police, ordered the clubs to be closed temporarily. The Assembly voted on 26 June to close those clubs recognized as dangerous and on 28 June to close all clubs. On 2 August, a decree on the right of assembly ordered that all clubs must make a declaration at the city hall or the prefecture of police, all meetings must be public, and no secret committees would be allowed. A representative of the police would attend each meeting, and any remarks that might disturb the public order or morality would be forbidden. Clubs must prohibit the bearing of arms, and no federation of clubs would be allowed.

According to Peter Amann, "Buoyant in March, sagging in April, compromised in May, the club movement did not survive the agony of June 1848. Already before the insurrection, the clubs were in rapid decline as activists, wearied by fruitless discussion, deserted. Harassed by an increasingly repressive government, the popular societies were forced to scramble for the limited number of private halls." (Public buildings had been closed to them.) Finally, a law of 2 April 1852 forbade any association, whatever its goal.

The clubs had been weakened by personal and political rivalries, by an absence of common goals, and by a lack of means for action. They were linked to the past by their structures and ideologies, but they pointed toward new directions that would not be realized for many years.

P. H. Amann, *Revolution and Mass Democracy* (Princeton, 1975); F. A. de Luna, *The French Republic under Cavaignac, 1848* (Princeton, 1969); A. Jouet, *Les clubs. Leur histoire et leur role depuis 1789* (Paris, 1981); J. M. Merriman, *The Repression of the Left in Revolutionary France, 1848–1851* (New Haven, 1978); R. Price, *The French Second Republic, A Social History* (London, 1972); D. Stern (Marie d'Agoult), *Histoire de la Révolution de 1848*, 3 vols. (Paris, 1851).

Jean-Claude Caron, trans. by E. Newman
Related entries: BARBES; BLANQUI, L.-A.; CABET; CLUB OF CLUBS; DEMONSTRATIONS OF 1848–1849; GARNIER-PAGES; HUBER; JUNE DAYS; LEDRU-ROLLIN; LONGEPIED; NIBOYET; RASPAIL; ROLAND; SOBRIER; SOCIETY OF THE RIGHTS OF MAN.

COAL INDUSTRY. In the decades after the fall of Napoleon, France's modest coal industry developed significantly; production topped 1 million tons in 1820 and 5 million tons in 1846. Yet during this same period Great Britain extracted some ten times this quantity annually. French mines could not meet the nation's needs, and France was forced to import annually a quantity equivalent to one-third to one-half of its own production, primarily from Belgium and Great Britain.

These imports increased sharply in the 1830s, when the July Monarchy abandoned the stiff tariff on coal established in 1816.

By the last years of the July Monarchy, the Loire was responsible for close to one-half of French coal production and the Nord for nearly one-third. Most of the remainder came from a number of smaller mines in central and southern France, including Grand-Combe (Gard), Blanzy (Saône-et-Loire), Commentry (Allier), and Decazeville (Aveyron). The isolation of many basins made transportation of coal costly. This restricted the spread of the use of coal in industry; coke did not surpass the use of charcoal in the production of iron until well into the Second Empire.

The First Empire had reaffirmed the state's ownership of all coal deposits and its right to authorize exploitation of them in return for a slight tax on production. Concessionaires had to follow specified rules and regulations in operating the mines, including the provision of immediate medical care for injured mineworkers. The state corps of mining engineers had jurisdiction over the mines, but this did not prevent many state mining engineers from taking leaves of absence to work for private mining firms.

Coal mining required significant investments. Of the twenty most highly capitalized industrial firms in France in 1840, eight were coal-mining companies, and another three were integrated coal mining and metallurgical enterprises. The largest firm in France, the Anzin Coal Company, had a capital of 50 million francs, three times that of the runner-up, Saint-Gobain.

The coal industry employed 30,000 miners in 1840. In order to ensure a stable and disciplined labor force, almost all firms provided a variety of services for their employees, generally financed by company contributions and deductions from workers' wages. In 1833 Anzin claimed that the pensions, free medical care, schools, and other benefits it offered were worth one-sixth of a miner's average annual salary. Some companies operating in remote areas created new communes near their pits, as in Decazeville and Grand-Combe.

During the first half of the nineteenth century, mining was a semi-skilled, artisanal occupation with a loose apprenticeship system. Although the period saw improvements in the control of water and fire within the mines, the jobs of the hewer and the loader changed little once firms established this initial division of labor. Some combination of men, women, children, and horses handled haulage, while the cleaning and sorting of coal above ground was left largely to women and children under adult male supervision. Conditions of employment varied greatly from region to region. Whereas miners in the Nord worked nine to ten hours daily during the late 1840s, their counterparts in the Loire produced twice as much coal during their twelve- to fourteen-hour workdays. Successful efforts by firms to substitute payment by production for payment by presence generated discontent among miners, as did the replacement in certain basins of subcontractors by company supervisors. The setting of wages, which accounted for over 40 percent of the sale price of coal, provoked several major and a number of smaller labor conflicts. The most important strikes took place at Anzin in 1833 and in the Loire in 1844 and 1846.

The French coal industry changed in several respects in the 1850s. Napoleon III broke up the monopolistic Loire Coal Company, thus temporarily reversing the concentration of coal production in a limited number of firms; the spread of railroads expanded the market for both French and imported coal; and the recently discovered extensive coal field of the Pas-de-Calais went into full-scale operation.

C. Fohlen, "Charbon et Révolution industrielle en France (1815–1850)," in *Charbon et Sciences humaines*, ed. Louis Trénard (Paris, 1966); R. G. Geiger, *The Anzin Coal Company, 1800–1833* (Newark, Del., 1974); B. Gille, "Les Plus Grandes Campagnies Houillères Francaises vers 1840," in *Charbon et Sciences humaines*, ed. Louis Trénard (Paris, 1966); M. Gillet, *Les charbonnages du nord de la France au XIXe siècle* (Paris, 1973); L. Murard and P. Zylberman, *Le petit travailleur infatigable* (Fontaney-sous-Bois, 1976); P. Stearns, *Paths to Authority* (Urbana, 1978).

Donald Reid

Related entries: ANZIN, COMPANY OF THE MINES OF; DECAZEVILLE.

COLLEGE DE FRANCE, a unique and prestigious research and teaching institute, independent of the University, preparing for no diplomas or degrees, whose courses are open to the general public. On the advice of his librarian, the humanist Guillaume Budé, in 1530 François I appointed six *lecteurs royaux*— two in Greek, three in Hebrew, and one in mathematics—to carry out advanced research in their fields and to report their findings in a series of lectures open to the public. The king intended that this Collège royal, later the Collège de France, should challenge the monopoly of higher education that the Sorbonne enjoyed; scientific methods and new areas of knowledge such as the physical sciences and ancient and Oriental languages should call into question the traditional disciplines, scholastic disputation, and the exclusive use of Latin. The institution flourished, survived the Revolution of 1789, consisted of twenty-one chairs in 1815, and expanded to twenty-eight chairs by 1852. For mathematical and physical sciences there were chairs in mathematics, astronomy, general and experimental physics, chemistry (changed in 1845 to mineral chemistry), natural history (changed in 1832 to natural history of unorganized bodies), medicine, natural history of organized bodies (new chair in 1837), anatomy (discontinued in 1832), and comparative embryology (new chair in 1844). The philosophical and sociological sciences included the law of nature and people and three new chairs: Greek and Latin philosophy (1832), history of comparative legislation (1831), and political economy (1831). Finally, the area that the Collège designated as historical, philological, and archaeological sciences comprised history and morality, Hebrew, Arabic, Turkish, Persian, Chinese, Sanskrit, Latin eloquence, Latin poetry, modern French literature, Slavic (new chair 1840), German (new chair 1841), South European languages and literatures (new chair 1841), archaeology (new chair 1831), and Greek (two chairs, reduced to one in 1832). Although practically all of the professors made important contributions in their fields, the best known to the general public were André-Marie Ampère for his experiments with electricity, Jean-François Champollion, who deciphered Egyptian hieroglyphics, Jean-Baptiste Say, the pioneer of laissez-faire economics in France, and Jules Michelet, for his lectures, history of the French Revolution, and other works.

Because of the Collège's renown and reputation for independence, governments sometimes intervened to dismiss scholars, create new chairs, or make appointments over the objections of the assembly of professors. By 1566 Charles IX had established the principle of nomination by the assembly of professors followed by appointment by the government, and this method was reaffirmed in a law of 1802. Yet before the Third Republic the Collège was never completely autonomous in the selection of its faculty. Between 1815 and 1830 the king appointed four professors despite the wishes of the faculty and dismissed one (the administrator, Louis Lefèvre-Gineau) for protesting these nominations and another (Pierre-François Tissot) for attempting to publish a history of the French Revolution. Tissot was reinstated following the Revolution of 1830, and the new government being receptive rather than hostile to classical economics, J. B. Say soon became the first holder of a chair in political economy. In Say's case as in many others, the initiative came from the government, and then the assembly of professors studied the suggestion, nominated a candidate, and awaited the government's appointment of the nominee. Under the July Monarchy the wishes of the assembly of professors were generally respected, but when the professors discussed converting a chair from anatomy to natural history, the government seized the opportunity to make an appointment to the new chair without consultation. This action discouraged the discussion of changing the discipline of a chair until 1880, for the professors, always zealous in the defense of their independence, feared losing control of appointments.

The Revolution of 1848 threatened to change the character of the Collège de France radically. In March the new government suppressed five chairs and created, without any consultation, eleven new ones which were to be held by prominent politicians such as Alphonse de Lamartine, Alexandre-Auguste Ledru-Rollin, and Etienne Garnier-Pagès. The new chairs were intended for the instruction of a carefully selected body of students who would attend an Ecole d'administration attached to the Collège de France. But this early initiative of the Republic was quickly abandoned as the republicans dealt with more urgent matters and the revolution ran its course; the five professors who had been dismissed regained their posts in the fall of the same year. The Ecole d'administration would have constituted a major diversion from the Collège de France's ancient purpose of furthering pure knowledge: the Collège would henceforth have had to assume the professional education of a discrete body of students. Yet although abandoned almost as quickly as it was founded, the Ecole d'administration served as a model for two similar schools founded later: the Ecole libre des sciences politiques in 1872 and the Ecole nationale d'administration in 1945.

Although the Collège de France survived the Revolution of 1848, as it had the Revolution of 1789, with the Second Empire came a return to severe censorship such as last seen under the Bourbon Restoration. Jules Michelet and Edgar Quinet had for several years expressed their republican and anticlerical sentiments freely in their crowded lecture halls, and Adam Mickiewicz used his lectures on Slavic literature to plead for Polish independence. The classes these men taught became political events rather than reports about pure scholarship. Controversy raged around Michelet and Quinet in particular, whose courses on the Jesuits aroused Catholics. Thus in March 1852 Napoleon III dismissed all three from their posts, and the professors who remained seem to have been wary of further expulsions, for there is no record of protest in the official minutes of their assembly. Ernest Renan was to be another illustrious victim of expulsion in 1864, not for his political views but for his factual treatment of the life of Jesus. Not until the Third Republic did the Collège regain and surpass the degree of autonomy that it had enjoyed under the July Monarchy.

Yet despite political vicissitudes over the course of its long history, the Collège de France has remained remarkably consistent with its original purpose: to encourage the most brilliant scholars to pursue original research and to report their findings freely to the public.

Annuaire du Collège de France 1981–1982: Historique (Paris, 1982); M. Bataillon, "Le Collège de France," *Revue de l'enseignement supérieur*, no. 2 (1962); C. Delangle, "*Histoire du Collège de France*" (thèse de troisième cycle, Ecole pratique des hautes études en sciences sociales, 1983); A. Lefranc et al., *Le Collège de France (1530–1930): Livre jubilaire composé à l'occasion de son quatrième centenaire* (Paris, 1932).

Robert J. Smith

Related entries: AMPERE; CHAMPOLLION; MICHELET; PUBLIC INSTRUCTION; QUINET; RENAN; SAY.

COMITE DE LA RUE DE POITIERS, also referred to as the Réunion de la rue de Poitiers, which later became known as the Party of Order, a group of conservatives who met at the Académie de médecine on the rue de Poitiers during the Second Republic and tried to influence public policy. While there is no exact date for the organization of this group, it apparently was formed immediately following the failure of the 15 May 1848 demonstration of radicals at the National Assembly, which resulted in a strengthening of the power of the notables in France. The April elections had weakened the radicals but at the same time had not encouraged the notables. Meetings were held at the Académie de médecine in the rue de Poitiers (hence the name) at least once a week. Many organizations at that time took the names of the streets or buildings where meetings were held rather than names identifying their political leanings.

Estimates of the number of members of the Réunion vary from 198 (in the Berryer papers in the Archives nationales) to 400 reported in the newspaper *La Presse*. Its composition changed during its brief existence, according to the affiliations of new deputies in subsequent elections. They were generally conservative deputies of the National Assembly and usually categorized as monarchists, legitimists, or moderate republicans. The first president was the martinet General Achille Baraguey d'Hilliers who had been recalled from Africa and then elected deputy from Doubs. His choice as president reflected a change in attitude of the notables who heretofore had avoided putting generals in positions of power. The vice-president was a lawyer, Jean-Didier Baze, from Lot-et-Garonne. Louis-René-Antoine Grangier de la Marinière, a deputy from Nièvre, was the secretary. Among distinguished members of the group were Adolphe Thiers, Henri de Larochejaquelein, Alfred-Frédéric de Falloux, Charles de Rémusat, Louis-Mathieu de Molé, Achille Fould, and Alexis de Tocqueville. Its strength lay in the influence or oratorical abilities of some of its members, especially Thiers.

The Réunion de la rue de Poitiers evolved from its beginnings as a defender of the economic system, which was being threatened by the short-lived Executive Commission, to a reluctant supporter of Eugène Cavaignac during the June Days and later of Louis-Napoleon. It had hoped to place members in Cavaignac's cabinet but failed as most of his appointees were *républicains de la veille*. All but one of his selections, Lazare-Hippolyte Carnot as minister of education, were accepted without resistance. The attack in parliament of Louis-Bertrand Bonjean, representing the rue de Poitiers group, on Carnot centered on the threat of socialism, and Carnot, after a fierce battle, stepped down, thus establishing the dominance of the Comité de la rue de Poitiers. Achille de Vaulabelle, named to replace Carnot, was acceptable to the group as being harmless despite his democratic leanings. However, he proved to be not so docile as had been anticipated. In addition to supporting Carnot's proposed educational reforms, he introduced some of his own.

Elections in the exercise of universal male suffrage throughout the summer of 1848, during Cavaignac's "state of siege," changed the composition of the National Assembly as well as the membership of the rue de Poitiers as more reactionary deputies were elected. D'Hilliers remained president of the group in spite of his disagreements with Cavaignac. Vice-presidents were Baze, Joseph Degousée, Falloux, Léon Faucher, and Fould. A former peer of France, General Joseph-Marcellin Rulhière, was secretary. Many former legitimist deputies returned to the Assembly, joined by Orleanists and other conservatives and representatives of the Left-Center and the dynastic Left.

Although Cavaignac's government is thought of as a very reactionary one, many social reforms were proposed, such as the progressive tax measures that Finance Minister Michel Goudchaux favored. Opposed by the rue de Poitiers, the proposals died as did the reforms in the educational system advocated by Carnot and Vaulabelle.

In September the rue de Poitiers opposed the selection of a president by the National Assembly and in October favored the election of a president of the Republic, seeing the establishment of a republic as a temporary necessity and the only way they might have some influence in the government. Cavaignac's popularity waned during the state of siege in the summer, and the tenuous relationship with the rue de Poitiers unraveled despite the government's purge of the radicals Louis Blanc and Marc Caussidière. The closing of radical newspapers pleased the Réunion until a legitimist paper was also closed down.

In September support for Cavaignac was further eroded by his proposal to send government representatives into the provinces to obtain information. In the face of determined opposition, Cavaignac canceled the project. Elections of deputies that month sent mostly conservatives to the Assembly, and moderate republicans, as well as Cavaignac, were disappointed and concerned. Five departments elected Louis-Napoleon.

Cavaignac lost ground in October when the Assembly approved the election of a president by popular vote. In September, on the other hand, his authority to continue seizure powers had been overwhelmingly approved. In October the climate had changed, and the powers were continued by the slimmest of margins, leading to a change of ministries and the inclusion of some monarchists in the cabinet, but not enough to satisfy the rue de Poitiers. On 19 October Cavaignac gave in, and the Assembly voted to end the state of siege. The parliamentary system of government remained intact. Final debate on a constitution that month led to its adoption in November, without opposition from the rue de Poitiers.

Cavaignac, who felt that a regular government should be elected and that his position would thus be strengthened, advocated an early election, which was opposed by the rue de Poitiers. Cavaignac won, and 10 December was set as the date for the election.

Until September Cavaignac had seemed the logical choice for president of the Republic, but Louis-Napoleon's stunning victories in the elections that month changed the picture. The rue de Poitiers was unhappy with both choices and considered putting up its own candidate, either General Nicolas Changarnier or Marshal Thomas-Robert Bugeaud. After having rejected that idea, it chose to back neither candidate officially, though it was courted by both political factions. Out of 200 attending the meeting where the decision was made, only 39 voted to choose a candidate. It thus lost a chance to have real political power. Some of its influential Orleanist members rejected Cavaignac because he would not give them the guarantees they demanded.

In a debate in the Assembly in November, Cavaignac won a victory when the deputies gave him a vote of confidence. Many rue de Poitiers representatives abstained from voting. Louis-Napoleon courted the committee and emphasized his stand on law and order. By 10 December many influential members of the committee openly supported him, including d'Hilliers, its president, Molé, and Thiers. He was also supported by most monarchist newspapers and people in the provinces whereas Cavaignac's chief support lay in the cities.

It is about this time that the Réunion de la rue de Poitiers evolved into the Party of Order.

F. A. de Luna, *The French Republic under Cavaignac, 1848* (Princeton, 1969); C. de Rémusat, *Mémoires de ma Vie: les dernières années de la monarchie, la Révolution de*

1848, la second République (1841–1851), vol. 4 (Paris, 1962); A.-J. Tudesq, *Les Grands Notables en France (1840–1849): étude historique d'une psychologie sociale*, vol. 2 (Paris, 1964).

Helen Castelli

Related entries: CARNOT, L.-H.; CAVAIGNAC, L.-E.; CONSTITUTION OF 1848; EXECUTIVE COMMISSION; PARTY OF ORDER; *LA PRESSE*; REPUBLICANS; VAULABELLE.

COMMISSAIRE, SEBASTIEN (1822–1900), republican, revolutionary, and political prisoner. Born in Dôle (Jura), Commissaire worked in the silk industry in Lyons, and was converted to utopian socialism after reading Etiénne Cabet's *Voyage en Icarie* in the 1840s, at which point he also entered the army. Stationed in garrisons in Metz and Strasbourg, Commissaire attempted to propagandize his fellow soldiers and participated in republican political organizations in the Haut-Rhin. He was a corporal in 1848, when two departments (Rhône and Haut-Rhin) elected him to the legislative assembly of the Second Republic at the age of twenty-six, along with two other radical noncommissioned officers, Ratier and Jean-Baptiste Boichot. Commissaire joined the Montagnard minority in the conservative assembly and participated in the 13 June 1849 demonstrations in Paris called to protest the sending of a military expedition to Rome to save the papacy from Garibaldi's revolutionaries. When the demonstrations were broken up by troops, Commissaire and other deputies gathered at the Conservatory of Arts and Crafts to issue a call for an armed uprising, where they were subsequently arrested. Tried with Jean-Marie-Joseph Deville (another deputy) by the high court at Versailles, Commissaire was sentenced to the prison at Belle-Isle with several hundred other republicans. Amnestied in 1859, he returned to Lyons and opened a clothing shop but was soon involved in the political opposition groups centered on the newspaper *Le Progrès*. A lifelong radical, his memoirs (1888) are a valuable source of information about radical politics in France in the mid-nineteenth century.

S. Commissaire, *Mémoires et souvenirs* (Paris and Lyons, 1888); R. Price, *The Second French Republic* (Ithaca, 1972); G. Weill, *Histoire du parti republicain en France* (Paris, 1900).

David Longfellow

Related entries: LEGISLATIVE ASSEMBLY; RASPAIL; ROMAN EXPEDITION.

COMMISSION DES RECOMPENSES NATIONALES (26 August 1830-October 1831), a commission created to administer the granting of public awards to the heroes of the Revolution of 1830 and of aid to victims of the revolution. The Commission des récompenses nationales was established by a royal ordinance of 26 August 1830 to receive and process claims from or on behalf of citizens who had contributed to the Orleanist victory in the Revolution of 1830. Subsequently it was specifically charged with recommending to the government the names of widows, orphans, and parents of the dead and of permanently disabled combatants who qualified for lifetime pensions and of wounded deserving of temporary support. The commission also was given the responsibility of determining recipients of the Medal of July or the Cross of July.

The commission received more than 20,000 claims and was importuned by so many eager claimants that armed guards had to be posted outside its offices. Before it was dissolved in October 1831, it had recommended the award of more than 1,100 lifetime pensions, support for 381 orphans until they reached the age of eighteen, 3,831 Medals of July, and 1,830 Crosses of July. Also on the commission's recommendation 274 combatants received commissions as sublieutenants in the army, and 590 were offered appointments as noncommissioned officers.

Local committees of recompense were established in thirty-nine departments. They recommended only five grants of financial aid but proposed the award of 59 medals and 145 crosses; the government approved 58 medals but only 37 crosses.

D. H. Pinkney, *The French Revolution of 1830* (Princeton, 1972).

David H. Pinkney

Related entry: CROSS OF JULY AND MEDAL OF JULY.

COMMISSION DU GOUVERNEMENT POUR LES TRAVAILLEURS. See LUXEMBOURG COMMISSION.

COMMISSIONS MIXTES. See MIXED COMMISSIONS.

LA COMMUNE DE PARIS (1848), newspaper of the clubs, particularly the Club of Clubs. The establishment of the Second Republic in February 1848 produced a spate of popular political clubs. By April about 200 had been founded in Paris. Many clubs tried to run their own newspaper, chiefly to print their own minutes. The *Commune de Paris* aimed to cover the activities of a number of clubs and was also the recognized mouthpiece of the society that attempted to organize the club movement, the Club of Clubs. Like all other newspapers emanating from this movement, it declined in popularity after the demonstration of 15 May 1848, but even then, with its founder Joseph Sobrier in prison, it continued to print 5,000 copies of each issue. The offices of the newspaper provided a useful rendezvous for revolutionary militants. Longer lasting than the *Voix des clubs*, the *Commune* was probably one of the most important journals of the springtime of 1848.

P. H. Amann, *Revolution and Mass Democracy: The Paris Club Movement in 1848* (Princeton, 1975).

Irene Collins

Related entries: CLUB OF CLUBS; CLUBS, POLITICAL; SOBRIER; *LA VOIX DES CLUBS*.

COMMUNISM. See CABET.

COMPAGNONNAGES, more-or-less secret societies of workers. Each of the rival *compagnonnages* included artisans from various skilled trades, and they fought bitterly against one another for control of jobs. Their goal was mutual assistance, finding jobs for members, and helping apprentices to learn their trade. They set wages, working conditions, and job qualifications, and they could force nonmembers or members of rival *compagnonnages* off their jobs or keep recalcitrant employers from finding workers. They also lodged and fed their members in *cayennes*, or mother houses, as they walked from town to town on the *tour de France* learning their trade. New members were admitted in secret rites similar to those of the Freemasons, although the *compagnons* claimed that their rites were more ancient. New *compagnons* rose from the rank of *aspirant* to *compagnon reçu* to *compagnon fini*, although the process varied among the different *compagnonnages*.

Compagnonnages existed before the Revolution and survived the police state of the First Empire. During the Restoration, they benefited from official tolerance and regained a certain amount of importance, but they never reached more than an elite minority of the artisans and only in about a dozen trades. The influence that the *compagnonnages* might have exercised was hindered by the inept and often violent battles between rival organizations, among whom the principal ones were the Devoirants or Devorants, and the Gavots, also known as the Renards de liberté.

   E. Coornaert, *Les Compagnonnages en France* (Paris, 1966).

                    Guillaume de Bertier de Sauvigny, trans. E. Newman
Related entries: FREEMASONRY; TOUR DE FRANCE.

COMTE, AUGUSTE (1798–1857), social philosopher. Self-proclaimed high priest of humanity, Auguste Comte devoted his life to the elaboration and propagation of the doctrine and ritual known as positivism. A Paris-based theorist, Comte launched positivism in the hope and expectation that it would resolve the social and intellectual chaos of his age. Although it was derided for its extravagant ritualistic trappings and limited in its influence during Comte's lifetime, positivism possesses a scope, rigor, and consistency that make it one of the major intellectual constructs in the history of French philosophy and social science.

   Born in Montpellier to a royalist, intensely Catholic family of modest means, Auguste Comte showed intellectual promise at an early age. While studying at the local lycée, Comte lost his religious faith and became a republican, although he also fell under the influence of Daniel Encontre, a professor of mathematics with encyclopedic interests and strong antidemocratic political views. In 1814 Comte entered the Ecole polytechnique, where he excelled scholastically and began to plan for an academic career. Sharing the liberal political sentiments of his associates, Comte demonstrated opposition to the repressiveness of the

Napoleonic and Restoration regimes. As in later life, his political activities led him into personal difficulties. He left the Ecole polytechnique following a student revolt in which he was implicated and helped organize a student organization that attracted the attention of the police.

While waiting to secure an academic post, Comte independently pursued studies in the natural and social sciences. In August 1817 Comte threw in his lot with Henri de Saint-Simon, dazzled by the older genius's intellectual scope and originality and drawn no doubt by Saint-Simon's offer of material support. Saint-Simon saw in the young student from the Ecole polytechnique precisely what he lacked: an orderly, rigorous mind informed by years of solid scientific training. As Saint-Simon's secretary for nearly seven years, Comte became familiar with the leaders of the opposition liberal press, whose demands for freedom of expression and smaller government budgets he warmly supported in a number of newspaper articles. Within a few years, however, Saint-Simon and Comte began moving out of the liberal orbit, collaborating on the outlines of a new industrial social system to replace the feudal society now relegated to the trashbin of history. The precise nature of that collaboration—from which both members clearly benefited—has long been a matter of unresolved, and probably unresolvable, controversy; partisans of both men have fought pitched battles over the paternity of the startling ideas that appeared in a series of joint publications. By 1824 the strain of intellectual, strategic, and personal differences led to a permanent state of alienation between Comte and Saint-Simon. Comte felt he had learned all he could from Saint-Simon and quarreled with Saint-Simon over the publication of Comte's "Système de politique positive," the first systematic statement of positivist principles.

Estrangement from Saint-Simon brought Comte fresh financial difficulties, compounded by marital problems that arose soon after his union with Caroline Massier in 1825. Comte managed to earn a small income during this period by offering private lessons and by writing for the Saint-Simonian journal, *Le Producteur*. But the major portion of his energies went into preparing a monumental "Cours de philosophie positive" that Comte proposed to offer in a series of seventy-two public lectures. Opened on 2 April 1826, the course drew a number of publicists, scientists, and associates from the Ecole polytechnique but was abruptly cancelled soon after it began when Comte suffered a nervous breakdown. The "Cours" was reopened on 4 January 1829 following Comte's recovery and successfully completed.

Publication of the *Cours de philosophie positive* in six volumes between 1830 and 1842 did little to enhance Comte's personal fortunes. He never managed to obtain the major academic appointment he craved and remained at the fringes of the academic establishment for the rest of his life. In the end, Comte had to settle for lesser positions, such as that of entrance examiner for the Ecole polytechnique. Even this relatively modest post was denied to Comte in 1844, after which he relied for a time upon subsidies offered to him by John Stuart Mill and other English admirers. In part the source of Comte's academic failure lay in his personal irascibility; in part it lay in his impolitic public statements and actions, one of which earned him a brief stay in prison.

Embittered by his failure and ultimately abandoned by his wife, Comte turned inward. By 1838 he gave up expanding his knowledge through reading and shifted the focus of his works from the objective system of natural objects to the subjective world of human needs and moral instincts. In 1844 Comte began transforming the early "Système de politique positive" into a far vaster work with the same title; it was published in four volumes between 1851 and 1854. A passionate love affair with Clothilde de Vaux, cut short by her death in 1846, buoyed his spirits for a time and helped inspire certain aspects of positivist ritual, in whose necessity he had long believed.

Donning the mantle of the high priest of humanity, Comte devoted the last years of his life primarily to the establishment of a positivist religion. In 1848, he organized the Société positiviste. Comte sought to propagate positivist doctrine and ritual among the public at large through a series of popular works and among the crowned heads of Europe through direct appeals. Positivism, Comte contended, was the only possible alternative to communism in the modern age. Comte supported Louis-Napoleon's coup d'état in the hope that a strong authoritarian government would be successful in quelling popular disorder and best equipped to institute a positivist "sociocracy." Visions of positivist rituals celebrated in Notre-Dame and of a positivist takeover of the Jesuits preoccupied him until his death in 1857.

Although Comte's thought was heavily influenced by the social philosophies of the Catholic counterrevolutionaries Louis de Bonald and Joseph de Maistre, positivism may said to derive from the attempts of the Enlightenment *philosophes* to come to grips with the political, social, and intellectual implications of the scientific revolution and the rise of capitalism. Like the *philosophes*, Comte believed that the course of modern society had made utterly obsolete the feudal ties that had bound people to one another and the superstructure of theology that had informed human thought since antiquity. Like the *philosophes*, Comte looked to the savant as the ultimate arbiter of human affairs and hence as the only possible source of a solution to the social and intellectual crisis occasioned by the collapse of medieval civilization. With the coming of the French Revolution, Comte thought, the crisis had reached a critical stage. The time had come to provide a definitive solution by consolidating human knowledge founded upon scientific principles within a single system of thought and by constituting a new normal social order in the light of this system. It was in the work of the Catholic counterrevolutionaries that Comte found a formal pattern to emulate in the composition of his positivist philosophy and his program for a positivist society; but it was from the *philosophes* that he borrowed the notion of reconstructing human knowledge and society on a purely scientific foundation.

Although Emile Littré and others have believed that the evolution of positivism could be divided into an earlier rationalist period and later emotive one, most scholars now see a single set of fundamental principles—enunciated when Comte was still in his twenties—governing all Comte's thought. In moving from the *Cours* to later works, it is now generally agreed, Comte changed only the focus of his philosophy, not its foundations.

The *Cours* represented Comte's attempt to explore the objective conditions of human existence—that is, the structure of the external world that impinges upon humanity. The only way in which the moral goals of humanity could be achieved, Comte thought, was to define first the realm of moral freedom through a scientific analysis of nature. Until the nineteenth century, Comte held, no completely adequate analysis of nature was possible insofar as societies had clung to the prescientific methods and concepts of the theological and metaphysical stages of historical development. Gradually prescientific methods and concepts were giving way to scientific or positive ones, first in those disciplines dealing with relatively simple objects (mathematics, then astronomy, then physics) and later in those dealing with relatively complex objects (chemistry, then biology, then social physics). With biology just having entered the positive stage of development, it now remained only for social physics to become a positive science before the ultimate system of human knowledge was essentially complete and humanity could march confidently into the positivist age.

In the *Cours*, Comte laid out the fundamental positive principles that constituted each of the major sciences and demonstrated their interconnections. It was pointless, he argued, to search for the ontological basis of phenomena or their causes, for these were unknowable; all science could establish were the regularities of their appearance by passing back and forth from the phenomena themselves to the invariable laws that governed them. Even the goal of unifying the sciences by subsuming all kinds of phenomena under one set of covering laws was dismissed by Comte as utopian. Although all the sciences had their origin in observation and although the knowledge acquired by the sciences of more complex objects rested on the knowledge acquired by the sciences of less complex objects, each science, Comte insisted, had its own methods of investigation, explanation, and proof. Comte particularly stressed this conclusion with regard to social physics; social facts were as distinct from biological ones as biological facts were distinct from those of chemistry. To be sure, social physics was closer in every respect to biology than it was to any of the other sciences. But it could not be directly derived from biology; still less could it effectively employ the quantitative methods used by the sciences of inanimate objects.

Having set out the general philosophical premises of positivism in the *Cours*, Comte, in his *Système de politique positive*, sought to establish social physics (now baptized with Comte's neologism *sociology*) on a broader and firmer foundation. Society, argued Comte, could be studied in both its dynamic and static states. As a dynamic entity, society had traversed the course of history in three major stages punctuated by two points of transition. The first theological stage corresponded to the age of antiquity, when man, acting upon the natural "fetishism" of his imagination, conjured up visions of a universe governed by divine beings and relied on conquest and slavery as the material basis of civilization. The second metaphysical stage corresponded to the Middle Ages, when mankind transmuted the gods of antiquity into the abstractions of scholasticism and attenuated the horrors of slavery by substituting for it the more benign forms of feudal servitude. The final positive stage corresponded to the modern age, when people began putting all knowledge on a sound scientific basis and supplied their material wants through the expansion of industry.

Approached statically, society appeared to Comte as a great being, which shaped the consciousness of all its members without destroying their individuality. Like other living bodies, society was composed of a unity of heterogeneous elements that, in the social realm, could be roughly divided into the superior spiritual and the inferior temporal sectors. By performing that function for which he was best suited by nature, each member of society contributed to the welfare of society as a whole in accordance with the principle of the division of labor. Although Comte recognized strict limits to the effects of social action on the natural realm, he believed that with the proper spiritual direction, society would be able, over the course of time, to so organize human energies that it would radically alter the social conditions of human existence. In part Comte looked forward to a major improvement in the material state of humanity. But he was far more concerned with the transformation of man's spiritual state, especially morals, perceiving in the repression of egotism and the enhancement of universal love the highest goals of civilization.

To this end, Comte, slipping into the subjective mode of reasoning through which the world was viewed from the standpoint of social need, sketched out in the *Système* and later works a positivist program for the "normal" state of society. The temporal sector of society would be composed of small republics— no larger than the provinces of the Old Regime—which would be overseen by bankers and major industrial leaders. The spiritual sector of society would be directed by priests, in particular the high priest, whose supreme duty would lie in administering a godless religion of humanity by an elaborate ritual Comte set out in painstaking detail. Thus organized, humanity would escape the chaos threatening to engulf it, joining harmoniously together in the ceremonial cult that had love for its principle, order for its basis, and progress for its goal.

Positivism, strictly defined, exercised little influence before Comte's death. Far less widely studied and publicized than, for example, Victor Cousin's eclecticism, it became generally known to the French reading public only during the Second Empire and Third Republic. Even then positivism's appeal was limited. Few could accept its doctrine as a whole, and still fewer were willing to practice its baroque ritual. It has been estimated that in the whole world, there were never more than a few hundred practicing positivists at any one time and no more than two thousand practicing positivists since Comte's day.

Although positivism attracted a substantial audience in England earlier than it did in France, a small segment of the French public had been exposed to positivist ideas by the reign of Napoleon III. The first person, aside from Comte himself, to discuss positivism publicly seems to have been a Dr. Henri de Blainville, a close associate of both Comte and Saint-Simon. In the 1840s, Emile Littré published a series of important pieces about Comte's work—some of them appearing in the newspaper *National*—which stressed the social implications of positivism. During the same decade, Comte reached out to the working classes through a series of public lectures on astronomy. The founding of the Société positiviste in 1848, which sought to spread positivism beyond the small circle of physicians, scientists, and former *polytechniciens* around Comte, lent the movement a measure of institutional stability, but this stability was undermined by dissension and splits among the faithful. The defection of Littré in 1852, arising in part out of Comte's embrace of Napoleon III, was especially damaging in that it robbed the movement of one of its most eloquent spokesmen and a possible successor to Comte as high priest. Even worse, Littré, having rejected positivist ritual and the entire subjective method of reasoning, lapsed into heresy by sketching out a rival version of positivism he believed to be more scientific. During the early Third Republic, the main force behind the dissemination of positivism in France was Pierre Laffitte, who lectured on positivism in the provinces and in Paris; in 1888 he drew audiences of more than five hundred at the Collège de France. By this time, positivist libraries and reading clubs had appeared in a number of French cities and towns.

Comte did make historically significant contributions to the social thought of his age by directing attention to the history of science and by defining sociology as an autonomous discipline. But Comte's direct influence on the major French intellectual figures of the nineteenth century is difficult to trace. Echoes of his thought may be found in the works of such scholars and social theorists as Ernest Renan, Hippolyte Taine, and Emile Durkheim, but these echoes are in most cases probably not a product of direct borrowing. Positivism, for all its idiosyncrasies, managed to incorporate within it some of the most widely held notions of the age: the universal applicability of scientific method; the possibility of explaining all individual phenomena with broad covering laws; society conceived as an interdependent organism; the inevitability of moral and material progress. When watered down by Littré and others, positivism came to represent in the public mind not the last best hope of humanity for universal reconciliation, as Comte had thought of it, but the ultimate statement of scientism. As such, it would become one of the most vulnerable targets for the philosophers and social scientists of the twentieth century.

P. Arnaud, Le *''Nouveau Dieu''—Préliminaire à la politique positive* (Paris, 1973); D. G. Charlton, *Positivist Thought in France during the Second Empire* (Oxford, 1959); H. Gouhier, *La Jeunesse d'Auguste Comte*, 3 vols. (Paris, 1933–41) and *La Vie d'Auguste*

Comte, 2d ed. (Paris, 1965); F. Manuel, *The Prophets of Paris* (Cambridge, Mass., 1962); W. M. Simon, *European Positivism in the Nineteenth Century* (Ithaca, 1963).

Thomas E. Kaiser

Related entries: BONALD; COLLEGE DE FRANCE; COUP D'ETAT OF 2 DECEMBER 1851; COUSIN; D'EICHTHAL; ECOLE POLYTECHNIQUE; JESUITS; MAISTRE; *LE NATIONAL*; SAINT-SIMON.

COMTE, FRANCOIS-CHARLES-LOUIS (1782–1837), publicist, lawyer, political journalist, coeditor of *Le Censeur européen* during the early Restoration era. Charles Comte, a member of the Paris bar, in collaboration with Pierre-Joseph Dunoyer, established *Le Censeur* in June 1814. To evade police suppression, this magazine appeared irregularly as discrete pamphlets and earned an enthusiastic following on the Left. His fame as a liberal journalist secure, Comte, as defense attorney, won his client's acquittal in the court-martial of General Rémy Exelmans. Comte rejected Napoleon's offer of the directorship of the *Moniteur*, but early in the Second Restoration Joseph Fouché, held over as minister of police, closed *Le Censeur* (September 1815).

An even stronger opposition voice, *Le Censeur européen*, with the original *Censeur* staff, appeared as a weekly in February 1817 and became a daily paper in June 1819. It was totally suppressed in June 1820 after a barrage of fines and prosecutions against its editors. Comte, for accusing the ultras of conspiring with the government, spent five months in La Force jail in 1817 and two months in 1820 for a similar offense. In 1821, marked for further prosecutions, Comte became an exile in Lausanne. Even there he was not safe from the ultras, to whom he had become a major adversary, and French diplomatic pressure led to revocation of his visa in 1823. The next refuge was in England, where he remained until 1826.

When he at last returned to France, he found himself disbarred and devoted his energies to the completion of a major work: *Traité de la législation ou exposition des lois générales . . .* (1827–35, 4 vols.). For this he later won the *Prix Monthyon* and other scholarly acclaim.

Under Louis-Philippe, Comte was given a legal post but soon lost it because of his uncompromising support of the growing dynastic opposition bloc of disaffected liberals. In 1831 and again in 1834 he was elected as a deputy from Sarthe. In 1832, he was made permanent secretary of the Academy of Moral and Political Sciences. Comte was the son-in-law of Jean-Baptiste Say, some of whose works he published posthumously.

E. Hatin, *Histoire de la presse* (Paris, 1859–61); *La Grande encyclopédie*, vol. 12.

Daniel Rader

Related entries: ACADEMY OF SCIENCES; *LE CENSEUR*; *LE CENSEUR EUROPEEN*; CHAMBER OF DEPUTIES; DUNOYER; FOUCHE; LOUIS PHILIPPE; *LE MONITEUR*; RESTORATION, SECOND; SAY.

CONCERT OF EUROPE, an expression commonly used in diplomatic and journalistic language since the Congress of Vienna of 1814–1815. It expressed the willingness of the great European powers, in the course of the nineteenth century, to settle the main international problems by establishing among themselves a consensus. The congresses and conferences occasionally held served to give visible and solemn expression to this basic intention.

Guillaume de Bertier de Sauvigny

Related entries: AIX-LA-CHAPELLE, CONGRESS OF; ROME, CONFERENCE OF; TROPPAU, CONGRESS OF; VERONA, CONGRESS OF; VIENNA, CONGRESS OF.

CONGREGATION, a Catholic philanthropic organization which many people erroneously believed was a secret society controlling the government during the Restoration. On 21 February 1801, in Paris, six students of law and of medicine founded the Congrégation (or Brotherhood) of the Holy Virgin under the direction of a former Jesuit, the abbé Dupuits. When Pope Pius VII came to Paris at the end of 1805, the association had about 180 members. Napoleon ordered its suppression in 1809 to punish it for having contributed to the diffusion throughout France of the papal bull that excommunicated those who had despoiled the Holy See. In 1814 Father Ronsin, a Jesuit, became the director of the reestablished Congrégation, and he turned it into a charitable society.

Its increasing influence aroused violent attacks; it was pictured as a secret political society that dominated the government, controlled who got government jobs, and spread a network of informers and agents throughout the country. This myth became part of the arsenal of anticlerical propaganda at the start of 1826 when François de Montlosier published his pamphlet, *Mémoire à consulter sur un système religieux et politique tendant à renverser la religion, la société et le trône*, and it became part of the standard history of the period after the fall of Charles X, thanks to historians like Achille de Vaulabelle. The publication of a book by Geoffroy de Grandmaison on the Congrégation in 1889 unmasked this polemic; this book, based on the archives of the society, showed that the Congrégation could not have had the political influence that its detractors had imagined. It seemed unlikely, however, that ill will alone could have created such a monster. This mystery was solved when the existence of a secret society, the Chevaliers de la foi, was revealed. Several leading members of that society were also members of the Congrégation, and consequently the very real activities and power of the clandestine Chevaliers de la foi could be attributed to an inoffensive religious society that operated openly in full view of the public.

G. de Bertier de Sauvigny, *Le comte Ferdinand et l'énigme de la Congrégation* (Paris, 1948); G. de Grandmaison, *La Congrégation* (Paris, 1889).

Guillaume de Bertier de Sauvigny, trans. E. Newman

Related entries: ANTICLERICAL CAMPAIGN; CHEVALIERS DE LA FOI; VAULABELLE.

CONGRESS OF AIX-LA-CHAPELLE. See AIX-LA-CHAPELLE, CONGRESS OF.

CONGRESS OF LAIBACH. See TROPPAU, CONGRESS OF.

CONGRESS OF TROPPAU. See TROPPAU, CONGRESS OF.

CONGRESS OF VERONA. See VERONA, CONGRESS OF.

CONGRESS OF VIENNA. See VIENNA, CONGRESS OF.

CONSEILS DE PRUD'HOMMES, literally, councils of wise men, or administrative boards with jurisdiction over industrial disputes. Napoleon introduced the institution, which had precedents in the guild tribunals of the Old Regime, in response to a petition from the Lyons Chamber of Commerce. The law of 18 March 1806 created a council for the Lyons silk industry and also authorized the government to set up similar councils in other manufacturing centres. Thirty-eight towns had councils by 1814 and sixty-two by 1830. The July Monarchy added only a few more, most notably in Paris, which finally got one for the metal trades in 1844 and three others for chemicals, textiles, and diverse industries in 1847.

Jurisdiction of the *conseils de prud'hommes* was limited to one or more industries in a community. They were authorized to settle differences between a manufacturer and his employees and apprentices over such issues as contractual obligations, wages, dismissal, or theft of raw materials. They could also settle disputes between manufacturers (for example, over the use of a trademark) or between workers (over the division of wages). A case coming before a council went first to a two-man conciliation board. If they failed to reconcile the parties, it went to the council as a whole, sitting as a board of judgment. Judgments were final when involving sums of under 100 francs; otherwise they could be appealed to the commercial courts. Most disputes ended in conciliation (94.6 percent of the 184,514 cases heard between 1830 and 1842). The councils, acting as police tribunals, could also judge the negligence of an apprentice or "any offense tending to trouble the order and discipline of the workshop" and impose a sentence of up to three days in prison. The councils also investigated contraventions of laws and regulations relating to manufacturing, and protected trademarks and property rights to new designs.

The *conseils de prud'hommes* included five to fifteen elected members, renewable by thirds every year, and serving without pay. There were representatives of both merchant-manufacturers and workers on the councils, but there was little real equality between the two groups. Employers always had one more representative than workers. Furthermore, "workers" meant only licensed workers—petty masters who paid a trade license (*patente*) and who themselves often hired wage labor. Foremen were counted among workers. Also, a single assembly, in which employers were usually the majority, elected the representatives when it demanded a restructuring of the councils and declared in February 1841 that "this tribunal does nothing for the workers, because it is too often the docile instrument of the masters."

The Second Republic introduced major reforms. The law of 27 May 1848 gave workers equal representation, allowed unlicensed workers to vote, and included foremen among the employers. It also created two electoral assemblies; employers nominated a list of their candidates from which workers made the final choice, and vice-versa. Louis-Napoleon Bonaparte modified but did not undo the reforms. The law of 2 March 1852 put foreman back among workers. The law of 1 June 1853 allowed employers and workers directly to elect their own representatives and gave the emperor power to name the president and vice-president of each council. On the whole, despite obvious shortcomings, the *conseils de prud'hommes* proved successful, although their importance tended to decline with the growth of trade unionism in the late nineteenth century. They still exist in France.

C. Binot de Villiers, *Manuel des conseils de prud'hommes* (Paris, 1845); C. P. Higby and C. B. Davis, "Industry and Labor under Napoleon," *American Historical Review* 53 (1947–48); F. Mollot, *De la competence des conseils de prud'hommes et de leur organisation* (Paris, 1842).

Michael Sibalis

Related entries: L'ATELIER; CHAMBERS OF COMMERCE.

CONSEIL SUPERIEUR DE L'INSTRUCTION PUBLIQUE, High Council of Public Instruction, variously named imperial, royal, or national council depending on the regime; a high council of academic experts having authority over various aspects of programs, diplomas, and administration of the public education system. Between 1802 and 1808 Napoleon organized the Imperial University of France, a highly centralized lay corporation possessing a monopoly over secondary and higher (and later primary) education in France. It was essentially a hierarchy of educational functionaries, of councils, rectors, and inspectors rigidly organized to enforce the state monopoly over schools, diplomas, certification, programs, and methods.

The university hierarchy consisted of a grand master (later minister of public instruction), the Council of the University, sixteen rectors at the head of regional academies, various inspectors, lycée officials, and others.

The Restoration transformed the council into a royal commission with five members. Under the July Monarchy the council was changed again to consist of twelve grand *universitaires*, each with lifetime tenure and each enjoying complete control over his specialty: hence Victor Cousin in philosophy, Louis Poinsot in mathematics, Louis-Jacques Thénard in science, Saint-Marc Girardin in history, and Abel-François Villemain in letters. Cousin and Villemain were ministers of public education from 1839 to 1844. In 1845, a new minister, Narcisse-Achille de Salvandy, enlarged the council and divided it into four sections. It continued to exercise great power, however, in view of the constant comings and goings of education ministers (eighteen between 1828 and 1842).

With the Revolution of 1848 and the coming of the Second Republic, the High Council was reformed and opened up. It consisted of seven members from legally recognized religious denominations, six delegates from the major state corporations, three members of the Institute, three from the private schools, and eight *universitaires (section permanente)*. Napoleon III (Second Empire, 1851 to 1870) disliked academic bureaucrats and abolished the permanent section in 1852.

P. Gerbod, *La Condition universitaire en France au XIX*e *siècle* (Paris, 1965); A. Prost, *L'Enseignement en France 1800–1967* (Paris, 1968).

C. Rod Day

Related entries: COUSIN; PUBLIC INSTRUCTION; VILLEMAIN.

LE CONSERVATEUR (1818–1820), right-wing newspaper of the Restoration. In 1818 the moderate ministry of Elie Decazes was vigorously attacked in journals that appeared at irregular intervals, thus escaping the police control prescribed for periodicals by the press law of 21 October 1814. Most of these semiperiodicals were of a left-wing nature, but during the summer of 1818 the ultraroyalist Eugène-François de Vitrolles obtained from the comte d'Artois 24,000 francs to found a semiperiodical that would attack the ministry from the Right. The *Conservateur* was launched in October 1818 with Chateaubriand as its chief editor. Vitrolles encountered enormous problems in dealing with his illustrious team of collaborators: Chateaubriand was arrogant and resented the slightest criticism, Félicité de Lamennais insisted on having a complete monopoly of articles on religion, the self-important August-François de Frénilly was piqued because Chateaubriand got more credit for the paper than he did, Villèle made no secret of the fact that he disliked the whole venture, and Joseph Fiévée quarreled with the group at an early stage and backed out. Chateaubriand and the various contributors insisted on handsome payment, and Vitrolles thought it necessary to rent expensive apartments. Fortunately, subscriptions rose rapidly from 3,000 to 8,500. The *Conservateur*'s expositions of political theory made heavy reading, but the personal popularity and brilliance of Chateaubriand ensured the success of the journal. The critical but strictly constitutional line adopted by the *Conservateur*, reminiscent of Chateaubriand's famous pamphlet *La Monarchie selon la Charte* (1816), was a source of embarrassment to the ministry.

When freer press laws were passed in 1819, the *Conservateur* launched bitter attacks on Decazes, accusing him of being in league with revolutionaries throughout Europe. When the murder of the duc de Berry in 1820 led to the introduction of censorship and the formation of a new ministry under Armand-Emmanuel de Richelieu, Chateaubriand was placed in a dilemma, for he was a personal friend of Richelieu but could not approve of the reactionary policies that the latter felt obliged to pursue, especially with regard to the press. Under these circumstances he persuaded the directors to dissolve the *Conservateur* in March 1820.

I. Collins, *The Government and the Newspaper Press in France, 1814–1881* (Oxford, 1959); N. E. Hudson, *Ultra-royalism and the French Restoration* (Cambridge, 1936); E. F. de Vitrolles, *Mémoires et relations politiques*, vol. 3 (Paris, 1884).

Irene Collins

Related entries: BERRY, C.-F.; CENSORSHIP; CHARLES X; CHATEAU-BRIAND; DECAZES; FIEVEE; FRENILLY; LAMENNAIS; PRESS LAWS; RICHELIEU; VILLELE; VITROLLES.

CONSERVATOIRE NATIONAL DES ARTS ET METIERS, National Conservatory of Arts and Crafts; a technical school created by a decree of the Convention on 13 October 1794 and maintained and developed by all succeeding governments. The Conservatory, which occupied the former buildings of the Abbey of Saint-Martin des Champs in Paris, included a museum that showed the applications of science to technology, models of all known machines, a library, some research laboratories, and courses to train and complete the education of engineers and technicians. During the Industrial Revolution of the nineteenth century it played a role in teaching the new technology to ordinary artisans.

F. B. Artz, *Technical Education in France* (Cambridge, Mass., 1966); E. M. Lévy, *L'Enseignement technique en France*, vol. 1 (Paris, 1900); A. de Monzie, *Histoire du Conservatoire des Arts et métiers* (Paris, 1949).

Guillaume de Bertier de Sauvigny, trans. E. Newman

Related entries: ECOLES NATIONALES DES ARTS ET METIERS; LA ROCHEFOUCAULD-LIANCOURT.

CONSIDERANT, VICTOR-PROSPER (1808–1893), utopian socialist activist and publicist and deputy in 1848. After attending the elite Ecole polytechnique, Victor Considérant entered the army engineers and was posted to Metz. There he first read the work of Charles Fourier. Completely captivated by the ideas of this socialist thinker, Considérant wrote an article for *Mercure de France* (13 March 1830), which led to a meeting with Fourier. Considérant then resigned his position in the army and became Fourier's most faithful disciple. They collaborated on the *Nouveau monde* and *La réforme industrielle*, the main organs of the *phalansteriens*. Fourier postulated that 810 types of people existed and that one male and one female of each type should be combined in what he called a phalanstry. These cells would be the building blocks for the perfect society. Fourier concentrated on love as the cure-all for social problems, and he ignored the seamier side of life—power. Later Marx would condemn these utopian ideas, and in the actions of Considérant, Marx's critique was quite accurate.

When Fourier died in 1837, Considérant emerged as the head of the Fourierist school of thought. Considérant took over direction of the Fourierist journal, the *Phalange*, and developed his own theories on *sociétaires*. Here Considérant wanted to combine work, talent, and capital for universal good. He moved away from the total emphasis on love and toward a critique of developing capitalist society. Although Fourier's ideas remained central, it was Considérant who popularized the idea of right to work that became the clarion call of the workers in the revolution of 1848. The new emphasis gave the phalansterians more of an interest in politics.

To further the aims of Fourierist ideas, Considérant founded a daily journal, *Démocratie pacifique*, in August 1843. For over six years this journal advocated socialist ideals. The staff of the journal also provided public lectures and even a library.

Although Considérant was a well-known socialist, the workers of Paris did not take him to heart in 1848. In the elections to the Constituent Assembly of April 1848, Considérant received barely 10 percent of the vote in the Seine. His reputation as a democrat, however, did lead to his election in the Loiret, where he was elected eighth of eight. As a deputy, he immediately confronted the problem of an idealist involved in revolutionary politics: how does one react to violence? Considérant never found a satisfactory answer.

He sat on the Labor Committee of the Assembly and its important subcommittee on the national workshops. Since he also was a member of the Luxembourg Commission, he was the only direct link between the antagonistic worker-backed commission and the monarchist-dominated assembly. Unfortunately, Considérant was not capable of bridging this gap by his appeal to understanding and cooperation. Being personally opposed to the implementation of socialism at the moment did nothing to help him. When people were willing to fight and die for their beliefs, his pacific appeals had little effect. Just prior to the outbreak of violence in June, he carried a petition signed by sixty members of the Assembly to the workers that blamed the current problems on nonhuman forces. The petition stated that all people had the right to live and work and that everyone must work together. The workers were unmoved, and the Assembly refused to publish this proclamation.

Considérant was never an effective member of the Assembly. He had not prevented Alfred-Frédéric de Falloux from issuing a report that condemned the national workshops. His position on the constitutional committee had no impact, and as a member of the Left his votes against the pursuit of Louis Blanc and Marc Caussidière, and for the right to work, were overriden by the majority. Only in his acquiescence to the behavior of General Eugène Cavaignac was Considérant in the majority.

In the struggle between the Assembly and Louis-Napoleon, the position of Considérant was clear: authoritarian executives were wrong. The *Démocratie pacifique* had supported Alexandre-Auguste Ledru-Rollin for president, and it became a vocal critic of Louis-Napoleon. Considérant voted against the Roman expedition, and it was this issue that led to his involvement in the events of June 1849.

After being elected to the new Legislative Assembly from the Seine, twenty-first of twenty-eight elected, he took his seat with the Montagnards. The actions of Louis-Napoleon so outraged Considérant that it was in the offices of the *Démocratie pacifique* that Ledru-Rollin, Félix Pyat, and others planned the insurrection of 13 June. When the call for a new Convention fell on deaf ears, he was pursued and eventually condemned by the high court of Versailles in absentia, as he had managed to slip into Belgium.

Considérant's career as a socialist activist was over. He spent the next twenty years attempting to found communities in the United States. La Réunion, along the Red River in Texas, failed with the outbreak of the U.S. civil war. Considérant returned to France in 1869 and lived in obscure poverty until his death in Paris in 1893.

M. Dommanquet, *Victor Considérant* (Paris, 1929).

Thomas Beck

Related entries: BLANC; CAUSSIDIERE; *LA DEMOCRATIE PACIFIQUE*; FOURIER; LUXEMBOURG COMMISSION; PYAT.

CONSISTORY, most important and comprehensive French-Jewish institution in the nineteenth century. Established in 1808 by Napoleon in imitation of the administrative organization of French protestantism, the Consistory was the official organization of Jewish congregations in France. It was made up of rabbis and laymen responsible for the administration of Jewish communities at the regional and national levels.

The system was hierarchical. The imperial decrees of 17 March and 13 December 1808 established a central consistory in Paris to head thirteen regional consistories. The central consistory was responsible for the supervision of all French Jews, especially the rabbis, and answered directly to the Ministry of Cults. The local consistories governed their Jewish communities but were ultimately responsible to the central consistory. A consistory was established in every department with a Jewish population of at least 2,000. Those having fewer were combined with other departments.

In the course of the nineteenth century, significant geographical and organizational changes occurred. The original decree established thirteen regional consistories, including seven in France proper—Wintzenheim (later Colmar), Strasbourg, Nancy, Metz, Paris, Bordeaux, and Marseilles—and six others in the Rhineland and northern Italy, which were then part of the Empire: Coblentz, Krefeld, Turin, and Casal. The 1810 annexation of central Italy brought the temporary addition of three new consistories, and in 1812 seven others were added with the annexation of Holland and more of Germany. All these outside France were lost in 1815, but new ones were created within France in Saint-Esprit (Bayonne) in 1846 and in Lyons in 1857. These were the last significant changes until after 1870, when demographical changes occurred because of the loss of Alsace-Lorraine.

Significant administrative reorganization also took place in the nineteenth century. In origin, three grand rabbis and two laymen of the central consistory were appointed by the government. The regional consistories, consisting of one grand rabbi and three laymen, were elected by twenty-five notables, named by the local prefects from among the highest taxpayers and most respected Jewish citizens in the district. Therefore, despite the fact that the head of each Jewish family was to pay dues to the consistories, most were disenfranchised. This often meant that entire Jewish communities went unrepresented. In 1844 important organizational changes were introduced that were to make the central consistory more responsive to the regional consistories and the latter more responsive to those whom they served. The central consistory was now to be composed of a *grand rabbin* (the chief rabbi of France) and a representative of each of the regional consistories. The regional consistories were to consist of a *grand rabbin* and five laymen to be elected under a considerably augmented definition of notables in accordance with changes in the French electoral system. The rabbi's influence was also increased in the changes of 1844 by giving him a veto over all religious matters. In 1848, after considerable agitation, every male Jew over twenty-five was declared a notable and given the right to vote. The Second Empire restricted suffrage again, but the Third Republic expanded it again in 1871, at least in regard to the election of lay members.

Until 1831, the Jewish consistories were not financially supported by the state. Since many members failed to pay their dues to the consistories, this caused serious hardship. Even the collection of such dues by the state treasury in return for a percentage of the income, beginning in 1816, failed to end the financial troubles of the Consistory. In 1831, Louis-Philippe incorporated the expenses of the Jewish religion into the national budget and legally made Judaism equivalent to Catholicism and Protestantism in the French polity.

The establishment of the consistories reflected the desire of Napoleon and the French state, on the one hand, to bring about the "moral and social assimilation" of Jews in France and, on the other hand, of Jewish leaders to regain some of the authority and autonomy Jewish communities had lost during the Revolution. The decree of 1808 exposed the primary goals of supervision and control that a state-imposed centralized organization of the Jewish cult would guarantee. The consistories were to ensure that no assembly for prayers should be formed without express authorization, to encourage the Jews in the exercise of "useful" professions and to refer to the authorities those who did not have an acknowledged means of livelihood, and to inform the authorities each year of the number of Jewish conscripts in the area. The central consistory's motto, "Religion and Fatherland," sums this up well. In return for official recognition by the state and equal French citizenship, Jewish leaders, in the name of French Jews, agreed to give up their economic, political, and, in the end, much of their religious distinctiveness. Throughout the nineteenth century consistorial leaders aggressively carried out their task of "regeneration," or moral and socioeconomic improvement, through immersion of French Jews in French language, culture, and mores, and by encouraging the acquisition of "useful" jobs.

The consistories' almost monopolistic control of Jewish institutions and their program of regeneration caused conflict and division within the Jewish community. The primary conflict was over the degree and pace of religious reform. The consistories had agreed to abide by the principles of the Great Sanhedrin, a supreme court of Jewish lay and religious leaders called by Napoleon in 1806 to prove that Jews could be good Frenchmen. Among the decisions, it provided for the exemption of religious observance for those performing military service. The Sanhedrin and later the consistories also promised to retrain Jews in useful trade and agricultural occupations. But in order for traditional-minded Jewish beggars and peddlers to practice useful trades, they would have to work on the Sabbath. These pressures, plus modern reforms in the daily festival and Sabbath services, frequently alienated Orthodox Jews while never fully satisfying reformers who wished to go even further in eliminating what they saw as anachronistic doctrines and practices of Judaism. The problem was particularly acute in Alsace, where many traditionally Orthodox Jews lived. With the institution of universal suffrage in consistorial elections, the Orthodox gained the upper hand in the Haut-Rhin in 1858. This led to the intervention of both the central consistory and the government, which annulled the elections.

After 1905, with the separation of church and state and the increased immigration of East European Jews into France, the consistories lost their monopoly over Jewish communal affairs; but to this day they continue to exercise important influence over the lives of French Jews.

P. C. Albert, *The Modernization of French Jewry* (Hanover, N. H., 1977); D. Feuerwerler, *L'emancipation des Juifs en France* (Paris, 1976); P. Guirard, *Les Juifs de France* (Paris, 1976); Z. Szajkowski, *Jews and the French Revolution of 1789, 1830, and 1848* (New York, 1970), and "Secular vs. Religious Jewish Life in France," *The Role of Religion in Modern Jewish History*, ed. Jacob Katz (New York, 1975).

Sanford Gutman

Related entry: JEWS.

CONSPIRACY AT THE WATER'S EDGE (CONJURATION DU BORD DE L'EAU) (1818), plot to overthrow the Richelieu ministry and install an ultraroyalist cabinet. By the summer of 1818 the ultraroyalists were becoming increasingly angry with several members of the cabinet, particularly Armand-Emmanuel de Richelieu, Laurent Gouvion Saint-Cyr, and especially the king's liberal favorite, Elie Decazes. In this context some ultras developed a plot against the cabinet and perhaps against the king himself. The plot surfaced on 23–24 June 1818. At that time a gendarmerie captain, Mesmay, a friend of General Simon de Canuel, revealed to the royal prosecutor, Jacquinot de Pampelune, a plot to kidnap the ministers after a cabinet meeting at Saint Cloud and incarcerate them at Vincennes. The conspirators would then impose on the king an ultraroyalist cabinet including Joseph de Villèle, Jacques-Joseph Corbière, François de La Bourdonnaye, Canuel, and François-René de Chateaubriand. This was to be carried out by a regiment of cuirassiers of the guard commanded by Auguste de Larochejaquelein, a guard infantry regiment under Anne-Pierre de Bertier de Sauvigny, and a regiment of Swiss guards barracked at Rueil. Other forces were to seize control of Paris and arrest certain officials. They may also have intended to depose Louis XVIII in favor of his brother Artois, the leader of the ultras, and perhaps to execute Decazes.

These plans were simultaneously revealed to Joseph Lainé by Lieutenant Pyrault, a former army officer who had served with Condé. Furthermore, the plot was soon to be carried out. Both informants made formal declarations before Nicolas-Francois Bellart, attorney general of the royal court of Paris. Further information indicated that Eugène-François de Vitrolles and Chateaubriand were involved in leading the plot. Chateaubriand especially was incriminated by a letter to him from Gabriel Donnadieu about the plot. The cabinet discussed the plot on 24 June and decided to keep the matter secret for a few days and to maintain police surveillance over the leaders. The cabinet was aware that since a Peer, Chateaubriand, was clearly incriminated, proceedings involving him would have to come before the Chamber of Peers. Investigation revealed that the affair also involved other associates of Canuel, including Charles-François-Cyprien de Rieux de Songy, Ange-Désiré Desfeux de Romilly, Paul-Louis-Fortuné Chauvigny de Blot, and a former chouan, Jean-René Chappedelaine. Various of the conspirators met daily on the terrace of the Tuileries gardens near the Seine—hence the name ''conspiracy by the water's edge.'' Other remarkable coincidences were revealed. The Swiss regiment at Rueil had twice held otherwise inexplicable exercises that took it to the gates of Saint Cloud on the days the council met, and Larochejaquelein's regiment had several times been called to alert.

By 29 June rumor of the plot began to circulate in Paris, and on 1 July two London newspapers, the *Times* and the *Morning Chronicle*, published letters from Paris about it. The cabinet now had to act. It decided to begin judicial proceedings, although trying to avoid involving Chateaubriand. By 2 July four conspirators were in custody, and on 6 July formal legal proceedings were begun. Those plotters who were arrested denied guilt but were kept imprisoned secretly. But the publication in pamphlets and newspapers of additional details aroused public interest and angered Artois. On 6 July he summoned some of the ministers and berated them. When the court investigation concluded on 3 November, there was insufficient evidence to try any of the accused, and so all charges were dropped. Curiously, this first large-scale plot of the Restoration was not against the monarchy but against the cabinet; it involved the army not the mob; and it was the work of the ultraroyalists, not the liberals or radical leftists.

E. Guillon, *Les Complots militaires sous la restauration* (Paris, 1895); L. M. Molé, *Le comte Molé, 1781–1855, sa vie, ses mémoires* (Paris, 1922–30); E. D. Pasquier, *Histoire de mon temps* (Paris, 1893–95); J. Peuchet, *Mémoires tirés des archives de la police de Paris* (Paris, 1838); A. Vaulabelle, *Histoire des deux restaurations* (Paris, 1874).

James K. Kieswetter

Related entries: BERTIER; CANUEL; CHATEAUBRIAND; CORBIERE; DECAZES; DONNADIEU; GOUVION SAINT-CYR; LA BOURDONNAYE; RICHELIEU; ULTRAROYALISTS; VILLELE; VITROLLES.

CONSPIRACY OF 19 AUGUST. See BAZAR CONSPIRACY.

CONSPIRATION DU BORD DE L'EAU. See CONSPIRACY AT THE WATER'S EDGE.

CONSTANT DE REBEQUE, HENRI BENJAMIN (known as BENJAMIN CONSTANT) (1767–1830), liberal politican, orator, journalist, and novelist. Born in Lausanne, Switzerland, the son of an officer in the Dutch service, Constant was intensely committed throughout his life to a love of liberty. The cosmopolitan intellectual rebuffed Jean-Jacques Rousseau's collectivist conclusions to defend a pure ideal of personal autonomy and the triumph of the individual over all authority, including the community's general will.

Proponent of a rationalistic and constitutional monarchy, Constant was attacked from all quarters in an era of extreme political polarization. His moderate position, which rejected all extremes to defend political liberty and individuality, earned him the scorn of enemies who often justly accused him of vacillation and lack of willpower (''Benjamin Inconstant''). But it was precisely his ability to see all sides of the problem from various perspectives that gave Constant's analyses great intellectual depth.

Constant arrived in Paris with Mme. de Staël on 25 May 1795 to defend the Directory. Voicing a plea for moderation, he urged all men of goodwill to rally to the defense of the Republic. As secretary of the Cercle constitutionnel, Constant supported an ideal of middle-class republicanism, which was anticlerical and anti-Jacobin.

Following Bonaparte's coup of 18 Brumaire, Constant served in the Tribunate during Napoleon's Consulate. His speeches critical of government proposals angered Napoleon, causing Constant's forced retirement in January 1802. Constant was the author of pamphlets critical of Napoleon's arbitrary government, including an attack on Napoleon even when he returned to France from exile on Elba and neared Paris in triumph. However, in a radical reversal rare in history, Constant served on Napoleon's Council of State during the Hundred Days. He was one of the principal framers of the Additional Act to the Constitution of the Empire. The act, which was popularly called ''*la Benjamine*,'' aroused little popular enthusiasm, and it was stillborn with Napoleon's military defeat at Waterloo.

During 1816 Constant benefited from his sojourn in England to observe the working of the House of Commons at first hand and to publish his great psychological novel *Adolphe*. This thinly disguised account of the break-up of his long liaison with Mme. de Staël hardly helped his political career in France.

Louis XVIII's removal of Constant's name from the list of proscribed persons and the new king's dissolution of the reactionary *chambre introuvable* opened the path for a parliamentary career for Constant. He was one of the leaders of the parliamentary opposition, serving from 1819 to 1830, except for sixteen months. Representing the Sarthe, Paris, and Alsace, he taught France the nature and process of parliamentary government. Constant was drawn to the *doctrinaires*, who were theorizing the principles of parliamentary practice in France. Although he inclined toward the political Left, Constant was an independent, whose works appeared in the *Mercure de France* and *La Minerve française*, the semiofficial organ of the liberal opposition.

As an orator, Constant was an eloquent opponent of threats to liberty. Thus he spoke out in opposition to the slave trade and supported the Greek war of independence.

Constant's balanced approach to political questions is demonstrated by his recognition of a need for limits on freedom of the press. He avoided the extreme position of defending license and realized the necessity of protecting society against incitement to murder, civil war, direct insults to the head of state, and connivance with an alien enemy. He held up the example of Great Britain as a moderate haven of press freedom. His arguments against censorship were eminently utilitarian. Burdened with a censored press, the government would tend to be linked with everything appearing in the newspapers. This would be inconvenient. Any critical remark by the editor would be thought to be inspired by the government. The final and distressing result would be a forced uniformity of thought, which is the plague of an official press. Replying to a claim that the golden age of French literature occurred during the heavy censorship of the epoch of Louis XIV, Constant reminded his countrymen of the baneful consequences of the Huguenot persecutions. A number of serious military and civil difficulties might have been avoided, he argued, if the Sun King had been better informed of the actual state of opinion in France and abroad.

Constant termed slavery a most atrocious crime. He called for severe punishment for the captains of slave ships on the model of the British. But his argument was eminently practical. By increasing the slaves in its colonies, France was populating its territories with potential enemies who would someday take a horrible revenge on those guilty of their degredation. Slavery was practically and morally reprehensible because it violated all the tenets of good government and thereby corrupted the dealer with the victim.

The focal point of Constant's thought was individual liberty. Morality required security, and interference with freedom undermined moral standards. Thus morality collapsed in a plague. And a modern plague of arbitrary government menaced human freedom.

Constant's arguments were emotional rather than intellectual. His love of freedom was based on casting his sympathies with the lot of others' sufferings, in the Greek meaning of "sympathy."

Constant was a man of talents beyond politics. Deeply pious, he wrote about the history of comparative religions. His novel *Adolphe* places him among the major pioneers of the psychological novel. His diaries reflect an intense inner life.

In his later years Constant was progressively isolated in the Chamber even while he enjoyed a great following outside parliament.

Although ill when learning of the 1830 Revolution, Constant was active during the three glorious days, visiting barricades and exhorting the people to overthrow the king. The new bourgeois king Louis-Philippe appointed Constant a councillor of state on 27 August 1830. Constant had lived to see the realization of his ideal of moderate constitutional monarchy and died in Paris 8 December 1830.

B. Constant, *Oeuvres*, ed. Alfred Roulin (Paris, 1957); P. Cordey and J.-L. Seylaz, *Actes du Congrès Benjamin Constant, Lausanne, Octobre 1967* (Geneva, 1968); J. Cruickshank, *Benjamin Constant* (New York, 1974); P. Deguise, "Etat présent des études sur Benjamin Constant," *L'Information litteraire* 10 (1958); H. Nicolson, *Benjamin Constant* (London, 1949); G. Poulet, *Benjamin Constant par lui-même* (Paris, 1968); G. Rudler, *Bibliographie critique des oeuvres de Benjamin Constant* (Paris, 1909).

James Chastain

Related entries: ACTE ADDITIONNEL; CENSORSHIP; COUNCIL OF STATE; *DOCTRINAIRES*; HUNDRED DAYS; *MERCURE DU XIX SIECLE*; *LA MINERVE*; STAEL.

LE CONSTITUTIONNEL, Begun in 1815; largest and most successful opposition daily paper of the Restoration; generally liberal; declined in July Monarchy but was revived in 1847. After several discouraging attempts between the Hundred Days in 1815 and 1819, *Le Constitutionnel* emerged as a stable daily newspaper and in a few years became the undisputed giant of the entire Restoration press.

During the Hundred Days it appeared as *L'Indépendant*, largely the creation of Antoine Jay. After the second Restoration, it was suppressed by Joseph Fouché but reappeared as *L'Echo du Soir*, which had merged with *L'Indépendant*. Another threat of suspension resulted in more titles: *Le Courrier* for a short period, then *Le Constitutionnel* and *Journal du Commerce*. In 1819 its permanent name was selected. Such title changes were accompanied by rotation of corporate directors and editors and the pretense of a new paper on each occasion.

After 1820, newspapers were subject to censorship and authorization but were no longer so vulnerable to total suppression. Jay had become a skilled pilot around these shoals, and his readers learned to interpret catchwords such as *congrégation*, evoking the alleged conspiracy of the clerical ultras, or *le système* to imply all of the Villèle ministry's chicanery. After 1821, the paper set the tone for the entire liberal opposition and allowed a voice to all sectors of the opposition except outright republicanism or outright Bonapartism, both of which were illegal under the Charter. There was always a tinge of Bonapartist-liberal suggestion, however, designed to compromise the patriotic pretensions of the ultras of 1814 by nostalgic references to imperial glory and nationalism. In 1817, the paper had been suppressed for printing an art review, against a censor's orders, dealing with a portrait that some gallery goers had declared to be of the son of Napoleon. Reborn as *Journal du Commerce*, the journal continued its hazardous career.

In the era after 1820 the *Constitutionnel* came into its own and rose to become the largest daily paper on the Continent by 1826 and solvent enough to survive judicial ordeals and make a profit. From a cost of 72 francs per subscription plus advertising revenue, the fifteen shareholders received a gross of 1.3 million francs in 1826 of which 400,000 francs went for overhead and wages, 400,000 for taxes, and 102,000 for postage, leaving an income per proprietor of about 25,000 francs. Among the earlier shareholders besides Jay were Charles Etienne, Louis Cauchois-Lemaire, and Jacques Laffitte. This group, representing wealth and a certain moderation, was faced with dissension when young Adolphe Thiers, newly arrived from Aix, was added to the staff. A coterie grew up around Thiers, who brashly promoted a more active polemic and a more directed policy. Thiers' faction was able to prevent Cauchois-Lemaire's bid to buy a controlling interest in the paper.

In the increasingly reactionary atmosphere of Charles X's reign, the paper exploited every opportunity to discredit that regime. Anticlerical articles, including news items about sinful priests, abounded and were always linked to a supposed nest of Jesuit conspirators. *Le Constitutionnel* was quick to sympathize with Chateaubriand when his *Journal des débats* entered the opposition ranks against Joseph de Villèle, a major rift among the royalists.

Although the paper's policy remained, as Leon Thiéssé called it, an opposition of publicity, not of overthrow, while respecting the king and the Charter, *Le Constitutionnel*'s staff and editors did not escape prosecution under the ultra government of Charles X. In December 1825, along with the *Courrier*, the *Constitutionnel* went on trial for its anticlerical editorials. The prosecutor cited twenty-three articles in which a Jesuit conspiracy was denounced and claimed that these writings together were incriminating under the tendency law of 1822. Both editors, defended by André Dupin, were acquitted because they had criticized Jesuit actions that were illegal: a victory for the opposition and a defeat for tendency.

Certainly, along with its new ally, the *Débats*, the *Constitutionnel* helped to overthrow first minister Villèle at the end of 1827. Not only the paper's unrelenting polemic under judicial fire but also its successful electoral propaganda were important factors. With Villèle out, the king was forced to temporize with a moderate regime, not being then prepared for another ultra ministry. Except for its brushes with the tendency law, the editors continued to escape indictment on specific press charges by careful wording. When co-owner Cauchois-Lemaire declared for the Orléans dynasty in 1827, he did so without his paper's recognition and was prosecuted as an individual. Yet the *Constitutionnel* repeatedly printed allusions to a change of dynasty, often invoking the parallels in England's revolution in 1688 but without mention of the French equivalent of William III: the duke of Orléans.

When the openly Orleanist *National* was founded in January 1830, it drew young talent away from the *Constitutionnel*, notably Adolphe Thiers. Younger, more aggressive spirits, republican or Orléanist, demanded a new direction impossible for the *Constitutionnel*.

Although *Constitutionnel* editors Antoine Année and Cauchois-Lemaire signed the manifesto of the journalists of 27 July 1830 against Jules de Polignac's edicts, the paper itself timidly acquiesced before the police power and did not appear again until 30 July when all was secure, with a scathing personal attack on the late king. The editors falsely declared that physical force had closed their press. The greatness of the *Constitutionnel* ended at this moment.

In the July Monarchy, the paper became the political voice of Thiers and supported the Orleanist position for better or worse through most of that decade. Dr. Louis Véron, a political chameleon and theater critic who also had helped create *La Quotidienne*, *La Revue de Paris*, and *Le Figaro*, became a codirector in 1838. No longer a paper ever ready to quarrel with the establishment, *Le Constitutionnel* lost prestige and subscribers, falling from 17,000 in 1830 to 9,000 in 1836 and a mere 3,300 in 1845. In 1847, Louis-Desire Véron, who regarded journalism as a business, used the profits from his successful publication of Sue's *Le Juif errant* to revive the paper. He was so successful that he was able to sell it five years later for nearly 2 million francs.

E. Hatin, *Histoire de la presse*, vol. 8 (Paris, 1859–61); C. Ledré, *La presse a l'assaut de la monarchie* (Paris, 1960); D. Rader, *The Journalists and the July Revolution* (The Hague, 1973).

Daniel Rader

Related entries: ANTICLERICAL CAMPAIGN; BONAPARTISM; CAU-CHOIS-LEMAIRE; CENSORSHIP; CHATEAUBRIAND; *LE COURRIER FRANÇAIS*; DUPIN, A.-M.-J.-J.; *L'INDEPENDANT*; JAY; *JOURNAL DES DEBATS*; LAFFITTE; *LE NATIONAL*; *LA REVUE DE PARIS*; SUE; THIERS; THIESSE; VERON.

CONSTITUTION OF 1848. Following the February Revolution and the election of a National Assembly by universal manhood suffrage on 23 April, the Assembly chose a committee to prepare a draft of a constitution for the new Republic. Among its eighteen members were former supporters of the July Monarchy (Odilon Barrot, Jules-Armand Dufaure, Alexis de Tocqueville) and republicans of various nuances (Armand Marrast, Louis-Marie de Cormenin, Victor Considérant, Félicité de Lamennais, the last of whom resigned). This committee prepared its draft by 19 June. After the civil war of June 1848, the fifteen committees of the Assembly discussed it, and a new draft was presented on 30 August. The Assembly then spent most of the next two months in exhaustive discussion before the constitution was formally accepted on 4 November by 739 votes to 30. Those who voted against it included a few monarchists (Pierre-Antoine Berryer, Henri de Larochejaquelein, Charles-Forbes de Montalembert) and several socialists (Jean-Louis Greppo, Pierre-Joseph Proudhon, Pierre Leroux). The constitution was promulgated at a ceremony on the place de la Concorde on 12 November.

In its final form, the constitution consisted of a preamble of 8 articles, 12 chapters, with 116 articles in all. The essential outlines were that France was to be "definitively" a republic, and "democratic, one and indivisible." This was to be a representative, parliamentary democracy based on direct universal manhood suffrage expressed by secret ballot; the *mandat impératif* of the tradition of direct democracy from the French Revolution was explicitly rejected.

While in its final form the constitution bears the imprint of its time and of the men who framed it, it is remarkable that there was little disagreement in the Assembly over most issues and that most of the first draft was retained despite the hardening of attitudes in the Assembly after the civil war (Paris was in a state of siege until 19 October). One reason for this may be that, as Adolphe Thiers remarked, the numerically dominant former monarchists regarded the constitution and the Republic itself as ephemeral. Hence the constitution reflects the ideology of Eugène Cavaignac's moderate republicans who formed the ministry during the second half of 1848.

This is apparent in a number of critical articles on the political process. There were to be no restrictions on eligibility to stand as a deputy apart from an age limit of twenty-five. A contentious issue from the July Monarchy was removed by making government officials ineligible to retain their positions if they were elected as deputies. Elections were to be held at the departmental rather than district (arrondissement) level, and voting was to take place at the cantonal rather than communal level. Both of these provisions were a deliberate republican attempt to lessen the influence of local notables over a massive and newly enfranchised electorate, as was the decision to allow slates as well as individual candidates. The ministers and 750 deputies in the three-year parliament were all to be paid. A proposal by Prosper Duvergier de Hauranne to create an upper house was defeated by 350 votes to 289, although the Assembly did introduce a consultative Conseil d'état chosen by itself.

The constitution guaranteed many fundamental civil liberties. The death penalty was abolished for all political offenses; slavery was abolished in the colonies, and the application of the constitution to the colonies was anticipated; the right of peaceful assembly was guaranteed, with a proviso of public safety; and the press was assured of freedom from censorship. The constitution committed the Republic to providing free education and the free administration of justice; all political and press offenses were to be tried by a jury; and henceforth all guilty verdicts were to require a two-thirds rather than simple majority. The constitution abolished all civil distinctions between citizens, ending titles of nobility.

There were, however, a number of significant elements of the constitution over which there was considerable disagreement or which reveal the extent of reaction within the Assembly to popular unrest. The constitutional committee, inspired by the example of the United States, had proposed that the president of the Republic be directly elected by the people. By September, when Louis-Napoleon Bonaparte was elected in five by-elections, this had become a political as well as constitutional issue. While Jules Grévy's amendment to replace the president with a premier elected by the Assembly was defeated by 643 to 58 on 7 October, the Assembly made a number of specific attempts to prevent the post being used as a stepping-stone to empire. The president was to be elected for four years and was not immediately reeligible. Although he was to name and dismiss ministers, ambassadors, military commanders, prefects, and other senior officials, he could not personally command the armed forces, nor could he suspend or dissolve the Assembly or alter the constitution, though he had a suspensive veto. The Assembly was to choose the president if no candidate won an absolute majority of the popular vote.

While the first draft of the constitution had explicitly ended the practice of *remplacement*, whereby a wealthy conscript could buy a substitute, the notables present in the Assembly, backed by a petition campaign, deleted reference to this by 663 to 140. Justices of the peace were now to be appointed rather than elected as in the draft.

Of central importance was the debate over the social obligations of the state. The right to work imposed on the Provisional Government in February by workers and met by the creation of the National Workshops had been ended by the dissolution of those workshops in June. The articles relating to social rights in the final version of the constitution are revealing of the moderate republicans' distinctive attitudes. In the preamble the constitution spoke only of fraternal assistance to those in need, whether by work programs or some form of charity. While article 13 guaranteed freedom of association and a role for workers in industrial arbitration, it again referred only to public works and to assistance for abandoned children and the sick and the old if families could not support them. The 19 June draft, on the other hand, had explicitly guaranteed work and assistance without reference to family help.

The initial draft had as its slogan "Liberty, Equality, Fraternity"; the final constitution added "Family, Work, Property, Public Order." Despite the opposition of radicals and some moderate republicans to the watering down of welfare provisions, Mathieu de la Drôme's amendment to reinclude the right to work was defeated by 596 to 187 on 14 September. A memorable debate pitted Thiers and de Tocqueville against Alexandre-Auguste Ledru-Rollin and Alphonse de Lamartine.

Revision of the constitution required a three-quarters majority in three separate votes a month apart. But before the coup d'état of December 1851 finally rendered the constitution redundant, it had already been violated in spirit and law. In direct opposition to specific articles, the French army was sent against the Roman Republic in 1849; education was not made free, except for the indigent; the law of 31 May 1850 disenfranchised one-third of the electorate; and the freedom of the press, as well as the right of free association, was increasingly infringed.

P. Bastid, *Doctrines et institutions politiques de la Seconde République*, 2 vols. (Paris, 1945); J. Cohen, *La préparation de la constitution de 1848* (Paris, 1935); E. N. Curtis, *The French Assembly of 1848 and American Constitutional Doctrines* (New York, 1918);

F. A. de Luna, *The French Republic under Cavaignac, 1848* (Princeton, 1969); A. de Tocqueville, *Recollections* (New York, 1956).

Peter McPhee

Related entries: BARROT, C.-H.-A.; BERRYER, P.-N.; CAVAIGNAC, L.-E.; CENSORSHIP; CHILDREN, ABANDONED; CONSIDERANT; DUVERGIER DE HAURANNE; GREVY; JUNE DAYS; LAMARTINE; LAMENNAIS; LA ROCHEJAQUELEIN; LEDRU-ROLLIN; LEROUX; MARRAST; MONTALEMBERT; NATIONAL WORKSHOPS; PROUDHON; PUBLIC WELFARE; THIERS; TOCQUEVILLE.

CORBIERE, JACQUES-JOSEPH-GUILLAUME (1766–1853), statesman. Born into a humble rural household in Amanlis, near Rennes, he gained considerable respect due to his talent as a barrister, and when he married a rich widow he fulfilled the conditions necessary to become a member of the Conseil général of the department of Ille-et-Vilaine, of which he became president. This led naturally to his election as a deputy in 1815. In the *chambre introuvable* he soon became a close friend with Joseph de Villèle. From then on his fortunes were linked with Villèle's, and he became an active orator in the royalist opposition to the governments of both Armand-Emmanuel de Richelieu and Elie Decazes.

In 1820 Corbière entered the second Richelieu administration as minister without portfolio but with the title of president of the Council of Public Instruction. He resigned with Villèle in July 1821, though he later returned to power with him as minister of the interior. His long tenure ended with that of his friend in December 1827. Corbière then entered the Chamber of Peers, from which, however, he was excluded after the Revolution of 1830, having refused to recognize the new king. A clever and pungent parliamentary orator, Corbière made a poor administrator because of his lackadaisical disposition and his harsh and boorish manners.

Guillaume de Bertier de Sauvigny

Related entries: CHAMBRE INTROUVABLE; DECAZES; RICHELIEU; VILLELE.

CORCELLE, CLAUDE TIRCUY DE (1768–1843), opposition deputy under the Restoration and the July Monarchy. Claude Tircuy de Corcelle was born into a family of the minor nobility in the region of Lyons in 1768. He intended to pursue a career in the French army, but while still a sublieutenant early in the Revolution he left France and joined the *émigré* army of the prince of Condé. Returning in 1799 he settled in Lyons and remained apart from public life until 1813, when he accepted appointment as lieutenant colonel of the National Guard of the department of the Rhône. During the Hundred Days he rallied to Napoleon and resumed his command in the National Guard, an act for which he was exiled by the restored Bourbon government in 1816. The banishment was lifted in the next year, and in 1819 Corcelle won a seat as deputy of the department of the Rhône. In the Chamber he became identified with the liberal opposition. He made himself the spokesman of the exiles of 1816, an outspoken defender of individual liberties, and an advocate of extension of the suffrage and freedom of the press. He lost his seat in the royalist reaction of the early 1820s, but in 1828 one of the electoral colleges of Paris returned him to the chamber.

In the debate on revision of the Charter after the Revolution of 1830, Corcelle proposed an amendment that would make the accession of Louis-Philippe to the throne conditional on popular approval. The proposal won little support and was quickly discarded. Corcelle nonetheless took the required oath of obedience to the revised charter and of fidelity to the king and continued to sit in the Chamber until 1834, the last three years as a deputy from the department of Saône-et-Loire. Although the regime had changed, Corcelle soon resumed his role as gadfly of the government, attacking especially the ministry's assumption of excessive power, the court's liberalities with its friends, and Louis-Philippe's pacific foreign policy. He retired to private life in 1834 and died in 1843.

Corcelle's son, Claude-François (1802–70), married Mélanie de Lasteyrie, granddaughter of Lafayette and sister of Mme. Charles de Rémusat. He served as deputy under the July Monarchy, the Second Republic, and the Third Republic.

Dictionnaire de biographie française, vol. 9 (Paris, 1933-   ).

David H. Pinkney

Related entries: CENSORSHIP; CHAMBER OF DEPUTIES; CHARTER OF 1814; ELECTIONS AND ELECTORAL SYSTEMS; FOREIGN POLICY OF LOUIS PHILIPPE; HUNDRED DAYS; NATIONAL GUARD.

CORNU, ALBINE-HORTENSE LACROIX (1809–1875), friend of Louis-Napoleon and woman of letters. Albine-Hortense Lacroix was born one year after Louis-Napoleon, the future president and emperor of France, who was her godfather. Her parents were in service to Queen Hortense, Louis' mother. The two children were playmates and lifelong friends, although Hortense broke off communication with Louis after the coup d'état of 1851, which she regarded as a betrayal of the liberal ideals they had held as youths and that she continued to hold. She denounced him as a traitor to the Republic, and the friendship was severed until he convinced her to renew it in 1863.

In 1834 Hortense Lacroix married a painter, Sebastien Cornu. While Louis was a prisoner at Ham, they visited him several times. She helped him obtain research materials and twice provided a haven for his mistress, Alexandrine, when she was pregnant with Louis' children. In 1850 she used her influence with Louis to obtain favors for several revolutionary radicals who had fallen into trouble with the police.

Her intellectual interests were in German philosophy and literature and Italian art. She published several translations and articles under the name Sebastien Albin, including *Ballades et chants populaires de l'Allemagne* in 1841 and "Essai sur l'histoire des arts en Italie" in the *Encyclopedie moderne* in 1848.

M. Emerit, *Madame Cornu et Napoleon III* (Paris, 1937); J. Ridley, *Napoleon III and Eugénie* (London, 1979); R. L. Williams, *The Mortal Napoleon III* (Princeton, 1971).

Gay L. Gullickson

Related entry: COUP D'ETAT OF 2 DECEMBER 1851.

THE CORONATION OF CHARLES X (May 29, 1825). Louis XVIII died 16 September 1824, and his brother, Charles X, whose views were more in tune with the institutions of the *ancien régime* than with the French Revolutionary legacy, ascended the throne. During the first six months of his reign, Charles sponsored the Indemnity Law and the Law of Sacrilege in the chambers and reopened wounds dating from the Revolution. The coronation ceremony did nothing to change the perception of the liberals that the new king was implacable in his hostility to the institutional changes inaugurated during the Revolutionary era.

Article 74 of the Charter of 1814 referred to the coronation ceremony, and Louis XVIII planned to be crowned. Early in his reign, however, the allied occupation dampened enthusiasm, and, after his announcement in 1819 of new plans for his coronation, physical infirmities made them impractical. Charles X had no comparable problems, and the ceremony seemed to provide a great opportunity for the royalists. Indeed, the major uncertainty seemed to involve the availability of the holy oil for consecration of the monarch. French kings since Clovis had been annointed with holy oil (or holy balm), and the legend was that this irreplaceable liquid had been sent from Heaven in the beak of a dove for the baptism and coronation of Clovis over 1300 years earlier. However, during the Reign of Terror, on 6 October 1793, an emissary from the National Convention shattered the *Sainte ampoule* on the pedestal of the statue of Louis XV at Rheims. It later developed that pious citizens who witnessed this scene reported that they had picked up some of the broken glass along with drops of the holy balm. This evidence of the continued existence of the precious fluid was accepted, and the Archbishop of Rheims, Jean-Baptiste de Latil, mixed the old balm with consecrated oil. On 16 May 1825, the *Moniteur* declared: "There remains no doubt that the holy oil poured on the head of Charles X will be the same that since the time of Clovis has consecrated French monarchs."

The coronation oath, as well as the holy oil, was much on the minds of the French during the weeks preceding the coronation ceremony. Would the Charter be mentioned in the oath? Would the oath be worded in a way to give recognition to changes brought by the French Revolution and the Charter of 1814? The Charter (Article 74) specifically stated that kings of France at their coronation must swear to "observe faithfully the present Constitutional Charter." Charles had been far from enthusiastic about this document in the past, but he agreed not only to the modification of the coronation oath but to the omission of several completely outdated oaths.

Plans for the coronation were elaborate. The *Administration des Postes* was ordered to pay the expenses of transporting members of the royal family to

Rheims, but all others were to pay the usual fare. In May an inventory of the crown jewels was completed for the Chamber of Peers and the Chamber of Deputies. It required thirteen large manuscript pages to list the diamonds, rubies, sapphires, opals, and pearls. There were 68,812 stones weighing a total of 18,750 carats and valued at 20,900,260 francs. A portion of this legacy is on display at the Louvre today.

Charles sent personal invitations to delegations of the Chamber of Peers and the Chamber of Deputies and included information as to available transportation, eating accomodations, and sleeping arrangements. The ten ministers of state were given a special invitation to attend the ceremony and assured that their expenses would be paid by the monarch. Since past coronation ceremonies had been in the hands of churchmen, the question arose as to whether members of the Chamber of Deputies and the Chamber of Peers should attend the celebrations following the ceremony. In fact representatives of all the great state bodies turned out in force. Peers and Deputies, prefects and mayors, the first president and the *procureurs-généraux* of the royal courts, representatives of the university and the institute, and members of the Orders of Saint-Louis, the Holy Ghost, and Saint-Michel, as well as the Legion of Honor, were on hand for every event.

The coronation ceremony really began during the early afternoon of 28 May with Charles' ceremonial entry into Rheims in the gilded coronation coach (under triumphal arches decorated with flowers). The king retired to the palace of the Archbishop of Rheims, Jean-Baptiste Latil, where he attended vesper services and listened to a sermon by the Archbishop of Sens, Cardinal de la Fare. The king, according to ancient custom, received city officials who presented gifts of champagne and Rousselet pears. The monarch, again according to tradition, pardoned and released some 128 prisoners.

Throughout the night of 28–29 May, the city of Rheims was in a state of commotion. By 5:00 A.M. crowds of people had gathered before the doors of the church, where they could see the portraits of the past kings of France decorating the columns of the cathedral. At 6 o'clock the doors were opened; the waiting throng quickly filled the seats. Toward 7:00 the diplomatic corps arrived and other foreign dignitaries made their appearances. Representatives of other religious groups were invited to the Catholic ceremony, and members of the Anglican, Calvinist, and Lutheran faiths were on hand, as were non-Christians such as Muslims and Jews. Modifications in the coronation oath were not the only concessions made by Charles. Four marshals of France, whose reputations were made while the king was in exile, participated in the ceremony. Jeannot de Moncey, Duke of Conegliano; Nicolas-Jean de Dieu Soult, Duke of Dalmatia; Edouard-Adolphe Mortier, Duke of Treviso; and Count Jean-Baptiste Jourdan carried the insignia of royal power during the ritual. The ceremony proper, which began at 8:00 A.M., was completed before noon and consisted of three principal parts. These three phases are briefly described in the order in which events unfolded on 29 May.

Charles was escorted to his place and after the completion of various preliminaries, the king, with his hands on the Gospels and what was said to be a fragment of the true cross, took the coronation oath. He repeated: "In the presence of God, I promise to my faithful people to maintain and honor our holy religion, as becomes the most Christian king and eldest son of the Church, to render honest justice to all my subjects, and to govern in conformity with the laws of the kingdom and the Constitutional Charter, which I swear to observe faithfully, so help me God. . . . " Soon after the king took the oath the ceremonial slippers, as custom dictated, were placed on Charles's feet, and the dauphin attached the spurs (which were immediately removed). Archbishop Latil then blessed what was called the sword of Charlemagne and presented it to Charles X. The king was armed.

The consecration of the king was the next important phase of the ceremony. Charles X was anointed with the "irreplaceable" holy oil, and this ritual has been described as follows:

> The king, conducted by two cardinals, sat down. The archbishop opened the reliquary containing the holy vial, and with the point of the golden needle he took out a portion which he mixed with consecrated oil. . . . The two cardinals opened the places in the king's garments for the unction and led his majesty to the altar where he knelt on pillows placed for the purpose. . . . The Bishop of Soissons took from the altar the holy oil and presented it to the archbishop, who took some with his thumb and anointed his majesty in the usual places. . . . First on the crown of the head, making the sign of the cross and saying "I anoint you in the kingship sanctified by God;" second, on the breast; third, between the shoulders; fourth and fifth, on the right and left shoulders; and sixth and seventh, on the back of the right and left arms. Each time the archbishop made the sign of the cross and repeated, "I anoint you in the kingship sanctified by God."

The consecration ceremony was similar to that at the coronation of Louis XIII in October 1610, when Cardinal François de Joyeuse had smeared the holy balm on his thumb and, making the sign of the cross on the top of Louis XIII's head, said: "I anoint you king with sanctified oil. In the name of the Father, the Son, and the Holy Ghost." He had then proceeded to anoint the king on the chest, between the shoulders, on each of the shoulders, and at the bend of each arm.

Following the consecration of Charles X, the third phase of the ceremony commenced in which the king received the insignia of office and was crowned. Charles, while kneeling, received from Archbishop Latil the scepter in the right hand and the hand of justice in the left. The Archbishop then turned to the princes of the blood and took from them what was described as the great crown of Charlemagne, which was placed on the king's head. The newly crowned Charles X was seated on the throne, and Archbishop Latil three times repeated the cry of *Vivat rex in aeternum* (May the king live forever) which, along with *Vive le roi*, was taken up by the entire audience. Inside the cathedral a thousand doves and other small birds were set free, while outside the church heralds scattered medals struck to commemorate the occasion. Trumpets blared and guns roared as the cathedral doors opened with a tremendous crash. The ceremony was over.

On 30 May at 10:00 in the morning, Charles, at the Hospital of Saint Mark began the ritual of curing the sick with the king's touch. Formed in two lines, 121 scrofulous patients awaited the king. Upon the forehead of each he made the sign of the cross while saying: "The king touches you, may God cure you." It was later reported that five of the sick had been healed. Interestingly enough, Louis XVI had touched 2400 during his coronation ceremony in 1775.

Charles X was not only the last king of France to participate in the coronation ceremony but probably the one who profited least from it. Essentially, it was a religious ceremony more appropriate for an earlier era, and the seeming dependency of Charles X on a clergy which played a central and dominating role sparked an anti-clerical campaign that continued until the king's overthrow in 1830. Sentences in the ceremony such as "Charles X, a man whom God has given us as king," were not in keeping with the restraints on his authority of the man-made Charter, which the monarch had taken an oath to obey. The legend of the holy oil, and the use of what was called a fragment of the true cross in the coronation oath (not to mention curing scrofula with the king's touch) went too far for substantial segments of the population.

At Rheims fervent royalists, some rewarded with titles, pensions, and decorations during the festivities, could hardly contain their joy. To Cardinal de la Fare the ceremony meant that the Lord had contracted a new pact with the monarchy. But in France as a whole the hoped-for burst of enthusiasm for Charles X and the kingship did not develop. Victor Hugo poked fun at a king lying prostrate at the feet of an archbishop, and Pierre Jean de Béranger's song on *Crowning Charles the Simple* made the old monarch a subject of ridicule. The *Constitutionnel*, critical as usual, pointed out that the ceremony fit the past better than it reflected the present. Charles X was portrayed on coins in the garb of a Jesuit, and endless tales were repeated about the immorality, intolerance, and arrogance of the clergy. The liberals, posing as the true interpreters and defenders of the revolutionary legacy, were using the media to discredit Charles X by portraying him as subservient to the most conservative elements in the state. Their attacks were continuous throughout his reign, and eventually they helped goad the king into signing the July Ordinances which cost him his throne.

V. W. Beach, *Charles X of France: His Life and Times* (Boulder, Colo., 1971); *Le Constitutionnel*, 3 June 1825; A. Delsart, *Sacre de S. M. Charles Dix* (Paris, 1825); J. P. Garnier, *Le sacre de Charles X et l'opinion publique en 1825* (Paris, 1927); R. Jackson, *Vive le roi: A History of French Coronations from Charles V to Charles X* (Chapel Hill, 1984).

Vincent Beach

Related entries: CHARLES X; CHARTER OF 1814; INDEMNITY BILL OF 1825; JESUITS; JULY ORDINANCES; LAW OF SACRILEGE.

COROT, JEAN-BAPTISTE-CAMILLE (1796–1875), major landscape painter. Camille Corot was born in Paris on 16 July 1796 to Louis-Jacques Corot, a cloth merchant, and Marie-Françoise Oberson, proprietress of a fashionable millinery shop. After schooling in Paris, Rouen (1807–12), and Passy (1812–14), Corot, who failed to distinguish himself in his studies, entered the textile business and remained there until 1817. From 1822, when Corot became the fortunate recipient of a stipend from his father, he devoted his life exclusively to the study and practice of painting. His choice of teachers, Achille-Etna Michallon (1796–1822) and Victor Bertin (1775–1842), revealed an affinity for classical landscapes in the quiet tradition of Nicolas Poussin (1594–1665). In 1825 Corot left France for a three-year stay in Italy, where the young artist encountered Théodore Carulle d'Aligny (1798–1871), a painter of classical landscapes whom Corot later considered his true teacher. Before his return to France, Corot exhibited two pictures, *Roman Campagna* and *Bridge at Narni*, at the Salon of 1827. Never a man to mix in politics or to show much interest in the events of the day, Corot abandoned Paris during the Revolution of 1830 for Chartres, where he painted a superb view of the cathedral. The remainder of Corot's largely uneventful life may be briefly summarized. He traveled widely, making two more trips to Italy, taking numerous tours of France, and visiting London. Although Corot did not attain genuine popularity until the 1850s, he won numerous prizes for works exhibited at the various salons, and he enjoyed a comfortable income from the sale of his pictures.

Corot received his first major award in 1833, a second-class medal for *Ford in the Forest of Fontainebleau* shown at the Salon. He also won medals at the Salon of 1848 and the Exposition universelle of 1867. His greatest triumph came in 1855, when he received the first-class medal for the canvases he had submitted, and the Emperor Napoleon III purchased *La Charrette: Souvenir de Marcoussis*. Although not the first time he had sold a work to an influential purchaser, this sale made Corot's popular reputation, and henceforth the demand for his pictures easily exceeded the supply. Recognition also came to Corot from other quarters; Charles Lenormant praised *Ford in the Forest of Fontainebleau* in the *Temps*, and Eugène Delacroix, Charles Baudelaire, and Jules Champfleury all accorded praise to Corot. Made a member of the Legion of Honor in 1846, he became an officer in 1867.

Although Corot does not neatly fit any of the categories into which critics and historians customarily place most nineteenth-century artists, he is often associated with the Barbizon school. Never having formulated any theories of art or painting, Corot was free to paint as he pleased and as his subject demanded. Many of his finest landscapes, particularly those dating from the 1820s and 1830s, fall within the tradition of landscape painting represented by Nicolas Poussin. In these pictures, Corot usually began with an actual scene, which he sketched in the spring or the summer, and then reworked it in the studio, imposing an idealized order on the parts of the original scene. The resulting painting, as in *View of Narni* or *Farnese Gardens in Rome*, conveys a captivating sense of serenity and harmony. In his later years, Corot painted arcadian landscapes peopled with nymphs and shepherds. These imaginary and sentimental scenes appealed to the imagination of the public and sold extremely well. The much-reproduced *Souvenir de Mortefontaine* serves as but one representative of this genre. In the last two decades of his life, Corot painted over 300 portraits and figure studies; only after his death did these works begin to attract critical attention. In the course of a lifetime of hard work, Camille Corot completed some 2,460 paintings, 100 prints, and 761 drawings.

Known throughout his life as a kind and gentle man filled with a youthful joy, Corot frequently shared his wealth with artists less fortunate than he. To give but one example of his generosity, he provided a cottage where the poverty-stricken Honoré Daumier could live out his years in peace. The quiet and modest life of Camille Corot ended in his studio on 22 February 1875.

G. Bazin, *Corot*, 2d ed. (Paris, 1951); E. Moreau-Nélaton, *Corot raconté par lui-même*, 2 vols. (Paris, 1929); A. Robaut, *L'Oeuvre de Corot. Cataloque raisonné et illustré, précédé de l'histoire de Corot et de son oeuvre*, 4 vols. (Paris, 1904–6); A. Schoeller and J. Diéterle, *Corot* (Paris, 1948).

Robert Brown

Related entries: BAUDELAIRE; DAUMIER; DELACROIX; *LE TEMPS*.

LE CORRESPONDANT. See LIBERAL CATHOLICISM.

LE CORSAIRE (1822–1852), liberal satirical and literary periodical; opposed government in the Restoration; radical Left in July Monarchy; called *Corsaire-Satan*, 1844–1847. *Le Corsaire* was one of the most durable of the literary satirical journals of its era. Although smaller than the popular *Figaro*, with an average subscription list of under 1,000, it was as widely quoted and as often involved in controversy. Well-known literary contributors flavored its columns with frequently ribald passages and outrageous lampoons of clerics and clericalism along with its customary political targets. In July 1829, the editor Jean-Louis Viennot, at the cost of a light sentence of fifteen days, received great notoriety and publicity from his prosecution for one of *Corsaire*'s witticisms. In defending his fellow editor, René-Théophile Chatelain of the *Courrier*, after his conviction for an anticlerical essay (26 June 1829), Viennot had compared Chatelain's judges to Maximilien Robespierre. Several months later, Viennot was sued for libel by Alphonse de Martainville, the quixotic editor of the ultra *Drapeau blanc*. In a feud between the journals, Viennot had questioned the ultras' patriotism during the fighting around Paris in 1815. Viennot had to apologize and pay a small fine in this rather amusing public affair. The satirical journals of the *petite presse*, usually monthly or weekly, were handled lightly by Restoration authorities. A notable exception was the 1829 prosecution of *L'Ancien album*. The *Corsaire* survived as a voice of the far Left under Louis-Philippe, constantly denouncing the increasingly severe treatment of journalists. In 1844, it merged with *Satan* and was called *Corsaire-Satan* for a few years. The journal was abolished by Louis-Napoleon.

C. Ledré, *La presse à l'assaut de la monarchie* (Paris, 1960); D. Rader, *The Journalists and the July Revolution* (The Hague, 1973).

Daniel Rader

Related entries: L'ANCIEN ALBUM; LE DRAPEAU BLANC; LE FIGARO; LOUIS PHILIPPE; MARTAINVILLE; ULTRAROYALISTS.

COTTAGE INDUSTRY. Between 1814 and 1852 at least three-quarters of the workers who were engaged in manufacturing were employed in small workshops with fewer than ten employees or in their own homes. Those who worked at home were participants in what is variously known as cottage industry, rural industry, domestic industry, and the putting-out industry. By 1814 the scale of cottage industry in many places had increased dramatically over what it had been in earlier centuries.

In traditional cottage industries, individuals or families produced goods like yarn or fabric partially for the family's own use and partially for sale in local markets or in exchange for goods and services they received from others in the village. People worked in their own homes with simple machines, such as spinning wheels, distaffs, hand looms, anvils, and hammers. In some putting-out industries, entire families participated in the production process, with children and often women preparing raw materials for final production by the men. For instance, in some regions women and young children cleaned and combed raw wool, which older children and women spun into yarn for men to weave. In other industries only one or two members of a family might be engaged in the production process, while other members engaged in nonrelated productive work such as farming. Women, for instance, might spin thread and weave ribbons while their husbands raised cows or grain crops.

In the late eighteenth and early nineteenth centuries, demographic growth and the opening of new colonial markets for manufactured goods encouraged urban merchants to increase production. As long as technology remained simple and urban populations relatively small, production could be increased by expanding the putting-out system. By 1814 in regions like Normandy, a majority of families were at least partially dependent on putting-out work in textiles for income. Spinning of cotton had moved into factories, but the weaving of cotton, linen, and wool, as well as flax and wool spinning, continued to be done in peasants' homes with traditional tools and traditional divisions of labor. Finishing processes were performed in the cities. The completed goods were sold in national and international markets. Large-scale cottage industries, which employed a substantial percentage of the population in a region, are called proto-industries. In many regions, this was an intermediate step between small-scale cottage industry and urban factory production. Some families who earned money in these large-scale cottage industries continued to alternate harvest work in argiculture with winter work in cottage industry. Other families withdrew from agricultural work altogether and formed a rural industrial proletariat.

Large-scale cottage industries engendered regional population growth by attracting immigrants and by encouraging early marriage and increased childbearing. The latter was especially the case when the cottage industry provided employment for children as well as adults. By 1852 some cottage industries such as hand weaving were declining in the face of machine-produced goods. The decline of a large proto-industry left the rural population unemployed and impoverished and resulted in large-scale urban migration.

Metallurgy (such as nail making), weaving, knitting, straw plaiting, glove making, and dressmaking were typical nineteenth-century cottage industries. Cottage industries thrived especially in subsistence agricultural regions located near market towns. The only regions that seem to have been almost completely hostile to the spread of putting-out industries were viticultural regions where work in the vineyards continued almost year round, making a seasonal division of labor between agriculture and cottage industry impossible for most families.

S. Chassagne, "La diffusion rurale de l'industrie cotonnière en France (1750–1850)," *Revue du nord* (1979); P. Deyon and F. Mendels, "Programme de la section A2 du huitième Congrès international d'histoire économique: La Proto-Industrialisation: Théorie et Réalité" (Budapest, 1982), *Revue du nord* 63 (1981); R. Lehning, *The Peasants of Marlhes* (Chapel Hill, 1980); F. Mendels, "Seasons and Regions in Agriculture and Industry During the Process of Industrialization," in Sidney Pollard, ed., *Region und Industrialisierung* (Gottingen, 1980).

Gay L. Gullickson

Related entries: AGRICULTURE; MIGRATION; NUPTIALITY; PEASANTS; POPULATION.

COTTU, CHARLES (1778–1849), lawyer, pamphleteer, and journalist. Charles Cottu was a lawyer at the Napoleonic Cour de Paris and at the Cour royal during the Restoration. In 1818 his publication *Réflexions sur l'état actuel du jury* led Louis XVIII to ask Cottu to make a study of judicial institutions in England as a basis for reform in France. In 1820 he published a work on the administration of criminal justice in England and later returned to England to study English penitentiaries as *sécrétaire générale* de la société royale des prisons. His early writings in the Restoration reflected a concern for individual liberty and a deep admiration for both the English jury system and freedom of the press, which he saw as guarantees of that liberty. This, plus his outspoken criticism of what he saw as the excessive political influence of Jesuits, the Congrégation, and other ultramontanes, and his resentment of the pretensions and former privileges of the old nobility, seemed to mark him as part of the liberal camp.

But by the early 1820s Cottu had become a persistent critic of liberals and *doctrinaires*. Even earlier he had held English primogeniture in high regard as an effective stabilizing force. Although Cottu's criticisms of Jesuits and the old nobility did not abate, he now emphasized the major threats to order posed by excessive liberty and a democratic Chamber of Deputies. To balance the latter and to offset the danger of revolution, he fervently argued for the creation of a new landed aristocracy by changing the Napoleonic Code to provide for primogeniture. When this proved impossible, he elaborated an admittedly bizarre scheme to create a landed aristocracy based on the electoral system of 1820. Cottu claimed that since the right to vote was the only privilege allowed by the new regime, the electors should become hereditary, thus joining landed wealth and heredity as the basis for the new elite. By 1829, however, Cottu felt that the only hope for stability in France was royal absolutism.

After the July Revolution, Cottu refused the oath to Louis-Philippe and retired to London. At the time of the trial of the ministers of Charles X (December 1830), he made a public appeal in their favor. He died in Versailles in 1849.

C. Cottu, *De l'administration de la justice criminelle en Angleterre* (Paris, 1820), *De le necessité d'une dictature* (Paris, 1830), *Les moyens de mettre la charte en harmonie avec royauté* (Paris, 1828), *Réflexions sur l'état actuel du jury* (Paris, 1818), and *Théorie générale des droits des peuples* (Paris, 1832); S. Gutman, "Justifications for an Aristocracy" (Ph.D diss., University of Michigan, 1976); D. Kelly, "Ultra-Royalism" (Ph.D diss., University of Wisconsin, 1964); J. J. Oechslin, *Le mouvement ultra-royaliste* (Paris, 1960).

Sanford Gutman

Related entries: CHAMBER OF DEPUTIES; CONGREGATION; *DOCTRINAIRES*; ELECTIONS AND ELECTORAL SYSTEMS; HEREDITY LAWS; JESUITS; LOUIS XVIII; REVOLUTION OF 1830; ULTRAMONTANES.

COUNCIL OF STATE, high administrative advisory council, dating from Napoleon I and maintained through the Restoration and July Monarchy. The term *council of state* apparently dates from the reign of Henry III, when it replaced the name *privy council* to designate the entire council of the king. This usage continued until the French Revolution. The modern Council of State, however, dates from a decree of 26 December 1799. The original Council of the Consulate included between thirty and fifty men, and in 1800 its members were ranked as councillors of state, masters of request, and auditors. It was initially organized into five administrative sections: finance, interior, legislation, marine, and war. Its primary function was to assist in the drafting of legislation and other government regulations. But it also had its own legislative and judicial functions—for example, serving as a supreme court of administrative justice in disputes between government agencies and between private citizens and the government. The council served as a forum for the leading administrators of the time, as well as a training ground for young men destined for other administrative posts. Certain posts such as the director generalship of roads and bridges were frequently assigned to members of the council.

Although the Constitutional Charter made no mention of the council, on 29 June 1814 Louis XVIII ordered its continuation. But the legacy of the Old Regime highly influenced it. While a majority of the members of the Restoration Council in 1814 were former imperial councillors, a large number were servants of the Old Regime who dominated their colleagues. It also included the princes of the blood. Furthermore the establishment of a high council curtailed its effectiveness even more. Thus by its organization and personnel, the first Restoration's council was relatively impotent. During the Hundred Days Napoleon restored it to its imperial status.

After Waterloo the council ceased to function until ordinances of 23 and 24 August 1815 revived it and modified its organization and personnel, deliberately attempting to break with its Old Regime heritage. It now met under the presidency of the king, the prime minister, or the minister of justice. Five committees—legislation, finances, marine and colonies, interior and commerce, and contentious affairs—were established. Napoleon's committee on war was dropped. Many of the imperial officials reappeared in the council. A required annual review of the thirty councillors and forty masters of request made them less irremovable. As under Napoleon, a council member who opposed the government could expect dismissal. In 1824 the rank of auditor was reestablished, and the princes reappeared on its personnel. A special ordinance was now required to dismiss a councillor, master of request, or auditor. Specific minimum requirements of prior experience were also established. The status of its personnel was divided into ordinary service (those actually working in the council) and extraordinary service (those working outside the council and administrative officials), as well as those given honorary status in either category.

Although the council was theoretically apolitical, its membership nevertheless reflected the wishes of the current government, the royal family, and various political factions, making it somewhat less stable and more subservient than Napoleon's council. Yet it still managed to function rather well within the spirit and practice of politics under the charter. Its functions from 1815 to 1830 were similar to the pre–1814 council. It assisted with preparation of laws and ordinances in all areas of government and decided disputes between the administration and individuals. Among its other duties were the regulation of religious orders and the adjudication of matters involving local jurisdictions. It provided unity and continuity in all aspects of administration. Nevertheless, it was attacked by the ultras as a Bonapartist institution and by the liberals as a monarchic abuse.

Under the July Monarchy the council initially continued as before. Changes, however, did occur. The proliferation of men in extraordinary service led in 1839 to the restriction of their number and the abolition of the honorific use of that category. The council came to serve increasingly as a support for the government. Although its authority decreased, its involvement in contentious matters greatly expanded. In 1845 the council was reorganized. The Second Republic's constitution maintained the council and transformed it into a powerful political, judicial, and administrative authority based on the assembly instead of the executive. Yet in March 1849 its judicial functions were largely abolished, and it was reduced more to providing apolitical professional and technical expertise, much the same emphasis it has maintained since.

L. Aucoc, *Le Conseil d'état avant et après 1789* (Paris, 1876); C. Léonardi, *Le Conseil d'état sous la restauration* (Paris, 1909); B. Olivier-Martin, *Le Conseil d'état de la restauration* (Paris, 1941); A. Regnault, *Histoire du conseil d'état* (Paris, 1853).

James K. Kieswetter

Related entries: BRIDGE AND ROAD SERVICE; CHARTER OF 1814; HUNDRED DAYS; LOUIS XVIII; ULTRAROYALISTS.

COUP D'ETAT OF 2 DECEMBER 1851, by which President Louis-Napoleon Bonaparte seized power. The coup was the culmination of two struggles: one between the president and his followers on the one hand and the dominant Party of Order in the Legislative Assembly on the other, and one between both these groups and the urban and rural supporters of the social and democratic republic.

Elected president of the Second Republic in 1848 by a massive majority, Louis-Napoleon had sought, notably during presidential tours of France in 1850–51, to present himself as a national savior at a time of economic depression and sociopolitical tension. However, the 1848 constitution, to which he had sworn fidelity, made the president ineligible for immediate reelection. In July 1851, a vote in the Assembly in favor of a revision to allow him to stand again passed by 446 votes to 278, a clear majority but well short of the three-quarters required for revision of the constitution. While those in favor of revision were from the Party of Order, Louis-Napoleon was able to distance himself from them by seeking, again unsuccessfully, to restore universal manhood suffrage, which the Assembly had curtailed in May 1850.

At the same time, Bonapartists and the Party of Order were disturbed by the social threat they saw in the surge of the Left since 1848 and the belief of the *démoc-socs* or *rouges*, as they were popularly known, that the legislative elections also to be held in 1852 would finally result in a peasants' and artisans' republic.

After July 1851, Louis-Napoleon began technical preparation for the coup, recalling Armand de Saint-Arnaud to be minister of war, appointing Maupas as prefect of police, and making sure that Charles de Morny, Victor de Persigny, and Emile-Félix Fleury were nearby. In choosing 2 December for the coup, he was commemorating Napoleon Bonaparte's coronation and the battle of Austerlitz; in calling the operation Rubicon, he was also claiming Caesar's mantle.

On the night of 1 December the national printery was seized, and the proclamations, which had been composed in fragments in scattered typesetting works, were posted at dawn the next day. At the same time Morny seized the Ministry of the Interior and arrested eighty democratic activists and twenty key deputies. Several hundred deputies from the Party of Order, among them Alexis de Tocqueville, Odilon Barrot, and Alfred-Frédéric de Falloux, met to declare the coup illegal but were dispersed or arrested. Many republican deputies began to call for popular resistance; this was centered on the Hôtel de ville and to the east but was soon quelled by troops.

It was in the provinces that resistance to the coup was greatest. While theoretically Louis-Napoleon had undercut popular opposition to his actions by dissolving a conservative assembly and reintroducing universal manhood suffrage, the rank and file of the Left were well aware that the coup had thwarted hopes for a radical victory in the presidential and legislative elections of 1852. In the week after the coup, up to 100,000 insurgents—chiefly peasants, rural laborers, artisans, and small traders—from 900 communities took up arms and temporarily seized control of nearly 200 towns and villages. Though there were protests in fifty-six of the eighty-five departments, the major resistance, including about thirty clashes with gendarmes and troops, was localized in thirteen departments in Provence (Var, Basses-Alpes, Drôme, Vaucluse, Ardèche), along the Mediterranean (Hérault, Pyrénées-Orientales, Gard), the Southwest (Gers, Lot-et-Garonne), and the Center (Nièvre, Yonne, Saône-et-Loire).

To repress this resistance, thirty-one departments were placed in a state of siege and, while fewer than 100 insurgents were killed, about 27,000 people from 2,000 communities were sentenced by special courts and several thousand deported to Algeria and Cayenne (Guiana). Large numbers of office-holders were dismissed—almost 450 mayors and deputies in the Ain alone—and over 100 republican newspapers were suspended or closed down. While large numbers of people accepted or supported the coup, the atmosphere of repression and fear meant that, in the plebiscite held on 20–21 December to ratify it, even insurgent areas voted in favor: 7,439,000 yes against 641,000 no, with about 1.5 million abstentions.

While Louis-Napoleon had made the coup against a Party of Order, which had refused to extend his powers legally, the extent of provincial resistance both pushed frightened notables into supporting him and served as a post-facto justification of his actions. The coup was now defended as a preemptive strike against the horrors of 1852.

M. Agulhon, *1848 ou l'apprentissage de la République* (Paris, 1973); T. R. Forstenzer, *French Provincial Police and the Fall of the Second Republic* (Princeton, 1981); T. W. Margadant, *French Peasants in Revolt. The Insurrection of 1851* (Princeton, 1979); K. Marx, *The Eighteenth Brumaire of Louis Bonaparte* (1852; New York, 1963); J. M. Merriman, *The Agony of the Republic* (New Haven, 1978); R. D. Price, ed., *Revolution and Reaction* (London, 1975); E. Ténot, *La Province en décembre 1851*, 13th ed. (Paris, 1869); E. Zola, *La Fortune des Rougon* (Paris, 1969).

                                                                                                   Peter McPhee

Related entries: BARROT, C.-H.-O.; CONSTITUTION OF 1848; COURS PREVOTALES; LEGISLATIVE ASSEMBLY; PARTY OF ORDER; PERSIGNY; REPUBLICANS; SAINT-ARNAUD; TOCQUEVILLE.

COURIER, PAUL-LOUIS (1773–1825), anticlerical polemicist, skeptic, classical scholar, journalistic gadfly, and pamphleteer. Of noble family, Courier disavowed aristocratic privilege and from his youth concentrated on Greek classical studies, of which he remained an impassioned scholar throughout his life. This was in odd contrast to a successful early career in the Revolutionary and Napoleonic armies, where he rose to become an artillery officer. Courier, however, grew sick of war after participating in the battle of Wagram (1809) and, upon retiring from the army, except for a period of study in Florence, spent much of his remaining life on the family estate near Tours.

With the Restoration, Courier again became active, with frequent visits to Paris and close collaboration with leading opposition writers and journalists, including Armand Carrel. Courier achieved a powerful reputation as a pamphleteer and editorial contributor to various journals of the Left, his articles appearing in the *Globe*, *Revue française*, and *Le Censeur européen* between 1816 and 1825. Not extreme in politics, Courier merely hoped for a better constitutional monarchy and focused his unique polemics on the aggressive clericalism in the ranks of the ultras. He quickly became the opposition's most vocal antagonist of the *parti-prêtre* and the Jesuits.

Courier's writings added force to the small *Gazette constitutionnelle des cultes*, which he helped establish. This journal offered articles on comparative religions, as well as direct attacks on the "secret government" of the church, and developed a running feud with its opposite number, *Le Mémorial Catholique*. The powerful *Constitutionnel* also served as an outlet for Courier's arguments.

During the intense reaction that ensued after the duke of Berry's murder in 1820, Courier served a short jail term (October-December 1821) for a pamphlet that brought him reknown: *Simple Discours de Paul-Louis*. Here he attacked the crown-sponsored plan to buy the palace of Chambord through public donations as a gift for the son and heir of the murdered duke. Typical of the gadfly Courier, he used his right under the Charter to republish a damning account of his trial, adding greatly to his audience.

Although known as a skeptic, Courier's humor and satirical style made him less the philosopher that this term implies and more of a latter-day Voltaire or, on occasion, a Holbach. His sharp dissections of clerical pomposity and religious hypocrisy ensured many editions, much popularity, and a continual war with the censors. Courier's death caused a scandal. He was shot in his own forest by two servants, but they were not brought to trial until 1830. The suspicion that he was martyred through the connivance of his enemies persisted among liberals for many years. Courier had a unique influence, but his role as scourge of the Jesuits was assumed by the comte de Montlosier, one of an extremely anticlerical group of ultra aristocrats.

Courier's courage as a writer in a time of repression, as well as his works on Greek literature, have established his place in nineteenth-century French intellectual life.

A. Carrel, *Oeuvres complètes de Paul-Louis Courier*, 4 vols (Paris, 1829–1830); C. Sainte-Beuve, *Causeries de Lundi*, vol. 6 (Paris, 1853).

Daniel Rader

Related entries: ANTICLERICAL CAMPAIGN; CARREL; *LE CENSEUR EU-ROPEEN*; *LE CONSTITUTIONNEL*; *LE GLOBE*; *LE MEMORIAL CATHO-LIQUE*; MONTLOSIER; *REVUE FRANCAISE*; ULTRAROYALISTS.

LE COURIER (1819–1820), *doctrinaire* newspaper of the Restoration. During the ministry of Elie Decazes the tactics adopted by popular liberal newspapers such as the *Constitutionnel* were criticized as factious and degrading by a small group of academic liberals known as the *doctrinaires*. The latter founded a new journal, the *Courier* (a spelling deliberately adopted from the English), which appeared daily from 21 June 1819 to 1 February 1820 under the editorship of Charles de Rémusat. The society of shareholders consisted of Prosper de Barante, Jacques-Claude Beugnot, François Guizot (whose wife Pauline de Meulan wrote articles for the journal), Auguste de Kératry, Charles Loyson, Charles de Rémusat, Pierre Royer-Collard, and Abel-François Villemain, probably the entire *doctrinaire* group. The writers in the journal worked hard at the business of defining liberty and constructing a technique of parliamentary politics, but Rémusat himself admitted that the public found the *Courier* boring, and the paper acquired so few subscribers that the founders lost their capital within a few months.

Irene Collins

Related entries: BARANTE; BEUGNOT; *LE CONSTITUTIONNEL*; *LE COURRIER FRANCAIS*; DECAZES; *DOCTRINAIRES*; GUIZOT; KERATRY; REMUSAT; ROYER-COLLARD; VILLEMAIN.

LE COURRIER DE LA MOSELLE (1829–1860s), regional republican newspaper. The republican *Tribune des départemens*, founded in Paris in June 1829, stimulated the appearance of several local and regional papers, including the *Courrier de la Moselle*, founded by Auguste Dornès at Metz later in the year. The editor was imprisoned for a month in 1830 for reproducing from the *Tribune* an article advising taxpayers to refuse to pay their taxes in order to bring down the Polignac ministry. In the early years of the July Monarchy, when all republican newspapers were frequently prosecuted and heavy fines imposed, the *Courrier* received financial aid from the Société des droits de l'homme. As a result of the Revolution of 1848 the *Courrier* suddenly found its position transformed from that of an opposition newspaper to the mouthpiece of the prefecture. Like many other such newspapers in the provinces, it supported Eugène Cavaignac (unsuccessfully) in the presidential elections in December 1848.

H. Contamine, *Metz et la Moselle de 1814 à 1870*, 2 vols. (Nancy, 1932); J. Julien, *Les journaux de la Moselle, bibliographie et histoire* (Metz, 1928); G. Perreux, *Au temps des sociétés secrètes* (Paris, 1931).

Irene Collins

Related entries: CAVAIGNAC, L.-E.; POLIGNAC; REPUBLICANS; REVOLUTION OF 1848; SOCIETY OF THE RIGHTS OF MAN; *LA TRIBUNE DES DEPARTEMENS*.

LE COURRIER DE L'EUROPE (1831–1833), legitimist newspaper of the July Monarchy. After the fall of Charles X in 1830, large numbers of former ultraroyalists continued to support his dynasty in the newspaper press. In 1831

Pierre-Sébastien Laurentie, a former editor of the *Quotidienne*, founded the ambitious *Courrier de l'Europe*. The paper was prosecuted three times during the first two years of its existence. In 1833 it fused with another legitimist newspaper, the *Rénovateur*.

C. Bellanger et al., *Histoire générale de la presse française*, vol. 2 (Paris, 1969).

Irene Collins

Related entries: CHARLES X; LEGITIMISM; *LA QUOTIDIENNE*.

LE COURRIER DES ELECTEURS (1829–1830), liberal journal. This weekly newspaper was founded in January 1829 by Jacques Sarrans as an offshoot of the *Courrier français*. Like the latter, it aimed its message at electors and elections, especially the Aide-toi society. It had 1,600 subscribers in 1830. In response to the advent of Louis-Philippe, the staff was changed, and the paper became more of a republican organ, changing its name to *Les Communes* and *Journal du programme de l'Hôtel de Ville*. In December 1830, it merged with the republicans' tiny *Révolution de 1830, journal des intérêts populaires*, which lasted until 1832, when it fell victim to government harassment.

C. Ledré, *La Presse à l'assaut de la monarchie* (Paris, 1960); D. Rader, *The Journalists and the July Revolution* (The Hague, 1973).

Daniel Rader

Related entries: AIDE-TOI, LE CIEL T'AIDERA; *LE COURRIER FRANCAIS*; LOUIS PHILIPPE; REPUBLICANS; *LA REVOLUTION*.

LE COURRIER FRANCAIS (1820–1846) liberal, anticlerical newspaper of the Restoration and July Monarchy. After the failure of the *Courier*, Auguste de Kératry founded the *Courrier français* in 1820. It at once adopted all the well-known prejudices of the liberal press. The first articles to be removed from publication by the censorship committee of 1820 were anticlerical articles appearing in the *Courrier français*. In April 1823 the newspaper was suspended for fifteen days for articles criticizing the war in Spain. In December 1825 it was prosecuted along with the *Constitutionnel* for a tendency to undermine the respect due to the state religion, but on this occasion the editor was acquitted, thanks to the Gallican prejudices of the magistrates. In acquitting the *Courrier français*, the court went further than it had done in the acquittal of the *Constitutionnel* by stating as a fact the illegality of ultramontane doctrines and religious orders that preached them. This was a bitter blow for the ministry of Villèle, whose party was already torn by religious dissension.

The *Courrier français* was never as popular as the *Constitutionnel*, probably because its anticlerical articles were considered too extreme. It never had more than 5,000 subscribers even when the anticlerical frenzy was at its height in France. The *Courrier*, however, was heavily subsidized by the banker Laffitte and could afford to ignore public taste. Immediately after the Revolution of 1830, its subscriptions rose to 8,750, partly because of its opposition to the previous regime and partly because of its demands for war on behalf of revolution in Belgium, Poland, and Italy. As time went on, however, it failed to compete with commercialized newspapers such as the *Siècle*, and by 1846 its subscribers numbered only 2,204.

C. Bellanger et al., *Histoire générale de la presse française*, vol. 2 (Paris, 1969); I. Collins, *The Government and the Newspaper Press in France, 1814–1881* (Oxford, 1959).

Irene Collins

Related entries: ANTICLERICAL CAMPAIGN; *LE CONSTITUTIONNEL*; *LE COURIER*; KERATRY; LAFFITTE; REVOLUTION OF 1830; *LE SIECLE*; SPAIN, 1823 FRENCH INVASION OF; ULTRAMONTANES; VILLELE.

COURS D'ASSIZES. See COURTS OF ASSIZE.

COURS PREVOTALES, special courts created by the law of 20 December 1815 to render swift justice for certain offenses, including political offenses, without appeal and without the juries required for regular criminal cases. Modeled after the *cours prévôtales* of the *ancien régime*, which included both civil judges and military officers, these courts operated for two years from the spring of 1816 to the expiration of their authorization with the end of the legislative session of 1818. Although the Constitutional Charter of 1814 authorized the creation of *cours prévôtales*, no steps were taken to introduce them until after the Hundred Days. They were given jurisdiction over political offenses defined by the sedition law of 9 November 1815. Following the practice of the *ancien régime*, they were also given jurisdiction over smuggling, vagrancy, and crime committed on the main highways (*grands chemins*).

One court was created in each department, consisting of a president and four judges, appointed by the government and drawn from the court of first instance of the department, and a provost (*prévôt*), a military officer at least thirty years of age and holding the rank of colonel, who also acted as a prosecutor. The organization of the courts was delayed for several months in an effort to staff the courts with politically reliable judges. There was no appeal from the sentences of these courts, which were carried out within twenty-four hours unless the court expressly recommended that the crown be given the opportunity to exercise the right of pardon.

The role of the *cours prévôtales* in the White Terror has often been exaggerated. In the two years of their operations, these courts heard 2,280 cases, of which only 265 were for purely political offenses, most of them involving sedition— shouts, speeches, and writings—and displaying the tricolor. Cases involving political offenses were numerous in the Rhône, the Hérault, and the Haute-Garonne departments, while twenty-seven departments tried none at all. Many of the sentences for political offenses fell within the three- to five-year range, although there were significant differences among individual courts in the severity of sentences, dependent on local conditions. A young woman of twenty-four was condemned to deportation by the court of the Yonne department in 1816 for having shouted "Vive l'Empereur! A bas les Bourbons." There were also grave miscarriages of justice involving the death penalty. In 1817 the Lyons court sentenced eleven persons to be executed for seditious assembly. The government did restrain overzealous *prévôts* from exceeding their jurisdiction. In spite of the bad reputation of the *cours prévôtales*, which resulted in their being banned by article 54 of the Constitutional Charter of 1830, the regular courts played a more active role in the legal White Terror than did the *cours prévôtales*.

An BB³ 123, 124, 125; A. Paillet, "Les Cours prévôtales (1816–1818)," *Revue des deux mondes* 4 (1911); D. P. Resnick, *The White Terror and the Political Reaction after Waterloo* (Cambridge, Mass., 1966).

Charles E. Freedeman

Related entries: CHARTER OF 1814; CHARTER OF 1830; HUNDRED DAYS; LAW OF GENERAL SECURITY; LAW ON SEDITIOUS SPEECH; RESTORATION, SECOND; WHITE TERROR.

COURTAIS, AMABLE GASPARD HENRI DE (1790–1877), general and politician. After graduating from the Ecole militaire, Courtais joined the army and served in many imperial campaigns. He was personally decorated by Napoleon. He was a colonel in the Hundred Days. He joined the Royal Guards during the Restoration but later resigned. In 1842, he was elected deputy for Montluçon and voted with the Left. He subsidized the republican newspaper *La Réforme*. He welcomed the Revolution of February 1848 with enthusiasm and was named to command the Paris National Guard, however, he proved a weak and unpopular commander. He was arrested and court-martialed after he failed to prevent the invasion of the Chamber on 15 May 1848.

L. Girard, *La garde nationale* (Paris, 1964) and *La IIᵉ république* (Paris, 1968).

Douglas Porch

Related entries: CHAMBER OF DEPUTIES; ECOLE MILITAIRE; HUNDRED DAYS; NATIONAL GUARD; *LA REFORME*; REVOLUTION OF 1848; ROYAL GUARD.

COURT OF CASSATION, the highest court for the civil and criminal jurisdictions. The Tribunal de cassation was created by the National Constituent Assembly in 1790 to hear the appeals from all the courts that were formerly heard by the Conseil des parties of the Conseil du roi. The Constitution of the Empire in 1804 changed its name to the Court of Cassation. The court was divided into three chambers, two for civil cases and one for criminal cases. Each chamber comprised fifteen *conseillers* and a president; a first president presided over the whole court. To render a decision, at least eleven members of a chamber had to be present. Representing the public interest (*ministère public*) were a *procureur général* and six *avocats général*, two for each chamber. Private parties involved in cases before the court could be represented by one of the sixty lawyers licensed to appear before the court.

The Court of Cassation was a court of final jurisdiction for questions of law only. Questions of fact could not be considered by the court, nor would the court hear a case until all lower appeals had been exhausted. If the court decided that there had been an error in the application of the law, the case was returned, not to the original court but to another court on the same level for retrial. In the event that the decision of the retrial court was also overturned, the Court of Cassation would render a definitive decision.

The chief purpose of the court was to interpret the law and to provide for a uniform application of the law throughout the country. It also functioned as a disciplinary authority for judges, having the power to censure, reprimand, suspend, or remove them for incompetence or misconduct. Elected during the 1790s, the members of the court were appointed for life by the chief executive under the constitutions of the Empire, Restoration, July Monarchy, and the Second Republic, but this did not prevent purges from occurring in 1815 and 1830.

A. Engelmann et al., *A History of Continental Civil Procedure* (Boston, 1927); A. Morillot, *La cour de cassation, conseil supérieur de la magistrature* (Toulouse, 1910).

Charles E. Freedeman

Related entries: CHARTER OF 1814; CHARTER OF 1830; CONSTITUTION OF 1848; COURS PREVOTALES; COURTS OF ASSIZE.

COURTS OF ASSIZE (*COURS D'ASSIZE*), criminal courts with juries established in each department by the Code of Criminal Procedure (1808). These courts tried the most serious offenses (*crimes*); lesser offenses, *délits* and *contraventions*, were tried by courts of first instance and justices of the peace, respectively. The assize courts, which met every quarter at the department seat, consisted originally of five judges (a president and four assessors) chosen by the president of the Court of Appeal (cour d'appel). Later the law of 4 March 1831 reduced the number of assessors to two. The president of the assize court was selected from among the judges of the Court of Appeal and the assessors from either the Court of Appeal or the Court of First Instance.

Juries, inspired by English practice and requested by some of the general *cahiers* of 1789, were first instituted in 1791. Under the Code of Criminal Procedure, only well-to-do or important persons were eligible to sit on juries. Lists of jurors were drawn up by the prefect. To be a juror, one had to be at least thirty years old and belong to one of the following groups: (1) the electoral college, (2) the 300 most heavily taxed residents of the department, (3) the top echelons of the civil service, (4) persons with university degrees, or (5) notaries, bankers, wealthy merchants, and those civil servants receiving a salary of at least 4,000 francs. The prefect selected sixty prospective jurors, from whom the president of the assize court chose thirty-six, which formed the pool from which the twelve jurors were subsequently selected, with both the prosecution and defense having the right to remove prospective jurors by challenge. The law of 2 May 1827 created an annual jury list from which jurors for the session list were to be selected by lot.

The prosecution (*parquet*) in the assize court was handled by a *procureur général*, or his assistant, and the baliff (*greffier*) of a court of first instance. The assize court heard the case only after a preliminary examination (*mis en accusation*), similar to indictment, in which the procedure was written and secret. The definitive trial before the assize court was oral and public. Decisions of juries and judges were rendered by majority vote, each group voting separately, with the juries deciding questions of fact and the judges questions of law. A simple majority was normally sufficient, but the size of the majority was changed several times between 1835 and 1853. The law of 9 September 1835 mandated secret balloting by juries.

Sentences were severe in an age that believed that harsh penalties were a deterrent to crime. The method of jury selection ensured a generally unsympathetic audience for crimes against property. Courts at first had little power of discretion over sentences, but the law of 24 May 1824 lowered to *délits* several offenses formerly classified as *crimes* and gave the courts the power to lower sentences in several types of cases where it was decided that attenuating circumstances existed. This discretionary power was further liberalized by the law of 28 April 1832. Appeals from the decisions of the assize courts were possible to the Court of Cassation but only on questions of law, not of fact.

Code d'instruction criminelle (Paris, 1808); E. Adhémar, *A History of Continental Criminal Procedure* (Boston, 1913).

Charles E. Freedeman

Related entry: COURT OF CASSATION.

COURVOISIER, JEAN-JOSEPH-ANTOINE (1775–1835), magistrate, deputy, and minister of the Restoration. Courvoisier was born at Besançon on 29 November 1775. He and his father emigrated, and he joined the army of Condé, where he earned the Cross of Saint Louis. He returned to France in 1803 and studied law. In 1808 he became a councillor-auditor in the court at Besançon. In 1815 the Bourbon government named him solicitor general to that same court, and in 1818 he became the attorney general of the royal court at Lyons. In the meantime, in 1816 the department of Doubs elected him to the Chamber of Deputies, where he served until 1824. As a deputy he initially supported the policies of the Richelieu cabinet, especially of Elie Decazes. In the fall of 1819 the Deputies chose him as one of their vice-presidents. At that time he proposed that the Deputies' address to the throne include comments supporting the inviolability of the Charter and opposing the preaching of the missionary societies which were then very active in France. When this proposal was rejected, he allied himself more closely with the Left. After the assassination of the duc de Berry, Courvoisier opposed the laws suspending individual liberty and giving the so-called double vote to the very wealthy. He now became a regular member of the opposition.

The 1824 elections did not return him to the Chamber, and he then devoted himself to his judicial duties. He also underwent a religious conversion, becoming a fanatical Catholic and changing his political views to a more conservative, although not extremely ultra, position. On 8 August 1829 he was nominated to be minister of justice in the Polignac cabinet, a rather obvious attempt to broaden the cabinet to the Left. His nomination was as surprising to himself as it was to public opinion. He hesitated before accepting, apparently fearing the government intended some violation of the Charter, which he indicated he would not support. He quickly had difficulties with other ministers, especially extreme ultraroyalists such as François de La Bourdonnaye. Yet Courvoisier played a major role in drafting Charles X's address from the throne to open the 1830 session that precipitated the conflict between crown and Deputies. However, he subsequently urged that Joseph de Villèle should replace Jules de Polignac in an effort to defuse the crisis. When that did not materialize, he opposed the use of extraordinary crown powers and opposed the dissolution of the Chamber on 21 April. Then he urged the cabinet to resign if it was defeated in the forthcoming elections, indicating that he would do so under that condition. He tried to mitigate the vengeance of the cabinet against the 221 deputies who voted the reply to the address. On 19 May 1830 he resigned from the cabinet rather than condone Polignac's avowed intention to oppose the newly summoned Chamber. Nevertheless, Charles X appointed Courvoisier to the Privy council and made him a minister of state when he resigned from the government. The July Revolution ended Courvoisier's public career, although he did testify for the defense at the trial of the former ministers before the Chamber of Peers. Courvoisier died at Lyons on 10 September 1835.

Archives parlementaires; P. Duvergier de Hauranne, *Histoire du gouvernement parlementaire en France, 1814–1848* (Paris, 1857–71); A. Robert et al., *Dictionnaire des parlementaires français* (Paris, 1889–91).

James K. Kieswetter

Related entries: DECAZES; DOUBLE VOTE, LAW OF THE; LA BOURDONNAYE; MISSIONS; POLIGNAC; THE 221; ULTRAROYALISTS.

COUSIN, VICTOR (1792–1867), philosopher and founder of the school of eclecticism, a synthesis of various philosophical doctrines. Born the son of a poor watchmaker, Cousin literally grew up in the streets of Paris until a fantastic turn of events rescued him from the future of an obscure apprentice. At the age of eleven, he came to the aid of a young bourgeois mistreated by his classmates, and the grateful Viguier family underwrote his education at the Lycée Charlemagne. The young vagabond sailed through at double speed, achieving two years of credits for every year he spent in school and garnering honors on the way.

Cousin's demonstrated brilliance led him to the Ecole normale, which had just opened in 1810, and after barely three years, he became a lecturer in philosophy and Greek. He described his introduction to philosophy as an illuminating experience that changed his entire life from the moment he heard Pierre La Romiguière speak.

In 1815, Cousin assisted Pierre Royer-Collard in the chair of modern philosophy at the Sorbonne. At first, he lectured on the Scottish philosophers, but he soon felt the magnetic attraction of the German philosophers. He acquainted his students with Kant, Schelling, and Jacobi; at the same time he was initiating himself into the intricacies of their thought.

It was, however, his meetings with Hegel that exerted the most influence. He introduced Hegel's thought to France, but Hegel himself remarked, upon reading the lectures for Cousin's course of 1828, "I provided him with the fish, and he has served it with his own sauce."

Cousin had a checkered academic career. University appointments were under governmental control, and his liberal views, as well as his lack of financial or family influence, resulted in the suspension of his courses between 1820 and 1827. He made profitable use of the interval, spending it in serious study and writing, working on editions of Proclus and Descartes and a translation of Plato, finally published in 1840, which he considered his finest accomplishment. Politically he fared little better in Germany, where he was incarcerated for six months and released only through the intervention of Hegel. Jean-Baptiste de Martignac restored Cousin to his position at the Ecole normale in 1828, and from 1830 to 1851 he was director of that institution. Although remembered as a teacher of philosophy, according to his former student, Jules Simon, he essentially quit teaching in 1830 and abandoned it entirely after 1837.

Cousin elaborated a popular philosophy that he called eclecticism, which reflected his own pattern of acquiring knowledge. Detractors denied him the title of philosopher with some justice, since he attempted to create a not-always-harmonious synthesis of the four classifications into which he had divided philosophic thought: idealism, sensationalism, skepticism, and mysticism. His teaching did, however, contribute positive impetus to the study of the history of philosophy.

The years from 1830 to 1848 mark the apogee of his career and an accumulation of honors: elected to the French Academy, named a peer of France, director of the Ecole normale, minister of public instruction (for eight months in 1840). He was master of philosophical instruction in France, which he controlled with an iron hand, until the revolution of 1848 and the subsequent unrest caused him to retire from public life in 1851.

Cousin constantly rewrote, so that his celebrated *Du vrai, du beau et du bien*, published in 1853, was a reworking of his *Cours de philosophie* (1836), which was itself a reworking of the course he gave in 1818. Other philosophical works include *Fragments philophiques* (1826), *Cours d'histoire de la philosophie* (1826), and *L'Introduction à l'histoire de la philosophie* (1829), which went through several reworkings to become *L'Histoire générale de la philosophie* (1863).

Cousin accumulated considerable wealth while living frugally in rooms at the Sorbonne. A lifelong bachelor, he developed a passion for women of the seventeenth century, which he indulged fully after his retirement. Although he is chiefly renowned as a philosopher, some critics feel that his most noteworthy achievements are the scholarly studies characterized by historical erudition and stylistic beauty that he produced during this period. They include *La Marquise de Sablé* (1854), *La Jeunesse de Madame de Longueville* (1853), *Mademoiselle de Scudéry* (1858), and a history, *La Société française au XVIIe siècle* (1856). He died of apoplexy while spending the winter of 1867 in Cannes with Merimée.

W. V. Brewer, *Victor Cousin as Comparative Educator* (New York, 1971); V. Cousin, *Course of the History of Modern Philosophy*, trans. O. W. Wight (New York, 1857); J. Simon, *Victor Cousin* (Paris, 1891, 1921); F. Will, *Flumen Historicum: Victor Cousin's Aesthetic and Its Sources* (Chapel Hill, 1965).

Shelby A. Outlaw
Related entries: ACADEMIE FRANCAISE; MARTIGNAC; ROYER-COLLARD; SIMON.

COUTARD, LOUIS-FRANÇOIS (1769–1852), general. Born in Ballon (Sarthe), he entered the army in 1787, distinguished himself in the campaigns in Italy, and advanced to the rank of colonel in 1803 and that of brigadier general in 1811, after serving in Spain and Portugal. A severe wound received in 1812 served to retire him from service in the field, but he had sedentary commands at Bordeaux and Pau. His refusal to serve Napoleon during the Hundred Days brought him a variety of rewards from the Restoration regime: the rank of lieutenant general and the commands of Besançon, Rennes, and finally of Paris (1822–30). He was elected as a deputy from the Sarthe in November 1827. For his loyalty to the Bourbons, he was cashiered in 1830.

H. de Riancey, *Le général comte Coutard* (Paris, 1857).

Guillaume de Bertier de Sauvigny
Related entries: HUNDRED DAYS; REVOLUTION OF 1830.

CREMIEUX, ISAAC-ADOLPHE (1796–1880), member of the Provisional Government in 1848. Born in Nîmes, Crémieux in 1817 became a lawyer and soon won a reputation for the legal defense of liberals and Bonapartists under the Restoration. He welcomed the July Revolution in 1830 but soon resumed his practice of defending individuals accused of political offenses; one was a former minister of Charles X, Martial de Guernon-Ranville, but most were editors of periodicals, including *La Tribune*, *Le National*, *La Gazette de France*, and *Le Charivari*. In 1831 he delivered the funeral oration for the abbé Henri-Baptiste Grégoire, who during the Revolution had championed the emancipation of Crémieux's fellow Jews. In 1842, Crémieux was elected to the Chamber of Deputies, where he sat with the dynastic opposition. Reelected in 1846, he participated in the 1847 Banquet Campaign for electoral and parliamentary reform. On 3 February 1848, Crémieux won the esteem of student opposition groups in Paris when he addressed demonstrators protesting the suspension of Jules Michelet and two other popular professors.

When three weeks later crowds invaded the Chamber of Deputies during the February Revolution, Crémieux was the sole nonrepublican deputy to be acclaimed a member of the Provisional Government, which he was one of the first to advocate after having earlier urged a regency. Crémieux also assumed the Ministry of Justice, and in April he was elected to the National Constituent Assembly. Retained as minister by the Executive Commission, Crémieux resigned on 7 June 1848, after opposing the move to prosecute Louis Blanc for alleged complicity in the demonstration of 15 May. Crémieux supported Louis-Napoleon Bonaparte for election to the presidency of France in December 1848 but soon turned against the new president. Elected to the Legislative Assembly in 1849, Crémieux sat with the left-wing republicans of the Mountain. He was temporarily imprisoned together with other opposition leaders during the coup d'état of 2 December 1851 and thereafter returned to private life and the practice of law. In 1864 he once again defended republican opponents of the Second Empire in the "Trial of the Thirteen," and in 1869 Crémieux was elected to the Legislative Body as an opposition deputy. One of the few to vote against the declaration of war on Prussia in 1870, Crémieux upon the overthrow of the Second Empire on 4 September 1870 became a member of the republican Government of National Defense. He once more became minister of justice and issued a decree granting French citizenship to the Jews of Algeria. Elected senator in December 1875, Crémieux played a minor role until his death in 1880.

F. A. de Luna, *The French Republic under Cavaignac, 1848* (Princeton, 1969); J. G. Gallaher, *The Students of Paris and the Revolution of 1848* (Carbondale, 1980); S. Posener, *Adolphe Crémieux*, trans. E. Golob (Philadelphia, 1940).

Frederick A. de Luna

Related entries: BANQUET CAMPAIGN; *LE CHARIVARI*; EXECUTIVE COMMISSION; *LA GAZETTE DE FRANCE*; GREGOIRE; JEWS; MICHELET; *LE NATIONAL*; PROVISIONAL GOVERNMENT.

CROSS OF JULY and **MEDAL OF JULY,** awards honoring participants on the victorious side of the Revolution of 1830. A royal ordinance 29 August 1830 authorized the striking of a medal to commemorate the Revolution of 1830. Subsequently known as the Medal of July, it was to be distributed to deserving participants in the revolution. A few months later, in December 1830, the parliament authorized a decoration for participants who had especially distinguished themselves. The Commission des recompenses nationales, which was charged with selecting the recipients of both awards, ruled that the cross should be given only to those whose roles in the revolution had been such that they would have paid with their lives had the revolution failed. The commission and the government interpreted this prescription generously and eventually awarded 1,867 crosses; 3,889 other participants received the medal.

D. H. Pinkney, *The French Revolution of 1830* (Princeton, 1972).

David H. Pinkney

Related entries: COMMISSION DES RECOMPENSES NATIONALES; REVOLUTION OF 1830.

CURIAL, PHILIBERT-JEAN-BAPTISTE-FRANCOIS, COUNT (1776–1829), general. The son of a notable citizen of Chambery (Savoie), he became French by the annexation of this province of the kingdom of Sardinia to the French Republic. His distinguished services in Italy and Egypt, as well as later at Austerlitz, were rewarded by a commission as colonel in the imperial guard. In this elite corps he rose to the rank of brigadier (1807) and general of division (1809). After Napoleon's abdication, he felt free to make obeisance to Louis XVIII. The king found it politically expedient to show some consideration to one of the chiefs of the glorious Old Guard. Thus Curial was made a peer with the title of count and appointed commander of the Nineteenth Military Division at Lyons. When Napoleon returned from Elba, Curial showed some hesitation in rallying to his cause; because of that Napoleon refused to have him back in his old command in the Guard and instead sent him to the distant Army of the Alps. For the same reason, Curial was promptly pardoned by Louis XVIII and reinstated in the Chamber of Peers. During the French expedition in Spain in 1823, Curial commanded with distinction a corps. Charles X made him one of the five chamberlains of his personal household, an exceptional honor for a former commoner.

J. Philippe, ''Le Lieutenant-général Curial,'' *Revue savoisienne* (1860).

Guillaume de Bertier de Sauvigny

Related entries: CHAMBER OF PEERS; CHARLES X; HUNDRED DAYS; LOUIS XVIII; SPAIN, 1823 FRENCH INVASION OF.

CUVIER, GEORGES-LEOPOLD-CHRETIEN-FREDERIC-DAGOBERT (1769–1832), zoologist and paleontologist. The son of an army officer in Montbéliard, Cuvier was originally destined for a career in teaching or the church, but his interest in natural science was stimulated by his studies at the Academy of Stuttgart (1784–88). As a tutor in Normandy, he studied marine life on the coast and made the acquaintance of the agronomist Alexandre-Henri Tessier (an *Encyclopedia* contributor), who introduced him to the naturalist Geoffroy de Saint-Hilaire. Under Saint-Hilaire's tutelage, Cuvier went to Paris in 1795 and soon became a member of the Society for Natural History and the Institute, then professor of natural history at the Ecole du Panthéon (1796) and the Collège de France (1801). By 1803, he was permanent secretary of the Academy of Sciences. Napoleon employed Cuvier as an inspector of public instruction, and he established the lycées of Nîmes, Bordeaux, and Marseilles, as well as the science faculty at the University of Paris, and universities at Genoa, Pisa, Parma, Siena, Florence, Turin and Rome (1806–13). Declining the Ministry of the Interior under the Restoration, Cuvier became a member of the French Academy (1818), a councillor of state (1816), and a *commissaire du roi* (working on the election laws of 1816 and 1820). He was made a peer shortly before his death.

Despite his long career in government and educational administration, Cuvier made important contributions to several branches of science. He was the author of several studies on the history of the natural sciences and added more than

13,000 displays and exhibits to the anatomical section of the Jardin des plantes. A pioneer in comparative anatomy, Cuvier studied the operation of organs and physical systems in vertebrates and mollusks and worked out the law of the correlation of organs, explaining the effects of modifications in related anatomical features. In paleontology, he was instrumental in establishing that fossils recorded the existence of extinct, as well as existing, species, and his anatomical theories permitted the reconstitution of the fleshy parts of fossilized remains. Although his studies were occasionally influenced by religious precepts (he rejected evolutionary theory in favor of catastrophism and estimated the origin of humanity at 4000 B.C.), his work on fossils, his mapping of geological epochs, and his classification system based on skeletal structure and differences in organs marked real advances in scientific knowledge.

W. R. Coleman, *Georges Cuvier, Zoologist* (Cambridge, Mass., 1964); G. Cuvier, *Règne animal* (Paris, 1816), *Leçons d'Anatomie comparée* (Paris, 1800, 1805), and *Recherches sur les ossements fossilés* (Paris, 1924); R. Dujarric de la Riviere, *Cuvier* (Paris, 1969); L. Roule, *Cuvier et les Sciences de la Nature* (Paris, 1926).

David L. Longfellow

Related entries: ACADEMIE FRANCAISE; ACADEMY OF SCIENCES; COLLEGE DE FRANCE; LAMARCK.

CUVILLIER-FLEURY, ALFRED-AUGUSTE (1802–1887), journalist and literary figure. Born in Paris in 1802, Cuvillier-Fleury studied at the Collège Louis-le-Grand, winning a prize for honors in rhetoric in 1819. He served for two years as secretary to Louis Bonaparte, the exiled former king of Holland, whom he followed to Rome and Florence. Returning to France, Cuvillier-Fleury joined the staff of the Collège Sainte-Barbe. In 1827 the duc d'Orléans appointed him as tutor to his son, the duc d'Aumale. Aumale subsequently retained Cuvillier-Fleury as his private secretary. He also was a frequent associate of Louis-Philippe and his family during the July Revolution and monarchy. In 1834 he became a regular contributor to the *Journal des débats* and supported the July Monarchy until its demise. Thus he benefited from a happy combination of personal conviction and professional opportunity. On 29 April 1845 Louis-Philippe named him an officer in the Legion of Honor. The following year he unsuccessfully stood for election in Guéret (Creuse) with official government backing and support. The 1848 Revolution, the Second Republic, and the Second Empire did not change his political persuasion. However, after 1848 he devoted himself to historical and literary works, including a biography of the duchesse d'Aumale, published in 1870, and the preparation of the correspondance of the duc d'Aumale, published in 1910–14. Cuvillier-Fleury's own *Journal intime* was published posthumously in 1903. It contained his extensive notes on the Orléans family from 1828 until 1851. He was a perceptive commentator on social and literary developments of the July Monarchy, the Second Republic, and the Second Empire. He became a member of the French Academy in 1866 and died in Paris in 1887.

E. Hatin, *Histoire du journal en France, 1631–1853* (Paris, 1853) and *Histoire politique et littéraire de la presse en France* (Paris, 1859); F. Hoefer, *Nouvelle biographie générale* (Paris, 1852–66); T. E. B. Howarth, *Citizen King: The Life of Louis-Philippe, King of the French* (London, 1961).

James K. Kieswetter

Related entries: ACADEMIE FRANCAISE; *JOURNAL DES DEBATS*; LOUIS-PHILIPPE.

D

DALMATIA, DUC DE. See SOULT.

D'ALTON-SHEE, COMTE EDMOND DE LIGNERES. See ALTON-SHEE.

DAMAS, ANGE-HYACINTH-MAXENCE, BARON DE (1785–1862), officer of the Empire and Restoration; Peer and minister of the Restoration. Born in Paris on 30 September 1785 to an old Burgundian noble family, Damas and his family emigrated to Germany and Russia. In 1795 he entered the Russian artillery school at Saint Petersburg and was commissioned a lieutenant in the Semonovski regiment of the imperial guard in June 1803. Wounded in the defense of Moscow in 1812, in October of that year he was promoted to colonel of the regiment of Astrakhan grenadiers. During the campaign in Germany in 1813, he rose to major general and distinguished himself at Leipzig, at Brienne, and before Paris in March 1814. In the First Restoration, he entered the French army as a maréchal de camp. At Napoleon's return in 1815, Damas, now a lieutenant general, accompanied the duc d'Angoulême to the Midi. After arranging the surrender of the royal army to Napoleon's forces, he followed Angoulême into Spain for the duration of the Hundred Days.

At the Second Restoration he received command of the Eighth Military District at Marseilles, where he remained until 1822. There he exercised extreme severity in his treatment of former imperial officials and earned the reputation of a devoted ultraroyalist. He commanded a division in the invasion of Spain. On 2 October 1823 Damas became a grand officer of the Legion of Honor. On 9 October Louis XVIII named him a Peer and on 19 October appointed him minister of war, a post for which he was utterly unqualified. On 4 August 1824 he resigned the War Ministry in a dispute over various measures demanded by the ultras, especially the forced retirement of several generals. But that same day he was appointed foreign minister to replace Chateaubriand, and he remained as interim war minister from 20 August 1824 until 29 September 1825. Damas was foreign minister until 4 January 1828, although the actual control and implementation of foreign policy was carried out by Joseph de Villèle, and Damas had little to do with it. When Damas did speak on foreign affairs, he was quite inept. In April 1827 Damas was one of the most adamant in demanding the complete disbandment of the National Guard as a result of its demonstrations on 29 April. Charles X held Damas in high esteem, and he was closely connected with the clerical party. Thus at the death of the duc de Rivière, the governor of the duc de Bordeaux, Charles appointed Damas to replace him. Damas' clerical and ultra connections later redounded to the disadvantage of Bordeaux. At the July Revolution Damas traveled with Charles and Bordeaux into exile. The new regime declared that he had resigned his army rank and placed him on the retired list. He remained abroad until the education of Bordeaux was completed. Then he returned to France, living in complete retirement from public affairs at Hautefort (Dordogne), where in 1846 he established a loan fund for workers. Damas died in Paris on 6 May 1862. His memoirs were published in Paris in 1922–23.

Archives parlementaires; V. Beach, *Charles X* (Boulder, 1971); M. L. Brown, *The Comte de Chambord* (Durham, N.C., 1967); A. Robert et al., *Dictionnaire des parlementaires français* (Paris, 1889–91).

James K. Kieswetter

Related entries: BORDEAUX; CHATEAUBRIAND; NATIONAL GUARD; SPAIN, 1823 FRENCH INVASION OF; ULTRAROYALISTS; VILLELE.

DAMBRAY, CHARLES (1760–1829), lawyer and statesman. The scion of an old family that belonged to the nobility of the robe, Dambray had a precocious career. At the age of twenty-eight he reached the high position of solicitor-general of the Paris Parliament. When this body was suppressed, he briefly left France, but he returned at the end of 1791 to live quietly on his Normandy estate of Montigny (Calvados). He was able to escape the Jacobin Terror. Not only that, but he made his house a staging post for royalists who were attempting to escape to England. During the Empire, though he was a member of the Conseil général of his department, he was an active member of the secret royalist society the Knights of the Faith, and he was able to correspond with the Pretender in England.

With the return of Louis XVIII, Dambray became chancellor and minister of justice. Because he was associated with the unfortunate policies of the First Restoration, the king could not reinstate him in the Ministry of Justice, appointing in his place François de Barbé-Marbois with the title of keeper of the seals. Dambray, however, kept the title of chancellor, which by tradition carried a life tenure. In May 1816, seeking to placate the ultraroyalists, Richelieu brought Dambray back to the Ministry of Justice, but with the new Chamber elected in the fall of 1816, such a presence ceased to be an asset, and Dambray was replaced by Etienne-Denis Pasquier in January 1817. Until his death, Dambray kept the title of chancellor and also that of the president of the Chamber of Peers, which went with the chancellor's office.

A. de Barante, *Souvenirs*, 8 vols. (Paris, 1890–1901); *Notice nécrologique sur M. Ch. Dambray* (Paris, 1830); *Moniteur universel*, 10 January 1830.

Guillaume de Bertier de Sauvigny

Related entries: BARBE-MARBOIS; CHEVALIERS DE LA FOI; PASQUIER; RICHELIEU; ULTRAROYALISTS.

D'ARGENSON, COMTE MARC-RENE. See VOYER D'ARGENSON.

D'ARGOUT, ANTOINE-MAURICE-APOLLINAIRE (1782–1858), administrator and statesman. The first steps of D'Argout's career were in the financial administration of Napoleon's empire. After 1814 he served in the prefectural corps: Basses-Pyrénées (1815) and Gard (1817). Elie Decazes made him a councillor of state and peer of France (March 1819). After 1830 he served in a number of ministries: Navy and Justice (November 1830), Commerce and Public Works (March 1831), Interior (October 1832), and Finances (January 1836). In 1836 he was appointed governor of the Bank of France, an office that he held for the next fifteen years. In January 1852 he was made a senator by Napoleon III.

G. Ramon, *Histoire de la Banque de France* (Paris, 1929).

Guillaume de Bertier de Sauvigny

Related entries: BANKING; CHAMBER OF PEERS; COUNCIL OF STATE; DECAZES.

DARU, PIERRE-ANTOINE-NOEL-BRUNO, COMTE (1767–1829), military administrator, peer of France, historian and poet, and patron of Stendhal. Pierre Daru was born in Montpellier on 12 January 1767, the son of Suzanne Periès and Noël Daru, secretary to the intendency of Languedoc. A brilliant student at the Military School of Tournon, operated by the Oratorian Order, Daru revealed early on a taste for poetry and history that would remain with him throughout his life. At the age of fifteen he began his administrative career, becoming a clerk at the intendancy of Languedoc. When the Revolution broke out in 1789, Daru welcomed it. Suspected of harboring sentiments favorable to England in May 1794, Daru lost his post and found himself first imprisoned, then placed under house arrest; while idle, he translated Horace and wrote a humorous *Epître à mon sans-culotte*, in which he demonstrated that a jailer is as free as his prisoner. With his release, Daru returned to his career with the army and served successfully in a succession of important posts. He found the first of many positions for his cousin Henri Beyle, the future writer Stendhal. A member of the Tribunat in 1802, Daru held numerous administrative positions during the Consulate and the Empire, becoming not only director of the administration of the Grande armée, but also minister of the administration of war in 1813. Napoleon had rewarded Daru for his faithful service by making him a count of the Empire in 1809. Following the abdication of the emperor in 1814, Daru returned to his estate of Bécheville and prudently avoided either supporting or plotting against the Bourbons.

Napoleon's return to France during the Hundred Days brought Daru out of retirement, and he became, at the request of the emperor, the minister of state charged with the administration of war. Daru promptly undertook the herculean task of raising and supplying a new army; the defeat at Waterloo interrupted his work, and he again withdrew from public life in July 1815.

Like many other former imperial officials who had chosen to follow Napoleon during the Hundred Days, Daru suffered some persecution during the White Terror. Soon, however, his sequestered property was returned to him, and he was permitted to dwell in peace at Bécheville. Moreover, he was not among those academicians removed from their seats when the Bourbons recreated the French Academy in 1816. By 1819, when Louis XVIII named Daru a peer of France, it was evident that the Bourbon regime wished his support. In the Chamber of Peers, Daru sat with the constitutional opposition, frequently defending individual liberties and freedom of the press, while opposing the intervention in Spain, the indemnity bill of 1825, and the Law of Primogeniture of 1826. His important work of 1827, the still useful *Notes statistiques sur l'imprimerie et la librairie*, served as a significant contribution to the successful liberal campaign against Charles de Peyronnet's proposed press laws. Daru also sat on a number of delicate commissions, including one empowered to examine the debts incurred by the royal family during the emigration.

Known throughout his life for his poetry and his translation from the Latin of Horace and Cicero, Daru returned during his last decade and a half to his early interest in poetry and history. In 1815, when his future in France was most uncertain, he undertook a seven-volume *Histoire de Venise*, a scholarly but popular history that went through four editions in the nineteenth century. His *Histoire de Bretagne* of 1826, however, did not duplicate this success. Daru's verse included *Epître à M. le duc de la Rochefoucauld sur les progrès de la civilisation* of 1824 and a didactic poem, *L'Astronomie*, written at the request of the scientist Laplace. Daru died at his estate on 5 September 1829.

H. de LaBarre de Nanteuil, *Le comte Daru, ou l'Administration militaire sous la Revolution et l'Empire* (Paris, 1966).

Robert Brown

Related entries: ACADEMIE FRANCAISE; CHAMBER OF PEERS; HUNDRED DAYS; INDEMNITY BILL OF 1825; PEYRONNET; PRESS LAWS; SPAIN, 1823 FRENCH INVASION OF; STENDHAL.

DAUMESNIL, PIERRE (1777–1832), general. A private in the armies of Bonaparte in Italy and Egypt, his singular courage allowed him to rise through the ranks. He was a major in the Imperial Guard when, at Wagram, he lost a leg. Napoleon made him a brigadier and gave him the command of the fort of Vincennes (April 1812). When the Allied armies entered Paris in March–April 1814, he rejected all demands to deliver the fortress, threatening even to blow up the tremendous supplies of gunpowder that he had in the vaults if any attack was attempted. Thus he kept the tricolor waving defiantly until he was satisfied that the change of regime was irreversible. Again, in July 1815, he put up a stubborn resistance; it was only a week after the return of the king that he accepted the raising of the white flag, but still he would not let the Prussians enter the fortress. With the complicity of French authorities and the Russian chiefs, he managed to deliver a small part of the great arsenal he kept in trust while holding out against the blockade until 15 November. Great was the popularity of "Old wooden leg" (*la jambe de bois*), as he was fondly called. However, because of his show of Bonapartism and his disobedience, he was put on retirement pay. Soon after the Revolution of 1830, he was given back the governorship of Vincennes, a lucky circumstance for the former ministers of Charles X, who were brought there after their trial in December 1830. The mobs that rushed to Vincennes thirsting to seize and lynch them were subdued by Daumesnil's appearance at the gate and a few firm words. He died in the cholera epidemic of 1832.

R. Baschet, *Le général Daumesnil* (Paris, 1938); H. de Clairval, *Daumesnil* (Paris, 1970).

Guillaume de Bertier de Sauvigny

Related entries: HUNDRED DAYS; RESTORATION, FIRST; RESTORATION, SECOND; REVOLUTION OF 1830.

DAUMIER, HONORE (1808–1879), caricaturist, painter, and sculptor. Born in Marseilles, Daumier moved with his family to Paris in 1815, where he grew up in poverty. In 1821 he was placed as a runner for a process server. In this apprenticeship he viewed the legal profession at close quarters. Later his father found him a training post in a bookstore in the Palais Royal, which allowed him to observe the more exalted and less pretentious aspects of the human situation. Thus Daumier's education was principally in the streets of Paris. Later it was these daily little comedies he had observed early in life that were depicted in some of his memorable works. Above all, Daumier was an artist who was close to the people.

By the mid–1820s, Daumier was studying art seriously. In 1825 he came to Belliard, a lithographer and printer of contemporary portraits.

The relaxation of censorship accompanying the July 1830 Revolution allowed Daumier the opportunity to turn his attention to political cartooning. Of his 250 lithographs produced between July 1830 and 27 August 1835, only 9 are not political in nature. In 1832 he began his association with *La Caricature*, which was edited by Charles Philipon.

Daumier's savage attack on Louis-Philippe, "Gargantua" (Loys Delteil, No. 54) resulted on 23 February 1832 in a prison sentence of six months and a fine of 500 francs. After leaving prison a public figure, Daumier joined a commune of political artists. Although Daumier himself was neither a militant nor a revolutionary, his close associates were often from the radical political Left.

The draconian censorship law (September Laws of 1835) forced Daumier to abandon politics as the essential theme of his lithographs. For the next forty years, he principally produced scenes drawn from daily life. These unique documents mirror the era, giving a sensitive depiction of the times. Honoré de Balzac recognized Daumier's genius for capturing the essential nature of the period, observing that Daumier had something of Michelangelo under his skin. Thus Daumier's lithographs give a complete tableau of society during the July Monarchy and the Second Empire, not ignoring the socioeconomic complexion of these bourgeois epochs.

Official censorship and heavy penalties imposed by the September Laws altered Daumier's style and subject matter, channeling his work into masterpieces of more gentle social satire. Daumier captured the essence of the age that is remembered for François Guizot's advice, "Enrichissez-vous!" In addition to the law courts and the theater, Daumier turned his attention to the business world. His Robert Macaire series depicted the prototype of the charming rogue who hovered about the fringes of the business world and stock market speculators. A certain sort of bourgeois had appeared in Paris, better known in the United States as a wheeler and dealer. Specializing in operations always bordering at least on the fraudulent, Robert Macaire's activities were drawn on Daumier's experience as a process server's runner.

In 1846 Daumier married and moved to modest surroundings on the Ile St. Louis. The banks of the Seine provided him with the main source of motives for his paintings. Daumier's atelier was a gathering place for his many friends, and his conviviality was a reflection of the great human warmth of an artist with a magnanimous heart. However, the stories of his fondness for wine are certainly exaggerated, as is proved by the enormous productivity and steady output of great works throughout his life. Daumier had a restless energy, a passion for long hours and constant work that made him a curious reflection of the bourgeois ethic. There is always something of Daumier in his works. His gentle satire often has a self-awareness, which made his humor so poignant. The characteristics of Daumier's lithographs were his love of humanity, his sympathy for the trivialities in the daily life of the common person. He derived his humor from the deflation of the self-satisfied.

Among his contemporaries, Daumier's reputation was based almost entirely on his caricatures. Although these lithographs afforded him a certain popularity and a modest means in keeping with his spartan standard of living, few individuals appreciated his genius. The exceptions were Manet, Jules Michelet, and Charles Baudelaire, who declared that a single stroke of Daumier's pencil had more value than all the paintings of the academic artists. Yet his paintings and sculpture were hardly known to contemporaries. This neglect was not alone the result of governmental censorship.

A more important force that made Daumier's painting and sculpture so rare was a subtle censorship of contemporary disapproval. Daumier's painting and sculpture were revolutionary. He painted in a unique and highly individual style, which was generally appreciated only after his death. Most of his known works of sculpture existed during his life only as the wax models, which were cast much later.

Equally important is Daumier's own personality. A fervent and lifelong republican, Daumier was an unassuming man of the people in his private and public life. His lack of pretension and self-satisfaction—the prime characteristics of the bourgeoisie he captured so well in his lithographs—and his misplaced sense of modesty probably caused Daumier himself to underestimate his own genius. Daumier lacked the sense of showmanship of a Robert Macaire, which is sometimes necessary in forcing an artist through to public recognition. This exemplary private character perhaps helps to explain the small number of his known paintings.

After the Revolution of 1848, Daumier again turned his attention to politics. He produced a hundred lithographs in 1848, which was an average output, although fewer than in 1847. Interested increasingly in painting, he was commissioned by the revolutionary regime for an allegorical picture of the Republic. What is probably a study for this painting exists, but the finished work was never delivered to the government.

The return of the pretender Louis-Napoleon to France in 1848 afforded Daumier an additional subject for satires to join the marvelous caricatures of Adolphe Thiers. Daumier's new character Ratapoil captured the brutality of Bonaparte's supporters from among the dregs of French society, those whom Marx termed the lumpenproletariat (ragged or criminal poor).

Characteristically, though, Daumier did not join the great number of Napoleon III's opponents in exile after the coup d'état of 2 December 1851. Embracing discretion as the greater part of valor and in keeping with his native sense of humor and realism, Daumier turned from politics as the inspiration for his art to describe the Gilded Age in witty and gentle works of satire. Daumier could amuse as he exposed the lack of good taste and the foibles of an era of injustice.

E. Bouvy, *Daumier: L'oeuvre gravé du maître*, 2 vols. (Paris, 1933); L. Delteil, *Honoré Daumier: Le peintre graveur illustré*, 11 vols. (Paris, 1926–30); M. Govin, *Daumier sculpteur (1808–1879) avec un catalogue raisonné et illustré de l'oeuvre sculpté* (Geneva, 1952); J. R. Kist, *Daumier: Eyewitness of an Epoch* (New York, 1979); O. W. Larkin, *Daumier: Man of his Time* (New York, 1966); Roger Passeron, *Daumier: Témoin de son temps* (Paris, 1979).

James Chastain

Related entries: BALZAC; BAUDELAIRE; *LA CARICATURE*; CENSORSHIP; COUP D'ETAT OF 2 DECEMBER 1851; GUIZOT; MICHELET; REPUBLICANS; THIERS.

DAUNOU, PIERRE-CLAUDE-FRANCOIS (1761–1840), cleric, deputy, jurist, legal and constitutional scholar. Born in Boulogne-sur-mer, Daunou was the son of a naval surgeon and was destined for a career in the clergy. Ordained a priest in 1787, he supported the Revolution and the Civil Constitution of the Clergy in 1791. Elected to the Convention (Pas-de-Calais) on 9 September 1792, Daunou served on the public instruction committee and effectively abandoned the Catholic church. Arrested as an opponent of the Jacobin *coup* (May-June 1793) in October, he remained in prison until November 1794. Returning to his seat in the Convention, he was a principal author of the Constitution of 1795. He was instrumental in founding the *écoles centrâles* and worked on reforms of the electoral laws, school organization, regulations on the press and in the national archives. Removed with the first third of the Council of Five Hundred (drawn by lot), he became director of the library of the Pantheon and helped organize the Institute. In Italy in January 1798 to write a constitution for the Roman Republic, he purchased books for the Pantheon library and the *Bibliothèque nationale* (including a substantial part of the papal library), and visited Pompei and Naples. Daunou was removed from office by Bonaparte, who resented his frequent criticisms of the Consulate. Daunou returned to his library work but was made archivist-in-chief under the Empire (15 December 1804). Refusing appointment as a councillor of state or chief censor, he traveled to Germany, Spain, and Italy to collect their state archives and returned to Paris with 157,586 cartons of papers (which were returned to their respective governments after 1814). Removed from his post at the archives as an ex-member of the Convention on 26 February 1816, Daunou became editor of the *Journal des Savants* and, with the aid of Elie Decazes, a professor at the Collége de France. He served one term as a deputy from Brest (1821–23) and became head archivist again after the Revolution of 1830, which he supported. A deputy again (1831–34), Daunou declined further election and devoted himself to his writing and research. His *Essais sur les garanties individuelles* (1818) was widely translated, and his *Histoire littéraire de la France, Biographie universelle*, and *Encyclopédie des gens du monde* were also greatly admired. Daunou was a long-time member of the Academy of Inscriptions and the Academy of Moral and Political Sciences.

A. Aulard, "La constitution de l'an III et la République bourgeoise" in *La révolution française* 38 (1900); H. Bernard, *Education and the French Revolution* (n.p., 1969); G. de Bertier de Sauvigny, *La Restauration* (Paris, 1955, 1963); J. Godechot, *Les Institutions de la France sous la Révolution et l'Empire* (Paris, 1951); G. Lefebvre, *Napoléon* (Paris, 1936); R. Palmer, "The Central Schools of the First French Republic," in *The Making of Frenchmen* (Waterloo, Ontario, 1980); A. Patrick, *Men of the First French Republic* (Baltimore, 1972); F. Ponteil, *Napoleon Ier et l'organisation autoritaire de la France* (Paris, 1956), and *L'oeuvre sociale et humaine de Napoléon* (Brussels, 1958); E. Seligman, *La justice en France pendant la Révolution 1791–1793* (Paris, 1913).

David Longfellow

Related entries: COLLEGE DE FRANCE; DECAZES.

DAVID, JACQUES-LOUIS (1748–1825), painter. Regarded as the embodiment of classicism in painting, David was virtual art director of France for over fifty years. Extending beyond painting, his influence reached far into the areas of interior decoration, fashion, furniture, and design and was reflected in the development of moral philosophy. His art became a complete break with the rococo tradition, and from this break modern art is dated by many historians.

David had his first drawing lessons with the rococo painter François Boucher, who was a distant relative. In 1766 David was admitted to the Academy as a student. He immediately forsook Boucher's fluffy rococo style in favor of the new neoclassicism. He painted classical motifs and forms to illustrate a strong sense of virtue he attributed to the ancient Romans. He was fierce in his desire for perfection in painting and in his passion for the political ideas that would inspire the French Revolution.

During the Revolution David participated actively in the political events that led to the overthrow of the monarchy and, as a Jacobin, was known as the "Robespierre of the Brush." He served with his close friend Maximilien Robespierre on the Committee of General Security and voted for the death of Louis XVI. After the fall of Robespierre, David in 1798 met Napoleon Bonaparte, and for the next seventeen years his painting passionately portrayed the cult of the emperor.

After the Hundred Days (20 March–22 June 1815) David fled to Switzerland and eventually retired to Brussels. He opened a studio and lived there in exile as an active influence in European art. In 1817 he painted *Cupid and Psyche* (Paris, Collection of Princesse Joachim Marat), *Telemachus and the Nymph Eucharis* (1818, private collection), the *Wrath of Achilles* (1819, private collection), and *Mars and Venus* (1825, Brussels, Musées des beaux-arts). These last works are of historical rather than artistic value and are very far from the classic beauty that Ingres, with his romantic temperament, was to produce. David thought that in these last works, especially his *Leonidas*, he had attained the true Greek ideal, but the spirit of the antique, only hinted at in these works, is held back by a Flemish overtone of detail.

Various dates are used to mark the point at which modern art supposedly began. One, used increasingly by historians, is 1784 when David finished his *Oath of the Horatii*. In this work a fundamental Renaissance tradition was seriously opposed for the first time: the use of perspective recession to govern the organization of pictorial space. It may be argued that David's work was crucial in developing ideas that led ultimately to twentieth-century abstract art. David did not actually abandon the tradition of linear and aerial perspective; he subordinated these by closing off pictorial depth by using such devices as a solid wall, a black area of neutral color, or a solid shadow. The result is an effect of figures composed along a narrow stage; these exist in space more by the illusion of sculptural modeling than by their location within a pictorial space that has been constructed according to the principles of linear and atmospheric perspective. David was reacting against the principles of perspective space as a method of representing depth. This space had to be closed off or denied in some manner before abstraction, which has no depth, could manifest itself.

Several contradictory factors mingle in David's art: from the early stern neoclassicism, he moved, in the Napoleonic pictures, toward a Venetian use of light and color, and yet later paintings of classical subjects show a rigid antiquarianism at odds with all the beauty of the Venetian. His portraits are always supremely well composed, yet his later classical subjects display a soft sweetening of style, perhaps due to the influence of his years of exile. He was indisputedly a great teacher, whose numerous pupils included Francois-Pascal-Simon Gérard, Anne-Louis Girodet, Antoine-Jean Gros, and Jean-Auguste-Dominique Ingres.

R. Cantinelli, *Jacques-Louis David, 1748–1825* (Paris, 1930); D. L. Dowd, *Pageant-Master of the Republic: Jacques-Louis David and the French Revolution* (Lincoln, Nebr., 1948); A. Humbert, *Louis David, peintre et conventionnel* (Paris, 1937); A. Maurois, *J.-L. David* (Paris, 1948); A. Thibaudeau, *Vie de David* (Paris, 1826); W. R. Valentiner, *Jacques-Louis David and the French Revolution* (New York, 1929).

Irene Earls

Related entries: GROS; INGRES; ROBESPIERRE.

DAVID D'ANGERS, PIERRE-JEAN (1788–1856), the greatest portrait sculptor of high romanticism. Born at Angers, he was the son of Pierre-Louis David, also a sculptor and carver. In 1808 he moved to Paris where he became a student of Philippe-Laurent Roland at the Ecole des beaux-arts. He won the Prix de Rome in 1811 and spent 1812–15 in Rome. David made a brief trip to London to study the Elgin marbles. On his return to Paris, he was awarded an important commission, which the dying Roland was unable to complete. The restored Bourbon regime planned a series of historical statues to line the Pont Louis XVI (now Pont de la Concorde). David executed a colossal statue of Condé in contemporary rather than classical dress, which marks the beginning of romantic treatment of historical subjects in sculpture. The plaster model was exhibited at the salon of 1817, and the marble (destroyed during World War II) was completed in 1827.

Over the next ten years, David d'Angers carried out various projects for public monuments, the most important being the memorial to General Maximilien-Sébastien Foy at Père Lachaise (1827). The artist became a member of the Institute in 1826 and later that year began teaching at the Ecole des beaux-arts. He believed that sculpture should glorify greatness and undertook a series of over five hundred medallions depicting (usually in profile) distinguished artists, writers, scientists, thinkers, and statesmen. He was as well a prolific maker of portrait busts. Notable are those of Lamartine (1828), François-René de Chateaubriand (1829), Johann von Goethe (1829), Pierre-Jean de Béranger (1829), Félicité de Lamennais (1839), and Honoré de Balzac (1844). His bust of Nicolò Paganini (1830–33) cast in bronze using the recently rediscovered lost-wax method exemplifies the romantic expressionism that David d'Angers pioneered. The modeling of the clay was retained in the finished bronze.

In 1832, the U.S. admiral Uriah Phillips Levy commissioned David to do a monumental bronze statute of Thomas Jefferson, which is now in the Rotunda of the U.S. Capitol. David's conception of a standing figure in modern dress in a naturalistic pose was the first monument of this type, a style that became so common in the nineteenth century that it is hard to realize how much David was departing from the prevailing classical norms. Another notable public monument is the one to Gutenberg done between 1837 and 1840 for Strasbourg. In 1833 David d'Angers undertook a tour of Germany with his wife (whom he married in 1831), Emilie Maillocheau, the granddaughter of the revolutionary Louis-Marie de La Révellière-Lépeaux. On this trip he added to his series of portrait medallions the likenesses of Alexander von Humboldt and Ludwig Tieck.

One of David's most famous public monuments is the pediment of the Panthéon. Louis-Philippe commissioned him to undertake this work in 1830, shortly after the July Revolution. David was to depict *Patrie* thanking her great men. *Patrie* is in the center handing out laurel wreaths provided by Liberty, while History records the names of those to be honored. Those honored for civic achievement are on the left, those for military achievement on the right. By the time the sculpture was executed, the political complexion of the regime had changed. Unhappy with the inclusion of such figures as the marquis de Lafayette and Jacques-Antoine Manuel, the government asked for changes, which David refused. The project, finished according to the original plans, was unveiled without fanfare in 1837.

An ardent republican, David was a supporter of the Revolution of 1848. He became mayor of a Paris arrondissement and deputy of Maine-et-Loire to the Constituent Assembly. His political career was cut short by his electoral defeat in 1849. After the coup d'état of 1851, David was arrested and sent into exile. He lived in Belgium and traveled in Greece and Italy. He returned to France in early 1853 and died in Paris in 1856. Always devoted to his native city, he sent copies of most of his works to the museum at Angers.

P. Fusco and H. W. Janson, *The Romantics to Rodin* (Los Angeles, 1980); H. Jouin, *David d'Angers* (Paris, 1878).

Sylvia Neely

Related entries: ACADEMY OF FINE ARTS; BALZAC; BERANGER; CHATEAUBRIAND; FOY; LAFAYETTE, M.-J.-P.-Y.-R.-G.; LAMARTINE; LAMENNAIS; MANUEL; ROMANTICISM.

DAVOUT, LOUIS-NICOLAS (1770–1823), Duc d'Auerstädt and Prince d'Eckmühl; marshal and minister of the Empire; peer of the Restoration. The son of an aristocratic officer, Davout was born on 10 May 1770 at Annoux (Yonne). He attended the military academies in Auxerre and Paris, graduating as a sublieutenant in 1788. He scandalized his fellow officers by adopting the Revolutionary ideas of the time. Nevertheless, his aristocratic background led to his forced resignation in 1793. But in October 1794 he returned to duty as a brigadier general in the army of the Moselle. He was subsequently assigned to Toulon to help organize the Egyptian campaign in which he participated. Davout became a loyal servant of Napoleon during this campaign and during the Empire he became a duke, a prince, and one of Napoleon's principal advisers.

In the Hundred Days Napoleon appointed Davout governor of Paris, minister of war, and a peer. Davout performed a remarkable feat of gathering supplies and men before Waterloo. After Waterloo he commanded the army in Paris and later the army of the Loire, ultimately surrendering Paris on 3 July on the order of the Provisional Government. He did, however, thwart an effort by General Gebhard von Blücher to capture Napoleon on 29 June. Davout did not swear loyalty to Louis XVIII until 1817, because the king had stripped him of all offices. In March 1819 he was named a peer of France but did not participate in public affairs. Davout died in Paris on 1 June 1823.

L. N. Davout, *Correspondance du maréchal Davout* (Paris, 1885); J. G. Gallaher, *The Iron Marshal: A Biography of Louis N. Davout* (Carbondale, 1976); A. G. Macdonnell, *Napoleon and His Marshals* (London, 1950).

James K. Kieswetter

Related entries: HUNDRED DAYS; WATERLOO, BATTLE OF.

DEBELLEYME, LOUIS-MAURICE (1787–1862), magistrate and prefect of police of the Restoration. Born in Paris on 16 January 1787, Debelleyme entered the bar in 1807 and earned a reputation for his ability and dedication. From 1814 to 1819 he served as deputy prosecutor at Corbeil, Pontoise, and Versailles. In 1821 he became investigating magistrate in Paris, in 1824 vice-president of the lower court, and prosecutor to that court in 1826. His conduct of these offices was marked by a high degree of moderation and independence. In handling the investigation of the 1827 massacre in the rue St. Denis, he found against the gendarmes. When the Martignac ministry sought to appease the liberals by replacing the ultraroyalist Guy Delavau as prefect of police, they appointed Debelleyme on 17 January 1828. In his eighteen months in office, he curbed many of the abuses of his predecessor, limiting political police activities and handling with discretion those he did implement, inspecting weights and measures, attending to the cleaning of the streets, abolishing various taxes, and introducing public omnibuses. He also provided charitable care for the genuinely indigent. He put many of the police in uniform, increased the number of constables, and reestablished the peace officers, all with beneficial results for public order. These measures made him popular with ordinary Parisians.

Debelleyme was elected to the Chamber of Deputies from the department of Dordogne in July 1829. When the Polignac ministry came into office in August, he resigned rather than lend his popularity to its support. Charles X protested his resignation and a few days later, on 13 August 1829, named him to preside over the civil court of the Seine. In the Deputies, Debelleyme sat on the Center-Right, and he refused to sign the address criticizing the king. However, when the July Ordinances appeared, in his judicial capacity he authorized newspapers to publish in spite of the prohibitions. He rallied to the July Monarchy, which gave him command of a battalion of the Paris National Guard. Although he had been defeated in the July 1830 elections, the by-elections in September 1831 returned him from the department of Seine. He lost again in 1834 but in November 1837 was elected from Ribérac (Dordogne), which subsequently returned him in 1839, 1842, and 1846. In the 1846 session he served as vice-president of the

Deputies. During his years in the Chamber, he generally supported the policies of the ministry. The 1848 Revolution ended Debelleyme's legislative career, but in 1856 Napoleon III appointed him a councillor in the Court of Cassation. He retired in January 1862, having earned an outstanding reputation as a magistrate. Debelleyme died in Paris on 24 February 1862. He had been a member of the Legion of Honor since 1821.

J. Bertin, *Biographie de M. de Belleyme* (Paris, 1863); H. Buisson, *La police son histoire* (Vichy, 1949); J. Peuchet, *Mémoires tirés des archives de la police* (Paris, 1838); A. Robert et al., *Dictionnaire des parlementaires français* (Paris, 1889–91); B. Saint-Edme, *Biographie des lieutenans-généraux, ministres, directeurs-généraux . . . de la police* (Paris, 1829); C. A. Sapey, *Notice sur M. de Belleyme* (Paris, 1862); G. Vapereau, *Dictionnaire universel des contemporains* (Paris, 1858).

James K. Kieswetter

Related entries: COURT OF CASSATION; DELAVAU; JULY ORDINANCES; MARTIGNAC; POLIGNAC.

DECAEN, CHARLES-MATHIEU, COMTE (1769–1832), professional soldier. Born near Caen, Decaen served in the marine artillery (1787–90) and was elected a sergeant of volunteers in 1792. Service at the siege of Mainz (1792), in the Vendée (1793) and under General Jean-Baptiste Kléber in Germany (1796) brought him promotion, and he became a general of brigade in 1796 and a general of division in 1800. His exceptional service at Hohenlinden (1800) led to appointment as governor of the French West Indies (1804–11), where he showed considerable administrative ability. On his return to France, he took over command of the Army of Catalonia from Marshal Etienne MacDonald and fought in Spain until Napoleon's abdication.

The Restoration government gave him the grand cross of the Legion of Honor and put him in charge of the Eleventh Military District (headquartered in Bordeaux). When Napoleon returned from Elba in March, Decaen's troops were eager to rally to the emperor, but the presence in Bordeaux of the duke and duchess of Angoulême (Louis XVIII's nephew and the surviving daughter of Louis XVI) created a crisis. Bordeaux was largely royalist (the duke was there to celebrate the first anniversary of the city's defection from the Empire on 12 March 1814), and the ducal couple, aided by the Baron Vitrolles, the provisional secretary of state, hoped to organize resistance. The approach of General Bertrand Clausel (an old colleague of Decaen from Spain and the newly appointed head of the Eleventh District) led to equivocation on Decaen's part when asked by the duchess if his men would fight for the Bourbons, and a subsequent attempt on her part to address the troops was shouted down by the garrison. The royalist leaders then left the city, and Decaen turned over his command to Clausel.

Decaen's action (or lack of it) wrecked his career. Assaulted by a crowd in Bordeaux, he was subsequently imprisoned for fifteen months after Waterloo and forcibly retired to Ermont until his death in 1832.

P. Mansel, *Louis XVIII* (London, 1981); E. Le Gallo, *Les Cent-Jours* (Paris, 1924); J. Thiry, *Les Cent-Jours* (Paris, 1943).

David Longfellow

Related entries: ANGOULEME, L.-A.; ANGOULEME, M.-T.-C.; MACDONALD; VITROLLES.

DECAZES, ELIE, DUC (1780–1860), prominent politician during the Restoration. The son of a middle-class family from Libourne (Gironde), he was first a lawyer and then a magistrate under the Empire, serving also as an intendant in the house of the Emperor's mother. During the Hundred Days, he courageously refused to take the oath demanded by Napoleon and was exiled from Paris. This act earned him nomination as prefect of police in Paris when Louis XVIII returned, and in that position he gained the king's admiration, so that Louis XVIII later called on him to replace Joseph Fouché as minister of general police. The growing favor Louis XVIII showed him made Decazes practically master of internal politics during the Richelieu ministry, and he inspired the tactic of combatting the ultraroyalist Right by enlisting the support of the liberal Left. When Armand-Emmanuel de Richelieu retired in December 1818, Decazes became minister of the interior in a ministry nominally presided over by General Jean-Joseph Dessolle, and he stepped up his policy of combatting the Right. By the end of 1819, however, he began to realize that the increasing influence of the Left was beginning to threaten both the crown and his own position. He wanted to reverse his policies, but Dessolle and two other ministers did not accept this about-face, and consequently the ministry had to be rearranged, this time with Decazes as president of the Council. He was preparing a new election law when the assassination of the duc de Berry on 13 February 1820 brought about his fall. The king, in despair over this forced separation from his "dear son," made him a duke and ambassador to Great Britain. When the royalists came to power in December 1821, Decazes' diplomatic career came to an end, and henceforth he would do no more politically than sit in the Chamber of Peers, where he generally defended the policies of the Center Left. He rallied without hesitation to Louis-Philippe, and from 1834 to 1848 he was *grand référendaire*, or president, of the Chamber of Peers. Because of the generosity of Louis XVIII, he had a large fortune, which he used, among other things, to create a center of mining and metallurgy in an isolated spot in the department of Aveyron, where a small city grew up that now bears his name: Decazeville.

E. Daudet, *Louis XVIII et le duc Decazes, d'après documents inédits* (Paris, 1899); R. Langeron, *Decazes, ministre du roi* (Paris, 1960).

G. de Bertier de Sauvigny, trans. E. Newman

Related entries: BERRY, C.-F.; DECAZEVILLE; DESSOLLE; FOUCHE; RICHELIEU; ULTRAROYALISTS.

DECAZEVILLE, a coal-mining and metallurgical center in the northwestern corner of the department of Aveyron. Duke Elie Decazes, for whom the town is named, became interested in the use of coke to smelt iron ore during his tenure

as ambassador to Great Britain in the early 1820s, and in 1825–26 he established
the Société anonyme des Houillères et Fonderies de l'Aveyron to exploit iron
ore and coal deposits in the Aubin Coal Basin. He soon found an excellent local
director in François Cabrol, an *enfant du pays*, former military officer, and expert
on British metallurgical technology. Until the Second Empire the company was
primarily a metallurgical firm and used most of the coal it extracted in its own
factories. Despite the protection given French iron from competition by the tariff
of 1822, the early years of Houillères et Fonderies were quite difficult. Sulphur
in the coal precluded the manufacture of high-grade coke; sulphur and phosphorus
in the local iron ore made it unsuitable for the manufacture of pig iron. The
company was forced to turn temporarily to other sources for ore and to smelt
the ore with charcoal. Overproduction of low-quality products exhausted the
firm's working capital in the mid–1830s. Plans to sell the enterprise to the Belgian
iron magnate John Cockerill in 1837 fell through only when he backed out at
the last moment.

A dramatic turnabout in the company's fortunes occurred in the late 1830s;
an upsurge in the demand for rails, a product that could be manufactured with
Decazeville's inferior iron, came to the rescue of the floundering company.
Decazeville's new preeminence was reflected in the share of rail production
allotted it in agreements among forges; it received 50 percent of the 13,000-ton
Paris-Orléans order of 1841 and two years later was given the leading position
in the five-company contract with the Compagnie du nord. The company's growth
was interrupted by the crisis of 1847–51 but resumed again under the Second
Empire. Between 1841 and 1854 the industrial complex at Decazeville expanded
from one forge to three; from six blast furnaces to ten; from twenty-six puddling
ovens to seventy-seven; from six steam engines providing 500 horsepower to
twenty-seven providing 1,600 horsepower. In 1856 production reached a level
unsurpassed at any other time during the nineteenth century: 33,458 tons of pig
iron, 16,304 tons of rails, and 4,175 tons of other iron products.

The Houillères et Fonderies was one of the largest industrial firms in France
under the July Monarchy. In 1840 it ranked fourth in capital behind Anzin,
Saint-Gobain, and Grand-Combe. During the Houillères et Fonderies' early
troubled years, prominent bankers on the board of directors arranged much-
needed loans, and in 1842 the firm became, with the aid of the Rothschilds, the
first French metallurgical firm to issue bonds. Self-financing played an even
greater role in the company's development; until 1845 all potential dividends
(5.2 million francs) were ploughed back into the firm.

The settlement that grew up around the mines and forges was designated the
commune of Decazeville in 1833; by 1851 the town's population had grown to
5,938. Although the firm originally depended heavily on British workers and
French workers from outside the area to staff the skilled positions in the factory,
it had some success in recruiting locally a stable labor force in the 1840s. Most
of the remaining British workers departed during the depression at the end of
the July Monarchy, leaving the native French population to experience the boom

of the mid–1850s and the bust of the early 1860s that followed the signing of the Cobden-Chevalier Trade Treaty.

D. Reid, *The Miners of Decazeville: A Genealogy of Deindustrialization* (Cambridge, 1985), and "The Origins of Industrial Labor Management in France: The Case of the Decazeville Ironworks During the July Monarchy," *Business History Review* 57 (Spring 1983); J. Wolff, "Decazeville: expansion et declin d'un pôle de croissance," *Revue économique* 23 (September 1972).

Donald Reid

Related entries: ANZIN, COMPANY OF THE MINES OF; COAL INDUSTRY; DECAZES; ROTHSCHILD FAMILY.

DECLARATION OF CAMBRAI. See CAMBRAI, DECLARATION OF.

LE DEFENSEUR (1820–1821), royalist literary, political, and religious periodical during the Restoration; the title was also used during the July Monarchy for a religious periodical. *Le Défenseur* was the short-lived successor to the more successful *Conservateur* (1818–20) and continued with nearly the same staff, François-René de Chateaubriand turning his attention more to the *Débats*. Among those who remained to edit the *Défenseur* were Louis de Boland, Joseph Fiévée, Félicité de Lamennais, and Eugéne de Genoude. Joseph de Villèle and even Jules-Armand de Polignac wrote for it occasionally, giving it all of the political flavors of the Right. Although it sometimes attacked the immoderate ultra polemicists of the *Drapeau blanc*, it joined the chorus that accused the liberals of fomenting the murder of the duc de Berry. It appeared at approximately weekly intervals.

E. Hatin, *Histoire de la presse française*, vol. 8 (Paris, 1859–61).

Daniel Rader

Related entries: BERRY, C.-F.; CHATEAUBRIAND; *LE CONSERVATEUR*; *LE DRAPEAU BLANC*; FIEVEE; *JOURNAL DES DEBATS*; LAMENNAIS; POLIGNAC; ULTRAROYALISTS; VILLELE.

DEGERANDO. See GERANDO.

D'EICHTHAL, GUSTAVE (1802–1886), successively, Auguste Comte's first disciple, a leading member of the Saint-Simonian sect, and a Parisian intellectual who never quite fulfilled the promise of his youth. D'Eichthal was a philosopher who considered his society to be in crisis but who also shared with many of his fellow intellectuals the belief, so strengthened by the dual revolution, that change was possible, that dreams could come true, that the crisis could be ended and utopia reached. He was thus a typical representative of those numerous schemers and visionaries in the France of the first half of the nineteenth century who planned a restructuring of society, new polities, and new religions. Among these dreamers, the best remembered are the so-called utopian socialists, but there were many others who dreamed of ending the period of transition in which they believed they lived. Most of these mystics have been forgotten; they acquired neither notoriety nor a following, and they lacked the insights of their more illustrious fellows. D'Eichthal was one of these. His aims were a widespread aspiration, his generous ideals and ardent seriousness were widely shared, his disappointments and failures those of many others who belonged to the romantic generation of 1830. Throughout his life and in all his different intellectual pursuits, there was a unifying thread. First as a Comtian, then as a Saint-Simonian, and afterward throughout his life, he believed mankind to be hesitating at the crossroads, thought he glimpsed the future path, and beckoned his reluctant contemporaries to follow him. He had a deep-felt sense of all-pervading existential crisis and sought to end it above all through devising a new synthetic religion, which would end the crisis of doubt, the alienation of man from himself and his fellows, and usher in an era of harmony.

D'Eichthal's family in the years immediately following Jewish emancipation in France were part of a small group of wealthy Jews who assimilated into Gentile society and achieved some prominence there and some of whom even abandoned Judaism. Gustave's father was a Bavarian banker who had set up on his own account in Paris in 1812. His brother Adolphe (1806–75) also became a successful merchant banker and the first Jew ever to be nominated as a regent of the Bank of France. D'Eichthal himself was one of the first Jews to attend the prestigious Lycée Henri IV, where he proved to be the outstanding pupil of his year. In 1817 he converted to Catholicism, but, though he left Judaism, his Jewishness remained an important aspect of his life because he continued to show a concern not merely for the future of Jewish communities but for Judaism. Thus as a Saint-Simonian he was partly responsible for the interest the sect took in Jewish questions. In 1836–37 he spent six months in Austria attempting to persuade the government there to grant equality to the Jewish communities of the Empire. In a number of his articles and books he, like other Jews of his time, and above all his friend, Joseph Salvador (1796–1873), attempted to show the contribution that Judaism had made to Christianity and, as a bridge between Christian and Muslim, might still make to civilization.

In the 1820s the young d'Eichthal, in common with many of his generation in Paris, was searching for a guide and a purpose. On two occasions he thought he had found the leader to follow and a set of beliefs that offered certainty. This was when he came under the spell first of Auguste Comte and later of the Saint-Simonians. He played a minor role in Comtism and a more significant part in Saint-Simonianism, two of the most influential nineteenth-century intellectual movements that had had more affinities with each other than they had bitter differences. He met Comte in 1822 when the latter was still struggling to make his name and to make ends meet. He became, at the age of eighteen, Comte's first disciple, spending most of 1823 with him. Although their relations subsequently cooled, it was d'Eichthal who suggested Comte give a series of public lectures to make his ideas more widely known and who, when Comte suffered his mental breakdown in April 1826, helped pay the medical expenses.

D'Eichthal first met Saint-Simon in 1823 and, though he was unimpressed by the philosopher, he was in contact with the group that after Saint-Simon's death in 1825 began to publish the *Producteur*, the first Saint-Simonian journal. It was not until July 1829, however, that he became fully converted. From then until November 1832, when he left the sect, he devoted himself wholeheartedly to Saint-Simonianism. He made a significant contribution to the movement, and the experience marked his life. He was one of the principal benefactors, giving 150,000 francs to the cause. He introduced the Saint-Simonians to Lessing, the German philosopher whose ideas influenced the evolution of the sect's religious ideas. He also helped spread the Saint-Simonian word, attempting to convert his lifelong friend, John Stuart Mill, and undertaking a much-publicized but unsuccessful proselytizing mission to England in 1831–32. More important, he played a part in the schisms and leadership changes. He was one of Prosper Enfantin's most devoted admirers and a staunch advocate of a new morality and women's equality when these questions led to divisive discussions. In the sect he found the security, faith, and mission he had been searching for. He was thus one of the last of the leaders to abandon the sect in 1832, and it is testimony to the electric atmosphere and emotional strain of those last months that immediately after he did so he suffered a major nervous breakdown.

The Saint-Simonian experience, however, left more permanent marks than this, for d'Eichthal's sense of mission remained for the rest of his life. For him the malady of his age was never just material and social but above all spiritual and religious, and he retained his faith in the Saint-Simonian metaphysico-theological theory of history and continued to believe that history was moving toward an imminent dénouement that would bring the crisis to an end. He therefore devoted much energy to the search for a religion that would reconcile and synthesize the three great religions of the Mediterranean basin—a grandiose task that was beyond his capabilities. He was not the only ex-Saint-Simonian to search for a new religion for all humanity; Jean Reynaud and Pierre Leroux also did so. For a brief moment in the heady days following the events of February 1848, d'Eichthal believed that the revolution heralded not only political and social change but the dawn of a new religious epoch. He even conceived the idea of a European "religious democracy," setting up a group to work for the creation of a new synthetic religion, and a number of other ex-Saint-Simonians joined him. The idea, however, was still-born, and d'Eichthal was always to feel that his religious writings were the least understood and appreciated of his writings.

He did have some successes in the 1830s and 1840s. Like others of his generation, he was attracted to Greece, whose civil war ended in 1832, and from September 1833 until June 1835 he was one of the numerous French collaborators of John Kolettes, Greek minister of the interior, and worked at restoring government finances. On his return to France, d'Eichthal became interested in the racial question. In part his inspiration came from contemporary debates on the abolition of slavery, but he treated the problem not in the narrow sense of freeing slaves but in terms of the rehabilitation of the Negro, of the respective qualities of black and white, and of the reconciliation of the two races. The slender volume, *Lettres sur la race noire et la race blanche*, that he and a collaborator published in 1839 brought d'Eichthal into contact with a heterogeneous group of savants from diverse disciplines, who in that year set up the Société ethnologique, the first purely scientific ethnological organization even to be formed. D'Eichthal played a significant part in the activities of these early anthropologists.

E. d'Eichthal, *Quelques âmes d'élite (1804–1912), esquisses et souvenirs* (Paris, 1919); P. Laffitte, ed., "Matériaux pour servir à la biographie d'Auguste Comte: correspondence d'Auguste Comte et Gustave d'Eichthal," *Revue occidentale*, 2e ser. (1896); B. M. Ratcliffe, "Crisis and Identity: Gustave d'Eichthal and Judaism in the Emancipation Period," *Jewish Social Studies* 37 (1975), "Gustave d'Eichthal (1802–1886): An Intellectual Portrait," in Barrie M. Ratcliffe and W. H. Chaloner, *A French Sociologist Looks at Britain: Gustave d'Eichthal and British Society in 1828* (Manchester, 1977), and "Saint-Simonism and Messianism: The Case of Gustave d'Eichthal," *French Historical Studies* 10 (1976).

Barrie M. Ratcliffe

Related entries: BANKING; COMTE, A.; ENFANTIN; JEWS; LEROUX; REVOLUTION OF 1848; SAINT-SIMON; SAINT-SIMONIANISM.

DELABORDE, HENRI-FRANCOIS (1764–1833), general. Born in Dijon, son of a baker, he had served for a few years in the lower ranks of the royal army when the Revolution opened for him, as for many others, the opportunities for a higher destiny. His rise in the military hierarchy was rapid, and he made contributions on so many fields of war. As early as 1793 he had reached the rank of general. Among the most important field commands he exercised later were those of an army corps in Spain (1809) and of a division of the Imperial Guard in Germany (1813), but he held also a number of sedentary territorial governorships. Louis XVIII granted him a generous pension of 10,000 francs while keeping him in active service. Thus he was commander of the Tenth Military Division at Toulouse when Napoleon returned. Unhesitatingly he rallied to the emperor and arrested Eugéne-François de Vitrolles, the royal commissionner. Napoleon rewarded him with a title of chamberlain and a seat in his newly formed Chamber of Peers. After the second return of Louis XVIII, Delaborde was listed among the nineteen military men who were to be court-martialed for their disloyalty in March 1815. But the military court was able to exonerate him through a legal quirk. He was thereafter unemployed and was cashiered in January 1820. His son Henri (1811–99) was to be known as a distinguished painter and art critic.

C. Mullié, *Biographie des célébrités militaires . . .* (Paris, 1851).

Guillaume de Bertier de Sauvigny

Related entries: HUNDRED DAYS; LOUIS XVIII; VITROLLES.

DELACROIX, FERDINAND-VICTOR-EUGENE (1798–1863), leading exponent of French romantic painting whose artistic talent was surpassed only by his influence. He was born to a notable family under circumstances that led to the supposition that his father in fact was the statesman Charles-Maurice de Talleyrand, whom he resembled. He began art studies in the Pierre-Narcisse Guérin studio, but more influential on his formation were the great masters whom he copied unceasingly in the Louvre. Although he never traveled in Italy, his style was marked by Michelangelo, the Venetians, and other great Renaissance masters.

Delacroix first caught the public eye with his *Dante and Virgil*, entered at the Salon of 1822 despite Guérin's protest. It was highly criticized but nevertheless purchased for the state, as was his subsequent *Massacre of Chios*. During these formative years, he developed friendships with Théodore Géricault and Richard Bonington. When he saw *The Haywain* at the Salon of 1824, he was so impressed by John Constable's use of color that he repainted the background of the *Massacre*, which was also displayed there.

In 1825 Delacroix visited England with Bonington and was inspired by the remarkable coloring of the English school, as well as the choice of subjects from literature and medieval history. With the painting of a subject drawn from Lord Byron's poem, *The Death of Sardanapalus*, he established himself as the leader of the French romantic school at the Salon of 1827.

Delacroix's *Liberty Leading the People* (1830) not only celebrated the victory of Louis-Philippe but was filled with the symbolism of the rallying cry of the romantics. They demanded above all freedom: freedom to express emotional reactions through art, to experiment with color, to give free rein to their imagination and poetic sensibility, to portray life and nature as they saw it, to reject slavish imitation of classical models and masters.

This insistence on freedom led Delacroix into direct conflict with the neoclassicists, resulting in many salon refusals and the denial of a chair at the Institute until 1857. Leader of the opposition was Jean Ingrès, and their quarrel came down to an insoluble conflict over the supremacy of line to color in painting. Ingrès was a superb and unemotional draughtsman, while Delacroix was a soul on fire, painting ardent, inspired, emotion-charged tableaux.

In 1832, Delacroix's travels in Spain and North Africa opened his eyes to a vivid and exotic new world. His *Algerian Women* (1834) and *Jewish Wedding* (1841) introduced the Oriental theme to French art with exciting repercussions among contemporary artists.

In addition to his striking innovations in color and subject matter, Delacroix transformed decorative painting. Despite Ingrès' iron control of the Institute, which refused Delacroix's bids for admission, he continued to receive important fresco commissions: the Palais Bourbon (1833–34), the Luxembourg library (1840–47), the Louvre Apollo Gallery (1850–51), the Hôtel de ville (1852–54), and the Church of Saint-Sulpice (1853–61).

Delacroix was immensely prolific and immensely versatile. He never married and devoted his entire life to his art, exhausting his limited energies in feverish bursts of passionate painting. When at last he succeeded to Hippolyte Delaroche's seat at the Institute in 1857, he had only six years to enjoy this success, and he spent those in an exalted frenzy of work. He incarnated for his century those Renaissance masters he admired so much. He was to French romanticism in art what Victor Hugo was in literature: a giant, incomparable. He was the originator of every great pictorial innovation in the nineteenth century. His later paintings had a strong influence on Renoir, and the loosening of his brushwork pointed toward expressionism. An excellent source of information on his life and works, as well as a record of developments in nineteenth-century art is his *Journal*, which he maintained from his twenties until shortly before his death.

E. Delacroix, *Journals* (1893, English trans. 1961); R. Huyghe, *Delacroix*, trans. J. Griffin (New York, 1964); G. P. Mras, *Eugene Delacroix's Theory of Art* (Princeton, 1966); F. H. Trappe, *The Attainment of Delacroix* (1971).

Shelby A. Outlaw

Related entries: BYRON; DELAROCHE; GERICAULT; HUGO; INGRES; ROMANTICISM; TALLEYRAND.

DELAROCHE, HIPPOLYTE (1797–1856), historical painter who combined classical style with romantic subject matter. Born to a family proud of his artistic talent, young Paul, as he was called, began his studies in Louis-Etienne Watelet's studio (1816) but soon became a pupil of Antoine-Jean Gros (1818). His first exhibited painting, *Josabeth saving Joas* (1822), brought him in contact with Théodore Géricault and Eugène Delacroix. Although he was much influenced by the latter, whose talent vastly overshadowed his, it was Delaroche who garnered commissions, wealth, and fame during his lifetime. Ironically Delacroix succeeded to a chair at the Institute only upon Delaroche's death.

This popular appreciation was due to Delaroche's conservative tendencies, which caused him to cultivate the *juste milieu*, which in this case may be simply another way of expressing mediocrity. His art marked the middle of the road between the careful technique of the neoclassicists and the dramatic historical subject matter of the romantics. He was drawn to tragic incidents, which he carefully prepared in wax images before painting the theatrical tableaux he had created.

He married Horace Vernet's only daughter and seemed never to have totally recovered from her early death, after which he turned almost exclusively to religious subject matter.

In 1837 he received the commission for the great painting of the hemicycle of the Ecole des beaux arts, which he conceived of as uniting all the great men in the history of art, with the feminine interest supplied by the muses who reign over the ensemble. He did not succeed in imbuing the figures with emotion or life, and he retained all his life a certain classical frigidity that was most apparent when isolated, as here, from dramatic subject matter.

For Delaroche, composition and light took precedence over historical accuracy. The romantic tableaux for which he is best remembered include *The Assassination of the Duc de Guise* (1835) and the *Children of Edward IV* (1831). He accumulated wealth and honors—the Légion d'honneur (1828), member of the Institute (1832), professor at the Academy (1833), and member of the academies of Amsterdam, St. Petersburg, and St. Luke—principally because he catered to the taste of the day and avoided shocking bourgeois sensibilities or creating original and controversial works.

N. D. Ziff, *Paul Delaroche: A Study in Nineteenth Century French History Painting* (New York, 1977).

Shelby A Outlaw

Related entries: ACADEMIE FRANCAISE; ACADEMY OF FINE ARTS; DE-LACROIX; GERICAULT; GROS; ROMANTICISM; VERNET.

DELAVAU, GUY (1788–1874), politician and prefect of police of the Restoration. Born in 1788 in the department of Maine-et-Loire, Guy Delavau studied law and in 1810 entered the bar. He specialized in criminal law. With the support of the Congrégation, of which he was a member, in 1815 he became a judge-auditor and in 1816 a councillor in the royal court. As a magistrate he demonstrated what some regarded as extreme harshness and partiality. On 20 November 1821, at the urging of the Congrégation, the Villèle ministry appointed him prefect of police. He remained there until 1828. Much to the outrage of the liberals, whom he persecuted, the new ultraroyalist prefect concerned himself more with political affairs than with the usual housekeeping duties of the prefecture, such as maintaining law and order and supervising the markets. Although he lacked concern for the details of his administration, he was responsible for some improvements in the police of Paris. In 1825 he was named to the Legion of Honor. Nevertheless, Delavau's subordinates on the police were not known for their integrity or probity, and his use of *agents provacateurs* was especially reprehensible. The liberals castigated him as a tool of the Jesuits, and he may have been a member of the Knights of the Faith. In 1828 he resigned, his departure being an effort by the Martignac government to appease the increasingly liberal public opinion. Jean-Baptiste de Martignac also simultaneously demoted him to the rank of councillor of state in extraordinary service. The Revolution of 1830 ended Delavau's public career. He lived thereafter in retirement, although he was involved to some extent in the 1832 legitimist conspiracy of the duchesse de Berry. He died in 1874.

H. Buisson, *La Police son histoire* (Vichy, 1949); J. Peuchet, *Mémoires tirés des archives de la police* (Paris, 1938); B. Saint-Edme, *Biographie des lieutenans-généraux, ministres, directeurs-généraux . . . de la police* (Paris, 1829); G. Vapereau, *Dictionnaire universel des contemporains* (Paris, 1858).

James K. Kieswetter

Related entries: BERRY, M.-C.; CHEVALIERS DE LA FOI; CONGREGA-TION; DEBELLEYME; MARTIGNAC; REVOLUTION OF 1830; ULTRA-ROYALISTS; VILLELE.

DELECLUZE, ETIENNE-JEAN (1781–1863), minor neoclassical artist, art critic for the *Journal des débats*, and patron of an important literary salon during the Restoration. Delécluze was born in Paris on 26 February 1781, the son of the architect Jean-Baptiste Delécluze. His early schooling, begun in 1789, was ended by the Revolution, with the result that Delécluze, who throughout his life read widely, received a somewhat haphazard education, allowing him to accept readily innovations in literature that he rejected in painting. Moved by a passionate desire to become an artist, he entered the famous atelier of Jacques-Louis David at the Louvre in 1796 and emerged a neoclassical painter of minor talent. Between 1807 and 1814, he did a number of canvases on such accepted themes as the death of Astyanax and the abduction of Europa. Although critics received kindly paintings he exhibited at the Salons of 1808, 1810, 1812, and 1814, and although he won several notable prizes, Delécluze exchanged his brush for the pen in 1814 and devoted the remainder of his long life to art criticism and literature. His *Louis David, son école et son temps* (1855) is still a valuable work that combines autobiography with a biographical study of the neoclassical master.

Fortunate to be financially independent, Delécluze devoted the years between 1814 and his death in 1863 to travel, art criticism, literature, and the Parisian salons. His travels, frequently during the Restoration in the company of his nephews Eugène and Adolphe Viollet-le-Duc, took him mainly to England and Italy; in the latter country, he nourished a love for the poetry of Dante. Delécluze published in 1843 the first translation of the *Vita nuova* and five years later supplemented it with a study of Dante. Begun in the *Lycée française*, his career as an art critic continued, upon the demise of this paper, in the *Moniteur universel*. In 1822, Delécluze became the art critic for the influential *Journal des débats*, a position he would retain for the remaining forty-one years of his life. Ever faithful to the neoclassical principles of art mastered in David's atelier, the critic spoke energetically against *la bourrasque romantique* and specifically attacked Eugène Delacroix and the artists who followed his lead. For Delécluze, Jean-Auguste-Dominique Ingres represented the true heritage of the school of David.

During the Restoration, Delécluze presided over an important literary salon that gathered in his bachelor apartment each Sunday afternoon. To it came such established luminaries as Stendhal and many of the younger romantics, men such as Paul-Louis Courier, Charles-Augustin Sainte-Beuve, Prosper Mérimée, Ludovic Vitet, Duvergier de Hauranne, François Mignet, Charles de Rémusat, and Paul-François Dubois (editor of the *Globe*), just beginning to make reputations for themselves in Paris. The habituees of Delecluze's salon, while receptive to many of the new literary currents, found discomforting the concerns of Victor Hugo's cenacle. They favored instead a liberal romanticism, a more realistic and less gothic version of the new literature mixed with political opposition to the Bourbon regime. Delécluze recorded for posterity valuable accounts of what transpired in his salon, and indeed at other noted Restoration salons, including that of the celebrated Mme. Récamier at the Abbaye aux Bois, in his *Souvenirs de soixante années* and the *Journal* of 1824–28.

A prolific author, Delécluze published, in addition to his journalistic pieces, a large number of works, ranging from art criticism and novels to historical studies and memoirs. The great critic Sainte-Beuve found his novel of 1832,

Mlle. Justine de Liron, worthy of much praise. A history of the arts and letters of the Middle Ages remained incomplete at the time of the author's death on 12 July 1863.

R. Baschet, *E.-J. Delécluze, Témoin de son temps, 1781–1863* (Paris, 1942); E.-J. Delécluze, *Dante Alighieri, ou la poésie amoureuse* (Paris, 1848), *Journal de Delécluze, 1824–1828*, ed. R. Baschet (Paris, 1948), *Louis David, son école et son temps* (Paris, 1855), *Mlle. Justine de Liron* (Paris, 1832), and *Souvenirs de soixante années* (Paris, 1862); C.-A. Sainte-Beuve, "Souvenirs de soixante années, par M. Étienne-Jean Delécluze," *Nouveaux lundis* 3 (Paris, n.d.).

Robert Brown

Related entries: COURIER; DAVID; DELACROIX; DUBOIS; DUVERGIER DE HAURANNE; *LE GLOBE*; HUGO; INGRES; *JOURNAL DES DEBATS*; MERIMEE; MIGNET; RECAMIER; REMUSAT; ROMANTICISM; SAINTE-BEUVE; STENDHAL; VIOLLET-LE-DUC.

DELESCLUZE, CHARLES (1809–1871), Jacobin republican journalist and conspirator during the July Monarchy and Second Empire. Born in the town of Dreux (Eure-et-Loire), Delescluze moved to Paris in 1830 to find a job as a law clerk and instead became involved in revolutionary politics. In 1831, he joined the secret republican society, the Amis du peuple, and participated in the insurrection of April 1834 (for which he was arrested but soon released). In 1836, the authorities accused him of plotting the assassination of Louis-Philippe, and he fled to Brussels to avoid arrest. He remained in exile for four years, earning his living as editor of the republican newspaper, the *Journal de Charleroi*, and by contributing articles to other republican journals in France. Returning to France in 1840, he moved to Valenciennes (Nord) and established another paper, *L'Impartial du Nord*.

With the outbreak of revolution in February 1848, Delescluze became the leader of republicans in northern France and received an appointment as commissioner of the Nord from the new government. Removed from this post in May 1848, he returned to Paris, where he served as both editor of *La République démocratique et sociale* and as general secretary of Solidarité républicaine (a republican club); however, the authorities implicated him in the insurrection of June 1849, and he once again had to escape to Belgium (and then on to England) to avoid prosecution. While in England, he founded *La Voix du proscrit*, an *émigré* republican newspaper, and he remained in close contact with his colleagues in France.

Delescluze returned to France following the coup d'état of 1851, hoping to plan the overthrow of Louis-Napoleon, but he was arrested and sentenced to Devil's Island. Amnestied in 1859, he reestablished himself in Paris and plunged back into active revolutionary politics. He became the spokesman for Jacobin republicanism through his new journal, *Reveil* (founded in 1868), and participated in the insurrections of October 1870 and January 1871. In February 1871, he was elected republican deputy from Paris to the National Assembly, although he resigned in March 1871 after the proclamation of the Paris Commune. The leader of the Commune's Jacobin wing, Delescluze served the city's revolutionary government in several capacities: as delegate for the nineteenth arrondissement, as member of the Committee of Public Safety, and, in the Commune's final weeks, as civil delegate of war. Already dying from tuberculosis, he was killed by Versaillais troops while defending a barricade on the last day of the Commune (25 May 1871).

M. Dessal, *Un révolutionnaire jacobin: Charles Delescluze, 1809–1871* (Paris, 1952).

Christopher E. Guthrie

Related entries: CLUBS, POLITICAL; COUP D'ETAT OF 2 DECEMBER 1851; LOUIS-PHILIPPE; REPUBLICANS; REVOLUTION OF 1848.

DELESSEPS. See LESSEPS.

DELESSERT, ABRAHAM-GABRIEL-MARGUERITE DE (1786–1858), peer and prefect of the July Monarchy. Born in Paris on 17 March 1786, Gabriel Delessert was the younger brother of Benjamin Delessert, the great philanthropist, and of François Delessert, deputy of the Restoration and July Monarchy. Having spent the years of the Terror in Germany and completed his education, Delessert returned to France in 1795. He joined his father's banking firm in 1808 and in 1814 served as adjutant commandant in the Paris National Guard, participating in the defense of Paris. In July 1815 he joined in protesting the order for the Guard to adopt the white cockade and was deprived of his commission.

During the Restoration he and his brothers participated in the management of the bank their father had founded, which had become one of the great banks of Paris. He also helped found the *caisse d'épargne* de Paris. He was actively involved in the July Revolution and henceforth devoted himself to politics. He became mayor of Passy on 1 August 1830. On 12 August 1830 he became colonel of the general staff of the Guard and was named to the committee to reorganize the National Guard of the kingdom. In 1832 he became a brigadier general. In this capacity he played a major role in suppressing the riots that erupted in Paris on 5 and 6 June 1832, demonstrating courage and moderation in the process.

Louis-Philippe appointed Delessert prefect of the department of Aube in February 1834 and then in November prefect of Eure-et-Loire. As prefect at Chartres (Eure-et-Loire) he made such a valiant effort to save the cathedral when it burned in 1836 that the citizens struck a medal in his honor from the metal of the melted bells. On 6 September 1836 he was appointed prefect of police of Paris and shortly thereafter councillor of state. As prefect of police, Delessert was responsible for significant improvements in streets, transportation, prisons, and relief. The moderation of his administration, which contrasted with previous prefects, was recognized by most factions. In recognition of his services Louis-Philippe granted him a peerage on 24 March 1844 and in April 1845 promoted him to the rank of grand officer of the Legion of Honor. It was largely Delessert who dealt with the planners of the banquet in February 1848 and who was instrumental in not executing certain previously agreed precautionary measures, including the arrest of various radicals. The February 1848 Revolution brought an end to Delessert's political career. He briefly fled to England, returning to France in August. He died at Passy (Seine) on 29 January 1858.

J. Balteau et al., *Dictionnaire de biographie française* (Paris, 1933-); H. Raisson, *Notice biographique sur la vie et les travaux de M. G. Delessert* (Paris, 1844); A. Robert et al., *Dictionnaire des parlementaires français* (Paris, 1889–91); M. B. Saint-Edme, *Biographie des lieutenans-généraux, ministres, directeurs-généraux, chargés d'arron-dissemens, préfets de la police en France* (Paris, 1829); J. Tripier le Franc, *M. G. Delessert* (Paris, 1859); J. Tulard, *La Prefecture de police sous la monarchie de juillet* (Paris, 1964).

James K. Kieswetter

Related entries: BANQUET CAMPAIGN; *CAISSES D'EPARGNE*; DELES-SERT, J.-P.-B.; NATIONAL GUARD.

DELESSERT, JULES-PAUL-BENJAMIN, BARON (1778–1847), financier, industrialist, deputy, and philanthropist of the Empire, Restoration, and July Monarchy. Benjamin Delessert (originally Lessert) was born on 14 February 1773 at Lyons, the son of an old Protestant family. He was the brother of Gabriel Delessert. After studies with Jean-Jacques Rousseau, in 1784 Delessert traveled to Britain, where he studied with Adam Smith and met James Watt. He returned to France during the Revolution, was conscripted into the army, and rose to the rank of captain in 1794. He served in Belgium under Charles Pichegru, but left the army in 1796 to take over his father's manufacturing interests and banking house in Paris, which ultimately became one of the leading financial institutions. In 1801 Delessert pioneered the establishment of a cotton spinning mill at Passy. He also established a refinery for sugar beets, whose success earned him appointment to the Legion of Honor and in 1812 the rank of baron of the Empire. In 1802 he became a regent of the Bank of France. In 1813 Delessert became commander of a legion of the Paris National Guard. During the Hundred Days he served as a member of Napoleon's lower chamber.

In September 1817 the department of Seine elected Delessert to the Chamber of Deputies, where he joined the liberal constitutional monarchists and became one of their leaders. In the Chamber he participated most extensively in debate and on committees dealing with various financial matters. In 1818 he helped introduce into France the English institution known as a savings bank and did much to popularize it. He served on the General Council of the Seine and on the Council of Commerce. Delessert's salon became one of the leading Protestant gatherings in Paris society. He was reelected to the Deputies in 1822 but was defeated in 1824. In 1827 Saumur (Maine-et-Loire) returned him to the Chamber and kept him there until 1842. Again he participated actively in debates on financial matters, opposing the national lottery and advocating the establishment of savings banks. In the July Revolution Delessert was one of the signers of the

Deputies' protest of 27 July against the July Ordinances. He was involved with Casimir Périer and other liberals in negotiating with Marshal Auguste de Marmont to end the shooting in Paris on 28 July. He was one of the deputies sent to work with the Peers and was influential in the ultimate Orleanist triumph. One of his first actions once the new government was established was to propose government compensation for the victims and property damaged during the Revolution. After the Revolution he served on the Chamber's committee to revise the constitution. For many years under the July Monarchy he was a vice-president of the Deputies. Finally in July 1842 he retired because of his health. Nevertheless, the people of his district still gave him a large vote at the polls.

In addition to his parliamentary career, Delessert was perhaps even better known as a financier and a philanthropist. In addition to savings banks, he helped to establish and support other institutions, such as a society to encourage industry and the Philanthropic Society. He also supported the sciences, arts, and letters. A member of the Academy of Sciences since 1816, he acquired a vast herbarium, including over 350,000 plants, which he left to the city of Geneva, and a large collection of 150,000 seashells. He owned an extensive art collection and a sizable library, which subsequently became part of the Library of the Institute. Delessert himself produced numerous published works on subjects ranging from botany to soup to savings banks. He died of a heart condition on 1 March 1847 in Paris.

Archives parlementaires; J. Bory, *La Révolution de juillet* (Paris, 1972); P. A. Cap, *Benjamin Delessert* (Paris, 1850); A. Robert et al., *Dictionnaire des parlementaires français* (Paris, 1889–91).

James K. Kieswetter
Related entries: CAISSES D'EPARGNE; DELESSERT, A.-G.-M.; MARMONT; PERIER.

DEMI-SOLDES, Napoleonic officers retired on half-pay during the Bourbon restoration. The need to scale down the vast armies of Napoleon in 1815 caused the government to retire 20,000 officers on half-pay. The belief common among partisans of the restored Bourbons that the *demi-soldes* were nostalgic for a return of Empire, a fear reinforced by the participation of some *demi-soldes* in a number of abortive plots to raise military revolts and in other antigovernment activity in the early years of the Restoration, caused these ex-officers to be subject to strict police surveillance. Following the successful Spanish campaign of 1823, when French troops remained loyal despite calls for them to side with Spanish liberals against their own government, the restrictive measures on the *demi-soldes* were considerably relaxed. About half returned to their farms, while others entered business or commerce or went abroad to train troops in Turkey or South America. About 5,000 *demi-soldes* were reintegrated into the army. By 1828, only 3,500 ex-officers were still collecting their half-pay. While the vast majority of *demi-soldes* successfully returned to their civilian occupations, a small number remained politically active, giving rise to a powerful myth of the *demi-soldes* as a large body of men dedicated to keeping the memory of the emperor alive and violently hostile to the Bourbon Restoration. The power of this myth was demonstrated in 1830 when King Louis-Philippe threw open the army to the *demi-soldes*, a move that caused great resentment among serving officers, who called them *les rentrés à la bouillotte*.

D. Porch, *Army and Revolution, France 1815–1848* (London, 1974); J. Vidalenc, *Les demi-soldes, étude d'une categorie sociale* (Paris, 1955).

Douglas Porch

Related entries: BAZAR CONSPIRACY; CARBONARI; LA ROCHELLE, FOUR SERGEANTS OF.

LE DEMOCRATE EGALITAIRE (1848), a short-lived newspaper linked to the Banquet Campaign. This newspaper was founded, ostensibly as a weekly, on 2 April 1848 with Edmond d'Alton-Shée, the nobleman hero of the banquet campaign, and Frédéric Gérard, former mayor of Montrouge, as owners and editors. D'Alton-Shée disappeared from the editorial board after the first issue, and the second issue, which appeared on 20 April, began with a declaration from Gérard in favor of the right of all men to subsistence. This was followed by an account of a popular banquet, which was said to have taken place in Paris on Sunday, 2 April, and was described as a new type of communion service. No further issues are known to have appeared.

E. Hatin, *Bibliographie historique et critique de la presse périodique française* (Paris, 1866).

Irene Collins

Related entries: ALTON-SHEE; BANQUET CAMPAIGN; REVOLUTION OF 1848.

LA DEMOCRATIE PACIFIQUE (1 August 1843–30 November 1851), the most successful Fourierist journal, which, under the editorship of Victor Considérant, developed a powerful critique of the iniquities and inefficiency of the market economy and the corruption and policies of the ruling elite of the declining July Monarchy regime. Many Saint-Simonians and Fourierists became journalists in the 1830s and 1840s, but whereas the Saint-Simonian sect broke up in 1832, the Fourierists were able, despite defections, to maintain their cohesion and a relatively high profile down to the end of the Second Republic. That they did so is in many ways surprising, since Charles Fourier (who died in 1837) had proposed that the principal remedy for the manifold ills that afflicted humanity would be the creation of phalanxes, which would displace existing society. Indeed, a minority of Fourierists continued to believe that the only goal of their movement should be the creation of such communities. There are two reasons for the survival of Fourierism as a political force in the face of the repeated failures of attempts to establish phalanxes in France and elsewhere. One is that the movement had a level-headed leader in Considérant. The other is that Fourierists, while they did not abandon their faith in the phalanx—

Considérant even asked Louis-Philippe to finance one—increasingly devoted themselves to criticizing contemporary society and to proposing a series of transitional reforms rather than just phalanxes. They did this in books and pamphlets but, above all, in the journals they set up from 1832 on.

Their first periodical, *Phalanstère*, set up in June 1832, changed its name to *Réforme industrielle* the following September and ran until the end of February 1834. A second journal, *Phalange*, was set up in July 1836 and appeared twice monthly until September 1840, when it began to be published three times a week. It was replaced in August 1843 by what was to be the most successful and influential of Fourierist papers, the *Démocratie pacifique*. The abandoning of the term *phalanx* for a title that indicated faith in universal suffrage and its achievement by peaceful means and the decision to publish the paper as a daily is indicative of the growing success of the Fourierist journal and the movement's increasing involvement with the political opposition. Considérant, indeed, had already been an unsuccessful candidate in the 1839 elections to the Chamber of Deputies and was to fail a second time in 1846. In November 1843, though, he was elected to the Paris Municipal Council and under the Second Republic was to secure a seat in the Constituent Assembly. By 1846 the paper, which appealed mainly to middle-class subscribers, had an average circulation of 1,665, which made it the twentieth of the Paris dailies, no mean achievement for a journal presenting the views of a minor political group.

The *Démocratie pacifique* owed its success to the journalism not only of Considérant (whose wife supplied funding for the paper) but of others like Désiré Laverdant (1809–84), Edouard de Pompery (1812–95), and Alphonse Toussenel (1803–85). In 1844 Toussenel published the best-known attack on the financial elite of the July Monarchy (*Les Juifs, rois de l'époque. Histoire de la féodalité financière*, 2 vols.). Indeed, the paper itself also owed its success and influence to its sustained critique of capitalism—which it condemned for its anarchy, wastefulness, and the social inequalities it engendered—and of the corruption and scandals of a political regime in decline. It was for one of these attacks that the paper was brought to trial but acquitted in 1847.

The paper welcomed the February Revolution and the proclamation of the Republic. In the following months it pressed for social reforms but continued to believe that they could be brought about peacefully. Its claim of 25 February that "all socialists are republicans and all republicans are socialists" expressed this optimistic desire for reform and reconciliation. Such, however, was not to be the course of events. The ill-fated demonstration in Paris on 13 June 1849 was planned in the paper's offices. With its failure and Considérant's flight into exile, the paper's influence and readership waned still further. It expired with the Second Republic at the end of 1851.

Barrie M. Ratcliffe

Related entries: CHAMBER OF DEPUTIES; CONSIDERANT; DEMON-STRATIONS OF 1848–1849; FOURIER; REVOLUTION OF 1848; SAINT-SIMONIANISM.

DEMONSTRATIONS OF 1848–1849, demonstrations that took place in Paris between February 1848 and June 1849, were usually the result of violent struggles between moderate republicans and antirepublicans on the one hand and socialist republicans on the other. On 25 and 26 February 1848, there were two demonstrations at the place de l'Hôtel de ville in Paris whose goal was to impose the red flag of the radicals on the Provisional Government as the national flag of France, replacing the red, white, and blue tricolor. Auguste Blanqui was especially anxious to impose this symbol, which would show that the revolution was more social than political, upon the Provisional Government. The socialist Louis Blanc also supported the red flag, but all the other members of the Provisional Government favored the tricolor. A compromise was reached: a decree of 26 February stated that the members of the Provisional Government and all other government authorities would wear a red rosette in their boutonnieres and that there would be a red insignia on every flagpole.

On 28 February workers demonstrated at the Hôtel de ville for a ten-hour day and the creation of a ministry of work. Louis Blanc, who may have instigated the demonstration, threatened to resign if the government did not create a commission for workers that he would preside over and whose goal would be the improvement of the lot of the working class.

Whereas demonstrations in Paris were clearly a struggle between social revolutionaries and those who wanted the revolution to be merely political, demonstrations in the provinces were less well focused. There were several large demonstrations of joy when the coming of the Republic was announced, but there were several instances, notably in the Nord, Normandy, and Champagne, when workers broke machines and tore up the railroad lines. There was very little destruction of property, and most of this was confined to the desecration of synagogues and of Jewish homes and businesses in Alsace.

The working class was not the only class to demonstrate. On 8 March 1848, shopkeepers and businessmen marched to the Hôtel de ville in Paris to ask the government to extend the due dates on their loans, a request that Etienne Garnier-Pagès refused despite the economic depression that had left many businessmen short of funds.

Meanwhile, the Parisian political clubs wanted to delay the elections of National Guard officers, which were set for 18 March, and the elections to the Constituent Assembly, which were set for 9 April. The Provisional Government, over the objections of Blanc, refused to delay the elections, but it did decree on 14 March that the old elite companies of the National Guards made up of well-equipped and wealthy men, the grenadiers and light infantry, would be disbanded. This decree, whose goal was to reduce the influence of the wealthy in the National Guard by mixing them into working-class units, met with resistance from the elite Guard units, who demonstrated against it on 16 March by marching in uniform, complete with their swords and wearing on their heads their bearskin buskins (thus, the march is called the demonstration of the bearskin buskins) but without their guns. Around 30,000 National Guardsmen went to the Hôtel de ville, which was defended by workers and students. A delegation demanding the repeal of the government's decree suppressing the elite units was coldly received by Armand Marrast, mayor of Paris. Meanwhile, the government had delayed the election of National Guard officers until 25 March.

On 16 March, the clubs of Paris made an appeal for a counterdemonstration the next day that would ask for a delay of the elections to the Constituent Assembly. Consequently, on 17 March about 100,000 to 150,000 workers, club members, and socialists left the Place de la Concorde at 11:00 A.M. singing the "Marseillaise" and the "Chant des Girondins" and cheering for Blanc and Alexandre-Auguste Ledru-Rollin. The organizers of this demonstration, the delegates of the workers of the Luxembourg Commission and the delegates of the clubs (including Cabet and Sobrier), presented a petition to the Provisional Government that asked for all troops to be removed from Paris so that they could not influence the elections. After a long discussion with Louis Blanc and Ledru-Rollin, who gave them nothing, the delegates left, and the demonstration moved on to the July Column in the Place de la Bastille. Finally, after difficult negotiations, the Provisional Government delayed the elections for officers of the National Guard until 5 April and those for the Constituent Assembly until 23 April. Thus the conservative demonstration of 16 March had gotten nowhere, but the government had been forced to yield to the leftist demonstrations of 17 March; this shows that the balance of power was still favoring the leftists. It should also be noted that the leftist demonstrators of 17 March were the elite workers of the working-class corporate organizations and not the poor, unskilled workers of the National Workshops; thus, the government had yielded to the elite artisans, not to the masses. Furthermore, the leaders of the clubs involved in the demonstrations supported the government; they had no desire to overthrow it.

As time went on, this goodwill began to wear thin for political and economic reasons. In the provinces there were incidents of machine breaking, attacks on chateaux, threats against foreign workers, and confrontations with the authorities. More serious conflicts took place when conservative areas like Bordeaux and Besançon refused to receive commissioners of the Provisional Government. In Paris there were numerous conflicts between the clubs and the moderate majority of the government and, within the Provisional Government, between the moderate majority on the one hand and Blanc and Albert on the other. Ledru-Rollin, who had the support of the clubs, appeared to be master of the situation and seemed to be merely waiting for the right moment to impose his ideas on the nation. Meanwhile the clubs, especially the Club of Clubs, were redoubling their activity as the elections approached, despite the attack against Blanqui (the so-called Taschereau affair). The socialists wanted the elections to be delayed again because their chances at the moment were not good. The Club of Clubs believed that just one big demonstration could obtain that adjournment, and Louis Blanc seems to have agreed. On 15 April Ledru-Rollin told the government that on the next day there would be a demonstration when the workers elected the officers of the National Guard. The demonstrators would march from the Champ de Mars to the Hôtel de ville. Their official demand was for "the organization of work into workers' cooperatives," but some clubists wanted the resignation of moderates in the government.

As planned, the demonstration moved off toward the Hôtel de ville after the election of the officers of the National Guard, with Etienne Cabet, François-Vincent Raspail, and others at the head of from 200,000 to 300,000 men. Ledru-Rollin, with the agreement of Lamartine, decided to beat the drums to call out the National Guard. Armand Marrast, mayor of Paris, was to prepare the defense of the Hôtel de ville, and General Nicolas Changarnier was to advise the government. The National Guard from wealthy areas began to shout, "Down with the communists!" and to utter threats against Cabet, Blanqui, Raspail, and even members of the government like Louis Blanc and Ledru-Rollin.

Thus when the demonstrators reached the Hôtel de ville, they found themselves facing Armand Barbès (an officer of the National Guard), the National Guard, the Mobile Guard, and even the students of the university and the professional schools. They were disarmed, insulted, and coldly received by an assistant to the mayor, and they left angry despite Blanc's assurances that this was all a misunderstanding. Lamartine had said that he was afraid of a plot to replace the Provisional Government with a Committee of Public Safety, like the one that the terrible Maximilien Robespierre had led during the first French Revolution. The National Guard, the armed bourgeoisie, were the victors of the day, and that night they tried to sabotage the meetings of the clubs. The clubs now began to think in terms of another revolution, and Ledru-Rollin, fearing this, tried unsuccessfully to arrest Blanqui.

The elections of 23 April 1848 were not disturbed, but when the results were announced, there were some violent demonstrations, such as those in Nantes, Nîmes, and Issoudun. In Rouen the workers, angry at the election results, rioted, the troops were called out, and on 25 and 26 April there were street battles that caused (according to the official figures) the deaths of 11 demonstrators, with 76 wounded and 250 arrested. In Limoges the workers, especially the raftsmen, attacked and disarmed the National Guard and formed, along with socialist bourgeois, a committee that would govern the city for more than two weeks until troops could reestablish order. By now, the government was dominated by antisocialist republicans.

The clubs were angry, especially the Centralization Committee that had succeeded the Club of Clubs. They again decided on a demonstration, this one ostensibly to bring to the Assembly a petition in favor of Poland on 12 May. Barbès and Blanqui, however, were reticent about the idea of a demonstration, especially one at the National Assembly, but the club members pushed them to act. The principal organizer of this demonstration was Aloysius Huber, president of the Centralization Committee of the Clubs. On 15 May about 150,000 clubists and workers, including workers from the National Workshops, met at the Place de la Bastille and moved toward the Concorde Bridge across the Seine to the National Assembly shouting, "Long live Poland!" and "Long live the Republic!"

The Assembly was not well defended because most of the National Guard was stationed on the Champs Elysées, and the Executive Commission decided not to redeploy them.

Consequently the few National Guardsmen on the Place de la Concorde were overwhelmed by the demonstrators, who crossed the Concorde Bridge to the National Assembly and, amid total confusion, invaded the meeting. Philippe Buchez, president of the Assembly, kept the meeting in session. François-Vincent Raspail went to the rostrum and read the petition, and then Barbès asked the demonstrators to leave. At that moment, Blanqui began to speak, first of Poland and then of the organization of labor and the misery of the workers. Barbès again mounted the rostrum and, after Ledru-Rollin and Blanc had tried to calm the crowd, he proposed that an army be sent to Poland financed by a tax on the rich.

Meanwhile, the Executive Commission sounded the alarm to call out the National Guard. Raspail left the National Assembly, but Barbès protested against the calling out of the Guard, and Huber, at about 4:15, proclaimed the Assembly to be dissolved. Barbès and Blanc were carried in triumph, but while Barbès gladly put himself at the head of the movement, Blanc refused to take part in this new revolution. The National Assembly emptied out after the list of members of a new Provisional Government (Barbès, Louis Blanc, Albert, Ledru-Rollin, Ferdinand Flocon, Marc Caussidière) had been read to it.

Barbès and Albert led the demonstrators toward the Hôtel de ville to install the new government, and they took it over without difficulty. But now the government began to organize repressive measures. Marrast, Alphonse de Lamartine, and Ledru-Rollin took charge of the dragoons, Mobile Guards, and National Guards who recaptured the Hôtel de ville and arrested Barbès and Albert. Blanc was insulted and threatened.

While the Assembly went back to work, the National Guard arrested Marie-Joseph Sobrier and Raspail, searched Cabet's house, and looked for Blanqui, and the prefect of police, Caussidière, was forced to resign. Three clubs were closed. Huber first hid, then was arrested and, once freed, exiled himself to England, although he later was to return to defend his actions. Blanqui was hunted down on 26 May. About four hundred were imprisoned and later brought before the high court of Bourges in March 1849. The club movement was decapitated, the Luxembourg Commission on labor was dismissed, and there was talk of closing the National Workshops; the socialists were in full retreat. Furthermore, after some Bonapartist demonstrations, the Assembly passed a law against demonstrations on 7 June: any participant in an armed gathering could be imprisoned if it did not disband after one warning. On 21 June the Assembly told all workers in the National Workshops under 25 to enroll in the army, and all others to prepare to leave Paris. On 22 June, hundreds of workers met at the Place du Panthéon and sent a delegation to see Alexandre-Thomas Marie, who received them coldly and threatened to evict them from Paris by force. When Pujol, the workers' delegate, brought back this news, the workers were angry. On June 23 they met at the Place de la Bastille to demand "Liberty or Death!" But the government, which had foreseen this insurrection, had made plans to suppress it.

The rebels, who had no leaders (these had been in jail since 15 May), began to build barricades in the east end of Paris. From 23 to 25 June they fought against about 50,000 soldiers (troops of the line, Mobile Guards, National Guards from the rich neighborhoods) commanded by Eugène Cavaignac, minister of war, who used cannon against them. On 24 June the Assembly pressured the Executive Commission to resign. Lamartine and Ledru-Rollin lost the most. Cavaignac became a dictator. By 25 June, the workers were losing. On that day, Monsignor Affre, archbishop of Paris, was killed, as was General Jean-Baptiste de Bréa, who was trying to negotiate with the rebels. The press lashed out at the insurgents. Cavaignac demanded unconditional surrender, and when the rebels refused these terms, the troops rushed the barricades on 26 June. The troops suffered about 1,000 dead and 2,500 wounded. More than 5,000 rebels were shot without a trial, especially at the Hôtel de ville. The Mobile Guard, composed of young workers and of young, uprooted rurals, was especially cruel. Gustave Flaubert, in his *Sentimental Education*, described the hatred between the combatants and the violence of the victors toward the vanquished. More than 15,000 were arrested; 6,374 were released, and 4,000 were transported to Algeria. The most serious cases were brought before military courts. The assassins of General Bréa were guillotined. The Assembly wanted to bring charges against Louis Blanc and Caussidière, who both had fled to Algeria. Following the June Days, the Assembly dissolved the National Workshops and closely regulated the clubs and the press.

These essentially Parisian days (despite a similar revolt in Marseilles) mark the defeat of the working class, both the poor in the National Workshops and the skilled artisans of the faubourg Saint-Antoine. The Republic, now decidedly conservative, put down riots in hundreds of towns, especially in the south and in the Massif central, between June and September 1848 against the 45 centime tax. These riots lasted into 1849 and sometimes took on a political coloration.

The last big demonstration in Paris took place in June 1849 and was provoked by French intervention against the republican revolution in Rome. The Mountain, and especially Ledru-Rollin, opposed this intervention and wanted to put the president and those ministers who had caused this violation of the constitution on trial. After the Assembly had refused, the Mountain organized a march on the Assembly with unarmed and ununiformed National Guards. This column, which marched along shouting, "Long live the Constitution!" and "Long live the Republic!" was dispersed by the cavalry. Some barricades went up, some representatives of the rebels were arrested, but Ledru-Rollin escaped. There were riots in some provincial cities like Lyons, and more than a thousand persons were arrested in the ensuing combats. Again, repressive measures were taken against the newspapers and the clubs, as well as against thirty-four representatives. Ledru-Rollin fled to England.

The final big demonstration on 13 June 1849 marked the defeat of the progressive republicans. Henceforth the conservative majority had a free hand. The streets would be calm until December 1851, even if from time to time the supporters of the Mountain would make themselves heard at election time. The demonstrations of 1848–49, tolerated at first, had later become the pretext for a systematic repression of socialists and communists that the government even seemed to welcome. This elimination of the Left created a political void that would later help to make the coup d'état of Louis-Napoleon Bonaparte a success.

M. Agulhon, *1848 ou l'apprentissage de la République (1848–1852)* (Paris, 1973); F. A. de Luna, *The French Republic under Cavaignac, 1848* (Princeton, 1969); R. Gossez, *Les ouvriers de Paris*, Bibliothèque de la Révolution de 1848, vol. 24 (1967); J. M. Merriman, *The Repression of the Left in Revolutionary France, 1848–1851* (New Haven, 1978); R. Price, *The French Second Republic, A Social History* (London, 1972); P. Vigier, *La vie quotidienne à Paris et en province pendant les journées de 1848 (1847–1851)* (Paris, 1982).

Jean-Claude Caron, trans. E. Newman

Related entries: AFFRE; ALBERT; BARBES; BLANC; BLANQUI, L. A; BREA; BUCHEZ; CABET; CAUSSIDIERE; CAVAIGNAC, L. E.; CHAN-GARNIER; CLUB OF CLUBS; CLUBS, POLITICAL; FLAUBERT; FLOCON; GARDE MOBILE; GARNIER-PAGES; HUBER; JUNE DAYS; LAMARTINE; LEDRU-ROLLIN; LEGISLATIVE ASSEMBLY; LUXEMBOURG COMMISSION; MARIE; MARRAST; NATIONAL GUARD; NATIONAL WORKSHOPS; PROVISIONAL GOVERNMENT; RASPAIL; REVOLUTION OF 1848; ROMAN EXPEDITION; SOBRIER; WORKERS' COOPERATIVES.

DEPLANQUE, LOUIS (?–?), journalist and politician active during the Second Republic. This collector of books participated actively in the February Revolution of 1848. He was president of the Popincourt Club and a member of the Club of Clubs, alongside Amable Longepied and Marie-Joseph Sobrier, and vice-president of the Revolutionary Committee. After the June Days of 1848 and the repressive laws against the clubs, he founded the *Journal des pauvres*, whose first number appeared in September 1848. This monthly republican newspaper, which saw itself as a partisan of order, work, property, and freedom, had Armand Marrast as a collaborator and Edmond d'Alton-Shée as a backer.

V. Bouton, *Profils révolutionnaires* (Paris, 1848–49); *Le Journal des pauvres*, no. 1, September 1848, B.N. 4 Lc^2 1952.

Jean-Claude Caron, trans. E. Newman

Related entries: ALTON-SHEE; CLUB OF CLUBS; CLUBS, POLITICAL; JUNE DAYS; LONGEPIED; MARRAST; REPUBLICANS; REVOLUTION OF 1848; SOBRIER.

DEPUTIES, CHAMBER OF. SEE CHAMBER OF DEPUTIES.

DEROIN, JEANNE (1805–1894), socialist and feminist. A Parisian seamstress who became literate through adult evening classes, Jeanne Deroin was one of a number of women on whom the special place of women in the thought of Charles

Fourier and Barthélemy Enfantin had a profound impact. Before 1848 she established, with great difficulty, a school for poor children. Profoundly religious in a pantheistic way, she had a vision of a cooperative, family-based society of small proprietors.

In 1848 she founded the Club for the Emancipation of Women and wrote for women's newspapers, in which she attacked Proudhon as well as the resort to insurrection. In 1849 she established, with Pauline Roland and Gustave Lefrançais, the Association of Socialist Teachers and, after her unsuccessful attempt to stand in the elections of May 1849, the Fraternal Association of Democratic Socialists of Both Sexes for the Liberation of Women. She published an important pamphlet on women and the law, containing the Saint-Simonian stereotype of women's civilizing mission, and taught at the Women's Mutual Education Society. Her most important work was in the area of workers' cooperatives; in October 1849 her plan for a Union of Workers' Associations became a reality when 104 associations accepted her program and appointed her a director. This program was a remarkably comprehensive plan for a self-regulating society of cooperative production and distribution, leisure and social welfare, which foresaw equality of work between the sexes and the abolition of cash exchanges.

On 29 May 1850, eighty police raided her office, and she, with eight other women and thirty-eight men, was arrested. She was imprisoned until 3 June 1851 after a famous trial in front of packed galleries. In the atmosphere of repression after Louis Napoleon's coup, she fled to England in August 1852, where she published three women's almanacs, and where she remained until her death. The story of the last half of her life remains to be told.

L. Adler, *A l'aube du feminisme: les premières journalistes (1830–1850)* (Paris, 1979); J. Maitron, ed., *Dictionnaire biographique du mouvement ouvrier français*, pt. 1 (1789–1864) (Paris, 1964–66); E. Sullerot, ''Journaux féminins et lutte ouvrière (1848–1849),'' in J. Godechot, ed., *La Presse ouvrière, 1819–1850*, ''Bibliothèque de la Révolution de 1848'', vol. 23 (1966).

Peter McPhee

Related entries: COUP D'ETAT OF 2 DECEMBER 1851; ENFANTIN; FOUR-IER; PROUDHON; ROLAND; SAINT-SIMONIANISM; WOMEN'S NEWS-PAPERS; WORKERS' COOPERATIVES.

DESBORDES-VALMORE, MARCELINE-FELICITE-JOSEPHE-DES-BORDES, MADAME (1786–1859), actress, singer and romantic poetess. Called the ''female Lamartine'' by some, the ''Mater dolorosa of poetry'' by an admiring Charles-Augustin Sainte-Beuve, the poetess Marceline Desbordes was born in Douai on 20 June 1786, the daughter of a painter of coats of arms. Because her father's profession disappeared during the Revolution, Marceline Desbordes and her three siblings grew up in poverty. The family nevertheless refused an offer of assistance from affluent relatives in Holland because it would have required conversion to Protestantism. A serious family quarrel led Marceline and her mother to depart, probably in 1801, for Guadaloupe, where they hoped to find shelter with relatives. By the time of this journey, her acting career had already begun. When the two women arrived in Guadaloupe, they found it in the midst of a revolution and their relatives ruined; shortly thereafter, Mme. Desbordes died of yellow fever, and Marceline returned to France after overcoming great difficulties. She resumed her career as an actress and debuted as an operatic singer, performing roles in André-Modeste Grétry's *Lisbeth* and Gaspare Spontini's *Julie, ou le pot de fleurs*.

Marceline Desbordes suddenly abandoned her promising stage career in 1808 to devote herself for the next five years to the great love of her life. This tempestuous love affair, one that would affect her for the remainder of her life and that would greatly influence her poetry, was with Henri Latouche, a minor romantic writer. From this union, which also caused her family to reject her, a child was born on 25 June 1810. When the affair ended in 1813, Marceline Desbordes returned to the stage; she did not, however, resume singing. That same year, her first poem, "Je vous écris," appeared in print. While on tour in Brussels, she met and married in 1817 an actor of mediocre talent, Prosper Lanchantin, called Valmore, to whom she remained devoted throughout her life.

Marceline Desbordes-Valmore's first book of verse, *Elégies et romances*, appeared in 1818. Many of the sentimental, melancholy, and highly personal poems in this collection, poems that won for her a small following in the mid–1820s when such delicate verse was the vogue, are addressed to a mythical "Olivier," the name given to Latouche in her poetry. During the 1820s, Marceline Desbordes-Valmore gave up acting and loyally followed her husband as he sought roles to perform in numerous provincial theaters. This decade also saw the birth of her three children, Hippolyte, Ondine, and Inès, two of whom died young. Her favorite, Ondine, whom Charles-Augustin Sainte-Beuve once had hoped to marry, died of tuberculosis at the age of thirty-one. After her husband's career as an actor finally ended in the mid–1830s, Marceline Desbordes-Valmore returned to Paris, where she remained for the rest of her life, a minor figure on a brilliant literary stage. More volumes of poetry—*Pleurs* (1831), *Pauvres fleurs* (1839), and *Bouquets et Prières* (1843)—reached print and she enjoyed a small government pension of 2,000 francs. To support her family, she continued to write, producing a large number of stories, novels, and children's poems. She died of cancer on 23 July 1859.

Following her death, Gustave Revilliod published at his own expense a volume of her uncollected verse; Sainte-Beuve, who had championed her verse in the 1830s and the 1840s, reviewed the volume in a famous *Lundi* of 12 August 1860. Nine years later, he devoted five of the *Nouveaux lundis* to Marceline Desbordes-Valmore, saying of her that "something set itself singing within her." Since the mid-nineteenth century, she has attracted a number of detractors and a larger number of admirers. Among the latter was Paul Verlaine, who included her in his volume of *Les poètes maudits*.

J. Boulenger, *Mme Desbordes-Valmore, sa vie et son oeuvre* (Paris, 1927); M. Desbordes-Valmore, *Oeuvres poétiques*, 4 vols. (Paris, 1886–1922); L. Descaves, *La Vie amoureuse de Marceline Desbordes-Valmore* (Paris, 1925), and *La Vie douloureuse de Marceline Desbordes-Valmore* (Paris, 1911); E. Jasenas, *Marceline Desbordes-Valmore devant la critique* (Geneva, 1962).

Robert Brown

Related entries: LAMARTINE; LATOUCHE; ROMANTICISM; SAINTE-BEUVE.

DESCHAMPS (DESCHAMPS DE SAINT-AMAND), EMILE (1791–1871), promoter and theorist of romanticism, critic, minor poet, short story writer, and translator. Anne-Louis-Frédéric Deschamps de Saint-Amand, known as Emile Deschamps, was born at Bourges on 20 February 1791, to Jacques Deschamps de Saint-Amand and Marie de Massaubré. His was a French Huguenot bourgeois family whose ancestry included at least two ministers of the Calvinist faith. His father held government posts administering public lands from the *ancien régime* to the Restoration, cultivated a strong interest in classical theater and poetry, and developed contacts with writers and members of the *Académie* despite the bitter experiences of the Terror. Mme. Deschamps died in 1800 soon after the birth of another son, Antoine-François-Marie, henceforth known as Antony (or Antoni). Not much is known of the childhood of the Deschamps brothers. They were raised by a servant whom they called Bonne and were consistently exposed in the late Empire and early Restoration to their father's literary eclecticism in one of the first regular informal groups that one may link to romanticism: the salon of Jacques Deschamps, rue Saint-Florentin. He welcomed both members of the old school and the young heretics who flirted with change. Emile's education by a clerical tutor at Orléans, though classical and Catholic, was fraught with Chateaubriand mysticism and with doses of fantasy and the supernatural. Although sensitive by nature, Emile displayed a happy, extroverted personality that complemented the quiet, morose, brooding attitude of Antony. The aristocratic Alfred de Vigny was perhaps Emile's closest childhood companion, and he often visited the son of his father's old friend, M. le chevalier de Vigny. Mme. de Staël's political, pedagogical, and literary ideas and Chateaubriand's brilliant writing style were thoroughly discussed in Jacques Deschamps' Salon, and they soon became Emile's idols. His adolescent years were filled with the elements of gothic literature and a special fascination for the old times going back to the Middle Ages. It is not surprising that he admired Gabriel-Marie Legouvé and Charles-Hubert Millevoye and that his first effort should take the form of troubadour poems. Although he respected tradition, his liberal attitude was enhanced by *De l' Allemagne*, which led him to admire Schiller and Goethe as well as André Chénier. Appointed to a position like his father's as the Empire waned, he helped defend the fortress at Vincennes during the sieges of 1814 and 1815.

About 1816, Emile Deschamps married Aglaé Viénot, daughter of a notary. She was a simple, charming woman, who for forty years would remain devoted to making his life and that of the father he worshiped comfortable and happy. Their relationship was more tender than passionate, and they remained childless.

In 1818, Deschamps worked at the *ministère des finances* with a childhood friend, Henri de Latouche, the liberal republican, already enjoying some literary success. His passion for the theater led to joint production of two plays. The second, *Tour de Faveur*, a satire of literary circles, was performed one hundred times. Henceforth, the two dedicated themselves to promoting the ideas of Mme. de Staël. They chose Chénier's *Idylles* to begin their campaign. Latouche edited and published them in 1819, and Deschamps had them read in his father's *salon*.

Toward the end of 1820, it became apparent that the true host of the rue Saint-Florentin (later rue Ville L'Evêque) salon was no longer Jacques Deschamps but his son Emile. Most of the poets who shared his liberal cosmopolitan attitude toward literature had acquired the habit of meeting at his home. Alfred de Vigny, Victor Hugo, Charles Nodier, Alexandre Soumet, Alexandre Guiraud, and many others, including several women, had become regulars. Early in 1823, when Hugo's *Conservateur littéraire* ceased publication, the Deschamps guests needed a journal, and the stars among them, with Emile in the lead (though truly a Voltairian classicist much more in tune with the Stendhal/Latouche/Delécluze liberals), founded *La Muse française*. In one of its late issues, Deschamps inserted a bold and witty response (*La Guerre en temps de paix . . .*) to Louis-Simon Auger's famous April 1824 speech condemning romanticism. The *cénacle* or *équipe* of *La Muse française* only lasted a year. In politics and literature, its members still represented too many different views, and Soumet's defection was more than it could bear. By a happy coincidence, Charles Nodier, whom Deschamps had long recognized as one of the romantic pioneers, had just been appointed librarian and was ready to welcome him and his companions to his Arsenal salon. During those crucial mid–1820s, Deschamps' voice, as literary critic of the romantic side, commanded the respect of his companions. By 1827, the conservative and liberal writers were united in Hugo's *cénacle* and, encouraged by the triumphs of the Shakespeare troupe in Paris that same year, had focused on the romantic drama to achieve their victory, Deschamps' role was to collaborate with Vigny to translate *Romeo and Juliette*. Unfortunately, though it was accepted at the Théâtre-français in 1828, it was not produced until many years later, having been preempted by Vigny's *Othello*. In any event, Deschamps was in some measure responsible for the Shakespeare vogue in the romantic group at that time. His interest was, however, much broader and his contributions to the cause became much more significant when he attained his full potential as a theorist with his *Etudes françaises et étrangères*, published in November 1828. He had translated Schiller, Goethe, and the *Romancero*, and now he provided one of the crucial manifestos of the romantic school, not the work itself (which, through translated poems, reaffirmed Mme. de Staël's efforts in favor of foreign literatures) but the preface that eloquently defends the new aesthetic as a natural, evolutionary phenomenon. It reinforced the *Cromwell* preface. Within a year, at least four editions had appeared. The author was admitted to the Legion of Honor, and his work won him the admiration and esteem of the great writers of his day. At the premier of *Hernani*, on that fateful February day of 1830, it is not surprising that Deschamps was one of the most vocal defenders of the new dramatic style.

After the political and literary victories of 1830, the school dispersed, and the former militants, having attained their goal of individual freedom, pursued their careers independently. Emile Deschamps was no exception. More than half his life still remained, and he trod a number of paths during those forty years. Until 1845, he is best described as a dilletante venturing into criticism of romantic art and operatic music and into music composition while maintaining his close friendships with Vigny, Hugo, Alphonse de Lamartine, and Alfred de Musset, whose works he evaluated. During that period, he also published poetry (1841) and a personal translation of *Roméo et Juliette* and one of *Macbeth* (both 1844).

The 1850s found Deschamps enhancing the ambiance of the imperial salons. He consoled himself of the loss of several *Muse française* colleagues by escaping into the world of prose fiction. He produced several short stories and novellas, some moralistic in the eighteenth-century style, some in the troubadour vein, and several were supernatural tales in the Nodier style.

Emile Deschamps' final years were spent in the elite intellectual society of Versailles. The death of his wife left him grief stricken and affected his health. He lost his sight and suffered much during that period, but he always retained his intellectual curiosity and his cosmopolitan love for the humanities. The young *parnassiens* even solicited his judgments on German and Slavic masterpieces. He obviously lacked the creative talent of a Hugo or a Musset, but the role he played in the triumph of romanticism, though secondary, was critical and essential.

J. Bertaut, *L'Epoque romantique* (Paris, 1947); R. Bray, *Chronologie du romantisme (1804–1830)* (Paris, 1963); H. Girard, *Emile Deschamps, 1791–1871* (Paris, 1921); L. Séché, *Le Cénacle de la Muse française, 1823–1827* (Paris, 1908).

Paul Comeau

Related entries: ARSENAL, SALON OF; AUGER; CHATEAUBRIAND; DE-LECLUZE; GUIRAUD; *HERNANI*; HUGO; LAMARTINE; LATOUCHE; LE-GOUVE; *LA MUSE FRANCAISE*; MUSSET; NODIER; ROMANTICISM; SALON D'EMILE DESCHAMPS; STAEL; STENDHAL; SOUMET; VIGNY.

DE SCHONEN, AUGUSTINE-JEAN, BARON (1782–1849), magistrate and liberal deputy of the Restoration and July Monarchy. Born at Saint-Denis on 12 February 1782, De Schonen studied law and in 1811 entered the imperial court of Paris as a judge-auditor. During the Hundred Days he served as solicitor-general, but the Restoration demoted him to a substitute's position. He became a leading member of the carbonari in the early 1820s. Nevertheless in 1819 he became a councillor in the royal court of Paris where his liberalism gained favor with the Left and the constitutional royalists. At the funeral of Jacques-Antoine-Manuel, his fellow carbonaro, in August 1827, De Schonen delivered an oration that smacked of revolution. In 1827 the fifth arrondissement of Paris elected him to the Chamber of Deputies by an overwhelming majority. In the Deputies he joined the liberal opposition, opposing the Polignac ministry and voting for the address criticizing the king in March 1830. Reelected by an even greater majority in July 1830, De Schonen became a dedicated leader of the July Revolution.

On 26 July at a meeting at the offices of the *National*, he suggested calling the people to arms and participated actively in the discussions among the deputies assembled in Paris. He was a member of the Provisional Municipal Commission of Paris and also of the commission to establish a provisional national government. In these capacities he vigorously demanded the dethronement of Charles X, rejecting the king's subsequent efforts at compromise. He also opposed the plans of the Orleanists. Nevertheless when the duc d'Orléans, as lieutenant general of the kingdom, sent a committee to Rambouillet to deal with the deposed Charles X, De Schonen was one of the two representatives chosen by the Deputies for this function. And he was one of the three commissioners who accompanied Charles to Cherbourg to supervise his departure from France. The July Revolution ultimately led to De Schonen's appointment as a colonel in the National Guard and as a member of the Paris municipal council. Louis-Philippe later named him attorney general to the Cour des comptes. He continued to serve in the Deputies until 1837, generally voting with the government. In October 1837 he was appointed to the Chamber of Peers, his acceptance outraging his liberal friends. The 1848 February Revolution removed him from public office, and he died in Paris on 4 December 1849.

Archives parlementaires; J. L. Bory, *La Révolution de juillet* (Paris, 1972); L. Girard, *Le Libéralisme en France de 1814 à 1848* (Paris, 1967); D. Pinkney, *The French Revolution of 1830* (Princeton, 1972); A. Robert et al., *Dictionnaire des parlementaires français* (Paris, 1889–91); P. Thureau-Dangin, *Le Parti libéral sous la restauration* (Paris, 1876).

James K. Kieswetter

Related entries: CARBONARI; MANUEL; MUNICIPAL COMMISSION; *LE NATIONAL*; POLIGNAC; PROVISIONAL GOVERNMENT.

DE SERRE. SEE SERRE.

DESHAYES, CHARLES (?-?), secretary of the Club of the Mountain in 1848. This Club of the Mountain met (infrequently) at the Chateau-Rouge in Montmartre in Paris. Deshayes was one of the two secretaries along with Laroche, and Dulaurier was the president. These three signed the declaration of principles of the club, which had been organized to prepare for the election of officers of the National Guard and of deputies to the Constituent Assembly.

Deshayes was also one of the commissioners of the Père Duchêne Banquet, a banquet where each participant had to pay 5 sous, which earned him a sentence of thirteen months in prison for embezzling more than 11,000 francs given to him by the banqueteers.

A. Lucas, *Les Clubs et les clubistes,* 2d ed. (Paris, 1851).

Jean-Claude Caron, trans. E. Newman

Related entries: CONSTITUTION OF 1848; NATIONAL GUARD; REPUB-LICANS; YOUNG (NEW) MOUNTAIN SOCIETY.

DESSOLLE, JEAN-JOSEPH-PAUL-AUGUSTIN, MARQUIS (1767–1828), general of the Revolution and Empire; peer, minister, and prime minister of the Restoration. Jean Joseph Dessolle (also sometimes spelled Dessole or Dessolles) was born at Auch (Gers) on 3 July 1767 to a noble family whose holdings included the bishopric of Digne. He entered military service before the Revolution and by 1792 was a captain in the army of Pyrénées-Occidentales. Although he lost his rank as a result of the law against former nobles, he was soon recalled to active duty and on 1 November 1793 was appointed adjutant general. During the Empire he became a general and councillor of state.

Dessolle was one of the first generals to abandon Napoleon in March 1814. On 1 April the French Provisional Government gave him command of the Paris National Guard and later of the line troops of the first military division. He helped influence Alexander I against a regency for the king of Rome. Artois shortly appointed him to the provisional Council of State. Then when Louis XVIII returned, he appointed Dessolle chief of the general staff of the National Guard and named him to the Order of Saint Louis and the Legion of Honor. On 4 June 1814 the king gave him a peerage. When Napoleon returned from Elba, Dessolle made a futile effort to stop his advance on Paris. Then Dessolle escorted the king as far as Béthune before returning to spend the Hundred Days on an estate near Paris.

Retaining his seat in the Peers at the Second Restoration, Dessolle voted for the death of Marshal Michel Ney. Although he resumed command of the Guard, he soon abandoned it but was appointed to the privy council. In the Peers he followed a moderate monarchist course but played little role in public affairs. He supported freedom of the press and Gouvion Saint-Cyr's army bill of 1818. On 28 December 1818 he became president of the Council of Ministers, with the portfolio of foreign affairs. He now became increasingly liberal in his views. Although he enjoyed Louis XVIII's confidence, Dessolle was really only a facade behind which Elie Decazes, the king's favorite, ran the cabinet. On 17 November 1819 Dessolle resigned from the cabinet in opposition to a proposed election law reform that Decazes had pushed. Decazes then became prime minister in his own right. Dessolle remained in the Chamber of Peers until his death on 2 November 1828 in Montluchet (Seine-et-Oise).

Archives parlementaires; P. Duvergier de Hauranne, *Histoire du gouvernement par-lementaire en France, 1814–1848* (Paris, 1857–71); E. D. Pasquier, *Histoire de mon temps* (Paris, 1893–95); A. Robert et al., *Dictionnaire des parlementaires français* (Paris, 1889–91).

James K. Kieswetter

Related entries: DECAZES; GOUVION SAINT-CYR; NEY.

DESTUTT DE TRACY, ANTOINE-LOUIS-CLAUDE, COMTE (1754–1836), major philosopher of the *idéologue* circle, senator (1799–1814), and peer (1814–36). Although from an old military and court noble family, Tracy sympathized with the moderate Revolution and emerged from eleven months in prison in 1794 to begin a new philosophical career. After his 1796 memoirs to the Second Class of the Institute, he became renowned for inventing "ideology" to define the science of ideas, including physical-mental relations, analysis of mental faculties in the style of Condillac, grammar, and logic. In a wider sense, ideology aspired to unify all the sciences, with special attention to morality, legislation, and political economy.

A strongly anticlerical agnostic and a rigid philosophical monist (more materialist in expression than Cabanis), Tracy endured the attacks of V. Cousin and other conservatives on sensualism after 1815. Yet he gained fame for his political and economic works. The first French editions of the *Commentaire sur l'Esprit des lois* (written 1805–7; U.S. edition, 1811; French, 1817 and 1819) omitted passages critical of monarchy and even paid lip-service to constitutional monarchy, but the book still inspired Restoration liberals. Distinguishing national representative governments that promoted equal rights from special governments protecting privilege, Tracy advocated a "democracy of enlightened reason." He even called for universal male suffrage, preferably expressed indirectly by electoral colleges without property qualifications. He remained a firm supporter of separation of church and state, divorce, and division of large inheritances.

The *Traité de la volonté et de ses effets* (written by 1811, published 1815 as vols. 4 and 5 of *Elémens d'idéologie*) defended a resolutely liberal economics, with property rights deduced from possession of personal faculties. Commercial exchange was the essence of society, and, following Adam Smith and J.-B. Say, the industrial entrepreneur was the heart of the body politic. Tracy attacked idle landowners and *rentiers* as threats to productivity and prosperity. He was aware of the dangers of inequalities of wealth and power, but he remained confident that private and public interests were reconcilable (hence the attacks by Marx in *The German Ideology* and *Capital*). Tracy opposed high taxation and high public debt as ruinous to citizens.

Since Tracy was inactive during the Hundred Days, he retained seats in the Académie française and as a peer. Close to the Lafayette circle, he knew some of the carbonari conspirators of 1820. In the Peers he opposed press restrictions, the indemnity to *émigrés*, and primogeniture. In July 1830, he was an aged figure in a silk suit who gave moral support to the insurgents at the barricades.

Tracy's disciples abroad included Thomas Jefferson and several Latin American revolutionaries. In France, his general philosophy and essay "De l'amour" inspired Stendhal, and his liberal politics influenced journalists such as the Fabre brothers and the Grenoble lawyer Joseph Rey. By 1836 *idéologue* philosophy gave way to positivism and *idéologue* politics to liberal republicanism. To Saint-Simon, Tracy's view of society was insufficiently organic, and Auguste Comte rejected individual psychology as a basis for social analysis.

A.-L.-C. Destutt de Tracy, *A Commentary and Review of Montesquieu's Spirit of Laws* (Philadelphia, 1811) and *Elémens d'idéologie*, 5 vols. (Paris, 1824–26); G. Gusdorf, *La conscience révolutionnaire, les Idéologues* (Paris, 1978); B. Head, *Ideology and Social Science* (Dordrecht, 1985); E. Kennedy, *A Philosophe in the Age of Revolution* (Philadelphia, 1978); S. Moravia, *Il pensiero degli Ideologues* (Florence, 1974); C. Welch, *Liberty and Utility* (New York, 1984).

Martin S. Staum

Related entries: CABANIS; COMTE, A.; COUSIN; FABRE, J.-R.-A.; FABRE, M.-J.-J.-V.; *IDEOLOGUES*; LAFAYETTE: REY: SAINT-SIMON; SAY; STENDHAL.

DIDOT. See FIRMIN-DIDOT.

DIVORCE, ABOLITION OF, effected by a law of 8 May 1816. Divorce, which had not been allowed under the Old Regime, was established and regulated by legislation adopted on 20 September 1792. It resulted partly from the general secularizing influence of the Revolution and from the assumption by the state of church functions such as the recording of births, deaths, and marriages. There was an immediate rash of divorces, and abuses resulted. But the number rapidly decreased. The National Convention somewhat liberalized the divorce legislation of its predecessor. Although many in the Council of State opposed it, Napoleon's Civil Code maintained divorce, perhaps because as early as 1802 Napoleon was thinking of a divorce from Josephine. But the allowable reasons were greatly reduced and the consequences made more severe for divorced persons. Judicial separation, as allowed under the Old Regime, was reestablished by law. Divorce, however, was prohibited for members of the Bonaparte family, except for Napoleon himself.

The Restoration of the Bourbons prepared the way for the abolition of divorce. The Charter made Roman Catholicism the religion of the state, thus greatly increasing the authority of canon law. The Charter also provided that the Civil Code and other existing laws were maintained unless legally abrogated or in conflict with the Charter. The opponents of divorce—the clericals, the conservatives, the Congrégation, and the ultraroyalists who demanded the restoration of church power—now had their chance. Led by Louis de Bonald and the *chambre introuvable*, they described divorce as an assault on society, morality, and religion. It was decried in both chambers, especially in the Deputies, as licentious, corrupting, pernicious, and a cause of infidelity. Even opponents of repeal hesitated to speak for fear of appearing antireligious. Consequently, having passed the Peers by a comfortable margin and the Deputies by 225 to

11, on 8 May 1816 a law was issued abolishing divorce in France. It even provided that in cases where a divorce had been decreed but had not yet been executed, the marriage was to continue. However, judicial separation was allowed for many of the same specific reasons that had previously been grounds for divorce. Divorce was not legalized in France again until 27 July 1884.

Archives Parlementaires; G. Thibault-Laurent, *La Première introduction du divorce en France sous la révolution et l'empire, 1792–1816* (Clermont-Ferrand, 1938).

James K. Kieswetter

Related entries: BONALD; *CHAMBRE INTROUVABLE;* CONGREGATION; ULTRAROYALISTS.

DOCTRINAIRES, independent or moderate royalists; moderate faction of the royalist party that split with the ultras in late 1815; generally supporters of the Charter and the policies of Louis XVIII. The extreme policies, especially the amnesty law urged by the ultraroyalists in late 1815 and early 1816, caused a group of moderates to split off from them. Led by Etienne-Denis Pasquier, Pierre-François de Serre, and Pierre Royer-Collard, this group took their cue from the organizational success of the ultras' *réunion Piet* and formed their own, the Club Saint-Honoré, so called because they rented a hall on the rue Saint-Honoré. The peers of this persuasion met at Cardinal Louis-François de Bausett's. In essence men of similar views dominated the cabinets from July 1815 until December 1821. Thus these moderates were natural allies of Armand-Emmanuel de Richelieu in his struggle with the *chambre introuvable* in 1815–16. Louis XVIII's support of Richelieu against the ultras gave these moderates a rallying point, and the 1816 elections gave them cohesion as well as a political victory. As the ministerial party from 1815 to 1821, the moderates enjoyed the use of the newspaper the *Moniteur*. They also influenced the *Journal général de France* and the *Archives philosophiques, politiques et littéraires*. Within the moderate royalist group, there were differences of opinion. Joseph-Louis-Joachim Lainé and Richelieu led the more conservative wing, Pasquier the Center, and Elie Decazes and Laurent Gouvion Saint-Cyr the liberals. With the advent of the liberal independent faction in the summer of 1817, these moderates became the Center party in the Chambers.

As early as 1816, however, there evolved within the moderate camp another faction nicknamed the *doctrinaires*. It was led by Royer-Collard, one of the most profound political thinkers of the Restoration. Its members included Camille Jordan, François Guizot, Prosper de Barante, de Serre, Victor de Broglie, and Charles de Rémusat. Guizot served as their chief publicist. The salon of the duchesse de Broglie became their meeting place. Because of the intellectual ability of these *doctrinaires*, they had influence far out of proportion to their numbers, not only within the Chambers and the moderate party but also with the general public as well. In 1819 the *doctrinaires* started the newspaper the *Courier*. Later, in the 1820s the *Globe* became their principal organ. They especially supported the ministries of Jean-Joseph Dessolle and Decazes in 1818–

19 and had a major role in the passage of the 1819 press law. But they turned against Decazes when he became more conservative in late 1819 and early 1820.

The moderate royalists, by contrast, did not drop their support of Decazes until after the assassination of the duc de Berry. The moderates supported the policies attempted by the second Richelieu ministry, including the Law of the double vote. They were even represented in the Villèle ministry by Christophe de Chabrol de Crouzol, minister of marine, but they were more comfortable with the Jean-Baptiste de Martignac cabinet. The *doctrinaires*, however, helped bring down this government when, by insisting on more liberal concessions than the king or cabinet would approve, they helped prevent adoption of Martignac's reform bill. Many of the moderates and *doctrinaires*, such as Pasquier and Royer-Collard, rallied to the July Monarchy. The factional designations of the Restoration, however, lost most of their meaning after 1830 and thus these men are henceforth found under other banners.

T. D. Beck, *French Legislators 1800–1834* (Berkeley, 1974); H. Bergasse, *Histoire de l'assemblée* (Paris, 1967); P. Campbell, *French Electoral Systems and Elections since 1789* (London, 1958); J. Crauffon, *La Chambre des députés sous la restauration* (Paris, 1908); P. Duvergier de Hauranne, *Histoire du gouvernement parlementaire en France, 1814–1848* (Paris, 1857–71); L. Girard, *Le Liberalisme en France de 1814 a 1848* (Paris, 1967); A. T. Vaulabelle, *Histoire des deux restaurations* (Paris, 1874).

James K. Kieswetter

Related entries: ARCHIVES PHILOSOPHIQUES, POLITIQUES, ET LIT-TERAIRES; BARANTE; BAUSSET; BERRY, C. F.; BROGLIE, A.; BROGLIE, A.-L.-V.; CHABROL DE CROUZOL; *LE COURIER*; DECAZES; DESSOLLE; *LE GLOBE*; GOUVION SAINT-CYR; GUIZOT; JORDAN; *LE JOURNAL GENERAL DE FRANCE*; LAINE; MARTIGNAC; PASQUIER; RE-MUSAT; RICHELIEU; ROYER-COLLARD; SERRE; ULTRAROYALISTS.

DOLLFUS, JEAN (1800–1887), manufacturer and economist. The son of a successful Alsatian manufacturer of calicoes and printed textiles in Mulhouse, Dollfuss became general manager of the firm and greatly expanded its operations. He was also an energetic advocate of free trade and tariff reform, even favoring the repeal of duties that benefited his industry. Active in the negotiation of the Cobden-Chevalier Treaty of 1860, which established de facto free trade between France and England, Dolfuss was a long-time mayor of Mulhouse and prominent philanthropist, particularly in the area of model workers' housing. A bitter critic of German annexation in 1870, Dollfuss refused all honors from the German government and used his election to the Reichstag in 1877 to campaign for the liberation of Alsace and Lorraine.

J. Dollfuss, *Plus de prohibitions* (Paris, 1853), and *De la Levée des prohibitions douanières* (Paris, 1859); D. P. Silverman, *Reluctant Union* (Pennsylvania State University, 1972); *Société Industrielle de Mulhouse, Histoire documentaire de l'industrie de Mulhouse et de ses environs au XIXe siècle* (Mulhouse, 1902).

David Longfellow

DOMESTIC INDUSTRY. See COTTAGE INDUSTRY.

DOMESTIC SERVANTS. Live-in domestic servants were a hallmark of the nineteenth-century middle class, and service constituted the largest nonagricultural occupational group for most of the century. Although the Revolution of 1789 did much to erode the image of the servant as aristocratic confidante, the rising wealth of the commercial and industrial middle classes provided expanding employment for live-in servants in the nineteenth century. In fact, live-in domestic servants became characteristic of the middle-class way of life before 1850. The number of urban domestic servants continued to increase in the early nineteenth century, stimulated by a period of intense urban migration, for servants were in the majority young, single females recruited from the countryside by the promise of available work, which included room and board. The category of domestic servants also continued to include many agricultural servants and even shop assistants or industrial employees before 1850, for both occupational tasks and conditions of work varied widely for early nineteenth-century servants.

Widespread complaints about servants' laziness, dishonesty, and sexual promiscuity were scarcely new, but they mark a middle-class fear of the outsider in the home and suggest that the intensity of the mistress-servant relationship was often hostile. Servants earned little more than room and board and were closely surveyed by careful employers. The work was hardly attractive, but positions were readily available and provided an opportunity to move into a large urban center without the difficulties of securing both job and lodging. Thus, the occupation remained the largest employer of women until 1906.

Meanwhile, the question of selecting servants and keeping them became so important for the middle classes that young middle-class women received as much advice on this subject as on the choice of a husband.

A. Chatelain, "Migrations et domesticité feminine urbaine en France, XVIIIe-XXe siècles," *Revue d'histoire économique et sociale* 47 (1969); M. Cusenier, *Les domestiques en France* (Paris, 1912); A. Martin-Fugier, *La place des bonnes* (Paris, 1979); T. M. McBride, *The Domestic Revolution* (London, 1977).

Theresa McBride

Related entries: AGRICULTURE; MIGRATION.

DONNADIEU, GABRIEL, VICOMTE (1777–1849), general of the Empire and Restoration and deputy of the Restoration. Gabriel Donnadieu was born in Nîmes to a Protestant family on 11 December 1777. As a youth he acquired a lasting devotion to the ideas of the Revolution. Enlisting as a cadet, he was commissioned a sublieutenant in 1791 and served in various units from the Rhine to the Vendée in 1792 and 1793. He especially distinguished himself on 6 February 1794 at the bridge at Tiffaughes where, with only a thirty-man platoon, he halted 3,000 Vendéans. Shortly after he was offered a promotion to major but declined because of his age. In his numerous battles, Donnadieu suffered so many wounds that in April 1797 he was given a medical discharge; however, he requested a return to active duty.

In November 1799 Donnadieu was posted as captain aide-de-camp to André Masséna and was promoted to major on 22 March 1800. He was arrested in May 1802 for plotting the death of Napoleon and was imprisoned first in the Temple and then in the chateau of Lourdes; however, he was amnestied and given the Legion of Honor in 1804. He returned to active duty, first with the army in the west of France and then in Spain where he served as colonel of a regiment in 1808. Napoleon named him a baron of the Empire in 1809 and in August 1811 promoted him to brigadier general and made him governor of the Hyères Islands. However, Marshal Nicolas-Jean de Soult ordered his arrest for an English-inspired attempt to foment rebellion in the army in Portugal. Although a court-martial acquitted Donnadieu, he was interned under police surveillance at Tours.

Donnadieu regained his freedom at the defeat of Napoleon and quickly offered his services to the Bourbons, who made him commander of the department of Indre-et-Loire and gave him the Order of Saint Louis. He spent the Hundred Days at Ghent and returned to France after Waterloo. Louis XVIII promoted him to lieutenant general in October 1815 and gave him command of the Seventh Military Division at Grenoble in December. There on 4 May 1816 Jean-Paul Didier hoped to launch a Bonapartist insurrection. When the prefect got wind of it and asked for military aid, Donnadieu flew into a rage, accusing the prefect of trespassing in the general's domain. But when Donnadieu realized the seriousness of the plot, he suppressed it with the utmost brutality, killing at least six in the affair and executing twenty-five after subsequent provost court proceedings. For his handling of this affair, one of the most despicable of the Restoration, Donnadieu was made a vicomte and a knight of Saint Louis. The relatives of his victims began action against him in 1819, resulting in his disciplinary confinement in the Abbaye. In 1818 he was involved in efforts to prevent the withdrawal of the Allied occupation army, and he was one of the leaders of the Conspiracy at the Water's Edge, a plot to arrest the cabinet and install an ultra ministry.

In November 1820 the department of Bouches-du-Rhône elected him to the Chamber of Deputies where he joined the extreme ultraroyalists, championing crown and church supremacy over the Chamber. His harsh attacks on the Richelieu ministry resulted in January 1821 in his removal from the list of active lieutenant generals. Among other things, he accused the government of having fomented all the insurrections of the early Restoration. The Villèle cabinet, however, recalled Donnadieu to active service, first as commander of the Fourth Military Division at Tours and then in 1823 in the army invading Spain, where Artois' influence obtained a command for him. He was, however, so insubordinate that Marshal Jeannot de Moncey removed him. Although he was reelected to the Deputies in 1824, he participated little in politics henceforth. He received the grand cross of the Order of Saint Louis at the consecration of Charles X in 1825. Donnadieu was not reelected in 1827, and the July Revolution ended his military career. He retired to Courbevoie (Seine) where he continued his polemics, writing pamphlets and addresses on various political subjects and the Grenoble affair. He incurred a fine and imprisonment for one particular tract that attacked Louis-Philippe. Donnadieu died in Courbevoie on 17 June 1849.

Archives parlementaires; H. Dumolard, *La Terreur blanche dans l'Isère. Jean-Paul Didier et la conspiration de Grenoble* (Grenoble, 1928); E. Guillon, *Les Complots militaires sous la restauration* (Paris, 1895); D. Resnick, *The White Terror and the Political Reaction After Waterloo* (Cambridge, 1966); A. B. Spitzer, *Old Hatred and Young Hopes* (Cambridge, 1971).

James K. Kieswetter

Related entries: CONSPIRACY AT THE WATER'S EDGE; RICHELIEU; SOULT; SPAIN, 1823 FRENCH INVASION OF; VILLELE.

DOUBLE VOTE, LAW OF THE. Presented in June 1820 by the second Richelieu ministry, the goal of the law was to weaken the liberal Left in the Chamber of Deputies by giving more weight to the votes of the richest electors, who were supposed to be the most conservative. The Chamber was to be composed of 430 members instead of the 258 now in place. The 258 previously elected by the electoral colleges of the departments would henceforth be elected by electoral colleges in each arrondissement, where all electors paying 300 francs in direct taxes or more could vote. The 172 new seats would be chosen from departmental electoral colleges or *grands collèges* formed by the one-fourth of those electors who paid the highest taxes. Thus the one-fourth of the electors who paid the highest taxes would vote twice: once in their arrondissement colleges and once in the departmental *grand collège*. In practice this double vote law attained its goal, bringing in a right-wing majority.

Guillaume de Bertier de Sauvigny, trans. E. Newman

Related entries: CHAMBER OF DEPUTIES; ELECTIONS AND ELECTORAL SYSTEMS; RICHELIEU.

DOUDEAUVILLE, AMBROISE-POLYCARPE DE LA ROCHEFOUCAULD, DUC DE (1765–1841), peer and minister of the Restoration. Born in Paris on 2 April 1765 to one of the greatest of French noble families, Doudeauville became a sublieutenant in the dragoons in 1781 and rose to major before he emigrated in 1792. After years of traveling in Europe, he returned to France during the Consulate. In spite of Napoleon's insistence, Doudeauville refused all public office except membership in the general council of the department of Marne. On 4 June 1814, however, the restored Bourbons appointed him to the Chamber of Peers. He remained inactive during the Hundred Days.

Returning to the Peers after Waterloo, Doudeauville joined the ultraroyalist faction, voting for the execution of Marshal Michel Ney and opposing liberal measures such as freedom of the press. In September 1822 he became director-general of posts, which shocked some who thought it demeaning. Yet in that office he demonstrated considerable administrative ability and instituted several significant reforms. Just before the death of Louis XVIII, Doudeauville became minister of the king's household, a post he occupied until May 1827. One of his first tasks in this post was to help plan the coronation ceremony of Charles X. Among other things he was responsible for the state's acquiring the estate of Grignon and establishing there a successful agriculture school. Although he was an ardent royalist and supporter and close personal friend of Charles X, he nevertheless differed with the policies of Charles and his governments on several occasions. He sharply criticized the government's handling of the events surrounding the funeral of his cousin, the duc de La Rochefoucauld-Liancourt, even writing to the king personally about it. He likewise opposed the abolition of the National Guard and resigned from his ministry when this was accomplished, concealing his apprehension from no one. He then devoted himself to charitable works, although in June 1830 he wrote to Charles X cautioning him against a coup. During the July Revolution he spoke in the Peers in opposition to the exile of the Bourbon family, and then in January 1831 he notified the president of the Peers that henceforth he would no longer sit in the Chamber. His name was then removed from the list of peers of France. Thereafter Doudeauville lived in retirement and died at Montmirail (Sarthe) on 2 June 1841. He left his memoirs, published in 1861–64.

Archives parlementaires; V. Beach, *Charles X* (Boulder, Colo., 1971); A. Robert et al., *Dictionnaire des parlementaires français* (Paris, 1889–91); D. Seward, *The Bourbon Kings of France* (New York, 1976).

James K. Kieswetter

Related entries: CORONATION OF CHARLES X; LA ROCHEFOUCAULD; LA ROCHEFOUCAULD-LIANCOURT; NATIONAL GUARD; NEY; ULTRAROYALISTS.

LE DRAPEAU BLANC (1819–1830), ultraroyalist newspaper of the Restoration. Founded in January 1819 as a periodical but quickly changing to a daily when more permissive press laws came into operation later in the year, the *Drapeau* expressed from the start the most extreme ultraroyalist views to be found in the whole of the Restoration press. Its editor, Alphonse Dieudonné de Martainville, had acquired a certain amount of notoriety as a playwright and actor before entering journalism, and he brought to his new profession an air of drama in such matters as, for example, the *Drapeau*'s banner headline: "Long live the king, anyhow!" The *Drapeau*'s vigorous, though somewhat tasteless, attacks on Elie Decazes, whose mildly left-wing policies it did not hesitate to declare responsible for the murder of the duc de Berry, were popular enough to increase the sales of the newspaper from an initial 2,000 to over 4,000 within a year. After the fall of Decazes, Martainville looked forward to extreme ultraroyalist policies from succeeding governments; but he was disappointed, first in the duc de Richelieu, who allowed the censorship committee of 1820 to remove a great many articles from the *Drapeau*, and later in Joseph de Villèle, whose successful attempts to deprive the *émigrés* of all claims to the restoration of their former lands by offering them financial compensation seemed to Martainville disgraceful. Martainville was not averse to taking subsidies from the government, however. Opposition to Villèle did not bring the *Drapeau* as many subscribers as opposition to Decazes had done, and its financial position was not strong. In 1824 it was bought over by a pro-government committee for the sum of 180,000 francs, and Martainville was retained as editor on the understanding that he would publish only minor criticisms of Villèle. When the *Drapeau* failed to support Charles de Peyronnet's press bill of 1827, the committee suppressed the paper. In August 1829 it was revived by Martainville with a subsidy from Jules de Polignac and loyally defended the July Ordinances. Its circulation was now only 622, however, and it ceased to appear of its own accord when Charles X abdicated. Martainville died from a stroke on 31 July 1830.

N. Burtin, *Un semeur d'idées au temps de la Restauration: le baron d'Eckstein* (Paris, 1931); I. Collins, *The Government and the Newspaper Press in France, 1814–1881* (Oxford, 1959); C. Maréchal, *Lamennais au Drapeau Blanc* (Paris, 1946); D. L. Rader, *The Journalists and the July Revolution in France* (The Hague, 1973).

Irene Collins

Related entries: BERRY, C.-F.; CHARLES X; DECAZES; INDEMNITY BILL OF 1825; JULY ORDINANCES; MARTAINVILLE; PEYRONNET; POLIGNAC; RICHELIEU; ULTRAROYALISTS; VILLELE.

DREUX-BREZE FAMILY. No fewer than four persons of that name and family reached some notoriety in the first half of nineteenth century. Henri-Evrard (1766–1829) was grand master of ceremonies in the court of Louis XVI. His name remains connected with the famous confrontation in the Estates General of 1789, when Gabriel de Mirabeau and Jean-Sylvain Bailly refused to obey the orders of the king, of which Dreux-Brézé was the carrier. He survived the Revolution without leaving the country and when Louis XVIII returned was reinstated in his office as master of ceremonies. He was also made member of the Chamber of Peers.

Scipion (1793–1845), son of Henri-Evrard, served in the last stages of the Napoleonic wars. In 1815, he followed Louis XVIII to Ghent and afterward served in the Royal Guard. In 1829 he succeeded his father in the office of master of ceremonies and in the Peers. After the Revolution of 1830, he chose to keep his seat in the Chamber of Peers, where he defended the legitimist cause.

Emmanuel-Joachim-Marie (1797–1848) had a versatile career: sometimes in the army (among other services he was in Spain in 1823), sometimes in the diplomatic service (he was attached to La Ferronnays' embassies in Russia and the great congresses), sometimes in court (he was a gentleman of the Chamber), sometimes simply traveling for his pleasure (one result was an interesting report on the military colonies of southern Russia, printed in 1826).

Pierre-Simon-Louis (1811–1893) entered the clergy, was active in promoting working-class welfare organizations, and became bishop of Moulins (1850), where he was to have more than one confrontation with both the imperial and republican administrations.

Duke de Noailles, *Eloge de Scipion de Dreux, marquis de Brézé, prononcé à la Chambre des Pairs* (Paris, 1846).

Guillaume de Bertier de Sauvigny

Related entries: LA FERRONNAYS; LEGITIMISM; ROYAL GUARD.

LE DROIT (1841–1860s), journal of the judiciary and trial courts, founded by Alexandre-Auguste Ledru-Rollin in 1841. *Le Droit* reflected two main components of Ledru-Rollin's career: his love of jurisprudence and his concern over injustice under Louis-Philippe. His earlier *Journal du palais* (1831–47) had been more limited to his profession, but *Le Droit* allowed freer exposition of actual trials and other verbatim legal accounts, especially those of journalists and politicians who suffered under the increasingly repressive regime. The editor's radical republican sympathies were often implied in *Le Droit* and led to his creation of the radical daily paper *La Réforme* in 1843.

A. Calman, *Ledru-Rollin and the Second French Republic* (New York, 1922).

Daniel Rader

Related entries: LEDRU-ROLLIN; LOUIS PHILIPPE; *LA REFORME*.

DROIT D'AINESSE. See HEREDITY LAWS.

DROITS REUNIS. Beginning in 1804, a single agency started to collect taxes on consumer goods, notably on alcoholic beverages, salt, tobacco, playing cards, public transport, and the stamping of objects made of silver and gold. These taxes were known as the *droits réunis*, and their increasing demands were largely responsible for the growing popular discontent with the Napoleonic regime. Consequently, upon their return to France, the Bourbons proclaimed, "No more conscription, no more *droits réunis*." But the needs of the Treasury were too great, and so only the name *droits réunis* was suppressed. The taxes remained and were called "indirect taxes," while the amount of certain duties was slightly reduced.

E. Allix and M. Leclercle, *Les contributions indirectes* (Paris, 1929); A. Rousset, *Histoire des impôts indirects* (Paris, 1883).

Guillaume de Bertier de Sauvigny, trans. E. Newman

Related entry: RESTORATION, FIRST.

DROUET D'ERLON, JEAN-BAPTISTE, COMTE (1765–1844), professional soldier, marshal. Drouet d'Erlon was born in Reims and entered the army as a private in 1782. Only a corporal in 1792, he became an aide to General François Lefebvre (who had also begun his career as a private soldier) and served in the Revolutionary armies of the Moselle, Sambre-and-Meuse, and England. Soon distinguishing himself, he was rapidly promoted and became a general of brigade in 1799. Decorated for service in the German campaign of 1800–1801, d'Erlon served in Napoleon's Grand Army as a general of division from 1803 to 1808 and held an independent command in the Tyrol in 1809. Created a count of the Empire and a grand officer of the Legion of Honor, he fought in Spain under Marshal Nicholas-Jean de Soult (1811–13) and participated in the defense of southern France against the duke of Wellington in 1814. D'Erlon accepted the Restoration reluctantly, though he was named commander of the Sixteenth Military District by Louis XVIII and was arrested on 3 March 1815 as part of a military conspiracy on behalf of the duke of Orleans. Released on 20 March, when Napoleon arrived in Paris at the start of the Hundred Days, d'Erlon rallied to the emperor, was created a peer on 2 June, and accepted command of I Corps in the Waterloo campaign. His troops failed to get into action at Quatre Bras or Ligny on 16 June, and his corps' assault on Wellington's position at Waterloo on 18 June was repulsed. D'Erlon was proscribed by the restored Bourbon government on 24 July, and he fled to Bayreuth in Germany. In May 1816 he returned secretly to France and participated in the S.-P. Didier conspiracy, returning to exile when it was detected and being condemned to death in absentia for his role on 10 August. The amnesty of 28 May 1825 included him, but he chose not to return to France until after the Revolution of 1830, when Louis-Philippe gave him command of the Twelfth Military District. He was responsible for repressing the duchess of Berry's Vendéan uprising in 1832 and served an undistinguished term as governor-general of Algeria in 1834–35. He was elevated to the marshalate on 9 April 1843.

D. Chandler, *The Campaigns of Napoleon* (New York, 1966); J. Drouet d'Erlon, *La Vie militaire* (Paris, 1844); H. Houssaye, *1815: Waterloo* (Paris, 1893); D. Porch, *Army and Revolution, 1815–1848* (London, 1974); G. Six, *Dictionnaire biographique des généraux et amiraux français de la révolution et de l'empire* (Paris, 1934).

David Longfellow

Related entries: BERRY, M.-C.-; HUNDRED DAYS; LOUIS PHILIPPE; SOULT.

DUBOIS, PAUL-FRANCOIS (1793–1874), journalist; educator; editor of the Restoration *Globe* (1824–1830), highly acclaimed periodical of the arts, sciences, philosophy, and political ideas; director of the Ecole normale supérieure, 1840–1852. If Paul-François Dubois had ever published his collected works, his importance in nineteenth-century French intellectual and political life would be more broadly proclaimed. A brilliant young student in his birthplace of Rennes, he taught successively at Falaise, Limoges, Besançon, and finally the Lycée

Charlemagne. Until 1823, he was an officer in the secret carbonari of Brittany. A gifted essayist and universal scholar, Dubois was always too busy to write the book he owed the world. He achieved great influence in two active careers, journalism and higher education, but he is best remembered for his editorial management of the *Globe*.

Le Globe began as a cultural magazine in 1824, although from the start it was seen as a weapon of the growing opposition to the ultra Right, led by the new king, Charles X, his reactionary ministers, the ultras, and the clericalists. In 1830 the *Globe* became daily and political, to the dismay of many purists, and joined in the new militant propaganda against the government. From the start, Dubois was the soul of this famous periodical. His initial partner, Pierre Leroux, did not play a major role in shaping policy. Most of the Globists were refugees from the academic purges of the Villèle ministry. Dubois himself was fired from his professorship of rhetoric at the Lycée Charlemagne. Other major contributors to the *Globe* who had been forced to resign from faculties but were too young to stand for the parliamentary chamber included Victor Cousin, Theodore Jouffroy, and François Guizot. Joseph de Villèle unwittingly added even more talent to the *Globe*'s staff by buying out the *Tablettes*, another literary magazine of the Left whose writers, including Adolphe Thiers, found a voice in the *Globe*. The roster of Globists reflects nearly all the literary and scholarly French genius of this period. Many, including Jean-Philibert Damiron and Charles-Augustin Sainte-Beuve, had been either teachers or students of Dubois. In fact, Sainte-Beuve lived next door to Dubois, and Victor Hugo lived only a few houses away.

Dubois' *Globe* stood for justice and freedom but its editor was anything but an ideologue. François-René de Chateaubriand, Hugo, Stendhal, classics, romantics, constitutionalists, republicans, Bonapartists: All found Dubois' forum to be above the cults and cliques that characterized most of the press. Dubois himself wrote many anticlerical articles, but even more were devoted to the examination of various Asian religions and cultures. His polemic never revealed the thin skin of a Chateaubriand, a Carrel, or a Guizot. When, in 1828, the Jesuits were found to be operating illegal seminaries, the entire Left denounced the matter as part of a great conspiracy. Dubois' editorial was different. He said he had no love for the Jesuits but that any cult or individual in France had the right, in his view, to open a private school and to expound its views freely. For this rare stoic nobility, Dubois and his *Globe* were praised throughout Europe by admirers including Goethe and Humboldt.

When the *Globe* became a political daily newspaper in 1830, it did not fall into a partisan niche. Dubois at last accepted and supported the growing Orleanist movement only as a practical compromise and without devotion.

On 10 March 1830, Dubois was indicted, along with the manager of the *National*, for editorials they had written in their respective journals in the previous month. The *Globe*'s article had been titled ''France and the Bourbons'' and certainly could not have been ignored by Charles X's minister Jules de Polignac because Dubois had struck at not only the current repressive ultra regime but at the roots of the Bourbon Restoration. Referring to the legitimacy of the Restoration as "compromised" at the start, he accused the Bourbons of breaking faith and placing the dynasty in jeopardy.

Under the rather liberal 1828 press law, trials were not only very public but very free in terms of the rhetoric allowed the defense. In addition, anything quoted or said in a trial could be endlessly reprinted in the press as a transcript. Dubois' trial was attended by the intellectual, artistic, and political elite, and Dubois was the charming and heroic victim. All the opposition papers reprinted every word, and the words the law had hoped to repress were broadcast a hundredfold. Dubois received a fine of 2,000 francs and a term of four months in Sainte-Pélagie prison: long enough to maintain his martyrdom but not truly oppressive. His cell was comfortable, and many admirers flocked to visit him, including Chateaubriand and Récamier. On the second of the July Days, he was set free as a hero by a joyous crowd.

While in prison, Dubois had also been deprived, as a felon, of his academic tenure and title. These were quickly restored by the new monarchy, and Dubois made use of them. The *Globe* was sold to a group of socialists and became one of several journals opposed to, and beleaguered by, the new July Monarchy. Dubois returned to the Ecole normale, where he established new academic standards and became its director from 1840 to 1852, and was also inspector general of public instruction. He also served, in the opposition again, as a deputy for several sessions, but he had never been a politician. One of many victims of Louis-Napoleon's coup d'état, Dubois was fired in 1852 and retired to Brittany. In April 1870, he emerged briefly to accept membership in the Académie. Vacherot said of him after his death four years later that no one in the University had ever left so deep a memory in the hearts of students or colleagues.

P. Gerbod, *Paul-François Dubois, universitaire, journaliste, et homme politique, 1793–1874* (Paris, 1967); A. Lair, "Paul-François Dubois," *Revue Bleue* 8 (1907); *Nouveaux lundis* vol. 13; *Portraits littéraires*, vol. 1; D. Rader, *Dubois of the Globe, Studies in Modern European History* (New York, 1956); C. Sainte-Beuve, *Causeries du lundi* vol. 6; E. Vacherot, *Notice sur Paul-François Dubois* (Paris, 1875).

Daniel Rader

Related entries: ANTICLERICAL CAMPAIGN; CARBONARI; CARREL; CHATEAUBRIAND; COUSIN; *LE GLOBE*; GUIZOT; HUGO; LEROUX; *LE NATIONAL*; POLIGNAC; PRESS LAWS; SAINTE-BEUVE; STENDHAL; *LES TABLETTES UNIVERSELLES*; THIERS; ULTRAROYALISTS; VILLELE.

DUBOUCHAGE, FRANCOIS-JOSEPH (1749–1821), naval minister, Viscount du Gratet. Dubouchage entered the military in 1763, rising to command a brigade of naval artillery in the West Indies in 1784 and at Brest in 1786. Promoted to *maréchal de camp* in 1792, he was named minister of the navy on 24 July. His advice to Louis XVI to resist the Revolution of 10 August more forcefully was ignored, and Dubouchage emigrated shortly after the fall of the monarchy, returning under the Directory. A devout royalist, he declined to serve Napoleon and was placed under surveillance in 1805 as a possible agent of the Bourbons. Welcoming the return of Louis XVIII, Dubouchage remained in Paris during the Hundred Days but was named minister of the navy under the Second Restoration. He purged his department of all Revolutionary and Bonapartist functionaries and proposed creating a naval academy in land-locked Angoulême to honor the king's nephew (the duke of Angoulême). Dubouchage's new appointees, loyal royalists but inexperienced naval officers, were typified by Hugues de Chaumareys (an *émigré* and veteran of the Quiberon disaster in 1795, who had not been to sea in twenty-five years), who was given command of the naval expedition to restore French control of Senegal. The resulting wreck of the frigate *Medusa*, with the loss of 155 lives (7–13 February 1816) was largely due to de Chaumarey's incompetence. When Dubouchage opposed Elie Decazes' proposed electoral reforms and sided with the ultra opposition in the Chamber in 1816–17, he was removed as naval minister on 22 June 1817. Elevated to the peerage, he remained a militant ultraroyalist until his death.

G. de Bertier de Sauvigny, *La Restauration* (Paris, 1955, 1963); A. McKee, *Death Raft* (New York, 1975).

David Longfellow

Related entries: DECAZES; ULTRAROYALISTS.

DUBOURG-BUTLER, FREDERIC (1778–1850), former Napoleonic army officer who briefly sought to assume command of the insurrectionary forces in Paris, 29 July 1830. "General" Frédéric Dubourg-Butler was a shadowy figure who moved briefly across the scene of the French Revolution of 1830. As a young man in the 1790s, he had joined the republican army. He continued to serve under the Empire and rose to a position on the staff of General Bernadotte. In 1814 he rallied to the Bourbons and was rewarded with appointment to the staff of the ministry of war. When Napoleon returned to France in 1815, Dubourg was among the faithful who accompanied Louis XVIII to Ghent, but his past associations apparently made him suspect to the ultraroyalists, and after the Second Restoration he lost his place in the army. The wish to avenge this ill treatment may have motivated his actions in July 1830.

On 29 July, dressed in a general's uniform, which, Louis Blanc reported, he purchased from a theatrical outfitter, he went to the Hôtel de ville in Paris, arriving in the interim between the flight of royal officials and the arrival of General Lafayette and the new Municipal Commission. There he found an editor of the liberal newspaper *Le Constitutionnel*, Evariste Dumoulin, trying to organize a centralized direction of the still leaderless popular insurrection. Dumoulin seized upon Dubourg as the military leader that the situation demanded, and Dubourg accepted the charge. He hastily organized a staff and began issuing orders. He had scarcely started, however, when Lafayette arrived at the Hôtel de ville to set up the command of the Parisian National Guard, soon followed by members of the newly appointed Municipal Commission. Dubourg immediately surrendered his position and his claims to power and receded into the obscurity from which he had emerged. In 1848, two years before his death, the republican government granted him an officer's pension.

L. Blanc, *The History of Ten Years, 1830–1840* (London, 1844); *Nouvelle biographie générale depuis les temps les plus reculés jusqu' à nos jours . . .* , vol. 40 (Paris, 1855–70).

David H. Pinkney
Related entries: LAFAYETTE; MUNICIPAL COMMISSION; NATIONAL GUARD; REVOLUTION OF 1830.

DU CAYLA, ZOE-VICTOIRE-TALON, COMTESSE (1784–1850), favorite of Louis XVIII. The daughter of a former magistrate, Du Cayla was introduced to the court of Louis XVIII when she separated from her husband. Beautiful and witty, she replaced Elie Decazes in the affections of the old king. She reconciled him with his brother, the future Charles X, and facilitated the coming to power of a right-wing ministry in December 1821. Louis XVIII showered gifts upon her, notably the little château of Saint-Ouen, which he had built for her. She helped to create the production of fine woolen goods at the royal factory of the Savonnerie. After the 1830 Revolution, she took refuge in the Netherlands, where she participated in the conspiracies of the duchesse de Berry against Louis-Philippe.

E. Perret, *La dernière favorite des rois de France, la comtesse Du Cayla* (Paris, 1937).

Guillaume de Bertier de Sauvigny, trans. E. Newman
Related entries: BERRY, M.-C.; DECAZES.

DUFAURE, JULES-ARMAND-STANISLAS (1798–1882), lawyer and politician. Jules Dufaure was born in Saujon (Charente-Maritime) on 4 December 1798 into a family that favored the Republic. His father, a former naval officer, sent him to the Lycée Charlemagne in Paris and then to the Paris School of Law, from which he graduated in 1820. He was a deputy from Saintes from 1834 to 1848. Soult made him minister of public works on 12 May 1839, but his ministry fell 1 March 1840. Dufaure attached great importance to the development of railroads and favored giving concessions to private companies.

Jules Dufaure did not participate in the political attacks against the regime in the late 1840s, but after the 1848 Revolution he rallied to the Republic and was elected a deputy first to the Constituent and then to the Legislative Assembly. Eugène Cavaignac made him minister of the interior from 13 October to 20 December 1848. Odilon Barrot gave him the same post the following year, and he held it from 2 June to 31 October. Hostile to Louis-Napoleon Bonaparte, Dufaure spoke out in opposition to the coup d'état and went back to the private practice of law.

G. Dubois, *Etude sur M. Dufaure* (Amiens, 1884); R. Poincaré, *Eloge de Dufaure* (Paris, 1883).

Jean-Claude Caron, trans. E. Newman
Related entries: BARROT, C.-H.-O.; RAILROADS.

DUMAS, ALEXANDRE (père) (1802–1870), a major dramatist and novelist of the romantic period. He was born 24 July 1802 in Villers-Cotterêts (Aisne). He died of a stroke on 5 December 1870 in Puys, near Dieppe. His father, Thomas-Alexandre Dumas Davy de la Paileterie, was an ardent republican who served as a general in Napoleon's army. His paternal grandparents were Antoine-Alexandre Dumas Davy, marquis de la Pailleterie, and Marie Cessette Dumas, a black slave. Much has been written about Dumas. Although he is best known today for his novels, he first gained fame for his immensely popular plays. In fact, as one of the first romantic dramatists, his place in literature rests on his theatrical pieces rather than on his novels. Altogether, he produced more than 300 works, including over 250 novels and 25 plays.

After his father's death in 1806, Alexandre was raised by his mother. Since Napoleon refused to grant her a widow's pension, the family had little income. Alexandre's limited formal schooling included tutoring in Latin, mathematics, and calligraphy. His early interests included dancing, fencing, shooting, riding, and the outdoors. Apprenticed at the age of fourteen to a local notary, he seemed destined for a career as a clerk. At age twenty, with the help of General Maximilien-Sébastien Foy, one of the leaders of the opposition, he obtained a position as a copyist with the duc d'Orléans.

Once in Paris, his friendship with Adolphe de Leuven and Amedée de la Ponce exposed him to the Parisian theater. At that time, melodrama and vaudeville were extremely popular and left their mark on the young author. His interests in the theater were discouraged by his superiors in the duke's secretariat. Alexandre, however, persisted in writing several unsuccessful efforts, many with the aid of other obscure writers living in Paris.

In 1824 he published his first known work, a thirty-eight-line poem, "La Rose rouge et la Rose blanche." That same year, he had a son, Alexandre, by his mistress, Marie Labay. Through his friendship with Charles Nodier he met Alfred de Vigny, Alphonse de Lamartine, Honoré de Balzac, Alfred de Musset, Prosper Mérimée, Eugène Delacroix, and, especially, Victor Hugo. In the fall of 1827, a performance of Shakespeare's *Hamlet* by an English company stimulated Dumas' desire to write his own plays. In July of 1828, he began writing *Henry III and His Court* for the Comédie-française. This work is regarded as the first romantic drama to be performed. The opening performance proved to be an enormous success. It ended Dumas' obscurity and freed him from the poverty of his early years.

After the Revolution of 1830, Dumas' republicanism strained his relationship with Louis-Philippe, the new king and former duc d'Orléans. Yet for Dumas, the next decade represented years of triumph as he emerged as one of the leading romantic dramatists enjoying wide popularity. The public seemed particularly interested in historical drama, especially plays about Napoleon. *Napoléon Bonaparte* drew large and enthusiastic crowds to the theater, despite its failure to impress the critics. His next effort, *Antony*, was a spectacular success. Its presentation on 3 May 1831 proved highly controversial, particularly because

Dumas' play with its theme of the adulterous wife challenged bourgeois notions of home, family, marriage, and chastity. Throughout the decade, he published a variety of other plays, which were well received by the public. In March 1831, he had a daughter, Marie-Alexandrine, by another mistress, Belle Krelsamer. In 1832, he wrote *The Tower of Nesle*, a play that had an enormous impact. Dumas was also involved in a street riot on 5 June 1832 that accompanied the burial of one of Napoleon's generals, Jean Lamarque. That incident strained further his relations with the king. Following the advice of friends, he left for Switzerland. His accounts of his travels in that country were published in various places, including the *Revue des deux mondes* and, collectively, under the title *Impressions de voyage en Suisse*. These works added substantially to Dumas' popularity. Dumas wrote for a middle-class public and is credited by some literary historians with having created two new and important dramatic forms: the historical drama and the modern drama. In 1837, upon the recommendations of Hugo and the young duc d'Orléans, he was made a chevalier of the Legion of Honor.

In the period 1829–43, Dumas, Hugo, and Vigny were the most successful and important of the French romantic dramatists. In the 1840s, Dumas turned his attentions increasingly toward the writing of novels. A superb storyteller, his novels were extremely popular and continue to be read today, while most of his plays are seldom performed. Most of Dumas' works were flamboyant and melodramatic, with history serving as a backdrop for romance or intrigue. Many of these novels were first published as serials in the *feuilletons* of the daily press. He published *The Three Musketeers*, *Twenty Years After*, and *The Viscomte de Bragelonne* in *Le Siècle*, *The Queen Margot* and *Joseph Balsamo* in *La Presse*, and *The Count of Monte Cristo* in the *Journal des débats*. Dumas often wrote several novels simultaneously, using the plots developed by his assistants as the basis for his finished work. His most important collaborator was Auguste Maquet, who is credited with the manuscript that inspired the first of Dumas' historical novels, *The Chevalier of Harmental*. Dumas produced so many works with the aid of collaborators that some of his detractors charged him with operating a literary sweatshop.

Literary critics have claimed that Dumas lacked style and subtlety and that his characters were neither real nor memorable. The public, however, treated these works more kindly than did the critics. Many of Dumas' historical novels reflect themes also contained in his plays, particularly the struggle between good and evil, the individual's search for glory, and the willingness to forsake all for friendship, love, or honor. His heroes are individuals, misunderstood by others, who revolt against society and its moral code. The success of his novels added considerably to the income gained from his plays. Dumas, however, spent money too easily and went bankrupt as a result of his construction of the elaborate château de Monte Cristo, which cost some 500,000 francs. He fled to Belgium in 1851 to escape his creditors. In that same year, he had another son, Henry Bauër. He eventually settled with his creditors and returned to Paris in 1853.

The Revolution of 1848 ended a period of affluence for Dumas and inaugurated one of relative penury for him. After the Revolution of 1848, Dumas continued to enjoy great popularity, but the quantity and quality of his work declined. Part of the reason rests with the increasingly poor health of the aging author, but part is attributable to the changing literary tastes of the French public. Romanticism continued to dominate the *feuilletons* of the Parisian daily press, while critics favored realism. A third explanation for Dumas' reduced productivity lies in the rupture of his friendship with his former collaborator, Maquet. Dumas never found an equally brilliant assistant. His later works include a collection of gothic tales of horror entitled *A Thousand and One Fantoms* (1849–50), and a series of novels based on his own childhood experiences published as the Villers-Cotterêts novels (1852–57). He also created a number of journals that had relatively short lives. The most notable of these were *Le Mois* and *Le Mousquetaire*. Widely traveled, he spent more than ten years in a variety of countries, notably Belgium, Italy, Russia, Austria, Germany, Spain, and parts of North Africa. These travels inspired a series of travelogues describing the customs and manners of the people he met. His later memoirs amount to some 3,000 pages in ten volumes, and the first two-thirds were originally published in serial form in *La Presse*, with the remainder published in his own daily, *Le Mousquetaire*. The close friendship that had existed between Dumas and his son cooled after 1848 as the latter disapproved of his father's sexual indulgences and, perhaps, suffered from professional jealousy. In 1869, the year before his death, Dumas, an excellent chef, completed his *Grand dictionnaire de cuisine*.

H. Clouard, *Alexandre Dumas* (Paris, 1954); A. Dumas, *Oeuvres completes* (Paris 1851); F. W. J. Hemmings, *Alexandre Dumas: The King of Romance* (New York, 1979); A. Maurois, *The Titans: A Three-Generation Biography of the Dumas*, trans. Gerard Hopkins (New York, 1957); D. Munro, *Alexandre Dumas père: A Bibliography of Works Published in French, 1825–1900* (New York, 1981); R. S. Stone, *Alexandre Dumas père* (Boston, 1976).

Roy E. Sandstrom

Related entries: FOY; *JOURNAL DES DEBATS;* NODIER; *LA PRESSE*; *LA REVUE DES DEUX MONDES*; ROMANTICISM; *LE SIECLE*.

DUMAS, JEAN-BAPTISTE-ANDRE (1800–1884), chemist and administrator. As a young man Dumas studied pharmacy and chemistry in the small town in southern France where he was born and in Geneva, to which he traveled in 1816. Moving to Paris in 1823 he obtained a junior appointment at the Ecole polytechnique and began giving evening classes in chemistry to adults at the Athenaeum.

His marriage in 1826 to the daughter of the director of the royal porcelain works at Sèvres strengthened his interest in the industrial applications of chemistry, and two years later he began the publication of his multivolumed *Traité de chimie appliquée aux arts*. In 1829 he cofounded the Ecole centrale des arts et manufactures.

Dumas' enthusiasm for applied chemistry was balanced by his deep interest in chemical theory, and many of his researches were devoted to resolving important theoretical issues of his day. Official recognition of his work came in a series of appointments, including professorships at the Ecole polytechnique (1835), the Ecole de médecine (1839), and the Sorbonne (1841). In addition, in 1840 he became one of the editors of the *Annales de chimie et de physique*.

Dumas worked extensively on the classification of chemical elements and organic compounds. Although skeptical about the existence of atoms, he nevertheless considered the atomic theory to be a valuable systematization of chemical knowledge, and he contributed to the revision of the atomic weights of a number of elements. His studies of animal chemistry, particularly those concerning digestion and nutrition, were criticized by the physiologist Claude Bernard as methodologically unsuitable applications of chemistry to the study of living phenomena.

With the Revolution of 1848, Dumas became active in politics. He served in the Legislative Assembly and was minister of agriculture from 1850 to 1851. Under the Second Empire he became a senator and was very active on the Paris Municipal Council, assisting Georges Haussmann in the modernization of the national capital. He retired from his teaching appointments in 1868 and in that same year was made permanent secretary of the Académie des sciences.

J.-B. Dumas, *La vie de Jean-Baptiste Dumas, par le général J.- B. Dumas son fils* (Paris, 1924); E. Maindron, *L'oeuvre de Jean-Baptiste Dumas* (Paris, 1886).

W. R. Albury

Related entries: ACADEMY OF SCIENCES; BERNARD; ECOLE CEN-TRALE DES ARTS ET MANUFACTURES; ECOLE POLYTECHNIQUE; LEGISLATIVE ASSEMBLY; PARIS FACULTY OF MEDICINE; REVOLU-TION OF 1848.

DUMESNIL, LOUIS-ALEXIS-LEMAISTRE (1783–1858), author and defender of the Gallican church during the Restoration. Born in the old Norman city of Caen on 10 September 1783, Alexis Dumesnil came from a family of magistrates with a tradition of devotion to the French monarchy. Not surprisingly, he served in the Royal and Catholic Army in the Vendée. After the uprising was crushed, Dumesnil joined the army of the Republic and fought in General Jean-Victor Moreau's last campaign; wounded, he returned to Caen. While convalescing, Dumesnil took part in an incident that brought upon him severe punishment from the government. As a result of frequent altercations between the people of Caen and an army unit stationed there, the townspeople, with Dumesnil at their head, expelled the troops. Participation in this incident not only brought Dumesnil under the supervision of the imperial police, it also gave him a reputation as a dangerous enemy of the Empire. Arrested and tried for his political activities, Dumesnil spent fifteen months incarcerated in the Temple before being taken in chains to Nancy.

For a brief time, Dumesnil resumed a military career, but he soon abandoned it for the serious study of religion and history. From this work, the first result appeared in 1810 and 1811, when Dumesnil published the first of three editions of *De l'esprit des religions* and the first of two editions of *Le Règne de Louis XI et de l'influence qu'il a eue jusque sur les derniers tems de la 3e dynastie*. Since the police considered the latter work hostile to the emperor, its publication occurred only after the removal of numerous offending passages; they were restored in the 1819 edition. Apart from a brief essay on Pascal, Dumesnil ceased writing, resuming only after the return of the Bourbons.

Greeting the First Restoration with enthusiasm, Dumesnil served the returned Bourbons as a royal commissioner in the Basse-Normandie, where he struggled to achieve recognition for the authority of the new king. During the Hundred Days, he took command of the royal volunteers of Caen and led them to Evreux, where they disbanded when the news of the king's departure from France reached them. Dumesnil then traveled to the Vendée, where he was arrested and imprisoned. Released only after the second abdication of Napoleon and the second return of Louis XVIII, Dumesnil led a small force to defend Cherbourg from the advancing Prussians.

Dumesnil's initial enthusiasm for the Bourbons soon waned, largely owing to the undue influence he suspected the ultra-Catholic Congrégation exercised over the government. He expressed his opinions with such vehemence that the government prosecuted him for an article published in the *Album* entitled "Tribulations de l'homme de Dieu." In this essay, the government perceived a vicious attack against the abbé Frayssinous, then grand master of the Université. Although Dumesnil paid a fine and served a month in prison, he nonetheless remained an outspoken advocate of the Gallican cause. In the mid–1820s, he had a role of some importance in the anticlerical campaign against the Congrégation, the Knights of the Faith, and the Jesuits. In fact, one historian has recently argued that Dumesnil launched this attack on suspected clerical influence with a vituperative pamphlet of October 1824 entitled *Considérations sur les causes et les progrès de la corruption en France*. In it he claimed that, since its founding in 1808, the Congrégation, which he compared with the infamous Catholic League of the sixteenth century, had schemed to impose a theocracy on France. In a second pamphlet published less than a year later, Dumesnil charged the Congrégation with using the jobs, funds, and awards at its disposal to undermine the new institutions of France. If these works of Alexis Dumesnil reached only a relatively small audience in 1824 and 1825, his thoughts and even some of his words were repeated by the comte de Montlosier in his popular and influential *Mémoire à consulter*, which went through eight editions in just a few weeks in 1825.

For the remainder of his life, Alexis Dumesnil continued to add to his impressive list of publications. His last works were a series of pamphlets published in 1848. Dumesnil died in Paris on 27 September 1858.

A. Dumesnil, *Considérations sur les causes et les progrès de la corruption en France* (Paris, 1824), *De l'esprit des religions* (Paris, 1810), *La Nation française et son roi appelés à juger de la conspiration permanente et progressive du parti jésuitique* (Paris, 1825), and *Le Règne de Louis XI et de l'influence qu'il a eue jusque sur les derniers tems de la 3e dynastie* (Paris, 1811; 2d ed., 1819); G. Lavalley, ed., *Des duellistes de Caen de l'an IV à 1848 et le bretteur Alexis Dumesnil* (Caen, 1914); A. Rabbe, ed., "Alexis Dumesnil," *Biographie universelle et portative des contemporains*, vol. 1.

Robert Brown

Related entries: ANTICLERICAL CAMPAIGN; CHEVALIERS DE LA FOI; CONGREGATION; FRAYSSINOUS; HUNDRED DAYS; JESUITS; MONTLOSIER.

DUMOULIN, EVARISTE (1776–1833), liberal journalist and political figure during the Restoration. After a youth inspired by Revolutionary ideals in the Gironde, Dumoulin became a successful businessman and, for avocation, pursued the study of mathematics and sciences. The prospect of greater independence through a literary career made him dissatisfied with his situation, however, when he had some verse accepted by a Bordeaux journal. Arriving in Paris in 1815, he quickly established friendships in journalistic and literary circles. He collaborated on a short-lived exposé paper, *Messager des chambres*, which was seized by police but reappeared in book form, and, at age thirty-nine, he became the youngest founding stockholder in the successful *Constitutionnel*. For this important liberal journal, he edited sessions of the Chambers and later added a section on theater notes. Like his newspaper, he was more a popularizer of taste than a classical critic.

He soon became associated with Benjamin Constant, Antoine Jay, and Pierre Tissot on the new *Minerve* (1818–20) and was active in the French version of the Carbonari, as were many other journalists of the time. A defender of imperial glory if not of Bonaparte, he published detailed accounts of the trials of Michel Ney, Antoine Drouot, and Pierre Cambronne (1815, 1816). In 1820 and again in 1827 he issued pamphlets attacking proposed press restrictions. All of this activity made him a popular gadfly of the Left, and he was prosecuted several times.

In the July Revolution, Dumoulin, not content merely to protest with other journalists, took sword in hand and joined the battle before the Hôtel de ville. Under Louis-Philippe he received a battalion command in the National Guard and other official sinecures, which allowed him considerable luxury.

A popular guest and liberal host, Dumoulin fell victim to a massive stroke on 4 September 1833 while feasting and drinking with friends in the office of the *Constitutionnel*.

F. Michaud, *Biographie universelle.* (Paris, 1811–28); C. Sainte-Beuve, *Causeries du lundi* (Paris, 1851).

Daniel Rader

Related entries: CARBONARI; CHAMBER OF DEPUTIES; CHAMBER OF PEERS; CONSTANT; *LE CONSTITUTIONNEL*; JAY; LOUIS PHILIPPE; NATIONAL GUARD; NEY; REVOLUTION OF 1830; TISSOT.

DUNOYER, BARTHELEMY-CHARLES-PIERRE-JOSEPH (1786–1862),
journalist and economist; founder, with Charles Comte, of the *Censeur* and the
Censeur européen. Born on 20 May 1786 in Carennac (Lot), Charles Dunoyer
belonged to an old noble family that was staunchly Catholic and devoted to the
French monarchy. The youngest son of Henriette de la Grange de Rouffilac and
Jean-Jacques-Philippe Dunoyer de Segonzac, Dunoyer was originally destined
to enter the Order of Malta. When the order was abolished during the Revolution,
Dunoyer's life was allowed to take a new direction. After receiving an early,
largely classical education from two aunts, both nuns of the Order of Saint Jean
de Malte, and the last Benedictine prior of Carennac, Dunoyer entered the Central
School of the Lot at Cahors. Because he showed an aptitude for the law, Dunoyer
received from the local prefect a scholarship that permitted him to attend the
Université de jurisprudence. In 1803, young Dunoyer arrived in Paris to begin
his studies. While a law student, he met Charles Comte, and the two men began
a friendship that would span their lifetimes. Comte and Dunoyer shared a distaste
for the Empire, which they saw as having deprived France of the political rights
won in 1789 and which they blamed for having deprived France of freedom of
thought, and a preference for the great works of the Enlightenment. They
particularly favored John Locke, Etienne de Condillac, Antoine-Louis-Claude
Destutt de Tracy, and Jeremy Bentham. After being licensed in the law, the two
young men found employment outside the government. While Comte devoted
his attention to the jurisprudence collection of Sirey, Dunoyer translated the
Novelles of a Byzantine emperor. Ultimately bowing to parental pressure, Dunoyer
tried to find suitable employment under the Empire. He served as a secretary to
an intendant in Spain and then in Holland.

Charles Dunoyer welcomed the fall of Napoleon and the return of the Bourbons;
he even joined an honor guard for the comte d'Artois. But his enthusiasm soon
waned, and he greeted the declaration of Saint-Ouen, which he found insufficiently
liberal, with a highly critical pamphlet. Soon Dunoyer joined with his friend
Comte to undertake the publication of the *Censeur* (1814–15), a notable liberal
newspaper of the First Restoration. In this journal, which had to appear in book
form to avoid royal censorship, the two young men advanced their own ideas
on the nature of constitutional government. During the Hundred Days, they
boldly refused to support the emperor. Following the disappearance of the *Censeur*,
Comte and Dunoyer launched the *Censeur européen* (1817–20). In this journal,
the two authors and their collaborators, most notably Henri de Saint-Simon and
Augustin Thierry, expounded the new economic theory of industrialism. Although
often prosecuted by the Restoration government, the *Censeur européen* managed
to survive until the sharp reaction that followed the assassination of the duc de
Berry.

With the final disappearance of the *Censeur européen*, Dunoyer became a
professor at the Athénée. His course of lectures became the basis for *L'Industrie
et la morale considérées dans leurs rapports avec la liberté* (1825). In addition
to a number of minor pamphlets, he also published his important ''Notice historique

sur l'industrialisme,'' a fundamental source for the origins of this economic doctrine. Dunoyer, finally, supported the liberal opposition with an occasional pamphlet. In July 1830, he made public the anger stirred in him by the publication of the July Ordinances. In the same issue of the *National* that carried the journalists' protest against the ordinances, Dunoyer published a letter in which he swore to pay no taxes until the ordinances were withdrawn.

Charles Dunoyer not only applauded the advent of the July Monarchy, he also served it well throughout the eighteen years of its existence. For seven of those years, Dunoyer served as a prefect, first in the department of the Allier and then in the departments of Mayenne and the Somme. He also sat as a member of the Council of State for some ten years. While in government service, Dunoyer continued to study, think, and write. He was named a member of the Académie des sciences morales et politiques in 1832, the year in which the Academy was reestablished. A revised and enlarged edition of *L'Industrie et la morale* appeared early in 1830 with the prolix title: *Nouveau traité d'économie sociale ou simple exposition des causes sous l'influence desquelles les hommes parviennent à user de leurs forces avec le plus de liberté, c'est-à-dire avec le plus de facilité et de puissance.* The third version of this work appeared in three volumes in 1845 with its final title: *De la liberté du travail ou simple exposé des conditions dans lesquelles des forces humaines s'exercent avec le plus de puissance.*

The Revolution of 1848 did not find a friend in Charles Dunoyer, and he showed no reluctance in publishing his views on republicanism. He even addressed a letter on the subject to Alphonse de Lamartine, the poet turned politician who played such a prominent role in the events of 1848. Despite his opposition to the Second Republic, Dunoyer remained, at the insistence of his colleagues, a member of the Council of State.

Although willing to serve the Second Republic, Dunoyer refused to remain in the government following the coup of 2 December 1851. The last years of his life he devoted to a book highly critical of the Second Empire; left unfinished at his death on 4 December 1862, this work was published clandestinely abroad under the title *Le Second Empire et une nouvelle Restauration.*

R. Adenot, *Les idées économiques et politiques de Charles Dunoyer* (Paris, 1907); F. Mignet, ''Notice historique sur la vie et les travaux de M. Charles Dunoyer,'' (Académie des sciences morales et politiques 1873); E. Villey, *L'Oeuvre économique de Charles Dunoyer* (Paris, 1899).

Robert Brown

Related entries: LE CENSEUR, LE CENSEUR EUROPEEN; COMTE, F.-C.-L.; COUNCIL OF STATE; DESTUTT DE TRACY; SAINT-SIMON; THIERRY.

DUPANLOUP, FELIX-ANTOINE-PHILIBERT (1802–1878), educator, writer, and bishop of Orléans. The small village of Saint-Felix (Haute-Savoie) was temporarily under French rule when, on 3 January 1802, the illegitimate child of a poor peasant girl was born. The identity of the father remained unknown; the general belief that he was of high social rank is confirmed by the fact that the boy was provided with an education in the best schools, much above the humble station of the mother. After brilliantly completing his classical studies in Paris he entered, in 1821, the famous seminary of St.-Sulpice. His first assignment as a young priest (ordained on 18 December 1825) was the teaching of religion (catechism) in the aristocratic parish of La Madeleine. He was so successful in this task that he soon became the favorite preacher and confessor for the high society of Paris, a standing that was notably increased when he was instrumental in arranging for the last-hour reconciliation to the church of the renegade bishop Talleyrand. In the meantime, Dupanloup had been shifted to the no-less-fashionable parish of St.-Roch. In September 1837 he was appointed director of the minor seminary of St.-Nicolas-du-Chardonnet, where he had himself received his classical education. Under his inspired leadership, the school gained a national reputation.

Throughout these first years of his career, Dupanloup had enjoyed the friendly confidence of his ecclesiastical superior, Archbishop Quélen, who appreciated, among other features, the attitude of hostile aloofness adopted by his young protégé in regard to Félicité de Lamennais and his group of brilliant disciples. But the successor of Quélen, Denis Affre (1840), was of another mind, and he removed Dupanloup from his school of St.-Nicholas to a seat in the chapter of the Notre-Dame cathedral. This kind of sinecure allowed Dupanloup to work in earnest on his great treatise *Education*, which was to be his main published work (6 vols., 1850–66), and also to enter more actively in the mainstream of the politico-religious controversies of the time. The most critical issue in those last years of the July Monarchy was that of the freedom of education claimed by Catholics in the face of the state's educational monopoly. With a series of brilliant pamphlets and a whirl of social activities, Dupanloup established himself as a leader of what could be called the Catholic lobby. In this struggle, the conservative he had been until then found himself joining hands with Charles-Forbes de Montalembert, the former beloved disciple of Lamennais; the two men became close friends, and some of Montalembert's liberalism rubbed off on Dupanloup. On the contrary he was repelled by Louis Veuillot's vociferous ultramontanism and reactionary politics; between those two talented writers and Catholic champions, there was to be a continuous and sometimes bitter feud.

The advent of the Second Republic (February 1848) gave Dupanloup an increased role in public affairs. As member of the extraparliamentary commission in charge of solving the legal problem of the freedom of education, he was the main author of the compromise that was finally embodied in the so-called Falloux Law. In the meantime he was made bishop of Orléans, a city close enough to the capital to allow him to combine his local pastoral duties with activities on the national scene in Paris. As bishop of Orléans he displayed his usual energy, applying all imaginable devices to revive Christian life and improve the quality and numbers of his clergy. The results, however, were not commensurate with the effort.

On the national scene, his stature was still growing. When Louis-Napoleon pulled his coup of 2 December 1851, Dupanloup was alone among the bishops present in Paris to urge French Catholics not to condone the violation of the constitution. The French Academy, by electing him to their fold in 1854, was honoring not only the talented orator and writer but also the fearless defender of the liberties of the church. Among many pamphlets published during those years, the most notable is *La Convention du 15 septembre et l'encyclique du 8 décembre*; in it he cleverly associated criticism against the emperor's Italian policies with an explanation of the famous *Syllabus*, blunting the unfortunate impact it had had on world opinion. The document was circulated around the world in several translations, and hundreds of bishops wrote their approval.

After unsuccessfully opposing the declaration of Papal infallibility at the Vatican Council of 1869, he was elected to the National Assembly in 1870, where he worked, again unsuccessfully, for a Bourbon Restoration. He died on 11 October 1878.

R. Aubert, in *Dictionnaire d'histoire et de géographie ecclésiastique* (Paris, 1912–38); C. Marcilhacy, *Le Diocèse d'Orléans sous l'épiscopat de Mgr. Dupanloup* (Paris, 1962).

Guillaume de Bertier de Sauvigny

Related entries: ACADEMIE FRANCAISE; AFFRE; BORDEAUX; COUP D'ETAT OF 2 DECEMBER 1851; FALLOUX LAW; LAMENNAIS; MONTALEMBERT; QUELEN; ULTRAMONTANES; VEUILLOT.

DUPIN, ANDRE-MARIE-JEAN-JACQUES (1783–1865), lawyer, magistrate, and important political figure during the July Monarchy; commonly called Dupin aîné. Born 1 February 1783 at Varzy (Nièvre), André Dupin was the son of Charles-André Dupin (1758–1843), a lawyer at the Parlement of Paris, magistrate, member of the Legislative Assembly, and subprefect of Clamecy. Having received an elementary education at home from his learned father, Dupin studied law in Paris during the Consulate and served as a solicitor's clerk. When the Schools of Law were reestablished, Dupin entered as a student, becoming first a *licencié* and then a doctor of law; he also studied theology and canonical law. In 1810, owing to his failure to win a competition for a professorship at the law faculties, he devoted himself to the bar, published several works, including a collection of Roman legal texts (the *Principia Juris*), and attracted the attention of prominent officials, notably the *procureur-général* Philippe-Antoine Merlin, who had Dupin appointed to a committee charged in 1813 to classify the laws of the Empire. Jean-Jacques de Cambacérès later named Dupin secretary of this commission.

During the Hundred Days, the voters of Château-Chinon selected André Dupin to represent them in the Chamber. Once in Paris, Dupin sat with the liberal faction, refused to support the Empire, opposed a post-Waterloo proposal to name the emperor's son Napoleon II, and rallied to the Bourbon cause. Although named president of the electoral college of the Nièvre by Louis XVIII, he failed to win election to the Chamber in the elections of July 1815 and, owing to the age requirements imposed shortly after, he became ineligible to stand for the Chamber until 1823. Dupin hence returned to the practice of law, embarking on a remarkable career that would soon bring him widespread fame as one of the leading opposition lawyers of the Restoration period.

Dupin commenced his career as an opposition lawyer by assisting in the unsuccessful defense of the celebrated Marshal Michel Ney, who, charged with treason, was convicted and shot. Other prominent figures prosecuted by the Bourbon government and defended by Dupin include General Armand-Augustin de Caulaincourt, charged with complicity in the arrest of the duc d'Enghien, the duc de Rovigo, and the famed liberal songwriter Pierre-Jean de Béranger. Dupin also conducted the defenses of newspapers like the *Constitutionnel*, accused in 1825 of having violated the law of tendency, and the *Journal des débats*, prosecuted in 1829. Both of these cases involved Dupin in the defense of the Gallican church from attacks by the ultramontanes and the Jesuits. Dupin also lent the comte de Montlosier assistance in his denunciations of the Jesuits. Finally, Dupin defended in 1823 the journalists Antoine Jay and Etienne de Jouy in a case that stirred up major questions concerning limits on freedom of discussion and the press. When the two authors published a biography of the *conventionnel* Jean-Baptiste Boyer-Fonfrède the government promptly indicted them; in his plea, Dupin vigorously defended freedom of discussion in historical matters. While taking a leading role in these and in many other cases involving both individuals and liberal institutions prosecuted by the Bourbon government, Dupin also served from 1817 as one of the legal counselors to the duc d'Orléans, the future King Louis-Philippe, and as his business agent. When the elections of 1827 were called, Dupin was thus well established as a defender of opposition and liberal causes, and he was closely tied to the Orléans family.

Dupin entered the Chamber of Deputies in 1827, and he took an increasingly important role there as an opponent of the regime of Charles X and an ardent defender of public liberties in the waning years of the Bourbon Restoration. He was in 1829, moreover, elected *batonnier* of the Parisian lawyers. In the political crisis of March 1830, which Charles X set off with his provocative speech from the throne of 2 March, Dupin had a major role. The king's speech provoked a bitter debate over the form of the Chamber's reply in which major questions about the nature of the Charter of 1814 were raised. Passed by a vote of 221 to 181, the Chamber's reply called on Charles to replace the Polignac ministry with one more acceptable to the Deputies. André Dupin numbered himself among the celebrated 221 and, in the elections of June 1830 that followed the king's dissolution of the Chamber, he won reelection as one of the 202 of the 221 returned as deputies. This stunning repudiation of Bourbon policies at the polls prompted Charles X to issue on 25 July the infamous July Ordinances.

André Dupin's part in the Revolution of 1830 began on 26 July, when, at the request of the editors of the *Constitutionnel*, he informed a group of perhaps a dozen journalists that the ordinances were illegal and that resistance to them was not only a right but a duty. When the journalists began to discuss possible forms of resistance, the prudent Dupin ordered them from his office. Nevertheless, on 27, 28, and 29 July, he actively participated in the events of the Revolution. On 30 July, he had a part in arranging for the duc d'Orléans to be invited to become lieutenant general of the kingdom and then in convincing his friend to accept the offer. On 31 July, Dupin helped draft the proclamation that announced the duke's acceptance of the invitation and that concluded with the notable phrase: "A charter will henceforth be a reality."

Dupin's essentially conservative interpretation of the July Revolution held that it had brought to France all the liberties compatible with her stage of historical development. The duc d'Orléans' address to the Chambers of 3 August 1830, rewritten by Dupin and François Guizot, reflected this desire to limit the consequences of the Revolution and to preserve the Charter. Dupin also successfully counseled the duke not to adopt the proposed title of Philippe VII, which would have made manifest a link to the deposed Bourbons, arguing that the duc d'Orléans had become king despite his ties to the Bourbon family. To the hurried efforts to create a firm basis for the new regime in the late summer and fall of 1830, Dupin lent a firm and willing hand, helping with the revision of the Charter of 1814, serving as a minister-without-portfolio in the Laffitte government, and advising the workers of Paris to shun all involvement in demonstrations and political clubs. On 23 August 1830, Dupin was named *procureur-général* at the Cour de cassation, a position that he would retain with but a few brief interruptions for the remainder of his life. Owing to this position and to his public utterances, Dupin rapidly became unpopular, and only the intervention of the National Guard saved his house from the crowd during the February 1831 riot of Saint Germain-l'Auxerrois. In 1832, Dupin became president of the Chamber of Deputies, an honor he would receive annually for the next eight years. Despite close political and personal ties to Louis-Philippe, he refused to become a minister, preferring to take an obstinate and inordinate pride in a political independence that he tried to maintain throughout the many complex political battles of the July Monarchy.

In the Revolution of 1848, the minor role Dupin played was conservative. Having failed to convince the Assembly to designate the comte de Paris as Louis-Philippe's successor, with the duchesse d'Orléans as regent, Dupin adroitly transferred his political allegiances and emerged as a supporter of the Republic, retaining, not coincidently, his position as *procureur-général*. Elected to the Constituent Assembly, he presided over the committee on legislation, contributed to the drafting of the Constitution of 1848, and took a conservative stance with regard to the National Workshops and the right to work laws. Out of a concern for law, order, and stability, Dupin supported Louis-Napoleon Bonaparte in the campaign for the presidency of the Second Republic. Beginning in June 1849, he served as president of the Assembly. By the end of 1851, Dupin, acutely troubled, like many other French political leaders, by the political turmoil of the day, favored a revision of the Constitution of 1848 that would prolong the powers of the prince-president. When the coup d'état of 2 December came, Dupin, not one of the leaders of the Second Republic imprisoned as a precautionary measure by Louis-Bonaparte, weakly protested and then ordered the Assembly to dissolve. Only when the new imperial government confiscated the lands of the Orléans family did Dupin resign his post. Five years later in 1857, he received it back, and, what is more, Louis-Napoleon named him to the Senate.

To his several careers as lawyer, magistrate, and politician, André Dupin added that of man of letters. A prolific author of dozens of legal books, speeches, and polemics, Dupin became a member of the French Academy in 1832 and of the Academy of Moral and Political Sciences in 1832. His *Mémoires* were published in four volumes between 1855 and 1861. André Dupin's long life ended in Paris on 10 November 1865.

A. Dupin, *Choix de plaidoyers en matière politique et civile* (Paris, 1823), *Libertés de l'Eglise gallicaine* (Paris, 1824), *La Révolution française* (Paris, 1830), and *Mémoires*, 4 vols. (Paris, 1855–61); C. Giraud, *Notice historique sur la vie et les travaux de M. Dupin aîné*, Académie des sciences morales et politiques, séance du 29 août 1876; Ortolon, *Notice biographique sur M. Dupin* (Paris, 1840).

Robert Brown

Related entries: COURT OF CASSATION; DUPIN, F.-P.-C.; DUPIN, S.-P.; GUIZOT; JAY; JOUY; NEY; SAINT-GERMAIN L'AUXERROIS, RIOT OF.

DUPIN, FRANCOIS-PIERRE-CHARLES, BARON (1784–1873), engineer, mathematician, politician, peer of France, and senator of the Second Empire. The second of the three Dupin brothers, Charles Dupin was born in Varzy (Nièvre) on 6 October 1784, the son of Charles-André Dupin (1758–1843). With the completion of his early education in the central schools of the Loiret and the Seine, Dupin entered the Ecole polytechnique in 1801, where his talent in mathematics and geometry caught the attention of Gaspard Monge and Lazare Carnot. Upon leaving this school, he commenced a career in naval engineering and worked over the next several years on the creation of the channel flotilla, in Boulogne, Anvers, and Genes and on the fortifications along the Dutch coast. He continued his work in mathematics, finding applications for some of his theories in the construction of ships. In 1807, Dupin went to Toulon, where he took part in the effort to rebuild the French fleet after Trafalgar. From Toulon, he went to the Ionian Islands, remaining there for five years and sharing in the creation of the Académie ionienne. His return to France delayed by a fever contracted in Italy, he spent the months of recovery working on essays in geometry that he presented to the Institut in 1813; in recognition of his achievement, the Institut named him a corresponding member. Back in Toulon, Dupin undertook a number of activities, including the creation of a naval museum and the publication of his *Architecture navale aux XVIIIe et XIXe siècles*.

Charles Dupin, who would serve the Restoration government in a number of technical capacities, who would be made a baron in 1827, and who would also figure prominently in the liberal opposition, welcomed the First Restoration and the proclamation of the Charter of 1814. His *Lois fundamentales de la France* of 1814 favored the creation of representative institutions. Like so many other Frenchmen, he then deserted the Bourbons to join the cause of the emperor in 1815, publishing a patriotic *Examen de l'Acte additionnel*. The defeat at Waterloo compelled him not only to propose a ceremony to honor those soldiers slain in the defense of the nation but also to suggest that France resume the war if a just peace was not obtained. Angered during the White Terror at the decree that proscribed, among many others, his friend and patron Lazare-Nicolas-Marguérite Carnot, Dupin protested against the government's action, offered to defend Carnot before the Chambers, and drafted a memoir in his behalf. Despite Dupin's activities, the Restoration government decided to assign him to the arsenal at Dunkirk. A visit to England in 1816, where he studied English military organization, gave him the materials for reports to the minister of the navy and the Academy of Sciences; the latter body elected him a member in 1818. When, however, Dupin published the observations made on his English journey in the *Force militaire de la Grande-Bretagne*, the government was not pleased, for it found Dupin's opinions far too liberal; his protests against efforts to censor his work led to a period of four years during which Dupin was out of favor. During the late teens, Charles Dupin had also issued a vigorous protest against a British proposal to prolong the occupation of France, and he had written several works, among them *Essai historique sur les services et les travaux scientifiques de Gaspard Monge*. Dupin returned to favor when the government named him professor of mechanics at the Conservatoire des arts et métiers, where he also taught applied geometry. He was named a baron in 1825.

Charles Dupin began in 1827 a ten-year career as a deputy and a forty-three-year career in French political life. Elected to the Chamber of Deputies, where he sat with the liberal opposition, he frequently made use of the new science of statistics in legislative debates, taking a special interest in matters relating to the navy and the public highways. Also in 1827, Dupin stirred a flurry of controversy with the publication of his *Forces électorales à la fin de 1827*. This pamphlet, which promptly went through eight editions and was promoted with enthusiasm by the liberal *Globe*, presented Dupin's reflections on the social and political effects of the aging of the French electorate. According to the figures he presented, electors sympathetic to the Revolution and the Empire would form a majority of the electorate after 1827. These thoughts later became part of his still-impressive *Situation progressive de la France depuis 1814*, a sophisticated study of the economic life of northern France. During the eventful year of 1830, Dupin favored military action in Algeria and was one of the famous 221 liberal deputies who voted for the reply protesting the royal address of 2 March 1830. Defeated largely due to government efforts in the elections of June 1830, Dupin was, however, returned to the Chamber of Deputies as a deputy from the Seine on 12 July 1830. He took but a minor role in the Revolution of 1830.

Between 1830 and 1837, when he was elevated to the peerage, Charles Dupin rendered the July Monarchy important service in the Chamber of Deputies, the Council of State, the Council of the Admiralty, and the Council of Agriculture.

In the Chamber, where his political stance became more and more conservative, he took a leading role in formulating the Law on the National Guard, in budgetary matters, and in questions concerning the military. In 1834, Dupin served for three days as the minister of the navy. Raised to the peerage on 3 October 1837, he involved himself in the upper house with questions concerning charity, child labor, and commercial relations with the colonies. One reward for Dupin's tireless devotion to the July Monarchy was appointment to the Legion of Honor.

The burden of his legislative duties did not prevent Dupin from publishing throughout the 1830s and the 1840s a number of important books, most of them dealing with economic questions, the condition of the working class, and colonial affairs. Upon its reestablishment in 1832, he was named to the Académie des sciences morales et politiques.

Dupin, who remained faithful to the July Monarchy until its fall, became an outspoken conservative critic of the Second Republic; after a brief hesitation, he decided to support the government of Louis-Napoleon in 1851. Elected to the Constituent Assembly in June 1848, he sat with the Right; while a deputy, he served as president of the Committee of the Navy, voted for the suppression of the National Workshops, spoke out against socialism, and supported the notion of a bicameral legislature. In the Legislative Assembly, he backed the expedition on Rome, the Falloux Law on education, and limits on universal suffrage. Following the coup of 2 December, Dupin chose to support Louis-Napoleon and was named to the Senate on 26 January 1852, where he vigorously participated in discussions concerning economic and religious matters. Long interested in industrial progress, Dupin served as head of the French delegation to the Universal Exposition in London and on the commission on the Universal Exposition of Paris. Retired from political life by the events of 4 September 1870, Charles Dupin died in Paris on 18 January 1873.

Dictionnaire de biographie française, vol. 12 (Paris, 1933); C. Dupin, Forces électorales à la fin de 1827 (Paris, 1827); A. Robert, E. Bourloton, and G. Cougny, Dictionnaire des Parlementaires français, vol. 2 (Paris, 1891).

                                                                                   Robert Brown

Related entries: ACADEMIE FRANCAISE; ACADEMY OF SCIENCES; ACTE ADDITIONNEL; ALGIERS, EXPEDITION TO; CARNOT, L.-H.; CHILD LABOR; DUPIN, A.-M.-J.-J.; DUPIN, S.-P.; FALLOUX LAW; MONGE; PUBLIC WELFARE.

DUPIN, SIMON-PHILIPPE (1795–1846), prominent lawyer and supporter of the Orleanist monarchy. Born in Varzy (Nièvre) on 7 October 1795, the son of the former deputy Charles-André Dupin, Simon-Philippe was the youngest of the three Dupin brothers, all of whom gained fame during the first half of the nineteenth century. His studies at the Collège de Varzy and the Collège de Clamecy completed, Dupin went to Paris, where he prepared for the law under the guidance of his elder brother, André. Having earned both a bachelor of laws and a doctor of laws, he joined the bar in 1816 and entered his brother's practice.

During the Restoration, Dupin established his reputation by successfully arguing a number of notorious cases, among them the case of the false count of Sainte-Hélène (1818), a defense of the *Constitutionnel* (1819), a defense of Captain Dequevauvillers, accused of complicity in a military conspiracy, and the celebrated case of the chevalier de Graviers (1820). When André Dupin entered government service following the July Revolution, Simon-Philippe took over his lucrative legal practice. Elected to the Chamber of Deputies in 1830, he resigned within a year, choosing to concentrate his energies on his flourishing legal career. Between 1831 and the early 1840s, Dupin became one of the most prominent lawyers of the July Monarchy, and he participated in several noteworthy cases. When Marshal Nicolas-Jean de Soult and Casimir Périer sued the *Tribune* for defamation, Dupin successfully argued their case. Further, he served the duc d'Aumale as legal counsel in the matter of the will of the duc de Bourbon. In these cases, and indeed in all his public statements, Dupin energetically defended Louis-Philippe and the July Monarchy. He also served the French legal profession, the city of Paris, and the Orléans government in a variety of capacities. He died on 14 February 1846 while on a trip to Italy for reasons of health.

A. Robert, E. Bourloton, and G. Cougny, *Dictionnaire des Parlementaires français*, vol. 12 (Paris, 1891); F.-J. Doublet de Boisthibault, *Philippe* Dupin (Paris, 1848).

Robert Brown

Related entries: BOURBON; CHAMBER OF DEPUTIES; *LE CONSTITU-TIONNEL*; DUPIN, A.-M.-J.-J.; DUPIN, F.-P.-C.; LOUIS PHILIPPE; PERIER; REVOLUTION OF 1830; SOULT.

DUPONT, PIERRE-ANTOINE (1821–1870), popular poet and republican songwriter. Born to a spurmaker (*éperonnier*) of Lyons, Pierre Dupont grew up in the countryside as the ward of a priest. After failing to accede to the life of the church, he was sent to Lyons to take up life as a silkworker or *canut*. Neither the life of an artisan nor working in commerce suited the young romantic idealist. His interest in poetry won the support of his grandfather, himself an author. At the same time as the publication of his first work, *Deux anges*, Dupont was drafted into the royal army. Because his work had won a prize from the Academy, his grandfather and his new literary friends in Paris were able to buy Dupont a replacement.

Taking up his true vocation, songwriting, Dupont was an instant success. He wrote of the countryside, the beauty of the trees, the noise of the wind in the pines, the cows in the fields. *Le Boeufs, Mère Jeanne*, and *Vigne* were popular in 1845–46, and the collection *Paysans: chants rustiques* was bought by the bourgeois for use with their pianos. Nature's secrets came to life in his songs, and among urbanites and rural folk alike the songs struck a responsive chord.

Besides writing about rustic tranquility, Dupont brought the life of the worker to the public in his songs. His *Les Ouvriers* (1846) was very popular, and it was on the lips of the workers in 1848. Dupont himself is known to have sung it at one banquet where the main speaker was Auguste Blanqui. Dupont's works dealt with the debilitating effects of poverty, a theme with which the workers could identify. His descriptions of individual crafts, like his songs about each type of tree, raised songs to the level of poetry.

Although Dupont was too much the humanitarian to be involved fully in politics, his socialist humanism did get him entangled in the events of the Second Republic. He had become good friends with Pierre-Jean de Béranger and associated with Victor Hugo, Henri Murger, Théophile Gautier, and Charles Baudelaire. Baudelaire had recognized his talents and lauded his devotion to liberty. Dupont could not write the battle songs for the workers, but he did try to keep them true to the Republic. His *Chant du soldat* said: "Soldiers—don't be gendarmes, support the people and their rights." He celebrated 1848 in *La Républicaine*, and in the fall of 1848 one song included the lines: "The Republic lives on despite all our errors and offenses. Her name shines high above us like a reflected glow of purple and gold." The events of 1848 also inspired *Chant du transporté* and *Adieux de Kossuth*.

This *poète populaire* did not please the prince-president, Louis-Napoleon, so Dupont was watched, threatened with arrest, and after the coup d'état of 2 December 1851 actually condemned in absentia to seven years of exile. Dupont had avoided arrest by slipping into Savoy, but he could not survive without his Parisian audiences, so in 1852 he pledged support of the regime and lived quietly thereafter in Paris. A simple man who cared for the people, Dupont had avoided all formal musical training in order not to dull his originality. He succeeded in this by bringing the qualities of his Christian-social-humanist spirit to life in songs of the countryside and everyday work. His work was collected in four volumes under the title *Chants et chansons* (Paris, 1854).

Le Grand dictionnaire universel du 19e siècle (Paris, 1866–90).

Thomas Beck

Related entries: BAUDELAIRE; BERANGER; BLANQUI, L.-A.; *CANUTS*; GAUTIER; SINGING SOCIETIES.

DUPONT DE L'EURE, JACQUES-CHARLES (1767–1855), judge and politician. Born at Neubourg (Eure) on 27 February 1767, he was the son of a merchant. In 1789 he became a lawyer at the parlement of Rouen. He held several administrative and judicial positions during the Revolution and the Directory. In 1809 Dupont refused to condemn royalists who had been falsely accused of attacking a stagecoach, though he had been pressured by officials to do so. This independent attitude earned him a loyal following, and he became one of the most popular and successful politicians of the Restoration and July Monarchy. In spite of his independence, he was named to the Legion of Honor in 1804 and became president of the imperial court of Rouen in 1812. In 1813, he was chosen as a delegate to the Legislative Body. He supported Joseph-Louis-Joachim Laîné's proposals of December 1813 asking Napoleon to accept the Allies' offer of the natural frontiers and demanding civil and political liberties.

Dupont served as vice-president of the Chamber of Deputies during the First Restoration but was suspected of devotion to the empire because of meetings with Lazare-Nicolas-Marguérite Carnot and Gazzani. At the elections of the Hundred Days in the Eure on 9 May 1815, a very small turnout chose Dupont as deputy. He received eighty-seven out of ninety-one votes. The Chamber of Representatives chose him to be vice-president, and he was among those objecting to the dismissal of the Chamber upon the return of the king. He was defeated at the elections of August 1815 and removed from the departmental council in 1816. In the elections of 1816, he was chosen a candidate on the third round by the arrondissement of Louviers but was not elected deputy by the departmental college. With the support of the duc de Broglie, Dupont was elected in September 1817, receiving 601 out of 963 votes on the first round. As the opposition candidate for vice-president of the Chamber, Dupont received only 15 votes.

Dupont was a solid and energetic supporter of the liberal cause in the Chamber. In November 1818, the reorganization of the court at Rouen was completed, and Dupont was removed from his post. Although judges were irremovable, their positions were secure only after reorganization by the government following the Hundred Days. This dismissal increased his popularity greatly since there was no charge of incompetence and since he was also denied a pension on the ground that he had completed only twenty-seven of the thirty years of service needed to qualify.

In 1820, Pierre-Jean de Béranger wrote a poem, "Le Trembleur," in which the poet humorously pretends to snub his friend Dupont for fear of the government. In the Chamber Dupont spoke against the Barthélemy resolution and in favor of the recall of the *bannis*. He urged abbé Grégoire to resign in 1819 rather than risk expulsion.

Dupont ran for reelection in November 1820 in the district of Bernay but lost to Lizot, 223 to 212. But he won at Pont-Audemer, by 301 votes out of 540. The voters of Seine, Seine-Inférieure, and Eure raised a subscription to purchase for him an estate near Beaumont-le-Roger to recompense him for his lost post and to make sure that he would retain his elegibility. He was one of a small group of deputies who participated in the carbonarist plots of the early 1820s, probably forming part of the *Haute vente*. He protested the expulsion of Jacques-Antoine Manuel from the Chamber of Deputies in 1823. Defeated at Pont-Audemer in the elections of 1824, he retained a seat in the Chamber when the voters of Paris chose him to replace General Maximilien-Sébastien Foy, who was elected in two districts and opted to represent Aisne. On 9 September 1827, a large political banquet was held at Bernay where he was one of the honored guests. In the elections of November 1827, Dupont was elected at Bernay (228 out of 348 votes cast), at Pont-Audemer (321 out of 434 votes cast), and reelected in Paris. He opted for Bernay.

In 1830 Dupont de l'Eure served on the committee that wrote the answer to the king's address and was one of the 221 voting in favor of the committee's document. In April 1830, a banquet was held at Bernay to honor him. Dupont was easily reelected at Bernay (236 to 87) on 12 July in the elections following the dissolution. He was at his home at Rougeperiers, near Neubourg, when the 1830 Revolution began. He hurried to Paris, arriving on the evening of 30 July. On 31 July, the Municipal Commission named Dupont to manage temporarily the affairs of the Justice Department. The next day, the duc d'Orléans, acting as lieutenant general, appointed him officially to head the Ministry of Justice. On 9 August, when Orléans came to the Chamber of Deputies to be made king, it was Dupont, in his official capacity, who handed him the text of the oath. The new king named him minister of state and keeper of the seals on 11 August.

Dupont's peasant-like honesty and forthrightness, which made him so popular with voters, was not designed to make his relations with Louis-Philippe easy. He turned down 25,000 francs that had been appropriated for each minister's initial expenses. His wife (whom he had married in 1818) instituted economies in the ministry and frequently entertained the lesser employees at dinner. He saw his primary goal as that of purging the magistracy. By the end of 1830, he had replaced 426 officials. In the cabinet, Dupont lined up on the Left with Jacques Laffitte. They supported the cause of Odilon Barrot, the prefect of the Seine, who had criticized the Chamber of Deputies after public disturbances in mid-October. Broglie and Guizot wanted to dismiss Barrot. The conflict resulted in a reshuffling of the cabinet (without Broglie and Guizot), Laffitte's nomination as president of the Council of Ministers, and Dupont's continuing at the Ministry of Justice.

The law of 12 September required all deputies who accepted paid government positions to stand for reelection. Dupont was reelected easily on 24 October and used his influence to have Barrot elected as a deputy from the Eure. Increasingly dissatisfied with the actions of the king and the Chamber, Dupont offered his resignation as minister on 26 December 1830, following the resignation of his close associate the marquis de Lafayette as commandant of the National Guard. His letter to the king expressed his dissatisfaction with the course of events, his long-held desire to resign, and the belief that he could do so with impunity now that the trial of the ministers was completed. The king, who had kept him as minister merely to placate popular opinion during the crisis, did not protest his decision.

In the election of July 1831, Dupont was elected at Bernay on the first round (198 out of 246 votes cast). He was elected vice-president of the Chamber on 1 August. He continued to oppose the direction of the government. By 1833 he was anonymous editor in chief of the *Revue républicaine*. In spite of a political position more radical than that of the voters of the Eure, his personal popularity with them continued undiminished. But in a by-election in the Eure in October 1833, he was unable to secure the victory of his candidate, Achille Treilhard, over his opponent, Narcisse-Achille de Salvandy. In November he was elected to the departmental council.

On 29 January 1834, Francois-Charles Dulong, one of Dupont's closest friends (rumored to be his illegitimate son), was killed in a duel motivated by politics.

Dulong was an attorney who represented the district of Verneuil (Eure). Following a heated exchange in the Chamber, a duel took place in which General Thomas-Robert Bugeaud killed Dulong. The latter's friend suspected a conspiracy. Devastated by the news, Dupont resigned from the Chamber in a letter that was an indictment of the regime. He accused the government of abandoning the principles of the July Revolution and going back to the men and methods of the Restoration. The government, he believed, should be based on the sovereignty of the people, not on "quasi-legitimacy."

Dupont ran again in the general elections on June 1834 following dissolution. Behind on the first round at Bernay, he withdrew but was elected at Brionne, 165 to 118. In early 1835, Dupont joined his political friends in founding a short-lived weekly political journal, *La Nouvelle minerve*. In an article entitled "De la Réaction," Dupont endorsed electoral reform as the first step needed to combat the counterrevolutionary forces. In the elections of November 1837, he was reelected at Bernay with 283 votes out of 336 cast. His name appeared in 1837 on a *Comité radical de Paris* without his knowledge. He decided not to withdraw it to avoid offending his friends. In March 1839, he was reelected at Brionne without opposition. Dupont continued the campaign for electoral reform by joining a group that advocated that all those who had a right to join the National Guard be electors and all electors be eligible.

At the elections of July 1842, the conservatives had announced that they would not run a candidate against the venerable Dupont, but they were forced to do so when the liberals presented him as a candidate in four districts. He was elected at Evreux (260 to 232 for Salvandy), Bernay, (205 to 170 for Le Prévost), and Brionne (329 out of 357 votes). He opted for Evreux. In April 1843, Dupont was injured in a carriage accident, and after that his attendance at the Chamber was less constant. In the elections of August 1846, he was a candidate at Evreux and at Brionne. He lost at the first (339 for Salvandy to 232) but won at the second (299 to 20).

One of the important banquets in the campaign for electoral reform took place at Neubourg on 12 December 1847 with Dupont de l'Eure as guest of honor. He was in the Chamber of Deputies on 24 February when the crowds stormed it. His name was on the list of seven people (decided upon by acclamation) who formed the provisional government. He was named president but served as minister without portfolio. He was included because of his popularity and his reputation for honesty and independence, but because of his age he made no contributions to policy decisions. On 27 February he led the procession on foot from the Hôtel de ville to the Bastille column and gave one of the speeches there.

At the elections of 23 and 24 April 1848 for the National Constituent Assembly, Dupont was elected in the Eure and at Paris (receiving second place with 245,000 votes after Lamartine's 259,800). He opted for the Eure. He stood for election to the Legislative Assembly in May 1849 but lost. After further losses in by-elections at Bouches-du-Rhône, Calvados, and Charente-Inférieure, he retired from political life and died on 2 March 1855.

A. Fortier, "Dupont (de l'Eure): La Révolution de Juillet 1830," *La Revolution de 1848* (1916–17); *Lettres inédites de Béranger à Dupont de l'Eure* (Paris, 1908); J. Vidalenc, *Le Département de l'Eure sous la monarchie constitutionnelle* (Paris, 1952).

Sylvia Neely

Related entries: BANQUET CAMPAIGN; BARROT; BARTHELEMY; BERANGER; BROGLIE, A.-L.-V.; BUGEAUD; CARBONARI; CARNOT, L.-N.-M.; GUIZOT; LAFAYETTE, M.-J.-P.-Y.-R.-G.; LAFFITTE; LAINE; MANUEL; MUNICIPAL COMMISSION; *REVUE REPUBLICAINE*; SALVANDY; TREILHARD.

DUPUYTREN, GUILLAUME (1777–1835), leading surgeon and professor of surgery, Hôtel-Dieu, and Faculty of Medicine, Paris. Surgeon in chief of the Hôtel-Dieu of Paris and clinical professor in the Faculty of Medicine from 1815 until his death in 1835, Guillaume Dupuytren was a dominant figure in the Parisian medical profession at the time when Paris ranked with Edinburgh as the most advanced medical center in the world. Dupuytren was born near Limoges in 1777, the son of a minor official of the parlement. After completing secondary schooling, he studied anatomy and physiology in Paris and in 1801 won appointment as *prosector* (*chef des travaux anatomiques*) in the School of Medicine. The next year he became a surgeon, second class, at the Hôtel-Dieu and in 1808 assistant surgeon in chief. Three years later a fiercely fought competition for one of the two chairs of operative medicine in the Faculty of Medicine in Paris ended in his elevation to a professorship.

Dupuytren conducted a large hospital practice and a lucrative private practice, attracted hundreds of students to his clinics, and actively pursued his researches. Louis XVIII in 1820 honored him with the title of baron, and Charles X named him his first surgeon and strongly—and successfully—supported him for election to the Academy of Sciences in 1825. The Revolution of 1830 cost Dupuytren his favored position with the court and the government, and in 1831, perhaps hoping to recover some political influence, he sought election as deputy from his native department, but he was defeated by a local country doctor. He resumed his exhausting schedule of practice and teaching, continuing until failing health in 1833 forced him to reduce his activities. He died in 1835, leaving an estate estimated at between 4 million and 7 million francs, an immense fortune for a physician in the 1830s.

Dupuytren wrote a number of scientific papers and books, and his students published several volumes of his clinical lectures, but he left no enduring mark on either surgery or anatomy. His reputation was based on his skill as a diagnostician and practicing surgeon and as a clinical teacher.

L. Delhoume, *Dupuytren* (Paris, 1935); H. Mandor, *Dupuytren* (Paris, 1945); *Nouvelle biographie générale*, vol. 15 (Paris, 1855–70).

David H. Pinkney

Related entries: ACADEMY OF SCIENCES; CHARLES X; LOUIS XVIII; PARIS FACULTY OF MEDICINE; REVOLUTION OF 1830.

DURAND, CLAUDE (1803–1895), republican songwriter. Claude Durand was a wealthy landowner in the heart of traditional royalist country. Under the July Monarchy, he had been on the municipal council of his commune, and in 1848 he became mayor. Favoring the Republic, he had asked for and failed to receive the support of his fellow citizens in the April 1848 elections to the Constituent Assembly as a candidate on the democratic-socialists workers' list. In May 1849 he again ran unsuccessfully, this time for the new Legislative Assembly. The son of a *vigneron*, Durand became famous for his "Chanson des vignerons," which he wrote as a campaign song for the by-elections of 10 March 1850.

"Chanson des vignerons" contained the following lines:

> Good villagers, vote for the Montagne
> There is the hope of poor vine growers
> For with it, good countrymen,
> Will disappear the taxes on drinks.
> In the hamlets, agricultural banks
> Will be especially for you, good peasants.
> Without charge also you will have schools
> And money at most at three percent.

For these words Durand was arrested for "an act of rebellion and the exciting of hate of one citizen against another." This republican of the Vendée, however, was acquitted by a jury in Napoléon-Vendée on 18 May 1850.

The coup d'état of 2 December 1851 brought Durand into action to defend the Republic. He attempted to raise an insurrection in his home town of Mauzé on 3 December, though his efforts were in vain. Managing to avoid arrest, he was nevertheless condemned in absentia to deportation to Algeria on 10 February 1852. Durand reappeared in Belgium, from where he journeyed to the isle of Jersey. His later songwriting was much influenced by his friendship with Victor Hugo during their mutual exile on Jersey.

Durand was permitted to return to Mauzé in 1856. He lived quietly during the remainder of the Second Empire, but when the war with Prussia began in 1870, his patriotic spirit was aroused. His song "Appel aux armes" won the praise of Hugo, Léon Gambetta, and Garibaldi. If the French government had followed Gambetta southward, Claude Durand would have been there to fight to the bitter end.

His works are collected in *Claude Durand et ses chansons* (Paris, 1886).
Le grand dictionnaire universel du 19e siècle (Paris, 1866–90).

Thomas Beck

Related entries: CONSTITUTION OF 1848; COUP D'ETAT OF 2 DECEM-
BER 1851; HUGO; LEGISLATIVE ASSEMBLY; REPUBLICANS; SINGING
SOCIETIES.

DURUY, VICTOR (1811–1894), historian, educator, and government minister.
The son of a worker at the Gobelins tapestry workshop and destined for a humble
trade, Duruy succeeded in winning admission to the Ecole normale supérieure
(ENS) in 1830. He graduated in 1833 and became professor of history at a
collège in Reims before accepting a similar post at the Lycée Henri IV he was
to hold for twenty-five years. A popular teacher, Duruy also wrote extensively
on ancient civilization and geography with special attention to younger readers.
Doctor of letters in 1853, he was appointed *inspecteur de l'académie* and *maître
de conférence* at the ENS in 1861 and inspector general of instruction at the
Ecole polytechnique in 1862. On 6 June 1863, Napoleon III (whom Duruy had
helped on his *Life of Caesar*) named him minister of public instruction. An
anticlerical and freethinker, Duruy worked to lay the foundations of a free public
school system that would make education nonreligious and compulsory. Duruy
helped to establish a degree of job security for lycée professors, reestablished
the *agrégation* and philosophy courses in the secondary schools, and established
departments of modern history in lycées and collèges. He reformed instruction
for public school teachers and the *baccalauréat*, conducted surveys on the state
of public schooling, and established the Ecole des hautes-études at the University.
The Falloux Law of 1852 had required communes to establish free elementary
schools (with various restrictions) while leaving free rein to private Catholic
instruction. The emperor blocked Duruy's proposal to make elementary education
compulsory, but the law of 10 April 1867 confirmed the principle of free primary
instruction, eliminated limits on numbers of students enrolled, and authorized
the establishment of courses for young women (accompanied by mothers or
maids) in town halls or lycées. Duruy's reforms, and his support for liberal
educational associations like the Society for Elementary Instruction, drew bitter
criticism from the Catholic church, Catholic deputies, and churchmen like Felix
Dupanloup, bishop of Orléans. When government losses in the elections of 1869
led Napoleon III to make concessions to his conservative opponents, Duruy was
dismissed (17 July 1869). He was made a senator and after 1870 returned to his
historical studies. Though Duruy often had to moderate his policies in the face
of clerical criticism, his work foreshadowed the educational reforms of the Third
Republic and the Ferry laws.

K. Auspitz, *The Radical Bourgeoisie* (Cambridge, 1972); V. Duruy, *L'administration
de l'Instruction publique de 1863 à 1869* (Paris, n.d.), and *Notes et souvenirs 1811–
1894*, 2 vols. (Paris, 1901); S. Horvath-Peterson, *Victor Duruy and French Education*

(Baton Rouge, 1984); J. Maurrain, *La politique ecclésiastique du Second Empire, 1852–1869* (Paris, 1930); J. Rohr, *Victor Duruy* (Paris, 1967); T. Zeldin, *Conflicts in French Society* (London, 1970) and *France, 1848–1945*, 2 vols. (Oxford, 1973, 1977).

David Longfellow

Related entries: DUPANLOUP; ECOLE POLYTECHNIQUE; FALLOUX LAW; PUBLIC INSTRUCTION; SOCIETY FOR ELEMENTARY INSTRUCTION.

DUVAL, ALEXANDRE-VINCENT PINEAUX (1767–1842), author of popular comedies during the Revolution, the Empire, the Restoration, and the July Monarchy. Born in Rennes on 6 April 1767 the son of a lawyer who was secretary to the Estates of Bretagne and the brother of Amaury Duval (1760–1838), Alexandre Duval led a restless life frequently filled with adventure. Leaving the collège de Rennes before completing his studies, he volunteered in 1781 for service with the French fleet that participated in the American War of Independence. Upon his return to France, Duval pursued a number of careers before 1789, none of them for long. During the first years of the Revolution, he earned a living by engraving portraits of revolutionary leaders. When the volunteers of 1792 rushed to the defense of *la patrie en danger*, Duval joined a company composed of writers and artists from the various French academies and served in the Argonne and at Jemmapes and Valmy. Returned to civilian life, Duval, with the exception of a brief imprisonment in the fall of 1793, resumed a career as a minor actor and as author of comedies of manners. With such plays as *Les Héritiers* and a comic-opera, *La Reprise de Toulon* (1795), Duval won considerable fame. His *Le Lovelace français, ou la Jeunesse de Richelieu* combined a historical setting with a denunciation of the licentious mores of the Old Regime. The successful *Edouard en Ecosse* (1802), in which Bonapartist officials discovered an attitude favorable to the Bourbons, brought Duval so much trouble that he left Paris for Rennes and then France for an extended journey that took him to Russia before he returned to France. Many of his plays in the ensuing years were based, like *Guillaume le Conquérant* of 1803, on historical themes. In 1808, upon the recommendation of Louis-Benoît Picard, Duval became director of the Théâter Louvois; between 1812 and 1815, he supervised the Odéon and the Opéra-Bouffe. Named to the Institut in 1812, Duval retained his chair in the reorganized Académie française of 1816.

During the Restoration, Alexandre Duval continued to write comedies and have them successfully performed. Owing to attacks on aristocratic pretensions in some of them, like *La fille d'honneur* (1818), Duval frequently became the object of attacks in the press by ultraroyalist critics. During the 1820s, he took a major role in the futile battle waged by defenders of classicism against the romantics. Later, in a pamphlet of 1833, Duval vehemently criticized Victor Hugo as the champion of romantic drama. From 1830 to his death on 9 January 1842, he occupied an official post at the Bibliothéque de l'arsenal. Published in nine volumes between 1822 and 1829, Duval's *Oeuvres complètes* contain, in addition to forty-nine plays, a large number of long and interesting prefaces.

C. Bellier-Dumaine, *Alexandre Duval et son oeuvre dramatique* (Paris, 1905); C.-M. Des Granges, *La Comédie et les moeurs sous la Restauration et la Monarchie de Juillet* (Paris, 1904); A. Duval, *Oeuvres complètes* (Paris, 1822–29); S. L. England, "The Characteristics of French Comedy during the Period 1815–1848," *Revue d'histoire litteraire* 41 (1934).

Robert Brown

Related entries: ACADEMIE FRANCAISE; HUGO; PICARD; ULTRA-ROYALISTS.

DUVERGIER DE HAURANNE, PROSPER (1798–1881), deputy, political writer, and historian. Under the Restoration Duvergier de Hauranne joined the *doctrinaire* school of the *Globe* and enthusiastically aided Louis-Philippe in his rise to power. In the Chamber of Deputies, which he entered in 1831, he became the zealous agent of Adolphe Thiers in his opposition to the conservative governments of Louis-Mathieu de Molé and François Guizot. He was one of the promoters of the campaign in favor of electoral reform and enlargement of the franchise, and this campaign finally carried away the July Monarchy.

Under the Second Republic he was an opponent of the prince-president, Louis-Napoleon Bonaparte, in both the Constituent Assembly and, later, the Legislative Assembly. The coup d'état of 2 December 1851 ended his political career. He consoled himself by writing a vast *Histoire du gouvernement parlementaire en France* (10 vols., 1857–72). In that book, the history of the Restoration is presented in great detail from a point of view that is Orleanist or moderate-liberal or *doctrinaire*. It is strictly a political history.

Guillaume de Bertier de Sauvigny, trans. E. Newman

Related entries: CONSTITUTION OF 1848; COUP D'ETAT OF 2 DECEMBER 1851; *DOCTRINAIRES*; ELECTIONS AND ELECTORAL SYSTEMS; *LE GLOBE*; GUIZOT; LEGISLATIVE ASSEMBLY; MOLE; THIERS.

DUVIVIER, GENERAL FANCIADE-FLEURUS (1794–1848), soldier. As a student of the Ecole polytechnique, he participated in the defense of Paris in 1814. He became one of the most distinguished Africains, noted for his scholarly interest in Algerian life and his archaeological digs. The founder of the zouaves, which he transformed from a regiment of Turkish mercenaries in the service of the dey of Algiers into one of Frenchmen dressed in native costume, he went native with a vengeance, insisting on dressing as the Algerians. He quarreled with his superior, Marshal Thomas-Robert Bugeaud, who detested intellectuals and polytechnicians, and left Algeria in 1841. He continued to attack Bugeaud in print, being especially critical of his use of the army in road building and of his neglect of a policy that would seek to make the Berbers the natural allies of the French against the Arabs. Elected as a deputy in 1848, Duvivier died defending the Hôtel de ville during the June Days of 1848.

A. de Colleville, *Notice biographique sur F.-F. Duvivier* (Cherbourg, 1848); C.-A. Julien, *Histoire de l'Algérie contemporaine* (Paris, 1964).

Douglas Porch

Related entries: BUGEAUD; ECOLE POLYTECHNIQUE; HUSSEIN; JUNE DAYS; REVOLUTION OF 1848.

E

L'ECHO FRANCAIS (1829–1847), monarchist and legitimist newspaper of the late Restoration and the July Monarchy. Several new right-wing journals were founded during the last years of Charles X's reign, including the *Echo français*, which appeared in January 1829. It accused the liberals of attacking not only the government of Jules de Polignac but the rights of the king and the dignity of the crown. After the fall of Charles X, the *Echo* continued to support the Bourbon dynasty. By 1846 it had only 2,000 subscribers, and in February 1847 it fused with two other legitimist papers, *La Quotidienne* and *La France*, to form *L'Union monarchique*.

C. Bellanger et al., *Histoire générale de la presse française*, vol. 2 (Paris, 1969).

Irene Collins

Related entries: CHARLES X; *LA FRANCE*; LEGITIMISM; POLIGNAC; *LA QUOTIDIENNE*.

ECLECTICISM. See COUSIN.

ECOLE CENTRALE DES ARTS ET MANUFACTURES, founded in Paris in 1829 by private initiative in order to train civil engineers, factory managers, builders, and, in the words of the prospectus, "to give to all who wished to take part in industrial specializations the necessary education both to appreciate its value and to watch over its development." The first class, in industrial physics, was given on 3 November 1829 to 140 pupils, all nonresident but uniformed, mostly aged between twenty to twenty-five years. The major force behind the new venture was Alphonse Lavallée (1797–1873), who was deeply concerned about the industrial situation of France in competition with other countries, together with Jean-Baptiste Dumas (1800–1884), a chemist who had been an assistant teacher at the Ecole polytechnique, Théodore Olivier (1793–1853), trained in mathematics, and Eugène Peclet (1793–1857), a former pupil and physics teacher at the Ecole normale supérieure. Lavallée rented a large house in the Marais district of central Paris, where the school remained until 1884. The three other founders contracted to teach, respectively, chemistry, geometry, and physics for twenty years with an annual salary of 3,000 francs. Teachers were engaged to give instruction in industrial mechanics, mining and building technology, industrial drawing, and other areas. Throughout the nineteenth century, the school maintained financial autonomy and paid for its upkeep from direct revenues without state support, although from its inception the foundation was placed under the protection of the Ministry of Public Instruction and, from 1835, under the aegis of the Ministry of Agriculture and Commerce. In 1857 the director and owner of the Centrale, Lavallée, gave responsibility for its management to the ministry on condition that its income remain completely separate from general revenues and be used exclusively for the institution. He remained as director until 1862. Graduates, known as *centraux*, were particularly influential in the development of the French railway system. The first graduate engineer, Jules Petiet, founded the Compagnie des chemins de fer du Nord with four other alumni. Numerous *centraux* reached positions of eminence in management and administration while retaining a loyalty to their former school, which maintained a high reputation for teaching and the ability to place graduates in good posts.

J. H. Weiss, *The Making of Technological Man: The Social Origins of French Engineering Education* (Cambridge, 1982).

David Higgs

Related entries: DUMAS, J.-B.-A.; ECOLE POLYTECHNIQUE; PUBLIC INSTRUCTION; RAILROADS.

ECOLE MILITAIRE (SAINT-CYR). Founded in 1803 by Napoleon, the Ecole spéciale militaire was moved from Fontainebleau in 1808 and installed in an old convent school, which dated from 1686, in the village of Saint-Cyr south of Paris. Originally, half of the places in the school were reserved for sons of officers, but from 1830 students were recruited by competitive examination. Although a limited number of scholarships were available, the school was fee paying. Following a two-year course at Saint-Cyr, cadets were ranked by order of merit and allowed to choose their initial assignment in the infantry or cavalry. (The top five cadets in each year's class traditionally went into the Staff Corps.) By the Second Empire, approximately half of the officers in the infantry and cavalry were Saint-Cyr graduates, the rest having been promoted through the ranks. The quality of the instruction at Saint-Cyr was considered extremely mediocre and the life of first-year cadets, constantly harassed by their seniors, arduous. These two factors no doubt contributed in great measure to the riotous behavior for which cadets were noted until well into the Third Republic. Several incidents of collective indiscipline prompted the French parliament in the July Monarchy to pass a law permitting the army to break cadets to the ranks to serve for five years as privates for severe infractions. Saint-Cyr was destroyed by the U.S. Army Air Corps in 1944 and subsequently rebuilt at Coëtquidan in Brittany.

D. Porch, *Army and Revolution, France 1815–1848* (London, 1974); E. Titieux, *Saint-Cyr et l'école spéciale militaire* (Paris, 1898).

Douglas Porch

Related entry: ECOLE NAVALE.

ECOLE MUTUELLE, a system of monitorial schools introduced during the early nineteenth century in which the older, more capable students taught the younger ones under the central direction of a master teacher. The monitorial method was developed in England by Joseph Lancaster and Andrew Bell in their charity schools in order to teach the rudiments of the 3 Rs, religion, and morality to large numbers of poor children as rapidly and cheaply as possible. After the peace of 1815, leading philanthropists in France, the baron de Gérando, the marquis de Jaucourt, and Georges Cuvier, organized the Société pour l'instruction élémentaire to popularize the method in France.

The new method appeared to be a means of educating large numbers of young people quickly with a minimum of trained teachers (of whom there were few in France). The principle of movement from group to group, each group being taught by a student monitor, allowed each child to work at his own level of ability in a given subject and relieved the tedium of sitting in one seat all day. The monitors were themselves being trained as teachers. In the process, French youth were to become literate, and France was to acquire a trained corps of teachers in a single generation.

Generally the system did not work well in France. The lack of well-trained masters, the scarcity of books and supplies, and the tendency of working-class parents to withdraw their children just as they were becoming well trained as monitors seriously weakened the system. The Catholic church was skeptical because it saw the method as an extension of the factory system in which the young would become cogs in the machine of industrial labor. It felt that religious education and other serious subjects would be neglected in a system in which children taught other children. It was also suspicious of the fact that the method was endorsed mainly by Protestants and by freethinkers.

M. Gontard, *L'Enseignement primaire en France de la Révolution à la loi Guizot, 1789–1833* (Paris, 1959); R. Tronchot, *L'Enseignement mutuel en France de 1815 à 1833*, 3 vols. (Lille, 1973).

C. Rod Day

Related entries: CUVIER; GERANDO; JAUCOURT; SOCIETY FOR ELEMENTARY INSTRUCTION.

ECOLE NAVALE, French naval college. First created in 1830, the school was held aboard a ship moored in Brest harbor. The school was traditionally called the *Borda* after the French mathematician and sailor Charles de Borda (1733–99). It offered a two-year course with a cruise in the summer. Between 1840 and 1913, the *Borda* was a three-tiered, masted wooden vessel. In 1935, it was transferred to permanent buildings on shore in Brest.

Douglas Porch

Related entry: ECOLE MILITAIRE (SAINT-CYR).

ECOLE POLYTECHNIQUE. Located in Paris, it was the most prestigious of the advanced training schools in nineteenth-century France, preparing students for artillery duty, military engineering, and branches of the public service. From its beginnings, the school was famous for pedagogical innovation in teaching mathematics, chemistry, and other sciences. Founded by a decree of the Convention (11 March 1794) to provide engineers to serve the Republic's war needs, it was placed under military discipline in 1804 with a governor and 300 male students aged between sixteen and twenty-three organized in battalions and living in barracks. Located in Paris to ensure that teaching staff could be drawn from the capital's intellectual elite, students examined in Paris rather than the provinces were more likely to be admitted during the first thirty years of the Ecole's existence. The student body was mainly Bonapartist in political sympathies prior to the Restoration, as was evident in 1814 and during the Hundred Days. The Restoration wished to uphold the Ecole's high intellectual standards but sought to purge those students with Bonapartist sympathies. A royal ordinance of 4 September 1816 reorganized the Ecole under the patronage of the nephew of Louis XVIII, the duc d'Angoulême. The entire student body was dismissed, although some were readmitted after new examinations and the replacement of a large part of the teaching and administrative staff. The commission that undertook the reorganization was presided by the mathematician and astronomer Pierre-Simon Laplace (1749–1827). The new governor was an artillery general. On 17 January 1817 the Ecole reopened with a relaxation of its military discipline, although students still lived in barracks and wore a distinctive civilian uniform with a top hat. After two years of training, students were commissioned into the artillery corps or the military engineering corps or went on to further training in other branches of the public sector like the Ecole d'application des ponts et chaussées. Daily prayers and regular attendance at Mass were required of Catholic students, and those obligations were resented. Throughout the Restoration, the students revealed themselves as mainly liberal in their political sympathies. In 1820 Etienne Arago, then a chemistry demonstrator, organized a carbonari cell (*vente*), which met until 1822. In July 1830 the polytechniciens played a prominent part in street fighting in the capital, especially at the attack on the Babylone barracks and the Louvre. One polytechnicien, Vaneau, was killed in the fighting. Jean-Baptiste Charras, expelled in early 1830 for singing the ''Marseillaise,'' was a leading combatant. He was later to return to service, became a war minister in 1848, and was arrested and deported in 1852. In 1830 the students were collectively commended by King Louis-Philippe. In the summer of that year, a commission presided by Arago suggested reforms in the Ecole, which were implemented the following November. Religious services inside the Ecole were suppressed and the number of hours when students were free to leave the buildings was increased, although barracks billeting and the wearing of the distinctive uniform continued, with all students now permitted to wear a sword. Student hostility to the July Monarchy was present in the 1830s and early 1840s. During the 1848 Revolution they were active in working for the Provisional Government. They formed a guard for Alphonse de Lamartine and were used to oversee food supplies. The internal organization of the Polytechnique underwent modification by the decrees of 1 and 25 November 1852.

A. Fourcy, *Histoire de l'Ecole polytechnique* (Paris, 1828); B.-C.-P. Marielle, *Repertoire de l'Ecole impériale polytechnique, ou renseignements sur les élèves... 1794 jusqu'en 1853 inclusivement* (Paris, 1855); Gaston Pinet, *Histoire de l'Ecole polytechnique* (Paris, 1887); T. Shinn, *Savoir scientifique et pouvoir social. L'Ecole polytechnique, 1794–1914* (Paris, 1980).

David Higgs

Related entries: ARAGO FAMILY; CARBONARI; CHARRAS; LAMARTINE; LAPLACE; PUBLIC INSTRUCTION.

ECOLES NATIONALES DES ARTS ET METIERS, arts and trades schools providing middle-level technical instruction in the mechanical arts for the sons of skilled artisans and workers. The Ecoles des arts et métiers were established by Napoleon at Châlons-sur-Marne in 1803 and Angers in 1811 on the model of an earlier school founded in 1788 by the duc de la Rochefoucauld-Liancourt near Paris. Napoleon wished to train skilled workers, mechanics, and foremen for the arms and mechanical industries. At first, demand for graduates was slack, and the schools had difficulty recruiting capable students, but the rise of the railway, machine construction, and metallurgical industries during the middle decades of the century opened up many professional opportunities and enabled the two schools to recruit from the most capable young people of modest origin coming up from the higher primary schools.

In 1832, the schools were placed under the direction of the Ministry of Industry and Commerce, where they remained until after World War I. Graduates had difficulty finding jobs until the late 1830s when a boom in railway building stimulated the machine construction and metallurgical industries and created great demand for mechanics and engineers. In 1843 a third school was opened at Aix-en-Provence near Marseilles to serve the rapidly growing industry of the south and southeast. Graduates usually began their careers as skilled workers, mechanics, foremen, and draftsmen, but most rose to positions as shop supervisors, production managers, and plant directors. A fair number went into business for themselves manufacturing machine tools and parts. Although the schools did not offer an engineering diploma until 1907, most graduates received the title through promotion on the job.

Three more schools were opened in Cluny (1891), Lille (1900), and Paris (1912). They received university status after World War II.

C. R. Day, *Education for the Industrial World: The Ecole d'Arts et Métiers and the Rise of French Industrial Engineering* (Cambridge, Mass., 1987), and "The Making of Mechanical Engineers in France: The Ecoles D'Arts et Métiers, 1803–1914," *French Historical Studies* (Spring 1978); A. Guettier, *Histoire des écoles des arts et métiers*, 2d rev. ed. (Paris, 1880).

C. Rod Day

Related entries: CONSERVATOIRE NATIONAL DES ARTS ET METIERS; LA ROCHEFOUCAULD-LIANCOURT.

ECOLES NORMALES PRIMAIRES, teacher-training schools established on a national level by the Guizot law on Public Education of 1833. During the eighteenth century, the teacher usually learned his craft through apprenticeship on the job. Professional qualifications did not exist, and the teacher simply hired out his services according to the reading, writing, and/or calculating skills that he could sell. A few had been trained by the Christian Brothers (*Frères de la Doctrine chrètienne*), an association of lay brothers that was the first in France to introduce the idea of professional training for the teacher. With their exile during the Revolution, organized teacher training came to a halt. The Ecole normale of Paris, opened in January 1794, soon became a casualty of the reaction against the Jacobins and their works. The Napoleonic law of 17 May 1808 calling for regional normal schools attached to major lycées (secondary schools) was never implemented. Many capable teachers abandoned their schools for more abundant opportunities in expanding state bureaucracies and in the military service.

In 1810 the first French normal school was established at Strasbourg by local officials on the model of the German normal schools. Although the school was a success, the idea did not spread elsewhere in France for several years. Most educators, from the Christian Brothers (who returned under Napoleon) to the advocates of the new monitorial method, favored teacher training through apprenticeship, the *école de stage*. Liberals disliked the normal school because the boarding school format (*internat*) too closely resembled the Catholic seminary and was too subject to state manipulation.

The relative failure of the monitorial method by the late 1820s and the small number of teacher-training programs run by the Christian Brothers led to renewed interest in the normal school. By 1823, the departments of the Meuse and the Moselle, located next to Alsace, had opened schools on the model of Strasbourg. In 1828 and 1829, Antoine de Vatimesnil, minister of education, encouraged other departments to do the same, and eleven responded. In 1830 there were fourteen normal schools; in 1832, on the eve of the Guizot Law, thirty-six; in 1837, four years after the law had made them obligatory on the departments, seventy-four.

The two-year program of the normal schools was designed for young men aged sixteen to eighteen and emphasized the advanced 3 Rs, some science and mathematics (especially applied geometry for surveying and mechanical drawing), notions of French history and geography, religion and morality, and practice teaching. For a time the regime of the schools was quite free and open, but conservative criticism caused the government to cut back programs and to enclose the school within walls of the *internat*, "half barracks, half monastery," as the normal schools came to be called.

Under the July Monarchy, the seventy-four or so schools averaged around 2,600 students in a given year, mostly the sons of farmers, village artisans, and schoolmasters. By the end of 1846, 9,200 graduates were on the job in a corps of about 40,000 teachers in France, and 8,000 had taken summer refresher courses in the normal schools. As graduates of the normal schools came gradually to replace the less competent older teachers, the quality of instruction in the villages and towns of France improved. Although threatened for a time during the reaction of the early 1850s, the normal schools survived. Under the Third Republic the departments were obliged to maintain normal schools for young women, and by the end of the 1880s there were about 160 such schools for men and for women in France.

C. R. Day, "Social Advancement and the Primary School Teacher: The Making of Normal School Directors in France, 1815–1880," *Social History, A Canadian Review* (May 1974), and "The Rustic Man: The French Schoolmaster in the Middle of the Nineteenth Century," *Comparative Studies in Society and History* (Winter 1982–83); M. Gontard, *La Question des ecoles normales primaires de la Révolution de 1789 à la loi de 1879* (Toulouse, 1964).

C. Rod Day

Related entries: BROTHERS OF THE CHRISTIAN SCHOOLS; *ECOLE MU-TUELLE*; GUIZOT LAW ON PUBLIC EDUCATION.

ECOLES PRIMAIRES PROTESTANTES, a system of schools belonging to the Reformed and Lutheran churches authorized as public under the terms of the education laws of 1816 and 1833. Prior to the revocation of the Edict of Nantes, the Reformed church of France possessed a flourishing system of schools. These disappeared under the persecutions of Louis XIV. During the eighteenth century, only clandestine schools, the *écoles buissonières*, survived as part of the outlawed *Eglise du désert*.

The Revolution restored the rights of Protestants, but their religious life suffered as a result of the secularism and free thought of the time. The religious awakening (*Le Réveil*) of the Restoration period, combined with help from the government, enabled them to rebuild their churches and to open schools. The Guizot Law of 1833 provided financial aid to their teachers and schools and support for their *écoles modèles* for the training of teachers. The law itself defined public education as essentially confessional, with each legally recognized faith allowed to have its own schools and school boards.

The Protestant schools grew rapidly, serving a Reformed church of about 500,000 members and a Lutheran church of around 250,000, located mostly in Alsace. After the loss of Alsace-Lorraine in 1871, the number of Lutherans in

France declined. At the time of the Ferry Laws of the early 1880s, there were about 1,500 Protestant schools. With secularization, these were merged into the public school system.

C. R. Day, "The Development of Protestant Primary Education in France under the Constitutional Monarchy, 1815–1848," *Canadian Journal of History*, no. 2 (1981).

C. *Rod Day*

Related entries: GUIZOT LAW ON PUBLIC EDUCATION; SOCIETY FOR THE ENCOURAGEMENT OF PRIMARY INSTRUCTION AMONG PROTESTANTS.

ECOLES PRIMAIRES SUPERIEURES, higher primary schools organized by the law on public education of 1833 (Guizot Law). The Guizot Law of 1833 required every commune of over 500 inhabitants to open an elementary school for boys and each city of over 6,000 to provide a higher primary school. The higher primary schools were apparently the idea of Victor Cousin, who had observed middle schools during his trip to Germany. They were designed for young men of modest origin aged twelve to fourteen who needed more than just an elementary education but who did not have the interest or the resources to study classical languages in the secondary boarding schools, the lycées, and collèges.

The higher primary school offered a three-year program teaching the 3 Rs, the elements of science and mathematics, surveying and linear drawing, French history and geography, and religion and morality. The program was mainly terminal in nature, and the graduates were expected to go to work on finishing their studies, usually as lesser clerks in business or government. Some did continue their studies either in teacher-training schools (*écoles normales primaires*) or in arts and trades schools (*écoles des arts et métiers*).

The schools did not do particularly well under the July Monarchy. There were 332 of them in 1837 (235 public and 97 private) with 9,414 students. By 1840 there were 455 (264 public and 191 private) with 15,285 students. Many parents preferred to enroll their sons as day students in modern programs in the *collèges communaux*, local secondary schools possessing more prestige than institutions associated with the socially inferior primary system.

The higher primary schools were not mentioned in the Falloux Law on public education of 1850, and they tended to disappear under the Second Empire. A few located in industrial areas survived as technical high schools. The Third Republic revived them on a national scale during the 1880s for boys and for girls. These schools did well until the 1930s when they were gradually assimilated by the lycées and, in some cases, by technical high schools. The *collèges d'enseignement secondaire* of the post World War II period are their heirs.

V. Cousin, *Rapport sur l'état de l'instruction publique dans les pays de l'Allemagne* (Paris, 1831); C. R. Day, "The Development of Higher Primary and Intermediate Technical Education in France, 1880–1870," *Historical Reflections* (Winter, 1972); S.-M.

Girardin, *De l'Instruction intermédiaire et de ses rapports avec l'instruction secondaire* (Paris, 1847).

C. Rod Day

Related entries: COUSIN; *ECOLES NATIONALES DES ARTES ET METIERS; ECOLES NORMALES PRIMAIRES*; FALLOUX LAW; GUIZOT LAW ON PUBLIC EDUCATION.

ECONOMIC CHANGE. Because of methodological difficulties and a paucity of statistics, the path to an understanding of French economic growth in the nineteenth century has always been a minefield. The nature, significance, and explanation of this growth have long been the subject of lively controversy among historians. There has recently been considerable rethinking and quantitative research on the problem, but it should not be supposed that the difficulties have been solved or that disagreements have ceased. On the contrary, and as is invariably the case in other historical controversies, new work has not simplified debate but made it more complicated.

What has happened, however, is that the view that dominated writing on French growth until about 1960, a view held above all by U.S. scholars, has been effectively challenged. This held that throughout the nineteenth century, France's economy at best grew only slowly and at worst stagnated and, in any case, failed to keep pace with the British and Belgian economies in the first half of the century and with the German in the second. The principal task historians set themselves was to explain this purportedly less than optimal performance, and they did this by proposing different clusters and priorities of so-called retardative factors. While some stressed the role of poor resource endowment, others suggested institutional factors or even social psychology and culture patterns. For the period down to 1850, indeed, the task of explaining slow growth seemed all the easier because the French economy emerged from the Revolutionary and Napoleonic periods with a number of weaknesses. The Revolution not only reinforced peasant ownership and thereby limited agriculture's capacity to change, but the dislocations and inflation of the 1790s led to a fall in industrial production of over a half by 1800. Although there was a remarkable industrial resurgence in the 1802–10 boom, the process of catching up with the British economy was more difficult after the fall of Napoleon than it had been in the 1780s. France's Atlantic economy had collapsed, and the most valuable part of the eighteenth-century empire (Santo Domingo) had been lost. At the same time, Britain's technological lead in heavy industrial and textile spinning had increased. French coal—and thus iron products—was more expensive than British, and French wage levels, though lower than across the Channel, were higher than the German. It is not surprising, then, that judged by some industrial indicators, France had fallen even further behind Britain by the middle of the nineteenth century. Per capita consumption of coal was six times, pig iron five times, and raw cotton nearly three times greater in Britain, and there were nearly five times as many steam engines per capita than in France. Although the gravity of the problems that the French economy faced in 1815 has not been questioned, long-standing strictures about poor economic performance thereafter certainly have. Two developments have prompted this challenge. One is the emergence of economic history as a discipline in France and the publication in the 1960s of the first quantitative studies of long-term French growth by researchers at the Institut de sciences économiques appliquées in Paris. The other is the adoption of more sophisticated approaches to what scholars increasingly realize is the complex and varied process of economic growth.

The use of these more sophisticated approaches has not led to a new consensus but to renewed debates. Some scholars question the models of industrialization used to evaluate the French experience. They argue that it is not helpful to judge French growth using the British case, since Britain's early industrialization and the competitive advantage some of its manufactures enjoyed precluded other economies following the same path. They add that French industrialists had advantages in other sectors—in high-quality textiles, for instance. In consequence, the process of industrial growth in nineteenth-century France was in important respects different from that in Britain. Comparing consumption of coal, iron, and raw cotton therefore may not be a suitable yardstick. Other scholars have gone further and, introducing value judgments, claim that the pace and nature of France's economic growth ensured a better quality of life for its citizens than did the more rapid process across the Channel. Still others have expressed reservations as to usefulness of national aggregates. In the France of the first half of the nineteenth century, indeed, national statistics hide wide disparities between sectors and regions and thus mask the changes that were taking place. Thus, though generalizations about agriculture have traditionally been based on that part of cultivated land held by inefficient peasant proprietors, this does not mean there was no dynamic sector or progressive region. Similarly, some of France's industrial regions were more progressive than others. A number of economic historians are even beginning to insist that economic growth is regional rather than national, and there is some truth to the assertion. The Nord and Pas-de-Calais, for instance, are in geological and geographical terms part of the Belgian industrial region. In the French cotton industry, the most important manufacturing region, with a third of all spindles, was Normandy, but it was Alsace, which despite its distance from the ports and its lack of coal, that was the most modern and dynamic area.

Even more important in challenging the validity of traditional strictures of French economic performance in the first half of the nineteenth century have been the quantitative analyses carried out by T. J. Markovitch, Jean Marczewski, Maurice Lévy-Leboyer, and François Crouzet. The slight differences in the growth indexes that these scholars have produced are to be explained by the fact that the statistical series available are not complete and by different methods used for computing general trends. Industry grew at an annual average rate of 2 percent between 1815 and 1913 (Crouzet, whose estimate of 1.6 percent is the lowest, has subsequently admitted that his figure is too low). Reconstructions of agricultural production also reveal steady growth. Lévy-Leboyer has calculated that the annual increase from 1815 to 1840 was 1.7 percent and that this rose to 2.62 percent down to 1865 (if the exceptionally poor run of harvests from 1850 to 1855 is omitted), only to fall back to the low rate of 0.26 percent a year down to 1900. Although it is possible that these figures are somewhat optimistic, they do indicate trends, and they do show that rates of growth in agricultural production were not far below those achieved in Britain and that per capita they were probably higher. The surprising picture that emerges from these two indexes is that, though British economic growth was faster through the century, the rates in Britain and France were about the same when judged on a per capita basis (and France's lower rate of demographic growth thereby taken into account).

Four major conclusions can be drawn from recent quantitative research. The first concerns the antecedents of nineteenth-century growth. From the 1720s to the 1780s French growth rates paralleled the British and in some instances were even higher (though the technical innovations that were being introduced into some British industries were not widely adopted in France). The Revolution and Empire, however, had a generally deleterious effect on the French economy, the remarkable spurt of industrial growth in the first decade of the new century notwithstanding. Second, the nineteenth century as a whole was one of moderate growth. Third, there was a deceleration in rates of both agricultural and industrial growth from 1860 to 1865, and the highest rates were therefore achieved in the first part of the century. It has even been claimed that there was an agricultural revolution at this time. As for industry, there remains a difference of opinion as to which decades saw peak growth. Crouzet finds that the highest rates of growth are to be found in the 1840s and 1850s. Others find them in the 1820–45 period. Fourth, and perhaps more controversial, it is argued that France had its own pattern of growth. It enjoyed competitive advantages in its lower labor costs (lower, that is, than in Britain), skills, and flair for design and finishing. French industrialists were thus able to excel in the production of high-quality consumption goods, like silks, prints, and mixed fabrics in textiles. And innovation proceeded downstream from finishing processes, as against the upstream pattern in Britain, where change came first in spinning and basic industries. At the same time, it seems that the trend toward large, integrated concerns was less marked in France, where handicraft and small-scale industries expanded alongside, and often in conjunction with, modern enterprise.

Recent work, then, has brought rates and patterns of French growth into sharper focus. However, though we have a clearer picture of the most important determinants of this growth, its explanation remains difficult. One reason is that there is no one generally accepted theory of economic growth that explains a complex process involving diverse elements, only some of which are measurable. Another is that for the French case, we still do not have sufficient data on crucial aspects like change in different economic regions. Yet another is that growth was not even between 1815 and 1850 but was rhythmed by the boom and slump sequence; the years down to 1820, 1827–32, 1837–41, and 1847–50, were all periods of depression. Motors of growth also changed. The railroad began to have a significant effect on capital formation and metallurgy (but not on goods transport until after midcentury) only in the 1840s.

We do, however, have a better understanding of variables that used to be regarded as insuperable barriers to growth. Historians now play down the importance of some of these retardative factors, like tariffs, banking, and transport. Thus, though problems remained, transport facilities certainly improved in this period. Between 1814 and 1846 7,000 kilometers of major highways and 22,000 kilometers of local roads were built. As a result and because of intensified competition and greater efficiency among haulers and competition from canals, the cost of goods transported by road fell by between a third and a half. The significance of this reduction can be gauged from the fact that roads carried over half the total goods traffic at midcentury. The canal network, too, was transformed by the completion of 2,900 kilometers of new waterways. Although some trunk railroads were completed (Paris-Orléans in 1842, Paris-Rouen in 1843, and the Northern line in 1846), railways carried only 11 percent of goods in 1850, as against over a third for the canals. Other barriers to growth, however, do retain much of the force that an earlier generation of scholars ascribed to them. There is evidence that in contrast to Britain and Belgium, France suffered from a shortage of coal. Although coal was not yet the vital sinew it was to become for French industry, its cost was high. Indicative of the failure of domestic supplies to keep pace with demand is the proportion of coal consumption that was imported: by midcentury 40 percent came from outside. More important, slow demographic growth acted as a brake on the pace of change. While it is true that population grew more rapidly in the first half of the century than it did in the second (an increase of 31 percent, 1801–51, as against a mere 9 percent in the 1851–1914 period), even this growth was still less than it was elsewhere. The significance for the economy of this slower growth is all the greater since demographic change at this time was largely an exogenous factor. The precocious slowing down of population growth was chiefly the result of an early adoption of family limitation that led to a falling birthrate.

We also have a better understanding of the determinants of industrial growth. Particularly important were increases in production and productivity in textiles since these industries were responsible for a fifth of industrial production by value. The dynamic textiles—wool, cotton, silk, and jute—had an annual average rate of growth of 2.3 percent from the 1830s to 1870s. Cotton went through especially rapid growth under the Restoration and steady growth during the July Monarchy. The chief stimulus for this came from the increasing purchasing power of the highly protected home market (only 20 percent of total production was exported). Domestic demand was also stimulated by the falling price of cotton goods, which resulted from cheaper raw cotton and rising labour productivity. The woolen and silk industries were similarly dynamic. Both of these textiles managed to increase their exports significantly. Thus the woolen industry, which exported 10 percent of its production in the early 1820s, had raised this to nearly a third by the 1850s. The metallurgical industry also enjoyed a high rate of growth; it has been calculated that iron output rose to an annual average of 5.5 percent between 1830–34 and 1860–64. This increase was encouraged by tariff protection and a growing demand for iron in the French economy. In the mid-1840s, for instance, rails for railways absorbed roughly a quarter of total bar-iron production. Increased output was achieved through both expanding charcoal smelting in small rural forges (up to 1837) and by the establishment of large, integrated concerns using coke for smelting and coal for puddling. By 1847 the seven largest of these firms were already responsible for nearly 40 percent of total iron production. The Second Empire was to consecrate the triumph of both coke and the large concern.

Agriculture, which in the early 1840s occupied just over half the active population and was responsible for 60 percent of the physical product (that is, agriculture plus industry), played a crucial role in economic growth. It played an equally important part in the generation of economic crises, as was shown by the impact on the economy of the poor harvests of, say, 1817 or 1846. It is nevertheless difficult to assess the importance of the agrarian sector as a source of capital or as a market for industry. Certainly the rural exodus accelerated. It increased from 473,000 in the 1830s to 849,000 in the 1840s. But this was due to a multiplicity of causes rather than just a release of agricultural labor. Agriculture, though, did manage to feed a growing urban population. From 1811 to 1851 urban population (defined as those living in cities of at least 3,000 inhabitants) increased by 50 percent. And despite the existence of great regional disparities, the sector managed a respectable global rate of growth. It did this by the continued spread of convertible husbandry—the crucial breakthrough in agricultural improvement before 1850—and of crops like the potato and sugar beet, and it did it mainly on large farms. French agriculture at this time has traditionally been regarded as being structured by myriads of small and unprogressive peasant holdings. There is some truth to this, but it is not the whole picture. Over three-quarters of farms were between 1 and 10 hectares, too small to support a family. Average size of farms, indeed, was only 12.5 hectares, as against a British average of 40. However, farms of over 40 hectares still covered nearly half the total cultivated area, and it was these that were responsible for much of the increasing production.

The history of French economic growth in the first half of the nineteenth century, then, has been radically revised by recent work. The fallacious clarity of earlier analyses of backwardness has been replaced by a new awareness of complex but accelerating growth in both the agrarian and industrial sectors. In 1850 France was still Europe's second economic power.

F. Braudel and E. Labrousse, eds., *Histoire économique et sociale de la France*, pts. 1, 2, and 3 (Paris, 1976); F. Caron, *An Economic History of Modern France* (New York, 1979); B. Gille, *Recherches sur la formation de la grande entreprise capitaliste, 1815–1848* (Paris, 1959); M. Lévy-Leboyer, *Les banques européennes et l'industrialisation internationale dans la première moitié du XIXe siecle* (Paris, 1964); S. Pollard, *Peaceful Conquest: The Industrialisation of Europe, 1760–1970* (Oxford, 1981).

Barrie M. Ratcliffe

Related entries: AGRICULTURE; COAL INDUSTRY; FOREIGN TRADE AND TARIFF POLICY; MIGRATION; POPULATION; SILK INDUSTRY.

EDUCATION, FREEDOM OF. See LIBERTY OF EDUCATION.

ELECTIONS AND ELECTORAL SYSTEMS. The electoral system of the Restoration and of the July Monarchy is called a *régime censitaire*. The word *censitaire* derives from a medieval term, *cens*, designating land rents. In order to qualify to vote, an elector was required to pay a certain level of direct taxes, the most important one being the *contribution foncière*, or tax on land. The other taxes taken into account in determining qualification were the *contribution personnelle et mobilière* (a poll tax and tax on residences), the *contribution des portes et fenêtres* (on doors and windows), and the *patente* (the tax on business).

The number of people qualifying to vote was small and varied from time to time. The 110,000 voters at the beginning of the Restoration had diminished to 89,000 by the end. Yet elections interested a much larger number of people. Members of the Chamber of Deputies were the only government officials chosen by election during the Restoration. These elections were the most significant political events that determined the course of policy and the fate of governments. Prefects were expected to produce satisfactory elections, as well as administer their departments competently.

Articles 35 to 42 of the Charter of 1814 established basic requirements for voting and office-holding. One-fifth of the Chamber of Deputies was to be elected every year for a five-year term. Electors were required to pay a direct tax of 300 francs and be at least thirty years old. To be eligible for election, a man had to pay 1,000 francs of direct taxes and be at least forty years old. Half of the delegation of each department had to have their political residence in the department. The king could dissolve the Chamber, and he appointed the presidents of the electoral colleges. Laws were to provide further provisions and details. The Charter was silent on the question of the mode of election, though its framers apparently assumed that there would be a two-step election process.

The Chamber of Representatives chosen during the Hundred Days was closed down as soon as Louis XVIII returned to France. Elections for a new chamber were held on 14 and 21 August 1815 with voting by the old Napoleonic electoral colleges plus additional voters named by the prefect of each department. According to the ordinance calling for elections, voters had to be twenty-one years old and deputies twenty-five. Primary colleges nominated candidates. Half of the deputies chosen by the departmental colleges had to be chosen from among these nominees. The result was the famous *chambre introuvable*.

When the government introduced an electoral law that called for indirect election of deputies, voters by right, and new age qualifications, the *chambre introuvable* amended the provisions substantially to give more power to rich landowners and decrease the power of those in official positions. The government let it be known that the bill was unacceptable, and the Chamber of Peers voted it down. A second attempt to pass a law satisfactory to the government also failed. With no electoral law, the Napoleonic colleges were convoked once again after the famous ordinance of 5 September 1816 dismissed the *chambre introuvable*. The prefects could again name voters to each college. A moderate Chamber was elected that docilely passed the new electoral law (*loi Lainé*) in February 1817. It departed from the traditional two-step voting and gave all voters thirty years old who paid 300 francs in direct taxes a place in the single departmental electoral college that chose the deputies.

If an electoral college numbered more than 600, it was divided into sections of no more than 600, each with its own bureau and vice-president. The president of the first section was president of the entire college. The college was limited in its functions. Only the president of the college (or a vice-president of a section) could make a speech. No debate was allowed. The first item of business was to elect a bureau consisting of a secretary and four *scrutateurs*. The following day, voting for deputies began. Each voter wrote on his ballot a number of names of eligible candidates equal to the number of deputies for the department. All sections voted for all candidates, and then the votes were totaled. The victor had to receive a total that was a majority of those voting and at least one-quarter plus one of those inscribed in the college. If the delegation was not complete after two rounds of voting, a third round (*ballotage*) was held in which voters were restricted in their choices to the top vote getters on the second round, twice as many names as there were slots to fill.

A fifth of the Chamber stood for election under this system in September 1817. Paris was part of the first series. Elections were repeated in October 1818 and October 1819, with increasing success on the part of the liberal opposition. After the election of the abbé Grégoire in 1819, the government sought a way of reforming the system to make liberal success less likely. In the reaction following the assassination of the duc de Berry, a new law was passed splitting the electorate into two parts. The old electorate would retain its vote, but instead of a departmental college, there would now be 258 arrondissement colleges each electing one deputy. The arrondissement colleges of a department elected the same number of deputies as had the departmental college previously. In addition, a new class of voters consisting of the one-quarter of the electorate that paid the highest taxes in each department was given a second vote. They constituted a departmental college that elected 172 additional deputies to an expanded Chamber. The victor's majority now had to consist of more than one-third of the number registered. This Law of the Double Vote (which passed the Chamber of Deputies by 154 to 93 on 12 June 1820) was first used in November 1820 when the fourth series was chosen by the new arrondissement colleges, and the *grands collèges* of all the departments met to select the additional delegates.

The government managed to reverse the electoral tide in the yearly elections between 1820 and 1823 in part because the censorship laws and laws on individual freedom limited the ability of the opposition to organize effectively. The general elections of late February and early March 1824 following the dissolution of the Chamber returned a strongly royalist Chamber that strove to preserve its gains by changing the law again to increase terms to seven years and decree general elections instead of yearly partial elections.

Elections were held again in November 1827 after the Chamber was dissolved. An invigorated opposition brought off a substantial victory. Its victory was even greater in the general elections of late June and July 1830 following another dissolution. Charles X refused to accept this result and issued his four ordinances, which ignited the Revolution of 1830 and led to his abdication. The ordinances suspended freedom of the press, dissolved the Chamber of Deputies, called for new elections, and ordained a new electoral law. The business tax (*patente*) was excluded from the totals of direct taxes to determine eligibility. Arondissement colleges were no longer to elect deputies directly but merely to present candidates to the *grand collège* which would elect the deputies, only half of whom had to be from among the candidates chosen by the arrondissement colleges.

The Charter of 1830, as revised by the Chamber of Deputies and issued by Louis-Philippe, lowered the minimum voting age to twenty-five and the age of eligibility to thirty. The amount of taxes to be paid was not specified in the Charter. The president of the electoral college was to be chosen by the voters, not appointed as previously. Deputies were chosen in general elections for five-year terms. The details of the electoral system were contained in the law of 19 April 1831, which set the number of deputies at 459, each elected directly by an arrondissement college. Taxes required for voting were lowered to 200 francs and for eligibility to 500 francs. In addition certain citizens paying only 100 francs were given the right to vote: members of the Institut and retired army and navy officers with pensions of 1,200 francs who had lived in the district for three years. If an arrondissement did not contain 150 qualified voters, additions up to that number would be made from those who paid the highest taxes. These changes almost doubled the number of voters from about 89,000 to about 166,000, one voter for 170 people.

These provisions remained unchanged for the duration of the July Monarchy, but the number of voters increased steadily because of the growth in population and wealth. By 1846 there were almost 241,000 voters. A new election in the case of a deputy who accepted a paid government position was stipulated in the Charter and regulated by the law of 12 September 1830. General elections were held in July 1831, June 1834, November 1837, March 1839, July 1842, and August 1846.

Under the July Monarchy deputies were not the only elected officials. Communal electors chose the members of the municipal councils. The mayor and his *adjoints* were appointed from among their number. One qualified to be a municipal elector by being among those paying the highest taxes or by filling a certain office or profession as defined by the law of 21 March 1831. In addition, departmental and arrondissement councils were elected according to the provisions of the law of 22 June 1833.

The voters of the Restoration and the July Monarchy were not representative of the general population. They were a small elite in which those whose wealth came from land predominated. The number of voters varied widely from one department to another, and the number of voters or candidates was not proportional to the population. Calvados with 2,400 voters and Finistère with 802 had approximately the same population under the Restoration. Some districts had trouble finding candidates who fit the requirements and who had the leisure or the money to leave their homes for the duration of the parliamentary session to accept an unpaid position as deputy. The law stipulated that if a department did not have fifty men who fit the eligibility requirements, the fifty largest taxpayers would be made eligible.

Official political parties did not yet exist, but there were organized efforts to promote candidacies. In the early years of the Restoration, national organization of the electoral opposition was rudimentary, but some local politicians constructed effective political committees to get out the vote. These local groups looked for inspiration to the deputies in Paris and followed political news avidly in opposition newspapers. This rudimentary political organization was dealt a sharp blow by the reaction of the 1820s and the success of the royalists at the polls. In 1827, the group Aide-toi, le ciel t'aidera began a more concerted effort to mount an effective electoral campaign. This successful organization survived the Revolution of 1830 but fell victim to the law of 1834 against associations. Its leaders, though, continued to function as a political opposition machine, in 1837 taking the name Comité central de l'opposition constitutionnelle. Under the July Monarchy, more voters and their greater sophistication led to more visible political campaigns and more newspapers and pamphlets devoted to politics. Electoral techniques, however, remained essentially the same as those pioneered during the Restoration.

The Left was always hampered in its effectivness by the variety of groups under that rubric: from radical republicans to rather conservative constitutional monarchists. In the elections of 1817, 1818, and 1819, the government unsuccessfully tried to create a middle alternative to the ultraroyalists on its Right and the motley collection of constitutional monarchists and former Bonapartists on its Left. Between 1820 and 1824, the ultraroyalists and moderate government supporters combined to defeat the badly split politicians of the Left, some of whom sought to overthrow the government in the abortive carbonarist plots. In 1827, a reinvigorated and united Left now faced a government harried by an ultra opposition. The victors of the Revolution of 1830 soon split into two camps: the government supporters made up of those who were content with what had been achieved and had no wish to go further, called the *résistance*, and the opposition consisting of those who saw the gains of the Revolution as only the first step in a process of greater reform, called the *mouvement*. A legitimist group existed as well, but it was far less important than the preceding groups.

The government enjoyed the advantage of a ready-made, permanent political machine consisting of the civil servants. Government employees at all levels were expected to work for the success of the ministerial candidates. The official candidate was carefully chosen and promoted. In the Restoration, the official candidate was often named president of the electoral college. Deputies were rewarded for their loyalty with paid government positions. Although the Charter of 1830 required that a deputy accepting such a position stand for election, most were reelected. Using the techniques at its disposal, the governments of the July Monarchy maintained effective control of the Chamber of Deputies until the end. As in 1830, it was a conflict over the electoral system that precipitated the Revolution of 1848: the Banquet Campaign demanding widening of the franchise.

The Revolution of 1848 instituted universal adult manhood suffrage in France, and this electoral principle, though circumscribed on occasion, was never to be denied henceforth. On 5 March 1848, the Provisional Government of the Republic called for elections for a 900-member Constituent Assembly. All Frenchmen twenty-one years of age residing in their communes for six months were eligible to vote. Representatives had to be twenty-five years old. Voting by secret ballot was to take place at the *chef-lieu* of the canton under the presidency of the *juge de paix*. The number of representatives per department was based on population: Seine had the most (thirty-four) and Hautes-Alpes the least (three). Each ballot contained votes for all the representatives of the department (*scrutin de liste* rather than single-member constituencies). Election was by plurality (not majority), but the candidate had to receive a minimum of 2,000 votes. Bowing to pressure from workers' clubs in Paris who feared the country was not yet sufficiently instructed in republican ways, the government postponed the elections from the original date of 9 April until 23 April.

Voter turnout for the first election held by direct universal suffrage was impressively large (7,835,000, or 83.69 percent of registered voters). Since well-organized political parties did not exist, exact breakdowns are impossible; however, it is possible to conclude that most of those elected favored monarchy. On the right were around 290 avowed monarchists (Orleanists and legitimists). The large center group, traditionally called moderate republicans, actually included only 230 who advocated republicanism before the revolution. On the left were 55 extreme republicans or socialists. The rest were former monarchists who went along with the Republic in hopes of averting disorder.

The principle of universal manhood suffrage was applied as well to the elections for municipal, arrondissement, and departmental councils (held in August 1848). Mayors of small communes were elected by the municipal council. In cantonal *chefs-lieux*, the mayor was chosen by the prefect from among the municipal councillors. Paris was an exception, administered by the prefect, not a mayor.

The Constitution passed by the Assembly on 4 November 1848 instituted an electoral system maintaining the essential features of that of March 1848. Unlike the preceding two-house legislatures of the constitutional monarchies, the legislative power was given to one Assembly consisting of 750 representatives. Representatives could not hold salaried public office but did receive compensation. They served for a three-year term and could be reelected indefinitely. The Constitution broke most radically with the past by giving executive power to a president to be elected by universal adult manhood suffrage for a four-year term. He could not be reelected. Presidents had to be native Frenchmen, at least thirty years old. Election required a majority of votes cast. If no candidate received a majority, the Assembly chose the president from among the five who received the most votes.

The first (and only) presidential election under this system was held on 10 and 11 December 1848. Although dividing cantons into several electoral districts made voting easier than in April, abstentions increased; 7,449,471 voted (abstention rate of 24.9 percent). The victor was Louis-Napoleon Bonaparte (Napoleon I's nephew) who greatly outdistanced the other four main candidates:

Louis-Napoleon Bonaparte	5,534,520	74.3% of votes cast
Cavaignac	1,448,302	19.4%
Ledru-Rollin	371,431	5.0%
Raspail	36,964	0.5%
Lamartine	17,914	0.2%

Louis-Napoleon Bonaparte's huge majority was the result of attracting diverse groups: conservative groups wanting order in the country, as well as those lodging protest votes against socializing tendencies, against current authorities (especially Eugène Cavaignac), and against notables of the past.

The elections for the Assembly were held on 13 and 14 May 1849 according to procedures outlined in the electoral law of 15 March 1849, which maintained the system of 1848 except for the stipulation that the victor's total had to equal one-eighth of the number of registered voters. Out of 9,937,000 registered voters, 6,750,700 voted (32 percent abstained). The results of this election showed a growing polarization in the country. The extreme Left (the Montagnards or démoc-socs) increased in strength to about 200 and received between 35 and 40 percent of the votes cast. The moderate republicans were reduced to fewer than 80 (with around 12 percent of the votes cast) while the Right (the Party of Order, made up of legitimists, Orleanists, and Bonapartists) won a handsome majority of almost 500 seats (with around half of the votes cast).

On 13 June 1849, the extreme Left mounted a march against the government and the majority of the Assembly, whom they accused of unconstitutional actions for sending the French army to Rome. The thirty-four members of the Assembly who had signed the proclamation calling for the demonstration were arrested or fled. In the wake of this event, laws limiting freedom of the press and suspending freedom of assembly were passed. Elections to replace the expelled members were held on 10 March 1850. Although the results were a gain for the Right of ten seats that had formerly been held by the extreme Left, the election of twenty-one republicans and the election on 28 April at Paris of Eugène Sue (reputed to be a socialist) frightened the Assembly into modifying the electoral law. The law of 31 May 1850, while maintaining the principle of universal suffrage, extended the residency requirement from six months to three years and stipulated that residency would generally be established by inclusion on the rolls of those paying taxes in a commune. The consequence was to disfranchise the very poor and large numbers of itinerant workers. Some 2,809,000 registered voters would be eliminated. The full application of the law never took place. The elections scheduled for 1852 were not held under this system but rather under the constitution written after Louis-Napoleon's coup d'état of December 1851. Facing the scheduled presidential election of May 1852 and unable to convince the Assembly to modify the Constitution to allow for his reelection, Louis-Napoleon took personal power and ended the electoral system of the Second Republic.

The Second Republic vastly expanded political participation and established freedom of the press, which brought about fundamental changes in the way politics was conducted. Clubs and societies mobilized the voters, and many new, inexpensive political newspapers spread their messages to the people, who were entering politics for the first time. After the June Days of 1848, censorship was reintroduced. New press laws required newspapers to post cautionary deposits and made seditious libel illegal. Political clubs were hampered by the law of 28 July 1848 and by police surveillance and persecution of their leaders. Further restrictive measures were taken after 13 June 1849, which signficantly hurt republican and socialist efforts at organizing the new political classes. In early 1849, sweeping changes were made in prefectoral personnel to ensure closer control over the electoral apparatus by the government's agents. The efforts of the Party of Order, increasingly fearful of Montagnard agitation, effectively eliminated or drove underground much of the organized political opposition before the coup d'état of December 1851. The repression following that event destroyed what was left of republic networks and societies.

F. B. Artz, "The Electoral System in France under the Bourbon restoration," *Journal of Modern History* 1 (1929); P. Bastid, *Les Institutions politiques de la monarchie parlementaire française (1814–1848)* (Paris, 1954); T. D. Beck, *French Legislators, 1800–1834: A Study in Quantitative History* (Berkeley, 1974); P. Campbell, *French Electoral Systems and Elections 1789–1957* (London, 1958); S. Kent, *Electoral Procedure under Louis-Philippe* (New Haven, 1937) and *The Elections of 1827 in France* (Cambridge, Mass., 1975); R. Rémond, *La Vie Politique en France depuis 1789*, 2 vols. (Paris, 1965–69); A.-J. Tudesq, *L'election présidentielle de Louis Napoléon, 10 décembre 1848* (Paris, 1965).

Sylvia Neely

Related entries: AIDE-TOI, LE CIEL T'AIDERA; BANQUET CAMPAIGN; CARBONARI; CAVAIGNAC, L. E.; CENSORSHIP; CHAMBER OF DEP-

UTIES; CHAMBER OF PEERS; CHAMBRE INTROUVABLE; CHAMBRE
RETROUVEE; CHARTER OF 1814; CHARTER OF 1830; CLUBS, POLITI-
CAL; DOUBLE VOTE, LAW OF THE; ELECTORS; GREGOIRE; JULY OR-
DINANCES; LAMARTINE; LEDRU-ROLLIN; LEGISLATIVE ASSEMBLY;
LOUIS-PHILIPPE; PARTY OF MOVEMENT; PARTY OF ORDER; REPUB-
LICANS; REVOLUTION OF 1830; REVOLUTION OF 1848; ULTRA-
ROYALISTS.

ELECTORS. Participation was limited to members who paid large taxes, and
individuals, not parties, were the basis of activity. Control by the leading classes
and a focus on political issues provided a basic unity to the entire period despite
the change of regimes in 1830.

The lower house was elected by a *censitaire* system. Originally the Charter
defined the electors as those males who were at least thirty years old and who
paid 300 francs in direct taxes. After the Revolution of 1830 the requirements
were changed to twenty-five years of age and 200 francs in direct taxes. These
restrictions produced an electorate of about 90,000 during the Restoration and
180,000 in 1831. With economic development and a subsequent rise in tax
payments, the number of electors expanded to nearly 250,000 by 1848. To be
eligible to sit in the Chamber of Deputies, a man had to pay 1,000 francs under
the Bourbons and 500 francs under Louis-Philippe.

The pivotal issues—freedom of the press and the electoral requirements—
were political, and fundamentally they represented one's position on the Revolution
of 1789. The Right was basically opposed to the Revolution, so when it was in
control, freedom of the press was severely limited and voting was restricted to
those with the wealth and leisure to engage in reflective thought about the needs
of society. For example, after the election of 1820, where the Right had triumphed
because of the reaction to the assassination of the duc de Berry, the Chamber
of Deputies passed the Law of the Double Vote. It gave the top 25 percent of
each department's electorate (measured by taxes paid) a second vote in order to
elect two additional deputies.

That system produced a single type of electorate, despite the expansion of the
franchise in 1830. The *censitaire* system yielded an electorate that was primarily
landed yet with a significant business group. Under the Restoration, the electorate
comprised 59 percent landed, 21 percent business, 10 percent professionals, and
11 percent government. The percentage of business types was much greater in
the north, and their percentage more than doubled in cities of over 20,000
persons. Even among those men who had the double vote during the 1820s, the
percentage of business types remained near 20 percent.

The new electoral law of the July Monarchy enfranchised the same basic
types. Even with the effects of economic change, the electorate in 1839 still had
57 percent landed and 25 percent business types. Government officials were a
smaller percentage, but the professions remained at 10 percent. The underlying

unity was landed wealth, with commerce and manufacturing playing a large role, especially in the north and in cities of over 20,000 persons.

While the system and the voters exhibited continuity, the type of men who were elected to the Chamber of Deputies varied with each change of political opinion. The men elected for their conservative ideas were clearly more attached to the land and the old nobility, whereas those who were favored for their liberalism were more likely to be professionals, especially lawyers, or businessmen and bourgeois.

Five distinct periods can be identified by examining the characteristics of the deputies: 1815–16, 1817–19, 1820–26, 1827–30, and 1831–48. In 1815–16 the ultras dominated, and therefore the deputies were landed (35 percent) and old noble (40 percent). With the success of the liberals in 1817–19, the type of man elected shifted so that the landed were now 25 percent and the old nobles just 21 percent. Deputies who were in the professions and in business composed just 16 percent of the deputies in 1815–16 but 26 percent in 1817. The contrasts were even greater for the elections of 1815, when the ultras won 78 percent of the seats, and 1819, when the liberals won 70 percent of the seats.

The assassination of the duc de Berry caused the voters to shift back to more conservative deputies. In the partial elections of 1821 and 1822 and then in the full election of 1824, the royalists won the day. The deputies elected in 1824 were 92 percent royalists, 43 percent landed, and 51 percent old nobles. Just 14 percent were in the professions or business. With the turn to the Left in 1827– 30, the type of man elected deputy changed again. In 1827, 30 percent were in the professions or business, and 44 percent were old nobles. The greater success of the Left in 1830 dropped the percentage of old nobles to 38, although many of the deputies elected in 1827–30 were old and had held positions in the government going back to the Revolution or even the Old Regime.

In the fifth period, the July Monarchy, a new generation of deputies made their appearance. These men were young, often having just begun a career under the Empire when disaster struck them. These would-be servants of Napoleon were more often bourgeois than the deputies of the Restoration, and they were about evenly split among landed, professionals, and businessmen. When the Right was truncated in the Revolution of 1830, the percentage of old nobles was halved. Professional and business deputies after 1830 jumped to nearly half of the Chamber. Although there was some backsliding during the July Monarchy, even in 1846 only 26 percent of the deputies were old nobles, and 40 percent were professionals or businessmen.

A key factor in the politics of the *censitaire* monarchies was maintenance of the accomplishments of the years 1789–91. Those among the electorate who favored this were more often located in the areas of France that were economically and socially advanced. Economic development was occurring primarily in the cities and in the north. These areas rejected Charles X and his perceived return to the Old Regime by voting Left in 1827 and 1830. Louis Phillippe seemed to have satisfied these voters' fears, since in none of the elections of the July

Monarchy would the north vote overwhelmingly for the Left as it had at the end of the Restoration.

The dissatisfactions with the politics and the politicians of the *censitaire* monarchies evidenced in the 1840s were more fundamental than the system could handle. The Revolution of 1848 rejected the *censitaire* system and ended an era of brilliant personal politics. The experience of the *censitaire* system left behind neither political organizational apparatus nor a large, politically educated population.

J. Barthélemy, *L'introduction du régime parlementaire en France sous Louis XVIII et Charles X* (Paris, 1904).; T. D. Beck, *French Legislators, 1800–1834* (Berkeley, 1974); J. J. Chevalier, *Histoire des institutions et des régimes politiques de la France modern, 1789–1958* (Paris, 1967); P. Duvergier de Hauranne, *Histoire du gouvernement parlementaire en France, 1814–1848* (Paris, 1870); S. Kent, *The Election of 1827 in France* (Cambridge, Mass., 1975).

Thomas Beck

Related entries: CENSORSHIP; CHAMBER OF DEPUTIES; CHAMBER OF PEERS; CHARTER OF 1814; CHARTER OF 1830; DOUBLE VOTE, LAW OF THE; ELECTIONS AND ELECTORAL SYSTEMS; PRESS LAWS; ULTRAROYALISTS.

ENFANTIN, BARTHELEMY-PROSPER (1796–1864), a thinker and major figure in the Saint-Simonian sect. Enfantin's career is doubly paradoxical. Although the originality and profundity of his intellect are questionable, he emerged as the dominant figure—as the charismatic leader—of a movement that between 1825 and 1832 attracted a group of brilliant young men. After the breakup of the sect, a handful of ex-Saint-Simonians remained faithful to him, but the rest of Enfantin's life was an anti-climax: he became a prophet without followers, a thinker unheeded by his contemporaries. After 1832, indeed, he became an embarrassment to many of the sect's former adherents, who had either disagreed with his religious and sexual theories or did not wish to be reminded of their youthful devotion to him. Indicative of this paradox is the attitude of Heinrich Heine, the German poet, who frequented Saint-Simonian meetings in the early 1830s. In 1835 Heine dedicated the French edition of his famous *De l'Allemagne* to Enfantin and later referred to him as "the most significant mind of the present day." By 1855 he had not only removed the dedication but in an unpublished note remarked that in his incarnation as Enfantin, God had made the supreme sacrifice: he had made himself ridiculous. Enfantin has even been an embarrassment to scholars of Saint-Simonianism, and though there are apparently two biographies of him, the one (by Jean-Pierre Callot) is frivolous, and the other (by H.-R. d'Allemagne) is little more than extracts of documents on Saint-Simonians after 1832. Enfantin is thus the great outcast of Saint-Simonianism. This is unjust.

Enfantin's role in the sect was of critical importance. In 1825 he was, with Olinde Rodriguès, the founder of the *Producteur*, the movement's first journal. He was responsible, indeed, for some of the most important articles on economic questions. It was he who suggested that the class structure of France could be gradually transformed by increasing death duties, abolishing collateral inheritance, and establishing a centralized banking system to ensure efficient distribution of capital. His writings on economics and finance, published in 1831 as *Economie politique et politique*, thus constitute a major source for understanding Saint-Simonian theories. His role in the elaboration of the group's theories from late 1828 onward, however, is difficult to determine. He gave few of the lectures that make up the *Doctrine de Saint-Simon*, and from then on ideas were collectively elaborated in increasingly emotional discussions at the sect's headquarters at the rue Monsigny. In these discussions participated not men with second-class minds but some of the most talented members of the generation of 1830. If his later writings are any yardstick, though, it would seem that Enfantin's intellectual contribution was limited.

It was not as a theorist that his contribution lay. It was in his daring, his charismatic qualities, his belief in his own destiny. From 1829 he increasingly imposed himself on the group and inspired the devotion of the majority of its members. How can this ascendancy be explained? One explanation is his physical presence. Contemporaries were in agreement about his "olympian beauty" (Maxime Du Camp), his charisma—Michel Chevalier was to call him "one of the great magnetizers who exist or have ever existed"—and his confidence and serenity amid the emotional confessions of faith, frenzied adulations of his followers, and impassioned debates. Another is his daring and courage. He dared broach discussions of man's psychic nature, relations between the sexes, religion, and the female messiah, who, he believed for a fleeting moment in the early 1830s, would join him in completing the new faith and ushering in the new society the Saint-Simonians dreamed of creating. He had the courage in the face of public ridicule in the early 1830s and indifference in the long desert he traversed for the rest of his life to remain faithful in his mission and yet to be resigned to his fate. But the explanation for the influence he exercised over the sect does not lie with Enfantin alone. It is also to be found in the adherents of the sect, in the atmosphere of the messianic sect that Saint-Simonianism became in the last months of its existence. He became the focus for the emotional needs of a group of alienated young men who, in the charged atmosphere of their communal life, first at the rue Monsigny and later at their retreat at Ménilmontant, believed they had found certainty and salvation in his person and in Saint-Simonianism. It was for these reasons that at the end of 1829 he and Saint-Amand Bazard, another early adherent, were named joint leaders—*pères suprêmes*—of the sect. By late 1831 differences between the two on sexual and religious theories reached a climax, and in November Bazard broke with the group. His defection was the signal for others, and by early 1832 Olinde Rodriguès also withdrew. Although Enfantin, by his demeanor and ideas, certainly helped provoke these schisms, it should be remembered that fissiparous tendencies are characteristic of messianic sects.

The theories being enunciated and the public attention the group was attracting frightened the authorities who in July 1832 brought Enfantin and two other leaders to trial on charges of immorality; convicted, they were sentenced to a year in prison. On his early release in August 1832, Enfantin and a handful of the faithful spent three years in Egypt. Their original aim was to find the female messiah. The result, though, was suffering and death from disease for some and the ending of Enfantin's active search for a priestly mate and his role as a prophet. Thereafter, though he continued to advocate some of the reforms Saint-Simonians had earlier proposed and though he published his mature philosophical and religious ideas, his creative and historical role had effectively ended. The tidal wave that had swept him to influence and notoriety ebbed and left him to languish.

In 1839 he accepted a position on the scientific commission the government set up to study the new colony of Algeria, and he published *Colonisation de l'Algérie* (1843). Although the work contained some remarkable insights, an appreciation of Arab culture, and bold policy proposals, it was ignored by government and public alike. In 1845 Enfantin again took up the idea of building a Suez canal that he had proposed to Méhémet Ali twelve years previously. An international consortium was even organized and studies of technical problems undertaken, but the midcentury crisis interrupted its activities. When the project was taken up again in the 1850s, it was Ferdinand de Lesseps who secured the concession, and he did so without Enfantin or his study group.

The 1848 Revolution momentarily rekindled Enfantin's ardor. In November 1848 he set up a nonpartisan journal, the *Crédit*, and secured the collaboration of Charles Duveyrier and other erstwhile followers. The paper never secured enough subscribers and ceased to appear in June 1850. Even his two major philosophical works—*La science de l'homme* (1858) and *La vie éternelle* (1861)—which he saw as the continuation of Saint-Simon's *Nouveau Christianisme* of 1825 and which certainly contained interesting reflexions, were only compilations of his letters, notes, and occasional pieces. Worse, ideas that three decades earlier might have seemed profound and revelatory now appeared pretentious and obscure. His last project, that for a scholarship and loan program for able students, launched in 1862, also failed to materialize. In fact, in only one domain did Enfantin achieve any modest success: as a railway promoter. In 1845 he was appointed to represent Lyonnais interests in the group of bankers and businessmen that was to secure the concession for the Paris-Lyons railroad. By his personality and diplomacy he helped consolidate the company and played a minor role in bringing about the fusion that created France's largest railway company, the P.L.M., in 1857.

In February 1853 Maxime Du Camp met Enfantin, then aged fifty-seven, for the first time. He found a man prematurely aged, slow in his movements, his hands shaking uncontrollably. Just before he died eleven years later, Enfantin wrote sadly of his loneliness, asking rhetorically of those ex-Saint-Simonians who had expected so much of him: "Qui de vous ne m'a pas un peu assassiné?"

He deposited his archives, containing 35,000 documents, at the Bibliothèque de l'arsenal in Paris. He still awaits his biographer.

S. Charléty, *Enfantin, morcaux choisis* (Paris, 1930); H.-R. d'Allemagne, *Les Saint-Simoniens (1827–1857)* (Paris, 1930); M. Emerit, *Les Saint-Simoniens en Algérie* (Paris, 1941); *Oeuvres de Saint-Simon et d'Enfantin*, 47 vols. (Paris, 1864–78).

Barrie M. Ratcliffe

Related entries: BAZARD; CHEVALIER; LESSEPS; MEHEMET ALI; RAIL-ROADS; REVOLUTION OF 1848; SAINT-SIMON; SAINT-SIMONIANISM.

L'ESPRIT PUBLIC (1845–1846), newspaper founded for profit during the July Monarchy. During the 1840s, many newspapers were founded as speculative ventures, hoping to exploit advertisements and serial stories. The *Espirit public*, founded by Charles Lesseps in 1845, had 3,649 subscribers in 1846. In the following year it fused with *La Patrie*, a newspaper that attacked the ministry of François Guizot without supporting any of the opposition groups.

A. Crémieux, *La Révolution de Février* (Paris, 1912).; E. Hatin, *Bibliographie historique et critique de la presse périodique française* (Paris, 1866; new ed., 1965).

Irene Collins

Related entries: GUIZOT; *LA PATRIE*.

ESQUIROS, HENRI-FRANCOIS-ALPHONSE (1812–1876), a radical democratic writer and politician who was elected to the legislatures of the Second Republic, the Empire in 1869, and the incipient Third Republic. Alphonse Esquiros was born in Paris on 23 May 1812. His assertion in 1834 that his birth coincided with the collapse of the Empire was an artistic invention. Esquiros' parents, Alexandre and Henriette Malin Esquiros, were fairly well-to-do members of the bourgeoisie. Esquiros was educated at the minor seminary of Saint-Nicolas at Conflans from 1827 to 1831. Influenced by Victor Hugo, he left the seminary in 1831 for the Jeune-France movement and a literary career. Although Esquiros eventually renounced Catholicism, he retained a spiritual, or at times spiritualist, dimension.

Esquiros' first literary accomplishment, a collection of poems entitled *Les Hirondelles* (1834), was praised by Victor Hugo. Esquiros then published two novels, *Les Magiciens* (1837) and *Charlotte Corday* (1840). In 1840 he published *Evangile du peuple*, a democratic commentary on the life of Jesus. It was well received by the extreme Left, but it cost Esquiros eight months in prison and a 500 franc fine. While in the Sainte-Pélagie prison, he wrote *Les Chants d'un prisonnier*. After his imprisonment, politics and social transformation became predominant concerns for him. With David d'Angers, Théophile Thoré, and Louis Blanc, he published the *Journal du peuple*, and with them, in January 1842, he signed a call for the organization of labor. His socialist sentiments imbued his 1842 *Vierges folles*, *Vierges martyres*, and *Vierges sages*, a trilogy on the history and conditions of women. He praised the Jacobin Convention in his two-volume *Histoire des Montagnards*.

Esquiros welcomed the establishment of the Republic in 1848. He championed the social republic on the podium and with his pen. He was an editor of *La Tribune nationale* from 26 February to April when it turned to the Right and the single issues of *Le Peuple*, *La République des arts*, and *La Montagne de la fraternité*, which appeared in March. After 26 April Esquiros was an editor of *La Commune de Paris*, the journal of the Club des clubs and Armand Barbès' Comité revolutionnaire. When *La Commune* ceased publication in the aftermath of 15 May, Esquiros edited *L'Accusateur public* from 11 June to 25 June.

After the June insurrection with which he had sympathized, Esquiros fled to England. When he returned to France in late 1848, he went to Marseilles. There he joined the Circle Marbeau and wrote for its *La Voix du peuple*, which he edited from 29 September 1849 to 17 May 1850. During this time Esquiros wrote the pamphlets, *Le Droit au travail: De son organisation par la réforme des institutions de crédit* and *De la vie future au point de vue socialiste*. On 10 March 1850, he was elected in a by-election to represent Saône-et-Loire. He took his seat on the extreme Left of the Assembly. When his election was invalidated along with those of his five fellow Montagnards, Esquiros was returned to the Assembly by the voters on 28 April. In 1851 he and his wife, Adèle Bettanchon, a radical feminist whom he had married in 1847, separated. During his exile, Esquiros had initiated a relationship with an English woman, Anne, which would last until his death. In 1849 Anne bore Esquiros a son, William, who died shortly after birth.

In 1851 Esquiros published *Les confessions d'un curé de village*, *Histoire des martyrs de la liberté* and the first volume of his *Les festes populaires*. At the time of the coup of Louis-Napoleon, Esquiros fled to England. While in exile Esquiros continued to write and in 1869 he returned to France and to radical politics. Elected to the Corps législatif, he opposed the government and voted against the declaration of war on Prussia. After 4 September he was named chief administrator of the department of Bouches-du-Rhône. He forbade the publication of the legitimist *Gazette du Midi* and expelled the Jesuits. He attempted to rally the south to the patriotic war but was disavowed by Léon Gambetta. Esquiros at first resisted the central government's decision to replace him but resigned on 3 November.

In 1871, with François Raspail, Esquiros published a journal of only one issue, *La République de Marat*, in which they called for the dissolution of the National Assembly and for revolutionary violence in defense of the Republic. He subsequently defended the Republic of Adolphe Thiers as the only alternative to a restoration of the monarchy. In 1875 he supported the constitutional laws. In his repudiation of revolution in favor of republican evolution, Esquiros was labeled a *républicain conservateur libéral*.

On 30 January 1876, he was elected to the Senate from the Bouches-du-Rhône. He took his customary place on the extreme Left and as his last political act signed Victor Hugo's proposal of full amnesty for all the communards. Esquiros died on 10 May 1876 at Versailles.

Dictionnaire biographique du mouvement ouvrier français, 2d pt. (Paris, 1968); H. Temerson, in *Dictionnaire de biographie française*, vol. 13 (Paris, 1975); J. P. Van der Linden, *Alphonse Esquiros, De la bohème romantique à la république* (Paris, 1948).

Bernard Cook

Related entries: L'ACCUSATEUR PUBLIC; BLANC, LOUIS; *LA COMMUNE DE PARIS*; *LE JOURNAL DU PEUPLE*; REPUBLICANS.

L'ESTAFETTE (1846–1858), radical newspaper of the July Monarchy, Second Republic, and Second Empire. This radical newspaper first appeared in government records in 1846, when it was listed as having 3,195 subscribers. In 1848 it welcomed the Second Republic but became more and more hostile to the personal authority of Louis-Napoleon Bonaparte. By the end of 1852, its readers had fallen to a mere 470. It had the temerity to continue expressing republican ideas during the Second Empire and was suppressed by the police in 1858.

Irene Collins

Related entry: REPUBLICANS.

L'ETOILE (1820–1827), ultraroyalist daily newspaper, merged with the *Gazette de France* in 1827; supported Joseph de Villèle. *L'Etoile* was edited by the marquis Antoine de Genoude during the 1820s, appearing every evening. This paper existed mainly to exalt the chief minister, Joseph de Villèle, and to defend his policies. In addition, *L'Etoile* defended the comte de Peyronnet, a member of Villèle's cabinet. Although often an embarrassment to both Villèle and Genoude, Peyronnet's vociferous ultraclericalism and absolutism made him a useful link with the more extreme Right. In July 1827, Villèle rewarded Genoude by making him owner of the *Gazette de France*, an old royalist paper that the minister had bought out in 1824 and Genoude had then edited. Genoude merged *L'Etoile* with the old *Gazette* to create a new *Gazette*. It was more successful than either antecedent, climbing from 3,500 subscriptions for both papers in 1824 to nearly 10,000 during the Polignac era in 1830.

N. Hudson, *Ultra Royalism and the French Restoration* (Cambridge, 1936); C. Ledré, *La Presse à l'assaut de la monarchie* (Paris, 1960); P. Thureau-Dangin, *Royalistes et Républicains* (Paris, 1874).

Daniel Rader

Related entries: LA GAZETTE DE FRANCE; PEYRONNET; POLIGNAC; ULTRAROYALISTS; VILLELE.

EXECUTIVE COMMISSION. The Executive Commission was a five-man committee that served as temporary executive authority in France between 10 May and 24 June 1848. The Constituent Assembly, which first met on 4 May, recognized the need to delegate executive power while it drafted a new constitution. But it was reluctant to choose a single head of government, who might prove too independent and too powerful. The Assembly therefore accepted a suggestion put forward by the moderate republicans and selected five men from its own ranks to act as a joint executive. These, in turn, were to name and supervise the ministers in charge of the government departments. The five chosen by secret ballot on 10 May were Francois Arago (with 725 votes), Etienne Garnier-Pagès (715 votes), Alexandre-Thomas Marie (702 votes), Alphonse de Lamartine (643 votes), and Alexandre-Auguste Ledru-Rollin (458 votes). The last was the only left-wing republican in the group; the Assembly included him reluctantly and only at the insistence of Lamartine, who wanted a government with some appeal to the Left and who was otherwise unwilling to accept election himself.

The Executive Commission took up residence in the Luxembourg Palace. This was a mistake, for it called to mind the despised five directors of 1795–99, who had also lived there. The commission met daily as a council of government to make policy decisions and to deal with administrative matters. It also consulted regularly with the ministers. The commission decided on 17 May not to attend sessions of the Assembly (of which they remained members) except when called upon to explain government policy or when the "interest of the Republic" required it. They wanted to present an appearance of unity and feared that to participate in debate and to vote would make evident any differences among them.

Intended to be a government of national conciliation, the Executive Commission was instead crippled and finally brought down by party conflict. The insurrection of 15 May delivered an early and fatal blow to the commission's prestige. The Right and many moderates blamed the government for failure to protect the Assembly against the crowd; the Left criticized the subsequent repression. In any case, the Assembly was determined to dominate political life by itself and failed to give the strong parliamentary support that the commission needed to govern effectively. Newspapers ridiculed the five members as "the pentarches," "the kings," and even "the new directors." Many condemend them as weak and indecisive, unable or unwilling to maintain order. This was unfair: minutes of the commission's meetings show great attention to the organization and the disposition of army, police, and National Guard in both Paris and the provinces. But the commission was also wary of provoking further revolutionary violence. Lamartine later described the dilemma in these terms: "These five men . . . felt themselves squeezed between the National Assembly, which demanded from them the immediate restoration of order, and the convulsive events of an immense revolution that required from them prudence and caution, for fear of bringing about an inevitable upheaval before they had the strength to resist it."

The Executive Commission saw the growing influence of Louis-Napoleon Bonaparte as a serious threat to the Republic. After his election to the Constituent Assembly on 4 June and the Bonapartist demonstrations in Paris on 12 June, the commission decided to deny Louis-Napoleon entrance to France. On 13 June, however, the Assembly overturned the decision by voting to allow Louis-Napoleon to take his seat. Lamartine complained: "The Assembly . . . ties our hands and then reproaches us for our weakness." He and Ledru-Rollin wanted the commission to resign; Arago and Marie were at first inclined to agree. But on 14 June, a full council of ministers rejected resignation by a vote of thirteen to five on the grounds that it would be wrong to abandon the responsibilities of power at a time of crisis.

The June Days destroyed the Executive Commission. On 23 June, the first day of the insurrection, the commission entrusted General Eugène Cavaignac with military command and itself supervised his suppression of the revolt. But the Assembly believed that so serious a crisis demanded a temporary dictatorship. On the morning of 24 June, the deputies proclaimed a state of siege and conferred full powers on Cavaignac. The Assembly rejected a motion to abolish the Executive Commission, but within minutes the five members tendered their resignation.

The memoirs of Garnier-Pagès provide a spirited defense of the Executive Commission and its historic role. Garnier-Pagès listed a number of laws proposed or planned by the government—few of which, however, were enacted. He expressed pride that the commission never yielded to the temptation to impose its waning authority by coup d'état, overlooking the fact that there was never sufficient support for such an action. He was perhaps on surer ground when he praised the good intentions that he and his colleagues had brought to an almost impossible political situation: "Around them all was darkness, confusion, traps, conspiracy, . . . reactionary and revolutionary zeal . . . But, measuring the full extent of the danger, they resolved to face up to it without hesitation or weakness, just as they had accepted their mission without personal ambition and without reservation."

Garnier-Pagès, *Histoire de la Révolution de 1848*, 10 vols. (Paris, 1861–72); C. H. Pouthas, *Les Procès-verbaux du Gouvernement provisoire et de la Commission du pouvoir exécutif, février-juin 1848* (Paris, 1950).

Michael Sibalis

Related entries: ARAGO FAMILY; CAVIAGNAC, L.-E.; CONSTITUTION OF 1848; DEMONSTRATION OF 1848–1849; GARNIER-PAGES; JUNE DAYS; LAMARTINE; LEDRU-ROLLIN; MARIE; NATIONAL GUARD; PROVISIONAL GOVERNMENT; REVOLUTION OF 1848.

F

FABRE, JEAN-RAYMOND-AUGUSTE (1792–1839), radical journalist. At the age of fourteen Auguste Fabre journeyed to Paris to be with his brother Victorin, who was achieving some notoriety as a poet. Auguste took up the study of painting, and later he shifted to medicine and military tactics. A devoted classicist like his brother, August soon became absorbed in the cause of Greek independence. In 1823 he celebrated the people's will to resist the Turk in his *La Calédonie, ou la guerre nationale*. Here and in a play he wrote two years later, which was to have opened at the Odéon until it was banned by the censor, liberty triumphed. In place of the banned play he wrote *Histoire de siège de Misolonghi* (1826), where his knowledge of military tactics even drew the praise of generals. During these same years, the brothers Fabre made a brief attempt to support their belief in classicism with the journal *La Semaine*.

Despite his conservative taste in art, Auguste was a firm advocate of republican government. He was one of those who viewed the new romantic ideas as being associated with the Middle Ages and kingship. For Fabre, the great ideas of the classical world of republicanism should hold sway once again. In the late Restoration, he joined the liberal electoral organization Aide-toi le ciel t'aidera with his friend Godefroy Cavaignac.

Only in June 1829 did Fabre become well known. In that month he and his brother became the editors of the new journal *Tribune des départemens* where the masthead proudly displayed the word *patriot* rather than the usual *liberal* or *republican*. In the first issue on 8 June 1829, they expressed their belief in utopian views: a decentralized federal republic where deputies and electors represented the true interest of the people. "Fabrists" scorned the idea that deputies were men of free will who need not represent the interests of their constituents. Since at the time it was common for well-known personalities to run for election to the Chamber of Deputies in any department where they could be successful, the ideas of the brothers Fabre were indeed unorthodox. The *Tribune* favored news of the provinces over that of Paris, and it raised up the

United States as the model nation with the hero of two worlds, the marquis de Lafayette, as the perfect patriot. Despite their worship of America, the brothers Fabre disdained bourgeois materialism, and by October 1829 they had lost their financial backing.

With the challenge of the Polignac ministry to meet, Auguste became involved as a leader of Parisian students in organizing possible military resistance. He helped in the stashing of weapons and the organization of primary assemblies for the coming constituent assembly. With the escalation of events in the spring of 1830, the Fabre brothers found new financial backing from a medical student, Morhéry, and from Lafayette himself. The *Tribune* reappeared in April.

When the July Ordinances were issued by Charles X in July 1830, Auguste Fabre was one of the Parisian editors to sign the protest published by *Le National* on 26 July. The *Tribune* itself did not appear on 26 or 27 July but not for a lack of effort on the part of Auguste. His publisher had prohibited publication without a bond of 200,000 francs to cover the likelihood that the police would destroy his presses. After searching two days for the money to cover such a bond, Fabre finally sought relief in the Commercial Tribune, where the judge, Louis-Marie de Belleyme, Jean-Baptiste de Martignac's prefect of police, ordered the paper to be printed.

Auguste took an active part in the fighting during the July Days. On 28 July he destroyed the telegraphic links between Paris and the rest of the world so that Charles X could not summon additional troops, and on 30 July he was on the barricades fighting with the people of Paris. From his vantage point, the selection of Louis-Philippe had not been sanctioned by the people. Fabre wanted citizens, not subjects, and he was uncertain that the Orléans could provide the proper government. The *Tribune* followed this ambivalent line under the editorship of the brothers Fabre until Victorin died on 29 May 1831, at which time Auguste ceased his involvement with the journal. They were replaced by the more extreme republicans Sarrat and Armand Marrast, and Auguste Fabre fell silent except to publish his work and views of recent events.

His *La révolution de 1830 et le véritable parti républician exposé de plan de ce parti en juillet; mémorial historique de la révolution de ses causes et des suites* (Paris, 1833) represents one of the best insights from those who felt betrayed by the Orleanist solution of the July Revolution. The problems that Fabre experienced in getting the *Tribune* published became one of the events cited by republicans to show that the Orleanists had never intended to have a revolution.

Le grand dictionnaire universel du 19e siècle (Paris, 1866–90); L.-G. Michaud, *Biographie universelle ancienne et moderne* (Paris, 1843–58).

Thomas Beck

Related entries: AIDE-TOI, LE CIEL T'AIDERA; CAVAIGNAC, G.-E.-L.; FABRE, M.-J.-J.-V.; JULY ORDINANCES; LAFAYETTE, M.-J.-P.-Y.-R.-G.; MARRAST; *LE NATIONAL*; REPUBLICANS; *LA TRIBUNE DES DEPARTEMENS*.

FABRE, MARIE-JACQUES-JOSEPH-VICTORIN (1785–1831), classicist and radical journalist. After studying in Lyons, Victorin Fabre settled in Paris in 1804. His abilities as a writer were soon appreciated in *Eloge de Boileau*, and his *Eloge de Corneille* (1808) won the *prix d'éloquence* from the Academy, the first of five that Fabre would win. As a promising young poet, his courageous rescue of his younger brother from the Rhône following a boating accident, where twenty-eight of the forty-two persons drowned, won him additional attention. Victorin was no admirer of the emperor, however, and he refused Napoleon's overtures to engage his talents in support of the Empire.

Fabre spent the years 1814–21 with his family nursing his sisters and his own frail health; in 1821 he returned to a changed Paris. The dominance of classical literature was gone. Mme. de Staël and the new ideas of the romantics were penetrating the cultural scene of Paris. Fabre struggled against this tide, most noticeably in his course, *Sur les principes de la société civile*, at the Athénée of Paris in 1823. The following year Fabre, along with his younger brother, Auguste, founded *La Semaine*, a journal of art criticism, to support their classical beliefs. It survived less than a year.

Along with his brother, Victorin became involved in politics at the close of the Restoration. In June 1829 the brothers Fabre founded the *Tribune des départemens* to express the "patriotic," as opposed to the liberal, point of view. Supporting the idea of a federal republic where elected representatives supported the opinions of their constituents rather than their personal opinions, the editors of the *Tribune* made the United States their model nation and the marquis de Lafayette their ideal leader. The *Tribune* failed in October 1829 when its financial backers withdrew over the Fabres' dislike for bourgeois materialism.

By April 1830 the political crisis caused by the dispute between Charles X and the Chamber of Deputies led the medical student Morhéry and Lafayette himself to reestablish the *Tribune* with the brothers Fabre once again as the editors. Victorin, despite his sickly constitution, was one of the young republican leaders of the July Revolution. Before leading the assault on the Swiss Guards at the Babylone barracks, he admonished his men to "be humane; that is your first duty." Like his brother, he opposed the Orleanist solution. His poor health led to his death on 28 May 1831.

Victorin Fabre's works were published as *Oeuvres de Victorin Fabre* (Paris, 1844–45).

Le grand dictionnaire universel du 19e siècle (Paris, 1866–90); L.-G. Michaud, *Biographie universelle ancienne et moderne* (Paris, 1843–58).

Thomas Beck

Related entries: CHAMBER OF DEPUTIES; CHARLES X; FABRE, J.-R.-A.; LAFAYETTE, M.-J.-P.-Y.-R.-G.; REPUBLICANS; REVOLUTION OF 1830; ROMANTICISM; STAEL-HOLSTEIN; SWISS GUARD; *LA TRIBUNE DES DEPARTEMENS*.

FABVIER, CHARLES-NICHOLAS, BARON (1782–1855), general and carbonarist conspirator. Fabvier was the son of a minor government official and was destined for a military career at an early age. After attending the Ecole polytechnique (1802), he entered the army as a lieutenant of artillery and was decorated for his service in Austria in 1805. Detached for service with General Auguste de Marmont (who became his principal patron in his military career) in Dalmatia, Fabvier subsequently served with the French military missions in Constantinople and Persia (1807–9). Returning to France by way of Russia and Germany, Fabvier assumed duties as an aide to Marmont (now a marshal) in Spain in 1811–12, where he was wounded. He fought in Russia with the Grand Army (and was wounded again before Moscow), in Germany in 1813, and in the final campaigns in France in 1814. Although he refused a command in Napoleon's army during the Hundred Days, he was active in organizing local and guerrilla resistance to the Allied invasion of eastern France (at Longwy and Metz) after Waterloo, surrendering his forces only in August 1815.

Although initially denied a command under the second Restoration, Fabvier was able to regain a post on Marmont's staff as a colonel. A friend of liberal deputies like the marquis de Lafayette, Maximilien-Sebastien Foy, and Jacques-Antoine Manuel, Fabvier published a pamphlet in 1817 criticizing government repression of sedition in Lyons. He was promptly retired on half-pay, tried for libeling government officials, and subjected to a 3,000 franc fine. Fabvier was deeply involved in liberal and carbonarist conspiracies against the Bourbon regime in 1820–22. The government was unable to uncover enough evidence to prove his complicity in the military plot of 19 August 1820, and charges against him were dropped, though he was fined for refusing to testify at the trial of the other conspirators. In December 1821 and January 1822 he traveled extensively in eastern France to organize the planned insurrection that was prevented by the arrest of the Belfort conspirators, and on his return to Paris he tried to devise a plan to save the four sergeants of la Rochelle from execution. Fleeing to London, Fabvier traveled to Spain on the eve of the French invasion in April 1823, fighting a hopeless skirmish with a small band of followers when French troops crossed the border. He next enlisted in the Greek war for independence from the Turks from 1823 to 1827, rising to command the Greek regular forces and traveling about Europe to raise money for the cause. Blamed for a defeat at the hands of the Turks for which he was not responsible, he left for Paris in September 1828 but returned to Greece with a legion of French volunteers later in the same year.

Fabvier fought in the Revolution of 1830 and was named commandant of Paris on 4 August and a grand officer of the Legion of Honor. He married the duchess of Frioul and retired until 1838, when he returned to military service as inspector general of infantry (instituting various reforms) and was promoted to lieutenant general. Elevated to the peerage on 23 September 1845, Fabvier was an occasional critic, but not an active opponent, of the July Monarchy. After the Revolution of 1848, he was retired from active service by the Provisional

Government. He accepted a brief appointment to reorganize the Danish army but returned to France as a deputy (Meurthe) to the Legislative Assembly of the Second Republic. Never an active republican, Fabvier remained a good liberal and refused to accept a military command under the Second Empire. After his death in 1855, he was widely honored in Greece for his service there.

A. du Casse, *Le Maréchal Marmont* (Paris, 1857); A. Debidour, *Le Général Fabvier* (Paris, 1904); P. Mansel, *Louis XVIII* (London, 1981); A.-F. Marmont, *Mémoires*, 9 vols. (Paris, 1857); W. Serieyx, *Le Général Fabvier* (Paris, 1933); A. B. Spitzer, *Old Hatreds and Young Hopes* (Cambridge, 1971).

David Longfellow

Related entries: BAZAR CONSPIRACY; CARBONARI; *DEMI-SOLDES*; ECOLE POLYTECHNIQUE; HUNDRED DAYS; LEGISLATIVE ASSEMBLY; MARMONT; PROVISIONAL GOVERNMENT.

FALLOUX LAW. (March 15, 1850), name taken from vicomte Alfred-Frédéric de Falloux, a liberal Catholic, who became minister of education on 20 December 1848 and appointed the extraparliamentary commission that drafted the law. The law is noteworthy for having given the church more influence in schooling, according it a role in secondary education like that the Guizot Law had entrusted to it in primary instruction, allotting the clergy a larger place on educational councils at the expense of lay teachers, and encouraging growth among private elementary schools.

Although the Falloux Law was a momentous event, it was not a sudden turning point. It followed a long Catholic campaign, generaled by Charles-Forbes de Montalembert, for "liberty of education," a principle promised by the Carnot project and then incorporated into the republican constitution (1848). Fears issuing from the Revolution of 1848 assured reduced autonomy for the University, and Louis-Napoleon Bonaparte seems to have promised liberty of education in return for Catholic support in the presidential elections.

The Falloux commission, an extraparliamentary one because leftists controlled the Chamber in 1848–1849, included Montalembert and Monsignor Dupanloup from the Catholic camp but also Adolphe Thiers, Victor Cousin, Saint-Marc Girardin, and the director of the école normale Paul-Francois Dubois, six representatives of the church (but only one cleric), nine from the University, and nine supposed neutrals, who actually tended to favor some form of liberty of education. Hardly anyone demanded monopoly for either the church or the state. It was a commission of moderates, for Falloux had deliberately excluded vocal anticlericals and Catholic extremists like Louis Veuillot and his episcopal allies.

Surviving verbatim records of the commission's debates reveal that although the law became renowned for its provisions concerning secondary schools, the dangers of elementary instruction preoccupied commission members. Therein has lain much of the historical controversy. The historiography has wrongly found in conservative arguments for restricting mass primary education the reasons for the passage of liberty of education at the secondary level. The two issues were distinct. Thiers, so concerned about socialistic tendencies among the lay *instituteurs* that he tendered a monopoly of primary schooling to the church only to find Montalembert, Dupanloup, and the Christian brothers having no part of it, insisted upon state supervision of secondary schools and was abashed that the final bill did not exclude the Jesuits from teaching.

Despite concern about elementary schools, the law affected them little. Both teachers and their training school (*école normale*) suffered more regulation; *enseignment primarie supérieure* disappeared—a backward step that explains in part the popularity of special secondary programs during the Second Empire—but the curriculum was expanded, a girls' school was required of communes of 800 or more, and teachers enjoyed a guaranteed minimum wage. In the secondary arena, the celebrated article 17 permitted anyone who was twenty-five years of age or older and had a *baccalauréat* or five years teaching in a recognized secondary school to establish a secondary school. The law further permitted any town to transfer its public *collège* to the clergy; so many did that the number of *collèges communaux* declined by 25 percent in the next decade when other secondary schools were enjoying substantial growth. Its silence was important too; it did not forbid schools run by the unauthorized religious congregations, the most notable of which was the Society of Jesus. Administratively, the law reduced the power of the *universitaires*. The new highest council for education consisted of seven clergymen (four Catholic), three representatives from private education, nine governmental officials, and eight lay teachers. It also granted governmental officials the right to inspect all schools and the state alone the right to grant the *baccalauréat*. Church and state each won rights from the teaching establishment.

As a result of the law, enrollment in Catholic secondary schools multiplied. By 1854 21,195 students attended an ecclesiastical school (about 20,000 in Catholic ones); by 1867, 36,924 attended one; another 20,000 to 25,000 enrolled in a minor seminary, most of whom had never glimpsed a priestly vocation. Private lay schools, taking advantage of the law, prospered too; their enrollment in 1854 was in fact twice that of Catholic schools, but such schools usually offered only a few years of secondary studies, and, unable to compete against the twin powers of church and state, they atrophied. Catholic schools sustained growth, however—a growth rate of 75 percent versus 34 percent for the whole secondary system 1854–67. For a time, church and state responded to social demand for more education with more schools. By the end of the Second Empire and the early years of the Third Republic, however, cooperation gave way to conflict as they competed for the same social groups. Anticlericalism and worries about competition from Catholic schools led to the abrogation of most of the libertarian provisions of the Falloux Law between 1880 and 1886. Granted a foothold, however, Catholic secondary education survived anticlerical legislation during the Third Republic and remains an important part of French secondary studies today.

In primary education, the results of the law are less sure. Catholic elementary schools expanded, but congregational schools had always made up a large part of the public sector. Girls' schooling expanded rapidly by 1863. The encouragement of private schooling certainly aided them, but women were seeking more education then, and the curve had been on the rise for a generation.

The Falloux Law was certainly not a victory for reactionaries; Louis Veuillot, *L'Univers*, and abbé Gaume vigorously opposed the law. A compromise, it permitted the church to operate schools while the state supervised them. The church conceded the state's right to supervise education; the state conceded the church's institutional right to conduct schools. It represented the center of French politics, a center too often missed in historians' captivation by the disputes of Catholic and anticlerical extremists. The growth of Catholic schooling during the Second Empire reflected the law's response to the age.

G. Chessenau, *La Commission extraparlementaire de 1849: Texte intégral inédit des procès-verbaux* (Paris, 1937); P. Harrigan, "The Social and Political Implications of Catholic Secondary Education During the Second Empire," *Societas* 5 (Winter 1976); J. Huckaby, "Roman Catholic Reaction to the Falloux Law," *French Historical Studies* 4 (Fall 1965); H. Michel, *La Loi Falloux* (Paris, 1926).

Patrick J. Harrigan

Related entries: BROTHERS OF THE CHRISTIAN SCHOOLS; COUSIN; DU-BOIS; DUPANLOUP; *ECOLES PRIMAIRES SUPERIEURES*; GUIZOT LAW ON PUBLIC EDUCATION; JESUITS; LIBERAL CATHOLICISM; LIBERTY OF EDUCATION; MONTALEMBERT; THIERS; VEUILLOT.

FALLOUX, VICOMTE FREDERIC DE. See FALLOUX LAW.

FAYETTE, DE LA. See LAFAYETTE, M.-J.-P.-Y.-R.-G.

FERDINAND VII, King of Spain. See SPAIN, 1823 FRENCH INVASION OF.

FERRAND, ANTOINE-FRANCOIS-CLAUDE, COMTE (1751–1825), magistrate, publicist, politician, and litterateur. Born in Paris in 1751, Ferrand descended from a long line of magistrates. His father was a lawyer at the Parlement of Paris, and Ferrand himself also became a lawyer serving at the Chambre des enquêtes. Joining with other *parlementaires*, he opposed the Maupeou reforms and was sent into exile with others. Again in 1787 and 1788 he supported the parlement against the monarchy but opposed the calling of the Estates General. Ferrand condemned the Revolution from the beginning. He emigrated in 1789 but returned in 1801 because of financial hardship and the death of his son. From this time until the Restoration, he continued an active literary career and also wrote several historical works, two of which were censured for suggesting the restoration of the monarchy.

Along with Chateaubriand and Sosthènes de la Rochefoucauld, he was part of the royalist delegation that called upon the Allies to return the Bourbon monarchy to power. His reactionary views were reflected early in the Restoration in his strong support of the Holy Alliance and in his participation in preparing the 1814 Charter. Ferrand headed the commission investigating the restitution of *émigré* land. A virulent opponent of all Revolutionaries, he even intimidated moderate royalists. In his speech calling for a substantial indemnity for *émigrés*, he distinguished between royalists of the *ligne droite* who had supported the king by emigrating at the start of the Revolution, and those of the *courbe ligne*, who stayed in France for all or part of the Revolution.

In the First Restoration, Ferrand held the title of minister of state. Later Louis XVIII nominated him interim minister of the marine, during which time he proposed a law that would have rescinded the abolition of the slave trade. After the Hundred Days, Louis XVIII appointed him a count and peer of France. Until his death in 1825 he actively followed the debates in the Chamber of Peers where, despite the great difference between them, he voted with both the Richelieu and Villèle ministries.

In his *Théorie des révolutions* (1817) and *Testament politique* (1930), Ferrand advocated a strong authoritarian monarchy. Unlike many other ultraroyalists, Ferrand was satisfied with the administrative centralization institutionalized by Napoleon because it gave the king the opportunity to appoint loyal prefects. To sustain further royal power, he opposed the law of military recruitment (1818) because it limited royal choice over military officers, supported the Gallican church against ultramontane and liberal attacks, and advocated a strong police force to guarantee public order.

J. F. Bluche, *L'origine des magistrats du parlement de Paris* (Paris, 1956); E. Droz, *Le comte de Modène et ses correspondants* (Paris, 1942); A.-F.-C. Ferrand, *Espirit de l'histoire*, 4 vols. (Paris, 1802), *Mémoires* (Paris, 1897), *Testament politique* (Paris, 1830), and *Théories des révolutions*, 4 vols. (Paris, 1817); J. Godechot, *La contre-révolution* (Paris, 1961); A. Mahul, *Annuaire nécrologie* (Paris, 1825); J. J. Oechslin, *Le mouvement ultra-royaliste* (Paris, 1960).

Sanford Gutman

Related entries: CHAMBER OF PEERS; CHARTER OF 1814; CHATEAU-BRIAND; HOLY ALLIANCE; HUNDRED DAYS; LA ROCHEFOUCAULD; LOUIS XVIII; RESTORATION, FIRST; RICHELIEU; ULTRAROYALISTS; VILLELE.

FERRONNAYS. See LA FERRONNAYS.

FERTILITY. Fertility in France showed a consistent decline throughout the period between 1815 and 1851, part of a general decline in fertility that began before the Revolution of 1789 in some parts of the country and continued into the second half of the century. The crude birthrate for the entire country declined from 31.3 per thousand in 1816–20 to 26.6 per thousand in 1846–50. While changes in proportions married may have contributed to this decrease in the crude birthrate, the principal reason for the change must have been the increasing adoption of controlled fertility within marriage. The spread of this within France during the first half of the nineteenth century sets the French experience apart from that of the rest of Europe, where the transition from natural to controlled fertility within marriage did not begin until the 1870s.

Within France, there were different regional patterns in the adoption of controlled fertility. In most of the country, the pattern was one of gradual, steady decline beginning at the end of the eighteenth century and continuing through the entire nineteenth century. In other regions, however, the decline appears to have begun in stages, with fluctuations in the level of marital fertility before the decisive decline actually began. A hesitation, and even backtracking, is visible in the trends of certain departments. This pattern was the experience of the departments in the west, the north, the east, the southeast, and the Pyrenees.

The explanation for this decline in marital fertility remains speculative. Classical demographic transition theory has stressed the role of demographic changes, especially declining mortality, and also broader socioeconomic changes connected with industrialization and urbanization. Verifying this theory with empirical data in France has proved difficult, at least partially because of the lack of usable data before the middle of the nineteenth century. The most recent and sophisticated study, however, has stressed that lower mortality appears to be associated with lower overall fertility, while higher income (land revenue) exerted an independent effect to lower marital fertility. Urbanization and industrialization, however, do not appear to play the role in France that transition theory assigned to them. The most likely explanation, therefore, is that change on a broad front, including increasing communication and secularization, effected the large-scale change in fertility behavior in France during the the first half of the nineteenth century. The difficulty of measuring these changes, however, makes confirmation of this explanation, or even refutation of it, unlikely.

The contribution of illegitimate or nonmarital fertility to the overall fertility trends in France during the first half of the nineteenth century was considerably less than that of marital fertility. In the country as a whole, illegitimate births made up around 5 to 7 percent of all births for the entire period from 1815 to 1851. In major cities such as Paris and Bordeaux, however, this figure could reach as high as 30 percent. While there is only sketchy evidence for an increase in illegitimacy after 1800, there are clearly regions in which illegitimacy was high (the north) and others in which it was low (Brittany, the Massif Central).

Explanations for levels and trends in illegitimate birth fertility have followed two directions. One explanation has emphasized the influence of a revolution in sexual attitudes, in which a wish to be free found expression in increased sexual intercourse outside of marriage, accounting for an increase in illegitimacy. Against this the argument is made that industrialization and urbanization helped to create a more mobile society in which the consequences of premarital sexual activity were less often legitimized by marriage. Both explanations have found difficulty in proving their contentions. The first, depending on attitudinal changes, lacks direct evidence for this change. The second posits an unchanging level of sexual activity, which is also difficult to prove.

E. Shorter, "Illegitimacy, Sexual Revolution, and Social Change in Modern Europe," in T. K. Rabb and R. I. Rotberg, eds., *The Family in History: Interdisciplinary Essays* (New York, 1971); L. Tilly, W. Scott, and M. Cohen. "Women's Work and European Fertility Patterns," *Journal of Interdisciplinary History* 6 (1976); E. van de Walle, "Alone in Europe: The French Fertility Decline until 1850," in C. Tilly, ed., *Historical Studies of Changing Fertility* (Princeton, 1978), and *The Female Population of France in the Nineteenth Century* (Princeton, 1974).

James Lehning

Related entries: MORTALITY; NUPTIALITY; POPULATION.

LA FEUILLE DU VILLAGE. See JOIGNEAUX.

FEUTRIER, JEAN-FRANCOIS-HYACINTHE (1785–1830), bishop of Beauvais and governmental minister. The son of an official in the Paris administration, he was one of the first students to enter the seminary of St.-Sulpice when it reopened in 1801. Cardinal Fesch, Napoleon's uncle and grand almoner, who had ordained Feutrier in 1809, took him in his staff as secretary general. So personable was the young priest that he was kept in his office when, in 1814, old Cardinal Talleyrand-Périgord succeeded Fesch as grand almoner. He was briefly demoted when he refused to take the oath of loyalty to the emperor in April 1815 but recovered his position with the second return of the king. His friend Quélen, in fact, managed the business of the *grande aumônerie*, and Feutrier, as his assistant, was then involved in all the delicate transactions involved in restoring the personnel of the French church, in accord with the spirit of the royalist restoration. Upon the death of Talleyrand-Périgord, who had jointly held the offices of archbishop of Paris and grand almoner, the two offices were separated. The new grand almoner, the cardinal-prince de Croy, dismissed Feutrier. Quélen, who had been made archbishop of Paris, took care of his friend Feutrier, naming him vicar general and pastor of the important Madeleine parish. Soon after, Feutrier became bishop of Beauvais (January 1825).

As such, his activites and public statements gave him the appearance of being an open-minded prelate. Therefore, in March 1828, he was offered the Ministry of Ecclesiastical Affairs in the place of Bishop Frayssinous, who had been identified with the conservative administration of Joseph de Villèle. One important concession demanded by the new liberal majority was the curtailment of the growth of clerical educational institutions, which tended to void the monopoly claimed by the state university. After long discussions, two ordinances were submitted to the reluctant Charles X. The first formally excluded Jesuits and other religious persons from the faculties of those ecclesiastical schools that would be allowed to operate. The second ordinance limited to 20,000 the number of students to be educated in these diocesan colleges, with provisions aimed at preventing the admission of children destined for secular careers. Feutrier, as minister of ecclesiastical affairs, had to countersign this second ordinance, and it was his duty to implement both ordinances. The rightist and clerical press heaped scorn and insults upon the unfortunate Feutrier, calling him a traitor, a Judas. His colleagues in the episcopate refused haughtily to submit to the law and even socially boycotted the minister. It took the intervention of Pope Leo XII to persuade the French bishops to submit to the legislation. Still, a few of them held out, and Feutrier emerged from all this turmoil with a tarnished reputation. As a sop, he received a peerage from the king (January 1829), but it could not compensate for the pain that he had suffered and was ill prepared to handle. When Charles X brusquely dismissed the so-called Martignac administration, Feutrier returned to Beauvais, but his health had deteriorated fatally, and he died suddenly in Paris, where he had come for medical consultation (27 June 1830).

A. Garnier, *Les Ordonnances du 16 juin 1828* (Paris, 1929); L. Pihan, *Notices biographiques sur les évêques de Beauvais* (Beauvais, 1900).

Guillaume de Bertier de Sauvigny

Related entries: CHAMBER OF PEERS; CHARLES X; FRAYSSINOUS; JESUITS; MADELEINE CHURCH; MARTIGNAC; QUELEN; TALLEYRAND; VILLELE.

FIESCHI, JOSEPH-MARIE. See FIESCHI PLOT.

FIESCHI PLOT, a plot to assassinate King Louis-Philippe during a military review of 28 July 1835. This was the most nearly successful of all the plots to kill Louis-Philippe. It was drawn up by two notable republicans, P. T.-F. Pépin and Pierre Morey, and to a lesser extent by Victor Boireau.

Joseph-Marie Fieschi was a Corsican born in 1790. Son of a shepherd, he had served in the army of Naples and spent ten years in prison (1816–26) for theft. He had come to Paris and held several jobs, including that of police agent, which he lost after he stole some silver in 1834. Then he met Morey, a saddler, and Pépin, a shopkeeper in the faubourg Saint-Martin, both of whom were members of the Society of the Rights of Man. Together with Boireau, a young working-class republican, they installed a series of twenty-four rifle barrels on a wood frame designed to fire in a series from low to high when the king appeared. The king was not hurt, but eighteen people, including Marshal Edouard-Adolphe Mortier, were killed, and about twenty were wounded.

Fieschi, wounded himself, fled but was arrested in a nearby house. His loquacity, contrasted with the taciturn Boireau, Morey, and Pépin, caused the public to turn against him while it admired his stoic co-conspirators. Despite his repentance, the Chamber of Peers condemned him to the punishment for parricides (a thumb cut off followed by decapitation) on 15 February 1836. Just before his execution, he said that he had warned Adrien-Barnabe Athanase de Recurt, Godefroy Cavaignac, and Auguste Blanqui about the plan. On 19 February, Fieschi, Pépin, and Morey were executed. (Boireau, condemned to twenty years in prison, would be amnestied in 1840 and would go to London.) All three tombs were covered with flowers by republicans until Henri-Joseph Gisquet, the prefect of Paris police, forbade it. The police were still chasing after peddlers and bookstores that sold the portrait of Morey in 1837.

This attempted assassination furnished a pretext for the September Laws of 1835, which restricted the freedoms of speech and of the press in France.

Cours des Pairs, *Attentat du 28 juillet 1835*, 6 vols. (Paris, 1836); *Mémoires de Gisquet, ancien préfet de police, escrits par lui-meme*, vol. 5 (Brussels, 1841).

Jean-Claude Caron, trans. E. Newman

Related entries: BLANQUI, L. A.; CAVAIGNAC, G.-E.-L.; CHAMBER OF PEERS; LOUIS-PHILIPPE; PRESS LAWS; RECURT; REPUBLICANS; SOCIETY OF THE RIGHTS OF MAN.

FIEVEE, JOSEPH (1767–1839), journalist and political figure. Fiévée, a prominent counter-Revolutionary newspaperman during the Directory and Napoleonic periods, had been a secret correspondent of Napoleon and was appointed prefect of the Nièvre in 1813, but his earlier association with the royalist underground enabled him to emerge as a leading ultra by 1815. His *Correspondance politique et administrative* (1815–19), a one-man journal, and his annual reviews of the parliamentary sessions were among the most widely read ultra publications during the period of royalist opposition to the Decazes ministry, which made Fiévée a right-wing hero by jailing him for three months in 1818. He was a major contributor to the most important ultra periodical, the *Conservateur* (1818–20). Together with Chateaubriand, Fiévée argued for a liberal royalism compatible with parliamentary institutions; he was especially identified with a program for administrative decentralization and the dismantling of the bureaucracy inherited from Napoleon. He was unique among ultra propagandists in being indifferent to religious issues. Fiévée's ideological moderation went together with tactical intransigence; he opposed Joseph de Villèle's cooperation with the Richelieu ministry in 1820, calling for a purely ultra government. His evolution from Right to Left was sealed with a pamphlet attacking Villèle and Chateaubriand's intervention in Spain in 1823, which went through five editions; Fiévée subsequently befriended the liberals and even contributed to the *Temps* in 1829–30, but he never regained the audience he had enjoyed as an ultra. He justified the Revolution of 1830 but quickly became disenchanted with its failure to make substantial reforms. Fiévée caused a final stir by publishing his secret letters to Napoleon in 1837. His other writings quickly fell into oblivion. Despite his failure to produce any work of lasting importance, Fiévée deserves to be remembered as one of the creators of the French liberal conservative tradition, in which Alexis de Tocqueville is the most prominent figure, and as one of the molders of French public opinion under the Restoration.

C.-A. Sainte-Beuve, ''Fiévée,'' *Causeries de Lundi* (Paris, 1852); J. Tulard, *Joseph Fiévée: Conseiller secret de Napoleon* (Paris, 1985).

Jeremy Popkin

Related entries: CHATEAUBRIAND; *LE CONSERVATEUR*; DECAZES; REVOLUTION OF 1830; RICHELIEU; SPAIN, 1823 FRENCH INVASION OF; *LE TEMPS*; TOCQUEVILLE; VILLELE.

LE FIGARO (1826–1842), left-wing newspaper of the Restoration and the July Monarchy. Founded in January 1826 by Etienne Arago and Victor Bohain as a literary journal, the *Figaro* first attracted public attention by changing from the support of classicism to the support of romanticism. Although romanticism was much patronized by right-wing groups, the *Figaro* remained left-wing in its political tendencies, and in 1829 it changed into a political daily in order to attacked the Polignac government. Bohain was condemned to six months' imprisonment and a 1,000 franc fine when the *Figaro* suggested that Charles X had been suffering from an affliction of the eyesight while choosing his ministers. After the fall of Charles X, the *Figaro* continued to entertain its readers with satirical attacks on monarchy, government, and church. A series of editors, including Henri de Latouche, attracted a large number of famous writers, among whom George Sand made her journalistic debut. The vigorous manner in which governments of the July Monarchy prosecuted opposition journals caused the *Figaro* to disappear for a month between February and March 1839 and to disappear finally in May 1842.

F. Ségu, *Le Premier ''Figaro''* (Paris, 1932) and *Un romantique républicain: Henri de Latouche* (Paris, 1931).

Irene Collins

Related entries: ARAGO FAMILY; CHARLES X; LATOUCHE; POLIGNAC; ROMANTICISM.

FIRMIN-DIDOT, AMBROISE (1790–1876), printer, publisher, and author; member of the Didot family. Ambroise Firmin-Didot belonged to the famous Didot family, printers, engravers, and publishers in Paris since the middle of the seventeenth century. The founder of this dynasty, François Didot (1689–1757), established a tradition of excellence by publishing fine books, including not only the Greek classics in translation but also the works of the abbé Prévost. His son, François-Ambroise Didot (1730–1804), the grandfather of Ambroise Firmin-Didot, inaugurated the famed Didot typeface and made important innovations in both the printing process and in the manufacture of paper. For the king of France, he printed in 1783 the elegant *Collection des classiques français destinée à l'éducation du Dauphin*. Next in the Didot line was Firmin Didot (1761–1836), scholar, printer, and engraver. He made the type for the

Epître sur les progrès de l'imprimerie (1784). During the Revolution, he continued to print fine books and undertook such government commissions as the printing of the *assignats*. Innovations in the printing process made by Firmin Didot permitted the mass production of less expensive books. Named printer to the Institut in 1811, he became in 1814 printer to the king. Thirteen years later, he turned his business over to his three sons, Ambroise, Hyacinthe, and Frédéric, devoting himself henceforth to politics. Elected to the Chamber of Deputies, he sat with the opposition, was one of the 221 who voted against the Polignac ministry, and, during the Revolution of 1830, signed a protest against the July Ordinances. Before he died in 1836, Firmin Didot had done much to help organize the July Monarchy, and he had attained such fame that his three sons obtained permission to use Firmin-Didot as their surname.

Born in Paris on 20 December 1790, Ambroise Firmin-Didot developed an early interest in classical languages and civilization. Especially attracted to Greece and the Greek language, he traveled there and in Asia Minor in 1816 and 1817, and, although he was disappointed by the reality he encountered, Firmin-Didot became an enthusiastic supporter of the Greek struggle for independence. At the insistence of his father, he and his brother Hyacinthe (1794–1880) took over the family business, which in the 1820s comprised a publishing house, a bookstore, a factory for the manufacture of paper, and a foundry for the casting of typefaces. Although expert in the making of type, Ambroise Firmin-Didot specialized in the publication of such monumental editions as the *Monuments de l'Egypte et de la Nubie* of Champollion (6 vols., 1835–72), the *Scriptorum graecorum bibliotheca* (62 vols., 1838–86), the *Thesaurus graecae linguae* of Henri Estienne (8 vols., 1831–65), the *Nouvelle biographie* (46 vols., 1852–66), and two editions of the *Dictionnaire de l'Académie française*. As a printer and publisher, Ambroise Firmin-Didot had to deal with the complex problem of the reform of French spelling, and he published an essay on this subject in 1867. An avid collector of books, manuscripts, paintings, and objets d'art, he took a particular interest in chivalric romances; the sale catalog of his collection amounted to seven volumes. Ambroise Firmin-Didot rounded out his career by publishing translations of Greek and Latin authors, studies of authors and books in his collection, and specialized works on aspects of the printing business. Finally, he served on various Parisian commissions concerned with the promotion of business and commerce, and he participated in the municipal government of Paris. He died on 22 February 1876.

Dictionnaire de biographie française, vols. 11 and 13; A. J. George, *The Didot Family and the Progress of Printing* (Syracuse, 1961); E. Werdet. *Etudes biographiques sur la famille des Didot* (Paris, 1864).

Robert Brown

Related entries: CHAMBER OF DEPUTIES; JULY ORDINANCES; POLIG-NAC; REVOLUTION OF 1830; THE 221.

FIRST BOURBON RESTORATION. See RESTORATION, FIRST.

FLAUBERT, GUSTAVE (1821–1880), novelist. Born in Rouen, his father a chief surgeon and clinical professor at the Hôtel-Dieu of Rouen and his mother the daughter of a doctor, Flaubert had solid bourgeois origins. He began his early writing during his school days. Instead of following the example of his brother Achille, a doctor at the hospital in Rouen, Flaubert read law but then broke off his studies after a nervous illness. For the rest of his life, he enjoyed the comfortable existence of a gentleman of letters, remaining a bachelor and devoting himself to his family and to literature.

Flaubert's literary method was a long and agonizing search of weeks and years for the single right word (*le seul mot juste*) to express precisely the mood or impression that would convey an idea. Working with great care and exactitude, he gathered copious notes while researching every detail, making certain that his facts were rigorously correct in the most insignificant (for us, but not for Flaubert) trivialities. No minutiae could be left without precise verification by exhaustive archival exploration, and nothing could be allowed to detract from the final product of the book. Flaubert moved with the skill and the precision of a surgeon, emulating that quality of clarity and precision that characterized men of the natural sciences. His goal was to create a style as precise as the language of science and as rhythmical as verse.

A rebel against his age, Flaubert satirized the social pretensions of his own social class. He despised them for their love of money, their general glorification of technology and machinery, and their widespread homage to private property. The positivists and patriots of the acquisitive spirit were ridiculed as petty materialists and conformists. Philistines were dangerous for their failure to appreciate the human value of the individual; they lost sight of humanity in the blind worship of the golden calf, which was the true deity of an age of improvement.

Flaubert had no more use for the vile masses than for the middle class. He observed that the multitude had no inherent virtue in becoming a majority, and their acquisition of power did not particularly increase human happiness or advance humanity toward the millennium. He warned that democracy based on universal suffrage might be no more than a snare and a delusion. The people could be all too easily flattered and tricked by professional politicians. He vented his disgust by turning irony on those seeking personal power. Yet the skeptical Flaubert distrusted the masses for the same reason that he hated the ruling classes: he revolted against all forms of tyranny.

His friend and correspondent George Sand objected in apprehension and in astonishment to what she perceived as Flaubert's social conservatism. Certainly, she protested, anyone who was sincere and disinterested or a victim of injustice was worthy of respect. But Flaubert failed to share Sand's optimism that change would necessarily make matters better. Turning his back on the pursuit of social action, Flaubert grappled with his age in order to denounce its faults and to criticize society with a pessimistic philosophy of revolt against order. However, Flaubert cautioned that social revolutionaries fell into the trap of attempting to propose an alternative that would most likely only make matters worse. Their search was ultimately utopian.

Neither the political process of his day nor revolution held any promise to Flaubert of improvement in the human condition. Distancing himself from all governmental forms, from his social origins, and from his times, Flaubert called into question all social relationships and reexamined society's foundations and moral codes.

In his own lifetime, Flaubert enjoyed little critical acclaim. His masterpiece, *Madame Bovary*, earned him the hostility of critics. Rejecting all schools and refusing to found one himself, Flaubert suffered in isolation. Even Emile Zola's proclamation that Flaubert was the father of realism brought only scorn from the would-be prophet. But the strongest attack came from official quarters, who publicly prosecuted him for immorality.

In a sense, there is a certain justice in the French government's indictment of Flaubert for publishing *Madame Bovary*. Flaubert had hardly transgressed public morals, as the court charged, but he had exposed the hypocrisy of the comfortable classes to public view. Stripping away the pretensions of the self-satisfied, Flaubert revealed the corruption of a society founded on pretension. The demoralizer tore away the veils concealing petty and sinister reality, conformism, religious pretense, and philosophical beliefs. He held up for public scrutiny actual conditions, stripped naked and deprived of disguises. Thus it is not surprising that the Sixth Chamber of Correctional Police judges gave the work a "severe reprimand." Flaubert had attacked the disease of his time with scalpel and lancet. He had written a ruthless diagnosis of social and moral criticism. It is also true that Flaubert belongs to a tradition of great moralists of the eighteenth century. Thus François Mauriac and Henri Guillemin have called Flaubert a "mystic without knowing it" and a "seeker of God in spite of himself." In the great anticlerical heritage of Voltaire, his actual objective as a demoralizer was moral: to rid the world of the degradation of hypocrisy and fanaticism.

Paradoxically, Flaubert enjoyed the friendship of Princess Mathilde, cousin of Louis-Napoleon. He even basked in official approval afforded by close proximity to the imperial entourage, welcoming the invitation to join Louis-Napoleon and his court for the excursion to Compiègne. His close relationship with his mother and family reflect the highly respectable bourgeois nature of Flaubert's personal life—as well as the supreme hypocrisy of the bachelor's affairs. These contradictions between Flaubert's private life and his works of literature illuminate his famous remark: "Madame Bovary, c'est moi" ("I am Madame Bovary"). His art was based on an intense self-examination; his castigations struck at his very own nature.

Living in comfortable bourgeois circumstances, Flaubert could enjoy the luxury of allowing his writing to meet his high standards of excellence. Not subject to the external financial pressure that plagued Dickens and Dostoyevsky, Flaubert was not forced to follow their example of dashing off (or unnecessarily extending an ending to squeeze out more installments) a work in order to stay a step ahead of creditors. Flaubert began writing *Madame Bovary* in September 1851, planning to be finished in eighteen months. Instead, writing took nearly five years. Even then he was not satisfied with the result, seeing it as containing "more patience than genius, and more labor than talent." Constructing his works slowly and deliberately, Flaubert's *Bouvard and Pécuchet* was unfinished with his death, yet he had devoted his last ten years to it and called it "the work of my whole life."

In the view of Flaubert, the time of heroes was past, and life was exposed as a failure. Truth and beauty were not to be found in absolutes but sought in fiction. Profoundly skeptical, Flaubert sought objectivity in composing a clear prose that could overcome the personality of the writer by a great intellectual effort, to transform the character by assimilating it to oneself. Yet even as he sought that objectivity, Flaubert can be observed behind his works in a delicate sensibility and humanistic sincerity.

V. Brombert, *Flaubert* (Paris, 1971); Gustave Flaubert, *Bouvard et Pécuchet* (1881), *Correspondance* (1884), *La Tentation de Saint-Antoine* (1874), *L'Education Sentimentale: Histoire d'un Jeune Homme* (1870), *Madame Bovary: Moeurs de province* (1857), *Salammbô* (1863), and *Trois Contes* (1877); M. Nadeau, *The Greatness of Flaubert*, trans. Barbara Bray (New York, 1972); J. P. Sartre, *The Family Idiot: Gustave Flaubert*, vol. 1 (Chicago, 1981); E. Starkie, *Flaubert: The Making of the Master* (New York, 1967), and *Flaubert: The Master* (New York, 1971); F. Steegmuller, *The Letters of Gustave Flaubert, 1830–1857* (Cambridge, Mass., 1980); A. Thibaudet, *Gustave Flaubert* (Paris, 1935).

James Chastain

Related entries: COMTE; ROMANTICISM; SAND.

FLOCON, FERDINAND (1800–1866), journalist and republican politician, son of an employee in the telegraph administration. Flocon was a carbonaro by 1823, and his ability as a stenographer gave him access to *Le Constitutionnel* and *Le Courrier français*, becoming an editor of the latter. He was also the author of anti-Jesuit pamphlets and of several novels. After the 1830 Revolution he joined the Société des amis du peuple and wrote for *La Tribune* before helping to launch *La Réforme*, which he edited from 1843 to 1848. The true nineteenth-century Jacobin, he was described by a contemporary as having Maximilien Robespierre's Declaration of the Rights of Man permanently in his mind and his pocket.

Flocon played an important role in the February 1848 Revolution and was a member of the Provisional Government. It was he who personally invited Marx to return to France, whence he had been expelled in 1845; Marx's high personal regard for Flocon was matched, however, by his critique of Flocon's politics. After his election to the Constituent Assembly, Flocon was retained by the Executive Commission as minister for agriculture and commerce, where the scarcity of his proposals bears testimony to the lack of attention most republicans had paid to rural problems. During the June civil war, he supported his old friend Eugène Cavaignac, seeing the rising as Bonapartist and antirepublican, and he helped to enact repressive laws, which he was later to regret bitterly.

Cavaignac did not retain him in the ministry, and Flocon moved again to the left, acting against the repression and moving a motion for amnesty on the last day of the National Assembly (26 May 1849). He was not elected to the Legislative assembly in May but almost won a by-election in the Hérault later that year. Flocon spent 1849–51 writing for *Le Démocrate du Bas-Rhin* and fled to Switzerland after the coup d'état of December 1851. He survived in Switzerland as a bookseller and translator while remaining in contact with other political exiles.

Dictionnaire de biographie française (Paris, 1933-); K. Marx and F. Engels, *Collected Works*, vols. 6–7 (London, 1976–77).

Peter McPhee

Related entries: CARBONARI; CAVAIGNAC, L.-E.; *LE CONSTITUTION-NEL; LE COURRIER FRANCAIS*; JUNE DAYS; MARX; *LA REFORME*.

FONTANES, JEAN-PIERRE-LOUIS, MARQUIS DE (1757–1821), author and administrator. Born in Niort to a Catholic mother and a Protestant father who was a well-to-do merchant, Fontanes had gained, before 1789, a literary reputation with various pieces of poetry and translations. As a journalist in 1792, he was suspected of counter-Revolutionary activities and had to go into hiding. After Thermidor he was given a teaching position and a seat in the newly formed Institut. But he was involved with the royalist party, and the purge of Fructidor 18 (September 1797) compelled him to seek refuge in London. There he met the young Chateaubriand, for whom he was to be the most devoted friend. When Bonaparte established his dictatorship, Fontanes, who had returned to Paris, was in a good position to help his friends, as he had become the lover of the consul's sister, Elisa. He himself did not lack the rewards of being close to the source of power: deputy to the Legislative Corps, presiding officer of this assembly (January 1804), grand master of the University (March 1808), senator (February 1810), and count. However, he voted for the deposition of the emperor (April 1814). Louis XVIII included him among the number of former senators to become peers, but he could not keep his position as the head of the University, the office of grand master having been abolished, with its functions assumed by a collective body. During the Hundred Days Fontanes conveniently kept away from Paris and thus was able to recover his seat in the Peers after the Second Restoration. There he supported the liberal-leaning policies of Elie Decazes, who had him rewarded with the title of marquis (31 August 1817). But in 1821 he seemed ready to follow a reactionary course with his friend Chateaubriand. Fontanes left the impression of being a kindly man who could adhere to the prevailing political currents without losing his dignity. He was also a supremely elegant writer though without a spark of genius.

R. Tessoneau, *Correspondance de Louis de Fontanes et de Joseph Joubert* (Paris, 1943); A. Wilson, *Fontanes, essai biographique et littéraire* (Paris, 1928).

Guillaume de Bertier de Sauvigny

Related entries: CHAMBER OF PEERS; CHATEAUBRIAND; DECAZES; HUNDRED DAYS; LOUIS XVIII; RESTORATION, FIRST; RESTORATION, SECOND.

FORBIN-JANSON, CHARLES-AUGUSTE-MARIE-JOSEPH, COMTE DE (1785–1844), abbé, Catholic missionary and bishop of Nancy. Born in Paris on 3 November 1785, Forbin-Janson initially entered government service rather than the clergy, becoming an auditor in the Council of State in 1805. But he ultimately turned to the religious vocation and was ordained a priest in 1811, serving as vicar-general at Chambéry. Although Forbin-Janson served Napoleon, he was genuinely a royalist. During the Hundred Days he was involved with others, such as Ferdinand de Bertier and Eugène-François de Vitrolles, who sought to rally royalist opposition in the south in collaboration with the duc d'Angoulême. Early in the Restoration he and the abbé de Bordeaux assisted the abbé Jean-Baptiste Rauzan in founding the Society of Missions of France to evangelize the lower-class masses of France with sermons, instruction, ceremonies, processions, and book burnings. But they became associated with the ultraroyalists, and thus opposition to the ultras redounded to the discredit of the missions and their leaders. Forbin-Janson and the Society of Missions were also linked to the Congrégation and the Knights of the Faith, whose leader, Ferdinand de Bertier, was a friend of his.

In 1817 Forbin-Janson went to preach Catholicism in Asia Minor, but he returned to continue his work in France and in 1823 became bishop of Nancy. Unfortunately he became so closely linked with the ultraroyalists and the monarchy that when the July Revolution erupted, he was forced to flee his see by the anticlerical rioting that followed. Only two other French prelates, the archbishops of Rheims and Besançon, were similarly treated. Forbin-Janson ultimately arrived in North America, where he evangelized in the United States and Canada from 1839 to 1841. In 1843, after his return to France, he established at Nancy the Oeuvre de la Sainte-Enfance, a missionary organization seeking to interest the laity in the redemption of Chinese children. Forbin-Janson died at the chateau de la Guilhermy near Marseilles on 12 July 1844.

A. Dansette, *Religious History of Modern France* (New York, 1961); De Rivière, *Vie de Mgr de Forbin-Janson* (Paris, 1892); A. Latreille et al., *Histoire du catholicisme en France* (Paris, 1962); P. Lesourd, *Un Grand coeur missionnaire, monseigneur de Forbin-Janson* (Paris, 1944), and *Histoire des missions catholiques* (Paris, 1937); C. S. Phillips, *The Church in France, 1789–1848* (New York, 1966).

James K. Kieswetter

Related entries: ANGOULEME, L.-A.; BERTIER, CHEVALIERS DE LA FOI; CONGREGATION; HUNDRED DAYS; MISSIONS; REVOLUTION OF 1830; ULTRAROYALISTS; VITROLLES.

FOREIGN POLICY OF LOUIS-PHILIPPE. The "citizen king" has had his share of detractors. In the area of foreign affairs, critics have claimed that Louis-Philippe possessed no clearly defined theme to his policies but merely reacted to events almost haphazardly. Louis-Philippe has also been taken to task for following the English lead instead of developing independent policies. His critics also assert that Louis-Philippe's pusillanimity pushed France into an appeasement posture designed to maintain peace regardless of the consequences for France.

An examination of the record, however, will refute these not completely consistent criticisms. In the Belgian Revolution, Louis-Philippe had France intervened militarily twice (1831 and 1832) in order to defend the Belgians from Dutch counterattacks. As a result, French influence increased in this neighboring region. When revolution erupted in the Papal States, Louis-Philippe again acted to defend the interests of France. Austrian troops entered the Papal States and readily suppressed the rebels. Since Austria was France's erstwhile rival in Italian affairs, Louis-Philippe believed that he needed to acquire some counterweight to this increased Austrian military presence in Italy. In 1832, he authorized the French fleet to hold a naval demonstration near the port of Ancona. Following this display of naval power, French troops occupied the city. Ancona was held until 1838 when both Austrian and French troops evacuated the Papal States. Under Louis-Philippe's direction, France in 1834 intervened in support of Anglo-Spanish efforts designed to terminate the Portuguese civil war. In 1847, the French navy cooperated with the British navy and the Spanish army in suppressing a rebellion against Portugal's queen, Doña Maria. These examples make it clear that Louis-Philippe did not cringe from the use of military force when he believed the situation warranted strong action.

While it was true that England and France periodically enjoyed harmonious relations during the age of Louis-Philippe, tension more often than not marked Anglo-French affairs. Viceroy of Egypt Méhémet-Ali's attempt to take control over the entire Ottoman Empire produced some friction between the French and the British. Given Britain's extensive interests in the eastern Mediterranean and the Middle East, the British viewed with considerable alarm any attempt to accomplish a radical reformation of the status quo in an area as strategically sensitive as the Ottoman Empire. The French, however, were friendlier to Ali's efforts. In fact, French officers and technical advisers served with Ali's troops. France believed that its special relationship with Ali's Egypt provided a necessary balance to Britain's influence in Mediterranean affairs. The British navy played a prominent part in suppressing Ali's revolt. As a result, French prestige suffered, and the Thiers ministry collapsed in October 1840.

The tangled skein of the Spanish marriages of 1846 also provided a focal point for Anglo-French friction. The marriages of the young queen of Spain, Isabella, and her sister, Louisa Fernanda, had international repercussions given the fact that they would determine succession rights to the Spanish throne. Adolphe Thiers' successor, François Guizot, worked feverishly in order to promote a choice of husbands who would be most beneficial for French interests in Spain.

Guizot hoped that Isabella would choose Don Francisco, duke of Cadiz, who was a member of the Bourbon family, and that Louisa Fernanda would select the duke of Montpensier, Louis-Philippe's fifth son. The British, especially Foreign Secretary Lord Palmerston, backed Don Enrique, duke of Seville, or Prince Leopold of Saxe-Coburg, who was related to Queen Victoria, as acceptable choices for Isabella. Under any circumstances, Palmerston wanted to prevent Montpensier from playing any part in the marriage arrangements. Guizot, however, proved to be a bit more persuasive than Palmerston. On 10 October 1846, Isabella wed Don Francisco, and Louisa Fernanda married Montpensier in ceremonies that were celebrated within moments of each other. Palmerston could not reconcile himself to this turn of events, which he regarded as yet another example of French treachery.

Louis-Philippe was driven from power by the February Revolution of 1848, which created the Second Republic. With the Bullen and Schmidt studies serving as indicators, it seems that historians are now ready to accept the fact that Louis-Philippe provided France with more than a mere eighteen-year interlude.

R. Bullen, *Palmerston, Guizot and the Collapse of the Entente Cordiale* (London, 1974); D. P. Schmidt, "The Foreign Policy of Louis-Philippe, 1830–1832: A Study in Interventionist Diplomacy" (Ph.D diss., Marquette University, 1976).

John W. Rooney, Jr.

Related entries: BELGIAN REVOLUTION OF 1830; GUIZOT; LOUIS-PHI-LIPPE; MEHEMET-ALI; REVOLUTION OF 1848; THIERS.

FOREIGN TRADE AND TARIFF POLICY. Until about the mid-1970s, scholars viewed the history of French foreign trade in the first half of the nineteenth century as one of failure and missed opportunities. Commercial policy, which was protectionist, was invariably condemned as having a nefarious effect on the growth of both trade and the economy in general. The contemporary debate on tariffs, between those who defended protection and those who pressed for more moderate duties, was presented as a conflict between the retrograde defenders of narrow sectional interests that enjoyed political power and crusading reformers armed with a vision and theories of economic liberalism. These traditional interpretations have recently been overthrown by historians who have adopted a more rigorous quantitative approach and freed themselves from the trammels of the theory of economic liberalism. These scholars have shown that in absolute terms and even as a proportion of European commerce, France's foreign trade expanded from the 1820s and grew even more rapidly from the 1840s. They have also revealed that the period down to 1860, when tariffs were protectionist, was also one when the French economy achieved its highest rates of growth for the nineteenth century and that the period of low tariffs after 1860 coincided not with even higher rates of growth but with deceleration of growth. As for the debates on commercial policy, scholars have demonstrated that protectionist theory was not the feeble hotchpotch of mercantilist arguments and the selfish defense of sectional interests that it has often been represented to be but rather a theory tailored to a situation where one trading partner—Great Britain—enjoyed an important technological lead in critical industrial sectors. Thus the most cogent of protectionist theories developed in this period, that published by the German economist Friedrich List in 1841, was first written for a French essay competition in 1838 and was much influenced by French protectionists. They have also revealed that the much-vaunted tariff reform campaign of the 1840s—that dominated by Frédéric Bastiat, Michel Chevalier, and export interest groups, especially in Bordeaux and Lyons—achieved but scant success and was in a state of collapse even before the onset of economic depression in 1847. Commerce and commercial policy, then, is a striking example of the way in which the application of new methods and approaches has led scholars to radically reassess older views on the French economy in this period.

Despite the loss of the most profitable parts of its eighteenth-century empire, the enforced intraversion of the economy during the Revolution and the Empire, and the preempting of some markets by British exporters and shippers, French trade recovered surprisingly quickly after 1820. The growth of foreign trade at first paralleled and, after 1840, was faster than that of the economy as a whole. While foreign trade was the equivalent of 13 percent of gross national product in 1830, this percentage had risen to 29 percent in 1850 and was to increase still further under the Second Empire. The explanation for this increase is complex. Imports, though, increased mainly because growing French industry needed more and more raw material and semimanufactured imports, and exports rose because exporters were able to conquer markets for high-quality goods like silks and woolens, *articles de Paris*, and the like and did so despite the high tariffs France's trading partners levied on its exports. Exports, indeed, increased more rapidly than did European and world exports, and France's share in international trade grew from around 10 percent in the 1820s to nearly 13 percent in the 1850s. Sixty percent of these exports consisted of textiles; at the midcentury, silk goods headed the list, followed by woolens, cotton goods, and wines. Nearly two-thirds of all exports went to Europe, and from the 1840s Britain became the principal market. The rate of growth of French imports paralleled that of exports. From 1825 to 1834, the annual increase by volume was 2.8 percent, while in the succeeding ten-year period it rose to 5.6 percent. Manufactured goods constituted a declining proportion of imports. Whereas they had made up about a fifth of imports by value in 1789, their share had fallen to 8 percent in 1830 and to 5 percent in 1860. In contrast, agricultural imports (that is, foodstuffs and raw materials for industry), which had made up just over half of imports in 1789, made up three-quarters by 1860. The most important of these were raw cotton and silk. Thus, while it can be argued that there were weaknesses in the pattern of French trade—its merchant marine carried but a small proportion of goods entering and leaving France's ports, for example—the period 1815 through 1850 was successful. There is, then, no truth in the claim (still repeated by Albert Broder in 1976), that this period was one of failed and missed opportunities.

It is by no means evident either that commerce or even the economy was held back by the tariff policy the government adopted. After a fleeting moment in 1814 when the First Restoration had erected moderate tariffs, policy in the first half of the nineteenth century was protectionist. The influx of British goods in 1814–15, and the economic crisis of the early years of the new regime, reinforced the arguments of those who demanded high tariffs, and legislation that gave effective protection was gradually enacted. The corn laws of 1819 and 1821 made cereal imports virtually impossible, and stockbreeders and even viticulturists were also given protective tariffs. At the same time a series of laws accorded protection to basic industries and textiles. Duties on coal, iron, and machinery were successively raised in the early 1820s, and the import of cotton yarns and cloths, shawls and silk goods, was prohibited. This tariff system reflected the political power enjoyed by the landowners—including owners of forests and mines—and powerful industrial interests, like the large metallurgical concerns set up in the 1820s, as well as an international economic situation where protectionist policies were being reinforced throughout Europe—the only breech being late in the period when the British adopted free trade—and where British iron and textile producers enjoyed an important competitive advantage in low-cost items.

This does not mean, though, that the French tariff system was without excesses and inconsequences. There were weaknesses in government encouragement to trade. In contrast to what was to happen under the Second Empire, scant funds were given to port modernization or to the steam shipping that began to develop on the North Atlantic in the 1840s. The government also failed to provide exporters with commercial intelligence. More important because of long-standing fears of British competition and because the economy was only emerging from the postwar depression, the tariffs adopted in the 1820s were too severe. Their severity, indeed, led France's trading partners to impose retaliatory duties on French goods. Besides, many industrialists, who supported the tariff in general but who needed imported coal, machines, or semimanufactures, were in favor of lower levies on these items. It was partly to remedy these drawbacks that there emerged a tariff reform movement.

Historians used to believe that the campaign to lower customs duties emerged only with economic prosperity and Britain's adoption of free trade in the 1840s. The campaign of that decade was indeed spectacular. The *Journal des économistes*, founded in 1841, campaigned for reform. The Association pour la liberté des échanges, modeled on the British pressure group, the Anti-Corn-Law League, was set up in 1846. Claude-Frédéric Bastiat published his *Sophismes économiques*, a vitriolic critique of protectionist policies, in 1846. However, the 1840s campaign did not lead to any reforms and succeeded only in provoking industrialists to a noisy defense of the existing tariff system. In reality, it was the earlier and lesser known campaign of 1831–36 that achieved some success. This reform movement coincided with and was fostered by the largely unsuccessful Anglo-French commercial negotiations of 1831–34 and an upswing in the trade cycle. It grew with the inquiry into prohibitions that Charles-Marie-Tanneguy Duchâtel, the minister of commerce, set up in 1834 and achieved modest success when parliament was induced to pass two tariff bills in July 1836. This legislation allowed the export of raw silk and the import of fine-count cotton twist, and it made slight reductions in dues on iron goods and major reductions in those on sea coal. Modest though they were, these reforms were the only significant tariff reduction before the Second Empire and the only reductions of any import that were passed by a French parliamentary body in the nineteenth century.

Apart from this minor reform, the tariff system of the first half of the century was that erected in the early years of the Restoration. The system was intended to serve two purposes. First, it was to provide revenue for the government and succeeded in doing so. Between 1816 and 1846 the annual yield from customs increased three times, and by 1846 customs revenue provided 11.5 percent of total government income. Second, the tariff system was also an economic instrument by which vulnerable interests were to be protected and growth fostered. Since a host of different factors enter into the determination of levels of international exchange and economic growth and given the imperfect development of communications and the national market in this period, it is difficult to assess the economic impact of the tariff. Most historians argue, however, that earlier scholars exaggerated the deleterious effects of the high tariffs since this was a period of rapid economic growth. Many also argue that tariff barriers afforded necessary protection to metallurgy, machine building, and the cotton industry, which were thereby able to take advantage of an expanding home market.

A. Broder, in F. Braudel and E. Labrousse, eds., *Histoire économique et sociale de la France*, vol. 3 (Paris, 1976); E. Lavasseur, *Histoire du commerce de la France*, vol. 2 (Paris, 1912); B. M. Ratcliffe, "Great Britain and Tariff Reform in France, 1831–36," in B. M. Ratcliffe and W. H. Chaloner, eds., *Essays in Trade and Transport* (Manchester, 1977), and "The Tariff Reform Campaign in France, 1831–1836," *Journal of European Economic History* 7 (1978); R. Schnerb, *Libre-échange et protectionnisme* (Paris, 1953).

Barrie M. Ratcliffe

Related entries: CHEVALIER; ECONOMIC CHANGE; *JOURNAL DES ECONOMISTES*.

FOUCHE, JOSEPH (1759–1820), Duke of Otranto, imperial minister of police; he played a major role during the Hundred Days and the Second Restoration. Born the son of a naval officer in 1759, Joseph Fouché received his education in schools of the Oratorians, prepared for a career as a teacher, and taught in Oratorian schools until 1792, when the order was abolished. Involved in Revolutionary activities, first in Arras and then in Nantes, Fouché was elected to the National Convention in 1792. While a member of the Convention, he voted for the death of Louis XVI, undertook various missions to the provinces, became a leading advocate of dechristianization, and took a major part in the bloody repression of Lyons in 1793–94. After surviving a bitter conflict with Maximilien Robespierre and having but a small role in the events of 9 Thermidor,

Fouché fell on hard times during the Directory. Participation in the coup of 18 Fructidor (September 1797) brought him back into favor and, with the assistance of the vicomte de Barras, he obtained diplomatic posts in Italy and Holland. On 20 July 1799, the directors made Fouché minister of police. A minor part in the coup of 18 Brumaire permitted him to stay in his new job. Between 1799 and 1810, Napoleon and Fouché maintained an uneasy relationship, one that, however, brought great honors and wealth to Fouché. Dismissed for secretly negotiating with the British in 1810, Fouché went first to Italy and then to the more remote Illyrian Provinces in 1813. Promptly chased from his new post by advancing Austrian troops, Fouché returned to France where, while at Avignon, he learned of the entry on 31 March 1814 of the Allied armies into Paris.

Fouché played a role of minor importance during the First Restoration, a somewhat greater one during the Hundred Days, and one of major significance in the transition to the Second Restoration. Having the notable misfortune to be absent from Paris when the crisis of early April 1814 commenced, Fouché hastened to the French capital, reaching it on 6 April, and took his seat in the Senate. Despite having helped convince the Senate to name the comte d'Artois, the brother of Louis XVIII, lieutenant-general of the kingdom in exchange for a few vague phrases about constitutional guarantees, Fouché received little gratitude from the restored Bourbons. Not only did he fail to obtain the ministerial post he coveted, he was also one of the fifty-four imperial senators omitted from the list of peers of France created by the king on 4 June 1814. Fouché's reputation as a *conventionnel* and regicide could neither be forgotten nor forgiven. Although he had little faith that the newly restored monarchy would last, Fouché did submit a paper to the government in which he analyzed its faults and proposed remedies. Meanwhile, he maintained clandestine contacts with leading figures of all political persuasions, including Charles-Maurice de Talleyrand and Clemens von Metternich in Vienna, Joachim Murat in Naples, Bonapartists in Paris, and, last but not least, Artois and the ultraroyalists. Early in 1815, Fouché involved himself in a plot, the nature of which is still obscure, by various Bonapartists and Orleanists to overthrow Louis XVIII and replace him either with a regency in favor of the king of Rome, Napoleon's only son, or with the duc d'Orléans, the head of the younger branch of the Bourbon family who was destined to become king of the French after the Revolution of July 1830. In motion when the news of Napoleon's return from Elba spread across France, the plot quickly disintegrated. As the emperor approached Paris and as Frenchmen loudly acclaimed his progress, the Bourbon government turned in desperation to Fouché, probably offering him the ministerial post he had earlier yearned for. Much too prudent to accept this offer, Fouché, who did not expect the new Napoleonic regime to last, cloaked his refusals with professions of loyalty to the throne. While Fouché awaited the emperor's arrival in Paris, L.-A.-F. Bourrienne (1769–1834), once Napoleon's private secretary and now director of police for the Bourbons and a personal enemy of Fouché, ordered his arrest; the wily Fouché easily outwitted Bourrienne's agents.

The night of the Emperor's return to Paris (19–20 March 1815) Fouché appeared at the Tuileries to offer his services; he asked for the portfolio of foreign affairs but had to content himself with resuming his old craft as minister of police. Having but little faith that the Bonapartist regime would long endure, he told the Baron Pasquier on 25 March that he expected the emperor to last no more than four months. Meanwhile, Fouché opened and maintained contacts with the English, the Austrians, the court of Louis XVIII, other royalists, and the liberal and republican foes of Napoleon within France. When directed to quell a royalist uprising in the western provinces, Fouché evinced a prudent moderation in his orders. A similar moderation was extended to the press only after the largely unsuccessful effort to silence *Le Censeur*. And on the occasion of the elections of May 1815, the minister of police did his best to ensure the return of liberal candidates largely unsympathetic to Napoleonic despotism; this chamber has even been called the *chambre de Fouché*.

Among the first to learn of the disaster at Waterloo, Fouché, who probably had not anticipated the suddenness of Napoleon's downfall, acted with dispatch to complete the demise of the Empire and to ensure a major place for himself in whatever new government France would have. Between 20 June and 8 July 1815, Fouché, never absent from the center of events in Paris, worked to guarantee that when Louis XVIII returned to his throne, he would owe Fouché an unforgettable debt of gratitude. Fouché saw as his first task the elimination of the emperor. Fearing that Napoleon would attempt to make himself a dictator, Fouché cleverly prepared members of the Chamber to greet the exhausted emperor with a demand for his immediate abdication. Both chambers also voted themselves in permanent session. Napoleon gave up his throne for the second time on 22 June 1815. Fouché's second task was to create a provisional government with himself as its head. The emperor's abdication in his hand, he appeared before the chambers and convinced them to appoint an Executive Commission, in effect, a provisional government, consisting of Lazare Carnot, Fouché, Nicolas-Marie Quinette, the duc de Caulaincourt, and General Paul Grenier. Fouché adroitly had himself named president of the commission and henceforth acted as if he possessed executive authority. Of the three possible governments that France could adopt in June 1815, the chambers, the army, and the people of Paris favored Napoleon II, while, almost alone, Fouché advocated the return of Louis XVIII and the Bourbons. Undaunted, Fouché distracted the chambers by asking them to write a new liberal constitution, and he eliminated the marquis de Lafayette, Benjamin Constant, and other prominent liberals by sending them off to negotiate with the Allies. Able to convince Napoleon to leave Paris and ultimately France, Fouché next opened negotiations with the royalists, using as an intermediary the baron de Vitrolles, whom Fouché had released from prison. Finally, Fouché arranged an armistice with the duke of Wellington and Gebhard von Blücher that stipulated the withdrawal of the French army behind the Loire. Fouché thus remained alone in Paris, the power to be reckoned with. Meanwhile, Louis XVIII, slowly making his way back to Paris, had reached Mons, where

Talleyrand joined him, and then journeyed to Cambrai, from where he issued the conciliatory proclamation of 28 June. As the king neared Paris, Fouché continued his negotiations with Talleyrand and Vitrolles, and he retained his contacts with Wellington. Finally, yielding to the urgings of his ministers, Wellington and even Artois, Louis XVIII reluctantly agreed to accept a cabinet in which Talleyrand became minister of foreign affairs and president of the Ministerial Council and in which Fouché took the Ministry of Police. On 6 July 1815, Talleyrand presented to the king his new minister of police. Chateaubriand has left an unforgettable and often-quoted characterization of this strange event. "It was vice leaning on the arm of crime; the trusty regicide [Fouché], on his knees, put his hands, which had pushed Louis XVI's head under the knife, into the hands of the brother of the martyred king; the apostate bishop [Talleyrand] was guarantor of the oath." On the next day, Fouché assembled the Executive Commission and, by cleverly misleading them with false statements about the Allies' intentions, convinced them to disband after making a pro forma protest.

Louis XVIII entered Paris on 8 July 1815, and he immediately undertook the formidable task of creating a workable government in the face of great difficulties. One problem impossible to avoid concerned the question of amnesty for those who had served the emperor during the Hundred Days, a group that included the regicide Fouché. On this subject Louis XVIII had already spoken in the Declaration of Cambrai, which promised amnesty to all who had not joined Napoleon until 23 March and who had abandoned the imperial cause before 8 July. The king had also promised that the chambers would make the final decision on the question of amnesty. Under intense pressure from the Allies, from public opinion, and from the ultraroyalists, Louis, having to forsake his promises, assigned Fouché the thankless task of listing those not eligible for amnesty. The minister of police duly compiled such a list, but it proved unsatisfactory. Of it Talleyrand said: "We must give the duke of Otranto credit for one thing; he did not forget any of his friends in drawing up the list." The amnesty decree, which was finally proclaimed on 24 July 1815, revoked twenty-nine peers and listed fifty-seven military and civilian leaders ineligible for amnesty. Fouché, to give the man his due, did much to assist the men threatened with death to leave France, supplying them with money and passports. Simultaneously with the concern over the amnesty question, France went to the polls (14, 22 August) to replace the Chamber of the Hundred Days that the king had dissolved on 13 July. Despite the efforts of Talleyrand and Fouché to ensure the election of a moderate monarchist chamber, the French elected the *chambre introuvable*, an assembly dominated by ultraroyalists. Among the first acts of the new chamber was to pressure Louis XVIII to dismiss Talleyrand and Fouché. On 15 September, the official paper, the *Moniteur*, announced that Fouché had been named minister to Dresden. A few days later, Talleyrand also resigned. Fouché remained in this post until deprived of it by the amnesty law of 12 January 1816, which exiled the regicides who had served Napoleon during the Hundred Days.

Fouché spent the remaining four years of his life in exile, dying in Trieste on 26 December 1820. His body, which was returned to France only in 1875, lies buried today in Père Lachaise.

Various memoirs purporting to come from the pen of Joseph Fouché appeared in the late teens and the early 1820s. Many of them, like *Les Mémoires de la vie publique de M. Fouché* (London, 1818), are fakes. The *Mémoires*, first published in 1824, have been made available in a scholarly edition by Fouché's biographer, Louis Madelin.

H. Cole, *Fouché: The Unprincipled Patriot* (New York, 1971); R. E. Cubberly, *The Role of Fouché during the Hundred Days* (Madison, Wis., 1969); J. Fouché, *Mémoires*, ed. Louis Madelin (Paris, 1945); H. Houssaye, *1815: La Seconde abdication—La Terreur blanche* (Paris, 1905); L. Madelin, *Fouché, 1759–1820*, 2 vols. (Paris, 1903) and "Les Mémoires de Fouché," *La Révolution francaise*, vol. 3 (1900); P. Robiquet, "La disgrace de Fouché en septembre 1815," *La Révolution française* 73 (1920) and "Fouché pendant les Cent-Jours," *La Révolution française* 71 (1918); S. Zweig, *Joseph Fouché: Portrait of a Politician* (New York, 1930).

Robert Brown

Related entries: AMNESTY BILL OF 1816; CAMBRAI, DECLARATION OF; CARNOT, L.-H.; CAULAINCOURT; *LE CENSEUR; CHAMBRE INTROUVABLE;* CONSTANT; HUNDRED DAYS; LAFAYETTE, M.-J.-P.-Y.-R.-G.; REICHSTADT; TALLEYRAND; ULTRAROYALISTS; VITROLLES.

FOURIER, FRANCOIS-MARIE-CHARLES (1772–1837), the most eloquent and thorough critic of the society of his day and the most imaginative yet least read and appreciated of the major crisis philosophers in the France of the first half of the nineteenth century. Two reasons explain why contemporaries and posterity have not given Charles Fourier the credit he deserves. One is that in his lifetime, he was a marginal and little-known figure, and, since we have little information on his life, he largely remains so. This son of a leading Besançon cloth merchant spent most of his solitary life in obscure commercial occupations, first as a merchant and then as a traveling salesman and even a clerk. Only after 1830 did he have the money and the support of admirers that enabled him to devote himself entirely to his writing. Fourier never married, apparently never made any lasting friendships, and though he saw himself as the savior of man was either ignored or ridiculed by his fellows. In the last years of his life, he patiently awaited the philanthropist who would finance the first phalanx—the new community Fourier had planned in the minutest detail—that he believed would usher in a new world of harmony. None ever appeared.

The drabness of his life and the disdainful silence with which most contemporaries greeted his publications contrasts with the richness and sensuousness of imagination and the humor and irony to be found in his complex writings. It is the nature of these writings, however, that is the second barrier to a proper appreciation of Fourier. The corpus of his writings, only a fraction of which was published in his lifetime, is enormous, for he wrote compulsively.

He began publishing articles in 1803, but his first work—*Théorie des quatre mouvements et des destinées générales* (2 vols.)—did not appear until five years later. Issued anonymously in Lyons but with a Leipzig imprint, it enjoyed no commercial success. His second two-volume work that elaborated, but did not alter, his theories was the *Traité de l'association domestique-agricole* (later *Théorie de l'unité universelle*) published in 1822. The best organized and most accessible of his books is *Nouveau monde industriel et sociétaire, ou invention du procédé, d'industrie attrayante et naturelle distribuée en séries passionnées* (1829), and the most bitter his last publication, *La fausse industrie morcelée*, which appeared in two volumes in 1835–36. All of these works, by both their form and their content, deter all but the most intrepid of readers. They are long and frequently tediously repetitive. Fourier takes liberties with pagination, with letters of the alphabet, some of which are put on their sides or turned upside down, and with words since his texts are littered with neologisms. More important, their content is forbidding. There is ample evidence that his critique of existing society and his blueprint for the future are, in part at least, a reflection of his personal experiences and proclivities. Thus his attack on the nuclear family reflects his own apparently unhappy childhood, while his condemnation of middlemen of all kinds reflects the frustrations of his own career. Even his tastes in food—his dislike of bread and his sweet tooth—influence the diet to be found in the phalanx. Fourier, moreover, was obsessed with numbers (the history of humanity has thirty-two phases; the ideal phalanx has 1,620 inhabitants) and with taxonomy (he classified no fewer than 810 human character types). But for many observers his most unacceptable and most damning trait was the poetic imagination that he apparently allowed to run amok in his writings. The most frequently cited instances of this are his claim that the planets are not mechanical bodies, as is usually supposed, but living organisms with their own sex lives and his forecast that once phalanxes had been established, new animals beneficial to humanity would evolve and the seas change to lemonade. These seemingly eccentric flights of imagination have traditionally posed problems for those who have tried to understand him and even for many of those who admired him. After his death, for example, his followers sought to suppress what they considered the unacceptable and superfluous aspect of his work. Other contemporaries, like Marx and Engels, and subsequently most scholars, followed their example, preferring to see Fourier as a vitriolic critic of captialist society, as the proponent of consumer and producer cooperatives and land banks, rather than as the projector of the phalanx or the cosmic dreamer.

In the 1960s, however, a radical reassessment of Fourier began. Scholars started to see previously neglected aspects of his thought as anticipations of contemporary liberation movements, like women's emancipation and the so-called sexual revolution. The last twenty years have thus witnessed a flurry of studies on Fourier and a new edition of his works, which includes the *Nouveau monde amoureux*, whose eroticism had previously prevented Fourierists from publishing it. Some scholars have gone even further and seen the essence of

Fourier not in the message he transmits but in the medium he uses and even the fertile imagination he possesses. Roland Barthes, for instance, sees Fourier's originality in his linguistic inventiveness; the medium becomes the message, and attitudes toward him have come full circle.

A theorist has to suffer the glosses on his work and the uses to which it is put by others, but none of these appraisals and reappraisals would have pleased Fourier, for two reasons. He believed he had found the secret of the universe, and he often compared himself to Newton. Whereas Newton had discovered the mechanics of nature, he, Fourier, had uncovered the mechanics of man and society. He was, to use another of his analogies, the Christopher Columbus of the new social world. Fourier, then, had a scientific solution for current ills. A second reason why he would not accept suppressions of parts of his work is that, given his anthropocentric vision of present and future society, he believed that how people organized society has an impact on the earth's climate, flora, and fauna and even on the universe. His critical analysis of the crisis of his time and the solution he proposed thus linked basic human drives at one end to the cosmos itself at the other. His was a total analysis.

Fourier developed a devastating critique of contemporary society, one that unquestionably influenced later socialist attacks on capitalism and bourgeois society. This critique had two aspects: a condemnation of the market economy and a denunciation of a society that not only failed to allow people to develop to their full potential and satisfy their physical and emotional needs but oppressed particular groups like the young, the old, and women. It must be admitted that his economic analysis lacks penetration. He was no economist, and there is no evidence that this autodidact ever read the economists of his day. He developed no analysis of class, and factory industry and the proletariat occupy no place in his discussions of existing conditions or in the phalanx, whose primary activity was to be agricultural. There are, however, insights in his criticism of the anarchy of production, of overproduction amid poverty, both of which resulted from the workings of the market mechanism. And there is ammunition for later critics of capitalist society in his attack on the nefarious proliferation of middlemen in the economy. In Fourier's analysis, this group included not only merchants and shopkeepers but financiers, stockbrokers, and speculators of all kinds. All were guilty of crimes ranging from trickery and the adulteration of goods to hoarding, speculation, and usury. Fourier claimed that as a child, he had early witnessed the dishonesty of middlemen but that he had come to understand the harm they did only when he discovered than an apple in a Parisian restaurant cost over a hundred times what it cost where it was grown. He even talked, probably only half-seriously, of this as the fourth historic apple after Adam and Eve's, the Greek Paris's, and Isaac Newton's. But his critique of the society of his time went beyond the economy. He believed that by its organization, its dominant ideology, and its coercive apparatus, society frustrated man's natural drives. This created unhappiness, prevented man from developing to his full potential and repressed feelings that were diverted into hostility and aggression. He began his attack with the nuclear family, the basic social institution. This he condemned because each family saw itself as competing with other families and was thus antisocial because the monogamous marriage locked partners and their offspring in emotionally unhealthy relationships. Above all, the nuclear family oppressed women (and even children). The prevailing ideology—like the middle-class ethos of sobriety, frugality, and restraint—and organized religion, which taught resignation in the face of suffering, reinforced a repressive social system. What made Fourier's criticisms all the more urgent was that he tried to show that the crisis was deepening, that oppression and exploitation were increasing, and even that the world's climate was deteriorating. What made his criticism all the more damning was that he promised that his scientifically organized phalanx would liberate man's passions and free oppressed groups like women and the old, who were marginalized and denied their sexuality in existing society. He even promised that those whose drives and sexual preferences society currently treated as eccentric or perverted would find fulfillment and acceptance in his harmonian world.

Like other crisis philosophers, Fourier believed that the solution he proposed for contemporary woes had two related advantages: it was scientific and could be adopted peacefully. It was scientific because he was the first to understand human needs and to plan carefully the phalanx to ensure that the new order would satisfy them. The creation of a world of phalanxes would not only redeem man, it would lead to wider changes, all to the good of man and the universe. These included a better climate and the evolution of new creatures—"antilions," "anticrocodiles"—which, rather than being harmful, would be willing helpmates for man. With a familiar horror of revolutionary upheaval and a faith in the power of persuasion, Fourier also believed that phalanxes could be established peacefully and painlessly. It is possible, however that the enduring value of Fourier does not lie in the scientific organization of the phalanx and still less in his optimistic belief that men could be persuaded to set it up but in the kind of libertarian society he wanted to create. This was to be a society without government or coercion and without the institution of the monogamous marriage. It was to have a progressive education system, complex work forces, and ceremonies so organized as to ensure that work would be a pleasure, that the most menial tasks would be seen as desirable and useful, and that individuals with the most varied interests and needs could find fulfillment. It was not to be a classless society, though, because Fourier felt that differences among individuals were necessary and beneficial. He thus retained private property and differences in wealth.

Despite the many disappointments he suffered during his lifetime and the inaccessibility of his writings, Fourier has not been without influence. Admirers attempted to set up communities along the lines he had proposed. In 1832 a phalanx was set up at Condé-sur-Vesgre (Seine-et-Oise), but it was ill organized—Fourier refused to recognize it—and quickly failed. A second experiment in Rumania in 1835–37 was also brought to an untimely end when peasants from neighboring estates angrily burned down the phalanstery. In the twenty years following his death, moreover, some thirty-five Fourierist communities were established in the United States. They, too, proved short-lived. Fourier exerted his greatest influence, however, not through his phalanx proposal but through his criticism of existing society. The Fourierist movement under Victor Considérant achieved some cohesion and prominence under the July Monarchy. In books and journals it reiterated and carried forward Fourier's criticism, developing the concept of a new feudalism of financiers and speculators, which corrupted and increasingly controlled the economy and government. He also exerted a more diffuse influence on later libertarian movements. For his analysis of women's condition in patriarchal society and his insistence that women's emancipation should be the yardstick of social progress, Fourier was read and admired by early feminists like Flora Tristan. By dint of his critique of all government and his desire to free man from any form of coercion, he has a respectable place in anarchist thought. By his recognition of the importance and complexity of the sex drive and the harmful effects of its repression, he anticipated later theorists and later—and ongoing—struggles. The progressive education he advocated—with its goal of developing the unique potential of each child, its postulate that children were human beings in their own right, its use of play and emulation as teaching tools, and its abolition of the classroom—is yet another indication of the insight into the human condition possessed by this most solitary and denigrated but most humanist of the major French crisis philosophers of the first half of the nineteenth century.

R. Barthes, *Sade, Fourier, Loyola* (Paris, 1971); J. Beecher and R. Bienvenu, eds., *The Utopian Vision of Charles Fourier, Selected Texts on Work, Love and Passionate Attraction* (Boston, 1971); F. E. Manuel, *The Prophets of Paris* (Cambridge, Mass., 1962); N.V. Riasanovsky, *The Teachings of Charles Fourier* (Berkeley, 1969); M. C. Spencer, *Charles Fourier* (Boston, 1981); T. Zeldin, *The Educational Ideas of Charles Fourier* (London, 1969).

Barrie M. Ratcliffe

Related entries: COMTE, A.; CONSIDERANT; *LA DEMOCRATIE PACIFIQUE*; MARX; SAINT-SIMONIANISM; TRISTAN.

FOUR ORDINANCES. See JULY ORDINANCES.

FOY, MAXIMILIEN-SEBASTIEN (1775–1825), general and liberal Restoration deputy. Born in Ham (Somme) and educated at an Oratorian collège in Soissons and the artillery academy at La Fère (1790), Foy entered the Revolutionary army in 1791 as a lieutenant. He served with distinction in Flanders and was promoted to captain before the representative-on-mission Joseph LeBon ordered his arrest for criticizing the excesses of the Terror (1794). Released after Thermidor, Foy fought in Germany (1795–97), Switzerland (under André Masséna, 1798–99), and Italy and the Tyrol (1800–1801). By 1802 he was a colonel, and as a moderate republican opposed Bonaparte's consolidation of his rule. His opposition to the consulate for life (1802) and the Empire (1804) and his association with Bonaparte's rival, General Jean Moreau, slowed his advancement, but he continued his military service in Austria (1805), Dalmatia (1806) and as a military aide to Horace-François Sebastiani in Constantinople (1807). In Spain (1807–13) he won promotion to general of division and served under Marshals Andoche Junot, André Masséna, Auguste de Marmont and Nicholas-Jean de Soult. He won Napoleon's favor by 1810, and his leadership in Spain provided some of the few bright spots in the long chronicle of French defeats at the hands of the duke of Wellington. Badly wounded (his fourteenth) in February 1814, Foy accepted the Restoration and was made inspector general at Nantes. Rallying reluctantly to Napoleon during the Hundred Days, he commanded a division at Quatre Bras and Waterloo and was wounded once more. Denied a command under the Second Restoration, Foy worked on his memoirs until he won election to the Chamber of Deputies in 1817 (from Peronne).

With General Jean-Maximin Lamarque, Foy became one of the prominent military members of the liberal opposition and probably its best parliamentary orator. While accepting the Restoration, he campaigned ardently in defense of the individual liberties contained in the charter and constantly recalled the glories of the Revolution and the Empire. Like Lamarque (and unlike liberal deputies like the marquis de Lafayette, Jacques-Antoine Manuel, and Marc-René de Voyer d'Argenson, Foy avoided the carbonarist conspiracies of 1822 and 1823, though he vigorously opposed attempts to limit freedom of speech and the press in their wake. An opponent of the Elie Decazes election law of 1820, the French expedition in Spain (1823), and indemnification of *émigrés* (1825), Foy championed Italian independence, the restoration of the tricolor, and an aggressive foreign policy. His eloquence gained him a wide popular following among opponents of the regime, and the sculptor Pierre-Jean David d'Angers carved an admired (and curiously neoclassical) nude statue of Foy at the tribune of the Chamber of Deputies. Reelected from three different constituencies (Paris, St. Quentin, and Vervins) in 1824, Foy made his last address to the legislature on 16 May 1825, denouncing the forced retirement of fifty-six Napoleonic generals. He died of a long-standing heart ailment on 28 November. His death was widely mourned, and more than 100,000 people followed the funeral procession to Père Lachaise, though there were no disorders (as at M. Lallemand's funeral in 1820 or Lamarque's in 1832). Casimir Périer delivered the funeral oration, and Francois-René de Chateaubriand expressed his respect. A public subscription to provide for Foy's five children quickly raised nearly a million francs.

V. Beach, *Charles X of France* (Boulder, Colo. 1971); G. de Bertier de Sauvigny, *La Restauration* (Paris, 1955, 1963); P. Cuisin, *Vie militaire, politique et anecdotique du general Foy* (Paris, 1826); M. Foy, *Discours* (Paris, 2 vols., 1826); M. Glover, *Wellington's Peninsular Victories* (London, 1963); J. Lucas-Dubreton, *La restauration et la monarchie de juillet* (Paris, 1926); P. Mansel, *Louis XVIII* (London, 1981); A. B. Spitzer, *Old Hatreds and New Hopes* (Cambridge, Mass., 1971); G. Weill, *Histoire du parti republicain en France* (Paris, 1900).

David Longfellow

Related entries: CHARTER OF 1814; DAVID D'ANGERS; DECAZES; LAMARQUE; SPAIN, 1823 FRENCH INVASION OF.

LA FRANCE (1834–1847), legitimist newspaper. This newspaper appeared daily from December 1834 to February 1847 under the subtitle *Organ of the Monarchical and Religious Interests of Europe*. Among its founders and editors were St.-Maurice, Verteuil de Feuillas, Fréderic Dollé, E.-P. Lubis, and Hippolyte de Villemessant (later famous as an editor of *Le Figaro*). The successor to *Le Brid' Oison* (1832–34), *La France* managed to build its average print run up from 957 in 1836 (175 provincial subscriptions) to only 1,438 in 1846 (1,065 subscriptions) despite a low yearly cost. This neglected paper was an important mouthpiece for the militant supporters of a Bourbon restoration, however. Its greatest success was to publish a series of fake but damaging letters from Louis-Philippe to foreign powers in 1841; it was acquitted, but on other occasions editors were fined or imprisoned. In February 1847 it fused with *La Quotidienne* and *L'Echo français* into *L'Union monarchique*, which became in 1848 the durable *L'Union*.

J. P. Aguet, "Le tirage des quotidiens de Paris sous la Monarchie de Juillet," *Schweizerische Zeitschrift für Geschichte* 10 (1960); C. Bellanger, J. Godechot. P. Guiral, and F. Terrou, eds., *Histoire générale de la presse française*, vol. 2 (Paris, 1969).

Peter McPhee

Related entries: L'ECHO FRANCAIS; LE FIGARO; LEGITIMISM; *LA QUOTIDIENNE.*

LA FRANCE CHRETIENNE (1821–1828), pro-Jesuit newspaper of the Restoration. Appearing twice weekly from January 1821 to February 1828, *La France chrétienne* supported the Jesuits and demanded more vigorous attacks upon the liberals. Joseph de Villèle found it an embarrassment, and it was suspended by the temporary censorship he imposed at the end of 1827. It disappeared entirely when François-Dominique de Montlosier's attacks on the Jesuits were referred by the minister Jean-Baptiste de Martignac to a parliamentary commission for investigation.

Irene Collins

Related entries: CENSORSHIP; JESUITS; MARTIGNAC; MONTLOSIER; VILLELE.

LA FRANCE MERIDIONALE (1829–?), Regional newspaper of Toulouse having a liberal influence in the south during the Restoration era. Of the sixty to seventy liberal provincial journals, *France Méridionale* was one of ten singled out by François Mignet for its steadfast courage in resisting Jules de Polignac's judicial persecutions in 1830. Its editor, Armand Dupin, was put on trial in March for merely reprinting a *Globe* editorial "France and the Bourbons," which had resulted in conviction of the *Globe's* editor. In a further attempt to destroy the *Méridionale*, its printer was also indicted, a form of intimidation commonly used in the provinces during Charles X's reign. Dupin received a six-month sentence and a fine calculated to destroy his small journal: 6,000 francs. A flood of donations from Parisians, including the *Globe's* staff, paid Dupin's fine and also supported his family during his confinement. The provincial press was crucial to Restoration electoral campaigns and was considered dangerous by Polignac's government.

Upon learning of the July Revolution, citizens of predominantly royalist Toulouse clashed in the streets until, on 4 August 1830, the liberal group behind the *France méridionale* formed themselves into a provisional city government and helped to restore peace during the transition of local authority.

D. Pinkney, *The French Revolution of 1830* (Princeton, 1971); D. Rader, *The Journalists and the July Revolution* (The Hague, 1973).

Daniel Rader

Related entries: CHARLES X; *LE GLOBE*; MIGNET; POLIGNAC; REVO-LUTION OF 1830.

FRANCHET D'ESPEREY, FRANCOIS (1778–1863), royalist and administrator of the Empire and Restoration. Born at Lyons on 14 December 1778, Franchet d'Esperey worked in the municipal customs service and fought the Revolutionaries during the 1793 siege of that city. He escaped to Paris where he joined the staff of the Directory of Combined Duties. He opposed the Empire. Being a devout Catholic—he later became a zealous member of the Congrégation—he joined the League of Devotion, a clandestine organization that circulated in France the forbidden pronouncements of Pope Pius VII, who was imprisoned by Napoleon. Franchet himself was arrested in 1811 for possessing copies of the papal bull excommunicating Napoleon. While incarcerated at Sainte-Pélagie, Franchet made friends with fellow prisoner Alexis de Noailles.

When the Bourbon Restoration freed Franchet, he became secretary to Noailles, accompanying him on mission to Lyons and to the Congress of Vienna. Franchet returned to France after Waterloo and was subsequently appointed chief of personnel at the Ministry of Posts, where he favored royalists untainted by involvement with the Revolution or Napoleon. In January 1822 the Villèle ministry appointed Franchet director of general police, nominally under the minister of the interior. This appointment he owed to his friendship with Mathieu de Montmorency and to the influence of the ultras, the Congrégation, the Knights of the Faith, and Frederick William III of Prussia. At the time of this appointment, he added "d'Esperey" to his family name of Franchet. He expanded the functions of his office far beyond the intention of those who created it, especially in the area of political police work. He supervised the political police, maintained files on suspects, wrote instructions for prefects, investigated political crimes, and supervised publishing, bookselling, and censorship. He also had authority over the prefect of police. He ardently persecuted those he regarded as enemies of crown and church yet surrounded himself with people of dubious reputation.

Franchet's conduct of his office was so obnoxious that the Martignac cabinet forced his dismissal on the king in 1828 and also separated him from the Council of State. Furthermore, during the Spanish campaign, Franchet was involved in shipping illegal supplies to the royalist guerrillas in Spain. He also conspired to attempt to discredit Armand-Charles Guilleminot, the former imperial officer serving as chief of staff to the duke of Angoulême for this campaign. The legacy Franchet left to his successors was one of hatred and scorn for the office he held, and it did nothing to endear his Bourbon master to the people. Nevertheless Franchet was named a councillor of state and member of the Legion of Honor in 1825, and after his dismissal from the police he became receiver general of the department of Nièvre. In early 1829 he was a leader of the effort to create a unified ultra opposition to Jean-Baptiste de Martignac, and he received a secret pension when Jules de Polignac came into power. At the same time Charles X issued his ill-fated ordinances on 25 July 1830, he also reappointed Franchet to the Council of State. At the July Revolution Franchet fled to England, where he joined Charles X. He then went to represent Charles at the Prussian court. He later returned to France, living at Versailles on pensions provided by the comte de Chambord and Napoleon III. Franchet died in Versailles on 22 June 1863.

J. Balteau et al., *Dictionnaire de biographie française* (Paris, 1933-); J. Peuchet, *Mémoires tirés des archives de la police* (Paris, 1838); Saint-Edme, *Biographie des lieutenants-généraux, ministres, directeurs-généraux . . . de la police* (Paris, 1829); A. Spitzer, *Old Hatreds and Young Hopes* (Cambridge, 1971).

James K. Kieswetter

Related entries: ANGOULEME, L.-A.; CHEVALIERS DE LA FOI; CON-GREGATION; MARTIGNAC; MONTMORENCY; NOAILLES; POLIGNAC; SPAIN, 1823 FRENCH INVASION OF; ULTRAROYALISTS; VILLELE.

FRAYSSINOUS, DENIS-LUC-ANTOINE (1765–1841), bishop and author. Frayssinous came from the Aveyron and was ordained as a priest in 1789 in the society of Saint-Sulpice. During the Empire he made a name for himself as a lecturer giving religious instruction to young students. The substance of these lectures is in his *Défense du christianisme ou conférences sur la religion* (Paris, 1825), which went through seventeen editions in France and was translated into several other languages. In 1822 he was consecrated bishop *in partibus* of Hermopolis and named grand master of the University. In August 1824 he became minister of ecclesiastical affairs and of public instruction. In this position, he tried to change the Napoleonic University system into a decentralized system more under the influence of the Catholic clergy. After the dissolution of the Villèle ministry, he was nevertheless able to stay in his post until March 1828. The 1830 Revolution caused him to leave France. He spent two years in Rome and then was called in August 1833 to be tutor to the duc de Bordeaux in Prague and in Gorizia. He returned to France in October 1838.

A. Garnier, *Frayssinous. Son rôle dans l'Université* (Paris, 1925).

Guillaume de Bertier de Sauvigny, trans. E. Newman

Related entries: BORDEAUX; PUBLIC INSTRUCTION; REVOLUTION OF 1830; VILLELE.

FREEMASONRY. The first group of Freemasons in France was organized in 1725 in Paris. The secret society grew rapidly during the eighteenth century, although it was blamed by conservatives for spreading Enlightenment ideas and allegedly fomenting revolutionary conspiracies. Many Freemasons were indeed active during the Revolution, and the order enjoyed a large measure of toleration under Napoleon. After the Restoration, Freemasonry was held in disfavor by the government. The movement clashed with the state on various occasions. Although lodges were ordered not to interfere in politics, members disobeyed, and a number of lodges were suspended. Louis-Philippe refused to allow his son, the duc d'Orléans, to become grand master after the 1830 Revolution, and an 1834 law made Masonic groups subject to strict police control. The Grand Orient, the major group of Freemasons, supported the 1848 Revolution, but the movement remained in a precarious position during the Second Republic and Second Empire. Later in the century, most lodges became affiliated with the Radical party, and Freemasonry was known for its ardent anticlericalism.

There were approximately 10,000 Freemasons in France in 1802 and double that number by the end of the century. Although the leaders were sometimes noblemen, most members came from the middle and lower middle classes. Shopkeepers, artisans, doctors, and journalists were among the common recruits. Lodges provided a social gathering place for members, and the rituals and ceremony became a sort of folklore for Masons. Freemasonry was thus one of the major voluntary organizations in nineteenth century France. The artisanal *compagnonnages* were influenced by the movement and adopted Masonic symbolism for their own uses.

M. J. Headings, *French Freemasonry under the Third Republic* (New York, 1949); J. Palou, *La Franc-Maconnerie* (Paris, 1964); D. Wright, ed., *Gould's History of Free-masonry*, vol. 4 (London, n.d.).

Robert Aldrich

Related entry: COMPAGNONNAGES.

FRENCH ACADEMY. See ACADEMIE FRANÇAISE.

FRENILLY, AUGUSTE-FRANCOIS FAUVEAU, BARON DE (1768–1848), journalist, deputy, and peer of the Restoration. Frénilly was born in Paris on 14 November 1768, the son of an old noble family much involved with the Enlightenment. He remained in France during the Revolution. As a member of an irregular royalist battalion, he was one of the defenders of the Tuileries on 10 August 1792. He hid in the provinces at Loches during the Terror and returned to Paris after the fall of Maximilien Robespierre. There he gathered the remnants of his fortune and collaborated with Mme. d'Houdetot in reviving the salons of the pre-Revolutionary literary society. For a while he was a member of an extreme royalist group known as the *muscadins*. He also occupied himself with agriculture at his chateau of Bourneville (Oise), which was noted for having one of the first flocks of merino sheep in France. Frénilly remained out of public life through the Empire. During the Hundred Days, he fled to England.

After the Second Restoration, Frénilly's family background and ultraroyalist political views led him into close association with the comte d'Artois. In 1817 he collaborated with John Stoddart, director of the *London Times*, in founding *Le Correspondant*, an Anglo-French literary publication that appeared from 1 August 1817 to 10 April 1818. He then was associated with François-René de Chateaubriand, Louis de Bonald, Joseph de Villèle, and others in establishing the ultra journal *Le Conservateur* in October 1818. There his ego brought him into conflict with Chateaubriand. After the fall of the Decazes ministry, the *Conservateur*'s main target, and the reintroduction of censorship, the paper ceased publication in March 1820 after printing seventy-eight issues. Frénilly, along with Bonald and Félicité de Lamennais, then established the *Défenseur*, a political, religious, and literary journal passionately expounding the philosophy of Lamennais. It appeared from 1 March 1820 to 27 October 1821.

Riding the wave of conservative political triumph, Frénilly was elected to the Chamber of Deputies by the department of Loire-Inférieure in October 1821. He was reelected in 1824 and served until 1827. In the Deputies he voted with the ultras, staunchly supporting the Villèle ministry. He actively served on several committees, especially those preparing addresses to the king. In February 1822 during debates on a new law to eliminate jury trials for press offenses, Frénilly attempted to deny virtually all the freedoms guaranteed by the Charter. In August 1824 Frénilly was appointed councillor of state, and in 1826 Charles X personally congratulated him on a speech on Saint-Domingue. On 5 November 1827 Frénilly entered the Chamber of Peers, where he opposed the Martignac cabinet as strongly as he had supported Villèle. As a result of his opposition, he was removed from the Council of State in November 1828, although the Polignac government recalled him on 25 July 1830. Upset by the July Revolution, Frénilly fled to Austria, where he joined Charles X and his court in exile. There he devoted himself to the literary pursuits that his political career had interrupted. He gathered material for an uncompleted parliamentary history of England, wrote various political tracts, translated Ariosto, and compiled his *Souvenirs*, which were published in 1908. Frénilly died at Gratz, Austria, on 1 August 1848.

Archives parlementaires; I. Collins, *The Government and the Newspaper Press in France* (Oxford, 1959); E. Hatin, *Histoire du journal en France, 1631–1853* (Paris, 1853); N. Hudson, *Ultra-Royalism and the French Restoration* (Cambridge, 1936); A. Robert et al., *Dictionnaire des parlementaires français* (Paris, 1889-91).

James K. Kieswetter

Related entries: CHATEAUBRIAND; *LE CONSERVATEUR*; DECAZES; *LE DEFENSEUR*; LAMENNAIS; MARTIGNAC; POLIGNAC; ULTRAROYAL-ISTS; VILLELE.

FRERES DE LA DOCTRINE CHRETIENNE. See BROTHERS OF THE CHRISTIAN SCHOOLS.

FRESNEL, AUGUSTIN-JEAN (1788–1827), physicist, who, with Thomas Young, pioneered in optics and did much to establish the wave theory of light. Fresnel was educated at home and at the Ecole centrale in Caen before entering the Ecole polytechnique in 1804. Despite a great deal of illness, he graduated with the highest honors and enrolled at the Ecole des ponts and chaussées. After receiving his degree, he became a government engineer. During the Hundred Days in 1815, he was suspended and placed under police surveillance for supporting the royalist cause. Napoleon, however, allowed him to return to Normandy, and on his way there he made the acquaintance of the French statesman and scientist François Arago, who advised him to spend his compelled leisure in the advancement of optics. Combining Huygen's principle that each point on a wave front serves as a new source of light and rediscovering Young's principle of interference, Fresnel gave the most complete description possible—prior to Maxwell's theory on the electromagnetic wave—of the phenomena of diffraction, refraction, and reflection. Fresnel, after explaining the phenomena relating to polarization of light by reflection, took up the investigation of double refraction. He explained this theory by the fact that light rays, if polarized in directions at right angles to each other, cannot interfere with each other, a theory that led him to theorize the transverse nature of light vibrations in 1821. During the last years of his short life, Fresnel became increasingly concerned with the existence and nature of a medium such as ether that could serve as a carrier of light waves. His so-called Fresnel partial-convection formula, later confirmed by Hippolyte Fizeau, was an important development in this field. He devised a method of producing circularly polarized light and promoted the replacement of mirrors with compound lenses in lighthouses. Although his work in optics received meager public recognition during his lifetime, Fresnel maintained that not even acclaim from distinguished colleagues could compare with the pleasure of discovering a theoretical truth or proving a calculation experimentally.

G.S. Lansberg, *Optika*, 4th ed. (Moscow, 1957); *Oeuvres complètes d'Augustin Fresnel* (Paris, 1866–1870).

Irene Earls

Related entries: ARAGO FAMILY; ECOLE POLYTECHNIQUE.

FREYCINET, LOUIS-CLAUDE DESAULSES DE (1779–1842), explorer and geographer of the Pacific. Born at Montélimar (Drôme) on 7 August 1779, Freycinet to some extent followed in the footsteps of his elder brother, Rear Admiral Baron Henri-Louis de Freycinet. The younger Freycinet joined the navy in 1793 and, sailing on the same ships as his brother, fought in several battles against the British. In October 1800 his brother took him along on an expedition, commanded by Captain Nicolas Baudin, to explore parts of Australia and Tasmania. On this voyage he was promoted to *lieutenant de vaisseau*. They explored Van Diemen's Land and discovered Port Montbazin and Port Dalrymple. Given command of the small schooner, *La Casuarina*, Freycinet continued his explorations. But missing a rendezvous with Baudin in his ship, *La Géographe*,

Freycinet nearly suffered disaster when his freshwater supplies were almost exhausted before reaching port. Continuing on to Timor after mapping parts of the coast of New Holland, both ships reached the Ile de France in August 1803. There the *Casuarina* was abandoned, and Freycinet and his crew returned to France in March 1804 on board *La Géographe*. After a brief subsequent voyage, poor health forced his return to Paris in September 1805. There he undertook to prepare maps and narration of the voyage to Australia. He finally completed this task in 1816 after several years delay due to the death of his collaborator, François Péron. Freycinet was promoted to *capitaine de frégate* in July 1811.

In 1817 the French government organized an expedition to circumnavigate the globe, studying the earth's shape, terrestrial magnetism, and meteorology, and exploring the Pacific and collecting scientific specimens. Freycinet commanded the corvette *Uranie* on this expedition, which left on 17 September 1817. He was accompanied by Louis-Isidore Duperrey and Jacques Arago. They sailed to Rio de Janeiro, the Cape of Good Hope, the Ile de France, the Ile Bourbon, and Dirk Hartog Island, conducting experiments, making observations, and filling in many gaps left from Baudin's expedition. Compiling extensive records on the island peoples he encountered, Freycinet then sailed to Timor and Papua, arriving on Guam in March 1819. Via Hawaii, Samoa, and New Guinea, he arrived at Sidney, Australia, in November and established an observatory for magnetism and gravity. He also studied the penal colony established in Australia.

His tasks accomplished, Freycinet sailed for France in December 1819. Rounding Cape Horn he encountered a severe storm that forced him away from Tierra del Fuego. Attempting to anchor in the Falklands for further experiments, the *Uranie* struck a large submerged rock on 14 February 1820. The ship was successfully beached, and most of the specimens and records were saved, but the ship could not be repaired. However, Freycinet managed to purchase a U.S. vessel, the *Mercury*, which arrived in the Falklands. Freycinet and his company reached Le Havre in November 1820 with copious records and biological specimens. In December Louis XVIII received him and promoted him to *capitaine de vaisseau*. Thereafter Freycinet devoted himself to the meticulous preparation and publication of his notes from the voyage. He was engaged in this task when he died of a coronary aneurysm at Freycinet, near Loriol (Drôme), on 18 August 1842. The published records of his *Voyage autour du monde* ultimately filled some thirteen quarto volumes and four atlases. He also left numerous other published works on navigation and science.

F. Frille, *Louis de Freycinnet, sa vie de savant et de marin* (Paris, 1845); F. Hoefer, *Nouvelle biographie générale* (Paris, 1852–66).

James K. Kieswetter

Related entries: ARAGO FAMILY.

FRIENDS OF THE FREEDOM OF THE PRESS. See SOCIETY OF FRIENDS OF THE FREEDOM OF THE PRESS.

FRIENDS OF TRUTH, SOCIETY OF. See SOCIETY OF THE FRIENDS OF TRUTH.

G

GARAT, DOMINIQUE-JOSEPH, COMTE (1749–1833), politician, orator, and writer. Garat was born in Bayonne and entered legal practice in Bordeaux in the 1770s. A prolific writer and a professor at the lycée in Paris before the Revolution, Garat seems to have been largely devoid of deep political principles and adapted himself deftly to follow the dominant political faction of the moment. He served incompetently as minister of justice from 1792 until the Terror. He returned to politics after Thermidor, then abandoned his professed republican principles to serve Bonaparte. Napoleon made him a count, a senator, a member of the Legion of Honor, and a teacher at the Institute. Although Garat became noted for his speeches in praise of Napoleon in the Senate (1805–12), he quickly abandoned him in 1814 and signed the act deposing him. Published elogia to the anti-Bonapartist general Jean Moreau, the duke of Wellington, and Alexander I soon followed.

Louis XVIII declined to make Garat a peer, but he was elected to the Chamber of Deputies (Tarbes) during the Hundred Days. Napoleon spurned his offers of assistance, and Garat returned to Bayonne after Waterloo, devoting himself to writing and embracing the Catholic church. He was reappointed to a chair at the Institute (October 1832) shortly before his death.

G. de Bertier de Sauvigny, *La Restauration* (Paris, 1955, 1963); J. Dawson, *Lakanal the Regicide* (Alabama, 1948); J. Godechot, *Les Institutions de la France sous la Révolution et l'Empire* (Paris, 1951); D. Jordan, *The King's Trial* (Berkeley, California, 1979); G. Lefebvre, *La Révolution française* (Paris, 1930).

David Longfellow

GARDE MOBILE, part of the National Guard of 1848. On 25 February 1848, the Provisional Government decided to recruit 24,000 men for a Garde mobile, or two battalions per arrondissement. These men would be paid, unlike the National Guards who were not, and it was hoped that this elite would prove more reliable in the maintenance of order than the regular battalions of the

National Guard. By June 1848, 16,000 men had been recruited and formed into nineteen battalions under the command of General Marie-Alphonse Bedeau. Although two battalions of the Garde mobile had cleared the Constituent Assembly of demonstrators on 15 May 1848, its heterogeneous recruitment and elected cadre gave the government some cause for anxiety. However, the large number of ex-servicemen among the Mobiles provided a certain solidity, so that when the revolution of the June Days of 1848 broke out, it was the Gardes mobiles, often acting spontaneously and without orders, who in the initial hours kept the revolution from spreading to many parts of Paris and allowed the army to concentrate for the counterattack. The garde mobile was disbanded after June 1848, but the name was revived in the reserve system established by the Niel Law in 1868.

L. Girard, *La garde nationale* (Paris, 1964).

Douglas Porch

Related entries: BEDEAU; JUNE DAYS; NATIONAL GUARD; PROVISIONAL GOVERNMENT; REVOLUTION OF 1848.

GARDE REPUBLICAINE, a largely ceremonial contingent of police. The garde républicaine first came to be called by this name in 1848. It grew out of the Gardes françaises of the *ancien régime*. After 1789, it went under various names: Garde municipale, Garde imperial (1802–13), Gendarmerie royale de Paris (1816–30), and Garde municipale de Paris (1830–48). A regiment of dragoons and one of infantry provided ceremonial guards for the Elysée Palace and various government bureaus, although troops of the Garde républicaine participated in the suppression of the June Days of 1848. Also in 1848, a band was established.

Douglas Porch

Related entries: JUNE DAYS; REVOLUTION OF 1848.

GARNIER, JEAN-LOUIS-CHARLES (1825–1898), architect. Too frail to follow his father's trade as a wheelwright, Garnier was able to enter the Ecole des beaux-arts at the age of seventeen, working during the day in various architects' offices (including that of Eugène Viollet-le-Duc). In 1848, he won the Prix de Rome with a plan for an arts and industries school. His drawings and reports on Greek, Roman, and Renaissance buildings in Italy attracted some notice, particularly a proposal for the restoration of the Temple of Aegina, but on his return to Paris, Garnier was only able to secure a post as architectural consultant to the fifth and sixth arrondissements. It was from this obscure position that Garnier entered the competition to design the new opera house, announced by Minister of State Alexandre Walewski in November 1860. Garnier's was one of five designs chosen from the original field of 170 and was selected as the final plan in the second round by the unanimous vote of the judges. Construction began in 1861 and was completed fourteen years (and 35 million francs) later. While Garnier would concede only that the site for the Opéra was poorly chosen, his Renaissance revival design (which the architect hoped would herald a new,

Second Empire style) excited lively controversy, particularly over the heavy use of ornamentation.

With his reputation established, Garnier went on to design the Music Conservatory and the Cercle de la librairie in Paris, hotels in Vittel and Bordighera, the tombs of Bizet, Offenbach, and Victor Massé (Paris), and the casino at Monte Carlo. His temporary constructions of the history of human habitation were one of the popular attractions at the Universal Exposition of 1889. Honors granted Garnier included the gold medal of the Royal Institute of British Architects (1886) and designation as a grand officer of the Legion of Honor (1895), the first time an architect had been appointed. Garnier wrote poetry and several architectural treatises and was interested in the problems of historical restoration.

C. Garnier, *L'histoire de l'habitation* (Paris, 1892) and with Ammann, *Le nouvel Opéra de Paris*, 2 vols. (Paris, 1878–81); G.E. Haussmann, *Mémoires du Baron Haussman*, 3 vols. (Paris, 1890-93); D. Pinkney, *Napoleon III and the Rebuilding of Paris* (Princeton, 1958).

David Longfellow

Related entry: VIOLLET-LE-DUC.

GARNIER-PAGES, ETIENNE-JOSEPH-LOUIS (1801–1841), liberal deputy. Born in Marseilles, Garnier-Pagès lost his father (Garnier) at an early age, and he and his twin brother Louis-Antoine were raised by a stepfather, whose last name (Pagès) they affixed to their own. Despite a difficult childhood, Garnier-Pagès was able to pursue legal studies and had become a respected Parisian attorney by the late 1820s. An active liberal opponent of the Restoration in the Aide-toi, le ciel t'aidera society, he helped to organize his neighborhood against the July Ordinances in 1830 and was disappointed that the revolution did not produce a democratic republic. Running for the Chamber of Deputies as soon as he was old enough to qualify, with financial support from his brother (a successful businessman), Garnier-Pagès was elected from the Isère in December 1831 and joined the small republican faction in the legislature. Although opposed to revolutionary conspiracies against the July Monarchy, he defended the insurrection of 5–6 June 1832 (funeral of General Lamarque) and pressed for social reforms, liberty of the press, progressive taxation, and (after 1840) universal suffrage, arguing that popular sovereignty was clearly implied in the Charter. An "opportunist" republican and a Freemason, Garnier-Pagès rejected socialism and violent political change, hoping suffrage could be extended through electoral reforms. At his death (probably from tuberculosis) in 1841, he was the recognized leader and spokesman of the republican delegation in the Chamber. His work was carried on by his brother, who helped organize the Banquet Campaign in 1848 and was mayor of Paris and minister of finance under the Second Republic.

S. Charléty, *La Monarchie de Juillet* (Paris, 1921); C. Ledré, *La presse à l'assaut de la monarchie, 1815–1848* (Paris, 1960); F. Ponteil, *La Monarchie parlementaire* (Paris, 1949); I. Tchernoff, *Le parti republicain sous la monarchie de juillet* (Paris, 1901); P.

Vigier, *La Monarchie de Juillet* (Paris, 1962); C. Weill, *Histoire du parti republicain en France* (Paris, 1900).

David Longfellow

Related entries: AIDE-TOI, LE CIEL T'AIDERA; BANQUET CAMPAIGN; CHAMBER OF DEPUTIES; FREEMASONRY; JULY ORDINANCES; LA-MARQUE; REVOLUTION OF 1830.

GASPARIN, ADRIEN-ETIENNE-PIERRE, COMTE DE (1783–1862), agronomist and politician; minister of the interior (1836–1837) in the Molé cabinet and in a transitional cabinet that fell after the riot of 12 May, 1839. Born 20 June in Orange (Vaucluse), Adrien de Gasparin was the son of an important politician in the 1789 Revolution who had been a regicide deputy, member of the Committee of Public Safety, and a supporter of Bonaparte at the siege of Toulon.

After service as an officer of dragoons during the Empire, Gasparin turned to agronomy, writing several veterinary studies during the Empire and the Restoration. These studies of land management were given prizes by the Institute and by several learned societies. It was not until after the Revolution of 1830 that he became interested in politics. He was named prefect of the Loire, then of the Isère, and elected a deputy from the Vaucluse. (He was not reelected in 1831). After the revolt of the Lyons silk workers in November 1831, Gasparin replaced the prefect of the Rhône, Louis Bouvier-Dumolart, and repressed the insurrection there of April 1834. As a reward he was made a peer on 19 April 1834. In April 1835 he became under secretary of state in the Ministry of the Interior, then minister of the interior on 6 September 1836 in the Molé cabinet. He was especially interested in almshouses, prisons, and insane asylums, and he helped draw up a new municipal law. It was he who ended the practice of marching prisoners along the roads chained together; henceforth they were transported in carts. He left the ministry on 15 April 1837 but became minister of the interior in a transitional government that took power 31 March 1839 and fell after the riot of 12 May 1839.

A grand officer of the Legion of Honor, member of the Institute in 1840, he presided over the Committee on Arts and Monuments. He returned to private life after the February Revolution of 1848 and refused the directorship of the National Agricultural Institute created at Versailles. (This institute was suppressed 27 September 1852.) Nevertheless, he was chosen to chair the jury on agriculture at the Universal Exposition of 1855. Afterward, his declining health forced his retirement to his estates in the Vaucluse, where he died 7 September 1862.

His brother, Auguste de Gasparin (1787–1857), was also a well-known agronomist and a deputy from the Vaucluse from 1837 to 1842.

Adrien's son, Agénor-Etienne de Gasparin (1810–71), was in charge of his father's office, *maître des requêtes* to the Council of State, and deputy from Bastia in 1842 (not reelected in 1846). He wrote books on the abolition of slavery and on Protestantism. His wife, Valéries de Gasparin (1815-?), wrote many books on Protestantism. His brother, Paul de Gasparin, was a deputy from Tarasçon (Bouches du Rhône) in 1846.

L. Blanc, *Histoire de Dix Ans, 1830–1840*, 5 vols. (Paris, 1841–44); *Nouvelle biographie générale*, vols. 19–20 (Paris, 1855–66).

Jean-Claude Caron, trans. E. Newman

Related entries: CHAMBER OF DEPUTIES; CHAMBER OF PEERS; COUNCIL OF STATE; LYONS, REVOLTS IN; MOLE; REVOLUTION OF 1830; REVOLUTION OF 1848.

GAUTIER, PIERRE-JULES-THEOPHILE (1811–1872), romantic writer and critic and the inspiration for the art for art's sake movement. Although born in Tarbes (Hautes-Pyrénées) on 30 August 1811, the son of Jean-Pierre Gautier (1778–1854), an official in the revenue service, Théophile Gautier grew up in Paris, where his family moved in 1814. As a youth, his favorite books were *Robinson Crusoe* and Bernardin de Saint-Pierre's *Paul et Virginie*. Although he began as a boarding pupil at the Collège Louis-le-Grand in 1822, he soon left to become a day student at the Lycée Charlemagne. While there, he made the acquaintance of Gérard de Nerval and Pétrus Borel. During the late 1820s, Gautier briefly studied art, and he began, like so many of his contemporaries, to write poems. In 1829, he met Victor Hugo, then the idol of the young Parisian literary elite. Fortunate to be present at the famous opening night of *Hernani* (25 February 1830) at the Théatre-français, Gautier recalled for posterity the brilliance of that evening in his *Histoire du romantisme* (1874). Outfitted in a celebrated red vest, he led part of the romantic claque that applauded Hugo's play. Five months later, Gautier published *Poésies*, a collection of adolescent poems that dealt with such themes as love and death.

Between 1830 and 1836, Gautier lived with enthusiasm the life of the romantic bohemian. With Philothée O'Neddy, Pétrus Borel, Gérard de Nerval, and others, he formed the Petit cénacle. An almost completely apolitical writer, Gautier began publishing in these years not only the first of his voluminous works but also the first sketches of his aesthetic doctrine of *l'art pour l'art* in the preface to *Albertus, ou l'âme et le péché* (1832), a narrative poem in the then-fashionable demonic style. The next year, in *Les Jeunes-France*, he poked gentle fun at the romantics and their way of life. Between 1834 and 1836, Gautier lived in the Impasse du Doyenné in a truly bohemian setting that attracted many of the writers, composers, and artists of the 1830s. From this period in Gautier's life dates *Mademoiselle de Maupin* and its famous preface, which took up the theme of *l'art pour l'art* first set forth in *Albertus*. In this manifesto, Gautier, who openly scorned bourgeois conventions, contended that art must be nonutilitarian and amoral and that in great art all thought must be subordinated to form. This aesthetic doctrine found as many supporters as it did opponents, and in the 1840s, a group of young writers, among them Théodore de Banville and Arsène Houssaye, bégan to champion Gautier's cause. Charles Baudelaire, who dedicated *Les Fleurs du mal* (1857) to Gautier, and Gustave Flaubert also recognized him as their master. Financial matters, particularly the need to support his parents and his two unmarried sisters, brought the bohemian phase of Gautier's life to an end.

Beginning in 1836, Gautier embarked on a journalistic career that would continue until his death. First for Emile de Girardin's *La Presse* (1836–55) and then for the official *Moniteur universelle* (1855–70), Gautier wrote over two thousand articles of criticism on the theater, the arts, and literature, and in them he elaborated at length on his aesthetic theories. The time and effort required to meet the daily demands of journalism did not prevent Gautier from writing successfully in a great number of fields. For the dancer Carlotta Grisi, the sister of his mistress Ernesta, he wrote the libretto to the famous ballet *Giselle* (1841) and to *La Péri* (1843). Of the great many plays that came from his fertile pen, the most notable are *Une Larme du diable* (1839), *Le Tricorne enchanté* (1845), *La Fausse conversion* (1846), and *Pierrot posthume* (1847). An indefatigable traveler, Gautier recorded his acute observations in a number of travel books; of these, *Un Voyage en Espagne* (1843) merits notice. His volume of poems, *Emaux et camées*, first published in 1852, contains the celebrated "L'Art," in which Gautier set down the rules adopted by the *art pour l'art* school. He also wrote short stories, which range from "Une Nuit de Cléopâtre" to "La Morte amoureuse," one of his many tales of the fantastic. Not to be forgotten is the romance *Le Capitaine Fracasse* of 1863.

Gautier, who found favor during the Second Empire with Napoleon III, had his hopes for high office dashed by the events of 1870. He also failed to win election to the French Academy. Gautier died on 23 October 1872 in Neuilly-sur-Seine.

A. Boschot, *Théophile Gautier* (Paris, 1933); T. Gautier, *A Romantic in Spain* (New York, 1926), *Le Capitaine Fracasse* (Paris, 1961), *Mademoiselle de Maupin* (Paris, 1966), and *Poésies complètes*, ed. René Jasinski (Paris, 1970); R. Jasinski, *Les Années romantiques de Théophile Gautier* (Paris, 1929); J. Richardson, *Théophile Gautier: His Life and Times* (New York, 1959).

Robert Brown

Related entries: ACADEMIE FRANCAISE; BAUDELAIRE; FLAUBERT; GIRARDIN, EMILE DE; *HERNANI*; HUGO; *LE MONITEUR*; NERVAL; *LA PRESSE*.

GAY, DELPHINE (MME. EMILE DE GIRARDIN) (1804–1855), celebrated writer and patron of fashionable intellectual life during the July Monarchy. Delphine Gay was born 26 January 1804 in Aix-la-Chapelle, the daughter of the famed Sophie Gay, who named her after Mme. de Stael's novel. While still in her teens, Delphine Gay easily won acceptance in sophisticated and elegant Restoration salons with her charm, her beauty, and her verse. Welcome in the salon at the Abbaye-au-Bois of the legendary Mme. Récamier, where aristocrats of the Old Regime and young romantics freely mixed, she recited there an ode on the coronation of Charles X. Also associated with the *Muse française*, the circle of royalist and Catholic romantics, she moved in the company of François-René de Chateaubriand, Victor Hugo, Alexandre Soumet, Alfred de Vigny, and others. Her earlier "Dévouement des médecins français et des soeurs de Ste.-Camille dans la peste de Barcelone" (1822) had won praise from the French Academy. Throughout the 1820s, Delphine Gay celebrated in verse many of the important public events of the day. To welcome the baron Gros' scenes from the life of Saint Geneviève in the Panthéon, she wrote "Hymne à Ste-Geneviève" (1825); to raise money for the Greek war of independence, she wrote "La Quête" (1825); and to mourn the loss of General Maximilien-Sébastien Foy, she recited "Vers sur la mort du Général Foy" (1825) at the funeral.

In the 1830s, Delphine Gay, who had married Emile de Girardin (1806–81), the enterprising creator of the mass press in France, presided over a salon that attracted the intellectual, artistic, and political elite of the July Monarchy. To her gatherings came Alphonse de Lamartine, Hugo, Alexandre Dumas, Alfred de Vigny, Honoré de Balzac, Théophile Gautier, and Eugène Sue, among others. For Girardin's *La Presse*, she wrote, under the name of the vicomte de Launay, "Le Courrier de Paris" (1836–48), a witty and gay but ultimately superficial serial novel in which she observed the glittering surface of the Parisian social scene. Author of such plays as *L'Ecole des journalistes* (1839), *Judith* (1843), and *Cléopatre* (1847), she wrote, among other works, *Lady Tartuffe* (1853), a comedy in prose, *La Croix de Bernay* (1846), and the novel *La Canne de M. de Balzac* (1836). Of all her works, Charles-Augustin Sainte-Beuve preferred *Le Lorgnon* (1832). During the June Days of the Revolution of 1848, she vigorously protested to General Eugène Cavaignac the arrest of her husband. Delphine Gay died in Paris on 29 June 1855. Of her, Victor Hugo wrote some beautiful if effusive lines in the *Contemplations*.

D. Gay, *Oeuvres complètes*, 6 vols. (Paris, 1860–1861); H. Malo, *La Gloire du vicomte de Launay* (Paris, 1925) and *Une Muse et sa mère. Delphine Gay de Girardin* (Paris, 1924); C.-A. Sainte-Beuve, "Madame Emile de Girardin," *Causeries du lundi*, vol. 5 (London, n.d.); L. Séché, *Muses romantiques: Delphine Gay* (Paris, 1910).

Robert W. Brown

Related entries: BALZAC; CAVAIGNAC, L.-E.; CHATEAUBRIAND; CORONATION OF CHARLES X; DUMAS, A.; FOY; GAUTIER; GAY; GIRARDIN, E.; GROS; HUGO; LAMARTINE; *LA MUSE FRANCAISE*; *LA PRESSE*; RECAMIER; ROMANTICISM; SAINTE-BEUVE; SOUMET; STAEL-HOLSTEIN; SUE, E.; VIGNY.

GAY, SOPHIE (1776–1842), prominent romantic salon hostess and minor novelist. Marie-Françoise-Sophie Michault de Lavalette was born in Paris on 1 July 1776, the daughter of a financier employed by the comte de Provence. Exiled during the Empire, she and her husband returned to Paris with the Bourbons in 1815. In her spacious home on rue des Mathurins, she hosted a salon that soon became a center of important social and literary influence. The hostess's wide circle of friends and acquaintances going back to the Directory flocked to her soirées to hear her enthusiastic reminiscences and to witness the energetic expressions of her penetrating wit. During those early Restoration years, she praised and encouraged the efforts of writers, among them especially Marceline Desbordes-Valmore, and pursued her own creative activities, producing two novels: *Anatole* (1815) and *Les Malheurs d'un amant heureux* (1818). Through her efforts Emile Deschamps secured the publishing services of Ambroise Tardieu for *La Muse française*. She continued throughout her remaining years to compose, producing more than twenty works, including several novels, such as *Un Mariage sous l'Empire* (1832), and two plays. She also contributed to several newspapers and founded a magazine, *Les Causeries du monde*.

Gay was practical enough to recognize that she lacked real talent and that her daughter, Delphine, had it. In 1823, at the age of seventeen, Delphine won the Academie française first prize in poetry. Sophie thus made a deliberate decision to exploit her daughter's talent and beauty and devoted the next eight years, those of the entire romantic conflict, to acting as promoter-manager-guide of the young writer's career. Thereafter, all her actions were intended to secure fame and success for Delphine through the right contacts in her own salon and others, and through poems appropriately written to celebrate carefully selected events. In 1824, the Parisian press acclaimed the young muse's first collection of poems, *Essais poétiques*. Two years later a tangible reward came. Delphine presented a copy of her *Nouveau recueil de poésies* to Charles X, and he rewarded her with an 800 franc pension. As her reputation increased, the constrictions of Sophie's salon became more obvious, especially with the loss of many of the mother's older friends and their replacement by the daughter's admirers. Not only were larger quarters needed, but the income suddenly interrupted by the 1830 turmoil had to be replaced. Her solution was to snare a husband for Delphine. The choice was Emile de Girardin, a wealthy, self-made giant of the journalistic world. They were joined in marriage in a grand ceremony at Saint-Roch Church in Paris on 1 June 1831. From that moment, the future of Sophie and Delphine was secure enough for Sophie to allow her salon to reduce its pace gradually and to permit Delphine to host the famous Wednesday gatherings at the Girardin salon. She did for July Monarchy political and literary figures what her mother had done for those of the previous regimes. Sophie Gay recalled in her *Salons célèbres* (1837) the ambiance of those of Mme. de Staël, the Empress Josephine, and several others. Her adventurous, picturesque life ended at the age of sixty-eight.

J. Bertaut, *L'Epoque Romantique* (Paris, 1947).

Paul Comeau

Related entries: ACADEMIE FRANCAISE; CHARLES X; DESBORDES-VALMORE; DESCHAMPS; GAY, DELPHINE; GIRARDIN, EMILE DE; *LA MUSE FRANCAISE*; REVOLUTION OF 1830; ROMANTICISM; STAEL-HOLSTEIN.

GAY-LUSSAC, JOSEPH-LOUIS (1778–1850), chemist and physicist. Gay-Lussac entered the Ecole polytechnique as a student in 1797 and, after graduating in 1800, began advanced engineering training at the Ecole nationale des ponts et chaussées. At about the same time, he began studying with the eminent chemist Claude-Louis Berthollet (1748–1822) at the latter's country house in the Parisian suburb of Arcueil. Gay-Lussac became Berthollet's assistant and was accepted for membership in the Société d'Arcueil, a prestigious scientific body that met at Berthollet's home.

Gay-Lussac was elected to the Institute in 1806. After holding various minor appointments at the Ecole polytechnique, he became professor of chemistry there in 1810. By this time he had also been appointed professor of physics in the Faculté des sciences (1808), a position he held until 1832, when he exchanged it for a chemical chair at the Muséum national d'histoire naturelle.

Gay-Lussac's principal research interest was the physics and chemistry of gases. During the course of his career, he collaborated with some of the most eminent scientific figures of his day, made balloon ascents to collect samples (1804), and traveled widely across the European continent. His most celebrated achievement, known as Gay-Lussac's Law, was announced in 1808 and stated that volumes of gases that combine chemically (such as hydrogen and oxygen in the formation of water) do so in simple, whole-number ratios.

For many years Gay-Lussac was co-owner and chemical editor of the important scientific journal *Annales de chimie et de physique*. He also showed a strong interest in industrial problems and investigated techniques of bleaching and the manufacture of sulfuric acid, developing the Gay-Lussac tower in 1827 to aid in this latter process.

He was offered a title by Charles X but refused to accept it. After the July Revolution, Gay-Lussac was elected several times to the Chamber of Deputies. In 1838 he resigned over an issue of principle. The following year Louis-Philippe appointed him to the Chamber of Peers, where he served as a spokesman for the interests of the chemical industry and agriculture.

E. Blank and L. Delhoume, *La vie émouvante et noble de Gay-Lussac* (Paris, 1950); M.P. Crosland, *Gay-Lussac: Scientist and Bourgeois* (Cambridge, Eng., 1978).

W.R. Albury

Related entry: ECOLE POLYTECHNIQUE.

LA GAZETTE DE FRANCE, royalist and legitimist newspaper of long duration. Since its origins in the seventeenth century, the *Gazette* had undergone many vicissitudes by 1814. It was one of the few newspapers that Napoleon, who hoped to attract the support of French royalists, had allowed to remain in existence during the Empire. At the time of the Restoration the *Gazette* declared its devotion to the monarchy with obvious sincerity. Throughout the reign of Louis XVIII, it supported moderate royalist policies and attracted approximately 6,000 subscribers. In 1824, however, there were rumors that the *Gazette* was about to oppose the policies of Joseph de Villèle, and in consequence it was bought up by a pro-government press committee established by the duc de La Rochefoucauld. The latter advised the suppression of the *Gazette* when the funds of the committee were running low, but instead Villèle handed the paper as a free gift to a friend, Eugène de Genoude, who in turn remained loyal to the minister after his downfall. Villèle continued for some time to hope for a return to office, and the *Gazette* in 1828 therefore campaigned for a revival of the conservative party that Villèle had led. This placed the paper in opposition to Villèle's successor Jean-Baptiste de Martignac, who found it a considerable embarrassment. Supported by the many officials whom Villèle had placed in office, its subscription list rose to nearly 10,000, and it remained until 1830 the only newspaper read regularly by Charles X.

After the abdication of Charles X, Genoude imposed a personal policy on the *Gazette*. He was sure that democracy would bring about a return of the Bourbon monarchy, unaided by politicians or armed rebels. He daily wrote articles advocating universal male suffrage, and no amount of advice from friends caused him to waver in his beliefs. Orleanist governments found the democratic policies of the *Gazette* just as unacceptable as the attitude of more traditional legitimist newspapers. By October 1832 the *Gazette* and the *Quotidienne* had between them undergone thirty-five prosecutions and accumulated fines of 47,650 francs and three years' imprisonment for their editors.

The *Gazette* showed commercial initiative in being one of the first newspapers to employ hawkers in the streets, but Genoude refused to publish serial stories when the latter were popularized by *La Presse*. He lowered the price of the annual subscription from 80 francs to 60 francs, but this alone did not result in large sales. By 1841 the *Gazette* had only 4,533 subscribers, and its income from advertisements was negligible.

In 1848 the *Gazette* welcomed the proclamation of universal male suffrage, confident that this would soon lead to the restoration of Henri V. It opposed the restrictive policies of Eugène Cavaignac, and hence found that a number of its issues were seized by the police. It welcomed the presidency of Louis-Napoleon Bonaparte, hoping that the latter would establish a pseudo-monarchical regime which would be a preliminary step to the restoration of the monarchy. In 1852 the *Gazette* was one of the fourteen daily papers that the new emperor Napoleon III allowed to remain in existence in Paris.

E. Biré, *La Presse royaliste de 1830 à 1852* (Paris, 1901); I. Collins, *The Government and the Newspaper Press in France, 1814–1881* (Oxford, 1959); N.E. Hudson, "The Circulation of the Ultra-Royalist Press under the French Restoration," *English Historical Review* 49 (1934); R. Pimienta, *La Propagande Bonapartiste en 1848* (Paris, 1911); A. Sirven, *Journaux et journalistes: La Gazette de France* (Paris, 1866).

Irene Collins

Related entries: BORDEAUX; CAVAIGNAC, L.-E.; CHARLES X; *L'E-TOILE*; LA ROCHEFOUCAULD; LOUIS XVIII; MARTIGNAC; *LA PRESSE*; *LA QUOTIDIENNE*; VILLELE.

LA GAZETTE DES TRIBUNAUX, important semiofficial daily paper devoted to court trials and legal matters, offering verbatim accounts; first published in 1825. Jean Achille Darmaing, the son of an ardent royalist, became a professor at St.-Cyr but was dismissed during the reaction of the early 1820s. Turning to journalism, he founded a successful newspaper dealing exclusively with the law, courts, and verbatim accounts of trials. The *Gazette des tribunaux*, first issued 1 November 1825, has endured through all later French governments. Darmaing took advantage of the press laws that allowed the transcription of public trials and concentrated on those dealing with political and press offenses. In its occasional editorials, the *Gazette des tribunaux* championed the ideals of Beccarian enlightened penal reform, publicizing the infamous penalties still allowed, such as the lawful but never used punishment for sacrilege under Charles X or cruel usage of slaves in the French colonies. Revolutionary and imperial codes had dealt a severe blow to the considerable progress in penal reform of the eighteenth century. Darmaing revived that old crusade and served as a conscience for the liberal judiciary and bar of Restoration France. Frequently the paper resorted to pure sentiment to make its point, as in its intimate interviews with the families of capital offenders. Darmaing opposed capital punishment as socially degrading as well as any imprisonment that was not rehabilitative. Another reason for the remarkable success of such a specialized daily paper (3,000 subscribers, larger than *Figaro*) was the spice of sex, humor, and gore sprinkled into many of the trial records.

Although the *Gazette des tribunaux* was editorially on the Left, it was respected enough for its accurate reportage that all factions quoted it as an official source: a *Moniteur* of the judiciary. Darmaing became a director of the Orleanist *Constitutionnel* a few years before his death in 1836, but the *Gazette des tribunaux*, in title and general function, has continued in successive French governments.

E. Hatin, *Histoire de la presse française* (Paris, 1859–61); D. Rader, *The Journalists and the July Revolution* (The Hague, 1973).

Daniel Rader

Related entries: LE CONSTITUTIONNEL; ECOLE MILITAIRE (SAINT-CYR); *LE FIGARO;* LAW OF SACRILEGE; *LE MONITEUR;* PRESS LAWS.

GENT, ALPHONSE (1813–1894), left-wing politician, journalist, and member of the Young Mountain during the Second Republic. Alphonse Gent began his political career as a young lawyer in Avignon (Vaucluse) where, during the 1840s, he became well known for his democratic views and active in an illegal republican society. Because of this background Gent was appointed *commissaire de la République* for the Vaucluse following the February 1848 Revolution. He held that position until the autumn of 1848, used it to get himself elected to the Constituent Assembly, and generally pursued a vigorous, if somewhat undisciplined, campaign for the "democratic and social Republic."

After reaction set in following the legislative elections of May 1849, Gent spent some time in Paris writing for a radical newspaper, *La Révolution démocratique et sociale*, edited by the future *communard* Charles Delescluze. Gent was picked up by the police as a suspect in the abortive insurrection of June 1849 but escaped prosecution and left Paris for Lyons. From his base in Lyons, Gent plunged into regional left-wing politics. He took the lead in organizing several secret societies into a loose network covering the Alpine region, the Rhône valley, Provence, and lower Languedoc—fourteen departments in all. These societies, however, were united only in opposition to the regime of the prince-president, Louis Bonaparte, and had only the vaguest political program in common. Gent had no program either apart from opposition, nor was he a particularly effective political organizer. Thus, the Young Mountain—as the network called itself—never turned into a serious political force. However, representatives of the secret societies did manage to convene once under Gent's leadership in June 1850 at the so-called Congress of Valence (Drôme). Nothing came of it. Police informers at the congress, one of whom Gent recruited himself, reported its proceedings and its membership to the authorities. In October 1850, Gent was arrested and tried the following spring in a celebrated case known as the conspiracy of Lyons. Convicted of attempting to foment rebellion, he and several of his associates were sentenced to transporation to Nuka-hiva in the Marquise Islands in the south-central Pacific.

Gent survived to serve the Government of National Defense under Léon Gambetta as super-prefect for the Midi in 1870, became a member of the National Assembly in 1871, a deputy in 1876, and a senator in 1882. His political perspective as an opportunist republican had not changed since the 1840s.

G. Renard, *La Deuxième république, Histoire socialiste de la France*, ed. J. Jaurès, vol. 9 (Paris, 1900–1908); I. Tchernoff, *Le Parti républicain au coup d'état et sous le second empire* (Paris, 1906).

Sanford Elwitt

Related entries: CONSTITUTION OF 1848; DELESCLUZE; REVOLUTION OF 1848; YOUNG (NEW) MOUNTAIN SOCIETY.

GEOFFROY SAINT-HILAIRE, ETIENNE (1772–1844), zoologist, paleontologist, and experimental embryologist. Geoffroy commenced his scientific career in 1793 at the age of twenty-one, when he was made demonstrator in zoology at the Jardin des plantes in Paris. Later in that same year the Jardin became the Muséum d'histoire naturelle, and Geoffroy was appointed professor of zoology with responsibility for the vertebrates, while his much older colleague, Jean Baptiste de Lamarck, was assigned the equivalent position for the invertebrates.

Geoffroy's friendly association with Lamarck lasted many years, with both scientists sharing the conviction that environmental changes could bring about the modification of species. Geoffroy's views on this point and on other related matters were strenuously opposed by Georges Cuvier, another colleague at the

Muséum, who had originally benefited from the patronage of Geoffroy but who later outstripped him in both public and scientific influence.

In 1798 Geoffroy sailed with Napoleon on the Egyptian campaign, returning to France after three years with an extensive natural history collection. In 1807 he was elected to the Académie des sciences, which Cuvier by then had come to dominate, and in 1809 he was made professor of zoology at the Sorbonne. In the following decades, he carried out fundamental researches in comparative anatomy, paleontology, and experimental embryology, which brought him more and more into conflict with Cuvier. Geoffroy's major work was his *Philosophie anatomique* (Paris, 1818–20), in which his principles of anatomical study were developed and defended.

The differences between Cuvier and Geoffroy were brought publicly to a head in 1830 when the Académie des sciences devoted a number of meetings to this controversy. Cuvier defended the view that species remain fixed through time and fall into groups based on very different forms of anatomical organization. Geoffroy's position was that species are modified by environmental influences acting upon developing embryos and that a single unitary plan of organization underlies all animal forms, with the more complex features developing out of the simpler ones. Cuvier's views were generally thought to have prevailed during this debate, and thereafter Geoffroy found the Académie des sciences increasingly less receptive to his ideas. After his death, some of his work was carried on by his son, Isadore (1805–61).

T. Cahn, *La vie et l'oeuvre d'Etienne Geoffroy Saint-Hilaire* (Paris, 1962); I. Geoffroy Saint-Hilaire, *Vie, travaux et doctrine scientifique d'Etienne Geoffroy Saint-Hilaire* (Paris, 1847).

W.R. Albury

Related entries: ACADEMY OF SCIENCES; CUVIER; LAMARCK.

GERANDO, JOSEPH-MARIE DE, BARON (1772–1842), publicist and administrator. Originally trained for the priesthood, Gérando narrowly escaped death when involved in the 1793 rising in Lyons against the Jacobins. He subsequently became important in the imperial administration of the Italian provinces (his family was of Italian origin) and in 1811 was awarded the *Légion d'honneur* and made a member of the Conseil d'état, a position he held until his death. In 1819 he was appointed as head of the Paris law faculty, and in 1837 Louis-Philippe appointed him to the Chamber of Peers.

Gérando was one of the founders in 1802 of the Société d'encouragement pour l'éducation industrielle; he remained one of the most prominent educationalists in France, and his work on the education of deaf-mutes (1827) became a classic. He was extensively involved with learned societies in the fields of education, industry, charity, and hospital reform, and he published prolifically in these areas. His most important book was perhaps the *Histoire comparée des systèmes de philosophie* (1804).

With Emile de Girardin, J.-B. Duvergier, and others, Gérando launched in 1831 the *Journal des connaissances utiles*, a monthly that sought to popularize agricultural reform and knowledge of the laws. At times subscriptions reached 130,000. Gérando was less successful in his desire to sustain paternalistic charity at a time when he saw the erosion of Christian morality in social relations; many industrialists regarded his proposals as an affront to individual liberty.

D. Johnson, *Guizot: Aspects of French History, 1789–1874* (London, 1963); *Nouvelle biographie générale* (Paris, 1855- 66).

Peter McPhee

Related entries: GIRARDIN, E.

GERARD, ETIENNE-MAURICE, COMTE (1773–1852), marshal of France. Born in Damvilliers (Meuse), he volunteered for the army in 1791 and served in the campaigns of 1792 and 1793 as a common soldier. He became a lieutenant after he fought at Fleurus, and, after an illustrious career, he was a general by 1814. Louis XVIII named him a chevalier of Saint Louis and gave him the Grand Croix of the Legion of Honor during the First Restoration and placed him in command of Belfort. He defected to Napoleon, who made him a peer of France during the Hundred Days. On 18 June 1815, at Waterloo, he was unable to persuade Emmanuel de Grouchy to march toward the sound of the cannon.

Obliged to go into exile by the Second Bourbon Restoration, he went to Brussels, where he was married. He came back to France in 1817 and retired to his estates. He founded the Society to Improve the Prisons in 1819. In 1822, the first arrondissement of Paris elected him to the Chamber of Deputies, where he sat with the opponents of the ministry. Not reelected in 1824, he was elected in 1827 in the Dordogne and in the Oise. He opted for the Dordogne.

He participated in the 1830 Revolution, rallying soldiers and National Guards to the revolutionary cause. Minister of war from August to November 1830 and raised to the rank of marshal, he was again elected a deputy. He then commanded the expedition to Belgium and engineered the capture of Antwerp (November-December 1832). In 1833, he sat with the Chamber of Peers. He was minister of war and president of the Council, succeeding Nicolas-Jean de Soult, from July to October 1834.

Retiring for reasons of health, he succeeded Edouard-Adolphe Mortier, killed in the Fieschi plot, as grand chancellor of the Legion of Honor in 1836. He succeeded Georges de Lobau as commander of the National Guard of the Seine from 1838 to 1842. A spectator rather than an actor in the February Revolution of 1848, he was named a senator by Napoleon III in January 1852. He died three months later.

L. de Chardon, *Maurice Gérard, le liberateur d'Anvers* (1973); *Nouvelle biographie générale*, vols. 19–20 (Copenhagen, 1966).

Jean-Claude Caron, trans. E. Newman

Related entries: BELGIAN REVOLUTION OF 1830; SOULT; WATERLOO, BATTLE OF.

GERICAULT, JEAN-LOUIS-ANDRE-THEODORE (1791–1824), early nineteenth-century artist, forerunner of the romantic style, and painter of *Raft of the Medusa*. Théodore Géricault was born in Rouen on 26 September 1791 into the comfortable bourgeois family of the lawyer Georges-Nicolas Géricault. After his family moved to Paris, the future painter attended the Collège Louis-le-Grand between 1806 and 1808. Géricault's artistic education and his apprenticeship as a painter began in 1808 when he became the pupil of Carle Vernet, a then celebrated but now forgotten painter of horses and battle scenes. Two years later, Géricault entered the atelier of Pierre-Narcisse Guérin (1774–1833), a minor neoclassical painter who served as an inspiring teacher to Géricault and other young artists, like Ary Scheffer, who would be a lifelong friend to Géricault. In Guérin's atelier, Géricault learned well the theory and practice of the reigning neoclassical style of Jacques-Louis David. The apprentice artist also spent long hours in the new art museum of the Louvre, then filled with the splendid plunder of Napoleon's campaigns, where he sketched the works of the Old Masters and reliefs from ancient Roman sarcophagi. Of the three pictures exhibited publicly by Géricault during his lifetime, two date from this period, both combining Géricault's passion for horses and his penchant for scenes of melodrama and adventure. The *Officer of the Imperial Guard*, a colorful, stirring, and heroic portrait of a mounted officer in the midst of battle, serves as a colossal image of the grandeur and energy of the Napoleonic spirit in 1812. Two years had passed, and the fortunes of France had been dramatically reversed when Géricault showed his *Wounded Cuirassier*, a somber picture that portrays a wounded cavalryman leading his horse from the scene and that evokes the tragic end of the Napoleonic wars. Military scenes fascinated Géricault for most of his life, and he completed a number of them, including several moving sketches of the retreat from Russia that focused on the struggle for survival of the wounded. The pathos of defeat, the sight of anonymous men caught up in events far beyond their control, the collective heroism of the unknown, the common man and his struggles against fate, themes that converged in *Raft of the Medusa*, were concerns that captivated Géricault from his earliest days.

One of the many young Frenchmen who welcomed the return of the Bourbons in 1814, Géricault enlisted as a *mousquetaire* and was present at the Tuileries Palace when Louis XVIII fled his capital at the approach of Napoleon in 1815. The young artist's enthusiasm for the Bourbons rapidly waned during the Second Restoration, however, and he was by 1817 closely associated with the liberal and Bonapartist opposition to the Bourbon regime.

To escape a tempestuous love affair with the wife of his maternal uncle, Géricault set out in 1816 to visit Italy, traveling primarily to Rome and Florence. Like so many other French artists before and after him, Géricault fell under the spell of the Italian people and countryside. More important, he viewed, studied, and eagerly absorbed such classic works as Michelangelo's frescoes in the Sistine Chapel, especially the *Last Judgment*, the works of Caravaggio and his followers, and those of Peter-Paul Rubens. Of Géricault's works from this Italian visit, some also reveal the vivid impression made on him by the sight of casts of the Parthenon frieze. A major project undertaken by Géricault for a large study of the *Corsa dei Barberi in Rome* remained unfinished, but the more than twelve major studies and innumerable drawings reveal the exacting work Géricault invested in his painting. While in Italy, Géricault also completed numerous drawings on traditional classical themes, including *The Triumph of Silenus* and *Hercules and the Bull*. Upon his return to France, Géricault resumed his affair, from which a son was born in August 1818. He also sought a subject for a painting that would both satisfy his ambition to paint a major work and his desire for something that would enthrall him.

The year of Gericault's return from Italy brought him into contact with not only the young Eugène Delacroix, on whom he would exercise a great influence, but also with the young liberal and Bonapartist opposition to the regime of Louis XVIII. Géricault's studio, located on the southern side of the Butte of Montmartre at 23, rue des Martyrs, adjoined that of Horace Vernet. In this new quarter of Paris called the Nouvelle Athènes, Géricault mixed freely with such prominent leaders of the liberal opposition as Colonels Maximilien-Sébastien Foy and Louis Bro, the politician Jacques Manuel, the notorious liberal songwriter Pierre-Jean de Beranger, and Antoine-Vincent Arnault, soon to be a biographer of Napoleon. In this atmosphere, Géricault continued to draw scenes from the Napoleonic wars, often focusing, as before, on scenes of wounded men. He also indicated his strong interest in contemporary affairs with a series of five sketches, the preliminary drawings for a major painting, depicting the murder of Antoine-Bernardin Fualdès; this crime was widely reported in the press as an instance of right-wing political terrorism. In the end, however, Géricault found this subject unsuited for the monumental picture he wished to compose.

Early in 1818, Géricault, after he read Henri Savigny and Alexandre Corréard's eye-witness account of the wreck of the *Medusa*, realized that he had chanced upon a subject that not only satisfied his desire to criticize the Bourbons and to express his passionate sympathy for the innocent victims of injustice but also stirred his artistic imagination. Commanded by an incompetent *émigré* with important connections, the French frigate *Medusa* ran aground off the coast of Africa on 2 July 1816. When efforts to refloat the *Medusa* failed, the captain ordered the ship abandoned, and the officers and the privileged passengers crowded in the six available lifeboats. Left to take their chances on a makeshift raft were 149 men and 1 woman. The lifeboats, which were to tow the raft ashore, cut it loose. For the next thirteen days while the raft drifted aimlessly at sea, its inhabitants, suffering horribly from the elements and from shortages of food and water, fought each other, struggled to overcome a mutiny, and resorted to cannibalism. When a searching ship finally located the raft, only fifteen people were alive, and, of them, five died shortly thereafter; hence, of the 150 who boarded the raft on 2 July, 140 had died. The French government, seeking to minimize the anticipated cries of outrage and anger, downplayed the incident. For political reasons of his own, however, Elie Decazes leaked the report on the disaster prepared by Henri Savigny, one of the survivors and the surgeon of the *Medusa*, to the widely read *Journal des débats*. Its publication on 13 September 1816 produced an immediate sensation, and the news of the shipwreck quickly became a weapon in the propaganda war waged by the opponents of the monarchy. Joined by Alexandre Corréard, Savigny expanded his report into a book published in 1817. It was the second edition of the *Naufrage de la frégate la Méduse* that captured Géricault's attention.

Having found a subject of suitable magnitude and importance, Géricault set to work with almost monomaniacal determination. He made every effort to learn as much as he could about the disaster by interviewing the survivors, by studying contemporary drawings, and by having the carpenter of the *Medusa* build for him a model of the raft. He also visited hospitals so he could observe the dying, and he traveled to the shore to study light and cloud formation. But this careful collection of details was by no means enough, and Géricault allowed his imagination to wonder how the great artists, particularly Michelangelo, Caravaggio, and Baron Gros, would have painted such a scene. Finally, he struggled to find the one instant in the story appropriate for his picture. After making numerous sketches, he settled on a moment when the survivors were desperately attempting to attract the attention of a passing ship. His preparations completed, Géricault devoted the next eight months of his life to transferring his ideas to a canvas that measured over sixteen by twenty-three feet. Completed in time for the Salon of 1819, the final version depicted in somber hues the frantic efforts of the fifteen half-starved, half-crazed survivors to attract the attention of a distant sail. Géricault succeeded in fusing a minute attention to realistic detail with an effective compositional device that in effect draws viewers of the *Raft* into the scene and makes them part of the tragedy.

Described in the Salon catalog as a painting of a shipwreck, Géricault's picture attracted considerable attention, most of it tinged with a political bias. Opposition newspapers praised the picture, while royalist critics condemned it. The *Raft* failed to win a prize in its category, and the French government declined to purchase the picture. Géricault fell into deep despair, emerging only to take the *Raft* to England in an attempt to make some money.

While in England in 1820 and 1821, Théodore Géricault turned from monumental plans for more grandiose pictures to the making of small canvases to which he transferred his sharp observations of everyday reality. In addition to the famous *Horse-Racing at Epsom*, Géricault's pictures were largely devoted to mundane scenes of the common people. Included among them were views of a public hanging, a portrait of an aged beggar, and a drawing of a paralyzed woman in a wheelchair.

The considerable financial success of Géricault's English trip notwithstanding, the last three years of life that remained to the artist following his return to Paris were filled with money problems, psychological torment, and painful physical suffering. In these years, Géricault again turned his attention to current political events, and he contemplated large works on the Greek war of independence, the emancipation of the slaves, and the opening of the doors of the prisons of the Inquisition. Dating from these same years also come Géricault's remarkable portraits of the insane. Finally, he completed a number of other notable works, including *The Limekiln* and a delicate and charming portrait of Madame Bro.

Theodore Géricault died after long suffering on 26 January 1824. His friend Ary Scheffer painted the deathbed scene. Largely neglected during the nineteenth century, Géricault enjoys today a reputation as one of the major French artists of the nineteenth century.

K. Berger, *Géricault et son oeuvre* (Paris, 1968); C. Clément, *Gericault: Etude biographique et critique avec le catalogue raisonné de l'oeuvre du maître* (Paris, 1879; rev. ed., New York, 1974); L. Eitner, *Géricault's Raft of the Medusa* (London, 1972); W. Friedlaender, "Géricault, Romantic Realist," *Magazine of Art* 45 (1952).

Robert Brown

Related entries: BERANGER; DAVID; DECAZES; DELACROIX; FOY; GROS; HUNDRED DAYS; *JOURNAL DES DEBATS*; MANUEL; SCHEFFER, A.; VERNET.

GILLE, CHARLES (1820–1856), Parisian corset maker, songwriter, and revolutionary republican. Gille, the most revolutionary of the working-class *chansonniers*, was born in Paris on 6 January 1820. His father died shortly after his birth, and his mother, a corset maker, taught the boy her trade. He had some formal education; he attended a mutual school from the time he was six until he was twelve, when his apprenticeship began. Besides being a corset maker, he had worked as a stock boy in a store pulling a hand cart around Paris and as a worker in a ceruse factory, subjected to the slow death of all others who worked with the white lead.

He began to write songs when he was sixteen, and by 1839, when he was nineteen, he was already celebrating his republican and liberal ideals in song. He became something of a lion in the *goguettes*, and he received admiring letters from Pierre-Jean de Béranger. He may also have been a member of the Nouvelles saisons, a republican secret society; in any case, he was named a lieutenant in the Republican Guard in 1848 by Marc Caussidière, who had been a leader of the Nouvelles saisons during the July Monarchy. What is certain is that he was president of the *goguette* Les Animaux, whose motto was: "Political songs are permitted; *un peut dire merde au roi*." When this *goguette* was raided and closed down by the police in 1846, Gille was arrested and sentenced to six months in prison.

When Gille got out of jail, Paris was in the midst of an economic crisis, and the price of bread was high. He blamed the government and wrote and distributed as widely as he could a new song, "Les accapareurs," or "The Hoarders", which blamed the high price of food on the speculators and ended: "there is no grain in the cottages. Let's make war on the châteaux!" In another song, "Aux riches," printed in 1844, Gille laid out his revolutionary socialist and anticlerical beliefs:

Hope for a better future! an old adage.
When I search the heart of the human race,
I see in the worker the serf of the Middle Ages,
Who himself is descended from the Roman slave;
Always there has been the same balance,
The weak are crushed under the heels of the strong.

I used to dream that Christianity
By proclaiming sweet charity,
Would snuff out egotism in all hearts
And save poor humanity,
But I have cursed the men in black robes;
They are sitting at dinner tables in their sanctuaries;
I used to have a God, I don't dare believe in Him anymore,
All my dreams have flown away.

You are trembling! the rumbling of this storm
Tells me: the people have raised up their heads again,
Truth wants to reign alone in the world:
Thrones, altars will crumble at the sound of its voice;
I will have my share of glory or of martyrdom,
Bard and soldier under your crenelated walls
I want to run, I was wrong to tell you
That all my dreams have flown away.

The 1848 Revolution was Gille's greatest triumph and his greatest sorrow. Appointed and then fired as a lieutenant of the Republican Guard, Gille was once again thrown into extreme poverty, selling his verses for 50 centimes per couplet to publishers like Eyssautier and Durand and receiving a little support from the publisher Vieillot. In "La République bourgeoise," he wrote:

What! the volcano has swallowed up its own lava,
And things now are like they were before!

Gille's natural sarcasm and bitterness increased as his situation and the revolution's worsened. On 24 April 1856, after paying a debt of 200 francs to a shopkeeper, he hanged himself in his room. For a long time, his *chansonnier* friends met on the anniversary of his death to honor him, and they were still doing so in 1876.

Gille published several collections of songs during his lifetime, and some of his songs were published in the working-class Saint-Simonian newspaper, *L'Union*, in the volumes of songs published by the *goguette* La Lice chansonnière, and by the *République lyrique*, a newspaper of the Second Republic devoted to song. Many others were printed on single sheets and sold for 10 centimes each, and these are available at the Bibliothèque nationale in Paris.

E. Baillet, *De quelques ouvriers poètes, Biographies et souvenirs* (Paris, 1898), and *La Chanson française, Le Pamphlet du pauvre (1834–1851)* (Paris, 1957); R. Brécy,

"Un oublié, Charles Gille, le plus grand des chansonniers révolutionnaires," *La Pensée* (January–February 1958); C. Gille, A. Letac, and E. Berthier, *Cent et une petite misères, oeuvre sociale* (Paris, 1846; 2d ed. 1848); C. Gille and C. Regnard, *La chanson de nos jours*, 2 vols. (Paris, 1844); C. Gille, ed. *Némésis lyriques par les auteurs les plus estimés* (Paris, 1846); J. Maitron, ed. *Dictionnaire biographique du mouvement ouvrier français*, vol. 2 (Paris, 1966); E. L. Newman, "L'arme du siècle, c'est la plume: The French Worker Poets of the July Monarchy and the Spirit of Reform," *Journal of Modern History* (1980) and *The French Worker Poets of the July Monarchy* (forthcoming); E. Thomas, *Voix d'en bas; la poésie ouvrière du XIXe siècle* (Paris, 1979); J. Touchard, *La glorie de Béranger*, 2 vols. (Paris, 1968).

Edgar Newman

Related entries: BERANGER; CAUSSIDIERE; *ECOLE MUTUELLE*; GARDE REPUBLICAINE; REPUBLICANS; REVOLUTION OF 1848; SINGING SOCIETIES; WORKER POETS.

GIRARDIN, EMILE DE (1806–1881), journalist and creator of the mass circulation press. Emile de Girardin was born in Paris on 22 June 1806, the offspring of an adulterous relationship between Adélaide-Marie Fragnan and Alexandre de Girardin. The irregular circumstances of his birth did much to create in Girardin a craving for wealth, power, and social acceptance. Dissatisfied with minor bureaucratic posts during the Restoration, he published *Emile* (1828), an autobiographical novel in which he spoke out about the plight of illegitimate children. Because he believed that both fame and fortune could be made in journalism, Girardin joined with Latour-Mézeray to found *Le Voleur* in 1828. Although little more than a collection of extracts from other papers, *Le Voleur* did well, and encouraged by this success, Girardin and Latour-Mézeray created *La Mode* a year later. Other projects, such as the short-lived *Garde-National*, did less well, but Girardin, never easily discouraged, always had new schemes to launch.

During the 1830s, Girardin had a major role in the creation of the mass circulation press in France. In the first year of the July Monarchy, he began by introducing the *Journal des connaissances utiles* to encourage, as one of his mottos boasted, the development in the masses of health, prosperity, and knowledge. For six years, the paper did just that, attracting thousands of subscribers and bringing to Girardin a handsome profit. Wealth and success in journalism, Girardin believed, came not from appealing to the elite but to the masses, and the fortunes of the *Journal des connaissances utiles* demonstrated that Girardin had mastered the formula.

The year 1836 is a symbolic one in the history of the French press, for in it Girardin not only launched his first mass circulation newspaper, the immensely successful *La Presse*, but he also killed in a duel Armand Carrel, editor of the *National* and, for many, the representative of the "old" press. Hence, it seemed that the age of the serious press with its sophisticated and serious readership had ended and that a new one, the day of the mass press, had begun. In June, Girardin, driven as ever by ambition and a desire to make a name for himself and to win social respectability, announced the imminent publication of *La Presse*, a new paper that he planned to sell for 40 francs a year, just half the current subscription price for other Parisian papers. He estimated that with a circulation of 10,000, he could make up his losses with advertising revenue, a miscalculation that ultimately forced him to increase the number of subscribers. Because it was to have a mass appeal, the character of *La Presse* differed from the usual Parisian journal of the mid–1830s. Girardin replaced the traditional sober emphasis on politics, philosophy, literature, and the arts with tidbits of scandal, gossip, and fashion, and he used publicity gimmicks to win the public's attention. His wife, Delphine Gay, writing under the name of the vicomte de Launay, contributed a popular *feuilleton*, "Le Courrier de Paris." But Girardin's true innovation, a veritable stroke of genius, was to supply the new reading public of the 1830s with the escapism, adventure, sentimentality, and romance they craved in the *feuilleton-roman*, the serial novel. In the *Presse* and its major competitors, *Le Siècle*, the *Constitutionnel*, and the *Journal des débats*, the masters of this genre, Balzac, Alexandre Dumas, and Eugène Sue, struggled to satisfy the public's seemingly insatiable demand. The popularity of these serial novels became in fact so great that the *Journal des débats* could attract, without having to lower its subscription prices, thousands of new readers with Sue's *Les Mystères de Paris*. By 1845, the circulation of *La Presse* had reached almost 22,500, a figure that gave it the third largest readership among the major Parisian dailies.

Although politics did not have a major place in the columns of *La Presse*, Girardin did support the July Monarchy until the mid–1840s. Then in 1845, the *Presse* published allegations that Guizot had used corrupt methods to introduce the *Epoque*, a new paper friendly to the government. Although unproved, the publication of these charges and the *Presse*'s hostility to Guizot helped undermine the July Monarchy. In the Revolution of 1848, Girardin had an influential part. On 24 February, because he had concluded that the Orléans dynasty could not survive, he went to the Tuileries Palace and, by so informing Louis-Philippe, helped convince him to abdicate. At this point in the Revolution, Girardin favored an Orléans regency in the name of the duchesse d'Orléans. On 26 February, when it had become clear that no such compromise was likely, he favored the establishment of a republic. Just four months later, on the eve of the June Days, Girardin ran afoul of General Eugène Cavaignac by suggesting that he was trying to make himself a dictator. Cavaignac retaliated by imprisoning the editor of the *Presse* and by closing the paper. Girardin remained in the Conciergerie until 5 July; the *Presse* did not resume publication until 6 August. In the elections held for the presidency of the Second Republic, the *Presse* supported Louis-Napoleon, not from any great faith in this nephew of the great Napoleon, but from hatred for his rival Cavaignac. Not long afterward, Girardin turned against Louis-Napoleon, and, as the *Presse* adopted this new political line, his paper's circulation fell by some 50 percent. Girardin finally sold his shares in 1856.

Within a decade, he had launched a new anti-Bonapartist paper, *La Liberté*, on 2 March 1866 and, within a year, it had gained a circulation of some 36,000. During the last two years of the Empire, Girardin supported the ministry of Emile Ollivier. Although he sold the *Liberté* in 1870, Girardin continued to manage during the last decade of his life a newspaper dynasty that included the *Petit journal* and *La France*. At the time of his death on 27 April 1881, Emile de Girardin was worth in excess of 8 million francs, proof that the age of mass journalism had arrived.

I. Collins, *The Government and the Newspaper Press in France, 1814–1881* (Oxford, 1959); M. Reclus, *Emile de Girardin* (Paris, 1934).

Robert Brown

Related entries: BALZAC; CARREL; CAVAIGNAC, L.-E.; *LE CONSTITU-TIONNEL*; DUMAS, A.; GAY, D.; GUIZOT; *JOURNAL DES DEBATS*; *LA MODE*; *LE NATIONAL*; *LA PRESSE*; *LE SIECLE*; SUE.

GIRARDIN, MADAME EMILE DE. See GAY, D.

GIROD, JEAN-LOUIS, BARON (1753–1839), and **GIROD, LOUIS-GASPARD-AMEDEE, BARON** (1781–1847), prominent magistrates and politicians; called Girod de l'Ain. Two politicians influential in the first half of the nineteenth century bore the name Girod de l'Ain. The elder was Jean-Louis Girod, born on 8 July 1753, who before the Revolution was a judge and then mayor of Gex (1780–91). Elected in 1791 the president of the Tribunal of the district of Nantua, he was arrested and imprisoned during the Terror. Regaining his freedom only after 9 Thermidor, Girod de l'Ain returned to public life, winning election to the Conseil des anciens and then to the Conseil des cinq-cents. An early supporter of Napoleon Bonaparte, Girod de l'Ain, named to the Corps legislatif by the Senate, received numerous honors during the Empire, becoming a member of the Legion of Honor (1807), a chevalier de l'Empire (1808), and a baron of the Empire (1809). Recalled by the emperor during the Hundred Days, he assumed the presidency of the Court of the First Instance of Paris. Between 1818 and 1820, Girod de l'Ain served in the Chamber of Deputies, where he became secretary and voted with the constitutional liberals. Owing to poor health, he retired from public life in 1820 and lived quietly until his death in 1839.

Louis-Gaspard-Amédée Girod, the eldest son of Jean-Louis Girod, was born on 18 October 1781 in Gex, where his father was the mayor. Trained as a lawyer, he followed this profession until 1806, when he entered imperial service, first as a prosecutor and then as a magistrate. Advocate-general of the imperial court in 1814, he signaled his abandonment of the imperial cause by signing a statement calling for the return of the Bourbons. Retained in his position during the First Restoration, Girod de l'Ain gave his support to Napoleon after the return from Elba and served as president of the court of the First Instance of the Seine; he also was elected to the Chamber of the Hundred Days. Temporarily returned to private life in 1815, he first sheltered and then defended General Antoine Drouot, winning an acquittal for him. Girod de l'Ain resumed his career as a magistrate in 1819. Elected to the Chamber of Deputies in 1827, he sat with the constitutional opposition. Chosen vice-president of the Chamber in 1829, he supported the liberal Martignac ministry, voted for the Address of the 221, and won reelection on 12 July 1830. Only on the last day of the July Revolution did he associate himself with the revolution; he then warmly supported the address to the duc d'Orléans. Appointed prefect of police on 1 August 1830, he took a major role in the restoration of order in the aftermath of the Revolution. Throughout the July Monarchy, Girod de l'Ain held a succession of important offices. In 1831, his colleagues in the Chamber of Deputies elected him their president. He also served Louis-Philippe as a minister and then as president of the Council of State, a body he had entered in 1831. The devotion of Girod de l'Ain to the July Monarchy was rewarded with a peerage and with the grand cross of the Legion of Honor. He died in Paris on 27 December 1847.

Biographie universelle, vol. 16; A. Robert, E. Bourloton, and G. Cougny, *Dictionnaire des parlementaires français*, vol. 2 (Paris, 1891).

Robert Brown

Related entries: CHAMBER OF DEPUTIES; CHAMBER OF PEERS; COUNCIL OF STATE; HUNDRED DAYS; LOUIS-PHILIPPE; MARTIGNAC; REVOLUTION OF 1830; THE 221.

LE GLOBE (1824–1832), liberal Paris newspaper. *Le Globe*, which first appeared on 15 September 1824, was founded by Pierre Leroux, Paul Dubois, Prosper Duvergier de Hauranne, Charles de Rémusat, and Achille de Jouffroy. It was initially devoted to philosophy and literature and participated on the side of the romantics in the struggle between classicists and romanticists. Although it eschewed direct political involvement, it impartially criticized and ridiculed all segments of the political spectrum. It achieved international renown and, with contributors such as André Ampère and François-Auguste Mignet, was the organ of many young intellectuals. After the fall of the Villèle cabinet in January 1828, the *Globe* became more political, ultimately serving as the chief voice of the *doctrinaires*. On 15 February 1830 it became a daily; it also adopted a larger, folio format and added the word *politique* to its previous subtitle, *Journal philosophique et littéraire*. Although its editors had now entered the political arena, they were less hostile to Charles X and the Polignac cabinet than other editors, such as those of the *National*. They sought to restrain the government rather than provoke it into a rash move. They did, however, begin to question the continuation of the dynasty. Essentially the *Globe* advocated neither the ideology of the Revolution nor of the Old Regime but rather a more moderate course. The *Globe* did not, however, lack for courage in attacking the king's speech from the throne in March 1830 and in opposing the July Ordinances. On the night of 26 July, the *Globe*, along with the *National* and the *Temps*, published without authorization its edition of 27 July containing the journalists' protest against the ordinances that Charles de Rémusat and Pierre Leroux helped to draft.

After the July Revolution so many of the *Globe*'s writers took jobs with the new government that it temporarily halted publication. Only Leroux and one editor, Charles-Augustin Sainte-Beuve, both disillusioned with the results of the 1830 Revolution, felt there was much left to fight for. By November 1830 they had become advocates of Saint-Simonian socialism. In January 1831 they adopted the subtitle *Journal de la doctrine de Saint-Simon*. This trend continued under the editorship of Michel Chevalier. Although the *Globe* did not attack the new throne, it criticized the social and economic results of the July Revolution. But the workers who struck for higher wages that fall showed little interest in the new doctrines advocated by the *Globe*. Finally, the editorship of Barthélemy-Prosper Enfantin degraded the paper, and, with its financial resources damaged by a fine, it published its last issue on 20 April 1832.

I. Collins, *The Government and the Newspaper Press in France, 1814–1881* (Oxford, 1959); E. Hatin, *Bibliographie historique et critique de la presse périodique française* (Paris, n.d.) and *Histoire du journal en France, 1631–1853* (Paris, 1853); C. Ledré, *La Presse à l'assaut de la monarchie* (Paris, 1960); D. Pinkney, *The French Revolution of 1830* (Princeton, 1972).

James K. Kieswetter

Related entries: AMPERE; CHEVALIER; *DOCTRINAIRES*; DUBOIS; DU-VERGIER DE HAURANNE; ENFANTIN; LEROUX; MIGNET; *LE NATIONAL*; REMUSAT; SAINTE-BEUVE; SAINT-SIMONIANISM; *LE TEMPS*; VILLELE.

GOBINEAU, ARTHUR-JOSEPH, COMTE DE (1816–1882), philosopher, historian, Orientalist, novelist, and diplomat; best known as a theorist of racism. Arthur de Gobineau was born in Ville-d'Avray on 14 July 1816, an ironic coincidence that irritated him throughout his life, for he resolutely opposed everything symbolized by the French Revolution. Although of bourgeois origins and impecunious circumstances, his family harbored noble pretensions. His father, an army officer with pronounced royalist beliefs, was forced into retirement in 1831. By this time, Gobineau's parents had separated, his mother taking him and his sister to Switzerland. There, at the College of Bienne, he studied German, the classics, and Oriental languages. In 1832, Gobineau's father had the children returned to Lorient, and he intended his son to prepare for a military career. Two years of study revealed young Gobineau's unsuitability for such a career; meanwhile, he continued his studies of the Orient.

In 1835, Gobineau went to Paris, where he hoped, in vain as it turned out, to receive assistance from his paternal uncle. Left to his own devices, he held a number of unimportant jobs and undertook some journalistic hackwork, all the while continuing his Oriental studies at the Collège de France. Through family connections, Gobineau began to circulate in legitimist political and literary circles. A notable friendship with Alexis de Tocqueville commenced about 1843, and from it resulted an important correspondence that continued until Tocqueville's death in 1859. A historical study of moral attitudes planned by Tocqueville, for which he engaged Gobineau's assistance, never came to fruition. During the 1830s and the 1840s, Gobineau wrote on political and literary topics for a number of journals, including *L'Unité* and *La Quotidienne*. In his political writings, he lamented the state of mediocrity into which France had fallen after having exchanged in 1830 its Bourbon king for liberal, democratic, and socialist ideas. Not only did Gobineau in his essays oppose the Orleanist regime, but he also assailed the timidity and irresponsibility of the legitimists. In the years before 1848, Gobineau also published an impressive number of literary works; these include *Scaramouche* (1843), *Le Prisonnier chaneux* (1844–45), *Jean Chouan* (1846), *Nicolas Belavoir* (1844–45), and *L'Abbaye de Typhaines* (1844–45). There is in these works enough merit to ensure Gobineau a minor niche in nineteenth-century literary history.

Gobineau greeted with repugnance the Revolution of 1848, for he feared it would lead to a renewal of Bonapartist despotism. In the *Revue provinciale*, which he edited with Louis de Kergolay, Gobineau had defended the idea of local political autonomy against the notion of a highly centralized state. Within the year, he had changed his mind and, after coming to believe that France required an authoritarian leader, became a supporter of Louis-Napoleon. Meanwhile, Alexis de Tocqueville had become minister of foreign affairs (June-October 1849), and he had appointed Gobineau as his secretary; when Tocqueville left office, Gobineau remained, thus beginning a diplomatic career that would last until 1877.

Gobineau decided in 1850 to write a work that would set forth his pessimism, developed during the 1830s and the 1840s and confirmed by the Revolution of 1848, about the future of a France and a Europe that had abandoned the old nobility and had turned political power over to the middle and lower classes in the name of democracy, liberalism, and socialism. The resulting *Essai sur l'inégalité des Races humaines* (1853–55) became not only the work with which Gobineau's name is inseparably linked but also a major source of racist theory for the late nineteenth and twentieth centuries. In the *Essai*, Gobineau, who thought of himself as an aristocrat and who adopted the title of count in 1855, endeavored to explain the decline of the European aristocracy, for tied with it, he believed, was the fate of civilization. Gobineau's work is, in many respects, a typical product of the mid-nineteenth century. He claimed, for example, to have utilized the scientific method in the composition of the *Essai*, and when he wrote an introduction to the second edition, Gobineau tied his work with that of Henry Thomas Buckle and Charles Darwin. Strong resemblances between the *Essai* and other scientific theories of culture popular in the eighteenth and nineteenth centuries do exist, but Gobineau's innate pessimism, his categorical rejection of the idea of progress, and his belief in the inevitable and irreversible decline of Western civilization isolated him from his more optimistic contemporaries. That Gobineau sought to explain the decline of civilization in terms of a deterministic philosophy of history centered on a single concept was also typical of his day and placed him in the company of Auguste Comte, Karl Marx, and others. Even the choice of race as the central thesis of the *Essai* drew on an idea that enjoyed a contemporary vogue, especially in France. In the *Essai*, Gobineau argued that three races—the Negro, the yellow, and the white—made up the human species. Of these three, the white race was superior because only it combined in harmonious proportions the twin attributes of physical energy and abstract intelligence. The white race was hence destined to conquer and rule over the two lesser ones. But, and at this point Gobineau's bleak pessimism becomes patent, such a conquest leads inevitably to a racial mixing and thereby to a decline in the superior race. Over the course of time, civilization must of necessity decline. Gobineau's message, far from being a political or social program of racial imperialism, was a cry of despair.

The profound pessimism Gobineau expressed in the *Essai* was confirmed during the remaining twenty-seven years of his life by observations made while on diplomatic service in France, Switzerland, Germany, and elsewhere and by the events of 1870–71 in France. He nonetheless continued to write, producing a steady stream of impressive books on the East, most written in the course of his diplomatic missions. These include *Trois ans en Asie* (1859), *Les Religions et les philosophies dans l'Asie centrale* (1865), *Histoire des Perses* (1869), and *Nouvelles Asiatiques* (1876). Other works from Gobineau's later years include the *Histoire d'Ottar Jarl* (1879), an attempt to trace his ancestry to a Nordic pirate, *Les Pléiades* (1874), a novel about youthful aristocrats, and *La Renaissance* (1877).

Largely unknown during his lifetime, Gobineau's racial theories attracted the attention of Richard Wagner in 1876. Through the influence of Wagner and his associates, Gobineau's ideas began to circulate in Germany. In 1894, his German enthusiasts founded the Gobineau Society to propagate racial studies. Gobineau's German disciples, of course, neglected his central thesis about the inevitable decline of civilization, focusing instead their attention on his ideas concerning the superiority of the white, Aryan race.

Arthur de Gobineau died alone in Turin on 13 October 1882.

M. Biddiss, *Father of Racist Ideology: The Social and Political Thought of Count Gobineau* (London, 1970); J. Buenzod, *La Formation de la pensée de Gobineau* (Paris, 1967); *Etudes Gobiniennes* (Paris, 1966-); J. Gaulmier, *Spectre de Gobineau*(Paris, 1965); A. de Gobineau, *Essai sur l'inégalité des Races humaines*, ed. Hubert Juin (Paris, 1967), *Gobineau: Selected Political Writings*, ed. Michael D. Biddiss (New York, 1970), and *La Renaissance*, ed. John Mistler (Monaco, 1947); A. de Tocqueville, *The European Revolution and Correspondence with Gobineau*, ed. and trans. by John Lukacs (Garden City, N.Y., 1959).

Robert Brown

Related entries: COLLEGE DE FRANCE; COMTE, A.; LEGITIMISM; MARX; *LA QUOTIDIENNE*; REVOLUTION OF 1830; REVOLUTION OF 1848; TOCQUEVILLE.

GOGUETTES. See SINGING SOCIETIES.

GONCOURT, EDMOND HUOT DE, (1822–1896) and **GONCOURT, JULES HUOT DE** (1830–1870), originators of realism and naturalism in the novel; also claimed credit for the vogue in Japanese and eighteenth-century French decorative art and decoration. Despite the difference in age and physical characteristics, these brothers represent a unique example of literary collaboration. They enjoyed the rare psychic intimacy of some twins that seems to have continued even after the untimely death of Jules, apparently a victim of tertiary syphilis. A small inheritance they received from their mother in 1848 liberated them financially, and they devoted their energies to the pursuit of literature.

Jules was slender, blond, an asthenic child of Paris, while Edmond was tall and dark, with the air of a musketeer. While Jules had an extrovert nature—gay and expansive though nervous and high-strung—Edmond was reserved, melancholy, and withdrawn. However, they had the common faculty of receiving exactly the same impressions from the exterior world. They began noting these impressions daily in their *Journal* in 1851, and Edmond took up the pen alone after Jules's death.

Important fragments of the *Journal* were published in the 1890s, but it was Edmond's intention that the unexpurgated version should appear twenty years after his death. In fact, due to unanticipated political and social pressures, the integral version did not appear until 1956. Although it is a biting, unpleasant work, significantly biased and frequently superficial, it is an inestimable witness to the world of art and letters of the last half of the nineteenth century.

Although the brothers tried their hand in theater, history, and fiction, it is the novel on which their reputation as innovators and stylists rests. After the publication of two novels, *En 18*** (1850), and *La Lorette*(1853), they concentrated for a decade on historical works of the eighteenth century, publishing *Histoire de la société française pendant la Révolution* (1854), *Histoire de Marie-Antoinette* (1858), *Portraits intimes du XVIIIe siècle* (1857–58), and *La Femme au XVIIIe siècle* (1862). When they returned to the novel, Edmond stressed its affinity with history: "History is a novel which has been lived; the novel is a history which could have taken place." They emphasized the importance of the document to historical research, but in literature it was the contemporary human document that fascinated them.

The Goncourts chose subjects from milieux with which they were well acquainted, but their novels were written as their lives were lived: as sensitive, probing observers of the intimate, unpleasant details of everyday life. The theme of the destructive female is dominant, and many novels were titled with a woman's name. Their writing was soon eclipsed by the prodigious productivity of Zola, but they nevertheless claim priority in naturalism with *Germinie Lacerteux* (1865). Other novels include *Charles Demailly Soeur Philomène* (1861), *Renée Mauperin* (1864), *Manette Solomon* (1867), and *Madame Gervaisais* (1869). Theirs is a curious combination of the crudest naturalistic document delivered with the most elegant refined style, which garnered the title *l'écriture artiste* and was primarily the invention of Jules.

They collaborated as two bodies with a common mind and soul. At dinner, one would often begin a sentence that the other would complete. They frequently would each write a chapter individually and then combine the best elements. Edmond took charge of structure and development, while Jules's delicate and sensitive nature suited best the pursuit of stylistic excellence. After Jules's death, Edmond published *La Fille Elisa, Les Frères Zemganno, La Faustin*, and *Chérie*, which bore such unmistakable marks of their mutual collaboration that Jules seemed to be spiritually, if not physically, present. Edmond blamed his creative fury for producing the stresses that broke his brother's always frail and high-strung constitution.

Edmond left an incredible legacy in the Goncourt Academy, which, in opposition to the French Academy's stultified and conservative posture, was to bestow an annual prize for a realistic novel of artistic merit. It was intended to recognize youth, boldness, innovation, and talent and to permit the author to work without financial pressure for a year. Distant cousins sought for six years to destroy the will, but it was ably defended by the young Raymond Poincaré, and the first prize was awarded in 1903. Although inflation has seriously eroded the financial benefit, the excitement that surrounds the award and the contagion that has spawned rival literary prizes has enhanced the prestige of the novel in a manner far surpassing Edmond's vision or even his imagination.

R. Baldick, *The Goncourts* (New York, 1960); A. Billy, *The Goncourt Brothers*, trans. M. Shaw (London, 1960); R.B. Grant, *The Goncourt Brothers* (New York, 1972); M. Sauvage, *J. et Ed. de Goncourt* (Paris, 1970).

Shelby A. Outlaw

GOUDCHAUX, MICHEL (1797–1862), banker, moderate republican, and minister of finance in 1848. A Jewish banker from Nancy, Goudchaux earned a considerable reputation among Parisian republicans during the July Monarchy through his articles in *Le National* favoring the nationalization of railroads and the establishment of voluntary workers' cooperatives. After the proclamation of the Republic on 24 February 1848, Goudchaux became minister of finance in the Provisional Government. As minister, his primary goal concerned the restoration of financial stability in France. For this reason he opposed the adoption of the red flag as the national emblem (arguing that it would cause the stock exchange to collapse) and proposed paying interest in advance on government bonds. This last proposal met with concerted opposition from other cabinet members, and, convinced that his policies were being undermined, Goudchaux resigned his post on 6 March 1848.

He unsuccessfully ran for a seat in the Constituent Assembly in April 1848, but he did manage to win a special by-election to the Assembly in early June. Deputy Goudchaux became highly critical of his former colleagues in the Provisional Government, voted for the dissolution of the National Workshops, and even fought on the side of the forces of order during the June Days. Impressed by his devotion to order and considerable financial skill, General Eugène Cavaignac reappointed Goudchaux minister of finance in his new government. Still intent on restoring financial stability, he successfully headed off a projected budget deficit by arranging a loan from the Bank of France but failed in his attempt to prevent future deficits by cutting government spending. Goudchaux, in an effort to shift the tax burden from the poor to the rich, also tried to introduce several tax reform measures: a tax on *revenu mobilier*, a graduated tax on inheritances, and the abolition of taxes on wine and salt. Determined opposition from the Assembly forced him to abandon these projects.

Goudchaux's career in the government came to an end in October 1848 when he resigned from office after the Assembly voted, over his objections, to investigate the finances of the Provisional Government. He returned to politics only once more before he died in 1862. In the 1857 elections to the Corps legislatif, he won a seat as a republican deputy from Paris. He gave it up, however, rather than submit to the requirement of swearing allegiance to Louis-Napoleon.

F.A. de Luna, *The French Republic under Cavaignac, 1848* (Princeton, 1967); R. Lazard, *Michel Goudchaux (1792–1862)* (Paris, 1907).

Christopher E. Guthrie

Related entries: BANKING; CAVAIGNAC, L.-E.; CONSTITUTION OF 1848; JUNE DAYS; *LE NATIONAL*; NATIONAL WORKSHOPS; PROVISIONAL GOVERNMENT; REPUBLICANS; WORKERS' COOPERATIVES.

GOUVION SAINT-CYR, LAURENT, MARQUIS (1764–1830), marshal of the Empire, peer and minister of the Restoration. Born at Toul (Meurthe) on 13 April 1764, Gouvion later added his mother's name, Saint-Cyr, to that of his father. He initially studied painting, traveling in Italy and working in Paris. He also tried acting. Appointed to the staff of the Paris National Guard, he supported the Revolution after 14 July 1789. After 10 August 1792 he enlisted in an artists' battalion and by July 1794 he was a provisional division commander. He demonstrated tactical ability and prudence in the campaigns in Germany and Italy. But he also was acquiring a reputation for jealousy and selfishness.

During the Empire, he always kept his distance from Napoleon and consequently was not included on the original list of marshals. He finally reconciled with Napoleon and became marshal during the Russian campaign of 1812. The retreating Emperor assigned him to hold Dresden, where he stayed until he was forced to surrender in November 1813. The Allies kept him a prisoner until peace was achieved.

Saint-Cyr returned to France where on 4 June Louis XVIII had already named him a peer. He lived in retirement until March 1815, when the king sent him to command at Orléans against Napoleon. Saint-Cyr abandoned his command when Napoleon arrived in Paris and, although the emperor summoned him, Saint-Cyr accepted no post during the Hundred Days. When the Bourbons returned after Waterloo, they appointed him minister of war. During his three-month tenure, he greatly mitigated the harshness of army reductions, preserving regimental traditions and protecting former officers as much as possible. He managed to abolish the military household of the king but had to accept creation of the royal guard. But he also ordered the court-martial of Michel Ney, although as a peer he voted for Ney's banishment rather than his execution. He resigned with the rest of the Talleyrand ministry on 25 September 1815. In 1817 Saint-Cyr, now a marquis, became minister of marine (23 February-11 September) and then served as war minister until 18 November 1819. He reorganized the army, increasing it to 240,000 men serving for six years under his famous 1818 recruitment law. Recognizing the damage done by the royalist reaction, he also regulated promotion, reserving two-thirds for seniority. He recalled many competent imperial officers to active duty and established a general staff. Thus he gave the Bourbon Restoration its first truly effective army. He also helped restore most of the marshals to their ranks and estates. Saint-Cyr resigned from the cabinet on 18 November 1819 out of opposition to a proposed electoral law. Henceforth he rarely appeared in the Peers, retiring instead to his estate to write his various memoirs. Saint-Cyr died at Hyères (Var) on 17 March 1830 and was given a state funeral at the Invalides.

Archives parlementaires; J. Gay de Vernon, *Vie du maréchal St. Cyr* (Paris, 1856); R. Humble, *Napoleon's Peninsular Marshals* (London, 1973); A.G. Macdonnel, *Napoleon and His Marshals* (London, 1950); J. Monteilhet, *Les institutions militaires de la France* (Paris, 1936) and *Histoire des diverses lois sur le recrutement* (Paris, 1902); D. Porch, *Army and Revolution, France, 1815–1848* (London, 1974).

James K. Kieswetter

Related entries: DEMI-SOLDES; ELECTIONS AND ELECTORAL SYSTEMS; HUNDRED DAYS; NATIONAL GUARD; NEY; ROYAL GUARD.

GOYET, CHARLES (1770–1833), liberal political leader of the Sarthe who organized the elections of the marquis de Lafayette in 1818 and of Benjamin Constant in 1819. Born in Vallon (Sarthe), he studied in Paris and then returned to the Sarthe where he became a follower of the local revolutionary leader Rigomer Bazin. When Bazin denounced the authorities in Le Mans for friendliness toward *fédéralistes* in 1794, the *représentant en mission*, Jacques Garnier de Saintes, had ten *bazinistes* (including Goyet) arrested. They were acquitted by the Revolutionary Tribunal in Paris.

Goyet's support of the *exclusif* party continued during the Directory, when the Jacobins of the Sarthe were noted for the originality of their political techniques. They spread their message through newspapers, plays, festivals, and the innovative *ambulance*, which involved processions to and banquets in neighboring towns. In the elections of 1798 Goyet was elected to the departmental council. An opponent of the Empire, Goyet devoted himself to his legal work as a lawyer at the *tribunal de commerce* of Le Mans. He resumed political activity during the Hundred Days. He was singled out as one of the most dangerous men in the department by the restored authorities. On 11 May 1816, the prefect of the

Sarthe, Jules Pasquier, arrested Goyet as an enemy of the government, but he was soon ordered released by the courts.

In 1818, Goyet began publishing a political newspaper, *Le Propagateur d'anecdotes curieuses et intéressantes*, which was designed to appeal to the unsophisticated readers of the Sarthe. It themes were official corruption and favoritism, anticlericalism, and the dangers of a revival of the Old Regime. Goyet organized political committees throughout the department and persuaded rural voters to exercise their franchise. In the elections to the Chamber of Deputies of 1818, all four of the candidates recommended by Goyet won election, including the prominent Lafayette, who had no previous connection with the department. The Sarthe, then, accounted for four of the twenty-four liberal deputies elected in 1818. At the by-elections of 1819 to fill vacancies, Goyet's choices were once again elected, including Benjamin Constant, who became an important spokesman for the liberal cause in the Chamber. Goyet maintained an extensive correspondence with the deputies of the Sarthe. He also urged liberals elsewhere in France to follow his examples of political organization.

The government fought back against his influence in various ways. The electoral law of 1820 gerrymandered the districts and undermined some of his organization. He was arrested for involvement in a conspiracy against the government. He was found not guilty in court, and the evidence appears to be that although Goyet was aware of carbonarist plots, he did not support them, preferring to confine his activity to electoral politics. In 1822, Lafayette, Constant, and the other two liberal incumbents lost their bids for reelection. Discouraged by the political climate of the 1820s and the liberal electoral losses, Goyet gave up active political organizing. He died at Pont-de-Gennes (Sarthe) in 1833.

B. Constant and G. de la Sarthe, *Correspondance, 1818–1822*, ed. E. Harpaz (Geneva, 1973).

Sylvia Neely

Related entries: ANTICLERICAL CAMPAIGN; CARBONARI; CHAMBER OF DEPUTIES; CONSTANT; ELECTIONS AND ELECTORAL SYSTEMS; HUNDRED DAYS; LAFAYETTE, M.-J.-P.-Y.-R.-G.; RESTORATION, SECOND.

GREGOIRE, HENRI-BAPTISTE (1750–1831), abbé, Revolutionary bishop of Blois, champion of minority rights, and lifelong republican. Born 4 December 1750 in Vého (Meurthe), the only child of devout petty bourgeois parents, Grégoire studied with both the Jesuits and the Lazarists and was ordained in 1775. As a pre-revolutionary cleric, he developed the interests he would pursue throughout his adult career: ecclesiastical reform, philanthropic causes, and agricultural improvement. He worked on a plan for clerical education, joined several philanthropic and scientific societies, and in 1788 received an award from the Metz Royal Society of Science and Arts for his *Essai sur la régénération des juifs*.

Elected to the First (or clerical) Estate of the three-house Estates General, Grégoire persuaded other priests to renounce their separate political status, and, once the unicameral Constituent Assembly was formed (June 1789), he championed various political, social, and religious causes.

As a reward for his Revolutionary fervor, in March 1791 Grégoire was elected to one of the bishoprics (Loire-et-Cher) left vacant by the refusal of most other bishops to accept the Civil Constitution of the Clergy. He returned to Paris in September 1792 as a member of the newly elected National Convention. He was absent during the trial of King Louis XVI because the Convention had sent him to organize the newly annexed Nice and Savoy. From there he wrote an ambiguous letter voting for the king's "guilt" but neglecting to recommend death, life imprisonment, or exile. This letter would be his undoing during the Restoration.

After the Convention disestablished the Constitutional church in late 1794, Grégoire and several other Constitutional clergy attempted to reorganize their church as a voluntary organization. In the legislature he fought dechristianizing policies and insisted on the right of free public worship. He and his colleagues edited a journal, wrote a code of conduct, and convened national church councils in 1797 and 1801. Despite their efforts, the Constitutional church attracted only a minority of Catholics, and it could not restore religious unity. Napoleon's 1801 Concordat with Pope Pius VII, which recognized that "the great majority of French citizens" were Roman Catholic, officially ended the Constitutional church.

In 1819 Grégoire was elected to the Chamber of Deputies as a symbol of republican opposition to the restored monarchy. Sentiment against supposed regicides was too strong, and he was denied his seat on technical grounds. Nonetheless, he continued to write and correspond concerning his favorite causes. He helped combat French colonists' plans to recapture the independent black state of Haiti and gave what assistance he could to Greek revolutionaries.

Grégoire's final days were troubled by the insistence of Hyacinthe Quélen, the archbishop of Paris, that he renounce the Civil Constitution before he receive the last rites. Ironically, even though Grégoire had severely criticized the July Revolution for betraying his republican hopes, it was due to King Louis-Philippe's intervention that he received the rites and, a few days later, was buried in consecrated ground.

P. Grunebaum-Ballin, *Henri Grégoire, l'ami des hommes de toutes les couleurs* (Paris, 1948); R.F. Necheles, *The Abbé Grégoire* (Westport, Conn., 1971).

Ruth F. Necheles

Related entries: CHAMBER OF DEPUTIES; QUELEN; REPUBLICANS.

GREVY, FRANCOIS-JULES-PAUL (1807–1891), french statesman, deputy during the Second Republic and Second Empire, president of the National Assembly, and president of the Republic under the Third Republic. Born in Mons-sous-Vaudrey (Jura) on 15 August 1807, Jules Grévy came from an old family of Franche-Comté favorable to the French Revolution. After a solid education, Grévy was admitted to the practice of law in 1833. During the July Monarchy he defended republicans, gaining special notoriety for his defense of the newspaper *Le National*.

Named general commissioner of the Republic in the Jura in 1848, he was elected a deputy there in March and sat on the left of the Assembly, but at the same time he always favored respect for the law. Consequently, the powers given to General Eugène Cavaignac in June 1848 seemed to him a danger for the Republic. When the 1848 Constitution was voted upon, Grévy proposed an amendment that would have eliminated the office of president of the Republic elected by universal suffrage and replaced it with a president of the Council of Ministers elected and removable by the National Assembly. This amendment was rejected as a result of the opposition of most deputies led by Alphonse de Lamartine. Violently hostile to Louis-Napoleon Bonaparte, Jules Grévy defended the powers of the Assembly on several occasions. He fought against the expedition to Rome to defend Pope Pius IX and against giving to General Nicolas Changarnier the double command over both the National Guard of the Seine and the first military division.

Elected to the Legislative Assembly, he continued to denounce all threats to public liberties and all attempts to establish a dictatorship. He tried to organize resistance to the coup d'état of 2 December 1851 but was arrested and imprisoned in Mazas. Once again a lawyer in private practice under the Empire, he was in the same year (1868) elected batonnier of the Order of the Bar and deputy from the Jura, crushing the official candidate. He was opposed to the Ollivier ministry and to the plebiscite of 1870.

After the fall of the Second Empire, he unsuccessfully asked for elections before the proclamation of the Republic. Elected a deputy in 1871, he called the Paris Commune a ''criminal insurrection.'' Yet he also refused his seat in the new royalist Assembly. He refused to support Marie-Edmé-Patrice de MacMahon's attempt to increase the powers of the president, and, in 1889, he was able to form his own ministry to govern the Republic. A moderate, he opposed both colonialism and a policy of revenge.

A. Dansette, *Histoire des présidents de la république de Louis-Napoléon Bonaparte à Charles de Gaulle* (Paris, 1960); D. Frémy, *Quid des présidents de la République* (Paris, 1981); B. Lavergne, *Les deux présidences de Jules Grévy* (Paris, 1966).

Jean-Claude Caron, trans. E. Newman

Related entries: CAVAIGNAC, L.-E.; CHANGARNIER; CONSTITUTION OF 1848; COUP D'ETAT OF 2 DECEMBER 1851; LAMARTINE; LEGISLATIVE ASSEMBLY; *LE NATIONAL*; NATIONAL GUARD; PIUS IX; ROMAN EXPEDITION.

GROS, ANTOINE-JEAN, BARON (1771–1835), painter, best known for Napoleonic scenes. Antoine-Jean Gros was born in Paris on 16 March 1771, the son of a painter. In 1785 he began to study under Jacques-Louis David, whose influence was evident in much of Gros' later work. In 1787 he entered the

Académie de peinture. After it closed in 1793, Gros, with David's help, went to Rome. In Genoa in 1796 he made the acquaintance of Josephine, who took him to Milan to paint a portrait of Napoleon, his hero. Napoleon received Gros well and commissioned him in the army so that he might accompany it in the field. Gros was present at the battle of Arcola and saw Napoleon plant the flag on the bridge, the incident he immortalized in his first great painting, *Bonaparte at Arcola* (1796). In addition to his now-established role as chief painter of Napoleonic history, Gros also was given the task of helping select Italian artworks to be sent to Paris as war tribute. The tact with which he accomplished this earned him the admiration of diplomats and Italian artists alike. Thereafter he returned to France and in 1798 exhibited his portrait of General Louis-Alexandre Berthier. Henceforth he devoted himself to depicting scenes of great valor or compassion, as in the *Pesthouse of Jaffa*, which created a stir at its exhibition in 1804. Here Napoleon was shown visiting and touching lepers, much as the kings of France had demonstrated their thaumaturgical powers.

In 1806 Gros completed *Battle of Aboukir*, which actually lionized Joachim Murat more than Napoleon. *Napoleon at Eylau* followed in 1808, depicting Napoleon in an almost deific pose amid the crowded figures that typified so many of Gros' other canvases. It earned him the Legion of Honor. His other major scenes of this type included *Meeting of Napoleon and the Tsar Alexander after the Battle of Austerlitz, Capture of Madrid, Battle of the Pyramids,* and *Battle of Wagram*. Napoleon subsequently commissioned him to decorate the cupola of the Pantheon, a project that was not completed until 1824 but earned him a barony from Charles X. But he never again repeated the great successes of *Jaffa* or *Eylau*.

During the Restoration, Gros enjoyed the favor of the Bourbons, painting works such as *Louis XVIII, Duchesse d'Angoulême,* and *Charles X,* as well as other portraits such as that of Mme. Récamier. When the Bourbons banished David, he chose Gros to continue the instruction of his students, and Gros made repeated but unsuccessful attempts to obtain the lifting of David's exile. Nevertheless, the Bourbons gave Gros the Order of Saint Michael, and in 1815 he was admitted to the Institute. David's insistence on classicism in the face of Gros' romantic tendencies led him in 1824 to attempt a more classical style for the ceiling of the Egyptian room of the Louvre. But this came at a time when romanticism was reaching greater development, leading to increasing criticism of his work. He attempted a comeback in 1835 with *Hercules and Diomeda,* and that year he was appointed a professor at the Academy. But the controversy and conflict swirling around him proved too much for his melancholy personality. On 26 June 1835 his body was found, drowned in the Seine at Meudon, presumably a suicide.

G. Dargenty, *Le Baron Gros* (Paris, 1887); J.B. Delestre, *Gros, sa vie et ses ouvrages* (Paris, 1867); H. Lemonnier, *Gros* (Paris, n.d.); J. Tripier le Franc, *Histoire de la vie et de la mort du baron Gros* (Paris, 1880).

James K. Kieswetter

Related entry: DAVID.

GUERNON-RANVILLE, MARTIAL-COME-ANNIBAL-PERPETUE-MAGLOIRE, COMTE DE (1787–1866), magistrate, deputy, and minister of the Restoration. Born on 2 May 1787 at Caen to an old Norman noble family, Guernon-Ranville enlisted in the Imperial Guard in 1806. His nearsightedness, however, soon led to his discharge. He then studied law in Paris and entered the bar at Caen. In 1814 he welcomed the return of the Bourbons and during the Hundred Days joined a volunteer company that ultimately served as guards of Louis XVIII at Ghent. His first official post was president of the civil court of Bayeux in 1820, where he speedily disposed of an extensive backlog of cases. His diligence in Bayeux earned him appointment as solicitor general in the royal court at Colmar in 1822 and as attorney general successively at Limoges in 1824, Grenoble in 1826, and Lyons in 1829.

On 18 November 1829, still relatively unknown nationally, he joined the Polignac cabinet as minister of public instruction and worship and grand master of the University. Although he was an avowed enemy of revolutionary ideas, he was a moderate monarchist and a supporter of the Constitutional Charter. As minister he generally refrained from politically motivated firings. He also worked to improve the conditions of teachers and to expand primary education. On 2 March 1830 the department of Maine-et-Loire elected him to the Chamber of Deputies. In the cabinet he advised Charles X to remain above the conflict between the Deputies and ministers and urged him to moderate the speech with which he opened the 1830 legislative session. In the Chamber Guernon-Ranville defended the king and opposed the Deputies' reply to the address from the throne. But in the Council he opposed the impending coup that had provoked that reply. He counseled the king against dissolving the Chamber, fearing that a new one might be worse to deal with. On 19 May, after the dissolution ordinance was published, he asked to be replaced in the cabinet and even suggested the formation of an entirely new ministry. In June he recommended lowering the suffrage tax requirement to 20 or 50 francs. Nevertheless, he was not reelected in the summer elections.

During the cabinet discussions leading to the July Ordinances, Guernon-Ranville spoke out against such extreme measures, opposing the use of the powers granted the king by article 14 of the Charter. But he ultimately signed the ordinances, apparently for the sake of conformity with his colleagues. Once the ordinances were issued, however, he opposed almost all concessions to the revolutionaries on 29 July, seeing the whole affair now as a struggle between legitimacy and revolution. He took the lead in suggesting measures to save the monarchy, proposing the transfer of the government to Tours. After the king and royal family had fled from Rambouillet, Guernon-Ranville walked to Tours, hoping to rejoin the king. But he was arrested there on 5 August and was returned to Vincennes on 26 August for trial by the Peers. The Peers sentenced him and his colleagues to life imprisonment. After five years incarceration at the chateau of Ham, he was released by amnesty in 1836. He returned to his estate of Ranville near Caen and lived in retirement until his death on 30 November 1866 in the chateau of Ranville. In addition to a learned work on the jury, he left a journal, published in 1873.

Archives parlementaires; V. Beach, *Charles X* (Boulder, Colo., 1971); J.L. Bory, *La Révolution de juillet* (Paris, 1972); A. Robert et al., *Dictionnaire des parlementaires français* (Paris, 1889–91).

James K. Kieswetter

Related entries: CHARLES X; JULY ORDINANCES; POLIGNAC; REVO-LUTION OF 1830.

GUINARD, JOSEPH-AUGUSTIN (1799–1874), ardent republican conspirator and deputy in 1848. Joseph Guinard was born shortly after his father was elected to the Council of 500 from the Lys. His administrator father adhered to the coup of Brumaire, was named to the Tribunat, and in 1804 became *directeur des droits réunis* for the Nord. Joseph attended the Collège de Sainte-Barbe, read with Godefroy Cavaignac, and became an ardent republican. Like other sons of Napoleonic officials, he became involved in the carbonari's efforts to overthrow the restored Bourbon monarchy in the early 1820s. Although Guinard took part in the plots of Nantes, Saumur, and Belfort, he avoided prosecution.

This liberal, generous bourgeois youth was part of the general staff of republicans in the July Revolution. He belonged to the liberal electoral organization Aide-toi, le ciel t'aidera, and he was one of the founders of *Le National*. He fought on the barricades with Godefroy Cavaignac, Jules Bastide, and C. Thomas, and he is credited with leading a column of workers from the faubourg Saint-Michel to the Tuileries, where they planted the tricolor. From his position as captain of artillery in the National Guard, he opposed the Orleanist solution.

Dedicated to liberty and to greater involvement of the people than the *censitaire* system of Louis-Philippe allowed, he was on the founding committee for the Society of the Rights of Man in 1832. In his opposition to the regime of the bourgeois monarchy, Guinard was one of the earliest persons to go beyond political demands to social concerns. These activities made him the target of several police pursuits, and in 1835 he was condemned to deportation for his part in the April plots. On 15 July 1835 he escaped from Sainte-Pélagie and fled to England.

By 1848 Guinard was again in Paris, where he resumed his position in the National Guard. It is men like Guinard who turned the National Guard from defenders of the regime into its undertakers. He led the National Guard in the taking of the Hôtel de ville, where he became one of the first to call for the Republic. For his dedication, the new Provisional Government named him vice-mayor of Paris. Some had wanted to make him prefect of Police, but Marc Caussidière had preempted that position. Guinard soon rose to second in command of the National Guard. He would support legal republicanism in the days ahead.

Guinard also became president of the Central Democratic Society, an offshoot of an electoral club founded in late 1847. The society was composed of upper-class moderate republicans, men who would just as soon keep the masses at arm's length. It became part of the club movement in the first months of the revolution, and like its president, it was fundamentally neo-Jacobin in sentiment.

In the elections of April 1848, the voters of the Seine sent Guinard to the Constituent Assembly, thirty-third of thirty-four elected. He took his seat on the Left, and his moderate position helped him to be elected fifth vice-president. Similar to other bourgeois republicans, Guinard became a tamed conspirator after the February Revolution. He was ambivalent about the fighting in June. As a commander of the National Guard and a close friend of General Eugène Cavaignac, he urged the attack on the faubourg Saint-Antoine, yet as a former fighter on the barricades, he was a reluctant fighter. Severely wounded, he nevertheless returned to the Assembly and continued his role as a moderate republican.

He voted against the reintroduction of caution money for journals, against the pursuit of Louis Blanc and Caussidière, for the abolition of the death penalty, and for the right to work. He also supported Cavaignac, although with the rise of Louis-Napoleon, Guinard moved leftward. He opposed the credits for the Roman expedition and voted for the accusation against the president. He left the legislature at the close of the Constituent Assembly in May 1849.

On 13 June 1849, Alexandre-Auguste Ledru-Rollin declared the government invalid and attempted to found a new Convention. As commander of the National Guard artillery, Guinard joined this attempt to save the Republic from the control of Louis-Napoleon. When the insurrection collapsed on 14 June, Guinard was arrested. The High Court of Versailles found him guilty of insurrection but innocent of conspiracy. Condemned to deportation, Guinard was sent to Belle-Isle.

In 1854 he returned to France, where he lived in retirement, except to act as one of the pallbearers for General Cavaignac in 1857. Guinard lived to see his son sit with the republicans in the National Assembly of 1871.

A. Robert and G. Cougny, *Dictionnaire des parlementaires français* (Paris, 1889–91).

Thomas Beck

Related entries: AIDE-TOI, LE CIEL T'AIDERA; BASTIDE; BLANC; CAR-BONARI; CAUSSIDIERE; CAVAIGNAC, L.-E.; CAVAIGNAC, G.-E.; CLUBS, POLITICAL; *DROITS REUNIS*; JUNE DAYS; LEDRU-ROLLIN; *LE NATIONAL*; NATIONAL GUARD; PROVISIONAL GOVERNMENT; RE-PUBLICANS; ROMAN EXPEDITION; SAINTE-PELAGIE PRISON; SOCI-ETY OF THE RIGHTS OF MAN.

GUIRAUD, ALEXANDRE (1788–1847), minor poet, playwright, and theorist of romanticism. Like Charles Nodier, Alexandre Soumet, and Stendhal, Guiraud is one of the transitional writers loyal to classicism but strongly tempted by romanticism. He was born on 31 December 1788 in Limoux, a village in Languedoc where his aristocratic family had fled in fear of a possible revolution. Although the source of their wealth, cotton manufacturing, linked them with the bourgeoisie, the family was fiercely Catholic and royalist, and Alexandre shared their beliefs. While a law student at the University of Toulouse under the detested Empire, he formed a lifelong friendship with his soul mate in politics and poetry, Alexandre Soumet; together they were known as the two Alexanders.

Guiraud's father died in 1806, forcing Alexandre to take over the family's cloth-making business. But he found time to write poetry, and in 1819 three of his early poems won awards from the Jeux Floraux Academy in Toulouse. His taste for literature, and the encouragement of Soumet, Victor Hugo, Alfred de Vigny, and others caused him to purchase a house in Paris on the rue Saint-Honoré, and during his stays in the city he would attend the salons of Emile Deschamps and Delphine Gay. His most successful tragic play, *Les Machabées*, premiered in Paris in June 1822.

Successive failures as a playwright brought Guiraud back to poetry. He helped to found the *Muse française* and, in its January 1824 edition, he wrote an article, "Nos doctrines," one of the first salvos of the classic-romantic war. Conciliatory in tone, it simply attempted to contrast classicism and romanticism and to justify the existence of both.

Between 1823 and 1825 Guiraud wrote his much-acclaimed elegy, "Le petit savoyard" (1823), *Poèmes et chants élégiagues*, and *Chants hellènes*. The last two, both published in 1824, reflected his concern for Spanish and Greek contemporary political events. He also collaborated with Soumet on *Pharamond*, an opera celebrating the coronation of Charles X, which led to his being made a baron and a member of the French Academy in 1826. By now he was also a classicist, as is illustrated by his choice of a Roman topic for his final play, *Virginie ou la Famille* (1827).

The Revolution of 1830 drove him from politics. Retired to his chateau in Limoux, he turned to romantic psychological novels: *Césaire* (1830) and *Flavien* (1835). He also wrote travelogues and articles in defense of human rights for the newspapers *La Gazette de France* and *La Revue européenne*. More socially conscious, he wrote a history of the human race in *La philosophie catholique de l'histoire* (1839). Other collections of poetry and a close friendship with Alfred de Vigny helped to occupy Guiraud until his death on 24 January 1847.

A.R. Hill, "A. Guiraud: Transitional Romanticist" (Ph.D. diss., University of Virginia, 1980); L. Seché, *Le Cénacle de la Muse française, 1823–1827* (Paris, 1908).

Paul Comeau

Related entries: GAY, D.; *LA GAZETTE DE FRANCE*; HUGO; *LA MUSE FRANCAISE*; ROMANTICISM; SALON D'EMILE DESCHAMPS; VIGNY.

GUIZOT, FRANCOIS (1787–1874), historian, political philosopher, and statesman. François Guizot was born in Nîmes on 4 October 1787, the son of a prosperous Protestant lawyer. During the Reign of Terror, the father, a federalist opponent of the government in Paris, was executed and his property confiscated, which may explain in part his son's uncompromising opposition throughout his life to popular government. In 1799 Mme. Guizot with her two sons moved to Geneva, and the young François completed his schooling in the cosmopolitan schools of that city, making his first acquaintance with English literature and political thought, a continuing influence in his life.

He came to Paris in 1805 and earned his living as a tutor and writer. He ingratiated himself with influential members of the city's intellectual elite and in 1812 obtained appointment as professor of modern history at the University of Paris. He favored the reestablishment of the Bourbon monarchy in 1814, and his friend Pierre Royer-Collard found him a position in the Ministry of the Interior. During the Hundred Days he accompanied Louis XVIII to Ghent and was rewarded after the defeat of Napoleon by appointment as secretary-general of the Ministry of Justice and *maitre des requêtes* of the Council of State. His moderate liberalism offended the ultraroyalists, and their protests led to his dismissal from the ministry in 1816. A year later he became a councillor of state, but in the royalist reaction of 1820 he again fell victim of the ultras. Dismissed from the Council of State, he returned to the university and taught until the government suspended his course in 1822.

Guizot then turned to writing as a means of support and in the 1820s wrote the first of the historical works that would win for him recognition as one of France's great historians: the first two volumes of his *Histoire de la révolution d'Angleterre* (1826–27), *Histoire de la civilisation en Europe* (1828), and *Histoire de la civilisation en France* (1830–32). He was a contributor to *Le Globe*, the leading liberal literary journal of the time, and in 1827 he was one of the founders and the first president of the liberal electoral organization, Aide-toi, le ciel t'aidera. In 1830 he entered a by-election in Normandy and won a seat in the Chamber of Deputies.

In March 1830 he was one of the 221 deputies who voted for a censorious reply to the king's opening address. Reelected in the general election in June, he was among the small group of deputies who in the July Revolution engineered the bringing of the duc d'Orléans to the throne. During the next eighteen years, he was in ministerial office for thirteen years, serving in eight of Louis-Philippe's seventeen ministries. As minister of public instruction, a position that he held for more than four years, he drafted and achieved passage of France's first basic law on primary education, the law of 28 June 1833, which required every commune to support a public primary school.

In October 1840 Louis-Philippe recalled Guizot from the ambassadorship in London, a position he had taken only eight months earlier, to join the ministry being formed by Marshal Nicolas Soult. For the next eight years Guizot was the minister of foreign affairs and the de facto head of the ministry. He gave France a resolutely conservative regime committed to maintaining peace abroad and order at home, to restricting political authority to the well-to-do, and to ensuring the material interests of the propertied classes.

The February Revolution of 1848 forced the king to dismiss Guizot. He had become a symbol of the regime's opposition to popular pressure for change and was thoroughly unpopular. He took refuge in England until the revolutionary wave had receded, but, back in France in 1849, he stood for election to the

Legislative Assembly. Defeated in that attempt he retired from politics and devoted his time thereafter largely to writing—on history, on religion, and his own memoirs. He died at Val Richer, his home in Normandy, on 12 September 1874.

F. Guizot, *Mémoires pour servir à l'histoire de mon temps*, 8 vols. (Paris, 1858–67); D. Johnson, *Guizot: Aspects of French History, 1787–1874* (London, 1963); C. Pouthas, *Guizot pendant la Restauration, préparation de l'homme d'etat* (Paris, 1925).

David H. Pinkney

Related entries: AIDE-TOI, LE CIEL T'AIDERA; COUNCIL OF STATE; FOREIGN POLICY OF LOUIS-PHILIPPE; *LE GLOBE*; GUIZOT LAW ON PUBLIC EDUCATION; REVOLUTION OF 1830; REVOLUTION OF 1848; ROYER-COLLARD; SOULT; THE 221.

GUIZOT LAW ON PUBLIC EDUCATION, the 1833 law dealing with primary education, named the Guizot Law after François Guizot, minister of public education from 1832 to 1835. This law required every commune in France having over 500 inhabitants to open an elementary school for boys, every city of over 6,000 people to provide a higher primary school (*école primaire supérieure*), and every department to maintain a teacher-training school (*école normale primaire*) for young men. The law also created a corps of primary school inspectors. It set a minimum wage of 200 francs per year for teachers and established more detailed regulations concerning teacher certification. A law of 1836 applied some of the provisions of the Guizot Law to the instruction of girls.

Although the law did not make education compulsory (fathers of families were not obliged to send their children to school) or free (only the poor attended free of charge) or secular (public schools were defined as confessional, each legally recognized religious group having its own school board), it did lay the groundwork for all three. The number of students attending elementary school rose from 2 million in 1835 to 3 million a decade later. The quality of teaching gradually improved as graduates of the normal schools began to replace older, ill-trained teachers.

The law established the primacy of the state over the church and local government in education while making some concessions to both. It greatly improved popular literacy in all but the most backward parts of France and laid the foundations for the introduction of universal public education fifty years later. The conception and formulation of the law were mainly the work of Guizot, Victor Cousin, and Ambroise Rendu.

M. Gontard, *L'Enseignement primaire en France de la Révolution à la loi Guizot (1789–1833)* (Paris, 1959); F. Guizot, *Mémoires pour servir à l'histoire de mon temps*, vol. 3 (1860); D. Johnson, *Guizot, Aspects of French History, 1787–1874* (London, 1963).

C. Rod Day

Related entries: COUSIN; *ECOLES NORMALES PRIMAIRES*; *ECOLES PRIMAIRES SUPERIEURES*; GUIZOT.

GUTTINGUER, ULRIC (1785–1866), minor novelist and poet, close friend of Sainte-Beuve, and older member of the conservative romantic faction. Albert-Arthur-Ulric Guttinguer was born at Rouen in 1785. His father, Jean-Ulrich, moved to Normandy from Switzerland and became a merchant and financier (*directeur du comptoir d'escompte de la Banque de France*) in 1806. Although his father was Protestant, his mother, Marie-Rose Filleul, was Catholic, and Ulric was raised as such in a sober, bourgeois atmosphere. At the age of nine he was sent to a boarding school in Paris, where the adolescent developed as a weak, extremely sensitive, and emotional young man lost in fanciful thoughts of consuming love. He remained guilt ridden from puberty, and his excess of passion would later conflict with a deeply religious nature. He revealed portions of himself during his youth in an unfinished autobiographical novel, *Albert, mémoires d'un cy-devant jeune homme*, some of whose passages were being composed at the same time as *René*.

Back in Rouen at the dawn of the Empire, the handsome Ulric spent several years enjoying to the fullest the life of a provincial *galant*. He finally chose the beautiful Virginie Gueudry, whose prominent father was able to provide a handsome dowry. They were married about 1810 and had two daughters by 1814. She was a very pious woman for whom Guttinguer had true affection. She gradually steered her husband toward a Christian life. They enjoyed only a decade of bliss; she died in 1819. Ulric was overwhelmed by her loss and spent ten more years (1819–29) trying to appease his sorrow with a series of intimate relationships. As a partisan of the conservative wing of romanticism, he was a contributor for *La Muse française* and was among the first during those years to become a regular at Charles Nodier's Arsenal. Later, as a charter member of Hugo's *cénacle*, he would join with Charles-Augustin Sainte-Beuve to produce his only work that has survived to a degree, a second autobiographical novel entitled *Arthur*, published in 1834 and 1836. It would reveal the stormy affairs of the merry widower. He abused most of his conquests, though he had some true affection for Alexandrine-Angélique Bouquet, nicknamed Elyse, from Honfleur, but his passionate love went to a married woman, Rosalie, who reciprocated for two years from 1826 to 1828. He was devastated when she firmly rejected him. Although he contemplated suicide, he consoled himself by pouring his feelings into poems published as *Receuil d'élégies* in 1829. He tried to erase her presence in 1830 through involvement in the construction of his famous chalet in an oak forest in Normandy at Saint-Gatien where many romantics would visit. That same year, he also renewed his ties with Elyse and brought her to the chalet, where she gave birth to their son, Gabriel, in 1833. They were married as he turned fifty in 1835. Throughout those trying years, he produced love poems while he went through a long conversion experience to Catholicism.

By late 1835, tired of Normandy, he moved his family to Paris, returning to the chalet only for vacations. Ulric Guttinguer lived for thirty more years sincerely attempting to lead a moral life but unable to forget Rosalie. His poems continued to serve as an outlet for his passionate deceptions. Two collections—*Fables et méditations* (1837) and *Les Deux Ages du poète* (1844)—appeared during that period. His was the life of a true romantic dominated and engulfed by love.

H. Bremond, *Le Roman et l'histoire d'une conversion* (Paris, 1925); L. Séché, *La Jeunesse dorée sous Louis-Philippe* (Paris, 1900).

Paul Comeau

Related entries: ARSENAL, SALON OF; HUGO; *LA MUSE FRANCAISE*; NODIER; ROMANTICISM; SAINTE-BEUVE.

H

HAURANNE, PROSPER. See DUVERGIER DE HAURANNE.

HAUSSEZ, CHARLES-LEMERCIER DE LONGPRE, BARON D' (1778–1854), Restoration prefect and minister. Haussez came from a royalist family in Neufchâtel (Seine-Inférieure) and was active in conspiracies against the Directory and the Consulate. Arrested in connection with the Cadoudal-Pichegru conspiracy in 1804, Haussez accepted the Empire after his release from prison but rallied to the Bourbons in 1814. A career bureaucrat under the Restoration, he was briefly a deputy (Seine-Inférieure, 1815–16) and then successively prefect of the Landes (1817), Gard (1819), and Isère (1820). Although a moderate and opponent of the ultras, Haussez energetically repressed carbonarist and Bonapartist organizations in Grenoble (where Joseph Rey first organized his Union) in 1821. Prefect of the Gironde (1824) and a councillor of state (1827), Haussez joined the Polignac ministry, after some hesitations, as minister of the navy and colonies (August 1829). He was the principal architect and planner of the Algiers expedition (1830), overriding the reservations of the army and navy and successfully fending off British efforts to interfere with the campaign until it had achieved its initial goals. The success of the expedition did not prevent his defeat in the legislative elections of 1830, and though Haussez had little to do with the implementation of the July Ordinances, he did sign the final proclamation. Stoned and injured in the July Revolution by the Parisian crowd, Haussez fled to England and was condemned to life in prison in absentia by the Court of Peers (April 1831). He returned to France under the general amnesty in 1836 and lived quietly until his death. Haussez wrote several works on the departments in which he served as prefect, and his memoirs contain valuable insights on the last days of the Bourbon Restoration.

V. Beach, *Charles X of France* (Boulder, 1971); C. d'Haussez, *Mémoires*, 2 vols. (Paris, 1896–97); H. Gaubert, *Conspirateurs au temps de Napoleon Ier* (Paris, 1962); D. Pinkney, *The French Revolution of 1830* (Princeton, 1972).

David Longfellow

Related entries: ALGIERS, EXPEDITION TO; CARBONARI; JULY ORDINANCES; POLIGNAC; REVOLUTION OF 1830; REY; ULTRAROYALISTS.

HENRY V. See BORDEAUX.

HEREDITY LAWS. During the Restoration attempts were made to restore a hereditary aristocracy, but the July Monarchy and Second Republic dismantled these efforts to limit legal equality.

During the Restoration a number of attempts were made to reconstitute a hereditary, landed aristocracy. The Charter of 1814 gave partial recognition of legal inequality by creating a hereditary Chamber of Peers and recognizing the existence of a hereditary, if nonprivileged, nobility. Supporters of a hereditary elite, however, wished to go further and successfully achieved the passage of a requirement for a landed *majorat* for titled nobles and hereditary peers (1817). In 1826 they unsuccessfully sought to pass a law on primogeniture. Too limited and insufficient to their purpose, these attempts had little more effect than to antagonize the supporters of the Revolution.

On 4 June 1814, "in the nineteenth year of his reign," Louis XVIII granted to the French a constitutional Charter, of which articles 24–34 defined the powers and functioning of the Chamber of Peers. An essential part of the legislative body, the Chamber was to be composed of two kinds of members, peers by right of birth and peers named by the king. The first category included the members of the royal family and princes of the blood. In the second category, the king could name an unlimited number of peers and appoint them either for life or hereditarily.

During the brief interlude of the Hundred Days, Napoleon departed from the example of Louis XVIII and proclaimed the peerage hereditary, male to male, by order of primogeniture in direct descendance of the first title holder. Napoleon also forbade transmittal of the quality of peer by adoption. The peerage was to be irrevocable.

When Louis XVIII returned to power in the Second Restoration, he followed Napoleon's example and by the ordinance of 19 August 1815 established that all peers already named and those to be named in the future would be hereditary, male to male, by order of primogeniture. In the case where there was no heir, the king reserved the right to authorize the transmission of the peerage in a collateral line. Article 4 of the same ordinance stipulated that letters patent were to be delivered to the peers in recognition of a noble title on which each peerage would be instituted. These titles included baron, vicomte, comte, marquis, and duc. Two years later the ordinance of 25 August 1817 ruled that the eldest son of a peer would take the next lowest title and the younger sons the title below the eldest brother.

A second part of the 1817 ordinance required the establishment of a *majorat de pairie*. The *majorat* was required for all peers, except ecclesiastical, who were named after 25 August 1817 and who wished to make their title of peer hereditary or pass it on to a collateral line. Following the example of Napoleon's *majorats d'empire*, Louis XVIII sought to create a true political aristocracy in the Chamber of Peers through what one commentator has described as "financial fiefs." Three classes of *majorats* were formed: those attached to the title of duc and requiring landed property producing at least 30,000 francs of net revenue; those attached to the titles of marquis or comte whose lands yielded at least 20,000 francs; and those attached to the titles of vicomte or baron whose net landed revenues amounted to at least 10,000 francs. The *majorats*, like the title of peer, were to be transmitted only in the male line by order of primogeniture except by special royal authorization.

Difficulties arose almost immediately over the interpretation of the 1817 ordinance and over the ability of many to meet the financial obligations. It was not clear, for example, whether the *majorat* had to be formed before becoming a peer or whether the appointment as peer recognized that the new peer had already met the qualifications. Ordinances of 1819 and after tried to clarify and considerably ease the requirements for the formation of a *majorat* in several ways. One could now form a *majorat* at a lower level than his personal title. A peer could also be exempted from forming a *majorat* unless he wanted it to be hereditary, or in some cases the eldest son would be allowed to form the *majorat* and then make the peerage hereditary. In 1823 the king even allowed certain pensions given by him to be acceptable as *majorats*. Thus, by the mid–1820s the formation of a *majorat* and a hereditary peerage was neither uniform nor clear.

Given the difficulties in forming *majorats* for the peers, one might think that the king would have wanted to end what was increasingly an empty proliferation of titles. Instead, in an ordinance of 10 February 1824 Louis XVIII decided that in the future all new titles of *noblesse* would become hereditary only after the constitution of a corresponding *majorat*. This gesture was intended to assuage the unhappiness of many ancient noble families who held no title and who now seemed to pale in dignity next to those with Napoleonic titles who had either never been officially ennobled or only recently so. This had come about because article 71 of the Charter had recognized the titles and noble status of both the new and old nobility while providing for ennoblement only by the will of the king. Intended to end the proliferation of titles, the 1824 ordinance did little to clear the more basic confusion between noble status and title or to end the divisions between the new and old nobility. The main effect of all these ordinances on *majorats* was more symbolic than practical. They brought disenchantment with a monarchy that was proliferating hereditary distinctions, albeit honorific, among Frenchmen who prized legal equality, without actually being sufficient to create the kind of hereditary aristocracy many conservatives sought.

This conclusion also characterizes the celebrated projected law of successions and substitutions. In his royal discourse of 31 January 1826, Charles X alerted the chambers of the need to end the division of property and to put the civil and political order in harmony with one another. On 10 February 1826 Charles de Peyronnet, the minister of justice, brought the projected law before the Chamber of Peers. Reflecting the views of the ultraroyalists, Peyronnet stressed the need to end the mobility of landed property, to consolidate the influence of families, and thereby to reensure social stability. He further argued that the progressive division of landed property was not only economically inefficient but, more important, contrary to royal government. The equal division of property among heirs, Peyronnet maintained, was more appropriate to democracy than to a monarchy that required an independent political class.

Although critics portrayed the projected law as an attempt to restore primogeniture, and thus hereditary privilege, the measure was actually more limited. According to the Napoleonic Civil Code, the lands of the deceased were equally distributed among his male heirs unless he specifically provided in his will that the disposable share (that part of his estate the Code allowed him to do with as he wished) go to the eldest son. (The disposable share could be as high as 40 percent of the property of the deceased.) The projected law sought to repeal certain clauses of the Civil Code. As finally amended, it provided that the disposable share of an estate of a proprietor who had paid 1,000 francs in taxes (the original bill called for 300 francs in taxes) would automatically succeed to the eldest son unless the proprietor had provided equal distribution in his will. A subsidiary provision would have allowed the substitution of someone else for the eldest son and would have made the succession of the disposable share good for two generations rather than one as provided for in the Civil Code. In effect, this substitution would have most frequently profited the eldest and his masculine heirs by order of primogeniture. The first, and most important part, of the bill failed. The second passed into law.

Critics charged that Peyronnet and the ultras were trying to recreate a privileged aristocracy made up of the feudal nobility. Even those who admired the English aristocracy argued that a landed aristocracy as envisioned by the proponents of the law would be an artificial plant on French soil. An aristocracy could not be abruptly created where it did not already exist. French history and customs, they maintained, knew only a feudal and courtesan nobility, not the independent, parliamentary aristocracy of England. Contemporary France would not abide replacing individual merit and virtue in civil society with privilege and accident of birth. The only privilege accepted by the Charter was the political institution of the Chamber of Peers.

The proposed law actually made no distinction between noble- and roturier-owned land; the criterion for determining the succession was to be wealth, not birth. Nor would the eldest gain special privileges beyond the opportunity to accumulate more wealth. The practical effects of the law would have likely been minimal. Only approximately 8,000 families would have been affected, and if these families continued the pattern already established in the Restoration, they would have chosen to divide their land equally. Only a very small percentage of even the wealthiest French families had chosen to use the option in the Civil Code that allowed them to will their disposable share to the eldest. Again, the issue of heredity had unnecessarily exacerbated the highly emotional and symbolic debate between new and old France, to little purpose.

Heredity was to become an important issue once again after the Revolution of 1830. This time many supporters of the revolution demanded the abolition of what they saw as the last major symbols of privilege, a hereditary monarch who claimed his power from divine right and the heredity of the peerage. The revolutionaries achieved their first demand—the elimination of the Bourbon monarchy—when the Chamber of Deputies declared the throne vacant and invited the duc d'Orléans to accept the revised Charter and become the new king of the French. The new Citizen King, Louis-Philippe, seemed to derive his power from the choice of the nation. That the new king would pass on his rule hereditarily seemed to be a contradiction to the principle of national sovereignty, but that contradiction was to become moot with the February Revolution of 1848.

The Chamber of Deputies decided to put off the elimination of the heredity of the peerage to less troubled times. A year later, on 27 August 1831, Casimir Périer brought before the Chamber of Deputies a proposal to revise article 23 of the new Charter. Périer, representing the government, proposed that the king have an unlimited right to appoint peers at his own discretion but only for the life of the appointee. Périer himself preferred the heredity of the peers. Like most other moderate supporters of the 1830 Revolution, Périer believed that heredity of the peerage would be better for political and social stability, would be a firmer support for a constitutional monarchy, and would provide a spirit of independence, which he saw as the best guarantee for individual liberty. But, he argued, the practical state of affairs had priority over the dictates of political theory. In other words, public opinion demanded the end of this last abridgement of civil equality, and he was willing to accede to that opinion.

The Chamber of Deputies overwhelmingly supported the abolition of heredity. Most deputies argued that French liberty depended on national sovereignty, not on an independent, hereditary aristocracy. Repeating some of the arguments against the proposed Restoration law on primogeniture, they also maintained that France was not England, that France had no truly independent aristocracy, and that this was not the time to create one. The Deputies therefore passed a revised version of Périer's proposal by a convincing margin of 386 to 40. The new law abolished heredity and limited the king's right to appoint peers to certain categories of notabilities. By the end of the year, the Chamber of Peers also recognized public opinion and voted the end of their hereditary rights.

The new law also foresaw the abolition of the peers' right to establish *majorats*. By 1831 only 78 *majorats* had been formed by peers and only 228 by nobles outside the peerage. The specific regulation of *majorats* was left to the law of 12 May 1835. This law prohibited the future constitution of new *majorats* and limited the duration of those already in existence to two generations. In order not to abridge those rights already acquired, an ordinance for October 1837 proclaimed that titles whose heredity depended on the constitution of a *majorat* would be recognized as hereditary even if the *majorat* had not yet been instituted by the title holder, as long as he was still alive, by 12 May 1835.

The July Monarchy also dismantled the governmental bureaucracy that supervised the registration of titles and letters patent of nobility. The *Conseil du sceau* was abolished, and all penalties for usurping titles were eliminated. On the other hand, Louis-Philippe tried to appease those enamored with hereditary distinction. For example, he regularized the ennoblements of those families of the Old Regime who were still in process when the 1789 Revolution broke out, and in 1839–40 he opened a Hall of Crusades at the Versailles Palace where the families of the medieval crusaders could display their coat of arms. Like Napoleon, he also granted a few hereditary titles and many titles for life. Although all men were now equal, Louis-Philippe maintained the illusory glamor of a hereditary peerage.

The advent of the Second Republic provided the final blow to hereditary distinction. The February Revolution abolished the nobility and noble titles, effective immediately, and article 10 of the Constitution of 4 November 1848 confirmed this double abolition. Finally, the *majorats*, despoiled of their titles since February 1848, were eliminated in a law of 11 May 1849. Afraid to abolish rights already granted, the Republic allowed transmission of a *majorat* to two generations in cases where the prospective inheritor had already been born before the promulgation of the law. Otherwise the lands were liberated into the hands of the possessor. By 1852 only twelve *majorats* remained.

By 1849 France no longer recognized hereditary distinction among its citizens (except those of gender) either symbolically or in law. The Restoration had feebly tried to amend the Civil Code and reintroduced distinctions. The July Monarchy suppressed the legal abridgements to the Code while retaining some symbolic recognition of titles. The Republic ended both symbol and reality. But in January 1852 the nephew of Napoleon I sought to regale his reign with symbolic distinctions and abrogated the decree of the Provisional Government of 29 February 1848. This returned the status of the nobility to the situation under Louis-Philippe. To this day French law recognizes noble titles while maintaining legal equality among its citizens.

P. Du Puy de Clinchamps, *La Noblesse* (Paris, 1962); S. Gutman, "Changing Conceptions of Elite," *The Consortium on Revolutionary Europe Proceedings* (Baton Rouge, 1978); A. Lardier, *Histoire biographique de la chambre des pairs* (Paris, 1829); M. Sarrazin, *Les majorats dans la législation française* (Paris, 1906); R. de Warren, *Les pairs de France*, 2 vols. (Paris, 1959).

Sanford Gutman

Related entries: CHAMBER OF PEERS; CHARTER OF 1814; CHARTER OF 1830; CONSTITUTION OF 1848; LOUIS-PHILIPPE; PERIER; PEYRONNET.

HERNANI (1830), romantic play by Victor Hugo that openly challenged the French classical tradition. In *Hernani* Victor Hugo chose to ignore both the quasi-divine three unities and the seventeenth-century rule of reason, seeking a more realistic treatment of plots and characters. As he had explained in his preface to *Cromwell* (1827), Hugo wanted to bring literary freedom to a new, modern theater where a mixture of tragic and grotesque moments and colorful and violent action, enhanced by picturesque scenery, would bring the theater closer to the people. *Hernani* was politically suspicious to the Bourbon monarchy, which tried to censure and discredit it. Thus, the battle of *Hernani* (February-June 1830) has become an event of historical significance as well. Young liberals exchanged insults and even physical assaults with the older and traditional patrons of the respectable Comédie-française during showtime.

Hernani is a tale of jealousy, honor, and love set in the Spain of 1519. Young Doña Sol is loved by her old tutor, Don Ruy Gomez, to whom she is betrothed. But she loves Hernani, an outlaw and a bandit, who returns her love with equal passion. Don Carlos, the king of Spain and candidate for the office of Holy Roman Emperor, also falls in love with Doña Sol. As the complex plot unfolds, each of Doña Sol's three suitors is forced by the rites of chivalry to protect one of his rivals from the third suitor, willing to risk the loss of his beloved rather than compromise his honor.

In the third act, which takes place at Don Ruy Gomez's castle, preparations are being made for the wedding of Ruy Gomez to Doña Sol. Hernani arrives disguised as a pilgrim and Ruy Gomez, who does not recognize him, grants him unconditional asylum. Don Carlos arrives and recognizes Hernani, but Ruy Gomez keeps his word and protects the outlaw. In gratitude Hernani gives Ruy Gomez a horn and promises that when the horn sounds he will forfeit his life.

Meanwhile Ruy Gomez sees that Don Carlos is also in love with Doña Sol. Enraged, he makes a pact with Hernani to kill the king. Don Carlos hears of this plot against his life, but when the cannon shots announce that he has become Holy Roman Emperor he magnanimously forgives his enemies and releases Doña Sol's hand to Hernani. In the fifth and final act Hernani and Doña Sol, blissfully married, encounter a mysterious masked man who has lingered in the palace after their wedding. Soon the sound of a horn interrupts the married couple; the masked man is Ruy Gomez, who has come to remind Hernani of his suicide promise. On hearing this Doña Sol takes hold of the poison and drinks along with Hernani. Finally, Ruy Gomez kills himself and falls upon the bodies of his two victims.

Hernani is a melodrama of great poetic beauty that enthralled the youth of 1830. More than a battle between two opposing literary schools, it articulated the revolt against the outmoded social conventions of the Bourbon gerontocracy.

G. Ascoli, *Le Théâtre romantique* (Paris, 1953); T. Gautier, *Histoire du romantisme*

(Paris, 1868); H. Juin, *Victor Hugo, 1802–1843* (Paris, 1980); P. Moreau, *Le Romantisme* (Paris, 1957).

Marcelle Maistre Welch

Related entries: HUGO; ROMANTICISM.

HOLBACH, PAUL-HENRI THIRY, BARON D' (1723–1789), Enlightenment philosopher, editor, translator, and man of letters. D'Holbach was celebrated in his own lifetime as the host of a philosophically diverse Parisian salon that flourished from the early 1750s until the early 1780s, attended by such Enlightenment notables as Denis Diderot, Friedrich-Melchior Grimm, Jean-François Marmontel, the abbés Raynal, Morellet, and Galiani, Jean-François de Saint-Lambert, Jean-Baptiste-Antoine Suard, and Claude-Adrien Helvétius. D'Holbach was known among his close friends and intellectual collaborators as the pseudonymous author of the most scandalous and thoroughgoing materialistic and atheistic works of the late Enlightenment, *Système de la nature* (1770) and *Le Bon-Sens* (1772), but the general public and the authorities of the *ancien régime* were unaware of his identity as a proselytizing atheist and identified him simply as a wealthy, well-connected, socially respectable patron of letters and the fine arts.

After d'Holbach's death, however, and in the wake of Jean-Jacques Rousseau's melodramatic condemnations of d'Holbach as a materialist and would-be persecutor of his person and reputation (in books 8 through 10 of Rousseau's *Confessions*), the wall of discretion that had protected d'Holbach's name began to crumble. By the dawn of the nineteenth century, the full story of his authorship, editing, translation, and patronage of notorious atheistic books was widely circulated. This knowledge would become common property through the influence of the many editions of A.-A. Barbier's *Dictionnaire des ouvrages anonymes et pseudonymes*.

As the *émigrés* of the French Revolution searched their memories of their lost society for the causes of their sufferings, they increasingly identified the philosophical radicalism of the Enlightenment—above all, its strains of atheism—with the political radicalism of the Revolution, and for many, the idea of a dark conspiracy involving the *philosophes* seemed a sure explanation of events. The most comprehensive of such accounts was the abbé de Barruel's *Mémoires pour servir à l'histoire du Jacobinisme* (1797–98), which described an alleged twenty-five-year conspiracy of *philosophes* and Freemasons that had culminated in the Revolution of 1789. For Barruel, the center of this conspiracy in Paris was the salon of baron d'Holbach, where strategy and propaganda were formulated to bring about the collapse of religion, morality, and royal government in France.

Although Maximilien Robespierre had denounced atheism as aristocratic and counterrevolutionary, and although, in fact, d'Holbach's reformist political philosophy had denounced revolution and mass politics in *La politique naturelle* (1773) and the *Système social* (1773), *émigré* and Catholic royalist thinkers came to accept the heart of Barruel's curious thesis. By the Restoration, d'Holbach, already detested by admirers of Rousseau, had become the object of widespread obloquy and the convenient focus of animosity toward the Enlightenment in general and materialism in particular.

In 1822, the influential and much-admired Mme. de Genlis, marquise de Sillery, published *Les dîners du Baron d'Holbach*, which, drawing heavily from Barruel and from Rousseau's portrait of d'Holbach's materialism and personality, combined these two strains of anti-Holbachian rhetoric. In Mme. de Genlis's work, d'Holbach's circle was depicted as the *machine de guerre* of a vast intrigue against France by the enemies of the Bourbon crown. Following instructions from Voltaire and Frederick II, baron d'Holbach, in Mme. de Genlis's account, organized the atheists of Paris into a center of Revolutionary activity that for a generation sought to sap the religious foundations of the *ancien régime*, undermine support for all established order by its publication of antireligious works, and prepare France for an anti-Christian political upheaval.

This view of d'Holbach and his coterie, rarely challenged, was brought into the scholarly mainstream and given official endorsement by the preeminent literary historian François Villemain, professor of French literature at the Université de Paris and, from 1839 to 1844, minister of public education. Villemain exercised a critical influence on nineteenth-century attitudes toward the French Enlightenment, and in his well-attended and widely read *Cours de littérature française* (first published in 1828 and reissued in 1840, 1841, and 1881), he gave credence to and further promulgated the description of d'Holbach as the leader of a sinister cabal of militant, revolutionary atheists who had precipitated the radicalism of the French Revolution. Although Villemain qualified the uniform condemnation of d'Holbach's circle urged by Barruel and Mme. de Genlis, describing such ultraroyalist heroes of the Restoration as Morellet and Suard as unwitting participants in its crimes, he insisted that d'Holbach presided over a society that planned and worked for the dechristianization, the destruction, and the pernicious reforms of the most rabid of the Revolutionaries. Atheism, Villemain sought to demonstrate, was no mere metaphysical doctrine but a threat to the stability and order of French government, society, and civilization.

By the end of the July Monarchy, d'Holbach's unmerited reputation as revolutionary plotter was firmly embedded in popular and academic literature. It received a final embellishment in the comte de Tocqueville's popular *Histoire philosophique du règne de Louis XV* (1847, two editions). Hervé-Louis-François Clérel, comte de Tocqueville, a distinguished administrator during the Restoration who became a *pair de France* (1827) under Charles X, enjoyed a major success late in his life with his philosophical history of the *ancien régime*. In de Tocqueville's rendering of d'Holbach and his role, all nuances and qualifications were eliminated, and the baron was presented as the leader of a Revolutionary order as disciplined as the Jesuits. D'Holbach, in this view, conducted a conspiratorial workshop where the individual *philosophes* of Paris were converted to atheism and organized into a coordinated effort to spread the atheistic and Revolutionary common creed.

This emphasis on d'Holbach's role as alleged host of a radical *cénacle* interfered with any serious encounter with the heart of his intended legacy to the nineteenth century, an atheistic philosophy centered on logical empiricism, a linguistic and scientific critique of theological claims, and a utilitarian condemnation of the consequences of theism. Further, d'Holbach's actual atheistic formulations were increasingly remote from even the antitheological themes of French thought in the first half of the nineteenth century. Already in the eighteenth century, d'Holbach's reliance on Newtonian physics as the model of nature was out of step with the more biologically based natural models of La Mettrie and Diderot; the vitalism of so much of nineteenth-century free thought was yet further removed from d'Holbach's conceptual world. Finally, d'Holbach had stressed the arbitrary nature of human knowledge, defending a materialistic language and ontology less on noetic grounds than on grounds of the historical and social consequences of philosophical choices; such a view of knowledge was increasingly inimical to the growing realism and positivism of nineteenth-century materialism.

A. C. Kors, *D'Holbach's Coterie: An Enlightenment in Paris* (Princeton, 1976) and "The Myth of the Coterie Holbachique," *French Historical Studies* 9 (Fall 1976); P. Naville, *Paul Thiry d'Holbach et la philosophie scientifique au XVIIIe siècle*, rev. ed. (Paris, 1967); V. Topazio, *D'Holbach's Moral Philosophy: Its Background and Development* (Geneva, 1956).

Alan Kors

Related entries: FREEMASONRY; JESUITS; ROBESPIERRE; ROUSSEAU; VILLEMAIN; VOLTAIRE.

HOLY ALLIANCE, a term used indiscriminately and applied to three entities historically distinct in their origins and natures.

1. The compact of the Holy Alliance was signed in Paris on 26 September 1815 at the initiative of Czar Alexander I. The idea of the Russian autocrat was that in order to avoid the return of disastrous conflicts, the leaders of the great European powers should forsake the practices of selfish and secular Machiavellian policies and seek guidance in the Christian gospel of universal brotherhood. In his thinking, he was encouraged by Julie de Krüdener, the enthusiastic pietist. The document the czar submitted in Paris during the peace conferences to the Austrian emperor and the king of Prussia was worded in high-flown religious language. Metternich was appalled, describing the compact as "that empty and sonorous monument." But neither his sovereign nor the king of Prussia dared refuse their signature. For Castlereagh it was nothing but "a piece of sublime mysticism and nonsense"; he could not recommend that it be signed by the prince regent because it could not be presented in Parliament, but he soothed the czar with written assurances that the prince was "united in heart and soul" with the noble intentions of Alexander. Such was also in substance the response of the U.S. government when it was approached in 1819. In the meantime, most of the European sovereigns, except the pope, had given some kind of formal adhesion to the compact, including even the Directory of the Swiss Confederation.

It must be strongly emphasized that this compact of the Holy Alliance was never considered as a formal treaty or binding diplomatic instrument but remained as a purely moral and personal statement of intentions from the heads of states. Never was it to be mentioned in any official transaction among the European chanceries, and Metternich insisted on that reservation.

2. The Quadruple Alliance was signed in Paris on 20 November 1815. Mainly conceived by Castlereagh, it was to be the realistic and effective underpinning for the nebulous compact of 26 September 1815.

3. The accession of France to the earlier Four Powers directory of November 1815, as a result of the Congress of Aix-la-Chapelle, produced the Quintuple Alliance, which, in the eyes of Metternich and Castlereagh would have no practical utility. The twin congresses of Troppau-Laibach (1820–21) brought about a deep revision of the nature and purpose of the alliance under the inspiration of Metternich.

The Quadruple Alliance of 1815 had as its primary objective the security of the system established by the congresses of Vienna and Paris. In addition, it implied a right to interfere in certain cases in the internal affairs of France. The new alliance of Troppau extended its scope to include the moral support and active defense of all "legitimate" governments.

According to the decisions proclaimed at Aix-la-Chapelle (15 November 1818), the enlarged Quintuple Alliance would intervene in the affairs of other states only on the request of their legitimate government, duly proffered by their representatives, whereas the protocol of Troppau (19 November 1820) asserted a right of intervention in all situations threatening the established order, listing even the gradual measures of coercion that could be used.

As England and also, less clearly, France dissociated themselves from these decisions, the alliance found itself reduced to its hard core of the three absolute monarchies: Austria, Prussia, and Russia. Because their sovereigns were also the first signatories of the compact of 26 September 1815, confusion often arises between the identity of the Holy Alliance and the new conservative league of the absolute monarchies. Metternich was partly responsible for the confusion when he had to invoke the Holy Alliance to keep the unpredictable czar in line, though he was most careful to banish the words *Holy Alliance* from all official transactions. In his mind and vocabulary, there was only *the* alliance, no more quadruple or quintuple.

The alliance was sorely tried but finally confirmed at the Congress of Verona. But the death of Alexander (December 1825) portended the end of the alliance. It came a few months later when Russia and England, seeking a solution to the knotty eastern question, entered into separate agreements (4 April 1826), followed in July 1827 by a three-power treaty with France, leaving Austria isolated with Prussia.

The notion of the Holy Alliance as a sinister league of reactionary powers was too useful a bugaboo for liberal propaganda, and it would long survive in popular thought and political literature.

G. de Bertier de Sauvigny, *La Sainte-Alliance* (Paris, 1972); M. Bourquin, *Histoire de la Sainte-Alliance* (Geneva, 1954); A. Phillips, *The Confederation of Europe* (London, 1914); H. Schmalz, *Versuch einer gesammteuropaichen Organisation* (Aarau, 1940).

Guillaume de Bertier de Sauvigny

Related entries: AIX-LA-CHAPELLE, CONGRESS OF; QUADRUPLE AL-LIANCE; QUINTUPLE ALLIANCE; TROPPAU, CONGRESS OF; VERONA, CONGRESS OF; VIENNA, CONGRESS OF.

L'HOMME GRIS (1817–1818), anticlerical, satirical newspaper of the early Restoration. The moderate ministry of Elie Decazes was attacked by a number of small satirical journals, including *L'Homme gris*, owned and edited by Amédée Féret and Nicolas-Joseph Creton. Prosecution in the law courts meant that the paper lasted barely a year (1817–18). It was replaced by *Le Nouvel homme gris*, founded by Jean-François-Cugnet de Montarlet and published with the collaboration of Louis Cauchois-Lemaire and Louis-Saturnin Brissot-Thivars. Like its predecessor, the new *Homme gris* was extremely anticlerical in tone. It, too, lasted barely a year (1818–19).

C. Bellanger et al., *Histoire générale de la presse française*, vol. 2 (Paris, 1969).

Irene Collins

Related entries: ANTICLERICAL CAMPAIGN; CAUCHOIS-LEMAIRE; DE-CAZES; PRESS LAWS.

HUBER, ALOYSIUS (1812–?), socialist conspirator, member of secret societies during the July Monarchy, and a leader of political clubs during the Second Republic. Born in Wasselonne (Bas-Rhin), Huber began as a tanner. Influenced by the theories of the socialist Pierre Leroux, he was quite active during the 1830 Revolution, when he went with a group of about fifteen to twenty people before the Municipal Commission to ask that the nation be consulted in the choice of a new political regime and that public liberty be guaranteed. Disappointed by the results of the revolution, he joined the Society of the Rights of Man and was sentenced to five years in prison for complicity in the Neuilly plot. Freed by the amnesty of 1837, he left for London but soon returned to Paris. Once again he was put in jail, this time for conspiracy to assassinate the king. Freed by the Revolution of February 1848, he returned to Paris, presided over the Alsatian Club, and was a member of the Society of the Rights of Man and the Club of Clubs. The Revolutionary Committee selected him as a candidate in the Parisian elections for the Constituent Assembly along with Armand Barbès, Louis Blanc, Marc Caussidière, Alexandre-Auguste Ledru-Rollin, Pierre Leroux, Pierre-Joseph Proudhon, François-Vincent Raspail, and others.

Huber played an important role in organizing the demonstrations of 15 May. It was he who led the clubs toward the National Assembly to deliver a petition in favor of Poland. He seized control of the rostrum and declared the Assembly dissolved. After the authorities had suppressed the resulting riot, Huber was arrested and then freed by the order of the mayor of the fourth arrondissement.

He fled to London, and consequently he was not tried along with those responsible for the uprising of 15 May. The former secretary-general of the Paris prefecture of police said that Huber had been a police agent since 1837. Huber returned to France to defend himself, and accused Raspail, Louis-Auguste Blanqui, and Caussidière of trying to defend themselves by accusing him in absentia.

The high court sentenced him to deportation on 12 October 1849. Imprisoned at Doullens and then at Belle-Ile, he was pardoned during the Empire and became a public works contractor. He continued to stay in touch with Proudhon.

L. Blanc, *Révélations historiques*, vol. 2 (Leipzig, 1859); *Dictionnaire biographique du Mouvement ouvrier français, 1789–1864*, vol. 3 (Paris, 1964–65); E.-J.-L. Garnier-Pagès, *Histoire de la Révolution de 1848* (Paris, 1861–72); G. Lefrancais, *Souvenirs d'un révolutionnaire* (Brussels, 1902).

Jean-Claude Caron, trans. E. Newman

Related entries: BARBES; BLANC; BLANQUI, L.-A.; CAUSSIDIERE; CLUB OF CLUBS; CLUBS, POLITICAL; DEMONSTRATIONS OF 1848–1849; LEDRU-ROLLIN; LEROUX; MUNICIPAL COMMISSION; PROUDHON; RASPAIL; REVOLUTION OF 1848; SOCIETY OF THE RIGHTS OF MAN.

HUGO, VICTOR (1802–1885), poet, playwright, novelist, prolific genius, leader and inspired guiding force of the French romantic movement. The character and personality of both his parents had much to do with the sheer strength, the burning ambition, the unflagging determination, the inner discipline, and the boundless vitality that were his own essential traits. His father, Joseph-Léopold-Sigisbert Hugo, came from a family of farmers and woodworkers from Nancy. From a simple soldier in the Beauvais Regiment in 1788, he earned a commission by 1790. As a dashing commandant, he met Sophie Françoise Trébuchet from Nantes and married her in a civil ceremony in Paris on 19 November 1797. Their marriage had begun to tear apart when Victor Marie Hugo was born at Besançon on 26 February 1802. Less than a year after his birth, his mother was romantically involved with the anti-Bonapartist General Victor Lahorie, and his father, a Bonapartist, with Catherine Thomas, henceforth the love of his life. In February 1804, Sophie Hugo, shortly after her husband's promotion to colonel, settled in Paris with her children. In 1811 Victor, as a student at the Collège des jeunes nobles, absorbed the impressions and visions that would profoundly influence his work and find expression in *Hernani* and *Ruy Blas*. He acquired a knowledge of Latin and Roman culture that would consistently reveal itself in all his literary production. Because of his frequent shifts between Paris and his father's assigned residences, coupled with his parents' troubles and outside interests, Victor's early education was unstructured, sporadic, and superficial. A multitude of ill-digested bits of knowledge flooded the imagination of the young poet at a time when splendid spectacles of Napoleonic glory offered ample visual stimulation.

In 1814, the final chapter of matrimonial crisis caused Sophie Hugo to move the children to another Paris address. While the divorce case was pending, the children reverted to General Hugo, who immediately boarded them at the *pension Cordier*. At thirteen, then, the budding writer began to study philosophy and mathematics, but, for nearly four years, he was really involved in a poetic apprenticeship. The walls of Cordier and of the Lycée Louis-le-Grand witnessed the rapid development of an ambitious bard. His classical training caused him to begin in 1816 by translating passages from Horace and Virgil and by composing a prose comedy and two classical tragedies in verse, *Athélie* and *Irtamène*. It was then, however, that he boldly declared, "Je veux être Chateaubriand ou rien," and began to pursue his own inspiration by invoking his memories of Spain, where he had lived with his father, in a prose drama, *Inez de Castro*. Though only a teenager, his spontaneous genius and tremendous confidence compelled him to tackle *Le Déluge*, the first of the broad epic topics he would confront during his life. What is most striking is the profusion of these early works which earned him a *mention* by the Académie française for an essay in 1817, gold flowers for two odes by the Académie des jeux floraux of Toulouse in 1819, and a stipend from the king in 1820 for his *Ode sur la mort du duc de Berry*. It was enough to bring to the fore a more pronounced royalist-Catholic zeal that would generate a series of these official *Odes*. In June of that year, as Victor was courting his childhood friend, Adèle Foucher, he turned to the novel, producing an initial version of *Bug-Jargal*, an exotic short novel illustrating the ravages of jealousy. For two years, Victor Hugo sharpened his critical judgment by studying Mme. de Stäel's *De l'Allemagne* and digesting the works of André-Marie de Chénier, Alphonse de Lamartine, François-René de Chateaubriand, Charles Nodier, and Walter Scott. His prizes had also produced contacts in the literary community. Alexandre Soumet, Alexandre Guiraud, and Jules de Rességuier, who had judged his poems in Toulouse, now became his friends in Paris and introduced him in the Emile Deschamps salon, where he witnessed the first romantic deeds and began a close friendship with Alfred de Vigny. In February 1821, he complemented that literary commitment with political and religious ones by joining the Société des bonnes lettres. His first collection, *Odes et poésies diverses*, was published in 1821 and earned its author a royal reward of 1,000 francs. This enhanced the wedding celebration held in October 1822. Within eight years, the Hugos would be parents of five children.

Hugo was confident that the choice of the dignified *ode* and his praise of classicism in his book's preface would ingratiate him with the ultraroyalists and pave the way for him as another Lamartine. He also helped to found in 1823 a new Catholic, ultra, romantic journal, *La Muse francaise*. In March 1824 appeared a second collection entitled *Nouvelles odes*, whose preface, one of the early manifestos of the great romantic debate, was an attempt to reconcile classicism with a revolutionary romanticism.

The death of Louis XVIII in September resulted in several benefits for the Hugo family. Its members had strongly supported the comte d'Artois, who as Charles X could now bestow rewards. The elder Hugo became a lieutenant general. In April 1825, both Victor Hugo and Lamartine became chevaliers in the Légion d'honneur, and Hugo and his friend and supporter Nodier attended the king's coronation at Reims in May. By 1826, Hugo, having proved himself as a poet and novelist, realized that it was urgent that he challenge the classical diehards and that he could do it only by showing true talent as a dramatist, so in August he started work on *Cromwell*.

Hugo's preface to *Cromwell*, which appeared in 1827, made him the leader of the young Romantics, and in his new apartment on the rue Notre Dame des Champs he played host to such young writers and artists as Honoré de Balzac, Alfred de Musset, Alexandre Dumas, Prosper Mérimée, Gérard de Nerval, Théophile Gautier, and Eugène Delacroix. Thus was officially constituted the famous *cénacle* of the romantic school with a leader, a doctrine, a meeting place, and even a publicity agent and critic in the person of Charles-Augustin Sainte-Beuve, recently befriended by Hugo, and sympathetic journals such as *Le Globe* and *Le Mercure*. For the first time, both republicans and monarchists could overlook their political differences to focus on literature. Hugo openly declared that he wanted to become the French Shakespeare and that *Cromwell* was in fact a Shakespearean drama. French audiences, which had rejected the presentations of an English Shakespearean troupe in 1822, applauded them when they were repeated in 1827.

Thus, Victor Hugo, at the age of twenty-five mature beyond his years, became the guide of the romantic movement, and his career entered a new phase. In 1829 he spent less than a month creating *Hernani*, which was promptly accepted by the Théâtre-français. The play depicted the love of two young people who, fighting tradition and social constraints, prevailed only in death. Despite bouts with the censors and with organized opposition in the audience, the play, whose premiere was held on 25 February 1830, ran for forty-five performances. Victor Hugo emerged a celebrity and romanticism a victorious aesthetic. His great novel, *Notre-Dame de Paris*, was published in March 1831.

Victor Hugo was a good father who adored his four children, but the demands and activities of an astonishingly successful career had caused him to neglect his wife. A love triangle with his close friend, Sainte-Beuve, as the rival, resulted. In 1831, Hugo had conquered fame as a writer, and the blow to his domestic happiness made him enter a period of more than a decade of intensive work on poems and plays. Henceforth, youthful exuberance gave way to somber reality as four books of verse and five historical dramas alternated during those adult years: *Les Feuilles d'automne* (1831); *Le Roi s'amuse* (1839), *Lucrèce Borgia* (1833), *Marie Tudor* (1833), and *Claude Gueux* (1834).

In 1841, Hugo was elected to the Académie française. His literary goals ostensibly achieved, he set out to attain political success. Caught up by Restoration attitudes, by the *Bonnes Lettres* philosophies, and Chateaubriand "fever," as well as influenced by his mother, Victor Hugo, to the age of twenty-five, had been a staunch royalist. However, by 1827, as he founded the *cénacle* and established the close friendship with Sainte-Beuve, his views had become markedly more liberal, and, out of loyalty to his father, he became a Bonapartist, contributing much through his writings during subsequent years to the Napoleonic legend of glory. During the 1830s, his political ideas evolved to the republican side, despite a sentimental attachment to the figure of the bourgeois king, and his concern for social issues increased. The idea of liberty was crucial to him, and his short novels reflected it. He even outlined in *La Presse* in 1836 a social reform program compatible with the Orléans monarchy. As a poet committed to and involved in France's progress, he was delighted when, following the accidental death of the duc d'Orléans in July 1842 and Hugo's sincere expression of sadness in an official speech as a close friend of the duchesse and as director of the Académie that year, Louis-Philippe invited him to visit the palace more often.

For the subsequent decade, Hugo's writing instincts compelled him to note, in a sort of gossip column format, descriptions and conversations of court happenings. The verbal sketches spanning the 1840–50 period were collected in an entertaining book, *Choses vues*. The author's only other literary project during that decade was a novel entitled at that time *Jean Tréjean* and then *Les Misères* (not to be published as *Les Misérables* until 1862), on which he spent most of 1847. His literary life really amounted to his duties at the Institute, including the probably unpleasant task of welcoming his wife's lover, Sainte-Beuve, to the Académie ranks just before his former friend had the boldness to publish his *Livre d'amour* of poems to Adèle Hugo.

His political life really began when Louis-Philippe signed a decree in April 1845 naming him a Peer of France. He made several key speeches in the upper chamber as a liberal monarchist on such subjects as literary and artistic property rights, social injustice, and the unrest of the masses. The events of 1848 were no surprise to him.

As the crucial drama of late February unfolded, Hugo's status abruptly changed when, on 24 February, the Chamber of Peers was dissolved. He favored democracy but preferred at that moment a liberal monarchy in the form of a regency by the duchesse d'Orléans. The plan was rejected, and he had no problem then siding with the republicans in the Provisional Government. The following day, he was elected provisional mayor of a Paris arrondissement. At the April general elections, Hugo, though not a declared candidate, received 60,000 votes but was not elected to the Constituent Assembly. In June, however, he won a by-election as a member of the moderate Right to a Paris seat in the Assembly by some 87,000 votes. He took his duties very seriously. One of his first speeches discussed the National Workshops and, though he helped the National Guard dismantle the barricades, he abhorred General Eugène Cavaignac's suppression of the June revolt. In August 1848, he helped his sons, Charles and François-Victor, and friends to found *L'Evènement*, a newspaper that supported the candidacy of Louis-Napoleon Bonaparte as president. Hugo had little confidence in Alphonse de Lamartine, feared Cavaignac, and hoped that he could become mentor to the nephew of the great Bonaparte as Mme. de Staël had tried to be to the uncle.

Although he was associated with the Right, Hugo often supported the Left in the Legislative Assembly to which he was elected on 13 May 1849. He opposed the Roman expedition, supported left-wing efforts to fight poverty, and expressed approval of the U.S. abolitionist movement. By 1851, he was aware of the intentions of the prince-president and his cohorts and he attacked him in his famous, passionate speech against *Napoléon le petit*. Both his sons were imprisoned in subsequent weeks. Still, Hugo was surprised by the swiftness of the December 2 coup d'état. As a member of the resistance committee, he moved from one secret refuge to another aided by his faithful mistress, Juliette, attempting at the risk of his life to organize the protestors. Finally accepting defeat, he was able, again with her help, to obtain a false passport and to flee to Brussels, where he arrived on 12 December. On 9 January 1852, President Bonaparte issued a decree condemning Victor Hugo to exile. Thus ended the busiest, most painful, and least literary decade of his life.

From the age of fifty for nearly twenty more years, Victor Hugo would complete his development and become a mature poet-philosopher. He began this second stage of his literary life by spending seven months in Brussels where, in 1852, he composed a scathing pamphlet, *Napoléon-le-Petit*, and *l'Histoire d'un crime*, an obviously biased description of the coup d'état that was not published until 1877. His compulsion to vent his wrath was irresistible for a time and he was haunted by the idea of crime and punishment. From his residence on the channel island of Jersey, he wrote *Les Châtiments*, a masterpiece of satirical verse begun in October 1852, shortly before the plebiscite that created the Second Empire, and published more than a year later in Brussels. During the winter of 1854, it circulated underground in France since Hugo was widely accepted in absentia as the leader of republican resistance.

In April 1869 Victor Hugo published his social novel, *Les Misérables*. The saga of Jean Valjean, in preparation for more than 15 years, depicted the lot of the downtrodden with as much realism as Eugène Sue, but it did so with a note of compassion and a plea for pity.

By the time he returned to Paris after Napoleon's fall in 1870, he had become a legend in the capital, which was enough to secure his election by 214,000 votes as a deputy following the Prussian siege. In the Assembly, he was a referee between the provisional government moderates and the radicals of the Commune. Since he had supporters in both groups, he had the trust of neither and, persisting in his idea of a United States of Europe, he resigned in frustration after only three weeks. After publishing his historical account of the humiliating events of the war and the siege, *L'Année terrible*, he sought peace and solitude in Guernesey. His active writing career appropriately ended in 1875–76 with his memoirs, *Actes et Paroles*, in three volumes. This creative activity revived his popularity enough for his election as a senator from Paris in 1876. He was a national figure more respected for his literary and social achievements than for his political effectiveness, but he continued to plead for amnesty for the *communards* and to defend liberty.

He died of pneumonia on May 15, 1885. His body lay in state under the *Arc de Triomphe*, his funeral was a national event, and his ashes were solemnly borne to interment in the *Panthéon*.

Victor Hugo overshadows most of the world's writers by his productivity, his versatility, his originality and his sheer talent. Though his dramas and novels contributed significantly to the development of those genres, his true greatness derives from his poetry. The awesome power of his vivid imagination, his creativeness, his sensitivity, his vision of the world as a world of contrasts brought him astounding success and recognition.

J.-B. Barrère, *Victor Hugo, l'homme et l'oeuvre* (Paris, 1968); E. Biré, *Victor Hugo après 1830* (Paris, 1891), *Victor Hugo après 1852* (Paris, 1894), and *Victor Hugo avant 1830* (Paris, 1883); R. Escholier, *Un Amant de Génie, Victor Hugo* (Paris, 1979); H. Guillemin, *Victor Hugo par lui-même* (Paris, 1951); J. P. Houston, *Victor Hugo* (New York, 1973); Mme. V. Hugo, *Victor Hugo raconté par un témoin de sa vie* (Paris, 1863); H. Juin, *Victor Hugo, 1802–1843*, vol. 1 (Paris, 1980); A. Maurois, *Olympio ou la vie de Victor Hugo* (Paris, 1954); H. Peyre, *Hugo* (Paris, 1972); J. Richardson, *Victor Hugo* (New York, 1976); P. Souchon, *Victor Hugo, L'homme et l'oeuvre* (Paris, 1949).

Paul Comeau

Related entries: ACADEMIE FRANCAISE; ARSENAL, SALON OF; BAL-ZAC; CAVAIGNAC, L.-E.; CHATEAUBRIAND; COUP D'ETAT OF 2 DE-CEMBER 1851; CORONATION OF CHARLES X; DAVID; DELACROIX; DUMAS, A.; *LE GLOBE*; GUIRAUD; *HERNANI*; LOUIS-PHILIPPE; *MER-CURE DU XIX SIECLE*; MERIMEE; *LA MUSE FRANCAISE*; MUSSET; NER-VAL; NODIER; *LA PRESSE*; RESSEGUIER; ROMAN EXPEDITION; ROMANTICISM; SAINTE-BEUVE; SALON D'EMILE DESCHAMPS; SOU-MET; ULTRAROYALISTS; VIGNY; VILLELE.

HUNDRED DAYS (23 MARCH–8 JULY 1815), the period of time between the First and Second Bourbon Restoration when Napoleon I returned from exile and took power. The phrase was coined by Gilbert de Chabrol de Volvic, prefect of the Seine, in his speech welcoming back Louis XVIII: ''A hundred days have passed since that fatal moment when Your Majesty left his capital.''

After Napoleon's defeat by the Allies and his first abdication (11 April 1814), the Bourbon monarchy was restored to France by the victorious powers to create a stable, nonrevolutionary, and nonaggressive government. The new king accepted a constitution, the Charter, modeled after the British system and giving substantial powers to a legislature elected by the wealthiest of the adult male citizens. There was opposition to the new government for political reasons and because it had been imposed on France by foreign victors.

Napoleon was forced into a pleasant exile on the island of Elba in the Mediterranean. He ruled his own little state, organized the construction of roads and a theater, and kept in touch with the unrest in France through foreign visitors and French and English newspapers.

On 5 March 1815 Napoleon and his followers arrived in four small ships on the south coast of France. The tricolor flag was flown. A proclamation was issued listing Napoleon's victorious battles and stating, "Soldiers you have not been beaten! . . . Your general [is] called to the throne by the voice of the people . . . come rejoin him." The Bourbon throne was called illegitimate, not having been established by the nation. Napoleon warned that the people were menaced by the possible return of mandatory church tithes and feudal rights and privileges. The king's soldiers, rather than resisting, cried "Vive l'Empereur."

Word of Napoleon's landing reached Paris on 5 March. A royal ordinance called him a rebel and traitor and instructed all government officials to pursue and arrest him. He was received in triumph by 2,000 peasants in Grenoble on 6 March. Soldiers refused to fire on him, and the city gates were opened. On 10 March Napoleon was welcomed in Lyons by a mob crying, "Long live the emperor," "Down with priests," "Death to royalists," and "Hang the Bourbons." The rapid and triumphal march continued north with garrisons joining him in town after town.

On 14 March 1815 Marshal Michel Ney, having promised the king to bring Napoleon back in a cage, met him and joined his forces. The liberal journals in Paris raged against Napoleon. Benjamin Constant called him "the man dyed with our blood." The liberal leader and hero of the American Revolution, the marquis de Lafayette, appeared wearing the white cockade of the Bourbons. As Napoleon approached Paris, the king, speaking to the legislature, said that although he was sixty years old, he would die in battle for his country and that "all the French love the Charter and I will maintain it." The duke of Blacas, who had lived with the king in exile in England, suggested that the king, in an open carriage surrounded by the legislators, should meet Napoleon on the road as "Attila would be driven back by such a procession." Calmer heads prevailed, and the king left Paris on 19 March 1815 and crossed the border into Belgium four days later. On 20 March Napoleon arrived in Paris. Some members of the royal family stayed in France, and the duchess of Angoulême tried to organize troops against Napoleon in Bordeaux, an act that the emperor said made her "the only man in the family."

A free press was reborn in Paris at this time, and Revolutionary demands not heard for twenty years reappeared. Hatred of the church and aristocracy was rampant. Heard were the cries, "Down with the priests" and "Aristocrats to the lampposts [hang them]." But Napoleon did not wish to restart the Revolution. He retained most of the king's top officers. Lazare-Nicolas-Marguérite Carnot, a famous Revolutionary, joined Napoleon's government and accepted the aristocratic title of count from him.

Napoleon had no coherent political program, however, considering himself above "factions." Under his previous Empire, the government had been a peculiar blend of egalitarian slogans and military dictatorship. The Empire was egalitarian, however, in that anyone who could serve Napoleon, regardless of origins or previous politics, could attain high position. Napoleon himself was seen as an example of a person from a lowly background (actually his family was minor nobility) whose talents had taken him to the top. But much of his appeal came from association with French military glory. At one time all of Europe, except England, had been under his power to some degree. France, Germany west of the Rhine, and parts of Italy comprised the French Empire ruled directly by Napoleon. He named his brothers kings of Holland, Westphalia (which he created in Germany), southern Italy, and Spain. He imposed alliances on the other continental countries. Compare this to the bland government of Louis XVIII, brought to France, according to some, "in the baggage train of the invading Allies."

Napoleon formed a commission to write a constitution. Carnot wanted a government based on a large suffrage, but most of the commission wanted the right to vote restricted to the "active citizens," who paid the most taxes—that is, the rich landowners in the country and the bourgeoisie in the cities. The final constitution was written by Benjamin Constant, a liberal who a month earlier had called Napoleon "Attila" and "Ghengis Khan." This constitution was called an Additional Act to the constitutions of the Empire, thus ignoring the short period of Bourbon Restoration. It included religious freedom, trial by jury, free press, and the right of the legislators to object to the king's ministers. There was a hereditary Chamber of Peers named by the emperor. The lower house of the legislature, the Chamber of Representatives, had 368 members elected from small districts, 238 from the departments, and 23 elected by commercial and industrial leaders.

This new constitution was practically a carbon copy of the Charter it replaced. There was a plebiscite on this constitution, and it passed overwhelmingly, but only about one-fourth of those eligible voted, and one-fourth of these were soldiers. There was also a very low turnout for the first election to the Chamber of Representatives. Eighty pure Bonapartists were elected, 40 ultra-Left Jacobins, and the rest were moderates.

There was little time for this government to operate. On 25 March the exiled king had signed the Allied treaty against Napoleon. On 18 June 1815 Napoleon was conclusively defeated at Waterloo by English troops commanded by the duke of Wellington and Prussians under Gebhard von Blücher. Napoleon abdicated three days later. A French Republic was out of the question, but there were several alternatives to a Bourbon restoration, such as Marshal Jean-Baptiste Bernadotte, Napoleon's son, and the liberal duke of Orléans. But Wellington, commander of the coalition forces in France, came out for Louis, and with the maneuvering of the brilliant opportunist Joseph Fouché, he was returned to the throne.

France was punished by the Allies for Napoleon's return by having its borders moved back to the 1790 lines rather than the 1792 borders given in 1814. In addition the victors demanded a 700 million franc (about $140 million) indemnity.

The restored king's first act was to issue a proclamation admitting previous mistakes, promising to uphold the Charter, and forgiving those who had gone astray (by supporting Napoleon). However, he refused to pardon those "instigators and authors of the horrible plot." This position was to play a role in the White Terror that followed.

G. de Bertier de Sauvigny, *The Bourbon Restoration* (Philadelphia, 1966); E. Lavisse, *Histoire de France contemporaine* (Paris, 1921).

Don Smith

Related entries: ACTE ADDITIONNEL; ANGOULEME, M.-T.-C.; BLACAS D'AULPS; CARNOT, L.-N.-M.; CHABROL DE VOLVIC; CHARTER OF 1814; CONSTANT; FOUCHE; LAFAYETTE, M.-J.-P.-Y.-R.-G.; LOUIS XVIII; NEY; RESTORATION, SECOND; WATERLOO, BATTLE OF.

HUNDRED SWISS. See SWISS GUARD.

HUSSEIN, DEY OF ALGIERS (1773–1838), defeated head of state in the French takeover of Algiers in 1830. Hussein came to Algiers from Smyrna as a merchant. He joined the militia and became the minister of the interior under Ali Pasha, whom he succeeded in March 1818. Hussein had a reputation for justice and religious toleration; however, his relations with France, and with its consul in Algiers, Pierre Deval, deteriorated progressively. Hussein took up a claim against the French government on behalf of two Algerian Jews, Bacri and Busnach, who demanded 14 million francs for having supplied Napoleon's armies in Egypt. The French government paid 4.5 million but refused to pay the rest, claiming that Bacri and Busnach owed money to French and Jewish merchants. Bacri and Deval were almost certainly working in collusion against Hussein, who wrote to Charles X asking for payment. When Hussein's letter was not answered, Hussein called in Deval and asked for an explanation. Deval insulted the dey, who hit him with his fly whisk. Both men attempted to minimize the incident, but the French government chose to make an issue of it. They blockaded Algiers from 1827 to 1829 at a cost of 20 million francs. When this produced no softening in Hussein's position, they sent an expedition of 27,000 sailors and 41,000 soldiers under Marshal Louis-Auguste-Victor de Bourmont in 1830. After a siege lasting approximately one month, Hussein surrendered Algiers on 5 July 1830. He was allowed to leave Algiers with his family and 10 million francs. After visiting France and Italy, he settled in Alexandria.

C.-A. Julien, *L'histoire de l'Algérie contemporaine* (Paris, 1964).

Douglas Porch

Related entries: ALGIERS, EXPEDITION TO; BOURMONT; CHARLES X.

HYDE DE NEUVILLE, JEAN-GUILLAUME, BARON (1776–1857), deputy, minister, and diplomat of the Restoration. Born at la Charité-sur-Loire (Nièvre) on 24 January 1776, Hyde de Neuville was the son of an English family who had fled to France during the 1745 Jacobite uprising. While a student at the Collège Cardinal-Lemoine in Paris, he participated in various counter-Revolutionary organizations, and at one point he went to Paris in a futile effort to save Marie Antoinette. In 1797 he was involved with the royalist club in

Clichy and after 18 Brumaire Hyde became one of the most active agents of the Bourbons, who made him their representative in Brittany. He even dared propose to Napoleon the restoration of the Bourbons. Accused of complicity in the "infernal machine" plot of 24 December 1800, he emigrated to the United States, arriving in New York in 1806.

Hyde returned to France in June 1814 and, having frequently risked his life for the Bourbon cause, was warmly received by Louis XVIII. The king sent him to England to negotiate peace with the United States and then to try secretly to arrange the transfer of Napoleon from Elba to a more distant exile. During the Hundred Days, which interrupted these latter efforts, Hyde joined the king at Ghent. After Waterloo he hastened to Paris, where he was instrumental in convincing various army commanders to support the Bourbons. His efforts earned him the Legion of Honor. In August 1815 the department of Nièvre elected him to the Chamber of Deputies where, although he spoke as an extreme ultra, he voted somewhat more moderately. In January 1816 the king named him minister to the United States, where he remained until 1821. There he negotiated a commercial treaty to settle conflicts over the Louisiana purchase treaty. Also, in spite of his own royalist convictions, he was quite solicitous about the welfare of various former imperial officers living in exile in the United States. The king rewarded him with the title of baron and the Order of Saint Louis and promoted him to grand cross of the Legion of Honor.

In November 1822 the Nièvre again elected him to the Deputies. He declined the Constantinople embassy to occupy this seat, resuming his ultra contribution as a follower of François-René de Chateaubriand. He especially demanded the suspension but not expulsion from the Chamber of the liberal deputy Jacques-Antoine Manuel. Hyde became ambassador to Portugal in 1823. During the abortive palace coup led by Dom Miguel in April 1824, Hyde supported King John VI and offered him the use of French troops. But Paris disapproved, and Villèle recalled him in December 1824. Returning to the Deputies, he became a harsh critic of the Villèle ministry, especially its Spanish policies. His criticism cost him his diplomatic pension. He also defended intervention in Greece and spoke on behalf of the *rentiers* who had been ruined by the Revolution. Two departments reelected him in 1827 on a broad base of support.

Hyde now became a major leader of the opposition to Joseph de Villèle and a member of the Agier group of royalist dissidents. Thus he contributed to Villèle's fall. To this end he even collaborated with various liberals. With Chateaubriand's backing, he became minister of marine in the Martignac cabinet. There he worked for freedom for the Greeks, improved the French colonial administration, and opposed the black slave trade. In early 1829 he tried to arrange the appointment of Chateaubriand to the cabinet. When he resigned his post in August 1829 at the fall of the cabinet, the king rejected him for a seat in the new ministry. Hyde thus joined the opposition to the Polignac government.

As a staunch supporter of the Charter, he attempted to prevent the impending debacle in 1830. The July 1830 elections returned him to the Deputies. There during the July Revolution he was the strongest supporter of the Bourbon family, speaking on their behalf on 30 July and protesting their dethronement until 7 August. When the final vote on dethronement was taken, he resigned from the Deputies and retired to private life. He continued only minor participation in political affairs, but in 1836 he went to visit Charles X and Bordeaux at Prague. The royalist club of the rue Duphot in Paris nominated him as a candidate in the May 1849 elections to the Assembly, but he received only a few votes. In 1851 he led the opposition to the democratic movement in Sancerre (Cher) that opposed Louis Napoleon's coup. Hyde de Neuville died in Paris on 28 May 1857. His *Mémoires et souvenirs* were published in 1888–92.

Archives parlementaires; H. Contamine, *Diplomatie et diplomates sous la restauration* (Paris, 1970); R. McLemore, *Franco-American Diplomatic Relations, 1816–1836* (Baton Rouge, 1941); A. Robert et al., *Dictionnaire des parlementaires français* (Paris, 1889–91).

James K. Kieswetter

Related entries: BORDEAUX; CHATEAUBRIAND; COUP D'ETAT OF 2 DE-CEMBER 1851; MANUEL; MARTIGNAC; POLIGNAC; SPAIN, 1823 FRENCH INVASION OF; ULTRAROYALISTS; VILLELE.

I

ICARIAN COMMUNISM. See CABET.

IDEOLOGUES, originally pejorative, then descriptive label for a circle of physicians, philosophers, and liberal writers active chiefly between 1795 and 1810, applicable to several significant survivors during the constitutional monarchy. In a memoir read to the Class of Moral and Political Sciences of the Institute on 20 June 1796, Antoine-Louis-Claude Destutt de Tracy defined ideology as a science of ideas in place of "psychology" or "metaphysics." He also subdivided it into rational ideology (theory of knowledge, mental faculties, habit, grammar, logic) and physiological ideology (relations of physiology to intelligence, character, mental and emotional states). Concurrently, his colleague and friend P.-J.-G. Cabanis read memoirs to the Institute later collected and expanded (1802) as *Rapports du physique et du moral de l'homme.* Cabanis and Tracy shared a vigorous anticlericalism and metaphysical monism (though critics misinterpreted it as mechanical materialism). They revised Etienne de Condillac's theory of knowledge and the mind and aspired to extend ideology to a naturalistic ethics and a post-Revolutionary science of society.

During the Directory the Tracy-Cabanis circle supported the moderate Republic against royalists and neo-Jacobins. Enthusiasts for the Brumaire coup, they broke with Bonaparte on civil liberties (such as the special courts of 1801) and on the religious revival. Although they called themselves ideologists, the derisive term *idéologue* appeared in the right-wing *Messager des relations extérieures* on 12 January 1800 and later in the works of François-René de Chateaubriand and statements of Bonaparte himself. Marx discarded the narrowly descriptive term to retain a pejorative connotation of *ideology* in his manuscripts of the 1840s. The open break between Bonaparte and the *idéologues* became evident in the purge of the Tribunate and suppression of the central schools in 1802 and in the abolition of the Class of Moral and Political Sciences in January 1803, even though the *idéologues* numbered only thirteen of seventy-two members and associates.

Scholars have loosely defined the *idéologues*, but one may suggest four empirical criteria: (1) an essential condition of authorship of a work of philosophy, grammar, literary history, physiology, ethics, legislation, or economics consistent with Tracy's goals, and conditions of personal or political affinity, (2) attendance at the salons of Mme. Helvétius, Cabanis, or Mme. Condorcet from 1794 to 1809; (3) editing or reviewing for *La Décade philosophique*, a sympathetic periodical; and (4) commitment to a moderate Republic after 1794. The core group, meeting three of the four criteria, consists of Tracy, Cabanis, C.-F. Volney, D.-J. Garat, P.-C.-F. Daunou, E.-J. Sieyès, P.-L. Ginguené, F.-S. Andrieux, M.-J. Chénier, F. Thurot, J.-M. Degérando, and physician P. Roussel. A peripheral group meeting two criteria includes P. Laromiguière, F.-P. Maine de Biran, P.-L. Roederer, J.-B. Say, F.-F.-W. Jacquemont, J.-A.-C. Gallois, C. Fauriel, and physicians P. Pinel, J.-J. Moreau de la Sarthe, J.-L. Alibert, and B.-A. Richerand.

After 1815 the surviving *idéologues* lost coherence as a philosophical movement. Degérando, Maine de Biran, and even the staunch Condillacian Laromiguière had long proclaimed their dualist inclinations. The philosophical ascendancy of Pierre Royer-Collard and Victor Cousin promoted acceptance of an active, immaterial soul. The reputation of Cabanis and Tracy as dogmatic materialists made them easy targets during the Restoration. Yet this was also the period of diffusion of Tracy's political and economic works and of Daunou's historical lectures at the Collège de France. In 1832 Guizot reunited the surviving *idéologues* with a younger group in the new Academy of Moral and Political Sciences. Some scholars have argued for a natural transition between *idéologue* philosophy and positivism and between *idéologue* political thought and post–1830 liberal republicanism.

A. Guillois, *Le salon de Madame Helvétius* (Paris, 1893); G. Gusdorf, *La conscience révolutionnaire, les Ideologues* (Paris, 1978); B. Head, *Ideology and Social Science* (Dordrecht, 1985); T. Kaiser, "The Idéologues" (Ph.D. diss., Harvard University, 1976); E. Kennedy, *A Philosophe in the Age of Revolution* (Philadelphia, 1978); S. Moravia, *Il pensiero degli Idéologues* (Florence, 1974) and *Il tramonto dell'illuminismo* (Bari, 1968); F. Picavet, *Les idéologues* (Paris, 1891); M. Régaldo, *Un milieu intellectuel*, 5 vols. (Paris-Lille, 1976); M. Staum, *Cabanis* (Princeton, 1980); C. Welch, *Liberty and Utility* (New York, 1984).

Martin S. Staum

Related entries: CABANIS; CHATEAUBRIAND; COLLEGE DE FRANCE; COMTE, A.; COUSIN; DAUNOU; DESTUTT DE TRACY; GARAT; GERANDO; GUIZOT; MARX; PINEL; ROYER-COLLARD; SAY; SIEYES; VOLNEY.

IMBRAHIM PASHA (1789–1848), viceroy of Egypt from September to November 1848. Imbrahim, son of Méhémet Ali, viceroy of Egypt, was born in Cavala (Macedonia) in 1789. He took up a military career and put down revolts by the Bedouins of Upper Egypt and then by the Wahabites of Arabia in the period 1816–19. After conquering the two holy cities of Mecca and Medina, he became popular and received the title of pasha.

At the request of Sultan Mahmoud II, Méhémet Ali sent his son and 20,000 men to fight the Greek rebels. Imbrahim took Navarino in 1825, ravaged Greece, and conquered Missolonghi (1825) before being defeated by the French, Russian, and English fleets at the battle of Navarino on 28 October 1827. Imbrahim, on his father's orders, signed the surrender asked for by General Nicolas-Joseph Maison and returned to Cairo.

In 1831 and 1832 Egypt conquered Syria with Imbrahim's help. This revolt against the sultan and against Constantinople alerted France and Russia, which imposed a peace treaty on the belligerents in 1833. The war broke out again, but the Austrians and the English intervened again in 1840 and forced Imbrahim to retreat. He now went for reasons of health first to Montpellier and then to Paris in 1845, where he was welcomed by Louis-Philippe. He also went to England.

His father abdicated due to ill health in September 1848, but Imbrahim, who was also ill, survived him by only a few weeks and died in Cairo on 10 November 1848.

P. Crabites, *Imbrahim of Egypt* (London, 1935); General Weygand, *Histoire militaire de Mohammed Aly et de ses fils*, 2 vols. (Paris, 1936).

Jean-Claude Caron, trans. E. Newman
Related entries: MEHEMET ALI; NAVARINO, BATTLE OF.

INDEMNITY BILL OF 1825, the attempt to settle the issue of properties confiscated during the Revolution. Charles X of France succeeded his brother, Louis XVIII, as king in September 1824. Before 1789, as the comte d'Artois, his compromising conduct with Marie Antoinette and his stubborn opposition to most efforts at reform contributed to the coming of the Revolution. In exile (1789–1814) the count was the leader of *émigré* nobles and prelates of the Catholic church, whose objective was to reverse the institutional changes inaugurated during the 1789–95 period and restore the throne and altar to their pre-Revolutionary status. During the reign of Louis XVIII, Artois was the leader of the ultraroyalist faction, which was very critical of the significant portions of the Revolutionary legacy incorporated in the Charter of 1814. Thus it comes as no surprise that when the comte d'Artois finally became king, the great measures of his reign were interpreted by many as constituting an attempt to restore the *ancien régime*.

On 3 January 1825, the ministry headed by the comte Joseph de Villèle presented bills to the Chamber of Deputies and the Chamber of Peers that were representative of those introduced during the reign. The first proposed legislation involved an indemnity to the *émigrés*, as well as compensation to the heirs of the proscribed Girondists and other victims of the Revolutionary confiscations. For many years the ultras had been protesting against the irrevocability of the sales of national property guaranteed by the Charter, maintaining that the *émigrés*, who had been despoiled during the Revolution, should either have their lands restored or be paid an indemnity.

Revolutionary legislation had legalized the confiscation of *émigré* property and that of other citizens who had seen fit, at one time or another, to oppose the faction in control at the moment. The various French governments of the 1790s, desperately needing cash, then sold the nationalized properties at reduced prices to relatively well-to-do peasants, to members of the moneyed middle class, and to out-and-out speculators. Those who had been dispossessed were bitter, and Napoleon, looking for support, attempted to placate some of those whose properties had been confiscated by permitting them the enjoyment of portions of their former estates. After his downfall in 1814, a law sponsored by the government of Louis XVIII returned such of the *émigré* properties as the state still controlled. The Charter, however, stipulated that "all property is inviolable, without any exceptions for that which is called national, the law making no distinction between them," and the purchasers of the national properties (those confiscated by the state during the Revolution) felt reasonably secure for the next few years.

The duc de Berry's assassination in 1820 triggered a rightward swing in French political life that had far-reaching consequences and eventually resulted in the reconsideration of the question of the confiscated holdings. Before the death of Louis XVIII four years later, a bill to compensate the *émigrés* bogged down in the Chamber of Peers after it had been approved by the lower house. The debates in the chambers were extremely heated, and old wounds, dating back to the Revolution, were reopened. Artois, who had increasingly assumed authority as Louis XVIII's health deteriorated, tried to silence the ultra press's opposition to the indemnity (the ultras demanded that the properties be returned to their former owners), and the dismissal of François-René de Chateaubriand as foreign minister was one of the by-products of this first serious attempt to reimburse the *émigrés*.

On 17 January 1825, Joseph de Villèle presented bills to the chambers that the government hoped would resolve once and for all the thorny issue of the confiscated properties. While one provided for the indemnity, another proposed a loan of a billion francs at 3 percent to finance it. One month later a committee of the Chamber of Peers reported on the bills to the full house. Immediately, debate waxed hot, and just about every event in French history since the time of Clovis was recalled as each faction reviewed the past in attempts to justify its position. The bill came under fire not only from members of the Left, who saw in the indemnity an effort to reward traitors, but also from the extreme Right, which normally questioned the legality of every Revolutionary change. François de la Bourdonnaye, a member of the ultra faction who was eager to embarrass Villèle, maintained:

If the so-called national assemblies were illegal, their decrees were null and void because they originated as acts of violence. Thus, these decrees have no validity since their enforcement ended with the violence which produced them. Thus, the *émigrés*, dispossessed in fact, but not by law, have legitimate claims to an indemnity.

La Bourdonnaye saw the measure as one validating the illegal confiscations of the Revolutionary assemblies, and he recommended that it be referred back to the committee for further study. The vicomte de Beaumont, as had la Bourdonnaye, argued that the restoration of Louis XVIII's rights in 1814 provided a legal basis for the restoration of properties to their former owners. He insisted that the indemnity should be paid to the purchasers and present holders of the former national (*émigré*) holdings and the lands returned to the families that had owned them before the Revolution. Another member of the chamber, Louis-Joseph Duplessis de Grénédan, went a step further, demanding that the properties be returned without compensation. It is interesting to note that he interpreted article IX of the Charter to mean: "All [legitimate] properties are inviolable without excepting those that one calls national." He maintained that the word *legitimate*, while not actually included in article IX, was in fact understood. Since he contended that the purchasers of national properties lacked valid titles, Grénédan demanded that former *émigré* holdings be restored to their original owners.

Liberals opposing the measure were very happy that some of the ultras found it convenient to oppose the indemnity. M. Devaux took the floor to ask why men who had fled their homeland should be treated as privileged creditors, while many who had remained in France and supported the Revolutionary changes lost not only their property but their lives as well. If the indemnity is intended "to pay a legitimate debt, it is not enough. If it is a gift, it is too much."

The vicomte de Martignac was strongly in favor of the indemnity, and he answered critics of the bill as follows:

> Every time the state contracts an obligation . . . society is expected to fulfill that obligation. . . . The unique question here, then, is to determine whether the state is obligated. . . . Now, it is the state which . . . ordered the confiscations, received the money, and spent the proceeds. Thus, it . . . owes an indemnity to those whom it has despoiled.

Speaking for the extreme Right, Bonald voted for the proposed law because he saw in it rigorous justice for the despoiled proprietors and a measure of pardon for those who had acquired confiscated holdings. What was more pleasing, in effect, than to give full legal rights to the purchasers of national property and make it possible for owners to sell their possessions at full value?

Charles used his influence to obtain passage of this legislation, hoping to reward those who had shared exile with him and seeking to strengthen the class that he considered the monarchy's chief prop. Indeed, as the *Drapeau blanc* pointed out on 11 March 1825, "The throne is occupied by an *émigré*, one of the princes who from exile addressed to these faithful servants those calls to which they have responded so nobly." And Chateaubriand, who favored the indemnity in principle but felt that the proposed measure gave Villèle too much power, pointed out: "It is for his brave companions in arms that he [the king] requests clothing. He asks for trousers for those old Bretons whom he has seen march in their bare feet around their future monarch, carrying their last pair of shoes on the end of their bayonets in order to be able to take the field for another campaign." The Chamber of Peers finally approved the bill by a vote of 221 to 130.

Many of the same arguments were repeated in the Chamber of Deputies where one of the most outspoken opponents of the bill, General Maximilien-Sébastian Foy, opposed the payment of public funds to *émigrés*, who numbered only one in a thousand in the nation. Not only had the former owners left France voluntarily, but once away they had begged foreigners to invade their homeland. Traitors to their country, they deserved to have their property confiscated, and he pointed out that many now claiming restitution could trace their ownership to gifts and grants to their ancestors after comparable confiscations of another era.

The comte de Villèle rose to defend the measure so close to his heart, explaining that all victims of the confiscations would be compensated whether they were *émigrés*, deportees, or the condemned. No special favors were being bestowed on the Parisian rich. And he asked what the fate of Louis XVIII and Charles X would have been had they remained in France during the Revolution. Obviously Villèle was of the opinion that most *émigrés* fled French soil to save their lives and had had no real freedom of choice. He pulled out the stops and exclaimed: "Our independence from the foreigner, our public liberties, the return of general peace, and the prosperity and happiness enjoyed by all, we owe to the emigration, which preserved our princes for us."

The bill passed the Chamber of Deputies by a vote of 259 to 154. An analysis of the results indicates that those who stood to profit financially from the bill generally supported it, while those with no direct pecuniary interest voted against it. As a matter of fact, 320 deputies, of whom some 266 held government posts, would receive compensation. As it turned out, a majority of the deputies voted for a bill that provided them with substantial sums from public funds. Many members of the Chamber had already received partial indemnification through the bestowal of high office and outright gifts by Louis XVIII and Charles X. Indeed, there was some substance to the charge that the government was being far too kind to the families of men who in many cases had fought against their country.

The companion bill to raise the money to pay the billion franc indemnity initiated sharp debates in the Chamber of Deputies and the Chamber of Peers but was finally approved. It was freely charged that bondholders would be cheated by the bankers as a result of the financial manipulations involved in the conversion of the *rentes*. The law, as finally approved, converted the 5 percent bonds into 3 percent at a rate of 75 francs. To liquidate the debt of 1 billion francs created by the indemnity law, Villèle divided it into five annual installments and paid it in 3 percent government bonds.

Actually the state had previously sold confiscated property valued at 1,297,760,607 francs, but property valued at 309,940,645 francs already had been returned to the dispossessed, leaving slightly less than a billion francs to be raised by the government. For those properties confiscated before 3 January 1795, special committees were assigned to study the situation in each department in terms of the depreciated *assignats*. For properties confiscated after 3 January 1795, the basis of valuation was established as twenty times the revenue of the properties in 1790.

The indemnity question penetrated to the very roots of French political and economic life. André Gain, whose work in this subject is definitive, estimates that 10 million people were concerned with the problem. Not only were the *émigrés* and their heirs most eager for compensation, but those who had purchased national property needed the confirmation of titles to their holdings, which only a final settlement could bring. The government had consistently sold these properties to individuals for sums below their true value, and it was time for this controversial issue to be resolved.

Government records listed 145,000 *émigrés*, but Gain estimates that the actual number approximated 200,000. Application for remuneration under terms of the indemnity law was made by 30,180 families; commissions created to handle these claims awarded compensation to 24,968. In addition, since nearly half the original owners were dead, claims of their beneficiaries were honored, and the number finally compensated totaled almost 70,000. Many of the exiles had owned no property, and others had managed to prevent confiscation of their lands. For France as a whole, awards averaged 45,904 francs, but variations from region to region were significant. The average payment was 3,458 francs in the Bas-Rhin; it jumped to 187,153 in the Rhône department. Those *émigrés* awarded less than 250 francs each were paid immediately, and those in this category constituted one-quarter of the claimants. The 987,819,962 francs eventually disbursed involved 452,072 properties. Gain includes some interesting statistics relative to the social classes represented by the *émigrés*. Of those receiving compensation, 32.1 percent were army officers of noble origin, 25.5 percent were nonmilitary members of the nobility, 26 percent were ecclesiastics, and 16.2 percent receiving payment belonged to neither the nobility nor the clergy. The duc d'Orléans, soon to become king Louis-Philippe, profited most from the legislation; he was awarded 12,704,691 francs. The duc de Montmorency-Luxembourg was second, but not a close one, receiving only 4,731,110 francs.

Interestingly, Charles X was not eligible for compensation under the terms of the new law. Although certain of his possessions had been confiscated, it had been established that personal holdings, once a prince assumed the responsibilities of kingship, became part of the domain of the crown. The Indemnity Law specifically excluded state property, and Charles requested that no claims be made in his behalf. However, creditors of the king, who had made loans to him and his friends during the long exile, filed claims, hoping to obtain payment of long-overdue debts. But their efforts were in vain, since the Council of the Prefecture of the Seine rejected these requests on the ground that the Indemnity Law did not apply to a prince who later became king. Charles and Villèle not only were eager to reward the faithful but hopeful that the recipients of the money would use it to buy land and restore the system of great proprietors so characteristic of the pre-Revolutionary era.

Charles X was extremely pleased by the passage of the indemnity bill; its final approval by the chambers was the greatest triumph of his reign. Indeed, it was the most important piece of legislation enacted during the Restoration era. The law gave security to the current owners of property confiscated by the state during the Revolution, and the value of these holdings was finally established at its true level. The *émigrés* and others who were indemnified could live in comfort in their old age, while peace had been restored to consciences disturbed for over a generation by problems created by the confiscations.

Villèle earmarked 100 million francs of the indemnity for a reserve fund, which he baptized ''the common fund,'' intended to compensate those who might be found at the conclusion of the liquidation to have been too scantily indemnified by the routine application of the law. This slush fund, on which so many *émigrés* had placed such high hopes, was the bond by which Villèle attached all these people to his government. Naturally, critics of the indemnity bill were unhappy with this and some of the other arrangements.

Charles X, in his speech from the throne on 3 January 1825, had described the indemnity bill as a means of healing the wounds left by the Revolution. He was right: the Indemnity Law was the most constructive and far-reaching legislation sponsored by Charles during his short reign as king. But the debates in the chambers had provided the liberals with an opportunity to attack the king and his supporters. Charles found himself riding the Revolutionary tiger from this time onward, and the government eventually was made virtually helpless by assaults on his ministers and his programs by the privileged middle class (or classes), which used institutions inaugurated during the Revolutionary era to destroy the regime. Just as the ultras distorted history in an attempt to damn the Revolutionary heritage, the liberals took advantage of any opportunity to exaggerate the dangers posed by the policies of Charles X.

V. W. Beach, *Charles X of France: His Life and Times* (Boulder, Colo., 1971) and *1825: The Decisive Year of Charles X's Reign* (Boulder, 1967); G. de Bertier de Sauvigny, *The Bourbon Restoration* (Philadelphia, 1966); A. Gain, *La restauration et les biens des émigrés*, 2 vols. (Paris, 1928); J. Mavidal and E. Laurent, *Archives parlementaires de 1787 à 1860*, 2d ser., vols. 42–45 (Paris, 1862–73).

Vincent Beach

Related entries: BERRY, C.-F.; BONALD; CHARTER OF 1814; CHATEAUBRIAND; FOY; LA BOURDONNAYE; LOUIS-PHILIPPE; MARTIGNAC; MONTMORENCY; NATIONAL LANDS; ULTRAROYALISTS; VILLELE.

L'INDEPENDANT (1815–1820), moderate newspaper of the Hundred Days and the Restoration. This agile newspaper first appeared during the Hundred Days. Its formation has been ascribed to Joseph Fouché, whose friends Antoine Jay and Jullien de Paris produced the first number at the beginning of May 1815. The paper professed respect for the Charter of 1814 but hostility to the royalists, whom it said had dominated events during the First Restoration. Napoleon was praised for giving France both liberty and honor. A tinge of anticlericalism added to the popularity of the newspaper, which acquired 3,000 subscribers within a month. When Louis XVIII was restored for the second time, the *Indépendant* declared its intention of defending the French people against reaction. It found excuses for the way in which officials had changed their loyalty from king to emperor and back again to the king within a short space of time, praised the army for defending the nation's honour at Waterloo, and defended General Charles de Labédoyère, condemned as a traitor for having transferred his allegiance from Louis XVIII to Napoleon during the Hundred Days. Hounded by the police for these views, the *Indépendant* escaped total extinction by changing its name three times within six months: from *L'Echo du soir* it became *Le Courrier* and then in October 1815 *Le Constitutionnel*. A new *Indépendant* appeared in support of the *Constitutionnel* in May 1819, but its vigorous left-wing views caused it to be attacked by the censorship established in March 1820. It fused with the *Courrier Européen* in April 1820.

E. Hatin, *Bibliographie historique et critique de la presse périodique française* (Paris, 1866, new ed., 1965).

Irene Collins

Related entries: CENSORSHIP; CHARTER OF 1814; *LE CONSTITUTION-NEL*; FOUCHE; HUNDRED DAYS; JAY; LOUIS XVIII; RESTORATION, SECOND; WATERLOO, BATTLE OF.

INDEPENDENTS, political party of liberal opposition to the Bourbon dynasty during the Restoration. The Independents were the real liberal opposition party of the Restoration. They were the last party to evolve, and included a variety of opponents of the Bourbon regime, such as republicans, Orleanists, and Bonapartists. Cautious in their initial moves, they did not begin to separate from the constitutional monarchists until the summer of 1817. After the elections in October 1817, which returned approximately twenty-five of them to the Deputies, they formed a distinct faction opposing the ministry. Their initial leaders were Casimir Périer, Jacques-Charles Dupont de l'Eure, and Jacques Laffitte, in whose salon they met to plan strategy and who helped finance their activities. In 1818 there emerged Jacques-Antoine Manuel and the marquis de Lafayette, the latter becoming the symbol they followed. Then in 1819 Benjamin Constant joined them and became their intellectual chief.

The Independents generally advocated individual liberty, anticlericalism, and popular sovereignty. Their numerous publications were special targets of government censorship. Among their best-known newspapers were the

Constitutionnel, the *Journal du commerce*, and the *Minerve*. They also corresponded regularly with affiliates in the provinces. Many of their members participated in the carbonari and other secret societies. The Bonapartists among them added a militaristic nationalism and were more prone to violence, especially military conspiracies. The 1818 elections gave them an additional twenty seats. At this time their rise and avowed opposition to the Bourbon dynasty caused Armand-Emmanuel de Richelieu to consider allying with the ultraroyalists. The Independents initially supported the Dessolle-Decazes ministry, but they demanded more liberalization of the press law than the cabinet would support. When Elie Decazes turned conservative in late 1819, the Independents turned against him. By late 1819 they had come to dominate liberal politics and showed their strength in opposing the 1820 press law and other exceptional laws. The 1820 election law, however, ensured their defeat, and in the November 1820 elections their strength was reduced.

The Independents nevertheless continued to arouse public opinion with issues such as their opposition to intervention against the Spanish revolution. But they were now denied access to political power by the Law of the Double Vote—by 1823 they had declined to only nineteen seats in the Deputies—and therefore some of them turned increasingly to conspiracies. The 1827 elections, however, gave them over 150 seats. They allied with the *doctrinaires* on some issues, and on others, in spite of their vigorous opposition to ultramontanism, they also allied with the ultras. Although the Independents attacked the Martignac cabinet, they ultimately agreed to support it in return for a bill to reform department and commune administrations. But the Independents contributed to the ministry's fall by pressing for excessive concessions. They staunchly opposed the Polignac cabinet and played a major role in passing the 1830 Deputies' address to the king. They also were extensively involved in the journalistic opposition to Charles X and the cabinet in the spring and summer of 1830. The July Revolution saw them splintered into their component groups, and after 1830 they no longer functioned as they had under the Restoration.

H. Bergasse, *Histoire de l'assemblée* (Paris, 1967); J. Crauffon, *La Chambre des députés sous la restauration* (Paris, 1908); P. Duvergier de Hauranne, *Histoire du gouvernement parlementaire en France, 1814–1848* (Paris, 1857–71); L. Girard, *Le Libéralism en France de 1814 à 1848* (Paris, 1967).

James K. Kieswetter

Related entries: CARBONARI; CONSTANT; *LE CONSTITUTIONNEL*; DECAZES; DESSOLLE; *DOCTRINAIRES*; DOUBLE VOTE, LAW OF THE; DUPONT DE L'EURE; ELECTIONS AND ELECTORAL SYSTEMS; *JOURNAL DU COMMERCE*; LAFAYETTE, M.-J.-P.-Y.-R.-G.; LAFFITTE; MANUEL; MARTIGNAC; *LA MINERVE*; PERIER; POLIGNAC; PRESS LAWS; RICHELIEU; ULTRAMONTANES; ULTRAROYALISTS.

INDUSTRY, COTTAGE. See COTTAGE INDUSTRY.

INGRES, JEAN-AUGUSTE-DOMINIQUE (1780–1867), principal champion of neoclassical art during the first half of the nineteenth century. Born on 29 August 1780 in Montauban, Jean-Auguste-Dominique Ingres was the son of

Joseph Ingres, an artist with a local reputation. For four years, he attended a school conducted by the Brothers of the Christian Doctrine (the Marists), but it closed when Ingres was but ten, and with it, to his later regret, Ingres' formal education ended. Lessons in drawing from his father kept Ingres busy until he entered the Academy of Toulouse in 1791, where he studied drawing, figure painting, and landscape painting and where he discovered the art of Raphael. While in Toulouse, Ingres supported himself by playing second violin in the orchestra of the local opera company; he retained a lifelong love of music. Six years passed before the young artist left for Paris with a letter of introduction to Jacques-Louis David, the most famed neoclassical painter of his day. David permitted Ingres to enter his large and famous atelier, and, impressed with his pupil's talent, the master assigned Ingres to paint the lamp in the famous portrait of Mme. Récamier. For reasons still unknown, David and Ingres soon parted company. Meanwhile, the young artist had entered works in several notable competitions between 1799 and 1801. A second-place award for his *Antiochus Sends His Son to Scipio* in the Prix de Rome competition followed a first-place prize from the Ecole des beaux-arts in 1799. In 1801, after managing only a second place in the preliminary competition for the Prix de Rome, Ingres' *The Envoys from Agamemnon* won the coveted award in September 1801. Owing to financial difficulties in France, Ingres could not take immediate possession of his award; as compensation, the government provided him with a studio and with a number of commissions. Important works from these years include *Bonaparte as First Consul* (1804), *Self-Portrait* (1804), portraits of three members of the Rivière family (1805), and the captivating *Napoleon I on the Imperial Throne* (1806). Ingres, who finally received his prize money in 1806 and immediately departed for Rome, missed the opening of the Salon of 1806 where his pictures were poorly received; critics described them as "gothic," "bizarre," and "revolutionary."

Ingres spent the next nineteen years of his life in Italy, the first fifteen in Rome and the last four in Florence. During the four years that his prize entitled him to at the French Academy in Rome, Ingres studied and copied the Old Masters, Raphael being an especial favorite, and painted several major works, including *Valpinçon Bather*, for shipment to France. When his tenure at the Academy ended, he remained in Rome, taking a studio at 40 Via Gregoriana. His *Jupiter and Thetis*, sent in 1811 to the Académie des beaux-arts, was poorly received. Nevertheless, owing to a friendship with two important officials, Ingres was able to support himself by painting commissioned portraits and other works. In 1813, he married Madeleine Chapelle, to whom he had proposed by letter without ever having met her. The fall of Napoleon had little impact on Ingres, and he stayed on in Rome, earning a meager living by doing portraits of English tourists; scorned by Ingres as mere trifles, these pencil sketches are highly valued today. He also continued to send paintings back to France for exhibition in the various annual salons. Almost without exception, these works, among which number the *Grande Odalisque* and *Roger Freeing Angelica*, were greeted by the critics with hostility. In 1820, at the invitation of the Italian sculptor Lorenzo

Bartolini, Ingres moved to Florence, where he studied and copied works by Titian and Raphael. On a commission from the Cathedral of Montauban, he undertook a large composition, clearly inspired by Raphael, on the theme of the *Vow of Louis XIII*. Back in France with this canvas for the Salon of 1824, at which Eugène Delacroix showed his *Massacre of Chios*, Ingres was no doubt astonished at his painting's success. Acclaim followed acclaim as Charles X decorated the artist with the cross of the Legion of Honor and as the Académie des beaux-arts elected Ingres a member. He opened a studio, and soon hundreds of aspiring artists flocked to study with him; among them was Eugène-Emmanuel Amaury-Duval, later to be Ingres' biographer. Between 1829 and 1834, Ingres became first a professor at the Ecole des beaux-arts, then its vice-president, and finally its president. From this period dates Ingres' marvelously evocative portrait of Louis-François Bertin, the director of the influential *Journal des débats*. His ten years in Paris came to an end when his *Martyrdom of St. Symphorian*, commissioned for the Cathedral of Autun, met with a poor reception at the Salon of 1834. Ingres requested and received the appointment as director of the French Academy in Rome. During his six years in Italy, Ingres produced several notable works, including *Odalisque with Slave*, *Antiochus and Stratonice*, commissioned by the duc d'Orléans, and *Virgin with the Host*. By this time, Ingres had been made into the symbol of the neoclassical school, just as his rival Delacroix had been elevated to representative of the romantic style.

In 1841, Ingres returned to Paris in triumph and remained there for the rest of his life. He painted numerous fine portraits, including those of Mme. d'Haussonville and the duc d'Orléans. His *Apotheosis of Napoleon I* was completed for the Salon of Napoleon III in the Hôtel de ville; it was destroyed in 1871 during the Commune. At the Exposition universelle of 1855, Ingres had a separate room where forty-three of his canvases were displayed. In 1862, he was made a senator. His last major work before his death in his Paris studio on 14 January 1867 was *Turkish Bath*. To his home town of Montauban, Ingres bequeathed the contents of his studio; the Musée Ingres now houses some 4,000 drawings, paintings, and the artist's notebooks.

E.-E. Amaury-Duval, *L'atelier d'Ingres* (Paris, 1878); E.-J. Delécluze, *Louis David, son école et son temps: Souvenirs* (Paris, 1863); R. Rosenblum, *Jean-Auguste-Dominique Ingres* (New York, 1967); G. Wildenstein, *Ingres* (London, 1954).

Robert Brown

Related entries: ACADEMY OF FINE ARTS; CHARLES X; DAVID; DE-LACROIX; *JOURNAL DES DEBATS*; LOUIS-PHILIPPE; RECAMIER.

INSTITUTION FOR BLIND YOUTH. The founder of the institution was Valentin Haüy (1745–1822), younger brother of a famous scientist who was a world authority on mineralogy. Valentin himself was a modest clerk in the French admiralty when he became interested in the plight of blind musicians who could be encountered at the time in places of popular revelry, clumsily trying to play various instruments. Haüy felt that if they could be provided with musical scores that could be read with their fingers, they could then study and memorize the pieces so that they could be properly performed. Thus he devised a system of signs presented in relief that could be rearranged like the characters in printing shops. The first results were so encouraging that the government of Louis XVI provided funds for a small establishment where twelve blind youths could be educated. The process of relief-letter types was soon applied to the production of books and other educational material. The National Constituent Assembly established Haüy's institution in a former religious convent, and later the Convention decided that there would be eighty-six pensioners, one for each department. But Haüy, for all his kindness, was a poor administrator, and the constant depreciation of the paper money he received from the government brought his institution close to collapse. Napoleon took drastic action: the faltering institution was merged with the venerable and well-endowed Hospital of the Quinze-Vingts, and Haüy was dismissed without compensation. But the needs and discipline required for the training of the young blind could not easily be reconciled with the way of life of the adult inmates. In February 1815 Louis XVIII ordered the total separation of the two institutions and gave a new site to that of the young blind, in a former college on the rue St.-Victor. Financial provisions were made for the maintenance and education of ninety boys and thirty girls. The young people, besides general education, would be also trained in various manual trades adapted to their condition. Music would receive special attention. An important development occurred in the 1820s when Louis Braille, a student in the institution, perfected a new system of representation of letters and other signs by combinations of dots in relief, the first idea of which had been proposed a few years earlier by a Charles Barbier. The so-called braille script, presented in 1829, made it much cheaper to produce books for the blind and was soon to be used worldwide.

At that time, however, the institution suffered from lack of sufficient resources, overcrowding, and unsanitary quarters. The government of Louis-Philippe finally financed the purchase in 1838 of a convenient plot of land, at the angle of the rue de Sèvres and the boulevard des Invalides, and better adapted facilities were built. In 1843, the institution was moved to a new site, where it remains today. At the time of transfer, the number of young students was 120 boys and 60 girls.

E. Guilabeau, *Histoire de l'Institution des jeunes aveugles* (Paris, 1907).

Guillaume de Bertier de Sauvigny

J

JACQUARD LOOM, improved silk loom developed by Joseph-Marie Jacquard (1752–1834). Jacquard was born in Lyons, the son of a master silk weaver. Apprenticed to a bookbinder and type founder as a boy, he used his savings to start a weaving *atelier* but went bankrupt in 1772. He worked subsequently for a lime merchant and served in the Revolutionary armies, returning to Lyons in the late 1790s and working on models for an improved silk loom in his spare time. In 1801, he won a medal at the Industrial Exposition in Paris for a preliminary design. Appointed to the Conservatory of Arts and Crafts by Lazare-Nicolas-Marguérite Carnot in 1803, he returned to Lyons the following year and took out a patent on an improved model. Despite the initial hostility of the weavers (who broke up several Jacquard looms), there were over 1,800 models in use by 1819. In 1806, in return for relinquishing exclusive rights to his invention, Jacquard was awarded a 3,000 franc pension and a 50 franc commission on each loom manufactured.

Jacquard's loom was designed to decrease labor costs in the industry by enabling a single weaver to produce elaborately figured fabrics, and his design refined earlier efforts by Basile Bouchon, Jacques de Vaucanson, and Breton. The primary shortcoming in the standard seventeenth- and eighteenth-century (or Dangon) loom lay in the difficulty of raising a complicated sequence of groups of threads in the warp (*chaine*) to permit the interweaving of a variety of colored weft (*trame*) threads to produce complex designs of flowers, foliage, stripes, or birds. An artisan weaving unfigured fabric (*étoffes unies*) or very simple patterns could use pedals to raise either even and odd threads (for *unies*) or up to seven or eight groups of threads, but the number of pedals that could be added to the loom was obviously limited. To weave elaborately figured fabrics, dozens or hundreds of groups of warp threads, attached by strings (*lisses*) to cords (*lames*), had to be raised (by pulling on the *lames*) in a prearranged sequence, by other workers, called *tireurs* or *tireuses*.

The key to cutting costs lay in finding an efficient mechanical means of pulling the *lames* in the proper order, without adding to the ever-present problems of tangling or breaking threads. In the eighteenth-century, Basile Bouchon had reduced the danger of human error by attaching metal rods to the *lames*, which were then inserted in a perforated board and pulled in an indicated order. Vaucanson and Berton in the 1750s had developed an automated loom, powered by a crank, in which the metal rods were pulled by a system of gears when they were in line with holes punched in a rotating cylinder. This loom worked poorly but provided the basic design that Jacquard would perfect after 1800.

In a Jacquard loom, the *lisses* attached to particular groups of threads were looped over hooks at the bottom of vertical metal rods, which were mounted in rows (and could number from 100 to 1,500) in a box solidly mounted above the *chaine*. A second hook at the top of each rod could engage a lever attached to a foot pedal under the loom so that by depressing the pedal, a weaver could raise all of the warp threads whose hooks were engaged by the lever. To enable the weaver to raise the proper *lisses* in the proper sequence, Jacquard attached a horizontally mounted pin (*aiguille*), backed by a spring, to each metal rod. The springs pushed each pin through a hole in a perforated board (the *planche aux aiguilles*) and into a corresponding hole in a perforated, rotating cylinder. When a pin penetrated both the board and the cylinder, it pulled its rod forward, the rod's hook engaged the lever, and the attached *lisse* would be raised when the weaver depressed his pedal. A roll of heavy paper (the *carton*), much like a piano roll, with holes cut to fit the pattern of *lisses* to be raised to weave a particular pattern, passed between the board and the cylinder (whose rotation advanced the *carton* in measured steps). When a pin passing through the board encountered a hole in the *carton*, it penetrated the cylinder, engaged its rod on the lever, and raised one *lisse*. If the *carton* had no hole corresponding to that pin, the pin did not advance, and its attached rod did not engage.

The resulting improvements were several. The *lisses* were raised automatically, and the *tireurs* or *tireuses* were eliminated. The design for a piece of fabric was imprinted in the perforations in the *carton* (which could be made as long as one wanted and by passing repeatedly over the cylinder could repeat the design), which meant that the weaver did not have to work from memory or stop to check how he had woven the design earlier. The *carton* also made exact reproduction of pattern possible, either at a later time or on more than one loom simultaneously. Although the Jacquard mechanism was now automatic, the loom was still hand powered, and the delicacy of silk thread and the complexity of designs prevented the addition of steam (and later electric) power until late in the nineteenth century. The Jacquard loom, however, could be operated by a less skilled or experienced weaver than the Dangon loom, which contributed to the social and economic grievances that disrupted the Lyons industry in the 1830s. With myriad improvements, the Jacquard system is still the basis of the modern silk loom.

C. Ballot, "L'évolution du métier lyonnais au XVIIIe siècle et la genèse de la mécanique Jacquard," *Revue d'histoire de Lyon* 12 (1913); J. Godart, *L'ouvrier en soie* (Paris and

Lyons, 1899); P. Hedde, *Parallèle de Vaucanson, Paulet et Jacquard* (Nimes, 1851); A. de Lamartine, *Vie de Jacquard* (Paris, 1864).

David Longfellow

Related entries: CANUTS; LYONS, REVOLTS IN; SILK INDUSTRY.

JACQUEMONT, VICTOR (1801–1832), traveler and botanist in India. Born in Paris on 8 August 1801, Victor Jacquemont was one of that group of French writer-scientist-travelers who stimulated French popular interest in foreign places, especially the lands of the East. Having studied science, especially botany, Jacquemont sought distraction from an unfortunate love affair by sailing to New York in 1826. After traveling in North America, he joined his brother Frederick, French consul in Haiti, in February 1827 and there collected an impressive amount of specimens. As a result the Jardin des plantes approved his request to undertake scientific travels for the French government in India and the Himalayas. He made contacts in England, became a member of the Asian Society of London, and sailed for India in August 1828.

Jacquemont reached Calcutta in May 1829. He spent several months studying languages and other subjects before setting out in November. He assiduously visited the major cities of India and was presented to the grand mogul at Delhi in 1830. He traveled into the Himalayas, penetrating as far as Beker and compiling a significant natural history collection, but he failed to enter Chinese territory. In 1831 he visited the Punjab, Lahore, and Cashmere, which had been closed to Europeans since 1663. He remained there for five months, making extensive scientific observations. He was offered the vice-royalty of Cashmere, which he declined. In February 1832 he departed for Bombay. But en route he suffered a debilitating attack of cholera. Jacquemont had scarcely arrived in Bombay on 9 October when he was stricken with a liver ailment and died there on 7 December 1832. His fame derived from the extensive collections he had acquired, from his correspondence from India published in 1834, and from the journal of his journey in India.

F. Hoefer, *Nouvelle biographie générale* (Paris, 1852–66); J. F. Michaud, *Biographie universelle ancienne et moderne* (Paris, 1854–65).

James K. Kieswetter

JANIN, JULES-GABRIEL (1804–1874), literary critic and novelist whose extraordinary contemporary fame was very short-lived. Born into a family of lawmakers, Janin, at the age of twenty-one, began his journalistic career at the *Figaro* and then moved to the *Messager*, before becoming editor for political news at the *Quotidienne*, which he left when it fell under the control of Jules de Polignac's ultra party. Janin found his true vocation when he was asked to substitute as theater review columnist in the *Journal des débats*. His weekly reports quickly achieved so much fame and popularity that during the next forty years, while not missing a single Monday issue, Janin entertained his faithful readers with the latest show in town, describing performances and performers in a witty and gossiping fashion, often at the expense of critical insight and accuracy. Nevertheless, his flamboyant style brought him the title Prince of Criticism (*Prince de la critique*). By the same token, Janin enjoyed the attention that he got as a result of his battles with writers and critics such as Alexandre Dumas, Théodore de Banville, Honoré de Balzac, and Désiré Nisard, who dared denounce his superficial judgments. Gustave Flaubert once said that Janin's blunders could fill an entire volume.

In 1858, Janin published his weekly dramatic reviews in six volumes in *Histoire de la littérature dramatique*, which brought the romantic era back to life in the midst of the positivist period. A tireless writer, he wrote short stories in Diderot's style and many novels with frantic and paradoxical imagery, such as *L'Ane mort ou la femme guillotinée* (1829) where he succeeded in parodying his contemporaries' taste for the macabre, or his *Contes fantastiques* (1831). Janin remained fond of short stories throughout his life. His *La Religieuse de Toulouse* (1850), *La Fin d'un monde et du Neveu de Rameau* (1861), *Béranger et son temps* (1866), and many more writings dealt with political or literary criticism, mostly generated by newsworthy events.

Finally, Janin's free translation of Horace (*La Poésie et l'éloquence à Rome*), and other similar paraphrases of Latin authors, brought him enough academic prestige to be elected to the Académie française in 1870, his first bid having been rejected in 1865. Interestingly, he followed Charles-Augustin Sainte-Beuve, one of the few great literary critics of his time, who had sensed Janin's real contribution to the recording of French literary history in his weekly editorials, in spite of his shortcomings as a literary critic.

P. Moreau, *Le Romantisme* (Paris, 1957); A. Piedagnel, *Jules Janin* (Paris, 1874); J. Place and H. Talvart, *Bibliographie des auteurs modernes de langue française, 1801–1949*, vol. 10 (Paris, 1950); A. Thibaudet, *French Literature from 1795 to Our Era*, trans. Lam Markmann (New York, 1967).

Marcelle Maistre Welch

Related entries: ACADEMIE FRANCAISE; BALZAC; DUMAS; *LE FIGARO*; FLAUBERT; *JOURNAL DES DEBATS*; POLIGNAC; *LA QUOTIDIENNE*; ROMANTICISM; SAINTE- BEUVE; ULTRAROYALISTS.

JASMIN (pseudonym of JACQUES BOE) (1798–1864), barber, wigmaker, and Gascon poet of Agen. The son of a tailor, Jasmin was born in Agen (Lot-et-Garonne) in 1798. He had some formal education in a seminary until he was expelled for stealing jam. He learned to rhyme, however, by participating in *charivaris*, the raucous and popular celebrations characteristic of premodern rural France. For fun, he began writing poems on the curling papers he used in his trade as a barber. One of his customers read them and encouraged him to publish them. In 1835, with the help of a group of local notables, the first of four volumes of Jasmin's *Papillôtos* (which means "curling papers" in Gascon) was published and quickly sold 5,000 copies, comparable to the sales of works by Honoré de Balzac and Victor Hugo. Jasmin was a star. Victor Hugo wrote to the Gascon

JASMIN

525

poet and praised his works while admitting that he could not read them. Lamartine wrote verses to him and called him "the sensitive proletarian Homer." When he performed his songs, he sang off-key, and when he read his poems, his gestures were ridiculous. Nevertheless, his fame was such that in 1842 King Louis-Philippe invited him to Paris and held an evening in his honor so that he could sing his songs and read his poems. The king decorated him and gave him a pension of 1,000 francs a year. The critic Charles-Augustin Sainte-Beuve and the romantic author Charles Nodier also received and praised him. In 1845 he was awarded the Legion of Honor, in 1852 he was crowned and given 5,000 francs by the Académie française, and finally in 1856 he was feted by his native Agen. Some of his poems were translated into English by Henry Wadsworth Longfellow. George Sand noted that he had been, along with Jean Reboul, one of the first worker-poets to achieve real glory.

Politically Jasmin was a true conservative in that he supported whatever existed. He praised every government that ruled France throughout his life, and every government in turn rewarded him. He extolled the Revolution of 1789, the glory of Napoleon, and the 1830 Revolution. Yet despite this appearance of opportunism, Jasmin was a man of principle. He truly believed that the July Monarchy was changing things for all Frenchmen, just as it had opened up opportunities for him. He was a protector of the arts, and in 1841 he wrote the deputy of his native Lot-et-Garonne on behalf of a jailed artist. He spent a great deal of time and energy giving benefit poetry readings for the poor and for his beloved Roman Catholic Church. He asked the poor for resignation and took care never to alarm the rich, but he spent much of his verse describing the misery of the poor and asking the rich to be charitable. He was a true revolutionary of the Center: he believed that things were changing for the better and that the selfish and materialistic world was, thanks to the July Monarchy and later to the Second Empire, becoming sensitive and caring. He died in Agen on 5 October 1864. Whereas most other worker poets had faded from the scene during the Second Empire, Jasmin was still immensely popular. The 1860 edition of his *Papillôtos* sold 20,000 copies.

V. Gélu, *Marseille au XIXe siècle* (Paris, 1971); Jasmin (Jacques Boé), *Les papillôtes de Jasmin, coiffeur*, 4 vols. (Agen, 1835–42), *Mes souvenirs*, trans. from Gascon into French (Paris, 1857), and *Oeuvres complètes*, 4 vols. (Paris, 1889); J. Maitron, ed., *Dictionnaire biographique du mouvement ouvrier français*, vol. 3 (Paris, 1966); E. L. Newman, "L'arme du siècle, c'est la plume: The French Worker Poets of the July Monarchy and the Spirit of Revolution and Reform," *Journal of Modern History* (1980) and *The French Worker-Poets of the July Monarchy* (forthcoming); L. Rabin, *Jasmin, sa vie et ses oeuvres* (Paris, 1889); E. Ripert, *La Renaissance provençal* (Paris, 1953); E. Thomas, *Voix d'en bas; la poésie ouvrière du XIXe siècle* (Paris, 1979); F. Tristan, *Le Tour de France, journal inédit, 1843–1844* (Paris, 1973).

Edgar L. Newman

Related entries: ACADEMIE FRANCAISE; BALZAC; HUGO; LAMARTINE; LOUIS-PHILIPPE; NODIER; REBOUL; SAINTE-BEUVE; WORKER POETS.

JAUCOURT, ARNAIL-FRANCOIS DE, (1757–1852), count, legislator and statesman. Scion of a noble Protestant family that had been able to survive honorably in the service of the king, Jaucourt was in 1789 colonel of a regiment of dragoons. He warmly embraced the Revolution and was elected president of the first departmental administration of Seine-et-Marne. The same constituency sent him as a deputy to the Legislative Assembly in September 1791. There he courageously defended the constitutional monarchy against the Jacobin faction. On 10 August 1792, he was arrested on the orders of the Revolutionary Commune. He would have lost his life with the other inmates of the Abbaye prison if Mme. de Staël had not managed to have him freed the day before the massacres started on 2 September.

Jaucourt hastened to seek a safe exile in Switzerland. He returned soon after the establishment of the Consulate of Bonaparte. Through the protection of Charles-Maurice de Talleyrand, he became a member of the Tribunate (1802), a senator (1803), and chief comptroller of the household of Joseph Bonaparte. Nevertheless, he later followed his friend Talleyrand in his underhanded opposition to the emperor and was among those senators who voted for the deposition of Napoleon on 1 April 1814. On the same day, he was elected as a member of the Provisional Government presided over by Talleyrand. Louis XVIII, upon his return, named Jaucourt a minister of state and a peer. During the absence of Talleyrand at the Congress of Vienna, Jaucourt held the portfolio of foreign affairs. In March 1815, he followed the king to Ghent, and upon the Second Restoration he briefly held the Ministry of Navy and Colonies. Thereafter, during the rest of his long life he sat in the Chamber of Peers and served on the boards of many charitable and community organizations of the French Protestant community, of which he was a prominent elder.

Correspondance du comte de Jaucourt . . . avec le prince de Talleyrand pendant le congrès de Vienne. Publiée par son petit-fils . . . (Paris, 1905); O. Douen, *Histoire de la Société Biblique protestante de Paris* (Paris, 1868).

Guillaume de Bertier de Sauvigny

Related entries: CHAMBER OF PEERS; HUNDRED DAYS; LOUIS XVIII; RESTORATION, SECOND; STAEL-HOLSTEIN; TALLEYRAND; VIENNA, CONGRESS OF.

JAY, ANTOINE (1770–1854), journalist and literary critic. A. Jay was educated by the Oratorian Brothers before studying law in Toulouse, where he passed the bar examination in 1795. He traveled several years in North America where he gathered notes for his *Nouveau journal de voyage* (1803). Director of the *Journal de Paris* in 1810 and lecturer at the Athenée, Jay was a member of the Chamber of Representatives and took part in the politics of the Hundred Days (1815). He joined the liberal Orleanist opposition when the Bourbon family was restored to power. Jay founded with Victor Jouy the *Constitutionnel* (1815), and the *Minerve littéraire* (1818). A regular member of Louis-Philippe's exclusive salon of the Palais royal, Jay collaborated with Etienne de Jouy, Antoine-Vincent Arnault, and Jacques de Norvins on the *Biographie nouvelle*, in which they counterattacked Joseph-François Michaud's royalist *Biographie* of historical characters. A slanderous remark sent Jay to prison, where he rejoined Jouy, who had been incarcerated for political reasons (1823). Together they published the *Hermites en prison* and, once released, the *Hermites en liberté* (1824), which portrayed the Parisian middle bourgeoisie during the Empire and Restoration regimes.

Favorable to moderate social changes, Jay was definitely hostile to literary and artistic innovations. A self-proclaimed champion of French classical aesthetics, he attempted to ridicule the romantic movement and its new principle of freedom of expression. In his most famous pamphlet, *Conversion d'un romantique* (1830), Jay caricatured Charles-Augustin Sainte-Beuve's *Pensées de Joseph Delorme*. Jay's critical essays collected in *Oeuvres littéraires* (1830) reflected the conservative taste and mentality of the French bourgeoisie apprehensive of bold changes. A member of the Chamber of Deputies from 1821 to 1837, Jay was elected to the Académie française under the Orleanist July Monarchy in 1832.

Berthelot, *La Grande Encyclopédie*, vol. 21 (Paris, 1886); P. Martino, *L'Epoque romantique en France, 1815–1830* (Paris, 1944); P. Moreau, *Le Romantisme* (Paris, 1957).

Marcelle Maistre Welch

Related entries: ACADEMIE FRANCAISE; CHAMBER OF DEPUTIES; *LE CONSTITUTIONNEL*; HUNDRED DAYS; JOUY; ROMANTICISM; SAINTE-BEUVE.

JESUITS. After suffering a humiliating dissolution in 1764, the Society of Jesus in France reappeared in 1814 humbly and rather stealthily. Only seven French ex-Jesuits remained, and one of them, Pierre Clorivière, was the prime mover in the reappearance. The Jesuits realized that Louis XVIII was cautious and not partial to the ever-controversial society; thus, they did not seek official recognition and were content to exist unobtrusively. For a while their demeanor brought moderate success.

As of 1815 the handful of Jesuit fathers had added some 60 novices; by the mid–1820s they numbered about 300. Their membership was small, but their reputation, especially as preachers and educators, was still great. They took over eight seminaries but could not satisfy well over 100 invitations to run residences, collèges, and other seminaries.

Charles X was ideologically favorable to the Jesuits, but even he was unable to do much for them. Indeed, in 1828 anticlericals, uneasy about the modest resurgence of the society, pressured him to issue an ordinance forcing all religious secondary schools to recognize the authority of the University of France and excluding from them teachers not in an approved teaching body. That ordinance eliminated Jesuits as teachers. Then came the July Days of 1830, during which crowds intimidated the fathers. As an immediate result fewer than 100 stayed in France, and those were in disguise and scattered. But this newest dispersion of the Jesuits was short-lived.

During the 1830s, in an atmosphere of religious indifference, the Jesuits returned, although not to their schools. After 1840, however, they again came under heavy fire. The high clergy opened the battle by trying to break the monopoly that the secular University had on education. Words then flew back and forth. The secularists not only defended the University but also turned their verbal guns against the Jesuits. Jules Michelet and Edgar Quinet led the attack in their lectures at the Collège de France. Pierre-Jean de Béranger and others joined in, but Eugène Sue surely best showed the nature of the campaign with his virulent novel, *The Wandering Jew*. On the Catholic side were parliamentarians such as Bishop Dupanloup and the comte de Montalembert and writers such as Louis Veuillot and La Croix de Ravignon, S.J., whose *The Existence and Institute of the Society of Jesus* was a leading document in his order's defense. Premier François Guizot tried to end the controversy by a new suppression of the society, but he secured (from the father-general in Rome and from the pope) only the dissolution of four houses, including the one in Paris.

The Jesuits thus quietly possessed some houses in 1848, when they managed to weather the latest revolutionary ferment. In 1850 new legislation, the Falloux Laws, brought freedom to teach. The fathers then were to experience three decades of peaceful development. But the vicissitudes that they had experienced for almost a century had not ended, as would be evident after 1870.

W. Bangert, *A History of the Society of Jesus* (1972); J. Bournichon, *La Compagnie de Jésus en France, 1814–1914*, 4 vols. (1914–22); M. Harney, *The Jesuits in History* (1941); J. Padberg, *Colleges in Controversy: The Jesuit Schools in France from Revival to Suppression, 1815–1880* (1969).

Charles R. Bailey

Related entries: ANTICLERICAL CAMPAIGN; BERANGER; DUPANLOUP; FALLOUX LAW; GUIZOT; MICHELET; MONTALEMBERT; QUINET; SUE; VEUILLOT.

LA JEUNE FRANCE (1829–1830), republican newspaper that first appeared in June 1829, edited by Eugène Plagniol, a prolific pamphleteer, and Alfred Franque. While it described itself as a newspaper of philosophy, literature, the sciences, the arts, and the theater, *La Jeune France* was noteworthy for its declared preference for a republic, defined only as the regime of civil liberties and the recognition of merit. Unlike most other republicans, its editors were hostile to Napoleon. Its issue of 15 June 1829 saw revolution as imminent, but the paper had folded before the 1830 Revolution, and Plagniol and Franque had moved on to *La Révolution* and *Le Patriote*, respectively.

C. Bellanger, J. Godechot, P. Guiral, and F. Terrou, eds., *Histoire générale de la presse française*, vol. 2 (Paris, 1969); G. Weill, *Histoire du parti républicain en France de 1814 à 1870* (Paris, 1900).

Peter McPhee

Related entries: LE PATRIOTE; REPUBLICANS; *LA REVOLUTION*.

JEWS. The regimes of the Revolution and the Empire, for a mixture of motives, brought about major changes in the legal condition of French Jews. In 1791, when emancipation was proclaimed, the legal disabilities that had long trammeled Jews were abolished. In 1808–9 the several hundred Jewish communities, which had lost the legal autonomy they had enjoyed before the Revolution, were reorganized in a centralized system of national and departmental consistories modeled on the administration already existing for Protestant sects. It was the period after 1815, however, that was the test of the meaning of these changes for Jews and Judaism. In this period, remaining barriers to complete equality were removed: in 1831 rabbis were made salaried officials like ministers of Christian cults, and in 1846 the *More Judaico*, a special Jewish oath, was abolished. Although anti-Semitism continued as an undercurrent and was even reinforced by criticisms of the supposed power of Jews in high finance by Pierre-Joseph Proudhon, Charles Fourier, and Fourierists like Alphonse Toussenel, and although there were instances of anti-Jewish riots in Alsace in times of economic and political unrest, the period down to 1850 was also one when anti-Jewish sentiment seemed to subside.

We know less about Jews in this time of relative calm but of accelerating change than we do about Jews in the Revolutionary and Napoleonic eras or in the phase marked by immigration, the recrudescence of anti-Semitism, and the Dreyfus affair from the 1880s on. The number of Jews in France at this time, for instance, is still not precisely established. More important, if we inevitably know a great deal about the attitudes and behavior of the visible and vocal assimilationist minority that made up the upper bourgeoisie, we know little about the vast majority of Jews who remained orthodox and orthopraxis. We know something about the consistories dominated by the elite; we know practically nothing about the *mynianim* (prayer assemblies) and mutual aid societies that existed outside official structures. There are even unresolved problems of approach, as to how scholars should view the assimilationist trend that was to dominate the Jewish community in the nineteenth century. Thus while earlier scholars saw assimilation as modernization and as desirable, some contemporary scholars, remembering nazism, the occupation, and Vichy, are more critical.

One thing is certain: scholars have tended to exaggerate the short-term impact of Jewish emancipation. Recent studies talk of the modernization of French Jewry and even the march toward assimilation that took place in the first part of the nineteenth century. However, it was not just legal equality that was to change the geographical distribution and the socioeconomic position of Jews but industrialization and economic development. It was the latter that would erode traditional Jewish occupations—like money lending and peddling—in Alsace-Lorraine where 80 percent of French Jews lived in the early century. Down to 1850, however, the pace of change, though it accelerated, remained modest. Scholars have also been led to exaggerate the process of assimilation because of a few spectacular instances of personal success. James de Rothschild achieved undisputed preeminence in finance. The Pereires rose to prominence as journalists and railway promoters. B. L. Fould, who had begun his career shining shoes, became a leading merchant banker. Olry Dupont began as a craftsman and ended up as a Parisian jeweler with an international reputation. Adolphe Crémieux enjoyed a distinguished career as a lawyer, first in Nîmes and then in Paris, and along with Michel Goudchaux, a Jewish banker, became a minister under the Second Republic. There is other evidence of upward mobility as a minority of Jews abandoned the lowest levels of trade and banking such as rag dealing and money lending for shopkeeping and wholesaling. There are even instances of Jewish communities whose occupational structure underwent radical change: in 1810 75 percent of adult males in the small Lyons Jewish community were peddlers, but by 1860 only 13 percent were. Such cases of rapid change are, however, exceptional. Even the Paris Jewish community, which produced the most remarkable examples of individual success, was no wealthier than Parisian society as a whole. Thus only 16 percent of Jews in Paris could be classed as bourgeois—the same proportion as for the capital as a whole—and perhaps 20 percent must be classed as indigent, which was a larger percentage than for gentile Parisians. At the midcentury, indeed, at least half of Parisian Jewish burials were at public expense because families could not pay funeral costs. Jewish populations in Alsace-Lorraine were probably even poorer, and improvement in their condition was certainly slower.

If increases in the wealth and social mobility of Jews in this period were modest, Jewish demographic growth and rate of migration to the towns were higher than for France as a whole. The Jewish community, which had numbered about 47,000 in 1815, had nearly doubled to about 89,000 in 1853, chiefly through natural increase rather than immigration. By 1853, however, Jews still constituted only 0.26 percent of the French population, a low density given that the European average was around 4 percent. Indeed, in only one department— the Bas-Rhin—did Jews constitute over 3 percent of total inhabitants (3.2 percent in 1861). There were also significant changes in the geographical distribution of the Jewish population. Jews remained concentrated in the three areas they lived in in 1815: the Ashkenazi communities of Alsace-Lorraine, which in 1815 made up 80 percent of the Jewish total; the mixed community in Paris with 6 percent; and the south, with the Sephardic communities in Bordeaux and Bayonne, and the Comtadin communities in Avignon, Carpentras, Marseilles, and Lyons, which together held 12 percent of French Jews. By 1853 only 62 percent of Jews lived in Alsace-Lorraine, and the proportion in the south had declined to 9 percent. Paris, on the other hand, had undergone spectacular growth. From about 3,000 in 1815, its community had risen to some 18,000 and was now a fifth of the Jewish total. The rate of urbanization of the Jewish population in general was high. In Alsace, where before the Revolution Jews had been prohibited from living in towns, Jews profited from the new freedom to move to cities like Colmar, Mulhouse, and Strasbourg.

There was also an acceleration in the process of cultural integration, and differences of dress and speech declined. Thus, if Yiddish and Judeo-Alsatian survived, Ladino and Chaudit, the dialects of the communities of the south, did not. At the same time, the ties between the wealthy and their communities were loosened as the rich moved out of Jewish quarters and into more bourgeois areas and as they adopted the behavior patterns of the gentile society in which they moved. If marriages outside the faith and conversions to Christianity still remained rare among the upper bourgeoisie, there was nonetheless a discernable relaxation in observation of dietary laws and the Sabbath and a growing indifference to religion.

The assimilation of wealthy Jews and the freer conditions of the period gave rise to what was to be an ongoing debate within Judaism. In contrast to what happened in Germany, this debate between orthodox and liberals did not lead to a schism. The positions were formalized in the 1840s, however, when the first permanent Jewish periodicals were established. The first of these, the *Archives israélites* founded by Samuel Cahen in 1840, represented the liberal cause. The second, the *Univers israélite* that Simon Bloch set up in 1844, was conservative. In general it was the rich and educated who favored reforms in ritual and strengthening lay power at the expense of the rabbinical. The majority wanted to retain existing religious practices and the power of the rabbinate. Since they elected and gradually secured lay control of the consistories, however, it was the assimilationist minority that was able to impose its will. In this period, though, it did so only gradually. Indeed, no coherent liberal doctrine and no uniform French rite emerged. What the reformers concentrated on instead was the elimination of those parts of ritual that they held to be undignified and out of step with Christian practices. In 1821 the Bordeaux synagogue organized a choir, and the innovation was subsequently adopted elsewhere. From 1831 the Paris consistory insisted that all sermons be in French, and other consistories followed its example. In the 1840s the organ began to be used, and initiation ceremonies for girls, modeled on the Catholic confirmation, began to appear. Regulations intended to improve circumcision practices had also been generally adopted by the middle of the century. Moves had even been made to develop a modern rabbinate with duties akin to those of the Christian clergy. All such changes were to accelerate after 1850. Janus-like, then, emancipation and greater toleration, together with economic development, offered Jews new opportunities and the possibility of greater integration into gentile society, but they also brought dilemmas and even crises of identity among the rich and tensions and conflicts within Judaism.

B. Blumenkranz, ed., *Histoire des Juifs en France* (Toulouse, 1972); P. Cohen Albert, *The Modernization of French Jewry: Consistory and Community in the Nineteenth Century* (Hanover, N.H., 1977); F. Delpech, ''L'histoire des Juifs en France de 1780 à 1840. Etat des questions et directions de recherche,'' in B. Blumenkranz and A. Soboul, eds., *Les Juifs et la Révolution française* (Toulouse, 1976); Patrick Girard, *Les Juifs de France de 1789 à 1860* (Paris, 1976); P. E. Hyman, ''Joseph Salvador: Proto-Zionist or Apologist for Assimilation?'' *Jewish Social Studies* 34 (1972); C. Piette, *Les Juifs de Paris (1808–1840): La Marche vers l'assimilation* (Quebec, 1983); B. M. Ratcliffe, ''Crisis and

Identity: Gustave d'Eichthal and Judaism in the Emancipation Period,'' *Jewish Social Studies* 37 (1975) and ''Some Jewish Problems in the Early Careers of Emile and Isaac Péreire,'' *Jewish Social Studies* 34 (1972); Z. Szajkowski, *Jewish Education in France, 1789–1939* (New York, 1980) and *Jews and the French Revolutions of 1789, 1830 and 1848* (New York, 1970).

Barrie M. Ratcliffe

Related entries: CONSISTORY; CREMIEUX; FOURIER; GOUDCHAUX; PROUDHON; ROTHSCHILD FAMILY.

JOIGNEAUX, PIERRE (1815–1892), agronomist, journalist, and republican. As a young man Joigneaux published articles strongly opposing the government of Louis-Philippe. In 1838 he was sentenced to four years in prison for his articles in *L'Homme libre*, a clandestine republican journal. After his release he founded several literary and agricultural journals, the most famous of which was the *Feuille du village*. His major interests were in spreading republican political ideals and good agricultural practices. He was named under commissioner of the republic at Chatillon by the Provisional Government in 1848 and was elected to the Constituent Assembly, where he served on the Commission of Public Works, voted with the extreme Left, and opposed the politics of Louis-Napoleon. Joigneaux was expelled from France after the coup d'état in 1851. He was the author of many books on agriculture.

Gay L. Gullickson

Related entries: AGRICULTURE; CONSTITUTION OF 1848; COUP D'ETAT OF 2 DECEMBER 1851.

JOINVILLE, FRANCOIS-FERDINAND-PHILIPPE-LOUIS-MARIE D'ORLEANS, PRINCE DE (1818–1900), third son of Louis-Philippe and Marie-Amélie. Born in Neuilly-sur-Seine on 14 August 1818, he studied at the Naval School of Brest and was named a naval lieutenant in 1836. He participated in the Mexican expedition of 1838. The prince of Joinville married the sister of the emperor of Brazil, Dom Pedro II, in 1843. A peer of France and vice-admiral in 1845, he followed the Orléans family into exile in England after the February Revolution of 1848. He visited the United States in 1861, and his son and his nephews fought in the Civil War. The prince of Joinville tried to participate in the Franco-Prussian War of 1870, but Léon Gambetta had him arrested and exiled to England.

Elected a deputy from the Haute-Marne in February 1871, the prince of Joinville was able to take his seat thanks to the abrogation of the exile laws. But he was not a candidate for reelection in 1876 and was dismissed from the naval reserve in 1886 by the law that excluded all pretenders to the French throne from public office.

J. P. Garnier, *Le drapeau blanc (la maison d'Orléans de 1787 à 1873)* (Paris, 1971); J. Lebreton-Wary, *Les Orléans d'hier et d'aujourd'hui* (1979).

Jean-Claude Caron, trans. E. Newman

Related entries: CHARTRES; LOUIS-PHILIPPE; MARIE-AMELIE DE BOURBON; NEMOURS; PARIS, COUNT OF; REVOLUTION OF 1848.

JORDAN, CAMILLE (1771–1821), *doctrinaire* royalist deputy of the Directory and Restoration. Born at Lyons on 13 January 1771 to a mercantile family, Camille Jordan was educated by various clerics. He first drew notice with his writings against the Civil Constitution of the Clergy. He was one of the leaders of the Lyons uprising against the National Convention in May 1793 and attempted to rally the neighboring areas to the royalist cause. When these efforts failed, he fled to Switzerland and England. In England he became acquainted with the leading *émigrés* and members of Parliament. He came to admire the English constitutional system. Jordan returned to Lyons in 1796 at the death of his mother. In April 1797, with the backing of Mme. de Staël in whose circle he moved, he was elected to the Council of 500 by the department of Rhone-et-Loire. He was one of the most conservative of the new deputies. A staunch opponent of the anticlericals, he was instrumental in repealing legislation against the nonjuring clergy and attempting to reestablish true religious freedom and separation of church and state. He also intervened to protect Lyons from repressive measures that the Directory sought. Jordan was included on the proscription list of 18 Fructidor, but he evaded arrest and fled to Basel. When Switzerland became unsafe, he moved on to Tübingen and Weimar, where he met Johann von Goethe, Johann von Schiller, Christoph Wieland, and Jean-Joseph Mounier, whose close friend he became. He returned to France in February 1800, albeit at first under police surveillance. Bonaparte may have sought his support. But when the question of the life consulate was placed before the people in 1802, Jordan published a tract exposing Bonaparte's ambitions and foreseeing the danger he posed to liberty. Obviously disqualified from public office, he devoted the years of the Empire to literature and philosophy and to the academy of Lyons.

Jordan's political career revived with the return of the Bourbons. As an avowed royalist, he was one of the representatives sent by Lyons on 30 March 1814 to the Austrian emperor, ostensibly to seek the restoration of the Bourbons but in fact to request a reduction of the requisitions inflicted on the city. In August 1815 he was appointed president of the electoral college of Lyons, but ill health prevented his active participation. However, in October 1816 the department of Ain elected him to the Chamber of Deputies, which chose him its president. In November 1816 he was also named to the Council of State. As a *doctrinaire* royalist he generally strongly supported the Richelieu cabinet but opposed the provost courts. He supported the 1817 election law and the use of the jury in press trials. During the 1818 election, Jordan published a *doctrinaire* proclamation rejecting any accommodation with the ultras and opposing the policies of the government. Thus after winning reelection in October 1818, he moved closer to the Left and became one of the leaders of the liberal constitutional opposition to the ministry. Jordan opposed the reestablishment of press censorship, the electoral system proposal, and all the exceptional laws of 1820. He especially opposed the Law of the Double Vote. This opposition in 1820 cost him his post on the Council of State. He simultaneously defended his liberal colleagues from attacks by the Right. The ordeal of the strenuous debates of 1819–21 and the assaults by the Right, however, ruined Jordan's already precarious health. He made his last speech in the Deputies on 30 December 1820. Typical of his disinterested eloquence, it was an effort to remove acrimonious partisanship from an address congratulating the king on escaping a bomb attack. Jordan died in Paris on 19 May 1821.

Archives parlementaires; P. Duvergier de Hauranne, *Histoire du gouvernement parlementaire en France, 1814–1848* (Paris, 1857–71); L. Girard, *Le Libéralisme en France de 1814 à 1848* (Paris, 1967); A. Robert et al., *Dictionnaire des parlementaires français* (Paris,1889–91).

James K. Kieswetter

Related entries: CENSORSHIP; CHAMBER OF DEPUTIES; COUNCIL OF STATE; *DOCTRINAIRES*; DOUBLE VOTE, LAW OF THE; ELECTIONS AND ELECTORAL SYSTEMS; RICHELIEU; STAEL-HOLSTEIN; ULTRA-ROYALISTS.

JOUFFROY, ACHILLE DE (1790–1859), marquis d'Abbans, legitimist, publicist and inventor. Achille de Jouffroy was a man of the past who attempted to reach into the future. He was a partisan of the Bourbons and a believer in divine right monarchy, absolutism, and ultramontanism. At the same time, he was a mechanic who experimented with steamboats and railway engines. None of his efforts, however, produced tangible results.

Jouffroy was from one of the great families of Franche-Comté. His father had developed the idea of propelling a boat with power generated by a steam engine and had first experimented with this novel idea on the Rhône River in 1776. He then journeyed to Paris to confer with Constantin Périer, the only other Frenchman to use steam power at that time, but Périer saw nothing useful in the scheme. After further developments with the Newcomen engine, Jouffroy père used one to propel a boat up the Rhône. This feat did not sufficiently impress the men of the scientific society of Lyons to win Jouffroy the necessary financial backing to continue his work. Thus this 1783 experiment failed, though it did draw the attention of the American Robert Fulton.

Achille de Jouffroy was born in the first year of the Revolution, the events of which his father strongly opposed. Jouffroy père emigrated, fought with the prince de Condé, and returned to France with the amnesty of 1800. Achille witnessed his father's second experiment at steamboating in 1816, but again the effort failed to gain sufficient financial backing to continue the work.

The younger Jouffroy was an early partisan of the *ancien régime*. He expressed his ideas in *Des idées libérales des français* (Paris, 1815), and by the 1820s he was a steady contributor of divine right monarchist views to *L'Observateur*. He also expressed his views in historical works (*Les fastes de l'anarchie*, 1820) and in drama (*Le Vampire*, 1820).

The July Revolution drove Jouffroy into exile. In London he founded the *Légitimité*, which was banned in France. He also continued to write on politics in *Avertissement aux souverains sur les dangers actuels de l'Europe* (1831) and

Adieu à l'Angleterre (1832). By 1832 he had abandoned his overt political opposition. He returned to France, and like many of his fellow nobles he retired to private life, divorced from the affairs of the July Monarchy.

For Jouffroy it was not agriculture that became his new pursuit but the vindication of the ideas of his father, who had died in the cholera epidemic of 1832. Jouffroy worked on new improvements for steam locomotion, and he applied them to steamboats and to the new railway engines. Trying to solve problems with the stability of railway engines, he proposed the addition of a third rail. He published his ideas in *Des bateaux à vapeur* (1839–41) and *Chemins de fer, système Jouffroy* (1844). None of his ideas proved practical.

Le grand dictionnaire universel du 19e siècle (Paris, 1866–90).

Thomas Beck

Related entries: LEGITIMISM; RAILROADS; REVOLUTION OF 1830; ULTRAMONTANES.

JOURDAN, JEAN-BAPTISTE, COMTE (1762–1833), soldier, marshal of France. Jourdan began his career as a soldier in the French army of the *ancien régime*, serving with the French expeditionary force in the American War of Independence. He left the army in 1784 but five years later joined the National Guards as a captain. By 1793, he was a general in command of the Armée du nord at the battle of Wattignies and in 1794 won the famous victory at Fleurus, afterward marching to Cologne at the head of his army of the Sambre et Meuse. He was replaced by Louis Hoche after he lost the battle of Würzburg in September 1796. A deputy in the Cinq-Cents, he gave his name to the recruitment law of 1798. Ambassador to the Cisalpine in 1801, *conseillier d'état* in 1802, he served in Naples and Spain, where he won the victory at Talavera de la Reina in 1809. In 1813, he was defeated at Vittoria. He rallied to Louis XVIII, who made him a peer of France in 1819. In 1831, Jourdan was asked to chair a committee on the reform of army recruitment. A partisan of a broad-based army, Jourdan proposed a period of five years' active service and two years in the reserve. However, during the subsequent debates, conservatives, fearful of the revolutionary inclinations of a broadly based, short-service army, pushed service time to seven years. No provision for a trained reserve was made. Thus, the Soult Law of 1832 was a defeat for the concept of service personnel. It established a small, long-service professional army without a trained reserve and set a pattern for military recruitment that contributed to the French defeats of 1870.

D. Porch, *Army and Revolution, France 1815–1848* (London, 1974); G. Six, *Les généraux de la Révolution et de l'Empire* (Paris, n.d.); R. Valentin, *Le maréchal Jourdan* (Paris, 1956).

Douglas Porch

Related entries: CHAMBER OF PEERS; LOUIS XVIII; NATIONAL GUARD; SOULT.

JOURNAL DE PARIS (1814–1827), liberal, then moderate royalist, then Villèlist newspaper of the Restoration. The *Journal de Paris* claimed descent from the first French daily paper, started in 1777. During the First Restoration and the Hundred Days, it was liberal, containing editorials by Benjamin Constant and Antoine Jay. In the Second Restoration, it became a moderate royalist organ serving the Decazes ministry. In 1824, the paper sold out to the Villèle government's "amortization" offer, at which time it had 4,000 subscribers. The *Journal de Paris* disappeared in 1827 in a merger with the *Gazette* of A.-E. Genoude, whose smaller *Etoile* was also absorbed. The merger gave the *Gazette*, as the sole Villèlist paper, a boost in circulation, as well as a more focused polemic. The title was revived in June 1829 in the *Nouveau journal de Paris* though with a very different political persuasion.

E. Hatin, *Histoire de la presse française* (Paris, 1859–61); C. Ledré, *La presse à l'assaut de la monarchie* (Paris, 1960).

Daniel Rader

Related entries: CONSTANT; DECAZES; HUNDRED DAYS; JAY; *NOUVEAU JOURNAL DE PARIS*; RESTORATION, SECOND; VILLELE.

LE JOURNAL DES DEBATS (1789–1944), prominent and influential newspaper of the Revolution, Empire, Restoration, July Monarchy, and Second Republic. Founded in 1789 with the object of publishing accounts of debates in the National Assembly, the *Journal des débats* established its importance with all succeeding governments, including that of Napoleon. The latter suspected the brothers Bertin, who had bought the paper in 1799, of royalist sympathies, but the prestige of the paper was such that he merely changed its title to that of *Journal de l'Empire* and appointed an official censor. As one of the only four national newspapers existing at the fall of Napoleon, the *Débats* had 24,000 subscribers, and Louis XVIII could count himself fortunate that it welcomed constitutional monarchy and prophesied prosperity for both bourgeoisie and aristocracy under the new Charter. As more newspapers were formed, the number of its subscribers declined to about 13,000, but it never ceased throughout the Restoration to be prosperous and influential. Its hero in politics was François-René de Chateaubriand: from 6 June 1824, when Chateaubriand was dismissed from office by Joseph de Villèle, the *Débats* made unrelenting war on the latter and led the assault that drove him from office in 1827.

In August 1829 the *Débats* joined the liberal press in denouncing the Polignac government and predicting reactionary measures. The elder Bertin was prosecuted for publishing an article that stated that all confidence between king and people was broken by the appointment of Jules de Polignac, but he was acquitted on a charge of attacking the royal prerogative after pleading that he had criticized merely the king's choice of ministers, not his right to choose them. The Bertin brothers hoped that Charles X would dismiss Polignac and save the Bourbon dynasty, but having remained loyal to Charles to the end, they compounded with his successor.

The *Débats* appealed to its readers for loyalty to Louis-Philippe on the grounds that he had saved France from republicanism. The paper had always prided itself on representing the upper middle class and the liberal aristocracy, and these groups now combined to form the governing class under the July Monarchy. The *Débats* drew most of its readers from this class, and throughout the reign of Louis-Philippe it served them well. Parliamentary debates were reported at length and with unusual accuracy, and the political events of the day were commented on in long, serious articles. Reporters were employed not only in France but in foreign capitals. The editorial staff was an impressive collection of men important in political and administrative circles, and the brothers Bertin were close friends of leading politicians such as Casimir Périer and François Guizot. The *Débats* thus enjoyed in France a prestige similar to that of the *Times* in Britain, though its subscribers never numbered more than 10,000 during the July Monarchy. When serial stories became an important feature of journalism, Armand Bertin (son of Bertin ''aîne'') paid large sums of money to secure Eugène Sue's *Les Mystères de Paris* and Alexandre Dumas's *Le Comte de Monte Cristo*; but the *Débats* still regarded politics as its *raison d'être*, and its refusal to lower its subscription rate from 80 francs a year signified a refusal to extend its appeal outside the narrow political elite of the July Monarchy.

At the outbreak of revolution in 1848, the *Débats* announced its allegiance to the new republican government in the interest, it said, of reestablishing law and order. Not surprisingly it supported Eugène Cavaignac after the June Days. Its allegiance was grudgingly transferred to Louis-Napoleon when the latter became president of the Republic, and though the *Débats* was allowed to continue publication after 1852, it was regarded by the police as secretly Orleanist.

I. Collins, *The Government and the Newspaper Press in France, 1814–1881* (Oxford, 1959); *Le Livre du centenaire du "Journal des Débats"* (Paris, 1889); A. Nettement, *Histoire politique, anecdotique et littéraire du "Journal des Débats,"* 2 vols. (Paris, 1838); A. Péreire, *Les Journal des Débats, politiques et littéraires* (Paris, 1924); A. J. Tudesq, *"Le Journal des Débats* au temps de Guizot,'' *Politique* (April–June 1959).

Irene Collins

Related entries: BERTIN DE VAUX, AINE; BERTIN DE VAUX, L.-F.; CA-VAIGNAC, L.-E.; CHATEAUBRIAND; DUMAS, A.; GUIZOT; PERIER; PO-LIGNAC; SUE; VILLELE.

JOURNAL DES ECONOMISTES (1841–1940), monthly journal espousing liberal economics and politics. Founded in December 1841 under the title *Journal des économistes: revue mensuelle de l'économie politique des questions agricoles, manufacturières et commerciales*, the *Journal des économistes* represented the views of liberal economists throughout the remainder of the nineteenth century. Because no voice existed for political economists, Michel Chevalier, Adolphe Blanqui, Hippolyte Passy, Charles Dunoyer, Louis Wolowski, and Frédéric Bastiat joined the publisher Gilbert Guillaumin to begin a journal to fill this need. As Louis Reybaud stated in the introduction to the first issue, someone had to represent the church of liberal political economy in the face of so many schisms, meaning the many new socialist proposals.

Adolphe Blanqui was the editor in 1842, followed by Hippolyte Dussard (1843–45) and then Joseph Garnier (1845–55). The journal was a strong advocate of modern professional and practical education, as opposed to the traditional classical one. It attacked the reforms of Narcisse-Achille de Salvandy (1845), which intended to strengthen education by allowing more freedom (mostly to the church) and by balancing classical and modern components of education. The editors of the journal also advocated free trade and maintained close ties with those holding similar views in England. Several of those in the bureau of the journal founded *L'Association centrale pour la liberté des échanges* in 1846. Trade, like property, was to the editors of the journal a right due everyone.

The journal's liberal line was evident from the first issue, where among numerous articles following laissez-faire economic analysis was a laudatory review of the sixth edition of Jean-Baptiste Say's *Traité d'économie politique*. The new move toward statistical analysis was also well represented in the journal. Alexandre Moreau de Jonnès and Louis-René Villermé were frequent contributors. The journal also closely monitored foreign economic developments.

As the founders had claimed, economics had matured enough to support its own professional journal. By the mid–1850s the *Journal des économistes* had 1,300 subscribers for its monthly volumes.

J. Sourris, *Le Journal des économistes: Principes et action d'une revue d'économie politique sous le second Empire* (Aix-en-Provence, 1959).

Thomas Beck

Related entries: BLANQUI, J.-A.; CHEVALIER; DUNOYER; SALVANDY; SAY.

LE JOURNAL DES OUVRIERS (1830), newspaper edited and published by workers; twenty-four issues, 19 September–12 December 1830. The paper's early numbers were confident that the July Revolution had created a government aware of the importance of "the working class which makes the wealth of the kingdom," but it became increasingly resentful at the lack of actual change. Its editors called for the death penalty, with mercy, for the ministers of Charles X, for intervention on the side of revolution in Belgium, and for protection of jobs. They called for the tax requirement for voting to be set at 100 francs so that workers' interests could be represented by master craftsmen and small employers. They expressed concern at mechanization and refused to use mechanical presses. The paper's subtitle was *A Popular Paper of Economics. Liberty! Public Order!* with a slogan from Voltaire emphasizing virtue rather than birth as the legitimate basis of social distinction.

B. N. LC² 1255 (incomplete collection); E. Dolléans, *Histoire du mouvement ouvrier*, vol. 1 (Paris, 1967); G. Weill, "Les journaux ouvriers à Paris (1830–1870)," *Revue d'histoire moderne et contemporaine* 9 (1907).

Peter McPhee

Related entries: BELGIAN REVOLUTION OF 1830; CHARLES X.

LE JOURNAL DES SANS-CULOTTES (1848), ephemeral newspaper during the Provisional Government of 1848. The Provisional Government of the Second Republic soon established almost complete freedom of the press. On 2 March 1848, stamp duties were suspended; on 6 March the hated September Laws of 1835 were abolished and the law requiring founders of journals to deposit caution money was provisionally suspended. Paris greeted this freedom by giving birth to more than 450 journals in a few months. Most of them covered only one small page and were printed in poor type on poor paper, but they demanded attention by the fearlessness of their views. The *Journal des Sans-Culotte*s was one of eighteen that took titles reminiscent of Jacobin days. It was published on crimson paper by Constant Hilbey, a former political prisoner, distinguishing itself from the *Guillotine*, which used red ink on white paper. Like most of these other productions, the paper lasted only a few weeks.

P. H. Amann, *Revolution and Mass Democracy: The Paris Club Movement in 1848* (Princeton, 1975); I. Collins, *The Government and the Newspaper Press in France, 1814–1881* (Oxford, 1959); H. Izambard, *La Presse Parisienne: Statistique bibliographique et alphabétique de tous les journaux . . . 1848* (Paris, 1853).

Irene Collins

Related entries: PRESS LAWS; PROVISIONAL GOVERNMENT.

JOURNAL DU COMMERCE (1819–1837), political and business newspaper, liberal and anticlerical in the Restoration; supported the July Monarchy; not directly related to a later paper, *Le Commerce* (1837–1848). The *Journal du Commerce* was the most business oriented of the liberal daily press of the Left in the Restoration era. Its specialty was financial and market news, but it openly and courageously promoted liberal ideas and backed liberal candidates for the Chamber. Its policy and some of its backers and writers were also involved with the *Courrier français*. The financier Jacques Laffitte had helped establish these and other opposition journals. *Journal du Commerce*'s founder-manager was François Bert, and its chief editor was François Larréguy. In the 1820s it had only about 2,000 subscribers, rising to over 4,000 during the July Monarchy.

Early in 1826, as a result of Joseph de Villèle's antipress campaign, the paper faced ruin when one of its editors, Cardon, was put on trial before the Chamber of Deputies, then strongly royalist. Cardon had written that the Chamber was "unfit to function legally," and under the law he was to be tried by that body. Cardon had served two previous short sentences and could now have received three years in prison and a 20,000 franc fine. Rich deputies of the Left, such as Casimir Périer, who defended him in vain, were prepared to pay his fine, but in a real victory for the free press and anti-Villèlism, Cardon's penalty was set at a mere token fine and thirty days in jail. This verdict was a measure not of liberal influence but of growing enmity for Villèle on the Right as well.

Another crisis in the career of this newspaper came in the fall of 1829 when it reprinted a document alleged to be the "Act of the Breton Association," a manifesto of Breton taxpayers, purportedly organized in Rennes to legally resist taxation by any illegally constituted government or in violation of the 1814 Charter. The new Polignac regime was thus put on the defensive, and the little *Commerce* was indicted, along with the *Courrier*, its sister newspaper, for "excitation of hatred and contempt for the King's government," among other charges. These papers had legitimately reprinted the alleged document but had added favorable comments. The trials became causes célèbres, and the useful publicity they offered the tax-refusal idea was augmented when the regime also tried several provincial papers for the same offense. The electoral club Aide-toi was behind the scheme and included most of the leaders of the opposition. After enormous legal publicity concerning these trials, François Bert of the *Commerce* and Valentin de Lapelouze of the *Courrier* were given minimum sentences of one month in jail. After three months of freedom on appeal, their cases were heard again. Both Parisian editors were acquitted by magistrate baron Séguier. The little *Journal du commerce* was hailed as the victor of a telling propaganda war against the ultra regime of Jules de Polignac, and the predecent of the court was carried elsewhere. Of two Parisian and six provincial journals indicted across the kingdom, three were acquitted in the first trial, three acquitted on appeal, and two provincial papers received only minimum penalties. Every word uttered at these hearings was legally reproduced in the opposition press.

When the July Revolution broke out in Paris, the *Journal du commerce*, along with the *Courrier*, again resorted to action to defy Polignac's edicts against the press. They sued their printers, who had denied their services out of fear, in commercial court but then ceased publication for two days. Bert and Larréguy also signed the journalists' manifesto against the edicts.

The paper had supported the cause of Louis-Philippe before the July Revolution and continued to do so afterward for a few years, moving toward the Left and opposing press restrictions such as the September Laws until its demise in 1837.

A successor paper, *Le Commerce*, under Charles Lesseps, replaced it in that year and continued a more independent political stance. It temporarily supported Louis-Napoleon Bonaparte in 1839 and joined the opposition journalists' protest of December 1841. *Le Commerce* ceased publication soon after the Second Republic was proclaimed.

C. Ledré, *La Presse à l'assaut de la monarchie* (Paris, 1960); D. Rader, *The Journalists and the July Revolution* (The Hague, 1973); C.M. de Salaberry, *Souvenirs politiques du comte de Salaberry*, vol. 2 (Paris, 1900).

Daniel Rader

Related entries: AIDE-TOI, LE CIEL T'AIDERA; BRETON ASSOCIATION; *LE COURRIER FRANCAIS*; LAFFITTE; PERIER; POLIGNAC; PRESS LAWS; ULTRAROYALISTS; VILLELE.

LE JOURNAL DU PEUPLE (June 1834–April 1842), important republican newspaper; 111 issues. The paper was founded by Auguste Dupoty, Audry de Puyraveau, Etienne Arago, Louis-Marie de Cormenin, Jacques-Charles Dupont de l'Eure, and the marquis de Lafayette; among its editors and contributors were

Godefroy Cavaignac, Louis Blanc, Félix Pyat, Théophile Thoré, Félix Avril, Savinien Lapointe, Pierre-Jean David d'Angers, and Henri Celliez. At first a monthly, the paper was a daily for a time in 1837, then thrice weekly in 1841 before a final vain attempt to survive as a daily in 1842. In 1836 it sold about 3,500 copies monthly and as a thrice weekly in 1841 about 3,000 per issue.

The paper was consistently democratic and argued that the chief aim of political action was the improvement of the position of workers, especially through producers' cooperatives and associations. It made sporadic efforts to attract articles from workers—for example, from the socialist boot maker Savary in 1838. It protested angrily at Adolphe Thiers' decision in 1840 to build new walls and forts around Paris and in 1838 published Flora Tristan's petition against the death penalty.

Dupoty attacked his republican rival, *Le National*, for supporting the reform campaign of the parliamentary opposition in 1839–41; instead he praised the strike wave of 1839–40, during which one of his editors had been arrested. To silence him, the government made its first and last use of a provision in the September 1835 press laws in order to accuse him before the Chamber of Peers of seditious articles leading to Quénisset's attempt on the duc d'Aumale's life in September 1840. Although there was an outcry in the opposition press at the lack of any substantive evidence, Dupoty was found guilty of moral complicity and imprisoned until May 1845.

The paper was taken over by Cavaignac, one of those sentenced after the rising of April 1834, and who had lived in exile in England since escaping from Sainte-Pélagie in July 1835. Despite a gift of 2,000 francs from his brother Eugène, later to be head of the executive in 1848, the paper failed. Many of its staff later wrote for *La Réforme*, founded in July 1843.

B.N. Lc² 1383; I. Collins, *The Government and Newspaper Press in France, 1814–1881* (Oxford, 1959); G. W. Fasel, "The French Moderate Republicans, 1837–1848" (Ph.D diss., Stanford University,1965); G. Sand, *Correspondance*, vol. 5 (Paris, 1969).

Peter McPhee

Related entries: ARAGO FAMILY; BLANC; CAVAIGNAC, L.-E.; DAVID D'ANGERS; DUPONT DE L'EURE; LAFAYETTE, M.-J.-P.-Y.-R.-G.; LAPOINTE; *LE NATIONAL*; PRESS LAWS; PYAT; *LA REFORME*; REPUBLICANS; SAINTE-PELAGIE PRISON; SOCIALISM; THIERS; TRISTAN; WORKERS' COOPERATIVES.

LE JOURNAL GENERAL DE FRANCE (1836–?), innovative newspaper of the July Monarchy. This politically indistinguished newspaper made two organizational innovations worthy of note. Appearing early in 1836, it was the first paper to be sold to subscribers at 48 francs a year instead of 80 francs. This innovation was copied with greater success by *La Presse*. The *Journal général* also printed its Paris edition in the middle of the morning and its provincial edition in the afternoon, so that it could summarize the official news appearing in the *Moniteur* on the day of its publication.

C. Bellanger et al., *Histoire générale de la presse française*, vol. 2 (Paris, 1969); E. Hatin, *Bibliographie historique et critique de la presse périodique française* (Paris, 1866, new ed. 1965).

Irene Collins

Related entries: LE MONITEUR; LA PRESSE.

JOURNAL UNIVERSEL (1815), or *Journal de Gand*, published at Ghent during Napoleon's Hundred Days; served as the semiofficial voice of Louis XVIII's monarchy in exile; biweekly. When Louis XVIII and his entourage escaped from Paris (20 March 1815) and the impending humiliation of Napoleon's return to power, they tried to establish a court in Lille, but a hostile reception drove them on into Belgium. There the new Dutch king would allow them sanctuary only in Ghent. Among the royalist faithful were several journalists, including Joseph-François Michaud, Louis-François Bertin de Vaux and his brother, Louis-François de Vaux aîné, and François-René de Chateaubriand. The Bertin brothers proposed a government newspaper to support the king and denounce Napoleon's usurpation under the title *Journal officiel*. King Willem, however, concerned over neutrality and his unstable control of the Belgians, considered this title inappropriate for an *émigré* paper, so it was first issued 14 April 1815 as *Journal universel*. This was quickly degraded to the *Journal de Gand* by French readers and journalists, who taunted the Bertins and Chateaubriand for their impotent diatribes against the restored imperial glory. The paper had a small format and appeared but twice weekly, a reflection of the frugal circumstances among the courtiers of Ghent. Its chief circulation was among its enemies, but it had a following in Tory circles in Britain and was occasionally quoted in the *Times*. The *Journal de Gand*'s last issue, on 22 June, crowed over the Allied victory at Waterloo and scorned the imperial army as French in name only. This unpatriotic swan song was not the work of Chateaubriand, who later claimed to have been on a holiday near Brussels and seized by purely French emotions when he heard the distant gunfire.

H. Houssaye, *The Return of Napoleon* (London, 1934).

Daniel Rader

Related entries: BERTIN DE VAUX, AINE; BERTIN DE VAUX, L.-F.; CHA-TEAUBRIAND; HUNDRED DAYS; LOUIS XVIII; MICHAUD; WATER-LOO, BATTLE OF.

JOUY, VICTOR-JOSEPH-ETIENNE DE (1764–1846), soldier, playwright, librettist, and social critic. Born at Jouy-en-Josas near Versailles on 19 October 1764, Jouy was the son of a cloth merchant who sold luxury fabrics to the retinue of Marie Antoinette. He was educated as a young man in the liberal atmosphere of the collège at Versailles directed by Antoine-Joseph Gorsas, where he learned to idolize Voltaire and devoured his writings. In this way young Etienne (family name) developed a quickness of mind, readiness of wit, and boldness of tongue that would earn the admiration of his contemporaries. At sixteen he was commissioned as a lieutenant in the infantry, serving in the American Revolution and in India. By the time that the Terror forced him into exile in 1793, he had become a major and collected a wealth of romantic tales that would serve him well in his literary career. He began writing vaudevilles in 1797. In 1800 he left the army and turned to writing full time. He composed the libretti of at least fourteen operas, one of which, *La Vestale*, won a prize when it opened at the Paris Opera in 1807.

It was as a journalist and social critic that Jouy made his mark. For twelve years starting in 1808, readers of the *Gazette de France*, the *Minerve*, the *Renommée*, and other newspapers were entertained by essays on Parisian society and life by "l'hermite de la Chaussée d'Antin," who also called himself "Guillaume le franc-parleur" during the Hundred Days and, at various times, "l'hermite de la Guiane," "l'hermite en province," "l'hermite en prison," "l'hermite en liberté," and "l'hermite au Louvre." These essays earned Jouy admission to the Académie française in 1815. He was a sought-after guest in Parisian salons, and the Bonapartist and liberal habitués at the salon of his mistress, Mme. Davillier, were delighted by his energy and wit.

As a member of the faction of diehard defenders of the classical style, he tried and failed to stem the rising tide of romanticism. By the 1830 Revolution his fame and fortune had ebbed, and he was grateful when King Louis-Philippe made him chief librarian at the Louvre. The admission of Alphonse de Lamartine to the Académie, the triumph of Victor Hugo's *Hernani*, and finally the admission of Victor Hugo to the Académie in 1841 were the final blows to Jouy and the classicists. He died in 1846 and was remembered as the Father of Social Reporting in France.

P. Comeau, "Etienne Jouy: His Life and His Paris Essays" (Ph.D diss., Princeton University, 1968); P. Martino, *L'Epoque romantique en France* (Paris, 1944); C. Pichois, "Pour une biographie d'Etienne Jouy," *Revue des Sciences Humaines* (April-June 1965).

Paul Comeau

Related entries: ACADEMIE FRANCAISE; *LA GAZETTE DE FRANCE*; *HERNANI*; HUGO; LOUIS-PHILIPPE; *LA MINERVE*; *LA RENOMMEE*; ROMANTICISM.

JULY ORDINANCES (FOUR ORDINANCES), the ordinances issued by Charles X on 25 July 1830 whose publication was the occasion for the outbreak of the Revolution of 1830. The Four Ordinances of 25 July 1830 emerged from a conflict between Charles X and the liberal majority in the Chamber of Deputies. It began on 16 March 1830 when the Chamber voted 221 to 181 in favor of a censorious reply to the king's address to the opening session of parliament two weeks earlier. The reply in effect informed the king that the majority in the Chamber had no confidence in his ministry, headed by Jules de Polignac, and asked him to replace it with a ministry acceptable to the majority. Charles's first response was to prorogue the chamber. In May he dissolved it and ordered new elections in June and July.

The king intended that the elections should return a majority favorable to the Polignac ministry, and he, his government, and the church used their powers and influence to ensure that result. The opposition conducted an active campaign to reelect the 221 deputies who had voted for the reply of 16 March. The opposition not only largely achieved its goal but increased its majority by nearly 50 seats.

Charles, convinced that the electors' defiance of his wishes and the pretensions of the deputies threatened the existence of the monarchy itself, accepted the advice of the majority of his ministers to use the emergency powers that, in their judgment, the Charter granted to the crown. Article 14 of the Charter authorized the king to issue ordinances "for the execution of the laws and the security of the state," and Charles assumed that this gave him authority to legislate without concurrence of parliament. Four ordinances were prepared in great secrecy, and on 25 July Polignac presented them to a meeting of king and ministry, where all present approved and signed them. They were published in *Le Moniteur universel* the next morning, preceded by a long "Rapport au Roi" justifying them.

The first of the ordinances suspended the freedom of the periodical press. The second dissolved the newly elected Chamber of Deputies. The third changed the electoral law, giving more weight to votes of rural landowners with the intent of reducing liberal representation in the chamber. The fourth ordered new elections in September. The second and fourth ordinances were clearly within the prerogative of the crown. The first and third, which altered existing laws, were of questionable legality.

Most immediately and vitally affected were journalists and publishers, and they were the first to react. On 26 July a group of them issued a proclamation charging the government with violation of the Charter, declaring their intention to defy the censorship imposed by the first ordinance, and calling on the deputies to resist the king's illegal act. After some hesitation, a handful of deputies did make moves to resist, but more immediately important was the popular reaction. Street crowds, moved in part by the journalists' inflammatory appeal, began violent action against police and troops, often with defense of the Charter as their rallying cry, and by the morning of 28 July Paris was in revolt.

The ordinances themselves were soon overshadowed by the larger issue of the survival of the Bourbon regime. On 29 July, in a belated attempt to recapture control over events in Paris, Charles authorized withdrawal of the ordinances, but his action was scarcely noticed in the fast-moving scene in the capital.

V. W. Beach, *Charles X: His Life and Times* (Boulder, 1971); *Le Moniteur universel*, 26 July 1830; D. H. Pinkney, *The French Revolution of 1830* (Princeton, 1972).

David H. Pinkney

Related entries: AIDE-TOI, LE CIEL T'AIDERA; CENSORSHIP; CHAMBER OF DEPUTIES; CHARLES X; CHARTER OF 1814; POLIGNAC; REVOLUTION OF 1830; THE 221.

JULY REVOLUTION. See REVOLUTION OF 1830.

JUNE DAYS (23–26 June 1848), an insurrection of Parisian workers against the government of the Second Republic, crushed by the army in the bloodiest street fighting in Paris before the Commune of 1871. The June Days grew out of the situation produced by the overthrow of the July Monarchy during the February Days of 1848. The insurgents of February, consisting mostly of Parisian workers, petty bourgeois, and bourgeois National Guardsmen, had created the Second Republic, with a Provisional Government dominated by moderate republican deputies and journalists but including a minority of radicals, one socialist (Louis Blanc), and one worker ("Albert"). While the economy, already in recession, plunged into depression, creating mass unemployment, the new government sought to introduce democratic reforms and felt constrained to respond to demands for social and economic as well as political innovations. The Provisional Government issued decrees limiting the working day and affirming the socialist principle of the right to work, and created National Workshops to provide jobs— or at least a dole—for the unemployed.

As the country prepared for elections—on the basis of universal manhood suffrage—to a National Constituent Assembly, Paris remained politically volatile. Scores of newspapers and about 200 new clubs appeared, some of which came under the leadership of renowned revolutionary militants such as Armand Barbès and Auguste Blanqui, whom the revolution had freed from prison. There were several massive street demonstrations in Paris, notably on 17 March and 16 April, which reflected dissatisfaction with the Provisional Government. The elections of 23 April, in which about 84 percent of adult Frenchmen voted, proved disappointing to the radicals and socialists of Paris. Although virtually all of the approximately 900 representatives claimed to be republicans, most were prosperous bourgeois who had not been republicans before February; and the Assembly soon demonstrated its relatively conservative majority by eliminating the Left of the Provisional Government from the new five-man Executive Commission on which Alexandre-Auguste Ledru-Rollin was the sole remaining radical. Dismayed, Parisian clubists and workers on 15 May mounted another large demonstration, which culminated in the invasion of the Assembly and the proclamation of a new Provisional Government, including Louis Blanc and other leftists. But the Executive Commission soon dispersed the demonstrators, arrested the most popular leaders—including Albert, Barbès, and Blanqui—and suppressed many of the clubs.

During the next five weeks, Paris remained in a state of tension, and a new, more violent confrontation between demonstrators and the government was widely expected. While sporadic agitation continued in the streets, Louis-Napoleon Bonaparte became suddenly popular, winning a by-election on 4 June. Attention increasingly focused on the National Workshops, which by mid-June had enrolled almost 120,000 jobless workers, most of whom were provided little productive employment. Meanwhile the government strengthened its defenses; Eugène

Cavaignac, one of the few republican generals in the army, was appointed minister of war and recalled more than 20,000 regular troops to the capital from which they had been ousted by the February Revolution. While rumors circulated that a huge working-class banquet planned in June would be the signal for a new insurrection, the government began to plan dispersal and eventual dissolution of the National Workshops. The uprising followed the government's announcement of plans to give registrants the options of removal to the provinces, enlistment in the army, or dismissal.

Several large gatherings at the place de la Bastille and at the Pantheon on 22 June and the morning of 23 June were followed by the erection of hundreds of barricades throughout eastern Paris. Instead of trying to prevent the construction of barricades, Cavaignac concentrated his troops in the center of the city before sending out columns against the major insurgent areas, a policy for which he was later severely criticized. Contemporaries were astonished to see that the insurgents seemed to be fighting without any recognized leadership; none of the prominent radicals or socialists backed the insurrection but instead supported the government. The areas of heaviest fighting were near the Grands Boulevards east of the porte Saint-Denis, from the Hôtel de ville east to the faubourg Saint-Antoine, and, on the left bank, the twelfth (now fifth) arrondissement, including the Latin Quarter and the faubourg Saint-Marcel. Regarding the National Guard as unreliable, General Cavaignac employed only the special Garde mobile in addition to the regular troops, and in another controversial policy did not hesitate to use cannon against the barricades. Fighting began around noon on 23 June; on the second day, frightened by reports that the insurgents were about to capture the Hôtel de ville, the Constituent Assembly declared Paris in a state of siege and placed full executive powers in the hands of General Cavaignac. By Sunday, 24 June, the tide seemed definitely to have turned against the insurgents, but bloody fighting continued in the faubourgs du Temple and Saint-Antoine. At the place de la Bastille, the archbishop of Paris was shot to death, apparently from the government side, as he was appealing to the insurgents to lay down their arms. The last barricade fell on 26 June.

Who were the insurgents? Some contemporaries identified them with the clubists and socialists or called them criminals and madmen, but more astute observers, including Alexis de Tocqueville, noted a distinct working-class character in the insurrection, and Karl Marx called the June Days the first great class struggle between the proletariat and the bourgeoisie. Although Tocqueville thought that the entire working class of Paris had supported the struggle, the best estimates of actual combatants range from 15,000 to 50,000, against whom were deployed 25,000 regular troops, 15,000 Gardes mobiles, and a few thousand Parisian National Guardsmen; in addition, more than 100,000 provincial National Guards arrived to support the government after most of the fighting was over. Casualties amounted to about 4,000 on both sides, of whom at least 1,500 were killed. In addition, about 15,000 Parisians were arrested, most of whom were later released;

4,348 were eventually designated for transportation, of whom 459 were shipped to Algeria early in 1850.

In recent years the social characteristics of the insurgents have been carefully analyzed by three independent researchers—French, English, and American—chiefly on the basis of lists of approximately 11,700 prisoners. Although their studies differ in detail, all conclude that the vast majority of the insurgents were workers. The most comprehensive analysis, that of Tilly and Lees, shows that most insurgents were artisans drawn from the building, furniture, or clothing trades; yet though only a minority were modern factory workers, proportionately more came from larger workshops in the metal, building, and transport industries than from the more traditional artisan elites. Sixty percent of the insurgents had belonged to either the National Guard or the National Workshops, though most members of both organizations abstained from the fighting. Most insurgents were residents of the poor sections of eastern Paris though they had been born in the provinces; only 4 percent were club members.

Recent research has done little to clarify the motivations of the insurgents of June. Most obviously they arose in protest against the impending dissolution of the National Workshops, and many barricades flew banners of the workshops, but there seemed to be a general intent to repeat the drama of February, to replace the moderate republican government with *la république démocratique et sociale* or even by a government headed by Louis-Napoleon Bonaparte; more profoundly, perhaps, the insurrection was a revolution of despair reflecting workers' disappointment over the failure to realize the hopes raised in February.

As for the government side, Marx argued that it deliberately provoked the uprising in order to crush the workers' movement, but no direct evidence supports this contention; indeed, there is evidence that the men in power feared such a conflict. Once the insurrection began, the Executive Commission and the Constituent Assembly staunchly supported Cavaignac's determination to crush it by force. Ledru-Rollin personally helped direct the repression, and not a single radical or socialist deputy, not even Louis Blanc, took the side of the insurgents. Instead, they were appalled at what they regarded as a violent assault on the embodiment of popular sovereignty, the National Assembly. But these political considerations were of importance only to those committed republicans who, though in charge of the government, were only a minority in the National Assembly and even less numerous in the country at large. There is abundant evidence that the insurrection stirred profound social fears; if anything the monarchists were even more eager to crush the insurrection than were the republicans. Outside of Paris all of the social classes in France, from the aristocratic notables through the layers of the bourgeoisie and the peasantry, and even some sectors of the urban working classes, vigorously supported the repression.

Some historians have regarded the June Days as the end of the French revolution of 1848 and the beginning of a reaction leading from the dictatorship of Cavaignac to the Second Empire. The June Days were indeed the climax of the workers' movement of 1848, and the brutal repression was accompanied and followed by various reactionary policies, including the closure of the National Workshops, continuation of the state of siege, the repression of the clubs and the socialist press, and the purge of Blanc and Caussidière. General Cavaignac remained in power for six months afterward but not as dictator; he became premier of a responsible republican government that continued to press ahead with democratic and even some mild social reforms, while the National Assembly adopted a thoroughly democratic constitution based on universal manhood suffrage. Yet both the insurrection and its repression had dealt the Republic a mortal wound, which became clear in December 1848, when Frenchmen of all classes overwhelmingly rejected the republican, radical, and socialist candidates in favor of Louis-Napoleon Bonaparte as their president.

P. H. Amann, *Revolution and Mass Democracy* (Princeton, 1975); F. A. de Luna, *The French Republic under Cavaignac, 1848* (Princeton, 1969); R. Gossez, "Diversité des antagonismes sociaux vers le milieu du XIXe siècle," *Revue économique* 6 (1956) and "Les Ouvriers de Paris, 1848–1851" (*thèse de troisième cycle*, University of Paris, 1963); P. McPhee, "The Crisis of Radical Republicanism in the French Revolution of 1848," *Historical Studies* 16 (1974); R. Price, *The Second French Republic* (London, 1972); C. Tilly and L. H. Lees, "The People of June 1848," in *Revolution and Reaction*, ed. R. Price (London, 1975); A. J. Tudesq, *Les Grands notables en France (1840–1849)*, 2 vols. (Paris, 1964).

Frederick A. de Luna

Related entries: AFFRE; ALBERT; BARBES; BLANC; BLANQUI, L.-A.; CAUSSIDIERE; CAVAIGNAC, L.-E.; CLUBS, POLITICAL; CONSTITUTION OF 1848; EXECUTIVE COMMISSION; GARDE MOBILE; LEDRU-ROLLIN; MARX; NATIONAL GUARD; NATIONAL WORKSHOPS; PROVISIONAL GOVERNMENT; REVOLUTION OF 1848; TOCQUEVILLE.

JUNOT, LAURE (1784–1838), Napoleonic noblewoman, memoirist, and member of the literary circles of the 1830s. Laure Junot, duchesse d'Abrantès, was a product of the French Revolution, a member of the Napoleonic elite, and a literary figure of the French romantic era. Focusing on France from 1789 until 1830, Mme. Junot authored twenty-four volumes of frequently gossipy, entertaining memoirs and a number of other fiction works and travelogues. Although her works should be regarded skeptically as historical documents, her characterizations of leading political and military figures and her observations of society are noteworthy and have been quoted frequently.

Born into a Corsican family with alleged ties to Byzantine royalty, Laure Junot was reared to appreciate the social graces of pre-Revolutionary French nobility, and during the Directory she was educated in her mother's popular salon where the Corsican society of Paris met, among them the youthful Napoleon Bonaparte. Her intimate contact with the Bonapartes, however, came in 1800 after her marriage to Napoleon's first aide-de-camp and commandant of Paris, Jean-Andoche Junot.

In 1805, Mme. Junot followed Junot to Portugal where he had been appointed ambassador. The following year, she played a role in the fusion of the two societies while Junot served as governor of Paris. But her life became embroiled in court intrigue and scandal allegedly with Metternich, and in 1810 she followed her husband to Spain, where he led a corps of the Army of Portugal. Her capacity there was no longer sheltered by diplomatic immunity, and she followed the troops to the frontiers of Portugal as an eye-witness to the horrors of the Peninsular War.

With her husband's death in 1813 and Napoleon's abdication, her life changed dramatically. Saddled by vast debts, she lived as a partial recluse for nearly fifteen years, except for brief, and fruitless, efforts to gain entrance into court society, where she hoped to find sympathy for her plight. Undaunted, she even corresponded with the pope, hoping for his intercession in her pension requests.

In 1826, Mme. Junot met the avant-garde writer Honoré de Balzac, who encouraged her to begin her literary career. Balzac had an insatiable desire to learn everything about the Napoleonic era. Meanwhile, he studied her and featured her as one of his fictional collaborators in *Physiology of a Marriage* (1829). Popular for her reminiscences and inspired by the events of the July Revolution, she prepared the first volume of her eighteen volumes on the Revolution, Consulate, and First Empire. Edited by Balzac and published by Lavocat, this first volume appeared in 1831. It was soon translated into English, Norwegian, and German.

In later years, the literary relationship between Balzac and Mme. Junot declined, as did the quality of her work. She turned to memoirs of the Restoration, music, and short stories. Published widely, her works were reviewed as both drivel and brilliance. Théophile Gautier called her the "duchesse d'Abracadabrantès" for her excursions into apocrypha; George Sand found her foreign publishing ventures "repugnant." Her friends included the marquis de Custine, Alexandre Dumas, Victor Hugo, François-René de Chateaubriand, and artists Gavarni (Sulpice-Guillaume Chevalier) and Pierre-Jean David d'Angers.

In spite of the success of Mme. Junot's memoirs and writings, ill health and poor money management plagued her. In 1838, she died in poverty and was buried in the Cemetery of Montmartre in Paris.

Bibliothèque Spoelberch de Lovenjoul, Balzac-Madame Junot correspondence (Chantilly, France); S. P. Conner, "Laure Permon Junot, duchesse d'Abrantès, 1784–1838" (Ph.D diss., Florida State University, 1977); L.-A. Junot, *Mémoires de Madame la Duchesse d'Abrantès: Souvenirs historiques sur Napoléon, la Révolution, le Directoire, le Consulat, l'Empire, et la Restauration*, 18 vols. (Paris, 1831–35), and *Mémoires sur la Restauration ou Souvenirs historiques de cette époque*, 6 vols. (Paris, 1835–36); H. Malo, *La Duchesse d'Abrantès au temps d'amours* (Paris, 1927) and *Les Années de Bohême de la Duchesse d'Abrantès* (Paris, 1927).

Susan Conner

Related entries: BALZAC; CHATEAUBRIAND; DAVID D'ANGERS; DUMAS, A.; GAUTIER; HUGO; REVOLUTION OF 1830.

JUSTE MILIEU, the motto and the goal of the ruling elite of the July Monarchy. This search for a "golden mean" was the guiding principle of the *doctrinaires* like Pierre Royer-Collard and François Guizot, who constituted the opposition of the moderate Left during the Restoration and the ruling party of the July Monarchy. In politics, the *juste milieu* avoided the extremes of royal absolutism and of popular democracy by leaving the right to vote open to rich property holders only. Political and social power thus occupied the middle ground between a closed society dominated by a hereditary aristocracy and democracy. The right to vote, which was given to only around 90,000 in the Restoration and 250,000 out of 33 million in the July Monarchy, would remain open to any men who followed Guizot's advice to "go get rich."

As a rule, the supporters of the *juste milieu* looked to the Charter of 1814 as an expression of their views. They were not always consistent; the *doctrinaires* in the *chambre introuvable* of 1815–16 favored the king's authority rather than the power of the Chamber of Deputies, but usually they wanted the king's ministers to be responsible to parliament. They also favored individual liberty, especially freedom of the press, but here again they would pass severe restrictions upon the press when they felt that it opposed them. They were most consistent in their support for the responsible, sensible propertied classes, the notables. Thus both Alexis de Tocqueville and Marx have seen the *juste milieu* as class oriented rather than issue oriented and as defenders of a narrow, selfish managerial class.

The *doctrinaires* of the *juste milieu* favored the Revolution of 1830 because they believed that Charles X had reacted against the Charter when he issued the Four Ordinances. Thus they saw the revolution as a conservative defense of the Charter against an attempt at right-wing revolution. Unlike leftists such as Marc-René de Voyer d'Argenson, Jacques Antoine Manuel, and the marquis de Lafayette, they wanted no further change after 1830, and their Party of Order fought against change throughout the July Monarchy. They set about writing histories that painted the bourgeois monarchy as the end result of all the struggles of the past: earlier revolutions were the inevitable result of humanity's longing for liberty, but now that the reign of liberty had come, all future attempts at insurrection must be suppressed. They thus became the embattled defenders of the social and political status quo, more and more out of touch with social and economic problems caused by the industrial revolution. Their constituency became so narrow that the February Revolution of 1848 would easily sweep them away.

V. Starzinger, *Middlingness: Juste Milieu Political Theory in France and England, 1815–1848* (Charlottesville, 1965).

Thomas Beck

Related entries: CHAMBRE INTROUVABLE; *DOCTRINAIRES*; GUIZOT; LAFAYETTE, M.-P.-J.-Y.-R.-G.; MANUEL; MARX; PARTY OF ORDER; ROYER-COLLARD; TOCQUEVILLE; VOYER D'ARGENSON.

JUSTICE AND LOVE, LAW OF. See PRESS LAWS.

K

KERATRY, AUGUSTE-HILARION, COMTE DE (1769–1859), man of letters, publicist, Gallican, liberal politician, peer of France. The young Auguste Kératry was a moderate partisan of the Revolution of 1789, despite the fact that his father was a delegate to the Second Estate from Brittany and his mother was a Duhamel de la Bothelière. Kératry had studied law at Quimper, and he petitioned the Constituent Assembly in support of equal inheritances, but politics was not his primary interest. In 1791 he published his first work, *Contes et idylles*, and he continued to write novels and religious works during the years of the Revolution. He barely escaped the persecution of nobles during the Terror. His neighbors twice saved him from Jean-Baptiste Carrier's orders for his arrest. Kératry was generally supportive of the Revolution, held local office, and lived quietly in Brittany.

Although Louis XVIII named Kératry as a councillor of the prefecture in Quimper, his political career began in earnest with his election to the Chamber of Deputies in October 1818. He was elected by the voters of the Finistère as a constitutional royalist, but he quickly became one of the greatest speakers of the opposition. His profound knowledge of literature, history, and religion was used in support of the liberals' resistance to the move to the right, especially after 1820.

The deepening conservatism of the regime caused Kératry to become involved in the carbonari's attempted insurrections in 1822. Along with the marquis de Lafayette, Marc-René-de Voyer d'Argenson, Benjamin Constant, and Maximilien-Sébastien Foy, he was listed in the provisional government of the rebels. Because of their parliamentary immunity and the refusal of those arrested to implicate any of these deputies, the deputies escaped any legal complications from the affair of Saumur and Belfort.

The electors of the first arrondissement of the Finistère returned Kératry to the Chamber of Deputies in November 1822. His literary talent was put to use in the mildly republican journal *Courrier français*, which he helped found. He fought the government of Joseph de Villèle, including its proposal to intervene in Spain. In the elections of 1824, although he increased his number of votes by 5, he lost 194 to 186 in the royalist landslide.

With the ascension of Charles X, the policies of the government turned back toward the *ancien régime*. In one important area, however, a significant change had occurred since 1789 that made it impossible to reestablish a unified royalist position: church relations. Because Napoleon had made peace with the church, the Republic and then the Empire had become the heir of Gallican traditions. Many opponents of the Revolution reacted by becoming supporters of the absolute power of the pope. Although this ultramontanism was dominant at court, many royalists did not share these views. Thus, when the king proposed new laws on church matters in 1825, a rupture developed in the royalist camp. Kératry, as a respected commentator on religious matters from the Gallican point of view, fully exploited the situation to the benefit of the opposition. From the pages of the *Courrier*, he preached the benefits of Gallicanism, even to the point of attacking the *Globe*'s stance on religious freedom. In March 1827, Kératry was prosecuted for his "Mensonges de M. de Villèle," which had appeared in the *Courrier*. The jury, however, failed to convict him.

With the popularity of his Gallican position, Kératry was elected in both the Finistère and the Vendée in the elections of November 1827. He chose to represent the electors of the Vendée, which he did by opposing Jean-Baptiste de Martignac and being among the famous 221 who voted for the response to the king in 1830.

His stance won him an easier victory in June 1830 than in 1827. This veteran of the Left, however, was not a republican. He was one of twelve deputies to deliver the nomination of Lt-General of the Kingdom to Louis-Philippe. Kératry spent most of his energy in the critical first days of the new regime ensuring that his views on religion found full expression. He is credited with having the famous phrase "Catholicism is the religion of the majority of the French" placed in the revised Charter. He was less successful in eliminating capital punishment for political crimes. Nevertheless, he was appointed to the Council of State, a move the electors of the Vendée approved in October 1830.

Kératry became a staunch supporter of the conservative majority. He maintained the correctness of hereditary peers, and in the elections of 1831 and 1834 he was returned to the Chamber of Deputies from the Finistère. Just prior to the elections of 1837, his devotion to Louis-Philippe was rewarded by his being named to the Chamber of Peers. He remained a loyal member of the Party of Order until the Revolution of 1848 caused him to resign all of his positions.

Just as in the Revolution of 1789, Kératry sat out the revolution in 1848. He returned to politics only with the elections of May 1849, when the citizens of the Finistère elected him thirteenth of thirteen deputies to the new Legislative Assembly. As the eldest member of the Assembly, he had the privilege of presiding at the opening session. From this position he vented his disdain for the republicans and became embroiled in a dispute with Alexandre-Auguste

Ledru-Rollin over the replacement of the military commander of the Assembly during the time since the adjournment of the Constituent Assembly. The furor subsided when Kératry apologized for his under-the-breath comments, but the dissonance of the Assembly did not. Kératry sat with the monarchist Right, opposed Louis-Napoleon, took part in the rue de Poitiers meetings, and retired after the coup d'état of 2 December 1851.

A. -H. Kératry, *Du culte en générale et de son état particulièrement en France* (1825), *Examen philosophique des considérations sur le sentiment du sublime et du beau* (1823), *Que deviendra la France? Pensée sur la situation actuelle* (1851), and *Voyage de vingt-quatre heures* (1800); A. Robert and G. Cougny, *Dictionnaire des parlementaires français* (Paris, 1889–1891).

Thomas Beck

Related entries: CARBONARI; COMITE DE LA RUE DE POITIERS; CONSTANT; COUNCIL OF STATE; *LE COURRIER FRANÇAIS*; FOY; *LE GLOBE*; LAFAYETTE, M. -J. -P. -Y. -R. -G.; LEDRU-ROLLIN; MARTIGNAC; PARTY OF ORDER; SPAIN, 1823 FRENCH INVASION OF; THE 221; ULTRAMONTANES; VILLELE; VOYER D'ARGENSON.

KNIGHTS OF THE FAITH. See CHEVALIERS DE LA FOI.

KOECHLIN, JEAN (1746–1836), pioneer cotton manufacturer. Jean Koechlin was the eldest of the nineteen children of Samuel Koechlin, one of the founders of the printed cotton industry at Mulhouse. At his father's death in 1771, Jean and two of his brothers established a new factory. Jean, however, soon left this enterprise to aid in the founding in Mulhouse of a commercial school that produced a horde of successful merchants in Switzerland and Germany. Subsequently Koechlin became director of a large textile plant at Wesserling, and a few years after that he helped establish a new calico factory at Bosserville, near Nancy. In 1802 he returned to Mulhouse, where he joined with his son Nicolas in the major textile firm known as Nicolas Koechlin et frères. At his death in 1836, Jean Koechlin left more than one hundred grandchildren and more than sixty great-grandchildren. He was significant for founding one of the major French dynasties of textile manufacturers and industrialists.

A. Brandt, "Une Famille de fabricants Mulhousiens au début du XIXe siècle, Jean Koechlin et ses fils," *Annales* 6 (1951); F. Hoefer, *Nouvelle biographie générale* (Paris, 1852–66).

James K. Kieswetter

Related entry: KOECHLIN, N.

KOECHLIN, NICOLAS (1781–1852), industrialist, entrepreneur, and liberal deputy of the July Monarchy. Born at Mulhouse on 1 July 1781, Nicolas Koechlin was perhaps the most successful of the sixteen children of Jean Koechlin, the textile manufacturer. After completing his education, Nicolas was initiated into commercial affairs in Hamburg and Holland, demonstrating tireless energy. He began on a small scale selling printed calico, and in 1802 he established the firm of Nicolas Koechlin et frères, which by the end of the Empire was quite prosperous. The Allied advance in 1813, however, closed his factories. After sending his family to Switzerland, Nicolas and two brothers fought for Napoleon throughout the campaign in France in 1814. This earned him the Legion of Honor in February 1814. He also carried out several special missions for Napoleon. During the Hundred Days Koechlin led a group of citizens of Mulhouse in guerrilla war against the Allies. After Waterloo he returned to the textile business, which he successfully revived. In 1825 he was responsible for building the new quarters of Mulhouse. He also participated in various liberal and Bonapartist plots against the Bourbons and was an active member of the carbonari.

In July 1830 the department of Haut-Rhin elected him to the Chamber of Deputies. Hastening to Paris on word of the July Ordinances, Koechlin was involved in the dethronement of Charles X and the selection of Louis-Philippe. In the debates on revising the Charter, he insisted that all of France should bear the burden of damage inflicted largely on the border provinces in wartime. He also supported the principle of equality among religious sects by advocating state payment of rabbis' salaries. Although initially a supporter of the Orleanist regime, he soon shifted to the opposition, following the general lead of Odilon Barrot. Koechlin was one of the instigators of the *compte rendu* of 1831, which was in reality a letter from Barrot to Koechlin himself. He was reelected in 1831, 1834, 1837, and 1839. In the Chamber he notably supported increasing political rights, granting pensions to the battalion of the island of Elba, and reforming customs in which he opposed prohibitive tariffs. He also served as a member of the general council of his department, as president of the Mulhouse chamber of commerce, and as a member of the general council of manufacturing under the Ministry of Commerce. In 1841 he resigned from the Chamber of Deputies in order to devote full time to building the railroad from Strasbourg to Basel, for which he had obtained a concession. He also was instrumental in constructing the railway from Mulhouse to Thann. In 1842, however, he stood for election again but was defeated by the conservative candidate, his own relative André Koechlin. Thereafter until the Revolution of 1848 he devoted himself to his business interests. The Provisional Government of 1848 appointed him commissioner for the department of Haut-Rhin. When the new republican prefect was appointed, Koechlin retired permanently from political life. Nicolas Koechlin died at Mulhouse on 15 July 1852.

Archives parlementaires; A. Brandt, ''Une Famille de fabricants Mulhousiens au début du XIXe siècle, Jean Koechlin et ses fils,'' *Annales* 6 (1951); L. J. Gras, *Histoire des premiers chemins de fer français* (Paris, 1924); A. Robert et al., *Dictionnaire des parlementaires français* (Paris, 1889–91).

James K. Kieswetter

Related entries: BARROT, C.-H.-O.; CARBONARI; CHAMBER OF DEPUTIES; CHARLES X; CHARTER OF 1814; HUNDRED DAYS; JULY ORDINANCES; KOECHLIN, J.; LOUIS-PHILIPPE; REVOLUTION OF 1830; REVOLUTION OF 1848.

L

LABBEY DE POMPIERES, GUILLAUME-XAVIER (1751–1831), liberal deputy of the Empire, the Hundred Days, and the Restoration. Labbey de Pompières was born on 3 May 1751 at Besançon. He joined the army and rose to the rank of captain before retiring in 1789. Quickly disillusioned with the Revolution, he was arrested as a suspect in 1793 and imprisoned for eighteen months. After his release, he became a member and president of the district council of Saint-Quentin. The Empire appointed him counsellor to the prefecture of Aîne where in 1812 he briefly replaced the prefect. In January 1813 he became a deputy from the department of Aîne in the Corps législatif, where he joined the opposition that arose in late 1813 and early 1814. He supported the dethronement of Napoleon and the restoration of the Bourbons. In the Chamber of Deputies in 1814, Labbey participated frequently in debate, evidencing his moderate sentiments by opposing such ministerial proposals as the reestablishment of censorship. In May 1815 he was reelected to Napoleon's Chamber, where he took little part in the proceedings.

Although Labbey was a constitutional royalist, after Waterloo he did not reappear in the Chamber until the Aîne reelected him in September 1819. Then he joined with the liberal opposition and, in spite of his age, took a vigorous part in debate. He spoke against the exceptional laws of 1820, against the proposed electoral system (Law of the Double Vote), and against the reestablishment of censorship. In budget debates he made the telling point of contrasting the 230,000 franc income of the archbishop of Paris with the 250 franc stipend of a country vicar. He equally opposed the policies of the Villèle ministry, supporting Jacques-Antoine Manuel and speaking against the Spanish campaign in 1823. Although he was defeated for reelection in March 1824, he was successful in August. Age only seemed to sharpen Labbey's opposition. He spoke out against indemnifying the *émigrés*, against the septennial law, against the sacrilege law, and against reestablishing primogeniture. He seized every opportunity to attack the Villèle cabinet. The November 1827 elections returned Labbey by a large majority.

In June 1828 Labbey proposed a formal accusation against the former Villèle cabinet for betraying the king and isolating him from the people. Although his proposal was favorably reported out of committee, the Chamber rejected it. The Martignac ministry was no less immune from Labbey's criticism, and the Polignac government suffered similar harassment. Having presided over the opening of the 1830 session, he was one of the 221 deputies voting the reply to the king's address. Reelected in June 1830, he was actively involved in the events of the July Revolution, meeting with other liberal deputies, personally urging the Parisians in several locations to resist, and pressing the republican cause at every opportunity. He quickly found the new Orleanist regime too conservative, and, having broken with the government majority in the Chamber, he simply ceased to appear. Labbey de Pompières died in Paris on 14 May 1831.

Archives parlementaires; P. Duvergier de Hauranne, *Histoire du gouvernement par-lementaire en France, 1814–1848* (Paris, 1857–71); L. Girard, *Le Libéralisme en France de 1814 à 1848* (Paris, 1967); A. Robert, *Dictionnaire des parlementaires français* (Paris, 1889–91).

James K. Kieswetter

Related entries: CENSORSHIP; CHAMBER OF DEPUTIES; DOUBLE VOTE, LAW OF THE; INDEMNITY BILL OF 1825; LAW OF SACRILEGE; MAN-UEL; MARTIGNAC; POLIGNAC; REVOLUTION OF 1830; THE 221; VILLELE.

LABICHE, EUGENE-MARIN (1815–1888), outstanding French comic dramatist of the Second Empire. Destined for the law, a profession totally foreign to his comic verve, Labiche was irresistibly drawn to the theater and published his first play in 1838 and his only novel the following year. He solemnly promised the parents of his future wife that he would give up the theater, considered a life of financial and moral uncertainty. A year later, however, his wife released him from the vow, which he gratefully acknowledged years later by dedicating to her the first edition of his complete works.

Although he had many collaborators, he seems to owe them none of the essential characteristics of his works: fine psychological penetration, spontaneous, exuberant gaiety, and a fund of common sense. A master of vaudeville, his work is nevertheless distinguished by unerring good taste, and for a brief time he raised that genre to something akin to literature. He greatly admired Molière, to whom his contemporaries compared him, as well as to Plautus and La Fontaine. Modern critical opinion is more conservative, and Labiche is valued chiefly for his excellent portrayal of bourgeois life under Louis-Philippe and the Second Empire. While the characters may be caricatured, the image of customs and manners is authentic.

Labiche borrowed many of his themes from Molière, and his best plays continue to provoke laughter because they are founded on universal truths about human nature. Labiche made a purposeful choice: "Of all the subjects which offered themselves to me, I have selected the bourgeois. Essentially mediocre in his vices and his virtues, he stands half-way between the hero and the scoundrel, between the saint and the profligate."

In 1877, after several plays had met with less than his usual success, Labiche decided not to attempt to outlive his glory and retired to Sologne. His lifelong friend, Emile Augier, convinced him to publish a revised and collected edition of his complete works. Although he wrote 162 plays, only 57 appear in the ten-volume *Thèâtre complet* published in 1878–79. The publication brought an unexpected triumph. Whereas public opinion had considered that Labiche owed his great popularity to the famous actors who had interpreted his plays, the critics now discovered that the caricatural style of low comedy affected by all the actors except Geoffroy had obscured the originality and finesse of Labiche's style and delineation of character.

This discovery opened the doors of the French Academy to Labiche in 1880, despite certain serious-minded members who considered him a frivolous choice. In fact, Labiche's work stands out in the nineteenth century, a welcome relief from both the heavy-handedness of romantic drama and the superficiality and suggestiveness of the farce in general.

The better-known works have been constantly utilized as school texts and include his first great success, *Le Chapeau de Paille d'Italie* (1851), *Le Voyage de M. Perrichon* (1860), *La Poudre aux yeux* (1861), and *La Cagnotte* (1864). Labiche enjoyed the honors that came to him near the end of his life with his usual modesty and quiet reserve, for the most part adopting the dress of a farmer and superintending the work on his rural estate.

H. Juin, "Eugène Labiche, la comédie des bourgeois," *Magazine littéraire*, n. 29 (June 1969); P. Soupault, *Eugène Labiche, sa vie, son oeuvre* (Paris, 1945).

Shelby A. Outlaw

LABORDE, ALEXANDRE-LOUIS JOSEPH, COMTE DE (1774–1842), politician, savant, and litterateur. Born in Paris on 17 September 1774, Laborde was the son of a French financier who was ennobled by Choiseul. The Revolution interrupted an excellent academic career, which probably would have led to a commission in the navy. Instead, he left France at his father's request before the beginning of the Revolution and went to Austria, where he served in the Austrian army. In 1797 he returned to France. For the next few years he traveled widely in England, Holland, Italy, and Spain and began the travelogues that were to occupy much of the rest of his life. These years of travel resulted in *Itinéraire descriptif de l'espagne* (1809) and his four-volume *Voyage pittoresque et historique en Espagne* (1807–18).

The war, however, distracted him from his projects and made it difficult for him to raise money. Therefore, in 1808, he entered political life and was named auditor to the Conseil d'état and later director of Ponts et chausées in the Department of the Seine. For his services he was appointed chevalier in the Legion of Honor in 1809, comte d'Empire in 1810, and in 1813 was elected as a member of the Académie des inscriptions et belles-lettres.

With the Restoration, Louis XVIII recognized Laborde's prior services by giving him the Croix de Saint Louis and reappointing him an officer in the Legion of Honor. Otherwise unoccupied, he went to England to study parliamentary institutions and a new movement for education of the poor in Lancaster known as mutual education. Returning to France, he helped found a French society to promote mutual education and became its director. Laborde reentered political life in 1818 as a member of the Conseil d'état under the more liberal government of Elie Decazes. In 1822 he was elected a deputy from the Seine and sat on the Center Left. Strongly opposing the invasion of Spain, he used his intimate knowledge of the topography to make the argument that the French cavalry would be destroyed. Opposing most of the policies of Joseph de Villèle, he was eliminated from the Conseil d'état in 1824 and failed to be reelected to the Chamber of Deputies. He was reelected, however, in 1827 in the liberal victory that swept Villèle from office and supported the more liberal Martignac ministry.

Although a liberal in the Restoration, Laborde greatly admired the English aristocracy and hoped that a similar aristocracy of landed wealth could be recreated in France. In *Des Aristocrates représentatives* (1814), he imagined that a hereditary aristocracy of great riches would not only provide for social stability by balancing the forces of democracy but would also employ its fortune for public works and such liberal causes as the reform of prisons, encouragement of education, abolition of slavery, and the improvement of agriculture. Unlike other liberals who sympathized with these causes, Laborde was willing to support primogeniture to create such an aristocracy. If sympathetic to such a liberal aristocracy, he remained critical of much of the old nobility and the absolutist tendencies of Charles X and the Polignac ministry. In 1830, Laborde became one of the leaders calling for popular opposition to the July Ordinances.

Rallying to the new regime, Laborde was rewarded by Louis-Philippe, who made him aide-de-camp and a member of the Conseil d'état. He was reelected deputy from the Seine in 1831 and 1834 and from Etampes (Seine et Oise) in 1837, remaining a deputy until 1841. Probably of greater importance to him at this time was the decision made by Louis-Philippe to turn the chateau de Versailles into a historical museum. In conjunction with this, Laborde decided to write a history and description of the chateau to assist visitors. The book with 800 engravings appeared in 1841 with the title *Versailles, ancien et moderne*. Laborde died the following year after a trip to Italy and Greece.

A. Beugnot and H. Passy, *Discours prononcés aux funerailles* (Paris, 1842); S. J. Gutman, "Justifications for an Aristocracy in the French Restoration" (Ph.D diss., University of Michigan, 1976); G. A. Kelly, "Liberalism and Aristocracy in the French Restoration," *Journal of the History of Ideas* 26 (1965); Alexandre Laborde, *De l'éspirit d'association* (Paris, 1821), *Des aristocrates représentatives* (Paris, 1814), *Itinéraire descriptif de l'Espagne* (Paris, 1809), *Paris municipe* (Paris, 1832), *Plan d'éducation pour les enfans pauvres* (Paris, 1815), *Versailles, ancien et moderne* (Paris, 1841), and *Voyage pittoresque et historique en Espagne*, 4 vols. (Paris, 1807–18).

Sanford Gutman

Related entries: BRIDGE AND ROAD SERVICE; COUNCIL OF STATE; DE-CAZES; *ECOLE MUTUELLE*; HEREDITY LAWS; MARTIGNAC; POLIG-NAC; SPAIN, 1823 FRENCH INVASION OF; VILLELE.

LA BOURDONNAYE, FRANCOIS-REGIS (1767–1839), comte de La Bretèche, ultraroyalist deputy, and peer of the Restoration. Born at La Varenne (Maine-et-Loire) on 19 March 1767 of a noble Breton family, La Bourdonnaye became an infantry officer in 1786. At the outbreak of the Revolution, he joined the Chevaliers du Poignard, noted for their monarchism. He was briefly arrested in early 1791 but emigrated in October and joined the army of Condé. He returned to France under the Directory but was forced to flee to Switzerland until 1802. In 1803 he was appointed to the general council of his department, becoming its president in 1813, and in 1814 he entered the municipal council of Angers. In August 1815 he won a seat in the Chamber of Deputies and immediately joined the extreme Right, becoming one of its leaders along with Joseph de Villèle and François-René de Chateaubriand. He advocated sanguinary measures allowing royalist vengeance and extending the proscription list of 24 July 1815, forcing the Richelieu ministry to produce its own amnesty measure. Henceforth La Bourdonnaye vigorously opposed the Richelieu government. He claimed that the cabinet's 1816 election law opened the door to greed and ambition. He passionately opposed the government's major proposals on individual liberty, freedom of the press, and army recruiting. When the Conspiracy at the Water's Edge was prepared in 1818, La Bourdonnaye was included in the ministry the plotters hoped to impose on the king. In the 1820 session he staunchly opposed the admission of the abbé Grégoire.

After the assassination of the duc de Berry, La Bourdonnaye proposed the suppression of seditious ideas and was instrumental in the downfall of the Decazes cabinet. He collaborated with the Left to attack the second Richelieu ministry even when other ultras cooperated with it. He was even hostile to the ultra cabinet of Villèle. In June 1822 La Bourdonnaye received the largest number of votes for the presidency of the Deputies, but Louis XVIII appointed Auguste Ravez instead. In 1824 he was one of the few ultras not appointed to preside over an electoral college. His opposition to the government extended even to breaking with his friend Chateaubriand when the latter became foreign minister in 1823. In February 1823 La Bourdonnaye took the lead in demanding the expulsion of the liberal deputy Jacques-Antoine Manuel for a laudatory remark about the French Revolution. He staunchly supported the 1825 bill to compensate the *émigrés* for their lost property, prophesying that things would then return to their pre-Revolutionary status. La Bourdonnaye and his colleagues even resurrected the defunct newspaper *L'Aristarque* to propagandize their arguments. In 1826, however, his dogmatic opposition to the government put him in the position of defending freedom of the press. The government sought to prosecute the liberal *Journal du commerce*. But La Bourdonnaye argued that such open opposition was a necessary check on representative government.

During the Martignac ministry, La Bourdonnaye once again failed to gain the presidency of the Deputies although he won a majority of the votes. In early 1828 he was considered for a ministry but was not appointed. During this period, he moderated his opposition and even settled his differences with Villèle, devoting himself to bringing down Jean-Baptiste de Martignac and his colleagues. In early 1829 he began collaborating with Jules de Polignac in the formation of a ministry, and in August he became minister of the interior, to the loud dismay of the liberals and public alike. As minister he introduced measures to regulate Paris butchers and improve the school of medicine, but he generally demonstrated his administrative incompetence and alienated his fellow ministers by his truculence. In November 1829 he resigned after Polignac became prime minister. The king thereupon appointed him to the privy council and made him a minister of state. On 27 January 1830 he was named to the Chamber of Peers. After the July Revolution La Bourdonnaye retired from public life, returning to his chateau at Mésangeau, near the town of Brain (Maine-et-Loire), where he died on 28 July 1839.

Archives parlementaires; N. E. Hudson, *Ultra-Royalism and the French Restoration* (Cambridge, 1936); R. Rémond, *The Right Wing in France from 1815 to de Gaulle* (Philadelphia, 1969); A. Robert et al., *Dictionnaire des parlementaires français* (Paris, 1889–91).

James K. Kieswetter

Related entries: CHATEAUBRIAND; CONSPIRACY AT THE WATER'S EDGE; COUNCIL OF STATE; DECAZES; ELECTIONS AND ELECTORAL SYSTEMS; GREGOIRE; INDEMNITY BILL OF 1825; *JOURNAL DU COMMERCE*; MANUEL; MARTIGNAC; PARIS FACULTY OF MEDICINE; POLIGNAC; PRESS LAWS; RICHELIEU; ULTRAROYALISTS; VILLELE.

LABRUNIE, GERARD. See NERVAL.

LACHAMBEAUDIE, PIERRE (1806–1872), republican fabulist and songwriter. Son of a *petit cultivateur* and veteran of the armies of the Republic, Pierre Lachambeaudie found his true calling early. He was expelled from the seminary in Sarlat (Dordogne) for writing a song. He finished his education in Lyons, and he then held a series of teaching positions in provincial schools. In 1829 he began to publish the first of the fables that would make him famous, *Essais poétiques*.

In the early 1830s he worked for the Chemis de fer de Roanne while writing for *Les Echos de la Loire*. His poetry reviews did not please his employer, so Lachambeaudie took up living with the Saint-Simonians of Lyons. He soon migrated to Paris, where he attended the reunions at the rue Montigny. With Mme. Gatti de Gramont doing the editing, the Libraire phalansterienne published his *Fables populaires* in 1839. The fables won a prize from the Academy, were an immediate success with the public, and went through six editions by 1849.

Lachambeaudie became involved in the events of 1848; he belonged to Auguste Blanqui's club and participated in the antigovernment demonstrations on 15 May. After the events of June, he was detained by the government, but his good friend and fellow songwriter Pierre-Jean de Béranger secured his release. The coup d'état of 2 December 1851 again drew Lachambeaudie into the political arena, and again Béranger interceded on his behalf. This time Béranger managed to have Lachambeaudie's sentence reduced from deportation to Cayenne to exile in Belgium. Lachambeaudie remained abroad until 1856.

Le grand dictionnaire universel du 19e siècle (Paris, 1889–91).

Thomas Beck

Related entries: ACADEMIE FRANCAISE; BERANGER; BLANQUI, L.-A.; COUP D'ETAT OF 2 DECEMBER 1851; DEMONSTRATIONS OF 1848–1849; JUNE DAYS; REPUBLICANS; REVOLUTION OF 1848; SAINT-SI-MONIANISM; WORKER POETS.

LACORDAIRE, JEAN-BAPTISTE, HENRI (1802–1861), a leading figure in the renaissance of Catholic thinking in France after 1815 and the most eloquent preacher of his day. The Catholic church in France faced a series of major challenges after 1789. The Revolution expropriated the church and imposed the Civil Constitution, and a gamut of socioeconomic and intellectual developments posed the problem of a decline of religious observance. Even the alliance of church and Bourbons forged from 1815 was broken by the July Revolution. Nineteenth-century French Catholicism, however, showed a capacity to adapt to changing circumstances. This responsiveness was early made possible by a renewal of clerical personnel and by the emergence of individuals like Charles de Montalembert (1810–70), Frédéric Ozanam (1813–53), Félicité de Lamennais, and Henri Lacordaire, who were to ensure that the church profited from the intellectual ferment and soul searching that took place in France in the first half of the nineteenth century. Lacordaire, then, has to be understood in this wider movement. Indeed, the precise role he played in the renewal of Catholic thinking is difficult to determine. Certainly, through his preaching and teaching, he sought to end the decline in religious observance, and, as an early liberal Catholic, he tried to reconcile church with century. He was, however, a complex and even paradoxical figure. He was a liberal, and yet throughout his life as a priest he secretly inflicted on himself a self-mortification of fastings, disciplines, and scourgings that seem out of step with his time. He was a lifelong believer in a constitutional monarchy, and yet in 1848 he sat on the extreme Left of the National Assembly. His sermons enjoyed an unprecedented success—as many as 10,000 packed into Notre-Dame Cathedral to hear them—and yet he was reserved and even cold in his personal relations, and, more important, he was no philosopher or theologian. It is not even easy to understand the popularity of his preaching, since his printed sermons—they were published in nine volumes in 1872—seem more a torrent of words and rococo metaphors than revelations of new ideas or divine inspiration.

Lacordaire did not come easily to his religious vocation. The son of a surgeon, his first intention had been to follow a professional career. He entered the Dijon law school in 1819 and, to complete his legal training, came to Paris in 1822. It was in the capital that he suffered a long spiritual crisis from which he emerged with renewed faith and a resolve to become a priest. Ordained in 1827, Lacordaire was to influence his time in four different ways.

First, immediately after and under the influence of the July Revolution, he joined with Lamennais and Montalembert in founding a new Catholic journal, *L'Avenir*. This proposed a series of liberal reforms, including abolition of the state monopoly of education and ending of press censorship. It also advocated that the right of association be granted to workers and religious congregations. Lacordaire played a leading role in the paper, writing thirty-eight signed articles and many more unsigned pieces. Although the journal was short-lived and its wider influence is difficult to gauge, it had a vital impact on Lacordaire's career. He accepted the Vatican's condemnation of liberal Catholicism in 1832 and abandoned journalism, but he did not abjure the liberal views he had expressed in the paper's columns. Equally important, though he was to break with Lamennais and even to publish a refutation of Mennaisian philosophy (*Considérations sur le système philosophique de M. de La Mennais*, 1834), he was always to remain suspect in the eyes of conservative Catholics.

Second, he undoubtedly exercised his greatest influence through the spoken word. Although he had already enjoyed considerable success at the pulpit of the chapel of the Collège Stanislas in Paris, it was from March 1835, when he first preached in Notre-Dame Cathedral, that he achieved lasting fame. The explanation for his success is to be found partly in his talents as an orator, and partly in the needs of the bourgeois and intellectuals who flocked to hear him. He opened his sermons not with the salutation "brethren," which had an outdated ring, but "Messieurs," and he also refused to follow the stylized sermon format that others used—text followed by exordium, divisions, and peroration. Instead he improvised. But above all, his warmth, emotion, and understanding of the perplexities and hesitations felt by many of his contemporaries struck a responsive chord in his listeners. He was thus successful in part because those who heard him needed him to be so. And there are other indications that the moment was propitious for a preacher like Lacordaire. Early in the 1830s Ozanam had pleaded for sermons that were less formal and dealt with more contemporary problems. Besides, there was an increase in religious observance under the July Monarchy, and there were other Catholic preachers who enjoyed success.

The third contribution he made to Catholicism was his reintroduction into France of the Dominican order. He was not the first to reestablish one of the old orders banished by the Revolution. Already in 1837 Dom Guérlanger (1805–75) had brought back the Benedictines, and he may have influenced Lacordaire's decision to join the Dominicans in 1839. But his decision was also a logical one, since his sermons reached but a select group and the return to France of an order devoted to duties of penitence and preaching promised to accomplish much more. Lacordaire completed his novitiate in the Dominican order in 1840 and from 1843 on began setting up houses in France. He proved no great organizer, however, and the successful implantation of the order was the work of others.

Finally, Lacordaire was the most prominent, and in his white Dominican habit the most obvious, churchman to take up politics and journalism in the first days of the Second Republic. In the general upswell of optimism immediately after the February Revolution, he returned to journalism, joining with Henri Maret (1805–84) and Ozanam to set up the liberal Catholic *Ere nouvelle*. He even stood as a candidate for the Constituent Assembly. Although he failed to secure election in the Seine department, he was successful in the Bouches-du-Rhône. He sat on the extreme left of the Assembly, but he only did so for eleven days. The 15 May invasion of the Chamber by the Parisian crowd dismayed him and convinced him that his excursion into politics had been a mistake. He resigned his seat three days later and soon withdrew from the *Ere nouvelle*. It was the last time he was to play any prominent role. He supported Alfred-Frédéric de Falloux's education reform of 1850 because it broke the University's monopoly. After Louis-Napoleon's coup d'état, he refused to give his Notre-Dame sermons because he felt it would be seen as tacit support for the new regime. He spent his remaining years away from the capital reorganizing the boys' college at Sorèze that his Dominican order had taken over.

P. Baron, *La jeunesse de Lacordaire* (Paris, 1961); J. R. Derré, *Lamennais, ses amis et le mouvement des idees à l'époque romantique (1824–1834)* (Paris, 1962); F. Lebrun, ed., *Histoire des Catholiques en France du XVe siècle à nos jours* (Toulouse, 1980); L. Sheppard, *Lacordaire: A Biographical Essay* (London, 1964); P. Spencer, *Politics of Belief in Nineteenth-Century France: Lacordaire; Michon; Veuillot*, 2d ed. (New York, 1973); R. L. White, *"L'Avenir" de La Mennais. Son rôle dan la presse de son temps* (Paris, 1974).

Barrie M. Ratcliffe

Related entries: L'AVENIR; CENSORSHIP; COUP D'ETAT OF 2 DECEMBER 1851; FALLOUX LAW; LAMENNAIS; LIBERAL CATHOLICISM; MONTALEMBERT; PUBLIC INSTRUCTION.

LACROIX, ALBINE-HORTENSE. See CORNU.

LAENNEC, RENE-THEOPHILE-HYACINTHE (1781–1826), physician. Laennec achieved early distinction in 1803 when he received the first prizes for medicine and surgery from the Paris Medical School. He completed his doctorate and entered private practice in 1804.

Under the influence of his teacher Jean Corvisart, Laennec took a special interest in diseases of the chest and in Corvisart's methods of investigating them through autopsy and percussion of the thorax. In 1816 Laennec was appointed physician at the Necker hospital in Paris, and in the same year he invented the stethoscope, making possible the technique of mediate auscultation. Direct application of the physician's ear to the patient's body (immediate auscultation) had previously been employed to investigate chest diseases. However, Laennec found that the use of a wooden cylinder as a listening device made the sounds of the heart and lungs much clearer to the physician's ear.

Laennec published his description of the stethoscope, together with case histories involving its use and his findings relating to lung and heart diseases, in his work *De l'auscultation médiate ou traité du diagnostic des maladies des poumons et du coeur fondé principalement sur ce nouveau moyen d'exploration* (1819). After the Restoration government's purge in 1822 of medical professors who were suspected of liberal or Bonapartist sympathies, Laennec was appointed professor in the Medical School and the Collège de France. His political acceptability to the Bourbon regime was guaranteed by his overt royalist sympathies and by his membership in the Congrégation. In 1823 he obtained a place in the Académie royale de Médecine, and in 1824 he was received as a chevalier of the Légion d'honneur.

Because of his political associations, Laennec was disliked by liberal medical students and professors, who were in a majority during the Restoration, and he was a particular target of attacks by François Broussais, who denounced him as a member of the *"partimédicojésuitique"* (medico-Jesuitical party). Laennec died of a chest ailment in 1826, shortly after completing the second edition of *De l'auscultation médiate*.

E. H. Ackerknecht, *Medicine at the Paris Hospital, 1794–1848* (Baltimore, 1967); R. Kervran, *Laennec: Médecin breton* (Paris, 1955).

W. R. Albury

Related entries: BROUSSAIS; COLLEGE DE FRANCE; CONGREGATION; CORVISART; PARIS FACULTY OF MEDICINE.

LAFAYETTE, GEORGE WASHINGTON DU MOTIER DE (1779–1849), politician. Son of the marquis de Lafayette, he was named for the American general. When his mother and two sisters went to join his father in his imprisonment at Olmutz in 1795, the young Lafayette sought refuge in the United States. He lived at Mount Vernon from 1796 through 1797. He returned to France in 1799 and joined the army. He fought with distinction in Italy, Austria, Prussia, and Russia and was aide-de-camp to generals Jean-Baptiste-Camille Canclaux, Pierre de Dupont, and Emmanuel de Grouchy. Denied promotion because of Napoleon's hatred of his father, he resigned in 1807. In 1802, he married Emilie de Tracy, daughter of the philosopher Antoine-Louis-Claude Destutt de Tracy.

During the Hundred Days he was elected to the Chamber of Representatives by the Haute-Loire, the department in which the ancestral Lafayette seat Chavaniac is located. He was a faithful assistant in all of his father's activities, working tirelessly behind the scenes to promote the liberal cause. In 1820, he ran for the Chamber of Deputies in the Haute-Loire but lost. In May 1822 he was elected in the liberal department of Haut-Rhin, receiving 97 out of 156 votes.

Lafayette took an active part in the carbonarist plots of the 1820s and traveled throughout the country organizing groups and planning insurrections. Losing in the elections of 1824, he accompanied his father on his triumphal tour of the United States in 1824 and 1825. In 1827 he was elected in the arrondissement of Coulommiers in Seine-et-Marne (178 out of 278 votes) and was reelected in July 1830. Supporting the new monarchy at first, he followed his father into the opposition of the extreme Left. He was reelected repeatedly during the July Monarchy. He helped edit his father's papers, which appeared in six volumes in 1837 and 1838. After the Revolution of 1848, Lafayette represented Seine-et-Marne at the Constituent Assembly, where he was chosen vice-president. He supported General Eugène Cavaignac and opposed the expedition to Rome. He was defeated at the by-election of Seine-et-Marne in July 1849 and died at Lagrange (Seine-et-Marne) on 29 November 1849.

A. Chaffanjon, *La Fayette et sa descendance* (Besançon, 1976).

Sylvia Neely

Related entries: CARBONARI; CAVAIGNAC, L.-E.; CHAMBER OF DEPUTIES; DESTUTT DE TRACY; HUNDRED DAYS; LAFAYETTE, M.-J.-P.-Y.-R.-G.; ROMAN EXPEDITION.

LAFAYETTE, MARIE-JOSEPH-PAUL-YVES-ROCH-GILBERT DU MOTIER DE (1757–1834), general and politician. Born at Chavaniac in Auvergne, Lafayette moved to Paris at the age of eleven. A rich nobleman, he married Adrienne de Noailles in 1774 and embarked on a military career. In 1777, at the age of nineteen, he left for America to make a name for himself in the struggle against England and to fight for liberty. He became a close friend of George Washington's, calling him his adopted father (his own father had died in battle against the British when he was two years old), and he tried to emulate Washington in France. The influence of American ideas, institutions, and personalities in Lafayette's life was substantial.

In France after the American Revolution, Lafayette advocated a constitutional monarchy. As a member of the Assembly of Notables of 1787, he was the first to introduce a proposal for a Declaration of Rights. After the fall of the Bastille, he was named commander of the National Guard of Paris. He supported the abolition of noble titles, dropped the title of marquis, and henceforth used only the title of general. But his attempt to chart a middle course, to create a constitutional monarchy with popular support, was unsuccessful. Unhappy with the increasingly radical policies of the Jacobins, he tried unsuccessfully to mount a revolt against them, and after the revolution of 10 August 1792, he left the country, was captured, and spent the next five years in Austrian captivity.

Napoleon tried to woo Lafayette by offering him the post of ambassador to the United States, but Lafayette refused to support what he considered an arbitrary regime. He explained his "no" vote in the plebiscite on the life consulate of 1802 by saying that he would support Napoleon when he established liberty. He retired to agricultural pursuits.

When the Bourbon regime was restored, Lafayette went to court to greet his old acquaintances Louis XVIII and the comte d'Artois. He quickly became discouraged by the attitudes of the returning *émigrés* and came to doubt Louis XVIII's willingness to accept the changes that had taken place since the Revolution. Nonetheless, when word came of Napoleon's return, Lafayette went to Paris to negotiate with officials to save the king in exchange for concessions on the king's part. He doubted the sincerity of the returning Napoleon's liberal pronouncements, but, encouraged by Benjamin Constant and Joseph Bonaparte and convinced that the Bourbons would be even less likely now to establish a liberal regime, he decided to participate in the government. He was elected to the Chamber of Representatives for Seine-et-Marne in May 1815 and was chosen a vice-president of the Chamber. He refused a peerage, refused to visit Napoleon, and was apparently planning ways of toppling the emperor. On 21 June, the day after the news of Waterloo arrived in Paris, Lafayette moved that the Chamber declare itself in permanent session. After Napoleon's abdication, Lafayette hoped to be named a member of the provisional government. Instead, Joseph Fouché managed to get Lafayette appointed to a commission to seek peace with the Allies, thus removing him from the scene of action. The commission was empowered to negotiate for the maintenance of Napoleon's son as head of state, but in fact when they met with the Allies at Haguenau, they stressed their flexibility and willingness to negotiate. Lafayette especially wished to avoid a restoration of the Bourbons imposed by the Allies, which he thought would mean a loss of national independence and partition of the country. During the Hundred Days Lafayette and other liberal opponents of the Empire learned to work with Bonapartists. They would combine to form the nucleus of the opposition group under the Restoration.

With the return of Louis XVIII, Lafayette retired to the relative safety and obscurity of Lagrange, his country home. He began to take an interest in politics again after the ordinance of 5 September 1816 and the passage of the electoral law of 1817. He was a candidate for the Chamber of Deputies from Paris in September 1817 but lost. In October 1818, he was a candidate for Seine-et-Marne. He lost, receiving only 32 percent of the vote. A week later, however, he was elected in a department to which he had no personal connections, the Sarthe, thanks to the organizing efforts of Charles Goyet. On the first ballot he received 569 out of 1186 votes (or 48 percent). On the second ballot he received 596 out of 1,055 (or 54 percent).

Lafayette had worked since 1817 with other politicians who called themselves *indépendant* to promote elections of the Left. Jean-Denis Lanjuinais, Marc-René de Voyer d'Argenson, Benjamin Constant, Lafayette, and others formed a committee to coordinate electoral activity. Lafayette was a member of the Société des amis de la liberté de la presse and encouraged political journalists of the left. In the Chamber, Lafayette spoke less frequently than another deputy chosen by the Sarthe, Benjamin Constant, but his fame ensured that his speeches were heard and commented on. His first speech on 22 March 1819 was to oppose the

François de Barthélemy proposal calling for changes in the electoral law. In the controversy surrounding the abbé Grégoire's election, Lafayette argued that Grégoire should not resign and refused to be a member of the delegation of liberal deputies who asked him to. He opposed the legislation introduced after the assassination of the duc de Berry and suggested in a speech on 23 March 1820 that the laws of suspects, censorship of the press, and elections were violations of the Charter, which dissolved the contract between the crown and the nation. This was his justification for his leadership in the carbonarist plots of the early 1820s. The government lacked sufficient proof to arrest him, but the prosecution linked his name to the conspirators in some of the trials. His letters stressed the theme that the party of privilege was locked in a struggle with the party of rights throughout Europe, and he supported revolutionary activity in Italy, Spain, and Greece.

In the elections of November 1822, he was not reelected in the Sarthe but was chosen by the arrondissement of Meaux in Seine-et-Marne, receiving 169 of the 312 votes cast. When in 1823 a detachment of National Guardsmen was sent to remove Jacques-Antoine Manuel (who had been officially expelled from the Chamber), Lafayette confronted them, amazed that the National Guard would do such a thing. The National Guardsmen then refused to carry out their assignment. Lafayette joined other deputies of the Left in boycotting the rest of the session. In the general elections of February 1824, he ran for reelection at Meaux and was defeated, 152 to his opponent's 184 votes.

Lafayette had long expressed an interest in revisiting the United States. At the invitation of the U.S. Congress, he traveled to America accompanied by his son, George Washington Lafayette, and a secretary, Auguste Levasseur, who later published an account of the memorable trip. Lafayette became the nation's guest, visited all twenty-four states, and was feted and celebrated everywhere he went. As one of the few surviving leaders of the Revolution and as a foreigner who had no particular regional identification, Lafayette was a potent symbol of union and disinterestedness in the divisive 1820s. For Lafayette, the acclaim was a personal vindication after his failures in conspiracies and elections. But the trip had a political purpose in France: it was a way of continuing to proclaim the virtues of republican government and free institutions in spite of the censorship and defeats.

Lafayette left Le Havre for the United States on 13 July 1824, arriving in New York on 16 August. After traveling in the East and commemorating the battle of Yorktown on 19 October, he visited Thomas Jefferson and James Madison in Virginia and spent some time in Washington, D.C. In February 1825 he began a long journey through the southern states, up the Mississippi and the Ohio rivers, through Pennsylvania and New York, arriving in Boston in time to commemorate the battle of Bunker Hill in June. After visits to New York, Philadelphia, and Washington, Lafayette left on 9 September 1825 for France, arriving on 4 October. In France, the trip was exploited for its political effect. Pierre-Jean de Béranger wrote a poem about it. A competition for the best poem to commemorate the trip was held. Lafayette helped to found the *Revue Américaine*, which featured articles on North and South America.

Much of Lafayette's property had been confiscated during the Revolution, and he received 325,769.90 francs of indemnity money in August 1826. He resumed his parliamentary career in 1827, winning a by-election at Meaux (Seine-et-Marne) on 23 June. He was elected on the second round, receiving 141 votes to André Tronchon's 139. On 24 August he delivered an oration at the funeral of Manuel. When Auguste Mignet was arrested for publishing his speech, Lafayette protested that he should be held responsible and that he disavowed none of his words. General elections were held in November 1827 after Charles X dissolved the Chamber. Lafayette was reelected at Meaux in the midst of success for liberals, again defeating Tronchon, 197 to 129.

During sessions of the Chamber of Deputies, Lafayette lived in Paris on rue d'Anjou Saint-Honoré, to which he moved in 1826. He held a salon there on Tuesday evenings. Much of his time was spent at Lagrange, where he received a steady stream of visitors, including numerous Americans. Throughout the Restoration, his views changed little. He called for a better organization of the National Guard, wider suffrage, direct suffrage, elected departmental and communal councils, and freedom of the press. While advocating constitutional monarchy for France, he supported republican governments in America and encouraged revolutionaries everywhere. In 1828 he was particularly pleased to see a French expedition embark for Greece, whose independence he had championed.

In August 1829 Lafayette revisited his ancestral home, Chavaniac, in the Haute-Loire and took the occasion to visit other locations in Auvergne, Dauphiné, and Lyonnais to rally the forces of the opposition. He was greeted with banquets and speeches reminiscent of his tour of the United States. A thousand copies of a pamphlet describing the trip were printed. In November 1829, Lafayette endorsed François Guizot's candidacy for a vacancy in the Eure. Lafayette was one of the 221 deputies endorsing the response to the king's address in 1830. After the dissolution of the Chamber, he was once again elected by the voters of Meaux, 264 to 72.

He was at Lagrange when news of the July Ordinances reached him. He hurried to Paris and participated in the 28 July meetings of deputies held at the houses of Pierre-François Audry de Puyraveau and Auguste Bérard. The next morning at a meeting at Jacques Laffitte's house, Lafayette informed the other deputies that he had been offered command of a reconstituted National Guard, and they endorsed his inclination to accept. They next proceeded to the election of a Municipal Commission after Lafayette turned down their offer to appoint the members himself. That afternoon, Lafayette and the commission (consisting of Casimir Périer, Georges de Lobau, Audry de Puyravault, Augustine-Jean de Schonen, and François Mauguin) took up their posts at the Hôtel de ville. Lafayette began to organize the National Guard, and on 30 July he declared that the royal family had ceased to reign.

The deputies meanwhile had been searching for a way to end the violence and agree on a future regime. On 31 July they offered the duc d'Orléans the position of lieutenant general of the kingdom. Lafayette sent Odilon Barrot to warn them that in order to retain public confidence, it was essential that they insist on certain guarantees from him before giving him power. When the duc d'Orléans arrived in Paris, the deputies presented him with a resolution specifying the public liberties he was to preserve. Then the duke and deputies marched to the Hôtel de ville to seek the support of Lafayette and the National Guard. The people inside the Hôtel de ville were suspicious, but when they heard the Chamber's resolution and Orléans' declaration that he supported it, they were won over. The crowds outside, however, were still shouting anti-Bourbon slogans. Lafayette seized a large tricolor flag, and he and the duke stepped onto a balcony. Lafayette's embrace of the duke changed the crowd's exclamations to cheers.

The crowd's acceptance of the duc d'Orléans as lieutenant general did not completely solve the problem of future leadership. Many of the radical revolutionaries feared accepting a new government that had not given specific guarantees. To satisfy them and himself, Lafayette called on the duke at the Palais-Royal on Saturday night. Their conversation convinced Lafayette that the duc d'Orléans shared his goals for the future of France. They agreed that what was best for France was "a popular throne surrounded by republican institutions, completely republican." (Lafayette did not say the sentence often attributed to him: "A popular throne is the best of republics.")

On 7 August the Chamber of Deputies approved the new Charter and voted to make the duc d'Orléans king. In the debate, Lafayette urged abolition of the hereditary peerage, but a decision on that was postponed until the session of 1831. The Chamber then marched to the Palais-Royal to inform the new king. Lafayette once again appeared with him on a balcony, to be cheered by the crowds.

Lafayette provided one other crucial service to the establishment of the new government. Named commanding general of the National Guard of the kingdom on 16 August, Lafayette played a key role in keeping the loyalty of the National Guard troops who guarded the Luxembourg Palace during the December 1830 trial of Charles X's arrested ministers. Large crowds gathered to shout "Death to the ministers," and the government feared the crisis could topple the new regime, especially since, to avoid antagonizing legitimists, it seemed essential not to sentence them to death. Lafayette placated the troops by suggesting that once this crisis was past, the government would move on to speedier reforms. Those who had no intention of doing that took the first opportunity to rid him of his source of power. The verdict on the ministers was announced on 21 December. On 24 December, the Chamber, which was deliberating the law on the National Guard, voted to do away with all commands extending beyond the level of the commune, thus eliminating Lafayette's command. Without waiting for the law to take effect, Lafayette immediately resigned. Louis-Philippe, who feared popular outrage, begged him to stay on, but he refused.

Lafayette's motives for this refusal were several. He had always opposed the concept of national command of the National Guard, and, he explained, with the crisis over he could resign in good conscience. He was obviously miffed at the Chamber's treatment. But he was also dissociating himself from the government, whose refusal to promote further reforms he deplored. On 18 January 1831 he was named a member of the departmental council of Seine-et-Marne. He accepted on the understanding that elections for such a position would be provided for soon. He spoke frequently in favor of French support for Belgium and Poland. On 5 June 1831 he was reelected deputy by the voters of Meaux (486 to 162) and was also selected by Strasbourg (117 to 92). He opted for Meaux. He argued successfully for the abolition of the hereditary peerage in the upper house in October 1831. He was named mayor of the commune of Courpalay (which included Lagrange) but did not keep this position long. He protested the severity with which the government suppressed the disorders at General Lamarque's funeral by resigning on 21 June 1832 from positions he held by royal appointment as mayor and member of the departmental council. He publicly accused Louis-Philippe of not fulfilling the promises he had made to him.

Completely alienated from the government, Lafayette believed that the attempted assassination of Louis-Philippe on 19 November 1832 had been staged by the police. On 3 January 1834 he gave his last important speech in the Chamber of Deputies, asserting that the promises of the July Revolution had gone unfulfilled and advocating freedom of speech and association. On 1 February he caught cold at the funeral of the deputy François-Charles Dulong, who had died in a political duel. Lafayette's recuperation was slow. On 9 May, an unexpected thunderstorm that came up while he was on a carriage ride brought on another chill. He died on 20 May 1834. The government gave him an official funeral, orchestrated to discourage popular demonstrations. He was buried next to his wife at Picpus Cemetery, in soil brought from America.

A. Bardoux, *Les dernières années de La Fayette* (Paris, 1893); E. E. Brandon, *A Pilgrimage of Liberty, a Contemporary Account of the Triumphal Tour of General Lafayette, through the Southern and Western States in 1825, as Reported by the Local Newspapers* (Athens, Ohio, 1944), and *Lafayette, Guest of the Nation, a Contemporary Account of the Triumphal Tour of General Lafayette through the United States in 1824–1825, as Reported by the Local Newspapers*, 3 vols. (Oxford, Ohio, 1950–57); E. Charavay, *Le Général La Fayette (1757–1834)* (Paris, 1898); J. Cloquet, *Recollections of the Private Life of General Lafayette* (London, 1835); R. M. Jones, "The Flowering of a Legend: Lafayette and the Americans, 1825–1834," *French Historical Studies* 4 (Fall 1966); A. C. Loveland, *Emblem of Liberty; The Image of Lafayette in the American Mind* (Baton Rouge, 1971); *Mémoires, correspondance et manuscrits du général La Fayette, publiés par sa famille*, vol. 6 (Paris, 1838); R. Rémond, *Les Etats-Unis devant l'opinion française, 1815–1852*, 2 vols. (Paris, 1962); F. Somkin, *Unquiet Eagle: Memory and Desire in the Idea of American Freedom, 1815–1860* (Ithaca, New York, 1967); B. Whitlock, *La Fayette*, 2 vols. (New York, London, 1929).

Sylvia Neely

Related entries: AUDRY DE PUYRAVAULT; BARROT, C.-H.-O.; BER-ANGER; BERARD; CARBONARI; CENSORSHIP; CHARTER OF 1814;

CHARTER OF 1830; CONSTANT; *DOCTRINAIRES*; ELECTIONS AND ELECTORAL SYSTEMS; FOUCHE; GOYET; GREGOIRE; GUIZOT; LAN-JUINAIS; LAFAYETTE, G.; LAMARQUE; MANUEL; MIGNET; MUNICI-PAL COMMISSION; NATIONAL GUARD; REPUBLICANS; REVOLUTION OF 1830; SOCIETY OF FRIENDS OF THE FREEDOM OF THE PRESS; THE 221; VOYER D'ARGENSON.

LA FERRONNAYS, PIERRE-LOUIS-AUGUSTE FERRON, COMTE DE (1777–1842), diplomat and governmental minister. During the Revolution, he emigrated with his family, and in London he became aide-de-camp and friend of the duc de Berry. In 1817 he was named minister from France to Copenhagen and in 1819 ambassador to Saint Petersburg. Consequently he took part at the Congress of Troppau, the Congress of Laibach, and the Congress of Verona. He became minister of foreign affairs in the government that replaced the Villèle ministry at the end of 1827. His actions prepared the French expedition to Morea and Greek independence. He was both devoted to the crown and sensitive to liberal aspirations, and he would have been able to play a decisive role in internal French politics if his health had not forced him at the start of January 1829 to leave the ministry. In February he accepted the post of ambassador to Rome, which had been left vacant by the resignation of François-René de Chateaubriand, but he refused to serve the July Monarchy.

A. Craven, *Récits d'une soeur. Souvenirs de famille* (Paris, 1866).

Guillaume de Bertier de Sauvigny, trans. E. Newman

Related entries: BERRY, C.-F.; CHATEAUBRIAND; TROPPAU, CON-GRESS OF; VERONA, CONGRESS OF.

LAFFITTE, JACQUES (1767–1844), banker, political leader, and minister. Jacques Laffitte was born in Bayonne, 24 October 1767, one of ten children of a carpenter. He worked in his native city as a clerk, first for a notary and then for a merchant-banker, until 1788, when he took a position as a bookkeeper with the leading Parisian banking house of Perrégaux. He rose to a partnership in 1806, and on the death of Perrégaux two years later the bank became Perrégaux, Laffitte et Cie., with Laffitte as the managing partner. The bank flourished under the Empire, and Laffitte accumulated a vast fortune. He was named a regent of the Bank of France and president of the Chamber of Commerce of Paris.

After the return of the Bourbons to France in 1814, he was appointed governor of the Bank of France. He served in the Napoleonic Chamber of Representatives during the Hundred Days but kept the governorship of the bank after Waterloo and played an important part in raising money to pay the indemnity demanded by the victors and in reestablishing the state's finances. He was elected to the Chamber of Deputies in 1816 and served in the Chamber throughout the Restoration with the exception of the years 1824–27. He usually voted with the opposition and became one of its prominent spokesmen, which in 1819 cost him his position as governor of the Bank of France. In the latter 1820s, he openly advocated the replacement of Charles X by the duc d'Orléans.

In the Revolution of 1830 he was the key figure in persuading the deputies to appoint the duc d'Orléans lieutenant general of the kingdom and then to offer him the crown. He served in Louis-Philippe's first ministry as minister without portfolio and as minister of finance. In November 1830 the king persuaded him to head a liberal ministry that could ride out the storm of popular protest raised by the government's handling of the trial of Jules de Polignac and the other former ministers. Once that danger had been passed, however, the king withdrew his support, and Laffitte resigned in March 1831.

He devoted the next several years largely to his business affairs. The financial crisis of the latter 1820s and early 1830s and inept management by his associates during his absence in government service forced the liquidation of Laffitte et Cie. and brought him close to financial ruin. By 1830, however, he had salvaged enough to establish the Caisse générale du commerce et de l'industrie, a pioneering joint-stock partnership intended to meet the growing demand for long-term credit not satisfied by the traditional banking houses. The Caisse failed in 1848, but it was a model for a number of important and successful banks established during the Second Empire.

Laffitte continued to sit in the Chamber of Deputies until his death in 1844. He broke with Louis-Philippe after 1830, charging that he had betrayed the Revolution of 1830.

Laffitte was proud of his rise from humble origins to high place, and he loved the plaudits of the crowd and the trappings of wealth and power. In 1818 he purchased the magnificent chateau de Maisons, built by François Mansart in the seventeenth century for René de Logeuil, president of the Parlement de Paris. He also acquired Mme. de Pompadour's former residence, the pavilion of Louveciennes, and the immense forest and estate of Breteuil in Normandy. In 1827 in a wedding celebration that was almost regal in its splendor, he married his daughter, Albine, to Napoléon Ney, prince de la Moskava.

P. Duchon, ed., *Mémoires de Laffitte (1767–1844)* (Paris, 1932); P. Duvergier d'Haur-anne, *Histoire du gouvernement parlementaire en France, 1814–1848*, vol. 10 (Paris, 1857–71); C. de Rémusat, *Mémoires de ma vie*, vol. 2 (Paris, 1958–67); P. Thureau-Dangin, *Histoire de la monarchie de Juillet*, vol. 7 (Paris, 1888–1900).

David H. Pinkney

Related entries: BANKING; CHAMBER OF DEPUTIES; HUNDRED DAYS; LOUIS-PHILIPPE; POLIGNAC; REVOLUTION OF 1830.

LAGRANGE, CHARLES (1804–1857), militant republican under the July Monarchy, deputy to the Constituent Assembly in 1848 and to the Legislative Assembly in 1849, deported after the coup d'état of 2 December 1851. Born in Paris, Charles Lagrange enrolled in the naval artillery while he was still quite young. He was arrested by his captain when he opposed the corporal punishment imposed on another sailor during a voyage to Brazil and was sent back to France in 1822, but he was not court-martialed. In 1823 he took part in the Spanish campaign despite his politics. He left the armed services in 1829 and became a wine salesman. He participated actively in the 1830 Revolution, and then, disappointed by the new regime, he joined the Society of the Rights of Man. In April 1834 he helped that society to lead the uprising of the Lyons silk workers, and consequently he was brought to trial before the Chamber of Peers, where he declared: "We now protest against your farcical prosecution just as we then protested against your bullets." Sentenced to twenty years in prison, he was amnestied in 1839. He was forbidden to go to Paris, but he went there anyway and became an editor of the newspaper *La Réforme*.

But it was not until the Revolution of February 1848 that his name became famous. He was said (although he always denied it) to have fired the pistol shot that provoked the fusillade of the boulevard des Capucines on 23 February 1848. Then he took part in the capture of the Tuileries, read the act of abdication of Louis-Philippe, and went to the Hôtel de ville, where he took command for several days. Elected to the Constituent Assembly in the supplementary elections of 4 June 1848 from the Seine Department, he was reelected to the Legislative Assembly in 1849.

Although his name was mentioned during the June Days of 1848, he took no part in the insurrection, but later he opposed the deportation of the revolutionaries and supported an amnesty. Sitting with the Montagnards, he asked for universal suffrage and the abolition of the death penalty. Lagrange was one of the sixty-five deputies expelled from the Legislative Assembly after Bonaparte's coup d'état of 2 December 1851. He went to Belgium, then England, and finally to the Low Countries, where he died at the Hague in 1857.

Biographie des neuf cents députés à l'assemblée nationale (Paris, 1848); A. Crémieux, *"La Révolution de Février, étude critique sur les journées des 21, 22, 23 et 24 février 1848"* (thèse d'état, Paris, 1912); J. Dautry, *1848 et la Seconde république* (Paris, 1957).

                                        Jean-Claude Caron, trans. E. Newman

Related entries: CHAMBER OF PEERS; CONSTITUTION OF 1848; COUP D'ETAT OF 2 DECEMBER 1851; JUNE DAYS; LEGISLATIVE ASSEMBLY; LOUIS-PHILIPPE; LYONS, REVOLTS IN; *LA REFORME*; REVOLUTION OF 1830; REVOLUTION OF 1848; SOCIETY OF THE RIGHTS OF MAN; SPAIN, 1823 FRENCH INVASION OF.

LAIBACH, CONGRESS OF. See TROPPAU, CONGRESS OF.

LAINE, JOSEPH-LOUIS-JOACHIM, VICOMTE (1767–1835), legislator and minister. Lainé, a lawyer from Bordeaux known for his talent as an orator, became a member of the Legislative Corps in 1808, and there at the end of 1813 he provoked the anger of Napoleon by denouncing in a courageous report the evils being caused by the war and the despotic regime. Under the Restoration, he was president of the Chamber of Deputies, and from May 1816 to December 1818 he was minister of the interior in the government of the duc de Richelieu, whom he aided with the greatest possible loyalty. Afterward, he continued as a deputy and then as a member of the Chamber of Peers, which he entered in 1823, to support the so-called Center Right.

E. de Perceval, *Un ennemi de Napoléon, le vicomte Lainé . . . et la vie parlementaire au temps de la Restauration* (Paris, 1926).

Guillaume de Bertier de Sauvigny, trans. E. Newman

Related entries: CHAMBER OF DEPUTIES; CHAMBER OF PEERS; RICHELIEU.

LALANNE, LEON-LOUIS-CHRETIEN (1811–1892), appointed director of the National Workshops on 27 May 1848 after the dismissal of Emile Thomas. A graduate of the Ecole polytechnique, Léon Lalanne had already begun what was to prove a brilliant engineering career that took him from helping to build the Paris-Sceaux line in 1846, through road and railway building in Switzerland and Spain, to the post of head of the prestigious Ecole des ponts-et-chaussées and a seat in the Senate. A moderate republican, he was appointed to the independent committee of inquiry into the National Workshops that the minister of public works set up on 17 May 1848 as a first step toward ending the scheme. As secretary of his committee, Lalanne proved to be a willing instrument of the minister, and it was for this reason that when a more pliable successor to Thomas was being sought, he was chosen. He immediately closed the political club for those enrolled in the workshops that the previous director had created and set about implementing the policies the government laid down: first, a reduction in the cost of the workshops, and then their closure. He thus organized the census of those enrolled that Thomas had been reluctant to undertake. Although this was still not complete by the time the June insurrection broke out, the fact that the census was being taken heightened workers' fear that the workshops were to be closed and was thus a contributing factor to the insurrection. However, it was also Lalanne who, on his own initiative, decided to continue to pay benefits to workers during the June Days. This decision had a significant result: it limited the participation of those enrolled in the workshops in this failed insurrection. He ceased to be a director when Eugène Cavaignac closed the workshops on 3 July. The subsequent government inquiry into the June Days praised Lalanne's administration, and in letters he published in the moderate republican journal, the *National*, he himself defended his role as faithful executor of government policies.

D. C. McKay, *The National Workshops: A Study in the French Revolution of 1848* (Cambridge, Mass., 1933); *Notice sur les travaux et titres scientifiques de M. Léon Lalanne* (Paris, 1876); A. Robert, ed., *Dictionnaire des parlementaires français* (Paris, 1891).

Barrie M. Ratcliffe

Related entries: CAVAIGNAC, L.-E.; ECOLE POLYTECHNIQUE; JUNE DAYS; *LE NATIONAL*; NATIONAL WORKSHOPS; REPUBLICANS; THOMAS.

LALLEMAND, M. (?–1820), university student and liberal martyr. In the aftermath of the duke of Berry's assassination (13 February 1820), the Decazes ministry, under ultra pressure, introduced bills restoring censorship, permitting the detention of suspects for up to three months on the order of three ministers and doubling the vote of approximately 23,000 rural electors paying more than 1,000 francs in taxes. The first two laws would lapse at the end of 1821, but the third would permanently strengthen the royalist majority in the Chamber of Deputies. The debate on the bill excited active opposition by liberal deputies (the marquis de Lafayette, Jacques-Antoine Manuel, Benjamin Constant, Jacques Laffitte, Marc-René de Voyer d'Argenson) and violent demonstrations by university students (mostly from the law and medical faculties) outside the Chamber in the first week of June. One student, Lallemand, was shot by the Garde du corps on 3 June, and his funeral (5 June) was the occasion of a massive student demonstration (organized by the liberals and the Friends of Truth), which included revolutionary slogans and appeals to the working-class districts of eastern Paris. A march on the Tuileries palace (where the Royal Guard had been massed under Marshal Jacques-Etienne MacDonald) was dispersed by a violent thunderstorm. The electoral law passed on 12 June, and student demonstrations ended on 15 June. While the demonstrations may have been an attempt to overthrow the Bourbon regime, the liberal leaders were frightened by the appeal to the lower classes, and student activism soon took the form of carbonarist conspiracies.

V. Ardouin, *Journal d'un étudiant en medicine et en sciences sous la Restauration (1817–1818)* (Paris, 1964); G. de Bertier de Sauvigny, *La Restauration* (Paris, 1955, 1963); P. Manuel, *Louis XVIII* (London, 1981); A. B. Spitzer, *Old Hatreds and Young Hopes* (Cambridge, Mass., 1971).

David Longfellow

Related entries: CARBONARI; CONSTANT; LAFAYETTE, M.-J.-P.-Y.-R.-G.; LAFFITTE; MACDONALD; MANUEL; ROYAL GUARD; SOCIETY OF THE FRIENDS OF TRUTH; ULTRAROYALISTS; VOYER D'ARGENSON.

LAMARCK, JEAN-BAPTISTE-PIERRE-ANTOINE DE MONET, CHEVALIER DE (1744–1829), naturalist and botanist, advocate of the idea of evolution through appetency and of inheritance of acquired characteristics. Born at Bazentin, Picardy, on 1 August 1744, Lamarck first sought a career in the clergy and then in the military. He subsequently studied medicine but became interested in botany instead. In 1778 he published a work on French flora in which he advanced the use of dichotomous characteristics for classification. This led to his admission to the Academy of Sciences in 1779 and the recognition of his work by Georges Buffon. He gained further fame collaborating on a botanical encyclopedia. Lamarck obtained the post of botanist to Louis XVI and in 1788 was appointed to the Jardin du roi (the present Jardin des plantes). In 1793 he became professor of zoology at the Museum of Natural History (the Revolutionary term for the Jardin), a post he held for the rest of his life. He specifically lectured on insects and worms, the study of which led him to introduce the term *invertebrates* to distinguish them from animals with backbones.

The study of invertebrates henceforth became Lamarck's specialty and the vehicle for expounding his views on evolution. An incisive observer, he made a detailed study of living and fossil invertebrates, especially of shells, and he introduced the classifications of crustacea, arachnida, and annelida. Along with Georges Cuvier, he was responsible for establishing the basic classifications of biology on the basis of comparative anatomy. Through his work on invertebrates, he developed his theories on evolution, which first appeared in his *Système des animaux sans vertebres* in 1801 and were elaborated in later works. He ultimately explained the evolution of animals by four basic principles: the idea that the size of an animal tends to increase up to optimum dimensions; the idea that the development of new organs results from a desire realized by the animal; the concept that the extent of development of such organs is related to their use; and the theory that such acquired organs or characteristics are inherited by the offspring of the individual that developed them. These concepts, the second and fourth of which were the most important for posterity, were completely developed by Lamarck in his *Histoire naturelle des animaux sans vertèbres* (1815–22). He subsequently asserted that these inherited characteristics changed slowly by adapting to the environment.

Lamarck suffered from impaired vision during the last years of his life and died blind and poverty stricken in Paris on 18 December 1829. His ideas, although frequently misunderstood, were of great importance in subsequent scientific and social thought. He especially was of influence on Marx and Engels. By extending his theories to the origin of man, he was a major forerunner of Charles Darwin.

R. W. Burckhardt, *The Spirit of System: Lamarck and Evolutionary Biology* (Cambridge, 1977); H. G. Cannon, *Lamarck and Modern Genetics* (Manchester, 1959); A. S. Packard, *Lamarck the Founder of Evolution* (New York, 1901); E. Perrier, *Lamarck* (Paris, 1925).

James K. Kieswetter

Related entries: ACADEMY OF SCIENCES; CUVIER.

LAMARQUE, JEAN-MAXIMIN (1770–1832), general and liberal Restoration deputy. Lamarque enlisted in the army in 1791 as a volunteer and rose to the rank of general of brigade by 1800. He served as chief of staff to the Army of Naples, was promoted to general of division in 1807, and led the assault on Capri in 1808. Subsequent service in Italy (1809), at Wagram, and in Spain (1810–13) was praised by Napoleon in his memoirs, and Lamarque was discharged at the Restoration (1814). Rallying to Napoleon during the Hundred Days, he was charged with putting down the royalist revolt in the Vendée (April–June 1815), a task he accomplished with a skillful combination of military action and offers of leniency. Proscribed at the Second Restoration, Lamarque returned in 1818 and, like other Napoleonic officers, refused to attend court until the death of Louis XVIII. Elected a deputy (Landes) in December 1828, he became a popular leader of the liberal opposition in the Chamber. A friend of the marquis de Lafayette, Lamarque served as the liberals' military expert and constantly advocated a war of revenge against the Allied powers, which had humiliated France in 1814–15. He opposed the union of Belgium with the Netherlands as a threat to French security and welcomed the Belgian revolution of 1830. He constantly lobbied for a strong French army with a minimum of civilian control. While Lamarque regarded the Restoration as a betrayal of the ideals of the Revolution, he was critical of fellow liberals who dabbled in revolutionary conspiracies from the safety of their seats in the Chamber.

After the Revolution of 1830, the Provisional Government sent him to the Vendée to maintain order, and his command stretched from Brittany to the Pyrenees. Returning to the Chamber, he soon came to oppose the July Monarchy's foreign policy, terming the failure to aid the Polish rebellion of 1830 as great a disaster as Crécy or Agincourt. He regularly advocated the replacement of the National Guard with a trained military reserve until his death on 2 June 1832. His funeral (5 June), which coincided with a Parisian cholera epidemic and an economic crisis producing widespread unemployment and high bread prices, was an opportunity for a liberal demonstration to counter the Orleanist rally at Casimir Périer's funeral on 16 May.

After a funeral service at the Madeleine, Lamarque's body was to be carried to the pont d'Austerlitz, where it would be embarked for burial in the general's home town near Bordeaux. The huge procession of supporters, political refugees from Spain, Poland, and Italy, and the largely republican artillery units of the National Guard sang the "Marseillaise" and called for the establishment of a republic. Violence broke out during speeches at the bridge, apparently provoked by the sight of an unnamed horseman in black who displayed a red flag. An attempt was made to carry the coffin to the Pantheon, and barricades were thrown up from the place des Victoires to the Jardin des plantes. The insurrection, though widespread, was leaderless (Lafayette and other liberal deputies having fled at the first signs of violence), and Louis-Philippe, after some hesitation, brought regular troops into the city under Marshal Georges Lobau. By the evening of 5 June the revolt had been confined to the fourth arrondissement (the rues Montmartre, St. Merri, Aubry-le-boucher, and des Arcis). On 6 June, units of the army and the National Guard wiped out the last vestiges of resistance in the cloister of the church of St.-Merri with artillery and the bayonet. The total number of dead was estimated at 800.

Louis-Philippe, in contrast to Charles X two years before, appeared frequently during the fighting to supervise operations, and the decree of martial law on 7 June was soon lifted. Arrested suspects were tried in the criminal courts, which handed down eighty-two sentences (the seventeen death sentences being commuted to deportation). The artillery units of the National Guard were disbanded.

Lamarque's funeral provided a providential opportunity for an insurrection that was to some degree spontaneous and based in economic grievances. The government's prompt action, so different from its behavior in the St. Germain l'Auxerrois riots in February 1831, and the king's energetic leadership eliminated any hope of success. The republican movement, however, was not crushed, and the formation of secret societies during the following year led to renewed violence in 1834.

G. de Bertier de Sauvigny, *La Restauration* (Paris, 1955, 1963); L. Girard, *La Garde nationale 1814–1871* (Paris, 1964); T. E. B. Howarth, *Citizen King* (London, 1961); J. Lucas-Dubreton, *La Restauration et la monarchie de juillet* (Paris, 1926); D. Pinkney, *The French Revolution of 1830* (Princeton, 1972); D. Porch, *Army and Revolution* (London, 1974); A. B. Spitzer, *Old Hatreds and Young Hopes* (Cambridge, Mass., 1971); I. Tchernoff, *Le parti republicain sous la monarchie de juillet* (Paris, 1901).

David Longfellow

Related entries: BELGIAN REVOLUTION OF 1830; FOY; LAFAYETTE, M.-J.-P.-Y.-R.-G.; NATIONAL GUARD; PERIER; SAINT-GERMAIN L'AUX-ERROIS, RIOT OF.

LAMARTINE, ALPHONSE DE (1790–1869), writer, politician, and diplomat. It must be emphasized that there were two Lamartines: the poet and the public figure. While his place in the vanguard of the romantic movement in French literature was firmly established in 1820 with his *Méditations poétiques* and strengthened with later publications, his public career is usually passed over, and he is dismissed as something of a dilettante who by chance came to head the government following the 1848 Revolution. In fact, he had a long and distinguished career as a diplomat and deputy.

Lamartine's family belonged to the lesser hereditary nobility because one of his ancestors had purchased a title in the seventeenth century. His maternal grandfather was a tax officer in the domains of the duc d'Orléans, while the grandmother was a governess in the duke's household. His mother was born in the palace at Saint-Cloud and reared in the household with Louis-Philippe. Thus, he was brought up in a staunchly monarchist as well as Catholic environment. He was educated at home and at schools in Lyons and Belley. Early exposure to liberal discussions of philosophy, literature, and court life, the Revolution, and emigration helped shape his attitudes and opinions. His first public service was as mayor of Milly from 1812 to 1815, at which time he was also mayor of Saint-Point.

Like many of his contemporaries, Lamartine suffered from *mal du siècle*, his poetry reflecting his real or imagined suffering. He drifted along for years with vague hopes of receiving a diplomatic post, gambling, wenching, dreaming, and writing—forever in debt. Financial problems were to beset him all his life. In 1820, when his *Méditations* brought him instant success, he was appointed attaché at France's embassy in Naples. There for only six months, he was bored by the routine activities and lack of social life.

This was a creative period for the poet, basking in his continuing literary popularity. In 1823 he and his wife, Marianne, moved to the Saint-Point chateau, a wedding gift from his parents, which he restored at great expense.

In 1825 Lamartine became second secretary at the French legation in Florence and served there for three years. Although the post was really a social one, he was very conscientious and resourceful and proved to be popular and influential at the court of Grand Duke Leopold, in spite of initial problems caused by what the Italians perceived as disparaging passages in his latest poem, *Le Dernier chant du pèlerinage de Childe Harold*, which dealt with the heroic death of Lord Byron in the cause of Greek independence. It led to a comic opera duel with Colonel Gabriel Pepe, who had attacked Lamartine in an article published in Lucca. After the duel, the two became good friends and were lionized by Florentine society.

A writing competition for attachés in 1825 gave Lamartine the opportunity to express some of his ideas on foreign relations. One of his observations was that Russia, a country born to conquer, was where the fate of the world was germinating.

When the minister left Florence in 1827, Lamartine became chargé d'affaires and was in fact minister without receiving the title, and at only half the salary. Though he carried out his duties diligently, he was irked that his skills were not properly recognized. In 1828 he resigned his post, and in 1830, following the Revolution, he resigned from the foreign service.

By 1828 Lamartine's letters reflected his fears of an impending revolution, with hints that he was thinking ahead of a career as a deputy. He returned to the life of a country gentleman, enjoying his popularity with peasants as well as his peers. In 1829 his fears of a possible revolution were deepened, and he refused an appointment in the Polignac ministry, which he considered too reactionary. That same year he was elected to the Académie française. In his eulogy of his predecessor, Lamartine broke with tradition and gave a political speech, defending the Charter and the monarchy.

His concern for France's predicament was reflected in poems written in 1830, beginning with *Les Harmonies poétiques et religieuses*. His *Contre la peine de mort: ode au peuple* (1830) marks his first public step into the strictly political arena. It shows his respect for humanity, his horror of bloodshed, and his fear of lack of judgment among the people. He pleaded for indulgence for the ministers of Charles X.

In October his "instinct of the masses," expressed in *La Politique rationnelle*, was not wishful thinking but a quality that was to carry him over seemingly insurmountable obstacles, especially in 1848. The ideas expressed in the essay were to be expanded upon in the Chamber of Deputies during his tenure there. This manifesto of the *homme politique* emphasized social considerations: free and universal education, especially for the poor; freedom of religion and separation of church and state; revision of the penal code with abolition of the death penalty; universal but proportional suffrage; a free press with the responsibility of being the voice for all people; and the need for a constitutional monarchy as a means of realizing the common good.

When the silk workers in Lyons revolted, Lamartine was called back to serve in the National Guard. The experience in putting down the revolt deepened his concern over the problems of an industrialized society, and he foresaw an inevitable social explosion. He felt there was a need for giving the working class pride in its work and the bourgeoisie willingness to accept reforms.

Lamartine's experiences on a journey to the Middle East in 1832–33 resulted in his writing *Voyage en Orient*, which reflects more his search for religious and political than poetic inspiration. The *Résumé politique*, published with the book, makes interesting reading. In it he predicted a void in the East on the collapse of the Ottoman Empire and foresaw the possibility of military confrontations there unless the European powers cooperated to find a solution. He suggested that protectorates be set up by various powers as a means of developing commerce and industry while preserving peace and respecting religion and customs. Turkey had to be preserved as a nation, he felt.

While in Beirut, Lamartine learned he had been elected in Bergues to the Chamber of Deputies. He returned overland to France, being delayed in Bulgaria by a near-fatal illness. His maiden speech in the Assembly in 1834 dealt with the Eastern question and established him as a persuasive orator.

For the next fourteen years, Lamartine fought for social reform and attempted unsuccessfully to organize a social party. His speeches and writings for years had a messianic tone, indicating his expectation of being called on as the man in reserve in France's hour of need, as indeed he was to be in 1848. Although a legitimist and conservative, his ideas were generally liberal, and his speeches were applauded in turn by the republican and conservative factions in the Assembly.

Although elected in 1834 in Mâcon to the Chamber, Lamartine chose to continue representing Bergues, where he was well liked. He realized that there was a certain amount of hostility toward him in Mâcon in spite of his being a member of the General Council there.

In 1835 Lamartine spoke out in favor of paying France's debt to the United States, incurred during the destruction of some U.S. ships during the Napoleonic era. The question had caused strained Franco-American relations for years and had been debated in the Chamber many times. His speech influenced the later decision to pay reparations.

In the same session Lamartine advocated the abolition of slavery (as he did again in 1836, 1838, 1840, and 1842) and voted for funds for the colonies' transition from an economy based on slavery to one based on a free society. He also spoke out on the lack of rehabilitation for convicts, on electoral reform, on the shocking infanticide rate, and on the disgrace of foundling homes.

Any impetus toward social reform that Lamartine's speeches might have generated was slowed almost to a halt by Fieschi's attempt on the life of Louis-Philippe. The reactionary September Laws of 1835 enacted then remained in force until 1848. While acknowledging that press reforms were needed, a militant Lamartine spoke out against the measures limiting freedom of speech and the press.

In the 1837 elections Lamartine won in Bergues, Mâcon, and Cluny. This time he chose to represent his home district Mâcon, a disappointment to his Bergues supporters.

The question of railroad development came up in 1838. Lamartine advocated that routes be under the direction of the state, with a systematic network. Although he was to continue his fight until 1850, he lost this round when the Chamber voted to leave the railroads to private companies, some of which failed later. In 1842 he suggested that government and private industry work together, and he accepted appointment as president of a commission to study the project.

In 1839 Lamartine was offered a peerage that could have assured him of an income that would solve his financial problems, but he preferred to remain a deputy and fight for social and political reform. He also turned down offers of ministerial posts, feeling he could not work with François Guizot who, as foreign minister, was to exercise real power until 1848. The offer of an ambassadorial post to London or Vienna was also refused.

Debates in the Chamber in 1840–41 dealt with the fortifications of Paris, which Lamartine vehemently opposed. Almost as though he could foresee the Paris Commune of 1871, he declared that the walls, while useless against a foreign invasion, could be a weapon in the hands of factions and a threat to freedom of deliberation in the Assembly. He preferred Frederick the Great's concept of mobile armies as a better means of defense and detached outposts instead of walls. His efforts were in vain; the Chamber approved the construction. He also favored the construction of the Suez Canal.

In 1842–43 Lamartine placed himself openly in opposition to Guizot but refused to sit with the Left. Now a popular speaker in his home region during legislative recesses, he advocated there and in the Chamber the creation of a democratic form of government through an orderly and peaceful achievement of democratic ideals without bloodshed. In the matter of labor unions, he opposed them but encouraged the development of industry. He hoped to prevent the wealthy from exploiting the workers by means of social legislation.

At Mâcon Lamartine and four colleagues founded a newspaper, the *Bien public*, published twice a week until 1848, when it was moved to Paris. It was a costly venture to which Lamartine himself contributed over 15,000 francs a year, but it furnished him a regular forum for expressing his political views. That same year, 1843, he began writing his monumental *Histoire des Girondins*, which was to achieve enormous popular success on its publication in 1847. Contrary to general criticism that the history was hastily written and not adequately documented, the fact is that the author was constantly reading memoirs and documents and interviewing survivors of that era. Nevertheless, there are many factual errors in the history. His financial position at this time was very precarious but would improve in 1844 with the advance sale of the history and his *Confidences*.

Lamartine continued his advocacy of freedom of education, especially the education of the least favored classes and the separation of church and state. It was to be another half-century before the separation was effected. Another social reform he kept fighting for was in the prison system. Condemning the policy of solitary confinement for those serving long sentences, he pleaded for deportation and rehabilitation of prisoners as more humane treatment. Concerned with the problems of workers, Lamartine proposed state intervention in matters of employment and wages of the masses. He believed that if a worker were fired or lost his job because his factory was closed, the state should provide temporary employment.

During the 1846 legislative session, Lamartine made thirteen speeches. He was not to appear on the rostrum again until January 1848. His speeches reflected his wide interests and concerns: opposition to slavery; support of savings banks and retirement funds for workers; support of the Maronites being massacred in Syria; opposition to a protective tariff, which he felt would adversely affect viticulture; advocacy of deepening of the Seine from Rouen to the sea for passage of larger ships; opposition to the monopoly of the Loire coal basin association, defending the right of the poor to buy cheap coal; and opposition to the high salt tax. Thus ended the most active, eloquent, and fruitful part of his parliamentary career. In August he was reelected in Mâcon by a large majority.

In spite of the success of the Girondins in 1847, it was a sad period for Lamartine because he could see that France was on the path to another revolution. In one letter he predicted that he would be "the leader of a new social order" with the fall of the monarchy, followed by a "revolution of contempt" and the Second Empire. At the same time as he was denying that he wanted a revolution, Lamartine saw political revolution as a vehicle for social change.

In spite of the Banquet Campaign during 1847, the king and his ministers were very complacent when parliament was reconvened in 1848. The undercurrent of opposition and dissatisfaction was to explode during the February Days of 1848, forcing the abdication of Louis-Philippe and the emigration of the royal family.

Ill, Lamartine stayed at home from 21 to 24 February but was kept fully informed about events in Paris. On word that an invasion of the Chamber was imminent, he got out of bed and walked alone to the Palais Bourbon where chaos reigned. During a heated debate on whether to establish a regency or a republic headed by a provisional government, Lamartine took the floor and in a brief speech advocated a provisional government, which would reestablish order, with elections to follow at once. In that way the people could choose their form of government.

For the duration of the February Days, Lamartine showed great personal courage in the face of real physical danger, especially during the march to the Hôtel de ville and the installation there of the Provisional Government, with Jacques-Charles Dupont de l'Eure as the figurehead president. His oratory on many occasions turned away anger and hostility and possibly prevented much bloodshed.

Following Lamartine's leadership, the Provisional Government called for the people's support and indicated its preference for a republic. The orator himself was named minister of foreign affairs, but—because of his leadership and Dupont's age—he was the real head of government. Decrees dissolved the Constituent Assembly, freed all political prisoners, and reassured the people that elections would be held as soon as order was restored.

Lamartine would not yield to the crowd's attempt to force adoption of the red flag, symbol of revolutionary struggles, and successfully argued that French prestige abroad would be greatly diminished if the tricolor were not adopted.

Under Lamartine's direction, other decrees were issued proclaiming the Republic, the abolition of the September Laws, and the establishment of public welfare institutions—measures that he had been pushing for years. National Workshops were created to deal with the enormous unemployment problems.

The Provisional Government was composed of two factions: a majority of conservatives and a minority of republican-socialists. As calm returned to Paris, the real revolution began: the attempt to change old and create new institutions. Lamartine's primacy reassured the notables and bourgeoisie because of his heritage and the revolutionaries because of his championship of social reform.

In addition to measures already passed, others were approved that reopened postal routes, declared freedom of the press, abolished all titles of nobility, provided help for orphans and those wounded in combat, created the National Mobile Guard, and planned for educational reform.

The United States was the first country to recognize the new government, and the revolution was accepted throughout France. In March Lamartine issued his "Manifesto to the Powers" to reassure other European nations that France wished to maintain harmonious relations with them. He refused to let France be drawn into entangling adventures in other countries or to become involved with schemes of various refugee groups stirring up trouble in France.

The early feeling of euphoria among rich and poor, conservative and radical, was gradually dispelled when each group realized its goals alone could not be achieved. Those who had rushed out early to pay their taxes in support of the government were soon disillusioned when they saw how much money was being spent to support thousands of workers. The economic crisis was the most serious one faced by the government, and it is to France's credit that it was the only European nation to try to help the workers. When the workshops were closed in June, Paris erupted in protest.

Rivalries and bitter party jealousies continued to increase. With the new freedoms, clubs and newspapers of all persuasions sprang up. In spite of the restlessness pervading France, Lamartine was at the height of his popularity and was elected in ten constituencies in April. In May the new, conservative Constituent Assembly was convened. Lamartine gave an accounting of the stewardship and accomplishments of the Provisional Government and reported on the conduct of foreign affairs and the successes of French diplomacy.

It is generally believed that Lamartine could have been chosen the sole executive head of the government then, but in spite of his vanity he did not want the honor. An executive committee of five, including Lamartine, was set up by the

Assembly. His insistence on Ledru-Rollin's inclusion and his negative reaction to the popular clamor for help for the Poles in their struggle for independence were factors in his coming fall from power. At the Fête de la concorde in May in honor of the new Assembly, Lamartine received the final homage of his public career. The crowd was enthusiastic in its adulation; however, it was increasingly apparent that the fire within him was dying, and his popularity beginning to wane.

Public agitation increased among factions opposing or favoring the abolition of the National Workshops. On 23 June there was a full-blown insurrection, and cries of "Down with Lamartine" were heard. The next day the Assembly invested General Eugène Cavaignac, the minister of war, with sole executive authority. Reaction had set in and continued to grow until it swept Louis-Napoleon into power in December.

The man of the hour in February had to suffer much verbal abuse and accusations of misconduct that summer. Accused of mismanagement of funds, he furnished figures to clear himself. In spite of his bitterness, Lamartine continued to express concern for the preservation of the Republic.

In September Lamartine proposed a unicameral legislature and the election of a president by universal suffrage. Some believe that had an election been held then, Lamartine would have become president.

In October Lamartine returned to a hero's public welcome in Mâcon. There were, nevertheless, cries of "Down with Lamartine" and "Long live the emperor" among the crowd. Unwilling to campaign, he was willing to accept the presidency had the vote gone his way in the election. To France's shame, he ran last in a field of five. The following May he was not even reelected in Mâcon, but two months later he won a by-election in Orléans and chose to represent that constituency although a repenting Mâcon also elected him soon thereafter.

Lamartine continued to serve his country until the coup d'état of 2 December 1851, but his heart was not in it. Life for him for the next twenty-one years was a constant struggle to earn enough by writing to pay his debts. He churned out histories, autobiographical works, plays, novels, poetry, and travel accounts. It is tragic that one who had contributed so much of himself and his means—spendthrift though he was—to French life should end his days in this way. The government made amends in a small way by awarding him a national recompense in 1867.

L. Barthou, *Lamartine Orateur* (Paris, 1916); G. Brereton, *A Short History of French Literature* (Baltimore, 1968); H. Castelli, "Alphonse de Lamartine: A Reevaluation of His Role in Nineteenth Century French Political Life" (Ph.D diss., University of Colorado, 1975); A. de Lamartine, *Correspondance de Lamartine*, ed. Valentine de Lamartine, 6 vols. (Paris, 1873–75) and *Oeuvres complètes de M. A. Lamartine*, 41 vols., vols. 37–40 constitute his *Mémoires politiques* (Paris, 1860–66); M. Toesca, *Lamartine ou l'amour de la vie* (Paris, 1969); H. R. Whitehouse, *The Life of Lamartine*, 2 vols. (Freeport, N.Y., 1969, reprinted).

Helen Castelli

Related entries: ACADEMIE FRANCAISE; BYRON; *CAISSES D'EPARGNE*; CAVAIGNAC, L.-E.; COAL INDUSTRY; DUPONT DE L'EURE; GARDE

MOBILE; GUIZOT; LEDRU-ROLLIN; LYONS, REVOLTS IN; NATIONAL WORKSHOPS; PRESS LAWS; PROVISIONAL GOVERNMENT; PUBLIC INSTRUCTION; PUBLIC WELFARE; RAILROADS; REVOLUTION OF 1848.

LAMBRECHTS, CHARLES-JOSEPH, COMTE DE (1753–1823), minister of the Directory, senator of the Empire, deputy of the Restoration. Born on 20 November 1753 at Saint-Trond in the Austrian Netherlands, Lambrechts studied law at Louvain, receiving his doctorate in 1782. He taught canon law there and became rector of the university in 1786. When the French invaded in 1792 and annexed his homeland, he supported the Revolution and became a naturalized French citizen. He served as a member of the municipal government of Brussels and later became president of the administration of the department of Dyle. On 27 September 1797 the Directory appointed him minister of justice, where he remained until 22 June 1800. He was once even considered a candidate for the Directory itself in 1799, but Siéyès was chosen instead. When Napoleon established his Senate, Lambrechts was in the initial group appointed on 24 December 1799. As a senator he opposed both the life consulate and the establishment of the Empire. Nevertheless, on 2 October 1803 Napoleon appointed him to the Legion of Honor and on 13 May 1808 named him a count of the Empire.

Lambrechts took the lead in the Senate in demanding the dethronement of Napoleon on 2 April 1814. Assigned to draft the document to accomplish the dethronement, he prepared a vicious attack on his former benefactor. Immediately appointed to the committee to draft a new constitution, it was Lambrechts who wrote the passage, "The French people freely summon to the throne Louis Stanislas Xavier, brother of the last king." During the Hundred Days he opposed the Acte additionnel. In the early years of the Restoration he did not participate in public affairs, until in September 1819 the department of Bas-Rhin elected him to the Chamber of Deputies. As a deputy he joined the liberal opposition, supporting the admission of abbé Grégoire and opposing the Law of the Double Vote. At his death in Paris on 3 August 1823, he left an endowment of 12,000 francs to establish a hospital for blind Protestants and 2,000 francs to the Institute for work on freedom of religion. The minister of the interior, Jacques-Joseph Corbière, rejected this latter sum.

Archives parlementaires; P. Duvergier de Hauranne, *Histoire du gouvernement parlementaire en France, 1814–1848* (Paris, 1857–71); A. Robert et al., *Dictionnaire des parlementaires français* (Paris, 1889–91).

James K. Kieswetter

Related entries: ACTE ADDITIONNEL; CHAMBER OF DEPUTIES; CORBIERE; DOUBLE VOTE, LAW OF THE; GREGOIRE; HUNDRED DAYS; SIEYES.

LAMENNAIS, FELICITE-ROBERT DE (1782–1854), until 1834 he spelled his name La Mennais; priest and the leading Catholic thinker of the Restoration whose political and social ideas led him first to liberal Catholicism and then to renounce his religion for a second vocation as social reformer. Judged by most traditional criteria, Félicité de Lamennais was a failure. Physically unprepossessing and invariably in poor health, he spent most of his life alone, and yet he longed for close friendships. An intellectual who ate little and slept less and who wrote massively, he sought to alter radically first the church and then society as a whole, and yet, apart from universal suffrage, he did not live to see any of the changes he advocated. He and his collaborators on the journal *L'Avenir* generated excitement among the younger clergy and controversy in the church by proposing a radical reorientation in church attitudes toward society and government. Yet his liberal Catholicism was doomed from the outset since both pope in Rome and episcopate in France believed that the best policies for a church still under siege were those that had worked in the past. Not only did *L'Avenir* and Mennaisian thought create no permanent movement, but Lamennais, at the age of fifty-two and after a prolonged and increasingly solitary personal crisis, was led to break with the church that had condemned his ideas. In the last twenty years of his life, he developed his democratic and reforming ideas in books and in journals. Yet though there were always those among socialist thinkers and workers' groups who admired him, he never gained a following. Twice elected to parliament in 1848–49, he proved a feeble orator and exerted no influence over the course of events.

Nevertheless, Lamennais' career is significant in three important ways. First, at the most general level, the principal preoccupations of all his writings show the impact the dual revolution—the French Revolution that had taken place and the industrial revolution that was beginning—had on French intellectual life in the first half of the nineteenth century. Second, and more specifically, Lamennais before 1834 was foremost among those who breathed new intellectual vigor into French Catholicism. By his desire to strengthen the pope's authority and thus give greater unity to the church, he was one of the first and most uncompromising of ultramontanes. By his desire to separate church and state and to ally church with liberalism, he was one of the first liberal Catholics. By his concern for the working classes, he was an early proponent of social Catholicism. Each of these was destined to be a major trend in the nineteenth and twentieth centuries. Third, at a more personal level, there is moral grandeur in the decision he took to break with the church and to follow the dictates of his logic and his conscience. His devotion to the cause of the moral and physical regeneration of the working classes that had been the most powerful reason for the break was to guide his subsequent career as a writer and activist. Indeed, in death as in life he was to remain faithful to the dictates of his conscience. Despite the entreaties of some, including the church itself, there was no deathbed recantation and, as he had wished, he was buried in an anonymous pauper's grave.

Ordained a priest in 1816, Lamennais quickly acquired renown as a leading Catholic intellectual and soon gathered around him at La Chesnaie, the property he owned with his brother in their native Brittany, a group of young clerics and laymen. In 1817 he published the first volume of his *Essai sur l'indifférence en matière de religion*. An immediate success, the work was held by many to be a masterpiece. An uncompromising condemnation of the Enlightenment belief in individual reason, which led inevitably to a decline in religion and an erosion of social stability, the work argued that society could avoid a repetition of the excesses and errors of the Revolutionary and Napoleonic eras only by accepting Catholic truth. Though not entirely original—Lamennais had been influenced by the Saint-Sulpicians—the work had the advantage of being powerfully written and being heartfelt, since he had himself long hesitated before taking up his vocation.

As early as the mid–1820s, however, this defender of the faith was developing more radical ideas concerning the church's relations with the state. Seeing the growing opposition to the regime, Lamennais came to the conclusion that the Bourbons would eventually be overthrown and that the church had to ally itself with the liberals. Liberalism alone, he believed, was flawed since religion was needed to cement the new order that was to be established. Such an alliance would thus ensure that both would triumph and that anarchy and despotism would be avoided. It was to spread such ideas that, immediately after the July Revolution, Lamennais and a group of friends set up the journal *L'Avenir*. This was not the first liberal Catholic periodical—the *Correspondant*, set up in 1829, had been the most important forerunner—but, by virtue of the status Lamennais enjoyed and the verve of collaborators like Lacordaire and Charles de Montalembert (1810–70), it was the most daring and successful. *L'Avenir* argued that the political conservatism of church leaders had alienated the people and proposed separation of church and state—a radical suggestion when at the time there was no major religion in Europe that did not have state support and no major state that did not have an official or semiofficial church—and freedom of education, arguing that parents had the right to educate their children as they saw fit. Such radical proposals raised a storm of opposition among the episcopate and conservatives, and when the journal ceased publication in November 1831, its three chief editors decided to take their arguments to Rome to seek papal approval. Such a mission was doomed to failure. Liberal Catholicism had secured no support among French bishops and had many opponents in the Vatican. Worse, Gregory XVI, the new pope, was himself a conservative who had recently faced an uprising in his own Papal States and who not only condemned the insurrection of the Poles, who were Catholics, against non-Catholic oppressors, but even refused to recognize Belgian independence. In August 1832 the pope issued the encyclical *Mirari vos*, which, without mentioning anyone by name, condemned liberal Catholicism. In the months that followed, Lamennais did not publicly retract his views, but he kept a docile silence that seemed to indicate submission. In private, however, he was recalcitrant and continued to develop his ideas. Not only did he come to believe that those who had seized power in July 1830 had stymied the revolution but that even universal suffrage would not be enough to eradicate social inequalities. He came to believe that he had a God-given mission to aid the working classes and that he could not carry out this mission from within a church that was incapable of change. In the course of 1833 he completed a work that was to signal his break—the *Paroles d'un croyant*—but not until April 1834 did he publish it. Deliberately written in an Old Testament style that was to give it popular appeal, this, his best-known work, was a moving indictment of the oppression of the working classes by kings and capitalists and a prophecy that an end to oppression was in sight. The moment was propitious, for the book's publication coincided with the failure of the Lyons uprising and the massacre of the rue Transnonain. *Paroles d'un croyant* went through eight editions within a year. Lamennais' defiance of the pope was also rewarded; the *Singulari nos* encyclical of July 1834 condemned not only his book but Mennaisian philosophy.

In the last two decades of his unexpectedly long life, Lamennais dutifully followed his new vocation as a proponent of political and social reform. He continued to explain and justify his break with the church, publishing a critique of Vatican policies (*Affaires de Rome*, 1836) and the diary he had kept during the long crisis from 1831 to 1834 (*Discussions critiques*, 1841). But he also attempted to talk directly to the working classes, publishing *Livre du peuple* (1837) and *Esclavage moderne* (1839), which again condemned the established order and announced its imminent demise. He also issued a new translation of the Gospels. Lamennais even played a minor role in politics. In 1835 he spoke in favor of the republicans on trial in the capital. In 1840 his short pamphlet, *Le pays et le gouvernement*, was such a violent critique of the government that he was imprisoned for a year. Although he played no important part in the events of 1848, a tired and deaf Lamennais found renewed enthusiasm, publishing *Le Peuple constituant* (27 February–3 July 1848), and sitting on the extreme Left of the National Assembly. The journal, *La Réforme*, which he founded the following year, lasted only a few weeks.

This period after 1834 was perhaps the loneliest and certainly the least successful of his career. The social and political message he preached was neither original nor incisive enough to attract more than a handful of followers. He continued to believe in the need for religion, but he refused to be a nineteenth-century Luther founding a new religion, arguing that a new Christianity would eventually emerge but that it could not be forced or fabricated. He criticized those who advocated equal remuneration, expropriating the property of the rich, and giving greater power to the state. But his own proposals were unoriginal. He argued that the way out of suffering and exploitation lay through universal suffrage, education, and workers' associations backed by mutual credit. Rather than by his ideas, it was by his example and personal sacrifice, by the warmth of his feeling and his language, that Lamennais attracted attention. But he attracted admirers rather than followers.

J.-R. Derré, *Lamennais, ses amis et le mouvement des idées à l'époque romantique (1824–1834)* (Paris, 1962); J.-B. Duroselle, *Les débuts du Catholicisme social en France (1822–1870)* (Paris, 1951); L. Le Guillou, *L'évolution de la pensée religieuse de Lamennais* (Paris, 1966); R. Rémond, *Lamennais et la démocratie* (Paris, 1948); P. N. Stearns, *Priest and Revolutionary: Lamennais and the Dilemma of French Catholicism*

(New York, 1967); R. L. White, *"L'Avenir" de La Mennais. Son rôle dans la presse de son temps* (Paris, 1974).

Barrie M. Ratcliffe

Related entries: L'AVENIR; BELGIAN REVOLUTION OF 1830; ECONOMIC CHANGE; LACORDAIRE; LIBERAL CATHOLICISM; LIBERTY OF EDUCATION; LYONS, REVOLTS IN; MONTALEMBERT; *LE PEUPLE CONSTITUANT*; SOCIAL CATHOLICISM; TRANSNONAIN, MASSACRE OF THE RUE; ULTRAMONTANES; WORKERS' COOPERATIVES.

LAMETH, ALEXANDRE-THEODORE-VICTOR DE, BARON (1760–1829), noble delegate to the Estates General, revolutionary, *émigré*, Napoleonic prefect, and opposition deputy under the Restoration. Alexander de Lameth was part of an illustrious family. His father, a general officer in the royal army, was married to the sister of Marshal de Broglie, and each of his three brothers had a prominent military and political career. Augustin (1755–1837) was a marquis who retired from his position as a brigadier general with the Revolution and later served in the Corps législatif from the Somme (1806–10). Théodore (1756–1854), a count, fought in America and had risen to the rank of colonel by 1789. Elected to the Legislative Assembly in 1791, he sat with the Right, voted against the war, and emigrated with the fall of the monarchy. Napoleon's amnesty brought him back to France in 1800, and he served the electors of the Somme in the Chamber of Representatives. Charles (1757–1832), a count, fought and was wounded at the battle of Yorktown (1781) and then served the comte d'Artois before being a delegate to the Second Estate in 1789. As a deputy from Artois, he sided with the Revolution and served in the army until the fall of the monarchy; he then emigrated until 1800 and returned to the army only in 1809. In 1829 he replaced his brother as a deputy from Pontoise (Seine-et-Oise). He voted on the Left with the 221, but later, as a supporter of hereditary peerages, he sat on the Right after the July Revolution.

Alexandre de Lameth followed in the path of his older brothers. He joined the royal army as a sublieutenant in 1777 and served with Rochambeau in America. On 5 April 1789 the nobles of Péronne selected him for the Estates General. On the night of 4 August 1789, Lameth was one of the first nobles to renounce his title, and he made the motion to use the lands of the church to solve the fiscal crisis.

The events of 1791 pushed Lameth toward a more conservative stance. By the end of the year he was firmly behind the monarchy. The outbreak of war caused him to be promoted to brigadier general and to be posted to the Army of the Nord. Like another veteran of the war in America, the marquis de Lafayette, Lameth went over to the Austrian side and was interned until 1795. The entire Lameth clan returned under the 1800 amnesty of Napoleon.

The talents of Lameth were put to use by Napoleon as a prefect. Napoleon rewarded Lameth with the Legion of Honor (1804), named him a baron of the

Empire (1810), officer of the Legion of Honor (1811), and *maître des requêtes* to the Council of State (1811).

Lameth fully accepted the restoration of the monarchy. He dropped the use of his title, baron of the Empire, returned to the army as a lieutenant general, and became prefect of the Somme. The events of the First Restoration, however, once again caused Lameth to shift his loyalty back to the emperor. He accepted appointment to the Chamber of Peers of the Hundred Days, although here he did more to defend royalists and support his old compatriot Lafayette than to aid the emperor. Nevertheless, any service to the emperor in 1815 was enough to ruin one's standing with the king. Lameth was excluded from the peers in August 1815, and he retired from the army in 1816.

This veteran of the Constituent Assembly returned to the legislature in the elections of April 1820. Contrary to the Right's expectations, not all the new double voters favored men of the Right. Those of the Seine-Inférieure had chosen Lameth, who sat with the constitutional opposition and fought the policies of Joseph de Villèle as a basic violation of the Charter. Lameth was not reelected in the royalist landslide of 1824.

By 1827 the political tides had shifted once again, and the electors of Pontoise (Seine-et-Oise) chose Lameth as their deputy. Like most other nobles, Lameth was extremely wealthy (his taxes were 1,999 francs in 1827), but unlike most of the rest of his order, he took his seat on the Left. His long public career ended with his death in 1829. His fellow opposition deputies Kératry, Casimir Périer, and Antoine Jay spoke at his funeral.

A. Lameth, *Histoire de l'Assemblée Constituante* (Paris, 1828–29), *Motion de M. Alexandre de Lameth, sur les parlemens* (1789), *Opinion sur les lois des élections* (1820), and *Un électeur à ses collègues* (1824); A. Robert and G. Cougny, *Dictionnaire des parlementaires français* (Paris, 1889–91).

Thomas Beck

Related entries: CHAMBER OF DEPUTIES; CHAMBER OF PEERS; COUNCIL OF STATE; DOUBLE VOTE, LAW OF THE; HUNDRED DAYS; JAY; KERATRY, LAFAYETTE, M.-J.-P.-Y.-R.-G.; PERIER; REVOLUTION OF 1830; THE 221; VILLELE.

LAMORICIERE, LOUIS JUCHAULT DE (1805–1865), general and politician. Lamoricière was probably the most brillant of the Africains. A graduate of the Ecole polytechnique, he participated as a sapper in the siege of Algiers in 1830. He became the first commander of the Arab Bureau established to administer the Algerian populations and was among the first French officers to learn the language, social organization, and customs of the native Algerians. His energy, as well as his astute use of intelligence, made him a particularly formidable general. He served in most of the major campaigns from the siege of Constantine (1847) to the battle of Isly (1844) and received the surrender of Abd el-Kader in 1847. A Saint-Simonian, he promoted the settlement of military colonies. Elected to the Constituent Assembly in 1848, he served Eugène Cavaignac as war minister after the June Days of 1848. Arrested and imprisoned in the fortress of Ham in 1851 because of his opposition to Louis Napoleon Bonaparte, he spent the years 1852–57 in exile. In 1860, he entered the service of the pope, only to be defeated by the Italians at Castelfidardo and forced to surrender.

A. Flory, *Le général de Lamoricière* (Paris, 1942); F. Hugonnet, *Français et Arabes en Algérie* (Paris, 1860); C.-A. Julien, *Histoire de l'Algérie contemporaine* (Paris, 1964); E. Keller, *Le général de La Moricière, sa vie militaire, politique et religieuse* (Paris, 1874); A. Rastoul, *Le général Lamoricière* (Lille, 1894).

Douglas Porch

Related entries: CONSTITUTION OF 1848; ECOLE POLYTECHNIQUE; JUNE DAYS; SAINT-SIMONIANISM.

LAMOTHE-LANGON, ETIENNE-LEON DE, BARON (1786–1864), administrator of the Empire, author of the Restoration and July Monarchy. Born at Montpellier on 1 April 1786, Lamothe-Langon's childhood was disrupted by the Revolution. In 1793 he was listed as an *émigré*, which he managed to have repealed only with some difficulty after the fall of Maximilien Robespierre. Henceforth he basically devoted himself to literature and published a collection of patriotic poetry against England in 1803. He entered the Council of State as an auditor in 1809, a position intended for the training of future administrators. In July 1811 he was appointed subprefect at Toulouse, where he dealt judiciously and humanely with famine-caused disturbances. In October 1813 he became subprefect at Leghorn, Tuscany, and was wounded in December defending Viareggio against the allies. Unemployed during the First Restoration, in May 1815 he became subprefect at Carcassonne, where he had to deal with royalist excesses. He resigned shortly after Waterloo, the target of much royalist enmity. In March 1819 he was appointed subprefect at Saint-Pons (Hérault) but was dismissed before he could assume office. This revived his interest in literature, and he never again returned to public office.

Lamothe-Langon is best remembered not for his prefectoral functions but as a romantic novelist and writer of false memoirs. Beginning with *Clemence Isaure et les troubadours* in 1808, his novels exhibited a vivid imagination and the subject matter typical of the romantics. This was followed by *L'Ermitage de la tombe mysterieuse* (1815), *Le Vampire ou la vierge de Hongrie* (1824), and *Monsieur le préfet* (1824), as well as many other works. Just as his novels catered to the popular taste, he became involved in writing pseudo-memoirs, which filled the gap left in public demand when real memoirs failed. In 1829–30 he published *Mémoirs et souvenirs d'un pair de France*. This led to *Mémoirs sur Louis XVIII* (1832–33), *Mémoirs de Napoléon Bonaparte* (1834), and others. Lamothe-Langon died in Paris in 1864.

N. Richardson, *The French Prefectoral Corps, 1814–1830* (Cambridge, 1966); J. Savant, *Les Préfets de Napoleon* (Paris, 1958); R. Switzer, *Etienne-Léon de Lamothe-Langon et le roman populaire français de 1800 à 1830* (Toulouse, 1962).

James K. Kieswetter

Related entries: COUNCIL OF STATE; HUNDRED DAYS; RESTORATION, FIRST; ROMANTICISM.

LANJUINAIS, JEAN-DENIS (1753–1827), count of the Empire, French statesman, jurist, and Oriental scholar. Lanjuinais led a broad-ranged political and scholarly life, which spanned the Old Regime, the Revolution, and the Restoration. He served in legislative assemblies of the Revolutionary and Napoleonic eras and later became president of the Restoration Chamber of Peers. But he was also an erudite man whose career included a law professorship at Rennes and independent scholarship in Oriental religion and philosophy.

Born to a comfortable bourgeois family, Lanjuinais studied law and became a counselor to the Provincial Estates of Brittany. From that position he became an active participant in the Revolution. In 1789 he was elected to be a deputy from Rennes to the Third Estate at the Estates General. There, he was an outspoken critic of the privileged orders and was one of the authors of the Civil Constitution of the Clergy. Altough initially supporting a constitutional monarchy with the balance of power in an elected chamber, he gradually came to advocate a moderate republic. As a deputy to the National Convention, in 1792 he supported sparing the life, if not the kingship, of Louis XVI but saved his strongest comments to criticize the Mountain and its encouragement of the crowds. Under the Terror he and his family were banished to his estate, but in 1795 the National Convention recalled him.

Although Lanjuinais opposed making Napoleon consul for life and later was critical of the Empire and its suppression of liberty, Napoleon still recognized Lanjuinais' popularity by first appointing him senator for life (1800) and then comte d'Empire (1808). Napoleon also named him to the Legion of Honor. During these same years he pursued his interest in Orientalism and in law, founding with other jurists the Academy of Legislation in Paris. For his studies on Oriental religion, he was elected to the Institut.

Lanjuinais had mixed feelings about the return of the Bourbon monarchy but decided to support it, hoping that it would help heal the wounds created by the Revolution. During the First Restoration he opposed the ultraroyalists at Rennes, where he had been named president of the electoral college by Louis XVIII, and in general fought all attempts to restrict the individual liberty of those charged with political crimes. Upon Napoleon's return, Lanjuinais refused to sign the Additional Act, but he served when chosen by the electors of Paris to the new Assembly. He was elected its president.

Louis XVIII reappointed him to the Chamber of Peers in the Second Restoration, and he was elected its president also. He sat and voted with the liberal Left, vainly voting against a guilty verdict for Michael Ney and then against condemning him to death. He supported a mixed government but with emphasis on the nation's being represented by an elected body. In the light of the return of the Bourbons, he was willing to acknowledge the need for some kind of aristocracy as long as it was given responsible functions in behalf of the nation, was controlled by law, and was open to all. The Chamber of Peers met these criteria for him, although he would have preferred that it not be hereditary.

His interpretation of the Charter was very liberal, and this put him in early opposition to the *chambre introuvable*. When the Decazes ministry came to power in late 1816, Lanjuinais supported the government's sponsorship of a liberalized electoral law and the military recruitment law of 1818. He also called for the return of those peers who had been proscribed for their participation in the Hundred Days.

In 1820, after the assassination of the duc de Berry, Lanjuinais again went into opposition. He ardently opposed the various attempts of the Villèle ministry to turn back some of the gains of the Revolution. A Catholic of Jansenist persuasion, Lanjuinais was also a strong advocate of religious liberty. Therefore, in his political writings, as well as in the Chamber of Peers, he expressed great concern about what he saw as the growing influence of the Jesuits and the reestablishment of clerical influence in public affairs. In 1825 he spoke against the indemnity bill, arguing that the public treasury could ill afford giving public funds to those who still held substantial landed property.

His last great battle was over the proposed law on primogeniture. Despite a heart attack in 1826, Lanjuinais came before the Peers once again to fight what he saw as a renewed attempt by the nobility of the Old Regime to gain despotic control over the people of France. In an earlier work, *Constitutions de la nation française* (1819), Lanjuinais had condemned the nobility as a lazy, selfish caste and as unnecessary to the monarchy of the Restoration as it was to that of the Old Regime. In 1826 he reminded his listeners and readers that the French nobility was not the English aristocracy. The latter may have had the interests of the people at heart, but the French nobility never served any useful purpose, not even as a bulwark against royal despotism. A revived nobility, recreated by primogeniture, would threaten representative government and individual liberty. He also argued against the law because of the privilege it gave to males, thereby putting women in perpetual tutelage.

Lanjuinais died in 1827, but not before he completed his translation of the *Bhagavad Gita* from Sanskrit.

E. Cappadocia, "The Liberals and Madame de Staël," *Essays Presented to Louis Gottschalk*, ed. R. Herr and H. T. Parker (Durham, N.C., 1965); B. J. Dacier, "Notice historique," Institut royale de France (Paris, 1829); G. A. Kelly, "Liberalism and Aristocracy," *Journal of the History of Ideas* 26 (1965); J.-D. Lanjuinais, *Constitution de la nation française* (Paris, 1819), *Discours contre le projet de rétablir . . . les privileges d'ainesse* (Paris, 1826), and *Oeuvres*, 4 vols., volume 4 of which contains his translation of the *Bhagavad-Gita* and his other writings on Indian literature, religion, and philosophy (Paris, 1832); V. Lanjuinais, "Notice historique," in *Oeuvres* (Paris, 1832); A. Lardier, *Histoire biographique de la chambre des pairs* (Paris, 1829); L. Sèche, *Les derniers jansénistes*, vol. 2 (Paris, 1891).

Sanford Gutman

Related entries: ACTE ADDITIONNEL; CHAMBER OF PEERS; *CHAMBRE INTROUVABLE*; DECAZES; HEREDITY LAWS; INDEMNITY BILL OF 1825; NEY.

LAPELOUZE, VALENTIN DE (?–?), journalist under the Restoration, a director of the *Courrier français*. A liberal, Lapelouze moved the *Courrier français*, a pro-government newspaper, into the opposition. He wrote both political articles and theatrical notes. His famous collaborators included Rable, Malleval, Denis-Louis Avenel, Isambert, Auguste de Kératry, Marc-René de Voyer d'Argenson, Adolphe and Auguste Blanqui, and Joseph Mérilhou who, after he became a prosecuting attorney under the July Monarchy, would later ask for the death penalty against Auguste Blanqui. Valentin de Lapelouze was also the editor of the poems of Jean Loret, a seventeenth-century chronicler.

Le Courrier, later *Le Courrier francais*, June 1819-March 1851; Dommanget, *Blanqui, des origines à la révolution de 1848* (Paris, 1969).

Jean-Claude Caron, trans. E. Newman

Related entries: BLANQUI, J.-A.; BLANQUI, L.-A.; *LE COURRIER FRAN-CAIS*; KERATRY; MERILHOU; VOYER D'ARGENSON.

LAPLACE, PIERRE-SIMON (1749–1827), mathematician who applied Newton's theory of gravitation to the solar system and developed the nebular hypothesis to account for the origin of the solar system. Pierre Laplace was born on 23 March 1749 at Beaumont-en-Auge in Normandy. He was the son of a peasant, but rich neighbors supported his study at the University of Caen. Laplace went to Paris, and, as a result of the support of Jean d'Alembert, whom he had impressed, he was appointed, at the age of twenty, professor of mathematics at the Ecole militaire. Teaching was not Laplace's forte. He is noted rather for his application of Newton's theory of gravitation to the solar system as a whole. He launched this life-long study with a 1773 paper stating the invariability of the mean motions of the planets. This work won for Laplace, in spite of his youth, associate membership in the Academy of Science. In 1786 he proved that changes in the mean motion of Jupiter and Saturn were periodic and self-correcting effects of gravitational attraction. In 1787 he also determined that variations in lunar acceleration were due to the eccentricity of the Earth's orbit.

In 1796 Laplace published *Exposition du système du monde*, a semipopular exposition of his study of celestial motion. The work also contained Laplace's nebular hypothesis. He hypothesized that the solar system had developed as a huge cloud of incandescent gas cooled and contracted. Successive rings, which separated from the edge of the cooling cloud, condensed into the planets and their satellites. The remaining contracted core formed the sun.

Between 1798 and 1825 Laplace published his five-volume *Traité de mécanique céleste*, in which he mathematically applied the theory of universal gravitation to the entire solar system. This work led Siméon Poisson to christen Laplace the Newton of France. In these volumes Laplace also contributed to the understanding of tidal oscillations.

Laplace did pioneering work in the theory of probability. In 1812 he published *Théorie analytique des probabilités* and in 1814 a popular introduction to this work entitled *Essai philosophique sur les probabilités*. Laplace applied analysis and infinitesimal calculus to probability theory. Much of this work was original and pace setting, but Laplace, in this area of his work, as well as in his cosmology, often neglected to give due credit to his antecedents.

Laplace made contributions to pure mathematics by applying generating functions to the solution of equations of finite difference and by expressing functions as definite integrals. His work in physics was also notable. With Antoine Lavoisier he invented a calorimeter to determine the heat generated by chemical reactions and human respiration. He developed a general theory of capillarity, explaining the inverse proportion between capillary rise and the diameter of the containing tube. In acoustics, Laplace attributed accelerations in the speed of sound to heat generated by vibrations. He also formulated the two elementary laws of electromagnetism.

Laplace possessed tremendous political flexibility. He was appointed to examine artillery students during the Old Regime. In 1795 he was appointed to the Ecole normale and then made an examiner at the Ecole polytechnique. Napoleon appointed Laplace minister of the interior in 1799. Laplace did not demonstrate any great talent for administration, and he was replaced after six weeks by Lucien Bonaparte. Laplace was, nevertheless, appointed to the Senate, of which he became vice-president in 1803. In 1806 Napoleon made him an imperial count. Laplace's opportunism led him successfully through the transition to the Bourbon Restoration. He voted for the end of the Empire and was made a marquis and peer of France by Louis XVIII. Laplace was elected to the Académie française in 1816.

In 1806 Laplace purchased an estate at Arcueil next to that of his friend Claude-Louis Berthollet. It was there that Laplace established the Société d'Arcueil to bring young intellectuals together periodically.

He died in Paris on 5 March 1827, survived by a wife and son.

H. Andoyer, *L'Oeuvre scientifique de Laplace* (Paris, 1922); E. T. Bell, *Men of Mathematics* (New York, 1937); C. Boyer, *A History of Mathematics* (New York, 1968); F. N. David, "Some Notes on Laplace," in J. Neyman and L. LeCam, *Bernoulli, Bayes, Laplace* (New York, 1965); R. Hahn, *Laplace as a Newtonian Scientist* (Los Angeles, 1967).

Bernard Cook

Related entries: ACADEMIE FRANCAISE; ECOLE MILITAIRE (SAINT-CYR); ECOLE POLYTECHNIQUE.

LAPOINTE, SAVINIEN (1811–1893), shoemaker, poet, and socialist politician in Paris. The life and poetry of Savinien Lapointe are an important source of insight into the mentality of urban artisans in France. A follower rather than a leader, Lapointe was usually (but not always) able to sense the trends that were in the air. He was naturally drawn to the ideas and the people most in vogue.

Lapointe was born in Sens (Yonne) in 1811 the son of a shoemaker. His family moved to Paris in 1814 fleeing the Allied invasion, and there he learned his father's trade. A republican, the young Lapointe fought at the barricades during the July Revolution of 1830 and in the Paris riots of 5–6 June 1832 sparked by the funeral of General Jean-Maximin Lamarque. He was placed under preventative arrest and held in the Sainte-Pélagie prison after the Paris riots of April 1834. In prison he read his favorite authors: Pierre-Jean de Béranger, Jean-Jacques Rousseau, and Lafontaine. He now had the leisure to try his own hand at writing poetry. In prison his politics changed; no longer a revolutionary republican, he had become a pacifist socialist. "No," he wrote in a phrase that would appear on the masthead of Jules Vinçard's Saint-Simonian socialist newspaper, *L'Union*, when it published its first issue in December, 1843, "we can no longer build our future on a barricade!" Society must be changed by creating producers' cooperative associations. These associations would enable the workers to take over the means of production peacefully and thus to build a just society in which workers would be rewarded for their labor and idlers would get nothing. Like most other French workers, Lapointe opposed communism and wanted to see private property preserved. But he demanded massive government aid to create producers' cooperative associations, and he asked for the nationalization of railroads and banks, the revision of France's tax structure, and the establishment of free public education.

Lapointe's social ideas and his talent as a poet brought him to the attention of the literary stars of the day. George Sand, who would later remember Lapointe as "one of the ten or twelve notable worker-poets," encouraged him, as did Eugène Sue, Léon Gozlan, Béranger, and Victor Hugo. Sue and Hugo visited Lapointe in his fifth-floor workshop on the Ile Saint-Louis; Hugo announced: "I have come to tell you that you are a poet." By 1838 his poetry was being published in several newspapers. In 1841 George Sand published some of his poems in the *Revue indépendante*, and Olinde Rodriguès, the Saint-Simonian socialist, included Lapointe's poems in his *Poésies sociales des ouvriers*, published in May 1841. During the 1840s his work appeared regularly in the working-class Saint-Simonian *La Ruche populaire* and in its successor, *L'Union*, as well as in the Buchezian *Atelier*. In 1844, Lapointe published, thanks to the help of Béranger, Sand, and his other generous protectors, *Une voix d'en bas* (A Voice from Below), his first volume of poetry. He was now something of a literary lion, regularly visiting his patrons Hugo and Béranger. The socialist Flora Tristan remembered that Lapointe was one of the dinner guests at Béranger's house when she dined there on 23 March 1843. "He greeted me," she said, "with the air of triumph of a vain sot who is proud to be seen dining at the home of a great poet. This boy has both a bad heart and a bad mind and will produce only mediocrities, for he does not feel the dignity of being a worker. He is so stuffed full of vanity that it's coming out of his eyes."

Lapointe's pride was typical of his class, and it helped to make France the most revolutionary country of the nineteenth century. Whereas Lapointe had impressed Flora Tristan as a vain sot proud only of his literary attainments, he quarreled and broke with George Sand over his pride as a worker. When Sand corrected an overly long alexandrine and advised Lapointe to count the beats of his poetry, he snapped: "So you don't like the common people, do you!"

Lapointe thus occupied the ambivalent position of all of the worker poets, with one foot in the workers' world and one foot in the heady world of France's literary superstars. Like most other workers he hankered after respectability; he dressed up in middle-class clothes for his photographs and dressed up his poetry in the middle-class style. His social protest took this line: he said that the working class, and not the bourgeoisie, was the more truly representative of middle-class values because they were honest, hard working, and decent, while the bourgeoisie were idle and debauched. Lapointe's respectability, his pride, and his ambition were all typical of his class. He was strongly nationalistic, and his pacifist principles were strained when the troops of Czar Nicholas I crushed the rebellion in Poland, which had always looked to France to protect it from its brutal neighbors. Lapointe was, in short, proud to be a worker, proud to be a poet, and proud to be French.

After the revolution of February 1848 had made France into a republic, Lapointe rediscovered his republicanism and wrote for radical newspapers like *La Vraie république* and *L'Organisation du travail*. He ran for the Constituent Assembly in April 1848 in his native Yonne department, but even the strong support of Béranger could not stem the conservative tide, and Lapointe, who had compromised himself by printing radical articles during the radical first phase of the revolution, was badly beaten. In 1850 he published another volume of poetry, *Les échos de la rue*. Louis-Napoleon Bonaparte's coup d'état of 2 December 1851 effectively silenced Lapointe's poetry, and he turned to publishing a professional journal for shoemakers and tanners. Ever sensitive to public opinion, Lapointe became an ardent Bonapartist. In 1856, Béranger advised him to leave shoemaking and take a job at the gas works. Lapointe remained an employee of the gas works for thirty years until an accident forced him to retire. He died at Soucy (Yonne) in 1893. Victor Hugo had said of Lapointe: "Men like you are beacons that light the way for others." No doubt Hugo had expected Lapointe to play a heroic role, spending the days bent over his shoes and the nights bent over his writer's desk. Lapointe was far less heroic and far more typical of his class: proud, respectable, and anxious to improve the lot of his class and, failing that, to live more comfortably himself.

S. Lapointe, *Une voix d'en bas, Poésies précédées d'une préface par M. Eugène Sue, et suivies des lettres adressées à l'auteur par MM. Béranger, Victor Hugo, Léon Gozlan, etc.* (Paris, 1844); H. D. Lockwood, *Tools and the Man, A Comparative Study of the French Workingman and the English Chartists in the Literature of 1830–1848* (New York, 1927); E. L. Newman, "L'arme du siècle, c'est la plume: The French Worker Poets of the July Monarchy and the Spirit of Revolution and Reform," *Journal of Modern History* (1980) and *The French Worker-Poets of the July Monarchy* (forthcoming); E. Thomas, *Voix d'en bas: La poésie ouvrière du XIXe siècle* (Paris, 1979).

Edgar L. Newman

Related entries: L'ATELIER; BERANGER; *L'ORGANISATION DU TRAVAIL*; *LA RUCHE POPULAIRE*; SAINT-SIMONIANISM; SAND; SUE; TRISTAN;

VINCARD; *LA VRAIE REPUBLIQUE*; WORKER POETS; WORKERS' COOPERATIVES.

LA ROCHEFOUCAULD, LOUIS-FRANCOIS-SOSTHENES, VICOMTE DE (1785–1864), ultraroyalist politician, later duc de Doudeauville. La Rochefoucauld made himself known as a fiery ultraroyalist in the *chambre introuvable*. Ambitious and scheming, he used the influence of Mme. du Cayla, the last favorite of Louis XVIII, to have himself named director des Beaux-arts in 1824. He made major improvements in the Louvre Museum and at the Opera. He left voluminous memoirs (5 vols.).

G. Cazenave, *Une camarilla sous la Restauration* (Paris, 1956).

Guillaume de Bertier de Sauvigny, trans. E. Newman
Related entries: ACADEMY OF FINE ARTS; *CHAMBRE INTROUVABLE*; DU CAYLA; LOUIS XVIII; ULTRAROYALISTS.

LA ROCHEFOUCAULD-LIANCOURT, FRANCOIS-ALEXANDRE-FREDERIC, DUC (1747–1827), aristocratic philanthropist, founder of the public savings banks. Since the days before the Revolution, he had devoted himself to social work and to creating in his domaine of Liancourt a model farm and a professional school that is the origin of the present Ecole des arts et métiers. A member of the National Assembly in 1789, he tried to reconcile his loyalty to the king with his devotion to the new ideas, but he was forced to leave France to save his head. A long stay in the United States led to his writing his *Voyage dans les Etats-Unis d'Amérique fait de 1795 à 1798* (8 vols.). After he returned to France under the Consulate, he encouraged new agricultural and industrial methods that he had studied in England, and he was also a proponent of vaccination against smallpox. Under the Restoration, he entered the Chamber of Peers and gathered a great number of benevolent activities into several institutions of welfare and public service. Most notably, he created public savings banks (*caisses d'épargne*).

J. D. de la Rochefoucauld, C. Wolikow, and G. Ikni, *Le duc de la Rochefoucauld-Liancourt* (Paris, 1980).

Guillaume de Bertier de Sauvigny, trans. E. Newman
Related entries: CAISSES D'EPARGNE; CHAMBER OF PEERS; ECOLES NATIONALES DES ARTS ET METIERS; PUBLIC WELFARE.

LAROCHEJAQUELEIN, HENRI-AUGUSTE-GEORGES, MARQUIS DU VERGIER DE (1805–1867), legitimist politician and supporter of Louis-Napoleon. Henry de Larochejaquelein had an impressive history to follow: noble heritage back to the Crusades, companions of Henry IV, father killed fighting the usurper Napoleon (4 June 1815). In recognition of the sacrifice of his father, Louis XVIII named the nine-year-old Henry a peer of France. Because of his age and later his refusal to swear allegiance to Louis-Philippe, Larochejaquelein never sat in the Chamber of Peers. Instead he followed the noble calling of the army. After attending Saint-Cyr, he began his military career as a sublieutenant in the fighting in Spain. Not satisfied with the quiet of the peace, he sought out battle in the service of the czar of Russia in the latter's efforts against the Turks.

For Larochejaquelein, the July Revolution was anathema, and upon his return to France he did his best to help the duchesse de Berry gain the throne for her son. For his efforts, the government attempted to condemn him to death, but a jury felt otherwise. Like many other royalist nobles, he returned to his lands in the 1830s. In addition to occupying himself with agriculture, Larochejaquelein experimented with *bateaux inexplosible* on the Loire. His involvement in politics was limited to an attempt to found a legitimist newspaper, which floundered when he quarreled with the famous legitimist lawyer and deputy Pierre-Nicolas Berryer.

By 1842 Larochejaquelein took the requisite oath to permit his participation in the political process. He had become a believer in the legitimism of universal suffrage as espoused by Antoine-Eugène de Genoude in the *Gazette de France*. Representing his legitimist convictions, he succeeded in being returned to the Chamber of Deputies by the electors of the Morbihan by just three votes. He took his seat on the Right and soon was recognized as the head of the militant legitimists. In 1844 he journeyed to pay homage to the comte de Chambord, for which the Chamber condemned him. Outraged at this infringement of his political rights, he resigned his seat, only to be returned by the electors of the Morbihan. They sent him to the Chamber of Deputies once again in 1846.

The Revolution of 1848 brought new opportunities to the legitimists. Rid of the ursurper Louis-Philippe, Larochejaquelein felt it was possible that universal suffrage would yield results favorable to the true monarch. Well enough known and brash enough to run for the Constituent Assembly from the Seine, Larochejaquelein was elected only in the Morbihan. There he finished fourth among the twelve deputies elected. Although he symbolized the disaster of the April elections for many staunch republicans, Larochejaquelein acted with some independence from the monarchist position. He voted against both the banishment of the Orléans family and the pursuit of Marc Caussidière, and he was one of just thirty deputies to vote against the new Constitution. The *Gazette de France* supported him for president, but the rural vote was preempted by Louis-Napoleon.

Larochejaquelein continued his legislative career in the elections of May 1849. During the Legislative Assembly, he met with the Catholic conservatives of the rue de Poitiers. The fundamental problem of the Second Republic for Larochejaquelein was the threat to peace and order from the actions of the Left. Since the hated Orleanists had been eliminated, any stable authority was now acceptable until the people could be convinced of the wisdom of restoring the Bourbons. Larochejaquelein thus became devoted to Louis-Napoleon. For such practical views, the new emperor rewarded the marquis by naming him to the Senate on 31 December 1852. In the Senate, Larochejaquelein became a champion of the church, and he favored a free press. He was awarded the Legion of Honor in 1856.

Larochejaquelein's verbal dedication to the legitimists' cause was supported in practice by his son. In 1871 the younger Larochejaquelein was elected to the National Assembly, where he voted with the legitimists in 1871 and again from 1876 to 1885.

A. Robert and G. Cougny, *Dictionnaire des parlementaires français* (Paris, 1889–91).

Thomas Beck

Related entries: BERRY, C.-F.; BERRYER, P.-N.; BORDEAUX; CAUSSIDIERE; COMITE DE LA RUE DE POITIERS; *LA GAZETTE DE FRANCE*; LA ROCHEJAQUELEIN; LEGITIMISM; SPAIN, 1823 FRENCH INVASION OF.

LAROCHEJAQUELEIN, LOUIS DE (1775–1815), brother of one of the glorious leaders of the great insurrection in the Vendée, he had himself fought in the ranks of the *émigrés*. In 1813–14, he participated in several royalist conspiracies, notably the conspiracy in Bordeaux. In 1815 he was one of the leaders of the royalist resistance in the provinces of the west against Napoleon and was killed while fighting heroically in one of the only serious battles of that campaign.

Guillaume de Bertier de Sauvigny, trans. E. Newman

Related entries: HUNDRED DAYS; LAROCHEJAQUELEIN, H.-A.-G.

LA ROCHELLE, FOUR SERGEANTS OF (1822), carbonarist military conspiracy. The conspiracy was centered in the Forty-fifth line infantry regiment, which was rotated in May 1821 from garrison duty in Dieppe and Le Havre to Paris, where the men were stationed in barracks in the rues St. Jacques and St. Jean Beauvais on the Left Bank, near the University. Several noncommissioned and junior officers, resentful of favoritism shown to royalist officers under the Restoration, came into contact with university students already active in carbonarist conspiracies and the Masonic lodge of the Friends of Truth. Meetings at the Hôtel de la Paix (behind St. Geneviève), the café Roi Clovis, and the local Masonic lodge (Les Amis de l'honneur) soon won several recruits from the regiment. The most prominent of these was Sergeant-Major Jean-François Bories, who joined the Friends of Truth and was soon organizing a carbonarist *vente* (twenty-member cell) among his fellow soldiers. Among his first recruits were sergeants G.-P. Goubin, J.-J. Pommier, and M. Raoulx and a private, Lefebvre. A captain, J. J. Massias (apparently the highest-ranking officer involved), also joined the carbonari at this time, though he was not a member of Bories' vente. Bories himself belonged to an intermediate *vente centrale* and may have been presented to the marquis de Lafayette and other liberal leaders by his student friends in Paris.

The Forty-fifth regiment was ordered to La Rochelle in January 1822, and Bories was directed to contact other carbonarist conspirators in the west, being provided with parts of paper cut-outs that would enable him to identify himself to sympathizers in Orléans, Niort, Poitiers, and La Rochelle. On 28 January, however, Bories was involved in a tavern brawl with members of the Swiss Guards regiment in Orléans and remained under arrest until the regiment's arrival on the coast on 14 February. Rumors of subversive activity and Captain Massias' public utterances had attracted the attention of the regiment's commander, Colonel V.-L.-A. Toustain, an ex-*émigré* and royalist, who notified the prefect of the Charente-inferieure (Pepin de Bellisle) and launched an investigation. One informant, a Sergeant Lefevre, provided an exaggerated account of the plotting in Paris in late 1821, and Toustain ordered Bories rearrested while notifying General H.-F.-J. Despinois (the commander of the Twelfth Military District) in Nantes. Despinois, who had been following the activities of ex-Napoleonic officers (principally General J.-B. Berton and Colonel J.-L. Alix) around Saumur, where another carbonarist conspiracy was active, took charge of the La Rochelle investigation and came to the city to conduct interrogations. A sergeant-major (A.-G. Goupillon) whom Bories and Raoulx had enlisted at La Rochelle soon revealed the dimensions of the conspiracy. The arrest of the Saumur conspirators on 25 February was followed by the detention of Sergeant Goubin (caught meeting with civilian radicals in Niort) and Sergeant Raoulx (caught disguised as a peasant) on 10 and 12 March, and Sergeant Pommier shortly after.

Goubin, Raoulx, and Pommier all confirmed Goupillon's initial revelations under interrogation by Despinois, though Bories refused all cooperation. The leads provided by their confessions enabled the police to make arrests of civilians and students in Paris, and the suspects charged in the Forty-fifth Regiment plot were tried in Paris for conspiracy from 21 August to 5 September 1822 (at the Palais de justice). The case drew large crowds of spectators, and the *avocat-général* who conducted the prosecution, Louis de Marchangy, demanded the death penalty. Pommier, Goubin, and Raoulx claimed their confessions had been extorted, and the defense tried to minimize the seriousness of the plot, but the presiding judge (de Montmerqué) denounced the defendants from the bench and threatened their attorneys with harsh penalties for any verbal attacks on the regime or public officials. Charges against Massias were dropped for lack of evidence, but the jury, after four hours of deliberation, found the four sergeants guilty and acquitted Goupillon for his aid in uncovering their activities. Seven other defendants were found guilty of the less serious offense of nonrevelation.

While the condemned men were imprisoned at Bicêtre, the Parisian carbonarists raised 70,000 francs to bribe their guards. A medical student, Guillier de la Tousche, approached the governor of the prison and a number of his officers, but this plot too was uncovered, and la Tousche and two officers were sentenced to three to four months in prison in November. Rejecting all appeals for clemency, the government ordered the executions by decapitation to take place in the Place de grève on the evening of 21 September 1822. Rumored plans to rescue the sergeants by a *coup de main* at the scaffold came to nothing, and the sentences were carried out, Bories being the last to die. Louis XVIII's decision to hold a concert and ball that same evening at the Tuileries to celebrate the birth of a grand-niece was seen by many as a deliberate gesture of contempt. The four sergeants were buried in the cemetery of Montparnasse, and their tomb became a site of republican observances under the July Monarchy and the Second and Third Republics.

The conspiracy and trial became a popular subject for works of fiction and plays, and Bories' heroism in the face of death was particularly admired. The date of the execution was marked by memorial services in the nineteenth century, and two cafés in the Latin Quarter bear the names of the Four Sergeants of la Rochelle.

P. Dethomas, *Le Procès des quatre sergents de la Rochelle* (Paris, 1912); H. Flaubert, "Le complot du 45e R. I.," *Aux Carrefours de l'histoire* (1957); L. Grasilier, *L'Aventure des quatre sergents de la Rochelle* (La Rochelle, 1929); Laboullaye et Jules, *Les Quatres sergents de la Rochelle* (Paris, 1831); J. Lucas-Dubreton, *Les Quatres sergents de la Rochelle* (Paris, 1929); A. Praviel, *La Conspiration de la Rochelle* (Paris, 1937); C. Robert, *Les Quatre sergents de la Rochelle* (Paris, 1849); A. B. Spitzer, *Old Hatreds and Young Hopes* (Cambridge, Mass., 1971).

David Longfellow

Related entries: BERTON; BORIES; CARBONARI; FREEMASONRY; MARCHANGY; SOCIETY OF THE FRIENDS OF TRUTH.

LATOUCHE, HYACINTHE THABAUD DE LATOUCHE (pseud. HENRI DE) (1785–1851), journalist, playwright, novelist, poet, translator, art critic, and promoter of romanticism. Hyacinthe-Joseph-Alexandre Thabaud de Latouche, later known as Henri de Latouche, was born 3 January 1785 at la Châtre in the Berry region. His was an old, distinguished, well-to-do family of the lesser nobility. But his ideas were liberal (he served as a subprefect during the Hundred Days), and consequently he was well positioned to reconcile political liberals (most of whom favored the classical style) with romanticism (which had at first been dominated by the royalist political Right).

As a poet (his *Le Mort de Rotrou* won an honorable mention from the Académie française in 1811) and playwright, he came to frequent the salon of Emile Deschamps, and here he decided to join the classic-romantic conflict. In 1819 he published the first critical edition of Andre-Marie de Chénier's poems, which Charles-Augustin Sainte-Beuve praised profusely. He published French national traditions and popular myths, translations of Shakespeare, Goethe, Schiller, and several other English and German authors from 1819 to 1823. Latouche was the editor of the *Mercure du XIX siècle* and the mentor who launched the careers of several romantic writers: his mistress Marceline Desbordes-Valmore and especially Honoré de Balzac and George Sand. His historical novel *Fragoletta* (1829) was the model for Balzac's *Les Chouans*. In fact, Latouche is responsible for Balzac's transition from the gothic novel to historical and realist fiction.

After the romantic victory and the July Revolution of 1830, Latouche, the diehard republican, returned to his career as a journalist, writing for the *Constitutionnel* and *La Pandore* and serving as editor in chief of *Le Figaro*. In his last years, his hotheaded temper mellowed, and he was able to renew his ties with Alfred de Vigny, George Sand, Jules Lefèvre, and Pierre-Jean de Béranger. Literary success had eluded him, but he had engineered the *rapprochement* of the conservative and liberal factions of romantics and had effectively guided the careers of some of the most talented of them.

F. Segu, *H. de Latouche et son intervention dans les arts* (Paris, 1931), *H. de Latouche, 1785–1851* (Paris, 1931), and *Un Maître de Balzac méconnu H. de Latouche* (Paris, 1928).

Paul Comeau

Related entries: ACADEMIE FRANCAISE; BALZAC; BERANGER; *LE CONSTITUTIONNEL*; DESBORDES-VALMORE; DESCHAMPS; *LE FIGARO*; *MERCURE DU XIX SIECLE*; ROMANTICISM; SAINTE-BEUVE; VIGNY.

LATOUR-MAUBOURG, MARIE-VICTOR-NICOLAS DE FAY, MARQUIS DE (1768–1850), general of the Empire; peer, ambassador, and minister of war of the Restoration. Born at La Motte de Galaure (Dordogne) on 22 May 1768, Latour-Maubourg entered the gardes du corps in 1789 and served as a cavalry colonel in the marquis de Lafayette's army. He emigrated in 1792 but did not join the *émigré* army. He returned to France during the Directory. He served as an aide to Jean-Baptiste Kléber on the Egyptian campaign and was badly wounded suppressing the revolt in Alexandria. Appointed to the Legion of Honor in 1802 and made a brigadier general in 1805, Latour-Maubourg participated in the Austerlitz campaign and in the Prussian campaign of 1806 where he took part in the battle of Jena. He fought in the 1807 campaign against Russia, commanding a division at Friedland. He was named a baron of the Empire in 1808. He went to Spain that year and remained until 1812, distinguishing himself in the battle of Cuenca and at the siege of Badajoz. During the invasion of Russia, he led a reserve cavalry corps and participated in the attack on the redoubts at Borodino where he was wounded. On the retreat from Moscow, he commanded the remnants of the cavalry guarding the flank of the Grande armée. In 1813 Latour-Maubourg fought in Germany at Dresden and Leipzig, where he lost a leg. He was named a count of the Empire on 22 March 1814. Nevertheless he supported the deposition of Napoleon. Although his service to Napoleon had been steady and reliable, it had not been outstanding.

At the Restoration, Artois appointed him to a commission to reorganize the army, and in June 1814 the Bourbons named him a peer of France. He took no part in the Hundred Days, but as a peer he sat in judgment on Marshal Michel Ney and voted for Ney's execution. He subsequently received the orders of Saint Louis and of the Holy Ghost and in 1817 was named a marquis. In early 1819 Latour-Maubourg went as ambassador to Britain. On 19 November 1819 he was appointed minister of war in the Decazes cabinet. As minister he effected a reorganization of the infantry. But he lacked political experience and was not a leading member of either the Decazes cabinet or the second Richelieu ministry, in which he remained as war minister. In the summer of 1820, liberal demonstrations broke out in Paris, and the ultraroyalists harshly criticized Latour-

Maubourg for not dealing more severely with the demonstrators. By the summer of 1821, the ultras were demanding that he resign to make room for Marshal Victor in spite of the fact that he had dismissed many former Napoleonic officers recalled to duty by Gouvain Saint-Cyr and had allowed royal favoritism to replace professionalism as the criterion for promotion. He did not, however, leave office until the entire Richelieu cabinet resigned in December 1821.

From 1822 until 1830, Latour-Maubourg was governor of the Invalides and remained in the Peers until he resigned at the time of the July Revolution. He remained loyal to Charles X throughout the Revolution, refusing to raise the tricolor in place of the white flag over the Invalides, the last one still flying in Paris. After resigning his offices, he briefly retired to Melun. When the followers of Charles X planned a comeback in late 1830 and early 1831, they offered a military command to Latour-Maubourg, who declined it. He was, however, involved in a legitimist committee in the summer of 1831, and in the spring of 1832 he may have been designated as the individual to replace the committees in a reorganization of the plot. Later in 1832 he became the legitimists' plenipotentiary in Paris. Having subsequently joined the Bourbons in exile, in 1835 he became governor of the duc de Bordeaux. Latour-Maubourg did not return to France until 1848 and died on 8 November 1850 at the chateau de Lys.

Archives parlementaires; J. L. Bory, *La Révolution de juillet* (Paris, 1972); M. L. Brown, *The Comte de Chambord: The Third Republic's Uncompromising King* (Durham, 1967); D. Porch, *Army and Revolution* (London, 1974); A. Robert et al., *Dictionnaire des parlementaires français* (Paris, 1889–91).

James K. Kieswetter

Related entries: BORDEAUX; CHAMBER OF PEERS; CHARLES X; DE-CAZES; GOUVION SAINT-CYR; LAFAYETTE, M.-J.-P.-Y.-R.-G.; NEY; REVOLUTION OF 1830; RICHELIEU; ULTRAROYALISTS; VICTOR.

LAUNAY, VICOMTE DE. See GAY, D.

LAW OF GENERAL SECURITY, law of 29 October 1815 permitting the arrest without trial of persons accused of conspiring against the Bourbons or against the security of the state. The months after Waterloo saw the outbreak of a royalist reaction, a widespread demand for the punishment of those responsible, and the restriction of conditions that had made Napoleon's initial success in 1815 possible. The Peers, the Deputies, and the cabinet ministers in varying degrees generally accepted the need for repressive legislation. Ultimately four repressive laws were passed: the law on general security, followed by a law on seditious speech, the reestablishment of the provost courts, and an amnesty law.

On 18 October 1815 Elie Decazes proposed the law on general security in the Deputies and stressed the urgency of adopting it. It suspended individual liberty by providing for the arrest and detention without trial of persons suspected of crimes against the person or authority of the king, the royal family, or the security of the state. It further required that persons suspect to a lesser degree be subject to political police surveillance. Pierre Royer-Collard, Etienne-Denis Pasquier, and a few others raised objections to the persecution of those who were merely suspect, to the type of detention allowed, to the ambiguities of the offenses, and to the extensive number of officials authorized to order such detention, which included even such minor functionaries as forest guards and parochial constables. But the Deputies rejected their proposed amendments, and the bill was quickly adopted by a vote of 294 to 56 on 23 October. The Peers approved it on 27 October almost without debate by a vote of 128 to 37. The king signed it into law on 29 October 1815.

Lacking the necessary safeguards, this law led to many immediate abuses. It expired with the next legislative session and in February 1817 was replaced by another law that was less vague, contained greater safeguards for those arrested, and limited the arrest authority to the president of the cabinet and the minister of police. The ultras vigorously opposed moderating the 1815 law. Yet another such law was adopted in 1820, albeit even more circumscribed than the 1817 version.

Archives parlementaires; P. Duvergier de Hauranne, *Histoire du gouvernement parlementaire en France, 1814–1848* (Paris, 1857–71); D. P. Resnick, *The White Terror and the Political Reaction after Waterloo* (Cambridge, 1966); A. T. de Vaulabelle, *Histoire des deux restaurations* (Paris, 1874).

James K. Kieswetter

Related entries: AMNESTY BILL OF 1816; CHAMBER OF DEPUTIES; CHAMBER OF PEERS; *COURS PREVOTALES*; LAW ON SEDITIOUS SPEECH; PASQUIER; ROYER-COLLARD; ULTRAROYALISTS.

LAW OF JUSTICE AND LOVE. See PRESS LAWS.

LAW OF SACRILEGE, law of 1824 providing the death penalty for desecration of Roman Catholic churches, especially of the consecrated wine and wafer. In the mid–1820s there broke out in France a rash of desecrations of Catholic churches that especially involved the profanation of the consecrated Host and of various sacred vessels. Under church influence, the regime had already abolished divorce and declared null in the eyes of God all marriages made during the Revolution. This new opportunity was seized by the ultras and clericals, those who wished to restore the church's power, who regretted the anticlerical measures of the previous thirty-five years and who in some cases sought to unite church and state. In 1824 the Peers adopted a measure providing the death penalty for certain thefts from churches. The ecclesiastical peers had unsuccessfully insisted on the inclusion of sacrilege in that law. When similar demands surfaced in the Deputies, the government withdrew the law. This concept was, however, the basis of a new proposal that the Peers began deliberating on 10 February 1825. It provided that the profanation of the consecrated Host would be punished as an act of parricide, and profanation of sacred vessels was to be punished by ordinary capital punishment. Death or forced labor was provided as punishment for various kinds of theft from churches. In fact the clericals had hoped to adopt the death penalty for the theft of anything from a church.

This proposed measure aroused extensive public outrage. The opposition in the Peers, led by Louis-Mathieu de Molé, Etienne-Denis Pasquier, Achille de Broglie, Jean-Denis Lanjuinais, and François-René de Chateaubriand, raised arguments against the death penalty, against the imposition of Catholic doctrine on non-Catholics and against recognition of sacrilege as a crime, which France had never before recognized. Even questions of theology were raised. The strongest defender was Louis de Bonald, who made his famous observation that the death penalty only sent one before one's natural judge. This led to considerable commotion in the Chamber and among the public. Ten ecclesiastical peers caused comment when they voted for the bill, arguing that while their clerical vows forbade them to apply the death penalty, their legislative office required them to participate in the adoption of laws. On 18 February 1825 the Peers adopted the measure by a vote of 127 to 92. Their only obvious major amendment was the replacement of mutilation before execution with a required public apology before the church in which the sacrilege had been committed. The Peers also, however, adopted the requirement of eye-witnesses to the crime for the application of the death penalty.

The Deputies took up the law on 11 April. More reflective of public opinion and political agitation than the Peers, the Deputies attacked the bill on political, social, religious, and ethical grounds. The most notable speech in opposition was by Pierre Royer-Collard, whose lengthy discourse denounced the measure on theological and historical bases. Although he could not stop the bill, he did arouse public opinion against it. Yet some extremely reactionary Catholic deputies even argued that the bill was too lenient. On 15 April the Deputies approved the government's proposal by a vote of 210 to 95, and Charles X signed it on 20 April. In fact the Peers' amendment requiring eye-witnesses effectively rendered the law unenforceable, and no one was ever convicted under its terms. In the minds of many, it did, however, stand as a symbol of the extent of subservience of the crown to the church. It helped to stimulate the anticlerical campaign of the 1820s and liberal opposition to Charles X. Certainly the Law of Sacrilege was one of the most infamous pieces of legislation of the entire Restoration period.

Archives parlementaires; J. H. Lespagnon, *La Loi du sacrilege* (Paris, 1935); G. S. Philipps, *The Church in France, 1789–1848* (New York, 1928); A. T. de Vaulabelle, *Histoire des deux restaurations* (Paris, 1874).

James K. Kieswetter

Related entries: BONALD; BROGLIE, A.-L.-V.; CHATEAUBRIAND; DI-VORCE, ABOLITION OF; LANJUINAIS; MOLE; PASQUIER; ROYER-COL-LARD; ULTRAROYALISTS.

LAW OF THE DOUBLE VOTE. See DOUBLE VOTE, LAW OF THE.

LAW ON SEDITIOUS SPEECH AND PUBLICATION, law of 9 November 1815 to punish writings, acts, and utterances aimed at overthrowing or weakening the authority of the king; one of the four repressive measures of this legislative session. On 16 October 1815 François de Barbé-Marbois, minister of justice, presented to the Deputies the draft of a law that defined various utterances and writings as seditious and established penalties for them. Under the current conditions, with France extensively occupied by the Allies, with the Bourbons shakily back on the throne, and with some Bonapartist sentiment still evident, the government felt that action was necessary. The committee of the Chamber and many individual deputies attacked the ministry's proposal. They found it too moderate, objecting that the acts in question were punished only as misdemeanors by police courts, not as felonies. The maximum punishment of five years' imprisonment, they felt, was too lenient. In fact the ultras used this opportunity to attack some of the ministry personnel who defended the bill. The Deputies' committee report, prepared by Etienne-Denis Pasquier, almost completely rewrote the proposal, adopting deportation as the basic penalty, under the jurisdiction of the provost courts, which were to be reestablished. Discussion in the Chamber was more reactionary, with some demanding the death penalty even for flying the tricolor. Others insisted on forced labor. These demands were rejected. But the maximum fine was raised to 20,000 francs, and even indirect provocation was made punishable. The Deputies finally adopted the law by a vote of 293 to 69.

In the Peers, however, there was considerably more opposition, with even François-René de Chateaubriand denouncing as barbaric a provision that might afflict *émigrés* who agitated for the return of their lands. As in the Deputies, there was some demand by the Peers for the death penalty. Nevertheless, the Peers adopted the measure on 7 November 1815, and Louis XVIII signed it into law on 9 November. It basically provided that acts, writings, and utterances that intended the overthrow of the monarchy or threatened the life of the king or royal family were punishable by deportation after trial in the assize courts and the provost courts as soon as they could be established. Furthermore other deeds that weakened respect for royal authority, such as invoking the name of Napoleon and raising the tricolor, were punishable by police courts as misdemeanors and carried up to five years' imprisonment and a fine of 20,000 francs.

Archives parlementaires; P. Duvergier de Hauranne, *Histoire du gouvernement parlementaire en France, 1814–1848* (Paris, 1857–71); D. P. Resnick, *The White Terror and the Political Reaction after Waterloo* (Cambridge, 1966); A. T. de Vaulabelle, *Histoire des deux restaurations* (Paris, 1874).

James K. Kieswetter

Related entries: AMNESTY BILL OF 1816; BARBE-MARBOIS; CHATEAUBRIAND; *COURS PREVOTALES*; COURTS OF ASSIZE; LAW OF GENERAL SECURITY; PASQUIER.

LE BAS, PHILIPPE (1794–1860), classical archaeologist and historian. At sixteen years of age Le Bas began his service in the imperial marines, served on the *Vigilant* and the *Diadème*, and then spent time in the Imperial Guard (in the third regiment of the honor guards). After having fulfilled these duties, he was, in 1820, during his residence in Rome, put in charge by Queen Hortense of the education of the young Prince Charles-Louis-Napoleon Bonaparte, the first nephew of the Emperor Napoleon I and later to become Napoleon III. Le Bas remained as tutor in the family until 1 October 1827. During his stay in Rome, he learned Greek from Boissonade and made the acquaintance of several Italian and German archaeologists. Upon returning to France, he earned his doctorate with superior marks and received his degree in 1829. Subsequently in 1830 he became professor at the Lycée Saint-Louis and then assumed the position of professor of history at L'Ecole normale superieure, a title he exchanged four years later for professor of Greek at the same school. In 1842 he was sent by the minister of public instruction on a two-year archaeological expedition to Greece and Asia Minor, where he collected more than 450 drawings and over 5,000 inscriptions. The publication of several parts of these precious documents was ordered by the government. They were published in 1848 under the title *Voyage archéologique en Grèce et en Asie Mineure*. Portfolios Le Bas had published himself greatly extended nineteenth-century archaeological research. Because of his success and popularity, he was elected to become a member of L'Académie des inscriptions et belles-lettres in 1838 and became the administrator of the Bibliothèque de l'université. Le Bas was also one of the authors of the *Dictionnaire encyclopédique de l'histoire de France* (12 vols.), the *Précis de l'histoire ancienne* (2 vols. in 12), and the *Précis de l'histoire romaine* (2 vols. in 12 published in several editions).

Nouvelle biographie générale, (Paris, 1852–1866); J. E. Sandys, *A History of Classical Scholarship*, vol. 3 (Cambridge, 1908).

Irene Earls

LEDRU-ROLLIN, ALEXANDRE-AUGUSTE (1807–1874), member of the Provisional Government and the Executive Commission and unsuccessful candidate for the presidency of the Second Republic in 1848; leader of the democratic socialist Mountain in 1849. Grandson of a celebrated physicist and prestidigitator of the eighteenth century and son of a physician, Alexandre-Auguste Ledru was born in Paris, where he studied law. Upon his admission to the bar in 1830, he added to his surname that of his maternal great-grandmother, Rollin, in order to avoid confusion with another lawyer named Charles Ledru. By 1832 Ledru-Rollin had joined the chorus of republican criticism of the July Monarchy and won attention by publishing a pamphlet denouncing the "massacre" of the rue Transnonain in Paris in 1834. He was chosen as defense attorney for Marc Caussidière in the mass trial of republicans that followed, and subsequently he defended various opposition periodicals while editing journals of jurisprudence. In 1839 he ran unsuccessfully for a seat in the Chamber of Deputies, but in 1841 he won in his campaign in the Sarthe to fill the seat of the late republican deputy Etienne Garnier-Pagès. He retained his seat from that time forward, winning a reputation as perhaps the most radical of the small contingent of republican deputies in the late July Monarchy. Ledru-Rollin also played an influential role in republican journalism as one of the founders and chief financial supporter of

La Réforme, a radical daily established in 1843 as a rival of the moderate republican *Le National*. In the columns of *La Réforme* as well as in the Chamber, Ledru-Rollin emphasized not only the typical republican goal of universal suffrage but also the need for certain social and economic reforms. At first contemptuous of the republicans of *Le National* for collaborating with the dynastic opposition in the 1847 Banquet Campaign for electoral and parliamentary reform, Ledru-Rollin by November had joined the campaign himself, speaking at banquets in Lille and other provincial towns. He was scheduled to speak at the final banquet planned for early 1848 in the Latin Quarter of Paris but withdrew after eighty other deputies announced they would attend only if Ledru-Rollin did not.

The street demonstrations of 22 February 1848, following a change of location and then the prohibition of the banquet, led to the revolutionary insurrection that brought down the July Monarchy. At first opposed to violence, Ledru-Rollin after the "massacre" on the boulevard des Capucines on the evening of 23 February urged the demonstrators to demand concessions beyond the dismissal of François Guizot. In the Chamber of Deputies on 24 February following the abdication of Louis-Phillippe, Ledru-Rollin was one of the first legislators to demand the creation of a Provisional Government, and he was included among the seven deputies thereafter acclaimed members of the government by the crowds of insurgents. Although he was the most radical of the deputies chosen from the Chamber, when four more members were acclaimed by crowds at the Hôtel de ville, Ledru-Rollin found himself outflanked on the left by Louis Blanc and the worker Albert.

Ledru-Rollin accepted the crucial Ministry of the Interior, where he assumed responsibility for organizing the election of a National Constituent Assembly based on the principle of universal manhood suffrage that he had championed since 1841. In attempting to propagandize the electorate in favor of the Republic, Ledru-Rollin removed most of the prefects, replacing them with *commissaires* of republican convictions, and also circulated a number of official bulletins exhorting them to seek the election of dedicated republicans. Before the elections were held on 23 April, the Provisional Government faced several hostile demonstrations, in one of which, on 16 April, Ledru-Rollin played a significant role by calling out the National Guard to defend the government. Elected to the National Assembly from three departments, Ledru-Rollin was the only radical among the five members of the Provisional Government retained in the Executive Commission, but he fell from power when the Executive Commission was supplanted by the dictatorship of General Eugène Cavaignac in the midst of the insurrection of the June Days. As reactionary forces reawakened thereafter, Ledru-Rollin found himself accused, along with Caussidière, Louis Blanc, and Pierre-Joseph Proudhon, of complicity in the *journée* of 15 May. Ledru-Rollin made effective use of his famed oratorical skills to defend himself and the record of the revolutionary governments, but the Assembly nevertheless voted to prosecute Caussidière and Blanc. The following month, Ledru-Rollin protested eloquently but in vain over the deletion of the right to work from the new Constitution. In the December elections to the presidency of the Republic, Ledru-Rollin was the candidate of the new organization of the radicals called the Mountain, and finished in third place, but with fewer than 400,000 votes to the 5 million of Louis-Napoleon Bonaparte.

During the spring of 1849, Ledru-Rollin proclaimed himself a socialist, and the Mountain, in which he was the most prominent figure, became a democratic-socialist coalition. In the elections to the Legislative Assembly in May 1849, the Mountain made remarkable gains, Ledru-Rollin himself winning in five departments. In opposition to the monarchist majority in the Assembly and to President Bonaparte, especially over the French expedition against the Roman Republic, Ledru-Rollin inspired a street demonstration in Paris on 13 June 1849. His own hesitation in joining the marchers lent credence to his perhaps apocryphal comment, "I am their leader; I must follow them." Government forces attacked the unarmed demonstrators and afterwards arrested the leaders of the Mountain, but Ledru-Rollin escaped to England. There he remained for more than two decades, loosely associated with other French exiles in London and publishing several pamphlets against Louis-Napoleon. As one of the most redoubtable leaders of the Left, Ledru-Rollin was excluded from the amnesties of 1859 and even of 1869 and was permitted to return to France only in 1870, by decision of the government of Emile Ollivier. In ill health, Ledru-Rollin played no part in the revolution of 4 September 1870; elected to the National Assembly in February 1871, he resigned his seat immediately. In 1874 Ledru-Rollin won election to a National Assembly for the last time, and his last speech, shortly before he died, was a defense of the principle to which he had devoted his entire public life, universal manhood suffrage.

A. R. Calman, *Ledru-Rollin and the Second French Republic* (New York, 1922); F. A. de Luna, *The French Republic under Cavaignac, 1848* (Princeton, 1969); R. Price, *The Second French Republic* (London, 1972); R. Schnerb, *Ledru-Rollin* (Paris, 1948).

Frederick A. de Luna

Related entries: ALBERT; BANQUET CAMPAIGN; BLANC; CAUSSI-DIERE; CAVAIGNAC, L.-E.; DEMONSTRATIONS OF 1848–1849; EXECUTIVE COMMISSION; GARNIER-PAGES; GUIZOT; JUNE DAYS; LEGISLATIVE ASSEMBLY; *LE NATIONAL*; PROUDHON; PROVISIONAL GOVERNMENT; *LA REFORME*; REPUBLICANS; REVOLUTION OF 1848; ROMAN EXPEDITION; SOCIALISM; TRANSNONAIN, MASSACRE OF THE RUE; YOUNG (NEW) MOUNTAIN SOCIETY.

LE FLO, ADOLPHE-CHARLES (1804–1887), general, politician, and diplomat. A graduate of Saint-Cyr, Le Flô spent much of his early career in Algeria. He was a severe critic of Marshal Bugeaud's mobile columns. In 1848, he was promoted to brigadier and elected deputy in the Constituent Assembly. An opponent of Louis-Napoleon Bonaparte, he was exiled following the coup d'état of 2 December 1851. He returned to France in 1857. In 1870–71 he served the Government of National Defense and subsequently became French ambassador to Saint-Petersburg (1871–79), where he gained the confidence of Czar Alexander II.

C.-A. Julien, *Histoire de l'Algérie contemporaine* (Paris, 1964).

Douglas Porch

Related entries: BUGEAUD; CONSTITUTION OF 1848; COUP D'ETAT OF 2 DECEMBER 1851; ECOLE MILITAIRE (SAINT-CYR).

LEGENDRE, ADRIEN-MARIE (1752–1833), mathematician who made significant contributions to the discipline through his work on differential equations, calculus, the theory of functions, the theory of numbers, and the method of least squares. His work on elliptic integrals supplied physics with its basic analytical tools. Legendre was born in Paris on 18 September 1752. From 1775 to 1780 he was professor of mathematics at the Ecole militaire in Paris, and in 1795 he was appointed professor at the Ecole normale. He was appointed to the Academy of Science in 1783 and held several minor governmental posts. Further public recognition of his accomplishments, however, was impeded by the jealousy of Pierre-Simon Laplace, who had probably appropriated some of Legendre's work.

In *La Figure des planètes* (1784), Legendre introduced the polynomials still known by his name. During the Revolutionary period, he participated in a number of notable geodesic projects and helped to prepare the metric system. In 1794 he published *Eléments de géométrie*, in which he rearranged and simplified many of Euclid's postulates. This work became the standard textbook of geometry in much of Europe. A translation was published in the United States in 1819, and it became the basic geometry text there as well.

In 1798 Legendre published *Théorie des nombres*, which contained his law of quadratic reciprocity. His *Nouvelles méthodes pour la détermination des orbites des comètes* (1806) introduced his method of least squares. His comprehensive three-volume *Exercises du calcul intégral* was published between 1811 and 1819. Legendre's most important work was his *Traité des fonctions elliptiques* (1825–32), in which he reduced elliptic integrals to the forms that now bear his name.

Legendre died in Paris on 10 January 1833.

C. B. Boyer, *A History of Mathematics* (New York, 1968); M. Kline, *Mathematical Thought from Ancient to Modern Times* (New York, 1972).

Bernard Cook

Related entries: ACADEMY OF SCIENCES; ECOLE MILITAIRE (SAINT-CYR); LAPLACE.

LEGISLATIVE ASSEMBLY (1849–1851), legislative body of the Second Republic whose internal divisions allowed Louis-Napoleon to win the battle for political control. Created by the Constitution of 4 November 1848, the Legislative Assembly embodied five of the six demands of the democrats of the day. It was elected by universal male suffrage, deputies were paid, representation was spread evenly across the country, voting was secret, and no property qualifications were required to vote. Only the requirement for one-year terms for deputies was not present; deputies were elected for three years. The Chamber consisted of 750 members, including eleven from the colonies. Government officials were not eligible to be deputies, thus solving a major complaint against the government of François Guizot. The Assembly convened itself and elected its own officers, and between sessions a committee of the Assembly functioned. The key issue of ministerial responsibility was left unclear. This was particularly unfortunate because the president was also elected by universal suffrage, and as such he could claim that he represented the people at least as much as did the Assembly.

The initial skirmish over political control went to the president. He had been elected on 10 December 1848 and took office immediately. The control of the administrative apparatus of the state was in Louis-Napoleon's hands. The Constituent Assembly, on the other hand, continued to sit until May 1849. While Louis-Napoleon cracked down on the social republicans by, for example, disbanding the *solidarité républicaine*, the Constituent Assembly sat powerlessly. The elections for the new Legislative Assembly were called for 13–14 May 1849.

The voters of France went to the polls in the midst of the controversy over Louis-Napoleon's dispatch of French troops to Rome to protect the pope. One view of the situation in Rome saw Catholic conservatives versus social revolutionaries; another saw social justice versus military support of reaction. Moderation in the election campaign was difficult to sustain. Republicans found conditions especially difficult because the government and the conservatives labeled all republicans as socialists, regardless of their actual opinions on social, as opposed to political, issues. The results of the elections were clouded by similar passions, although the results seem clear to historians.

The conservatives actually won an overwhelming majority. Unfortunately, their conservatism took three forms, each incompatible with the other two. Two hundred deputies were dedicated to the restoration of the Bourbon monarchy, and many would die before allowing any illegitimate Orléans back on the throne. For many of these legitimists, a Bonaparte would be preferable to an illegitimate Orléans. Two hundred deputies supported the Orleanist solution, which for them was the true embodiment of responsible liberal government. To the Orleanists, only those capable of running society should be allowed to participate in politics, though everyone was an equal citizen. Finally, Alfred-Frédéric de Falloux and Charles de Montalembert led about fifty deputies who were dedicated to the church above all.

These 450 conservatives achieved their success primarily in the north (except in the Nord itself), Normandy, the west, and the Vendée. They did well particularly in wheat-growing and other prosperous farm areas, although, as André Tudesq has shown, no simple geopolitical relationships existed. Not all conservative victories were in the countryside. The Committee of the rue de Poitiers, which selected the Catholic slate of candidates, had backed 18 winners in the 28 seats for the Seine. With this large number of conservatives in the Assembly, the number of *grands notables* increased from previous legislatures.

Abstentions ran to nearly 40 percent of the electorate. Whether they hurt the conservatives or the radicals is unknown. The suspicion has always been that the efforts of Louis-Napoleon to repress social republicans made it most likely that republicans stayed away from the polls, despite the use of the secret ballot. Nevertheless, the radicals were excited by the results. After their crushing defeat in April 1848, the elections of May 1849 seemed to mark a comeback for the social Republic.

Alexandre-Auguste Ledru-Rollin, who had done dismally in the presidential election, was elected in five districts and polled 720,430 votes compared to just about 800,000 for all moderate republicans elected. Ten democrats won in Paris, although the best had 30,000 fewer votes than the victorious conservatives. Nationally, historians have counted 180 democrats and 75 moderate republicans. Urban areas were partial to these men of the Left, as were the Rhône-Saône valleys, Alsace, the areas of the center west and north of the Central massif, and less so the Nord and parts of the Midi. Eleven workers gained election, but generally the republicans were members of the legal profession (seventy-six) and the other liberal professions (fifty one).

When the Assembly convened on 28 May 1849, the deputies faced the issue of the Roman expedition and the imposing position of Louis-Napoleon. Odilon Barrot, the long-time opposition deputy under Louis-Philippe, continued to lead the ministers. Since he had majority support in the new assembly, no immediate problem arose over the issue of ministerial responsibility.

The first crisis arose from the demands of the Left that the president be censored because he had exceeded his powers in handling the Roman expedition. On 12 June 1849 Ledru-Rollin demanded that the Assembly condemn the president. His request was refused, and on the following day he and his followers declared the Assembly and the president to be outside the law. A new Convention was called for. This attempt at insurrection by the Montagnards failed. Thirty-four deputies were arrested, and these and many others citizens were condemned by the High Court of Versailles. This rash action by the Left solidified opinion in favor of the forces of order, with the president, not the conservatives in the Assembly, being the chief beneficiary. The Assembly on 9 August passed a law giving the government wide powers to declare a state of siege. Despite the personal preferences of many deputies, the Bonapartist solution seemed right for the moment.

With the problem of the Roman expedition still festering, Louis-Napoleon acted on 31 October 1849 by dismissing Odilon Barrot and declaring that he, a Bonaparte, now ruled. He would henceforth choose his ministers as he, the prince-president, saw fit. The Assembly was unable to offer effective opposition due to its many irreconcilable factions and gave way. While trying to resist the full implications of this act by the prince-president, the Assembly was pushed into action by the successes of the Left in by-elections. The Assembly responded by passing a number of acts that most historians have found significant.

The conservatives looked to the future and passed the Falloux Education Law on 15 March 1850. Here the forces of order inserted the church into the battle to combat the leveling influences of socialism. The Assembly now placed the priest over the lay teacher in the schools in order (according to Karl Marx) to increase the power of the bourgoisie, which made up the dominant class in the Assembly. It is little wonder that the worker, whose life so few *curés* understood, felt the Assembly was a living social reaction.

On 10 March 1850 by-elections were held to replace those deputies ousted in June 1849. Despite the pressure of the government against the Left, the social republicans were triumphant in twenty-one of the thirty-one elections. Such success led the Assembly to approve a new electoral law (31 May 1850). This law kept many in the lower classes from voting by instituting a three-year residency requirement, whereby residency could be established only by being on the tax rolls. The minimum age was also raised from twenty-one to twenty-five. Approximately 3 million of the 9.5 million voters were excluded, and those eliminated lived in the social republican strongholds. Voter rolls were reduced 62 percent in Paris, 51 percent in the Nord, 43 percent in the Loire and the Seine-Inférieure, and 40 percent in the Rhône. The Assembly had violated the Constitution, while the prince-president reaped the benefits.

The next target of the forces of order was the press. Long bothered by its freedom, the conservatives again supported the power of the government. The press law of 16 July 1850 reestablished the practice of caution money and stamps for small journals and newspapers, and the law of 30 July 1850 reintroduced censorship on the theater.

The sparring between the Assembly and the prince-president continued through 1851. On 28 May 1851 the Assembly refused to alter the constitution to prolong the term of the president, although the measure received 448 votes. On 2 December 1851 the prince-president initiated his own solution with the disbanding of the Legislative Assembly and the takeover of the entire operation of the government.

The task of the Assembly had been to consolidate the Republic. The irony is that monarchists were elected to do the job. The Assembly was crippled from the outset by two fundamental flaws: its powers in relation to the president were unclear, and it was composed of two antagonistic groups that could not work together. By playing to the desire of the majority for order, President Louis-Napoleon had been able to win the struggle for control. For those who had wanted a social republic, the hope for success had been even slimmer because the task of governing had also been given to landowning bourgeois.

P. Bastid, *Doctrines et institutions politiques de la second république*, vol. 2 (Paris, 1945); A. Tudesq, *Grands notables en France (1840–1849)* (Paris, 1964).

Thomas Beck

Related entries: BARROT, C.-H.-O.; COMITE DE LA RUE DE POITIERS; CONSTITUTION OF 1848; COUP D'ETAT OF 2 DECEMBER 1851; FALLOUX LAW; GUIZOT; LEDRU-ROLLIN; MONTALEMBERT; PARTY OF ORDER; PRESS LAWS; REPUBLICANS; ROMAN EXPEDITION; *SOLIDARITE REPUBLICAINE*.

LEGISLATIVE BODY (CORPS LEGISLATIF), window-dressing legislature of the last year of the Second Republic and for the Second Empire. After the coup d'état of 2 December 1851, Louis-Napoleon revamped the legislative branch of the government. The Constitution of 14 January 1852 created a bicameral legislature, with the lower house being the Corps législatif. Its 261 members were elected by universal male suffrage for those at least twenty-one years old. Deputies were distributed by department; each represented 35,000 persons and served for six years. The colonies lost their representation. Louis-Napoleon thus appealed to democratic sentiments, since these requirements removed the restrictions imposed by the Legislative Assembly in 1850.

The prince-president also took a step back from democratic rule by removing the stipend for being a deputy (it was restored in 1853) and by ending the ability of the legislature to control its own existence. He convened, adjourned, and dissolved the Corps at his pleasure. The sessions were supposed to be annual and to last for three months; with a dismissal new elections were to be held within six months. Deputies could not be ministers, prefects, subprefects, judges, councillors of state, or military officers.

The deputies were not expected to be independent sources of political power. All candidates had to swear allegiance to the prince-president; once elected, deputies had no initiative in the legislative process. Their job was to discuss and pass upon the laws proposed by the Council of State, a body appointed by the executive. The Corps could not amend proposals without approval of the Council of State. Further, the Corps could not accept petitions from citizens as the Chamber of Deputies had done. The deputies could not even play to the public in their discussions because the press was not allowed to publish the proceedings. Instead the president of the Corps, an appointee of the prince-president, lived in the assembly building with a yearly salary of 10,000 francs and supplied the press with a summary of the proceedings. Sessions, however, were open to the public. Finally, no organized political life developed within the Corps. Each bill was examined by seven *bureaux* of randomly selected deputies. Then each *bureau* elected a reporter, and this group of seven reported to the full Corps. The random nature of this committee structure and the fact that every bill was examined by every deputy limited any development of organization or expertise in one area.

Election of the deputies was closely controlled by the prefects. The government endorsed its own set of candidates, all opposition was discouraged, and anything approaching republicanism was severely repressed. Most opposition leaders had been exiled on 9 January 1852, and nine of every ten journals publishing in 1848 had been closed by the time of the elections of 1852 (29 February–14 March). The governmental pressure was extremely effective; only seven opposition candidates were successful. Three of them—General Eugène Cavaignac, Jacques-Louis Hénon, and Hippolyte Carnot—elected by the republicans of Paris, refused to take the required oath and forfeited their seats. One opposition deputy, Audren de Kerdrel of Fougères, represented legitimist opinion.

Given the ground rules, it is not surprising the two sessions of 1852 (29 March–28 June and 25 November–3 December) were dull procedural affairs. The second extraordinary session was called just to make way for the Empire. Only Charles de Montalembert attempted to raise the deputies from their stupor. Conditions in the Corps remained bland through the life of the terms of these first deputies.

After the elections of 1857, more spark appeared, and after 1860 the emperor began to liberalize the system. Like the Corps législatif of the First Empire, this Corps has aroused little interest in historians due to its lack of independence. At best, the deputies can show the type of person who was pushed to the fore by the Second Empire. Until now, however, no study has been done on this subject. The workings of the Corps also did nothing before the final, more liberal, years of the Empire to develop parliamentary government, modern political parties, or an appreciation for electoral politics that are necessary for every democracy.

F. Ponteil, *Les Institutions de la France de 1814 à 1870* (Paris, 1966).

Thomas Beck

Related entries: CARNOT, L.-H.; CAVAIGNAC, L.-E.; CHAMBER OF DE-PUTIES; COUNCIL OF STATE; COUP D'ETAT OF 2 DECEMBER 1851; LEGISLATIVE ASSEMBLY; LEGITIMISM; MONTALEMBERT; REPUB-LICANS.

LEGITIMISM (1830–1883), a political movement designed to put the elder branch of the Bourbon dynasty back on the throne after its overthrow in the July Revolution of 1830. In the face of both revolutionary upheaval and a movement to crown Louis-Philippe, the head of the Orleanist or cadet branch of the royal family, Charles X abdicated on 2 August 1830 in favor of his ten-year-old grandson, the duc de Bordeaux (who in 1843 would take the title the comte de Chambord). Charles's action was to no avail. Louis-Philippe ascended the throne. Charles and his family went into exile. And within several weeks of the July Revolution, hundreds of prominent officials, including prefects and subprefects, military officers, magistrates, and members of the two parliamentary chambers, rather than swear an oath of allegience to an Orleanist king, resigned and returned to their country estates and town houses, in the dramatic *émigration intérieure*. During the July Monarchy (1830–48) there were several farcical plots by leading legitimists to overthrow Louis-Philippe, the most important of which was the badly planned, poorly coordinated, and ultimately unsuccessful effort in the summer of 1832 to incite large-scale revolts around the duchesse de Berry, mother of the young duc de Bordeaux, in the strongly legitimist south and west. Generally, however, rather than working actively against Louis-Philippe, legitimist notables withdrew from that prominent role in public life, at least at the national level, which was their right as members of the propertied elites. During the Second Republic (1848–52) legitimists reappeared in public life on the national level, driven, by fear of socialism and of political democracy, into a loose coalition known as the Party of Order. The Party of Order comprised several groups of propertied notables, including Orleanists. The elections of May 1849 for the Legislative Assembly proved to be a victory for the Party of Order and for legitimists, who won almost two hundred seats. Attempts, however, to merge legitimism and Orleanism in preparation for the reestablishment of the monarchy failed, largely because of personal differences between Chambord and the Orleanist princes but also because of differences between the legitimist counterrevolutionary mentality and outlook and that of Orleanism. With the advent of the Second Empire in 1852, legitimists again withdrew from the national scene, only to reappear briefly at the beginning of the Third Republic. After the Orleanist-legitimist victory in the elections of February 1871 for the National Assembly, another unsuccessful effort was made to unite legitimists and Orleanists, preparatory to the reestablishment of the monarchy. With the death of the childless Chambord in 1883, the elder branch of the royal family came to an end. And so did legitimism. Most legitimists now acknowledged the right of the Orleanist leader, the comte de Paris, to ascend the French throne.

Legitimism was much more than simply a political movement on behalf of Charles X's successor. It identified itself closely with the defense of the old, rural, landed nobility, but it also received much support from bourgeois landowners. Fully half of the legitimist deputies in the National Assembly of 1871 were bourgeois. And, most notably in the west and the south, legitimism could also appeal widely to the popular classes. As evidenced by Lyons and many of the cities of the Midi, legitimism could be very much an urban phenomenon. Legitimism was possessed of a counterrevolutionary mentality and ideology. But it was a mentality and an ideology with regional variations, reflecting the fact that legitimism consisted to a considerable extent of regional movements led by aristocratic and bourgeois notables who, if not prominent on the national stage, were powerful in their own regions and identified themselves with the particular interests of their regions. Thus in the Midi legitimism could be intransigently opposed to the advances of capitalism and industrialization, while in the Nord or in Lyons it could be more accommodating. Legitimists could be advocates of the most modern techniques, notably in agriculture. And some of the most advanced and sophisticated industrial enterprises in France were owned by legitimists. But generally legitimism was a negative movement of protest characterized by fear of the modern world: of individual liberty, democracy, the centralized bureaucratic state, capitalism, and industrialization. The political, social, and economic program of legitimism consisted not so much of practical proposals on how to alter or reverse the course that nineteenth-century France was taking as of wistful, romantic dreams about a lost world of paternalist, communitarian institutions in some unidentifiable pre-Revolutionary past. Legitimists derived most of their ideas from the previous generation of Catholic, counterrevolutionary writers, notably Louis de Bonald and Joseph de Maistre.

M. L. Brown, *The Comte de Chambord* (Durham, 1967); R. L. Locke, *French Legitimists and the Politics of Moral Order in the Early Third Republic* (Princeton, 1974);

C. T. Muret, *French Royalist Doctrines since the Revolution* (New York, 1933); R. Rémond, *The Right Wing in France from 1815 to De Gaulle* (Philadelphia, 1966); A.-J. Tudesque, *Les grands notables en France, 1840–1849* (Paris, 1964).

David M. Klinck

Related entries: BERRY, M.-C.; BONALD; LEGISLATIVE ASSEMBLY; MAISTRE; PARTY OF ORDER; REVOLUTION OF 1830.

LEGOUVE, GABRIEL-JEAN-BAPTISTE-ERNEST-WILFRID (1807–1903), dramatist and moralist, a pioneer in women's rights and the education of children. The son of poet Gabriel Legouvé, he was orphaned at the age of five, but a considerable fortune and the careful tutoring of Jean Nicolas Bouilly provided him with a thorough education and a love of literature. He received a prize from the French Academy for a poem in 1829.

While still a student, he sent a projected dramatic plot to Eugène Scribe. Later the popular playwright, who had been asked by the Théâtre de la république to write a play for the great star, Rachel, invited the collaboration of Legouvé. The young writer had previously offered her his *Médée*, which she had refused. Nonetheless, he found a perfect subject in *Adrienne Lecouvreur*, carried out the research, and wrote the first two acts. When Rachel refused the play, it was Legouvé who persuaded her, stressing the importance of the female lead. It was an unqualified success when it appeared in 1849, but Rachel refused to continue after twenty-five performances.

Subsequent collaboration produced *Les Contes de la Reine de Navarre* (1850) and *La Bataille de dames* (1851). Had he remained in Scribe's shadow, Legouvé would doubtless be a forgotten contributor, but his lectures at the Collège de France (1847–48) on *L'Histoire morale des dames*, published in 1848, revealed him as a budding moralist. He was much in demand as a lecturer, and he employed the podium as a propagandist for women's rights and advanced education for children. He was genuinely appalled that women were blamed for the very ignorance to which the prevailing morality of the society had condemned them.

Legouvé's ideas, widely circulated in *La Femme en France au XIXe siècle* (1864), *Messieurs les enfants* (1868), *Conférences parisiennes* (1872), *Nos filles et nos fils* (1877), and *Une Education de jeune fille* (1884), exercised considerable influence. He was an advocate of physical training. He campaigned for an affectionate, natural upbringing for children but later avowed a kind of helplessness at reconciling a relaxation of authority with the resultant tyranny of the child.

Legouvé was elected to the French Academy in 1855, chiefly on the fame of his *Médée*, published that year. After the death of Désiré Nisard in 1888, he became the father of that body. He was raised to the highest degree of the Légion d'honneur in 1887 and held for many years the post of inspector general of female education in the national schools. His *Soixante ans de souvenirs* (1886–87) is an excellent example of autobiography.

H. Koon and R. Switzer, *Eugène Scribe* (Boston, 1980); E. Scribe, *Théatre choisi* (Paris, 1932).

Shelby A. Outlaw

Related entries: ACADEMIE FRANCAISE; COLLEGE DE FRANCE; SCRIBE.

LEMAITRE, FREDERICK (1800–1876), renowned actor of romantic melodramas. Called the Talma du boulevard, Frédérick Lemaître was born in Le Havre on 21 July 1800, the son of an architect. Perceiving his son's talent, Lemaître's father took him to Paris and enrolled him in the Conservatoire, where young Lemaître received a thorough classical training. Despite the recommendation of the famed actor Talma (1763–1826), the Odéon refused in 1819 to engage him, and Lemaître spent the next four years of his career acting with less than notable success on the stages of Paris' less prestigious theaters. He even played a lion in *Pyrame et Thisbé* at the Théâtre des variétés-amusantes. Lemaître's first major opportunity came in 1823 when he acted in *L'Auberge des Adrets* at the Ambigu-Comique. Booed in his opening performance of this melodrama, he turned a potential disaster into a personal triumph and made his reputation by transforming the villain of the play into a comic caricature. By 1830, Lemaître had solidly established himself on the French stage.

Lemaître, who liked to dazzle his audiences with novel and dramatic interpretations and with passionate, often excessive, outbursts on the stage, reached the height of his popularity between 1830 and 1850 when, with Marie Dorval (1798–1849) and Bocage (Pierre-François Touze, 1797–1863), he dominated the performance of melodrama and romantic drama. His more notable roles included such overwhelming successes as *Robert-Macaire* (1834), Victor Hugo's *Lucrèce Borgia* (1833) and *Ruy Blas* (1838), and Alexandre Dumas' *Kean, Richard d'Arlington*, and the *Alchimiste*. His performance in *Ruy Blas* probably marks the high point of his art and fame. After midcentury, Lemaître's reputation declined, and he died in 1876, largely forgotten and in poverty. In addition to his career as an actor, Lemaître authored three works: *Prisonnier amateur* (1826), *Vieil artiste, ou la Séduction* (1826), and *Robert-Macaire* (1834).

L.-H. Lecomte, *Un comédien au XIXe siècle. Frédérick Lemaître*, 2 vols. (Paris, 1888); E. Silvain, *Frédérick Lemaître* (Paris, 1926).

Robert Brown

Related entries: DUMAS, A.; HUGO; MACAIRE; TALMA.

LEMERCIER, JEAN-LOUIS-NEPOMUCENE (1771–1840), dramatic author with republican sympathies. A victim of the generalized aristocratic neglect of children, Lemercier suffered a mild right-sided paralysis. Nonetheless, his origins and his noble godparents helped launch an early literary career when a tragedy he wrote at the age of sixteen, *Méléagre*, was performed before Marie Antoinette in 1788. His *Tartuffe révolutionnaire* was forbidden by the Directory after five performances, foreshadowing future political difficulties.

Lemercier mingled with other fashionable figures at the salons of Mme. Tallien and Josephine de Beauharnais, where he developed a friendship with Bonaparte. In 1797, his *Agamemnon*, a mediocre tragedy in verse, was acclaimed as a masterpiece. Following a bitter public letter written by the envious Jean-Sébastien Mercier begging the public not to confuse their names, Lemercier henceforth used his third name exclusively and even named his daughter Népomucie.

Lemercier created a new literary genre in 1800 with *Pinto, ou la journée d'une conspiration*, the historical comedy, a precursor of romanticism. Its success was of short duration. Bonaparte apparently viewed it as a commentary on his rise to power. Lemercier perceived Bonaparte's political ambitions and expressed his disapproval candidly at Malmaison. In 1801, he refused 10,000 francs from Bonaparte. Although he accepted the Légion d'honneur in 1803, the execution of the duc d'Enghien intervened before he gave the oath required by law, and on the day Napoleon crowned himself emperor, Lemercier returned his brevet and informed Napoleon that, the Constitution having been changed, he considered his Légion d'honneur nullified.

Napoleon retaliated by closing the theater to Lemercier, depriving him of goods and property, and humiliating and persecuting him. In 1813, the Conseil d'état took advantage of Napoleon's absence to indemnify Lemercier for "nine years of misery and ruin."

Lemercier had no more sympathy for the Restoration and fared little better under it. His earlier censured plays were performed with little success, and except for the *Panhypocrisiade* in 1819, a satirical poem hesitating between epic and verse drama, he produced a great deal without any noteworthy success.

Elected to the French Academy in 1810, Lemercier consistently opposed Victor Hugo and the romantics, although his *Christophe Colombe* (1810), a *comédie shakespirienne*, was a distinctly romantic effort. Its many innovations provoked such disturbances that one person was killed and future performances had to be guarded. It was Lemercier's tragedy to suffer from the restrictions of classical style without having the talent or courage of a true innovator. Victor Hugo, who succeeded him at the Academy, respected the man without admiring the author. Charles-Maurice de Talleyrand paid him the finest compliment: "He walks through mud in white silk stockings, without a stain."

J.-L.-N. Lemercier, *Pinto*, ed. Norma Perry (Exeter, N.H., 1976); G. Vauthier, *Essai sur la vie et sur les oeuvres de N. Lemercier* (1886).

Shelby A. Outlaw

Related entries: ACADEMIE FRANCAISE; COUNCIL OF STATE; RO-MANTICISM.

LEMONTEY, PIERRE-EDOUARD (1762–1826), man of letters, minor Revolutionary figure, and historian. Born in Lyons on 14 January 1762 the son of a merchant, Pierre-Edouard Lemontey prepared for a legal career and entered the bar of his native city in 1782. Preferring a life of literature and the salon to that of the law, he soon became a typical eighteenth-century provincial man of letters. Two of his eulogies, one on Peyrèse in 1785 and the other on James Cook in 1789, won literary prizes from the Academy of Marseilles. On the eve of the Revolution, Lemontey revealed his liberal opinions by defending in a 1787 essay the right of Protestants to full political rights. In the days immediately preceding the Revolution, he helped draft the *cahier* of the Third Estate and served in the new municipal government of Lyons. Elected to the Legislative Assembly in 1791, he sat as a supporter of the constitutional monarchy, becoming first its secretary and then its president (December 1791–January 1792). Following the events of 10 August 1792, Lemontey returned to Lyons; during the course of the insurrection there, he fled to Switzerland. Returning to France in 1795, Lemontey served briefly as a local official, but because he recognized that he lacked the temperament for the tumultuous and violent political life of Lyons, he resigned and moved to Paris to resume life as a man of letters.

During the last years of the Directory and throughout the Consulate, Lemontey devoted himself to letters and published a number of light and witty works. An opera, *Palma, ou le Voyage en Grèce*, performed in 1798, met with a modest success; a second opera, *Romagnèsi*, however, failed. In 1801, he published *Raison, folie; chacun son mot*, later praised by Stendhal, which contained a chapter on economics that explored the potentially harmful political and social effects of the division of labor so highly praised by Adam Smith. By 1804, Lemontey had obtained from the Napoleonic regime enough sinecures to ensure for him a comfortable income. Having become censor of the theaters, he had the audacity to alter not just the language but entire scenes of the great French classical plays. In return for his lucrative positions, Lemontey celebrated the establishment of the Empire with *La Famille du Jura, ou Irons-nous a Paris?*, lavished praise on the imperial armies in *La Vie du soldat français*, and welcomed the birth of the king of Rome with *Thibaut, comte du Champagne*. Napoleon also commissioned Lemontey to write a history of France since Louis XIV and provided him with both a pension and access to the government's archives, including those held in the Ministry of Foreign Affairs. Possibly complete in 1816, the book remained in manuscript, for there was little chance of publication for a volume dealing with the decadence of the French monarchy.

With the Restoration, Lemontey tried to accommodate himself to the new government in an effort to save his several positions. For reasons of economy more than for political revenge, the Bourbon government deprived Lemontey of all but his position as censor of the theater. Nevertheless, between 1814 and 1818 he attempted to live in peace with the restored monarchy. In 1818, his attitude and his intellectual position changed dramatically. Evidence of this new stance came with the publication of the *Essai sur l'établissement monarchique de Louis XIV et sur les altérations qu'il a éprouvées pendant la vie de ce prince*. Lemontey's book, a great and controversial success in 1818, has been praised as one of the first good histories written during the nineteenth century. Extensive in its use of original documents, the *Essai* traced the origins of the Revolution back to the absolutism of Louis XIV and thereby opened a new path for the study of the French monarchy. Because Lemontey emphasized the continuity between the monarchy of the Old Regime and the institutions created by the Revolution, his book stands as a worthy predecessor of Alexis de Tocqueville's *L'Ancien régime et la Révolution*. Largely on the merits of this historical work, Lemontey won election to the French Academy in 1819.

Encouraged by the reception accorded the *Essai*, Lemontey undertook the completion of a sequel, *Histoire de la régence*. Completed at the time of his death in 1826, the book was not published until 1832 because the comte d'Hauterive, the archivist at the Ministry of Foreign Affairs, had Lemontey's notes, papers, and manuscripts seized. François Mignet, who became archivist in 1830, ordered the release of Lemontey's possessions. Stendhal, who greatly admired Lemontey, also claimed both that the author was afraid to publish his work and that the Jesuits had tried to destroy the manuscript. The book, nonetheless, met with a poor reception. Other works published by Lemontey during the Restoration include *Des avantages de la caisse d'épargne et de prévoyance, ou les Trois visites de M. Bruno* (1819) and *Etude littéraire sur la partie historique de Paul et Virginie, accompagnée de pièces officielles relatives au naufrage du vaisseau le St-Géran* (1823). After a year of illness, Pierre-Edouard Lemontey died on 26 June 1826.

Biographie universelle, vol. 24; P.-E. Lemontey, *Essai sur l'établissement monarchique de Louis XIV* (Paris, 1818), *Histoire de la régence et de la minorité de Louis XV* (Paris, 1832), and *Oeuvres*, 7 vols. (Paris, 1829–32); B. Réizov, *L'Historiographie romantique française, 1815–1830* (Moscow, n.d.).

Robert Brown

Related entries: ACADEMIE FRANCAISE; MIGNET; REICHSTADT; RESTORATION, SECOND; STENDHAL; TOCQUEVILLE.

LERMINIER, JEAN-LOUIS-EUGENE (1803–1857), professor of comparative law at the Collège de France, journalist, political figure, and author of many works on legal theory and history, German culture, and literature. Raised and educated in Strasbourg and Germany, Lerminier became a leader in the legal field by his mid-twenties. A practicing lawyer, teacher, and contributor to *La Thémis* and the *Globe*, he built a legal system synthesizing the German historical approach with the rationalism of French codification. The novelty of this system and its possibilities as a proto-social science, as well as his popular style, quickly made Lerminier a hero of the university world, more inspiring, it was said, than François Guizot or Victor Cousin.

In the 1830s Lerminier published the bulk of his work, including *Introduction générale à l'histoire du droit* (1829), *Philosophie du droit* (1831), *Lettres philosophiques adressées à un berlinois* (1832), *De l'influence de la philosophie du XVIIᵉ siècle sur la législation et la sociabilité du XIXᵉ* (1833), *Cours d'histoire des législations comparées* (1835–36), *Etudes d'histoire et de philosophie* (1836), *Dix ans d'enseignement* (1839), and especially *Au-delà du Rhin* (1835), which established his claim to be Mme. de Staël's successor. During this period as well he became one of Paris's premier journalists, moving successively from major work for the *Globe, Bon sens, Le Droit*, and finally the *Revue des deux-mondes*, whose editorial policy he shaped. These journals (though he contributed to many more) mirrored Lerminier's political metamorphosis from St. Simonian to populist, constitutionalist to Orleanist. This final shift brought him to the height of his career when he became a consultant to Louis-Philippe, received the Legion of Honor, and was selected as *maître des requêtes* to the Conseil d'état.

Adherence to Orleanism brought Lerminier down. Having built his career in great measure on a romantic, dashing style in lecturing and journalism, he appeared to have deceived his audience, which overlooked the conservative principles espoused in his legal philosophy. The honors bestowed on Lerminier in 1838 were followed by rioting at the Collège de France (the greatest since the days of Peter Ramus, it was said) and a smear campaign in the press, many of whose members envied Lerminier's meteoric rise. Once mentioned with Victor Hugo and Jules Michelet as the savant of his generation, he became a figure of derision, an anathema to former friends like George Sand, Alfred de Vigny, and Charles-Augustin Sainte-Beuve. Because his career pattern of opportunism, success built on talent, and ephemeral fame were so paradigmatic, he remained intriguing to writers like Honoré de Balzac and Stendhal, who immortalized him in *Lucien Leuwen* and *Illusions perdues*. For all that, his last works—*De la liberté scientifique* (1849), *De la littérature révolutionnaire* (1850), *Tablettes européens* (1849), and *Histoire des législateurs et des constitutions de la Grèce antique* (1852)—passed with him into oblivion.

B. G. Smith, "The Rise and Fall of Eugène Lerminier," *French Historical Studies* 12 (Spring 1982).

Bonnie G. Smith

Related entries: LE BON SENS; COLLEGE DE FRANCE; COUNCIL OF STATE; COUSIN; LE DROIT; LE GLOBE; GUIZOT; LA REVUE DES DEUX MONDES; SAINTE-BEUVE; SAINT-SIMONIANISM; SAND; STAEL-HOLSTEIN; VIGNY.

LEROUX, PIERRE (1797–1871), utopian socialist. Pierre Leroux was one of the most influential, prolific, and in some ways the most unusual of the utopian socialists who populated the literary and political worlds of the late Restoration and the July Monarchy. He combined several talents and vocations: philosopher, poet, inventor, journalist, and political activist. Leroux's influence extended from republican secret societies to the salons of literati habituated by such as Victor Hugo and George Sand. He put his stamp on the peculiarly French romantic socialism of the era.

Originally headed toward the elite Ecole polytechnique and an engineering career, the premature death of Leroux's father, which plunged the family into poverty, changed the young man's life. Forced to earn a living, he found a job working for a stockbroker. However, in a mood that prefigured his subsequent career, Leroux soon quit, finding life as a manipulator of money distasteful. He worked briefly as a mason and then found the entry into his vocation as a type-setter for a publisher that put out liberal and occasionally republican pamphlets.

In 1824 Leroux founded his own newspaper, the *Globe*, in which he promoted the liberal ideas fashionable among opponents of the Restoration monarchy. But his own political perspective evolved rapidly, and by the end of the decade the *Globe* had achieved a European-wide reputation as a leading journal that combined literary and philosophical discussions with considerations of the social question, chiefly the relationship among classes, their history, and the social effects of industrialization. During this period Leroux came under the influence of Saint-Simonian ideas, which he carried with him throughout the remainder of his career. Leroux was most deeply affected by Saint-Simon's last work, *Le Nouveau christianisme*, which called for the creation of a religion of humanity to replace Christian orthodoxy and to serve as a foundation for social unity. Specifically this religion was scheduled to replace class tensions by common spiritual bonds. Neither Saint-Simon, nor Leroux after him, supplied this religion with much concrete content; it remained a mystical and metaphysical construct surrounded by romantic vapors and harbored the sort of utopian visions of human perfection through spiritual renewal in which Leroux specialized. But through its propagation in the pages of the *Globe*, which had become the official Saint-Simonian organ by 1830, the religion of humanity and associated utopian projections deeply influenced middle-class radicals and intellectuals seeking paths to social peace.

In 1831, Leroux left the Saint-Simonian church founded by Barthélemy Enfantin and Saint-Armand Bazard and turned over the *Globe* to another acolyte, Michel Chevalier. At the same time, Leroux placed a certain distance between himself and the Saint-Simonians. Although he retained his faith in the core of the doctrine, ''all social institutions should aim towards the moral, material and intellectual improvement of the most numerous and poorest classes,'' Leroux rejected the authoritarian and elitist strains in the Saint-Simonian movement. Moreover, its formalized and bizarre cult practices repelled him. What remained, however, was the quest for harmony, symmetry, and mystical exaltation. This occasionally took some strange forms, as when Leroux advanced his theory of reincarnation and actually calculated the average number of times an individual had been reborn (405) and the number of years spent on earth (27,500). In the same vein, his discussion of the organic unity of the human ecology, by which inert matter provided essential nourishment, dwelled on the culture of beans fertilized by human excrement in flower pots. Nevertheless, his point was a serious one and had political implications: the interdependence of all forms of human activity and the unnatural condition of the exploitation of man by man. From this position it was but a short step to political activism.

Leroux became involved in the secret societies that proliferated during the late 1830s and the 1840s and in the movement for a democratic and social Republic. He focused his political efforts on the Société des droits de l'homme, a bourgeois association that counted among its members many of the republican luminaries of the July Monarchy: François-Vincent Raspail, Godefroy Cavaignac, Marc Caussidière, and Marc-Etienne Dufraisse, among others. Politically radical, the Société did not have much in the way of a concrete social program. Leroux brought to the Société his particular vision of an egalitarian, democratic—but unfocused—socialism. While an enemy of bourgeois privilege and a harsh critic of capitalism, Leroux, like his contemporary Etienne Cabet, eschewed class struggle. Drawing upon Jean-Jacques Rousseau, Maximilien Robespierre, François-Noel Babeuf, as well as his own Saint-Simonian background, Leroux envisioned a society of equal citizens held together by the natural forces of human solidarity. Because he believed in the essential continuity and uninterrupted flow of history—that is, a nondialectical philosophy of history—Leroux insisted that harmony, not struggle, was humankind's natural state and prescribed destiny. For him, socialism represented not the negation of individualism but the absorption of the individual within the larger body of citizens. All of this was to come about not through political struggle but by way of religious conversion. In other words, socialism meant salvation, a moral transformation to some higher, mystical condition.

This fog-enshrouded mysticism notwithstanding, Leroux was a penetrating critic of contemporary France. He denounced the regime of formal equality and the philosophers, such as Victor Cousin, who defended it, for, as he repeated, all Frenchmen were not equal. One law existed for the rich, who could get away with all sorts of crimes, and another for the poor, who were the victims. Typical of the other utopian socialists of his time, Leroux founded an experimental community in Boussac (Creuse) of eighty persons, each of whom received the same wage; all profits were destined for reinvestment in agriculture. By this he intended to solve the problems of the proletariat. The colony did not prosper, although it did attract the attention of a cluster of wandering romantic writers and musicians from France and Germany; even Franz Liszt took an interest.

Despite the fact that Leroux specialized in utopian schemes and mystical constructions, he was never politically idle. When the Republic was proclaimed in Paris on 24 February 1848, he proclaimed it in Boussac three days later and was elected mayor of the municipality. He stood for election to the Constituent Assembly as a deputy from the Creuse but lost. In June 1848, he took a seat in the Assembly as a deputy from Paris. Following the slaughter of workers in the June Days, Leroux gained national attention after delivering an impassioned speech in the Assembly defending the workers and denouncing his old comrade from the Société des droits de l'homme, Godefroy Cavaignac. Leroux took part in the deliberations on the Constitution for the Second Republic and became the object of considerable derision among his colleagues when he proposed that the Constitution include reference to the principle of the Trinity, or the "Triad," as he called it. Even in the hurly-burly of politics, Leroux remained consistently faithful to his social religion, but events had passed him by.

Leroux sat in the Legislative Assembly in 1849 where he identified himself with the Left, or the Mountain. But he refused to associate himself with the

Mountain's call for insurrection in June 1849. Leroux did not believe in violence. Instead he worked the fringes of the various secret society plots and conspiracies during the next two years. Finally, with the police after him, he joined Cabet and Louis Blanc on the island of Jersey where they set up a community similar to the one in Boussac. During the 1860s Leroux lived from hand to mouth, earning a meager living from the sale of some of his books and benefiting from the generosity of his fellow typesetters who organized several collections on his behalf. They and other workers had never forgotten his defense of their rights in 1848 or his vocation as a self-styled peaceful revolutionary. Leroux died in Paris during the Commune, the great civil war that he devoted his life to preventing.

D. O. Evans, *Le Socialisme romantique* (Paris, 1948); M. Leroy, *Histoire des idées sociales en France*, vol. 3 (Paris, 1946); I. Tchernoff, *Le Parti républicain sous la monarchie de juillet* (Paris, 1901).

Sanford Elwitt

Related entries: BAZARD; BLANC; CABET; CAUSSIDIERE; CAVAIGNAC, G.-E.-L.; CHEVALIER; COUSIN; ECOLE POLYTECHNIQUE; ENFANTIN; *LE GLOBE*; HUGO; LISZT; RASPAIL; ROUSSEAU; SAINT-SIMON; SAINT-SIMONIANISM; SOCIETY OF THE RIGHTS OF MAN; YOUNG (NEW) MOUNTAIN SOCIETY.

LEROY, GUSTAVE (1818–1860), brushmaker, democratic and socialist *chansonnier* in Paris. Leroy was known as one of the gods of the *goguette* and has been called the most gifted *chansonnier* of his time. Born in Paris on 6 October 1818, Leroy grew up without a father. His mother could not afford to send him to school, but Mme. Saque, the famous tightrope walker, gave him some instruction. By the time he was thirteen, it became possible to send him to school. In the *pension* where he was placed, the students every Friday recited verses from the works of Corneille, Racine, Voltaire, and other classic writers. This gave him a taste for poetry, which carried over into his first trip to a *goguette*. Leroy had already tried his hand at songwriting, but the works he heard there were so good that they seemed beyond his powers. Just as he was about to quit writing, he sold his first song and then several others to an organ-grinder, and soon his name was posted along with the names of other well-known *chansonniers* like Charles Gille. This impressed "my mother, my child, my friends, even those who detest me. That's why I'm a *chansonnier*."

Leroy sang at the *goguette* Les Enfants du temple, at Les Animaux (where Charles Gille was president), at the Amis de la vigne, at the Assommoir, and at Les Infernaux, where he was elected president in 1840. Whenever he entered a *goguette*, handsome and well dressed, there was a burst of loud applause, and when he sang in his husky voice, the victim of his pipe and of the fog of pipe smoke that shrouded every *goguette*, there was silence, and people stood up to get a better look at him. He wrote about four hundred songs, which he sold in small collections for 40 centimes or sold to publishers like Eyssautier and like Durand for 50 centimes per couplet. He also wrote original melodies for some of his songs. All of this brought him little money but lots of glory. As Leroy wrote in a song that was published in *La voix du peuple*, a collection of songs published in 1844: "For the poor man the *goguette* is the center of culture / that the Louvre Museum is for the rich man! / Go there, all of you bards of the working class!!!"

Leroy was delighted by the 1848 Revolution and took some credit for overthrowing the July Monarchy by means of song. He tried to cash in on his popularity by running for the Constituent Assembly with the support of the working-class Buchezian *L'Atelier* in 1848, but he was not elected. From here on things got worse. Saddened by the June Days of 1848, he supported Alexandre-Auguste Ledru-Rollin's monumentally unsuccessful campaign for the presidency of the Republic in December 1848. In 1849, he attacked the government of Louis-Napoleon Bonaparte in a song, "Le Bal et la guillotine," for which he was fined 300 francs and imprisoned for six months for stirring up hate and distrust of the government of the Republic by a published work. He tried to live by writing during the Second Empire, but little that he wrote during that period has survived, and his career as a *chansonnier* seems to have been snuffed out along with the *goguettes*. He died in poverty in Paris on 14 April 1860.

In politics, Leroy was a revolutionary who opposed revolution. He admired the Revolution of 1789 and celebrated Bastille Day and the triumphs of freedom and the republican armies in *La Voix du peuple*, published in 1844. Yet in the same volume he published this song:

> What is this! People are pouring out of the working-class suburbs,
> The populace is rioting,
> Townsmen and soldiers are cutting one another's throats,
> Over one single word: liberty.
> Frenchmen, let's save our fire for more praiseworthy wars.
> Little birds, make love not war.

He favored French intervention in Poland, and he sang of liberty, the first Republic, the glories of the Empire, the three glorious days of the 1830 Revolution, and the disappointment of the people in its result. He spoke out against laws that curtailed the freedom of the press, and he wrote songs in favor of the socialist ideal that everyone had the right to a decent job at decent pay. He was, however, not a communist, and in "Les Députés de 48," he wrote:

> I'm not an ardent communist,
> I don't want what isn't mine;
> I am at war against the big capitalist,
> Who coldly speculates on the products of our labor.

The solution, then, was the creation of producers' cooperative associations, which would give the workers ownership of the means of production and control over the products of their labor. Leroy as a young man had complete confidence in the power of the press and in the power of song to spread his ideas. When he lost this, his creative life ended.

> For us the press is a powerful resource.
> You know, it is like gunpowder,
> When you strike it, it gives off a spark.

H. Avenel, *Chansons et chansonniers* (Paris, 1889); E. Baillet, *La Chanson française, Le Pamphlet du pauvre (1834–1851)* (Paris, 1957); C. Gille and C. Regnard, *La Chanson de nos jours*, 2 vols. (Paris, 1844); J. Maitron, ed., *Dictionnaire biographique du mouvement ouvrier français*, vol. 2 (Paris, 1966); E. L. Newman, "L'arme du siècle, c'est la plume: The French Worker Poets of the July Monarchy and the Spirit of Revolution and Reform," *Journal of Modern History* (1980) and *The French Worker Poets of the July Monarchy*, forthcoming.

Edgar L. Newman

Related entries: L'ATELIER; CONSTITUTION OF 1848; GILLE; JUNE DAYS; LEDRU-ROLLIN; REVOLUTION OF 1848; SINGING SOCIETIES; WORKER POETS; WORKERS' COOPERATIVES.

LESSEPS, FERDINAND-MARIE, VICOMTE DE (1805–1894), diplomat and financier who built the Suez Canal and failed to build the Panama Canal. Lesseps spent all but three years of his professional career down to 1849 outside France. This career can be divided into two parts. The first, from 1825 to 1848, saw him rise in the consular service from assistant vice-consul at Lisbon to consul general at Barcelona. In the second period, from 1848 to 1849, his career suddenly changed gear: he was promoted to the prestigious post of ambassador to Madrid and in May 1849 sent to Rome as minister pleni-potentiary charged with negotiating an agreement with the republican government there. This second mission proved a failure. He was recalled and reprimanded for failing to follow instructions. His pride wounded, Lesseps resigned from the service and retired to his country estate. He not only published a 132-page defense of his mission to Rome, but nearly forty years later he again lengthily explained his action in his autobiographical recollections. It was the end of his diplomatic career, though, that launched his second career as an international financier: late in 1849 he began to plan the Suez Canal that was to be his greatest achievement. As both diplomat and financier, Lesseps remains a controversial figure. Scholars still do not agree on his responsibility for the Panama scandal or for the failure of his mission to Rome in 1849. Pierre de la Gorce, in his classic *Histoire de la deuxième République* (1887), was strongly critical of his conduct at Rome, but his most recent French biographer, Georges Edgar-Bonnet, exonerates him from all blame.

Lesseps' choice of career in 1825 was inevitable. Since 1740 members of his family, which originated from Bayonne, had worked in the consular service. His father and his uncle were consuls, and both his brothers spent at least part of their careers working for the Foreign Ministry. It was his paternal uncle, Barthélemy, who initiated Lesseps in the service during a two years' apprenticeship in Lisbon, and his father completed his education at Tunis from 1828 until 1832. This latter year was a significant one, for Lesseps then began five years' service in Egypt, first as vice-consul at Alexandria and then as consul at Cairo. These were more important than most consular posts because the Egypt of Méhémet Ali, though under the suzerainty of the Porte, was undergoing rapid economic change, and Frenchmen were playing important roles in the country's administration. They also offered Lesseps his first opportunity to distinguish himself: Alexandria and Cairo were struck first by an outbreak of the plague and then by cholera, and he displayed enough courage and ability while organizing relief to be awarded at the age of twenty-nine the cross of the Legion of Honor. His spell in Egypt marked his life in a second way: Lesseps came into contact for the first time with plans for a Suez canal. He read the memoir drawn up by Jean-Baptiste Lepère, one of Napoleon's engineers, met Adolphe Linant de Bellefonds, an engineer who had been in Egypt since 1818 and who also made studies for a canal, and discussed the project with Barthélemy Enfantin, who spent three years in the country from 1833 to 1836. Lesseps also struck a friendship with Méhémet Ali and with his youngest son, Saïd Pasha, whom he taught to ride. When the latter unexpectedly came to power late in 1854, he was to invite Lesseps to return to Egypt and to grant him the Suez Canal concession.

For five years after his spell in Egypt, Lesseps vegetated in minor postings in Rotterdam and Malaga. His appointment in 1842 as consul at Barcelona, however, was to change the course of his career. The Catalan capital was not only Spain's leading port and industrial city but the scene of an insurrection in November of that year. During the revolt and the government's siege of the city, Lesseps organized the embarcation of over a thousand French nationals and Spanish refugees and for a time acted as a negotiator between the two sides. Although the Spanish authorities criticized his actions, the French government rewarded him by making him an officer of the Legion of Honor and promoting him to consul general. His conduct in the crisis, then, brought him public attention and was one factor in his sudden and unanticipated promotion to the diplomatic corps in April 1848.

Alphonse de Lamartine, the foreign minister in the Provisional Government, adopted a prudent policy and appointed tried diplomats rather than new men. Lesseps was one of these. He was first sent as ambassador to Spain with orders to improve relations and thus protect the Pyrenean border in the event of war with other powers. Lesseps worked well with Manual Narvaez, the Spanish prime minister, but his task was facilitated by British encouragement of opposition groups and the subsequent expulsion of the British ambassador. Early in 1849, however, Lesseps was recalled to Paris and given a delicate mission to Rome. The situation in the Papal States was complex, his instructions ambiguous, and his mission unlikely to be successful. A nationalist revolt in Rome had forced the pope to seek refuge in Naples and had brought to power a government with Mazzini as its most flamboyant and intransigent leader. It was believed in Paris that the republican government in Rome did not have popular support and that Pius IX could be persuaded to grant political reforms. Both suppositions proved erroneous. On 30 April republican forces inflicted heavy losses on the French expeditionary force when it attacked the city. In the wake of this defeat, Lesseps was sent to Rome to negotiate. Although by the end of May he had finally reached a tentative agreement with the Roman government that would have permitted French troops to occupy the city, he was recalled to Paris. Once there and by virtue of a hitherto unused clause in the new constitution that made public officials accountable for their actions, Lesseps was brought before the Council of State. By a vote with only one dissension, this body reprimanded him. There is reason to believe, however, that this decision was unjust.

The instructions Lesseps had received before his departure were vague, and no further instructions had been sent to him. Besides, while he was in Italy, elections in France had strengthened the conservative majority in the Assembly and thus opposition to the Roman republic. This political change in Paris helps explain not only Lesseps' recall but the authorization given to the French commander outside Rome to attack the city again. The Left opposition in the Assembly, led by Alexandre-Auguste Ledru-Rollin, was not only stridently critical of this second attack that once again violated the guarantee of the liberty of peoples in the French Constitution but even organized a mass demonstration in the capital. It was immediately before the violent parliamentary debate on the Roman question that the government, needing a scapegoat, decided to bring Lesseps before the Council of State.

Lesseps had certainly been guilty of overoptimism in believing that he was capable of carrying out a mission when he was ignorant of conditions on the spot and insufficiently aware of conflicting interests in France. But he was, above all, a victim of changed political circumstances in France and of an impossible situation at Rome. French policy there, indeed, was to prove a failure.

E. Bourgeois and E. Clermont, *Rome et Napoléon III, 1849–1870* (Paris, 1907); G. Edgar-Bonnet, *Ferdinand de Lesseps: Le Diplomate, le créateur de Suez* (Paris, 1951); F. de Lesseps, *Ma mission à Rome, mai 1849* (Paris, 1849), "Notice sur mes services diplomatiques," *Revue d'histoire diplomatique* 71 (1957), and *Recollections of Forty Years*, 2 vols. (London, 1887); I. Scott, *The Roman Question and the Powers, 1848–1865* (The Hague, 1969); A. J. P. Taylor, *The Italian Problem in European Diplomacy, 1847–1849* (Manchester, 1934).

Barrie M. Ratcliffe
Related entries: CONSTITUTION OF 1848; COUNCIL OF STATE; ENFANTIN; LAMARTINE; LEDRU-ROLLIN; MEHEMET ALI; PIUS IX; ROMAN EXPEDITION.

LES LETTRES NORMANDES (1817–1820), irregular left-wing newspaper of the Restoration. Léon Thiéssé's *Lettres normandes* was one of the first journals to evade the police control that the law of 21 October 1814 prescribed for periodical publications by appearing at irregular intervals. Its articles were weighty and discursive and included every shade of left-wing opposition, including bonapartism (which during the early years of the Restoration was akin to republicanism). Eleven volumes, having more of the appearance of a book than a newspaper, appeared between September 1817 and September 1820. The semi-periodical nature of the publication did not preclude prosecution in the law courts, and in February 1820 the director, Léon Thiéssé, and the editor, Foulon, were condemned to one month's imprisonment and 1,000 francs fine for an article criticizing the commemoration of the death of Louis XVI. The censorship established in March 1820 cut out so much material from the *Lettres* that the journal ceased publication later in the year.

A. Crémieux, *La Censure de 1820 et 1821* (Abbeville, 1912).

Irene Collins

Related entries: BONAPARTISM; CENSORSHIP; REPUBLICANS; THIESSE.

LIBERAL CATHOLICISM, a movement that attempted to reconcile Catholicism with political liberalism. It accepted the early years of the French Revolution and advocated separation of church and state but emphasized the church's rights as an independent corporation within society. Like social Catholicism, liberal Catholicism represented a Catholic attempt to relate constructively to social and political change of the nineteenth century. While social Catholicism focused on problems emanating from industrialism, urban growth, and laissez-faire economic philosophy, liberal Catholicism responded to the political ideology of the Enlightenment and the consequences of the French Revolution. It tried to reconcile the notion of a divinely established church with civil rights, representative government, a neutral or secular state, and a society in which most members did not owe primary allegiance to the church. Its roots lay deep: in the church-state strife during the French Revolution, in reaction to the throne-altar union during the Bourbon Restoration, in protest to Jean-Baptiste de Martignac's ordinances of 1828, which restricted the church's educational role, and in concern about the church's role after the Revolution of 1830.

Dominant Catholic opinion had rejected the Revolution and even the Concordat of 1801 because the latter was "imposed" on the church. In the first years of the Bourbon Restoration, a few Catholics began to search for a new role for the church in modern society. Even Vicomte Chateaubriand in a re-edition of his *Essai sur les révolutions* asserted that Catholicism and liberalism were not incompatible. Both *Le Catholique* (1826) and *Le Correspondant*, journals published by a Danish-born converted Jew, Baron Ferdinand d'Eckstein, stressed freedom rather than dominance for the church in society. Becoming disenchanted with the monarchy, Félicité de Lamennais by 1826 was predicting its fall and looking for a union of Catholicism and liberalism to "restore society on its real bases." The plight of Catholic minorities of Belgium, Poland, and Ireland, who suffered civil disabilities because of their religion, troubled increasing numbers of French Catholics, who noted that the Catholic minority had struck an alliance with secular liberals in Belgium. Legislation in 1828 restricting religious schools, which secular liberals like Benjamin Constant opposed, encouraged both Catholics and Protestants to demand freedom of education as a civil right and to organize a lobby, Société de la morale chrétienne, for that end.

If liberal Catholicism had a lengthy gestation period, it was born in 1829 along with Félicité de Lamennais' *Des progrès de la Révolution et de la guerre contre l'église*, which sold 6,000 copies in two weeks, and *Le Correspondant*, the main organ of liberal Catholicism for most of the century. From a theocratic ideal stressing the authority of the pope and the need for a Christian basis for society, Lamennais concluded that both princes and secular liberalism had failed. A new insight that distinguished him from reactionaries and from his earlier writings was his confidence that in a free exchange of ideas, Christianity would emerge victorious. Once the clergy acquainted itself with the modern spirit, the ''people'' would freely reestablish the reign of religion. Like John Stuart Mill, Lamennais believed in the triumph of truth amid free discussion (though he believed rather different truths). This marked a sharp break with Rome's old notion that error had no rights. In the same year, *Le Correspondant* called for freedom of education, of the press, and of religious association.

Liberal Catholicism reached fruition in France where three streams met. Those who, like Lamennais, wanted separation of church and state because the state was no longer ''Catholic'' joined with those who defended Catholics' civil rights from anticlerical governments, and a newer group, surrounding Charles-Forbes de Montalembert, who thought the church had been compromised by prior political associations. Mere weeks after the July Revolution, *Le Correspondant* argued that the Bourbon cause was lost; it was now necessary to save religion.

Although its life was a brief thirteen months—October 1830-November 1831— the daily newspaper *L'Avenir* was the great forum for liberal Catholics. A cooperative venture of Lamennais, Henri Lacordaire, and Charles de Coux, quickly joined by Montalembert, it was dominated by Lamennais. Using Lockean phraseology, it asserted that certain natural rights of liberty existed: freedom of conscience and religion (from this followed separation of church from state), education, press, and association. It also called for democratization and decentralization of government. Implicit in the argument was a strong notion of progress and confidence in the compatibility of learning (*science*) and faith. Confident in the generosity of fervent Catholics, it challenged the clergy to renounce governmental salaries. Its ultramontanism offended Gallicans; its call for separation worried both the episcopacy and the Vatican; its political liberalism alienated legitimists. Attacked by the prestigious *L'Ami de la religion*, it was condemned by three influential bishops—Cardinal de Rohan, Msgr. d'Astros, and Msgr. Clausal de Montals—and banned in a number of dioceses. Shaken by episcopal sanctions and with their subscription list of 2,000 young clergy threatened, the editors voluntarily suspended publication, journeyed to Rome, and appealed to Gregory XVI. Although a pious man, Gregory had been an isolated monk before his election during suppression of liberal uprisings in the Papal States. His encyclical *Mirari vos* condemned the ideas of *L'Avenir*.

Lamennais broke with the church, while the other editors submitted in 1834; *L'Avenir* never published again.

During the next decade liberal Catholics remained on the defensive, with massive transfers of priests occurring from 1836 to 1842 for disciplinary purposes. Many liberal Catholics turned to introspective intellectual matters, contributing to a resurgence of Catholic letters in France.

Liberal Catholics returned to center stage in the mid–1840s, led by Montalembert and allied with some not-so-liberal Catholics, to fight a battle for public opinion in favor of liberty of education—notably the right of the church to operate secondary schools—a battle won in 1850 with the passage of the Falloux Law. The accession to the papacy of the reputed liberal Cardinal Mastai (Pius IX) in 1846 and the February 1848 Revolution in France added weight to their cause. Msgr. Parisis in "A Problem of Conscience" de-emphasized the condemnatory passages of *Mirari vos*. *Le Correspondant* welcomed the February Revolution, the French episcopacy supported the Provisional Government, and fifteen priests were elected deputies.

Superficial Catholic unity dissolved, however, over two issues: social reform and educational unity. Three groups emerged. One, including Henri Maret, Frédéric Ozanam, Henri Lacordaire, and Philippe-Olympe Gerbet, advocated social reform and democracy in their journal *L'ère nouvelle* (1848). Others, like Montalembert and Bishop Dupanloup writing in *L'ami de la religion*, adamantly opposed socialism but favored the libertarian provisions of the Falloux Law. A third reactionary group, whose most famous spokesmen were Louis Veuillot and abbé Joseph Gaume, insisted on the political and social dominance of the church.

Liberal Catholics, most of whose roots lay in the upper-middle class or in the aristocracy, feared democracy. Although *L'Avenir* mentioned social reform and Lacordaire and Ozanam were bridges between liberal and social Catholicism, social and political questions were kept separate. In the short term, liberal Catholicism unwittingly gave a lift to ultramontanism because Rome decided disputes. In the longer term liberal Catholics came to distrust the papacy and insist on a narrow definition of papal authority.

French liberal Catholics were pioneers, anticipating many trends within the church. Their ideas about church-state relations, government within the church, the importance of the educational role of the church, and the relevance of the role of a church as a social, as well as religious, institution influenced Catholic policy and became a departure point for church-state discussions for at least a century. The *ralliement*, a half-century after the death of *L'Avenir*, was its resurrection.

J. Cabanis, *Lacordaire et quelques autres: Politique et religion* (Paris, 1982); A. Dansette, *Religious History of Modern France*, vol. 1 (New York, 1961); A. Latreille and R. Rémond, *Histoire du Catholicisme en France*, vol. 3 (Paris, 1962); G. Weill, *Histoire du catholicisme libéral en France, 1828–1908*, (Paris, 1909).

Patrick J. Harrigan

Related entries: L'AVENIR; CHATEAUBRIAND; CONSTANT; DUPAN-LOUP; FALLOUX LAW; LACORDAIRE; LAMENNAIS; LIBERTY OF ED-

UCATION; MARTIGNAC; MONTALEMBERT; PIUS IX; SOCIAL CA-
THOLICISM; SOCIETY OF CHRISTIAN MORALS; ULTRAMONTANES;
VEUILLOT.

LIBERTY OF EDUCATION, the cry during the July Monarchy of opponents
of the state-controlled University's monopoly of secondary and higher education.
They achieved partial victory with the Falloux Law of 1850, which permitted
both private and public high schools to operate. The church's role in schooling
became a bitter issue in France with the Revolution. Most influential Catholics
then from abbé Audurein (*Una gens una mens*, 1790) to Chateaubriand opposed
any alternative to clerical domination of schooling. After Napoleon bestowed an
effective monopoly of postprimary schooling on the University, Catholics vied
with others for control of the University. Only after the Ordinances of 1828
ended clerical power within the University and further restricted the operation
of private schools did a new group of liberal Catholics assert themselves,
demanding not a clerical monopoly of schooling but the right of Catholics, as
citizens, to conduct private schools. The leadership came from Catholic laymen
and priests rather than from the episcopacy. Church-state issues became a matter
of public concern rather than one decided by secular and clerical princes.

Both Félicité de Lamenais and *Le Correspondant* were calling for liberty of
education within months of the ordinances. The call resounded through liberal
Catholic circles during 1830, accompanied by the demise of the Bourbon
monarchy, revision of the Charter, and news of a Catholic-liberal alliance in
Belgium; it was one of the natural rights enunciated by the liberal Catholic daily
newspaper inaugurated that year, *L'Avenir*. The suspension of *L'Avenir* and the
subsequent condemnation of its liberal principles by Pope Gregory XVI in *Mirari
vos* (1832) put liberal Catholics on the defensive. During the 1830s Catholic
journals and bishops reflected a traditional position: public schools were institutions
of pestilence. In a country without religious schooling, students might better be
ignorant. By 1836 Charles-Forbes de Montalembert was rallying liberal Catholics
to a more constructive approach and defining liberty of education as an issue
that could find support among liberals of whatever stripe. At the same time,
Mgr. Affre of Paris was making confidential overtures to the government for a
position for the church within secondary schooling. A series of bills delicately
approached the issue, with none resolving it. Catholic dissatisfaction with Abel-
François Villemain's abortive project in 1841 opened a period of great public
debate in 1843–44, dramatic years when Catholic militancy and unity marched
together in acceptance of the liberal heritage of the Revolution and notions of
progress. Montalembert and his associates shrewdly turned secular liberal
philosophy against liberals, argued that the government was abridging rights
guaranteed in the 1830 Charter, and directed his appeal to the moderate, literate
public.

Three major public statements asserted the principle in 1843. In September
Louis Veuillot's *L'Univers* printed a public letter to Villemain; in October

Montalembert published *Du Devoir des catholiques dans la question de la liberté de l'enseignement*; in December, after visiting two weeks in Liège with the architect of the Catholic campaign in Belgium, Mgr. Van Bommel—a campaign that Cardinal de Bonald had called French Catholic attention to in 1841—Mgr. Parisis published *Liberté de l'enseignement* about the same time that the resurrected biweekly *Le Correspondant* took up the issue. In March 1844 *L'Univers* released a confidential letter of Mgr. Affre to Louis-Phillipe, which prompted the public adherence of fifty-six bishops to its contents. Bishops had formerly been reluctant to enter public debate because a few wanted a Catholic monopoly, some feared that lay leadership on any question would ultimately weaken their authority, some believed in traditional church-state diplomacy, and some found public debate demeaning. They joined Montalembert's bandwagon reluctantly but did so out of frustration from governmental neglect of pastoral protests, legal restrictions on episcopal convocations, and loathing of the "godless" University, which seemed to encourage publications like Jules Michelet's anticlerical *Jésuites* (1843). In 1844 Montalembert, supported by Parisis but not most bishops, founded a committee for the defense of religious liberty, which worked as a modern political lobby in the election of 1846 and managed to gain the adherence of about one-third of the elected deputies to the principle of freedom of education. Montalembert briefly rallied bishops, clergy, and laymen alike under the flag of liberty of education.

With success came division. Although Montalembert from his writings in *L'Avenir* in 1831, in his *Lettre à M. Villemain* in 1839, his statements in 1844, and his reaction to the Falloux Law of 1850 consistently demanded genuine freedom for Catholics—a sentiment shared by men like Henri Lacordaire, abbé (later bishop) Felix Dupanloup, Father Ravignan, a Jesuit Superior, and Frédéric Ozanam—others coveted more. Veuillot, Nicholas Deschamps, a Jesuit, and abbé Combalot, among others, viciously attacked the "atheistic" University and wanted dominance for the church (Mgr. Parisis had both his liberal and reactionary moments). If the episcopacy (save for Clausal de Montals and Parisis) had intervened cautiously and infrequently (Montalembert described bishops as "cowardly"), public debate loosed the extremists. The excesses of militant Catholics led to a reaction by liberals and a resurgence of anticlericalism. In two works—*De la pacification religieuse* (1845) and, after an audience with the newly elected Pope Pius IX, *Etat actuel de la question*—Dupanloup attempted a compromise, polemically attacking members of the University but conceding its right to conduct schools, state surveillance of schools (public or private), and past mistakes of the clergy. This conflict was not one simply between church and state or religion and irreligion. Practicing Catholics in the Chamber (including ministers Villemain and Salvandy) opposed freedom of education. François Guizot, a Protestant, Adolphe Thiers, and some of the liberal press (*Le Globe* and *La Presse*) were sympathetic. A few bishops, some Catholic teachers, and many chaplains within the University defended the University at the same time that colleagues were damning it. The issue involved interpretations of the Charter, attempts to reconcile church-state relations, resistance to monolithic rights of any dominant institution—clerical or secular—and parental rights versus corporative rights. Older divisions and prejudices deflected attention from these central issues and focused attention on extremists in both camps. Intelligent, moderate debate gave way to vicious and ridiculous claims by Catholics and anticlericals alike.

The Falloux Law of 1850 granted the church the right to conduct secondary schools and reduced the power of the University. Another law in 1875 allowed the church to found universities. In winning a battle, proponents of liberty of education found themselves in a war. Within the Catholic camp, Montalembert and Dupanloup would politely decline Thiers' offer of a monopoly of schooling for the church (an offer precipitated by Thiers' fear of social revolution after 1848) and welcome the Falloux Law. Veuillot, abbé Joseph Gaume, and the Assumptionist Order adamantly opposed the law for not giving sufficient power to the church. Internal divisions within the French church were drawn along similar lines for a quarter-century. Increased clerical influence in education remained a bitter pill for anticlericals to swallow. The Ferry Laws (1880–82) and, ultimately, separation in 1901 would return monopoly of higher schooling to the state and extend it to the elementary level.

L. Grimaud, *Histoire de la liberté d'enseignement en France*, 6 vols. (Paris, 1944–54); J. Moody, "The French Catholic Press in the Education Conflict of the 1840's," *French Historical Studies* 7 (Spring 1972); G. Weill, *Histoire du catholicisme libéral en France, 1828–1908* (Paris, 1909).

Patrick J. Harrigan

Related entries: AFFRE; ANTICLERICAL CAMPAIGN; *L'AVENIR*; CHA-TEAUBRIAND; DUPANLOUP; FALLOUX LAW; *LE GLOBE*; GUIZOT; GUIZOT LAW ON PUBLIC EDUCATION; LACORDAIRE; LAMENNAIS; LIBERAL CATHOLICISM; MICHELET; MONTALEMBERT; PIUS IX; *LA PRESSE*; PUBLIC INSTRUCTION; SALVANDY; THIERS; VEUILLOT; VILLEMAIN.

LILLE, COMTE DE. See LOUIS XVIII.

LISZT, FRANZ (1811–1886), composer and musician. Liszt was born in 1811 to the family of an estate official for the Esterhazys, his father Hungarian and his mother German. Religious and musical interests were strong in the family. He moved to Vienna in 1821 to study with Antonio Salieri and Carl Czerny (and claims to have been kissed by Beethoven) but in 1823 went on to Paris, where he quickly became established as a leading performer in fashionable salons. By the early 1830s he had established himself as the foremost keyboard virtuoso and during the next two decades achieved a fame no other performer succeeded in matching in the nineteenth century. As the lion of the most prestigious salons and the sponsor of the most sought-after public concerts, he showed a canny ability to use musical and social trends to his advantage, rather as Leonard

Bernstein has done in our day. In some ways he was the creature of the burgeoning music business, since the publication of his works in editions easy enough for amateurs to play was the secret to the scale of his notoriety and his wealth. Most of these pieces were glib and brilliant variations on opera tunes everyone heard at salons, designed to make an effect upon the increasingly large and powerful pianoforte. He owed the breadth of his fame as well to the distances he traveled giving concerts in minor courts and small towns as well as major cities all the way from Moscow to Lisbon.

Yet there were other dimensions to Liszt than this one. Unlike any other major virtuoso of the epoch (Chopin had so limited a public career he should not be considered a virtuoso), he developed an extremely varied set of musical interests beyond the commercial idioms of salon music. Not only did his opera variations have far more musical substance than was conventional—the *Don Juan* Fantasy on Mozart's opera most strikingly of all—but he also performed a wide repertory of music by Mozart, Beethoven, J. S. Bach, and Domenico Scarlatti. He stayed in touch with the emerging classical music world and in 1842 made a concert tour into the hinterlands of Eastern Europe to raise money for a monument to Beethoven in Bonn.

The balance among his interests shifted drastically at midcentury. In 1848 he moved to Weimar as the music director of the court of Saxe-Coburg-Meiningen, a position he had held in absentia for six years, and in so doing he gave up his career as virtuoso pianist almost completely. While he had written so-called serious music before this, he now focused his attention on abstract genres (the B minor sonata, for example), symphonic poems (*Tasso*), and religious music (the cantata *Die Legende der heiligen Elisabeth*). His religious interest resurfaced while he was trying (unsuccessfully) to obtain an annulment of the former marriage of his lover Princesse Carolyn Sayn-Wittgenstein, and he proceeded to enter a convent outside Rome briefly and take minor secular orders. This direction in his life fit closely with the previous influence of both Alphonse de Lamartine and Félicité de Lamennais, and with his musical interest in medieval and Renaissance music.

The restlessness of his mind and the power of his personality manifested themselves as well in the role he took as a champion of progressive music after midcentury. Even more than Wagner, he began the whole idea of a musical avant-garde. From his bastion in Weimar, he tried to rally the composers and listeners sympathetic to the most forward-looking tendencies in composition, chiefly free-form (the symphonic poem) and chromatic harmony (the departure from clear tonal bases). He waged his campaign in a highly partisan way, which gave him and his followers the reputation of being troublemakers. The sense of an avant-garde he established was carried on by Arnold Schoenberg and Anton Webern in Vienna at the turn of the century.

Journal of the American Liszt Society; A. Loesser, *Men, Women and Pianos: A Social History of the Piano* (New York, 1951).

William Weber

Related entries: BEETHOVEN; CHOPIN; LAMARTINE; LAMENNAIS.

LOBAU, GEORGES MOUTON, COMTE DE (1770–1838), general of the Empire; peer of the Hundred Days; deputy of the Restoration; and deputy, peer, and marshal of the July Monarchy. Born at Phalsbourg (Meurthe) on 21 February 1770, Mouton enlisted on 1 August 1792 and by the end of the year had risen to captain. Under Napoleon he became a staff officer and Comte de Lobau. In 1814 Mouton (who had dropped his title and begun using his family name again) was freed after the peace and returned to France where the Bourbons named him to the Order of Saint Louis and made him inspector of infantry. During the Hundred Days Napoleon named him a peer and gave him command of the Sixth Corps of the Army of the North. At Waterloo Mouton played an important role, but he was unable to halt Friedrick von Bülow who outnumbered him by three to one. While trying to rally his retreating troops, he was wounded and captured by the English. Exiled from France by the ordinance of 24 July 1815, Mouton stayed in England and Belgium until he was permitted to return in 1818. He remained in retirement until in 1828 the department of Meurthe elected him to the Chamber of Deputies, where he sat until 1833. Prior to 1830 he voted with the liberal opposition. During the July Revolution he participated in the meetings of the liberal deputies who sent him as one of their delegates on 28 July to try to convince Auguste de Marmont to halt the shooting. On 29 July he was named a member of the provisional Municipal Commission, which was instrumental in advancing the Orleanist cause. Lobau was one of the more conservative members of this commission. Louis-Philippe gave him command of the Paris National Guard on 27 December 1830, and the following May he dispersed a Bonapartist demonstration in the place Vendôme by using fire hoses, thus avoiding bloodshed. This brought him appointment as a marshal of France on 30 July 1831. He also helped quell the Paris uprisings in June 1832. On 27 June 1833 he was elevated to the peerage. Lobau died in Paris on 27 November 1838 of the effects of an old wound.

Archives parlementaires; J. L. Bory, *La Révolution de juillet* (Paris, 1972); D. Pinkney, *The French Revolution of 1830* (Princeton, 1972); A. Robert et al., *Dictionnaire des parlementaires français* (Paris, 1889–91).

James K. Kieswetter

Related entries: CHAMBER OF DEPUTIES; HUNDRED DAYS; LOUIS-PHI-LIPPE; MARMONT; MUNICIPAL COMMISSION; NATIONAL GUARD; REVOLUTION OF 1830; WATERLOO, BATTLE OF.

LOI FALLOUX. See FALLOUX LAW.

LONDON, TREATY OF (1827), a treaty between the Greek rebels and the Turkish-Egyptian armies, guaranteed by Russia, England, and France, that led to Greek independence. The uprising of the Greeks against Turkish domination, which began in the spring of 1821, was dragging on in an increasingly atrocious and indecisive manner while European opinion was becoming more and more favorable to the rebel cause. The governments of Russia and England at last got together in the Protocol of Saint Petersburg (4 April 1826) and demanded that the dispute be mediated. The protocol between the power that had been the pillar of the conservative Alliance and the power that had detached itself from that alliance seemed to Clemens von Metternich to be an act of treason. His discomfort was aggravated when France joined the two signatories of the protocol by means of a true treaty, which was signed in London 6 July 1827. The Allies, resolved to impose an armistice, went on to establish a sea blockade that prevented the Turco-Egyptian forces from carrying on their war of extermination. The naval battle of Navarino (20 October 1827) was followed by a Russo-Turkish War and finally by Greek independence.

Guillaume de Bertier de Sauvigny, trans. E. Newman
Related entries: METTERNICH; NAVARINO, BATTLE OF.

LONGEPIED, AMABLE (1796–?), revolutionary, leader of various societies and clubs. Born in Paris in 1796, Longepied was a schoolteacher. He was secretary of the Society of the Friends of the People in June 1832, and it was he who had the *Tribune* publish a notice on 4 June 1832 saying: "The members of the Society of the Friends of the People are asked to meet Tuesday at 9:00 A.M., Place du Louvre, for the funeral of General Lamarque."

Active during the July Monarchy, he is known especially for his role in the February Revolution of 1848. At that time he presided over the Revolutionary Committee, Club of Clubs, which wanted to unify the Parisian clubs, and become the principal defender of the Republic. Armand Barbès, Marc Dufraisse, Marie-Joseph Sobrier, Pierre-Joseph Proudhon, and Etienne Arago were the most notable members. Longepied worked, as he said at the meeting of the Clubs of Paris on 26 March 1848, so that "the Clubs of Paris and of the nearby suburbs would unite."

He was a member of the commission that went to the home of Alexandre-Auguste Ledru-Rollin, minister of the interior, to get funds so that delegates could be sent to the provinces in order to work in the forthcoming elections to the Constituent Assembly. Ledru-Rollin gave him more than 100,000 francs. But Longepied was arrested on 15 May and accused of instigating the riot at the National Assembly. He was denounced because of the use he had made of the funds Ledru-Rollin had given him.

He was freed, rearrested in June 1848, then freed again in August. He was linked to the socialist workers, and his name appeared on their lists of socialist electoral committees in June 1849. He opposed the coup d'état of December 1851 and tried to organize armed resistance, and he himself fought at the barricade of the Carré Saint-Martin. He was sentenced in absentia to deportation to Algeria.

Dictionnaire biographique du mouvement ouvrier français, 1789–1864, vol. 3. (Paris, 1966); Garnier-Pagès, *Histoire de la Révolution de 1848* (Paris, 1861–72); A. Longepied and Laugier, *Comité révolutionnaire, Club des Clubs et la Commission* (Paris, 1850); D. Stern, *Histoire de la Révolution de 1848*, 2 vols. (Paris, 1850).

Jean-Claude Caron, trans. E. Newman

Related entries: ARAGO FAMILY; BARBES; CLUB OF CLUBS; CONSTITUTION OF 1848; COUP D'ETAT OF 2 DECEMBER 1851; DEMONSTRATIONS OF 1848–1849; LAMARQUE; LEDRU-ROLLIN; PROUDHON; REVOLUTION OF 1848; SOBRIER.

LORAIN, PAUL (1799–1861), teacher, administrator, and author. A graduate of the Ecole normale, Lorain taught high school in the provinces. Later he taught at the Ecole normale and at the Faculty of Letters, and he finished his career as rector of the Academy of Lyons. He published a textbook history of the United States and translated contemporary British novelists into French, but his major publication was *Tableau de l'instruction primaire en France* (Paris, 1837). That work, based on the first extensive national inquiry into French primary schooling and following upon the Guizot Law, painted a negative picture of French schooling and has greatly influenced French historiography of education. The work, unfortunately, is biased, excerpting negative examples from inspectors' reports and generalizing from them. Lorain's own notes often do not sustain his textual argument.

Patrick J. Harrigan

Related entries: GUIZOT LAW ON PUBLIC EDUCATION; PUBLIC INSTRUCTION.

LA LORGNETTE (1824–1826), literary, satirical, and political magazine; became *Le Mentor*, 1826–1828. *La Lorgnette* and its immediate successor, *Le Mentor* (January 1824–August 1828) was one of that group called *la petite presse*, which masqueraded as purely humorous or literary magazines but were effectively political through their use of satires, allegories and innuendoes. They were accused of sedition in an 1825 ministerial report, which listed *La Lorgnette* along with *La Pandore* and *Le Corsaire*. Both the 1822 Law of Tendency and the earlier law of July 1821 were aimed in part at checking the impudence of these journals.

C. Ledré, *La presse à l'assaut de la monarchie* (Paris, 1960).

Daniel Rader

Related entries: LE CORSAIRE; PRESS LAWS

LOUIS XVIII (1755–1824), king of France. When he was born on 17 November 1755 in Versailles, there seemed to be scant chance that he would one day bear the crown of France. Louis-Stanislas-Xavier was the third in line of the four sons born from the marriage of the only son of Louis XV with Marie-Josephe of Saxony. His father died in 1765 and his mother a few months later, leaving the young princes under the contrasting tutelage of their debauched grandfather and of the austere duc de la Vauguyon. By that time the eldest brother, the duc de Bourgogne, was also dead, and thus the title of dauphin (heir to the throne) fell to the duc de Berry, who became king in 1774 with the title Louis XVI. Upon this event, Louis-Stanislas-Xavier, comte de Provence, was to be styled Monsieur according to the custom of the French court. Earlier, in May 1771, at the age of sixteen, he had been married to Marie-Josephine, daughter of Victor-Amédée, king of Sardinia and Savoy. They were not a happy couple. Marie-Josephine was not stupid but was definitely ugly. After two aborted pregnancies, Louis ceased to show any interest in her, and the unfortunate princess was left to seek solace in the bottle and the dubious affections of one of her ladies in waiting, a Mme. de Gourbillon. During the long years of exile, Marie-Josephine had to follow her husband except for a few years when she was able to stay with her parents in Turin, but she had no part in the activities of her husband and was little more than a cumbersome piece of luggage in his train. Her death in 1810 in England was hardly noticed outside of the royal circle. As for Monsieur, he made a show of keeping a mistress in title, a comtesse de Balbi, who could entertain him with her wit, if not in bed, because Louis' physical constitution did not allow him to enjoy very many sexual pleasures. In addition to this deficiency, he suffered also from a malformation of his hip joints, which kept him away from such aristocratic pursuits as dancing, fencing, riding, and hunting. This circumstance, combined with an epicurean appetite, soon added to his physical handicaps that of a growing obesity.

As compensation Louis developed an exceptional knowledge and taste for literature and art. With the sizable income he enjoyed, he was able to gather around himself a small court of his own in his palace of the Luxembourg in Paris and his countryside residence of Brunoy. There he entertained writers, poets, artists and collected paintings and other pieces of art.

Monsieur could hardly conceal his frustration at being confined to the role of a useless drone when he thought of himself as being more capable of governing the kingdom than his brother Louis XVI. Queen Marie-Antoinette, sensing his ambition, showed her dislike and her distrust, and he retaliated by encouraging or inspiring some of the public attacks on her character. The convening of the Assembly of Notables in 1787 provided an opportunity to show his political capacities. As president of one of the seven committees, he contributed to the dismissal of Charles-Alexandre de Calonne, the minister of finances, and cautiously built up for himself the image of an enlightened prince favorable to reform.

In keeping with this attitude, he chose to remain with the royal family throughout the first phases of the Revolution, whereas his younger brother Charles, comte d'Artois, had left the country after 14 July 1789. When the king himself resolved to escape from Paris, Monsieur decided to do likewise on the night of 20–21 June 1791. Luckier than his brother, who had taken the road toward the eastern border and was arrested at Varennes, Monsieur, having taken the northern road toward the Belgian frontier and traveling with only one companion while disguised as English merchants, reached the safety of Mons and Brussels. The story of this rather scary escape was to be recounted much later by Louis himself in a booklet printed in 1822: *Relation d'un voyage à Bruxelles et à Coblentz*. In that Rhineland city, Louis and his brother Artois were provided a residence by their uncle, the bishop-elector of Trier. Around them gathered a number of *émigrés*, and they assumed the role of leaders of the counter-Revolution; a small army was organized under the command of their cousin the prince de Condé, and they strove to persuade the European powers to invade France and restore the old monarchy.

These activities were most compromising for the king in Paris who, in spite of his official disavowals, was suspected of keeping in touch with his brothers. When the French Legislative Assembly declared war upon the Austrian monarch (April 1792), the princes and their small army entered France with the Austro-Prussian forces under the duke of Brunswick. They were able to stay but a few days in Verdun until the defeat of the invading army at Valmy compelled them to retreat to Liège and Aix-la-Chapelle. At the end of December, the king of Prussia allowed them, after disbanding the Condé army, to take residence in Hamm (Westphalia). A few weeks later they received the news of their brother's execution in Paris. Monsieur then proclaimed himself regent for his nephew, the captive young Louis XVII. In November 1793, he left Hamm with the purpose of going to Spain, but he stopped in Turin at his father-in-law's court. In May 1794, he established himself in Verona, where he was to remain until the Venetian government, under pressure from the French Republic, compelled him to depart (April 1796). In the meantime, the death of Louis XVII (June 1795) had allowed the regent to claim the title of king of France, while, out of respect for the sovereigns who harbored him, he was designated as the comte de Lille. His life during the years to come was that of an exile, bounced from place to place according to the whims and policies of the European powers: Rastadt in Baden, Blankenburg in the duchy of Brunswick (1796), Mittau in Russian Courland (Latvia) (1798), Warsaw (1801), again Mittau (1804), and finally England (1807), where the prince regent rented for Louis a spacious and safe residence at Hartwell House, near Aylesbury, about forty miles from London.

During these years, the exiled monarch kept busy on two levels. First, he maintained around himself the external trappings of royalty, as much as the subsidies provided by the British and other governments would allow. Second, he produced a constant stream of correspondence with foreign powers and royalist partisans in France and all over Europe, issuing pompous manifestoes whenever the circumstances seemed to call for such, as, for instance, when Napoleon made himself emperor. Earlier, Bonaparte had approached Louis, suggesting that he might be given a substantial living in exchange for a formal renunciation of the throne. "He is mistaken," answered Louis, "if he believes he can induce me into a transaction upon my rights. Far from it, these rights, if they could be questioned, find themselves confirmed by this very initiative. . . . I want always to be able to say, as Francis I said: 'We have lost everything but honor.' " At the end of 1812, when the mayor of London extended an invitation to attend a celebration for the defeat of Napoleon's armies in Russia, Louis refused, saying,

"Never shall I nor any prince of my family rejoice at an event in which two hundred thousand Frenchmen perished." And he begged the victorious czar to be generous toward his prisoners.

The invasion of France by overwhelming Allied forces in the first weeks of 1814 provided a chance for the restoration of the Bourbon dynasty. But among the leaders of the coalition, only the British had at first a clear idea that such a solution would be the best way to ensure a durable peace in Europe. It was under the protection of Wellington's army that the white flag of the old monarchy was first raised in Bordeaux (March 12). This first event helped Charles-Maurice de Talleyrand convince Czar Alexander I to favor the Bourbons when Allied troops entered Paris (31 March). The imperial Senate itself, after proclaiming the deposition of Napoleon, recognized the expediency of recalling to the throne the brother of the late king, but it stated that he would not be recognized unless he would swear acceptance to a hastily concocted constitution. According to this document, the king, as in 1791, would be only the first officer of the executive branch of government, holding his power from the free choice of the nation. Louis cleverly foiled this pretension. Avoiding any commitment, he landed in Boulogne (24 April) and proceeded slowly to Paris, receiving enthusiastic demonstrations along his route that served to strengthen his hand. When he reached Saint-Ouen (a northern suburb of the capital) he issued a declaration in which he maintained the principle of his divine, or historic, right to the throne while appeasing the Revolutionaries by retaining the basic institutions of the previous regimes. He then was able to make a solemn entry into Paris (3 May).

The two most important pending problems were soon resolved: that of the peace between France and the Allies by the first Treaty of Paris and that of the nature of the future regime by the Constitutional Charter. Many elements of distrust and discontent soon surfaced, however, and these encouraged Napoleon to attempt his comeback of March 1815. As the former emperor made his way from the Mediterranean shores to Paris, corps after corps of the regular army defected to his side. Louis XVIII had to choose between risking all by staying in his Tuileries palace—a stoic attitude that would have been highly embarrassing for his adversary—or a less dignified retreat to safety out of France. The king decided he would not become a hostage or a bargaining pawn in the hands of Napoleon, and on the night of 20 March 1815 left Paris. He had hoped at first to establish himself in the fortified city of Lille, but the attitude of the garrison compelled him to cross the border, and he settled in Ghent, waiting for the outcome of the military contest.

After the decisive battle of Waterloo, Louis XVIII hastened to reenter his kingdom, issuing from Cambrai a declaration aimed at appeasing the anxieties of the various factions of the nation. Thanks to the clever manipulations of Joseph Fouché, the Second Restoration came as a bloodless and smooth transition. Thus, on 8 July, Louis XVIII found himself back in his palace. Invoking the fiction that the Allied powers had fought Napoleon, the usurper, but not the French nation, Louis XVIII strove to limit the exactions of the victorious armies, which, almost 1 million in number, sought retribution by occupying over two-thirds of the territory of France. The most telling action of the king was when he prevented the Prussians from blowing up the bridge of Iena in Paris, threatening that he would have himself carried out upon it.

The second Treaty of Paris (20 November 1815) was to be much more onerous than the first one of 1814. The internal situation was also much worse; the last dramatic events had opened a deep rift in the nation. All those who had actively supported the last adventure of Napoleon were now branded as disloyal and became enemies of the regime, while faithful royalists demanded punishment for the traitors. Many felt that the king was too lenient on this score; they were dubbed ultraroyalists. This tendency prevailed in the legislative elections held in August 1815. Under the pressure of the so-called *chambre introuvable*, the king had to dismiss Talleyrand and the other ministers whom he had accepted upon his return in July, and he appointed as president of the council the duc de Richelieu. This new administration tried to moderate the royalist reaction, the so-called White Terror, but in doing so it lost the confidence of the majority of the elected Chamber. In September 1816 Louis XVIII, under pressure from the Allies, dissolved this legislative body. A new election provided a working majority, which labeled itself constitutional. The material and moral reconstruction of the country proceeded satisfactorily. Richelieu was able to obtain the full independence of France at the Congress of Aix-la-Chapelle.

After this major achievement, Richelieu retired, and real power passed into the hands of Elie Decazes, the able intriguer who since 1815 had gained the confidence and affections of Louis XVIII. By his efforts to conciliate the enemies of the Bourbon monarchy (liberals and Bonapartists), Decazes enraged the ultraroyalist faction, which had the support of the king's brother and heir, the comte d'Artois. The tragic death of the duc de Berry provided a pretext to pressure Louis XVIII into dismissing his favorite. Richelieu was recalled; legislation was passed to curtail the press and to establish a new electoral system, the so-called double vote, designed to ensure the dominance of the most conservative elements in French society. At the same time, the old king fell under the spell of a clever woman, the comtesse du Cayla, who managed to influence the king in favor of various ultraroyalist policies. In December 1821, Richelieu was compelled to resign; he had incurred the displeasure of both the rightist and leftist oppositions with his overcautious external policies. The new ministry was composed of men devoted to the king's brother. In this government, the comte Joseph de Villèle, minister of finances, soon emerged as the leading personality. His colleague for foreign affairs, the famous romantic author François-René de Chateaubriand, had pushed the reluctant Villèle into a military intervention in Spain to restore the absolute power of King Ferdinand VII against the liberal government established after the Cadiz *pronunciamiento* of January 1820. The venture was a complete success; it demonstrated to Europe the restoration of France's military and political power, and it also served to bolster the regime by demonstrating the loyalty of the army and exposing the fallacies of liberal propaganda.

During the last months of his life Louis XVIII, weakened by increasing infirmities, took only a distant interest in government; still he maintained with an inflexible will the ceremonial rituals of the monarchy. His death on 16 September 1824 was the last peaceful one of a French monarch in his palace.

Louis XVIII inspired respect and even awe with his pungent wit, his unflappable composure in the face of great adversity, and his contagious belief in the almost supernatural majesty of his office. But he could hardly be loved. Very early in his life he had developed a cold, calculating, selfish, and deceitful character. His public utterances lacked spontaneity; he was always acting a part, that of the king as he conceived it. Except for the ceremonial aspects of his office, he seemed bored by the day-to-day operation of government, and thus he fit fairly well the role of a constitutional monarch, though he still considered himself to be an absolute ruler. His greatest contribution was through his ability to adjust the traditions and trappings of the old monarchy to the new social order born from the Revolutionary and Napoleonic eras. To his credit remains the fact that his reign, initiated amid frightful disasters, ended with a pacified, independent, and prosperous country.

P. Mansel, *Louis XVIII* (London, 1981).

Guillaume de Bertier de Sauvigny

Related entries: AIX-LA-CHAPELLE, CONGRESS OF; BERRY, C.-F.; CAMBRAI, DECLARATION OF; CHARLES X; CHARTER OF 1814; CHATEAUBRIAND; DOUBLE VOTE, LAW OF THE; DU CAYLA; ELECTIONS AND ELECTORAL SYSTEMS; FOUCHE; PARIS, SECOND TREATY OF; PRESS LAWS; RESTORATION, SECOND; RICHELIEU; SPAIN, 1823 FRENCH INVASION OF; TALLEYRAND; ULTRAROYALISTS; VILLELE; WHITE TERROR.

LOUIS, JOSEPH-DOMINIQUE, BARON (1755–1837), an abbot during the *ancien régime* and member of the Parisian upper class; best known for his work as finance minister during the Bourbon Restoration. His political career began in 1779 with the purchase of an office in the Parlement de Paris and continued until 1832. Baron Louis was in the diplomatic service under Louis XVI, served Louis XVIII three times as finance minister (1814, 1815, 1818–19), and—following the July Days of 1830—was called back by Louis-Philippe. He was succeeded by Jacques Laffitte in November 1830 when there was a reshuffling in the cabinet following unrest in the clubs and the streets in October. When Casimir Périer was called in on 11 March 1831 to bring order out of chaos, he would accept only Baron Louis as minister of finance to try to repair the damage done by Laffitte in that office.

As a member of the Council of State in 1813, with a fine reputation in financial circles, Baron Louis was considered but passed over by Napoleon in favor of Louis-Mathieu de Molé to put into effect his plans for raising money. A close friend and protégé of Charles-Maurice de Talleyrand, Louis worked with Archbishop Mâlines to win the support of Napoleon's generals in 1814 and served as commissar of Talleyrand's Provisional Government during the Hundred Days.

As the first minister of finance during the Restoration, Louis has been both praised and maligned. Ultraroyalists condemned him for his proposal to sell 864,850 acres of national forests, land that had been church property, and to confiscate lands of the *émigrés* that had not been sold. Their opposition to the plan prevented its realization until 1820. Other so-called penny-pinching measures alienated various segments of society, but he was not to be deterred in his determination to bring order out of financial chaos in France and to regain the respect of the victorious Allies.

The minister's first steps to bring money into the treasury were to sell off 10 million francs worth of Napoleon's gold and jewels and to issue bonds. The fact that the government securities (*rentes*) kept increasing in value reflects the confidence of the banks and the public in the government. Louis was also able in time to obtain foreign loans at low interest rates.

The government of Louis XVIII inherited an estimated deficit of 750,000 francs, including arrears in payments accruing during the Empire. Baron Louis' budget estimate for 1814 was 826 million francs. All existing taxes were expected to net 520 million in 1814 and more in 1815. He anticipated a balanced budget in 1815, based on income and a reduction in expenditures.

This was not to be, however, because of Napoleon's return in 1815 and the burden placed on the government after the Hundred Days by the indemnities imposed by the Allies and the cost of maintaining the occupying forces in France until 1818. Now the government deficit rose to 695 million francs. Added to this were 140 million for the annual payment on the war indemnity (the indemnity totaled 700 million), 135 million for the foreign troops, and 525 million for the annual budget. The Finance Ministry was faced with a staggering figure of about the equivalent of $299 million. Baron Louis was determined that all debts be acknowledged and payment for them be budgeted. By 1827 there was a surplus in the budget as a result of his efforts and those of his successors.

Working on the bureaucratic foundation laid during the Empire, Louis, in drawing up the budgets for 1814 and 1815, insisted on the retention of the indirect taxes (*droits réunis*) levied under Napoleon on alcoholic beverages, playing cards, vehicles, tobacco (a state monopoly), and salt. Monsieur (comte d'Artois, who became Charles X) had promised the abolition of these taxes during the seventeen days preceding the return of Louis XVIII in 1814. In addition, there were tax stamps required for legal documents, *patentes* paid by professional men and manufacturers, and taxes on post office profits. Most imported items were subject to customs duties. Income from these sources was estimated at 113 million francs. These taxes led to many protests, including "tavern wars." Talk in the quarter of a million bars and taverns was instrumental in influencing public opinion.

Direct taxes, the determinant of qualifications of electors and officeholders, were continued. These were paid on personal property, land, and doors and windows. In an average year, direct taxes could bring in 291 million francs.

Thousands of military officers had their pay reduced by half, and about a quarter of a million men were demobilized by Pierre Dupont de l'Etang, the minister of War. Provisions in the Fontainebleau Treaty that provided for substantial income for Napoleon and some of his men were ignored. The budget for roads and public works was reduced, but parliament granted an annual income for life of 25 million francs to the royal family. In addition, the royalist household guard of 6,000 men was reinstated at an estimated cost of 20 million francs. All this occurred while roads and bridges were deteriorating and unemployment was severe all over France. About 15,000 government jobs alone were abolished.

Parliament passed the budgets without much opposition. While the upper classes expressed their confidence in the new regime and invested money in government securities, the common people were disturbed as they had been led to believe that their taxes would be lowered. Royalists were angry because of the government's insistence on paying the debts inherited from the Empire. Baron Louis was undisturbed by the opposition as he had a singleminded determination to make the government solvent and restore it to the good graces of the European community.

The baron was a member of the exile ministry of Louis XVIII at Ghent during the Hundred Days when strict economic measures were imposed. He was finance minister under Talleyrand in the early months of the Second Restoration, resigning his position in September 1815 when Talleyrand's ministry fell following the election of the so-called *chambre introuvable*. He was succeeded by Louis-Emmanuel Corvetto, who remained until the end of 1818 when Baron Louis was called back once again, this time to serve in Richelieu's cabinet. Through his expert handling of finances, France became a solvent nation and once again took a respected place among the European nations. He resigned in November 1819 and was among those working to defeat Joseph de Villèle's faction in 1827. He was recalled by Louis-Philippe in August 1830 following the fall of Charles X in the July Revolution. In October the ministry resigned, and Laffitte became finance minister. The financial situation in France steadily worsened.

Prior to 1831, budgets had included block grants to the ministries for their expenses. A law passed in January 1831 required that the budget of each ministry be broken down to show where the monies were to be spent. Funds appropriated for one area could not be transferred to another. Only the government could approve an increase in funds to cover unanticipated expenses. Thus the deputies could call into question any expenditure.

When Casimir Périer came in to head the government in 1831, Baron Louis returned as finance minister to render his final service to France. In March 1832 a terrible cholera epidemic swept through France, claiming Périer as one of its victims. Baron Louis, now a weary old man, was replaced by Jean Humann in the duc de Broglie's cabinet.

G. de Bertier de Sauvigny, *The Bourbon Restoration* (Philadelphia, 1966); M. D. R. Leys, *Between Two Empires* (London, 1955); J. H. Stewart, *The Restoration Era in France: 1814–1830* (Princeton, 1968).

Helen Castelli

Related entries: CHAMBRE INTROUVABLE; CHARLES X; *DEMI-SOLDES*; *DROITS REUNIS*; HUNDRED DAYS; LAFFITTE; PERIER; RICHELIEU; ROYAL GUARD; TALLEYRAND; ULTRAROYALISTS.

LOUIS-PHILIPPE (1773–1850), duc d'Orléans, head of the house of Orléans, and king of the French. Louis-Philippe d'Orléans was born in Paris on 6 October 1773, the first son of Louis-Philippe-Joseph, duc d'Orléans, head of the younger branch of the Bourbon family. The father, like the preceding ducs d'Orléans, had royal ambitions, and he made his Parisian residence, the Palais-Royal, a gathering place of subversive opponents of Louis XVI's government. He entrusted the education of his children to the comtesse de Genlis, his learned ex-mistress who was an admirer of the *philosophes* and of Rousseau. She imbued her charges with the ideas of the Enlightenment, instructed them in ''useful'' knowledge (history, geography, foreign languages), and took them on visits to workshops and farms. The young Louis-Philippe emerged from this regime well read, industrious, and convinced of the benign power of human reason.

Not surprisingly he greeted the Revolution of 1789 with enthusiasm. He joined the Jacobin Club and the Parisian National Guard and in 1792–93 served in the republican armies. He became involved in General Charles-François Dumouriez's plotting against the Republic, and when Dumouriez fled to the Austrian lines on 4 April 1793, Louis-Philippe fled with him. His father, who had been elected to the National Convention and had changed his name to Philippe Egalité, was charged with complicity in the conspiracy of Dumouriez, convicted, and executed.

After 1793 Louis-Philippe spent twenty-one years in exile. In 1800 he settled in England as a pensioner of the British government and declared his allegiance to the exiled Bourbon pretender to the throne, Louis, comte de Provence. In 1808 he married Marie-Amélie, daughter of the Bourbon king of the Two Sicilies, and from 1810 until 1814 he lived in Sicily. He refused to serve in the *émigré* or Austrian armies, but he would have taken command of a Spanish army fighting the French in Spain in 1810 had not the British government imposed its veto.

He returned to Paris with his family in 1814. When Napoleon reappeared on the scene the next year, the Orléans did not accompany the court to Ghent but fled to England, which aroused Louis XVIII's suspicions that Louis-Philippe was perhaps maneuvering to replace him. Orléans did not return to France until 1817. Louis XVIII continued to be suspicious of his politics and ambitions, but, though the duke had friends in the liberal opposition to the government, there is no evidence that he engaged in political activity detrimental to his Bourbon cousins before July 1830.

In July-August 1830, when Charles X lost control of his capital, Orléans' supporters induced the deputies in Paris to declare the throne vacant and to invite

Orléans to occupy it. On 9 August 1830 he took an oath to abide by the revised Charter and became Louis-Philippe I, king of the French. Once on the throne, he was eager to rule, as well as to reign. He never openly defied his ministers or the majority in the Chamber of Deputies, but he did use intrigue and corruption to ensure amenable ministers and a friendly majority, and he tried to minimize the role of the president of the Council of Ministers. In 1840 he found in François Guizot a first minister who shared his views on royal and ministerial powers, and together they governed France for eight years. They gave the country a stable government, order at home, and peace abroad, and they fostered an atmosphere congenial to investment and economic development. On the other hand, their rigid opposition to political reform alienated important elements of the population, and when in February 1848 a street demonstration turned into insurrection, they found themselves with little effective support. The king's dismissal of Guizot failed to appease the opposition, and on 24 February Louis-Philippe abdicated in favor of his grandson, hoping, in vain, to save the crown for his family.

Louis-Philippe and his family again took refuge in England, and he lived there until his death on 26 August 1850.

P. de La Gorce, *Louis-Philippe, 1830–1848* (Paris, 1931); T. E. B. Howarth, *Citizen King: The Life of Louis-Philippe, King of the French* (London, 1961); *Mémoires de Louis-Philippe, duc d'Orléans, écrits par lui-même*, 2 vols. (Paris, c. 1973, 1974); P. Vigier, *La Monarchie de Juillet* 4th ed. (Paris, 1974).

David H. Pinkney

Related entries: CHARTER OF 1830; CHARTRES; FOREIGN POLICY OF LOUIS-PHILIPPE; GUIZOT; JOINVILLE; MARIE-AMELIE DE BOURBON; NEMOURS; PARIS, COUNT OF; REVOLUTION OF 1830; REVOLUTION OF 1848.

LOUIS, PIERRE-CHARLES-ALEXANDRE (1787–1872), physician. Having received his doctorate in medicine at Paris in 1813, Louis emigrated to Russia after the Restoration and practiced there for seven years before returning to France around 1823. He was soon appointed to positions in several of the main Parisian hospitals and became a member of the Académie royale de médecine (1826), but he never received a professorship in the medical faculty.

As one of the principal opponents of F.-J.-V. Broussais, Louis attacked his adversary's medical doctrines with detailed statistical analyses of clinical successes and failures. Louis' numerical method, although mathematically unsophisticated, nevertheless gave statistics a central role in medicine for the first time. A series of Louis' statistical articles appearing in 1828 made a strong case against the effectiveness of bloodletting as a therapy and thus undermined confidence in Broussais' favorite method of treatment. These articles were later collected together for publication under the title, *Recherches sur les effets de la saignée dans quelques maladies inflammatoires, et sur l'affection de l'émétique et des vesicatoires dans la pneumonie* (1835).

In 1832 Louis founded the Société médicale d'observation to pursue clinical research on a statistical basis. This society flourished for twenty years under Louis' leadership but went into decline after the founder's retirement in 1854. The value of clinical statistics continued to be debated during Louis' lifetime and was disputed by such eminent figures as Claude Bernard, but the statistical approach was eventually accepted as a mainstay of clinical research by the end of the nineteenth century.

Despite his failure to obtain a professorship in the medical faculty, Louis enjoyed a reputation as a brilliant clinical teacher in the hospitals and attracted a strong following among foreign students. His popularity was especially high among medical students from the United States, the most famous of whom was Oliver Wendell Holmes (1809–94). American medicine continued to show evidence of Louis' influence well into the twentieth century.

E. H. Ackerknecht, *Medicine at the Paris Hospital, 1794–1848* (Baltimore, 1967).

W. R. Albury

Related entries: BERNARD; BROUSSAIS; PARIS FACULTY OF MEDICINE.

LOUVEL, LOUIS-PIERRE. See BERRY, C.-F.

LUXEMBOURG COMMISSION, a body formed after the 1848 Revolution to deal with the problems of the working class. It had no legal power. When a march by armed workers on 25 March 1848 forced the Provisional Government to decree the right to work and the organization of labor, the government's response was to establish National Workshops and a Commission du gouvernement pour les travailleurs. The latter, presided over by Louis Blanc and the worker Albert from the Provisional Government, was to be an assembly of workers' delegates to formulate proposals to the forthcoming National Assembly; it was to meet in the Palais du Luxembourg, the former seat of the Chamber of Peers.

While the establishment of the Luxembourg Commission may be seen as a means by which the government diverted Louis Blanc's, Albert's, and other workers' energies into a blind alley, in fact it is of considerable importance in the history of 1848 and of the labor movement, notably in the political organization of workers' corporations. The electoral base of the commission was the Paris trades, and the election of delegates often created corporations in hitherto unorganized areas.

Within the commission, Louis Blanc's role was somewhat patriarchal. Only one-third of the workers' delegates were actually to sit on the commission, with the others attending periodic general sessions. There was also a permanent committee with only ten workers alongside Blanc, Albert, and well-known economists such as Charles Dupont-White and Frédéric le Play. Blanc saw the government as taking the initiative and the workers' delegates fulfilling an essentially consultative role.

Beyond generating theoretical discussion of a new economic order based on producers' cooperatives, the commission also came to play a role in negotiations during industrial disputes, usually imposing regulations favorable to workers. As the one elected government body before 4 May, the commission formed a type of assembly of labor within which workers began to elaborate a theory of the state as a federation of trade corporations.

The high moment for the commission was 17 March when, in response to a hostile demonstration by elite companies of the National Guard the day before, the delegates were able to mobilize up to 200,000 marchers, mainly behind their trade banners, in support of the Provisional Government and of a postponement of the national elections. Although the latter were delayed a fortnight in response to the marchers' pressure, the commission remained poorly organized and distributed copies of its slate of candidates only late in the campaign. This list was composed of the four radicals from the Provisional Government, twenty of the candidates proposed by the Paris trades, and ten socialists; in all only six were elected.

On the basis of Louis Blanc's alleged involvement in the attempted seizure of power on 15 May, the National Assembly closed down the commission. The delegates attempted to maintain a presence by founding a society of united corporations and the *Journal des travailleurs* (six issues, 4–25 June). After the June civil war, employers began ignoring the industrial agreements previously imposed by the commission. A committee of Luxembourg delegates resumed activity for the by-elections in September and organized a banquet attended by 2,000 workers on 13 November. There were smaller versions of the Luxembourg Commission in Lyons, Marseilles, Lille, Nantes, Reims, St.-Quentin, Valenciennes, and elsewhere.

L. Blanc, *La Révolution de février au Luxembourg* (Paris, 1849); J. Chapelle-Dulière, "Le 'socialisme' de Frédéric Le Play (1806–1882), membre de la Commission du Luxembourg en 1848," *Revue de l'institut de Sociologie, Université libre de Bruxelles* (1982); R. Gossez, *Les ouvriers de Paris*, vol. 1: *Bibliothèque de la Révolution de 1848* (1967); W. R. Sewell Jr., *Work and Revolution in France* (Cambridge, 1980).

Peter McPhee

Related entries: ALBERT; BLANC; JUNE DAYS; NATIONAL GUARD; NATIONAL WORKSHOPS; PROVISIONAL GOVERNMENT; WORKERS' COOPERATIVES.

LYONS, REVOLTS IN (1831–1834), the last of a century-long series of labor disturbances in the city's silk industry, France's largest urban artisanal trade. The Lyons silk weavers had organized work stoppages in 1744 and 1786, and the decade from 1787 to 1796 had drawn the artisans deeply into Revolutionary politics in support of their economic grievances. The uprisings of 1831 and 1834 marked the final efforts of France's most militant preindustrial work force to secure decent incomes and a voice in the management of an industry in which their influence had steadily declined.

The eighteenth-century silk *fabrique* in Lyons had employed more than 30,000 of the city's 150,000 inhabitants and was organized as a royally regulated *communauté*. The industry was dominated by 300 to 400 silk merchants (*maîtres-marchands*), who provided commissions and employment for nearly 6,000 master weavers (*maîtres-fabricants*) who worked at hand-powered looms in family workshops scattered in particular neighborhoods of the city. The merchants sold finished silk fabric (particularly the expensive *façonnés*, whose intricately woven patterns were the industry's finest product) on the national and international luxury textile markets. Although the weavers were dependent on the merchants for orders and work, they were also employers themselves—of the army of journeymen, apprentices, shop assistants, and wage laborers who made up the bulk of the industry's work force. Largely literate and educated, highly skilled in the mastery of a complex and demanding craft, the weavers suffered the domination of the merchants with difficulty. Merchant control of the *communauté*'s committee of syndics (*maîtres-gardes*), who maintained quality of production and adjudicated disputes between merchants and weavers, and the *maîtres-marchands'* efforts to eliminate the small class of weavers who attempted to market their own fabric (*maîtres fabricants pour leur compte*), had provoked the 1744 strike, which was broken by royal troops and confirmed merchant ascendency in the industry.

A second source of weaver resentment lay in the payment of piecework rates for individual commissions. Though these were fixed by law in a table of rates, or *tarif*, merchants regularly paid lower prices in an effort to cut their costs and improve their competitive position in the silk market. The 1786 work stoppage (*la révolte de deux-sous*) was an attempt to raise piecework rates and to force the merchants to abide by them, but it too failed. These long-standing grievances were exacerbated by the irregular fluctuations of the luxury textile trade, which was subject to changes in fashion and interruptions in international commerce and could produce sudden business slumps and high unemployment. These recurrent crises reduced hundreds of weavers to near misery and increased their determination to win fairer treatment from the merchants.

A long recession in the textile trade, beginning in 1787 and lasting for more than a decade, helped to push the weavers into political organization after 1789. They successfully excluded the merchants from the *communauté* elections of delegates to the city's secondary assemblies during the elections for the Estates General in the opening year of the Revolution. Using their newly found political and electoral power, the weavers secured a new *tarif* in 1790 and expelled the merchants from the *communauté* in May 1791. While the Constituent Assembly abolished guilds and royally regulated corporations and passed the Le Chapelier law to prohibit artisanal labor organizations in 1791, the weavers were able to elect sympathetic politicians to the Lyons city government and preserve their rudimentary labor movement. A de facto alliance with the Lyons Jacobins brought an increase in *tarif* rates in 1793 and drew many weavers into the administration of the Terror in the city in 1793–94. The civil war and repression in Lyons, however, further disrupted the already moribund industry, and the weaver movement was crushed after Thermidor.

Although the Empire established new *tarifs* in 1808 and 1811 and government orders, the Continental System, and the return of political stability helped to restore some of the industry's former prosperity, there was a severe business downturn in 1810, and full recovery was not achieved until the Restoration.

By the 1830s, several major changes in the industry were apparent. The silk trade was still Lyons' largest (employing 40,000 of the city's 175,000 residents in 1833), but weavers' workshops were increasingly concentrated in the city's suburbs—the Croix-Rousse, Guillotière, Brotteaux, and Vaise—and less in the city center. The abolition of the old *communauté* meant that weaving was no longer restricted to Lyons itself, and merchants in search of cheaper labor had created a growing cottage industry in the surrounding countryside. The old legal distinction between master weavers (though this term was still used informally) and less-skilled journeymen (*compagnons*) had also disappeared, and the latter (always a minority of the weaving population in the eighteenth century) now equaled the former in numbers. The new regulatory bodies created by the Empire— the Chamber of Commerce, the Commercial Court, and the *Condition public* (which maintained quality controls)—were dominated by the merchants, as the old bodies had been. Weavers particularly resented their minority status on the Conseil de prud'hommes, which had taken over many of the functions of the old syndics, and resolved financial disputes involving less than 100 francs between weavers and merchants, usually in the merchants' favor. The Le Chapelier law, and additional restrictions on worker organization in the Napoleonic Code, were strictly enforced, and the *canut* (as the nineteenth-century silk worker was termed) now carried the *livret*, which listed his employers, debts and other obligations. With the exception of a few wealthy weavers owning seven to twelve looms who might aspire to merchant rank, the *canut* found himself sinking to the level of a wage laborer, threatened by poorly paid women and rural weavers, and still subject to periodic economic slumps from which he had little protection.

Despite their apparent powerlessness and declining status, the weavers retained a strong sense of their own self-worth and a distinctive popular culture based on shared work, language, and customs. The merchants' habitual disregard for the *tarifs* and their willingness to reduce piecework rates to the lowest possible levels also established a community of interest between older weavers and *compagnons*, and their mutual problems were discussed in cafes and secret meetings. When a slump in production at the beginning of 1831 brought the usual threat of poverty and unemployment, the *canuts* organized protest demonstrations in February and circulated a petition demanding increased representation on the Prud'hommes. The petition was ignored, and the demonstrations were dispersed by the National Guard, but a weaver protective association (Society of Surveillance and Mutual Indication, organized in 1827) helped organize a second petition in October, demanding a new *tarif*. The new prefect of the Rhone, Bouvier Dumoulard, was sympathetic to the request and ordered weaver and merchant representatives to negotiate new piecework rates. A preliminary agreement was arrived at on 31 October, and its terms were immediately printed in a newly established weaver newspaper, *Echo de la fabrique*. Encouraged by their success, the *canuts* organized a General and Mutual Association and proclaimed their intention of making the merchants abide by the new *tarif*, but the merchants generally ignored it, and some withheld commissions for new work to indicate their displeasure at any attempt to fix the cost of labor.

The weavers responded with a strike on 21 November, and when National Guard units composed largely of merchants and their clerks fired on demonstrators, a general uprising began. Municipal officials and Dumoulard ordered their armed forces to withdraw from the city the next day, but the prefect tried to reach an agreement with the weavers and appointed a council of sixteen *canuts* to help maintain order. Although the weavers' economic grievances were clear, they had no political program to implement, and the arrival of royal troops under Marshal Nicolas-Jean de Soult on 2 December found the city peaceful and the *canuts* ready to return to work. About 550 people had been killed and wounded on 21 and 22 November.

Dumoulard, whose temporizing was seen as a principal cause of the disturbances by the national government, was removed from office and replaced by Adrienne Gasparin (formerly prefect in Grenoble). Gasparin was directed to prevent any further outbreaks, and an upturn in business orders in March 1832 helped to calm the industry. But while Gasparin introduced a few minor reforms (increasing the number of weavers who could vote for the Prud'hommes and opening a *caisse des prêts* to provide loans for artisans), he replaced the new *tarif* of 31 October 1831, which the weavers had assumed would be enforced, with nonbinding guidelines. Gasparin was also convinced that the weavers had been incited by Lyons' small republican party, a group of largely bourgeois radicals organized in a chapter of the Society of the Rights of Man. In fact, the Lyons republicans were faction ridden and few in number and do not seem to have made any sustained effort to seek support among the *canuts* at the time of the strike.

The weavers continued to organize on their own. New mutualist societies (the Society of Mutual Duty and the Society of Ferrandiniers) recruited several hundred weavers and included organization in support of the *canuts*' 1831 demands with their more traditional efforts to provide accident, old age, and unemployment funds. Like the republican societies, mutualist associations were organized in chapters of twenty or fewer members, which technically exempted them from article 291 of the Law on Associations, which applied only to larger groups. The city and departmental administrations infiltrated police spies into both groups and arrested mutualist leaders when they could be identified. While some mutualists experimented with plans for cooperative weaving enterprises (grouping *canuts* in profit-sharing "central houses" to compete more effectively with rural cottage weaving), and some links to the equally suspect republicans may have been established in 1832–33, suggestions that the weavers embraced a socialist or radical political ideology in this period appear unfounded. The weavers pragmatically sought the same reforms in the existing industry that had united

them for nearly a century: a fair and binding *tarif*, greater voice in the direction
of the *fabrique*, and a modest chance for upward mobility. Although these
demands were often colored by a nostalgic evocation of the regulated *communauté*
of the eighteenth century (in which the weavers' rights and privileges, however
frequently violated, were clearly spelled out), it seems equally inaccurate to
suggest that they were bound by a reactionary guild mentality.

Strikes by cobblers, tailors, and wheelwrights in the fall of 1833 indicated
that artisanal activism in Lyons was far from dead, and a sudden slump in the
textile trade in February 1834 brought the usual collapse of piecework rates in
the silk *fabrique*. The Society of Mutual Duty, whose executive committee
elections had brought a majority of militant younger weavers into office, called
for a strike on 14 February but emphasized the nonviolent character of the planned
work stoppage. The strike succeeded in idling all 25,000 of the city's looms and
lasted for eight days. The merchants, alarmed at the success of the strike,
hurriedly drew up a new *tarif*, but Gasparin, convinced that the weavers were
only agents of a larger republican conspiracy, blocked its implementation. Forced
to return to work by shortages of money and food, the weavers saw five of their
leaders arrested and scheduled for trial on 5 April. In April word also arrived
of the July Monarchy's introduction of a bill modifying the Law on Associations
to include all organizations with twenty members or fewer, which threatened
mutualist and republican societies alike. When noisy demonstrations on 5 April
forced the postponement of the trial until 9 April, Gasparin and the commander
of the military district (General Aymard) hurriedly massed 13,000 soldiers around
Lyons. Scattered acts of violence between soldiers and demonstrators on 9 April
rapidly escalated, and weavers and other artisans erected barricades in their
suburban neighborhoods. Shortages of arms, the lack of any plans for a concerted
uprising, and the relative isolation of the weaver strongholds from the city center
doomed the insurrection before it began. On 11–12 April, the army bombarded
the sections of the city in which the revolt was concentrated and stormed the
barricades, mopping up the last vestiges of resistance by 14 April. Most artisans
had never joined the uprising, which was crushed at a cost of 350 casualties.
Of 500 participants arrested by the authorities, 90 percent were unmarried
compagnons under forty, about 40 percent of whom were silk workers. Only a
handful of republican lawyers and teachers were included in the total. News of
the revolt provoked less serious disturbances in Arbois, Grenoble, Lunéville,
and Vienne and sparked the disastrous republican uprising in Paris on 13–14
April, which resulted in the rue Transnonain massacre.

The scattered violence was used to justify a massive government crackdown
on republican and mutualist societies, opposition newspapers, and critics of the
regime. Fifty-two of the Lyons rebels were brought to Paris in March 1835 for
the mass trial before the Chamber of Peers. While the Paris and Lyons republicans
attempted to convert the proceedings into a dramatic political indictment of the
government, the weavers and other artisans indicted generally refused to speak
in their own defense and were sentenced to terms of prison or deportation of

from one to twenty years. Repression in Lyons crippled mutualism for a decade and ensured merchant domination of the increasingly rural and decentralized industry. Many weavers turned to Icarian or Fourierist utopian socialism in the 1840s, and the 1834 uprising marked the last major disturbance in the *fabrique* before the mechanization of the industry in the 1890s replaced the hand-loom artisan with a factory labor force.

The Lyons revolts of 1831 and 1834 have been seen by many commentators and historians (Karl Marx among them) as the opening shots of the long war between modern capital and labor, but such analyses overlook the overwhelmingly artisanal and preindustrial character of the silk industry in the early nineteenth century. These easily repressed insurrections can be better understood in the context of the century-long struggle by France's most militant craftsmen to safeguard their livelihood and identity in that nation's most conservative textile trade.

J. Aguet, *Les Grèves sous la Monarchie de Juillet, 1830–1847* (Geneva, 1954); J. Alazard, "Le mouvement social et politique à Lyon entre les deux insurrections de novembre 1831 et d'avril 1834," *Revue d'histoire moderne* 16 (1911); R. Bezucha, *The Lyon Uprisings of 1834* (Cambridge, Mass., 1974); F. Dutacq and A. Latreille, *Histoire de Lyon de 1814 à 1940*, vol. 3 of *L'Histoire de Lyon* (Lyons, 1939–52); M. Garden, *Lyon et les lyonnais au XVIIIe siècle* (Paris, 1970); J. Godart, *L'ouvrier en soie* (Lyons, Paris, 1899); A. Kleinclausz, *Histoire de Lyon*, 2 vols. (Lyons, 1948); D. Longfellow, "Silk Weavers and the Social Struggle in Lyon during the French Revolution, 1789–1794," *French Historical Studies* 12 (1981); M. Moissonnier, *La Révolte des canuts* (Paris, 1958); E. Pariset, *Histoire de la fabrique lyonnaise* (Lyons, 1901); F. Rude, *Le mouvement ouvrier à Lyon de 1827 à 1832* (Paris, 1944) and *C'est nous, les canuts* (Paris, 1977); G. Sheridan, "The Political Economy of Artisan Industry: Government and the People in the Silk Trade of Lyon, 1830–1870," *French Historical Studies* 11 (1979).

David Longfellow

Related entries: CANUTS; CHAMBER OF COMMERCE; CONSEILS DE PRUD-'HOMMES; COTTAGE INDUSTRY; GASPARIN; MARX; NATIONAL GUARD; SILK INDUSTRY; SOCIETY OF MUTUAL DUTY; SOCIETY OF THE RIGHTS OF MAN; SOULT; TRANSNONAIN, MASSACRE OF THE RUE.